BOOKS BY PETER GAY

Reading Freud: Explorations and Entertainments (1990)

Freud: A Life for Our Time (1988)

A Godless Jew:
Freud, Atheism, and the Making of Psychoanalysis (1987)

The Bourgeois Experience: Victoria to Freud
Volume II   The Tender Passion (1986)

Freud for Historians (1985)

The Bourgeois Experience: Victoria to Freud
Volume I   Education of the Senses (1984)

Freud, Jews and Other Germans:
Masters and Victims in Modernist Culture (1978)

Art and Act: On Causes in History—Manet, Gropius, Mondrian (1976)

Style in History (1974)

Modern Europe (1973), with R. K. Webb

The Bridge of Criticism: Dialogues on the Enlightenment (1970)

The Enlightenment: An Interpretation
Volume II   The Science of Freedom (1969)

Weimar Culture: The Outsider as Insider (1968)

A Loss of Mastery: Puritan Historians in Colonial America (1966)

The Enlightenment: An Interpretation
Volume I   The Rise of Modern Paganism (1966)

The Party of Humanity: Essays in the French Enlightenment (1964)

Voltaire's Politics: The Poet as Realist (1959)

The Dilemma of Democratic Socialism:
Eduard Bernstein's Challenge to Marx (1952)

The Cultivation
of Hatred

The Bourgeois Experience

VICTORIA TO FREUD

VOLUME III

The Cultivation of Hatred

PETER GAY

W·W·NORTON & COMPANY · NEW YORK · LONDON

First Edition

The text of this book is composed in 10.5/13.5 Bembo
with the display set in Centaur
Composition and manufacturing by The Haddon Craftsmen, Inc.
Book design by Antonina Krass

Library of Congress Cataloging-in-Publication Data
(Revised for vol. 3)
Gay, Peter, 1923–
The Bourgeois experience.
Vols. 3– published: New York:
W. W. Norton, 1993–
Includes bibliographies and indexes.
Contents: v. 1. Education of the senses—
v. 2. The tender passion—v. 3. The
cultivation of hatred.
1. Middle classes—Europe—History—
19th century. 2. Middle classes—United States
—History—19th century. 3. Sex customs—
Europe—History—19th century. 4. Sex
customs—United States—History—19th century.
5. Sex (Psychology) 6. Love. 7. Aggressiveness
(Psychology) 8. Psychoanalysis and culture.
I. Title.
HT690.E73G39 1984 306.7'094 83–8187
ISBN 0-19-503352-3 (v. 1)
ISBN 0-393-03398-8 (v. 3)

W. W. Norton & Company, Inc., 500 Fifth Avenue, New York, N.Y. 10110
W. W. Norton & Company Ltd., 10 Coptic Street, London WC1A 1PU

1 2 3 4 5 6 7 8 9 0

Contents

The illustrations will be found following pages 244 and 404.

Was ist das, was in uns lügt, mordet, stiehlt? Ich mag dem Gedanken nicht weiter nachgehen.

Georg Büchner to his fiancée, Minna Jaegle, ca. *1835*

Le sentiment de la destruction inné dans l'homme: on dirait que c'est un animal mal doué et homicide de nature.

Edmond and Jules de Goncourt, Journal; mémoires de la vie littéraire, *November 16, 1859*

The joy of killing! The joy of seeing killing done—these are the traits of the human race at large.

Mark Twain, Following the Equator, *1897*

The Cultivation
of Hatred

Introduction

The scars that aggression has left on the face of the past are indelible. Wars and rumors of war, class struggles, clashes between religious denominations or racial and ethnic groups, rivalries for place and power in politics or business, the hatreds generated by nationalism and imperialism, the ravages of crime, the confrontations of private life from marital discord to family feuds—all these, and more, offer persuasive testimony that aggression has supplied most of the fuel for historical action and historical change. The search for the origins, meanings, and implications of aggressiveness—threatening or adaptive—has always been, and must always be, a pressing preoccupation for local magistrates, social reformers, military planners, and political theorists. But beyond that, this book will show that aggression acquired singular salience for the Victorian bourgeoisie, as poignant for the participants as it has proved puzzling for the historian.*

Nineteenth-century observers, early and late, had few doubts that the human is an aggressive animal. "What is it in us," the German playwright Georg Büchner rhetorically asked in a letter of 1835, "that lies, murders, steals?" and he refused to stay for an answer: "I do not want to pursue the thought any further."[1] He did not want to pursue it because the depressing reply—human nature really is like that—seemed painfully obvious to him. A quarter of a century after Büchner, the Goncourt brothers, experimental novelists, consummate snobs, and sour chroniclers of their time, said it again, flatly: "The sentiment of destruction is innate in man."[2]

---

*"Victorian" is used in this book as a synonym for "nineteenth-century." There were "Victorians" before Victoria and after; the long nineteenth century ran from the defeat of Napoleon in 1815 to the outbreak of the First World War in August 1914. What is more, traits we rightly consider characteristic of the Victorians were not confined to Great Britain.

To most good nineteenth-century Christians, the conviction that mankind is inherently wicked—greedy, sensual, mendacious, aggressive—came naturally. And to unbelievers, the immensely influential ideas of Herbert Spencer and of Charles Darwin, more often misunderstood than understood, seemed to offer irrefutable philosophical and scientific rationales for mankind's essential, inexpungeable combativeness. Around the turn of the century, William James summed up post-Darwinian opinion when he observed that "ancestral evolution has made us all potential warriors." In his view, bigotry, dogmatism, the lust for dominion—"the baiting of Jews, the hunting of Albigenses and Waldenses, the stoning of Quakers and ducking of Methodists, the murdering of Mormons and the massacring of Armenians"—demonstrate "that aboriginal human neophobia, that pugnacity of which we all share the vestiges."[3] A few years later, the subtle German sociologist Georg Simmel reiterated this broadly based consensus: in his principal work, *Soziologie,* he assumed that the human mind is endowed with a "fighting instinct," an "inborn need to hate and fight."[4] Those who had reservations about this popular verdict were in a small minority.

The majority had a point: whether an essential human endowment, an acquired trait, or a fleeting, unpremeditated response to provocation, aggression in some form seems to be necessary to the most self-effacing of human creatures.* The proverbial humble subaltern who never raises his voice with his equals, let alone his superiors, will abuse his wife or, as a last resort, kick his dog. To each his, or her, own aggression. But beyond this sure ground is the vast, far from wholly charted domain of enigmas. Aggressive acts, to begin with, are not all primitive pugilism, wanton cruelty, or routine murder. They range across a broad spectrum of verbal and physical expression, from confident self-advertisement to permissible mayhem, from sly malice to sadistic torture. They emerge as words and gestures—less fatal, to be sure, than physical violence, but little less unmistakable. To flaunt one's possessions or overcome one's rivals in love is an act of aggression no less than to provoke a duel or invade a neighboring country. The practice of invidious social comparisons is awash with aggressive impulses. So is the delicious occupation of gossip, and so, even more, is the battlefield of competition in sports, politics, trade, or the race for prizes in art, literature, and science. Besides, as will emerge, the sort of aggressiveness a culture rewards or deprecates, legalizes or outlaws, obviously depends on times and circumstances, on perceived risks or advantages, on social habits of rebelliousness or conformity.

*For rival theories of aggression—including the psychoanalytic, on which I have drawn in this text—see the Appendix.

What is more, many aggressive acts are reactive; a reputable school of social scientists has committed itself to the proposition that the most dependable trigger of these acts is frustration.[5] And the theorists offer some persuasive evidence; aggressions are often enough a means of self-defense. The surly, often intemperate responses of American sermon writers and editorialists to the moderate political program that feminists drew up in 1848 at their convention in Seneca Falls, New York—the delegates could barely be persuaded to ask for the vote—were a nervous plea to preserve time-honored styles of thinking from what these fearful critics perceived as the menace of radical subversion. The no less intemperate responses of late-nineteenth-century academic art critics to Impressionist paintings were quite as nervous. What is more, aggressive feelings are not identical with aggressive acts; the feelings are often unconscious, well below the threshold of awareness, at once cause and consequence of buried inner conflicts. The expression of other feelings, less successfully repressed, may be dampened down by fear, prudence, well-rehearsed lessons in decorum, or the censorious prodding of the superego. They may issue merely in a scowl or a muttered sarcasm—or a neurotic symptom. The impulse to aggression often materializes, when it does materialize at all, distorted and disguised, recognizable only by those alert to the devious ways of the mind.

The nineteenth century understood intuitively, decades before Freud proposed theoretical formulations to account for it, that while culture must police aggression no less energetically than sexuality, there are territories in which the writ for emphatic self-assertion runs without challenge, to general applause. But the proper place and the proper boundaries for aggression remained problematic all through the age. Many Victorian bourgeois, in many situations, took specific forms of aggressive expression as a hard-won privilege to be cheerfully enjoyed; more of them, more of the time, perceived such forms as an acute danger to be anxiously warded off. In an age of drastic upheaval in virtually every dimension of life from finance to transport, morals to politics, art to architecture, the problem of aggression proved just another, if critically important, ground for confusions, hesitations—and controversies.

In fact, much like the members of other literate societies, but more than most, the nineteenth-century bourgeoisie engaged in continuous, often acidulous debates over the moral nature and adaptive properties of aggression. These altercations were bound to be most ferocious when nation clashed with nation, class with class, interest group with interest group, but they proved only marginally less spirited when fought out over subtler issues. These controversies suggest that many Victorians were alert to the varieties of aggressiveness and stood ready to attack or defend one or another of its manifestations. But, as this book will document, conscious and contentious attitudes toward aggression coexisted with aggressive ideas and acts that were not recognized as such. In that situation—and it was frequent—the historian's hindsight must serve to clarify what in its own time remained obscure.

In carrying on their heartfelt disputes, Victorians developed what I shall call alibis for aggression: beliefs, principles, rhetorical platitudes that legitimated verbal or physical militancy on religious, political, or, best of all, scientific grounds. And this makes for more complications. These justifications were intended to blunt criticisms as they portrayed middle-class culture launching on the world attacks that deserved nothing but praise. Were assertions of control over raw materials and high finance, business organization and sanitary hazards, far-flung communications and scientific mysteries not purely constructive activities? True enough: we can appropriately call Victorian bourgeois aggressive not merely because their hunt for profits and power exacted grave social costs from sweated labor, exploited clerks, obsolete artisans, or maltreated natives, but also because they expended energies to get a grip on time, space, scarcity—and themselves—as never before. For all their defensiveness, some of these aggressive acts turned out to be purely beneficial. Still, it must be admitted—and many Victorian cultural critics did admit—that in doing their strenuous, often ruthless, work, these campaigns for mastery, in which the inventive and purposeful nineteenth century excelled, bent and broke resistance and trampled on time-honored ways of living, exacerbating tensions between the powerful and the powerless, the rich and the poor. They exhibited the familiar fact that aggression, no matter how benign in intent or result, leaves bruised casualties in its wake.

Yet the insistence on the positive nature of at least some aggressiveness was more than mere self-serving apologetics. We have come to recognize that just as children's burgeoning sexual energies act as an educator for life, their aggressions rehearse their capacities and trace their boundaries. Saying no, refusing help, pushing out elbows, serve not merely to establish necessary limits but, often enough, to widen them. Taking charge of a sandbox can be a healthy testing of one's powers rather than an anguished cry for attention. And adults for their part can, and often do, act aggressively not merely to insult, maim, or kill. The woman's movement of the nineteenth century, the pugnacity characteristic of its humor, and its forceful campaigns to master self and nature, shows how aggressiveness, suitably sublimated, could be enlisted to conquer a world without brutalizing it. But whether a certain act is constructive or destructive can never be conclusively determined. What a target of aggression may resent as an unwarranted blow, the aggressor may defend quite sincerely as essential to survival. An act of aggression is a transaction, and how it is judged obviously depends on the perspective of the participants. Who is to decide? Asking about the gored ox is not enough.

These difficulties do not arise just because aggressor and victim are almost bound to disagree. Many aggressors cannot really know whether they are actuated by constructive or destructive impulses. The two are so thoroughly intertwined that most likely both have had their share in prompting action. Certainly the defense mechanisms that psychoanalysts have shown to be essential to all mental endowment produce layers of mixed motives. The wish to injure others can be sublimated into aesthetic or scientific productivity; the horror at one's murderous desires may, in reaction, generate a consuming love for all living beings. Freud once drily noted that when pacifists were youngsters, they probably enjoyed torturing animals. This is not cynicism, but the awed recognition of human complexity. I shall explore these subtleties in the pages that follow.

It is important to state in these introductory pages that while I have concentrated on the varieties of aggressiveness in nineteenth-century middle-class culture, I am tacitly presupposing a measure of collaboration, and of clashes, between sexuality and aggression. The two are instinctual allies and adversaries. Pure specimens of aggression are as rare as pure specimens of love. That was no secret to the romantics; Heinrich Heine was not the only one to revel in provocative oxymorons like "sweet cruelty," the "voluptuousness of revenge" and "cruel tenderness." And William James would observe that "the closest human love incloses a potential germ of estrangement or hatred."[6] He, like his predecessors, recognized that the dynamic confrontations of love and hate are at once an opposition and an interaction. The sexual boasting of a Don Juan, the ungainly sentiment of jealousy which mingles envy, rage, and a sense of loss in a volatile mixture, the Oedipus complex with its delicate, unstable amalgam of longing and rejection, all document the continuous interplay of love and hate.

This interplay is fundamental to human experience. Civilization itself, with its exigent demands on individuals and the individuals' efforts to gratify their desires, is an interminable contest, only intermittently peaceful, between Eros and its great adversary, aggression. Freud's working habits informally exhibit this tense intimacy: after he had published his *Interpretation of Dreams* late in 1899, he worked alternately on a book about jokes and a book about sexuality, keeping both manuscripts on his desk and taking up the one or the other as his inclination moved him.[7] He thus dramatized the mutual engagement of what he would later single out as humanity's most interesting innate urges, and the ease with which one of them may gain, and then lose, ascendancy over the other.

As a study of aggression in the Victorian century, this book stands on its own. But since the interaction of aggression with Eros is a fact of human life, it can also be read as part of a larger enterprise, as the third volume in an extensive exploration of bourgeois culture in these years. The previous volumes show that the enigmas posed by the erotic sensibilities and actions of the Victorian bourgeoisie are intriguing and intractable enough.[8] But they pale before the conundrums awaiting the historian who tries to discover the defining qualities and characteristic effects of aggression in the decades from Victoria to Freud. This book is an attempt to open at least some of the locked doors barring access to our aggressive nineteenth-century past.

BOURGEOIS EXPERIENCES, III

Mensur—the Cherished Scar

Around 1900, the English actor, playwright, and editor Jerome K. Jerome translated memories of an agreeable bicycle tour through Wilhelmine Germany into a travel report, *Three Men on the Bummel,* that speaks eloquently to the basic theme of this book: the cultivation of hatred. The phrase is, of course, a play on words, but that is precisely its claim to seriousness. Humans, pugnacious animals that they are, cultivate their hatreds because they get pleasure from the exercise of their aggressive powers. But the societies in which they live cultivate hatred in precisely the opposite way, by subjecting bareknuckled aggression in most of its forms to stern control; they rein in violence before it destroys everything. This second type of cultivation is a matter, literally, of life and death. And the *Mensur,* the German student duel, is a superb instance of the clash between the two meanings of cultivation, an exercise in aggression checked by accepted rules.

A few years before he published his book on that German "stroll"—*Bummel*—Jerome, a strenuously cheerful essayist, had established a national, even international, reputation as a genial student of human nature with *Three Men in a Boat.* There he had recalled an excursion, half-sentimental and half-humorous, taken with two friends and a dog up the Thames from London.[1] In its successor about Germany, featuring the same cast of characters (except for the dog), Jerome set sentimentality aside and gave his humor, normally gentle and even a little saccharine, a certain edge. He was, after all, an Englishman observing Germans, with wry amusement and real affection but not without asperity.

Indulging himself in a few invidious if relatively benign comparisons, he depicted the Germans as hardworking, pedantic, servile to authority, almost comically law-abiding. Even German birds and dogs knew their place: birds refused to nest in birdhouses not provided by the government; dogs obeyed signs warning them off the grass, slinking away from forbidden terrain with tail between their legs. All this was meant to be lighthearted. But then, in a methodical, almost leisurely exploration of a student duel, Jerome abandoned humor altogether and reported his reponses with a mixture of clinical detachment, moral censoriousness, and confessional intimacy.

Not unexpectedly, Jerome was very severe on this Teutonic blood sport. As an Englishman, he was disposed to share the disgust expressed by the *Saturday Review*. "Duelling," it had pronounced in 1858, "belongs to a coarse and barbarous state of society," or is, at the least, a grave symptom of "a deep social disorder." The weekly attributed the survival of the duel among the French, so polished in general, to the burden that the despotic regime of Napoleon III had imposed on his country: "If men cannot talk and settle debatable questions by argument and free speech, they have recourse to the vulgar reasoning of sword and pistol." In the United States, the duel was still common because that nation, though superficially different, was precisely like France in being a tyranny, a "demagogic" despotism.[2] A few months later, the weekly returned to duelling in France with the same contemptuous curl of the lip: authors "of a lower grade," notably playwrights and drama critics, were engaging in ugly "literary duelling," assaulting one another in furious disputes, and then turning to more lethal weapons to settle their quarrels.[3]

The combats the *Saturday Review* had in view, to be sure, involved two grown men shooting at one another, shooting to kill. But Jerome thought little better of students fighting with sabers, despite the comparatively innocuous outcome of their ritual exercise. The Germans, he wrote, have persuaded themselves that the Mensur is eminently useful in building character: "There is no brutality in it—nothing offensive, nothing degrading. Their argument is that it schools the German youth to coolness and courage." Jerome would have none of these transparent rationalizations. The student, he argued, echoing German critics of the practice, would show more courage in refusing a challenge than in honoring it; after all, "he fights not to please himself, but to satisfy a public opinion that is two hundred years behind the times." Far from infusing him with virtue, "all the Mensur does is to brutalize him." Perhaps at universities like "aristocratic" Bonn or cosmopolitan Heidelberg, student duels might be formal, ceremonious, even rather picturesque. But everywhere else, they "combine the ludicrous with the unpleasant." So uninviting, in fact, was the "celebrated" German Mensur that Jerome urged his "sensitive reader to avoid even this description."[4] Nothing else in *Three Men on the Bummel* even remotely resembled the horrors he was about to unfold.

Having secured his audience by warning it off, Jerome launched into his report. Contemporary memoirs and realistic fiction confirm its accuracy. "The room is bare and sordid; its walls splashed with mixed stains of beer, blood, and candle-grease; its ceiling, smoky; its floor, sawdust covered. A crowd of students, laughing, smoking, talking, some sitting on the floor, others perched upon chairs and benches, form the framework." The combatants, goggled and wrapped in protective cushions, confront one another, looking most ungainly. "The umpire takes his place, the word is given, and immediately there follow five rapid clashes of the long straight swords." For Jerome, at least, the fight had "no movement, no skill, no grace." Quite simply, "the strongest man wins; the man who, with his heavily-padded arm, always in an unnatural position, can hold his huge clumsy sword longest without growing too weak to be able either to guard or to strike."[5]

While the duel lacks all tension or charm, "the whole interest is centred in watching the wounds. They come always in one of two places—on the top of the head or the left side of the face." And they provide an appalling spectacle. "Sometimes a portion of hairy scalp or section of cheek flies up into the air, to be carefully preserved in an envelope by its proud possessor, or, strictly speaking, its proud former possessor, and shown round on convivial evenings." As one might expect, from every wound there "flows a plentiful stream of blood. It splashes doctors, seconds, and spectators; it sprinkles ceilings and walls; it saturates the fighters, and makes pools for itself in the sawdust. At the end of each round the doctors rush up, and with hands already dripping with blood press together the gaping wounds, dabbing them with little balls of wet cotton wool," but inevitably, as soon as the duellists begin the next round, "the blood gushes out again, half blinding them, and rendering the ground beneath slippery." The combatants' appearance grows more and more bizarre. "Now and then you see a man's teeth laid bare almost to the ear, so that for the rest of the duel he appears to be grinning at one half of the spectators, his other side remaining serious; and sometimes a man's nose gets slit, which gives to him as he fights a singularly supercilious air."[6]

But the wound, of course, the cherished scar, is the thing. The point of the whole exercise, after all, is to "go away from the University bearing as many scars as possible"; for this will ensure the duellist the envy of fellow students, the admiration of desirable maidens, and, in the end, "a wife with a dowry of five figures at the least." That is why "the actual fighting is only the beginning of the fun. The second act of the spectacle takes place in the dressing-room." The so-called doctors presiding there are for the most part medical students, "coarse-looking men" who seem "rather to relish their work" and who cheerfully inflict as much punishment on their victims as possible. This is a crucial part of the ritual. "How the student bears the dressing of his wounds is as important as how he receives them. Every operation has to be performed as brutally as may be, and his companions watch him during the process to see that he goes through it with an appearance of peace and enjoyment. A clean-cut wound that gapes wide is most desired by all parties. On purpose it is sewn up clumsily, with the hope that by this means the scar will last a lifetime."[7] Only a permanent scar bestows permanent benefits.

Jerome doubted that this ceremony had anything to be said in its favor. Certainly, "upon the spectators it can and does, I am convinced, exercise nothing but evil." He submitted his own responses in evidence. "I know myself sufficiently well to be sure I am not of an unusually bloodthirsty disposition." At the beginning, "before the actual work commenced, my sensation was curiosity mingled with anxiety as to how the sight would trouble me"; then, "as the blood began to flow, and nerves and muscles to be laid bare, I experienced a mingling of disgust and pity. But with the second duel, I must confess, my finer feelings began to disappear; and by the time the third was well upon its way, and the room heavy with the curious hot odor of blood," more primitive sensations claimed primacy. "I wanted more."[8]

This is an extraordinary confession. With its frank admission of an emerging complicity, it probes to unsuspected depths normally buried aggressive urges, lured from their lair in the unconscious to find gratification in an alien cultural style. To the uninitiated the Mensur was, as Jerome had noted, brutal, repellent, pointless, so childish and irrational as to be bewildering, at times savagely funny. Its only value to the observer who had freed himself from hypocrisy, Jerome thought, was to remind him that "underneath our starched shirts there lurks the savage, with all his savage instincts untouched."[9] To be sure, this was not an original insight. But Jerome invested accepted nineteenth-century generalities about human nature with, almost literally, the flesh and blood of concrete experience.

For all its unappetizing, rather sordid drama, the evidentiary value of the Mensur for the student of the nineteenth-century bourgeoisie is not immediately apparent and calls for some reflection. It was an extravagant institution. More savage forms of duelling, combats to the death, had of course long been customary throughout Europe and, especially in the first half of the nineteenth century, in the United States. One thinks of Alexander Hamilton, shot to death in 1804 by Aaron Burr; or of the poignant fate of Alexander Pushkin, who made his great novel in verse, *Eugene Onegin,* hinge on such a fatal encounter and then himself fell in a duel a few years later. The age saw other talented young victims—and lucky survivors: the Russian poet and novelist Mikhail Lermontov was killed in a duel in 1841, four years after Pushkin; Heinrich Heine, stung by insulting looks and anti-Semitic remarks, fought a number of duels as a student and lived to tell the tale. In the antebellum South, where parents trained their sons to face death if necessary to defend their gentlemanly honor, so jealously guarded and so easily offended, possibly fatal duels were the accepted method of settling disputes touching on one's manhood.

Nor did army officers and their imitators have a corner on the issuing and acceptance of challenges. The charismatic German socialist theorist and politician Ferdinand Lassalle died in 1864 in what was billed as an affair of honor—a dispute over a woman. Just a few years earlier, the radical French journalist and novelist Jules Vallès, then an impecunious young writer, survived such an encounter, seriously wounding his adversary, a close friend. Certainly for the imaginative literature of the day, pistols at thirty paces was a welcome dramatic device, especially if the protagonists were military men. When Colonel Brandon, in Jane Austen's *Sense and Sensibility,* told the sensible Elinor Dashwood that he had fought a duel with the worthless charmer and vicious seducer Willoughby, she "sighed over the fancied necessity of this; but to a man and a soldier, she presumed not to censure it."[10] In *Nicholas Nickleby,* Dickens disposes of one of his less admirable characters, Lord Frederick Verisopht, through a duel. Arthur Fletcher, the hero of Trollope's *The Prime Minister,* regrets that he cannot shoot Ferdinand Lopez, the mysterious man whom the woman he loves seems to prefer—but then, duels had been outlawed in Britain by mid-century.

Yet they continued to make news, and stories, on the Continent. Maupassant has a duel in his novel *Bel-Ami.* Theodor Fontane makes a duel serve as the tragic climax of his best-known novel, *Effi Briest.* Chekhov employs a duel with mortal outcome in his unique offhand way in *The Three Sisters.* Some of Schnitzler's most mordant stories revolve around duels fought and duels evaded: his justly famous interior monologue, "Leutnant Gustl," depicts an Austrian officer frightened out of his wits by the prospect of his imminent, so wasteful death in a duel, and saved at the last moment by the timely demise of his opponent. Most of the continental writers who injected duels into their fictions did not approve of them. But they treated them as commonplace, at least in certain circles.

A relatively bland version of such confrontations, the Mensur was the duel tamed, reduced to almost laughable routine. Hence being tolerant about it was easier, even for outsiders. While the Mensur was largely a Teutonic phenomenon, the excited response of foreign visitors strongly suggests its general, if largely subterranean, appeal. More than half a century before Jerome had discovered the intoxicating pleasure of watching blood being shed, another English tourist, William Howitt, thought that his countrymen, watching German student life, would doubtless find two things most repugnant: "the Beer-duel, and the Sword-duel." Yet this same observer, though a Quaker, decided that the Mensur was really a civilizing sport, one of those splendid cultural defects designed to drive out far worse evils, "a sort of discipline which the students exercise amongst themselves, and thus banish every ruder and not seldom dangerous explosion of passion."[11] If there was widespread, mounting opposition to officers' or journalists' taking the law into their own hands, the student duel, that specialized Teutonic exercise, found approving echoes in many places.

But were they bourgeois echoes? The aggressive posture of student duellists, their meticulously regulated military bearing and their elaborate code of honor, strongly hint at the aristocratic origins of the sport. But it had not remained the private preserve of Junkers from Prussia or barons from southern German states. It was an aristocratic survival taken over into an increasingly bourgeois society. After all, in the nineteenth century, *Bürger,* too, insisted on their honor. When, in 1841, Heinrich Heine resented an insulting comment by the banker Salomon Strauss—both men of course were Jewish, at least by origin—and challenged him to a duel, Heine's publisher, Julius Campe, encouraged him in this dangerous course. "Better dead than dishonored," he told his favorite author.[12]

Young German bourgeois, filled with notions of honor, crowded into the nineteenth-century universities. The scions of noble houses did attend these universities in proportionately greater numbers than other young Germans, but even in the fashionable seats of learning that they preferred—Heidelberg and Bonn—they rarely exceeded one in six among the student population. Especially in years of burgeoning enrollments, their number would hover at one in ten, or, at some universities, one in twenty. The bulk of the German student body was drawn from the affluent and, even more, the educated middle strata— the *Besitzbürgertum* and the *Bildungsbürgertum;* it was common for university graduates to expect their sons to follow in their footsteps. To be sure, aristocrats were overrepresented in the exclusive *Corps,* and indeed in the slightly more "democratic" fraternities, the *Burschenschaften.* But they rarely outnumbered their bourgeois fellows even in the most select of these clubs. A few of the most prestige-laden *Corps,* such as the Saxoborussia at Heidelberg and the Borussia at Bonn, were the playgrounds of young aristocrats, but they too enrolled a sizable share of respectable commoners.[13]

The bourgeois slashing at one another's faces in intimate companionship with their aristocratic brethren were, to be sure, far from ordinary middling burghers; they were the enterprising, the prosperous, the assiduous social climbers. And in their turn, they set the tone for the German middle classes, which, even more than the English, dearly loved a lord. Despite their fascination with technology, modern Germans persisted in rescuing and reviving disturbing elements from a faraway past. The snob, the parvenu, the insecure, found something irresistible in their titled drinking, parading, and fighting companions who condescended to hearty demonstrations of ostentatious equality. The pathos of young men perched on the edge of seductive new social possibilities, usually egged on by their proud, anxious, and ambitious parents, was keen and far from pleasant to behold. Borrowed hauteur could be as brutal, and as comical, as the real thing.

This state of affairs was common talk, taken for granted. In 1914, the outspoken and witty Social Democratic deputy Hermann Wendel entertained the Reichstag, to the applause of his party comrades and to general hilarity, with a devastating portrait of the German bourgeois as gentleman. In contrast with their English counterparts, Wendel observed, the German middle classes had not succeeded in infiltrating private morality and the general way of thinking. Instead, "the bourgeois class has been feudalized and militarized." The ideal German whom the bourgeois seem to cherish most is not "the honorable *Bürger*" but the "dashing gentleman with the upturned mustache." The deputies, inescapably reminded of the martial, and upturned, mustache of Kaiser Wilhelm II, laughed heartily.[14]

In Germany, Wendel continued, "a young businessman does not want to look like a young businessman, but, if possible, like a lieutenant in mufti." The most impeccably bourgeois young man buys himself a monocle and affects the kind of twangy speech associated with Prussian royalty. Hence, "it is not surprising that the bourgeoisie has offered no energetic opposition to the duel; rather, with its morbidly retarded class consciousness, it has adapted itself to this bad habit precisely because it is feudal." He reminded his listeners that an anti-duelling league had been formed a decade or so earlier, but at its founding session the motion compelling all members to refuse challenges had been defeated. Even principled opponents of the duel did not want to lose the privilege of duelling![15] The hilarity which, the stenographer noted, punctuated Wendel's caustic vignette suggests that his criticism of the feudalized German bourgeoisie had hit home without being excessively disturbing. It was a truth about the German middle class that everyone could more or less recognize and accept.

Cynics took such disparagement further. To their minds, fraternities essentially served aspiring bourgeois to establish connections that would prove useful later on, in the commercial, professional, or marital marketplace. Social prestige, political preferment, rapid promotion in business, were the rewards expected from the organized camaraderie fostered in alcoholic embraces and sealed with jagged facial mementos. Max Weber, who as a student at Heidelberg had drunk and duelled with the best of them—his youthful face, swollen and scarred, amply attested to his dissipated ways—later dismissed the fraternity business with a single disdainful name. The duelling fraternities, he wrote, were nothing but insurance companies devoted to the advancement of their members: *Avancementsversicherungsanstalten.*[16]

Of the three groups into which the student population was traditionally divided—scholars, careerists, and cavaliers—it was mainly the last, the swaggering *Kavaliere,* who had the funds and the inclination to join fraternities that took pride in fighting for their honor. Most scholars were too busy studying and too disdainful of what they thought uncivilized absurdities, to find mindless beer bouts, fashionable uniforms, and sanguinary episodes in any way appealing. And the sizable number of students known derisively as *Brotstudenten*—those who studied strenuously for the civil service examinations, to earn their bread later— were too poor, too compulsive, and in any event not socially eligible for the expensive and extravagant fraternity life. Hence it was a strutting minority that performed the Mensur, students who were influential at the university and who fully, and justly, expected to be no less influential in later years. The ability of nobly born students to form the style of their fraternity, and through that, of their university, was the triumph of status over statistics.

The popular image of the nineteenth-century German university, then, end-lessly polished with slight variations in tinted postcards, sentimental sheet music, quaint restaurants, lachrymose novels, and sensational reports of duellers punished or on rare, shocking occasions, mortally wounded, was a distortion of university realities. But what matters here and deserves to be reiterated is that most members of the highly visible student aristocracy who gave shape to these misty celebrations were sons of academics or scientists, financial magnates or secondary school teachers, especially teachers in the elite schools strong in the classical languages, the *Gymnasien.* Humor magazines like *Simplicissimus,* and political outsiders like the orators of the Social Democratic party, liked to savage the *Corps* and the *Burschenschaft* student, grossly swollen with beer or almost anorexic in his willowy decadence, blasé, stupid, afraid to be seen sober or with a book, incurably ignorant yet always dressed to a fault in his fraternity gear. It was a collective caricature, but—no one can deny—as telling as it was funny.

The *Corps* student was not just fatuous, involuntary fodder for uncompli-mentary wits; he and his brethren made up the pool from which Germany, for decades before Jerome witnessed his Mensur, drew not only its generals and its cabinet ministers, but its bankers, civil servants, university professors, medical specialists, and trial lawyers. Addressing the Bonn *Corps* in 1891, Kaiser Wil-helm II expressed the hope that "one of these days many officials and officers will spring from your circle. How many distinguished men," he exclaimed, "we have sitting here among us: scholars, officials, officers, and businessmen!"[17] It was an exuberant and tactless pronouncement, typical of the Kaiser, for its tendentious singling out of the *Corps* at the expense of the *Burschenschaften.* Yet even this emperor was constrained to number among the elite he prized not merely his beloved officers but also bureaucrats, to say nothing of academics and businessmen.

Bourgeois, then, were prominent among the students belonging to duelling fraternities. When the great historian of Christian dogma Adolf von Harnack was a student at the University of Dorpat, he joined a "progressive Landsmann-schaft" and found that "the members were drawn from the sons of noble families, circles of the so-called literati (members of the free professions) and commercial circles. While the aristocrats in fact largely determined the style of life, there was no aristocratic narrowness, but genuine liberality." Earlier, at Heidelberg in the 1840s, the eminent physician and physiologist Adolf Kuss-maul had felt himself, once elected to full membership in the Corps Suevia, as one of "the student knighthood, in which princes and barons, sons of officials and of farmers, honored one another as free and equal *Burschen*."[18] These glow-ing recollections may be slightly questionable, but in fact a number of these bourgeois knights did end up with an aristocratic *von* in their name, acquired through money, a fortunate marriage, or even merit. And most of the rest, who remained like their fathers good bourgeois decorated with cherished facial scars, took places of prominence and power in German society.

The intense controversy that the Mensur generated in the press, in the pamphlet literature, and in German legislatures makes it all the more a part of the nineteenth-century bourgeois experience. To be sure, young aristocrats who had grown up with the honor code of their caste had few doubts about its value and enduring validity. Even after duelling had become a blatant anachro-nism and, late in the century, began to lose the persuasiveness of a living tradition, it retained the compelling force of an obsessive habit. In *Effi Briest*, Fontane captured the fossilized quality of this cultural survival: Baron von Instetten, its protagonist, kills a former lover of his wife's in a duel fought not out of rage or jealousy—the affair had happened long ago and had been patheti-cally short—but from an inherited sense of obligation he dare not question. Some foreign observers, such as William Howitt, might find the Mensur a supreme educational experience; apologists, foreign or domestic, liked to paint it as a school for life. But many middle-class Germans—students and professors among them—were not quite so sanguine about the civilizing mission of the student duel. Its advocates were vehement, tenacious, and extremely influen-tial, but its critics, far from being mere eccentrics or radicals, never gave up.

In the late eighteenth century, with the German university on the verge of its spectacular career, a group of students at Jena, under the impress of enlightened ideas, had vigorously polemicized in behalf of the suspension or expulsion of persistent duellers. And in 1782, the poet August Niemann called the Mensur a desecration of patriotism; the true hero, he maintained, never lifts his sword except in defense of his insulted fatherland. There was a brief vogue, too, for the *Schokoladisten*—a group of students so called for their notion that all disputes can be amicably settled over a cup of hot chocolate. Goethe was not alone in applauding their efforts. But though the movement generated sympathetic resonances in other universities, the anti-duelling campaign ultimately, and predictably, failed. Students who wanted to duel would not do without it. As late as 1882, the American scholar and feminist M. Carey Thomas, then completing her doctorate in Zurich, reported to her mother that Swiss students who belonged to strictly outlawed duelling clubs, and faced fines and prison for being caught saber in hand, would travel all the way to Germany to do their fighting.[19]

Yet pacific views never wholly disappeared from student debates. A nonviolent, nonaggressive substitute, the court of honor designed to settle disputes touching on a student's honor, gained a certain currency in the course of the nineteenth century. Religious student associations like the devout Protestant and Catholic fraternities and clubs devoted to hiking or serious debates explicitly banned the Mensur on principle; other organizations, like the *Reform-Burschenschaften* of the 1880s, deprecated the rage for duelling but insisted on retaining in their statutes the institution of challenge and *Satisfaktion*. In a controversy over the Mensur at the end of the century, the historian Georg von Below, known for his opposition to duelling, called for its abolition. He spoke only for a minority. It may be, wrote the legal scholar Heinrich Geffcken, that although "inner honor" cannot be touched by anyone apart from ourselves, "outer honor," the *Ehre,* is "the surrounding world being aware of our value," and needs to be defended. The student duel will not disappear until there is another way of restoring insulted honor, for "like the old Germans, we, too, want our *Ehre* intact."[20] This was also the position of a reform-minded professor like Adolf von Harnack, who attempted to civilize the *Burschenschaften* from within.

When Harnack took up the reforming cause in the last decades of the century, his arguments were wholly familiar. So were those of the abolitionists. The *Schokoladisten,* after all, go back to the late eighteenth century, and as early as 1828, Johann Nepomuk Ringseis, a distinguished physician and professor at Munich, had told an audience at his university that the Mensur was worse than irrational; it was a perversion of honor, an affront to every law-abiding citizen, and a downright dishonorable pursuit for students of medicine, theology, and law, called by their professions to heal, reconcile, and inspire submission to lawful authority. The causes of duels, Ringseis argued—"drinking, quarrelling, and insult"—made them peculiarly unsavory. Yet, aware that his opinions were unpopular, he sugar-coated them with patriotism: "Let every individual endeavor to outstrip the others, every organization the others, our university all others in knowledge, in morals, in obedience, in glowing love to King and Fatherland. I call you, my friends, to such a noble contest"; and he invoked his listeners' "honor, the fame of our university, the fame of the Fatherland, and of our King."[21]

Stirring talk this, and a touching effort to find a moral equivalent for duelling in more peaceful strife. But while the laws were with Ringseis, his arguments made few converts. University authorities were inclined to interpret the students' right to their free way of life most generously and connived with them by looking the other way. Sometimes, especially after particularly riotous behavior or a fatal duel, they did feel compelled to enforce whatever anti-duelling regulations were on their books. But usually the devotees of the Mensur kept on slashing at one another undisturbed, while popular writers' everywhere, English, French, and Italian no less than German, expatiated on the romance of the duel.

The Mensur retained its appeal in large part because its champions took care to advertise its long and honorable past. Yet its impressive-looking feudal pedigree was highly suspect. Of the debates it would engender, those about its history were among the most intemperate. According to one historian whose fidelity to the duelling fraternities stands beyond question, the honorable practice of challenging one's adversary to a serious fencing contest emerged first in medieval German cities, was adopted by the nobility, and later was embraced by students. The Mensur may have been born, in short, a bourgeois institution. In the 1890s, George von Below, with his anti-duelling axe to grind, offered a different pedigree: the Mensur, he insisted, was not originally German at all, but had been invented in the corrupt and decadent French court of Henry III and then exported to French-oriented German states. Whatever the elusive truth— and it remains elusive after diligent researches—the prized credentials, at once aristocratic and Teutonic, that lent the Mensur its prestige among the heirs to commercial or industrial fortunes were of uncertain origin at best. Possibly they were forged.[22]

This much seems beyond dispute: like so many institutions reeking with tradition, Germany's nineteenth-century duelling fraternities were in essence relatively modern—barely recognizable offspring of medieval corporations. Similarly, the *Komment,* an obsessively detailed set of rules regulating German fraternity men's dress, mannerisms, drinking sprees, courtships, and reasons for feeling affronted, had its remote ancestor in the far less elaborate rules governing late-medieval student life.[23] But whether freshly minted, skillfully adapted, or authentically old, the customs of students, aristocratic and bourgeois alike, were inescapably invaded by history. Most of the *Landsmannschaften,* parochial associations of students from particular regions of the old German Empire, were reorganized around 1800 into the *Corps,* which in turn united into overarching cartels both within and among universities. Their members regarded themselves as a painstakingly selected elite and stretched their imaginations to lend their status the highest possible prominence. They co-opted new members with care and secretive ceremonial, developed intricate procedures governing sociability, and created distinctive dress, notably the conspicuous colored cap and the military-looking sash. They spent money beyond the capacity of most fathers' bank accounts. Each *Corps* student solemnly undertook to preserve lifelong loyalty to his corporation, scrupulously obey the *Komment* in all matters of comportment, dress, and drink, and uphold collective honor by standing ready to fight duels that would solidify friendships, display courage, and avenge insults.

By reducing all aspects of conduct to rule, the nineteenth-century *Corps,* with their superb claim to be speaking for all students, professed to raise the ethical, social, and at times even intellectual standards of German students. The cultivation of hatred comes to the fore at this point in all its paradoxical character: by prescribing stern, unbreakable laws for combat, which is to say aggression, these fraternities claimed to be—and in some measure actually were—civilizing naked pugnacity. The *Corps* looked down on the notorious drunkards, ruffians, dandies, and wastrels who had given German university life a bad reputation in the eighteenth century, and undertook to reform undisciplined excesses. It is an ironic twist of history, but perhaps unavoidable, that the kinds of uncivilized behavior initially to be shunned became in time models to be imitated; they came to be seen as supremely chic and tough, as aspects of a praiseworthy anti-intellectual public demeanor—provided they took place under the aegis of a fraternity.

Whatever moved university *Corps* to fight duels, they were scrupulously unpolitical. A primitive patriotism and no less primitive loyalty to the ruling dynasty was all they demanded and permitted. To be sure, the social station, or social aspirations, of their members virtually compelled the *Corps* to grow into defensive, aggressively conservative institutions. The aristocrats naturally wanted to keep the privileged position they enjoyed, the bourgeois members wanted to acquire it. But so prominent a socialist politician as Wilhelm Liebknecht remained a member of his *Corps* all his life no less than did Otto von Bismarck.[24] There is no evidence that Karl Marx retained any yearning for the Trier Tavern Club, a drinking and duelling fraternity he joined at Bonn, but it is amusing to recall that like so many other bourgeois, Marx engaged in a duel, and bore a scar over his left eye in witness.[25] Peaceful or bellicose in later life, conformist or rebellious, student of law, medicine, or theology, the *Corpsier* was bound by the sacred statutes of his fraternity to do his fighting on the duelling grounds. Politics had nothing to do with it.

In contrast, the *Burschenschaften* entered the history of political aggression right from their birth in the nineteenth century. The first of them was founded in the aftermath, and as a direct consequence, of the defeat of Napoleon I, who had for a decade cowed German princes, humiliated German armies, and carved up German territories to suit his convenience. The *Burschenschaften* were creatures of exhilaration mixed with despair: exhilaration aroused by the allied campaign against France, in which students had played a notable and courageous part; despair over the political settlement at Vienna following Napoleon's fall in 1815, a settlement which forcefully tried to restore the Old Regime and to stuff the twin demons of nationalism and democracy back into the bottle of prerevolutionary institutions. As early as 1811, Friedrich Ludwig Jahn, "Turnvater Jahn," the demagogic father of organized calisthenics, had knit bodily fitness and patriotic language reform into a program for national unity, and had worked out a program for an organization that would purify student life, supersede the parochial *Corps*, and draw its membership from a larger pool.

Late in the spring of 1815, after several false starts, students at the University of Jena translated the ideas of Jahn and his fellow ideologues into reality. While the fraternity they founded took over the rules that had governed eighteenth-century associations now largely disbanded, its ethical and political program was the response of enthusiastic youths to the romantic, radical currents of their own day. The slogan the Jena fraternity adopted was as terse as it was revealing: "Freedom, Honor, Fatherland." These three resounding nouns summed up the students' sense of their mission: to bring about the drastic enlargement of the political public combined with the unshackling of new ideas, to foster honorable conduct in all dealings private and public, and to make propaganda for a German national state. Any historian looking for a "rising bourgeoisie" need look no further. The *Burschenschaft* was evidently most timely: students elsewhere rapidly imitated their colleagues at Jena, and soon German universities were nests of highly politicized fraternities, aggressive to the core and panting for action.

Of the three elements in their slogan, Honor was from the beginning the most sensitive. Despite the supposed aristocratic roots of the duel, the fraternities did not want it to prevent the democratization of student life: all, except unconverted Jews, should be welcome. Not even that single restriction was strictly enforced everywhere: Heine was admitted to a *Burschenschaft* in Bonn during the winter semester of 1818–19, six years before his baptism. Like the *Corps,* the *Burschenschaften* rejected the time-honored brutality of student combats that had only too often ended with the death of one of the duellists: these were untenable, downright perverted, interpretations of *Ehre*. Honor was, in their book, a spiritual condition, a noble self-perception not to be irresponsibly invoked to dignify drunken brawls or to secure "satisfaction" for imaginary provocations. At the same time, the early fraternity men took the regulated duel to be an indispensable ingredient in their moral education; it was manly, hence irresistible to romantic young men imbued with notions of medieval chivalry and inordinately sensitive to what was due them. They called for the purification of student combat rather than its elimination. Fraternities that rejected the Mensur never secured the prestige of their more militant competitors.

While Honor imposed delicate tasks on fraternities, Freedom and Fatherland proved troubling to politicians. The authorities of post-Napoleonic Europe, under Metternich's skillful and anxious tutelage, read the radical nationalistic rhetoric of the organized students as a threat not lightly to be ignored. Then events propelled the fraternities into the battlefield of real life. The murky reservoir of philosophical notions provided by exalted lecturers supplied them with manly sounding political notions in which the line from thought to action was straight and short. One of the most seductive alibis for aggression was the conviction, imbibed from favorite professors, that a principled, honorable rebel is entitled to take the law into his own hands and punish the enemies of freedom. The inciters' justification for the release of aggressive impulses was often fairly technical in tone; simplified, it wrought havoc in muddled youthful minds.

At first, the most zealous among the students and their handful of professorial allies remained content with speeches and parades. In October 1817 (the tercentenary of Luther's nailing his theses to a church door in Wittenberg and the fourth anniversary of the decisive allied victory over Napoleon at Leipzig), some five hundred of them launched the much-described Wartburg Festival. It was an orgy of poetry readings, patriotic addresses, nationalist sloganeering, fervent Germanic prayers, and book burning, a heady collective initiation into politics, unprecedented in Germany's fragmented lands.[26] Its principal result was the plan for a national and nationalistic cartel of student fraternities. It was founded at Jena precisely a year later.

The defenders of order found all this very ominous, savoring of a demagogic conspiracy to subvert the legitimate authority so painfully restored after two decades of revolutionary upheaval. An isolated murder, an appalling exemplar of what anarchists would later call propaganda of the deed, gave new, stronger grounds for anxiety. In March 1819, the theology student Karl Ludwig Sand stabbed to death the playwright and editor August Friedrich von Kotzebue, melodramatically dispatching him as a "traitor to the Fatherland." It was no secret that Kotzebue, a vituperative polemicist against nationalistic and democratic ideas, had been supplying the Russian government with information about radical students; he was the perfect victim on whom to practice the notion that the end sanctifies the means. It was more than a linguistic accident that the *Burschenschaft* with whose aims Sand identified himself called itself the *Unbedingten*—the "Unconditionals." Such commitment was death, almost literally, on pity or compromise. Beheaded before a sympathetic, even hysterical crowd, Sand was rapidly promoted into a martyr to the cause for which he had sacrificed his life. His fatal gesture was forgotten in what was hailed as the piety and justice of his intentions.* The purity of his conviction, one theologian told Sand's mother, wiped out the crime. Antinomianism, the privileged ideology of a few publicists and their impulsive youthful admirers, was proving contagious.

The repressive Karlsbad Decrees that the confederated German states issued late in 1819 on the urging of Metternich encapsulated the response of nervous rulers intent on preserving what wild idealists seemed bent on destroying. A savage press law stifled political criticism and crippled the voicing of questionable opinions; a commission empowered to investigate subversive activities went into action; professors suspected of stirring up labile students and fostering unwelcome modern notions were dismissed or transferred. The *Burschenschaften* were dissolved; so were the *Corps*. The revolt of the young had provoked the furious response of the old; aggression, even the intimation of aggression, was energetically repressed by counteraggression. For more than two decades, at least until Friedrich Wilhelm IV ascended the Prussian throne in 1840, fraternities of all descriptions vegetated as more or less innocuous drinking societies or carried on some of their old political debates, their drinking—and their duels— in clandestine hideouts, shadowed by persistent, thoroughly realistic worries about detection and its possible consequences.

The University of Göttingen of the mid-1820s, Heine's time there, is a case in point. It boasted no fewer than seventeen secret "clubs" that practiced duelling as though the Karlsbad Decrees had never been. On occasion, the authorities chose to notice: in 1821, Heine himself was banished from the university for half a year for a duel. In his *Harzreise,* a witty compound of travel report and nostalgic reminiscence, he recalled a chance encounter with some Göttingen students; their dinner talk began "as usual" with "duels, duels, and again duels."[27]

Eduard Wedekind, later a liberal lawyer and politician, Heine's close friend

---

*In a nostalgic gesture redolent with unconscious irony, the executioner built a garden house with the remains of Sand's scaffold, a secluded place where members of suppressed fraternities would later meet.

during his Göttingen years, filled his diaries with circumstantial reports of drunken excesses, nasty challenges, and collective bouts. "The previous semester," he noted in April 1824, "was extremely stormy here; not only many duels, as never before, but also very dangerous ones." One duellist "even had his nose hacked off." A number of these Mensuren were fought with the wicked crooked saber, without protective gear, and even without provocation. When the university authorities explicitly threatened to suspend anyone caught fighting under these conditions, Wedekind reported, duelling continued with heavier precautions and less lethal weaponry. Though he was a sensitive poet and diligent reader, Wedekind's primary concern seems to have been the "scandals" that had to be settled by means of a Mensur, fought in remote spots to escape the vigilance of the alert beadles. He had no reservations about the sport itself: "Our duellists are all devilishly courageous." One of his acquaintances had been a student at Jena, where he had had the "misfortune" to kill a doughty fighter from Heidelberg, "which he took very much to heart." Wedekind added ingenuously that "the killer is a very nice fellow." At moments he showed traces of anxiety, but what apparently worried him more than the possibly crippling or lethal outcome of a Mensur was the expense—the fees one had to pay once sentenced to the *Karzer,* that more or less comfortable student jail, and the bill of the physician who stitched up the combatants and was obviously entitled to payment more substantial than that of a mere medical student.[28]

In a handful of German states, notably Bavaria, the most combative of duelling fraternities could count on the protection of the ruling prince, but other states, notably powerful and worried Prussia, enforced the Karlsbad Decrees with pedantic, at times imaginative conscientiousness. A few quixotic outbursts of political activism on the part of students and professors, brave but wholly pointless, would bring efficient prosecution and draconian sentences. Police spies, university authorities, and government officials effectively frustrated whatever political aspirations a student might harbor. But even they could not wholly check duelling. The boldest spirits continued to find ways to fight, persuaded that their fraternities were schools of patriotism, or simply unprepared to tone down their exuberance. Their pugnacious style easily survived the challenge of progressive students who, in the mid-1840s, gained some following with their call for the complete abolition of the duel. The Mensur remained irrepressible.

It would survive decades of political vicissitudes in the German lands. In March 1848, in the wake of the February Revolution in France, revolutionary outbreaks swept across many German states, including Prussia; earnest proposals for a united Germany under a constitutional ruler occupied debaters for at least another year before failing pathetically. But during all the decades of political prudence and victorious reaction that followed, old fraternities flourished and new ones were spawned. The fraternities, and the Mensur, survived too the founding of a united German Reich in 1871. Yet German student life from 1848 to the outbreak of the First World War became a spectacle of increasing complexity and rapid change. Tradition-bound *Corps* and *Burschenschaften* were forced to compete with brash new associations. Students' fraternal orders were beset by financial crises and ideological disputes, responding to cultural needs and political imperatives.

After the creation of the Reich, the most divisive issue was the question of anti-Semitism; the endemic anti-Jewish bias of earlier days had rarely claimed the status of a principle or of racist conviction that it now acquired. But increasingly the most bigoted fraternity members found Jews unworthy of settling disputes of honor by means of the duel; they regarded them as incapable of giving "satisfaction"—*satisfaktionsunfähig*. Some fraternities did accept Jews as members: Theodor Herzl, thoroughly assimilated and not yet committed to Zionism, practiced and duelled four hours a day as a member of the Burschenschaft Albia at Vienna, until an anti-Semitic incident drove him to resign. Other Jewish students responded to social anti-Semitism by founding fraternities of their own. Like their gentile counterparts, they quarreled over matters of principle; toward the end of the nineteenth century, with the birth of Zionism, these splits became incurable. And, emulating the very fellow students they found most objectionable, many of the Jewish fraternities, bourgeois all of them, declared themselves in favor of the Mensur.[29]

Some Jewish students, then, demanded—and got—satisfaction. A cartoon in *Simplicissimus* in 1898, a classic in the satirical weekly's vicious style, makes cruel fun of German Jews awkwardly adapting to the duelling culture. The scene is the living room of an evidently prosperous family. Its inhabitants—father, mother, son—are unmistakably Jews; their unathletic build and hooked noses attest to that. Over the sofa, crossed foils hung with ribbons are mute witnesses that the son of the house belongs to a duelling fraternity. The miserable owner of the weapons slouches on the sofa, holding his mother's hand. His head and his nose are heavily bandaged; he has obviously received some solid hits. The mother, in a German tinged with Yiddish, is trying to soothe the head of the household, who is angrily pacing up and down: "Now stop scolding and grumbling, Löb Baruch. A Mensur is an affair of honor, and you don't know anything about that. That's not your line of trade."[30]

More seriously, the need to prove their courage, a quality that anti-Semites steadfastly denied them, drove Jewish students to espouse the Mensur with uncommon conviction, just as it produced a remarkable number of tough

Jewish boxers.* In 1886, in a manifesto addressed to their fellows at the University of Breslau, a group of Jewish medical students explicitly called for "physical training" to enable Jews to display valor. "We have to fight with all our energy against the odium of cowardice and weakness which is cast on us. We want to show that every member of our association is equal to every Christian fellow student in any physical exercise and chivalry." In 1904, a Jewish student was four times as likely to be involved in a duel as his gentile counterpart.[31] A *Schmiss* on the face of a Jewish student had particular poignancy: the scar was a symptom of defense, a proof of bravery, an assertion of equal status and manly self-respect.

In short, despite all the anti-duelling regulations on the books and all the earnest anti-duelling polemics, the Mensur remained a popular, and always the most spectacular, form for student aggressions. Its conventions and rituals changed, but by mid-century all its regulations were in place. Feudal violence had survived into disciplined modern Germany; good German bourgeois, at least many upper-class bourgeois, had adopted with a will an aristocratic alibi for aggression. It was not damaged by the fact that its feudal pretensions were inauthentic in the extreme, and that the forms of knightly honorable conduct mattered far more than its substance.[32] The *Schmisse,* for whose sake presumably well-bred young men endured nights of sweating anticipation, torments of fear lest they show fear, and painful, often disfiguring episodes, were, for most of the nineteenth century, outward badges of outward show. They were, whatever else they might be, emblems of aggression indulged, witnessed, suffered. For what real purpose?

As usual, pure cynicism like Max Weber's illuminates only fragments of the matter. Adolf Kussmaul, typical in this respect of many Germans recording memories of their "student knighthood," sprinkled his autobiography with the names of the good friends he had made during his university years; bourgeois nearly all of them, they had gone on to become physicians, scientists, and government officials, and proved themselves men of real merit and deserved

*There is abundant anecdotal evidence that Jews duelled bravely and skillfully. One of these was Carl Koller, famous for his discovery of cocaine as an anesthetic. In 1885, a young physician and lieutenant in the reserves, he became involved in an altercation with another physician, also a lieutenant, over the treatment of a patient in the emergency ward. The latter called Koller a "Jewish swine," whereupon Koller boxed his ears. The necessary outcome: a duel with foils, to continue until one of the combatants was unable to go on. Koller wounded his antagonist. Among the many letters of congratulation he received was one from his friend Freud. See Hortense Koller Becker, " 'Coca Koller': Carl Koller's Discovery of Local Anesthesia," *Psychoanalytic Quarterly,* XXXII (1963), 300–73.

eminence. In their *Corps* and their *Burschenschaften,* the sons of bourgeois jostled up against the sons of landed aristocrats and enjoyed—at least some of them did—a sense of intimacy and equality.

In fact, reminiscences both published and unpublished, and the university novel, at once sentimental in tone and photographic in portraiture, strongly suggest that the principal attraction of student associations was fraternity in its widest, most deeply emotional connotation. Offering fellowship and occasions for communal regression, the *Corps* and the *Burschenschaften* functioned as antidotes to adolescent anxiety, loneliness, often fearful isolation, and a relief from studies perceived as arid and repetitious drill. The distinguished philosopher and pedagogue Friedrich Paulsen recalled that in the early 1860s he had joined a fraternity at Erlangen from a variety of rather indistinct motives: "A vague notion that the *Burschenschaft* stood for Germany's unity and grandeur, combined with the feeling of the emptiness of existence." Companionship was easygoing and without particular content; there was little heavy drinking, much stress on studying—"one was proud of those who made a place for themselves"—and a good deal of jocular, somewhat primitive *Gemütlichkeit.* Paulsen dutifully practiced his fencing every day, and found the weekly *Mensuren* "an exciting diversion." He fought only three times, without giving outstanding performances, but also, very much like Jerome later, "not without a certain susceptibility to the allure of the bloody game."[33] For Paulsen, duelling was not a thrill to be enjoyed and remembered for its own sake; rather, it served his pressing need for fellowship. Like many others, he saw fraternal life as a kind of rescue operation, a substitute for the home he had lost.

In the golden glow of recollection, student days, very much including the *Mensur,* were transfigured into an irretrievable time of pure glory, the very summit of life. This idealization was anything but forced. The generous support that Old Boys poured out to enable their sons to repeat the experience testifies to that. They enthusiastically swallowed histories of their fraternity, faithfully subscribed to its magazine, dressed up in its colors for long-drawn-out sentimental reunions, and surrounded themselves at home with engravings and memorabilia recalling their drinking bouts, torchlight parades—and fencing exploits. These Old Boys were the most gullible customers in the nostalgia market.

But all their sincere tributes to long-vanished years, enjoyed in tranquil, sometimes tearful retrospect, leaned heavily on the work of repression. Authoritative accounts, and the rare candid autobiography, show students facing recurrent crises with nail-biting nervousness or tremulous bravado. They had much to worry about: final examinations, the wrath of parents confronted with extravagant bills from boot makers or liquor dealers, and the ever-present threat of a paternity suit from a wronged local beauty. Nor was the Mensur the unambiguous pleasure it came to seem through the haze of memories. Only the strongest, most adept, or most suicidal truly enjoyed the fighting all the way. Stilpe, the protagonist of a satirical novel by Otto Julius Bierbaum, says of his university days, "Sometimes there are Mensuren. I won't deny that this little agitation amuses me. If you drink five cognacs beforehand, you become astonishingly valiant and heroic and let them split your skull." After a little more experience, Stilpe conscientiously amends his recipe. "My saber Mensur," he confesses, "was not really first class. I had overestimated the cognac. One must definitely have port wine to hand." Proffered with Bierbaum's characteristic light touch, this describes a prevalent method of acquiring—temporarily—some necessary boldness.[34]

Even novels unashamedly celebrating fraternity life acknowledge the anxiety. Walter Bloem's *Der krasse Fuchs* shows Werner Achenbach, the hero, anticipating his first ordeal with an inquisitive, almost voyeuristic jubilation in his heart. At the Mensur itself, however, all turns dark before his eyes, and he has to force himself not to vomit.[35] Such fictional accounts are faithful representations of all-too-familiar experiences, deeply felt and in general quickly repressed. They explain why alcohol was so often called to the rescue. Even Gregor Samarow's *Die Saxoborussen*—a novel about the most exclusive Heidelberg *Corps,* possibly more adulatory still than Bloem's exercise in prettifying memories—has the hero's closest friend prescribe the remedy of spirits. "Drink a glass of water with cognac," he quietly implores as he bandages his friend's arm in preparation for the Mensur and sees him turn pale, "it will strengthen and warm you."[36] In the end the hero determines to rely on will power alone, but alcohol was freely available to those who did not quite trust themselves to perform with the required stylish stoicism the counterpart to aggression unleashed.

Official histories, apologists, and university fiction dwell with demonstrative coolness on duels in which lips are cut through and cheeks are slashed for several inches, ear lobes hit the sanded arena and blood gushes until the hapless, happy duellist is virtually covered with it. But behind this cultivated, carefully acquired *savoir-faire* lurks a kind of intoxicated joy, a sadistic urge escaping repression mixed with naked anxiety. Perhaps, as Bierbaum drily put it, one got used to this sort of performance as a poodle gets used to being bathed.[37] But for many duelling students, especially before their sanguinary bath became routine, the lust for robust action was tempered, often outweighed, by the sheer barbarity of the proceedings, to say nothing of the fear of pain and the fantasies of mutilation. This is what made the warm sentiment of fraternity so indispensable: it gave the youthful duellist, saber in hand, the sense that he was not alone, and that others had survived the ordeal.

No wonder these intimate associations of like-minded young men sharing memorable moments of excitement and embarrassment provided the sturdy foundation for lifelong friendships and uncritical backward glances. There was nothing clandestine about these adolescent affections: fraternity periodicals, *Corps* reunions, and, once again, the fiction depicting student life, made much of these manly attachments. Consider Werner Achenbach once more. He takes pity on a much admired *Corps* brother, Klausner, who, though he has been consistently brave and faultless in battle, has fought one unlucky Mensur and is suspended from all honorable posts in his fraternity for two weeks. Visiting the profoundly humiliated Klausner, Achenbach finds him resigned to his fate, even though he had respectworthy reasons for his failure; he had got engaged to be married the night before, and his mind was not on combat. Bloem does not dwell on the irony of Klausner's situation: one powerful motive for heroism in the duel was to win the woman of one's dreams, yet precisely in dreaming on love, Klausner has forfeited honor, even if only temporarily. A willing, submissive victim, he insists that he had no excuse; one must accept the judgment of one's peers as one accepts the verdict of a court.

Klausner, in short, is no rebel; he has no quarrel with the system, though he recognizes its unjust and cruel side. But his resignation only intensifies Achenbach's regard. As the two students talk with increasing intimacy about fraternity life and their youthful infatuations, their rapport blossoms. "And as the youths looked into each other's eyes when they said farewell, the smooth bark of the *Corps* student's customary constraint loosened itself in their young-young hearts. Suddenly they were in one another's arms." This sentimental moment flusters them, but only slightly. Both men, Bloem does not mind writing, felt warm and strong in their hearts: "They had become something better in that hour than brother *Corpsmen*. They had become brothers."[38]

To gauge the prevalence of overt homosexuality among German students is impossible, and it is pointless to try, but certainly the kind of fervent mutual identification Bloem depicts with such innocent pathos left visible traces on many lives. In the world of the student fighting his Mensur, women figured only as tender and pallid worriers and as elusive prizes, objects of longing fantasies. The ideal of premarital chastity, to which a number of fraternities explicitly subscribed, only tightened the passionate hold of adolescent males on one another. Crushes, the novelists and psychologists of the age firmly insisted, were for girls alone. But there was a good deal of the crush in the shy, inarticulate adulation that many a first-year postulant felt for the senior *Bursche* whom he served only too gladly—that forceful leader of men, so accomplished in reciting the commands at ritual drinking bouts, so adept at handling his weapon at the Mensur, so splendidly brusque with the wide-eyed *Fuchs* who eagerly ran his errands, carried his sword to the duelling ground, and only wanted, some distant day, to become like his ideal.

While the adolescent fantasy of manliness, the virile self-display of fighting young animals in the presence, and for the gratification, of their peers, informed the duellist's erotic economy, a more adult love loomed in the distance. By the late nineteenth century, a small but emphatic literature insisted that the true nature of the Mensur was biological: it was an elaborate mating dance, with the maturing male preening in excited search of a female. According to this view, the women were, so to speak, militant by proxy; they fully approved of their men's resort to arms to settle questions of honor. William James was only echoing a current commonplace when he declared that "the woman loves the man the stormier he shows himself."[39] Fiction about the Mensur—the evidence from real life is skimpy in the extreme—is full of young women praying for their brave, honorable fighting suitor as they wait, hands twisting a tear-stained handkerchief, at home.

Some Teutonic maidens appear to have had a special taste for this controlled mayhem, reserving their love for those who excelled in it. Jerome calmly reported the popularity of the man with a *Schmiss* among eligible young ladies. And in his novel *Stilpe,* Bierbaum playfully confirmed the association of mutilation with love. "Recently a youth fought with our chosen weapon," says Stilpe. "He was terribly frightened, but would not let himself be turned away," battling on until he had received a hit in the face that would leave a scar. "Later he confessed to me that he had fought 'for love.' " Had his opponent, Stilpe suavely inquires, dared to lay a hand on his fiancée? " 'Oh, no,' he said, 'my fiancée only wants me to have a good-looking *Schmiss*.' " Bierbaum comments, invoking mythical German heroines and romantic German forests, "That is how heroically the daughters of Thusnelda are inclined. Don't you hear the rustling of the oak forest?" The best thing about the Mensur, Bierbaum has Stilpe say, "is the smell, the most delightful mixture of iodoform, phenol, cognac, and a little sweat. It works on me like an aphrodisiac. But it is possible that I am a little perverted. Bloodthirstiness and lust! Give me your heart to guzzle, Laura! I love you."[40] In the Mensur, the most fundamental drives were indissolubly intertwined in-all-too human contradictions: the scar, in all other contexts a sign of failure, became the passport to success; aggression stimulated love, and love, aggression.

This was a characteristic adolescent compound. And even the apologists for fraternity life acknowledged that the Mensur was a noble, if painful, ingredient in the student's preparation for a wider world. No less an authority than Kaiser Wilhelm II was sure that *Corps* life stamped each member with its spirit forever by "steeling his strength and courage." The duel, he maintained, had been

widely misunderstood; it was the modern counterpart of the medieval tournament, "inculcating the degrees of fortitude necessary in the outside world."
The controversial literature, far more furious and vituperative, made the same
point over and over. "I have witnessed many student duels in my life," exclaimed one polemicist, Heinrich Rosenberg, in a pamphlet directed against a
Franz Josef Egenter, who had dared to question their pedagogic and moral
value, "but the duellists that Herr Egenter depicts I have never seen at a Mensur. Those I have seen were happy, healthy, honest young people, who measured their dexterity at arms with one another, without any further rancor.
They did not confront each other with murderously glittering, bloodthirsty
eyes; they took their places with a jest and when the whole thing was over, it
was all forgotten."[41] The *Akademische Monatshefte,* the official organ of the
Corps, naturally agreed that the duelling corporations gave young men the true
direction and the best education for life. One could hardly expect them to say
anything else, but their boast was widely credited. Nor was it wholly absurd.
There must have been troubled and fearful adolescents who managed to fight
down crippling anxieties by exposing themselves to the real but circumscribed
risks of the Mensur. Defying their fears by seeking out the situation that most
frightened them, they found that in the right setting, counterphobic conduct
can pay rich dividends.

For centuries, men had fought duels to erase an insult to their honor, but the
insult provoking a Mensur all too often was a purely formal pretext. Students
did not duel to avenge a slight; rather, they sought—or manufactured—a slight
in order to duel. The Mensur seemed the proper way of allowing the untried
young man to stand tall among his fellows; as schoolboys might engage in
pissing contests or, when they got older, in competitive masturbation, so many
students found it essential to fight in order to be seen as virile, as stoical, as
enterprising. Klausner tells Achenbach, "Look, for us *Corps* students, the Mensur is not a sport, a play with weapons," but an "educational tool." The student,
saber in hand, is "supposed to prove that he is indifferent to bodily pain,
disfigurement, even serious wounds or death." And Klausner proves his point,
soberly, without boasting, at the Mensur he fights to reclaim his good name, in
the presence of his closest associates.[42] The most shameful thing a duellist could
do was to retreat; to turn tail—*kneifen*—invariably generated universal contempt. Nothing could be more adolescent than this effort to seek identity with
one's fellows as the royal road to acceptance and stature.

Adolescence, certainly in modern middle-class culture, is a tempestuous
time, exciting and excited. It is a time for testing and experimentation, a time
that replays childhood dramas and revives childhood passions. The sexual and
aggressive feelings that the child has been taught to regard as improper and

wicked, feelings pushed out of awareness, now return, almost literally with a vengeance. Expressive behavior, awkward, violent, often irrational, directed against everyone including oneself, seems less a choice than a fate. Physiological maturation allows fantasies of sexual triumphs to turn from futile and vague dreams into precise and accessible possibilities. The same holds true of aggression: rebellion against parental authority, impossible, almost unthinkable, in one's early years, now appears in the adolescent's grasp. But grandiose vistas of omnipotence and mastery are shadowed by the frightening nightmare of fiasco. Hence the adolescent's new powers become a source of conflicts and anxieties, as the desire to retain childish love objects stubbornly confronts the desire to discard them, and aggression is woven into the texture of burgeoning sexual fantasies. Homoerotic attachments, the notorious crushes to which the pubertal youth is susceptible, do more than yield erotic pleasure; they serve as a safe haven from the pressures and perils of adult love for women.[43]

The adolescent, then, is enmeshed in unsettling conflicts. Hence that extravagant oscillation of moods and the no less extravagant mixture of defiance and conformity that stamp so much behavior at this time. For the adolescent, the appetite for victory in the oedipal battle, reappearing in new and more urgent manifestations, is as dangerous as defeat, perhaps more dangerous. Hence the search for experience is likely to be complicated by a search for punishment, which in extreme cases may end in disguised, or open, suicide.

From this perspective, the Mensur appears to be brilliantly conceived to deal with the ravages of puberty. To be sure, even in Germany, the vast majority of humans, male and female, had to cross the minefield of adolescence without the benefit of a ritual duel. But then, other rites of passage awaited them, in school, in the family, in the streets. And many of these rites, whether ingeniously devised ordeals or coarse hazing, were exercises in exquisite cruelty visited on the aspirant to adulthood, justified in the eyes of those who administered them as necessary steps across the threshold to maturity. Yet the Mensur combined prohibitions and permissions, punishments and rewards, suffering and pleasure, with peculiar felicity. It provided ceremonials for establishing manliness, tests and substitutes for sexual prowess, and, with its obsessively prescribed rules of procedure, a dependable framework within which youths could master the aggressive feelings that swamped them. Better still, the Mensur inflicted enough pain to gratify the most exacting superego.

In short, furnishing an arena for the simultaneous assertion of autonomy and dependency, the Mensur gave sons who battled for their colors the chance to gratify and at the same time defy their fathers. Preparing for respectable careers and voicing patriotic sentiments that closely followed paternal practices and ideals, the *Burschenschaftler* proved a most pliant, conventional rebel. He was a bourgeois incarnate, sowing his wild oats to prescription and with an eye to later safety. It is surely no accident that Social Democrats critical of the German *Bürger* should characterize him as retarded and should see the Mensur, justly enough, as a political institution (or, better, an introduction to a political posture) that permitted aristocratic pretensions in an increasingly democratic age. The Mensur was the codification of adolescence; it was one way—not the only, or the best—for certain nineteenth-century bourgeois to regulate their aggressions. It was scarcely a prescription for personal or political maturity. More than most social arrangements disciplining pugnacity, the Mensur was a living paradox, and one immensely instructive in the contradictory ways of cultivating hatred. Devised to fence in the spirit of aggressiveness, it also fostered that spirit: it controlled violence and canonized it.

⮞ ONE ⮜

Alibis

Every culture, every class, every century, constructs its distinctive alibis for aggression. And each of these defensive stratagems has its history. Most are sheer replicas of time-honored rationalizations, or subtle variations on them; only a handful ever manage to be truly innovative. The Victorians, too, seeking respectable excuses for hitting out in word and act, borrowed much and originated little; several of their principal justifications for freedom from constraint had a long, if not always honored past. Still, what the nineteenth-century bourgeoisie added to, or amended in, traditional reasons why certain pugnacious activities are appropriate, ethical, even commanded by nature, amounts to a recognizable cultural style. Hence an atmosphere compounded of familiarity and novelty pervades the alibis for aggression on which Victorians liked to rely.

The prehistory of these nineteenth-century rationales is in fact extremely diverse. Of the three singled out here—there are, of course, others—the first, the case for competition, spread out from a modern biological theory to pervade the economic, political, literary, even private life of the Victorian decades; the second, the construction of the convenient Other, was a compound of relatively recent pseudoscientific "discoveries" and habitual agreeable prejudices; the third, the cult of manliness, was a nineteenth-century adaptation of the aristocratic ideal of prowess. Varied as this menu of self-justification proved to be, all provided collective identifications, serving as gestures of integration and, with that, of exclusion. By gathering up communities of insiders, they revealed—only too often invented—a world of strangers beyond the pale, individuals and classes, races and nations, it was perfectly proper to contradict, patronize, ridicule, bully, exploit, or exterminate. All three rationales had the same effect; they cultivated hatred, in both senses of the term: they at once fostered and restrained it, by providing respectable pleas for its candid exercise while at the same time compelling it to flow within carefully staked out channels of approval.

Just what sort of community such alibis for aggression create and cement must obviously vary with time, place, opportunity, and the competing pressures of particular interests. Nor do they always point in the same direction; especially in moments when social or international tensions are becoming acute, one alibi is likely to contradict its rivals, or uneasily coexist with them. Which one prevails depends on which identification—religious, racial, regional, economic, or cultural—wins the battle of divided loyalties. The nineteenth-century family of alibis for aggression was rarely free of internal discord and, often enough, open to doubts.

Nor were these rationales etched in stone. A patriot might discover pacifism in the midst of war, an anti-Semite astonish himself by learning to value his Jewish acquaintances. It is precisely their mobility that makes these alibis valuable clues to the murky, largely unconscious domain of intimate human needs and anxieties. All constituted licenses to unleash feelings of aggression, but they arose from, and were fed by, widely dispersed subterranean reservoirs and found the most differentiated public expression. Some began as propaganda evolved by a governing elite or self-serving ideologies to justify greed, sadism, or racial bigotry. Others rested on what was considered the most scientific information available. Still others were adaptive convictions; the old saying that not all of a paranoid's enemies are necessarily imaginary applied in the nineteenth century. However egotistical the permissions the Victorians gave themselves for indulging in pugnacity, at least a few of them were rational responses to social disorder, religious parochialism, or political chicanery. Valid generalizations from experience, they could, in culture as in a court of law, withstand the most clear-eyed and skeptical scrutiny. Reasonable or tendentious, they could be something better than a cynical excuse for doing something selfish or nasty that one found profitable.

This diversity only serves to complicate the understanding of nineteenth-century bourgeois culture. To complicate it still more, the alibis developed to make the Victorians feel comfortable made many of them feel exceedingly uncomfortable at times. Most forcefully in their century, with the exigent bourgeois conscience holding an impressive array of temptations to vehemence in check, some alibis became sources not of self-satisfaction but of self-laceration. Many among the most energetic bourgeois—perhaps not John D. Rockefeller or Andrew Carnegie, but others—found their schemes for unfettered activity inhibited, at times lamed, by their censorious superego. The Victorians knew this: by the turn of the century, it had become a platitude that aggression against others seemed to be turning into aggression against the self. Beatrice Webb observed that she was living in a time when "men of intellect and men of property" had developed "a new consciousness of sin," a "collective or class consciousness" about obligations to those less fortunate than themselves. No doubt George Bernard Shaw was exaggerating in his patented manner when he looked back in 1912 to recall that "the great conversions of the XIX century were not convictions of individual, but of social sin. The first half of the XIX century considered itself the greatest of all centuries. The second discovered that it was the wickedest of all the centuries."[1] In actuality, the contrast was not quite so sharp; permission for the acting out of aggressive impulses had been withheld more and more since the Renaissance. Certainly by 1800, the stern call for self-control, especially among the respectable middling orders of society, was stringent indeed. In 1858, more than fifty years before Shaw's pronouncement, the brilliant English man of letters Walter Bagehot could observe that "the unfeeling obtuseness of the early part of this century was to be corrected by an extreme, perhaps an excessive, sensibility to human suffering in the years which have followed."[2] The point was that many of Bagehot's contemporaries did not think their sensibility excessive, and translated inchoate self-reproach into private philanthropy, campaigns to organize social services, or crusades for political reform.

There is no need to be sentimental about the pathos of nineteenth-century bourgeois inner life. The age was, as its critics charged with ample evidence, hospitable to cold-blooded merchants, callous manufacturers, indolent bureaucrats, corrupt politicians, and uncharitable administrators of charities. But thoughtful, edgy bourgeois were increasingly troubled during the Victorian decades by whether it was fair to keep those who worked with their hands docile and ignorant, the better to facilitate the pursuit of entrepreneurial profits, and whether it was fair to keep excluding small property holders or respectable workingmen from the privileges of citizenship. Devout Christians intent on spreading literacy to enable everyone to read the Bible found somewhat incongruous allies among secular reformers equally bent on the same program with the very different aim of admitting members of responsible but disfranchised classes to the political public.

Facing a muddled present and an uncertain future, then, Victorians everywhere engaged in prolonged, emotional, normally inconclusive, and often fascinating disputes on every issue touching on aggression. As the combative language of controversy attests, the age took its conflicts seriously, and some of the most interesting among them were over the question of whether the bellicosity that one alibi or another legitimized was really necessary or justifiable. The very titles of polemical writings, especially in the touchy domain of religion, hint at struggles to the death; witness Andrew Dickson White's uncompromising *History of the Warfare between Religion and Science* and John William Draper's no less uncompromising *History of the Conflict between Religion and Science*. And the most excited participants in nineteenth-century debates, whether over religion or other controversial issues, felt entitled to treat their adversaries as worse than merely lost sheep: Dissenters fighting Anglicans, Protestants fighting Catholics, Orthodox Jews fighting Reform Jews, unbelievers fighting believers, all invoked without any qualms their favorite alibis for aggression. Still, they had to face those with more pacific opinions, mediators and skeptics and compromisers who were made uneasy by all this heat and who suspected most justifications of hatred to be mere self-serving rationalizations.

Indeed, none of the favorite nineteenth-century rationales for aggression was without its detractors; the attempts to resolve conflicts within each contentious camp generated further conflicts, new acts of aggression. Parties formed, as nineteenth-century bourgeois battled over the justifications for corporal and capital punishment, the tactics permissible in politics in a century of democratization, the right of women to effective self-assertion in the home and in the world, the legitimate limits to the knife thrusts of humor, the most effective method for diverting free-floating pugilistic impulses into socially profitable energies. Even pacifists showed themselves to be aggressive in behalf of peace, thus further enriching the explosive mixture of a culture at war with itself. To be sure, certain viewpoints dominated bourgeois culture in the nineteenth century, but all were contested; everything—well, nearly everything—was open.

I. The Apotheosis of Conflict

It was a striking feature of nineteenth-century culture that influential justifications for aggression relied on what their partisans advertised as scientific proof. The alibi that conflict is necessary and desirable greatly benefited from such claims. Its apologists proudly asserted that the case for untrammeled competition, whether in the economic, the social, or the military domain, was susceptible of demonstration. To be sure, the pleaders for racism also appealed to science. So, less plausibly, did defenders of the manly ideal, despite all the aroma of medieval romance and instinctual urges emanating from it. But Victorian champions of conflict had weighty scholarly testimony on their side, especially after 1859, when Charles Darwin published his *Origin of Species*. This master-

piece proved even more unsettling than he had expected, thanks in part to the
support that enthusiastic followers brought to the debate. Extravagant and
sometimes unscrupulous polemicists, determined to kidnap Darwin's biological
theories for use in their political nostrums, perched as it were on the shoulders
of the most celebrated and most controversial scientist that the Victorian century produced. By the 1880s they were generally known by the capacious and
oversimplified title "Social Darwinists."

Presumably scientific arguments in behalf of conflict were part of a more
comprehensive strategy. Anti-feminists intent on reserving public aggressiveness for men by barring women from colleges and universities insisted that they
were not being self-serving defenders of venerable male privileges, but were
acting on medical information. After all, women's brains are demonstrably
smaller than men's; adult women bleed once a month, thus incapacitating
themselves for strenuous intellectual work.

The appreciation of rivalry in human affairs, whether as a positive force or an
inescapable doom, reaches of course back to antiquity. Justifications of egotistical self-assertiveness found much potent support late in the century in Darwin,
but there was nothing new about the proposition that life is a perpetual struggle
to the death, in which the strongest and best survive. Tennyson's terrifying,
much-quoted line from *In Memoriam* about "Nature, red in tooth and claw"
had struck many a responsive chord. That poem was published in 1850. Two
years earlier, in the *Communist Manifesto,* Karl Marx and Friedrich Engels had
tersely announced that conflict pervaded all human society, past and present.
All history, the two proclaimed in ringing tones, is the history of class struggles.*

For centuries in fact, it had been a commonplace that, the Book of Ecclesias-
tes to the contrary, the race *is* to the swift and the battle to the strong. Thomas
Hobbes's savage portrayal of life in the state of nature as solitary, poor, nasty,
brutish, and short was blunt in the extreme, but however subversive Hobbes's
political thought, his assertion that humans are one another's natural enemies
surprised or offended few in the seventeenth century. More than a hundred
years later Adam Smith, seeking to dismantle mercantilistic paternalism, endorsed competition as an eminently constructive social force. It "can never hurt
either the consumer," he asserted stoutly, "or the producer."[1] His much-
quoted conceit of the invisible hand, intended to prove the social usefulness of
selfish activity, could be interpreted as removing the sting of immorality from

---

*It is well attested that Marx proposed to dedicate the first volume of *Kapital* to Darwin as a
token of his admiration; Darwin's name does not appear on the dedication page only because he
politely declined the honor.

the ruthless fight for one's place in the economic sun. A careful reading of his classic *Wealth of Nations* reveals that Smith assigned to the state indispensable regulatory functions, but nineteenth-century ideologues converted him into the icon of free competition and played down his humane philosophy.

When, on the threshold of the nineteenth century, Thomas Malthus proffered his appalling predictions for mankind, his readers found them shocking principally because of the mathematical form into which he had cast them. The irresistible sexual urge, Malthus reasoned, compels populations to multiply at a geometric rate, and since the food supply can grow only at an arithmetical rate, their numbers inevitably outrun that supply. At the other extreme from the high-flying theories of progress that Enlightenment enthusiasts like Condorcet had advanced, Malthus's gloom read like a responsible return to despair after a brief season of irrational hope. His pessimism was no innovation. "That the first want of man is his dinner, and the second his girl," John Adams noted caustically in 1814, "were truths well known to every democrat and aristocrat, long before the great philosopher Malthus arose, to think he enlightened the world by the discovery."[2] It was Malthus's pseudoscience, not his glum outlook, that was new.

Malthus diluted his original forecast in later editions of *On Population,* granting that "moral restraint"—late marriage and sexual abstemiousness—might reduce population pressure on available subsistence. But he kept the specter of overpopulation and its horrific consequences alive and lent it portentous authority over much of the nineteenth century. If he was correct, any attempt by the state or private philanthropy to relieve misery—and thus to check potential aggression—must be futile. There was every likelihood that humans would continue to fight over scarce resources and eventually find themselves decimated by poverty, disease, and war.

Hopeful social engineers, to be sure, rejected, or at least smoothed down, the sharp contours of such bleak prognoses. Herbert Spencer, widely considered an oracle of ruthless evolution, explicitly took issue with Hobbes for exaggerating human wickedness and egotism.[3] Still, as the nineteenth century went on and skepticism about the soothing, healing message of Christianity spread, there seemed to be nothing beyond a nature hostile or at least supremely indifferent to humankind. The vision of the world as a battleground, a blood-spattered arena fit only for gladiators, enjoyed general currency long before Darwin and his devotees had written a line. It was in his boyhood, around 1840, that James Fitzjames Stephen, publicist, judge, historian of the English law, and principled conservative, awoke to the truth that man is a combative animal. Eton, with its violence, he recalled, "taught me for life the lesson that to be weak is to be wretched, that the state of nature is a state of war, and *Vae Victis* the great law of nature."[4] He did not need Darwin to learn this lesson. The difference was that with the spread of Social Darwinist notions, apologists for aggressiveness would propound such views with unshakable confidence.

The century, then, did not have to wait for Darwin to find its scientist of strife. Herbert Spencer, the most avidly read promoter of competition, was actually not a Darwinian at all. His first book, *Social Statics,* appeared in 1850, almost a decade before Darwin agreed to make his evolutionary theory public; it contained the essential ingredients of what a later generation would ungratefully call Social Darwinism. "Pervading all nature we may see at work a stern discipline, which is a little cruel that it may be very kind," Spencer declared. This "state of universal warfare maintained throughout the lower creation, to the great perplexity of many worthy people, is at bottom the most merciful provision which the circumstances admit of." The destruction of the decrepit and infirm ends their existence before it becomes a burden, and makes room for a younger generation.[5]

Without blinking, Spencer saw the adaptive "purifying process" that eliminates "the sickly, the malformed, and the least fleet or powerful" at work among humans quite as much as in the animal kingdom. He acknowledged that it went against the grain to see an incompetent artisan go hungry, a sickly laborer suffer destitution, widows and orphans left to wrestle for their very lives. But he was undeterred: "When regarded not separately but in connexion with the interests of universal humanity, these harsh fatalities are seen to be full of beneficence—the same beneficence which brings to early graves the children of diseased parents, and singles out the intemperate and the debilitated as the victims of an epidemic." People unable to face these realities were, in Spencer's judgment, "spurious philanthropists."[6]

The leeway such reasoning created for self-centered, aggressive sentiments and actions hardly needs comment. It powerfully insinuated indifference to deprivations and resistance to any attempts at alleviating them. Spencer tersely summed up this doctrine in the facile slogan he coined in 1862, "the survival of the fittest," a slogan that virtually preempted all debate. Indeed, for several decades, across Europe and, far more, in the United States, Spencer's reputation as a "towering intellect" eclipsed that of his contemporaries. Some thought him the greatest living philosopher, perhaps the greatest of all time, at least the equal of Newton.[7] Even Darwin, who disliked Spencer's self-centeredness and spurned his deductive style of argumentation as useless for his own work, warmly admired his gifts.[8] Spencer's numerous and prominent devotees, in their glowing certitude, saw Darwin as merely swimming in his wake.

To call Spencer a Social Darwinist, then, is to deprive him of whatever credit he deserves for popularizing a favorite nineteenth-century alibi for aggression.

This mislabeling seems a fitting irony. Spencer was a philosopher who read very little, a sworn positivist unwilling on principle to examine the other side of any issue. Though a prophet preaching the survival of the fittest, he was a lifelong bachelor and contributed nothing to the propagation of the race. Saddest irony of all, before his death in 1903, despite his apparently solid eminence, his reputation began to fade until he became largely a historical curiosity. Except in the United States, in the arena of contending ideas Spencer's were proving unfit.

But what makes Spencer a representative Victorian of supreme interest is that he was no slave to doctrine, not even his own. However committed to the blessings of competition, he did not deny the need to civilize hatred. As a young man, impatient with religious belief and a devotee of science, he worked out an all-embracing system resting on a few simple tenets—tenets he never substantially modified. Society is an organism, an integrated network of institutions, in perpetual movement toward ever higher differentiation; the elemental tendency of evolution is from simplicity to complexity, from homogeneity to heterogeneity, and, significantly, from egoism to altruism. And the compelling agent of change is natural selection, which guarantees that the fittest survive.

Despite his ardor for the implacable laws he had discovered, Spencer showed himself sanguine about the world. The signs of the times indicated to him that an era was approaching when the shackles of prejudice would be shaken off, when reason and truth rather than feelings and the worship of precedent would become men's guide. Not lacking self-esteem, Spencer was confident that his laws would eventually provide realistic standards for human conduct, enabling it to fit ever more smoothly to cultural needs. The industrial society Spencer saw being born before his eyes would raise individualism to perfection and establish true personal liberty, compatible with the liberty of all. His cheerfulness partially evaporated in his later years, but for much of his life Spencer equated evolution with improvement. "Progress," he wrote in *Social Statics,* is "not an accident, but a necessity."[9]

The program implicit in so sweeping a theory is by its nature mainly negative, with a thoughtful passivity as its paramount lesson: the task of government is to stay the hand of meddling politicians. Intelligent legislators must work to repeal all pseudohumanitarian laws and dismantle all pseudohumanitarian institutions. They must indeed be cruel to be kind. Echoing the natural-rights theorists of earlier generations, Spencer never put his case more plainly than in *Social Statics.* To prevent some from buying beer in order to keep others from getting drunk is to assume that such intervention will do more good than harm, a palpable error of judgment. To tax the incomes of the many to pay for exporting human casualties to the colonies for a second chance is an equally palpable error. The state should refrain from regulating trade with foreign countries, the banking system, public housing, or sanitary conditions. Nor, he suggested ominously, should it try to ameliorate the situation of the poor. Violating natural laws, which is to say Spencer's laws, in the name of compassion must only produce greater misery later.

This is the Spencer everyone quotes, but it is not all of Spencer. Explicitly, vehemently, he objected to the indiscriminate application of his iron-fisted evolutionary laws in domains where they did not belong. As he was aware, his principle that the inferior must be eliminated by the superior appeared to make him an ally of heartless robber barons, even their spokesman. He was unwilling, though, either to evade or to accept moralistic indictments. He had an answer ready to hand: the struggle for existence in advanced cultures only generates an increase in benevolence. Had he not insisted in his first book that "the desire to command is essentially a barbarous desire"?[10] Even though he described himself as a determinist, Spencer saw no inconsistency in defending the utility of private charities: in modern industrial societies compassionate activities are a legitimate aspect of social conduct. What men need is realism without cruelty, a felicitous combination of philanthropic energy with philosophic calm.

This humane side of Spencer, strictly circumscribing his famous alibi for aggressive competition, pervaded his writings through the decades. Benevolence had its innings as early as *Social Statics* and as late as *Facts and Comments,* a gathering of splinters and second thoughts he published in 1902, the year before his death. In these last words, he firmly took his distance from the coarse utilitarianism of rapacious contemporaries: "I detest that conception of social progress which presents as its aim, increase of population, growth of wealth, spread of commerce"; it slights quality for the sake of quantity.[11] Prosperity is not enough. In short the best-known, best-loved advocate of individual liberty and economic competition found some uses for the noble submergence of self in the service of others.

To be sure, in opposing state-sponsored education, Spencer retained his old affection for the law of supply and demand. The lower orders should "get culture for their children as best they may, just as they are left to get food and clothing for them"; for then "the children of the superior will be advantaged: the thrifty parents, the energetic, and those with a high sense of responsibility."[12] Yet—and this lesser-known Spencer is as characteristic as the familiar one—in a long, emotional essay, "Re-Barbarization," he worried over a new primitivism that ran counter to the social evolution that had reined in warlike sentiments and military organization and, with that, produced a welcome growth of freedom. He found the evidence for this development indisputable: the nasty combativeness of contemporary politics and the rebellion of organized churches against civil authorities.

Writing in the midst of the Boer War, Spencer brooded about an unexpected enthusiasm for fighting among patriotic poets, divines, sportsmen, journalists, and members of rifle associations. This fervor struck him as peculiarly unpleasant in that odd religious phenomenon, the Salvation Army. With its very name, its officers, its mottoes, it was spreading "military ideas, military sentiments, military organization, military discipline." The results were in the newspapers daily: the illegal and spiteful violence offered opponents to the Boer War, a violence unchecked by the guardians of the law. England had become "a fit habitat for Hooligans." Spencer found the prospects troubling: "On every side we see the ideas and feelings and institutions appropriate to peaceful life, replaced by those appropriate to fighting life." The chauvinist excitement that fed Englishmen's craving to reduce foreign enemies to abject submission struck him as particularly deplorable. Imperialism, indeed, rests on a delusion. "The exercise of mastery inevitably entails on the master himself some form of slavery, more or less pronounced." This apparent paradox he defended as the simple truth.[13]

These pacific attitudes were not the sentimental eruptions of a fading pedant. Spencer was frequently in the company of reformers; it is often forgotten that in Social Statics, that exemplary statement of his thought, he had eloquently pleaded for the rights of women. In 1882, having finally accepted pressing invitations to the United States, he astonished a railroad executive by preaching to him "the gospel of relaxation." And when he gave a major address at a dinner in New York, he astonished his audience no less by criticizing, after some polite flourishes, the "over-devotion to work" of his hosts. After all, "life is not for learning nor is life for working, but learning and working are for life."[14] He did not want the alibi of competition made into a fetish. His listeners should have expected it; he had long held such views.*

Vintage Spencer this, unfortunately obscured by his sloganeering. It was, after all, typical of him to call consistently for "a higher standard of international justice." Had he not damned the desire to command as barbarous? He was as caustic about chauvinism as he had been about male supremacy and audaciously

---

*Nor should Andrew Carnegie have wondered at Spencer's response to industrial America, supposedly the supreme incarnation of his philosophy. Carnegie had been instrumental in promoting Spencer's visit to the United States, and even lured him to Pittsburgh. A tour of a Carnegie steel plant left him almost, but not quite speechless. "Six months' residence here," he told his host curtly, "would justify suicide." Joseph Frazier Wall, *Andrew Carnegie* (1970), 386.

disdained the name of patriot for himself: "To me the cry—'Our country, right or wrong!' seems detestable."[15] When in 1885 Émile de Laveleye, a Belgian sociologist, accused him of being "anxious to see the law of the survival of the fittest and of natural selection adopted in human society," Spencer demurred. Intent on avoiding any misunderstanding, he insisted: "Aggression of every kind is hateful to me."[16] This firm disclaimer was inconsistent with his essential doctrine, but it strikingly demonstrates once again Spencer reflecting the tensions pervading the Victorian alibi for aggression to which his name is linked.

The same intriguing complexities enlivened the thought (and even more the reception) of Darwin. In 1859, not unexpectedly, a middle-class culture still strongly committed to churchgoing offered spirited resistance to what seemed to be Darwin's canonization of godless competition. When the *Origin of Species* was published, the *Saturday Review,* in an unusually lengthy commentary, at once acknowledged the alarms of the pious and sought to exorcise them: "Although it is certain that Mr. Darwin's views will cause painful anxiety to many who will regard them as hostile to the truths of Revelation, we cannot share in that anxiety." After all, "except in a single brief and somewhat obscure paragraph, Mr. Darwin has avoided all reference to the origin of the human race," even though "in his future work he can scarcely fail to be explicit upon that point."[17] The reviewer was prescient; in 1871, in *The Descent of Man,* Darwin would repair this signal omission.

Still, with the assimilation of Darwin's ideas and some adroit pious readings, the anxiety of the devout soon lost much of its force. As early as 1867, Walter Bagehot, a shrewd reader whom Darwin was to quote with approval, noted that "while at first some objection was raised to the principle of 'natural selection' in physical science upon religious grounds," the objection was "passing away; the new principle is more and more seen to be fatal to mere outworks of religion, not to religion itself."[18]

In truth, Darwin's subversive theories won converts with impressive rapidity; after all, the idea of evolution, though in a more pious guise, had been in the air for a century. Looking back to the late 1860s, Henry Adams described the repute of these theories as virtually untouchable: "Unbroken Evolution under uniform conditions pleased every one—except curates and bishops." He might have added that even curates and bishops would make their peace with the new, dangerous doctrines. "Natural Selection," Adams thought, had become a substitute religion, "a dogma to be put in the place of the Athanasian creed." He recalled that "evolution from lower to higher raged like an epidemic. Darwin was the greatest of prophets in the most evolutionary of worlds." Adams exaggerated little. The eminent American botanist Asa Gray, an indefatigable defender of Darwin against the charge of atheism, easily co-opted the theory of natural selection as one more testimony to God's intentions for mankind. A sprinkling of other scholarly clerics and reverent scientists took this comfortable eclecticism further. To be sure, in Catholic France, objections to godless Darwinism were more tenacious, but by 1882, on Darwin's death, even some pious French writers could concede that his *Origin of Species* contained nothing "in contradiction to the idea of a superior order and a supreme will."[19]

By then, numerous Christians had come to terms with the enemy. As early as 1873, in his *Darwinism and Design,* George St. Clair, a devout geologist and engineer, recruited Darwin's theories as proof that the Almighty had planned the universe at once wisely and beneficently. And Freud, who studied with the persuasive German philosopher Franz Brentano at the University of Vienna in the mid-1870s, noted that his teacher believed in God and Darwin at the same time.[20] In 1893, in his Lowell Lectures, the Scottish theologian Henry Drummond was bringing no news, then, when he told his listeners, "Evolution is seen to be neither more nor less than the story of creation as told by those who know it best"; it was "the method of Creation."[21]

Still, these ecumenical interpretations of Darwin did not remain uncontested. Unbelievers objected that they took the edge off Darwin's incomparable theories; it was precisely the scandalous anti-Christian drift of evolutionism that made it so irresistible to them. They saluted it as a triumph of reason, a prop for progress, a call to action against superstition and reactionary clericalism. The prolific zoologist Ernst Haeckel, Darwin's most assiduous and influential German disciple, valued his master in large part because, he thought, his evolutionary doctrine had definitively discredited the Christian religion. In his most widely read book, *The Riddle of the Universe,* published in 1899 and almost immediately translated into English, Haeckel praised Darwin, as he had so often before, for being the most compelling scientist of his century. And he took pleasure in seeing the century end on a note of increasingly vehement conflict between science and Christianity.[22] There was no room for religion in such talk, except for the religion of evolution.* Other irreligious disciples of Darwin, though generally more restrained, happily subscribed to this assessment. Unreconstructed religious believers shared it as well, though obviously with far less pleasure.

Despite all the pacific gestures, then, the philosophical and theological impli-

---

*In his adoring biography of Haeckel, Wilhelm Bölsche made excited propaganda for Haeckel's blasphemous Darwinian pantheism. Virtually alone, he claimed, Haeckel had fully grasped Goethe's song about the God-Nature: "All-Nature. And he himself in that Nature. All-Evolution. And he himself in this Evolution." *Ernst Haeckel. Ein Lebensbild* (1900), 5.

cations of Darwinism generated persistent controversy. Its possible political and social implications were more controversial still. Admirers of Darwin's writings felt entitled to cannibalize them with impunity as they ventured to enlarge his theory about the evolution of species into a universal explanation of—and program for—human affairs. Adroitly, they appealed to what they called Darwin's conclusive demonstration that progress results from a ruthless struggle of all against all. Industrious searchers for usable passages supporting aggressiveness could easily find them in the master's writings. "As many more individuals of each species are born than can possibly survive," he had asserted, "and as, consequently, there is a frequently recurring struggle for existence, it follows that any being, if it vary however slightly in any manner profitable to itself, under the complex and sometimes varying conditions of life, will have a better chance of surviving and thus be *naturally selected*."[23] Social theorists in search of an authoritative foundation for their ideas thought they could make good use of this bracing generalization.

After Darwin published *The Descent of Man*, these theorists felt all the more justified. In that text, Darwin criticized "civilised men" for doing their "utmost to check the process of elimination" by building "asylums for the imbecile, the maimed and the sick," by instituting poor laws and having physicians "exert their utmost skill to save the life of every one to the last moment." In consequence, "the weak members of civilised society propagate their kind," and this, Darwin was inclined to believe, served mankind ill: "No one who has attended to the breeding of domestic animals will doubt that this must be highly injurious to the race of men." Hence, he could commend "open competition for all men" and caution against preventing "the most able" either "by laws or customs from succeeding best and rearing the largest number of offspring."[24] Darwin never repudiated this vision of men in combat, whether over food, females, or more impalpable prizes. And there is no evidence that he ever paused over these callous and remarkably superficial speculations.*

Such spirited and gratuitous sallies were rare, however, and Darwin more than matched them with pronouncements of a less pugnacious order. The debates over alibis among the Victorians, which, we know, were ubiquitous,

---

*Toward the end of his life, in July 1881, Darwin told William Graham, a professor of jurisprudence in Belfast, that he stood by these vintage Social Darwinist convictions: "I could show fight on natural selection having done and doing more for the progress of civilisation than you seem inclined to admit." He reminded Graham of the way that "the more civilised so-called Caucasian races have beaten the Turkish hollow in the struggle for existence," and, looking to the near future, he predicted that "an endless number of the lower races will have been eliminated by the higher civilised races throughout the world." Ronald W. Clark, *The Survival of Charles Darwin: A Biography of a Man and an Idea* (1984), 206–7.

did make their appearance in Darwin's own work, but in general, he was reluctant to draw inferences for social policy from his historic discoveries about evolutionary mechanisms. Unfortunately for intellectual precision—and for society—his disciples overlooked, or overcame, that reluctance with sovereign ease. From the late 1860s on, readers of Darwin took so virtually self-evident the rationalizations they thought natural selection furnished for hard-nosed self-assertion. At the very least, it offered welcome reasons for calculated failures in charity. Vigorous, often deadly, competition was nature's chosen instrument for progress. To resist it was pointless. Darwin himself had been less primitive than this.

Despite the controversies surrounding Darwin's ideas, the luster of his fame, though for a time under attack, survived into the twentieth century undimmed, in Britain as abroad. Darwin was that uncommon exception, the prophet honored in his own country. At first, some of the attention lavished on him was rather wry; as his ideas began to spread among the educated British public, imaginative writers took wicked pleasure in satirizing them. The crude notions that mankind is the offspring of monkeys, and that there is a mysterious missing link between humans and animals awaiting discovery, seemed irresistibly funny. And not only funny: novelists like Benjamin Disraeli, Charles Reade, and Wilkie Collins, as well as a host of lesser authors, invented unlovable adherents to Darwinism. Rent by perplexities about life's meaning, these characters were driven to suicide or, at the least, made fools of themselves at dinner parties, spouting nonsense about man's humble descent and inviting devastating rebukes from articulate pious adversaries.*

In these fictions, Darwin's acolytes are depicted as presumptuous, pedantic, and repulsive; when they are not vicious they are boring and preposterous. But as Darwinism was assimilated into Britain's intellectual climate, and, one suspects, as the repetitive lampoons grew tedious, novelists took a more conciliatory line. Almost from the beginning, pious writers with a taste for biology, such as Charles Kingsley, had cautioned that ignorant ridicule of evolutionism was both unworthy and unproductive; with like-minded colleagues, Kingsley sought a compromise, exploring routes to a possible alliance between God and Darwin. These efforts proved inadequate: some decades later, H. G. Wells

---

*See also the curious novel *The Outcast,* in which Winwood Reade, a speculative historian and earnest student of Darwin, paid a rather odd tribute to his own loss of religious faith after reading the *Origin of Species.* The novel records the appalling fate of an amiable, intelligent, scholarly, profoundly religious young man who, upon reading Malthus on population and, worse, Darwin on the origin of species, begins to question his cherished Christian beliefs, goes hopelessly insane, and hangs himself.

pronounced the Christian religion and Darwinian naturalism to be incompatible, and came out in favor of Darwin.

Not to be outdone, writers dealing in facts rather than fictions kept Darwin's name before the public. For some decades, British social theorists who had purloined his ideas flourished little less than the master himself. When in 1894 the diligent autodidact Benjamin Kidd, in his fashionable *Social Evolution,* wove a veritable romance around the "stern facts of human life and progress," he was speaking for a generation of British Social Darwinists. In his view, modern industrial society was animated by mental qualities like the love of action, and the appetite for strenuous labor was linked with the craving for success. Kidd was confident that competition had not slackened among advanced societies and was not likely to diminish in the future. Progressive nations paid a price, he thought, for their overflowing energy, notably great nervous friction and severe stress, but this was a price worth paying.[25]

British writers had no corner on such convictions. The French developed their own partisans, foremost among them Clémence-Auguste Royer, Darwin's able and opinionated translator. She larded her version of the *Origin of Species* with anticlerical and free-trade comments of her own. "The social question for every living organism," she wrote, "is in reality simply another name for the universal struggle, the *struggle for life* of Charles Darwin."[26] Royer's tendentious liberties with his text made Darwin uneasy, but Darwin himself made French readers uneasy enough. And while French economists and philosophers solemnly debated the case for and against Darwinism, novelists and playwrights gave the dispute wider publicity. Like their British counterparts, several of them, then fashionable and now mostly forgotten, exploited the dramatic possibilities of Darwinism by inventing protagonists at odds with conventional—and praiseworthy—bourgeois rectitude. Equating Social Darwinism with science, science with materialism, and materialism with amorality, they built up a rogues' gallery of spectacular criminals liberated from the constraints of Christian ethics. These sinners, victimizing others or themselves as they preached the foolishness of religion and the supremacy of *la lutte pour l'existence,* did what they wanted because they wanted to do it. In despair, they killed themselves, or, even worse, they murdered their spouses in order to take up with more attractive sexual partners.

Among these literati, Alphonse Daudet deserves special attention. In his novel *L'Immortel* in 1888, and a year later in his play *La Lutte pour la vie,* he domesticated the dominant British Darwinian slogan by baptizing one of his fictional villains a "*struggle for lifeur.*" The critic Gustave Geffroy, reviewing Daudet's drama favorably, noted that "Darwin's formula became a public danger the day it spread among the middle classes as the scientific justification of the long-condemned axiom 'might makes right.' " Paul Bourget's much-discussed novel of that year, *Le Disciple,* a key document in the spreading French counter-revolution against *struggleforlifeurs* and against science in general, featured a seduction, a suicide, and a murder, terrible events all set into motion by the teachings of a Darwinian philosopher. A year later, in 1890, the new supplement to Larousse's *Grand dictionnaire du dix-neuvième siècle* listed *struggleforlifeur* and several variants for the first time.[27] The term, and the notions clustering around it, had arrived in France. Yet liberal novelists like Anatole France and philosophers like Ernest Renan protested against the convenient twisting of scientific theories in behalf of religious propaganda. The debate they heated up with their objections only served to broaden the spread of Social Darwinist notions among the French public.[28]

Émile Zola's obsessive preoccupation with science, and his rather mechanical application of a deterministic credo in his work, intensified this debate further. The most famous and most interesting French novelist between Flaubert and Proust, formidable in his productivity, Zola portrayed his characters as helplessly caught in the toils of heredity, acting out a destiny laid down for them by their forefathers. But they are not mere puppets obediently mouthing the lines that physiological fortune has written for them; they find themselves acting in an arena of competing forces, struggling to survive and if possible prosper. Like himself, some of his most eloquent fictional characters are readers of Darwin and look upon life as a battle to the end. In his twenty-volume Rougon-Macquart cycle, a sweeping panorama of French life during the Second Empire, he depicted that battle pervading society—bloody strikes, bestial peasants, seductive courtesans, adulterous bourgeois. Zola, better than anyone else, dramatized the alibi that aggression is an irresistible natural force. Humans are aggressive because their very nature compels them to be.

In *Au Bonheur des dames,* Zola enlisted even the department store, then an emerging power in merchandising, to testify to the deadly conflict that lies at the heart of things. The novel was Zola's "poem of modern activity."[29] Octave Mouret, the energetic, unscrupulous, but attractive owner of a new Parisian department store, arouses the erotic cupidity of his female customers with an array of modern advertising stunts and irresistible sales, and in the process ruins the small anachronistic shop across the street. Mouret is a Darwinian fighter, enjoying every moment of commercial combat. "Action contains its own reward," he says. "To act, to create, to fight against the facts, to conquer or be conquered by them, all human joy and health are in that!"[30] The quite unequal competition with his flyblown, underfinanced rival is for Mouret a kind of war, and Zola openly declared himself Mouret's partisan. He did not regret the demise of the small retail stores. "I shall not weep for them," he wrote in a memorandum to himself. "On the contrary: for I want to show the triumph of modern activity." It was "too bad" about those old, often interesting little shops, but they were bound to go under, "crushed by the colossus."[31] If even competition among clothing stores stood under the sign of the universal struggle for existence, the pictures in the minds of many Frenchmen and Frenchwomen, whether approving or not, were likely to be Social Darwinist.

Popular writers in the German and the Austrian empires were no less receptive to the great debate. True, in German society, where even self-defined liberals strongly supported state intervention, Darwinian or Spencerian talk about the survival of the fittest never achieved the kind of ascendancy it was to reach in the United States. But despite the countervailing ideology of state paternalism, a troop of popularizers kept their versions of Darwin's ideas before the educated public. Haeckel, who functioned as the supreme commander in his campaign for general enlightenment, was ably seconded by his disciple Wilhelm Bölsche, a rhapsodic historian of love. Oddly enough, Haeckel paired the rhetoric of Social Darwinism with progressive political ideas, even as he underscored his allegiance to a philosophy of tough-minded struggle by earnestly denouncing Social Democrats for their mad fantasies about general brotherhood and equality.[32]

Haeckel was one of a large company, though many of the others were far more conservative. Especially after the founding of the German Empire in 1871, ambitious historians of culture launched bulky guides to the human past. Tracing the struggle for existence from primitive times to the present, they visibly gloried in the clamorous clashes they discovered everywhere. In 1875, in a two-volume "cultural history in its natural development to the present day," Friedrich von Hellwald recorded on page after page his conviction that the struggle for existence, whether as relatively mild economic competition or as outright warfare, has reigned at all times and in all places. Even in the highest cultures, victory is to the stronger and "as a rule, even in civilized society, the stronger is also the better." Similarly, Julius Lippert, whose equally massive cultural history of humanity secured a certain following, detected the earliest expression of the struggle in prehistoric times and found its utility undiminished in the present.[33]

Thus German and Austrian writers cheerfully accepted the universal rule of combat and decried the sentimentality of reformers who would disarm aggressive man. Yet not all were ferociously single-minded; some displayed surprising hesitations and second thoughts. Perhaps the most interesting of these was the anthropologist Otto Ammon, who spoke with two voices. Like others of his vintage he enjoyed hammering away at socialists with Social Darwinist arguments. And in his most ambitious venture, a treatise on the social order and its natural foundations, he labored to substantiate the claim that society obeys natural laws which reformers breach to everyone's damage. In selecting individuals for prominence and power, therefore, society must prevent the incompetent from rising and promote the competent to their proper station. One way to achieve these ends is to institute hurdles like apprenticeships and exacting examinations. Even competition that leads to bloodshed is beneficial to humanity, for "war is the highest and *most majestic* form of the struggle for existence, and indispensable." Yet Ammon had his qualms: at times in life's competition, the ablest, the most ethical, and the most intelligent are outmaneuvered by the tricky and the unscrupulous. Weeds are often stronger than the plants they displace.[34] It is a wry tribute to the intricate issues raised by evolutionism that a Social Darwinist extremist like Ammon should still discover its laws to have unexpected—and undesirable—consequences.

While these learned, long-winded scholars reached a limited public, Friedrich Nietzsche schooled far more fellow Germans in the militant philosophy of life. The soil had been prepared for him; in 1885, noting that a quarter of a century had passed since Darwin had published the *Origin of Species,* Georg von Gizycki, in a rather tortuous essay on Darwinism and ethics, said flatly, "The great majority of scientific investigators no longer doubt the correctness of the biological theory of evolution" that Darwin had "first demonstrated through impressive inductive proofs." The time was near when evolutionism would be "recognized, like the heliocentric theory of Copernicus, as a constituent part of modern thinking as such."[35] He was right, and for Germans it was Nietzsche who proved him right.

Nietzsche was not a biologist; he was, rather, a cultural aristocrat expected by his public to supply the longed-for antidote to current conformity, prudence, vulgarity, and materialism. This thinker, who philosophized with the hammer, extolled the will to power, and sang the superman, was the anti-bourgeois warrior par excellence to his ecstatic admirers, most of them solid bourgeois themselves. In a much-quoted passage in *Beyond Good and Evil,* one of many like it, Nietzsche summed up the case: to renounce aggression is to embrace a base outlook that gives up on life and endorses its decay and dissolution. "Life itself is *essentially* appropriation, injury, overwhelming of the alien and the weaker, oppression, hardness, imposition of one's own form, incorporation, and at least, at its mildest, exploitation." Exploitation is confined neither to perverted nor to primitive societies. Rather, it "belongs in *essence* to the living, as an organic fundamental function," a "consequence of the essential will to power, which is in fact the will of life."[36] This was not a philosophy for middling merchants or prudent bureaucrats.

Readers sympathetic to Nietzsche would point out that his thought was anything but an invitation to brutality or racist oppression, even though selected passages in his work, taken out of context, sounded fierce enough. But whether understood by the attentive or misread by the superficial, Nietzsche's philosophy was a signal contribution to the perception of all life as a tumultuous struggle for existence—without any guarantee that the fittest would survive. Nietzsche secured a hearing with his gift for aphorisms and poetic expression, coupled with his tragic personal fate: his philosophy exploded in Germany with a most unphilosophical uproar in the early 1890s, shortly after he had gone mad and fallen silent. But it was mainly Nietzsche's subversive, psychologically penetrating rejection of unheroic Christian ethics that substantiated the claim to his originality. After all, as early as 1871, the year of Darwin's *Descent of Man,* the new edition of Büchmann's *Geflügelte Worte,* a compendium listing felicitous German sayings, had begun to include "struggle for existence" as a well-worn slogan.[37]

Nothing would be easier than to present multiple testimonials, with only marginal national variations, to the virtues of aggressiveness and inevitable conflict. But nothing would be harder than to reduce their most emphatic version, Social Darwinism, to a consistent line of thinking; the confusions inherent in that doctrine as a cultural rationalization are beyond repair. The appearance of unanimity, or at least of a broad consensus, among its leading spokesmen is an illusion, generated by a handful of glib advocates who specialized in boisterous and easily remembered pronouncements. They papered over discord with a handful of resounding and endlessly reiterated, suitably vague maxims touting the survival of the fittest, maxims that served the cause well because they were short and seemed profound; their pithiness made thinking superfluous. So-called practical men—American tycoons like Andrew Carnegie, John D. Rockefeller, James J. Hill—used them with easy familiarity, casually copying each other and themselves.[38] As the Statue well says in Shaw's *Man and Superman,* "A good cry is half the battle."

But it was only half the battle. The divisions among Social Darwinists were incurable. Some took their instances of natural selection from the fiercely competitive marketplace. Others saw all society as an arena for cruel combat between healthy, gifted individuals and sickly, inferior specimens. Still others, pushing the logic of necessary warfare all the way, described a world torn apart by fatal confrontations between rising and fading civilizations or between master and slave races. The social and economic policies that Social Darwinists proposed ranged no less widely. Some were content with advocating free trade and denouncing what they called self-defeating private philanthropy; others, harder men, rejected on principle government aid to the poor and unfortunate; still others promoted draconian eugenic measures to preserve valuable human qualities by preventing the defective from breeding; and a handful of extremists played with the joyful prospect of apocalyptic military confrontations.

While many were willing, then, to wait upon events to sort out those fit to survive from those destined to go under, others, less sanguine, thought it necessary to help history along. Their gloomy attitude further complicated what was called Social Darwinism; from its earliest days, the essentially optimistic vision of the Spencerian plea for competition was shadowed, and curiously reinforced, by a pessimistic version. Modern Cassandras believed that nature, icily indifferent, blindly destroyed what should be preserved. The French anthropologist Georges Vacher de Lapouge spoke for these despairing ideologues when he somberly predicted that the "chimera" of progress would soon vanish: to analyze the process of social selection must lead to the most unequivocal pessimism. The future would belong—if one was lucky—to the mediocre.[39]

With their curious mixture of cheer and gloom, Social Darwinists never held the whole public in the palm of their hand. A vocal opposition, less adroit in devising memorable slogans but intellectually far from negligible, gave them no quarter. Broadly speaking, the interminable arguments over the Social Darwinist justifications for aggression mobilized three distinct parties: the fundamentalists, who toiled to apply the doctrine of the struggle for existence more or less literally; the liberals, who interpreted the terrible law of natural selection as a call for action to counter or at least soften its consequences; and the skeptics, who insisted that Social Darwinists of whatever stripe had misread, or drawn wholly unwarranted inferences from, the theory of evolution.

This sketch map suffers the defects of easy legibility. It fails to record unexpected alliances among adversaries and slights the crosscurrents of feeling in the more sophisticated. After all, even as a variety of Social Darwinists borrowed isolated passages from his writings, Darwin himself took the side of their detractors. Early in 1860, just after his *Origin of Species* had been published, he reported to the eminent geologist Charles Lyell, "I have received in a Manchester newspaper rather a good squib, showing that I have proved 'might is right' and therefore that Napoleon is right, and every cheating tradesman is also right."[40] If Marx could say that he was not a Marxist, Darwin could say, with equal justice, that he was not a Darwinist, certainly not a Social Darwinist—most of the time.

Darwin was not alone in treating the tendentious interpretations of his thought with reserve. The troop of doubters was sizable and diverse; it included unreconciled Christians, suspicious sociologists, contentious socialists, and, most telling of all, careful students of Darwin's writings. Serious efforts to discover a reasonable application of Darwin's thought to society began soon after the *Origin of Species* appeared. Prominent among these are the spirited speculative essays that Walter Bagehot published in 1872 under the title *Physics and Politics*. The ideas bearing the label "natural selection," originally offered to explain animal evolution, might, he thought, work for human history no less. Though much about that history remained obscure, Bagehot felt secure enough to suggest that "those nations which are the strongest tend to prevail over the others; and in certain marked peculiarities the strongest tend to be the best." What is more, in each nation the "most attractive tend to prevail," and for the most part the attractive are the best. The triumph of stronger over weaker nations is not invariably gained in a peaceful contest. Indeed, in earlier times, during the "fighting age," the foremost engine of progress was war, and then "the best nations conquered the worst; by possession of one advantage or another the best competitor overcame the inferior competitor."[41]

This reads like an early version of pitiless Social Darwinism. But Bagehot provided his own demurrer: there is no reason why the struggle for existence, though fundamental to progress, must degenerate into violent confrontations. War served progress in the past, but the nineteenth century is an age of discussion; war has fortunately given way to constructive debate and rational decisions. In any event, Bagehot's affection for the bellicose character is never unequivocal: "War both needs and generates certain virtues," but they are not the highest virtues; they are, rather, "preliminary virtues, as valour, veracity, the spirit of obedience, the habit of discipline." In fact, those countries that foster discussion most are also the most progressive. The fighting age had fastened on men the bridle of law and had frozen habits into a solid "cake of custom"; now, "a government by discussion, if it can be borne, at once breaks down the yoke of fixed custom."[42]

One beneficial effect consequent upon the crumbling of the "cake of custom"—it became a famous phrase—is, Bagehot added, the decline in bigotry; a second, the openness to new ideas; a third, the creation of a new kind of human being at once spirited and controlled, vital and reasonable, a creature of *"animated moderation."* Let others, like Carlyle, interpret this development as a weakening of energy; Bagehot read it as a welcome sign that "the hereditary barbaric impulse is decaying and dying out."[43] Though worried about the democratic tendencies of his age, Bagehot was a man of hope: he saw human advancement as a progression from conflict to cooperation, from impulsiveness to rationality. In short, aggression can be—and in civilized times ought to be—sublimated.

Bagehot died in 1877, at fifty-one. Had he lived another sixteen years, he would have welcomed the most powerful defense of the century against politi-cized readings of Darwin's work, a famous lecture by Thomas Henry Huxley on the relation of evolution to ethics. Huxley, Darwin's most loyal and most effective lieutenant, was a spectacular catch for the opponents of Social Dar-winism. His authority was enviable; speaking for Darwin from the beginning, he had faced down princes of the church and recalcitrant biologists alike. And he had never shared the convictions of Darwin's most tendentious interpreters. Now, in 1893, after devoting earnest thought to the issue, Huxley offered his case against Social Darwinism to the general educated public. "Let us under-stand, once for all," he said bluntly, "that the ethical progress of society de-pends, not on imitating the cosmic process, still less in running away from it, but in combating it." Nature is neither teacher nor friend; it is, rather, implaca-bly the "headquarters of the enemy of ethical nature." The struggle for exis-tence among humans is anything but adaptive; natural selection is as kind to the criminal as to the good citizen. "The thief and the murderer follow nature just as much as the philanthropists." Hence it is counterproductive to seek instruc-tion from nature in weighing moral or political decisions. Reasonably enough, Huxley observed that the debate swirling around the application of Darwin's thought to society had been badly compromised by the all too widely credited misunderstanding of that unfortunate slogan, the survival of the fittest; it was *not* synonymous with the survival of the best. Evolutionary ethics, Huxley con-cluded, is nothing better than a fallacy.[44] He was saying to anyone who would listen that the alibi Social Darwinists had invented for aggression was, in a word, invalid.

In the United States, too, where Spencer and Darwin had been popularly interpreted as extreme advocates of combat, opponents were not silent. From the 1880s on, the maverick American sociologist Lester Frank Ward made a strong case against the application of the Social Darwinists' notions to social theory and political practice. The blind evolutionary forces we see at work in nature are distinct from those evolutionary processes that reasonable humans subdue to their purposes. "The *laissez faire* school has entrenched itself behind the fortifications of science," and worked with a mixture of truths and errors. Its adherents are right to argue that "social phenomena are, like physical phe-nomena, uniform and governed by laws," but wrong to argue, quite illogically, that therefore "neither physical nor social phenomena are capable of human control." In fact, "all the practical benefits of science are the result of man's control of natural forces and phenomena which would otherwise have run to waste or operated as enemies to human progress." Nature left to itself is prodi-gal and irresponsible in the extreme; hence intelligently planned social legisla-tion is the only sure way to progress.[45] This was a formidable assault on the defenders of competition. By appealing to reason as opposed to nature, Ward's critique went to the very heart of Social Darwinism, which, whatever its form, declared nature supreme.

Nor were the opponents of Social Darwinism the only ones to raise questions about the legitimate reach of this alibi. William Graham Sumner, Spencer's best-known and most discriminating American disciple, could hardly be expected to share Ward's skepticism about aggressiveness. But, following his British master, he carefully differentiated between acceptable and unacceptable acts of aggression. Not that Sumner ever hesitated about the value of the struggle for existence. Born in 1840 into a respectable working-class family, he never disowned the ideal of strenuous work and hardy self-denial that he had absorbed in his boyhood. Briefly an Episcopalian minister after graduating from Yale, he converted to sociology in 1872 and was appointed at his alma mater to a new chair in political and social science. Once in place, he quickly acquired and never lost an impressive authority over the undergraduates as he rasped out his message that "the world owes nobody a living."[46]

Soon his influence spread beyond Yale. Schooled as a persuader in the pulpit and at the lectern, Sumner spent his life preaching in the classroom, in the lecture hall, in magazine articles, in books. The texts for his sermons were unvaried: the struggle for existence dominates all human encounters, whether in the empty spaces of America or the crowded terrain of Europe; the competition in which man pits himself against nature is a merciless affair; talk of natural rights is claptrap, noble sentiments are only comical effusions, the essential lesson the science of sociology imparts is that state intervention in evolutionary processes almost always leads to disaster.

Sociology, as Sumner conceived it, had to return always to the self-evident truth that human nature, like external nature, is swamped in conflict. The human animal is activated by four elemental springs of action: hunger, sexual desire, vanity, and the fear of ghosts.[47] One motive force that pushes people into society—altruism—is conspicuously missing from Sumner's list. Rather, to his mind, self-preservation is fundamental; it is in the cause of self-preservation that the battles take their start. Nature, anything but sentimental, does not exist to serve humanity. Before her tribunal "a man has no more right to life than a rattlesnake; he has no more right to liberty than any wild beast; his right to the pursuit of happiness is nothing but a license to maintain the struggle for existence, if he can find within himself the powers with which to do it." The consequences a legislator must draw from such a vision are bound to be bleak: "In civilized society the right to live turns into the guarantee that he shall not be murdered by his fellow-men." Unlike Ward, to whom nature appeared wasteful, Sumner saw it as niggardly in the extreme: "Perhaps the most fundamental fact which makes this world a world of toil and self-denial is that two men cannot eat the same loaf of bread." It is the scarcity of resources that makes for perpetual combat. "If we do not like the survival of the fittest," Sumner told an appreciative audience, the Free Trade Club, in 1879, "we have only one possible alternative, and that is the survival of the unfittest." No wonder Sumner could confess to an "extreme prejudice against State interference."[48]

All this sounds perfectly straightforward. Sumner's contemporaries, admirers and critics alike, read his ideas as support for unregulated capitalism, a hunting license for an aggressive business culture. After all, Sumner was unabashed in his championship of private property and his fondness for the very rich, whom he hailed as the product of natural selection. It is perfectly true, he admitted, that millionaires live in luxury, but their existence is good for society. His affection for the rich was, he protested, in the service of his far stronger affection for the middle class: "The reason why I defend the millions of the millionaire is not that I love the millionaire, but that I love my own wife and children, and that I know no way in which to get the defense of society for my hundreds, except to give my help, as a member of society, to protect his millions."[49]

The rich are valuable, too, as an antidote to social reformers, for whom Sumner reserved his most unmitigated scorn. His conservative critique of rationalistic reformers echoes the famous strictures of Burke. Ideals "are necessarily phantasms. They have no basis in fact." Provocatively he titled one of his most-quoted essays, dating from 1894, "The Absurd Effort to Make the World Over." It concludes with a contemptuous image of a man sitting down "with a slate and pencil to plan out a new social world," surely "the greatest folly of which a man can be capable."[50] Liberty, Sumner's great ideal, is incompatible with equality. To enforce peace between labor and management is therefore a dubious blessing; in the long run, social antagonisms will give way to harmony, but never through conscious planning.[51]

And yet, like Spencer before him, Sumner showed marked irritation over the possible abuse of his teachings. He refused to extend them to international relations, let alone to war or imperialism. Not that Sumner was a sheep in wolf's clothing. His passion for competition and his esteem for privileges won in combat were unstinted and undisguised. But his true hero was the hardworking, tax-ridden, ordinary citizen whom he called, in a rather pathetic formulation, the "Forgotten Man"—a patient victim of the philanthropists and humanitarians who, intent on turning the poor and the weak into "social pets," compel him to pay for their sentimental and hare-brained schemes. Sumner's Forgotten Man—and, not to overlook her, the Forgotten Woman—are responsible bourgeois who spend their lives working and voting and saving and, above all, paying. Sumner saw them as infinitely superior in character to, and infinitely more useful than, the plutocrat, that modern excrescence stamped by a narrow-minded attachment to money-making and the pursuit of unsavory political deals.

In short, Sumner was anything but an apologist for raw pugnacity. He condemned America's imperialistic designs on its neighbors as "a case of genuine political earth hunger," a "project of pure outrage, cruelty, and aggression." Earth hunger is the most primitive of emotions, "the wildest craving of modern nations," serving both national vanity and economic expansionism. The imperialism fueled by such appetites is the chase after "all the old baubles of glory, and vanity, and passion." To pursue them only adds "another to the long list of cases in which mankind has sacrificed the greatest blessings in pursuit of the greatest follies." A sane policy would be to recognize that the states of the globe form a "great family of nations, united by a growing body of international law."[52]

Following out this line of thinking in an acerbic essay of 1898, Sumner charged that the American public, infatuated with the Spanish-American War, was overlooking its baleful consequences—the abandonment of American for Spanish ideals, the very ideals the United States had been founded to oppose. Nor was the war a fair fight: "My patriotism is of the kind which is outraged by the notion that the United States never was a great nation until in a petty three months' campaign it knocked to pieces a poor, decrepit, bankrupt old state like Spain."[53] Sumner took a high-minded sporting view of international conflict, but he plainly preferred peaceful competition among nations to war. For him, the lust for conquest is at once uncivilized and stupid. His advocacy of aggression stopped at the outer edges of the economic struggle.

Sumner conceded that men may seek to escape war for sordid reasons like cowardice, but he denied the motives for war any grandeur or nobility. With no love for "humanitarianism and flabby sentimentalism," he nevertheless detested politicians who prescribed war as a "handy remedy" for the presumed "vices of industrialism and the evils of peace." To prepare for war on some general principle of human nature is only to invite it—just another instance of how abstract ideas ruin policy: "If you want war, nourish a doctrine. Doctrines are the most frightful tyrants to which men ever are subject, because doctrines get inside of a man's own reason and betray him against himself. Civilized men have done their fiercest fighting for doctrines," and all of these doctrines, whether religious or political, are "nothing but rhetoric and phantasms."[54] Aggressiveness must be debunked, not coddled; most talk about manliness is a transparent fraud. These attitudes, strongly held and consistently expressed, expose once again the nuances of bourgeois alibis for aggression in Victorian days. The most determined critic of Social Darwinism could not have assailed it more effectively than Sumner did.*

As we have seen, the international debate over Social Darwinism was far more than an academic exercise. French novelists and playwrights who borrowed its slogans, and writers with a facility for words, from Nietzsche to Sumner, gave it extensive circulation. The French critic Gustave Geffroy was surely right to observe in 1889 that the doctrine had found a home among the middle classes. No wonder: effective agents were spreading the word. Among these were the worriers over depopulation whose pamphlets flooded France and Germany after the Franco-Prussian War. Following the unforeseen debacle inflicted on the French by Prussian arms in September 1870, French students of decadence, including amateur demographers, assailed the growing use of birth control by their fellow citizens. Contraception, these doomsayers argued, prevented solid bourgeois families from raising the able-bodied soldiers who would avenge the shame of Sedan and wrest the lost eastern provinces—Alsace and most of Lorraine—from the militaristic Huns across the Rhine.[55] German alarmists for their part did not find the French panic reassuring. They were bound to acknowledge that their birthrate was well ahead of that of their late enemy; the notorious French two-child, or one-child, family had not yet made many converts, even among prosperous Germans. Still, the German population was growing at a decreasing rate, while the Russians massed on the eastern borders were making babies in unwelcome numbers. The threat to Germany on battlefields to come seemed too obvious to be ignored. After all, the struggle for existence was an elemental and ubiquitous struggle over numbers, and the wars of the future were being won and lost in bed—now. Nor were the prophets of catastrophes, whether French or German, troubled by population statistics alone. What about the physical condition of potential fighters, more of them stoop-shouldered, concave-chested, nearsighted than any recruiting sergeant liked to see?

These years of anxiety were also the heroic years of eugenic research, as self-assured in tone as it was slipshod in techniques. It generated heated talk about scientific breeding; widely read, and widely misunderstood, reports like Richard Dugdale's study of the Juke family caused unnecessary alarm. They

---

*Assailed—and mocked. Sumner feared that rhetorical phantasms gain access to young minds and fester there. In an essay exploring the publications to which the boys of his time were regularly exposed, he objected to the way that all-too-popular tales of adventure inculcate the martial spirit. See "What Our Boys Are Reading" (1880), *Earth-Hunger and Other Essays,* ed. Albert Galloway Keller (1913), 375–76.

seemed to confirm that people of low average intelligence, and even more the moronic, were reproducing themselves in frightening numbers, while respectable men and women of good stock were involved with their selfish pleasures, their youthful figures, their vacation trips abroad, far more than with patriotically making children for their country's armies. Fear of what Theodore Roosevelt would call "race suicide" was in the air.

A handful of best-selling American novelists, Jack London their undisputed leader, sent the same message. His tales—compelling, scarcely disguised dramatizations of his raw-boned evolutionary determinism—made the brutal naturalism of his master, Zola, appear almost tame in comparison. The heroes and victims of Jack London's adventure stories, whether men or animals, act out his savage sense—it scarcely deserves to be called a philosophy—that life is warfare without pity ending only in death. The stories are embodied alibis for literally mortal competition.

An avid and indiscriminate reader, London took Spencer as one of his inspirations. But he scarcely needed the libraries he swallowed in search of a truth to believe in. An intrepid sailor, reckless war correspondent, socialist orator, and at the same time, a racist trumpeting the blond Teutonic superman, a victim alike of the Alaska gold fever and of drink, he lived and gloried in the Darwinian battlefields he obsessively explored in his writings—a thousand words a day and more. Civilization was to him a thin veneer, with the lust for blood pulsing just beneath. Men and dogs in extreme situations, at sea, at war, in the frozen North, realize their destiny only after they have learned to kill. No writer ever shouted for virility more joylessly; yet for some years, his following was immense. By the time he died of a morphine overdose in 1916, bloated and worn out by debauchery, he had spread his tales of the unchecked lust for aggression to the millions.

So did Frank Norris, a far more interesting writer, but like London deeply in debt to Zola and like London essentially enamored of the pseudoromantic cult of the war of all against all. His message, uttered through his protagonists, is the doctrine of every man for himself. This selfishness, basic to human nature, drives "the weakest to the wall, the strongest to the front."* The need for aggression is its own alibi. Yet, significantly, all of Norris's bluster barely conceals a pervasive anxiety, the dread specter of collapse. Life is that "great, mysterious force that spun the wheels of Nature," driving "before it the infinite herd of humanity, driving it on at breathless speed through all eternity, driving

---

* *Vandover and the Brute* (written in 1895; published posthumously in 1914), 251. The character who voices these views, Charlie Geary, is the villain of the tale. But in Norris's universe, in which the higher and the lower are in perpetual conflict, Geary's "philosophy" has much of the truth.

it no one knew whither, crushing out inexorably all those who lagged behind
the herd and who fell from exhaustion, grinding them to dust."[56] The hypnotic
repetition of key words and short phrases that is his stylistic signature was
designed to embody the deadly struggles fundamental to all life. Actually, his
view of the world was more intricate, but in these musings and in his character
portrayal he transmitted a particularly moody and simplistic form of Social
Darwinism to the novel-reading public.

Notions of this sort were also common among those too busy to read novels.
They came easily, we know, to magnates like Carnegie and Rockefeller, who
were acting out the alibi of merciless competitiveness in their own careers. Yet
their professions, however sincere, could not escape an interesting paradox. In
his business practice, Carnegie greatly preferred mergers and monopolies to
what he and his fellow combatants liked to call "cutthroat competition." So did
Rockefeller; competition was wasteful and had to yield to modern industrial
organization. Candidly he noted in his reminiscences that "the day of individual competition in large affairs is past and gone." No doubt, "the chief advantages from industrial combinations are those which can be derived from a
cooperation of persons and aggregation of capital."[57] These powerful representatives of Darwinian competition had not reckoned with the fact that one result
might be its own demise, and that they might be instrumental in bringing this
demise about.

And the actions of Carnegie and Rockefeller complicated the alibi of aggressive conflict in yet another way. Having sufficiently demonstrated their capacity
for aggressiveness in the great economic wars, they devoted as much time and
ingenuity to giving away what they had amassed as they had devoted to amassing it. They had not changed their mind about the blessings of aggression; both
men, the most liberal donors of the late nineteenth and early twentieth centuries, saw their philanthropic activities as perfectly consistent with the view of
life that had permitted them to become millionaires many times over. As they
endowed libraries, supported medical research, founded universities, all after
soliciting expert advice, they took great pride in being scientific philanthropists—prudent and sensible investors in the future of humanity.

No doubt, their private motives were far more tangled, far less logical, than
this simple, appealing picture might suggest. In 1868, already a rich man at
thirty-three, Carnegie noted in a much-quoted private memorandum that "no
idol is more debasing than the worship of money." And he promised himself to
give up its pursuit in two years, lest he be degraded "beyond hope of permanent
recovery."[58] It was a pledge he broke, but in 1891, when he declared that he
and his kind must pour their wealth into worthy causes, he observed that the
very rich, taxed with opulent living, might "find refuge from self-questioning

in the thought of the much greater portion of their means which is being spent on others."[59] His own slogan was, the man who dies rich dies disgraced. It is hard to visualize Andrew Carnegie ridden with severe guilt feelings, but clearly a long-held and scrupulously nourished sense of responsibility—to all but his competitors—informed his actions as a philanthropist. To be sure, his detractors had a point when they attributed far from purely creditable motives to this donor of thousands of public libraries. After all, most of the libraries ostentatiously bore Carnegie's name and must have gratified his thirst for recognition. But vain or not, Carnegie explicitly perceived his lavish ventures into organized benevolence as a means of helping those willing to help themselves. That was the rationale for his policy of donating funds for a library building alone, compelling the locality that had successfully applied to him to buy the books and provide the upkeep.

Indeed, the famous pair of articles jointly titled "The Gospel of Wealth,"[60] in which he delineated his creed of giving, offered a veritable banquet of the Social Darwinist commonplaces that had guided (or rationalized) his rise to eminence as America's steel baron. We read, as we have often read before, that the price society pays for the growth of large-scale manufacturing is steep but worth paying and that the law of competition is impossible to evade. Anarchists and socialists are the enemies of civilization, while "Individualism, Private Property, the Law of Accumulation of Wealth, and the Law of Competition" are quite simply "the highest result of human experience," and the man who fosters them is "the highest type of man, the best and most valuable of all that humanity has yet accomplished." Giving alms rewards vice and fails to relieve virtue. The respectable poor are one thing, the spongers another. Indeed, a comfortable beggar is "more dangerous to society, and a greater obstacle to the progress of humanity, than a score of wordy Socialists." Hence, the indiscriminate charity to which millionaires lend themselves is a more consequential crime than miserliness.[61] Carnegie's program was consistent with this hardheaded attitude. As a rational millionaire he could endow great universities, free libraries, innovative hospitals and laboratories, beautiful parks, useful meeting halls, health-giving swimming baths, and last (indeed, least) churches. All other philanthropic methods were folly.[62]

The institutions bearing Carnegie's name in the United States, Scotland, and elsewhere document his commitment to Spencer's fundamental principles. Like Spencer (and, for that matter, like Sumner), Carnegie refused to extend approval of competition to its apotheosis. He was in fact a fervent peacemonger, persuaded that the day an "International Court is established will become one of the most memorable days in the world's history."[63] The competitors Carnegie had broken on his climb to the top, the union men he had

outmaneuvered and outgunned, the employees he had pitted against one another for the sake of improving efficiency and increasing profits, might ruefully
add some darker touches to Carnegie's genial self-portrait as a benevolent and
beneficent autocrat. But his philanthropic enterprises and his distaste for war
allowed Carnegie to feel satisfied that he had managed to confine his Social
Darwinist alibi for aggression within sensible limits.

Comparable intricacies mark the actions of John D. Rockefeller. His comments about the right kind of business partners and subordinates attest to his lust
for fighting. He liked associates who were not only "interesting and quick-
minded men" but also "full of vigor and push." But he too was no pure Social
Darwinist: just as Carnegie carried traces of his youthful Scottish radicalism
through life, so Rockefeller remembered his Baptist roots; he tithed himself
years before he embarked on a career as a philanthropist to match Carnegie.
Wealth alone, he once said, does not bring happiness. "What most people seek
cannot be bought with money." Nevertheless, the dogmas of commercial aggressiveness held him securely in their grip. He denied that he had ever gone
"ruthlessly" after his competition and tried "to ruin it by cutting prices or
instituting a spy system,"[64] but the record testifies against him. Besides cutting
prices and using industrial espionage, he corrupted pliant state legislators to
sabotage efforts at regulating the oil industry, formed trusts to evade legal prohibitions against monopolies, and quietly bought periodicals critical of him and
converted them into mouthpieces for Standard Oil; in short, he did all the
things he vigorously denied doing. Like any robber baron, he acted as though
economic inequality were divinely ordained and hence justified the most callous acquisitiveness.

He rationalized his tactics as necessary corollaries to the Spencerian laws of
competition. Apologists for Standard Oil energetically seconded him; their
voices, bought and unbought, were loud. Their company's rivals, they argued,
resorted to the same shady tactics whenever they had the opportunity, a defense
that only underscores the muckrakers' indictment of late-nineteenth-century
industrial and financial America as an uncharted jungle, with John D. Rockefeller one of its two or three most insatiable predators. For his own part, Rockefeller's allegiance to the theological and scientific license granted to commerce,
red in tooth and claw, permitted him to assert more than once, quite sincerely,
that his immense riches were a kind of loan from the Almighty.[65]

That was the notorious side of Rockefeller's aggressiveness. The other side,
increasingly conspicuous in his later years, led him to aim at very different
targets: the scourges of ignorance and disease.[66] He persuaded himself that he
must explore all avenues for spending, lavishly yet prudently, most of the riches
he had accumulated. "I know of nothing more despicable and pathetic than a

man who devotes all his waking hours to making money for money's sake," he wrote, sounding like Carnegie, and he meant it. He was propelled by a heady amalgam of religious and secular motives: in his mind the Baptist's God and Spencer's nature opportunely blended into one. Rational assistance, he concluded, would give pleasure to donor and recipient alike. The "field of scientific philanthropy," he concluded, sounding as though he had read Carnegie to good purpose, had securely established one insight: "The only thing which is of lasting benefit to a man is that which he does for himself. Money which comes to him without effort on his part is seldom a benefit and often a curse."[67]

Rockefeller's spectacular rescue of the obscure and failing University of Chicago, like his establishment of a munificently endowed foundation, demonstrate that for him philanthropy was economic management for noneconomic purposes. He designed his giving to elicit the cooperation of other millionaires, and whole communities, in good works. The Rockefeller Foundation loftily announced its purpose to be the enhancement of "the well-being of mankind throughout the world"; this meant supporting medical research, higher education, and agricultural productivity. Recipients showered Rockefeller with tokens of gratitude, but there were critics, mainly socialists, who wondered whether it might not have been cheaper and less destructive to prevent him and his like from getting so rich in the first place and allocate through public bodies the wealth rescued from their clutches.

Socialists were not the only ones to denounce the robber barons. Early in 1907, President Theodore Roosevelt included Rockefeller among the "great and powerful malefactors" whom he held responsible for the panic then gripping the stock market and endangering the survival of important lending institutions. And he more than once denounced Carnegie, sometimes by name, as one of those contemptible "peace-at-any price, universal-arbitration" idealists.[68] It was in the cards that the most ardent partisans of alibis for aggression would at times vituperatively attack one another.

The United States was the favorite arena for the battle over the proper range of conflict. William Graham Sumner, Jack London, John D. Rockefeller were, of course, all Americans; Andrew Carnegie prospered mightily in the United States; and Herbert Spencer sold far better there than in any other country. The conspicuousness of Americans in the exploration of the Social Darwinist alibi for aggressive competition was somehow poetically just. After all, the nineteenth-century United States was, Tocqueville had recognized as early as the 1830s, the future. That youthful, expansive colossus blessed with vast tracts of unsettled territories, seemingly inexhaustible natural resources, streams of hungry, venturesome immigrants, and a comparatively thin cover of traditional restraints, was an unmatched laboratory for social combat. That combat reached epic proportions in the western territories, with its ready resort to force and lynch law. But it was only marginally less stirring across the rest of the continent as a growing nation struggled to absorb, perhaps to tame, the dizzying rise of banking and railroading, industry and commerce. Bursting with energy and beckoning rewards, the United States offered unprecedented opportunities to the bold and the unscrupulous. If Carlyle's militaristic sobriquet "captains of industry" applied to anyone, it applied to the iron-fisted conquistadors who carved out gigantic corporations from New England to the barely settled West—the Pennsylvania Railroad, United States Steel, Standard Oil. These were men who discovered uncharted tracts of economic openings and were not afraid to seize them.

Whether or not they resorted to the slogans of Social Darwinism, these men obviously found its enthusiasm for the pugnacious spirit highly congenial. They were bent on conquering wealth and power by any means, at any cost—to others. Hence they could hardly expect their claim to a monopoly on untrammeled aggressiveness to go unchallenged. Makers of wealth, they were makers of victims no less, and the victims—hordes of small businessmen and farmers, helpless consumers, to say nothing of working men, women, and children— looked for a champion powerful enough to speak and act on their behalf. That champion, in the absence of an experienced trade-union movement with ample financial reserves, could only be the state. For decades the struggle would be unequal. Some American state and federal legislators (quite apart from those in the camp of the Carnegies from an authentic, or corrupt, identity of interests) found themselves in a race with men of ruthless energies, impressive resources, and the best lawyers that money could buy. No wonder the drafters of restrictive laws limped after those who made their legislation necessary. It was only the passage of time, scandals too blatant to be ignored, the long recession of the 1870s and 1880s, and increasingly vocal public pressure that belatedly forced governments into action.

These were precisely the decades, Lester Frank Ward wrote sarcastically, when advanced industrial societies were beginning to put an inglorious end to the reign of *laissez-faire*. While free-trade propagandists were struggling to keep their dogmas alive, Germany was nationalizing the railroads and enacting protective tariffs, France was retaliating with tariffs of its own and subsidizing shipowners, Britain was taking over the telegraph and passing laws making education compulsory, and the United States was considering some of these desirable remedies for economic chaos. The idea that the free market, the theater for unchecked mutual aggression, is totally self-regulating had proved to be something of a self-serving superstition. "The whole world has caught the contagion," Ward wrote, "and all nations are adopting measures of positive legislation."[69]

He was right enough about Europe. Bismarck's Germany adopted pioneering social insurance in the 1880s, and other countries followed suit. Several decades before, during the heyday of economic liberalism and the exploitation of labor in mines and factories, Britain had introduced at least some protective legislation for workers; toward the end of the century its network of such laws became extensive and enforceable. But Ward's gleeful appraisal of the American situation was premature. There were a few signs, no more, during the administrations of Grover Cleveland that the tycoons' aggression was generating counteraggression—regulatory statutes and commissions—but it remained hesitant and inadequate. Stung by these modest ventures in restraint, the great entrepreneurs vigorously responded by seeking out a rationale that would keep their sovereignty intact.

They found it in an unforeseen place, the Fourteenth Amendment to the United States Constitution. Ratified in 1868, during Reconstruction, this amendment had been principally intended to protect blacks from discriminatory treatment. But by the 1880s, company lawyers and complaisant federal judges were interpreting the ringing and imprecise clauses that prohibited states from violating "due process of law" as a shield against legislation that would regulate employers' practices in hiring labor or setting wages and hours. Laws affecting matters of this kind, they contended, interfered with "liberty of contract," and were thus unconstitutional. The Supreme Court, a bulwark of social conservatism and economic liberalism, was disposed to side with them. In 1905, in the *Lochner* case, the Supreme Court invalidated in a 5 to 4 decision a New York statute limiting the workweek in bakeries to sixty hours. In a famous dissent, Mr. Justice Holmes criticized the majority for reasoning from "an economic theory which a large part of the country does not entertain." He objected to this masking of economic preferences with constitutional rhetoric. "The Fourteenth Amendment," he wrote in a memorable sentence, "does not enact Mr. Herbert Spencer's *Social Statics*."

Holmes's terse dictum essentially revealed Social Darwinism as partisan rationalization in its claim, against all the evidence, that employers and employees negotiate with each other as equals. But tone-setting Americans, in high places, rejected Holmes's plea—it was, after all, a dissent. Coarse though the essential doctrine of Social Darwinism proved to be, increasingly under attack though it found itself toward the end of the nineteenth century, its devotees continued to muster subtle arguments to sustain it. But their lawyerlike adroitness does not fully explain its staying power. It survived so tenaciously because it gratified a perennial psychological need: the primitive urge to split the world into heroes and villains, persons and policies wholly good and wholly bad. Only racism could compete with it.

2. The Convenient Other

Nothing seems more natural than the ease with which humans claim superiority over a collective Other. It is an immensely serviceable alibi for aggression, solidifying the bracing sense of one's merits—or assuaging the secret fear of one's imperfections. The discovery that outsiders are dogged by grave, perhaps repulsive defects grants, as it were, permission to think angry thoughts and commit hostile acts. Defying persuasive evidence, French anti-Semites of the late 1890s continued to believe that Captain Alfred Dreyfus must be a German agent, simply because he was a Jew. Thus they unwittingly demonstrated the psychological dividends that the reassuring split between friend and enemy is bound to yield to all but the most sophisticated minds.

They invented nothing; the slanderers of Dreyfus were acting in a modern version of an ancient drama. The Hebrews of Old Testament times believed that Abraham's covenant with the Lord set them apart from lesser mortals. The Egyptians of the Old Kingdom took their fertile land as proof that the creator-god Re had singled them out in preference to the miserable Asians. The Greeks thought themselves better than the barbarians. Nor were self-serving comparisons confined to ethnic or national groups; Pericles in his funeral oration extolled Athenians at the expense of Spartans, for their exemplary political ways, their pursuit of wisdom and beauty. The animus was always the same: whether nation, province, or city, whether religion, class, or culture—the more one loved one's own, the more one was entitled to hate the Other.

Through the centuries politicians had exploited this human trait. In the knowledge that hatred can be cultivated with a purpose, they constructed enemies in order to bolster domestic concord.* In 1861, understanding how help-

*In the late sixteenth century, baffled by the seemingly interminable religious wars between Catholics against Huguenots, the French statesman Pomponne de Bellievre proposed to reestablish harmony among Christians by unleashing a crusade against the Turks. "It is not possible to preserve the domestic peace except by a foreign war." European states are like stomachs requiring a diet of infidels. Raymond F. Kierstead, *Pomponne de Bellievre: A Study of the King's Men in the Age of Henry IV* (1968), 34–35. Shakespeare put this counsel into the mouth of the dying Henry IV, who in his final interview with his son, prince Hal, urges him to "busy giddy minds / With foreign quarrels," to make the people forget the murder of Richard II. *2 Henry IV,* act 4, sc. 4. Shakespeare's contemporary Robert Burton observed that "in a Commonwealth, where is no publick enemy, there is, likely, civil wars, and they rage upon themselves." *The Anatomy of Melancholy* (1621; ed. Floyd Dell and Paul Jordan-Smith, 1927), 212.

ful it would be to have a hateful Other to hand, Secretary of State William Seward suggested to President Lincoln that he could reunite the war-torn nation by provoking a foreign war.[1] Schemes of this sort were borrowed from manipulative predecessors, and venerable alibis—religious parochialism, for example, which the philosophes had already gleefully exposed in the eighteenth century—continued to be favorites.

Another timeworn legacy was the urgent sense of a mission to civilize—that is to say, Christianize—unenlightened heathen tribes overseas or the unwashed heathen poor at home. The old-fashioned, self-assured Victorian proclamations of duty to the world had tangled emotional roots and no less tangled political consequences. They could serve as a cloak for imperialistic military or commercial designs, but Victorians were also driven by personal devils to be exorcised by self-destructive ventures abroad, by unimpeachable benevolence, by active feelings of guilt over one's privileged position—or by a mixture of them all.* For centuries, the conviction that Christians had a divine call to convert the world had animated believers, who mounted crusades and gave them their prayers, their money, even their lives; it gained new strength in the nineteenth century, as missionaries spread across the globe in ever larger numbers. But the most interesting reasons the nineteenth century advanced for feeding collective narcissism were modern. It injected what it touted as scientific rationales for hating or despising outsiders. What came to dominate these rationales for aggressiveness was the argument from race.

At their most innocuous, the racist theories that released so much socially acceptable aggression in the Victorian age were a cluster of mutually contradictory notions and biological or historical speculations. But their dubious stature did not keep these grandiose claims for "Aryan" or Celtic racial excellence from being virtually irresistible. Freud's analysis of the inescapable coexistence of affectionate and hostile emotions, first advanced in the mid-1890s, sheds some light on the power of racist argumentation. It strongly suggests that racial pride and racial hatred are a special case of a universal psychological stratagem: projection. Freud thought it beyond dispute that a religion of love must necessarily be a religion of hatred as well. But he had more to offer than this Enlightenment commonplace. In a long clinical memorandum of early 1895, he argued that so far as they are not justified by real exploitation or real persecution,

*From a psychoanalytic perspective things were even more intricate. The rage to improve the world whether it wanted improvement or not, usually called benevolence, was, often enough, what Freud called a reaction formation—a defense mechanism that converts aggressive feelings into their opposite and thus masks them. The most determined anti-aggression is often aggressive in origin.

people making an enemy will adopt the psychological maneuver of projection. They defend themselves against their unacceptable thoughts or wishes by expelling them from their own mind into the outside world, onto the convenient Other. This mechanism provides a highly supportive way of living with one's failings; it permits the denial that one is subject to these failings in the first place and then opportunely rediscovers them in strangers or adversaries, real or imagined—students in a rival university, members of a gang disputing one's turf, alien immigrants working at low wages, Protestants in a Catholic country, conspiratorial Freemasons, capitalist malefactors of great wealth, or the gypsy poisoners of wells.

In his medical practice, Freud came to discover the imaginative and flexible mechanism of projection in patients suffering from paranoia, in other neurotics, and in "normal" people. He offered the instance of an alcoholic who "will never acknowledge that his drinking has made him impotent. However much alcohol he can tolerate, he cannot tolerate this insight. So his wife is the guilty one—delusions of jealousy and the like." Such a stratagem, and others, Freud observed, work for groups no less than for individuals.[2] Later, he would add the provocative idea that the bond holding groups together is erotic in nature; he always took love seriously. But the essential outlines of projection as a privileged excuse for oneself and fuel for aggressive action were in place in his psychoanalytic theorizing during the founding years.

One reason the gambit of projection works so well is that it is largely unconscious; to make a point of feeling distinctly superior to "quarrelsome Irishmen" or "shopkeeping Englishmen" or "sexually uninhibited Latins" is to deny, unjustly but with perfect sincerity, that one harbors belligerence or greed or lust, wishes at once exciting and shameful. Once the transposition from self to others has been made, the search for villains is bound to prove an agreeable diversion from self-reproach. And the aggressive acts that follow are likely to be all the more furious because a certain measure of uneasiness may be surging up from the depths. Can it be that one is no better than one's victims? It is a terrible thought, to be kept at bay.

There were those in the nineteenth century, before psychoanalysis, who recognized this mechanism. Anton Chekhov, that perceptive observer of the human scene, saw it all. In a prescient letter to a friend, the writer and publisher Alexei Suvorin, he diagnosed the campaign of the anti-Dreyfusards as an instance of projection—without using the word. "Dreyfus is an officer, so the military became defensive. Dreyfus is a Jew, so the Jews became defensive." So "there was talk of militarism, of Yids. Such utterly disreputable people as Drumont" (a noisy French anti-Semite) "held their heads high. Little by little, a messy kettle of fish began stewing, it was fueled by anti-Semitism, a fuel that reeks of the slaughterhouse. When something is wrong within us, we seek the cause from without and before long we find it: it was the French who messed things up, it was the Yids, it was Wilhelm." In short, "Capitalism, the bogey-man, the Masons, the syndicate and the Jesuits are all phantoms, but how they ease our anxieties!"[3]

Unconscious projection, to be sure, was not the only tactic at work in the making of scapegoats. As Marxists, anti-slave-trade reformers, and liberal anti-imperialists contended at the time, with a show of justice, much indignant combativeness was a cynical camouflage for self-interest. But projection held center stage. Ethnic pride and ethnic anxiety were, in many, indistinguishable. Despite all their claims to higher status, whites found themselves envying blacks their presumed sexual potency; "Aryans" envied Jews their fabled cleverness; Europeans envied Americans their legendary enterprise. The sequence was simple and effective: "I am bad / I am not bad / *You* are bad," or "I am in-ferior / I am not inferior / *You* are inferior."

This drama of psychological self-defense made racist ideas and racist language the weapon of choice in the Victorian years, especially after 1850. Yet with all that the nineteenth century did for racist argumentation, its earliest modern form, the obsession of sixteenth- and seventeenth-century Spaniards with pure blood—*limpieza de sangre*—had already exhibited the fantasies that would afflict it throughout its prosperous career. The Spaniards' mania for purity, which deprived Spain of the services of able men tainted with "Jewish blood," created a festering atmosphere of suspicion and launched the fiction of blood as the carrier of racial qualities.[4] Englishmen discovering blacks in Africa in these centuries were only marginally less credulous than the Spaniards, though a cosmopolitan minority among them learned to draw distinctions between the inhabitants of North and West Africa, and even to appreciate the natives on their own terms.*

These touches of sensible relativism were soon swamped by the rage for classification. In the late 1730s, the celebrated Swedish naturalist Carl von Linné

*One captain of an English slave ship, Thomas Phillips, observed in 1694 about African natives that he could not "imagine why they should be despis'd for their colour, being what they cannot help, and the effect of the climate it has pleas'd God to appoint them. I can't think there is any intrinsick value in one colour more than another, nor that white is better than black, only we think it so because we are so, and are prone to judge favourably in our own case, as well as the blacks, who in odium of the colour, say, the devil is white, and so paint him." Winthrop Jordan, *White over Black: American Attitudes toward the Negro, 1550–1812* (1968), 11. Phillips sounds like the thinker of the eighteenth-century Enlightenment, to whom this reasonable relativism appealed greatly; Voltaire observed in an essay on beauty that a toad finds another toad beautiful.

tried to bring system into the chaos of human variations; he identified four distinct races, separated by color. His even more celebrated French contemporary the comte de Buffon discovered six races, and also disagreed with Linné by insisting that racial characteristics are open to environmental influences. The debate on racial differences—their number and nature—was on its way, and soon intensified. When, in 1775, the German anatomist Johann Friedrich Blumenbach devised his epoch-making catalogue of human races, he placed each of the five he found—Caucasian, Mongolian, Ethiopian, American, and Malay—in its own region of the globe. But he saw mankind as one; distinguished from the animals by upright posture and the capacity to reason, it can change. Race theorizing had not yet become racism. That was to be the contribution of nineteenth-century speculative thinkers and social scientists, all too often one and the same.

Propagators of racist dogmas found theirs a hard lot; each had to contend with the equally dogmatic theories of his competitors. Monogenists, whether devout or irreverent, saw all races as distinct branches of a single tree; their adversaries, the polygenists, argued that each race had been made by a separate act of creation. Around 1800, the pioneering French paleontologist Georges Cuvier traced races back to Ham, Shem, and Japheth; his successors, for the most part disdaining such Old Testament pieties, preferred to classify races by the shape of the head or, more traditionally, the color of the skin. Whatever their views, they dragged consequential moral and social judgments in their train. Extremist nineteenth-century politicians, those great simplifiers, would put a favorite racist theory to work as though it were unambiguous and firmly established. They were more certain than the theorists from whom they borrowed.

But despite its scientific-sounding credentials, this easy way of dividing up the human world did not conquer public opinion quickly, or without opposition. For decades the racists were slowed down by the clear-eyed objections of the enlightened and the humane. In 1813, Benjamin Constant had lucidly exposed the aggressive animus behind appeals to a racial past. "Our fanatical reformers," he charged, "confuse chronology to revive hatreds or to keep them alive." In the past, people had gone "back to the Franks and Goths to sanction oppressive distinctions"; nowadays, they were busy tracing the same pseudohistory to find other "pretexts for oppressions."[5] Indeed, for a number of years, self-praise continued to take old-fashioned forms; it was the fuzzy notion of national character that gave grounds for pride. Around 1830, François Guizot, in an imposing cycle of lectures on the history of civilization (by which he meant, largely, the history of France) displayed considerable impatience with German historians and their French disciples. They had overestimated the impact of the Teutonic barbarians—that is, of their racial qualities—on France's national character. Guizot saw that character as a felicitous, slowly evolving mixture of Roman, Christian, and certain Teutonic elements, and he refused to dwell on "the puerilities of learned patriots."[6] But as he denounced the puerile mysticism of racial thinking, he yielded to fervent chauvinism instead. At times other countries might be ahead of France, but surely his own was both center and focus of European civilization.[7]

Even after mid-century, becoming hesitations marked some of those who would later use the vocabulary, though not the venom, of race. In the early 1860s, Hippolyte Taine, the influential literary critic and conservative historian of the French Revolution, laid it down in his authoritative *Histoire de la littérature anglaise* that culture is shaped by three elements—*race, milieu,* and *moment.* This did not commit him to the proposition that human racial "innate and hereditary dispositions" are decisive or permanent. He was speaking, rather, of national character, for him a more elastic concept than race.[8] Even so, entering the field after racism had gathered momentum in learned and journalistic circles alike, Taine took much of it for granted. He sprinkled his history with the sort of word painting that race theorists specialized in. And even if, to Taine's mind, racial qualities are susceptible to change, they do have a way of persisting; their future is determined almost entirely by the properties inherent in the "primitive stock." His Saxons were tough, cold-blooded, drunken, brutal, slow to love, "pre-eminently adapted for endurance and enterprise."[9] This is the vocabulary, and some of the reasoning, that mid-nineteenth-century biologists, anthropologists, and historians were beginning to use to bestow formal dignity on timeworn biases. Later racist doctrinaires would set aside Taine's reservations and turn the alien race into the most persistently conscripted bogeyman of the age.

Race was everywhere by mid-century. During a long career as political novelist and cultural commentator, Benjamin Disraeli consistently proclaimed the central role of race.* In 1870, looking back at his novel *Coningsby,* he noted that in his day "the general influence of race on human action was universally recognized as the key to history."[10] The Scottish anatomist Robert Knox, an influential theorist, sounded much like Disraeli: "Race is everything in human history." He meant what he said: "Race, or hereditary descent, is everything; it stamps the man."[11] Theorists of race amassed veritable mountains of evidence, ranging from the weight of brains to the size of noses, from legends of migration

---

*Disraeli's conviction demonstrates that in his day, "race" could be enlisted to support a wide variety of positions; for him, it was essential to show that the Jewish "race," the mother of Christianity, had made valuable contributions to civilization. See Robert Blake, *Disraeli* (1967; ed. 1968), 193–97.

to imputations of tribal attributes. They thought themselves entitled to draw far-reaching consequences from the skull measurements gathered in surveys, pitting the dolichocephalic, or long-headed, races against the brachycephalic, or rounded-headed. They propagated their anthropological notions drugged with massive but essentially meaningless accumulations of data. Watching the spectacular triumphs that physicists, chemists, and astronomers were celebrating, the students of man, in tight alliance with the Social Darwinists, retailed more absurdities in the name of science than their peers ever perpetrated, before or since. Aggression was the gainer.

Its most effective promoter was comte Arthur de Gobineau. His *Essai sur l'inégalité des races humaines,* published in the early 1850s, was widely admired. Elaborating Knox's sweeping assertion at exhausting length, he wrote as if all civilization did indeed depend on race. Studying the origins of his "agitated modern world," Gobineau had come to see the "ethnic question" as paramount. Racial inequality was the key to history. A more fundamental determinant of human identity than geography, class, or religion, race explained everything.[12]

For all the contrasting cultural traditions from country to country, for all the developments from decade to decade, nineteenth-century racial thinking was remarkably uniform. Particular historical experiences—the immigration of East European Jews into the Habsburg empire or the emancipation of the slaves in the United States—no doubt lent that thinking distinct national colorations. Still, its essential notions ran across Western civilization with the heat and speed of a brush fire; what united racists was far more significant than what divided them. And it was the conviction that racist thinking rested on science that made for intimate affinities, even in the rhetoric.

The procedures of Paul Broca, who founded the Anthropological Society of Paris in 1859, are representative for his international tribe. Broca, a surgeon by profession and craniometrist by obsession, owned the truth before he set about to demonstrate it. He *knew* that women are inferior to men, and, with even more certainty, that blacks are inferior to whites. He knew, too, that the most dependable way of documenting these rankings was to measure brains, for brain size is surely correlated with intelligence. Accordingly, across the years, he and his school stuffed untold scores of skulls with lead pellets to determine their capacity, and weighed the brains that illustrious personages had willed to the cause. The results of these zealous (and honestly reported) researches often threatened to embarrass the investigators. While the brain of the great Cuvier weighed an impressive 1,830 grams and that of the novelist Ivan Turgenev even exceeded 2,000 grams, other eminent men had evidently done their work with far lighter cerebral equipment: the founder of phrenology, Franz Josef Gall, for one, had made do with only 1,198 grams. Worse, it turned out that some professors' brains were smaller than those of some convicted criminals.[13]

But these findings did not deter, even if they disturbed, the craniometrists. Their theories were a matter of faith; faced with inconvenient measurements, they would retreat to hastily improvised positions, keeping their conclusions intact by complicating their criteria. They acted like the early-modern astronomers who managed to retain the increasingly implausible Ptolemaic theory by adding epicycles to their map of the solar system. Brain weight alone, Broca and his school eventually felt compelled to admit, does not wholly determine intellectual capacity; the shape of the brain, the richness of its convolutions, and other variables may also influence the results. But what had been plain at the beginning remained plain at the end, at least to Broca's satisfaction: races must be ranked. He was not surprised to find his own race securely lodged at the top of the ladder. More than once, proud of his scientific sophistication and contemptuous of mere dogmatists, Broca exposed the danger of self-serving inferences in the delicate matter of racial grading: "It is a natural tendency of men, even among those most free of prejudice, to attach an idea of superiority to the dominant characteristics of their race."[14] He did not apply this penetrating observation to his own method. He knew, and he did not know; plainly the stakes were high.

In retrospect, then, for all the anthropologists' professed devotion to cool quantification, their theories of race were nothing better than organized rationalizations of prejudices. They rested on superficial observations, facile conjectures, farfetched hypotheses, and self-promoting fantasies. If Social Darwinism embodied a largely illegitimate set of inferences from a legitimate scientific theory, racism embodied a wholly illegitimate set of inferences from illegitimate pseudoscientific assertions. The racists of course did not see it this way. Had they not been patiently developing their theories for decades? Early in the century, prestigious students of man had begun to elevate patronizing platitudes about racial qualities into so-called laws of human nature, and the tribal stereotypes that had served as rallying points in earlier ages were soon overtaken by the new obsession with race.

Despite their diligence and mutual support, though, nineteenth-century anthropologists could never devise a definition of race they could all accept. Some of them limited the range of the term to the most visible physical divisions among humanity; others, taking race to be dependent on culture, did not hesitate to speak of an English race or a race of journalists or of lawyers.* But

_____
*The practice of attributing racial characteristics to various groups was accepted enough for so discriminating a writer as William James to distinguish the "Latin races" (which think of sin in the

while they threw about "race" with an abandon that should have made lex-
icographers blush, all agreed on one essential: individuals with common ancestors carry in their blood inherent and indelible characteristics and capacities that
link them to other individuals sprung from the same racial family tree. The most
neutral use of the word "race" could not conceal the invidious element lurking
in the background; it was hard to resist the implication that a particular cluster
of qualities gave one race an edge over others. And as modern anti-Semitism
demonstrates, this implication was very hard to refute: if a Jew displayed certain
undesirable traits, these were evidence for an incorrigible racial endowment; if
no amount of research turned up the slightest trace of them, that showed they
were cleverly hidden—the cleverness being itself typical of the Jewish race.
Rhetoricians of race played with profit an old verbal game: Heads I win; tails
you lose.

Besides arguing with one another, race theorists also argued with themselves,
often awkwardly; they changed their minds as their imagination flourished or
their researches expanded. Early in the century, aspiring to the ideal of simplicity without disregarding the claims of complexity, the French naturalist Isidore
Geoffroy Saint-Hilaire offered a dual ranking of races, with sets and subsets.
Later on, in Britain, Thomas Henry Huxley followed suit, after some hesitations. In 1865, he listed eleven human races, but five years later he drew up a
more intricate scheme composed of five primary races and fourteen secondary
ones. In 1873, the zoologist Ernst Haeckel, whom we have encountered as
Germany's most authoritative popularizer of Darwin, listed twelve races, but in
1879, dissatisfied with the neatness of his formulation, he raised the number to
thirty-four.

One dramatic instance of such self-correction was the intellectual odyssey of
the eminent German orientialist and Oxford professor Friedrich Max Müller.
More than any other scholar, Müller, in his heavily attended lectures, put the
"Aryan race" on the map around 1860. But by the late 1880s, he ruefully
deplored what he had previously advocated and declared that "Aryan" could
refer only to a linguistic quality. It was really most annoying: "To me an
ethnologist who speaks of Aryan race, Aryan blood, Aryan eyes and hair, is as

---

plural and as a stigma "removable in detail") from the "Germanic races" (which think of "Sin in
the singular, and with a capital S"). *The Varieties of Religious Experience: A Study in Human Nature*
(1902), 134. While such imprecise usage took some of the edge off the term, those speaking of
"race hatred" and predicting "race war" were not disposed to weaken it. To complicate matters
further, racial categories were often confused with class categories, so that one snobbery sustained
another. See Philip Mason, *Prospero's Magic* (1962).

great a sinner as a linguist who speaks of a dolichocephalic dictionary or a brachycephalic grammar."[15]

It was too late; the value-laden racial epithet "Aryan" was off on its independent career. It conjured up a tall, fair-haired, blue-eyed, loyal, family-loving but warlike race, its manly—and womanly—members sharply contrasting with the Semites, who threatened to subvert civilization with their unhealthy offspring, mercantile outlook, and decadent modernism. By Müller's time it was becoming plain that racist thinking satisfied an appetite beyond the need for scientific accuracy. It licensed aggression.

Certainly not all researchers were quite so scrupulous, or obsessive, as Huxley and Müller. Many, in their ardor for the explanatory potency of the concept, discovered races and confidently wrote their history, patchy, evanescent, or downright imaginary though their evidence might be. The serious students of linguistic history or ethnic traditions were swamped by enthusiasts who made propaganda for the excellence of the Anglo-Saxons or their rivals, the Celts. The disputes of these enthusiasts were not well-mannered academic debates but exercises in unabashed self-congratulation—or, at times, perverse self-abasement. British and, following them, American anthropologists and comparative philologists, to say nothing of cultural historians, elaborated the myth of the sturdy, freedom-loving, energetic Anglo-Saxon race that entitled them to despise those of "mixed" or "lower" origins. The devotees of the Celts, for their part, found glimmers of their own admirable race in France, in Wales, in Scotland, and—though this was more problematic—in Ireland, and took pride in the poetic genius the race so beautifully displayed. After their defeat in the Franco-Prussian War, some of the French came to deplore their Celtic heritage, as they pathetically pitted it against the vigor of German Teutons and English Saxons. This was a deadly game that everyone could play, both ways.

Partisans of the Anglo-Saxon race made much of little; those of the Celts made more of less. The Anglo-Saxonists' favorite text was Tacitus's *Germania,* written some eighteen centuries before, an indispensable source book for polemicists seeking reasons to praise northern Europeans at the expense of lesser—shorter, darker-skinned, less pugnacious and more abstemious—mortals. They borrowed, too, from the fanciful comparative sociology of Montesquieu, who in the mid eighteenth century had tracked the origins of England's free institutions to the German forests. On the basis of such testimonials, Anglo-Saxonists offered circumstantial accounts of early English history. To them it exemplified the triumph of the Teutonic tribes—Jutes, Angles, Saxons—who had brought Britain the blessings of self-government in the dim past and had handed down their unmatched worthiness intact through the centuries. These mutually reinforcing clusters of historical fantasies fostered the comforting thought that Anglo-Saxon virtues gave the modern English and Americans a decisive advantage over their neighbors and potential enemies. On the other side the Celticists, building on vague references to northern tribes culled from ancient Roman historians, drew up their own catalogues of desirable racial qualities, hoping thus to create a counterweight to the boasts of their Anglo-Saxonist competitors.

Across the century, virtually all those who studied linguistic history, skeletal remains, or head shapes banked on the proposition that race is best when it is purest. But to the degree that rationality still flickered among them, they could hardly deny that the history of the world was a history of invasions and consequently of intermarriages. With few exceptions, race theorists concluded that such mingling, unless it occurred among racially identical clans, was calculated to drag civilization down the slippery slope of decadence. In his influential treatise, Gobineau explicitly, and tautologically, observed that "a nation perishes under social scourges because it is degenerate, and it is degenerate because it perishes." He did not intend to minimize the responsibility for social decay of other social ills such as fanaticism, luxury, immorality, and irreligion, but he declared the mixture of the superior white race with the inferior yellow and black to be the most pressing problem of the age. Liberals who subscribed to the dogma of fraternity, he asserted, were contradicting one of the oldest and soundest of human convictions—that the races are essentially unequal. Those who pretended they were really free of a secret aversion to crossbreeding were hypocrites.[16] In the hands of Gobineau and his followers, the survival of the fittest had somehow turned into the survival of the unfittest. The racist alibi for aggression shifted to pessimism; once the attribute of a triumphant conqueror, aggression was transformed into the self-protective policy of great races in danger.*

*The parallel to the shift from buoyancy to gloom among Social Darwinists is close. Significantly, so well educated and clever a politician as Henry Cabot Lodge, the powerful Republican senator from Massachusetts, could not resist employing racist arguments even though he did not fully believe them. Perceiving the millions of immigrants from southern and eastern Europe to be a threat, he spoke as a pragmatic racist in his campaign for restrictive legislation. On March 16, 1896, he told his colleagues, honestly enough, that there is "no such thing as a race of original purity according to the divisions of ethnical science," but quickly added that there are "artificial races," made by "climatic influences, wars, migrations, conquests, and industrial development." And when these artificial races were permitted to mix, the "lower" would outdo the "higher." Barbara Miller Solomon, *Ancestors and Immigrants: A Changing New England Tradition* (1956), 115–16.

The mounting gloom of race theorists suggests that a dynamic ingredient in all this projection disguised as theorizing, all this slander in the name of scholarship, was an almost uncontrollable anxiety over the direction of modern civilization. It was an anxiety fed by ubiquitous conflicts in an unstable time. The French feared the impact of their low birthrate on the recruitment of future armies to fight the Germans; Americans worried about the massive influx of immigrants thought less desirable than the hitherto relatively homogeneous population; aristocrats could not reconcile themselves to the spectacular gains of democracy; the patricians of fading elites hated the parvenus who were conspiring to displace them from the pinnacles of power; Englishmen grew nervous over the invasion of Irish workers in their sprawling industrial cities; the members of newly organized labor movements resented those who would restrict their activities; conservatives were dismayed by the widespread appeal of socialist ideas, which if victorious must mean the death of civilization.

In short, group after group contrived to discover enemies everywhere. Some of these were real enough, but the favorite enemy was another race. Jeremiahs envisioned a race war to the death, though their scenarios varied: Anglo-Saxons against Celts, Aryans against Semites, Europeans against Asians, whites against blacks. "Indian-hating," Herman Melville wrote in *The Confidence-Man* in 1857, "still exists; and, no doubt, will continue to exist, so long as Indians do."[17] When Melville wrote, America's Indians were largely unable to exact revenge. But other despised "races"—the Irish in England or the Jews in Russia—still survived to fight, and suffer, another day. By the end of Queen Victoria's reign, the repercussions of these massive projections had already made a shocking record.

Among late-nineteenth-century purveyors of racist anxiety, the anti-Semitic French social scientist Georges Vacher de Lapouge is among the most instructive. A professor at the University of Montpellier and a self-styled "anthroposociologist," he energetically championed the transcendent virtues of the "dolicho-blond Aryan race," worried about its travail in modern polyglot culture, denounced the "Semites," and predicted a terrible blood bath to come. In the 1890s, when he began to write, there were some sixty thousand Jews in France, two-thirds of them in Paris—a mere two-tenths of one percent of the French population. After the pogroms of 1881 in Russia, a substantial number of refugees augmented that total, but the bulk of France's Jews had come to consider themselves French. Anti-Semitic propaganda to the contrary, they were neither concentrated in, nor dominated, commerce and banking, but spread out across the liberal professions and the arts. Lapouge, despite his claims to scholarship, had no interest in figures that contradicted his thesis, and no trust in assimilated Jews. His racism was unequivocal: "The blood one brings along in one's veins upon birth one keeps all one's life." To him, "race, nation, are everything." That Kaiser Wilhelm II should have esteemed Lapouge as "the only great Frenchman" attests to his prestige in powerful circles and to his salience as a symptom for his day.[18]

In his best-known treatise, L'Aryen: Son rôle social, Lapouge celebrated homo Europaeus, the Aryan, and singled out the Jew as his "only dangerous competitor." The book is larded with all the fetishes of the race theorist: cephalic indexes, sketches of skulls, charts and numbers. It struck him as trustworthy evidence for his racist theories that the Jews, though wanderers over the earth for many centuries, had never changed. They were now, in modern France, Poland, or Hungary, just as they had been in ancient Babylon and Egypt. Whatever their looks, "everywhere they are the same, arrogant in success, servile in misfortune, crafty, extremely dishonest, great hoarders of money, of remarkable intelligence, yet at the same time incapable of creating anything"— and always "odious."[19] And he comfortably noted that whatever persecutions they had undergone the Jews had brought on themselves. In his bald caricature, the link between the imputation of unalterable racial qualities and the alibi for aggression is direct.

Fortunately, Lapouge soothed himself, the Aryan's "intense combativeness" has made him not only "a military and industrial conqueror but also a free man," both "aggressive" and a "model soldier."[20] But this optimism was a whistling in the dark: the future was clouded. While Jews lacked the military virtues, their "prodigious aptitude" for speculation and crooked dealings, coupled with their high birthrate, made their domination of France, perhaps of all Europe, extremely probable. He feared that a bad race would win out over its betters. Lapouge refused to give up all hope: the great struggle for world mastery was at hand, and surely the large nations, with their immense resources, would triumph. But it would be a bloody conflict. "One shudders at the human hecatombs the future has in store."*

In predicting race wars, Lapouge and his fellows supported the cause of more or less naked aggressiveness. At times it became naked indeed. In 1890, in Problems of Greater Britain, a bulky, widely appreciated treatise on the British Empire, the Liberal politician Sir Charles Dilke foresaw a decisive racial confrontation between the Russian and the British peoples. Fortunately, Dilke

---

*L'Aryen: Son rôle social (1899), 476, 481, 500. "Political science," Lapouge announced, wrapping himself in the mantle of the scientific student of society, "prefers the reality of Forces, of Laws, of Races, of Evolution to the fictions of Justice, Equality, Fraternity." Socialists and clericals might form a reactionary alliance against the "barbarian" Darwinists, but the future belonged to the social scientist who could face the unvarnished truth. Ibid., ix, 514.

thought, the largely Anglo-Saxon British Empire would win out, since it had preserved all the best racial qualities: "Courage, national integrity, steady good sense, and energy in work such as are perhaps unknown elsewhere."[21] There were moments in history—and Dilke evidently thought this was one—when aggression is on the side of the good battalions.

His was still relatively tame talk. E. A. Freeman, the most prestigious among the Teutonic school of English historians, was far more vociferous. He paraded what he frankly called his "Aryan prejudices" with a freedom that invites quotation. A profitable lecture tour in the United States in 1881–1882, which gave him abundant opportunities to observe race relations, only supplied fodder for his already pronounced racist attitudes. "This would be a grand land," he wrote a friend from New Haven, "if only every Irishman would kill a negro, and be hanged for it." This sentiment was, he thought (not wholly without cause) "generally approved," though few expressed it quite so brutally. To Freeman, "niggers" resembled "big monkeys dressed up for a game," mere "half-men, and still more half-women," or "hideous apes whom Darwin has clearly left unfinished." The Jews, Freeman thought, were more human in appearance but scarcely more admirable. They "controlled the press of half the world" and were only too sharp in their commercial dealings. These genial convictions permitted Freeman to take a light-hearted view of the pogroms that were then outraging humane opinion across Western civilization: "The Russians have punched some Hebrew heads irregularly."[22] These pronouncements were not eccentric; Freeman was neither crank nor outsider. His sponsors in American universities were distinguished, and his appointment in 1884 as Regius Professor of Modern History at Oxford must disarm any question about his respectability. Even some among those who found Freeman's racism anathema responded to his fervid Anglo-Saxonist enthusiasm.

In Britain and the United States, then, in Germany, in Italy, and elsewhere, race theorists by the score, some more excited than others, busied themselves with sticking pins into selected opponents. Race stereotypes shifted with perceived needs, but they persisted, growing more and more vicious. In the 1850s, English political cartoonists had caricatured the Irishman as the alcoholic, childlike, relatively innocuous Paddy. After the Irish secret Fenian Brotherhood had struck terror into English populations with isolated acts of terrorism, the cartoonists redrew him, abandoning haughty humor for slashing defamation. In 1882, in one of John Tenniel's cartoons for *Punch,* he appears as a ferocious Frankenstein's monster, a gorilla-like creature complete with fangs, a masked Caliban wielding a wicked knife.[23] As social observers recognized at the time (though, of course, without the psychoanalytic vocabulary), projection at its most savage reduced the Other to subhuman stature. And to deprive him of his humanity authorized the most uncontrolled aggression against him. If Freeman thought the "nigger" a mere monkey, anti-Semitic orators, increasingly racist from the 1870s on, reduced the Jew to vermin.

Such denigration was convenient; after all, extermination of a lesser species need arouse no guilt. As early as 1846, the American diplomat and man of letters James Russell Lowell had unmasked and mocked this mental stratagem in his famous *Biglow Papers*. Speaking of the attitude Americans had adopted toward the Mexicans they were then fighting, he wrote:

> Afore I come away from hum I hed a strong persuasion
> Thet Mexicans worn't human beans,—an ourang outang nation,
> A sort o' folks a chap could kill an' never dream on 't arter,
> No more 'n a feller'd dream o' pigs thet he hed hed to slarter.[24]

More than half a century later, in 1901, in a brilliant exposé of British war propaganda against the Boers, the iconoclastic economist J. A. Hobson quoted these lines and applied them to the way the gutter press was poisoning the minds of its readers against their South African adversaries.[25]

Racist name-calling could sink to astonishing depths. In 1913, Dr. Vladan Djordjević, a Serbian politician and expert in public health, characterized Albanians as bloodthirsty, stunted, animal-like, so invincibly ignorant that they could not tell sugar from snow. These "modern Troglodytes" reminded him of "prehumans, who slept in the trees, to which they were fastened by their tails." True, through the millennia, the human tail had withered away, but "among the Albanians there seem to have been humans with tails as late as the nineteenth century."[26] Racists had been letting their imaginations roam like this for decades.

Admittedly Tenniel and Djordjevic were extreme. But in late-nineteenth-century racist talk the extreme was often the normal. And it touched millions of lives; the subject was never the private preserve of cloistered scholars or perverse dilettantes, of anthropologists infatuated with their skull measurements or bureaucrats justifying the unjustifiable. The theories spawned by intellectuals found resonance among the general public, including the middle classes, because they dovetailed with their self-interest and, even more, with their anxieties. Racism appealed to merchants and workingmen feeling threatened by foreigners and to settlers in colonies with overwhelmingly black populations.

At times, as in the notorious Eyre episode, talk turned into action. The affair, which cruelly divided British opinion in the mid-1860s, had a tangled prehistory. After the British Empire had abolished slavery in 1833, and after trying years of adjustment, sugar planters in Jamaica had fallen on hard times. They had not been generously compensated for their losses from emancipation, and many of them were financially overcommitted. Obstinately they refused to diversify their crops despite declining markets, devastating droughts, and pressing competition from other sugar-producing colonies. Most damaging of all, they could not keep the black freedmen, who preferred to cultivate their own crops, on their plantations. In December 1849, Thomas Carlyle weighed in with a diatribe, "Occasional Discourse on the Negro Question," in which he canvassed the planters' situation. For two decades he had been the scourge of mindless, heartless industrial society, but now his crankier side was emerging. The planters, he noted, were suffering under regrettable labor shortages, and, he added, writing as usual at the top of his voice, several million of them were on the verge of starvation. Yet, to his disgust, his "PHILANTHROPIC FRIENDS" were not interested in their hard lot, but seemed moved only by the plight of "our interesting Black population."[27]

To Carlyle's mind, the hypocritical benevolence that gave the English philanthropist, that "sad product of a sceptical Eighteenth Century," such pleasure, was wasted. Blacks were incurably lazy, drunken louts who would far rather swill their rum and and blackmail the white settlers for higher wages than work in the sugar plantations. In a typical paradox, Carlyle thought that the blacks had a perfect right to be forced into doing competent work. Otherwise they would just be idle. "Sitting yonder with their beautiful muzzles up to the ears in pumpkins, imbibing sweet pulps and juices; the grinder and incisor teeth ready for ever new work"—this was the level of Carlyle's analysis, lending racism the dubious assistance of his feverish and quirky eloquence.[28]

Carlyle's invective against "philanthropism" enjoyed the flattery of imitators. Strong-minded conservatives borrowed the rude insults he aimed at English liberals and missionaries, for their "rosepink Sentimentalism" and their cavalier disregard of misery among the British poor in favor of remote "brothers." These were the men who believed in the pedagogic value of flogging, severity with undeserving spongers, and racial inequality.[29] But not everyone admired Carlyle's outburst; it provoked a heated rebuttal from John Stuart Mill, a formidable liberal debater. Mill had long admired Carlyle the prophet, but he could not let this nasty effusion pass by in silence. Carlyle, he pointed out, was championing the brutal right of the strongest and the most "damnable" doctrine that "one kind of human beings are born servants to another kind."[30] Certainly in Jamaica, even after the abolition of slavery, most whites subscribed to that doctrine and felt frustrated at their inability to enforce it, while their "free" laborers continued to feel like slaves.

Edward Eyre stepped into this Jamaican minefield in 1862. He had acquired a good deal of experience with dark-skinned races as a sheep grower and administrator in Australia, New Zealand, and other British outposts. But as governor of Jamaica, a post he officially assumed in 1864, he proved inflexible, imperious, and arbitrary. When, in October 1865, a rebellion broke out among the island's blacks, he could neither control his responses nor restrain his troops and suppressed the uprising with unmitigated ferocity. Almost 450 natives were shot without trial or hanged after a perfunctory court-martial; some 600 were flogged, and about 1,000 houses, many of them flimsy huts, were burned to the ground.[31] Most scandalous of all, a prominent, talkative, difficult local magistrate, an educated mulatto named William Gordon whom Eyre held responsible for the revolt, was executed after illegal proceedings.

The news, above all the manner of Gordon's death, hit a raw nerve in Britain. While an official commission severely censured Eyre for his handling of the uprising, a fascinated public was divided. A Jamaica Committee, driven by John Stuart Mill's determination to have the governor tried for murder, faced a well-organized Eyre Defense Committee, quite as determined to establish that he was innocent, even that his conduct was meritorious. Each party recruited prominent personages, celebrities to conjure with: Eyre's infuriated prosecutors mobilized Darwin, Huxley, Spencer, the philosopher T. H. Green, and the legal scholar A. V. Dicey; his indignant defenders could drop such names as Ruskin, Dickens, Tennyson, and Carlyle. The controversy divided friends far more used to fighting shoulder to shoulder; politicians, writers, artists, newspapers and periodicals took sides, many of them prepared to question the others' facts and motives. The casualties were wounded only by words, but the bitterness rankled.

In the end the Jamaica Committee lost the venomous debate—Eyre escaped prosecution—but the cause of understanding the racist alibi lost even more. Some of Eyre's most uncompromising detractors virtually apologized for their stand. The positivist lawyer Frederic Harrison acknowledged, "I have no more liking for black men than for Baptists." And E. S. Beesly, a radical professor of history at the University of London, wanted it understood that he was "no negro-worshipper. I don't consider a black man a beautiful object." To be sure, some blacks might have abilities and a good character, "but there can be no doubt that they belong to a lower type of the human race than we do." Even Huxley was moved to make plain that he had joined the Jamaica Committee not from "any particular love for, or admiration of the Negro," but because a careful reading of the record had convinced him that Eyre had violated the law.[32] They might differ decisively on the proper limits of aggression, but the two contending parties had more in common than they thought.

The Eyre case focuses attention on the arena in which much late-nineteenth-century racist discourse was translated into deeds: the colonies. Dissenting voices, true anti-imperialists on secular or religious grounds, grew fainter with each decade. By the 1880s, it was accepted wisdom that the higher races were destined to expand and to rule over their inferiors in continents not yet fully opened to the West.[33] Even the new great powers, the United States among them, took to this sincerely felt propaganda with a will. As Americans awoke to the recognition that they could compete with other serious players in world politics, they devised intoxicating slogans like "manifest destiny" to justify their expansionism. Imperialism was nothing less than a sacred duty imposed on the higher races. This, of course, was the lesson of Kipling's overworked verses in "The White Man's Burden," which thousands found memorable, verses that urged the white man to take up his heavy destiny and send the best of his race into "exile" to serve their "captives' need." That need was, it seems, imperative: "in heavy harness," the white man must wait on his "new-caught, sullen peoples, / Half-devil and half-child." The last line is scarcely a flattering portrait of the lucky beings the white man was obliged to raise to a higher level of civilization.

This call to duty was the dominant refrain of imperialistic rhetoric through-out these decades. In his best-selling *Our Country* of 1885, the prolific American divine Josiah Strong praised the Anglo-Saxon race for its genius at colonizing and argued that its sterling qualities fitted it to impose its blessings on lesser, more shiftless races. In fact, Strong foresaw a *"final competition of races, for which the Anglo-Saxon is being schooled."* The "result of this competition of races will be the 'survival of the fittest.' "[34] The italics were emphatically Strong's, and his borrowing from Spencer exhibits how heady the blending of Social Darwinism with racism could be.

The final competition that Strong and others foresaw would most likely be fought out in the empires that the British and French, Belgians and Germans, Portuguese and Americans were amassing or consolidating in Africa, Asia, and the West Indies. But while there would be tense confrontations among the great powers for contested territories, the most ferocious bloodletting would be between colonizers and the natives they were struggling to subdue. Cruelty and brutality are an old story; the nineteenth century did not invent atrocities. On the contrary, in significant ways its record compares favorably with the record of its predecessors and that of our own century. But this was an age of frantic colonization, with major—and would-be major—powers engaged in a race for terrains they coveted for their minerals or their strategic location. Whether sent out on official missions or working on their own account, adventurers could operate with relative impunity. In remote, little-known and little-visited regions, they satisfied their aggressive needs with abandon. And more: missionaries and explorers often mixed sexual excitement with their sheer aggressiveness. Homoerotic travelers admired the bodies of the local men, and lascivious heterosexuals admired those of the local women, reporting home about naked breasts, legs, and buttocks worthy of the artist's pencil.

The conduct of these colonial conquistadors, marked by arrogance at best and only too often by outright sadism, was adaptive—from their perspective. Men willing to vegetate in harsh tropical climates, to treat with alien and often antagonistic peoples, and to face deadly diseases, were by the nature of their work self-selected types. The bush, the jungle, the tribal village, were no place for the timid merchant, the domesticated bourgeois. What was wanted were athletic, often enough self-destructive, counterparts to industrial buccaneers, ruthless men with an outsized sense of self whether authentic or carefully nurtured. Carl Peters was among the most notorious; restless, ambitious, inordinately vain, and self-absorbed far beyond the bounds of the normal, he was the loudest, most indefatigable advocate of a German empire in the 1880s. In 1884, he founded the Society for German Colonization to propagate his impassioned program, one his government viewed with ambivalence. But this did not inhibit his aims, which he publicized in the best Social Darwinist style. Colonial policy, he wrote in 1886, "is and remains the ruthless and determined enrichment of one's own people at the expense of other, weaker peoples."[35]

The history of nineteenth-century aggression is partly a history of pathology, and the share of pathology among enthusiastic racist colonizers was impressive. Interestingly enough, what made some of these freebooters angriest at the indigenous tribes in their path was "insolence." Peters, for one, was plagued by the thought that natives might somehow be laughing at him. Late in the 1880s, he led two expeditions to eastern Africa, concluding treaties of annexation with local chieftains. He found the negotiations irritating, almost literally maddening. The most autocratic severity was the only acceptable stance: he had learned that it was impossible to get on with the natives without recourse to corporal punishment. Only uncompromising firmness could stop black natives from robbing and cheating the white man; they despised any show of kindness as a sign of weakness. "If I give a black chief an ox, he will be immediately inclined to take away my whole herd; but if I give him a blow with my whip, he will be on the contrary inclined to make me a present of oxen."[36]

Taking loss of face personally, Peters and his like experienced native "insolence" as a dire narcissistic injury. It was in defense of their integrity that colonizers had to take the strictest measures. "I have found," Peters wrote, recalling military expeditions in eastern Africa against tribes that had never seen a white man, "that these peoples are impressed only by manly energy and, in certain cases, by ruthless force."[37] Presumably intended to impress others, the adventurers' display of manliness showed how badly they needed it to impress themselves.

Peters has been called a psychopath, not without reason. But the sensitivity to slights from natives was a trait he shared with saner colonizers. In 1867, analyzing the Jamaican planters' response to the rebellion two years earlier, Charles Roundell, secretary of the investigating commission, shrewdly observed that they had "resented" the uprising "as a kind of personal insult." And there was Sir Leander Starr Jameson, Cecil Rhodes's confidant, whose name will forever be attached to his quixotic raid on the Boer colony of Transvaal designed to further Rhodes's ambition for power over all South Africa. Jameson justified draconian measures against obstreperous South African natives— burning down their villages and killing them wholesale—on the ground that they had been "impertinent and threatening."[38]

What legitimated these distant barbarities in the home countries is as important to the historian as the barbarities themselves, and more complicated. The unadventurous Belgian, British, and German bourgeois, who would have been misfits in the tropics, naturally had no direct experience with the "discipline" their compatriots were enforcing in exotic climes, but if they chose, they could read about it in the daily newspapers or in radical exposés. Yet many of them had been schooled to indifference, to a sort of silent complicity, by the soothing implications of racist doctrines. Their complaisance rested on the anodyne called self-interest, but not on that alone. Adventurers wanted to secure glory, politicians prestige, and military planners naval bases; entrepreneurs wanted profitable concessions, and missionaries Christian converts. And it was all so far away.*

Hence in the early 1880s most Belgians, apart from a few indignant socialists, cheerfully acquiesced in the formation of the Congo Free State, the private empire Leopold II had patched together in central Africa, skillfully maneuvering among the great powers that were carving up the "dark" continent. As long as their king was taking full responsibility and paying all the bills, his subjects could resort to the comfortable psychological mechanism of denial; they could live as though they knew nothing of the monopolies in ivory and rubber the

---

*For a characteristic instance of how those who stayed at home could deceive themselves about distant realities, see E. Jung, writing in a German family weekly about his country's colonial aspirations. He describes the "peaceful competition of nations" in Africa, and notes that merchants from the expansionist countries have settled in the "dark continent" to "exchange products of European industry for articles from those lands, to open up new markets, and to conquer new lands for civilization." "Deutschlands Colonialbestrebungen. Deutsche an der Westküste von Afrika," *Die Gartenlaube*, XXXII (1884), 609.

royal owner of the Congo state had introduced. They could remain quite as ignorant of atrocities against the natives toiling—and often dying—for his personal gain. In the early 1890s, ugly reports began to filter through to Europe, accusing Belgian officials and the "sentinels" who supervised native workers of flogging their charges, sometimes to death, of punitive shootings and ingenious mutilations. But these rumors did not arouse public opinion. It was best not to know.

Some of the disciplinary orgies that Leopold's men staged must have given pleasure for their own sake. But their underlying cause was far less the sadism of a few soldiers and administrators drunk with absolute power than the king's unremitting quest for cash. As in other colonies heavily dependent on mines and plantations, the issue in the Congo was productivity, or rather, its lack.[39] Leopold was dancing on the edge of bankruptcy, and the instruction he gave his agents—maximize profits—left little leeway for laxity or humane scruples. The king was endowed with an enviable gift for self-deception: when he first learned of the abuses, he was horrified and ordered them to be stopped, but he did not rescind his economic policy. And it was this policy that made the atrocities virtually inescapable.

In 1904, as embarrassing investigations of the king's Free State multiplied, a British consul on the spot found their accusations credible.[40] Yet it was not until four years later that the Belgian government annexed his plaything, after authoritative reports had confirmed that the most frightful accusations were not the fantasies of left-wing cranks or tender-minded philanthropists, and informed public opinion in other countries had loudly denounced Leopold's African regime.

The imperialistic mood, which blinked at such behavior and even found plausible reasons to defend it, also pervaded the German political public around the turn of the century. Germany had come to the colonial race late and reluctantly. But once ensconced in the scattered African regions that the British and French had not thought worth taking, German settlers moved efficiently to reduce the tribes inhabiting their new domains into servants of their interests. In 1904, in German Southwest Africa, this policy produced an explosion that reverberated all the way to Berlin. The Hereros, an agricultural people who had had the land to themselves until the Germans came, rose in force. One of the army officers most deeply implicated, naturally a zealous apologist for his country's colonial policies, described the reasons for the outbreak with deliberate blandness: the principal cause of the rising had been the "*hatred of the Hereros against foreign German domination.*" That hatred "naturally grew and grew as German influence spread and, with that, the native element was pushed back."[41]

What this officer smoothly called the spreading of German influence had amounted to stealing the Hereros' one prized asset, their cattle, by driving the people from their grazing lands or cheating them through deceptive barter arrangements. When the Hereros, their patience exhausted, rebelled against their German masters, they killed over a hundred settlers, though, gallantly enough, they spared women, children, and other foreigners. The Germans retaliated mercilessly. Relying on modern firepower, reinforcements from home, and a new commander, General von Trotha, they virtually annihilated the tribe. After the revolt had been suppressed, the official report congratulated the German command for its ruthlessness. The troops had hunted down the Hereros like so many wounded beasts, and realized von Trotha's aim, "to destroy the rebellious tribes with streams of blood and streams of money."[42] The casualty figures show that he had realized it only too well; by 1906, three-quarters of the eighty thousand Hereros were dead—shot, hanged, starved to death—or in exile, and the survivors, once rich in cattle, were miserable beggars.

General von Trotha's explicit strategy of terror, congenial to a man of his character and predictable from his previous record, documents once again the liberating power of the racial alibi. He proclaimed that the German forces would take no prisoners, and he signed himself, "The great general of the most powerful Emperor."[43] His language was to become notorious, but von Trotha knew that Wilhelm II, that most powerful emperor, was following developments in Southwest Africa closely and fully approved of his savagery. Some German politicians, though, found it unpalatable or, in any event, too expensive. Opposition deputies—members of the Catholic Center party, Progressives, and Social Democrats—asked questions in the Reichstag, caviled at the mismanagement of the punitive expedition, and hinted at corruption. But they did not capture public opinion.

True, von Trotha was recalled in 1905—too late for the Hereros—and the debate over German conduct in Southwest Africa simmered on. But it ended two years later with a graphic vindication of the government in elections that strengthened its hand and cut the Social Democratic presence in the Reichstag nearly in half. During the election campaign, the government's colonial policy was among the dominant issues of partisan combat. The usual critics criticized it, the usual supporters of the government supported it; liberals and socialists faced, as they so often did, conservative bourgeois and the most politically vocal aristocrats. On the hustings, the defenders of officially sanctioned aggression resorted to chauvinist appeals with more than customary intensity. To impugn the reputation of hard-working German settlers, or of the heroic German force that had rescued them from savages, was unpatriotic. To raise uncomfortable questions about the conduct of von Trotha was to love the Hereros better than one's fellow Germans. In contrast, to applaud German expansionism was to participate in the country's effort to stand tall among the great nations. The "colonial idea," as the Social Democratic strategist Karl Kautsky ruefully commented after his party had been trounced at the polls, had far more "recruiting power" than his party had expected. Manliness compounded with racism was a hard combination to run against.[44]

But it is worth repeating that the widely credited racist pseudoscholarship could not escape the vigorous questioning that was the hallmark of the bourgeois century. Unrepentant skeptics—some of them left-wing politicians, some of them well-trained anthropologists, some of them independent-minded philosophers—were alert to the opportunism and the irrationality that lurked in narcissistic self-definitions. The age that carried the disease of scientific racism also provided sustained efforts at finding an antidote; late in the century, empiricists and liberals intensified the skeptical questions that had never quite died out.

In 1872, in a book attempting to link biology to politics, Walter Bagehot shrewdly cautioned against the innumerable abstract principles that had been "eagerly caught up by sanguine men, and then carefully spun out into books and theories, which were to explain the whole world." A realistic view goes against such abstractions. The young and the unwary may be impressed by such systems, "but cultivated people are very dubious."[45] Some indeed were. In 1878, the German anthropologist Robert Hartmann, a professional student of African tribes, alerted his colleagues to the unhelpful caricatures of blacks with which enthusiastic but ill-trained travelers were seducing the lay reader. Richard Burton's distortions, illustrated with hideous "Nigger mugs," Hartmann said severely, could only create a "veritable devastation in half-educated and confused minds." Two years before, in his monograph on the Nigriter, Hartmann had already dismissed the whole racist case as nonsense: "The Aryans are an invention born in a scholar's cell." In 1886, Gabriel de Mortillet, a respected French anthropologist, reiterated this polemical agnosticism in the prestigious *Bulletin* of the French Anthropological Society. As for the Aryans, he said, "I do not know what they are."[46]

After the turn of the century, in 1902, William James joined the chorus of unbelievers. He described the sense of mission animating imperialists of the Anglo-Saxon or Celtic persuasion as a kind of religion, and not a commendable one: "Certainly the unhesitating and unreasoning way in which we feel that we must inflict our civilization upon 'lower' races, by means of the Hotchkiss guns, etc., reminds one of nothing so much as of the early spirit of Islam spreading its

religion by the sword." Four years later, James's colleague at Harvard the philosopher Josiah Royce tied race theories squarely to aggressiveness, where they
belong: "Our so-called race problems are merely the problems caused by our
antipathies."[47]

Perhaps the most authoritative among the late-nineteenth-century critics of
racism was Salomon Reinach, the prolific French archaeologist, classical
philologist, and historian of religion and art, whose mastery of the literature was
unsurpassed. A rationalist in the style of the Jewish Enlightenment, he was filled
with contempt for his devout brethren, but he never denied his heritage. Hence
racism held a special meaning for him. But scholarship rather than defensive
rage guided his pen. In 1892, in a lively, virtually exhaustive survey of modern
speculations about the Aryans, he acknowledged that investigation into their
origins was still, for science, "the order of the day." A fascinated public was
following the issue "with ardor." But he noted that from the beginning of the
century, linguists and anthropologists had differed over both the physical appearance of the prehistoric Aryans and their place of origin. Most visualized
them as tall and blond; others were sure they had been brunette and stocky. The
majority placed the Aryans' origins in Asia; others preferred Scandinavia or
eastern Germany. A few had restricted the name "Aryan" to a group of languages; most scholars enlarged it to signify a race. Reinach praised a handful
among these impassioned publicists as learned and sober, but denigrated the
overwhelming majority as excited and dogmatic. No matter how resounding
their academic diplomas, they were sheer amateurs and their results showed
it—hence the "scientific dilettantism" that disfigured nearly all contributions to
the debate. Reinach permitted himself to wax sarcastic even about Paul Broca,
"the learned professor." Nor was Broca his only victim. Reinach dismissed one
author for publishing a "little prehistoric novel" and another for injecting
"chauvinism" into scientific discourse. The trouble was that while one really
knew nothing about race—the cacophony of mutually exclusive theories, each
advanced with enviable confidence, should prove that—people had persuaded
themselves that they actually know a good deal. In short, it is "a gratuitous
hypothesis" to speak of "an Aryan race" at all.[48]

Even William Graham Sumner, for all his tough Social Darwinism, lent his
support to the anti-racist school. In 1903, he analyzed the phenomenon of
invidious comparisons in an essay remarkable for its psychological penetration.
For centuries, Sumner pointed out, savage Indian tribes had been no less ethno-
centric than literate citizens were now. Each tribe had seen itself as a race
favored by the gods. Drawing on this ethnographic observation, Sumner generalized about the interplay of love and hate: the cohesion binding a group
together is complemented by hostile feelings against the Other. "Any group, in

order to be strong against an outside enemy, must be well disciplined, harmonious, and peaceful inside; in other words, because discord inside would cause defeat in battle with another group."[49] Freud would say it not much better.

One might dismiss Sumner's argument for the utility of mixed feelings as pure Darwinian functionalism. But artless though the reasoning may be, Sumner's observations are solid enough: "There are two codes of morals and two sets of mores, one for comrades inside and the other for strangers outside, and they arise from the same interests. Against outsiders it was meritorious to kill, plunder, practice blood revenge, and to steal women and slaves." Sumner did not hesitate to identify religion as a prominent ingredient in this double standard; religion authorizes making war on the stranger. It had "always intensified ethnocentrism; the adherents of a religion always think themselves the chosen people or else they think that their god is superior to all the others, which amounts to the same thing."[50] Sumner, to be sure, was not a religious man. But his recognition that religion is a source of hatred found echoes among the pious as well. William Gladstone, as devout a Christian as lived in the Victorian age, acknowledged sadly in 1877, "The very worst things that men have ever done have been done when they were performing acts of violence in the name of religion."[51]

Jean Finot, a French magazine editor and humanitarian author, made the same case in 1905 in a heartfelt treatise against the rising tide of racist thinking. That thinking, he asserted, had begun innocently but grown into a scourge. On the international stage, the so-called science of race made invidious comparisons among nations; at home, perhaps even worse, it "preaches hatred and discord." Finot denounced the racists' unjustified claims to the support of science, which only lent respectability to destructive impulses. Preaching the necessity of hatred, it gave our secret bloodthirstiness free scope. It was, in a word, an alibi for the ugliest aggression. "In the name of science, people today talk about the extermination of certain peoples and races, as well as of certain classes." White Americans, he said, flaunt their superiority over blacks; Germans want to exterminate the Poles; Russians preach against the Yellow Peril; Turks massacre Armenians. "Pretexts to tear one another to pieces have become countless." And all in the name of science. "Of 1,000 educated Europeans," unfortunately "999 are persuaded of the authenticity of their Aryan origins," even though nobody has ever been able to prove such a lineage. Race theories were slipshod, internally inconsistent, and mutually incompatible; bluntly, Finot derided the whole Aryan business as a simple lie.[52]

In short, both before the turn of the century and after, a troop of vocal dissenters threw doubts on all racist claims. In analyzing the psychological roots of pseudoscientific bigotry, they gained a certain distance from self-satisfied assertions of racial superiority. Victorian novelists, philosophers, and students of man—a few of them in any event—carried on the work of the Enlightenment, with new, more refined diagnostic instruments. In 1903, in his novel *Sur la pierre blanche,* Anatole France spoke for this party: "The anti-Semites kindle the rage of Christian peoples against the Jewish race, and there is no Jewish race."[53] He was in accord with the sociologists and psychologists who cut through the impulsions to legitimize hatred to discover more adequate and more generous perspectives on group characteristics. That these critics took decades to convert presumably thoughtful men and women to their views, and failed outright with many of them, was due to the undeniable psychological fact that racist thinking provided pleasure. And, as Freud observed more than once, people are extremely reluctant to give up whatever gives them pleasure.

Hence the flood of tendentious conjectures about the glorious "Aryan race" could not be stemmed by the best-informed and most energetic scoffers. Even Reinach's critique of the mania for racial explanations—light in touch, moderate in tone, and devastating, one might think conclusive, in its marshaling of evidence—was about as effective as a popgun against a tank. Nor did sober treatises make much more of an impression on a public intoxicated with race. Race theorists had in their corner cherished and firmly held opinions.

The dilatory acceptance of Franz Boas's impressive rebuttals of racism demonstrates how hard it was to dampen the enthusiasm for racial confrontations, perhaps even race wars. Boas began his precise investigations into race in the 1890s. Addressing both his colleagues and an educated lay public, he rejected the favorite notion that racial traits are essentially stable. He could find no reliable evidence for this essential prop of racist thinking. Severe in his methods and prudent in his findings, Boas was a social scientist who followed the evidence wherever it led. He knew that "an expected result may influence an observation."[54] Broca had said the same thing, but unlike Broca, Boas let his observations influence his results. In an epoch-making short paper laden with graphs and charts, published in its final form in 1912, he reported that the children of immigrants to the United States differed markedly from their parents in height, weight, and even head shape. The last of these, the cephalic index, was the most sensitive indicator for Boas, since it was the most fashionable. Doing his research in a scientifically selected variety of populations, he increasingly appreciated the impact of the environment on human traits. Though he did not ever discount the share of heredity in the making of character, the role of nurture loomed ever larger in his thinking. During some four decades of teaching—he was appointed professor of anthropology at Columbia

University in 1899—Boas dominated and largely shaped American anthropology, and his students spread his healthy agnostic style of thinking on race across the academic world.

And yet: even though Boas enjoyed great influence among the experts, his findings did not noticeably diminish racial discrimination in housing, employment, education, or entertainment facilities, let alone the choice of a marriage partner. One good place to gauge the depth and persistence of racist feeling is the post–Civil War American South.[55] Obviously, in the antebellum years, few whites—and few blacks—ever doubted that God had appointed the white race to be master. Yet, save for some notable exceptions in its small cities, the South had not known racial segregation. Household slaves lived and labored, on a familiar if deferential footing, in the houses of their masters. Some of this intimacy was intimate indeed; it found expression in the presence of mulattoes, more visible in the towns than on the plantations. In short, for good and practical reasons, segregation was virtually unthinkable. Southern whites and blacks before the Civil War might be described as together but not equal.

Jim Crow, which underscored white supremacy by establishing legal segregation of the races in transportation, facilities, schools, housing, and places of entertainment, was in fact a Yankee invention. Early on, Tocqueville had observed in some astonishment, "The prejudice of race appears to be stronger in the states that have abolished slavery than in those where it still exists; and nowhere is it so intolerant as in those states where servitude has never been known."[56] The move of Jim Crow below the Mason-Dixon line after Emancipation ran up against ingrained Southern habits. Banishing blacks to the rear of streetcars and to separate waiting rooms, giving a black witness in court a separate Bible to kiss, and all the rest of the humiliating legislation, struck many Southerners, including unimpeachable conservatives, as ludicrous.

Indeed, a few audacious Southern liberals called for nothing less than a total end to racial discrimination. In *The Silent South,* published in 1885, the novelist George Washington Cable, a former Confederate soldier, insisted that the South could aspire to free and honest government only after it had realized the ideal of complete racial equality in employment, politics, and the administration of justice.[57] And Lewis H. Blair, a Virginia businessman and reforming politician with Southern credentials as impeccable as Cable's, argued in 1889 in an incisive, vehement little book that the South was poor because blacks were kept down. To elevate the black into a partner in the efficient production of wealth simply made good sense; to keep him down and teach him servile satisfaction with his lot was as shortsighted as it was immoral. But to give the black his due meant abandoning segregation. "The negro must be allowed free access to all hotels and other places of public entertainment; he must be allowed free admittance to all theatres and other places of public amusement; he must be allowed free entrance to all churches, and in all public and official receptions of president, governor, mayor, &c. he must not be excluded by a hostile caste sentiment." Blair was categorical: "In all these things and in all these places he must, unless we wish to clip his hope and crush his self-respect, be treated precisely like the whites, no better, but no worse."[58]

Blair's views, like Cable's, were admittedly radical, and they attracted little support. But they were not completely out of tune with Southern sentiment. A state as unimpeachably Southern as South Carolina did not segregate blacks and whites on railroad cars and streetcars until the very end of the century. And only at about this time did Southerners fully endorse Jim Crow. "God Almighty drew the color line," said the Richmond *Times* in 1900, calling for rigorous segregation, "and it cannot be obliterated."[59] These were relatively new accents. What C. Vann Woodward has called the "capitulation to racism" was an awkward, very gradual affair, abetted—in fact accelerated—by Northerners yielding to racist doctrine.[60] When, in 1896, in the notorious *Plessy* v. *Ferguson* decision, the United States Supreme Court endorsed the "separate but equal" doctrine, segregation had the blessing of the country's most irreproachably national spokesmen, Northern and Southern alike.

Again science—or what was called science—had done its bit for racism. The scores of earnest, presumably responsible treatises defending Jim Crow suggest just how prevalent and respectable race stereotypes had become. "All along the line," Woodward writes, "signals were going up that the Negro was an approved object of aggression." They were, these signals, "permissions-to-hate."[61] Their counterparts in Europe generated equally intensive popular support. And it was the confident way this literature licensed aggression that made the alibi, much like its companions—competition and manliness—so seductive and so dangerous for the bourgeois century.

3. Manliness: Ideal and Trauma

Unlike other nineteenth-century rationalizations for the cultivation of hatred, the cult of manliness depended less on science than on tradition. Far from being a modern invention, it attested to the resilience of aristocratic ideals. However sincerely Edmund Burke, writing in 1790 against the French Revolution, might mourn the death of chivalry, it remained very much alive. But Victorians democratized the courtly ideal of prowess, watering it down from a showy trait natural in the select few to an attribute highly commendable in middle-class men. In an age of waning opportunities for noble heroism, a bourgeois equivalent seemed needed. Those whom Baudelaire called, only half jokingly, the heroes of modern life exhibited prowess not on the battlefield but in the countinghouse, in the energetic but bloodless tournaments of commerce, industry, and politics.

One way of defining the modern meaning of manliness is to contrast it with the concurrent virtue of womanliness. Indeed, without the cult of womanliness, which was central to nineteenth-century bourgeois culture, the alibi for manly aggression remains incomplete. But as we shall see in chapter 4, the precise meaning of that virtue too was increasingly in question as the century went on. The alibi of manliness proved at best an uncertain mechanism for the liberation of aggressive impulses. Some publicists, to be sure, crudely celebrated manliness as sheer robust exhibitionism. Not long after mid-century, in a paper on heroism, the pugnacious English divine Charles Kingsley, chief of the muscular Christians, wondered out loud "whether the policeman is not demoralizing us; and in proportion as he does his duty well." He found it plausible that "the perfection of justice" and "the protection of body and goods" would "reduce the educated and comfortable classes into that lap-dog condition in which not conscience, but comfort, doth make cowards of us all," and would make the lives of the majority "mean and petty, effeminate and dull."[1] Men, he believed, needed a more strenuous environment than Victorian comfort provided.

The worry that the cultivated were growing (or had already grown) effeminate troubled many observers throughout the age, across Europe and the United States. In 1831, the year before his death, the aged Goethe, neither a good Christian nor particularly bellicose, had already deplored the decline of manliness. Looking over some modern etchings with Johann Peter Eckermann, his Boswell, he called attention to what was palpably missing in them all: "*Männlichkeit.*" He urged Eckermann to remember that word and underscore it.[2] Some seventy years later, William James echoed Goethe. Worried over what he thought the waning energies of the middle classes, he dramatized his point by pitting them against classical antiquity. "The Greeks had not made the discovery that the pathetic mood may be idealized, and figure as a higher form of sensibility. Their spirit was still too essentially masculine for pessimism to be elaborated or lengthily dwelt on." Surely the Greeks, who had kept "lachrymosity" within bounds, "would have despised a life set wholly in a minor key." Modern races were "more complex, and (so to speak) more feminine than the Hellenes" of the classical age.[3]

This tendentious comparison recalls the famous explosive harangue that William James's brother Henry gave to the male—exceedingly male—protagonist of *The Bostonians,* the Southerner Basil Ransom. An angry and in his harsh way

an attractive hero, Ransom scarcely represents the innermost feelings of his
author, a bundle of sensitivities if ever there was one. But he does represent the
manly ideology, which he expounds with excited adjectives, indicting as "feminine" his "nervous, hysterical, chattering, canting age, an age of hollow
phrases and false delicacy and exaggerated solicitudes and coddled sensibilities,"
all of them mortal enemies of "the masculine character, the ability to dare and
endure, to know and yet not fear reality, to look the world in the face and take
it for what it is."[4]

The Bostonians is fiction, not a sociological treatise; Ransom is a figure in a
novel, not a detached student of bourgeois culture. But his diatribe has a certain
diagnostic value: it sums up the case for manliness with eloquence and economy, and with the vituperativeness that the nineteenth century relished. Other
troubled students of contemporary culture heartily restated Ransom's lament.
In 1895, in his acceptance speech to the Académie française, the novelist and
essayist Paul Bourget told the other Immortals that the modern spirit was suffering from a sickness of the will, from nihilism and pessimism. Melancholy—
that most unmanly of diseases—was the maladie du siècle.[5]

By the turn of the century, this virile contempt for the spineless bourgeois
had grown into an international campaign. Otto Julius Bierbaum, that mild
German satirist with sardonic things to say about the Mensur, was only one of
many bourgeois-baiters in those years to scoff at the "philistine who loathes
everything that is out of the ordinary, distinctive, multicolored." The bourgeois was "the embodiment of all that is mediocre, and is made up of nothing
but the common, of the sand-papered, of sheer grayness." What eluded this
pathetic creature, unable to see that "danger is the spice of life," were the uses
and pleasures of aggression. The nineteenth-century philistine did not dare
acknowledge the great Darwinian truth that "struggle" is the supreme element
in human existence.[6]

Just after 1900, in his massive treatise on adolescence, the American psychologist G. Stanley Hall took the same tack. Boys must train their capacities in
"wrestling, fighting, boxing, dueling, and in some sense, hunting," thus emulating in their lives the animal world, which "is full of struggle for survival." He
welcomed schooling in "man-making" as a defense against "degeneration, the
essential feature of which is weakening of will and loss of honor. Real virtue
requires enemies, and women and effeminate and old men want placid, comfortable peace, while a real man rejoices in noble strife which sanctifies all great
causes, casts out fear, and is the chief school of courage." A few years later, in
1906, the French political theorist Georges Sorel, then in his revolutionary
syndicalist phase, despaired of the flabbiness of the "timorous humanitarian
middle class"; he proposed as an antidote that radicals pump up bourgeois

bellicosity, lest the class struggle lose all its savor and cleansing proletarian violence become a redundant exercise. In a treatise posthumously published the following year, the Austrian military judge and political scientist Gustav Ratzenhofer inveighed against the pacifism "propagated by women of both sexes," and warned against the "sad, culturally damaging" inability "to use force where force is appropriate."[7] The sexual innuendo against the effeminate bourgeoisie, an old rhetorical tactic, had lost none of its savor.

All could agree, furthermore, that manly men could safely count on women finding them irresistible. In one of his late novels, *The Duke's Children*, Anthony Trollope introduces Francis Oliphant Tregear, a young lover and, alas, a younger son in a family with recent pretensions to gentility, as intelligent, confident, and supremely good to look at: "He was dark, with hair that was almost black, but yet was not black; with clear brown eyes, a nose as regular as Apollo's, and a mouth in which was ever to be found that expression of manliness, which of all characteristics is the one which women love the best." Lady Mary Palliser, the duke of Omnium's daughter, loves this paragon, and defends his suitability, for all his poverty and comparatively undistinguished family connections: "He is a gentleman, highly educated, very clever, of an old family—older, I believe, than papa's. And he is manly and handsome; just what a young man ought to be. Only he is not rich."[8] What does impecuniousness matter in face of stunning looks and virile deportment?

In this age, desperate to control the passions, Don Juan, that fatal collector of mistresses, was out of place. Novelists like Trollope offered a safe, domesticated kind of Don—a handsome, appealing, in a word manly suitor. While Tregear and his fictional fellows leave little doubt that Trollope's century fancied a manly man, they were innocent bourgeois versions, lovers whom respectable men could identify with and good women could desire. Early in the century, in his singular dreamlike tale about Don Giovanni, in which fantasy and reality are curiously blended, E. T. A. Hoffmann had still hinted at the demonic power traditionally attributed to the Don Juan of song and story. Within the tale, the singer taking the title role is a "strong, magnificent figure," with "a prominent nose, penetrating eyes, softly formed lips" and "a face of manly beauty."[9] Later authors preferred to show their manly protagonists intent not on seduction but on matrimony.

Bourgeois, of course, also valued other qualities that made a man attractive to a woman: the right family connections, a good living in the church, promising economic prospects, perhaps a university degree. But good looks were far from negligible. In 1852, the American travel writer Grace Greenwood, crossing to Europe on the "gallant" steamer *Atlantic,* found herself at a table with Otto Goldschmidt, a well-known pianist and husband of the celebrated singer Jenny

Lind. He fascinated Greenwood, "not only as a man of genius, but of rare refinement and nobility of character." Yet, significantly, her sketch of him dwelt not on these qualities but on his appearance. "He is fair, with hair of a dark, golden hue, soft, brown eyes, thoughtful even to sadness. I have never seen a brow more pure and spiritual than his. Yet, for all its softness and youthfulness, Mr. Goldschmidt's face is by no means wanting in dignity and manliness."[10]

Greenwood's sensitive and discriminating description of Jenny Lind's attractive husband, who resembled Hoffmann's Don Giovanni with his softly formed lips, raises the suspicion that in the nineteenth century, the meaning of "manliness" was infected with incurable imprecision and subject to dispute. Alibis for aggression were far from unequivocal; one single, apparently simple word stood for diverse fantasies, meant many things to many men—and women. Hence it should occasion no surprise that one observer could call Oscar Wilde "manly," while another saw him as "unmanly."[11] Like the cloud with which Hamlet drove the courtier Polonius to comical despair, manliness looked sometimes like a weasel, sometimes like a whale.

Examples of "manly" as a term of genial, more or less unfocused approval are virtually inexhaustible from the beginning of the age to the end. A few must stand for many. In 1811, alluding to a quarrel between Lord Byron and his friend Thomas Moore that almost drove them to a duel before Byron deliberately cut it short, Samuel Rogers applauded Byron for being "candid & manly." Byron took this comment as a compliment for his readiness both to face danger and to abort it.[12] At mid-century, in his great *Römische Geschichte,* Theodor Mommsen admired the "manly eloquence" and "manly handsome appearance" of his cherished Julius Caesar. Around the same time, the French journalist Louis-François Veuillot found the identical quality in the political pamphlets of the journalist and playwright Auguste Romieu, who had thrown in his lot with Louis Napoleon: "One cannot say more things in fewer pages, nor say them with a more manly eloquence."* Thomas Babington Macaulay extolled the English yeomanry of the late seventeenth century as "an eminently manly and truehearted race," while Walter Bagehot observed in *Physics and Politics* that nations which gained "a little progressiveness" in exchange for "a great deal of hard manliness" had found themselves among the shipwrecks of his-

---

*Mommsen, *Römische Geschichte,* 3 vols. (1854–56; 2nd ed., 1857), III, 445, 446; Veuillot, in *L'Univers* for April 1851, quoted in Adrien Dansette, *Louis-Napoléon à la conquête du pouvoir* (1961), 318. Mommsen's term is *männlich;* Veuillot's is *mâle.* Both of these adjectives can simply refer to the male of the species, but are normally understood as terms of praise denoting vigor and force.

tory.[13] He was speaking for a wide consensus: one gave up one's manliness at considerable risk.

Novelists, especially English novelists, scattered this epithet with almost dizzying abandon. In *Martin Chuzzlewit*—to give but one instance—"manly" surfaces at least ten times. Young Martin Chuzzlewit's temper is "free and manly," and the righteous characters confronting the villain Pecksniff, that smooth fraud, look "so gallant and so manly beside him"; later, Dickens has John Westlock ask Tom Pinch for "a manly and straightforward answer" to a delicate question.[14] Impressionistic as they were about this admirable trait, Dickens and and his fellow novelists knew what their readers wanted—a manly hero marrying a womanly heroine. Humorists and philosophers, too, used the term freely. In the early 1860s, in one of the verses in *Bab Ballads,* W. S. Gilbert conjured up shades that were haunting him:

> Ghosts that hover about the grave
> Of all that's manly, free, and brave.[15]

Almost forty years later, learning that his friend John Ropes had died, William James mourned "old J. C. R.," with "his manliness, good-fellowship, and cheeriness, and idealism of the right sort."[16] Clearly, in the bourgeois century, manliness was not in short supply.

In these instances and many more like them, writers expected to be understood even though they did not—or, for that matter, could not—lend the epithet any settled significance. Often enough, "manly" worked as an affable platitude, a vague term of approbation, rather than a graphic characterization. When Hurrell Froude, as a youth, tortured his younger brother James by holding him by his heels and stirring up the muddy waters of a stream with his head "to make him more manly," one can understand, if hardly applaud, his pedagogic objectives. But when the object of this drastic training in virility searched all his life for "a positive, manly, and intellectually credible explanation of the world," it is not immediately clear just what kind of philosophy he was aiming at.[17] Perhaps one has some idea just why Henry James complained about the want of manliness in Burne-Jones's canvases, as one visualizes the willowy, often boneless, male figures populating these paintings.[18] But it is hard to fathom Thackeray's intentions when he admires in Robert Fleury's salon paintings "the *manliness* of the artist."[19] Since Thackeray was no friend to heroics, one may conjecture that what he recognized as the élan of Fleury's technique combined with a sturdy human sympathy moved him to adopt the vocabulary of manly ideologists usually so uncongenial to him.

The liberal application of the term to works of art and literature leaves little doubt that in the nineteenth century, "manliness" was at least in part an aesthetic category. Typically, just before 1800, the great German romantic critic Friedrich Schlegel praised an essay by Friedrich Schiller for being "definite, compressed, unornamented, and manly."[20] Schlegel was chiefly commending a terse and confident style, and his sort of compliment prospered throughout the Victorian years. Macaulay, in an early essay, singled out Machiavelli's "judicious and candid mind," which "shows itself in his luminous, manly, and polished language."[21] Later, at the turn of the twentieth century, Theodor Gomperz, an eminent Austrian philologist and historian of Greek thought, reported to a friend that he had just greatly enjoyed reading Gustav Frenssen's new novel, *Jörn Uhl*, "a manly, authentically German book."[22] For Gomperz, *männlich* summoned up the stubbornness and determination of the peasant hero in face of the intemperate, intolerant peasantry that surrounded him.

As though such verbal gymnastics were not confusing enough, Victorians extended manliness to women. Writing to his thirteen-year-old daughter Margaret, lonely and depressed far from home at an English school, William James tried to boost her morale by applauding her resolve: "I believe you have been trying to do the manly thing under difficult circumstances."[23] Samuel Smiles, the apostle of self-help, thought he was paying the doughty anti-feminist journalist Eliza Lynn Linton a compliment when he addressed her as "my most manly of your sex." Nor did it clarify matters that Victorians should at times give "manliness" a wry, derisive edge. Waxing sarcastic about the grandiloquent American general Fladdock in *Martin Chuzzlewit*, Dickens scoffs at his "manly breast."[24] In his novel *Sybil*, Disraeli notes that "a schoolboy's ideas of the Church then," just before passage of the Reform Act of 1832, "were fat livings, and of the State rotten boroughs. To do nothing and get something formed a boy's ideal of a manly career."[25] Serious as those endowed with manliness liked to be, they could appreciate the term's amusing side.

In fact, Heinrich Heine enlisted claims to "manliness" to mock the Germans slavishly "freeing" themselves in 1813: "When God, snow and the Cossacks had destroyed Napoleon's best forces, we Germans received orders from on high to free ourselves from the foreign yoke and we flamed up in manly wrath because of the servitude we had borne too long, and we thrilled to the good melodies and bad verses of Körner's songs, and we conquered our freedom; for we do everything commanded by our princes."[26] This confirms what we have noted before: if a woman could be manly or a real man laugh at "manliness," the ideal covered far too extended a terrain to be a truly reliable alibi for aggression.

To be sure, nineteenth-century writers made valiant efforts to lend this elusive ideal some substance, but their usages were incompatible with one another.

In 1848, during the race for the presidency of France, the liberal politician A. J. S. Dufaure commended one of the candidates, General Cavaignac, for his "*mâle*" qualities: "In the choice it must make, the nation must entrust itself to a past beyond reproach, an unchallenged patriotism, a resolution manly, energetic, already tested in the service of the Republic rather than to futile and deceitful promises." Manliness and energy are here inextricably yoked together.* Again, William Morris, bitterly lamenting his feeling of helplessness before depression and the dread of artistic sterility, confessed to a friend, "It seems so unmanly."[27] The manliness that Morris feared he lacked is easy to tease out: he was ashamed that he could not muster, in face of psychological travail, the tight-lipped stoicism that so many of his contemporaries prized as a man's peculiar endowment. And in a series of essays on courage, the prolific French publicist Charles Wagner identified "manly honour" with the sturdy refusal to capitulate to sensuality or take "advantage of the love of a pure girl". Here manliness means virginity.[28] These were brave but largely futile stabs at concreteness.

One implication of the epithet was relatively uncontroversial: its bearing on character. Thomas Carlyle depicted Cromwell as winning over the city of London in 1647 with his "noble manful *simplicity*."[29] For his part, Georg Ebers, a learned German Egyptologist and author of popular historical romances, recalled the headmaster of his *Gymnasium* as having been "earnest, thoroughly natural, able, strong, reliable, rigidly just, free from any touch of caprice," and "every inch a man."[30] In 1877, when Woodrow Wilson was a student at Princeton, his father sought to console him for failing to be admitted to an oratorical contest by invoking his strength of character. He rejoiced in his son's failure, he wrote, because it would show "the stuff you are made of." After some days of feeling discouraged, Woodrow would "arise with new resolution," with a stronger purpose, "prophetic of a noble and honorable manhood." It was a resounding, if a little pathetic exhortation, pure wishful thinking: "I know you. You are capable of much hard mental work, and of much endurance under disappointment. You are manly. You are true. You are aspir-

---

*Dansette, *Louis-Napoléon*, 250. Manliness might simply means "superiority." In Theodor Fontane's novel *Frau Jenny Treibel*, Frau Schmolke, a trusted long-time servant, tells her master's daughter Corinna Schmidt, the attractive heroine hesitating between two possible husbands, "You must get a smart man, one who is in fact smarter than you are—by the way, you aren't that smart—and who has something manly . . . before whom you have respect." *Männlich* here appears as an impressive, statuesque, almost threatening characteristic that a woman can only admire and never herself attain. *Frau Jenny Treibel* (1892), in *Sämtliche Werke*, ed. Edgar Gross et al., 24 vols. (1959–75), VII, 151 [ch. 14].

ing."[31] It was hard work being manly; it was harder work still being a manly man's father—or son.

Middle-class thinking about manliness was not merely ambiguous, but at times prudent and subtle as well. For many, the manly stance worked to support women's yielding acquiescence, and Victorian society did much to turn this ideology into a self-confirming prophecy.* But many others explicitly saw manliness as a happy balance between aggressiveness and discipline. In 1907, in a book on education for manliness, the German educator Ludwig Gurlitt first defined it as "the epitome of all the virtues that are the essence of a genuine man, such as truthfulness, courage, endurance, fidelity, nobility," and then quickly retreated, suggesting that such perfection was not a realistic goal. Real men were complicated, all-too-human, and not all of them were generals or aggressive statesmen; Bismarck was manly, but so were Goethe and Schiller, Beethoven and Wagner. Two years later, the German educator Friedrich Wilhelm Foerster singled out "firmness combined with kindness and self-control. That is the true flower of vigorous manliness." Indeed, "firmness is not generated by brutality and toughness; on the contrary, exaggerated external nerve is always a sign of lacking inner firmness, betrays a concealed fear and insecurity." This was a widespread view. Even G. Stanley Hall, for all his flamboyant paean to virility, disliked "overpugnacity." This is what Thackeray had in mind more than half a century earlier in his famous preface to *Pendennis*. His hero had experienced sexual temptation and risen above it: "He had the passions to feel, and the manliness and generosity to overcome them."[32] The authentic manly man, in this view, was at once self-assertive and self-controlled. Those who applauded tough talk about the manly male never dominated the debate; they were extremist in the party of virile aggressiveness.

Many propagandists for manliness, then, made room for tender touches, not so much as man's protective patronage for unworldly, weak-kneed females, but for the sake of tenderness itself. They saw nothing wrong with expressive emotional gestures, far from taboo even in the proverbially tight-lipped northern Protestant climes. A manly tear or two was acceptable to signalize an irreparable loss or celebrate a longed-for reunion in life no less than in fiction. Husbands could perform domestic offices at the crisis of childbirth or during a wife's illness, and perform them without apology, with a twinge of self-consciousness perhaps but without embarrassment. A man was not necessarily effeminate

*The relation between this manly stance and the Victorian concept of womanliness is discussed in chapter 4.

because he put down his sword, enjoyed reading poetry, or wept at a concert. Even the eugenicist Francis Galton, for all his tough-minded view of the human animal, could pay his tribute to complexity. In a lecture before the Sociological Society, listing desirable masculine qualities like "health, energy, ability" as well as "manliness," he quickly added "courteous disposition."[33] In turn, women could make their weight felt in the world, could be unflinching in their charitable endeavors as they encountered appalling poverty or disfiguring disease. They could disprove current commonplaces about woman as a limp doll without losing their reputation for womanliness. Ruskin's much-copied portrait of woman as the yielding queen content with presiding over the hearth while her consort brought home bleeding trophies from the combat zones of finance, industry, or politics, was a wish more than a fact.

At times it was not even a wish. On this score, the writings of Thomas Hughes, probably the most compelling popularizer of manliness at mid-century, are exceptionally revealing. His *Tom Brown's Schooldays,* a jolly and sentimentalized portrait of Rugby, the public school Hughes had attended and never quite outgrew, embodies the benign middle-class version of the manly prototype to perfection. It roused the reading public to enthusiastic response; almost everyone, not just nostalgic public-school graduates, found entertainment and reassurance in Hughes's good-tempered, philistine pages. *Tom Brown's Schooldays* made Hughes—lawyer, radical member of Parliament, Broad Church Anglican, Christian propagandist—a national celebrity almost overnight. From its first appearance in 1857, the book piled up edition after edition, dozens of printings in Britain and the United States, and translations into the major European languages.[34]

Tom Brown's manliness, Hughes alerts his readers in the opening pages, is a worthy inherited trait. "The Browns are a fighting family. One may question their wisdom, or wit, or beauty. But about their fight there can be no question." They are fiercely loyal to one another, dogmatic in their opinions, firm in adversity, and innocent of snobbishness. Young Tom, a good Brown in this as in all else, is a "robust and combative urchin," an acclaimed sportsman from his boyhood. He wrestles, goes fishing, and plays football; he excels in the sport of back-swording, an English village version of the Mensur, fought with sticks, which draws blood and leaves painful welts. It is characteristic of the book's pugilistic atmosphere that the chapter in which Tom is first introduced to Rugby centers on a lovingly depicted melee, a strenuously contested football match.[35]

Tom Brown's world is a world of decency, independence, informality, of self-sacrifice and authentic inward religious faith, of games hard fought and honestly won. It is a world without women, except, of course, for "dear mamma," who is always in Tom's heart, even when—especially when—he is far from home. At one critical moment, when he regains consciousness after being tortured by brutal schoolmates until he faints, his first word is "Mother!"[36] This is the exception that is no exception; Tom's love for his mother, the one woman in his life until, much later, he falls in love with a woman his own age, only guarantees the purity of his manliness.

Not unexpectedly, concern about manhood is steadily on Thomas Hughes's—and Tom Brown's—mind. The village boys who are young Tom's companions before he goes away to school are "manly and honest." And in a grand oration to his schoolmates at Rugby, the much-admired Old Brooke warns them that, whatever they may hear, "drinking isn't fine or manly." Hughes's frequent authorial interventions, little homilies all, are exercises in selling manly convictions and conduct. "Play your games and do your work manfully," he exhorts his readers, and "aquit yourselves like men then; speak up, and strike out if necessary for whatsoever is true and manly, and lovely, and of good report." For Hughes, the unsurpassed exemplar of human excellence, a model to his pupils and the world, is Rugby's famous headmaster, Dr. Thomas Arnold. His "manly piety" had transformed the school, and his weekly sermons had incarnated the Christian masculinity Hughes now sought to inculcate in others. Arnold had taught his boys to strive "against whatever was mean and unmanly and unrighteous"; he had made a moral difference even to those among his pupils too young and too inexperienced to grasp all his message. Tom Brown would walk away from such inspiring occasions filled with good intentions.[37]

This was something of a departure from the unadulterated doctrine of Christian manliness for which Hughes's good friend Charles Kingsley was famous; it offered impressive scope to the "feminine" element in the manly man's character. In *Tom Brown's Schooldays* he cast doubt on the naive admiration of the brawny male animal, which he saw as a forced and facile caricature of virtuous masculinity. He had not linked the manly to the "lovely" for nothing. Most of his readers were content; many thoughtful Victorians in Hughes's day came to suspect the automatic association of manliness with activity and womanliness with passivity.*

---

*In 1915, attempting to bring clarity after decades of inconclusive debates, Freud noted that it seemed "indispensable to be clear that the concepts 'masculine' and 'feminine' " are "among the most confused in the sciences." *Drei Abhandlungen zur Sexualtheorie* (1905; addition of 1915), in *Gesammelte Werke,* ed. Anna Freud et al., 18 vols. (1940–68), V, 121n; *Three Essays on the Theory of*

In *Tom Brown at Oxford,* published four years after his classic celebration of Arnold's Rugby, Hughes continued this subtle retreat from his friends the muscular Christians. He still applauded "the brotherhood" who from the 1850s on had lustily invigorated religious life in Britain. They were chivalrous and Christian men, he contended, a marked improvement over those he chose to call the "musclemen." The mindless athlete was sadly ignorant of his body's real purposes, "except some hazy idea that it is to go up and down the world with him, belabouring men and captivating women for his benefit or pleasure, at once the servant and fermenter of those fierce and brutal passions which he seems to think it a necessity, and rather a fine thing than otherwise, to indulge and obey." True, young men "will have fits of fighting, or desiring to fight with their poorer brethren, just as children have the measles. But the shorter the fit the better for the patient."[38] Hughes was, largely implicitly, taking his distance from the fighting Browns, who, it would seem, remained fixated on adolescence all their lives.*

To recognize fits of fighting as essentially tied to puberty was a shrewd perception. True manliness came to mean, for Hughes and others, rising above boyish exploits, above adolescence. In his incursion into popular biblical exegesis, *The Manliness of Christ,* published in 1879, he refined his ideal of manliness even further, seeking to elevate the mundane to the level of divinity. This was not an eccentric enterprise: religious faith—and for some, religious doubt—was a crucial emotional, as well as social, experience for bourgeois in the Victorian age. As Hughes reports in the introduction, the little book had grown out of readings he had conducted on Sunday afternoons at the London Working Men's College, which he had helped to found. He had been troubled to learn that the Young Men's Christian Association was failing to reach rough working-class youths, notorious for their impiety and intemperance, because its "tone and influence" seemed "to lack manliness." Those scornful of the Y.M.C.A. attributed this presumed effeteness to its pallid vision of Christianity,

---

Sexuality, in *Standard Edition of the Complete Psychological Works,* tr. and ed. James Strachey et al., 24 vols. (1953–74), VII, 219n. It was an opening he did not fully explore; while some of his observations throw brilliant light on this vexed topic, he unfortunately followed, on occasion, the common usage.

*Some of Wilkie Collins's protagonists are no less outspoken. In 1869, Collins lent his support to the pacific party with *Man and Woman,* one of the most didactic of his thesis novels. Its villain, Geoffrey Delmayn, is a long-distance runner of unmatched prowess and melodramatic viciousness; he is stupid, coarse, and an inveterate seducer. The caricature is too extravagant to be persuasive, but Collins's intentions are unmistakable: he is pillorying athleticism as a violation of civilized values.

its habitual appeal to "men's fears—to that which is timid and shrinking rather than to that which is courageous and outspoken."[39]

Hughes himself took a far more cordial view of London's organization for young Christians than this, but he felt compelled to admit that its reputation for inculcating "weakness," however unjustified, was rampant, and crippling to its missionary campaigns. Hence he thought it urgent to make people recognize "manliness as the perfection of human character"—and Christ's character and life as the incarnation of that perfection.[40]

In Hughes's revisionist life of Christ, the Savior bestrides the scene as a warrior wrestling manfully with an assortment of evils—priestly arrogance, devilish temptations to desert his calling, distrust and mean derision, sordid betrayal and cruel death. It is an unsophisticated recital; as in *Tom Brown's Schooldays,* good and evil confront one another in unrelieved contrast. Hence Hughes easily enlists martial metaphors in the cause: "We are born into a state of war; with falsehood and disease and wrong and misery, in a thousand forms, lying all around us, and the voice within calling on us to take our stand as men in the eternal battle against these." This is what Christ did, faithful to the truth that was in him. His reputation for meekness and his shocking collapse in the garden of Gethsemane have given him a reputation for unmanliness. But they fade before his sublime fortitude, until at the end he emerges "as the true Head of humanity, the perfect Ideal, not only of wisdom and tenderness and love, but of courage also."[41] His manliness was, literally, incomparable.

Hughes's Christ, the perfect Being, is endowed with more than just a soldier's bravery; he also incorporates wisdom, love—and sensitivity. In an introductory chapter of *The Manliness of Christ,* Hughes carefully differentiates between manliness and courage, and elevates the first over the second. Courage, a quality that some animals share with humans, embraces persistence and disdain for safety or ease. Manliness is more inclusive; it also entails tenderness and thoughtfulness. "A great athlete may be a brute or a coward, while a truly manly man can be neither."[42] Animal courage may be purified through the worthy motive of self-sacrifice, as in the admirable suicidal heroism of military men under fire. But manliness is a spiritual rather than a physical quality in essence, and its supreme test is unswerving loyalty to truth, maintained against the most determined and most powerful adversaries.[43]

All this is fairly primitive stuff, no doubt, relying on exhortation and repetition rather than analysis. And it does continue to assign primacy, however qualified, to the military virtues: Hughes's Christ is the Perfect Headmaster on the rugged playing fields of an unregenerate world. Still, by introducing these finer shadings, Hughes threw a bridge to a countertradition stirring in some of his contemporaries. That style of thinking, tenderhearted, aesthetic, downright "feminine," surfaced paradoxically enough in the most pugnacious—and probably most troubled—of Hughes's allies, Charles Kingsley himself. To be sure, in public Kingsley was firm. His pugnacity, and his way of identifying those who held views different from his as enemies of true Christianity, legitimized his pleasure in combativeness and served as an alibi for virtually unsublimated aggression.* At the same time, he left himself open to the suspicion that his insistence on manliness was a mask for its opposite. Indeed, even as he swore unceasing strife against personal temptations, public degeneracy, and religious error, Kingsley did not escape "feminine" emotions. As he inveighed against what he derided as the effeminacy of High Church and Roman Catholic clerics, he was obscurely worrying over possible symptoms of effeminacy within himself.[44] It was his tender side that allowed Kingsley to complicate his definition of heroism by adding, alongside its muscular qualities, justice, restraint, modesty, and the readiness for self-sacrifice.[45]

Interestingly enough, Elizabeth Barrett Browning was taken with Kingsley for displaying precisely that tender touch. "Few men have impressed me more agreeably," she wrote in 1852 upon meeting him for the first time. "He is original and earnest, and full of a genial and almost tender kindliness which is delightful to me." His ideas might be "wild and theoretical in many ways," but she found him a "good and noble" man. And she later confided to her close friend the poet and playwright Mary Russell Mitford that she rather admired Kingsley. " 'Manly,' do you say? But I am not very fond of praising men by calling them *manly*. I hate and detest a manly man." If she found Kingsley neither hateful nor detestable, that must have been because she saw in him qualities the world did not see. "*Humanly* brave, true, direct, Mr. Kingsley is—a moral cordiality and an original intellect uniting in him."[46] Kingsley was apparently more appealing, more polished—and more pacific—when talking in the drawing room than when writing pamphlets at his desk or exhorting his audiences from a lectern. Such advocates of the manly ideology could give its adversaries a measure of comfort.

---

*Some of Kingsley's contemporaries saw this clearly. In 1860, W. R. Greg, a liberal commentator on English culture, described Kingsley as "fearfully pugnacious," one of the two "most combative writers" of the age, the other being Carlyle. "Nature sent them into the world full of aggressive propensities." Astutely, Greg observed, "It must be delightful to array all the energies of the old Adam against the foes of the new. What unspeakable relief and joy for a Christian like Mr. Kingsley, whom God has made boiling over with animal eagerness and fierce aggressive instincts, to feel that he is not called upon to control these instincts, but only to direct them." Thus he can permit himself to hate "with a perfect hatred," to act as "a war-horse panting for the battle." "Kingsley and Carlyle" (1860), *Literary and Social Judgments* (1873), 116–17.

That ideology could give them, too, a clue to a derisive diagnosis. Adversaries of manliness in most of its meanings thought it not just a menace but a mask. By mid-century, they were reading it as a striking instance of personal pathology translated into social prescription. Its partisans, like Kingsley, seemed to be palming off psychological problems as a law of human nature. Perhaps the most intemperate advocates of manliness were so vehement only because they had something to hide: a physical defect, erotic hysteria, or small-boy helplessness in an adult world beset by frightening women.

This was certainly Thackeray's conjecture. In 1848, in *Vanity Fair,* before the cult of manliness had reached its height in Britain, he pointedly suggested that the conspicuous display of strength so common in proclamations of manliness might be a symptom of weakness. Why was it that since "time out of mind, strength and courage have been the theme of bards and romances"? Beginning with the *Iliad,* "poetry has always chosen a soldier for a hero." Perhaps it was "because men are cowards in heart that they admire bravery so much, and place military valour so far beyond every other quality for reward and worship?"[47] It was a good question.

Others raised it as well. Writing to a close friend in 1860, the tormented Austrian poet and novelist Adalbert Stifter confessed, "Since the present-day world situation is one of weakness, I flee to strength and depict strong humans, and that strengthens me."[48] A few years later, the *Westminster Review,* a journal noted for its support of radical views, traced man's definition of woman as a domestic goddess to sheer male panic: "The possibility that women, if adequately educated, may develop powers adapted to employments monopolized by men, has led to a jealousy for female delicacy and elevation above work which is a little suspicious: men have never made an outcry against women's entering upon any occupation however hard or 'degrading,' unless that occupation were one in which they would compete with men!"[49] Perceptive Victorians, then, were subverting manliness, as it were, from within. Was the alibi not part of a male defense against female aggressiveness? Was it not transparently self-serving? Probably men had invented it in the pious hope that they were the lords of creation, subtly driven on by the fear that they were not.

Beyond exposing the tendentious origins of the manly doctrine, beyond showing appreciation for men's "feminine" qualities, the nineteenth century developed an explicit anti-heroic world view that rescued the Enlightenment's cosmopolitan and pacific program into their own time. Echoing such celebrated critics of the military ideal as Voltaire, they made professional heroics a subject of open derision. Impressive numbers of bourgeois were deserting the venerable aristocratic standard of manly prowess, banishing heroics to the opera house or the sports stadium, and setting up in their place a new ideal embodied in the undramatic domestic lives of ordinary mortals, the reassuring moderation of homely themes, the rationality of tempered emotions. Safety and sanity seemed to them infinitely preferable to the warrior's militancy, rational and peaceful bourgeois preferable to bellicose noblemen.

Leaders in this historic revaluation of values were novelists like Thackeray and Trollope. Self-inflated men of importance wearing fancy uniforms and spouting pugnacious rhetoric became favorite targets. Satirists, of course, have always been deflaters of heroics. To cut swaggering mortals down to size, to expose the pretense of greatness and false glamor, has been their trade since the time of the ancient Greeks. They stand for the reality principle at work, puncturing the childish worship of omnipotence. The operettas of Jacques Offenbach and of Gilbert and Sullivan—*La Grande Duchesse de Gérolstein, La Belle Hélène, Iolanthe*—lightheartedly undermining the heroic ideology, sent up stupid generals, self-important officials, corrupt heroes, lecherous gods.* In a late mock-sermon, Thackeray again offered a psychological explanation for hero worship and further subverted it. His text was an "old dictum" associated with Oxford dons, "ALL CLARET *would be port if it could!*" It showed that laudable ambition only too often degenerates into vanity, pretense, and self-seeking.[50]

No wonder Thackeray could write what he called *A Novel without a Hero*. He may have intended this subtitle for *Vanity Fair* as a sardonic commentary on his flawed characters—the most flawed of whom, Becky Sharp, flourishes impenitently to the end—or as a sigh of relief at so human a universe. In either reading, he put the ideology of manliness at a discount. True, Thackeray gave the protagonist of *Pendennis* a "manly heart," but Pendennis is not free of oddly assorted, quite "feminine," admixtures: he is "kind, ardent, and hopeful" as well as "generous and manly and self-denying"; indeed, a man "with all his faults and shortcomings, who does not claim to be a hero, but only a man and a brother."[51] When Thackeray did have a hero, like Henry Esmond, his heroic

---

*Thackeray commended English painters of the early 1840s for painting "from the heart more than of old, and less from the old heroic, absurd, incomprehensible unattainable rules." Thus "a gentle sentiment, an agreeable, quiet incident, a tea-table tragedy, suffices for the most part their gentle powers." As for antiquity, allegory, or heroism, "we have wisely given up pretending that we are interested in such, and confess a partiality for more simple and homely themes." Mario Praz, *The Hero in Eclipse in Victorian Fiction* (1952; tr. Angus Davidson, 1956), 219–20. Witness, too, the mock heroics in George Bernard Shaw's pitiless lampoons in *Arms and the Man* and other comedies. In 1909, protesting the banning of his "crude melodrama," *The Shewing-Up of Blanco Posnet,* Shaw described its characters as "a little community of violent, cruel, sensual, ignorant, blasphemous, bloodthirsty backwoodsmen, whose conception of manliness is mere brute pugnacity, and whose favorite sport is lynching." Clearly, they were not his ideals. "Blanco Posnet Banned by the Censor (Printed Statement issue to the Press on 22 May 1909)," *The Bodley Head Bernard Shaw: Collected Plays with Their Prefaces,* 7 vols. (1970–74), III, (1971), 801.

qualities manifested themselves in his overcoming sexual temptations, and "holding fast to honour, duty, virtue."*

Thackeray was a sardonic physician to society. But Trollope's unheroic heroes, like those of Flaubert and Fontane, attest that one did not have to be a satirist to detest the cult of manliness. In short, try as they might, muscular Victorians, Christian or otherwise, could not persuade everyone that the complicated ideal of manliness was really quite elementary. If even Thomas Hughes could acknowledge that "a great athlete may be a brute or a coward," more polished minds than his would push the perception of complexity further. Witness Leslie Stephen's psychological sketch of Macaulay: "No reader of Macaulay's works will be surprised at the manliness which is stamped no less plainly upon them than upon his whole career. But few who were not in some degree behind the scenes would be prepared for the tenderness of nature which is equally conspicuous."[52] For Stephen, Macaulay's well-concealed sensitivity and vulnerability, known only to his intimates, far from compromising his firm, impressive, manly public presence, only enriched it.

Hans von Bülow, brilliant conductor and piano virtuoso, wit and neurotic, displayed the same understanding. A young musician, Eduard von Welz, whose career he had been fostering with paternal solicitude, was involved in a disagreeable incident at a student concert in Munich. A spectator had brashly insulted the music students in the hall, and they had demanded, and received, "satisfaction"—whether an apology or a duel is not clear. In any event, Bülow congratulated Welz on his conduct and then launched into an excited assertion of professional dignity: "The times are now over when artists and those who unfortunately limp after them the most—the musicians, particularly distinguished for their lack of character—were lackeys, milksops, rabbits, molluscs. As servants of a consecrated profession, they have the right, in fact the duty, to make themselves respected in their person as well." In his generous enthusiasm, Bülow waxed exalted: "The religion of Bach, Beethoven, and Wagner demands from its apostles first of all 'manliness.'"[53] But Bülow, as a German aristocrat no stranger to the duel, was not bloodthirsty. He wrote Louise von Welz, young Welz's mother, "He who knows how to bridle his tongue and to overcome his passions is stronger than he who takes cities by assault."[54] For Hans von Bülow, then, as for Leslie Stephen and indeed for Thomas Hughes,

---

*The words are Charles Kingsley's, in "Heroism," *Sanitary and Social Lectures and Essays* (1880), 252. "This was what Mr. Thackeray meant—for he told me so himself, I say—that it was possible, even in England's lowest and foulest times, to be a gentleman and a hero, if a man would but be true to the light within him." Ibid. Thackeray's self-appraisal, and Kingsley's endorsement of it, only underscores the complexity—and, I must add, the essential innocuousness in many hands— of the manly ideal in the nineteenth century.

manliness was a Janus-faced deity, looking toward contrasting aspects of human nature. Relatively civilized and in its way civilizing, manliness was severely limited in its support for naked combativeness.

These fairly benign readings of manliness were an enlightening distance from the cultivation of hatred that characterized societies devoted singlemindedly to the cult of honor—enlightening because the contrast throws light on bourgeois attitudes. That cult, particularly at home in aristocratic and primitive societies, lived on into the nineteenth century, especially in the antebellum American South, in the lands bordering the Mediterranean, and, of course, in the German academic subculture that gloried in its duels. In these cultures, touchiness on the great matter of honor was extreme. All significant aspects of life—rites of passage, social intercourse, the choice of a mate, orders of rank and precedence, even commercial transactions—were meticulously regulated and subject to obsessively enforced rituals. Affronts, whether real or trumped up, had to be avenged with the most extreme remedies at hand: ostracisms, duels, lynchings, vendettas. Men felt compelled to display and continuously reaffirm their manhood from the time they were striplings, to prove their hardihood, their sheer physical strength, and their tenacious endurance of the bodily suffering that their risk-seeking lives necessarily entailed. For societies living by heroic codes, prestige was the cherished aim, pain the necessary test, disgrace a perpetual threat; autonomy was sacrificed to the good opinion of others. In these cultures, society was the superego.

The value they placed on manliness was extraordinary. In June 1861, as the American Civil War was heating up, Lucius Quintus Cincinnatus Lamar, a prominent secessionist, justified the conflict by invoking the *Iliad* and, not unexpectedly, the crucial difference between the male and the female: "The fight had to come. We are men, not women. The quarrel had lasted long enough. We hate each other so—the fight had to come. Even Homer's heroes, after they had stormed and scolded enough, fought like brave men, long and well." His very regrets appealed to the imperatives of heroism: it was a failure of manliness that had forced the need for its most emphatic display. He recalled the scandalous scene on the floor of the Senate in 1856 when the South Carolina congressman Preston Brooks had beaten the Massachusetts senator Charles Sumner into insensibility for insulting Brooks's uncle. If, Lamar said sarcastically, "the athlete Sumner" had only "stood on his manhood and training and struck back when Preston Brooks assailed him, Preston Brooks's blow need not have been the opening skirmish of the war. Sumner's country took up the fight because he did not."[55]

It is a curious argument. Surely a single brutal episode did not cause the Civil

War. But it is psychologically revealing in that it exhibits the residual authority of the aristocratic, classical—or primitive—code in the nineteenth century. That code was, in fact, so thoroughly ingrained that many women, especially in the American South, heartily endorsed it and perpetuated it from generation to generation, though they were themselves often its victims. Exhorting their sons never to forget their honor and to die fighting rather than live retreating, they were modern versions of the fabled Spartan mother who enjoined her sons never to be caught with wounds on their backs.[56]

To be sure, like other mothers and wives handing on the precious canon of manly conduct, these Southern women did reject the mindless resort to violence. That was a sign of immaturity, not bravery, and violated the exacting ideals they tried to live by. Yet they were prepared to countenance—seemed practically determined to provoke—perilous situations in which their men's lives were at risk. Like other mothers of heroes these women made demands that put almost intolerable strains on their sons, fearful as those must have been of losing maternal approval. To still the fear of failure, these youths, perpetually on trial, were bound to adopt an antagonistic stance toward possible rivals or adversaries, and to treat the most trivial comments, the most casual gestures, as grounds for ferocious self-assertion.

Woman was at the heart of this chivalrous militancy. Heroes engraved their mother's or their wife's image on their conscious, and, more than they knew, a far more ambivalent image on their unconscious mind. And the obligations were mutual. With all their silent anxieties and hatreds, men could permit no doubt that just as they must not let their women down, the women they loved must in turn live up to the highest possible standards. Their women had to be strong in their meekness, worthy of adulation, quick to acknowledge male superiority, and ready to sacrifice time, effort, their own desires, to their men. Significantly but not surprisingly, a girl's unchastity and a wife's infidelity were the gravest crimes inscribed in this code. A woman's shame stained the reputation of the men to whom she belonged—her son, her husband, her brothers—until the stain was erased, by aggression.

Yet precisely in the matter of sexual conduct, that most delicate point of manly honor, this creed provided for transgression, unofficially but authoritatively. Infractions of the sexual ideal were as carefully regulated as the provisions for its observance. One supreme test of manliness, after all, apart from that of tolerating pain without flinching, was erotic exhibitionism.[57] A youth proved his manliness by drinking, swearing, fighting, and fornicating. Sexual triumphs were so many trophies the adolescent collected on the road to manhood; each of his performances verified the virility by which he and his cohort set great stock—presumably because they needed such verification over and over. The escape from these conflicting commitments to sexual purity and sexual impurity lay in finding one's pleasure with outsiders, those too alien or too lowly to be eligible as marriage partners.

In comparison, the indulgent bourgeois commonplace about young men needing to sow their wild oats was pale indeed. The private lives of middle-class men show this platitude in action: schoolboys would frequent brothels, young bachelors would engage in illicit romances with shopgirls or, if they were raffish and affluent enough, with ballet dancers. The touching, doomed love affair that Thomas Mann's young Thomas Buddenbrook carries on with a charming, oriental-looking salesgirl in a flower store, until family pressures force him to give her up, is a telling fictional representation of uncounted liaisons in real middle-class life.[58] Even so, the struggles of the manly bourgeois for trophies in sports, in politics, in war, in love, seem positively civilized compared with the desperate efforts to triumph in cultures in which the writ of honor ran undisputed.

Nineteenth-century campaigns to complicate and civilize manliness repelled and infuriated its unreconstructed champions. They fought back; they could hardly do anything else. Impious scoffers at old-fashioned manly virtues were, they believed, corroding the very fiber of their world. Evidence of decay lurked everywhere: a palpable loss of religious faith, the shameless advocacy of free love, agitation to lure women from their domestic destiny, a decreasing birthrate among the bourgeoisie. Hence the counterattacks inevitably liberated some ominous feelings and proposed some ominous policies. Manly orators like Theodore Roosevelt spoke in the most combative accents as they defended virility in an effete age. But even among less emphatic and less excitable controversialists, the rehabilitation of aggressive manhood hovered near the perilous edge of anti-intellectualism, even of brutality. Near-panic over decadence, and its counterpart, the celebration of the warrior's virtues—increasingly noisy, increasingly bleak, late in the century—led to calls for the most desperate remedies. In the background of these denunciations and celebrations, and only too often in the foreground as well, lurked the enemy to be despised, corrected, defeated: the materialistic, unmanly bourgeois.

Thanking Sir Henry Taylor late in 1868 for his "able pamphlet" *Crime and Its Punishment,* Kingsley predicted that Taylor's advocacy of a "just and rational treatment of crime" would find noisy opposition, largely due to "the effeminacy of the middle class which never having in its life felt bodily pain (unless it has the tooth-ache) looks on such pain as the worst of all evils. My experience of the shop-keeping class (from which juries are taken) will hardly coincide with yours. You seem to think them a hardier and less dainty class than our own. I find that even in the prime of youth they shrink from (and are often unable to bear, from physical neglect or training) fatigue, danger, pain, which would be considered as sport by an average public schoolboy."[59]

This is an instructive text. Kingsley saw the nineteenth-century middle class—especially the lower middle class—which took so much pleasure in reading about heroic adventures, as unprepared to pay the cost that strenuous ideals exacted. The sneering epithet "dainty" only underscores his manly disdain for tenderhearted shopkeepers. One perceptive liberal editor and commentator, W. R. Greg, described this posture well. Kingsley, much like Carlyle, he wrote, is "contemptuous and abusive" to his "adversaries far beyond the limits of taste, decency, or gentlemanly conduct."* One wonders—and some of their contemporaries did wonder—why they needed to fight so hard.

The challenge to the spiritual deterioration of the once self-respecting bourgeoisie was not confined to anxious denunciations. On suitable occasions orators sought to recall the middle class to its manly habits by celebrating the heroes whose sacrifices an ungrateful century was disposed to forget. Addressing veterans of the Civil War on Memorial Day, 1884, Oliver Wendell Holmes, Jr., deploring the selfishness and baseness of his time, sounded the manly alert once again: "High breeding, romantic chivalry—we who have seen these men can never believe that the power of money or the enervation of pleasure has put an end to them." Happily, "New England is not dead yet. She still is the mother of a race of conquerors—stern men."[60] This sort of rhetoric, appropriate to a commemoration of soldiers slain in war, was appealing enough to shape public attitudes beyond its immediate occasion. Holmes's declamations could become grounds for policy; the anxiety over womanish traits—one's own or those of one's culture, a distinction often hopelessly blurred—appeared a standing invitation to political and military swagger.

In retrospect, then, manliness was a potentially volatile compound of desperate restraints and ferocious desires barely held in check, the whole ready to burst into flame if combined with other alibis for aggression. Self-protective propaganda in behalf of the virile male grew markedly more strident with the passing decades. The nineteenth-century ideology of manliness had a history of its own, a history of mounting defensiveness and vulgarization and of regression to more uninhibited verbal brutality and more militant postures. It became the

*Greg, "Kingsley and Carlyle," 118. Kingsley was by no means consistent in his appraisal of the bourgeoisie. In 1872, speaking in Birmingham on "The Science of Health," he observed, "One cannot walk the streets of any of our great commercial cities without seeing plenty of men, young and middle-aged, whose whole bearing and stature shows that the manly vigour of our middle class is anything but exhausted." *Sanitary and Social Lectures,* 25. Such inconsistencies are like so many warnings against slighting human complexity.

servant of diplomatic bullying, imperialistic adventures, and the insouciant resort to arms. Yet not without a struggle: for much of the age, even beyond Queen Victoria's death, manliness was, as we have seen, a debatable ideal.

4. T.R.: Extremist of the Center

Alibis for aggression are collective cultural phenomena; they flourish or wither in the public domain. But at times they are incarnated in a single commanding personage. Perhaps no figure spanning the decades from Victoria to Freud acted out nineteenth-century alibis for aggression more instructively, and more entertainingly, than Theodore Roosevelt. "Never," said H. G. Wells, "did a President before so reflect the quality of his time."[1] Exhibiting—virtually epitomizing—the lust for competition, fashionable racial attitudes, and the ideal of manliness, he became a classic symptom of bourgeois aggression at work and, at the same time, a model of how to bridle that aggression and make it into a viable instrument of democratic politics.

Representative though he might be, T.R. was extraordinary in everything—and irresistible. Forever boyish, appealing and offensive, at times preposterous but always worth watching, he was a self-appointed warrior for righteousness. Deploring his own age as unmanly and all too pacific, he made himself into a willing throwback to an age when men were men and women adored them for it.

This self-image led him to separate himself at times from the class into which he had been born. In the 1880s, the reluctance of his prosperous friends to enter the political arena aroused his manly contempt. "The wealthier, or, as they would prefer to style themselves, the 'upper' classes, tend distinctly to the bourgeois type, and an individual in the bourgeois style of development, while honest, industrious, and virtuous, is also not unapt to be a miracle of timid and short-sighted selfishness." What Roosevelt patronized as the "commercial classes" were, he thought, "too selfish to be willing to undergo any trouble for the sake of abstract duty." Their offspring were if anything even worse, "too much engrossed in their various social pleasures to be willing to give up their time to anything else."[2]

Preaching and at times practicing his pugilistic ideology, Theodore Roosevelt brought the bitter traumas of his childhood to the White House with him. But he grew into a personality too considerable to be judged as a mere victim of his neuroses. This is not to slight the haunting presence of T.R.'s early years. As a boy, born in 1858 into a prosperous New York family, he was subject to frequent, severe, and frightening attacks of asthma.* It is an ailment that leaves its victims feeling utterly helpless, gasping for breath as if on the verge of drowning. Theodore Roosevelt's picturesque and excessive vitality, his Faustian inability to be content with the worlds he had conquered, his untiring, in the end monotonous, insistence on manliness and man's duty to serve on the front lines of life, deserve the analysis they have received. They appear like a desperate struggle with an all-too-familiar sense of impotence, a reiterated (because never wholly convincing) proclamation of fitness that will enable him, the asthmatic, to survive the next attack. For T.R., with his father's urging, did his manly best to battle his uncertain health.

It is part of T.R.'s enduring fascination that he was a perennial paradox—a sickly boy who forced himself to become a passable athlete, a voracious reader who preferred the great outdoors to his upholstered chair, an author who would rather box than write, a patrician who chose to descend to the gutter of politics, a self-advertised reformer whose accomplishments were relatively modest, a fanatic for healthful exercise who died prematurely of a coronary embolism at sixty. And as we have just seen, he was by descent and morality a quintessential bourgeois who took pleasure in standing up as the scourge of his class.

His exhibitionistic vigor that ever demanded to be proved—a demand exacerbated by his need to wear glasses—aroused in him, and inflated, the all-too-human striving for "power after power," which, as Hobbes tells us, ceases only in death. "The strenuous life," a phrase and more than a phrase that T.R. virtually patented, was his solution to the harsh conundrums that existence presented to him. Ceaseless activity kept anxiety and—more important—depression at bay. Enlisting Horace's famous epigram about black care, he once said, "Black care rarely sits behind a rider whose pace is fast enough."[3] Spurred on by, and internalizing, his father's approval, he lifted himself by his emotional bootstraps, earnestly practicing what psychoanalysts call counterphobic behavior: conscious of what he feared most, he acted as though he were not afraid and discovered that the fear disappeared—at least from his awareness.†

Whatever his submerged motives, a good portion of the ideology Theodore

---

*In a careful study of T.R.'s asthma, David McCullough has been able to rule out genetic factors and allergens as causes; he observes that the attacks almost invariably took place on Sundays, thus strongly suggesting psychological roots to be sought in Roosevelt family dynamics. *Mornings on Horseback* (1981), ch. 4.

†"There were all kinds of things of which I was afraid at first, ranging from grizzly bears to 'mean' horses and gun-fighters; but by acting as if I was not afraid I gradually ceased to be afraid." Theodore Roosevelt, *An Autobiography* (1913), 54.

Roosevelt advocated—and lived—was deliberate and self-generated. In his *Autobiography,* as unintentionally revealing as it is amiably self-serving, he candidly describes himself as a "nervous and timid" boy who comforted himself with fantasies of fearless exploits. At nearly fourteen, he was involved in an episode that, he claims, changed his life. After one of his asthma attacks, he was sent off to a resort, by himself, to recuperate. On the stagecoach taking him there, he met a couple of boys about his own age, far more active and mischievous than he. Easily spotting his vulnerability, they tormented him without mercy; he "finally tried to fight them," T.R. reports, and "discovered that either one singly could not only handle me with easy contempt, but handle me so as not to hurt me much and yet to prevent my doing any damage whatever in return."[4] The experience propelled him from pathetic wishing for strength to its cultivation: he took boxing lessons, to good effect. This reminiscence reads like a screen memory, condensing into one striking recollection what must have been a series of humiliations that darkened his young life.

His unappeasable urge to convert passivity into activity became the organizing force in Theodore Roosevelt's character. More than one of his biographers has observed that he was always volunteering.[5] But there was something compulsive in that volunteering, an urge that drove him to court risks and danger. He was impetuous and at moments, some feared, a little mad. That is why Henry Adams, the most sardonic witness to the Washington scene, trembled for his friend—and his country—when in the fall of 1901, upon the assassination of President William McKinley, Vice-president Theodore Roosevelt was catapulted into the presidency. The new president, Adams later recalled, brought to his office an air of "pure excitement." It was worrisome: "Power when wielded by abnormal energy is the most serious of facts, and all Roosevelt's friends know that his restless and combative energy was more than abnormal. Roosevelt, more than any other man living within the range of notoriety, showed the singular primitive quality that belongs to ultimate matter—the quality that mediaeval theology assigned to God—he was pure act."[6] Yet when T.R. left the White House in March 1909, Adams shook hands with him and declared, with rare emotion, "I shall miss you very much."[7]

Fortunately for Theodore Roosevelt and—though this is more controversial—for the United States, Adams's character sketch is hyperbole masquerading as analysis; Adams was usually more interested in being witty than in being just. Much of T.R.'s pure act turned out to be pure talk. As a seasoned politician confronting the realities of partisan infighting and economic pressures, he was often enough content with image rather than substance. In September 1902, during the crippling coal strike that threatened to bring the country to its knees, Roosevelt's intimate friend Senator Henry Cabot Lodge of Massachusetts, aware that the executive had few legal powers to avert catastrophe, asked him, "Is there nothing we can appear to do?" T.R., recognizing the imperative need to retain his image as a decisive doer, must have asked himself that question more than once. When during his presidency he indulged in his favorite pastime, hunting, he was nervous about the negative publicity that failure to hit his quarry might entail.[8] With all his insistence on manliness, he often reversed his own famous motto; he would speak loudly and carry a small stick.

It was in character that Theodore Roosevelt should perceive his first venture into public life, around 1880, as a test of his manhood. At this time, his circle thoroughly despised politics. "The men I knew best were the men in the clubs of social pretension and the men of cultivated taste and easy life," he remembered. "When I began to make inquiries as to the whereabouts of the local Republican Association and the means of joining it, these men—and the big business men and lawyers also—laughed at me and told me that politics were 'low'; that the organizations were not controlled by 'gentlemen'; that I would find them run by saloon-keepers, horse-car conductors, and the like, and not by men with any of whom I would come in contact outside; and, moreover, they assured me that the men I met would be rough and brutal and unpleasant to deal with."[9] His friends did not perceive that this one-time weakling with poor eyesight, this amateur boxer fresh out of Harvard, could take these snobbish cautions only as heady incentives, virtual aphrodisiacs.

Politics, the fastidious Henry Adams declared, is a harsh business; "its methods are rough; its judgments rougher still." But precisely that attracted Theodore Roosevelt. He decided that he would desist if the venture proved quixotic, but "certainly would not quit until I had made the effort and found out whether I really was too weak to hold my own in the rough and tumble." Joining a political club was like entering the boxing ring, a trial of strength. It was more: a bid for mastery. He told his friends that if they and the politicians had nothing in common, "it merely meant that the people I knew did not belong to the governing class, and that the other people did—and that I intended to be one of the governing class."[10] He wanted—needed—to be in charge, at the controls.

His spectacular career, which reads like a race for the world's record in scrambling up the rungs to power, abundantly documents Theodore Roosevelt's appetite for battle. He was elected to the New York state legislature at twenty-three, and quickly made a name for himself as he repeatedly defied the *laissez-faire* orthodoxy he had imbibed at Harvard. He never knew much about economics, but he distrusted the convenient Republican dogma that protective social legislation violates the sacred laws of nature. The labor leader Samuel

Gompers, with whom T.R. toured the filthy, unsanitary hovels of New York's tobacco workers, found his "aggressiveness and evident sincerity" memorable.[11] After an overwhelming double tragedy—his mother and his wife died within eleven hours of each other—he sought solace, as he would, in action. Beginning in 1884, he spent three years in the West as a rancher, savoring his free and hardy life, breaking horses like a real cowboy, killing buffalo and grizzly bear, all the while toughening his body. He returned to marry again, and served in turn as a civil service commissioner, assistant secretary of the navy, colonel of the Rough Riders fighting in the Spanish-American War, governor of New York, briefly vice-president, and finally president of the United States. He was all of forty-three when he moved into the White House.

In all these roles, he was himself: hyperactive, exceedingly visible—and audible. As assistant secretary of the navy, he bypassed his more pacific superior, Secretary John D. Long, to get Commodore George Dewey, spoiling for battle, appointed commander of the American naval forces in the Pacific; that accomplished, he eased Dewey's way toward confrontation with the Spanish fleet in the Philippines. Loudly calling for war with Spain, he took the reluctance of President McKinley and other peace-minded politicians to join in his flag-waving almost as a personal insult. When the battleship *Maine* was blown up in February 1898 in Havana harbor and no American declaration of war followed immediately, he protested that he felt "humiliated and ashamed." Fearful that military action might elude him, he told everyone that he must get away from Washington; he did not want to be among the "armchair and parlor Jingoes."[12] In this spirit he organized a cavalry regiment, the Rough Riders, once war was finally declared, and took them to Cuba. There they went from triumph to triumph; the finest moment, by his lights, came when he and his men stormed San Juan Hill, and, as he later boasted, he killed a Spaniard with his own hands.

Of course, T.R.'s killings were generally not of the physical variety; rather, he scattered them among the millions of words he wrote, published, delivered as speeches—one sheer act of aggression after another. He composed and dictated innumerable letters, among them little treatises of attack or self-exculpation—or both at once. He wrote scores of magazine articles and printed lectures and more than a dozen books, all bearing his unmistakable imprint. His first book, *The Naval War of 1812,* begun before he graduated from Harvard, was a revisionist assault on an author who had covered the topic before. This sort of attack, to be sure, is typical of the novice establishing credentials, but it was particularly typical for him. When he aimed to wound he lashed out, by mail or in print, with no regard for decorum. After breaking with his long-time political ally the Progressive Amos Pinchot, he wrote him, "Sir: When I spoke of the Progressive Party as having a lunatic fringe, I specifically had you in mind. On the supposition that you are of entire sound mind, I should be obliged to say that you are absolutely dishonorable and untruthful. I prefer to accept the former alternative. Yours Truly."[13] He did not care what the *New York Times* said about him (he insisted) because such papers, "both in their editorials and in their correspondence, lie in response to the demands of the big corporations," and "make their bread and butter by so doing."[14]

Private correspondence was a favorite vent for denunciations of this sort. He wrote F. S. Oliver, a British author he had never met, that he had no use for William Graham Sumner because "he is a college professor, a cold-blooded creature of a good deal of intellect, but lacking the fighting virtues and all wide patriotism, who has an idea that he can teach statesmen and politicians their duty." Influential industrialists who lobbied against his proposals to regulate railroad rates were "conscienceless speculators" making "foolish and hysterical speeches," corrupt men alternately arrogant and "literally in a panic frenzy." Critics of his naval policies were "malevolent enemies of the navy" and "timid fools" and "conscienceless scoundrels." Adversaries like Harriman or Rockefeller exhibited "worse than recklessness." T.R. even conscripted a rarely used word to express his animosity toward these millionaires: "scoundrelism."[15]

A man who wrote like that, no matter how sincere his protestations that he thrived on candid debate, was reaping emotional rewards beyond the pleasures of reasoned argument. Elihu Root, an adviser and cabinet member who knew T.R. well and liked him, called him a fighter "completely dominated by a desire to destroy his adversary."[16] He found name-calling exhilarating. Obviously, he was not aware just how comical he was being when he complained that extreme reformers who painted real abuses in garish colors were guilty of "overstatement."[17]

This, then, was the man who translated the dominant nineteenth-century alibis for aggression into the call for the strenuous life. His was not a subtle concoction; steady reiteration—one can safely take illustrative texts from every decade of his career—made it predictable. Yet each ingredient had its highly personal nuances for him. Consider manliness, which was his signature. Like other partisans of this problematic trait, he thought it an essential element of good character and feared that pampered modern living was damaging it fatally. "One of the prime dangers of civilization," he told an audience at the University of Berlin in 1910, "has always been its tendency to cause the loss of virile fighting virtues, of the fighting edge. When men get too comfortable and lead too luxurious lives, there is always danger that the softness eats like an acid into their manliness of fibre."[18]

This was one reason why he so heatedly endorsed the sport of hunting, especially the hunting of wild game that exposes the hunter to mortal danger. It forces him "to show self-reliance, resourcefulness in emergency, willingness to endure fatigue and hunger, and a need to face risks"—the very traits that Theodore Roosevelt thought were sadly fading in the bourgeois culture of his day.[19] The specter of "unmanliness" preyed on his mind. It meant evading stern, disagreeable, dangerous duties. That is why the young T.R. plunged into politics, practicing the manly virtues and displaying his courage, moral no less than physical. After all, as he told the English historian and public servant George Otto Trevelyan, life is war, "a long campaign where every victory merely leaves the ground free for another battle."[20]

But manly devotion to this warfare was not to exclude affection, kindliness, and the virtues of scholarship; on this important scruple, Roosevelt was at one with Thomas Hughes. In October 1903, in a letter Hughes might have written in his later years, he told his son Kermit that he was glad to hear he was playing football. But, he immediately added, "I should be very sorry to see either you or Ted devoting most of your attention to athletics, and I haven't got any special ambition to see you shine overmuch in athletics at college." For one thing, athletics took too much time. "But I do like to feel that you are manly and able to hold your own in rough, hardy sports. I would rather have a boy of mine stand high in his studies than high in athletics, but I could a great deal rather have him show true manliness of character than show either intellectual or physical prowess." This was, he confessed, a "dreadfully preaching letter." But evidently the subject was on his mind, for two days later the doting father wrote to his son Ted that while he was proud of his pluck playing football, he worried a little that he might be injured. "I believe in rough, manly sports," he said, but then cautioned, "I do not believe in them if they degenerate into the sole end of any one's existence." He deprecated "over-athleticism" in general, and concluded his little sermon with a ringing pronouncement: "Athletic proficiency is a mighty good servant, and like so many other good servants, a mighty bad master."[21]

When Ted was a little boy, T.R. took distinct pleasure in boasting about his son's "most warm, tender, loving little heart." Yet he would quickly add, as though to forestall misunderstanding, that Ted was "a manly little fellow too."[22] His attitude toward his boys reflects his attitude toward himself. T.R. willed himself all his life to be a pugilist, but with a heart of gold; "I am not naturally at all a fighter," he once confessed.[23] He declared that he detested a bully, and he was perfectly sincere. Still, the warm sensual glow of aggressive feelings, the pleasures of blind rage, never quite left him. "Every man who has in him any real power of joy in battle, knows that he feels it when the wolf begins to rise in his heart; he does not then shrink from blood and sweat, or deem that they mar the fight; he revels in them, in the toil, the pain and the danger, as but setting off the triumph." After all, the "virile, fighting instinct" made life worth living.[24] These are the accents of Jack London. But this instinct, he worried, was largely lacking in the degenerate bourgeoisie of his time. Nor did he forget sexual innuendo as he surveyed that degeneracy: "An advanced state of intellectual development is too often associated with a certain effeminacy of character." Those capable of "holding a high ideal," he insisted, admired "manliness and womanliness"—two traits that were, to his mind, clearly distinct.[25]

It was in prizing militant manliness as essential to survival that Theodore Roosevelt joined forces with the Social Darwinists. Like others of that persuasion, he spoke derisively of the "foolish sentimentality of stay-at-home people, with little patent recipes and those cut-and-dried theories of the political nursery which have such limited applicability amid the crash of elemental forces."[26] T.R. never doubted that "sentimentality, mock humanitarianism, and hypocrisy" were no less ruinous a remedy for society's ills than the disease of cold-blooded egotism.[27] He might have been quoting William Graham Sumner, the professor he so detested. When, in his second term as president, he moved to the left of his earlier legislative program and advocated federal regulation of industry, commerce, and banking, he rationalized his "radicalism" as a crusade against privilege and plutocracy. Predatory industrialists and railroad magnates made real democracy impossible, and only the power of the federal government deployed against them could restore the necessary balance. But whichever tack Theodore Roosevelt thought it right to take, he kept the image of deadly struggle before him.

The same image controlled his defense of war as an imperative element in life. Not an impassioned militarist, he made things simple for himself by distinguishing between just and unjust wars. The latter are terrible, to be shunned; the former are necessary, to be fought without regard to cost: "Tyrants and oppressors have many times made a wilderness and called it peace. Many times peoples who were slothful or timid or short-sighted, who had been enervated by ease or by luxury, or misled by false teachings, have shrunk in unmanly fashion from doing duty that was stern and that needed self-sacrifice." No doubt, "the peace of tyrannous terror, the peace of craven weakness, the peace of injustice, all these should be shunned as we shun unrighteous war."[28] So much for Andrew Carnegie and his peacemongering! When in the late 1890s T.R. pressed for war with Spain and volunteered to do his part, he protested that he was in dead earnest. "I am not acting in a spirit of recklessness or levity, or purely for my own selfish enjoyment," he exclaimed in April 1898, not long before he took his Rough Riders to Cuba.* No doubt, Theodore Roosevelt's conscience was exacting. But one cannot forget his joy in feeling the wolf rising in his heart.

None of this is to deny that T.R. had repeated attacks of good sense. He was too well-read, too much his own man, to adopt Social Darwinist doctrines uncritically; too shrewd to accept the biological metaphors that social theorists liked to conjure with—the rise, maturity, and death of civilizations, for example—as more than analogies.[29] Reviewing Benjamin Kidd's dogmatic *Social Evolution,* he found it a "suggestive but a very crude book," excessively committed to the advantages of competition and the survival of the fittest. "In civilized societies the rivalry of natural selection works against progress."[30] T.R.'s version of Social Darwinism, felt far more than articulated, was in its eccentric way as sophisticated as the doctrine could be. There is wry poetic justice in the fact that in 1906, this sturdy warrior, active in settling the Russo-Japanese War, should be awarded the Nobel Peace Prize.

In his affection for a third favorite alibi for aggression, the convenient Other, Theodore Roosevelt was close to most of his contemporaries. He displayed his nationalism in the boisterous pride he took in being an American; his voluminous history *The Winning of the West,* begun when he was just out of Harvard, displays his affection for the uncouth pioneers who bravely protected, and boldly extended, America's frontier against cruel Indians and clever French and English settlers. Not until his last years did he grow willing to recognize a special relationship between his country and Britain; his distaste for transatlantic marriages yoking American heiresses to British aristocrats was fierce and vocal. But his chauvinism was as moderate as one could expect in someone so vigorously committed to manliness.

Nor was Theodore Roosevelt more of a racist than most of his fellow Americans; he was, in fact, less of a racist than many. He snobbishly dismissed Latin Americans who displeased him with their sharp dealings over the Panama Canal as "Dagos," and dealt with them as though he were a benevolent but firm teacher compelling a class of unruly boys to behave. They were "contemptible little creatures" and "jack rabbits" who needed a lesson. More obviously still, he never had the slightest doubt that blacks "as a race and in the mass" were

---

*"I don't want to be shot at any more than anyone else does; still less to die of yellow fever. I am altogether too fond of my wife and children, and enjoy the good things too much to wish lightly to hazard their loss, or to go away from my family; but the above is my duty as I see it." T.R. to Alexander Lambert (his friend and physician), April 1, 1898, *The Letters of Theodore Roosevelt,* sel. and ed. Elting E. Morison, with John M. Blum and Alfred D. Chandler, Jr., 8 vols. (1951–54), II, 808.

"altogether inferior to the whites." He thought little better of southern and eastern Europeans. If there was one issue about which he felt most strongly—and he felt strongly about many issues—it was the pernicious practice of birth control, which was crippling the superior races in their contest with their inferiors, virtually depriving them of the next generation. For them to avoid having children was criminal. That ominous phrase "race suicide" was often on his lips and under his pen. Seeing large families gave him hope—in 1899 he was delighted to meet a couple, named Tower, with their seventeen children—but he continually worried over "the diminishing birth rate among the old native American stock."[31] The lower races, after all, were breeding like rabbits. He and his second wife, Edith, did their part: they had six children.

At the same time, this champion of the superior Anglo-Saxon races believed that the American ethnic melting pot was a source of strength, and he strenuously objected to the maltreatment of Japanese immigrants in California. What is more, he invited a black educator, Booker T. Washington, to dinner at the White House. This cost him valuable support in the South, and he did not repeat the blunder. As president, he also heatedly protested against the techniques, clever or vicious, used in Southern states to keep blacks from voting. He noticed no inconsistency between his racial and his presidential attitudes: his supreme task as the Great Umpire, he believed, was to see justice done even to the lowly. Nor did he notice that his was not a wholly disinterested protest; after all, when blacks did vote, they tended to vote Republican. T.R. never allowed himself to recognize his partisan moves as partisan: the Democrats would be bad for the country, and to keep the Republicans in power was, he frequently observed, a patriotic duty.

There was, then, a good deal of loud and agitated motion in Theodore Roosevelt's life. As president, he rapidly gained a reputation as a courageous trustbuster. To be sure, his administration's sensational—and successful—prosecution of the Northern Securities Company, a gigantic holding company, helped to establish a climate of federal regulation on which later presidents would capitalize. But T.R. initiated far fewer antitrust suits than William Howard Taft, his less flamboyant successor. He would thunder, in his private letters and public pronouncements, against irresponsible millionaires, but these malefactors, far from going to jail or forfeiting their fortunes, remained as influential and as wealthy as ever.

Again, though refusing to compromise with labor leaders he thought bent on violence, T.R. presented himself as an intrepid defender of the workingman. His ideal, which he thought he was realizing admirably, was that of the fair-minded protector of the people, hovering above the frays of selfish special interests. In the last of his annual messages to Congress, he paraded once again his aspiration to supreme impartiality: "Both the preachers of an unrestricted individualism, and the preachers of an oppression which would deny to able men of business the just reward of their initiative and business sagacity, are advocating policies that would be fraught with the gravest harm to the whole country. To permit every lawless capitalist, every law-defying corporation, to take any action, no matter how iniquitous, in the effort to secure an improper profit and to build up privilege, would be ruinous to the Republic and would mark the abandonment of the effort to secure in the industrial world the spirit of democratic fair dealing. On the other hand"—there was always another hand for President Theodore Roosevelt—"to attack these wrongs in that spirit of demagogy which can see wrong only when committed by the man of wealth, and is dumb and blind in the presence of wrong committed against men of property or by men of no property, is exactly as evil as corruptly to defend the wrong-doing of men of wealth."[32] No matter how declamatory his speeches and how firm his announced intentions, he was the supreme extremist of the center.

As that sort of extremist, T.R. was steadily at war on two fronts: against male-factors of great wealth and against radicals preaching subversion; against what he liked to call the pacifists who would weaken the navy and against bellicose jingoes who would plunge the world into unjust wars; against sentimentalists who would disregard the hierarchy of races that nature had laid down and against bigots who would persecute blacks and Japanese. He may have had more than a touch of the demagogue in him, but during his second term he could earnestly declare: "I abhor a demagogue as much as I abhor a corruption-ist." Characteristically, he reflected that the French Revolution had been at once just and unjust; the oppression of the people had been extreme, but the response of the reformers had been excessive.[33] It was no wonder that to radicals he appeared a conservative, and to conservatives, a radical.

But to speak of T.R. as perpetually engaged in wars on two fronts is to overlook a supreme struggle he fought on a single front—the struggle against appetite let loose. Theodore Roosevelt, that man of force and impulse, was a defensive rationalist. With obsessive regularity, especially during his second term, he inveighed against "the dark and evil passions of men," the "evil passions of envy and jealousy and hatred," the "basest passions of the human soul."[34] The men who excited these passions deserved to feel the full force of the government's restraining hand. He was pitting aggression against aggres-sion.

This sounds like a prescription for paralysis or at best a merely reactive use of power that responds to outrages threatened or perpetrated by others. But there was much more to T.R.'s public career. His presidency went far beyond mere noise. The Square Deal could claim more than a few modest successes; part of T.R.'s legislative program to control abuses in the meat-packing, railroad, and steel industries and to protect the country's natural resources became law. His administration was the first to inject the federal government into a labor dispute. And he proposed social legislation farseeing enough to be rejected, legislation that would not go onto the books until the New Deal. There were occasions, even, when he entertained the seditious notion that women deserved the vote. His friend Henry Adams, we know, thought him nearly mad, and indeed, at times he talked and acted as though driven by hidden pathological urges. Yet on balance it was the prudent rather than the rash uses of aggression that marked his career, of vital energies harnessed rather than let off the leash.

❧ TWO ❦

Pathologies

In mid-April 1865, just after he learned that President Lincoln had been assassinated, Charles Holmes wrote to his beloved Annie, whom he was then courting. His letter was filled with uncharacteristic rage, and his somewhat uncertain spelling and punctuation were not improved by his unmanageable feelings. "I hardly know how to address myself to the pleasant duty of writing to you to day," he wrote. His appetite for revenge, he recognized, left no room in him for the working of Eros. "The terrible affliction that has fallen so suddenly upon our unhappy country so fills and monopolizes my thoughts that I am unfit for the sweet intercourse of love. My soul is full of grief and bitterness and hate and vengance."[1]

Not even the Civil War had aroused him to such a pitch. He could speak with some authority about that war; a successful manufacturer in the northeastern states, he had volunteered for active duty and served as a colonel. "Through all this long and rancorous struggle both in its political and military aspects if I know my own heart I have not cherished one feeling akin to hate or vengance toward the misguided men who at home and in the field have sought the nations life—if I know my inner self my breast has through it all had only the angels of pity and mercy for its tenants."[2]

From all we know about him, this is a fair self-appraisal; Holmes's favorite epistolary modes were the affectionate and the lyrical. But now he had shunted the angels of pity and mercy aside, "and there is a stranger there dark stern relentless and implacable and I welcome him with all the ardor yes with all the affection that a Lover might his chosen one and to his guidance I yield my Soul and heart and strength untill the day shall come when there shall not be left one venomous reptile of the whole brood who shall dare to show his head." His love temporarily swamped by hate, he had his punitive fantasies working over-time.[3]

Holmes modestly disclaimed any intention to advertise himself "as the champion of my countrys cause or imagine myself a David to slay this Goliath single handed," but "where I have been silent I will speak and speak at the promptings of that Stranger in my heart where I have counseled and exercised forbearance I will counsell and exercise relentless persecution   where I have pitied I will be unpitying   where in my limited sphere and capacity I have counselled and exercised Mercy I will to the extent of that sphere and capacity counsell and exercise vindictive and uncompromising war   I will know no distinction between traitors at home or in the field   I will work for the discomfort and ruin of both   I will loose no opportunity to work them evil   I will rejoice when calamity befalls them   I will mourn when they are not afflic-ted   I will hope for their death and be merry over their graves." Unable to requite his president's death directly on the body of the assassin (and, he darkly hinted, the assassin's many accomplices), he discharged his frustrated appetite for revenge to Annie.[4]

Then, the paroxysm over, Holmes stepped back for a moment. "You may think you have made a discovery now," he told his wife-to-be, "and gained an insight into some characteristics which I have heretofore kept hid from you. Well I have made a discovery too   three days ago I would have as soon believed myself capable of being myself an assassin as of feeling as I now do toward any human being but this occasion can not be measured by any former experience   nor are the feelings excited by and belonging to this occasion any measure of a mans general character." He then proceeded to place the "foul murder" of Lincoln on the larger, less intimate, stage of history. It much resem-bled, he wrote, that "vain and impotent" attempt to "drown the voice of truth and progress" eighteen centuries before with "cries of crucify him, crucify him." And in conclusion, almost as though embarrassed by his epistolary fit—though not too embarrassed to send it off—Holmes reached for a new sheet of paper "for something pleasanter and more congenial," and began a new letter, complete with the customary salutation: "My Dear Annie."[5] He had forced himself back to his normal posture.

The news that his president had been fatally shot provided Charles Holmes with two shocks rather than one: the poignancy of his loss and the savagery of his response. With unselfconscious self-awareness, he registered the fact that while he was mourning, he was not melancholy: he was furious with an inten-sity that astonished him. More than many other human beings, Holmes usually kept his destructive impulses in check and out of sight—even from himself. But this historic catastrophe released an urgency to avenge the injury, which he took as a deep personal insult. He could permit ferocious hostility to invade his awareness because he was certain that he was right, and this conviction constituted a license for a punitiveness so extreme, so uncontrolled, that it seems just a trifle mad.

1. In Search of Civilized Rationales

Charles Holmes, an obscure nineteenth-century bourgeois pouring out his rage, affords a rare and welcome glimpse into the ways that aggressive emotions could liberate themselves from civilized constraints. Of course, his vindictiveness was confined to paper. And it is worth noting that in the midst of his manic rehearsal of the revenge he wished to visit on the evildoers who had conspired to murder his president, he could distance himself from his unaccustomed vehemence. Like other reasonable nineteenth-century bourgeois, he was dimly aware that hatred, even apparently justified hatred, could degenerate into pathology. His hesitations point to a pervasive uncertainty in respectable nineteenth-century culture about licensed punitive aggression. And most aggression *was* punitive, whether in the family, at school, at work, in the army, on the streets, in the law courts. As elsewhere, so in this vast domain, a century in search of clarity was persistently divided.

This search was naturally of particular interest to the bourgeoisie, especially to substantial property owners. "The state," Goethe commented coolly early in the nineteenth century, "is interested only in seeing that property is certain and secure; whether it is lawfully held concerns it less."[1] Most offenses—childish pilferage, casual theft, small-scale fraud, planned robbery—had long been perpetrated by those who wanted against those who had. Even at the time, mercantile Britain was notorious for leading the way in draconian retribution against those who appropriated other people's property. In the late seventeenth century, the list of capital crimes contained about sixty items; some seventy-five years later, when Sir William Blackstone made a count, the total had risen to 160; by 1820, it amounted to roughly 220. Nearly all these additions to the fatal register were designed to repress various forms of theft, forgery, or grand larceny—this last defined as stealing an object worth more than twelve pence. Humane judges might instruct juries in such a way as to avoid a death sentence, and humane juries often refused to convict, but the message of the law was unmistakable.

No one doubted that impulsive crimes—acts of drunken agitation or vindictive fury—were committed far more frequently by the poor than by the comfortable. Hence, those earnestly working to map the proper domain of punishment could hardly leave class out of account. In 1872 Ernest Bertrand, a councillor at the court of appeals in Paris, published a substantial statistical study comparing the morality of various classes in France. The crimes of the agricultural classes, he concluded, generally arise not from cupidity, but from violent passions—"outbursts of rage, the spirit of revenge, domestic dissensions, quarrels in taverns." The urban working classes are less violent than their country cousins, and specialize in crimes against public order, such as rioting, and crimes against property.[2] The figures he compiled only confirmed self-satisfied bourgeois perceptions; the invidious distinctions he drew between the criminal lower orders and the respectable middle class were familiar to all. But self-interest did not wholly govern middle-class thinking about crimes and punishments. While those who advocated, or welcomed, the death penalty for even petty crimes against property belonged to the middle classes, so also did the members of juries who refused to convict patently guilty thieves. Like the most intractable spokesmen for the severe repression of crime, its most energetic critics were good bourgeois.

The question was how to define pathological excesses in the campaign against crime and distinguish them from the sensible, even necessary, infliction of pain. Some reformers called for the abolition of flogging or of the death penalty; others sturdily defended both. Whatever their rhetoric, neither party, nor for that matter their victims, seriously doubted that dealing out pain gave pleasure, mainly to the aggressor. Yet though this sound psychological intuition put a number of accepted punitive practices into doubt, it could not discredit the supreme principle of punishment. Humanitarian reformers never envisioned abandoning collective regulated repression of evildoers; they thought it self-evident that society must protect itself against agents of disorder or subversion. Even the gentle libertarian anarchist Prince Kropotkin found it necessary to propose punishing incorrigible loafers in the communist society of the future, by isolating them from their fellows.[3] In 1889, Louis Günther, an ambitious academic German historian of retribution, claimed the "modern"— which is to say, humane—point of view for his own, but quickly added, "We believe that there is a limit" the philanthropist should "take care not to cross. It is the people's sense of justice." To affront that sense would only oblige him to "overturn what he has so hastily created."[4] In short, the recognition that punishments were only too often an alibi for unacceptable, even deranged vengeance might narrow, but could not eradicate, their claims to legitimacy.

These claims lived off impeccable, venerable credentials. The fable of man's

Fall, laid down in Genesis, retained much of its authority throughout the nine-teenth century; the fear of hell was still very much alive. Many Victorians, like their ancestors, read the biblical tale as a terrible saga of disobedience and retribution. For unpardonable transgression—unpardonable, that is, in the eyes of their creator—Adam and Eve, and all their descendants, had to pay with the loss of sexual innocence and with a life of labor, pain, and mortality. The world into which God had thrown humankind was for many Victorians a kingdom of punishment. The fate of Cain, like that of Sodom and Gomorrah, reinforced this stark view of the human condition. The God of the Hebrews, of St. Augustine, of Calvin—and of Gladstone—was a God of vengeance, an exacting master who doled out mercy sparingly. In the scriptural texts as the severe pious continued to read them, the divinity figured as a stern, punitive judge, even as sophisticated Unitarians, relaxed Anglicans, and liberal Jews ventured to rede-scribe him as a magnanimous probation officer.

Much like their biblical counterparts, the Greek myths that educated Vic-torians absorbed in school were tales of mortal offenses and appalling retaliation. The divine, titanic, and royal criminals whom Homer and the Greek tragedians so memorably dramatized amassed a sizable catalogue of sensational transgres-sions: not merely theft and adultery, but incest, castration, the treacherous murder of spouses, and horrifying cannibalism. Preserved for posterity by gen-erations of epic poets, dramatists, and philosophers, these myths survived in nineteenth-century theater and poetry, painting, sculpture, and popular speech, imparting the somber lesson that twist as humans will, punishment is woven into the texture of their lives. Whether biblical or classical, they emphasized a single majestic circular sequence: violation of order, meting out of punishment, restoration of order. Punishment acted as the mandatory instrument for mend-ing the rent that crime had torn in the social fabric. Only in comedies did the wicked get away with murder.

These founding myths were saying, in effect, that while retribution had proved indispensable to the survival of human society, it had also produced the most drastic upheavals. Freud's highly debatable exercise in speculative prehis-tory, *Totem and Taboo,* published just before the First World War, underscores the message that Greeks and Christians had domesticated in Western civiliza-tion. In this startling fable for a bourgeois age, Freud reconstructed what he regarded as the decisive episode in human history, arguing that in some remote past, sons had banded together to overthrow their all-powerful, sexually om-nivorous father, the tyrant they hated and loved. They had killed the patriarch and eaten him, only to discover that he proved more powerful in death than in life and that their impulsive act of self-liberation had produced an irreversible mutation in their existence. They had won freedom from the shackles of prehistoric dependence and obedience, only to confine themselves by their parricide and their parricidal meal within a mental prison of their own making. Remorsefully, they felt compelled to shoulder the burden of guilt feelings and, with that, of sexual self-denial. The superego and its child, civilization, were born. From then on, social institutions would inhibit the most deeply held human desires, above all the wishes to commit murder and incest. Freud, in short, argued that human civilization had sprung from a monstrous crime. His modern version of the founding myth amounts to a stunning paradox: constraining civilization is at once a punishment and the necessary condition for its continued existence.

Even prehistorians who have rejected Freud's imaginative construction concede that through the ages societies have devised ceremonial repetitions of a primeval felony, usually sacrificing an animal or some other symbolic substitute for the original victim.[5] Often the hapless criminal has been, quite literally, made into the sacrificial object; in the code of the Roman republic, as Theodor Mommsen observed in his great history of Roman penal law, punishment was a sacred act: "The verdict is the handing over of the convicted offender to a god."[6] Such ceremonial sacrifices, whether a meal consumed in a primitive religious orgy or a sophisticated reenactment like the Catholic mass, were solemn new editions of the old master plot: crime, punishment—and survival. It was a cycle that the nineteenth century never wholly rejected.

In the Victorian age, as through the centuries, legislators, lawyers, and philosophers placed rationales for punishment, though with subtle nuances, under three comprehensive rubrics: retribution, deterrence, and rehabilitation. Of these the harshest, retribution, most clearly reveals the psychological rewards that the chastisement of misdeeds brings to all but the perpetrator (and at times also to the perpetrator)—even if many advocates of this justification deny, at times in injured tones, that it is simply an apology for revenge.

Late in the eighteenth century, Immanuel Kant, a robust partisan of retribution, set forth its function explicitly: "Every deed that offends a man's right deserves punishment, whereby the crime is *avenged* upon its perpetrator (not merely the injury made good)." To be sure, God alone has the right to take vengeance; it is man's duty to refrain from returning hostility with hatred, and to appeal to "the world-judge" for vengeance. After all, "a man has enough guilt of his own to be very much in need of forgiveness." But if punishment may not "be inflicted out of hatred," it still must be inflicted; whoever allows a murderer to escape execution becomes his accomplice, covered with blood guilt.[7] This line of reasoning was no doubt a sincere deduction from Kant's categorical moral doctrine—the criminal must be punished not for the sake of society, or for his own reformation, but because he deserves it. Yet though Kant professed not to feel the *frisson* of seeing criminals getting their just deserts, others taking his line were less austere, more open, in enjoying the sufferings of the wicked.

The aggressive craving for reprisals often underlay the other rationales— deterrence and rehabilitation—no less, though more deviously; the hidden or unconscious reasons for punishment were far more complicated, often far less benevolent, than the justifications apparent to orderly minds. Devices of deterrence that philanthropists praised as infallibly humane often came to look, in their own century, like disguised ways of gratifying the punitive passions. Similarly, the kinds of rehabilitation that many eloquent reformers supported were exposed, deservedly, to searching criticism. In some hands, they turned out to be nothing better than alibis for indulging the urge to get even.

Despite the mixed motives of its professional avengers, what set the nineteenth century apart was a pronounced effort to discover rational and charitable grounds for punishment. Historians, lawyers, and editorial writers taking pride in their progressive age liked to offer the decline of licensed vindictiveness in proof. In 1860, in a bulky prize-winning treatise, Claude-Joseph Tissot, a prolific French psychologist and historian of philosophy, traced cultural attitudes toward punishment back to antiquity and exuberantly concluded that they had undergone an upward evolution toward rationality and decency. The history of punishment was, to his mind, a history of the mounting willingness to forgo the emotional dividends of revenge. In the remote past, punishment had been motivated first by vengeance, then by the law of talion—an eye for an eye. But under the influence of Christianity and, most happily, of enlightened eighteenth-century ideas, the philosophy of punishment had climbed to ever higher stages, until now, in the late nineteenth century, civilization had achieved "justice tempered by compassion and kindness."[8] It was a cheerful picture, calling for self-congratulation.

Some years before Tissot, Thomas Babington Macaulay had composed an extended, fiercely Whiggish, tribute to the restraint of vengeful passions that his polished age had achieved. "It is pleasing to reflect," he wrote in his *History of England,* proudly comparing the nation of his own day to the England of 1685, "that the public mind of England has softened while it has ripened, and that we have, in the course of ages, become, not only a wiser, but also a kinder people. There is scarcely a page of the history or lighter literature of the seventeenth century which does not contain some proof that our ancestors were less humane than their posterity. The discipline of workshops, of schools, of private families, though not more efficient than at present, was infinitely harsher. Masters, well born and bred, were in the habit of beating their servants. Pedagogues knew no way of imparting knowledge but by beating their pupils. Husbands, of decent station, were not ashamed to beat their wives." The kindliest of gentlemen would travel long distances to see prisoners whipped and criminals executed. Possibly—Macaulay was, as it were, protecting his rear—exaggerated forms of nineteenth-century compassion had "produced some ridiculous and some deplorable effects." But "the more we study the annals of the past, the more shall we rejoice that we live in a merciful age, in an age in which cruelty is abhorred, and in which pain, even when deserved, is inflicted reluctantly and from a sense of duty."[9]

Macaulay was letting his well-known enthusiasm for the march of progress run away with his critical perception of current realities. But few in his time would have denied that civilized societies had begun to enforce a marked reduction in acceptable cruelties. For some decades, the humane reformers—or those who persuaded themselves that they were humane—had had the upper hand in the making of policy. But they roused anxious and angry voices in opposition, arguing that this so-called humanity had gone too far. Macaulay himself, that unimpeachable liberal, was plagued by doubts about the unchecked philanthropic impulse. In March 1846, commenting in the House of Commons on petitions for mercy to save several convicted insurrectionists from the sentence of transportation for life, he described these appeals as "the natural reaction against that barbarous penal code which had been in force in England during the past century," a reaction that had led to "such a sort of effeminate feeling in the country, that there was hardly a case of atrocity with respect to which they would not have thousands of persons petitioning for mercy, if the house gave any encouragement to the practice." His fellow members of Parliament greeted this sally with "hear, hear."[10] There was something almost irresistible about being manly in public.

"Effeminate"—with this sexual innuendo, Macaulay found himself in the unexpected company of Thomas Carlyle, the Cassandra of modern industrial society. At mid-century, in "Model Prisons," one of his crankiest performances, Carlyle denounced recently built English jails as characteristic of a decaying culture. He worried over sentimental philanthropists who wanted to "cure a world's woes by rose-water." Carlyle was coming to be regarded as eccentric, but in his derisive campaign against weak-kneed reformers, he spoke for indignant conservatives—and, as we have just seen, for some tough-minded liberals.

Whatever their position on this sensitive issue, all could agree that a society's way with its offenders is the touchstone for the level of civilization it has reached. This dictum, itself a sign of a new sensitivity to suffering and a new preoccupation with crime and punishment, became an international cliché. "In order to be able to form a sound judgment on the moral state of a people," said

Louis-Mathurin Moreau-Christophe, a French inspector general, in 1837, "history must find a way into the prisons."[11] Carlyle had no difficulty with the dictum, but employed it to denounce, not applaud, the reformers: the way his age treated criminals was a cause for alarm; they were being coddled at the expense of their victims. In 1850, pursuing his dogged diagnosis of contemporary society, Carlyle went to visit one of the "exemplary or model kind" of prisons—it was Millbank Penitentiary, anything but exemplary—and sardonically pronounced it to be "excellent." He found the building clean, the food superlative, the work productive, the exercise wholesome, the prison governor imbued by the "method of love"—and he was appalled: "Hopeless forevermore such a project. These abject, ape, wolf, ox, imp and other diabolic animal specimens of humanity, who of the very gods could ever have commanded them by love?" These prisons were palaces: "No Duke in England is, for all rational purposes which a human being can or ought to aim at, lodged, fed, tended, taken care of, with such perfection."[12]

Later that year, in the last installment of *David Copperfield,* Charles Dickens closely paraphrased his admired Carlyle, savagely lampooning the new prisons as triumphs of hypocrisy and ineffectiveness. Visiting a model penitentiary, the hero encounters among the inmates the two principal villains of the novel; they are as vicious as ever, but great favorites with the administration and the inspectors for their pious cant and their humble way of finding fault with the cuisine. Looking at the dinner the prisoners are about to be served, Copperfield wonders at "the striking contrast between these plentiful repasts of choice quality, and the dinners, not to say of paupers, but of soldiers, sailors, labourers, the great bulk of the honest, working community; of whom not one man in five hundred ever dined half so well."[13] This was inaccurate reportage and heartless satire, but biting editorials and "humorous" commentary in *Punch* attest that Carlyle and Dickens spoke for a far from negligible point of view. We hear a humorous echo of it in W. S. Gilbert, who entered the debate in 1885 with his humane Mikado, "a true philanthropist" intent upon letting "the punishment fit the crime," and making

to some extent
Each evil liver
A running river
Of harmless merriment.[14]

Considering his curmudgeonly temperament, Gilbert was doubtless lampooning the humanitarians rather than the rigorists. In any event, he found strong support in public opinion.

Nor was this censure of unmanly humanitarians confined to Britain. In the early 1860s, in a treatise on German criminal law, the distinguished jurist Gustav Geib leveled a barrage of accusations against the Enlightenment's spirit of reformist jurisprudence: it exhibited, he said, contempt for tradition, unwarranted self-confidence, "philanthropic-cosmopolitan ardor," zeal for humanitarian causes curiously mixed with ruthlessness in practice, uncritical enthusiasm for everything grand and beautiful combined with an unwillingness to do serious research, the whole "dissolving in empty phraseology and vague emotional reasoning." So much for the moral and intellectual style of nineteenth-century philanthropists, the heirs of the Enlightenment! The legal scholar who quoted those provocative words in 1891, Professor Zucker of Prague, feared that the same charges might one day be leveled against the legal theorizing of the Victorians; they were at once so soft-minded and pugnacious, so unhistorical and ruthless with tradition.[15]

Zucker had reason to worry; the champions of tradition spoke up freely and angrily. Bismarck was only the chief among Germany's politicians who were already echoing Geib's derisive diagnosis. In 1870, during a strenuous debate on capital punishment in the North German Reichstag, he took the floor more than once, in his familiar aggressive style. Unwilling to rest his case for the executioner's axe on pragmatic or ethical reasons alone, he denounced the abolitionists as mealymouthed and of "sickly disposition." They seemed more intent on indulging the criminal than protecting his prey. These philanthropic jurists, too weak to shoulder their awesome responsibilities, struck him as symptomatic for the "sicknesses of our time." Their argumentation, he said— one can hear his manly contempt—was a "mess of false sentimentality."[16]

This name-calling did not deter the reformers, who drew confidence from the time-honored credentials for their psychological and legal analyses. As so often, we cannot understand nineteenth-century ideas without glancing back at their eighteenth-century roots. Early in that century, Montesquieu had outlined a legal system that would establish a "just proportion between punishment and crime," and in the 1760s, Cesare Beccaria, the most celebrated jurist of the age, had repeated Montesquieu's call, advocating "a proportion between crimes and punishments."[17] As these names attest, Victorian efforts to move away from the principle of retribution and toward the deterrence and rehabilitation of offenders were a legacy of the radical wing in the secular eighteenth-century Enlightenment.

The plea for humanity and self-restraint in punishment was, of course, not the monopoly of unbelievers, as the philosophes had claimed. Early on, devout Christians had fought in the vanguard of prison reform and for a redefinition of permissible official aggressiveness, and in the nineteenth century they were more active still. In the 1830s, looking back at the age of the Enlightenment in their terse historical outline of developments in penitentiary systems, Gustave de Beaumont and Alexis de Tocqueville gave credit to the Pennsylvania Quakers, who had consistently protested against "the barbarous laws which the colonies had inherited from the mother country," and succeeded in abolishing in their home state "the death penalty, mutilation and the whip."[18] They could have added John Howard, a spartan, conscience-ridden Nonconformist whose campaigns against the shocking insanitary conditions of prisons in his day, both in Britain and elsewhere, provoked some shamefaced remedial action.* Religious or nonreligious, Victorian reformers retrieved Enlightenment schemes for social betterment and put their own stamp on them.

Their most admired model was Beccaria. His treatise of 1764, *Dei delitti e delle pene,* was quickly translated into several major languages; it retained its authority for a century. "His arms," said Jeremy Bentham, "were of celestial temper."[19] Punishment, Beccaria conceded, is an inescapable social sanction, since man is by nature aggressive. The laws must repress the "despotic spirit" alive in everyone. But the only rational and effective way of guaranteeing social order is to prevent crime rather than punish it, and where punishment is unavoidable, to ascertain the smallest amount of pain it is necessary to inflict. Anything more is "tyrannical." Torture is a relic of savagery unworthy of a civilized age, and so is the death penalty. Triumphantly summarizing his case in a hundred pages, Beccaria concluded that any punishment falling afoul of his principle is a sheer act of violence.[20] The whole liberal Victorian program for penal reform is contained in his denunciations and recommendations. The nineteenth-century reformers were Beccaria's legitimate, grateful, and inconsistent heirs.

The Enlightenment's program linked two impulses for reform: humanitarianism and social engineering. It virtually identified the passion for decoding the human condition with the passion for improving it. High-minded and strenuously informal teachers of virtue, among them Addison and Steele in the *Spectator* and *Tatler,* and their imitators on the Continent, inculcated self-respect in their bourgeois readers and trained them to polite piety, generosity to inferiors, and the civilized treatment of women, children, servants, and criminals. The politics of decency won intrepid and influential converts.

It needed them. In France, the legal code still in force was the *Ordonnance*

---

*It is symptomatic of the complexities of this history that Howard, the great humanitarian, was also one of the most insistent advocates of exceedingly rigorous prison discipline, especially of the isolation of inmates from one another.

criminelle of 1670, a halfhearted revision of late-medieval and early-modern enactments. Most of it seemed to be, in Voltaire's concise verdict, "directed solely to the ruin of the accused."[21] It treated sins as crimes and crimes as sins, protected property against thieves and rioters with pitiless rigor, retained torture as a device for securing valuable information and avenging the offended deity, and prescribed ferocious punishments for a sizable inventory of offenses. Trials were ritualistic combats in which the prosecution held all the weapons. Few legal codes elsewhere were more lenient or more rational. In that atmosphere, the philosophes launched assaults on entrenched customs and codes, implicitly and quite often explicitly calling for the restraint of hatred in the name of reason. Montesquieu argued for shortening the roster of crimes; Lessing advocated dropping laws restricting the access of Jews to civil society; Helvétius developed the subversive ethical principle of the greatest good for the greatest number; Voltaire spent years rehabilitating the victims of judicial murders; Rousseau presented the claims of children for adult consideration; Kant proposed a plan for world peace; Bentham demonstrated the advantage of evaluating all social policy by the unconventional calculus of pleasures and pains.

The limits of human betterment, the philosophes asserted, are largely those imposed by ignorance. Admittedly, to understand is not automatically to reform; too many "sinister interests," as Bentham called them, impede the progress of rationality. But reform presupposes understanding. This reasoning brought into play the second impulse for drastic change, social engineering. Most philosophes envisioned rational study of the human animal as a first step toward what David Hume had called "the science of man."[22] Aspiring Newtons of the mind worked toward a dependable psychology that would equip reformist statesmen to expose abuses, attack superstitions, remedy injustices— and deal with transgressors in ways at once benevolent and sensible. In the Victorian century these pioneering probes spawned new professions, expert practitioners called sociologists, political scientists, economists, and criminologists. The last of these names was popularized in the late 1870s by Paul Topinard, a prominent French criminal anthropologist and the famous Broca's successor as general secretary of the Anthropological Society of Paris.[23] Vengeful aggression, too, was to yield to scientific understanding and treatment.

For decades, nineteenth-century philanthropists across a broad spectrum of religious and political convictions called for that scientific understanding, intent as they were on exposing current Old Testament harshness in the law as pathological. The fact that aggressiveness is a human trait, they argued, should not stop society from inhibiting it, limiting it to acute emergencies. By the time

W. S. Gilbert made fun of making punishment fit the crime, social thinkers far more solemn than he had long been calling for proportionate penalties, basing their case on utilitarian as much as on compassionate grounds.

One of the Enlightenment's legacies to the Victorians was the debate over human nature. It loomed large in the great canvass of the rationales for punishment, as reformers struggled with the touchy question of revenge as an alibi for aggression. Nineteenth-century specialists on crime and punishment, a rapidly growing tribe, almost all agreed that the exigent impulse creating the greatest difficulties for attempts to rescue human nature from the consequences of inborn bellicosity was the lust for revenge. Where the specialists sharply differed from one another was over the psychological and legal implications of this apparently indelible trait.

Even those Victorian jurists, then, who urged civilized societies to resist the disposition to aggression, found themselves forced by their prized realism to acknowledge, grudgingly, the human appetite for revenge. Speaking for the reformers, Tissot asserted that vindictiveness is "a lively and profound feeling," the "thirst for vengeance" a basic psychological need to return injury for injury. Louis Günther, that modern, and by his lights progressive, student of retribution, also felt compelled to recognize this all-too-human endowment: whatever position we take on the real purpose of punishment "in our enlightened and humane time," everyone must admit that the "first impulse to punish an injustice springs from the characteristic of human nature to take revenge for wrongs and injuries undergone." Georg Jellinek, who described crime in fashionable sociological language as a "*social product*" and "*a chronic illness of the social body*," still admitted that "among the ethical ideas of the nations perhaps none has played a larger role than that of retaliation. Precisely because it is profoundly involved with our sensual nature, there has been a great temptation to see it as an eternally valid law of the divinity and the world," a temptation the great religions have not resisted.[24]

Though most nineteenth-century students of the mind and of jurisprudence were critics of vindictive penalties, their psychological theories supplied congenial ammunition to their adversaries. The defenders of venerable rationalizations for punishment offered much the same diagnosis as the opponents, though radically different prescriptions. James Fitzjames Stephen, for whom society was little better than a jungle in which humans are forever at one another's throats, pleaded for retribution as essential to the legal system. He shared the philanthropists' conviction that the lust for revenge is a deeply rooted human emotion, but he did not grant this fact of life with reluctance; he applauded it. The most candid and forceful opponent of the democratizing tendencies which, he feared, afflicted the Britain of his day, Stephen was sure that in "morals as well as in religion there is and must be war and conflict between men." The consequences for the punishment of criminals seemed to him self-evident: British law might be excessively harsh, but once brought into play, it had to satisfy the implacable appetite for revenge. Criminal acts receive punishment not just because they are dangerous to society, but also because this gratifies "the feeling of hatred—call it revenge, resentment, or what you will—which the contemplation of such conduct excites in healthily constituted minds." Criminals should be hated, and their punishment should express that hatred.[25] This is the frankest justification that the century produced for legalized aggression against malefactors.

Stephen was in good company. Kant, we recall, had postulated that society had a duty to give criminals what they deserve. In the mid-1840s, Moreau-Christophe took vehement exception to the activities of the prolific prison official and reformer Charles Lucas: "It is *criminal* heresy to say that a penalty does not represent *vengeance,* that punishment should not involve *suffering.*" After all, "*vengeance,* in this case, is a synonym for *justice.*" And in the early 1880s, the widely read German philosopher and psychologist Hermann Lotze rejected all high-flown talk of a divine commission to punish, or an obligation to negate the negation of right, or even a duty to rehabilitate the offender. Punishment will not improve the criminal, but will help us, the victims and the onlookers, by satisfying the "lively indignation" we feel as long as retribution has not been dealt out to the transgressor. The need for revenge alone gives the state the right to inflict pain.[26] Human nature, as Stephen, Moreau-Christophe, Lotze, and their allies across the Western world never ceased to insinuate, is too steeped in its aggressive needs to permit the legitimate joys of revenge to go unsatisfied. The reformers could not in all honesty reject this view entirely; they agreed, reluctantly, with their stern opponents that the human is an aggressive animal. But they refused to accept the consequence the conservatives drew. The law, they believed, must try to control and master, rather than celebrate, this primitive hatred.

2. Between Prisons and Pathos

Nineteenth-century applications of eighteenth-century Enlightened doctrine proved to be partial—often resourceful and compassionate, more often erratic, even counterproductive. The aggressive repression of malefactors changed with only glacial speed. What had started out as a noble campaign to undo anachronistic practices of a harsher past, to contain and in the best sense rationalize official aggressiveness against malefactors, yielded some impressive results. But in the struggle against the savage and arbitrary treatment of convicted criminals, bourgeois indignation, which had served so well in the transatlantic crusade against the slave trade, made a difference only after painful delays. The destitute young in Britain and elsewhere, sleeping under bridges and recruited into gangs of thieves—Dickens's *Oliver Twist* was not altogether fiction—were particularly slow to benefit from Victorian humanitarianism, even though their lot had engaged anguished sympathy since the beginning of the century. Social activists, anticipating governmental committees of inquiry, had repeatedly and frankly described the harrowing existence of youngsters driven to stealing from sheer hunger—to little purpose.

In fact, to judge from a troubled article by W. R. Greg in the *Edinburgh Review* in 1855, little had happened for more than half a century to relieve an appalling situation—except that strong feelings had been aroused. True, the energetic and humane educator Mary Carpenter, founder of the famous "ragged schools" for poor youngsters, agitated in their behalf, and with some success. But reviewing official and private reports on juvenile offenders, Greg bleakly noted, "For more than two generations—ever since, indeed, attention had been awakened and reflection aroused upon the matter,—no Judge of unblunted sensibility ever presided over an Assize, no Magistrate of ordinary feelings of compassion or rectitude ever sat at Quarter Sessions, without having to pass sentences which revolted his humanity and lay very heavy on his conscience. Children were repeatedly brought for trial, of twelve, of ten, of *seven* years of age,—so small that they had to be lifted up in the arms of the gaoler before the Jury or the Bench could see them,—so young that it was impossible for anyone really to regard them as responsible moral agents, or proper victims of the law,—conscious, indeed, that they were in a state of hostility with the community at large, but scarcely conscious of guilt in being so—of whom it was notorious that they were trained to depredation, acting under parental authority, and often under parental threat."[1]

The writer conceded that "their guilt was undeniable; the necessity of stopping them in the career of such guilt undeniable too; the propriety of punishing such guilt, according to received notions, equally indisputable." But received notions were wrong. "Judge and magistrate knew perfectly well that to whip these wretched infants, and then turn them back upon their homes, was to inflict wholly gratuitous and unprofitable suffering—was simply to restore them to a course of inevitable crime, to be re-commenced on the morrow, with

greater caution, perhaps, but with added skill." Imprisoning them was, as everyone knew, even worse. "Yet year by year, Session after Session, Judges and
Magistrates, fathers themselves, with tears in their eyes and a heavy nightmare
in their hearts, conscious that they were acting wrong, knowing they were
doing mischief, went on sentencing these young vagabonds to gaol, because it
was their duty, or, at least, their function to do so, because law and fact left them
no alternative."[2]

This moving plea for compassion captures the Victorian reformist impulse at
its highest pitch. But in light of the stiff penalties that magistrates kept handing
out to youngsters caught stealing food or firewood, one wonders how many
tearful, nightmare-ridden British judges the writer had really seen. Indeed,
nearly all seem to have been dry-eyed and to have slept soundly. So, it would
appear, did judges in France. Appalled by the precocity of thieving children,
they delivered moralizing harangues, but sent the little convicts to La Roquette,
an experimental prison for boys opened in Paris in 1838, where the inmates
were kept in solitary confinement in tiny cells and died in shocking numbers.
Beyond doubt, an ingrained class disdain reinforced this callousness. The young
offenders, most of them boys, were almost entirely from the rural and urban
working population; they belonged to the lower orders, which, as all but the
most rabid philanthropists knew with certainty, were strangers to the finer
feelings. Still, irate bourgeois reformers expected that their moral outrage
would force traditional legal habits to yield sooner or later.

In sovereign disregard of humane outbursts, the law yielded later, not sooner.
To be sure, reformers could record occasional triumphs. One of their most
stirring victories came in 1832; animated by remnants of reforming enthusiasm
that Louis Philippe's regime had not yet stifled, the Chamber of Deputies
provided French juries with the option of taking extenuating circumstances
into account, substantially shortened the list of capital crimes, and rather
grandly outlawed branding and mutilation as the "odious debris of barbarism."[3]
But through the 1850s and for decades more, French children were sent to
prison, and British children of twelve or fourteen convicted of minor crimes,
mainly petty larceny, continued to be sentenced as adults. In 1851, in Oxford-
shire, Daniel P., fourteen, illiterate, was sentenced to serve six months' hard
labor in a house of correction and to be whipped once in the first month and
again in the fifth. His offense was pocketing a cotton handkerchief worth
sixpence. Again, in the early 1870s, a pair of brothers—one of them fifteen, the
other twelve—stole a bag of bread and butter worth sixpence; they were sentenced to a month in prison at hard labor, followed by four years in a reformatory school. Sometimes, instead of committing these children to prison, the

magistrates ordered them to be whipped, meticulously specifying the number of strokes.* The alibi for this sort of aggression against miserable youngsters must have seemed ironclad.

To be sure, in the 1850s Parliament started to make some provision for offenders under sixteen. It instituted reformatory schools for first offenders in 1854, and eked them out three years later with industrial schools for children in danger of sinking into a life of crime. In that year, 1857, England boasted thirty-four reformatories holding nearly 1,900 inmates, of whom, the *Saturday Review* reported with evident distaste, some 500 were "little Papists." The weekly took special note of the Roman Catholic reformatories because it feared them as "denominational or proselytizing" centers.[4] They were dour institutions in which the convicts were fed badly and worked hard. It was only in 1887, with the Probation of First Offenders Act, that magistrates were permitted to let adolescent petty criminals go; not until 1908 did the Children Act prohibit the jailing of anyone under fourteen. It had been a long time.

Throughout much of the century, great reform campaigns produced little more than the replacement of coarse kinds of cruelty by subtler ones. As so often, the United States took the lead in innovations and confusions alike. Beginning around 1820, it developed two distinct types of incarceration. The Pennsylvania plan, or "separate" system, decreed the total isolation of each inmate from all others at all times. In contrast, the Auburn plan, or "silent" system, first tried out in New York State and widely copied, permitted convicts to work in company during the day, but forbade them to speak to, or look at, one another, and enforced the silence, when deemed necessary, with the whip. The two systems were in furious competition for public attention and funds. Advocates of the Pennsylvania plan accused their rivals of inhumanity and inconsistency; advocates of the Auburn plan, armed with plausible statistics, returned the compliment by accusing their rivals of inhumanity and consistency. By the 1840s, both American models had conquered Europe. But these transatlantic triumphs, far from stilling the debate over penal policy, only intensified it, to no one's complete satisfaction. In 1856, after more than three decades of muddle and continual controversy across the Western world, the *Saturday Review* could observe that at least in Britain, "the whole subject of the adaptation of punishment to crime" had been dealt with "fragmentarily, in-

*See Pamela Horn, *The Victorian Country Child* (1974), ch. 11 and Document M. Nor did they order this matter better in France: in that country, in 1875, there were almost ten thousand minors in prison; in 1890, 3,378 boys and 558 girls under sixteen were convicted of a variety of crimes. The country experimented with a variety of substitutes for prison for juveniles, but it did not establish special courts for them until 1912. Patricia O'Brien, *The Promise of Punishment: Prisons in Nineteenth-Century France* (1982), 110–11, 125–31. The figures for other countries were no smaller.

consequentially, and empirically." What was needed was principles and theories.[5]

It was an odd judgment. Certainly the country had not failed to speculate about punishment; it had suffered, if anything, from excessive theorizing. And even more than in Britain, in the United States and France, theorists had seen their notions translated into legislation and into buildings—the new model prisons. From about 1820, for some three decades, countries in the old world and the new erected massive fortresses to hold their criminal populations, strongholds expensive to build and expensive to run, all of them tributes to modern principles. Most reformers, it seems, were too quick to expand casual impressions into dogmatic generalizations and to elevate conjectures about human nature into pseudoscientific propositions. Earnestly fashioned to spread rational humanity, the new science of penology proved neither wholly rational nor consistently humane.

Evidence for its problematic nature emerges in the opinions of articulate prison officials and reformist amateurs. In 1831, during their visit to the United States to investigate the country's much-praised penitentiaries, Tocqueville and Beaumont interviewed Elam Lynds, the founder of Sing Sing. Lynds was the virtual inventor of the silent system. A tough old soldier, known as a disciplinarian, he calmly told his French visitors—who were greatly impressed— that he regarded whipping, the sole punishment he meted out to recalcitrant prisoners, as "the most effective and at the same time the most humane punishment, for it never injures the health and forces the inmate to live an essentially healthy life." Again, in his best-selling serial novel Les Mystères de Paris, Eugène Sue, noted for his political sympathies with the disinherited and the unfortunate, balanced his rejection of the death penalty with the proposal that murderers be blinded and committed to solitary confinement for the rest of their days. And in 1864, a German journalist walked through a prison for youths from six to twenty that reformers had established in Paris some thirty years earlier. He was horrified by the separate system still largely in force behind these dank and gloomy walls at a time when it was being discarded elsewhere. He was no less horrified by the enthusiasm that the prison official accompanying him mobilized in defending his domain. There was no way of persuading that man of its "exquisite cruelty." The German visitor found this resistance very illuminating: "There was the explanation why my companion liked the prison. Once a thinking and feeling being, he had become a machine."[6] These were chilling attitudes, far from unknown among progressive spirits in the first half of the nineteenth century.

Though their remedies could be draconian, the reformers' humanitarian intentions were impeccable, their motives, at least their conscious motives, pure. This paradox emerges perhaps most instructively in the English philosopher Jeremy Bentham and the American enthusiast Samuel Gridley Howe. In his long life—born in 1748, he died in 1832—Bentham took the Enlightenment's view of man and its radical program into the Victorian century. Cheerfully acknowledging his debts, he carpentered his utilitarian system together from the hedonistic psychology of Helvétius and the rationalistic penology of Beccaria, adding touches of his own. Beginning as a single-minded critic of English law, he converted himself into a democrat in midcareer, but always retained an authoritarian streak; he could be invoked as a prophet of *laissez-faire* or of state intervention. The struggles over economic and social policies that marked the Britain of the Victorian decades, years after he was gone, sometimes look like bouts of Bentham against Bentham.

This ambiguity pervades Bentham's legal thinking. As a disrespectful young savant, he mapped, with quickly growing scorn, what he denigrated as the labyrinth of English jurisprudence. His contempt for historical precedent complete, he treated Blackstone's monumental and authoritative *Commentaries on the Laws of England* of the late 1760s as a masterpiece of obfuscation and an apology for reigning abuses.* All the legislator needs to know is that men are governed, and should be governed, by two masters, pleasure and pain, and that they seek the one while they flee the other. Working with this knowledge, he can propel society toward the greatest happiness for the greatest number.

It was as an enlightened scientist of man that Bentham proclaimed the need to reduce the human lust for punishment to sane levels. His aphorisms on vengefulness belong among the pioneering modern attempts to analyze aggression and to master it. "Men punish because they hate; crimes, they are told, they ought to hate."[7] The desire for revenge may have its uses; it generates the energy to pursue the criminal. But the extreme punishments now in place only overbalance the victim's pain against the pleasure that society squeezes from his sufferings. "Whence originated the prodigal fury with which the punishment of death has been inflicted?" he asked, and answered his own question: "It is the effect of resentment which at first inclines to the greatest rigour; and of an imbecility of soul, which finds in the rapid destruction of convicts the great advantage of having no further occasion to concern one's self about them."[8]

Bentham did not rule out the death penalty and other harsh penalties, but he

*Lawyers, Jeremy Bentham wrote, are "a passive and enervate race, ready to swallow anything, and to acquiesce in anything; with intellects incapable of distinguishing right from wrong, and with affections alike indifferent to either; insensible, short-sighted, obstinate; lethargic, yet liable to be driven into convulsions by false terrors; deaf to the voice of reason and public utility; obsequious only to the whisper of interest, and to the beck of power." Preface to *A Fragment on Government* (1776; ed. F. C. Montague, 1891), 104.

objected to their casual employment. It was one thing to recognize, even to cherish, the power of the passions; it was quite another for legislators to yield to them. Man, he warned, is naturally inclined to punitive brutality.[9] This was one reason for humanizing the criminal law. Another, no less weighty, was that English law, incalculable and hence arbitrary, offended reason. The legislator and the judge who prescribed the noose or the rod literally did not know what they were doing—always, with Bentham, a cause for stern reproach. His reasoning had all the warmth of a logician analyzing a syllogism; he justified his proposals for radical legal and constitutional reform far more on the grounds that they were economical than that they were compassionate. Yet, as one of his nineteenth-century admirers, John Stuart Mill, put it, he offered ideas by which "the yoke of authority has been broken."[10]

The career of Samuel Gridley Howe illustrates the migration of this reformist style across the Atlantic. Howe collected good causes the way more frivolous mortals collect stamps. Born in Boston in 1801, he was trained as a physician at Harvard Medical School, but in 1824, inspired by Byron, he sailed off to assist the Greeks in their uprising against Turkish overlordship. He fought, organized relief, and remained for six years, punctuating his stay with visits back home to raise thousands of dollars for starving Greek patriots. Upon his return to Boston he discovered a cause of a very different sort, the blind, for whom he founded an innovative school. Later, he became interested in relieving the pathetic condition of idiots, hitherto thought beyond help. An effective lobbyist, he managed to wrest appropriations for his causes from the state of Massachusetts. It is hardly necessary to add that he was a zealous abolitionist orator.

But prisons raised especially intimate echoes for Howe. In early 1832, he had spent some six weeks in solitary confinement in a Berlin jail; he had been caught working, typically, for the continuing resistance of Poles to the czarist regime, which had largely crushed their rebellion the year before. For long years he was a faithful member of the Boston Prison Disciplinary Society, but in the mid-1840s he broke with its leadership over their enthusiastic partisanship for the Auburn plan. It was an aggressive move characteristic for Howe. Finding himself outvoted and his minority views denied room in the society's annual report, he went public with a substantial pamphlet to atone for what he now damned as his former blind discipleship. Point for point, he compared the Auburn with the Pennsylvania plan, disparaging the first and extolling the second. He found the prisons run on Pennsylvanian principles far more consistent and effective in deterring crime, and far more compassionate than their competitors. The "separate system" was misnamed, for it was not a solitary system: it "checks no impulse of the social nature; it encourages the prisoner to talk,—it only takes care that he talks not with bad men; it invites him to give confidence and to indulge affection, but it introduces into his room such persons only as will have a good influence over him."[11] On this issue Howe, the principled progressive, sounded much like Carlyle, the principled reactionary.

Howe's case was flawed beyond repair. His figures and anecdotes comparing the lot of prisoners under each of the American schemes were purely impressionistic and probably less reliable than those his opponents supplied.* What matters more is that this consistent humanitarian could not visualize the horrors haunting the penitentiary of his choice; he could not imagine a less fearsome system that might effectively deter crime and reform the criminal. Few, if any, blamed Howe. He was, and remained, the great humanitarian. In 1891, when Franklin B. Sanborn published the first full biography of Howe, he did so in a series on American reformers, and subtitled his life, in characteristic Victorian fashion, *The Philanthropist*.

This, then, was the cultural climate in which a professional prison administrator like Lynds must be judged. He was only one among many, in the United States and in Europe, who reacted against the penal methods prevalent in the eighteenth century: erratic and hence unpredictable procedures—the death penalty freely imposed, transportation to tropical colonies, which was only a sentence of death in another form, branding, and public whipping. Other venerable punishments were equally unacceptable, some of them because their effect on the malefactor was so uncertain. As Bentham recognized, if someone popular with the crowd was put in the pillory, he might become a momentary hero; someone else—a government informer or a homosexual—might be pelted with muck and beaten to death by a furious, drunken mob.

Eighteenth-century places of detention had been no better. Indiscriminate depositories for the indigent, the aged, the mad, those awaiting trial and those convicted, they were managed by corrupt wardens and exploited by greedy contractors; overcrowded and filthy, they gave fever and starvation their lethal opportunities. It had become a trite, if virtually inescapable, metaphorical habit to call prisons schools of crime or, a touch more elegantly, seminaries of vice. They had been, said Samuel Gridley Howe, looking back in 1845, "loathsome cesspools into which was thrown all that was foul and corrupt."[12] No wonder the early-nineteenth-century reformers felt a little smug as they pressed for

---

*One vigorous English critic of both these systems, Henry Mayhew, a dramatist, editor, and crusading journalist, made a revealing statistical comparison between England's "unreformed" prisons and the "model" prison of Pentonville, which approximated the Pennsylvania prototype. He found that while in eight years, from 1842 (the year of Pentonville's founding) to 1850, some 5.8 out of every 10,000 inmates went insane in the "unreformed" prisons, some 62 per 10,000 did so in Pentonville. This would give Pentonville a lead of more than ten to one. Mayhew and John Binny, *The Criminal Prisons of London and Scenes of Prison Life* (1862), 103–4.

more humane criminal trials, more rational penalties, more salubrious prisons.

Drawing their invidious comparisons with the past, then, tough-minded Americans and their European followers had good reasons for the conviction that their experiments with isolating prisoners were preferable alternatives, even if they included the threat, and all too often the reality, of the whip. To them, this cruelty must have seemed kindness. Even those, like French experts on penology, who could not accept the corporal punishment of inmates thought the segregation of prisoners a vast improvement over the callous and haphazard old ways. Doubtless it was, in some measure. But the pitiless prison regimen, the pressure for silence and subservience, the monotonous round of unvarying meals, perfunctory exercise, compulsory prayer, and tedious, ill-paid work, drove convicts to rebellion, insanity, and suicide. Penitentiaries became engines of society's revenge, places for almost naked aggression. Something had gone wrong somewhere.

What had gone wrong was the consistent application of a mechanical environmentalism, an unscientific reaching for a science of human nature coupled with an undercurrent of anxious pessimism about the human animal. The label of shallow optimist, which their opponents liked to fasten on Victorian humanitarians, was far from appropriate. Many of them were shallow, perhaps, but few were optimists. Actually, nineteenth-century ways with the legacy of Enlightened ideas proved to be something of a detour. The philosophes, it is often forgotten and worth reiterating, were not naive about the human prospect; most of them, though not all, retained a solid, at times snobbish, skepticism about the capacity of the lower orders to live without superstition and to curb their unruly desires. Yet they were less troubled than the Victorians would be by fear of the seething caldron of egotistical, at times murderous, passions concealed in all men and women, passions needing to be contained lest they explode into destructive action.

Hence a Victorian conservative like James Fitzjames Stephen was far from eccentric in viewing humans as a pack of pugnacious and selfish hounds. And this meant, in the collective diagnosis that early-nineteenth-century reformers took as almost self-evident, that prisons of the old type must necessarily fail to reclaim the guilty. Throwing convicts together, they could only encourage criminals to persevere in their wicked ways. The only possibility of rehabilitation lay in separating the evildoers as completely as human ingenuity could manage: contact produces contagion, and since it is far easier to keep bad habits than to acquire good ones, isolation is the necessary precondition for uprooting the first and cultivating the second. Beaumont and Tocqueville put this commonly held view with impressive economy: "Two depraved persons kept in the same place must corrupt one another: they are separated. The voice of their passions or the hurly-burly of the world have dazed them or led them astray: they are isolated and thus brought back to reflection. Their contacts with the wicked have perverted them: they are condemned to silence. Idleness has depraved them: they are made to work. Misery has brought them to crime: they are taught an occupation. They have violated the laws of their country: a punishment is inflicted on them. Their life is protected, their body hale and unscathed, but nothing equals their moral suffering. They are unhappy; they deserve to be. Having become better, they will be happy in the society whose laws they respect." This "is the whole system of the American penitentiary."[13] After short delays, it was that of most European penitentiaries as well.

The envenomed pamphlet wars between advocates of the Pennsylvania plan and of the Auburn plan were over marginal rather than fundamental differences; they agreed that bad company must fatally infect those who have remnants of goodness left in them. It followed from the psychology to which both parties subscribed that strict prison discipline had a double function: it served as a defensive strategy and as a pedagogic device. It protected the prisoner, and the prison, against laziness, insubordination, and riots, and it provided a living lesson in steady work habits and self-control. Unvaried and dependable regimentation would inoculate prisoners with virtues they had not acquired at home or in the streets. The penitentiary routine was to be a kind of remedial superego; it would generate or strengthen a guilt-inducing and socially adaptive conscience.

The work schedule on which prison directors everywhere insisted was an indispensable part of the plan; it forced prisoners to make some money for the penitentiary, always welcome when government inspectors came around, and it kept them from going insane with, or literally dying of, boredom. Best of all, work inculcated productive habits that would stand released prisoners in good stead when they faced the world. It has often been observed that the values the model prisons were intended to cultivate were bourgeois values: thrift, seriousness, regularity, hard work, self-discipline—above all self-discipline. All life, the reformers agreed, even life outside prison, is a battle of vulnerable good against powerful evil; all life is a hard school of character.

While the prison reformers leavened their forbidding estimate of human nature with the hope that they might make the penitentiary into a place of redemption, many among them were haunted by doubts as to whether this was a realistic aspiration. When Beaumont and Tocqueville asked Lynds if he really expected the "reform of a great number of prisoners," Lynds soberly told them that he did not. "Nothing, in my opinion, is rarer than to see a convict of mature age become a religious and virtuous man." He had little faith in the "counsels of the chaplain, or the meditations of the prisoners." His confidence in the conduct of well-behaved prisoners was equally limited: "The worst subjects make excellent prisoners." The only improvement Lynds thought one had a right to hope for was that "a great number of old convicts do not commit new crimes"; they became good citizens simply because they had learned a "useful art" in prison, "and contracted habits of constant labor."[14]

So impassioned a believer in progress as Samuel Gridley Howe was at times moved to admit, after years of labor in the vineyard of prison reform, that the rehabilitation of convicts, the "most important object of imprisonment," had "never yet been attained in any satisfactory degree in any prison, under any system." He poignantly added that skepticism was rife, and, alas, only too justified. Hence he threw himself onto the future, the "almost limitless power of the human intellect, when directed by human love."[15] These, he knew, were slim reeds, but faith in them was typical of his age.

By mid-century, even this modest trust in the new penal departures had faded. Empirical researchers, mainly experts serving on government committees who paraded increasingly credible facts and figures, questioned the defensive self-appraisals of doctrinaire reformers. High hopes were followed by deep disillusionment. Politicians and criminologists worried that the criminal population seemed to be growing and that persistent offenders were not made any less persistent by the most modern methods of incarceration. There was much talk of professional criminals not deterred by whatever penalties the state could think up. "Punishments, of whatever sort," said the Saturday Review, "operate very slightly indeed as a check upon this class in the pursuit of their calling, or in the continuance of their previous course of life."[16] The portentous word "recidivism" became a familiar, menacing term in editorials and statistical surveys on crime. Apparently, too many felons graduated from prison only to commit new felonies. Significantly, a few audacious penologists were recommending alternatives to incarceration, and governments began to test them—to suspend sentences and parole prisoners. And at last, they paid some attention to that most harrowing of phenomena, the young offender. As the first experiments, centering on prison reform, appeared on the verge of failure, new experiments in penology were pressing toward center stage.

They got their chance in the second half of the century with the fruitful, though still tense, collaboration of legal and medical experts. In 1886, a group of French scholars advertised this alliance by founding the Archives d'anthropologie criminelle to facilitate the joint work of "physicians, jurists, professors of criminal law, and magistrates." Such a coalition was not unprecedented; cooperation among these specialists had grown more intimate from the 1860s on, but its beginnings antedated the discoveries of Darwin, and the hard-won recognition

of medical experts, by some decades. The adhesive that bound these professionals together was the vexed question of a defendant's mental state during a
criminal act. Late in the eighteenth century, scores of English defendants had
pleaded insanity, and in several cases physicians had been called to testify. Then,
early in the nineteenth century, a handful of venturesome specialists and judges
made the link between mental medicine and legal proceedings explicit, and the
alliance between two ancient professions flourished. Medical schools showed
marked interest in medical jurisprudence, and in 1811, a Napoleonic decree
assigned the psychiatric expert a place in determining criminal responsibility.
By the mid-1820s, ambitious French physicians specializing in mental ailments
were urging their diagnosis of "monomania" on the courts in intriguing murder cases.[17] And in 1838 Isaac Ray, the most prestigious forensic psychiatrist in
Victorian America, published his famous *Treatise on the Medical Jurisprudence of
Insanity,* which he lived to revise repeatedly.

But it was a trial rather than a treatise that made the difference. Following a
sensational murder in 1843, English judges laid down the much-praised, much-
criticized—and much copied—M'Naghten rules. From then on, students of
the field would use that year as a decisive marker. The M'Naghten rules and
their interpretations domesticated in modern jurisprudence a view of human
nature first adumbrated by Plato. It saw the mind as a highly vulnerable system
of peremptory passions subjected to rational controls that at times break down,
then permitting destructive urges to govern behavior.

Suffering from delusions of persecution and imagining that he was being
followed by spies, M'Naghten had killed Edward Drummond, Sir Robert
Peel's private secretary, in the misapprehension that his victim was the prime
minister. For all his morbid suspiciousness—he would today be diagnosed as a
paranoid schizophrenic—M'Naghten was not obviously insane; he had
behaved normally in his business and private affairs. Yet his lawyers, "able and
zealous counsel," impressed the court with "the more sound and humane views
of insanity which have resulted from modern inquiry."[18] Persuaded, and carefully steered by the judge's instructions, the jury decided that M'Naghten's
delusions were exculpatory and found him not guilty on grounds of insanity.

The problematic decision made the country, including Queen Victoria, exceedingly uneasy; it seemed to offer legal shelter to the most savage of criminals.
Accordingly, the lord chancellor invited a panel of judges to clarify the issue
before the House of Lords by answering some pointed questions. Their responses were the so-called M'Naghten rules, which defined insanity as the
inability to tell right from wrong, an instance of reason gone astray. Inadequate
though they soon showed themselves to be, these rules stood firm; they would
govern American no less than British trials almost unchallenged for many

decades. Their only supplement was the "irresistible impulse" rule, adumbrated soon after. By recognizing emotional incapacity as a defense, this rule suitably broadened the rationalistic M'Naghten criteria, permitting juries to find innocent a murderer who was not necessarily bereft of his reason but was, rather, at critical moments helplessly delivered over to his aggressive needs.

The trickle of legal rethinking swelled into something of a flood in the mid-Victorian decades. In 1871, in the preface to the fifth edition of his classic treatise, now thirty-three years old, Isaac Ray observed with evident satisfaction that since the book was first published, "an unprecedented degree of attention has been given to the Medical Jurisprudence of Insanity, and been followed by a remarkable improvement of its condition. Treatises upon it have multiplied, the chapter devoted to it in general works on Medical Jurisprudence has evinced a better conception of the subject, medical journals have freely and frequently discussed the questions it has raised." Even more gratifying was the fact that physicians had not been the only ones to change their minds. "The bench and the bar have yielded more or less to the progress of ideas, and, in spite of some attempts to maintain the old landmarks, they have, on the whole, liberally responded to the requirements of science." Best of all, "society, too, has become more tolerant of innovations upon the time-honored philosophy of crime, and more willing to accept the conclusions of science."[19] As Ray saw the situation in the early 1870s, the program of the Enlightenment had been modernized through the authoritative findings of specialists in mental functioning— and malfunctioning. Compassionate experts, armed with impressive, recently acquired scientific knowledge, were making propaganda in behalf of the good cause and influencing the general public to discard, or at least modify, its prejudices about the wickedness of all lawbreakers.

Ray's backward glance was well-informed, his sunny optimism premature. The rise of the expert, while it often produced a consensus, also triggered fierce clashes. Reformers continued to be exposed to the sniping of conservatives unreconciled to humanitarian penology, but they were kept quite as busy battling one another. It seems ironic that the invasion of criminology by outside authorities should have exacerbated disputes over penal policy instead of settling them, but the irony is not unexpected. After all, the second half of the Victorian age was the time of brash Social Darwinism and cocksure racial theories, of measuring skulls and weighing brains—in short, a time of bold, untrustworthy theorizing about the human animal. As we have seen, the piles of statistics that indefatigable researchers gathered about presumed racial characteristics proved everything and therefore nothing. What social scientists and physicians were sure they knew about mind and body far outran what they really knew, and their theorizing regularly violated the essential criteria of scientific method. Hence the modern discipline of forensic psychiatry too, though civilized in its aims and, usually, in its results, was a guessing game dressed up as a science, the disputes it generated only too often dialogues of the deaf.

Still, by late in the century, the courts were increasingly disposed to take into account physicians' expert testimony. Inescapably, occasional boundary disputes arose between the ancient profession of law and the young profession of psychiatry struggling for recognition. But they paled before an impressive readiness on the part of both to act in concert. Their cooperation was cemented by the clear understanding that the law remained, as it had always been, the senior partner. Judges retained firm control over their domain. The trouble lay elsewhere: the conclusions of the various sciences were in serious, at times irreparable, conflict with one another. As criminologists exploited and reinterpreted Darwinian ideas, they found that the associated anthropological doctrines kept shifting ground. To put a complicated matter simply, the quarrel was over the respective roles of nature and nurture.

For Victorian reformers confronting the disheartening statistics of crimes and criminals, the strongest hope—to the extent that they allowed themselves hope at all—lay in an appeal to environmentalist psychology, the psychology that had been so indispensable a prop of the Enlightenment's program for human betterment. To be sure, however imprecise they were about the mechanisms of heredity, nineteenth-century social scientists insisted, more and more with the passing decades, on its influence over the course of mental life. Mad-doctors, psychiatrists, alienists—whatever they called themselves in the Victorian decades—mental healers welcomed information about a patient's syphilitic father or alcoholic aunt and would feature it prominently in their case histories. By the 1860s, most of them "knew" that one inherits insanity, a disposition to degeneracy, and criminal inclinations as one inherits skin color. Progressives could not seriously quarrel with this line of reasoning, whether from a residual trust in the biblical doctrine of original sin or from the sober recognition that inborn human passions do indeed seem exigent, hard to govern. But they found comfort in the thought that heredity might have only limited powers, with part of every mortal's fate dependent on what society—the family, the school, the workplace—inscribes on the slate of his mind across the years.

If so, the wicked are not born wicked, and attempts to reclaim transgressors are not a pure waste of time, whatever seasoned, cynical prison directors may say to the contrary. Humanitarians could be buoyed up by the observation that kind-hearted determinists, both devout and secular, granted at least some elbow room to the work of the environment and the possibility of improvement. Even some Social Darwinists, after all, harbored surprisingly reformist notions, and a few nineteenth-century students of crime managed to be determinists and political radicals at the same time.

The most spectacular representative of such a riven ideology was doubtless the embattled Italian criminologist Cesare Lombroso. He claims attention because he beautifully documents once again how hard his century found it to redraw the old map of legitimate aggression against transgressors. Lombroso's criminology, like that of others, was deeply enmeshed in politics. Born in 1835, trained as a physician, surgeon, and psychiatrist, he made himself into a most controversial authority on forensic medicine. He received his final accolade in 1906, three years before his death: the University of Turin, where he had taught for thirty years, appointed him to a chair of criminal anthropology obviously tailored to him. But he had tasted fame and controversy much earlier, from 1876 on, with his massive, fervently debated treatise studying delinquent man from a variety of perspectives, *L'uomo delinquente studiato in rapporto alla antropologia, alla medicina legale ed alle discipline carcerarie.* Its most memorable innovation, the key idea for which Lombroso is remembered, was summed up in a terse phrase: "born criminals."[20] In an eccentric application of evolutionary doctrines, Lombroso argued that criminals are criminals from birth and recognizable by atavistic physical features, throwbacks to a more primitive stage of human development or even to animal nature.

Lombroso's characteristic criminals are stigmatized by an asymmetrical face, prominent jaw, apelike long arms, extra fingers or toes, an inability to blush, and abnormalities in the brain; the heavy tattoos covering the bodies of so many of them spoke to Lombroso as eloquent testimony to their regression. The startling revelation that criminality is inborn overwhelmed him in 1870 as he dissected a notorious Italian brigand and came upon a revealing oddity in his skull. It was a dazzling moment.* The rest would be commentary—and partial retreat.

A self-styled empiricist, Lombroso refused to base his far-reaching assertion on a single instance or on metaphysical speculation; in years of research he observed and dissected untold numbers of criminals, avidly collected the art work of delinquents, and magisterially directed investigations by his loyal adherents. To no one's surprise, least of all his own, he found what he sought. But he was too shrewd—too scientific, his admirers would say—to claim universal

---

*"At the sight of that skull, I seemed to see all of a sudden, lighted up as a vast plain under a flaming sky, the problem of the nature of the criminal—an atavistic being who reproduces in his person the ferocious instincts of primitive humanity and the inferior animals." In Maurice Parmalee, "Introduction to the English Version," Lombroso, *Crime: Its Causes and Remedies* (1899; tr. Henry P. Horton, 1911), xiv.

application for his revelation. Offenders displaying the telltale stigmata of the born criminal substantiated his theory; offenders who did not display them had to be grouped under other rubrics: Lombroso conveniently called them habitual or occasional criminals or criminals from passion. In edition after edition of his *L'uomo delinquente* and in satellite publications, he gradually reduced his estimate of the percentage of born criminals in the total population of offenders. Again, in a study of the causes and remedies of crime published in 1899, he offered a pedantic, exhausting catalogue of the physical and social causes of crime: climate, geography, race, population density, alcoholism, education, religion, wealth and poverty, and much else. In short, his theory was infallible, fitting all exigencies.

Lombroso's desertion of biological determinism was never complete; he insisted all his life that born criminals are beyond help. But he saw the others as certainly open to rehabilitation. Indeed, social reform was always one of his pivotal preoccupations. The spirited cavils of his French critics notwithstanding—they accused him of paralyzing all efforts at reform with his determinism—Lombroso was a zealous anticlerical, a good democrat, an advocate of carving up Italian estates in behalf of destitute peasants, even a socialist. Leaning heavily on humane reformers all the way back to Beccaria, he advocated keeping punishment to the minimum necessary for deterrence, liberal probation policies, penalties appropriate to each individual criminal (always a talking point for him), reduced prison terms for "emotional offenders," and attempts to reclaim felons for society. The only exceptions, of course, were his favorites, the born criminals, who resisted all efforts at reform. If these incurables, after imprisonment, transportation, and hard labor, repeated heinous crimes for a third or fourth time, there was "nothing left but the last selection, painful but sure,—capital punishment."[21] These evildoers tried the patience of Lombroso, a persistent champion of progress, beyond endurance.

Not surprisingly, so supple a theorist roused his contemporaries to extremes of esteem and disdain. Havelock Ellis respectfully relied on Lombroso and his "so-called Italian school" as the leading experts. Even more uncritical, Hippolyte Taine, his most famous French admirer, thanked Lombroso privately for having "shown us fierce and lubricious orang-utans with human faces." It was evident that "if they ravish, steal, and kill, it is by virtue of their own nature and their past." Other French social scientists sharply dissented. The social psychologist Gabriel Tarde picturesquely denounced Lombroso's school for being "mentally intoxicated with the wine of the natural sciences." If it is to avoid the excesses of "philosophical alcoholism," it must "still eat the dry, substantial bread of the historical and social sciences."[22] The German psychiatrist Paul Näcke, a prolific writer on mental ailments and other delicate subjects, accused

Lombroso of hunting degenerates as though this were a sport.*

The critics had a solid case. Lombroso and his followers styled themselves positivists to underscore their commitment to hard-nosed science and distinguish themselves from the "classical" criminologists they were attacking. But their loyalties to scientific method were shallow and their proceedings self-confirming. Students of crime anxious to rescue Lombroso's reputation were reduced to saying that while he offered unacceptable answers, he deserved credit for having raised the right questions.

That is about as much as can be said for Lombroso. His criminology was a symptom rather than a solution, a symptom characteristic of a time—I cannot repeat this too often—when old attitudes toward crime had been shattered forever by the nineteenth-century disciples of the Enlightenment. The problem was that none among the experiments with prisons built on rational principles, pleas of diminished criminal responsibility, and substitutes for the death penalty, had proved satisfactory. "Why are our penal methods so helpless and discomfited in face of the criminal population?" asked W. Douglas Morrison of Her Majesty's Prison at Wandsworth in 1895. "Why do the combined efforts of legislators, judges, police, and prisons produce so few practical results? Is it because the social disease with which these agencies are grappling is beyond the reach of human skill, and will continue to rage with unabated virulence so long as social life exists?" Morrison did not think so. "All that the failure of our present methods succeeds in establishing is the immediate and imperative necessity of placing our whole penal system upon a more rational foundation." The world was not facing "an incurable disease in the body politic."[23] A revealing metaphor, this; it hints that the perception of crime as a social disease was winning converts. So does Morrison's point that setbacks in the application of modern penal methods were simply signs of inadequate reasoning: the cure for the failures of science was more science. The humane implications of this intellectual temper lay on the surface: crime deserves not to be avenged but to be treated.

It was no wonder that traditionalists, and even moderates, greeted such dec-

*See Paul Näcke, "Die Kastration bei gewissen Klassen von Degenerirten als ein wirksamer socialer Schutz," *Archiv für Kriminal-Anthropologie und Kriminalistik,* III (1900), 59. Näcke's grasp of science was no more secure than that of his adversary. Witness the anti-Semitic invective he leveled against Lombroso; adopting a criticism of Lombroso by the American brain anatomist E. A. Spitzka (whom Näcke praised for being a rare exception to the usual American naiveté), he wrote, "L. has only rarely chosen to comply with strict scientific demands; he has preferred being a 'guerillero,' and probably also considers this in his semitic vanity (many a semitic trait can be documented in his writings!) far more original." "Kleinere Mitteilungen. Ein interessantes amerikanisches Urtheil über Lombroso," ibid., X (1903), 287.

larations with troubled skepticism. For one, Louis Proal, a French criminologist, statistician, judge, and edgy writer on crime, protested in 1890, "If punishment is replaced by treatment and the prison by the asylum, then society's security is compromised and honest people are turned over to wrongdoers."[24] His arguments were perfectly commonplace: the state must exercise control over people who have no control over themselves; to pretend that brutal victimizers are really pathetic victims is no way of fulfilling that supreme duty. In his treatise on crimes of passion, Proal announced that "poor humanity is largely composed of weak and feeble creatures, slaves of mere passion and instinct."[25] Humans, susceptible to the tyranny of passion and instinct, need elevated models—and prisons.

Proal was speaking for a party in retreat. A social scientist like Lombroso might arouse the contempt of a social scientist like Tarde, but these bitter professional rivals were nevertheless partners in the effort to civilize the legal process by applying reason in efforts to guide fallible human nature. These criminologists were quarreling about means, not about ends. The 1880s and 1890s saw the emergence of an imposing array of recruits to serve the good cause, most of them building on earlier ventures: journals appealing to lawyers and psychiatrists, international congresses arguing out the latest findings, translation projects bringing the classics of criminology to new readers, organizations like the German Society for Social Reform taking a particular interest in juvenile offenders and their rehabilitation. All were designed to damp down aggressive impulses, especially the lust for revenge, in legislators, prosecutors, judges and juries—and the newspaper-reading public. An ungrateful posterity might denigrate the achievements of this crusade as uncertain, even dubious, but the crusaders were devoted, industrious, and by their lights—often enough, too, by ours—humane.

Among these late-Victorian attacks on aggression, Hans Gross's journal, *Archiv für Kriminal-Anthropologie und Kriminalistik,* with its zest for the scientific study of man in the service of reform, typifies the civilizing aspirations of the time. But its editor made his *Archiv* into a refreshing exception by tempering that zest with a heartfelt refusal of certainty. Criminologists, Gross told his subscribers in September 1898, in the first number, simply did not know enough, and had to master too many fields, to permit themselves the luxury of the dogmatism that characterized Lombroso and his uncritical admirers.*

*As its title page proclaims, Gross edited his journal "with a number of experts." Considering that the demands on the criminologist were so diverse that they could only be addressed—though never wholly satisfied—by a team of specialists, Gross built the *Archiv* into a forum for a generous assortment of voices and interests. Contributors, many of them physicians, published thoughtful

Gross, an Austrian prosecutor, judge, and professor of criminal law who remained chief editor of the *Archiv* until his death in 1915, first secured a professional reputation in 1883, with *Handbuch für Untersuchungsrichter,* a lucid and comprehensive manual for examining magistrates, which made his long and varied experience with criminal cases available to other forensic investigators. Deploying an impressive repertory of specialties from chemistry and microscopy to ballistics and above all psychology, the *Handbuch* forcefully illustrates Gross's conviction that the science of "criminalistics"—the term is his coinage—must be an interdisciplinary science or it will be nothing. The *Archiv* was the destined product of such thinking. Its very name, incorporating criminal anthropology and criminalistics, advertises Gross's aim of marrying the human sciences to the study of crime and punishment. What held his eclectic brew together was a commitment to the psychological analysis of misfits and criminals, and, with a few glaring exceptions, a compassionate attitude toward the offenders, normally from the lower orders of society. For the editor of the *Archiv* and most of his authors, all bourgeois professionals, to understand much meant to forgive much.

In general, Gross kept his opinions to himself, but at times he thought it necessary to intervene. Yet even when he felt compelled to demur, his editor's conscience wrestled down his moral objections. Troubled by Paul Näcke's ruthless proposal that the most desperate "degenerates" be castrated, he nevertheless published the piece, accompanying it with a gentle editorial dissent.* And some years later, disagreeing strongly with an article recommending that criminal penalties against homosexual acts be dropped, he published it too, stating in a foreword his liberal principle: "I believe that interesting pieces should be published."[26] Gross and his contributors were all seekers together.

They spoke for a cultural style that was beginning to prevail, even though it continued to arouse skepticism and had failed as yet to uproot traditional severities. Conditions arousing bourgeois indignation were still abundant. There were still many, as there had been from time out of mind, who would not check their vengeful aggressive appetites at the sight or even the report of an

---

essays on the relation of guilt to punishment, unconscious motives and criminal justice, sensational trials of sexual offenders, prostitution and psychopathy, the psychopathology of the arsonist. Shorter notices kept subscribers up to date on recent publications and entertained them with intriguing items from across the world.

*See Hans Gross, "Anmerkung des Herausgebers," to Näcke, "Die Kastration," ibid., III, 58n. Näcke's proposal was exceptional for the *Archiv* but not for the times. He quotes from an assortment of American physicians advocating castration of certain insane criminals. One Dr. Gordon of Wisconsin described a bill to that effect proposed in Michigan as "strictly a humane, just, progressive, and scientific measure. It should meet the approval of all Christian people." Ibid., 82n.

offense, appetites that only the report—or far better, the sight—of retribution could assuage. They still found something intensely satisfying in the Lord's tough-minded, evenhanded instructions to Moses in the law of talion that was to govern the children of Israel—primitive as it was, or precisely because it was so primitive. But a mounting number of legislators and preachers, social scientists and editorial writers, wondered whether the old arguments for retribution were not simply an egotistical defense of illicit, largely unacknowledged pleasures. Thus, Victorians continued to narrow the territory of acceptable aggression.

It is symptomatic of their voluntary self-denial that in the 1890s sociologists could treat crime, with sovereign neutrality, as a social phenomenon. The great French sociologist Émile Durkheim—who cited Lombroso only to refute him—defined crime as a perfectly normal, really inevitable, break in social solidarity, while the pioneering German sociologist Ferdinand Tönnies explicitly separated the sociological concept of crime from ethical considerations. It is even more symptomatic that the *Freie Bühne,* a German periodical founded to advocate naturalism in drama and fiction, should give house room in its very first volume of 1890 to articles on "social," and on the "new," jurisprudence. One of these told its readers that the idea of crime as a social phenomenon had become self-evident: it was modern and eminently practical. People had come to see that "the struggle against crime, and the removal of its preconditions, is our goal."[27]

By the time these words were published, then, there was substantial support for the proposition that if psychiatrists certified a failure of mental controls, courts should take their views into account. To requite a madman's or madwoman's aggression upon another human being by the legal counteraggression of severe punishment—or any punishment—was unkind; perhaps it was irrational, even pathological. It seemed more and more plausible that liars, thieves, forgers, even rapists and murderers, might be hostages to hopeless poverty, domestic neglect, or mental imbalance. Rule-breaking and lawbreaking might have social and psychological causes that made offenders only partially responsible for their acts, or not responsible at all. In this new mood, many bourgeois traded the savage thrill of acting out their vengeful impulses in favor of less intense but more refined pleasures.

3. The Bourgeois Conscience at Work

Some of the most audacious attempts in the nineteenth century to redescribe the delights of primitive vindictiveness as instances of pathology centered on the somber ritual of capital punishment. Across the decades, the case for the abolition of the death penalty found mounting support among the respectable. Comparing the cultural style of his time with that prevailing half a century earlier, the English journalist Alexander Shand suggested in 1888 that "society is no longer satisfied to lock up its wild animals, or hang them out of hand."[1] He was speaking of Britain, but his observation held with local variations for the rest of Western civilization. Actually, late-Victorian society was still hanging or guillotining its "wild animals," but more rarely and more hesitantly than in earlier days. Beccaria's electrifying plea of 1764 for the abolition of the death penalty had always had its unreconstructed critics, but with time the approving voices grew louder.

For some decades the opponents of capital punishment worked on the margins of social protest, rallying a small if determined cadre of supporters. The vast majority still shared the views of Kant and Goethe, those exemplary champions of human dignity and self-realization, who stood by capital punishment as essential to the social order. "If he has murdered," wrote Kant about the convicted felon, "then he must *die*." Goethe for his part mused wryly that he would have nothing against the abolition of death, but that if the death penalty were abolished, the repeal would not last, since "self-help will immediately emerge: vendetta knocks at the door."* Still, by the time Queen Victoria ascended the throne in 1837, the abolitionists were making themselves heard. Having raised capital punishment to a major grievance, they started journals, founded societies, held meetings, and lobbied lawmakers. Across the years, they covered Western civilization with a network of abolitionist organizations. Perhaps the first of them was the Society for the Diffusion of Knowledge Respecting the Punishment of Death and the Improvement of Prison Discipline, founded in England in 1809 by a Quaker, William Allen, a reputable chemist and public-spirited citizen. It was an active group; in 1831, as the issue was being debated in Parliament, its London branch, the Committee for the Diffusion of Information on the Subject of Capital Punishments, brought out a series of five compelling pamphlets immortalizing rousing speeches by abolitionists in

---

*Immanuel Kant, *Metaphysik der Sitten*, part II, "Das öffentliche Recht," *Werke in sechs Bänden*, ed. Wilhelm Weischedel (1960–64), IV, 455; Johann Wolfgang von Goethe, "Maximen und Reflexionen," nos. 110, 111, *Goethes Werke*, ed. Rich Trunz, 14 vols. (1948–69), XII, 379. In his respected, widely quoted, polemic against the death penalty, Albert Friedrich Berner, professor of law at the University of Berlin, borrowed this maxim of Goethe's—without explicitly citing him—only to dismiss it: the assertion "that the family of the murdered must obtain atonement through the bloody sacrifice of the criminal," and that otherwise "vendetta is knocking at the door," is to advance a notion perhaps appropriate to a country like Corsica but not to Germany. *Abschaffung der Todesstrafe* (1861), 10–11.

Parliament and out. One of these publications provided a chilling comparative view. Using heavy Gothic letters for the word "Death," it listed the scores of capital felonies in England for which American courts were sentencing criminals only to fines or short stints in jail.

Allen's society soon enjoyed the company of like-minded lobbies. By the 1870s, Belgium had its Association pour l'abolition de la peine de mort; Italy its informative *Giornale per l'abolizione della penna di morte;* London its Howard Association. Massachusetts, New York, and Philadelphia each had a Society for the Abolition of Capital Punishment. And there were others—exchanging information, recruiting important personages, propping up the morale of fellow warriors and, in moments of defeat, their own.

The struggle over the death penalty preoccupied lawyers, politicians, journalists, pastors, psychiatrists, to say nothing of a sizable contingent of amateurs, pen ready to hand. They published their speeches, their sermons, their statistical surveys, their collected letters to the editor. They made or consolidated reputations by entering the debate with striking proposals: in 1822, François Guizot, already a well-known historian, caused something of a sensation with his *De la peine de mort en matière politique,* in which he advocated the abolition of capital punishment for political offenders. Many of these abolitionists were disinterested, concerned not with personal reputation but with the good of the cause; some of them wrote anonymously, as did "A Barrister of the Middle Temple," who in 1831 tried to influence the debate in Parliament over reducing the list of capital crimes with an urgent plea, *Anti-Draco; or, Reasons for Abolishing the Punishment of Death, in Cases of Forgery.* The nineteenth was a century in which thousands of small local printers set in type whatever was thrust upon them, and the protracted public disputes over the death penalty gave them almost as much business as the inflammatory issues of temperance, slavery, the vote, and that international fountain of trouble, the conflict between secular and church schools.

The prodigious volume of this literature attests to the ardent feelings that the ritual of putting criminals to death aroused in nineteenth-century bourgeois culture—on both sides of the fence. The abolitionists were leading an impassioned crusade against no less impassioned resistance, and not all of their triumphs were secure or permanent. In 1847, after years of high-pitched debates in the legislature and other public forums, the state of Michigan abolished capital punishment, but for more than a decade, the victorious abolitionists had to beat back strong, almost successful efforts to reintroduce it. The state of Maine, which did away with the death penalty in 1876, reinstated it in 1883, only to reaffirm its original decision four years later. And Rhode Island, which had joined Michigan in 1852, restored the death penalty thirty years later, though only for someone already under a life sentence committing a murder. Switzerland showed itself quite as sensitive to the emotional crosscurrents swirling about this delicate business. In 1874, the Swiss federal government abolished capital punishment. But after a rash of murders and of protests, it called a plebiscite on the issue, and in accordance with the results, granted individual cantons the option of reintroducing the death penalty—a dubious privilege of which seven among the country's twenty-two cantons availed themselves.

It was evident, then, that partisans of hanging had no reason to give up without a fight. Mobilizing support among skeptical, ambivalent, and anxious citizens everywhere, they slowed the abolitionist movement or forced it into compromises. At times they defeated it. In 1872, a year after its founding, the German Empire—with Bismarck's explicit and energetic support—included in its criminal code the death penalty for attempts on the emperor's life and for premeditated murder. This reversed an abolitionist trend in a number of smaller German states, including Baden and Saxony, which had removed capital punishment from their arsenals of legal revenge. The assassinations of several prominent personages and heads of state, an English Quaker pamphlet noted in 1883, had "undoubtedly produced a strong wave of reactionary opinion, in favour of capital punishment, during the past few years, both in Europe and America."[2]

The fate of Charles Julius Guiteau, whose only claim to fame is to have assassinated President James A. Garfield in 1881, exemplified the Quakers' warning. It is a riveting and revealing story, showing a civilized society in search of a sacrificial victim. A self-appointed patriot, Guiteau shot the president in obedience to "divine pressure." He was a manic scribbler of political manifestoes and letters to public figures, a flamboyant failure with a substantial record of petty dishonesty, bizarre schemes, and violent mood swings. He was certainly insane; his anguished father called him fit only for a madhouse. Alienists, including the celebrated George M. Beard, author of *American Nervousness* and other treatises on neurasthenia, thought so too; and defying the public's unconcealed appetite for revenge, they said so. Whether arguing from common sense, pronouncing him a typical case of tainted heredity, or diagnosing symptoms of emotional illness, they declared Guiteau not responsible for his crime.

As incompetent a marksman as he had been in everything else, Guiteau had only wounded the president at close range, and there was intermittent hope that Garfield might recover. His long agony, from the shooting on July 2 to his death on September 19, cemented the popular intransigent position that Guiteau must pay with his life. The trial was an exhausting series of duels between counsel and experts on opposing sides; Guiteau and his lawyers enjoyed ample opportunities to state his case and, quite incidentally, document his mental state. For his noisy, frequent, irrelevant, though not incoherent, interruptions during the proceedings (and the childish poetry he wrote after his conviction) consistently confirmed to anyone not determined to hang him that he was hopelessly psychotic. But only professional psychiatrists, challenging the conservative medical establishment of the day, pleaded for Guiteau's acquittal on grounds of insanity.

His defenders knew that theirs was a lost cause; no demonstration of Guiteau's madness could make any difference to the outcome of the trial. Clerics gravely orated about a mortal sin that only the work of the hangman could atone; editorial writers and politicians warned against the "sentimental twaddle" that would leave this monster alive to infest the earth and encourage others to act on their murderous urges. There were threats on his life, and one of his guards shot off a gun at him. Significantly, it took the jury, thoughtfully coached by the judge's instructions, only an hour and five minutes to convict.

Not even the irresistible impulse doctrine could provide much support for the insanity plea; while Guiteau shouted during the trial that his "free agency" had been destroyed and that he had been "overpowered," there was evidence that he had pondered his moves with care. But it was not legal technicalities that doomed Guiteau, nor was it legal precedents that made appeals to spare his life, all the way to President Arthur, exercises in futility. Garfield's death guaranteed Guiteau's death; the doctrine of a life for a life still showed substantial vitality. Commentators at the time observed that if the president had lived, or if Guiteau had shot some insignificant fellow citizen to death, he would have been committed to an insane asylum without fail. But public parricide, rousing as it did the most complicated feelings, could not go unavenged—not yet.[3]

Two debates taking place in the years just before the First World War, one in the French legislature and the other in the pages of a German periodical, demonstrate the precariousness of the abolitionists' progress. For several months in 1908, the Chamber of Deputies rehearsed once again the familiar arguments for and against the guillotine. Public opinion had been inflamed by several spectacular murders and by the widely advertised fact, ruefully acknowledged by the abolitionists, that homicides had been on the increase for a decade. It had been whipped up further by the conservative press, and not by its gutter dailies alone, with grisly details and excited editorials calling for the retention of capital punishment in the face of tenderhearted, misguided humanitarianism. For a year and more, sarcastic anti-abolitionist cartoons had entertained and frightened readers. One of them depicted a murderer comfortable in his cell, complete with bottles of wine and a fatherly jailer; another showed an assassin caught knife in hand, his victim lying not far off, protesting to the policeman trying to arrest him that he would write to his deputy.[4]

The controversies dividing the legislators touched on the highest principles
and the most practical issues; the left offered noble orations reminding deputies
of the duty incumbent on civilized humanity, while the right countered with
warnings that social order was in mortal danger. Both sides battled over statistics, which proved, according to some, that the death penalty acted as a deterrent against further crimes, or, according to others, that it did nothing of the
kind. In December, the abolitionists were thoroughly defeated, by a vote of 334
to 210; the guillotine would keep up its decisive work.[5]

Meanwhile, contributors to the *Archiv für Kriminal-Anthropologie und Kriminalistik* had been wrangling over the question of abolition of the death penalty in
the German Empire. Not all articulate citizens of imperial Germany had rested
content with the government's decision to include the death penalty in its
arsenal of social self-defense. Hans Gross, editor of the *Archiv*, consistently
called for the abolition of beheading for political offenses. In 1902, he went
further, denouncing the "injustice, unmodernity, and dangerousness" of capital
punishment and proposing its absolute abolition after a transitional phase. His
intervention came as an editorial comment on an article by a contributor from
Prague, Ernst Lohsing, who argued the same case on the ground that under
capital punishment, innocent persons could be—and, alas, had been—put to
death. A response by the indefatigable Paul Näcke in the same year called this
posture into question. He had no use for the argument that capital punishment
deters crime, but advocated its retention *"in most exceptional cases"* on Social
Darwinist grounds. The sentimental "giddy humanitarianism" of the day, he
warned, kept alive inhuman specimens, virtual animals, sexual monsters like
Jack the Ripper, whom society should put out of harm's way. While " 'judicial
murder' " was always distressing and shameful, its incidence amounted to only a
derisory proportion of executions and was no argument for their abrogation.[6]

Lohsing, of course, wasted no time in replying to Näcke—the *Archiv* welcomed these contentious confrontations. He reiterated his abhorrence of a legal
system that put unjustly condemned people on the block and disputed Näcke's
contention that there are ways of recognizing the sort of monster that infallibly
deserves death.[7] He returned to the fray in 1911, shortly after a convention of
German jurists produced a majority for the death penalty, turning its back on
the declaration of an earlier convention, in 1863, which had unequivocally
called for the elimination of capital punishment from any future legal code.

For Lohsing these belated second thoughts by the jurists were nothing better
than a tragic emotional return to a cruel anachronism. He supported his plea
with an affecting description of a hanging that had left no one dry-eyed as the
convict, sentenced to death for a brutal murder, embraced the pastor and the
prosecuting attorney, made his peace with God, and then called out to his

mother as the executioner was tightening the noose. This pathetic presentation necessarily provoked a rejoinder, and it came the following year from a Dr. Schüle, an associate professor of forensic medicine at the University of Freiburg, who objected to Lohsing's bad taste, defended capital punishment, and called for more statistical studies. "Lohsing's arguments," he concluded, "will, I think, convert few supporters of the death penalty." He was right. Lohsing responded, justifying his anecdotes and reiterating the reasons he had offered before.[8] But the death penalty remained on the books.

Still, a sheer recital of the countries in retreat from capital punishment documents far more victories for the abolitionists than defeats. Even those Swiss cantons that restored the death penalty carried out no executions. In Britain— which, we know, once claimed primacy for its savage penal code—the catalogue of capital offenses steadily shrank, after slow, often ungraceful tinkering. By 1914, only murder, high treason, piracy with violence, and destruction of public arsenals and dockyards were punishable by death. The last two of these were quaint survivals from a vengeful time; murder was virtually the only offense for which British courts would invoke the specter of the cord. And perhaps half, at times less than half, of all death sentences were carried out.* The current against killing killers was running ahead of the letter of the law.

Other countries recorded comparable shifts in legal enactments and public opinion, reflecting a tentative, almost experimental disposition toward mitigating or abrogating the death penalty. The checkered legal map of the United States in the Victorian age graphically displays these unresolved conflicts. By the 1890s, only Wisconsin had joined Michigan and Maine in repealing capital punishment. The other states kept the death penalty in their criminal codes, but some of them had not imposed it for decades, and many allowed juries to recommend a lesser sentence. As in Britain, so in the United States, a conviction did not guarantee execution. Conforming to an international trend, most American states had drastically trimmed the catalogue of capital crimes; individuals hanged or electrocuted were far outnumbered by those lynched. In 1892, twelve persons were convicted of first-degree murder in California, but not one of them was executed, while in Massachusetts, two men were convicted of that crime, of whom one was hanged.[9]

Europe was no different. In 1906, Austria-Hungary retained only two capital

---

*See W[illiam] F[eilden] C[raies], "Capital Punishment," *Encyclopedia Britannica* (11th ed., 1910–11), V, 280. In 1831, English courts handed down 1,601 death sentences, of which only fourteen were for murder. Twelve of the murderers were executed, but only fifty-two of the others, a sign of how absurd most of the other death sentences had come to seem even to the authorities. In 1862, when the courts handed down twenty-nine death sentences, twenty-eight were for homicide. And of these just more than half, fifteen, were carried out. Ibid.

crimes in its penal code: high treason against the emperor and the most atro-
cious kinds of murder. Even earlier, the death penalty was reserved there almost
exclusively for killers. France, too, while retaining the death penalty for seven
crimes, was fiercer in law than in fact; in 1887, for example, of 240 persons
convicted of capital offenses, 210 were spared because of extenuating circumstances, and only 6 of the remaining 30 went to the guillotine. Other countries—Sweden, Denmark, Belgium—also eliminated capital punishment except for the gravest of offenses, like murder and treason, and actually executed
few of those convicted. Humanitarians had good reason to welcome such humane compromises, but naturally they were even more gratified by abolition of
the death penalty altogether. Romania and Venezuela did so in 1864; Portugal
in 1867, the Netherlands in 1870, and Italy in 1880.* The rage to punish, to
gratify the passionate need to expend one's vindictive feelings against transgressors, seemed to be abating in bourgeois culture.

With the passing decades, the literature the abolitionists produced grew as
monotonous as it grew massive. In the mid-1860s, the Swedish reformist law
professor K. D'Olivecrona called the abolition of capital punishment one of
those issues that "cannot fade away." But intensity of feeling had to substitute
for originality of argumentation. Some fifteen years later, an English partisan of
abolition, Francis Bishop, opened a debate on the proposition "Thou shalt not
kill" with the disheartened admission that "the Capital Punishment controversy is one that can lay no claim to any charm of novelty." But this did not stop
him from issuing his statement. As long as the battle was only half won—and it
never was wholly won—more pamphlets would be published, no matter how
repetitious. "For many years," Paul Näcke mused in 1902, "not a single new
argument has been offered concerning the death penalty either pro or con."[10]
Yet he too thought it worth his while to add a few words on this thoroughly
ventilated issue. Only the psychoanalytic theory of unconscious guilt would
throw fresh light on the motives of criminals—and of those who made it their
business to punish them with death.

One can hardly blame the pamphleteers; there were only so many arguments
the abolitionists could marshal. What is more, the founders of the movement
had largely preempted them. The very title of Benjamin Rush's pioneering

---

*See ibid., 280–81; for France, see the Howard Association pamphlet *Official Statistics and
Reports (1890) on Capital Punishment* (1890), 1. Decreasing proportions of the death sentences were
actually carried out. In Austria-Hungary between 1853 and 1873, 880 individuals were convicted
of murder and 102 of these were hanged; between 1875 and 1900, with 2,085 convictions for the
same crime, 81 were executed; while between 1900 and 1903, the figures were 180 convictions
and just 9 hangings. Craies, "Capital Punishment," 280–81.

pamphlet of 1792, *Considerations on the Injustice and Impolity of Punishing Murder by Death,* already adumbrated the two rationales for abolition that would practically monopolize the controversy for a century and more: the death penalty is inhuman and it is ineffective. A pamphlet of 1844 by one John Howard is typical: *Capital Punishment, Unjust and Inexpedient.* Except for a few complicating touches, the polemics that had accumulated by the end of the nineteenth century just offered reiteration. Nor could the defenders of the death penalty diversify the debate; they did little more than dispute the charges of inhumanity and ineffectiveness.

The moralistic nineteenth century naturally found the first of the rationales for abolition, the ethical argument, eminently worth pursuing. Just as naturally, that argument often appeared in religious garb; as we have seen, in many upright circles the authority of scriptural quotations had not waned between the age of Samuel Johnson and the age of Queen Victoria. Unfortunately, all parties could exploit the Bible, a well-stocked and miscellaneous treasure house, with equal profit. Still, the devout valued Scripture too highly to do without it. Literally hundreds of divines speaking for a wide spectrum of denominations burdened printers with sermons criticizing or justifying the death penalty, hoping to reach and perhaps persuade an audience larger than their own congregation.[11] And as in war, so with capital punishment, all of them confidently invoked the divine blessing for their party alone.

What they said was what less pious controversialists were saying, only in more elevated tones and with more quotations from the sacred Book. In 1842, taking as his text the sixth commandment, the Reverend William Patton deployed convenient, well-tested biblical texts for his paradoxical reading of "Thou shalt not kill" as an authoritative alibi for capital punishment. Quoting Leviticus 24:17, "He that smiteth a man so that he die shall be surely put to death," Patton declared it "not possible to express, in more explicit terms, the mind of God in this matter." Humans could only read and obey. In the same year, the Reverend John N. McLeod, pastor of the Reformed Presbyterian Church in New York and evidently one of Patton's admirers, concurred. Utilizing his dialectical and philological skills, he proved to his own satisfaction that the New Testament the abolitionists liked to pillage for their misguided purposes did not repeal the Old Testament injunction that the shedding of blood must be repaid with the shedding of blood. "The ordinance for capital punishment was given to the world at the dawn of its new existence" and had never been repealed. Capital punishment was "prescribed by God."[12] What else needed to be said?

Very little. Four years later, Joseph F. Berg, a voice from the Patton-McLeod camp, made his case for the divine displeasure with murder by arguing that God had addressed his commandment "Thou shalt not kill" only to murderers, not to the public servants who prosecuted them and put them to death. Quoting a dictum from Numbers to which Patton had also resorted—the repertory of handy passages was visibly limited—Berg insisted that "the Bible is altogether against the total abolition of the punishment by death."[13] Not content just to shore up his case with biblical quotations, Berg aggressively met his antagonists on their own ground. Pious abolitionists had long treasured the tactic of criticizing their opponents for relying on the cruel, discredited Jewish code of an eye for an eye that the advent of the loving Savior had set aside. Berg, who had quoted St. Paul as well as Exodus, thought he could make short work of that cavil: "It is sufficient to remind the reader," he reminded the reader, that Jesus' much-quoted injunctions to love even one's enemies were intended only for "the adjustment of private injuries."[14] Around 1870, a tough-minded German pamphleteer, Moritz Müller, published a broadside arguing, right in its title, that "the saying, the death penalty is a sin before God and man, is nothing more than empty chatter."[15] The proponents of capital punishment denied that Jesus' gospel of love could be read as an alibi for abolitionist sentiments. There were times when the state must sacrifice a body to save a soul.

These aggressive moves enjoyed wide currency among angry men who, like Charles Dickens in his later years, had no use for making pets of prisoners and for the tears that humanitarians shed over the last moments of a murderer while they dismissed his victim from their moral discourse.[16] In 1843, in his famous three-day debate with the abolitionist J. L. O'Sullivan in New York, the zealous American Presbyterian divine George B. Cheever helped to set the tone: "When the Savior says, Thou shalt love thine enemies, it is the same benevolence which speaks, The murderer shall surely be put to death. When God says, Resist not evil; Recompense to no man evil for evil; Vengeance is mine, I will repay, says the Lord."[17] Cheever seemed honestly amazed, even indignant, at the obtuseness—or Scholastic cleverness—of his adversaries.

Abolitionists mining Scripture to support radically opposite conclusions only document the hackneyed saying that when two read the same book they are not reading the same book. They liked to quote a telling passage from the Sermon on the Mount: "Ye have heard that it hath been said, an eye for an eye and a tooth for a tooth. But I say unto you, That ye resist not evil; but whoever shall smite thee on thy right cheek, turn to him the other side." To reinforce the critical distinction Jesus had drawn in this dictum, A. D. Mayo roamed around the New Testament for confirming quotations, and found them with ease. Even the Old Testament yielded to his debater's tactics.[18] But while nineteenth-century divines both supported and attacked capital punishment, their allegiances were far from random. Somewhat predictably, the theologi-

cally conservative Protestants—Presbyterians and Baptists, Lutherans and Anglicans—were likely to defend the death penalty, while liberal denominations
like the Unitarians and, of course, the Quakers, were almost bound to oppose
it. In an irascible polemic against the defenders of capital punishment, the
American physician Henry S. Patterson denounced "the clergy" as "the sworn
champions of the gallows," and pitted "the Christian spirit," the glorious "law
of love" preached by Jesus, against "priestcraft" which has "influenced the
minds of the superstitious, weak, and priestridden."[19] Patterson's excited critique was not unfounded, though he would have been more persuasive if he
had been more discriminating and exempted some denominations from his
strictures.

Secular polemicists proved only marginally less elastic than the preachers.
Nearly all the abolitionists who rested their case on philosophical rather than
theological arguments appealed to the ideals of the Enlightenment as they
damned the death penalty for violating the dignity of man. Many of them
launched their publications with a ceremonial invocation to their patron saint,
Beccaria, who had dispensed with religious rhetoric in his pleas for the humane
treatment of human beings. Characteristically, Charles Lucas, the most prominent and persistent of nineteenth-century French abolitionists, gave the principle of the "inviolability of human life" the highest priority. In half a century of
thundering against the death penalty, he remained faithful to this conviction
and this rhetoric. In 1827, in a prize-winning volume on the penal system and
capital punishment, he asserted that "issuing from the hands of the Creator, our
duty to everyone is to respect the existence of our fellow creature." In 1873,
still intent on defending the sacredness of life, he criticized the proposal to
discuss capital punishment at an international conference on the penitentiary
question; linked though the two issues were, they had to be separated if justice
was to be done to each.[20]

Most writers who invoked human dignity and the inviolability of human life
damned capital punishment as unworthy of civilized communities. Victorians
willing to deny themselves the satisfaction of what Kant had called the appetite
for revenge tried to persuade their contemporaries that they should do no less.
To them, the death penalty was a sad reflection on the character of those who
tried to vindicate it, to say nothing of those who enforced it without any visible
qualms. In an emotional attack on these traditionalists, the barrister Charles
Neate, member of Parliament for the town of Oxford, reminded his readers in
1857 that barbarities were still on Britain's law books. The judge who announces to a "wretched culprit in the convulsions of terror, supported by a
goaler on either side, in a voice as clear as silver and as hard as steel," that the
next morning the sun would rise on his death—Neate pointedly noted that he

had witnessed this scene—was nothing better than a "rhetorical butcher." Significantly, Neate was alert to the sadistic side of this legal murder: there were judges in the British system "to whom the pain of passing sentence of death has been not unmixed with pleasure."[21] The psychologically astute among the abolitionists made much of the discreditable gratification that people derived from tormenting others.

They found an added impressive reason for diagnosing the death penalty as a species of social and, all too often, personal pathology: the obstinacy of its defenders in the light of appalling evidence that more than once the wrong person had been hanged. Abolitionists prized anecdotes about lethal miscarriages of justice and passed them down from generation to generation. In a widely read and repeatedly revised book first published in the mid-1850s, *Vacation Thoughts on Capital Punishment,* Charles Phillips, an English barrister and public servant, recited a harrowing catalogue of such irreparable mistakes. The *Saturday Review* complained in its lordly way that Phillips was only repeating commonplaces that had been conclusively refuted. Nor was it impressed by his plea that humane Christians should not murder murderers, or his assertion that statistics proved the inefficacy of capital punishment. That punishment "is valuable" not just as a deterrent "but as a standing protest against a whole mass of weak and dangerous untruths."[22]

Yet, just as conservatives were not converted by abolitionists, abolitionists were not discouraged by conservatives. Following in Phillips's footsteps and drawing on him as an authority, the German jurist Karl Josef Mittermaier, an internationally respected specialist in criminal law, tersely cited wrongful hangings in Italy, Ireland, France, and Britain. "The cases in which innocent persons are condemned to death and are executed are becoming ever more common, so that their innocence can be demonstrated only after it is too late." A few years later, D'Olivecrona quoted an English jurist, Sir Fitzroy Kelly, to the effect that in the nineteenth century so far, seventeen innocent persons had been sentenced to death in England, and eight of these had been hanged. And near the end of the century, the Howard Association noted that "in some cases it has been *proved* that *innocent* persons have been sacrificed through the irrevocable nature of Capital Punishment." One instance it cited had occurred in 1874, when "a man in Pennsylvania, on his death-bed, confessed himself the perpetrator of a murder for which an innocent man, R. Lewis, had previously been hanged at Merthyr Tydfil." Unfortunately, "both jurors and judges are very fallible"; indeed, in many cases "there are grave reasons to *fear* that innocent persons have been put to death by judicial mistake."[23] The death penalty, in the abolitionists' view, was not just arbitrary and barbaric; it was unforgivably stupid.

The weighty charge that modern justice relying on the death penalty had fatally miscarried with uncomfortable frequency throws a bridge from the abolitionists' point that capital punishment is inhuman to their point that it is ineffective. To be sure, from the very outset, its defenders had argued, to quote the German pamphleteer Moritz Müller, "Only death gives complete security, since prison or banishment can be evaded." In fact, the fear of being hanged was the "sword of Damocles" Lombroso wanted to see suspended over the head of hardened criminals.[24] But skeptics had their rebuttal ready; the facts eloquently proved that far from deterring crime, capital punishment was bound to increase it, for the spectacle of public executions only roused murderous instincts. Franz von Holtzendorff, a liberal Prussian aristocrat and professor of law at the University of Munich, put the matter plainly: every crime publicly discussed awakens the all too human instinct of aggressive imitation; the death penalty "becomes exemplary for new murderous crimes."[25] Abolitionists liked to cite statistics showing how many convicted murderers had attended executions.

Paradoxically, a lavish menu of capital offenses seemed to encourage crime in yet another way; it saved indisputably guilty criminals from being convicted— witness early-nineteenth-century England. Blackstone had already objected some decades before that compassionate victims would not press charges, compassionate juries would not find the accused guilty, compassionate judges would not visit the full weight of the law on a convicted felon. In 1830, while Peel was in the Home Office consolidating and humanizing criminal statutes, more than a thousand English and Scottish bankers petitioned him to work toward the abolition of the death penalty for various acts of forgery. "A more lenient law," they earnestly prayed, would give them the "protection" they needed and ironically could not now obtain under the draconian statutes.[26] Not that the petitioners were interested solely in their financial well-being; a number of them were sympathetic to abolitionist efforts. Nor was their position necessarily hostile to the reformers' case. After all, it was a staple of abolitionist propaganda that greater humanity in penal legislation and greater certainty in securing convictions would enlarge, rather than shrink, the prison population. The petitioners, in short, being human, attacked the vexed problem of punishment with mixed motives. In 1854, after a particularly disturbing case in which a child murderess had been acquitted in England, one contemporary commentator noted, "The feeling against capital punishment is spreading among the class of men from which common juries are taken; and sooner or later the executive will be compelled to devise the means of inflicting severe secondary punishment."[27]

This complication was not the only unexpected aspect of the great debate. Oddly enough, the conservatives who wanted the death penalty retained as a deterrent showed themselves, quite unwittingly, more optimistic about human nature than the reformers who wanted it deleted from the legal code. They saw potential criminals rationally calculating the consequences of their actions, while abolitionists warned against the bloodthirsty beast insecurely caged within all humans. At the very least, the reformers insisted, appealing to anecdotal evidence as proof, partisans of the deterrent effect of capital punishment were blind to the powerful irrational component in human behavior. "Soldiers march gaily to battle with the certainty that many of them must fall," the famous American abolitionist Edward Livingston argued in the 1840s. "Those who commit a crime, punishable with death, always proceed with the hope that they will avoid detection."[28]

In addition to psychological analysis, abolitionists enlisted dry statistical summaries to show that capital punishment was no deterrent. In 1894, Congressman N. M. Curtis prepared a report, awash with numbers and tables, for the House Judiciary Committee. As a severe critic of American criminal law, "the bloodiest code in the world," Curtis could not refrain from making his numbers boost his argument. True enough, abolition had led to an increase in murders in Colombia and Ecuador, but this handful of exceptions apart, he found the record most encouraging. "The penalty of death has not been abolished in Belgium," he noted, "but since 1866 it has not been executed," and still the figures showed grave crimes decreasing in that country. The same was true of the Netherlands, where the abolition of capital punishment had produced no increase in crime. And in Portugal, which had done away with the death penalty in 1867, the number of homicides had diminished.[29] These countries were proof that the death penalty was not a necessary deterrent—surely reason enough for the United States to go and do likewise.

By the time of Curtis's report, the choice was no longer simply between the retention of capital punishment and its abolition. The reformers' indictment of public executions as a maker of criminals had given rise to a contentious side issue that was proving an acute irritant for them. Early in the century, some logical and sensitive spirits had begun to wonder whether it would not be sensible to end these sordid festivities and execute convicted criminals in private. Already in the 1820s, some American writers described the official observance of revenge as inexpedient, demoralizing, and wasteful, calculated to make "a hundred persons" worse while just "one is made better by a public execution. Rioting, drunkenness, and every species of disorderly conduct prevail."[30]

The proposal to sequester executions from the multitude appealed to the more adroit champions of capital punishment; relegating the ceremony to the somber seclusion of a prison courtyard would eliminate its orgiastic aspects while leaving the death penalty intact. In short, the state's aggression against malefactors would be rendered invisible but continue to operate. This was a compromise with an increasingly squeamish public opinion that unrepentant defenders of the death penalty thought they could afford. But abolitionists, though repelled by the heartless theater of public hangings, thought private hangings no better. As early as 1835, the eloquent American reformer Robert Rantoul, Jr., argued that "there is no form of execution free from insuperable objections. Public executions are on all hands confessed to be demoralizing. Private executions are equally, perhaps more objectionable, from their odious and anti-republican character and from the temptations and facilities which they might under peculiar circumstances offer for the most dreadful abuses."[31] Only total abolition would serve justice. In France, Charles Lucas endorsed this stance. He noted in 1848 that while a substantial minority had been unable to persuade the Prussian legislature to abolish the death penalty, that legislature had decreed almost unanimously that executions be private, as though it was rather ashamed of itself. "What can, after this, be the future of a penalty that condemns human justice to blush for it, and to hide itself as it commits its murder, like the murderer it punishes?"[32]

Quite as dismissive and far more suspicious, English abolitionists denounced the proposal to move executions to some inaccessible spot as a shabby trick by unreconstructed advocates of legalized killing. It was, Richard Cobden told a meeting of like-minded reformers late in 1849, a "new dodge." Significantly, his fellow radical John Bright detected the old lust for revenge lurking behind this new display of delicacy: its proponents were driven on by "a mere longing to put someone to death." And William Ewart, the most energetic champion of abolition in the House of Commons, alerted his sympathetic listeners that private hanging was nothing more than an "evasion of the main principle for which they were agitating."[33] For Ewart and his fellows, the point was to unmask this apparently humane proposal and to continue battling for true abolition.

Understandably, the idea of private executions found support across a wide range of opinion, even if many conservatives remained unimpressed. In 1856, the *Saturday Review*—not surprisingly—argued for the retention of public hangings because they gave crowds an opportunity to witness "not only a death, but a shameful death." Granted, the assembled masses, "the lowest class of society," displayed a "morbid curiosity" and were guilty of "indecent conduct." But this was merely an incidental and remediable side effect. More than a decade later, in 1870, when a republican French deputy introduced a bill to convert the guillotining of felons into a private ceremony, he faced the objection that this would unduly disregard "salutary fear and the satisfaction of the public's need for vengeance."[34] It was a textbook response of conservatives threatened by innovators they despised as effeminate sentimentalists.

Still, many manly nineteenth-century bourgeois came to deplore the way public executions degenerated into lighthearted carnivals, occasionally into riots, their original purpose forgotten. Hangings were meant to serve as a terrifying warning and, even more important, as a solemn ritual in which a community made itself whole again by purging itself of a transgressor. In one of his imaginative flights, Dickens called the hangman "the Finishing Schoolmaster." But in reality, an execution had long since become anything but a didactic performance. Mobs of spectators, often numbering into the thousands, drunk with alcohol no less than with the occasion, cheered or jeered the condemned felon, and got into fistfights. Hawkers peddled crudely printed poems, nearly all of them barefaced inventions, describing the crime about to be expiated or retailing the criminal's last words. Pickpockets plied their trade under the eyes of the police.

Nor was it only the idle and the disreputable who took pleasure in the spectacle; while the poor cherished executions as entertainments and counted them among their constitutional rights, a sizable smattering of good bourgeois and sophisticated aristocrats also came to watch. The affluent did not have to mingle with the mob; they arrived in coaches and rented, at a substantial price, windows that overlooked the scene. And they reveled in the event no less, if less boisterously, than those in what the *Saturday Review* had patronizingly described as the lowest class of society.

To judge from the responses of witnesses capable of calibrating their emotions and recording them with plastic precision, the immediate effects of public vengeance were uncertain and unpredictable. They document once again the explosive admixture of erotic impulses in aggressive behavior. Sometime around 1815, the German playwright, actor, and novelist Karl von Holtei, then an adolescent, witnessed the execution of two women convicted of murder. He never forgot the scene, and described it in his autobiography with every gruesome particular, as though finally to exorcise the memory. Executions, he wrote with bitter sarcasm, assailing his respectable fellow townsmen for relishing so perverse a show, were a "popular folk drama" that good people thought "most diverting." The two culprits had managed to postpone their fate by lies, false confessions, and pregnancies in prison; this delay had made his fellow citizens "lust greedily after their blood." To find places from which to see, "tender-hearted" women "accompanied by their tender progeny and amply provided with victuals of all sort" had set out for the place of execution the night before, "in droves."[35]

Young Holtei had been invited to inspect the instruments of torture, "the utensils of justice, from the wheel to the 'damper,' " the rope that, pulled tight around the "delinquent's" neck, was designed to keep the victim from screaming. The murderesses were to be strapped to the wheel, which would break their bones; then they would be strangled. He looked at these "objects," Holtei noted, his guilt feelings unassuaged, "with a peace of mind and an indifference that shocks me even today." Of the execution itself, he could recover only a few "pictures from the delirium into which curiosity, horror, and disgust plunged me in those morning hours—but those forever." He did not fail to observe, though, and to remember, that the younger of the felons was a well-endowed beauty. As she was carted to her execution, she kept screaming at the mob, protested her innocence, and hit out at the Capuchin priest who was patiently praying for her. "She tore her dress from her shoulders, and the sight of her lascivious charms filled me with boyish fear." Sitting on a friend's shoulder, he saw it all, heard the bones break, and fainted. It took a year for "the impress of this butchery to fade enough to let me sleep again." What never faded, though, "and will never fade," was the sight of a gentle-looking woman just in front of him, who, "while the wheel moved blow by blow, calmly ate a large slice of buttered bread."[36] This awful mixture of visual and oral pleasures, added to his adolescent sexual excitement and fear, was too much for him. When, a few years later, Byron watched the guillotining of three robbers in Rome, the spectacle made him tremble until he became hardened to it, though not quite: "I would have saved them if I could."[37]

He would have saved them if he could—it was this humane impulse, conquering the aggression liberated by the sight of bloodshed, that breathed life into the growing opposition to public executions. Two much-quoted journalistic accounts of a hanging at Newgate in 1840, one by Thackeray and the other by Dickens, worked for the movement, for they reached a far larger public than Byron's letter and Holtei's autobiography. The two novelists attended the execution of François Courvoisier, a Swiss butler who had killed his employer, Lord William Russell. Thackeray was shocked by the sight of the stocking cap being pulled down over Courvoisier's face. For a time, the scene weighed on his mind, "like cold pudding on the stomach." The article he wrote was as meticulous and unsparing a piece of observation as he had ever done—complete with the criminal's "wild, imploring look" and "pitiful smile," the hangman's deft way of twisting Courvoisier's body into position. And he was candidly self-observing: "I am not ashamed to say that I could look no more, but shut my eyes as the last dreadful act was going on, which sent this wretched, guilty soul into the presence of God." Much like Holtei before him, he felt ashamed of his indifference. "This is the 20th of July, and I may be permitted for my part to declare that, for the last fourteen days, so salutary has the impression of the butchery been upon me, I have had the man's face continually before my eyes." He could visualize the hangman at work, "with an easy air, taking the rope from his pocket," confessed that he felt "degraded at the brutal curiosity which took me to that brutal sight," and prayed to "God to cause this disgraceful sin to pass from among us, and to cleanse our land of blood." The scene had traumatized but not silenced him.[38]

Dickens, who had arrived early to observe the building of the scaffold and the arrival of the mob, concentrated his disgust on the spectators. "I did not see one token in all the immense crowd of any emotion suitable to the occasion. No sorrow, no salutary terror, no abhorrence, no seriousness, nothing but ribaldry, debauchery, levity, drunkenness and flaunting vice in fifty other shapes." He was appalled at his fellow creatures; he had never thought they could be "so odious."[39] This was written six years after the event, when Dickens still firmly rejected the death penalty; three years later, he retreated to the convenient compromise of opposing only public hangings, a position that earned him the vocal hostility of abolitionists disappointed at losing so famous and articulate an ally.[40] But Dickens's regression to a licensed vindictiveness makes him a vivid exemplar for a century confused by contradictory signals and no less contradictory desires, eager for a new humanitarianism yet reluctant to dismiss the old severity and the old enjoyments.

Arrangements in country after country display this ambivalence. Britain abolished public hangings in 1868. France executed fewer and fewer felons, but kept the guillotine in public view, attracting thousands of the curious and the bloodthirsty; around 1900, however, the government did make the lethal knife less accessible to the crowd, transferring it to a remote section of Paris. In the German Empire, the condemned was beheaded in a prison courtyard in the presence of a few select witnesses. "By daybreak, while Berlin still is slumbering"—*Die Gartenlaube,* that favorite family weekly, described the scene—"the executioner performs his bloody, terrible duty, and only the feeble sound of the death knell announces to those nearby that a human being is being led to death! A few hours later, and the gigantic city, as it awakens, has already been informed that the sentence has been carried out, for glaring red official placards on public pillars proclaim the decapitation of the murderer. And through every street and alley, into the most distant nooks and corners, runs news of the bloody atonement of a bloody deed. The news flies through criminal circles, too; it finds its way through the strongest prison and penitentiary walls into the most remote cells, spreading shock and terror and sowing an impressive seed."[41] The suggestion that private executions have their deterrent effect dominates this highly colored account, and that is precisely why abolitionists distrusted such reports.

This word painting suggests, too, that the death sentence, whether administered in public or in private, powerfully engaged the Victorian imagination.
After the emergence of a large-circulation press, sensational trials and their
aftermath enjoyed lavish journalistic attention. Murder became good copy; so
did a hanging. Major writers—poets and novelists—were gripped by the topic
no less. In 1839 and 1840, William Wordsworth, long since cured of his youthful revolutionary fervor, composed a series of fourteen sonnets defending the
death penalty. Some two hundred capital crimes had been stricken from the
English criminal code in 1837, and reformers, still unsatisfied, took the shifting
atmosphere as an opportunity to press for complete abolition. But Wordsworth
urged the legislators' duty to protect the social fabric and to place "well-
measured terrors in the road / Of wrongful acts." Vividly depicting the prisoner
during his last days on earth, Wordsworth showed him stung by remorse,
shedding tears as he welcomed death.[42]

But the abolitionists had less mawkish, more eloquent spokesmen, the most
notable being Victor Hugo. Haunted by obscure private terrors to which he
returned obsessively, Hugo made abolition of the death penalty his great cause.
It was as though he had to exorcise death wishes and death anxieties of his
own.[43] Looking back, he anchored his impassioned campaign in a troubling
recollection of an episode he had witnessed in Paris as an adolescent. It was a
memory that condensed into one unforgettable moment early disturbing impressions: cadavers of hanged criminals he had seen on his youthful travels,
prisoners he had seen in chains, the guillotine at the Place de Grève.

In a letter he wrote more than forty years later, he recalled that on one fine
summer's day in 1818 or 1819, as he walked across the square of the Palais de
Justice, his attention was captured by a crowd gathered around a post. A very
young woman, just a girl really, was fastened to it, encumbered with an iron
collar around her neck and a signboard on her head identifying her as a petty
thief. Then the hangman stepped forward, red-hot iron in hand, and branded
the girl on her naked shoulder. "I still have in my ear, after more than forty
years, and will always have in my soul, the horrible scream of that suffering
being." Her torment focused his latent hatred of cruelty and sublimated it into a
decision. "To me, she was a thief, a martyr. I left the place determined—I was
sixteen—to battle against the evil actions of the law."[44] He would assail the
death penalty for more than half a century almost to the day of his own death in
1885, pleading for its abolition in the Constituent Assembly in 1848, appealing
for clemency in letters to judges and legislators in Britain, Switzerland, and
Mexico, spurring on like-minded crusaders whenever he heard of their efforts.

Hugo's first and possibly most formidable blow in his war on the guillotine
was a short novel of 1829, *Le Dernier Jour d'un condamné*. It was widely praised,

far beyond France, quoted and paraphrased by poets, novelists, and pamphleteers, and soon translated into English. For decades, in the United States and
elsewhere, abolitionists singled it out as the most compelling plea for their cause
that the age had produced. It haunted Dostoevsky both before and, even more,
after his brush with execution; it impressed Zola and helped him to discover the
moral mission of literature.[45]

Hugo's early novel was a literary tour de force, a marvel of imaginative
identification with the musings and wrenching fears of a convict facing the
guillotine the next day. It sent precisely the sort of philanthropic message that
the likes of Carlyle found so deplorable; its engrossing pages invited fellow
feelings with criminals at the expense of their victims. Indeed, the world of that
victim, in which the condemned man had once lived and worked and married,
and gone wrong, seems far away; Hugo takes good care to remain silent about
the nature of his protagonist's crime and never mentions his name. Instead, he
sketches agonizing reflections, horrifying hallucinations, unrealistic cravings for
life, fantasies of revenge, and heartrending encounters. When his time has
almost run out, the convict's three-year-old daughter, who has not seen him for
a year, is brought to him for a last visit. She is "lively, rosy, with large eyes, she
is beautiful." But she does not recognize him, calls him "monsieur," and tells
him her father is dead—"he is in the earth and in heaven." When he asks her if
she wants him to be her father, she rejects his desperate overture: "No. My
father was much handsomer." And when she shows him that she can read, she
spells out his sentence of death, which her nursery maid, who sits weeping in a
corner of the cell, had bought for a few pennies.[46]

In this set piece, with its calculated effects, pathos verges on bathos. But the
ground has been well prepared. Hugo's doomed protagonist is articulate, extraordinarily observant, even witty in his morbid way; the record he compiles
of his moods and impressions, his daydreams, his very nightmares, are those of
an educated and sensitive man. Hence his anguish over the irreparable alienation from all he has loved, when his little girl treats him as a stranger, appears
credible enough. In any event, Hugo had not aspired to literature alone; he
wanted his intensely subjective text to work as a political statement. "It is the
strangest book you can read," Zola judged in 1860, in "a long rigmarole" about
Hugo's novel. "A thrill of terror seizes you from the first line: one goes through
all the anguish of the miserable creature, one climbs onto the scaffold with
him." He was not about to criticize Hugo for "shattering" the reader this way:
"He had but one aim: to render the death penalty odious; do you want him to
write an idyll? He has taken the shortest route, to address himself to your heart,
to your nerves, to make your hair stand on end, to move you to pity" and to
terror. "When one wants the end, one must want the means."[47] If Hugo had

read this letter, he would have nodded in agreement.

In fact, Hugo explicitly affirmed such intentions in the preface he added to the novel in 1832. "The author can now confess, indeed loudly avow, the political idea, the social idea that he wanted to popularize under this innocent and candid literary guise." *Le Dernier Jour d'un condamné* is "nothing but a plea, direct or indirect, as you like, for the abolition of the death penalty." Hugo linked this seminal reform to the historic revolt against the Old Regime, of which traces still remained. "The social edifice of the past rested on three pillars, the priest, the king, the hangman. Long ago, a voice said: The gods are gone! Recently, a voice was raised and shouted: The kings are going! It is time now that a third voice is raised and says: The hangman is going!"[48] This remained Hugo's cry. One of the most forceful among his extraordinary confessional drawings—they are so many messages from the underground—depicts a cadaver dangling from a gallows, his face an undefinable blotch. At the bottom Hugo has inscribed a word that evokes the suffering Christ: *Ecce*—"Behold!" He is Everyman as victim until the hangman goes.[49]

A hundred years of inconclusive debate over capital punishment could not resolve an unsettling tension that had troubled Victorian bourgeois culture from the beginning. Profiting from more than two centuries of state-building, nineteenth-century governments had confirmed their monopoly on aggression, which included the sole right to prosecute, sentence, and punish transgressors. Private armies were a thing of the past, and vendettas had been outlawed. A few survivals from aristocratic times—remnants of police power over their peasants for Prussian Junkers, duels settling disputes of honor in military circles, illegal death sentences meted out by lynch mobs—made no significant inroads on the state's ultimate authority. All of these were anachronisms, disapproved of, if at times countenanced by, good bourgeois. The modern state was aided in its duties of protecting lives and safeguarding property by a notable efflorescence of the cultural superego among the middling orders. The mounting internalization of guilt could only ease the state's ability to keep order. It was aided, too, by the radical reappraisal of criminal behavior which held social and familial problems responsible for illegal acts. The criminals the reformers put in the dock were loss of religious faith, households without love, and even more, unemployment, destitution, illiteracy—in a word, the social question.

But that social question proved intractable. Had nineteenth-century governments been confident that order was secure, they could have directed their unprecedented authority over punishments toward leniency; they could certainly have afforded to abolish the death penalty. But they were not confident. Since the French Revolution, with the dizzying, irresistible spread of urbanization and industrialization, turmoil rather than calm had been the norm in state after state. Or so it seemed to nervous observers at the scene; the prevailing mood among politicians, legislators, and judges was one of foreboding. A beset-ting fear of the revolutionary masses gnawed at respectable hearts; threatening subversives took the guise of Irish laborers recruited for English factories, French provincials looking for work in Paris, brawny rustics migrating to the growing industrial centers of the German states. The legend of the "dangerous classes," men and women turbulent in their essence, given to strikes, pillage, rapine, and murder, seems to have been launched in the France of the July Monarchy in the 1830s. It was an effective fable, widely adopted as truth, and it prompted the authorities, already in a repressive mood, to move against the press, spy on and tightly control the meetings of socialists and other dangerous folk, and, of course, call for keeping or reintroducing draconian punishments—just in case. Collective anxiety neuroses could only benefit the hangman.

But the defensive orgy was countered—and it is this crosscurrent that pro-duced the tension—by the bourgeois spirit of moral sensibility and fellow feel-ing, whether fed by Christian forbearance or Enlightened rationalism. At the very time when law-and-order officeholders and journalists, from Bismarck to writers for the *Saturday Review,* defended capital punishment as indispensable to public safety, abolitionists offered statistical and moral arguments in rebuttal. The numbers provided their rationale, and the indignation their fervor. As almost nothing else, except slavery, had done in the Victorian century, the death penalty, exercising emotions even more than reason, put the bourgeois conscience to work.

4. The Pleasures of Pain

The hardworking bourgeois conscience, intensely preoccupied with the death penalty, was only marginally less exercised by flogging, one of the Victorians' favorite "secondary" punishments. Increasingly, both came to seem pathologi-cal forms of acting out aggressive needs. The domestic ideal that had appointed the father an absolute ruler and made corporal punishment a preferred means of training character was on the wane. In 1891, in a much-quoted treatise on domestic education in eighteenth-century Germany, Gustav Stephan told with visible disapproval horrifying story after horrifying story about fathers—and mothers—beating their children for trivial infractions or, for that matter, just to keep their already cowed offspring properly subdued. "Tender fathers letting children have their way must have been rare."[1] Tender fathers never flogging their children must have been rarer still.

Stephan's text is evidence that times were changing. But reluctantly—the German humor magazine *Fliegende Blätter,* which spiced political with cultural commentary, published cartoons depicting corporal punishment with approval, especially as it was meted out at home, right into the early twentieth century.[2] And in the comical fables of Germany's favorite humorist of the age, Wilhelm Busch, fables he provided with breezy illustrations, the cane is virtually omnipresent. Busch briefly records one notable exception, a mild-mannered father who holds to the principle that blows are superficial and spiritual punishments alone touch the heart.[3] But that naive, indulgent soul is plainly a figure of fun, to his son and to Busch's readers alike. The others in his works do what ordinary fathers and teachers did elsewhere: they beat their children, or their pupils, with little mercy, with no hesitation, and with pleasure.

A short catalogue drawn from Busch's humorous verse tales will convey the flavor: a father deals out "the most urgent moral admonitions" on his son's behind because he carelessly ruined an expensive new pair of trousers. An inebriated young man, tottering home from the tavern and dropping into a ditch, thrashes his dog for protecting him too eagerly from those who would rescue him. A peasant, after trying everything else, belabors his calf for obstinately refusing to move along the road. An uncle unhesitatingly takes a cane to his fourteen-year-old nephew because the precocious youth has dared to steal a kiss from a lady the uncle fancies for himself. A teacher flogs a seven-year-old boy in his care for stuffing his pipe full of evil-tasting hair. A farmer takes his whip to two boys who have been stealing his apples, thoroughly enjoying himself—Busch points out that he becomes "cruelly cheerful" as he discovers the culprits. Even a gentle Papa loses patience with his two sons and raises his cane to discipline them in time-honored fashion.[4]

The champion among Busch's flogging automatons, as absurd as that indulgent father who will not lift a finger to his son, is one Master Druff, whose rule is to flog children before they have committed any outrage whatever; it makes them fresh and lively. The sheer monotony of these vignettes in which pedagogues resort to their favorite—really their only—remedy for youthful transgressions securely anchors these writings in Victorian culture. And for Busch, a professional pessimist, finding a rationale for flogging children, certainly boys, presents no difficulty. Since human nature is tainted, since virtue is unpleasant and goodness only wickedness left uncommitted, humans need and fully deserve punishment. They deserve it, as his Master Druff would say, even if they have not done something wrong: they will. Busch recalls that he was once beaten as a child, and unjustly so. But, he reports—significantly without a word of protest—those who chastised him had their alibi handy: "Can't do any harm!

This beating is for whatever we don't know about!" To Busch's mind, quite characteristic for his age, aggression breeds and should breed counteraggression. Defiances of authority must be repressed by its firm, impressive assertion.[5] And caning remained the most familiar, and most familial, form of correction, recommended as a harmless and indispensable way of establishing or restoring mastery.

This view was not a German monopoly. *Punch,* too, in occasional cartoons on the subject, bathed it in a benign light. In Boston in the 1860s, a schoolmaster, H. H. Lincoln, could assert that "physical pain, inflicted by a kind-hearted teacher, is a self-sacrificing act." The flogger's venerable platitude, "this hurts me more than it does you," condensed a socially acceptable sentiment. Beating pupils was to Lincoln's mind "a disagreeable duty" which, though unpalatable, proved "elevating in its tendencies upon the moral nature."[6]

Lincoln's alibi, like Busch's beating scenes, is free of middle-class ambivalence on the subject, and shows none of the reservations that the compassionate expressed about beating apprentices and recruits, servants and slaves, even the young. But his unapologetic apology—at least he had the grace to call the duty of flogging disagreeable—unintentionally suggests that protests had begun to have their effect. Some years earlier, in 1847, Lyman Cobb, a well-known American author of school books and persistent opponent of corporal punishment, had claimed that there was perhaps "no question which has agitated the public mind, during the last eight or ten years, more than the subject of Corporal Punishment."[7] He was exaggerating, but by the time he wrote, the issue was distinctly on the agenda of reform.

As time went by, abolitionists grew more confident and more outspoken. Not long before the First World War, Henry Salt, a principled English vegetarian, social satirist, humanitarian, and self-confessed faddist, characterized the stern disciplinarians as "flagellomaniacs."[8] Few critics of flogging took so radical a line, but more and more parents and teachers came to think that he might be right. Salt was, after all, in a noble—if subversive and largely subterranean— tradition: back in the sixteenth century, Montaigne had forcefully argued that while boys should be brought up to be "lusty and vigorous," this in no way commended the panacea of flogging to him. On the contrary, it would be much more fitting if their classes were "strewn with flowers and leaves than with bloody stumps of birch rods!" Montaigne went beyond moral indignation to psychological analysis: "The mother of cruelty is cowardice."[9] He understood that a show of strength is all too often a symptom of weakness.

Salt, more penetrating than most of his contemporaries, endorsed Montaigne's diagnosis. Seeing through conventional rationalizations, he made a persuasive case, in blunt letters and caustic poems, that there is something sick about floggers. "As the miser craves for treasure," his "Hymn of the Flagellomaniacs" begins,

> As the drunkard craves for grog,
> So we crave for morbid pleasure—
>   Something sentient to flog!
>
> Give us juvenile offender,
>   Truant oft from school or church,
> Yet for prison cell too tender:—
>   Ah! to brand him with the birch!

He pushed his derisive assessment further still. The flogger finds a more exquisite joy in seeing his victims' bloody stripes than in all the other forms of aggression he can let loose against the defenseless:

> All the tortures—hanging, burning,
>   Cropping, thumbscrew, boot, and rack—
> Pale before our fevered yearning
>   For the bare and bleeding back.[10]

For Salt, then, corporal punishment in all its forms exhibited with blinding clarity the all-too-human pleasure in inflicting pain. Lyman Cobb might piously insist that "no parent or teacher *can* take pleasure in hearing the cries and entreaties, and in seeing the writhing of those who are whipped."[11] Salt knew better. In view of its continuing popularity and the high-flown pedagogical, even theological rationales offered in justification, he thought caning an incomparable instance of the pathology of everyday life.

One formidable source of resistance to its cure was the teaching profession, especially in England, the United States, and Germany. More than once in the nineteenth century, trained pedagogues in these countries faced down demands from irate parents, worried physicians, or reform-minded school superintendents that they stop beating their charges. Infuriated by these incursions into their proper domain, and intent on protecting their prestige as members of a respected guild, the teachers rejected the pleas with scorn and turned the quarrel into a dispute over turf. They knew better than these amateurs what was good for children, and they irritably defended their right to keep on doing what they had always done.

One of these conflicts erupted in Boston in the mid-1840s. For seven years,

the magnetic and controversial educational reformer Horace Mann, secretary to
the Massachusetts Board of Education, had troubled the pedagogues under his
aegis with an onrush of voluminous, hectoring annual reports and unsettling
innovations, as he struggled earnestly, even desperately, to make the school
system serve the new democratic age. He called on legislators, parents, and
educators to improve school attendance, library holdings—and teachers' competence. Those who instruct the young are to have an "enlightened conception" of the nature and duties of their office.[12]

Mann was prepared to spell out his meaning in what the teachers thought
insulting detail. In 1844, they struck back, making corporal punishment one of
the issues on which to take a stand against their inconvenient chief. Several
Boston pedagogues published intemperate pamphlets defending the practice;
ministers of the gospel, unable to stay out of the fray, irrelevantly accused Mann
of damnable secularism. Replies followed remarks; rejoinders tumbled over
replies. The most aggressive defense was the collective effort of thirty-one
Boston teachers, *Remarks on the Seventh Annual Report of Hon. Horace Mann,*
which heatedly justified the uses of punishment "in tangible shape, the actual
rod," for maintaining school discipline. In his reply, Mann, never one to mince
his words, questioned not merely the teachers' ideas but their character. They
were men with but one program: "Authority, Force, Fear, Pain!" An old-
fashioned rhetorician, Mann intoned this unholy quartet over and over, and
added other capitalized charges. "Not Duty, Affection, Love of Knowledge,
and Love of Truth" characterized these teachers, "but Power, Violence, Terror, Suffering!" The only remedy they seemed to know was "the cowhide and
birch" and "the strong arm that wields them!"[13] Here, sixty years before Salt,
was Salt's diagnosis of floggers as people who dress up perverse pleasures in
elevated justifications.

The controversy did not go away, in Boston or elsewhere. In the late 1860s,
more than three hundred citizens petitioned the Boston School Committee to
abolish corporal punishment in the public schools. They had been stirred into
action by the whipping of a sixteen-year-old girl in Cambridge, and the School
Committee's defense of the action as perfectly proper had not pacified them.
The signers included the president of Harvard, Thomas Hill, the eminent poet
Henry Wadsworth Longfellow, the no less eminent botanist Asa Gray, and an
imposing array of other educators and professional men. Greater Boston's
teachers, unimpressed, took this intervention in very bad part. They voiced
their intransigence at public meetings and in publications, deriding the petition
as "a singular exhibition of a species of presumption." Questions of school
discipline should be left where they belonged, with "the *class* of teachers and
the *class* of committee men." For its part the School Committee, unable to

ignore so distinguished a parade of protesters, took a more politic line: it replied that the petition "has had its proper effect upon our minds." But it quickly nullified this concession: the petitioners' case had been compromised "by the knowledge that this movement was the offspring of a temporary excitement, and of a just and proper indignation, rather than of deliberate, calm conviction."[14] The Committee was of course deliberate and calm.

Opponents of corporal punishment might interpret this halfhearted acknowledgment as a welcome token of progress, but the results of 1867 were the same as those of 1844. The School Committee informed the petitioners in choice Benthamite language that it had been compelled "reluctantly" to decide that " 'the greatest good of the greatest number' demands, that the Board should continue to authorize the exercise" of corporal punishment, "under proper restrictions." To be sure, teachers too quick with the rod must be censured or if necessary discharged after a careful investigation. The Board would protect youngsters against prejudice or cruelty, but thought it unsafe to disregard the realities of youthful nature: "The pupils in our schools are not all seraphs." Bad boys must be made to respect authority; failing that, they will "grow up a curse to society." Indeed, "ungoverned, unrestrained, wilful boys, become turbulent, violent, and vicious men." Hence corporal punishment is valuable and necessary. Its "abolishment would bring great and lamentable evils upon them and upon the public welfare."[15] The fear that small sinners unchecked would ripen into great criminals shadowed educators as it did other Victorians.

It shadowed Germans no less. In 1876, at the first national convention of teachers, one of their number, Julius Beeger of Leipzig, lectured a plenary session on the subject of school discipline to enthusiastic applause. Beeger firmly disclaimed any kinship with ironhanded disciplinarians, but felt impelled to warn his listeners against the conspicuous defects of the generation under their care: "*rudeness* and *savagery, idleness* and *craving for pleasure,* and *insubordination,*" all of them disquieting "cancer sores on the body of society." Their immediate causes were plain: the wars of the 1860s, followed by the indecent ease of making a fortune after the founding of the Reich. But educators could not escape censure, since they had countenanced insubordination and precociousness. This, coupled with excessive freedom granted by indulgent parents, had made pupils lazy, impolite, godless, and rebellious.[16]

One casualty of "unenergetic education," Beeger said, was the noble ideal of manliness. "Misunderstood humanistic principles" were producing moral decay. His listeners rewarded this sally against sentimentalists with shouts of "Bravo!" No doubt these "aberrations" were the work of "well-meaning

teachers and pedagogic authors, liberal politicians and progressive governments"—precisely the individuals and institutions that had fired up the bourgeois conscience against harsh punishments in the first place. In decrying flogging as a relic of barbarous times, humanitarians had saddled pedagogy with
fateful errors. The discipline of the rod was the surest method for eradicating
evil youthful dispositions. Pity for the poor pupil being caned was misguided
compassion.[17]

Quoting an authority guaranteed to secure the approval of his audience,
Beeger recalled what Bismarck had told critics of the death penalty: "Gentlemen, you are showing great sympathy for the murderer; but you say not one
word about the inexpressible torments of his miserable victim." For Beeger, the
struggle to retain corporal punishment was a vindication of cherished traditions;
his address a spirited defense of territory that teachers had long claimed as their
own. It spoke to the anxiety aroused (in the words of other German educators)
by the "silken" *Zeitgeist,* which had generated a "modern mollycoddling and
effeminization," or by the "moral anemia that was paralyzing the seriousness of
justice and the arm of authority."[18] Manliness called for more manly measures.

The applause for Beeger was not unanimous. Two years after his triumphant
performance, the publicist Eduard Sack threw a fierce response at him and his
partisans. A dedicated democrat and pugnacious anticlerical polemicist, Sack
was perfectly at home with the furious tone. He was proud of having had one of
his assaults on the educational establishment banned in the dukedom of Bruns-
wick-Lüneburg. In his critique of the "flogging pedagogues," he described
Beeger as "one of the most knowledgeable teachers in Germany"; this very
eminence, Sack noted, made a counterblast all the more urgent. He charged
Beeger and those who applauded his oratory with failing to profit from generations of pioneering educators, beginning with Rousseau and Basedow, and he
deplored their eagerness to "break" the spirit of the young—"a terrible
word!"[19] In a rhetorical vein favored by the reformers, Sack tried to overpower
his readers with shocking anecdotes about exemplary floggers, especially pious
teachers of religion who drummed the sacred truths into their charges by wielding stick and cane, boxing ears, and slapping faces. Almost gleefully, he offered
depressing proofs that teachers of religion flogged more often and more painfully than teachers of secular subjects.*

---

*In other countries, too, observers made a point of singling out clerics as the worst offenders in
the flogging department. In 1874, an English daily, *The World,* argued editorially that a "careful
investigation" would "bring to light many instances of ill-judged severity" on the part of clergy-
man-teachers. "Our grounds for this suspicion are, that clergymen are in all relations of life, as a
body, less merciful, less ready to make allowances for human frailties, than laymen. . . . To them
there is no such thing as a little sin," and "like captains of men-of-war, [they] are apt to become

Sack also touched on a pervasive irony of corporal punishment in nineteenth-century society. He recognized that the law of the cane was class-bound. Offenders belonging to the "higher orders"—army officers or landowners—were explicitly exempted from corporal punishments.[20] Indeed, the enactments and regulations with which Prussia experimented after adopting its new legal code in 1794 graphically exhibit this bias. The "head of the house" had the right to chastise his wife, parents their children, masters their servants, landowners their peasants, employers their apprentices, teachers their pupils—chastise them with the rod. To be sure, the code provided that beatings must be "moderate," and through the decades the Prussian state made efforts to limit the right of inflicting pain with cane or strap. But these were halfhearted moves and suggest the pressures of class interests on presumably generally valid principles of law.

Not surprisingly: nearly all influential German bureaucrats and legislators stemmed from social strata intent on perpetuating their privileges. Yet, as Sack also noted—and this is the irony—in the school the flogger put welts on the backs of the rich as of the poor. Decades before, Heine had ruefully recalled how French and Latin had been beaten into him; sourly he had celebrated the egalitarianism of the cane: "Surely nothing more humiliates the proud master of the earth, the high spirit who dominates the seas and investigates the laws of the stars, than corporal punishment. The gods, in order to dampen down the blazing arrogance of humans, created flogging."[21] Sack commented that it was in this barbaric practice alone that he could detect any democracy in his Germany.

Sack, of course, categorically rejected all corporal punishment as degrading and futile. Not all humanitarians were quite so uncompromising. Around the turn of the century, the German philosopher Bartholomäus von Carneri, not a partisan of cruelty, observed that the nervousness of two-year-olds could be "stifled in the germ" by "a little slap applied at the right moment, in cold blood." But the century abounds in anecdotal evidence that a beating aroused misgivings even among bourgeois families that did resort to it, under extreme provocation. Like the Boston pedagogue H. H. Lincoln, they thought flogging a distasteful duty at best. In September 1847, Gladstone recorded in his diary that he had just had "a painful office to discharge—that of whipping Willy," his oldest child. Willy, then seven, had been guilty of unruly inattention to his tutor. But immediately "after the infliction, I spoke to him as having paid his forfeit & sent him to reflect & pray & then come & kiss me." It was almost as though the father needed his son's forgiveness. The little boy understood the

---

despotic." Ian Gibson, *The English Vice: Beating, Sex and Shame in Victorian England and After* (1978), 73.

implicit message: "Even *during* the infliction he did not seem to have the least anger or resentment against me wh[ich] shows his good *naturel*."[22] Many fathers and mothers in his century thought as Gladstone did. Parents taking up the cane this hesitantly were ripe for the reformers' crusade.

In the course of time, that crusade made important recruits, but like the struggle against the death penalty, it recorded only limited successes. And like that struggle, it too saw countries clambering back from the abyss of reform they had skirted in moments of political effervescence. In the revolutionary year 1848, the Habsburg empire abolished physical chastisement of offenders, which its laws had precisely regulated down to the appropriate number of stripes. Yet only four years later, ostentatiously reembracing the old regime, Austria restored the penalty, thirty strokes for recidivists, twenty for certain offenses by servants, apprentices, and day laborers. Elsewhere, though, reforms were more lasting. "Corporal punishment," wrote Morrill Wyman of Cambridge, Massachusetts, in 1867, "has been steadily retreating before civilization, and is now practised in the school and in the family only."[23] This claim was more a hope than a fact, a stratagem designed to spur on his country, lagging behind advancing humanity, to catch up with other civilized societies.

Wyman had diligently gathered proofs for his progress report. He had asked European diplomats in Washington how matters stood, and printed their answers in full. The Netherlands, its ambassador told him, prohibited such punishment. "If, very exceptionally, an instance of it occurs, the authorities immediately intervene." The French virtually defied him to find a public school in their empire in which a teacher was allowed to beat a child. The Austrians, he learned, never resorted to the cane, but would briefly imprison the most unruly pupils and expelled the unmanageable. As for Prussia, its minister to Washington informed Wyman that "no corporal punishment is allowed, by law or by practice, to be inflicted upon any pupil in the public schools of Prussia," unless the parents request it. Americans, Wyman said with lifted finger, should take note.[24]

There is good reason to distrust most of these sanguine bulletins. The gravamen of Julius Beeger's complaint, we recall, was not that corporal punishment had been outlawed in German schools, but that liberal officials and meddling parents were continually intruding and, with their reprimands or lawsuits, clamping unreasonable restraints on the disciplining of pupils. It is true that German states like Prussia and Bavaria—in the Empire, keeping order in schools remained their responsibility—were consistently enforcing and increasingly tightening those restraints. Most of them defined excessive punishment as maltreatment that might leave lasting injuries. In Saxony, the regulations permitted a teacher to reach for the cane only after warnings and all milder penalties had failed and the pupil had shown impudent resistance to correction. Even then only "moderate corporal chastisement" was permissible, "always inflicted in a manner that is appropriate and seemly, and does not endanger the health."[25]

Early in the twentieth century, several German states redefined "appropriate" corporal punishment once more and almost stayed the hand of the flogger altogether. In Bavaria, an edict of 1909 emphatically cautioned teachers in primary schools against "transgressing the right to chastisement." In Prussia, a regulation of the same year confined corporal punishment to pupils in the lowest three grades, and permitted it there only after the master in charge or the headmaster had been informed. In schools, one Prussian commentator noted in 1910, "the bounds are drawn narrowly."[26] German faces were still slapped, a good many German backs still beaten raw, as a teacher's rage, whether self-generated or provoked, escaped through the protective network of bureaucratic rules. But toward the end of the Victorian age, most German teachers had to secure discipline with watchful outsiders looking over their shoulders. The floggers no longer had things their own way.

They lost much of their dominion even in England's illustrious public schools. In 1859, the *Saturday Review,* a stalwart champion of flogging, had cheerfully observed, "That this punishment is still in vogue at public schools proves incontestably that the large mass of the upper and middle class are not inclined to proscribe it."[27] And flogging was left untouched by the 1861 royal commission that thoroughly investigated the operations of Eton, Harrow, Rugby, and their fellow institutions. But sensibilities were turning more delicate, even among the English gentry; without much fanfare, in the midst of calls for real men to govern the British Empire, headmasters and teachers administered beatings more sparingly, and in greater privacy, than they had before the 1860s. Henry Salt, an Etonian and from the late 1860s for more than a decade a master at his school, was still a maverick in refusing to have one of his pupils thrashed at the request of the boy's mother, who had "sent her son to Eton to be flogged."[28] But by the time of this historic refusal, Salt's aversion to beatings no longer seemed a scandalous defiance of virile morality.

The English public schools, and the small preparatory schools that sent their graduates to them, were the nurseries of the English elite. They trained clergymen, dons, entrepreneurs, government officials. All but one member of the 1861 royal commission had attended the very institutions they were now studying. But these schools were enigmas to outsiders. Foreign educators, even those—perhaps especially those—who knew them at first hand, were baffled and not a little displeased. In 1867, in their report on British secondary education, two reputable French experts, Jacques Claude Demogeot and Henri

Montucci, attributed the persistence of that "old and degrading custom" of flogging to its status as a hoary tradition. Coming from a country that strictly outlawed corporal punishment in the schools, they did not find this long standing a valid excuse for its survival. "*Flogging*"—they used the English word—"is scarcely proper and scarcely decent." In his famous report on England, Hippolyte Taine voiced the same aversion. Though he praised the public schools for producing well-informed and indeed spirited graduates, he found the popularity of flogging among pupils hard to understand, and the role of headmaster-executioner shocking. "There is scarcely a headmaster in France who would accept a salary of a hundred or a hundred fifty thousand francs at that price."[29]

It was admittedly odd, and the answer must lie in the secret emotional world of the public schools. Harrow, Rugby, Winchester, and the rest were democracies both anarchic and authoritarian. Especially at Rugby, in Dr. Arnold's reforming reign, much of the discipline, including corporal punishment, was in the students' hands. The boys lived in a state of near-war with their masters, kept in check by time-honored obligations and by love. Each public school prized its unique customs, observed arcane rituals, obeyed an elaborate code of conduct that condemned new boys to abject slavery to the older boys and tolerated—even fostered—imaginative pranks and fierce, almost daily, battles. The headmaster was the key to the whole, at once inimitable ideal, fair-minded judge, and supreme enforcer. His ministrations remained a powerful ingredient in the mixed memories, resentful and rapturous, that accompanied Old Boys through life, often dictating the shape of their adult sexual pleasures.* When these memories waned, they went into hiding in the unconscious.

To say that handiness with the cane was requisite for presiding over an English public school is only a modest exaggeration. Headmasters flogged their pupils for crimes real and imagined, grave and slight: for boyish escapades, for fighting, for making disrespectful jokes, for drinking ale, for ostentatiously resisting authority, for failing to construe a passage in Greek, for just having a suspicious look about them. John Keate, the beloved headmaster of Eton early in the century, would reach for the birch because, as he liked to say, he saw guilt in a suspect's eyes. Like many adepts, he was a true democrat in the business of chastising; one of his former pupils recalled that he had "no favourites and flogged the son of a duke and the son of a grocer with perfect impartiality."[30] Diminutive—Gladstone, who was at Eton under Keate, gave him at most five

---

*At times these memories served not as expressions of sensuality, but as a defense against it; we know from Gladstone's diaries that when he found himself aroused by licentious literature or by the attractions of the prostitutes he befriended in order to reform them, he would flagellate himself.

feet one—he was a figure of unmatched authority. "Keate the master of our existence," Gladstone exclaimed, "the tyrant of our days!"[31] But the stories that circulated about his ready punitive responses ignored the lasting adolescent affection that survived, and in some men battened on, memories of the "sanitary correction" they had received at his hands.* And they obscure the fact that many of Keate's colleagues were quicker than he to flog their charges, more capricious, and literally more hard-hitting.

It is instructive to note how few parents protested against this child abuse or transferred their boys to some less barbaric institution. The practice must have somehow matched their wishes, which barely conceal a curious mixture of indifference, tough-minded educational ideology, and, at times, unconscious hatred. On the rare occasions when a headmaster or teacher beat a pupil to death or, which happened more often, crippled him for life, there was an evanescent scandal. But for most families—we recall the mother of Salt's pupil—one reason for sending the little savages to school was to have their spirit broken and reduced to disciplined docility.

In a largely religious culture, it helped that the Bible supplied quotable passages supporting physical punishment. So did the overworked alibi for flogging from Samuel Butler's *Hudibras,* "spare the rod and spoil the child." Headmasters and teachers, after all, were only doing in school what most fathers—and less often, mothers—had done at home, with full confidence in the benefits of the birch. It was not flagellomanes alone who wistfully recalled their boyhood whippings, which, they were sure, had done them no harm and probably a lot of good. To have one's child flogged by professionals was one way of converting parental passivity into activity, at least vicariously.

However fond of caning, Thomas Carlyle had some reservations about the practice; Teufelsdröckh's pedantic teacher in *Sartor Resartus* knew "of the human soul this much: that it had a faculty called Memory, and could be acted on through the muscular integument by appliance of birch rods." More characteristically, James Fitzjames Stephen thought that some humans simply deserved "the gallows, the gaol, or the lash."[32] Until the outlook slowly changed, "all education," the publisher C. Kegan Paul charged in his memoirs, "was driven in with the cane." From the long distance of old age, he recalled with undiminished distaste and pardonable hyperbole the ignorant, incompetent, and irasci-

---

*Yet in 1841, at a dinner celebrating the fourth centenary of Eton, the cheer for him, Gladstone recalled, "was indescribable. Queen and Queen Dowager," who had been toasted before, "alike vanished into insignificance. The roar of cheering had a beginning, but never satiety or end." When Keate finally struggled to his feet, he was too overcome with emotion to speak. "It was certainly one of the most moving spectacles that in my whole life I have witnessed." John Morley, *The Life of William Ewart Gladstone,* 3 vols. (1903), I, 44–46.

ble masters in his school, Ilminster. The only discipline they knew was "furious flogging for the majority" coupled with "the grossest favouritism for a few."[33]

The casual allusions to flogging in English fiction from Austen to Meredith offer substantial confirmation that Kegan Paul's indictment had its roots in reality.[34] We recall the schoolboys in Kipling's *Stalky & Co.* who regularly escape or do not escape whippings. In fact there were in that world, armed with canes and the will to use them, dispensers of corporal chastisement who make Wilhelm Busch's and Rudyard Kipling's luxuriant inventions appear pallid in comparison. A notable representative of these tyrants was the Reverend H. W. Sneyd-Kynnersley, headmaster of St. George's at Ascot, an expensive and exclusive preparatory school he had founded. Among artists with the birch in Britain and on the Continent, Sneyd-Kynnersley stood out. In his short career as a flogger—he died in 1886, at the age of thirty-eight—he must have bent many a twig out of shape. His school boarded some forty pupils, mainly the sons of prosperous middle-class parents; some of his charges later achieved eminence, among them Roger Fry, the prolific art historian, critic, and painter who domesticated the Post Impressionists in Britain.[35] Winston Churchill suffered through two miserable years at St. George's in 1883 and 1884, entering when he was seven, only to be removed from Sneyd-Kynnersley's tender care after the boy's loving nanny noticed the stripes on his body and insisted that his parents send him elsewhere.

Self-willed, given to fits of temper and picturesque outbursts of rage, Churchill would steal sugar from the pantry and once, memorably, took his headmaster's straw hat and kicked it to pieces. For these acts of boyish aggression, all of them looking like desperate pleas for the attention his parents did not give him, he could safely count on superior counteraggression; he was flogged often. To be whipped by the headmaster was an expected and, for all but a few unbroken spirits, an accepted part of the routine. One particularly obstreperous boy, a born rebel, was flogged so often that his classmates, marveling at the patterns on his back, nicknamed him "Stars and Stripes."[36]

Roger Fry, who enjoyed (if that is the word) the dubious privilege of being head boy for years, assisted at many of these "executions," and never forgot them.[37] Sneyd-Kynnersley, as Fry recalled him, was "something of a dandy," with "an aquiline nose and angular features" and red side-whiskers. Of "meagre intellectual culture," a "bigoted and ignorant high church Tory," he felt inferior—with good reason—to teachers of any intelligence, and usually replaced them with "imbeciles." Despite his handicaps, or because of them, he was vain, proud of the social ascendancy that his "aristocratic connections" lent him, and "very much the gentleman." His snobbishness did not keep him from being "genuinely fond of boys"; he would take them on skating expeditions in the winter and excursions to Eton in the summer, sweetening the occasions with welcome treats like "high teas and strawberries and cream." On Sunday afternoons, he read from such classics as Wilkie Collins's *The Moonstone* and Dickens's *Pickwick Papers,* faultless choices. No wonder even rebellious pupils praised him for enlisting their imagination "like a pianist playing his instrument."[38] He was a very seductive man.

But Sneyd-Kynnersley, who liked boys, also—we are not surprised—liked to beat them. On the first morning of school, Fry recalled, he "explained to us with solemn gusto" that he "reserved to himself the right to a good sound flogging with the birch rod." The assembly held every Monday morning, as the school gathered to hear tutors' reports, regularly supplied fresh fodder for Sneyd-Kynnersley's pleasures. After "a moment's awful silence," he would intone the names of the miscreants of the week. Then the two top boys would escort them to the headmaster's study. "In the middle of the room was a large box draped in black cloth and in austere tones the culprit was told to take down his trousers and kneel before the block over which I and the other head boy held him down. The swishing was given with the master's full strength and it took only two or three strokes for drops of blood to form everywhere and it continued for 15 or 20 strokes when the wretched boy's bottom was a mass of blood." Most of the victims endured the flogging with "fortitude," but some would struggle and howl until Fry was "almost sick with disgust." He does not say what disgusted him more—the executioner's lust for blood or the victim's treason to schoolboy stoicism.[39]

One execution remained etched on Fry's mind. It involved "a wild red-haired Irish boy, himself rather a cruel brute, who whether deliberately or as a result of the pain or whether he had diarrhoea, let fly. The irate clergyman instead of stopping at once went on with increased fury until the whole ceiling and walls of his study were spattered with filth." Fry speculated that for once Sneyd-Kynnersley was embarrassed, since, assisted by a pet pupil, he cleaned up his study himself.[40] And he wondered whether his headmaster, freely exposing his joy in maltreating the pupils he loved, was not perverted in his habits. Though acquitting Sneyd-Kynnersley of being homosexual, Fry thought that the headmaster's "intense" pleasure in these floggings was "even excited by the wretched victim's performance."[41] By 1886, the year Sneyd-Kynnersley died, the educated had words for the behavior of such torturers and of those who derived pleasure from being tortured by them: sadism and masochism.

These two technical terms are windows into the literary culture of educated Victorians: Richard von Krafft-Ebing, the distinguished Austrian psychiatrist who popularized "sadism" and coined "masochism," was, of course, invoking the names of two writers. They were well chosen; the marquis de Sade really was a sadist and Leopold von Sacher-Masoch a masochist. Both rehearsed in their lives what they later fixed onto the page, practicing before they preached. And, it is worth remarking, neither was a bourgeois.

Here their resemblance ends. Sade was more the stenographer of his fantasies and his orgies than a compelling stylist. Those trying to rescue him from his reputation as the prince of pornographers have discovered a philosophy in his work, but it amounts to no more than an incoherent amalgam of atheism and satanism badly soldered together. Sade calls upon humans to obey nature, which is vicious at its very heart, and at the same time to rebel against it by outraging it.[42] Youthful dissipation, marriage for a fortune, expenditure of money he did not have to secure the indulgences he coveted, extramarital liaisons—this, though not exactly an average way of life, was in no way alien to his aristocratic caste. But Sade's specialty, the sexual escapades he recorded and far outdid in his fictions, set him apart. Scandal followed scandal. He became notorious for taking a prostitute home to flog her mercilessly. Later he went further, arranging an obscene bacchanalia with harlots hired to have themselves whipped by him and whip him in turn, and to watch him engaging in a variety of homosexual couplings.

Spending many years in prison, Sade employed his hated involuntary leisure to write the novels that secured him a posthumous reputation and eventually a name in the lexicon of psychiatry. They are extravagant productions in which his sexual reveries run riot, celebrating all conceivable and some inconceivable vices: large-scale orgiastic lesbian, homosexual and incestuous parties, mass poisonings and arson, fiendish cannibalism, virgins fed to savage beasts, murder machines that kill scores of victims on command, ingenious torture chambers, debauches that would satisfy the requirements of the most hard-boiled coprophiliac or necrophiliac—all in the service of orgasm.

Of his sizable output, the twin novels *Justine; ou, Les Malheurs de la vertu* and *Histoire de Juliette, sa soeur,* published and revised in the 1790s, remain the best known. Sade hammers home their message on page after page, in volume after volume. Justine is punished for every virtuous act she performs—but, unable to believe that life can be so heartless and unfair, she never stops trying to do good. That is why she is repeatedly raped, subjected to horrifying sexual indignities, branded as a thief, whipped nearly to death. In all too blatant contrast, her sister Juliette, prostitute, poisoner, mass murderess, perhaps the most vicious young woman in fiction, prospers in all she does and delights in all the vices she tastes. In the end, Juliette and her friends send Justine outside during a thunderstorm and are pleased to see her struck dead by lightning. Nature itself has smiled on vice.

For almost self-evident reasons, Sade's writings were censored and driven from the bookstores, so in the nineteenth century his following was small; it consisted largely of professional pornographers who pillaged his work without shame, and a handful of rebellious spirits like Flaubert and Baudelaire in France, Swinburne and Monckton Milnes in England. To the bourgeois century, Sade was almost totally alien. But sadism was not; nor was masochism.

The two are intimately related. Sneyd-Kynnersley, giving pain, was also giving pleasure: sadist that he was, he made masochists.* In a powerful passage in his *Confessions,* familiar to many Victorian readers, Rousseau had graphically sketched his growing sexual excitement at the age of eleven as a motherly woman in charge of him resorted to well-deserved corporal punishment. The time came when Rousseau asked for it.† Undetermined numbers of his English admirers relived, and corroborated, the effects of this famous erotic initiation; being caned became not a chastisement to be dreaded, but a stimulant to be anticipated. Swinburne, an Etonian who immortalized his masochistic proclivities in forthright autobiographical novels and poems, was only the most notorious on an impressive list of public-school boys who grew to lust after corporal punishment and to need it in their adult sexual life as an addict needs a daily dose. By late in the century, French writers were calling this yearning for the birch "the English vice." But as a mere look at Proust documents, if documentation is needed, this manner of securing sexual relief was no monopoly of upper-class Englishmen, or of Englishmen in general. Masochism is a perversion accessible to all humans.

Like sadism, it had a living model. But unlike Sade, Leopold von Sacher-Masoch, the Austrian aristocrat who (much to his irritation) gave masochism its name, never had to go underground. Even after his reputation drooped toward the end of his life, his readers, at once shocked and fascinated, did not quickly desert him. From the 1850s to the 1880s, he was a productive, well-regarded novelist and playwright with a certain following among the naturalistic authors of his day. Until his obsession compelled him to caress masochistic scenarios, he took his subjects from the Austrian past and the Galician countryside where he had spent much of his youth. But his best-known "fiction" was *Venus im Pelz;*

---

*I am not suggesting that masochism always involves a simple direct orgasmic response to pain; we are right to assume that in the mind nothing is ever really simple. In fact, as recent psychoanalytic research has stressed, "pain," in the words of Charles Brenner, may be "the condition rather than the source of sexual pleasure." "The Masochistic Character: Genesis and Treatment," *Journal of the American Psychoanalytic Association,* VII (1959), 205.

†"I had found in pain, even in shame, an admixture of sensuality which left me with more desire for, than fear of, a repetition by the same hand." Jean Jacques Rousseau, *Confessions* (1781–88), in *Oeuvres Complètes,* ed. Bernard Gagnebin, Robert Osmont, and Marcel Raymond, 4 vols. (1959–69), I, 15 [book I].

published in 1869, the first coherent, and the most startling, transcription of his sexual fantasies. Thereafter, while he sometimes deviated from his favorite topic, he never strayed far from the one-sided war between woman and man.

Sacher-Masoch's scantily disguised account mirrors his erotic predilections. A worldly young man finds sexual bliss in being enslaved and soundly whipped by a voluptuous, unmerciful, and majestic woman, who asks a more virile lover to spice up the melodrama by assisting her in tying up, humiliating, and flogging the narrator. The moral Sacher-Masoch wanted to enforce with his tale is that "the woman, as nature has created her and as she attracts the man nowadays, is his enemy and can only be his slave or his despot, *but never his companion.*"[43] Having delivered himself of this bit of wisdom, the narrator professes himself cured of his self-abasing perversion.

This may have been the lesson the protagonist learned from his passive love affair; it was not the lesson his inventor learned for himself. Sacher-Masoch drew up elaborate contracts with the women whose despotism he courted, specifying his abject submission to them as long as he was not required to violate his honor as an aristocrat. Evidently reproducing some prized early erotic impressions, he demanded, in fiction and in life, that the woman who would master and maltreat him wear furs. A latter-day Rousseau, in one reminiscence he attributed his fetishistic obsession to memorable experiences with a domineering, ferocious, and carnal aunt; she had seduced and beaten him, indelibly joining these two acts into a single fount of sexual ecstasy. But the reading matter of his childhood suggests that his overpowering aunt only served fantasies already securely in place; as a boy Sacher-Masoch had swooned with voluptuous pleasure over the varied and horrific tortures that Christian martyrs had had to undergo. Passively experienced cruelty and lustful pleasure blended into one. This was scarcely an ideal of bourgeois love, but victims of Sneyd-Kynnersley and his fellows proved that it served some of them very well.

Sadism and masochism are interesting pathologies in the catalogue of human aggressiveness gone wrong, for they constitute the supreme paradox in sexual life: a relationship in which pain gives pleasure—keen erotic pleasure.* In both, aggression is sexualized and sexuality given over to aggression, turned toward others in the sadist and oneself in the masochist. The two perversions almost never exist in complete isolation from one another. "A sadist," Freud, one of

*Strictly speaking, "sadism" and "masochism" denote a marriage of violence and sexuality, but both terms have often been used rather more loosely for extreme forms of aggressiveness against others and the self. Freud himself was not exempt from this rather confusing conflation—one instance is his category of "moral masochism."

the pioneers in the study of this pathology, noted in 1905, "is always a masochist, too, at the same time." He added, reasonably enough, that "the active or
the passive aspect of this perversion may be more strongly developed in him and
constitute his predominant sexual activity." Sadists and masochists harbor unconscious countercurrents. Those who seek orgasmic climaxes by beating others may develop an appetite for having themselves beaten for the same purpose,
but one orientation or the other is likely to dominate their quest for gratification.[44]

The uneasy sense that love can consummate an unholy union with hate,
though usually in milder forms, had agitated poets and moralists for centuries.
Late in the seventeenth century, the duke de La Rochefoucauld hinted as much
in his celebrated aphorism that we find something not displeasing to us in the
misfortunes of our best friends. Some two hundred years after him, Dostoevsky,
whose novels are populated with a chilling array of sadists and masochists,
restated this perception as he observed the "strange inward glow of satisfaction
which is always found, even among his nearest and dearest, when disaster
suddenly strikes."[45] Years before psychoanalysts fixed on ambivalence as a fundamental fact of mental life, it was no secret that one may envy and hate those
one loves most.*

Some thoughtful Victorians were ready to see this incongruous alliance as a
general phenomenon. In 1843, no doubt prompted by his own self-punishing
disposition, Gladstone wondered in his diary, "Has it been sufficiently considered, how far pain may become the ground of enjoyment, How far satisfaction
and even an action delighting in pain may be a true experimental phenomenon
of the human mind."[46] This was a well-grounded surmise. The *Saturday Review*, scarcely an introspective organ of opinion, speculated about this mysterious side of human nature a few years later. Reflecting on some intriguing recent
murders, it observed that "the very sight of physical pain stimulates and exas-
perates the torturer, and one act of cruelty begets another." No doubt, "the
very act of inflicting pain produces a certain sense of physical pleasure in inflict-

---

*While these disillusioned dicta were silent about the sexual element in sadistic and masochistic
inclinations, the early-nineteenth-century romantics had an inkling of it; witness their fictional
lovers who discover tormented amalgams of bliss and anguish in their amorous adventures. In an
early poem Heinrich Heine celebrates this unlikely alliance as he imagines a lustful stone Sphinx
embracing the lover who has kissed her into life and tearing him with her leonine claws: "En-
chanting torture and delicious woe / The pain, like the joy, beyond measure." Baffled, the poet
asks Eros to explain this paradox: "O love! What does it mean / That you mingle with deathly
torments / All your felicities?" "Vorrede zur dritten Auflage," *Buch der Lieder*, in *Sämtliche
Schriften*, ed. Klaus Briegleb et al., 6 vols. (1968–76), I, 14–15. See Peter Gay, *The Bourgeois
Experience*, vol. I, *Education of the Senses* (1984), 205–6.

ing it, and the mind thus distorted and brutalized seeks for a wholeness and completeness in exhausting the terrible varieties of another's sufferings.''[47] The *Saturday Review* apparently did not know that this physical pleasure was in essence sexual, but the psychiatrists who began to focus on the perversions in the 1880s would probe more deeply.

The most authoritative of these was the Austrian Richard von Krafft-Ebing, professor of psychiatry and forensic expert. His classic *Psychopathia Sexualis* of 1886, which initiated the scientific investigation of sadism and masochism, was an estimable publishing success. Its technical language and the discreet lapses into schoolboy Latin for particularly captivating vignettes of sexual misconduct lost it no readers. Soon translated into English, steadily revised and enlarged, the treatise reached its eleventh edition in 1901, only fifteen years after first publication. By then the work had a firm position as the authority on sexual perversions. Havelock Ellis relied on it, and so did Freud.[48] What Freud did in his epoch-making *Three Essays on the Theory of Sexuality* of 1905 was to complicate the issue. He insisted on treating sadists and masochists as suffering human beings; far from forming a distinct species, they are neurotics who exhibit in their florid behavior the sexual conflicts all "normal" humans conceal in their unconscious. It was a sobering thought, for which the most psychologically acute poets and novelists had not quite prepared the Victorians. But two cultural symptoms of pathological aggression, violence against women and violence against the self, attest that in one form or another sadism and masochism were very much alive in that age.

They were alive even among the respectable classes. Bourgeois in the Victorian decades largely took it for granted that crimes against women—rape, wife beating, sex murders—were confined to jaded aristocrats and, even more, coarse laborers and illiterate peasants. "Men of education and refinement," the essayist and historian J. W. Kaye said flatly in 1856, "do not strike women."[49] On the other hand, bourgeois never tired of saying that men lacking education and refinement did strike women. Tennyson, in *Maud,* has a brutish, sexually vicious lower-class type:

> And the vitriol madness flushes up in the ruffian's head,
> Till the filthy by-lane rings to the yell of the trampled wife.

In his naturalistic novels, Zola drew similar portraits for his readers, at greater length and with a more heated vocabulary; his primitive, uninhibited working-class and peasant males sate their sexual hunger whenever, wherever, and however they please. Such social reportage, presumably neutral in its realism, amounted to an imputation of sexual guilt to whole classes. While serving the voyeuristic needs of bourgeois readers, it could also give them a comforting sense of collective innocence. The animalistic behavior typical of "ruffians" was, many hoped, a pathology that visited only the most neurotic specimens in the civilized classes.

Actually, scattered anecdotal and statistical evidence indicates that bourgeois had no cause for complacency about the business of violence against women. Any wholesale self-acquittal had to ignore some uncomfortable facts. Between 1837 and 1901, the years of Queen Victoria's reign, some 480 murderers were executed in England, and 127 of these were men who had killed their wives, while some 30 more had murdered a mistress; these convicted felons included small entrepreneurs, men of leisure, and (to no one's surprise) physicians.[50] While few of their fatal assaults fall under the rubric of sex crimes—they were mainly summary ways of discarding an inconvenient spouse or inheriting her money—the most spectacular killer of the century, known as Jack the Ripper, was a sex murderer in the purest sense. In 1888, he killed and savagely mutilated five or perhaps six London prostitutes. He was never brought to justice and his identity was never established, but the conjecture that he was a man of education—possibly of refinement—is consistent with the little dependable material that has survived.

The middle classes, then, were far from innocent. Bourgeois husbands beat their wives even during pregnancy, compelled them to have sex just after childbirth, raped or sodomized them.[51] A physician who had worked at the penitentiary in Waldheim, Germany, studying the records of fifty-three males convicted of sex crimes—rape, fornication with minors, incest—discovered, in the company of a large majority of lower-class felons, one teacher, two owners of a bakery, and one owner of a cheese dairy—some 7.5 percent of the whole.[52] The controls over destructive aggressive passions that were a mainstay of middle-class self-definition in the nineteenth century broke down more often, and more disastrously, than good bourgeois liked to believe.

A further complication, for Victorians and their chroniclers, was the fact that until the 1860s, and in some societies even later, an uncertain gray area in the law and in cultural opinion gave men disposed to be harsh, even vicious, to women ample opportunities to vent their aggressive impulses. As feminists charged, a culture dominated by males freed husbands to be financially exigent, sexually tyrannical, even physically abusive. Respected moral authorities—divines and judges—would advise victimized wives to try persuasion, prayer, and above all patience. But in a number of countries, this dominant style was under attack; court decisions successively narrowed a husband's right to intimidate, let alone beat, his wife. Hesitantly, bourgeois families translated the ideal of the wife as competent partner from feminist tracts into mundane practice. In England, violent quarrels habitually started by the husband, or his irrational demands for household service, became sufficient grounds for a legal separation.[53] As elsewhere, maltreating a woman became less rewarding, even risky.

Rape was a more vicious abuse of women than wife-beating, but harder to document. True, law codes everywhere stigmatized it as a heinous crime. "The dastardly cowardice of this outrage," the Massachusetts legislator Robert Rantoul, Jr., wrote in 1835, "as committed against those who have a natural claim on the stronger sex for protection, the depth of depravity which it indicates, its atrocity, as being more cruel towards the party injured than murder, confer upon it the most malignant character in the black catalogue of guilt."[54] American Southerners expressed the same horror, largely animated by the self-serving conviction that rape was committed almost by definition by black men on white women. But the Yankee reformer's indignation indicates that racist preconceptions were not the only conscious motive for damning rape as an outrage worse than murder.

The problem lay in establishing the rapist's guilt. Dostoevsky's depraved Svidrigaylow in *Crime and Punishment,* taunting a potential victim, spoke for the age: " 'Force' is very difficult to prove."[55] For painfully obvious reasons, the prey of rapists were reluctant to come forward. They were unwilling to reexperience their ordeal in a packed courtroom, to advertise their ruined reputation—their virginity gone—and to expose themselves to lewd jokes. Their violator, they feared, would claim that they had countenanced, in fact ardently welcomed, his sexual overtures, and they had no appetite for being heard with smiling incredulity, if not scorn. It turns out that their anxieties were excessive, but they were not irrational. Many a judge and juror—is it necessary to remind ourselves that in the Victorian era they were all men?—knew in his bones that women are provocative, exploitative, and mendacious: they say no but mean yes, sham resistance to make themselves more alluring, display their charms to rouse men's sexual appetites. Unflattering stories about women's vengefulness, and their lively imaginations, abounded.*

*The reality, as we shall see, belied these tales. Yet many vicious crimes went unreported or unavenged. In 1858, the *Saturday Review,* indignantly discussing the case of a respectable "monster" named Johnston, jailed for refusing to provide for the upkeep of his daughters, commented, "Whenever any extravagant instance of domestic cruelty comes out in the annals of a police court, it is only an accident which reveals a long course of brutality and unnatural persecution. The wife goes on through years of silent suffering—the children are beaten, or starved, or subjected to all manner of unspeakable evil—and no complaints are uttered." "The Johnston Case," *Saturday Review,* VI (October 9, 1858), 351. And the notion that the sexual abuse and rape women did report were largely imaginary was fed by the medical literature. Thus in 1899, in a characteristic

If rape were simply the impatient, explosive gratification of exigent sexual pressures, one would wonder why nineteenth-century bourgeois ever resorted to it. They had easy, less degrading ways of satisfying their urges. The affluent could keep a mistress or visit a high-priced brothel. They could exploit servants at home, clerks in their offices, woman workers in their factories. In the colonies that imperialism had opened up to Western civilization, the business agents, government officials, and military personnel could slake their amorous appetites with natives. Offering bribes, promising marriage, threatening with dismissal, bourgeois Don Juans in places of power held all the trumps in the sexual game. But rape is no tribute to Eros; in the violation of women, sexuality is not the twin of aggression but its servant. Rape is essentially a rabid display of raw power and towering rage; only the true sadist who must use coercion to reach orgasm rapes for sexual reasons. Domestic frustration, that convenient and plausible alibi, figures least among the impulses that drive men to do sexual violence to women. And so the bourgeois century had its respectable rapists, who for reasons often unknown to themselves ravished women—and children—in savage displays of pathological aggression.*

Some observers were unnerved. In 1841, in a study of French convicts in the prison ships at Toulon, Hubert Lauvergne judged that "rape has, beyond possibility of doubt, infected all parts of the body social." The ships "hold only the most impure and the grossest delinquents." This was not disinterested sociology; a fervent phrenologist committed to the proposition that faith is the one secure bridle on filthy passions, Lauvergne wanted to show that such appalling crimes blossom in a society cursed by "the overthrow of the religious, moral and political order." Documenting his dismay, he cited a Jew who had raped his

---

anecdote, a Dr. Altmann told of a sixteen-year-old German girl who had accused her stepfather of having "forcibly used her sexually." The accused, a man of unblemished reputation, spent ten days in prison while the authorities investigated. But court physicians found the accuser to be a virgin, and it turned out that she often dreamt of men and had dreamt her stepfather's assault as well. "Traum statt Wirklichkeit," *Archiv für Kriminal-Anthropologie und Kriminalistik*, I (1899), 334–36.

*One set of official statistics leaves no doubt that the sexual molestation of children was far more frequent than that of women, and the numbers, as well as the proportions, grew steadily worse. Thus in the *département* of the Seine, which includes Paris, 57 rapes of women were prosecuted between 1825 and 1838, while there were 153 prosecutions of the same crime against children. Between 1867 and 1880, the first group doubled, to 101, while the second leaped almost ninefold, to 1,291. Albert Bournet, *De la criminalité en France et en Italie. Étude médico-légale* (1884), 115. From then on, these proportions remained fairly stationary, with the relative number of offenses against adults slowly rising. In the fourteen years between 1886 and 1900, there were 201 prosecutions for "*viols et attentats à la pudeur sur adultes*," while prosecutions for the same assaults on children stood at 1,586. See Maurice Yvernès, "La Justice en France de 1881 à 1900," *Journal de la Société de statistique de Paris*, XLIV (September 1903), 301.

daughter, forcing her to submit by striking her with a knife: "This kind of rape, under the domestic roof, is becoming more and more common."[56]

There is no way to confirm, or discredit, this alarmist critique of godless nineteenth-century culture. Many rapes went unrecorded, and in any event, nineteenth-century crime statistics were too undifferentiated to permit really informed conjectures; they never cleanly separated out middle-class sex offenders from criminal drifters and licentious peasants. Victorian "moral statisticians" (as serious investigators of crime, prostitution, and population trends called themselves) did have enough information to conclude that the incidence of sex crimes was higher among the literate than the illiterate classes of society. And they blamed the spread of "instruction," which merely imparts technical skills and is a yawning gap away from "education," which infuses pupils with moral ideals. "Unhappily," Dr. Albert Bournet wrote in 1884, in a substantial comparative study of crime in France and Italy, "to the degree that instruction is popularized, the moral sense seems to weaken." Sadly, "sexual passions"—he meant those visited on women and children—"grow overexcited by their very satisfaction."[57] These rough surveys might reassure the middle classes, for they revealed that while men with only primary schooling were more likely to commit sexual assaults than those with no schooling at all, they were also far more likely to do so than those with more advanced education. But the Victorians could not deny that there were in their midst pillars of the community criminally assaulting young, often innocent women.

Unsavory though nineteenth-century bourgeois found the subject, they made few attempts to repress this unhappy fact of contemporary life. The learned medical and sociological literature on rape was admittedly skimpy; pundits generally shied away from it.[58] But even if they had attempted to mount a conspiracy of silence, novelists and reporters would have reminded them. To be sure, some victims of fictional rape were of the lower orders, like Zola's handsome and sturdy peasant Françoise in *La Terre,* violated by her gross brother-in-law Buteau. But heroines of the privileged orders were not immune. The noblewoman in Heinrich von Kleist's striking novella *Die Marquise von O . . . ,* an honorable widow, inexplicably finds herself pregnant. Advertising for the father that she may marry him, she discovers that she was raped by a brave, appealing aristocratic Russian officer, ironically after he had saved her from precisely that fate at the hands of marauding troops. Against all probability, Kleist has the couple marry happily in the end.

Other fictions were deliberately more ambiguous. The scene in which Thomas Hardy's Tess loses her virginity, less extravagant than Kleist's astonishing melodrama, remains hard to read. The rich and rakish Alec d'Urberville, who has been making advances to the innocent Tess, takes advantage of her when he finds her resting after their night ride in the woods.[59] Hardy at once defies and placates his prudish readers; his evasions leave the critical moment in misty uncertainty—did Alec used rough persuasion rather than outright force? But however we read the passage, he hints at a most unsavory consummation.

In contrast, in a stark novella of 1890, the Austrian writer Marie von Ebner-Eschenbach, in her time a famous storyteller valued for her realism, makes the victim's passionate collusion clear. Her *Unsühnbar* is a harrowing tale of unforgivable adultery and fatal remorse. The young countess Maria Wolfsberg, propelled into an arranged marriage, yearns after an early suitor, Felix Tessin, as irresistible a seducer as Hardy's Alec d'Urberville. After a long absence, Tessin returns to renew his verbal assaults on Maria's virtue, and at last she confesses her feelings for him. Elated, Tessin embraces her, and she does not resist. "Two drunken humans had lost all consciousness of honor, duty and fidelity; the world and every memory sank away from them."[60] It is her share in this erotic debauch that makes the crime *unsühnbar*—"inexpiable."

While Ebner-Eschenbach and Hardy burden the seducer with ultimate culpability for victimizing the woman he professes to love, they leave an aura of moral indefiniteness hanging over the decisive sexual encounter. The women they portray may—or may not—have failed in their duty to resist male aggression. But though its tone is discreet, John Galsworthy's *The Man of Property* of 1906 leaves no saving incertitude at all. Soames Forsyte, the protagonist of this opening novel in the Forsyte cycle, practices as a solicitor and displays refined tastes in art and society. But, to his growing distress, his marriage to the mysterious Irene is unhappy; she is very beautiful but very remote. She takes to sleeping in a separate bedroom and locking the door. One night, baffled beyond bearing by her reserve, starved for her affection, and (justly) jealous of another man, Soames enters Irene's bedroom, for once unlocked, and rapes her.

Galsworthy eschews that ugly verb, but tells the reader just what happened: "The morning after a certain night on which Soames at last asserted his rights and acted like a man, he breakfasted alone." Sitting by himself, he recalls "the overmastering hunger of the night before" and wonders if he had been right to yield to it. An "intolerable feeling of remorse and shame" overcomes him, and yet, was not this woman, who had treated him so unkindly, "his lawful and solemnly constituted helpmate"?[61] Yet his offense is, like that of Ebner-Eschenbach's Maria, inexpiable. Galsworthy's fiction conjures up the night side of a bourgeoisie that at times lets its aggressive fantasies erupt into real crime.

The middle-class public that did not read novels had the daily papers. And there they would discover that prevailing wisdom to the contrary, a rapist did not always go unpunished. A rapidly growing mass press provided news of trials for rape and took care to enliven it with titillating particulars. This reportage, leaving much but not everything to the reader's fantasies, was to many troubling. In fact, in Germany, where the courts excluded unauthorized spectators from these cases, one cultural critic worried that hints in the press at unspeakable outrages could only "arouse the reader's imagination." For its part, the London *Times* scattered stories about sexual violence in its law columns among mundane offenses like wife-beating and robbery. In one year alone, 1850, it reported at least a dozen rapes or attempted rapes. Most of the accused were men with reputations to uphold: a ship's broker, a furrier's son, a prosperous tailor, a commercial traveler, a rich farmer, even a clergyman. When a particularly engrossing case of rape was on the docket, the courtroom was crowded and local gossip lively. In Leamington, one trial with colorful local touches "excited," the *Times* reported, "very great interest in the town" and "throughout the neighbourhood." Again, "a great deal of excitement," we read about the trial of a clergyman accused of the same offense, "has prevailed in the town during the day."[62] Cases of rape, especially with a man of wealth or reputation in the dock, served as popular entertainment, almost as good as a hanging.

Most newspaper reports of rape consisted of a story from one to four or five inches long; then coverage faded as other crimes claimed journalists' attention. At times, newspapers failed to follow up the initial report beyond recording that an accused had been remanded to prison or freed on bail. But when a trial boasted unusual features or controverted testimony, it might drag on for days, even weeks, and then the press followed it with lip-licking delight. One such trial involved a charge of rape against Joseph Solomons, son of Moses Solomons, a London furrier. The drama had begun when the victim, "a young innocent-looking girl, aged 17, named *Fanny Harnsworth,*" was charged with stealing a victorine, a kind of fur scarf, worth some three shillings. The accused, evidently a spirited young woman, insisted that this absurd complaint would never have been brought "if it had not been for Master Joseph." She testified that he had come "to her bed room at night and had taken improper liberties with her, and effected his purpose." When she complained to Master Joseph's mother, she was told, coolly, "I suppose he did not kill you." Upon investigation, the examining magistrate found the stories told by the Solomons family contradictory and undependable and dismissed the case against Fanny Harnsworth.[63]

This gave her lawyer his opening; he charged Joseph Solomons with rape. Master Joseph had apparently had his way with Fanny more than once, forcibly silencing her. Naturally "the court was crowded by persons anxious to hear the proceedings" as the case continued. Young Solomons was freed on bail totalling two hundred pounds, a sum the magistrate, clearly suspicious, promptly doubled. He was right; after trying some transparent stratagems—attempting to bribe Fanny Harnsworth, describing himself as too ill to appear—Master Joseph, a jury trial only days away, skipped the country, forfeiting his bail. While the magistrate issued a warrant for the defendant's arrest, "the case was thus suddenly brought to a close, to the mortification of a crowded court."[64] This was one way for justice to be frustrated.

What happened to Fanny Harnsworth we do not know. But throughout the proceedings, the magistrates made their sympathies with a young servant girl perfectly evident. Repeating the victim's testimony about Mrs. Solomons' callous response, one of them observed, "A more disgusting remark than that made by the prisoner's mother I cannot conceive." Nor were the courts in general particularly tenderhearted toward the accused, even when they were clerics. The "reverend defendant" Robert Abercrombie Johnstone, rector of West Horndon, Essex, charged with raping his young domestic servant, was remanded to jail until the police found his elusive accuser. He was acquitted after she was detected in perjury, but if her damaging testimony had been truthful, Johnstone would have been convicted and punished.[65]

Job Lawrence, a married itinerant vendor who had amassed a fortune of about £1,500, did not fare so well. Charged with having "feloniously ravished" a nineteen-year-old servant girl of impeccable reputation, he offered in defense that he had been too drunk to know what he was doing. But after several hours of deliberation the jury found him guilty, though of a lesser charge—"an assault with intent to commit a rape." This verdict spared Lawrence transportation to a penal colony, an outcome virtually guaranteed if he had been convicted of full-fledged rape, but it did not save him from two years at hard labor.[66]

The English legal system, with its presumption of innocence and burden on the prosecution to prove its case, did work in favor of some defendants almost certainly guilty as charged. A tailor named Henry Digby was accused of "having acted in an indecent manner towards two little girls, the one between 14 and 15, and the other between 12 and 13 years of age." The alderman hearing the case was not impressed by the prisoner's abundant tears, nor by his claim that he was being victimized by a conspiracy of the girls' family and friends. On the contrary, he was persuaded that the "fellow" had "long been attempting to pollute the minds of the children, and that he deserved being punished." But since "there were circumstances in the case which he was convinced would prevent a jury from convicting," the alderman regretted that he could do no more than impose a bail of forty pounds on the defendant to ensure his good conduct for the coming year. When the rapist was guilty beyond a reasonable doubt, however, retribution was harsh and instantaneous. In a curt note, the *Times* reported in October 1850 that one David Harrington, aged thirty, convicted "upon the direct evidence, of a felonious assault" on a girl of eight, was "sentenced to be transported for life."[67]

One last entry may round out this catalogue of pathological aggression: suicide. Self-murder amply earns its place in this study, for it dramatizes the Victorians' heartfelt attempts to extend the range of permissible hatred by redefining what had long been thought transgressions of divine law and grave offenses against the state as instances of pathology. Prompted by fresh modes of thought and fresh opportunities for action, they linked self-destruction to other grave matters as they engaged in debates about ethical judgments, scientific understanding, and social policies.

For a millennium and a half, the church had condemned suicide as a sin, and in the early-modern period, following its lead, states had added it to the roster of crimes. The earliest Christian theologians, prompted by the heroism of martyrs taking their own life to avoid being raped or forced to renounce their faith, had hesitated to discard the Stoic and Epicurean doctrine prizing suicide as a dignified exit from life. But St. Augustine demolished this equivocation by declaring the human body holy. "Certainly, he who kills himself is a homicide."[68] In succeeding centuries, Christian councils spelled out what St. Augustine's categorical denunciation of self-murder implied for believers. Nor did the Anglican church and Protestant sects retreat from this severity after the Reformation; the impulse to self-destruction was a temptation from the devil. Hence they deprived a suicide of the religious rites and Christian burial to which ordinary mortals, lesser sinners, were entitled. The French code of 1670 specified that the suicide would be subjected to a humiliating mock trial, his property forfeited to the state, and his body dragged naked through the streets face down and hanged as if he were an infamous felon. It was a primitive retaliation that remained on the books through the eighteenth century. Aggression against the self was punished by counteraggression from the state.

The philosophes, followers of Roman thought in this as in so much else, vehemently objected, insisting on man's right to choose his own way and his own time to die.* But since much of the nineteenth century, for all its princi-

---

*The law put Voltaire into a state of philosophical rage: "The republic will do very well after my death, as it has done very well before my birth. I leave it on the chance of not finding a better one. But you! What madmen you are to hang me by the feet when I am no longer alive! And what thieves you are to rob my children!" *Prix de la justice et de l'humanité* (1777), in *Oeuvres complètes,* ed. Louis Moland, 52 vols. (1877–85), XXX, 543. He was speaking for most of the Enlightenment and in the tradition of Montaigne's essays. He was in tune, too, with David Hume, whose essay "Of Suicide" was first published in 1777, the year after his death. "A man, who retires from life, does

pled unbelievers, remained in the shadow of piety, many bourgeois never caught up with these Stoic sentiments. The fact that wicked French revolutionaries had eliminated suicide from the penal code did not exactly endear such a pagan notion to Victorian legislators and journalists, to say nothing of clergymen. Still, the age witnessed a striking, conflict-ridden evolution of thinking about self-murder. To judge from the many suicides in its novels, punitive judgments did retain a certain vitality. Mr. Merdle in Dickens's *Little Dorrit* is a consummate swindler who does away with himself when his financial empire is on the verge of collapse; we shall not miss him. Others among Dickens's suicides—Ralph Nickleby and Jonas Chuzzlewit—are villains whose death the reader is invited to greet with relief. But even the painful end of Emma Bovary, in whose descent into adultery and catastrophe the reader may take a sympathetic if clinical interest, is the predictable punishment for indulging her luxuriant imagination. And Anna Karenina, the adulteress, a figure of stature and the casualty of a cold marriage, pays, though tragically, for her transgression.

Nevertheless, having been denounced for centuries as a sin and a crime, suicide was reclassified twice during the 1800s, and for many was freed of moral stigma. First, Victorians discovered it to be the pathetic outcome of mental derangement. Then, after profiting for several decades from this diagnosis, suicide joined juvenile delinquency, prostitution, and crimes against property as a social problem. Naturally, these shifts did not follow the same rhythm or produce the same results everywhere. Indeed, much like the struggles over the death penalty, ecclesiastical and legal disputes over suicide intensified late in the century as churches mounted counterattacks against impious liberalism. More or less in vain: though incomplete and inconsistent, these reclassifications made significant inroads on public opinion.

The diagnosis of suicide as the most desperate resort of mental illness became fashionable around mid-century and opened the door to humanitarian efforts at prevention. It made legal revenge against self-murder appear unkind, even barbaric. This in turn reinforced a much older disposition to mercy; sympathetic clerics and judges had long clutched at verdicts of incurable melancholy or momentary insanity to free suicides from moral responsibility and hence from mortal sin. Now the Victorian decades became the classic age of the

---

no harm to society. He only ceases to do good," Hume said. He thought it "a kind of blasphemy to imagine that any created being can disturb the order of the world or invade the business of providence!" In short, "that suicide may often be consistent with interest and with our duty to ourselves, no one can question, who allows that age, sickness, or misfortune may render life a burthen, and make it worse even than annihilation." "Of Suicide," *Essays,* in *The Philosophical Works of David Hume,* ed. T. H. Green and T. H. Grose, 4 vols. (1875; ed. 1882), II, 413, 412, 414.

insanity defense for suicides, in tandem with the same defense for homicides.[69] French specialists took the lead. In 1822, the alienist Jean-Pierre Falret, though unlike many of his fellow physicians a religious man, argued that self-destruction often results from inherited mental disease. In 1838, the celebrated Étienne Esquirol, pioneer in the study of "monomania," endorsed this view with a substantial chapter in his influential *Des maladies mentales:* "Suicide offers all the characteristics of mental alienation, of which it is really nothing but a symptom"; it results from "delirium of the passions or madness."[70] This diagnosis held the profession captive for decades.[71] The contention that the very act of suicide is trustworthy proof of irrationality became a favorite weapon in the arsenal of what the pious feared was an army of godless doctors on the move.

While clerics and laymen continued to wrangle over the sanity of self-murderers, social scientists, that modern breed of experts, invaded the debate and radically altered its terms. If the redescription of suicide as madness made legal retribution appear cruel, its redescription as a social problem made such retribution irrelevant. Victorian sociologists studying suicide faced formidable obstacles: flawed and fragmentary statistics, inadequate criteria to distinguish deliberate from accidental death, persistent underreporting that protected the good name of affluent suicides, incompetent police work, unclear categories of motives.* But undaunted, searching for general laws of behavior, the sociologists imposed a severe scientific agenda on themselves. Concentrating on a single subject, Émile Durkheim observed in the preface to his classic *Suicide* of 1897, "one can discover real laws that prove, better than any dialectical argument, the possibility of sociology"—laws that are preferable to "the common theories of moralists."[72]

To establish the study of society as a science was the sociologists' program. And in analyzing suicide as a social pathology subject to general laws rather than a religious or moral failing, they undermined accepted alibis for aggression. But the impediments to scientific neutrality were greater than Durkheim and his colleagues recognized.

Ideally, the pursuit of science, of sociology no less than of physics or biology, is unencumbered by moral, let alone religious, commitments. It is by defini-

---

*"The material" on suicides "is very scattered, so that it is hard to collect"—thus the well-known conservative German political economist Adolf Wagner, in *Statistisch-anthropologische Untersuchungen der Gesetzmässigkeit in den scheinbar willkürlichen menschlichen Handlungen* (1864), 103; "all statisticians confess the impossibility of getting precise data"—thus the Italian professor of psychological medicine Enrico Morselli, in *Suicide: An Essay on Comparative Moral Statistics* (1879; tr. 1882), 9; "the statistics on suicide provide only a scanty shaft of light into some dark aspects of the problem of causes"—thus the German economist Hans Rost, in *Der Selbstmord als sozialstatistische Erscheinung* (1905), 3.

tion, in the best sense of that equivocal term, value-free. Unfortunately, the sociologists' irrepressible penchant for social criticism and social reform—a legacy, like the passion for the human sciences, from the Enlightenment—often interfered with their realization of that ideal. To the extent that they smuggled into their analysis of self-murder an agenda for contemporary society, they opened their work to the reproach of tendentiousness. More often than was comfortable, the figures that crowd their reports threatened to become not the basis of their self-assured generalizations but ornaments for them. With all their training as statisticians, all their methodological sophistication, they found it hard to shake off ideologies pushing them to propound conclusions they had actually reached on political or religious grounds.[73] The humane impulses that lent their research its energy often prevented them from seeing their field steadily and whole.

Most nineteenth-century social scientists, in fact, found prescribing for industrial society quite irresistible. It was, to their minds, the fatal breeding ground of personal disorganization, of which suicide was only the most drastic symptom. The fault lay with an age that had fostered secularism and thus demolished the bulwarks against amorality and deadly mental states. Their panic over mounting suicides blended into other panics—over falling birthrates, habitual criminals, domestic immorality. And this conjunction only fed their alarm. In 1881, in his study of suicide, Thomas Masaryk, social scientist, cultural critic, and Czech nationalist, noted that the annual total of acknowledged suicides across Europe was at least 22,000. Worse: that number probably represented less than half of the suicides actually carried out. Projecting these figures into the future Masaryk was dismayed: "Imagine what the numbers will be in a decade or a half-century!"[74]

Students of suicide writing from a denominational perspective, especially Roman Catholics, had no doubts as to its causes. "People often neglect to implant a sense for genuine religiosity, authentic love of humanity and of justice in the child's heart," wrote A. Baer, a Berlin physician, in a "social-hygienic study" of children's suicides. True piety "provides the desperate and the despondent with a firm support. The consecrated breath of healthy religious life flows from the parents to the child and is woven into all his feeling and thinking." Hans Rost, in his statistical inquiry into self-murder, extended this pious analysis to all of contemporary society, adding a touch of fashionable anti-Semitism: "Social democracy, the liberal and not least the *modern* Jewish world view have moved *the center of gravity of being into worldliness.*" This has left masses of people vulnerable to self-destructive anguish. The best antidote is faith: "*Each confessional of the Catholic Church is an anti-suicide bureau.*"[75] Just as counter-revolutionaries after 1800 blamed the subversive Enlightenment for the French

Revolution, so counterrevolutionaries a century later were blaming Victorian positivists and atheists for what they deplored as the demoralization of contemporary society.

Perhaps the most persuasive critic taking this tack with Victorian culture was Thomas Masaryk. His widely praised monograph on suicide, *Der Selbstmord als sociale Massenerscheinung der modernen Civilisation,* obliquely testifies to his deep inner turmoil. Born a Catholic but with an independent turn of mind, he was prey to agonizing religious conflicts between the time he completed his book on suicide and the time he published it. By 1880, he had converted to Protestantism. Yet he did not revise his study with his newly acquired religious convictions in mind, but firmly remained more critical of the post-Reformation era than of the medieval centuries. Whatever the impact of his mental struggles on his thinking, the Masaryk who indicted the culture of his time was trying to see the situation as a sociologist interested in mass phenomena. Since at bottom humans never really change, it must be cultural influences that bless some ages with a low suicide rate and curse others with a high one. Hence it can only be "the sickness of our century" that accounts for the steadily rising figures. One can explain the social phenomenon of suicide simply as "a tragic result of the prevalent irreligiosity of the masses." In short, *"suicides are the bloody sacrifices of the civilizing process."*[76]

Émile Durkheim's *Le Suicide* shows that unbelievers could reach the same dismal conclusions. It shows, too, that Durkheim was an extraordinarily elusive thinker. A thoroughgoing secularist and convinced anticlerical, he concentrated in much of his best work on the social force of religion; a faithful adherent of the French Third Republic, he left it largely to others to enter the political fray; a professional social scientist to the bone, he imported strong convictions into his treatises; a good liberal, he was enamored enough of the ideal of close social cohesion to color his liberalism with authoritarian touches. *Le Suicide* reflects, and does not resolve, these tensions. Diagnosis and prescription at once, it aims to understand what Durkheim called "the general malaise" that was besetting the Europe of his day. His was "a critical period."[77] And he thought he could offer helpful suggestions toward navigating it safely.

Durkheim, however, disdained playing the faith healer. Like the philosophes more than a century before him, he expected that neither dogma nor tradition could bring relief. In an energetic declaration of faith in science, he asserted that "science, far from being the source of the evil, is its remedy and the only remedy at our disposal." He exhorted his readers to "beware of treating it as an enemy!"[78] Only by working with purely sociological methods will the student of society come to recognize the one dominant reality that disfigures contemporary life: the corrosive effect of modern individualism on social cohesion.

Suicide is the supreme insult to that irreplaceable solidarity. It is offered when society is inadequately represented in individuals, because it curbs them excessively, does not curb them enough, or curbs them in destructive ways. All these failures betray a disharmony between social regulations and the needs of society's members.[79]

Not even the most devoted readers of Durkheim's brilliant and controversial treatise on suicide deny that his analysis leaves important questions about self-destruction unresolved, notably the relation of psychological springs of action to the social forces that close in on every individual. What matters here is the place of Durkheim's work in our historical understanding of aggression in the nineteenth century. With iron consistency, Durkheim adopted the Enlightenment's conviction that knowledge is the supreme clue to action, is in fact itself a form of action. Marx once notoriously accused philosophers of merely wanting to understand the world when the point was to change it. Durkheim was not the traditional philosopher Marx was deriding. However inconclusive his answers, he redefined more effectively than anyone else in the Victorian age the nature and the limits of pathology. And working to discover the right kind and amount of repression in the service of social health, he redefined aggression.

✾ THREE ✾

Demagogues and Democrats

I. Redefinitions

It should be plain by now that the Victorian age was an age of redefinitions. Competition was secularized; race, dramatized; manliness, democratized. Sins became crimes; crimes, diseases; diseases, social problems. Probably the most spectacular beneficiary of this radical rethinking was politics. The competition for place and power, once the jealously guarded preserve of rival aristocratic factions, was turned first into an aspiration, then into a serious claim, of middle-class burghers—provided they were male. These developments raised important questions about the very nature of aggression, its proper boundaries, and the numbers (and requisite qualities) of the players entitled to participate in political activity.

Politics is a deadly serious contest played by rules differing from society to society, but ranking, whatever form they take, among the supreme fictions governing modern public life. At its best, it is an exemplar of aggression channeled in the service of rational self-interest or realistic public ideals. The aggressive drive, we know, is not synonymous with hostility. Suitably sublimated it may, and in politics often does, fuel pacific self-assertion, eschewing the tempting pleasures of destructive impulses. A pogrom may serve politicians, but it is not politics. And as a pivotal human experience, part self-promotion and mass entertainment, part economic calculation and authentic statesmanship, politics is thoroughly modern.

This is not to say that the nineteenth century invented the game; its remote origins go back beyond recorded history. In one of his early papers, Freud quotes an unnamed English author to the effect that the man who first flung an epithet at his enemy instead of a spear was the true founder of civilization.* He would have been quite as justified to call that distant culture hero the true founder of politics. But its growth was slow. True, partisan pronouncements by propagandists and tactical maneuvers by officeholders are an old story. They feature in the class struggles tearing apart ancient Rome, the combat for authority pitting medieval emperors against the papacy, the assertion of Parliament's rights against the Stuart monarchy in early seventeenth-century England. Shakespeare's history plays form one long exhibition of such combats. But all these resembled warfare far more than the nonviolent duel that is politics: they were fought out, and were more or less expected to be fought out, amid slaughter. A few seventeenth- and eighteenth-century states, most impressively England, saw the emergence of a political culture, but the most prominent ingredients of politics—a legitimate opposition to the holders of power, effective freedom of the press and of association, a widespread right to participate in free elections—were offspring of the French Revolution and of industrialization. For politics requires a fairly sophisticated technology of communication and transportation, a high level of literacy, and the rather genial expectation of an inborn capacity for responsible conduct. With all its envenomed controversies, all the determined efforts to manipulate or frustrate the expression of dissent, the Victorian age was the political age incarnate.

It was aware of its advantages. Early in the nineteenth century, in 1819, Benjamin Constant spoke out against the common idealization of ancient politics. Born in Lausanne and educated in England and France, he was on his way to making himself France's most intelligent, if at times erratic, liberal political theorist and politician. In an astute lecture, he contrasted ancient with modern views of liberty, and invited his audience to free itself of ancestor worship. Among the Greeks, the individual might be sovereign in public matters, deciding freely on peace and war, but as a private person he was virtually a slave, constrained, watched, controlled in all his movements. Even Athens, a republic freer than any other Greek commonwealth, had resorted to ostracism, that most pernicious and arbitrary of practices. All ancient society had been cruel, almost

---

*See Sigmund Freud, "On the Psychical Mechanism of Hysterical Phenomena" (1893), in *Standard Edition of the Complete Psychological Works,* tr. and ed. James Strachey et al. (24 vols. (1953–74), III, 36 (not included in *Gesammelte Werke*). For his part, the principled libertarian Herbert Spencer saw the origins of organized society not in the sublimation of aggressiveness, but in its exercise. "Be it or be it not true that Man is shapen in iniquity and conceived in sin," he wrote in 1884, "it is unquestionably true that Government is begotten of aggression and by aggression." *The Man versus the State* (1884), 44.

invariably at war, with repressive institutions to match. The vaunted freedom of
the ancient Greek had amounted to his right "to interrogate, remove from
office, condemn, plunder, exile, kill his magistrates and his superiors."[1] Thus
the politics of antiquity had been far more an acting out than a sublimation of
aggression. Constant's point was well taken. Alliances of ambitious men, primitive versions of political parties, had struggled for supremacy in ancient Athens;
but as the notorious condemnation of Socrates shows, their struggles were
bound to end in unpolitical resolutions. And so were later efforts, for centuries.
Blood remained their argument.

That argument rested on the hoary but long-credited contention that constituted authority alone understands, and alone acts to realize, the true needs of a
society. Almost by definition, kings—or, in republics, magistrates—serve their
state; factions only serve themselves. Hence, down to the eighteenth century—
and into the nineteenth—opposition implied intrigues, conspiracies, even the
threat of insurrection. As long as the ancient principle "The ruler can do no
wrong" went unchallenged, the situation could hardly be otherwise. What
solid grounds could loyal subjects ever have for discontent? The question cast
dissent in the lurid light of selfishness or treason. Merchants might humbly
petition for relief from financial burdens, divines handy with the pen might take
the risk of publishing pamphlets urging the state to change its course, but these
tame complaints apart, aggression in the public arena had to remain the monopoly of those in power.

This fiction of infallibility was necessarily supplemented by the fiction of evil
advisers—a classic instance of a defensive stratagem that makes unacceptable
hostile feelings acceptable by displacing them onto less awe-inspiring targets. A
ruler hedged with divinity soared far above fallible humanity in anointed perfection. But he could be victimized by conniving ministers, or misinformed
through wicked designs. Then, his reason obscured, he might allow corrupt
courtiers to sway his judgment. One consequence of this convenient psychological fiction was that in the infighting that marked virtually every regime,
absolute or constitutional, before the French Revolution, political rivals treated
one another as enemies deserving punishment rather than as honorable public
servants advocating misguided policies. Hence the behavior of a figure like
Richelieu toward his less fortunate rivals: after he rose to power in the 1620s as
Louis XIII's chief minister, he had his opponents exiled or executed, thus
exercising a cruelty which, he coolly thought, was kinder than the misplaced
clemency that permits the scourge of disorder to invade the body politic. Richelieu cultivated his hatred with a vengeance, but in an accepted style.

Before the rise of modern politics, the public—and not the illiterate, undisciplined mob alone—would vent its rage without pity on ministers who had been

discredited, or simply defeated. Lapses in leadership, or just the loss of royal favor, frequently entailed the end not merely of a career but of a life. In the seventeenth century and after, states could correct failure only with the most extreme vindictiveness, allowing, even encouraging, victors to visit their rage freely upon the defeated. In the early 1640s, eager to strike at King Charles I, the Long Parliament condemned by bills of attainder his two principal advisers, the earl of Strafford and William Laud, archbishop of Canterbury, both responsible for unpopular policies, and sent them to the scaffold. The peaceful democracies that flexed their muscles during the Victorian decades started their pacific careers in blood and defiance.

Early in the eighteenth century, the familiar habit of dividing the world of power into heroes and villains began to wane, slowly. In Britain, fallen ministers were still proscribed and often sought safety in exile. But bribery, or the sheer passage of time, could restore their civil rights. In France, a minister dismissed was still a minister "disgraced," but this normally meant no more than condemnation to the boredom of his provincial estates and his family's company. Still, the century offered vivid reminders that the old need for gratifying vengeful passions had not yet wholly given way. In 1719, shortly after the death of King Charles XII of Sweden, Baron Görtz, his immensely influential and generally detested principal adviser, was tried by a kangaroo court intent on convicting him, and unceremoniously decapitated; R. N. Bain, the late-Victorian historian of Sweden, while granting that Görtz had been unscrupulous and arrogant, called his execution "certainly a judicial murder."[2] That sort of thing, he implied, was no longer necessary in his own age, the enlightened nineteenth century. He was right. By Bain's time inconvenient politicians were neither executed nor exiled; in Britain, they might be got out of the way by elevation to the House of Lords. Though drenched in pugnacious rhetoric, politics developed institutions permitting contenders for power to engage in a duel that all would survive and most, sooner or later, might turn to their profit.

Bourgeois avidly watched, and often actively worked for, this great redefinition of legitimate public aggression—not, as will emerge, without bruising conflicts. In the United Provinces and in the free cities dotting the Holy Roman Empire, burgher patricians and oligarchs had for some centuries exercised power or seriously contested aristocratic and clerical supremacy. And in parliamentary systems like Britain's, leading bourgeois, especially after they had left sordid commerce behind for the ranks of the landed gentry, had long enjoyed the status of political actors. But bourgeois demands for political rights grew more general and more clamorous after the French Revolution. Pierre Paul Royer-Collard, a middle-of-the-road liberal philosopher and politician, spoke not merely for early-nineteenth-century French bourgeois but for their fellows elsewhere when he asserted that "all interests can find their natural representation" in the middle class; the upper classes "need to dominate," while the lower orders are unfitted for public life through "ignorance, habit, and want of independence."[3] Metternich's system repressed such claims after 1815, but at the same time only intensified the bourgeois appetite for politics.

Observers were well aware that this was a class appetite. Small contingents of well-read travelers recorded the fine social distinctions then governing political aggression; Alexis de Tocqueville was not alone in seeing his civilization gripped by a "great revolution," a revolution that assured "the prevalence of the bourgeois classes and the industrial element over the aristocratic classes and landed property." To visitors, the United States, that young giant, seemed to incarnate the great revolution, the democratic consummation toward which European societies were traveling too, though more reluctantly. Writing a friend from upstate New York in June 1831, Tocqueville insisted that the "democratic tendency" he was studying was irresistible everywhere. The United States was doubtless in the vanguard, but other countries, including his own France, were fated to move "toward a democracy without limits."[4]

Reflecting on recent history, the progressive German historian and literary critic Georg Gottfried Gervinus echoed this judgment: "The movements of this century are supported by the instincts of the masses" now beginning to "take the lead in politics." In contrast to Tocqueville, he was not disposed to worry over this development, and his assessment is a measure of just how far the more venturesome among bourgeois intellectuals had come by mid-century: "Individualism and self-reliance have become too strong in man, not to loosen the existing political notions and institutions, not to dissolve exclusive corporations and all that assumes the character of a state in the state, and not to level all differences of caste and class." Later, in 1869, the German historian and liberal nationalist politician Heinrich von Sybel confirmed what was by then a commonplace. "In our old Europe," he wrote a friend, "the march of time progresses irresistibly in democratic paths. It is not to be stopped, and which human who considers his fellow humans capable of perfection would want to stand in the way of its direction?"[5]

The clamor for democracy necessarily remained highly differentiated. Its vehemence, its realism, and its program varied with distinct cultural styles and political opportunities. Observers thought they could measure these differences by comparing the diverse fortunes of the bourgeoisie. The United States was endowed with a substantial and powerful middle class of professional men, merchants, and rentiers, but the masses—this much struck the studious tourists who crossed the ocean—had moved beyond patrician control to popular politics. In contrast, France seemed wholly at the mercy of its bourgeoisie. "In

1830," after the revolution had brought the Orleanist Louis Philippe to the throne, Tocqueville noted in his memoirs, "the triumph of the middle class had been definitive and so complete that all political power, all prerogatives, the whole government found themselves enclosed and as it were huddled up within the narrow limits of that single class."[6]

By contrast, the British middle classes, though anything but timid, allowed the nobility to maintain most of its time-honored prerogatives. And the *Bürgertum* in the German states appeared relatively undemanding in the political sphere or, when demanding, unsuccessful. The bourgeoisie's road to power was anything but straight and never easy. Germany managed to delay the accession of the *Bürgertum* until well into the twentieth century, while Britain astonished the world with the spectacular resilience of its aristocrats. In 1845, the young Friedrich Engels had thought that "the ruling class is, in England, as in all other civilized countries, the bourgeoisie." But half a century later he amended this crude generalization, wondering at the "meekness" with which the "wealthy middle class" had left "the landed aristocracy in almost exclusive possession of all the leading government offices."[7] The history of nineteenth-century middle-class claims to political self-assertion, then, registers delays and defeats; but it registers, too, the infiltration of middle-class politicians, or at least middle-class interests, into places of power.

For the middle classes, the prospect of power was more enticing than the prospect of democracy. Their ambivalence about the looming triumph of popular politics, the supreme issue of the age, was perfectly understandable; it presented them with dangers no less than opportunities. Which of these would prevail, whether it was rational for a bourgeois to join the democrats or to oppose them, was not always apparent. The decision depended on his judgment, his political convictions, to say nothing of his position in the middling orders. The term "bourgeois," after all, covers a wide terrain; what was in the interest of a banker or a rentier might not be in the interest of a small merchant or a professional man.* Nor did observers find it easy to conjecture just what form the democracy of the future would assume. Tocqueville, for one, would not commit himself to a prediction whether the political avalanche of his time would prove a supreme good or a supreme evil. "The clearest fact," he wrote his brother late in 1831, "is that we are living in a time of transition, but whether we are going toward liberty or marching toward despotism, God alone knows precisely."[8] He was right to be cautious, for it would turn out that the outcome was rarely clear-cut. The age would see the rise of the new Caesars—

---

*For further details about the composition and role of the nineteenth-century bourgeoisie, see Peter Gay, *The Bourgeois Experience*, vol. I, *Education of the Senses* (1984), 21–35.

political leaders at times in league with bourgeois, more often with their adversaries—who would impose despotism in the name of liberty.

Few in the nineteenth century doubted that politics was laden with risk, yet most thought it the road to grand solutions that might change men's lives for the better. "Vain hope," Thomas Carlyle jotted in his journal in October 1831, "to make mankind happy by politics!" But in his disenchantment with political action, to him just another instance of the "mechanical temper" he despised, he was speaking for a minority.[9] And so, the middling orders, whether reading about politics in their newspapers, promoting it in clubs, or practicing it by seeking office, faced the advent of democracy, that supreme end toward which the redefinition of public aggression was steering, with a complex mixture of delight and outrage, hope and anxiety.

2. The Long Birth of Political Culture

Legitimate opposition had existed in European politics for more than a century before the term entered common usage. Addressing the House of Commons in 1826, the radical Whig Sir John Cam Hobhouse amused his colleagues by lightheartedly coining the phrase "His Majesty's Opposition." It secured wide circulation, and once its significance as a terse statement of a fundamental political idea was appreciated, its origin as a joke was forgotten.[1] Early in 1845, Disraeli could praise to the House of Commons the "wholesome" and "salutary check of a constitutional Opposition." He complained not that the opposition was factious, but, on the contrary, that conditions for its healthy working were not propitious enough. Again, after a fierce debate in November 1852, Lord Palmerston reminded the House of Commons that theirs was an assembly of gentlemen and that "we who are Gentlemen on this side of the House should remember that we are dealing with Gentlemen on the other side."[2] The principle of politics as aggression sublimated is exemplified in Palmerston's generous observation.

The process that Disraeli and his fellow member of Parliament thought uncontroversial for countries boasting free institutions differed in kind, then, from the clashing of cabals that had dominated the public scene for centuries: crown princes eager to mount the throne plotting against their anointed fathers, militant nobles with armed retainers asserting their rights, authentic or spurious, to supremacy against their prince, a favorite minister clamoring for his ruler's ear in savage rivalry with other favorites. These duels were more or less naked struggles for power or (which was much the same thing) for influence over the powerful; they followed no securely instituted rules that would ensure an untroubled transition in an office or an untroubled change of course.

Even if holders of power could not prove that their critics had committed treason, they could charge them with fomenting faction. In the early eighteenth century, when the foundations of modern politics were laid down, denouncing faction became a fashionable way of smearing one's antagonists. Viscount Bolingbroke, intent on discrediting the English Whig oligarchy then in power, proposed the self-serving remedy of a fatherly patriot king floating above factions—a party to end parties.[3] Bolingbroke's political fantasies matter because they enjoyed considerable vogue among the makers of the United States Constitution; in the *Federalist* papers, James Madison and Alexander Hamilton displayed vocal distaste for faction, a vice or disease which, they thought, is almost bound to destroy liberty.[4] For the Founding Fathers, the vigorous dissension of parties raised the specter of chaos.

Though a brilliant exercise in political advocacy, on this point *The Federalist* looked to the past, not forward to the nineteenth century. But some of its authors' contemporaries were slowly making party respectable. David Hume, though still lamenting the passions that factions generate, had welcomed the gradual reduction in the temperature of political rhetoric in Britain and acknowledged that parties, if in fundamental accord, might prove necessary in a parliamentary regime.[5] Edmund Burke completed the revolution in political perception that Hume had started. Admittedly a partisan and active player in ongoing disputes, he rose above current cant to larger realities. Trying to lift the old curse on faction, he famously defined a party as "a body of men united, for promoting by their joint endeavors the national interest, upon some particular principle." Partisanship, he admitted, could degenerate into narrowness and bigotry, but at best, a party, though disposed to push its own advantage, would do so without resorting to proscriptions.[6] No proscriptions: this was the crucial point. For Burke the political process was a pacific contest among groups equally committed to the general welfare.* These are almost Victorian accents.

---

*This was the ideal; the reality was often more squalid. The history of the eighteenth-century antecedents of nineteenth-century politics attests that, much like other cultural phenomena, the very institution designed to cultivate hatred by refining it could actually support its escalation. The political process handed enraged combatants ready targets for the exercise of hostile passions. Parliamentary elections in Hanoverian Britain and the American colonies repeatedly deteriorated into little more than cynical, drink-sodden exercises in open bribery, no less open influence peddling, or brazen harassment. Influence, money, alcohol, the heady momentary social alliance between upper-class candidates and lower-class public, voters and nonvoters alike, could provide grounds for support more solid than a candidate's stand on matters of policy, or even his character. Until well into the Victorian years, and not always even then, temperate and honest political conduct was an aspiration far more than a fact.

The recipe for sublimating aggression into debates and elections was tried out first in the British Parliament and in the Congress of the recently founded United States. Yet, paradoxically enough, the French Revolution, certainly no stranger to proscriptions, played an epoch-making, if profoundly ambiguous, role in the invention of modern politics. This is a book about the nineteenth century, but the history of that century, especially its political history, is incomprehensible without a sustained glance at that eighteenth-century upheaval the French Revolution. Several generations of Victorian statesmen and poets and social reformers attested to its reverberations, mainly with anxiety. "The answer to every democratic suggestion," wrote Henry Adams about the United States in the age of Jefferson, "ran in a set phrase, 'Look at France!' "[7] This held true for Europe quite as much. In 1848, when Marx and Engels asserted in their *Communist Manifesto,* that a specter was haunting Europe, they meant the restive proletariat. They would have been more telling if they had recognized that specter as the shadow of the French Revolution. The political and cultural history of the long nineteenth century begins not with Victoria, or even Napoleon, but with Mirabeau and Robespierre.

The Old Regime in France had developed a rudimentary political culture, nourished on provincial academies, reading circles, subversive literature, a professional tribe of lawyers, all spreading a brooding aura of serious discussion. Yet French politics was limited to verbal civil war among the privileged, punctuated by food riots, as defensive nobles and assertive royal officials competed for power. The Revolution put the ordinary citizen on the political stage, or, more precisely, allowed (often compelled) the ordinary man to see himself as a political actor. In rough and ready ways, the accelerating tempo of memorable days—revolutionary *journées*—amounted to a liberation of untested political energies, an unprecedented political education.

The struggles between successive revolutionary assemblies and the royal government, and the internecine quarrels among revolutionaries, underscored the unexpected strength of that vague, increasingly active force known as public opinion. Assembly delegates and royal ministers alike discovered the charms of popularity and cultivated it, further enlarging the circle of public involvement. Other lessons in politics, even more instructive, followed from the vacillating resistance of the Crown to the imposition of popular sovereignty, the highly publicized opposition to the Revolution by foreign governments, and, later, the forging of an effective fighting force with the draft of thousands of young Frenchmen.

Admittedly, the education was chaotic at best. Frenchmen found themselves called upon virtually every day to make hard decisions about new threats and new possibilities—decisions about how to respond to decrees, what policy to support, which politician to proscribe, whom to hate most. Torrents of pamphlets and broadsides, more than the most diligent could read, let alone digest, swept the country, all asserting the general public's right to a measure of public aggression. This propaganda swamped political newspapers, political clubs, and political demonstrations, and, with its conflicting recipes, proved more confusing than enlightening. Here was what Tocqueville would call, provocatively, a new religion, the religion of politics.

Certainly the rhetoric of revolution, dramatized in secular emblems and meticulously managed festivals, placed politics at the heart of things. Late in August 1789, the Declaration of the Rights of Man adopted by the National Assembly issued a formal invitation to politics to those who had never received one before. It included among the "natural, inalienable, and sacred rights of man" the right of all "to concur personally, or through their representatives," in the making of the laws. All must be "admissible to all public offices, positions, and employments, according to their capacity, and without other distinction than that of virtue and talents."[8] Even if this left the precise shape of the political public in doubt, it was seductive talk.

Equally seductive was the indictment of Louis XVI, which made "the French people" the king's accuser, charging him with treason against "the French people." So was the proclamation the Convention issued "to the French people" on January 23, 1793, two days after his execution, which carefully deployed this rhetoric to underscore the share of all French citizens in the act of regicide—beneficiaries all, accomplices all.* Even after St. Paul's doctrine that the powers that be are ordained of God had lost much of its luster, even after revolutionaries were exhorted not to feel apologetic about subverting venerable authority, many recognized that *this* sort of aggression was an awesome responsibility. Significantly, those supporting so radical a remedy for their country's ills rationalized it on the revolutionary ground that the people alone are truly sovereign. Hence the people alone are empowered to set aside whatever historical or religious claims the reigning dynasty may advance. Indeed, through all the vicissitudes of the Revolution, orators insisted on the right of French citizens to express their views freely and to have them reflected in official policy. In April 1793, Robespierre proposed a new declaration of rights guaranteeing

---

*The regicides proceeded neither casually nor frivolously. No doubt they found it easier to kill a king than had those who ordered the execution of England's Charles I in 1649. But like the earlier execution, the later one, imposed on a fearfully divided country, brought into play all the apologetic machinery, all the forensic ingenuity, that the parricides could muster. Like Charles I, Louis XVI lost his head after a ponderous public trial marked by wrangling over the very competence of the tribunal appointed to try the sovereign; like the execution of Charles I, that of Louis XVI was witnessed by crowds moved to frivolity, or tears, by the enormity of the spectacle.

peaceable assembly and a free press.[9] The Old Regime at its most benign had never sounded like this.

Incessant talk about the New Man, political man, was cant but more than cant.* The visual proofs that politics now belonged to everyone were ubiquitous; the execution of the king of France had been anticipated, and was followed, by strenuous efforts to find emotionally satisfying substitutes for paternal authority. Marianne, Everywoman, flaunting or wearing the Phrygian liberty cap, became the badge of the new France, a political France.[10] And, as the new figures in the seats of power attested, the democratization this majestic commoner embodied was more than symbolic. The nobles, who had virtually monopolized the leading positions before the Revolution, almost disappeared from the scene. Local government was metamorphosed as ennobled judges and aristocrats of ancient lineage gave way to educated commoners, to attorneys and prosperous merchants; later, as revolutionary events kept circulating new elites, it was the turn of humbler middle-class citizens. To be sure, numerous bourgeois became victims of the Revolution. Some financiers went to the guillotine; some professional men were seriously inconvenienced by the abolition of corporations and universities that had once guaranteed them a corner on their lucrative trade. Nevertheless, while the Revolution was no bourgeois conspiracy, by and large those who replaced noblemen in managing public affairs were bourgeois notables.

Yet on the great matter of politics, the Revolution sent grossly inconsistent signals. The supreme agent of political education, it also drastically subverted that education. Contradictions between liberal bills of rights and oppressive practices, between humane professions and savage actions, were so blatant that all but the most infatuated partisans were deeply troubled. The story of Europe's disillusionment with events in France, events at first so thrilling, needs no retelling; Kant's unswerving support of the Revolution in all its incarnations was exceptional.†

In 1789, many foreigners, especially in England, had sounded precisely like

---

*The New Woman did not fare so well: the Jacobins in particular were vehemently opposed to women in public life; despite the protests of brave, isolated feminists like Condorcet and Olympe de Gouges, they ordered all women's organizations dissolved, and eventually sent de Gouges to the guillotine.

†In faraway Königsberg, aging but alert, Kant found events in France through all the turbulent decade appealing enough to merit praise. The revolutionaries, he thought, were correctly regarding citizens humanely, not as means but as ends. Not even the atrocities of the Terror could shake his Jacobinism. All the horrors the French had undergone, he told a colleague, were as nothing compared to what they had suffered in the Old Regime: "The Jacobins probably did right in all their actions." Jacques Droz, *L'Allemagne et la Révolution française* (1949), 158.

Kant. They shared Wordsworth's feeling that it was bliss in that dawn to be alive. The spectacle of a neighboring country throwing off absolute monarchy, breaking with superstition, declaring its devotion to freedom—in short, striving to become more English—was of absorbing interest, moving and grandiose. France, as Burke noted in November 1789, was presenting the world with an "astonishing scene." But sanguinary incidents like the "second" revolution of August 10, 1792, which effectively checkmated the royal power, the massacres of prisoners in Paris a month later, and, even more, the execution of Louis XVI, converted sympathizers into opponents of the new "oppressor."[11]

The revolutionaries gave their disenchanted supporters good grounds for dismay; their transgressions against the political ideals they had so proudly broadcast—had in fact called into being—were fundamental. Having solicited the general citizenry to enter the arena of politics, they violated its one indispensable ground rule by treating opponents as enemies, dissenters as traitors. The same factious politicians who had promised to broaden the right to aggression now monopolized it. In the hypertrophy of politics that marked the Revolution throughout, zealots enlisted daily life in the service of civic education. Every detail of apparel and manners became telling testimony that distinguished the good citizen from the wicked counterrevolutionary—what newspaper one read, what clothes one wore, what name one adopted, what plays one applauded.*

If being out of step even in matters of taste was a token of political perfidy, failure became a symptom not of bad luck or sheer incompetence, but of treachery. There were so many ways of betraying the Revolution, whether one unfairly distributed food rations, clumsily dismantled badges of royalty on public buildings, ineptly fought military campaigns. The Other was a hoarder of grain, an "aristocrat," a conspirator secretly serving the pope or the counterrevolutionary exiles. One of Benjamin Constant's most provocative contributions to nineteenth-century liberal thought was the perception that freedom for politics must include freedom from politics; he saw that a free citizen requires a protected domain of privacy into which the state, or the mob, has no right to intrude.

The self-appointed guardians of political virtue elevated denunciation into a patriotic duty. From 1789 on, the unbalanced Jacobin Jean Paul Marat consistently advocated the most drastic remedies against the "sacrilegious cabal" pant-

---

*When in the fall of 1793 the Comédie Française put on an adaptation of a Goldoni drama that stern republicans found excessively aristocratic and hence disloyal, the Jacobin journal *Feuille du salut publique* denounced the audience for its "truly monarchial luxury." Emmet Kennedy, *A Cultural History of the French Revolution* (1989), 179.

ing to destroy the work of the Revolution. But presumably more rational Girondin leaders were no more moderate. And Robespierre, too, though in the beginning more prudent, used "faction" as a term of abuse with abandon, excluding the Other from the circle of reasonable and decent citizens.[12] Obviously one man's patriotism was another man's factionalism. The charges a politician leveled against his rivals could be thrown back against him, and often were. Almost anything could become grounds for suspicion, arrest, and perhaps the guillotine: advocating price controls or their abolition, thundering against the excessive power of Paris over France or defending it, voting to exile Louis XVI or to execute him. Hence the stability that a true political environment envisions and supports was unavailable to the revolutionaries. "The Enemies of those who now reign," Gouverneur Morris observed in late 1792, "treat them as they did their Predecessors, and as their Successors will be treated."[13] The Revolution was eating not only its children, but its fathers as well.

Not all revolutionary bloodshed was barbarism unleashed or pure paranoia. The assemblies and committees that governed France from 1789 on were under mounting pressure from mobilized Parisians who were learning how to lend their political wishes proper weight. Nearly all the memorable *journées* of the Revolution obeyed the logic of street politics. "It seems probable that those who possess Paris will dictate to the others," Gouverneur Morris wrote.[14] The pressures that local mobs brought to bear were partly caused, certainly exacerbated, by intractable economic and military problems: from the spring of 1792 on, France was at war with most of Europe and faced armed resistance to its enactments and exactions at home; in the effort to make everything new, the government had disrupted markets and destroyed traditional bodies that had long provided education, charity, and justice. Nor did France's new leaders have enough time, or enough ingenuity, to fill the vacuums they had made. Anxious improvisation, coupled with inexperience and attacks of panic at bad news from the domestic and foreign fronts, nurtured a militant stance of massive, often convenient outrage in which extreme measures were not the last resort, but the first. It is not without significance that most of those guillotined during the Terror were sentenced to death in combat zones—in the northeast, where allied troops were trying to fight their way through to Paris, and in the Vendée, the center of counterrevolution.

Still, not all of the victims were caught in the turmoil of military action; the deadly habit of equating mistakes or disagreement with capital transgressions took its toll. In this poisonous climate, the political ideal of recognizing the opposition as human could hardly be expected to flourish. Nor did it quickly recover after that summer's day of 1794 when Robespierre and his allies were eliminated by the very method they had employed against their adversaries—

the guillotine. Terror did not cease; red terror was succeeded, often outdone, by white terror. And for all its intermittent successes, the floundering Directory that labored to rule France from 1795 on veered between corrupt compromise, cynical manipulation, and harsh repression. Hence many Frenchmen found satisfaction in that historic day of November 1799—18 Brumaire—when Napoleon Bonaparte seized power. Many distrusted the ambitious general, and hoped he would merely serve as a transitional figure. But he had warm partisans to cheer him. "He appeared like a savior," the philosopher and liberal politician Charles de Rémusat recalled in 1818.[15]

To be sure, the token resistance to Bonaparte's coup d'état by the French political public, so active and so volatile during the revolutionary years, was no gauge of his true popularity. The repressive measures favored by the government he dislodged had smothered virtually all resistance, and the excesses of the revolutionary decade, coupled with the unexampled intrusion of politics into daily life, had generated a hankering for stability. Still, Bonaparte, triumphant, self-crowned, the deliverer who cleverly exploited public weariness, was too shrewd to rely on the emotion of relief alone. He knew that the gift of adulation, easily granted, could be as easily withdrawn. So after seizing power, he took no chances. Henceforth, he proclaimed, the only political activity permissible was the activity he could sponsor or control; the only public voice that really counted would be his own. To secure his rule against all challenge, Bonaparte stifled political expression instead of cultivating it. During his decade and a half at the summit of French affairs, he utilized and invented an imaginative repertory of tactics: concessions, diplomacy, cajolery, censorship, bribery, repression, and murder. On the rare occasions when Napoleon mentioned political opposition, he denounced it. All it did, he told his brothers, was to "discredit the authorities in the eyes of the people." As for himself, he refused "to be a man of party."[16]

Napoleon Bonaparte's reign was, of course, more than a collection of political—or, rather, antipolitical—techniques. It left its indelible imprint on France, to say nothing of the rest of Europe. He gave the French Revolution permanence by superintending the drafting of a new civil code, though in domestic law he retreated from it. He improved the status of the Jews by decree. He strengthened administrative centralization. He propagated the rhetoric of careers open to talent. And he exported his ideas and his edicts to the countries his armies conquered, leaving a legend, and a legacy, that Europe's politicians would wrestle with for half a century. But from the perspective of the long birth of political culture, his reign was a fifteen-year interlude, a detour in the march of what Tocqueville would later call the democratic revolution. For the political impulse survived even Napoleon's radical surgery. Once awakened, the craving for political self-assertion, for a share in sovereignty, proved indestructible.

Indestructible, but tortuous and paradoxical. There is not space enough to recite all the milestones of early-nineteenth-century politics, but its vicissitudes in the countries boasting legal parties—notably the United States, Great Britain, and France—are of particular interest. The paradoxes of party politics were most conspicuous in the United States, where the tension between dogma and experience would be resolved, slowly and painfully, in favor of experience. Leading Americans were extremely hesitant to accept the idea that parties could represent irreconcilable but equally respectworthy views. The Founding Fathers were true eighteenth-century men in assuming that by and large each problem soliciting the statesman has only one good solution. Factious by nature, men are bound to debate alternatives, but their verbal confrontations should crystallize in a policy that all rational citizens can loyally support. The speeches and writings of George Washington, down to his Farewell Address, form an anthology of consistent anti-faction sentiments. As the country's first president, he visualized himself as above party and urged others to follow his example.

But while Washington sought to propel the political culture of his fellow Americans toward the ideal of unanimity, the realities of public life pushed them in the opposite direction. As politicians in the newly founded republic struggled to mold domestic and foreign policies, quarreling over the divisive issues of finance, federal powers, and attitudes toward revolutionary France, they kept applying the psychological strategy of splitting: I am a staunch patriot, you are a factious politician. With unabated zest, Hamiltonian Federalists denounced Jeffersonian Republicans as seditious agents of France, and the Republican minority retaliated with equally choice compliments. The demagogic Alien and Sedition Acts, passed in 1798 during the presidency of John Adams, suggest that political hostilities had risen to collective paranoia. Arbitrary, draconian, and blatantly partisan, they authorized drastic action against suspect foreigners and the Americans consorting with them. More, they opened the way to the prosecution of writers, publishers, and ordinary citizens for broadcasting (or even holding) sentiments that did not tally with the Federalists' notions of loyal carriage.

The United States was not France. No alien was deported under the acts, and though a handful of printers and publishers—all of them Jeffersonians—were arrested and convicted, Republican newspapers carried on their factious campaigns almost unobstructed; in 1800, they helped to secure Jefferson's election to the presidency. It could hardly be otherwise: the American political public, though still besieged with resounding calls for the purge of all traitors, had been forged in a school that knew no Bastilles and no Terror. In 1791, after the addition of the Bill of Rights to the Constitution repaired what had been a glaring oversight and cleared a path for the free exchange of ideas, virtually all the skeptics had fallen into line. In this climate, no matter how sincerely American politicians—including Jefferson—deplored the malady of faction, the emergence of modern political parties was only a matter of time.*

Their growth was accompanied by critics sniping at them from lofty positions recalling eighteenth-century views. In 1838, in the midst of the Jacksonian period, the popular writer of frontier novels and part-time political theorist James Fenimore Cooper, an emphatic political libertarian, was still lamenting the very existence of parties and their undeserved good repute. Political parties, far from being essential to liberty, were instruments of error that led to "vicious, corrupt and unprofitable legislation," and propelled corrupt and incompetent men into power.[17] The longing for the days of the Founding Fathers, when presidents were—or at least tried to be—above party, was showing astonishing resiliency. Despite this uneasiness, by the time Cooper voiced his heartfelt denunciations, political parties were accepted actors on the American political stage. Not unexpectedly: the soil had been in preparation since the founding days. When William James wrote a friend some sixty years later, "The only serious permanent force of corruption in America is party spirit," he was fighting a hopeless rearguard action.[18]

The British insertion of opposition into the political process was, characteristically, more chaotic. Britain, it seems, acquired the two-party system in a fit of absence of mind. Politicians continued to throw about the old names "Whig" and "Tory"; the epithets could assume any coloration a speaker chose to give them. In any event, the divisions were no longer fatal; faction was no longer a danger. Party cohesion, party organization, party responsibility were still in the future. But Britain was ready for them even before the Reform Act of 1832.

---

*"The structural features of American society," Richard Hofstadter has written, "were exceptionally favorable to a moderate course of political development. Property was widely diffused. The political public was a large one, resting in part upon this propertied base and in part upon a generous suffrage." What is more, it was "a literate public, and a large portion of it was accustomed to taking part in political life. It was proud of its rights, alert to violations of them, and suspicious of authority." While the rhetoric dividing citizens over the proposed constitution had been "couched in high and inflammatory tones," the urge toward conciliation and compromise once the document had been adopted proved irresistible. *The Idea of a Party System: The Rise of Legitimate Opposition in the United States, 1780–1840* (1969), 75–76, 77, 79.

In Britain and in the United States freedom slowly broadened, from precedent to precedent. France underwent a far more mercurial political history. The country was compelled to work through the trauma of the Revolution and the countertrauma of Napoleon; the claims for the right to political self-assertion that the first had earnestly planted, the second had tried to uproot. Benjamin Constant, writing while Napoleon was at the summit of his power, pithily analyzed the devastating consequences of his regime for French political life: "When a free country enjoys neither freedom of the press nor political rights, the people will wholly detach itself from public issues. All communication between those who govern and those who are governed is broken." To be sure, "the authorities and its partisans can regard this as an advantage. The government encounters no obstacles. Nothing contradicts it." But the results! "It acts freely—but it alone is alive and the nation is dead."[19] One historic if largely unintended effect of the Restoration that followed Napoleon's fall was a revival of the nation's political impulse.

It was, though, a revival within the narrowest limits. Louis XVIII, brother to the martyred Louis XVI, set in Napoleon's place on the French throne by the victorious allies, proved far more intent on managing the French public than on developing its political culture. "The application of ideas of equity, moderation, even of humanity to politics"—thus Rémusat characterized the Restoration—"was still, so to speak, in its infancy."[20] The monarchy that the Charter of 1814 established was an ill-assorted amalgam of nostalgia and realism, with nostalgia increasingly dominant, especially after 1824, when the king's pious and intransigent younger brother mounted the throne as Charles X. Resistance to popular politics, let alone popular sovereignty, came naturally to this king, who was not much more awake to the facts of modern life than the rest of his tribe. But the six-year reign of Charles X definitively proved how futile it was to try bringing back the eighteenth century. For all its relative calm and financial stability, the very passion for control in the Restoration attests to a deep-seated anxiety over instability and to the primitive level of its political self-awareness.

Control meant imposing stiff property qualifications that trimmed the voting public down to tax-paying, affluent, mainly landowning Frenchmen, and an intricate system of indirect elections that tightened the hold of property and prominence more securely still. This electoral strategy gave some 72,000 Frenchmen the vote and entitled a select handful of 16,000 "reliable" subjects to compete for seats in the Chamber of Deputies. Nor was the regime prepared to give a voice to the young: voters had to be at least thirty years old and deputies at least forty. Control meant, further, that the king's servants really were his servants, responsible to him alone. And control meant, finally, an owlish watch over the press by censors and the police, armed with stringent libel laws designed to prevent newspapers and periodicals from dropping into bad habits of carping, let alone real opposition. Playing on fatigue with politics and fostering self-interest was a surefire recipe for reducing the tensions of political life to a safe minimum.*

But a soporific is not a poison. Constricted as the circle of the political public remained, alert as the king's servants were to their task of seducing or intimidating the electorate, the heavily compromised freedom of thought and action that characterized the Restoration still provided some surprises. The elections of August 1815 returned a majority of nostalgic Ultraroyalists to the Chamber of Deputies, reactionaries on whom not even a solid Bourbon like Louis XVIII could count. In the chamber itself, the deputies—Ultras, loyalists, liberals, a few Bonapartists—grouped themselves into distinctive clusters which, though still unorganized and far from coherent, resembled parties in the making.

Rather hesitantly, then, the political education of Frenchmen resumed. "France has entered upon the course of liberty," exclaimed François Guizot, journalist, historian, statesman, then at the beginning of his political career, in a pamphlet of 1821 defending the right to opposition in France. "One can delay its progress, one will not check its thought." The legacy the restored Bourbons must learn to live with is the "victory of the Revolution" over the old regime.[21] Guizot was no democrat. He called for the unshackling of political life yet warmly endorsed the constitutional order; legitimizing an opposition did not imply unregulated license for free expression.

Guizot spoke for others who had accepted the Revolution. But not for them all; drawing divergent lessons from their political experiences, the liberals under the Restoration were far from unanimous in their opinions and tentative in their alliances. While Guizot wanted to protect the state from vilification by the extreme left and, even more, by unreconciled Ultraroyalists, Benjamin Constant employed his prolific pen to promote the apparently paradoxical view that an unshackled press is the most effective way to public peace. At the same time, in true eighteenth-century style, he deplored the "spirit of party," which, he feared, exalted passion at the expense of reason. Much like Constant, Charles de Rémusat, looking back on the interminable debates over freedom of the press, declared that issue the great question of the age, and, less troubled about fac-

*In August 1819, Count Gustaf Löwenhielm, the Swedish ambassador to France, tallied up the results: "No one talks politics," he wrote. Admittedly, "there are some agitators, but they are not very successful. Exhaustion and self-interest guarantee peace and quiet." Löwenhielm to Count Karl Otto Palmstierna, August 1819, Guillaume de Bertier de Sauvigny, *The Bourbon Restoration* (1955; tr. Lynn Case, 1966), 288.

tionalism, commended uninhibited political activity as the citizen's best safeguard.[22] And while the superb parliamentary orator Pierre Paul Royer-Collard,
with his moderate royalism, was more conservative than his allies, he acknowledged that democratic forces deserved to be handled sympathetically. In short,
groping for a stable and rational political order, French liberals found strict
consistency eluding them.

One conviction, though, they all shared: the right to opposition is fundamental to a decent civic order. For them, Napoleon's unforgivable crime was
that he had demolished opposition wherever he found or suspected it, producing a regime of lies, hypocrisy, and silence. They found Charles X only marginally more tolerable, and in 1827, three years after his accession, Guizot, Rémusat, the aging Lafayette, and other liberals, formed a committee to counteract
royalist electoral propaganda and intimidation. Careful to stay within the law, it
published brochures and handbooks informing voters of their rights and instructing them how to register. And, with hardworking subsidiaries in fifty-six
of France's *départements*, it added some 15,000 voters to the electoral lists—no
small accomplishment. The name of this organization, a political action committee more than a political party, was nothing less than inspired: *Aide-toi, le
Ciel t'aidera*—"Heaven helps those who help themselves." Borrowing this old
adage to designate a rudimentary political machine, its organizers displayed the
will to politics at work; French liberals were asserting their right to legitimate
aggressiveness in the contest for public power.

Indeed, the pathetic end of Charles X's reign was a tribute to the vitality of
the sorely tried French political spirit—and to his obtuseness. The king and his
favorite advisers thought he could rule as though the last thirty-five years had
never happened. He granted indemnities to former émigrés, not lavish enough
to satisfy them but too lavish for his liberal and radical subjects. He cultivated
the church, stimulating never dormant anticlerical sentiments. He listened to
courtiers distinguished mainly by their hatred of the Revolution and all its
works. He blandly disregarded the implications of high bread prices. Then, in
1829, snubbing his subjects, he appointed as ministers men whom most of the
French detested. He would have done well to ponder an ominous comment in
the *Journal des débats:* "Thus, once again the tie of love and trust which united
the people to the monarch is broken!"[23] It did not occur to him, seduced by
diplomatic and military successes, that without that tie, politics must become
jungle combat.

Aching to enact his fantasy as an absolute monarch, Charles X unwittingly
provoked the political opposition into action. In March 1830, 221 deputies,
facing down 181 loyalists, voted to send an address to the king pointedly reminding him that the necessary concord between crown and people was now

lacking. The polite rhetoric masked an assault on the royal privilege of selecting his own ministers. Stung, Charles dissolved the chamber and called for new elections in July. The results were a stunning setback; the opposition overcame the usual electoral chicanery and gathered fifty-three new recruits. Here was the editorial in the *Journal des débats* translated into votes. The king's response amounted to a virtual coup d'état; he decided to set the election results aside. On July 25, his government proclaimed the notorious four ordinances muzzling the press, further narrowing the electorate, dissolving the chamber, and again calling for new elections. It was Charles's most concerted attack on politics, and his last.

The opposition was ready. Others took fire from its fervor, and politics moved from the electoral process to the strident editorials of opposition newspapers and to the streets of Paris. In three Glorious Days—*Les trois Glorieuses*—all was over. Charles X abdicated, and the Orleanist Louis Philippe was elevated to the French throne. The upheaval had been as costly as it had been rapid: some eight hundred of the Parisian demonstrators and barricade builders, and some two hundred of the royal troops, had been killed. But the victors hailed the event as a triumph of politics and expected a substantial reward: the rehabilitation of political life.

The rehabilitation proved incomplete, the reward disheartening. In the making of modern French political culture, the July Monarchy played a vacillating role. It aroused great expectations, but in the course of its eighteen-year life, it satisfied few. At the outset all was smiling promise: the new charter took care to call Louis Philippe, in a far-reaching gesture toward popular sovereignty, "King of the French"; it set its seal of approval on the spirit of '89 by adopting the tricolor as the nation's flag, ostentatiously relegating the Bourbon's fleur-de-lys to the dustheap of history; it reduced the king's share in the making of legislation; it undertook to free the press and the publishing trade by expunging censorship from the books; and it deprived Roman Catholicism of its status as the country's official religion, revived during the Restoration, instead tactfully calling it the faith professed by the majority of the French. At first glance, then, the Orleanist regime appeared to incorporate, or at least approximate, the bourgeois ideals that such liberal journalists and historians as François Auguste Mignet thought essential to a good state, a regime "in which rights are respected, laws are by consent, speech is free and public opinion consulted," in which, in short, politics would be not a charade but a reality.[24]

But the liberals' triumphs in the July Monarchy were almost as deleterious to a vigorous political climate as their failures had been in the Restoration. Hopeful and ambitious young intellectuals like Guizot and Adolphe Thiers, who had been in the forefront of the liberal opposition in the 1820s, took the revolution of 1830 as an opportunity to run the state instead of attacking it. Having got more or less what they wanted, they were determined to keep it. Quite unintentionally, they documented one of the principal vicissitudes in political life: with something to conserve, liberals in office discover a distinctly conservative streak. Occupying a broad center known, not without some self-satisfaction, as the *juste milieu* or "golden mean," these young liberals struck out at enemies right and left, unreconciled legitimists and discontented republicans alike. Rémusat, who watched the Orleanist monarchy from the inside, would glumly lament the "timid spirit animating the men of 1830." Especially in the first years of the regime the liberals could have launched and realized great projects, but "we were so happy, so anxious to establish a government, that we put all our ambitions into preserving it and into showing all our wisdom in making it last."[25] For these liberals, the sublimating of aggression meant a paralysis of the critical will.

Hence, although the July Monarchy was not without a creditable if limited record in education, transport, and economic development, its policies amounted to a sustained sequence of self-protective gestures. Its leaders ferociously repressed working-class uprisings in Lyons and Paris. They reintroduced laws crippling the press, with Daumier and his publisher, Philipon, among their most famous victims. They were satisfied with roughly doubling the minuscule electorate of the Restoration, to about 166,000—hardly a generous enlargement of the political public, still a mere 3 percent of all Frenchmen over twenty-one. These strategies kept the political elite homogeneous and the France of the July Monarchy "a combination of bureaucracy and plutocracy."[26] Its exclusiveness and defensiveness did little to sustain, let alone advance, France's political culture.

Without planning to do so, however, it contributed to the political education of the French middle class, largely by providing a privileged arena for infighting. The bourgeois character of the July Monarchy has been overdrawn; to caricature Louis Philippe, with his unostentatious bearing, his model family life, and his umbrella, as the bourgeois king par excellence, has proved irresistible. To be sure, after the revolution of 1830, France's nobility, which had partially reclaimed the centers of power in the favorable climate of the Restoration, retreated to its country estates or the social whirl in Paris. As fewer and fewer nobles occupied seats in the legislature, the prefecture, and the town hall, bourgeois officeholders tightened their grip. Still, excluding the bulk of the middle class from access to office, the regime remained a narrow oligarchy of notables—government of the few, by the few, for the few. Most political activity was confined to cautious grumbling and occasional outbursts of indiscreet rage. "The petty bourgeoisie of all degrees," Karl Marx noted in 1850, "were completely excluded from political power," just as if they were peasants or workingmen.[27]

Marx's observation was just enough, even obvious. Somewhat less obvious were the subtler lines of distinction he drew among the middling orders in the July Monarchy, even as he overstated their political influence as a class: "It was not the French bourgeoisie that ruled under Louis Philippe, but *one section* of it, bankers, stock-exchange kings, railway kings, owners of coal and iron mines and forests, a part of the landed proprietors that rallied around them—the so-called *finance aristocracy*. It sat on the throne, it dictated laws in the Chambers, it distributed public offices, from cabinet portfolios to tobacco bureau posts." On the other hand, "the *industrial bourgeoisie,* properly so called, formed part of the official opposition," growing all the more resolute as the "autocracy of the finance aristocracy" became "more unalloyed." Journalists, manufacturers, wine growers, intellectuals, bourgeois all, were ranged together against the ruling oligarchy.[28]

One might add that bourgeois squabbled with bourgeois not only from self-interest but also about attitudes. Witnessing the devastations of the industrial revolution across the Channel without appreciating its possible benefits, many French bankers and businessmen vigorously opposed accelerating its pace at home. But other bourgeois were perfectly willing to ease conditions of investment, and contemplated with pleasure a rapidly growing railroad network and large-scale industry. Some entrepreneurs in the 1840s deserted the party of caution for the party of risk taking. During the July Monarchy, French bourgeois practiced politics within set limits, as much as they dared, in the legislature and salons, in the press and economic policy.

Louis Philippe's reign, after all, was not a dictatorship; opposition voices, despite the impediments the laws and the police threw in their way, managed to make themselves heard. But the overall effect of these brakes on serious political debate was chilling. Partisan struggles in the Chamber of Deputies were vehement and elections were frequent, but the atmosphere reminded more than one observer of the silence that had characterized the Restoration. Some, politely, called it political tranquility. Others were less cheerful. In March 1846, Léon Faucher, then an opposition journalist, recorded that "in this country, the political spirit is dead, has been for several years; all people can think of is to enrich themselves and build railroads."[29] The regime of Louis Philippe is proof, if further proof is needed, that political culture requires a fare more nourishing than verbal wrangles and manipulated voting.

As before, though, obituaries were premature. Almost precisely two years after Faucher had lamented the death of politics, the country erupted in an explosion of activity that left it, and the rest of Europe, gasping. In a dizzying four years, France was a monarchy, a republic, and an empire. In February 1848, Louis Philippe was sent into exile and the Second Republic, complete with universal suffrage, was proclaimed; during four bloody days in June the masses who had secured the February Revolution on the barricades were mowed down. In December, Louis Napoleon Bonaparte, the emperor's nephew, once an outlaw, was elected president of the republic, a state he solemnly swore to uphold at his installation, cynically undermined in the following months, and mercilessly destroyed on December 2, 1851. His coup d'état put an end to political effervescence in France, and, with that, to political freedom. In his empire, confirmed precisely a year later, talk about the death of politics, or at least about its paralysis, would be more appropriate than it had been under Louis Philippe.

By this time, the French had acquired, and were regularly corroborating, a reputation for political instability. Within the short span of sixty years, they had lived under a dozen constitutions, two republics, two royal dynasties, and two empires. Brave reaffirmations of politics ended over and over with its demise.* The age of parties was at hand even in France, but the obstructions that faced parties, and not in France alone, show that the future of responsible political culture was still precarious.

3. Modern Caesars

In the course of the nineteenth century, democratic politics on the march faced some formidable obstacles, none more formidable than the thriving cult of personality. From 1800 on, two self-appointed French emperors, Napoleon I and Napoleon III, played the political game by rules that turned it into a bad joke. And by mid-century, the Prussian politician Otto von Bismarck had

*In 1855, the *Edinburgh Review* put the despotic French in their place: "A Parliamentary Government is a government of political parties." This involves the integration of the Other into the political process, with untrammeled speech outside parliament, open public meetings, and freedom of the press—all rights that Englishmen have long enjoyed. True, contemporary authoritarian regimes are far from brutal, and protect persons and property. But they are despotic in preventing politics from breathing, as they suppress all criticism in the legislature. Such repression foists hypocrisy on the public, which must pretend to approve, or at least refrain from censuring, what it abhors. Admittedly, a constructive opposition is hard to come by. "Accusation is more stimulating than defence: eulogy is flat and uninteresting." A responsible opposition must strive to offer not just cavils but realistic options, but these tasks require moderation. [G. C. Lewis], "Art. I.—*Hansard's Parliamentary Debates.* (New series)," *Edinburgh Review*, CI (January 1855), 1–20 passim. Though not mentioned by name, the real target of this essay in comparative government is Napoleon III, with whom the educated British public seemed obsessively preoccupied.

begun to test his powers. The prosperity of these outsized figures is an irony of nineteenth-century history. They made themselves masters precisely during massive social and economic transformations whose servants they should have been, and in large part were. Even Bismarck, a statesman at the rudder of events if anyone ever was, described himself as the instrument of forces larger than himself. Yet he and the two Napoleons appeared to vindicate the old-fashioned theory that it is the towering individual who makes history. To social theorists like Tocqueville and Marx, intent on identifying the larger forces causing historical change, the hero worship that Carlyle propagated in his lectures and biographies appeared hopelessly anachronistic. But in ways that Carlyle did not anticipate, heroes—or, many thought, great villains—indelibly marked the age.

Some of the Caesars strutting on the nineteenth-century stage, notably Napoleon I and Napoleon III, defined their ideology across several decades. It seemed, on the surface, massively inconsistent. On the one hand, they aspired to absolute authority; on the other, they exercised that authority—they said—not merely for the sake of the people, but in their name and under their watchful eyes. They professed the sincerest regard for ordinary men as the sole source of legitimate power, posturing as supreme servants holding authority on trust, whom their masters, the political nations, could with one stroke dismiss.* So much for oratory; in the cold light of political reality, this posture provided an alibi for an autocrat's monopoly on public aggression. Yet at bottom there was no contradiction. Caesarism was a logical, if problematic, element in the democratization of politics.

Naturally, the precise form and fate of the Caesarist regimes varied, depending on each nation's political traditions and historical events as much as on the Caesar's character. Quite as naturally, the verdicts of contemporaries also varied. Some thought Caesarism a mere detour, or a strictly temporary phase, in the redefinition of political aggressiveness. Others saw it as an essential ingredient in modern democracy, woven into its very texture. This much seems beyond dispute: Caesarism was too conspicuous a political phenomenon, too closely involved with seismic shifts in public authority, to be dismissed as merely a disease of the body politic. If it was a pathological form of popular sovereignty, it was also more than that; the doctrine stands as an incongruous but viable amalgam of aggressions with erotic undertones.

---

*Anyone who knows anything about Bismarck will recognize that this collective profile does not fit him in the way it fits the two Napoleons. Bismarck, to sum up a cluster of attitudes—they were attitudes rather than a systematic political philosophy—was a Prussian monarchist whose loyalties were profoundly traditional. But as the following pages will show, he had unexpected, striking, and fundamental affinities with the Caesars of his time.

The effectiveness of that alibi did not depend on the profits the Caesar bestowed on his supporters. His most ardent disciples rose above calculation. They were bound to one another in a passionate fraternity and to their leader in blind, loving submission. It is this dual amorous bond that helps to resolve the apparent contradiction inherent in the Caesarist form of domination: it is an erotic democracy drawing its authority from a no less erotic hero worship. The faithful follower yields up all aggression against his fellows and, needless to say, against his leader in return for satisfying emotional intimacy and permission to visit aggressive impulses on those who reject, or are excluded from, his happy political family. Thus the Caesarist virus spread. By the 1880s, after the French Caesars had left the stage and Bismarck was nearing retirement, more and more domineering politicians—Georges Boulanger in France, Joseph Chamberlain in England, Francesco Crispi in Italy—seemed to be infected with it. The paradox of absolutist aspirations in a democratizing age remained to haunt late-nineteenth-century politics.

The self-serving pronouncements of the modern Caesars and their servile publicists found approving echoes among contemporary historians. These professionals mattered to their culture, for in the Victorian days respected historians spoke to a wide educated public ready to listen. Now they were seeking to rehabilitate the first Caesar and restore him to his rightful place in history. Their verdicts on the legitimacy of his aggressive career had political implications.

To be sure, past centuries had granted Caesar heroic, almost mythical stature. Brutus was the faithless parricide; Dante, as everyone knows, had dropped him into the very pit of frozen hell as an infamous traitor, as irredeemable as Cassius and Judas. But Shakespeare had already drawn a more complex, more tormented figure, and the French Revolution had been the time for Brutus—the lover of freedom who, setting aside personal affection, did not hesitate to strike down the tyrant. Parricides were in fashion then, for obvious reasons. Even earlier in the eighteenth century, lives of Cicero and histories of the Roman republic had depicted Caesar as an ambitious dictator, a subverter of republican institutions. The nineteenth century, more intent on order than on revolution, drastically modified this reading. Looking back in 1907 as he reflected on his *Caesar and Cleopatra,* George Bernard Shaw recalled that at mid-century and even after, Brutus had been the hero and Caesar the dubious character. But in the early 1870s, after the debate had been agitating learned circles for some decades, the eminent French educator and historian Victor Duruy observed that while the tradition of a virtuous Brutus still had its adherents, faith in that tradition was "very much shaken in Caesarian Germany and free England."[1]

One of the historians to shake it was Duruy himself. In his *Histoire des Romains et des peuples soumis à leur domination* of 1843, he took a revisionist line, defending Caesar against his detractors. Only three years earlier, the ashes of Napoleon I had been returned to France from St. Helena, to frantic public excitement. Caesar's champions were making themselves heard. Some had anticipated Duruy: in 1832, in a series of articles on the Roman emperors, Thomas De Quincey, that most intuitive of essayists, had made an original, rather unsettling plea for Caesar. He not only discovered suggestive resemblances between Caesar and Napoleon I but displayed the erotic dimension of the Caesarist appeal with a shocking metaphor. Julius Caesar had not destroyed Roman greatness: "Peace, hollow rhetoricians! Until Caesar came, Rome was a minor; by him she attained her majority." He had committed a beneficient rape. Critics said that Caesar had "deflowered the virgin purity of her civil liberties." But he had thereby "caused her to fulfill the functions of her nature," raising Rome from "the imperfect and inchoate condition" of a mere female to the "perfections" of a woman. Thus this "godlike man" had matured a nation.[2] Far from protesting against her sexual violation, passive Rome, overpowered by the virile male, had profited from it—and gloried in it. Leadership, in this account, is the most brutal, almost unsublimated, exercise of manliness in action.

This was strong stuff, and few controversialists, if any, followed De Quincey in celebrating political leadership as a violent sexual melodrama. What many did come to value was the constructive order which, to their minds, Caesar had imposed on Rome after decades of civic turmoil. In his *Histoire des Romains,* Duruy mentioned Napoleon I, that modern Caesar, in passing, but gave the original preference over the copy. "His mind and manners had a fascination that one other great ruler of men has also possessed; but in Caesar this was allied with a natural elegance that Napoleon was never able to acquire." For Duruy, "Caesar was the most complete man Rome ever produced."[3] And in the mid-1850s, this reverent assessment was buttressed by the formidable scholarship of Theodor Mommsen. In his brilliantly written *Römische Geschichte,* Mommsen saluted Caesar as a patriot of genius, manly orator, thoroughgoing realist, tactful statesman, and, most important, democratic monarchist. This last formulation, above all, put the highest possible gloss on Caesarism as the happy blending of two apparently incompatible political systems.[4]

Mommsen towered over the field. Some students of Caesar, like J. A. Froude, simply paraphrased the master.[5] Still, unanimous about nothing, the nineteenth century had its dissenters from the growing consensus about Caesar as the savior of Rome. Among the most eloquent was Goldwin Smith, soon to be appointed Regius Professor of History at Oxford. In 1856, he reviewed, negatively, lectures in which the positivist philosopher Richard Congreve praised Caesar for laying the foundation of a beneficent "imperial despotism." Reviving eighteenth-century assaults on faction, Congreve saw Caesar's rule as a relief from partisan conflicts. Unpersuaded, Smith bracketed Congreve with "an advanced and slightly terrorist school of philanthropists" impatient with "the checks and responsibilities of a constitutional system." Congreve, he charged, sympathetic with a "demagogic tyranny for the future," was rewriting the past, tendentiously. The empire Caesar had created "remains, in our eyes, what it was before,—a tyranny which perhaps Rome had deserved." Smith trusted "that humanity will never see its like again."[6]

Mid-nineteenth-century France, which, after all, had had two Caesars to observe at close range, generated very similar salutary skepticism. In 1867, in *Théorie du progrès,* Henri de Ferron, a specialist in French government, warned against Caesarism as a threat to civilization. Capitalists were calling for the tyrant in fear for their property; men in search of tranquility were looking to find "refuge in the arms of despotism." Anticipating Lord Acton's most-quoted aphorism, Ferron cautioned that "all men, heads of state like simple mortals, have a despot within themselves. One can hardly cite two men in the last three thousand years who, in possession of real power, have not abused it. Which makes absolute power necessarily evil."[7]

Smith and Ferron did not lack respectable company, but the drift of nineteenth-century opinion was toward Caesar—if not always toward Caesarism. Some admirers at least kept past politics and present politics apart. By mid-century, though, this was increasingly hard to do; Mommsen, the most scholarly of historians, scattered contemporary references through his history of ancient Rome. And it had become virtually inevitable to think of Napoleon III as one wrote, or read, about Julius Caesar. Louis Napoleon was then, as he has been since, treated as the classic representative of the genre.* But he had a recent as well as a distant model, his uncle Napoleon I. For all the original touches he lent his imperial rule, Napoleon III always remained a nephew.

---

*Walter Bagehot, in a brilliant essay of 1865, had this wily emperor in mind when he analyzed the phenomenon: "Julius Caesar was the first who tried on an imperial scale the characteristic principles of the French Empire,—as the first Napoleon revived them, as the third Napoleon has consolidated them." The "notion of a demagogue ruler" goes back to the ancient Greeks, but "on the big page of universal history, Julius Caesar is the first instance of a democratic despot. He overthrew an aristocracy—a corrupt, and perhaps effete aristocracy, it is true, but still an aristocracy—by the help of the people, of the unorganised people. He said to the numerical majority of Roman citizens: 'I am your advocate and your leader: make me supreme, and I will govern for your good, and in your name.' This is exactly the principle of the French Empire." "Caesarism As It Existed in 1865" (1865), *Literary Studies (Miscellaneous Essays),* ed. Richard Holt Hutton, 3 vols. (1st ed., 2 vols., 1879; 2nd ed., 1902–05), III, 72–73.

Whatever else Louis Napoleon Bonaparte learned from his uncle, his preoccupation with Julius Caesar is particularly arresting. It is at its most notable in the two-volume *Histoire de Jules César* he published in 1865, with his name on the title page—a claim no more trustworthy than others he made throughout his political career. The catastrophic end of his empire was just five years away, but *Jules César* shows no signs of anxiety, let alone panic. It is a lavish tribute to the inspiring democratic dictator of antiquity and, no less, a gracious bow to Napoleon I, who, he knew, had devoted precious time to the praise of Julius Caesar.[8] Shortly after that modern Caesar had taken power in November 1799, Louis de Fontanes, a minor poet and agile politician, had already celebrated his country's new master with a sycophantic pamphlet virtually deifying him as greater even than the greatest captain of antiquity: "Every hope attaches itself to his glory and his life. Happy Republic, *if he were immortal!*"[9]

The infatuation thus launched outlived Napoleon's reign. In tedious exile, sentenced to inaction, he dwelt moodily on Julius Caesar. For the ex-emperor, who had no weapons left but words, biographical and autobiographical obsessions swam together into one self-aggrandizing fantasy. In 1808, in a famous conversation at Erfurt, he had told Goethe that Caesar would have rendered humanity happy if he had only been given time to carry through his magnificent projects. Now, on St. Helena, as he kept refining the legend he wanted posterity to adopt, he applied this verdict to himself, discovering pleasing similarities between himself and "that great man." Like Caesar, he had reformed the legal code, beautified his capital with grandiose projects, created a new, worthy nobility, treated his enemies magnanimously. And like Caesar, he had been cut off prematurely, and that was a disaster for the world. Marcus Brutus, raised on the rigid Greek distaste for tyrants, had failed to recognize the legitimacy of Caesar's authority—the will of the people. Here Napoleon touched the core of the Caesarist persuasion. Had he not, a Caesar for the nineteenth century, realized the best the revolutionary program had to offer? Was he not a man of peace offering hope to enslaved Europe, guiltless of the crimes his enemies were imputing to him? Napoleon answered these rhetorical questions as he dictated a wordy commentary on Caesar's writings.[10] And exculpating himself by exculpating his precursor, he left his nephew a tempting legacy.

To that nephew, Caesar was "an eminent genius," one of those "privileged beings who, from time to time, appear in history like luminous beacons." His phrasing broadly hints that though too modest—or too crafty—to mention his own name, he thought himself worthy of being counted in the rare company of historic beacons. Napoleon III was pleading his own case when he professed to be troubled by historians so busy denigrating superior men that they failed to appreciate their motives, their achievements, and their great designs. Were they not consistently belittling *him*? Borrowing his uncle's reasoning, he denied that Caesar had aspired to supreme power when he marched off to Gaul or that he ever craved the mantle of royalty. Superficial historians baying at his heels had always sadly misjudged him. Far from instigating disorder in Roman society, Caesar had actually made himself its "indispensable pilot."[11] The parallels Napoleon III wanted the reader to draw were only too blatant.

But while he idealized Caesar, Louis Napoleon identified far more intensely with Caesar's nineteenth-century successor. In his best-known formal portrait, by Jean Hippolyte Flandrin, Napoleon III stands amidst pointed attributes: a bust of Napoleon I crowned with laurel conspicuous on his right and the Napoleonic eagle in the background. How much Louis Napoleon's identification with his uncle was a calculating exploitation of his magical family connection, how much an unplanned, unconscious need, is impossible to settle; the two motives made a mixture not to be unraveled. Napoleon III, his contemporaries complained, was a riddle. In 1865, Pierre Vésinier, a mordant, outspoken radical journalist who cordially disliked the emperor, called him a "modern Sphinx," and the epithet has stuck.[12] Louis Napoleon wrote a good deal, but he said very little about his inner life. His writings include technical treatises and topical pamphlets: a manual on artillery and a plea for tariffs to support home-grown beet sugar, a project for a canal in Nicaragua linking the Atlantic and Pacific oceans, and scattered self-serving reflections on politics and history. They include, too, a sizable harvest of speeches and letters, short and banal. He gave away very little of himself.

What he did insist on giving away, as publicly as possible, was his affection for his immortal uncle; it served him as an unmatched alibi for aggression. His sentiment was rooted in childhood impressions and nurtured in years of exile. Born in 1808 to Napoleon's brother Louis and Hortense de Beauharnais, daughter of Napoleon's first wife, Josephine, Louis Napoleon Bonaparte was steeped in the imperial ambiance. At thirteen, when his tutor broke the news of the emperor's death on St. Helena, he precociously acted the part of one who bears an illustrious name and a heavy responsibility. "When I do wrong," he wrote his mother, "if I think of *this great man,* I seem to feel his spirit within me bidding me to make myself worthy of the name *Napoleon.*"[13] Whether spontaneous, contrived, or inspired by his tutor, the letter suggests that the uses of the resounding name he bore were not lost on him.

Dramatizing this family piety, he made a sentimental pilgrimage to Waterloo, the battlefield where his uncle's doom had been sealed; wholly in character, eight years before, he had made another pilgrimage, no less sentimental. Kneeling at the banks of the Rubicon, the river Julius Caesar had illegally crossed to march into immortality, he filled with its water a bottle he had thoughtfully brought along.[14] From his adolescence, self-consciously, Louis Napoleon linked his destiny with two Caesars.

He played his heritage for all it was worth, but in some part of himself, he was in earnest—Napoleon I was his ego ideal. Adoration and manipulation went hand in hand. In 1836, in a quixotic attempt to seize power fated to collapse within two hours, he tried to mobilize troops for a march on Paris by invoking his uncle's charismatic name. Three years later, he published his first extended essay in political polemics, the *Idées napoléoniennes,* a paean to the person, the works, and the legacy of the emperor. An astonishing publishing success that made his name known to thousands across Europe, the little book was a cleverly conceived bid for public recognition. It reads like the verbal equivalent of a coup d'état, as though its author vaguely imagined he might ride to power on the shoulders of the great Napoleon, whose signal achievements he applauded, prettified, and in part invented. What Guizot had called, in 1821, "the yoke of a memory," the worship of Napoleon I, was no yoke for his nephew, but a prop for self-elevation.[15]

The *Idées,* and its introductory statement, *L'Idée napoléonienne,* added a year later, set the stage for a new edition of modern Caesarism, a highly sophisticated cultivation of hatred in the service of political ambitions. Louis Napoleon invidiously compared the moral and civilizing progress under the emperor with the instability of the Restoration and the July Monarchy. Both had failed to consolidate the gains of the Revolution. Today, in depressing contrast to the days of the Empire, "corruption on one side, lies on the other, and hatred everywhere—that is our condition!" Napoleon I, arriving on a turbulent scene, had recognized his historic role as that of "the *testamentary executor* of the revolution." Exacting though his task had been, he had accomplished his mission by reconciling order with liberty.[16]

Intent on arousing nostalgia for that modern Caesar, Louis Napoleon stressed his intimate rapport with ordinary Frenchmen. Napoleon I, always responsive to the people, had built his dynasty on the identity of interests between ruler and ruled. That this great idea should have won the sympathy of the masses was only just. His envious detractors notwithstanding, Napoleon had been a man of peace, reformed his country's finances and its laws, promoted industry and agriculture, fostered education and foreign trade. His greatest goal had been liberty; the smoke of battle that hung over his reign should mislead no one. "The emperor's eulogy is in the facts." And just in case the reader might miss his underlying message, Louis Napoleon suavely insinuated his own claim to stand in the succession to this giant. The point was not to copy his actions but to rule in his spirit. In ringing capitals, he apostrophized the great man sleeping at

St. Helena: "FREE PEOPLE EVERYWHERE WORK TO BEGIN YOUR WORK ANEW."[17] That key democratic word, "people," could not have been more conspicuous.

Louis Napoleon took care to suppress the fact that his uncle's love affair with the common people had been one-sided, on his part a grand deception. A cynic about human nature, convinced that men are moved by fear and self-interest and ruled through their vanity, Napoleon I had adopted his erotic posture with his subjects as a highly conscious strategy. "So long as I hold my place in the heart of the masses," he said, "I need not worry about the leaders; and if I had only the leaders in my favor, of what use would they be to me against the torrent of the masses?"[18] For him, demagogy was high policy. Goethe, an enthusiastic member of the Napoleonic sect, was not alone in paying naive tribute to this populist element in Napoleon's recipe for ruling. "For all his greatness," he told Eckermann, "even Napoleon did not disdain popularity."[19] What Goethe failed to recognize—and Louis Napoleon failed to mention— was the essential mendacity of the emperor's posture.

In its omissions, as in its assertions, the *Idées napoléoniennes* was a stirring piece of self-promotion. But in 1840, the year after its publication, its author made a second attempt at a military coup, no less fantastic than the first. In justification, he conjured up the shade of the emperor; picturesquely, but with a modicum of psychological plausibility, he described himself as sensing that shade urging him forward and speaking through him. The voice should have advised him to stick to assaults with the pen; he was captured and put on trial. On the stand, he exploited his priceless exposure with a rousing reiteration of his respect for popular authority: "I stand before you the representative of a principle, a cause, a defeat. The principle is the sovereignty of the people; the cause is the cause of the Empire; the defeat, Waterloo."[20] The judges, unimpressed, sentenced him to perpetual captivity in the fortress of Ham. There he vegetated comfortably for almost six years, until he escaped to England. Fortress life was boring but not solitary; he wrote articles for the press, corresponded with his admirers, fathered two children with a local mistress, and brooded on the glory that must surely await a Napoleon.

He got his opportunity sooner than he, or his loyal lieutenants, had thought possible. In September 1848—he was still in England—he was chosen to sit in the assembly drafting a constitution for the republic that had emerged after the February Revolution. Confident of his mission, he returned to France to popularity, controversy, and some ridicule. In December he was elected president of the Second Republic in a stunning triumph, garnering 5.5 million votes, some three times as many as all his competitors together.[21] And during his campaign for the presidency—in fact, throughout his career as a speechmaker and pamphleteer, whether exile, prisoner, deputy, president, or emperor—he declared his debt to the people more assiduously than his uncle ever had. His Caesarism never discarded the populist mask. During the political campaigns in the summer and early fall of 1848, he appealed to his masters, the voters, in honeyed tones. Again, once seated in the legislative assembly, he reassured his fellow deputies that he wanted only to serve. "How little those who accuse me of ambition know my heart!" Only the good will of his "fellow citizens" consoled him for the vicious attacks on his person. These were canny forensic performances, making him all the more formidable as a presidential candidate.[22]

They were as repetitive as they were canny. In early December 1848, during the closing days of the national campaign, he promised his "dear fellow citizens" in a manifesto outlining his platform that whatever the results of the election, he would "bow to the will of the people."[23] And once elected president, he remained faithful to his repertory. He effusively expressed his gratitude to the millions who had voted for him, and implored them to discard factions. Such an appeal was, no doubt, a politician's commonplace. But for Louis Napoleon it had theoretical implications: as president of all the French, he was determined to float above parties. Accordingly, dissenters could be reproached for being "factious"; that term of abuse simply would not die.

The very cloudiness of the Napoleonic oratory made him many things to many men. One electoral manifesto, typical for his partisans' use of his diffuse but engaging appeal, promised that "the nephew of the great man, with his magic name, will give us security, and save us from misery." As Marx wrote in his sneering and perceptive way, "Just because he was nothing he could signify everything save himself."[24] Thousands of voters delighted in his crude caricature of a program; thousands of rustics could not tell Napoleon I and his nephew apart.* And so, outlaw, rebel, conspirator, far from prepossessing, an orator of modest talents, the professional nephew sailed into the presidency on his name alone. It was ironic that he should have been the beneficiary of the universal manhood suffrage the Second Republic had so proudly enacted. Frenchmen by the millions, far more than had ever participated in a political act before, declared themselves for the new Caesar.

---

*"They wanted a Bonaparte, man or mummy did not much signify." James Augustus St. John, *Louis Napoleon, Emperor of the French: A Biography* (1857), 273. St. John had little faith in the political judgment of the majority: Louis Napoleon took advantage of "that superstition of the French military classes for his uncle's memory, which really partook of the nature of idolatry." Ibid., 182–83. Four years after, an anonymous English writer let his indignation boil over: "The elections for the presidency gave proof of an instability and ingratitude in the French people which no previous example in history can exceed." *A Glance at the Causes and Effects of the Revolutions in France since 1847* (1852), 41.

The Warder Collection

Walter Bagehot, the brilliant English political economist, political essayist, and editor of *The Economist*

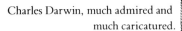

Charles Darwin, much admired and much caricatured.

Radio Times Hulton Picture Library

Yale University Library, Manuscripts and Archives

William Graham Sumner, more complex a fighter for Social-Darwinist ideas than often thought, around 1890.

Theodore Roosevelt, armed to the teeth as a hunter in Colorado in 1905, in his second term as president.

F. A. Townsend, "Smithson Junior (as the homily ends...)," *Punch* (1911). Neatly illustrating the persistence of flogging into the twentieth century, the invasion of schoolboy discourse by modern science, and the benevolent view that *Punch* takes of the whole business.

SMITHSON JUNIOR (as the homily ends and the real business is about to start): " Please, sir, is it sterilized ? "

1846   1886

"Our Medical Students," *Punch* (1886).

THE NEW TYRANNY

"Of course you needn't *Work*, Fitzmilksoppe;
but *Play* you *must* and *shall*."

"The New Tyranny," *Punch* (1889).
Manliness forces games on everyone.

John Keate, headmaster of Eton in the early nineteenth century, a famous but beloved flogger. From John Chandos, *Boys Together* (1984).

Tom Brown and his friend Harry East successfully attack the school bully, Flashman. H. M. Brock, illustration for 1913 edition of Thomas Hughes, *Tom Brown's Schooldays* (1857).

Sunday services in the prison chapel at Pentonville. Henry Mayhew and John Binny, *The Criminal Prisons of London and Scenes of Prison Life* (1862). The extremes to which jailers went to keep prisoners separate from one another.

The execution of the poisoner William Palmer, June 14, 1856. Note the packed crowd, including children. From David D. Cooper, *The Lesson of the Scaffold* (1974).

Wilhelm Scholz, Bismarck masterfully handling the snake of politics. From Horst Kohl, ed., *Bismarck-Gedichte des Kladderadatsch* (1874).

"Louis Napoleon riding through the Boulevards." The popular president of France showing himself to the people, June 13, 1849. The coup d'état is only two and a half years away.

Die neuen Amazonen.

Theekesselpauker.

Husaren = Lieutenant.

Scharfschütz.

Küchendragoner — Unteroffizier.

General en chef.

Fähndrich der Pantoffelgarde.

L. Burger, "The New Amazons," *Fliegende Blätter* (1853). Typical of the periodical's anti-feminist stance, and part of a more widespread campaign to make fun of the "new woman."

IN THE SIXTIES

IN THE SEVENTIES

IN THE EIGHTIES

IN THE NINETIES

PAST AND PRESENT

"Past and Present," *Punch* (1891). Women grew more active in sports and less encumbered in dress.

FICTION—PRESENT STYLE

GERTRUDE: "You never do anything now, Margaret, but go to all sorts of Churches, and read those old Books of Theology. You never used to be like that."

MARGARET: "How can I help it, Gerty? I'm writing a Popular Novel!"

Everard Hopkins, "Fiction—Present Style," *Punch* (1892). Woman novelists, in the magazine's rather condescending view.

GEORGE SAND

The great George Sand in her later years, from a portrait by Thomas Couture

True, a few Cassandras cautioned against a Bonaparte in power and a new authoritarianism in the wings. But Louis Napoleon's past and his rumored ambitions were swept aside by a rush of nostalgia for the Napoleonic legend, fed by eulogists like Victor Hugo and, indirectly, by the unpopularity of his competitors. He was the chosen favorite not of the bourgeoisie, but of the church, of unlettered and unpolitical peasants, of those who accepted his populist rhetoric as a political promise. Once elected president, Louis Napoleon continued to deploy precisely this rhetoric, seeking to persuade the country that he was in charge, and vigorous criticism, disloyal. In June 1849, after surviving peaceful, almost timorous demonstrations against his regime and some tough talk of insurrection, he issued a ringing proclamation against the "few factious men" who had dared to "raise the standard of rebellion against a legitimate government because it is the product of universal suffrage."[25] Ineffectual insurrections in Paris and Lyons gave him another opportunity to pose as the nation's savior, elected to defend his people's life and property.

During elaborately orchestrated progresses through his domains, he dwelt on the popular basis of his rule. Whether reviewing troops or visiting exhibitions, toasting cities at festive dinners or inaugurating a new section of the rapidly spreading French railroad network—these occasions were favorites with him— he reiterated yet again his simple message. He liked to call himself "the recognized Leader of this great nation" and to remind his audiences that it was they who had "given me Power," they who had imposed that "heavy burden" on his shoulders.[26] He liked to portray himself as the natural adversary of rightwing and left-wing extremists, and whenever possible spoke in his people's name. That in December 1848 his "people" had in effect voted to disfranchise themselves was still hidden in the future.

Not for long. Louis Napoleon chafed at the provision that limited the president to a single term. Knowledgeable acquaintances like Tocqueville suspected from the outset, rightly, that he would try to evade this constitutional check.[27] Adroitly, at times desperately, Louis Napoleon schemed to rally the country to his uncle's banner. In late October 1849, he told the legislative assembly in a characteristic plea, "The name of Napoleon is in itself a whole program. It wants to say: at home, order, authority, religion, the people's well-being; abroad, national dignity. This is the policy, inaugurated by my election, which, with the aid of the Assembly and the people, I want to see triumph."[28] Accordingly, from the first months of his presidency, Louis Napoleon moved to tighten his control over French public life. He struck at the heart of political activity, especially at the radical republicans, or Jacobins, his prefects could detect and his gendarmes terrorize. A battery of laws suppressed left-wing political clubs and unpalatable newspapers. These were not wholly unpopular moves; the legislature's anxiety about subversion at times even outran the president's.

In this atmosphere, Louis Napoleon launched assault after assault on the legacy of '89, perverting the political education of the French in the process. In May 1850, he accepted a new electoral law, massively curtailing the suffrage, that struck some 30 percent of the electorate—Thiers called them "the vile multitude"—from the rolls with cleverly devised clauses. The law was not part of his program, but it played into his hands. And as though to underscore his departure from the revolution, once again imitating his uncle, he worked toward a politic rapprochement with the church. Profiting from the blessings of Bonapartist auspices, old religious orders secured thousands of recruits, new religious orders began to mushroom, recently silent churchmen again found their voice. The Falloux Law of 1850, granting clerics the privilege of opening secondary schools, further bolstered Catholic influence. Religious and legitimist extremists were still dissatisfied, but they had less to be dissatisfied about.

As the president maneuvered his way through his term of office, the prospect of May 1852—which would bring elections for a new president and a new legislative assembly—began to oppress citizens fearful of revolution. Driving themselves to attacks of panic as they painted the mirage of a sanguinary Jacobin regime on the wall, they found the threat of a legitimist counterrevolution innocuous in comparison. Late in 1851, the virulent publicist Auguste Romieu, who had made his name some months before with a pamphlet calling for a new Caesar, deftly played on these apprehensions with a brochure bearing the incendiary title *Le Spectre rouge de 1852*. Louis Napoleon could only welcome such publicity, as he did his best to inflame public anxieties. He warned of a "demagogic conspiracy" and of secret societies working to "extend their ramifications into the smallest townships." Party men, "insane, violent, incorrigible," had "made a rendezvous for 1852, not to build but to overturn."[29] These forecasts were self-fulfilling prophecies; making the situation appear more ominous than it really was, the president exacerbated the political paranoia.

Hence Louis Napoleon's coup of December 2, 1851, which laid the threat of May 1852 with a single stroke, was a logical move. It was not a giddy inspiration, or the response to an emergency; he had been assembling his team of conspirators for some months. In the early morning of December 2, he completed what the repression of the previous three years had well begun. There was not a trace of amateurishness this time; the president and his accomplices deftly mobilized their resources, and encountered practically no opposition. The proclamation they posted on walls all over Paris was a consummate exercise in Caesarist propaganda. "IN THE NAME OF THE FRENCH PEOPLE" it announced that the legislative assembly had been dissolved and universal suffrage restored. And it summoned the French people to the polls to endorse or reject Louis Napoleon's action.

Inevitably, his favorite populist rhetoric pervaded the usurper's address to "the people of France" on this fateful occasion. In private, his cynicism was complete: three days after, he told the reactionary Spanish theologian Donoso Cortès that he drew a distinction between universal suffrage as the "source of power" and as the "habitual basis" of government. "I don't mind being baptized, but that is no reason for living in the water."[30] In public, he naturally sounded very different. He charged that criminal plots against "the power I hold directly from the people" had reached into the legislative assembly. And he promised that if he was denied a majority of the votes, he would convoke a new assembly and hand it back the mandate the people had earlier bestowed on him. The constitution promulgated in January 1852 explicitly provided that "the President of the Republic is responsible to the French people, to which he always has the right to appeal."[31] As so often, the Caesar's aggressiveness masqueraded as obedience to the electorate.

On the morning of the coup, the president's troops had arrested inconvenient politicians in a civilized way, even with a certain humor. But two days later, when army commanders learned that barricades were going up in Paris, they decided to teach the cadre of activists the only lesson they were trained to impart. Hundreds, builders of barricades and unlucky bystanders, including dozens of bourgeois—the precise number will never be known—were killed in Paris. And in the provinces, where principled democrats rose in a brave but futile attempt to reverse the irreversible, hundreds more were shot out of hand and nearly 27,000 political prisoners rounded up, of whom some 10,000 were subsequently transported to the colonies.

This excessive response was out of tune with the prudent actions that had characterized the coup itself. But not all was rational in this latest assault on French political culture; Louis Napoleon had summoned magical thinking to his aid. The very date sounded avuncular echoes. Precisely forty-seven years earlier, on December 2, 1804, Napoleon Bonaparte had crowned himself emperor and—an added fillip—precisely one year later, he had won a decisive battle at Austerlitz. In Louis Napoleon's choice of date, showmanship blended with superstition, itself now an alibi for aggression. When he converted his newly minted ten-year presidential term into the imperial dignity, there was something predictable about the date of the coronation—December 2, 1852.

Sizable segments of the bourgeoisie remained aloof from this pious charade, or went into the opposition. "At this moment," the comte de Montalembert, Catholic publicist and editor, wrote a political ally a week after the coup, "Bonaparte has against him all the orators, all the sophists, all the lawyers, all the bourgeois, and all the traveling salesmen, that is to say, all the representatives of Voltairianism and of democracy. He has for him all that remains of the *sane,* of the disciplined or the *disciplinable* in the nation, the army and the peasants."[32] No doubt, "all the bourgeois" was an overstatement. But middle-class anti-clericalism and a residual loyalty to revolutionary ideals, especially among professional men, gave many a bourgeois pause. Well-informed foreigners, too, especially Englishmen, disapproved of December 2; they saw its aggression against free politics as an exemplar of a tyrant at work.

Systematically stifling political expression and political organizations, the dictator refined repression into an art. His regime fined and jailed editors, writers, and printers; shut down newspapers and publishing houses that offended its sense of what was proper for French readers to know; proscribed radical pamphlets, songs, broadsides, and almanacs. Under the emperor's benevolent eye, the state rigorously regulated political clubs and authorized local officials to ban them; the policeman who attended their meetings, listening stolidly but attentively, became a regular feature of their precarious existence. Any occasion that independent spirits might turn into a moment of political self-expression—a funeral, a banquet, a fair, planting a liberty tree— invited police interference. And all this while, the harassment of political opponents, the deportation of suspicious-seeming foreigners, and the purge of unreliable public officials went on.[33]

It was, of course, all dressed up to look perfectly legitimate. Louis Napoleon kept his promise to permit—virtually to compel—the French electorate to register its approval of his coup. This technique, too, the nephew had learned from his uncle. Prominent in the first Napoleon's repertory of self-protective and self-promoting modes of seduction, significant for the redefinition of political activity then under way, was the "appeal to the people"—the plebiscite—a device he used three times between 1800 and 1804 to tighten his grip on France. To no one's surprise, he won each of these votes with overwhelming and incredible majorities, having employed cajolery, manipulation, intimidation, and, just to make sure, massive fraud.[34]

Louis Napoleon proved an apt pupil. Catholic spokesmen urged an affirmative vote; the minister of the interior instructed prefects across the country to exercise their influence to ensure correct results; military officers did their duty, haranguing their men about the blessings of December 2. With opposition voices largely silenced, with the fear of reprisals in the air, the outcome was guaranteed. But a completely free and honest election would have given similar results, shaving only modest numbers from the 7.5 million votes Louis Napoleon received, as against some 650,000 against him. "There has been terror," George Sand wrote to Mazzini, "but the people would have voted as it has without this."[35] Louis Napoleon was truly the people's choice. Some of his enemies would not forgive him. Victor Hugo, who had been the emperor's devotee until the coup turned him into a savage critic, sent forth a stream of invective from the safety of exile. Hugo's Louis Napoleon was a contemptible figure, *Napoléon le petit*. Still, though Hugo's ferocious lampoons amused many, they persuaded few.

The plebiscite was Louis Napoleon's most emphatic act of Caesarism. Inviting the people to ratify his absolute authority under democratic suffrage, he swept aside time-honored claims of divine right, dynastic title, or historic prerogatives. And after he assumed the imperial title, he did not change his democratic tune in the least. In 1858, speaking at Cherbourg at the dedication of an equestrian statue of Napoleon I, he once again defined the government he headed as "resting on the will of the masses" and therefore "the slave of no party."[36] And in his will, of 1865, speaking of his only son, he managed to squeeze into a single sentence the two salient ideas that had shaped his political career—Napoleonism and populism. "Let him never forget," he admonished, "the motto of the head of our family, Everything for the French people."[37]

If these reiterations sound monotonous, they were—more or less by design. Louis Napoleon was one of the first nineteenth-century politicians to grasp and exploit the propagandistic potential of sheer repetition. He wanted, and found, the slogans that people could remember. Like Voltaire a century before him, he knew how inattentively people read and listen, and how often one must make one's points before they sink in. With unvaried incantations that celebrated his faith in popular sovereignty and his stewardship of his illustrious uncle's legacy, Louis Napoleon advertised the essential differences that set him apart from other political leaders. This self-presentation proved a splendid asset with a large, often politically naive electorate.

The charisma Napoleon III borrowed from Napoleon I was all the more potent because his professions were not completely empty or simply tactical. In his youth, he had absorbed a flock of progressive notions about the advantages of technology, mainly from Saint-Simonian social theorists, and he believed some of his own propaganda. He dragged cautious manufacturers and bankers into the industrial age, stimulating economic growth by presiding over the formation of a flexible banking system, drastically reducing tariffs, and supporting the expansion of France's railroad network. There was a certain substance, then, beneath the shadow of his carefully cultivated popular image.

The most enduring of his domestic initiatives was the making of modern Paris. In 1853 he appointed Georges Eugène Haussmann prefect of the Seine. Competent, aggressive, and strongly backed by his emperor, Haussmann rebuilt much of the old city—a rabbit warren of isolated neighborhoods, crooked streets, decrepit houses, and unsanitary plumbing. In almost two decades of incessant demolition and construction a new capital emerged, an almost literally unrecognizable showcase that boasted delightful parks, handsome boulevards, and salubrious sewers. Daumier, in print after print, recorded the bafflement of couples unable to find their house after a short absence, and he was using only modest artistic license.

The emperor's reasons for plunging into such a vast public-works program were, as usual, overdetermined. Widening the streets and demolishing obstructive dwellings could serve as insurance against the building of barricades and facilitate the deployment of government troops. It also did much for the sheer beauty of the city; judging from plans Louis Napoleon had drawn up long before he could do more than dream of power, the aesthetic impulse was very much alive in him. All this planning, moreover, vitally assisted the circulation of people and vehicles; in the new Paris, traffic could flow far more easily from one section to another than it had before. And, of course, this feverish, ruinously expensive circus provided bread for masses of Parisians; in the 1850s and 1860s, about one in five Parisian workingmen was employed in the building trades. When, early in 1870, Haussmann was dismissed and the project, much of it completed by then, ground to a halt, Parisian workers groaned at the end of a splendid bonanza.[38]

As dictator and as emperor, grown prudent, Napoleon III did not trust speechmaking alone, or for that matter popular policies, to secure his regime. The press laws, harsher than those of Louis Philippe, were buttressed late in 1852 by censorship of the stage. Even more high-handed were the government's strategies for depriving universal manhood suffrage of real meaning. Despite the emperor's solemn assurances that his reign rested on the people's assent alone, his officials shamelessly managed elections, taking the suspense out of voting in the most gratifying way—gratifying to the government. The administration fielded "official" candidates, who received every legitimate and illegitimate assistance that local functionaries could devise. Election districts were gerrymandered, and ballot boxes stuffed. Restoration politicians had employed similar techniques, but then, they had never professed allegiance to that democratic fetish, popular sovereignty.

Sheer aggression supplemented the dirty tricks. Arrests, threats, violence, served where pressure proved insufficient.* Careers could ride on how one

---

*After the elections of 1857, one opposition candidate, the poet François Ponsard, reported, "Mayors, police commissioners and rural gendarmes made the rustic herd vote as they pleased. They arrested the people who carried my voting papers and tore my placards to pieces; they grabbed my voting papers from the hands and even in the houses of the peasants, and made all sorts

voted. The stealth with which the emperor initiated his diplomatic and military ventures—in Russia, in Italy, in Mexico, in Africa—further widened the chasm that repression and manipulation had first opened between governors and governed. All rulers, not just autocrats, claim foreign policy as their privileged domain, but Napoleon III kept his plans not only from the public and the legislature but from his ministers as well. In domestic matters he was no less secretive.

Yet, as the first imperial decade neared its close, Napoleon III did introduce traces of parliamentary practices into his authoritarian regime. For once he refused to follow his revered uncle, who had only intensified political repression with the passing years.* For all the casualties his troops had left behind in December 1851, all the curbs on opinion he had openly sponsored or tacitly approved, he was too humane to be a consistent Caesar. And he had a promise to keep: in earlier days, he had solemnly announced that liberty would follow once authority had done its work. Now he began to aim at what well-meaning observers, in obvious relief and with understandable hyperbole, called a "liberal empire." It was not an empire for the liberal bourgeoisie; the clergy and its conservative supporters retained their commanding influence, and the emperor crept toward liberty at a glacial pace. In 1859, he amnestied those convicted of political crimes, and most of the exiles came home—though not Victor Hugo. In 1860, he granted the legislature permission to debate the imperial address in the presence of his ministers. And in 1861, to everyone's amazement, he submitted his budget to the legislature and had it vote appropriations item by item.

Understandably, Napoleon's critics did not trust this slow conversion to constitutionalism.[39] Yet, astonishing his detractors, the emperor continued to expand his concessions. As he co-opted some of his most vocal antagonists, he was retreating from a monopoly on aggression and taking bold steps toward repairing the political process he had done so much to damage. In January 1870, he invited the fiery republican orator Émile Ollivier to form a cabinet. This was the revival of politics in action, the ultimate accolade to the principle of free opposition. Ollivier, lawyer and self-proclaimed realist, had worked within the system, the "liberal empire," for several years; now, like an English politician resuming office after an electoral victory, he was in charge. In May, Napoleon

---

of threats against them; they promised mayors fairs, churches, roads and relief for those flooded the year before." Alain Plessis, *De la fête impériale au mur des fédérés, 1852–1871* (1973), 191.

*The nephew also parted company with the uncle in one other domain: Napoleon III was a nationalist, romantic in his intensity; some of his foreign interventions, especially in Italian affairs, were aimed at bringing about a unified nation-state. Napoleon I had redrawn the map of Europe with little regard for national identity within his artificial constructions.

III resorted once again to his favorite populist device, a plebiscite, calling on the political public to ratify his experiments. The result was gratifying: well over 7 million voted their approval, over against a mere 1.5 million registering displeasure.

Yet within less than half a year, the empire was only a memory. A fatal mixture of rash foreign initiatives by Napoleon III and German pressure toward unification propelled him into a disastrous war.[40] Contrary to the emperor's and his country's confident expectations, Prussia brusquely displayed its superiority in the field. During the catastrophic defeat at Sedan on September 2, the ailing emperor was captured, and two days later a new French republic was proclaimed. It was the third in eighty years. The Caesarism of Napoleon III, though more flexible than that of his uncle, had been neither popular enough nor authoritarian enough to endure. And the principal engineer of Napoleon's fall, Otto von Bismarck, minister-president of the North German Federation and prime minister of Prussia, proved a far stronger player in the game of Bonapartism than the aging politician after whom it had been named.

For the historian of nineteenth-century aggression, overt or controlled, Otto von Bismarck offers unrivaled materials. His long dominance elevated his psychological symptoms to historic stature. He was too pugnacious to let his aggressive impulses lie fallow, too shrewd to give them their head. A late starter but quick study, Bismarck was not a primitive who equated politics with brute force. We have already observed, and will observe again, how diverse the styles of aggression can be. Bismarck explored nearly all of them, with bluster and suavity, spontaneous outbursts and calculating tactics. And since he acted on the largest possible stage—Prussia, Germany, Europe—making a historic difference, his aggressiveness was highly visible. Nor is this Bismarck's only use for the historian of aggression. His acknowledged "natural appetite for combat" gave him much pleasure, but also, though he barely knew it, many uneasy moments.[41] Bismarck's inner conflicts shed light on how people learn—or fail—to tame the lust for fighting.

Bismarck's political aggressiveness worried his mentor, the arch-conservative Leopold von Gerlach. Might his disciple be an admirer, even something of a student, of that incarnation of illegitimate rule, Louis Napoleon? In 1857, writing to Gerlach, who had the ear of Friedrich Wilhelm IV, Bismarck good-humoredly denied the charge.[42] He was then forty-two and Prussia's delegate to the federal German diet. His conscience was clear: surely he did not identify with Caesars old or new. He saw himself as a tough-minded servant of the Prussian monarchy, pursuing its interests with implacable logic.

Bismarck's disclaimer addressed the most momentous question a Prussian diplomat could face after 1848: how to navigate between his country's two great continental rivals, France and Austria. It also provides access to Bismarck's much-debated realism, a political stance exemplary for aggression pressed into the service of clearly perceived, though not necessarily admirable, strategic goals. He protested to Gerlach that he was no more an advocate of the French than of the Austrians and gently reproached him for *"ignoring the realities"* in foreign policy. It was not a mistake he proposed to make. The "fight against the revolution" was, to be sure, his governing principle, but he would not subordinate the "interests of my fatherland" to personal likes and dislikes.[43] Bismarck was liberating himself from the shackles of rigid ideology that he might maneuver freely among friends and enemies at home and abroad. He always liked to keep his options open. But they were *his* options: if Bismarck's twin masters, realism and royalism, were not always compatible, he found a convenient resolution to any tension their clash might generate; he simply identified any policy he favored as the most rational advice he could offer his king. To follow his star was the paramount show of loyalty.

Yet he had no illusions of omnipotence. Bismarck was well aware that he did not determine the course of nineteenth-century Germany single-handed; that is why he firmly denied politics the status of a science. Certainly Bismarck's early career gives no hint of Caesarist inclinations. He had always been a partisan of the powers that be. In his boyhood, he had toyed with the subversive notion that a republic might be the best form of government, but his "historical sympathies" had firmly remained "on the side of authority." Significantly, even then Brutus had been, "to my childlike sense of justice, a criminal."[44]

Only half a Junker—his mother came from a prominent family of non-noble officials—he entered public life more ostentatiously aristocratic than the real article. There could be no compromise with the nineteenth century; at his debut in 1847 as a deputy in the Prussian diet, he placed himself unhesitatingly among the supporters of the unreformed old regime and spoke for legal and financial privileges that more flexible aristocrats stood ready to abandon. He rejected the merest hint of parliamentary government, tax reform, or secularism. He vehemently objected to the admission of Jews to the civil service, in a long speech full of "bitter things," on the ground that Prussia was, after all, a Christian state. His report to his fiancée on these interventions shows him characteristically brisk and self-assured. The twenty-five speakers who had advocated Jewish emancipation had all "proffered the same sentimental sanctimoniousness" and "boring humanitarian drivel."[45] Neither sentimental nor boring, he took his speech as an opportunity to exhibit aggressiveness in full force.

Bismarck's conduct during the March days of 1848 was exemplary for a rising young reactionary. Prussian liberals, infected by the revolutionary winds blowing from France and Italy, had called for a constitutional regime. After a bloody clash between troops and demonstrators in Berlin, Friedrich Wilhelm IV, anxious to prevent worse incidents, yielded to the liberals' demands. Appalled at this craven betrayal of monarchist principles, Bismarck hatched a fantastic plot to restore the authority of the Prussian crown. It would have forced the king's abdication in favor of his young nephew, delivering a puppet into the hands of an ultraconservative camarilla. Bismarck's blueprint included teaching the rebels a sanguinary lesson. This was not the last time he recommended violence as an instrument of policy. "Blood and iron" was on his mind years before he explicitly formulated his ferocious slogan.

His very words repay study. Bismarck's pugnacious and picturesque language is flavored with metaphors from the hunt and the deadly duels of war. To be sure, warlike images must easily occur to anyone who talks of politics. Certainly fierce political rivals like Gladstone and Disraeli did not spare one another, at least in private. But in public they preserved a decorum that Bismarck refused to honor. His oratory had a particular combativeness, and his plans often matched his words; there were times when extreme policies seemed reasonable to him. In March 1852, he threatened the populations of large cities with extinction. They were led by "ambitious and mendacious demagogues," he told them bluntly, in a typical outburst. Should the cities rise up once again as they had four years before, the Prussian people would "know how to reduce them to obedience, even if they should wipe them from the face of the earth."[46]

Later, in 1874, in his fourth year as chancellor of the Empire, he aimed similar emphatic language at the Catholic Center party. Worried that it might form an alliance with the Social Democrats, he interpreted the suspected move as revealing a desire to "devour the German cadaver," a cannibalistic craving he hoped would remain ungratified: "Before that happens, Germany will have shot both tigers."[47] Four years after that, he told the Reichstag deputy Robert von Benda, a leading National Liberal, that he really did not care what political parties thought or did: "I am going my way; whoever goes with me is my friend, who goes against me is my enemy—to the point of annihilation." This instructive outburst underscored what he had said of himself: "When I have an enemy in my power, I must destroy him."[48] He meant it, even if the semiconstitutional political arena into which fate had thrown him frustrated his fondest desire.

That desire was to fight. With engaging candor, he freely confessed to a bellicose disposition, that "natural appetite for combat." One observer perceptively described Bismarck the young deputy in 1848 as a "tall, rigid, somewhat obese figure with blond beard and a scanty head of hair; he does not speak fluently but pushes out his words as in suppressed rage over the revolution and the revolutionary assembly." Except for a few contrite comments to his wife, there are few signs that he consciously regretted his rage, by no means always suppressed; some years before publication of the *Origin of Species,* he offered a kind of Social Darwinist rationalization for political mayhem: "Great crises form the weather that fosters Prussia's growth in that we exploit them fearlessly, perhaps even quite ruthlessly."[49]

Ruthlessness was for him the law of life. Philosophizing in retirement, he told a gathering of academics that as a woodsman he recognized strife as a governing force in all beings, from insects to birds of prey to humans. It was in character for him to see "the hunter's life" as "really natural to man." Yet his passion for combat was a psychological necessity more than a philosophical principle; dividing the world into allies and enemies provided him with an alibi for his pugnacity. No wonder the crowd of his enemies grew as that of allies shrank. "In office," he wrote in 1873, "it will be lonely around me, the longer the lonelier; one's old friends die off or become enemies, and one doesn't acquire any new ones." Political melees were a continuation of warfare by other means, implacably fought out on a "battlefield."[50]

In the course of his illustrious career—deputy to the Prussian diet, ambassador to the Germanic Diet at Frankfurt, envoy to Russia, prime minister of Prussia, chancellor of the German Empire—Bismarck fought on many battlefields, approaching each confrontation as though it were for the highest stakes. In 1872, during the early days of his quarrel with the Catholic Church, the *Kulturkampf,* he emphasized the government's readiness to *"fight"*; mobilizing his troops against subversive Jesuits at home and the imperialist papacy abroad, he urged that whatever the government chose to do, it must not show the white flag. One had to be active, in a word, aggressive, on principle: "Passivity is taken for weakness and is weakness." Again, in the following year, intent on suppressing Social Democratic agitation by strengthening censorship of the socialist press and surveillance of socialist organizations, he insisted that "the government must not remain passive in this fight."[51]

At least in his rhetoric—and, it is safe to conjecture, in his fantasies—he wanted conclusive resolutions, no concessions, even if in the end reality, his master, forced compromises on him. As he told Robert Lucius von Ballhausen, one of the few officials he trusted, "Better an end with terror than a terror without end." Every political goal had to be pursued with the utmost energy. *"If I stay in office,"* he told his colleagues in 1877, *"I want to take the Kulturkampf to its utmost end, an end to which perhaps not all those present will want to go with me."*[52]

This gladiatorial posture left traces across Bismarck's extensive track record.

His urge for fighting was more than a mere tic; it could rise to a thirst for blood. In September 1848, when a revolutionary resurgence in Berlin seemed possible, he expressed regret to his wife that "unfortunately" blood was not likely to flow. Not long after, he lamented the feebleness of "our government of castrati," who failed to satisfy his desire for drastic action against "barricadists." Again, in March 1886, in an excited outburst at a cabinet meeting, he insisted that the government must show its seriousness about licensing saloonkeepers; if necessary, it could set the constitution aside, but at all events, one had to make "war to the knife." He thought that many of his plans remained just that—plans—because most of his colleagues lacked the grit to follow his lead. No wonder he admired the English grudgingly, for their "manly self-assurance."[53] Manliness was a quality he valued, hoped he possessed, and needed to demonstrate.

He gave that quality robust expression by calling his enemies bad names. Bismarck's oral aggressiveness was not eccentric in a blunt age, but he gave way to it more passionately than other orators. He derided opponents not just as wrong but as egotistical, even vicious; he read their efforts as intended not to redirect policies, but to subvert the government. The liberals of 1848 were engaged in a "swindle." The Prussian bureaucracy had been "corroded by the cancer of republican-pagan education." The emergence of the First International was less a clue to economic grievances than a symptom of a "disease pervading the whole civilized world." Those who dared to disagree with him in the bureaucracy, on the floor of the Reichstag, or in the newspapers were practicing "demagoguery," or—a favorite epithet—acting as "enemies of the state."[54]

The Reichstag, which provoked Bismarck year after year, gave his gift for invective the largest possible scope. It was a "growling dog," which "loves its diseases and takes them for merits." It was populated by "professional deputies," who with their "incompetence and megalomania," were far worse than the rest of the population. The Austrians, too, whose dominance over German affairs he furiously resented and delighted in shaking off, were frequent targets of his inventive vocabulary. In 1854, incensed by what he chose to regard as Austrian duplicity, he called it "this Jewish mixture of cowardice, greed, and impudence." And the press, to which he paid close attention all his life, was a chief enemy—except, of course, for the docile papers he had bought. "The art of printing," he wrote in 1850, "is the chosen implement of the antiChristian."[55] In short, Bismarck did not mind voicing his hatreds.

Topping his list of the hateful was Eduard Lasker, a courageous, popular, extremely persuasive left-wing National Liberal deputy who often challenged and sometimes thwarted him. Bismarck denigrated his political ideas as "Laskerei," and called him doctrinaire and a "stupid Jew-boy."[56] Not even Lasker's death in early 1884 appeased him. When Lasker died in New York on an American tour, the House of Representatives voted a resolution of sympathy to be transmitted to the Reichstag. Far from conveying the message, Bismarck returned it to the sender, and instead harangued the Reichstag with a caustic speech filled with reproaches, distortions, pitiless denunciations of his late rival and all his works.[57] It was almost as though Bismarck blamed Lasker for dying and thus depriving him of more combat.

For a professing Christian, he was remarkably unforgiving. In 1849, he visited a cemetery in Berlin and walked past the graves of the Berlin demonstrators killed in the March revolution of the previous year. Writing to his wife, he asked her to pray for him, for "I grow so worldly here, and so angry, when you are not with me." He had found himself unable to forgive the dead, even though history had exposed their liberal dreams as castles in the air. "My heart was full of bitterness" against an "idolatry" that celebrates the memory of these "criminals." It infuriated him to see the inscriptions on the crosses over their graves, "boasting of 'Freedom and Right,' a mockery of God and men."[58] His grudges died only with his own death.

For decades the reality of Bismarck, victim of his temper, had very limited public circulation. His millions of admirers imagined him as complete master of himself, a statesman who trusted in intuition enriched by experience. Only a few intimates knew that he bought his almost legendary self-confidence at an exorbitant price. At moments of extreme stress—he would disclose some of them candidly enough in his classic memoirs—he broke down and dissolved into hysterical tears.[59] Beneath the steely surface of Bismarck the leader in charge lurked an interesting warfare between striking out and holding in, between impulse and inhibition. This persistent conflict is, of course, everyone's lot. But it is obviously more consequential in decision makers, and there is good evidence that Bismarck fought it out more vehemently than most.

Bismarck's fury repeatedly manifested itself in physical symptoms, one of the costs of aggressiveness bottled up. In 1847, irritated by the Prussian diet, he confessed to his fiancée that "sometimes I feel like smashing windowpanes, glasses, and bottles." Years later, aroused by Austrian "perfidy," he suffered from "continual attacks of bilious vomiting." Accusing others of fostering political excitement, he lived in an aura of excitement himself. "I am suffering, from morning to night, with bilious sickness from the mendacious, slanderous insincerity of the opposition and its obstinate, malicious willfulness." Full of ferocity and lacking adequate opportunities to show it, he thought himself ready to burst. In mid-January 1871, just after the German Empire had been proclaimed at Versailles, he reported to his wife that "the emperor's birth" had been a difficult one. "As obstetrician, I had several times the urgent need to be a bomb and to explode so that the whole building would fall into ruins." Bismarck's fantasies of world destruction were close to the surface. Writing to his sister in 1848, he admitted honestly enough, as was his habit, that there was a "choleric element in my nature."[60] He gave it much exercise.

Unlike pugnacious spirits who enjoy battling for its own sake, though, Bismarck wanted to fight because he wanted to win. Victory mattered more than popularity; he could approvingly quote Cicero's pugnacious exclamation, *Oderint, dum metuant*—"Let them hate as long as they fear." The urge to come out on top, to be first, to take command, remained with him as a goad long after his stormy, often unhappy youth. Like others, he carried childhood conflicts into adult life. His conscious feelings about his parents were complicated enough; it seems certain that his unconscious feelings were still more complicated. He told his fiancée that he really loved his father, a Prussian Junker boasting the most faultless pedigree. He did not tell her that he idealized that indulgent, ineffectual man far beyond merit, as though to stifle any trace of scorn for an aristocrat who, during the outpouring of Prussian patriotism in 1813 in the war against Napoleon, had stayed at home. In contrast, he confessed to a deep-seated hostility to his mother, handsome and intelligent, ambitious for him, chilly rather than affectionate, and characterized by a "cold rational clarity." It is ironic but natural; his mother's share in forming Bismarck's character and launching his career was far larger than his father's, but he never thanked her for it. Rather, he tried to manage the trauma of an unloving mother by engaging in a lifelong hunt for reassurance and uncritical affection, and in its counterpart, a search for gratifying objects to hate.[61]

As a youth, defying his mother's far-reaching plans for him, he had been indifferent in his studies. When he plunged into raucous student life at Göttingen and Berlin, he did what lesser young men did less well than he, carousing— and duelling.[62] All his life he took pride in having fought—and, he asserted, won—twenty-five duels; the only hit he suffered, he claimed quite inaccurately, was an unfair sally. The Mensur seemed virtually made for him. After leaving the university he drifted for years, from impiety to piety, from one civil service post to another, from Berlin to his family estates. All he knew then was that he must be master. In a much-quoted letter, he likened "the Prussian bureaucrat" to a musician in an orchestra, "whether he plays the first violin or the triangle"; but he wanted to make music "the way I find good, or none at all." In early 1845, when he was twenty-nine, he told a friend of his youth, "I have never been able to stand superiors." It was only to be expected that he was prey—as he admitted—to a "storm of untamed passions."[63] The point was to tame them. That was the most grueling battle of all.

What made Bismarck into the formidable statesman rather than a hulking political bully was his ability to win that battle much of the time. He managed to cultivate his hatreds in both senses of the phrase, sublimating them into prudent policy. He told Leopold von Gerlach in the 1850s, we know, that policy is best made in disregard of personal sentiments; *raison d'état* is a stern master. In 1866, after Prussia's decisive victory over the Austrian army at Königgrätz had put a quick end to the war between the two countries, Bismarck pressed for a generous peace. He envisioned a settlement that would guarantee Prussia's hegemony over the northern German states but leave Austrian territory intact. His king, Wilhelm I, angrily demurred. He had been reluctant to enter a war against the Habsburg empire; now, persuaded of the enemy's perfidy, he wanted revenge on Austria and its allies—slices of land, heavy reparations, perhaps a humiliating parade of the triumphant Prussian troops through the streets of Vienna.[64] But Bismarck calculated the implications of Prussia's victory far more clearly than his rather limited chief. He wanted Prussia's dominance, not Austria's ruin. Only after an exhausting squabble did Bismarck win his point. A united "small" Germany was not far in the future.

When its time came, in January 1871, Bismarck repeated his performance of the moderate statesman in action; he assured anyone who would listen—journalists, foreign diplomats, Reichstag deputies—that his country had no territorial ambitions and wanted only peace. At useful moments, especially when the military budget came up for debate, Bismarck could rattle the saber with the best of demagogues and proclaim war in sight. But he was perfectly serious about Germany's needs and intentions; he knew that for the military, diplomatic, and economic welfare of his country restraint was the most rational policy.

It was not a policy he could consistently sustain. When his urge to control men and events was unsatisfied, he felt his self-image threatened and regressed to pugnacity. His vehement, often mean-spirited speeches in the Reichstag, and interviews he gave friendly journalists attest that the storm of untamed passions to which he had confessed in his youth continued to rage. So do his reiterated threats to resign, symptoms of collapse as much as tactical maneuvers. So, too, do his intermittent illnesses, more psychosomatic than diplomatic, that kept him on his estates, far from Berlin, for months. So do, most of all, his tireless schemes to overthrow the constitution he had sworn to uphold.

Bismarck's projects for a coup d'état were no mere farfetched, desperate fantasies. He took them seriously and caressed them through the years. There were moments when he professed a measure of sympathy with the parliamentary form of government. He could sound envious of the English, who in his judgment had more or less realized that ideal. Germany, with eight or ten parties competing and with selfish political leaders, had not. "Parliamentarism," he told the author Moritz Busch in 1886, "works only when just two parties wrestle with one another and take turns, and where the legislators are well-to-do, not egotistical, have no need to be ambitious for themselves. I am no absolutist. Parliamentarism is good, even with us, as a veto against the will of an uncomprehending government and bad monarchs, as criticism."[65] But these musings were uncharacteristic; for the most part, Bismarck was absolutist enough, especially when he could deploy his favorite psychological device of equating loyalty to his king with getting his own way. Then he could safely denigrate his opponents as traitors.[66] He was only being consistent when he denounced party politics as a disease.[67]

These attitudes accompanied him through life. When he thought out loud about a coup to men in his confidence, it was clear that he saw himself not as a revolutionary but as the prop of order. He treated the instrument of government as precisely that—an instrument, to be used and discarded, just as he used and discarded his subordinates.* As early as 1862, while the constitutional struggle between the Prussian monarchy and its legislature was heating up—it would end four years later with a signal triumph for Bismarck—men in his circle covertly discussed the "possible need of a Brumaire." They did so with Bismarck's full approval. In 1884, exasperated after a heated debate in the Reichstag, he suggested to his cabinet that they should let the legislature persist in its folly until "it is in our gunsights." At the same meeting, he voiced hopes for a putsch by the Social Democrats and proposed to "permit the material for further conflicts to develop more." Robert Lucius von Ballhausen, who recorded these remarks, noted that Bismarck was "calm and resigned as he usually is not after conflicts of this sort," and shrewdly interpreted his chief's unaccustomed serenity as an indication that "he is considering serious, far-reaching plans."[68]

This was the *politique du pire*, the strategy of hoping for the worst to make dramatic, unconstitutional responses inescapable. As late as March 2, 1890, some two weeks before the young emperor Wilhelm II forced him into retirement, Bismarck discussed with his ministers measures against the Reichstag that would protect the imperial prerogative against the stubborn political opposi-

---

*"I can still hear him saying," the French archaeologist Salomon Reinach reported of Mommsen speaking about Bismarck, *Diese Menschenverachtung!*"—"This misanthropy!" Albert Wucher, *Theodor Mommsen. Geschichtsschreibung und Politik* (1956), 191n.

tion.[69] Yet unlike Louis Napoleon, Bismarck was never to enjoy the 18 Brumaire of which he spoke so often, with such longing. He was unlike Louis Napoleon in other ways as well, too original to become a mere disciple of anyone. But for all his fierce Prussian patriotism, all his contempt for the urban masses, the pressures of politics were strong enough to make him purloin certain techniques from the radical Bonapartist rhetoric of popular authority. As his early conservative mentors had feared, he was a supreme opportunist; his Christian professions markedly contrasted with his practice as a statesman.

It was Bismarck's lifelong opportunism—he preferred to call it flexibility—that allowed him to exploit the nationalistic fervor of ordinary Germans. Some four years before Bismarck entered the Prussian diet, Louis Napoleon had laid down the rationale for manipulative populism: "Have no preoccupation other than the good of the country and above all have no fear of the people; they are more conservative than you are!"[70] In his experiments with writing constitutions and electoral laws, Bismarck fully expected this to prove true. In 1859, he amazed the liberal politician Victor von Unruh by telling him, "The sole reliable, lasting allies that Prussia can have, if it conducts itself accordingly, are the German people."[71]

Impenetrable as Bismarck tried to make his maneuvers, his liberal critics feared his populist inclinations. In 1863, the prominent Progressive deputy Hermann Schulze-Delitzsch observed that the Prussian government under Bismarck's leadership was "trying to mobilize for their side the very classes they have at other times held up to the propertied as a dread apparition." The masses as ally of the Junkers—nothing, the liberals said nervously, could be more Bonapartist than this.[72] Three years later, in March 1866, Bismarck validated their anxiety. On the eve of war with Austria, he proposed a German parliament to be elected by universal manhood suffrage, and justified this astonishing step on the ground that plain men are reliable monarchists. He professed to have no doubt whatever: "In the moment of decision, the *masses will stand by the monarchy*," no matter what political line it may be following.[73]

Karl Twesten, a respected Progressive deputy and political pamphleteer, reacted promptly: "Bismarck is thinking of a Napoleonic regime with universal suffrage and similar tricks." Theodor von Bernhardi, historian and shrewd political insider, agreed. "With universal suffrage," he told Albrecht von Roon, then Prussia's minister of war, "we are falling into a pure imitation of France—into Caesarism." He had been aware for some time that by passing draconian laws against the press, the Bismarck cabinet was parroting, even outdoing, the regime of Napoleon III.[74]

Of course, like other modern Caesars, Bismarck scorned liberal demands for an authentic parliamentary system, in which the prime minister is responsible to the legislature and must bow to the majority. He expected—or hoped—that his own system would put the Hohenzollerns' power above challenge. Bismarck's conversion to universal manhood suffrage, in short, was not a sign of his political education; rather, he was appropriating a device to checkmate the liberal middle classes pressing for participation in politics. "In a country with monarchical traditions and loyal sentiments," he frankly told Count von Bernstorff, Prussia's ambassador to London, in April 1866, "universal suffrage would lead to monarchical elections by eliminating the influence of the liberal bourgeois classes." Even more frankly he confessed to the Saxon plenipotentiary von Friesen that he was aiming to *bring down parliamentarism by means of parliamentarism.*" Nor did he give up this manipulative strategy after he had become chancellor. In 1878, he told King Ludwig II of Bavaria that "the voters are friendlier to the government than are the Reichstag deputies."[75] The educated middle strata, priding themselves on their cultivation, were nothing better than troublemakers, bearers of revolution.

While Bismarck recognized that there were bourgeois on whom he could count, his favorite deputies were loyal peasants. The worst kind of parliament was one that had "become moderately liberal," for that would demand reforms one could hardly refuse to enact.[76] These splinters of political wisdom date from 1866, when Bismarck was reflecting on the shape that a constitution of Prussia and northern Germany should take, but they remained a dependable guide to his designs—and his hatreds—on the domestic front. In the mid-1860s, Engels told Marx that since Bismarck had made his "suffrage universal *coup,*" the German bourgeois would accept it "after a little struggle, for after all, Bonapartism is the real religion of the modern bourgeoisie." Since these bourgeois were not capable of governing directly, "Bonapartist semi-dictatorship" would be "the normal form." The material interests of the upper bourgeoisie would manage it all even against the protests of the rest of the middle class.[77] That was being too clever, but during the 1860s, as Bismarck appeared to be the only farseeing and effective German player at the chessboard of European politics, the overwhelmingly nationalistic German public, including most bourgeois, did go over to him in droves. Good liberals who had strenuously objected to Bismarck's political style deserted their ideals for the promise of a Reich they had dreamt of for half a century.

The active politicians among them were aware that Bismarck's high-handed policies—providing funds for the military, repressing free speech, and mounting costly wars—violated the Prussian basic law over and over. But all this, Bismarck's new recruits said, though unfortunate, was a modest price for national unity. It was appropriate that the party with whose support Bismarck began to govern Germany was called the *National* Liberal party. The religion of Bismarck's worshipful followers was success embroidered with Christian verbiage, much like Bismarck's own religion. That success, when it came, no doubt brought conspicuous benefits to broad segments of the bourgeoisie, just as it did to broad segments of Germany's other classes. Yet in more than two decades of dominance, Bismarck could never silence an opposition led by politically conscious liberal bourgeois and that astonishing newcomer on the German scene, the Social Democratic party.

The alliance that Bismarck had sought to forge between the common people and the imperial power did not hold. His condescending trust in the bulk of lower-class voters proved to be his most portentous miscalculation. The urban proletariat conducted itself in ways he could never understand, let alone sympathize with. They were disturbingly unlike that rural "healthy element" in German society, the docile peasants on his estates, whom Bismarck had taken to be representative. What he knew of industrial workers he had learned mainly in 1863, in confidential conversations with Ferdinand Lassalle, authoritarian state socialist and founder of the first German workers' party. Lassalle had reassured Bismarck that the masses were perfectly ready to support a "social dictatorship" by the Prussian monarchy as long as it functioned in the interest of the lower classes. But Lassalle, we know, died in 1864 in that most aristocratic of deaths, a duel, and the Social Democratic party traded Caesarist notions for the incendiary theory of class struggle. Laboriously educating themselves in the realities of political life, the Social Democrats matured into Bismarck's most vociferous critics.

Though strapped for funds, rudimentary in organization, and under steady harassment, the Social Democrats prospered. By 1877 they polled almost half a million votes in elections to the Reichstag, 9 percent of the total. Starting from nowhere, the party had grown into the fourth strongest in the country. Bismarck's mode of dealing with this menace from the left was typical of him—and reminiscent of the French Caesars: an amalgam of sticks harshly applied and carrots haughtily offered. Nor does the resemblance end there. Bismarck's way of seizing his opportunity recalls the responses of the Napoleons to the openings that good fortune threw their way. Like them he reacted promptly. Like them he attacked enemies he wanted to destroy rather than those deserving condemnation. Like them he was not above lying.

One of his most notorious fabrications was intended to eliminate the Social Democratic party. In May 1878 a mentally unbalanced young man shot at Kaiser Wilhelm I. He missed, and though he had clearly acted on his own,

Bismarck welcomed the incident as the cue for a stringent anti-socialist law.*
The bill was hastily thrown together and plainly irrelevant, and the Reichstag
rejected it. Then in June luck gave Bismarck another chance—a second attack
on the emperor's life. This time the aged monarch was wounded. Defying the
evidence, the government claimed that the assailant had admitted being a Social
Democrat. The lie did its work well; Bismarck dissolved the Reichstag and the
subsequent elections gave him a majority for the law he wanted. For twelve
years, until its repeal, Germany's Social Democrats had to campaign under
appalling handicaps: their congresses were outlawed, their newspapers confiscated, their meetings dissolved on the slightest pretext. One cannot help thinking of Consul Napoleon Bonaparte; in December 1800, he had exploited a
bomb thrown by royalists to suppress the Jacobins, who had nothing to do with
the attentat.

So much for the stick; in the 1880s, Bismarck added the carrot. The imperial
message of 1881 noted that "social damage" can be cured not just by repressing
"Social Democratic excesses," but also by "the positive fostering of the workers' welfare."[78] Concretely, this meant what conservative critics denounced as
state socialism: in 1883, sickness insurance; in 1884, accident insurance; in 1889,
old-age and disability insurance. These measures instituted admirable social
experiments that other countries would imitate, but as political gestures they
were total failures. Except for a setback in the elections of 1881, the Social
Democratic party kept enlarging its delegation to the Reichstag; in 1890, the
last year of the anti-socialist law, it garnered almost a million and a half votes (19
percent of the total) and thirty-five seats. This showing was all the more spectacular in light of the conditions under which, we know, Social Democrats had
to campaign. When Wilhelm II dismissed Bismarck in March 1890, it was as
though the times had passed the old chancellor by. The new German emperor,
vain, self-assertive, unpredictable, aching to assert his authority, seemed determined to prove that two Caesars are like two tenors in a small opera company.
One of them must go, and it had to be Bismarck.

This, then, was the ironic fate of the master politician whom Max Weber
would not hesitate to qualify as a Bonapartist in the most unflattering sense of
that slippery epithet—a Caesarist demagogue plain and simple. Weber described Bismarck as an unscrupulous hoarder of power, intolerant of the slightest show of independence, ruthlessly playing off classes against each other to
maximize his own influence over Germany's affairs.[79] Looking back amidst the

---

*The complexities of politics in imperial Germany cannot be our business here, but it is worth
noting that in proposing this law, Bismarck was striking not only at the Social Democrats but at the
National Liberal party, with which he had so far been allied.

horrors of the First World War, he grimly summed up Bismarck's legacy: a German nation *"without any political education whatever,* far below the level it had already reached" in the decades before his accession. "And above all, a nation *without any political will whatever."*[80]

Theodor Mommsen's verdict was as scathing and all the more crushing; after all, as an active liberal politician he had in the 1860s welcomed Bismarck's strategic moves toward a united Germany, and his paean to the Roman Caesar remained unforgettable. But there was, for Mommsen, no comparison between the creative popular statesman of antiquity and his power-hungry modern German counterfeit. Bismarck had consistently dismissed the strictures of Mommsen, who sniped at him for years, as typical for a cloistered pedant so deeply immersed in antiquity that he had no eye for contemporary political realities. As he said in private and in public, he had no respect for "political children and doctrinaire scholars."[81] But Mommsen's judgment could not be so easily shunted aside. In 1902, a year or so before his death, he wrote a friend, memorably, "Bismarck has broken the nation's back."[82] He was exaggerating; the health of the German political nation was not in quite so parlous a state as that. But his curt verdict is a far from inappropriate epitaph for Bismarck's legacy.

In the late 1860s, Bismarck had coined a famous aphorism: "Politics is the art of the possible." The saying is less banal than might appear at first glance. It tersely sums up the stance of which Bismarck was very proud—his realism. But though he had been more adaptable than the two Napoleons, in the face of the pressures for democratic politics he had not been realistic enough. That the empire he had created almost singlehanded outlived him by less than three decades must be laid in large part to his designs, his policies, and his limitations. Even this most brilliant of modern Caesars could not leap over his shadow. The future of democracy lay elsewhere.

4. Human Nature in Politics

The key conundrum for Victorian politics was the franchise. Only manipulators of the Caesarist persuasion knew no hesitation. Through the century, country after country witnessed interminable disputes about just who was entitled to participate in the political process. They were anything but disinterested; ideologues schemed to reshape electorates to bolster their supporters and exclude their critics. But some of the debaters rose above such tendentious stratagems. Unwilling to identify the special interests of their class with the general welfare, they reflected about human possibilities and human limitations. At the highest level of discourse, for a Tocqueville or Bagehot, views on the vote were views on man's capacity for autonomy and for harnessing aggression. Could reason in the public service triumph over the brute need for self-assertion? By 1908, when the brilliant political scientist and social psychologist Graham Wallas published *Human Nature in Politics,* a pioneering study of nonrational elements in political choices, the question was still far from answered.

Like other contentious nineteenth-century matters, the role of human nature in politics had already been canvassed in the previous century, during the Enlightenment. As impassioned social pedagogues, the philosophes linked political rights to education. Their two questions—just how wide to draw the circle of instruction, and how wide to draw the circle of the enfranchised— were really a single question. They confronted, after all, some intractable realities: even in advanced England and France most people were barely literate or wholly illiterate. But, committed to the preeminence of nurture over nature, they discarded Plato's myth about humans being different in their essence— some of noble metal by nature, some base. Instead they adopted Locke's more optimistic view that the mind of every human is at birth a blank slate, upon which experience will inscribe habits, desires—and political opinions. At home with this vision, they wondered just how educable the uneducated might be. The political rights of what some philosophes liked to deride as the *canaille* depended on the resolution of this perplexity. They did not all resolve it in the same way.*

And they handed it on to the nineteenth century, which discovered all over again that the well-to-do and the educated are not always rational, and the poor and uneducated not necessarily emotional, helpless victims of their brutish needs and fears. "A lawyer or a doctor," Graham Wallas noted, "will on quite general principles argue for the most extreme trade-unionism in his own profession, while he thoroughly agrees with a denunciation of trade-unionism addressed to him as a railway shareholder or ratepayer."[1] It was a telling illustration, but the question of just how to determine the precise proportions of reason and passion in politics remained a vexing one. While the philosophers

---

*Some, like Helvétius and Holbach, argued that ignorance alone causes the animal-like surrender to the lower passions so typical of the poor. To educate them would be to remove all obstacles to intelligent political activity. But they were in a minority; the view of human nature that held sway in their century was that of Voltaire, who scattered sarcastic bon mots about the lower orders among his letters and his published writings. It is doing society a favor, he insisted, to keep the lower orders religious; once they understand that He will not punish them for their actions, they will give themselves over to debauchery and crime. Voltaire himself, it should be noted, eventually moved beyond these barbed remarks; his final verdict on the "masses" was more nuanced, less class-bound.

had been able—or, rather, in the absence of political power, had been doomed—to play speculative games as they explored the workings of human nature in politics, nineteenth-century social theorists, editorial writers, and makers of constitutions were driven to translate theoretical generalities into practical provisions.

But whether gentlemen talking politics in coffeehouses or legislators drafting statutes for an electoral system, whether liberal opponents of monarchical absolutism in Great Britain or impatient philosophers in France, few were democrats calling for universal suffrage—except of course the Caesars, for reasons of their own. Most thought pure democracy the counterpart to the sole rule of a king: an invitation to tyranny. It is revealing that Victorian political thinkers were ready to go back to Aristotle for his demonstration that a mixed government—one that happily blends elements of monarchy, aristocracy, and democracy—is best. They wanted institutions that would check the pressures from one segment of society with counterpressures from the others. The fact that constitutional regimes almost universally resorted to a two-house legislature vividly attests to the intellectual prestige that the old idea of mixed government continued to enjoy throughout much of the century.*

The most obvious implication of this idea was that only men owning property should be authorized to enter the fenced-in domain of political culture. Precise definitions necessarily varied, as lawgivers and pamphleteers wrangled over the fine points of just how much property, and what kind, is sufficient to give its holder a stake in the country. There was little dispute over imbeciles, children, prisoners, servants, paupers, and women; for reasons nearly everyone thought too self-evident to need discussion, none of these deserved a voice in the country. The controversies were over more substantial citizens like thriving workingmen and small property owners, and over a possible distinction between the right to vote for one's representatives and the right to be one of them. But, with all the dissension, the principle that major exclusions are necessary to guarantee a rational political culture retained its vitality everywhere. Venturesome democrats who campaigned for the abolition of property qualifications were a subversive minority, troublemakers in the style of their predecessor Tom Paine. Until the revolutions of 1848 they were barely respectable.

The logic of the argument for property tests was simplicity itself. "The true reason of requiring any qualification with regard to property in voters," Sir

---

*A locus classicus is, of course, *The Federalist*, the series of papers written in 1787–88 by Alexander Hamilton, James Madison, and John Jay to sway the voters of New York to support the proposed constitution of the United States.

William Blackstone contended, "is to exclude such persons as are in so mean a situation as to be esteemed to have no will of their own."[2] A man earned the suffrage, he was not born with it—unless, of course, he was born to wealth. The franchise, noted Teofron Säve, a Swedish writer, "is a mandate that the state confers on such persons as are qualified to fulfill it, and it is not a right that is due a person merely because he is born or is a citizen." Säve wrote after 1866, the year Sweden adopted drastic reforms that curtailed the hegemony of its notables. And as late as 1896, when less than a third of all Swedish males had the vote, the conservative Rudolf Kjellén warned against "a politics that seeks to place power in the hands of all." That, he thought, "is as perilous as it is rootless, for it involves a violation of the order of nature and the organic body of the community of the people."[3] Such rhetoric was a common refrain across the Western world.

This aristocratic position struck its supporters as a self-evident alibi for limiting the vote to the substantial and the established. During the tense exchanges that preceded the passing of the British Reform Act of 1867, its most outspoken opponent, the influential Liberal politician Robert Lowe, linked "inequality" to "the order of Providence"; in familiar accents, he insisted that it was "the wisdom of the State to make its institutions conform to that order." Even unimpeachable reformers denounced universal suffrage as destructive of the social fabric, offensive to the very nature of the human animal. In 1842, as the House of Commons was debating a Chartist petition for broad electoral reforms, Thomas Babington Macaulay declared that while he could support the secret ballot and other Chartist demands, he must reject its centerpiece, universal suffrage. "My firm conviction is that, in our country, universal suffrage is incompatible, not with this or that form of government, but with all forms of government, and with everything for the sake of which forms of government exist; that it is incompatible with property, and that it is consequently incompatible with civilisation."[4] In the same vein Odilon Barrot, a prominent liberal politician in the reign of Louis Philippe, held the saying *Vox populi, vox Dei* to be "the most dangerous and the most despotic absurdity that has ever emerged from a human brain. If you want to ruin a state, give it universal suffrage."[5]

There is no need for further examples. Most Victorians thought this view solidly anchored in what Kjellén called the order of nature, and Lowe called the order of Providence. The France of the Restoration, as we know, specified in its charter the requisite gender, wealth, and age of voters and of deputies. Of the more than 8 million adult Frenchmen, less than 1 percent comprised the *pays légal*. The July Monarchy of Louis Philippe liberalized these numbers with a moderation verging on timidity. The taxes a man paid to qualify as a voter were reduced; so was the age of those eligible to sit in the legislature. The modest result was a less than threefold increase in the electorate, with the privilege of the vote bestowed on just under 3 percent of French males. When, in February 1848, triumphant revolutionaries proclaimed universal suffrage, they enlarged the *pays légal* from a narrow oligarchy to a democracy—of men, not women. Where there had been some 250,000 voters, there were now, suddenly, 9 million. We have seen how ambiguous a windfall this revolutionary act proved to be once Louis Napoleon learned how to use it. But the leap had been taken, and it remained a spur to some, a nightmare to most.

The United States alone progressed toward universal manhood suffrage with prodigious though uneven steps. As early as 1829, the New York *Workingman's Advocate* had solemnly warned that "it is a dangerous thing to sneer at universal suffrage in this republican country." In France one could talk derisively of *canaille,* and in England "of the *mob* and the *swinish multitude.*" But "this is neither France nor England."[6] By the 1840s, living with a crazy quilt of widely divergent electoral laws, Americans were proudly making the democratization of the suffrage their favorite political issue. As Charles Dickens's *American Notes* and *Martin Chuzzlewit* attest, ridiculing this self-satisfied democratic republicanism was easy. But even as Dickens was writing, and whatever the aptness of his sour remarks about American boastfulness and American philistinism, states were erasing the property and tax qualifications inscribed in their constitutions. Well before the Civil War, the United States was a democracy—with the blots of unenfranchised women and blacks—and had vindicated Tocqueville's prediction.

The progress of the suffrage in Belgium was less dramatic and hence more typical of the age. After the defeat of Napoleon, the allies had forced the Belgians into an unwanted union with the Dutch. But in the fall of 1830, inspired by the July revolution in neighboring France, Belgian clerics, proletarians, and bourgeois formed an unorthodox alliance and shook off Dutch rule. They promptly wrote a constitution that provided for a powerful monarch and guaranteed civil rights. Just as promptly, they enacted legislation specifying that to be eligible to vote, one had to pay a certain amount in direct taxes, the required sum varying with the district. And they introduced an innovative electoral qualification: proof of working in a liberal profession as "a guarantee of political competence."[7]

Intoxicated with their liberalism, the makers of the new Belgium took pride in its being more democratic than any other European state. But the country was at best comparatively democratic; its complicated electoral provisions, restricting the vote to one out of about thirty males, protected the elite from what it perceived as the docile masses who would slavishly vote as their betters told them, or paid them, to vote. "The more we lower the property tests," observed

Joseph Lebeau, a prominent liberal politician, as the constitution was being formulated, "the more aristocratic the elections we will have."[8] This fear of the swinish multitude, not as a revolutionary force, but for its reactionary potential, remained a compelling deterrent to a wide franchise, and not in Belgium alone. Before 1848, it did not take much to be the most democratic state in Europe.

In Belgium, though, as elsewhere, agitation to enlarge the franchise went on unabated. The campaign was often supported, even led, by bourgeois liberals looking beyond their concrete class interests to a political culture shared by all—well, almost all. But resisters to democracy long retained the upper hand; and in some states, such as Prussia, they invented transparently self-serving rules to abort it. Prussia's electoral law of May 1849, a pillar of the pseudoconstitutional structure substituted for the real article promised to the rebels the year before, was in most of its provisions perfectly conventional and resembled statutes across Europe. It specified that elections be indirect and open; voters would choose electors who then selected, without the protection of a secret ballot, their representative in the Chamber of Deputies. An independent spirit balking at an elector favored by the authorities was putting his livelihood at risk. Another clause in the statute, virtually unique to Prussia, was designed to secure beyond challenge the power of the landed Junker aristocracy and their allies: the voters of each electoral district were divided into three classes, according to the amount of taxes paid; those who paid a third of all the taxes had as much voting power as the middling people paying the second third, or the masses paying the rest.

The scheme had its apologists. "I cannot consider it just and reasonable," one Prussian aristocrat, Baron Adolf Senfft von Pilsach, argued, "that a simple working man has as much voice as his employer who hires hundreds or thousands like him, gives them bread and feeds their families."[9] Ironically, this clever system proved not clever enough; by the early 1860s, as Prussia's impressive economic strides made bankers, industrialists, and businessmen into millionaires, a new breed of men—parvenus all, the aristocrats sneered—captured the presumably unconquerable bastion of the *Chamber*. They took the lead even in the third electoral class because the lower orders, despairing at how little their votes mattered, tended to stay at home on election day.* Many new men of power were, perhaps surprisingly, liberals; Bismarck hated them as the distilled bourgeoisie, the organized revolution. Whatever its unintended results, there

---

*In 1861, the first electoral class had 159,000 voters; the second, 454,000; and the third, 2,750,000. A voter in the first class, in short, had seventeen times the weight of one in the third. Otto Pflanze, *Bismarck and the Development of Germany*, 3 vols. (1990), vol. I, *The Period of Unification, 1815–1871*, 224–25.

was no nonsense about democracy in the Prussian electoral system. Still, it remained intact right up to the collapse of the empire in 1918, sitting awkwardly with the universal suffrage law governing elections to the Reichstag. Obviously, the history of the franchise is a history of anomalies.

The most interesting of the fierce and seemingly interminable debates about the suffrage were conducted not between absolutists and constitutionalists, but between liberals and democrats. After all, partisans of absolutism held views so clearly irreconcilable with the ideal of popular sovereignty that they found any compromise with the advocates of a wide and effective suffrage virtually unthinkable. In contrast, nineteenth-century liberals, on principle committed to a genuine constitutional order, a lively electorate, and diligent experiments in political education, proved worthy adversaries for democrats working to enfranchise the bulk of the adult population.

The issue that divided liberals and democrats was plain: if the consent of the governed is to be at all meaningful, if they are to weigh the acts of their governors and join in the making of laws through their representatives in a legislature that is better than a charade, they must be rational creatures capable of rising above willful self-interest. Was it reasonable to demand disinterested restraint from day laborers and peasants doomed to lives of unending drudgery on the edge of starvation? Could human nature overcome illiteracy, exhaustion, indifference, the centuries-old habit of submissiveness punctuated only by riots? Could one fashion into competent citizens the holders of a little property or small craftsmen who work with their hands, men who read, if they read at all, the Bible or some scandal sheet?

Most liberals in most countries thought not, and wove an elaborate network of rationalizations in defense of a relatively narrow electorate. French liberals of all stripes did so more elaborately than others. Their reasoning, often defensive in the extreme, suggests how traumatized they had been by a decade of revolution followed by the rule of Napoleon and, after that, times of riot and insurrection. Even those to the left of Guizot—those who saluted, and worked to perpetuate, the ideals of '89—had qualms about the unlettered being active in politics. Madame de Staël had said it more bluntly than most; put political power into the hands of the propertyless and you will get "the government of crime."[10]

Benjamin Constant had tormented himself in the same liberal and antidemocratic cause. He had pleaded for popular sovereignty and in the 1820s hinted that Restoration France would do well to widen its franchise: the right to vote should not be tied to a proven interest in political life; rather, the vote should be the *cause* of public spirit. At the same time, Constant had justified existing property qualifications on the well-rehearsed ground that the poor cannot be independent; they cannot afford to offend those for whom they work. Only those with a modicum of property are educated enough, and enjoy sufficient leisure, to make rational decisions in public matters. This line of reasoning left an important opening for the advocates of universal suffrage: education is the key to the making of citizens. It was an opening of which Constant was aware, one he did not live long enough to explore. In any event, among most French liberals, fear of the plebs outran their hopes for it. To give the masses the vote was to invite chaos.

Tocqueville elaborated this position as he worried about the "tyranny of the majority" looming over democratic cultures. And Guizot, reflecting on politics both as a historian and as a minister, thought every society, including his own, equipped with a natural elite which, with its brains and its public spirit, had the right—indeed, the duty—to speak for those less well endowed with the political virtues. It was all a matter of competence, and competence was always in limited supply. Recalling the revolution of 1830, he described the masses as an inadequate bulwark against loyalists conspiring to restore the discredited Bourbons.[11] That at least was being candid; Guizot wanted an electorate he could rely on. Hence he was skeptical about the Second Republic under the presidency of Louis Napoleon: the "idolatrous cult" of "democracy" had become a talisman invoked by all parties. He professed to support the new political order, but it was a bourgeois regime he had in mind, one that boasted the middle classes as its fundamental element. Optimists about human capacities might hail the rapid shift toward mass rule, but Guizot was not among them. Let everyone examine himself deeply; he will discover "an incessant war between good and bad inclinations, between reason and caprice, duty and passion." This combat makes democracy the agent of disorder, for it is the "unleashing of all human nature," including egotism and the revolutionary spirit. True, "democratic France owes much to the emperor Napoleon," but that was not a compliment: Napoleon had both embraced democracy and scorned liberty.[12] Indeed, Guizot thought, the two were incompatible.

As late as 1872, after the Second Empire had given way to a shaky Third Republic, Hippolyte Taine rehearsed the old antidemocratic arguments in a carefully reasoned pamphlet on the best electoral system. His country, he was convinced, had made ill use of universal suffrage. The troubling truth was that most Frenchmen were unfit for active citizenship; of each twenty eligible to vote in his day, the large majority were peasants or workingmen living on farms or in villages, ignorant, unpolitical, often indifferent to elections, many of them unable to name their deputy. Only three out of twenty—shopkeepers, master craftsmen, small entrepreneurs—could claim "demi-bourgeois" status, and only three more were cultivated and prosperous. The implications were obvious—for Taine: the "political education of the masses" requires indirect elections, with voters choosing local electors who, in turn, choose the legislature.[13]

Most German liberals were no less anxious. Talk of the barely controllable masses ran through their polemics like a leitmotif and set the tone for the controversies over the right to political participation. In 1830, the Rhenish entrepreneur and liberal politician David Hansemann noted, at a time of revolutions elsewhere, "The first danger is an uprising of the lower popular class."[14] The German revolutions of 1848 only exacerbated this political nervousness. In that year, a Cologne socialist, Andreas Gottschalk, a Jewish physician who practiced among the poor, observed that among his Rhenish fellow bourgeois, the very word "republic" was synonymous with "robbery, murder, and Russian invasion."[15]

Not surprisingly, the heartfelt debates in the Frankfurt parliament of 1848 were dominated by liberals, not democrats. Convened to write a constitution for a Germany that did not yet exist, most delegates canvassed once again the fatiguing arguments against universal suffrage. A handful of democrats protested, in vain. "Do you really believe," one asked rhetorically, "that bureaucrats in the states, or professors, here much praised, are freer than workers?" Another pointed out that while independence is indeed a desirable quality in a voter, what really counts is "independence of mind" rather than affluence. Still another cautioned that to exclude any responsible male from the electorate would pit citizen against citizen. The liberals were not to be moved. The masses, they argued, were simply politically immature, with no independent will of their own. Hence it would be dangerous to give them the vote. Interpreting events to support their stand, liberal delegates pressed recent history into the service of their cause. Months of revolution across Europe had sobered even the enthusiasts among them. "Who put absolutism into Napoleon's hands, who made him into an unlimited hereditary emperor?" one delegate asked, and he answered his own question: "Universal suffrage." These were illuminating reservations. "The aristocracy should be given no means," one delegate urged, presciently enough, "to govern through the masses." Such would-be founders of a constitutional state were worrying about Caesarism.[16]

More than a decade later, in 1862, the historian Heinrich von Sybel laid out the liberals' program from the same defensive posture: "It is our wish, by establishing a liberal and national regime, to appease spirits and prevent a revolution." Some seven years after, just before the creation of Bismarck's Empire, he warned that the powerful democratic movement was edging toward the abyss of radicalism. As long as "education and ethics are not yet equally developed among all men"—and that would still take a very long time—"it is folly to talk of an absolute equal right to political power, a universal right to vote, an inborn human right to legislative power." Since the working class obeys its passions and is easily seduced, votes for all would only keep the old regime in power or inaugurate a reign of demagogues. Complete equality could only produce "the wretched alternation of anarchy and dictatorship, of popular and military tyranny."[17] The German disputes reveal once again that the principal issue dividing liberals and democrats was human nature in politics.

That issue was confronted most persistently, and most instructively, in Britain. A string of reform acts—in 1832, 1867, 1884, and 1885—reinforced by important acts in 1870 and 1872 moving toward general education and granting the secret ballot, make nineteenth-century British history appear like a preordained march of democracy, step by judicious step. The reality was more complicated and more fascinating. It was political theater of the highest order, with splendid orations and close votes, heroes and villains abruptly trading places; an absorbing melodrama played out in Parliament, election campaigns, and floods of pamphlets, and in salons, clubs, the political press, and public meetings. The decades of reform left no aspect of the redefinition of public aggression untouched. And they were rife with surprises: the Reform Act of 1867 was pushed through not by Gladstone's Liberals, but by Disraeli's Conservatives.

The Great Reform Act became law in 1832 because the people who counted and made themselves heard wanted it. Early in 1831, when the clamor for parliamentary reform reached fever pitch, Earl Grey, then prime minister, acknowledged that the pressure had become irresistible: "With the universal feeling that prevails on this subject, it is impossible to avoid doing something; and not to do enough to satisfy public expectation (I mean the satisfaction of the rational public) would be worse than to do nothing."[18] Ever since the twin menaces of the French Revolution and Napoleon's assault on Europe had dragged Britain into costly and exhausting wars, the country had lived in an atmosphere of great expectations. The industrial revolution had already left its impress, generating technological unemployment and intensifying the misery of the laboring poor. Hunger provoked petitions, marches, strikes, the destruction of machinery—manifestations the government suppressed with rigor, even ferocity.

Not all was gloom. While political economists and political theorists tried to think their way through their country's unprecedented situation, economic changes brought prosperity to the well-placed and the enterprising. And at the Home Office, Sir Robert Peel was rationalizing the English criminal law, dragging it into the nineteenth century. The radicals who had dreamt of introducing the spirit of '89 had been silenced, but the call for reform—in tariffs, the poor laws, the statutes disfranchising Roman Catholics, the prohibitive taxes that crippled the press—did not abate. And the House of Commons became the focus of the discontent. Reforming action could be taken only in Parliament, and only after Parliament itself had been reformed.

In isolated districts, such reform had, as it were, already taken place; the political education of the public varied as wildly as did the right to vote in Britain's haphazard electoral system. The Westminster constituency in London was a model of advanced political consciousness, a foretaste of democracy to come. The breadth of its franchise was exceptional; its ten thousand voters included not only physicians, lawyers, and businessmen but artisans and marginal merchants—unenfranchised nearly everywhere else in Britain. Since 1807, the democrats controlling the Westminster constituency's informal but potent political clubs had sent two radicals to the House of Commons, where they spoke out, a tiny and noisy minority, for far-reaching electoral reform.

The dominant figure in this democratic enclave was Francis Place, a prosperous London tailor. Place is of interest as an exemplar of the new political man rising from the ranks. He had made enough money to amass an impressive library and enjoyed enough leisure to read it, but he was too energetic to remain a bookish onlooker; he sought out the leading lights among Britain's progressive intellectuals, and corresponded diligently with politically minded workingmen, aspirants to office, and social theorists. The cabinet's panicky and repressive responses to popular unrest infuriated him. He trusted the political sagacity of ordinary people far more than that of the politicians governing—or misgoverning—the country.

Place's radicalism outran public opinion, even the program advanced by the reforming minority in Parliament. But with his persistence he revitalized the political education of the British public. So did, in his own eccentric way, the orator William Cobbett, an odd combination of demagogue, radical, and nostalgic reactionary. Cobbett traveled across England delivering to appreciative audiences his simple, rather ominous plea for a wider franchise: the country had to undertake political reform if it wanted to escape a revolution.[19] In Birmingham the Political Union was formed to push for the cause. The discontented were learning to organize themselves peacefully, striding toward constructive political aggressiveness. Another step came in 1830, when the duke of Wellington resigned as prime minister upon being defeated in the House of Commons on the very issue of parliamentary reform. Unlike his predecessors in the same quandary, King William IV felt powerless either to keep Wellington in office or to choose a successor the Commons would not support. Responsible parliamentary government, its rudimentary beginnings going back to the eighteenth century, was finally on its way.

The reformers were determined to recruit those sound, middle-class elements whom Earl Grey singled out as the "rational public." In 1831, in a lengthy, excited, widely reported speech to the House of Lords, the radical Henry Brougham, recently created Baron Brougham and Vaux, extolled the wealthy segments of the "middle classes." Those "hundreds of thousands of respectable persons" were "the genuine depositaries of sober, rational, intelligent, and honest English feeling." Though perhaps unable "to round a period, or point an epigram," he told their snobbish detractors, they were "solid, right-judging men," and "above all, not given to change." One could feel safe with "the bold, rational, judicious, reflecting, natural, and because natural, the trustworthy opinions of those honest men." To "dream of carrying on any Government in despite of those middle orders of the State" was unthinkable. Since middle-class radicals pressing for the vote made the establishment very nervous, the most reassuring thing Brougham could say about them was that they would "neither be led astray by false reasoning, nor deluded by impudent flattery."[20]

One might be inclined to discount this hymn of praise to English industrialists, bankers, and businessmen; Brougham was notorious as the most boisterous spokesman in the extreme wing of the Whigs.* The Lords did discount it, defeating the proposed reform bill by a majority of forty-one. But calmer spirits said the same thing in calmer tones. Earl Grey defined "the middle classes" as those "who form the real and efficient mass of public opinion, and without whom the power of the gentry is nothing." Like other members of Parliament who supported the bill he made it plain that when he spoke of the "people" who deserved the vote, he meant not the drunken mob, not the barely literate poor, but "the great majority of the respectable middle classes of the country."[21] It was among these serious, responsible merchants and professional men that sufficient amounts of property and intelligence, two guarantors of stability, were to be found. The bourgeois cause had its aristocratic spokesmen.

The Reform Act of 1832 went some way toward vindicating the claims of the upper middle class. True, with its detailed and intricate provisions, it took only a cautious stab at transforming the political public. Governance remained essentially in the hands of the old oligarchy. Many voters continued the familiar pattern of choosing candidates the magnates told them to choose, not so much

---

*It is a symptom of how far nineteenth-century politics had been able to sublimate aggression that Brougham, who, with his sweeping rhetoric, ambitious plans, and inconsistent leadership, had made himself something of a nuisance to his followers—to say nothing of his opponents—was reduced to relative harmlessness by being promoted to the House of Lords in 1830. As we saw at the beginning of this chapter, a century earlier he would most likely have been banished to his properties; two centuries earlier he would have gone to the scaffold.

from fear of reprisals as from residual trust in their betters; the old deferential society survived very much intact.[22] Yet the act reduced glaring inequities among electoral districts, assigned greater though still inadequate weight to the propertied living in Britain's largest cities, and eliminated some of the most scandalous abuses that had made recruitment to the unreformed House of Commons so comfortable and so predictable an affair. By adding half a million voters to the rolls, it nearly tripled the voting public. But the strongest impact of the Great Reform Act was symbolic; even if personnel and policies changed only marginally, it signalized that the era of undisputed oligarchic dominance might be nearing its end.

What mattered was that the bill had become law; this sufficiently demonstrated that practices once thought beyond possibility of amendment were not untouchable after all. Yet the first massive revision of the 1832 act only came a full generation later, in 1867. The second reform act was not an abrupt explosion of accumulated grievances but the culmination of a lengthy campaign, a necessary elaboration. Opponents of the 1832 act had been right to argue, when they evoked the dread apparition of democracy, that once begun, the work of chipping away at the dominance of the peerage and the gentry would surely continue.

By the mid-1860s, when the agitation for reform displayed the excited urgency that reminded veterans of the furor in 1831 and 1832, much had happened to alter the contours of Britain's political culture. In 1858, after heartsearching debates, disabilities for Jews were lifted, as they had been lifted for Catholics three decades before. This was not a triumph of the bourgeoisie, or an assault on the privileges of property. All that Jewish emancipation meant for the moment was that Baron Lionel de Rothschild, who had been elected to the House of Commons by the City of London, could take his seat without being compelled to take an oath "on the true faith of a Christian." Still, the vote to admit Rothschild and his coreligionists to the privilege of parliamentary service was a recognition that religion and politics could be separated, even in a country with a state church, and that anxiety about diversity in the political public was abating.

Four years earlier, in 1854, the oligarchic network, still profiting from the accident of birth and the favor of connections, had received a blow no less cruel than that of parliamentary reform. In a historic report, two distinguished public servants, Sir Charles Trevelyan, an official in the Treasury, and Sir Stafford Northcote, a Tory member of Parliament, recommended a subversive overhaul of the British civil service. Their most radical proposal was that civil servants be recruited and promoted on the basis of competitive examinations. In the end, most of the reforms, which struck terror into the hearts of the lazy, the over-age, and the undeserving, took long years to implement, but some were enacted promptly. The shock of forcing talent on public office reverberated for decades; it was still acute enough in the 1880s for W. S. Gilbert to make an elaborate joke in *Iolanthe* of peers being selected by "Competitive Examination." Early in the century, Viscount Melbourne, accomplished politician and fatherly adviser to the young Queen Victoria, had praised the exclusive Order of the Garter because "there is no damned merit in it." By imposing damned merit on the civil service, high-minded Victorian improvers were broadening the scope of political demands. And within Parliament, agitation continued. From 1852 on, proposals to strengthen the reforms initiated in 1832 repeatedly reached the floor, brought forward by an incongruous alliance among advanced Whigs: prosperous and influential brewers, heirs of rich merchants, professional malcontents, and reform-minded country gentlemen.[23]

The motives driving these reformers were the usual mixture: fear of social unrest and hope for co-optation. For enthusiastic agitators, hope for what Walter Bagehot called the "education of the public mind" outweighed fear of revolution.[24] By the early 1860s, even the prudent Gladstone had become convinced that English workingmen had proved their political maturity. To his mind they had established their right to political participation by their capacity to curb, and sublimate, their passions. "What are the qualities which fit a man for the exercise of a privilege such as the franchise? Self-command, self-control, respect for order, patience under suffering, confidence in the law, regard for superiors." English workingmen had displayed these qualities—splendid bourgeois virtues all—during the hard winter of 1862 in a "signal," even "illustrious" manner.*

Like other British politicians of his day, Gladstone was a moralist, and reformers wrapped their case for a new reform act in an ethical imperative. It was this moral politics that animated the authors of *Essays on Reform,* which appeared in the spring of 1867, while the debates were at their most heated. The contributors, among Britain's best young minds, insisted that a new act was essential to the political education of the British nation. They had no patience

---

*Speech of May 11, 1864, Peter Stansky, *Gladstone: A Progress in Politics* (1979), 100. So widely read a writer as Herbert Spencer had shown his democratic colors as early as 1850, in his first book. His reasoning was essentially negative: "Whoever demurs to the enfranchisement of the working men on the ground that they are immoral, is bound to point out a constituency which is *not* immoral. When it is alleged that the venality of the people renders them unfit for the possession of votes, it is assumed that some class not chargeable with venality may be found. But no such class exists." *Social Statics; or, The Conditions Essential to Human Happiness Specified, and the First of Them Developed* (1850; American ed., 1865), 246. Since he believed in equality for women, his call was for truly universal suffrage.

with Caesarism. One of them, George C. Brodrick, liberal journalist and editorial writer for the London *Times,* put it plainly. At its most paternal, despotic government is as degrading morally as it is ruinous economically; its real viciousness "consists not in its wilful neglect of popular interests, but in its contempt for popular opinions, in treating the people as passive materials for benevolent superintendence."[25] This was the issue: the political competence of the lower orders.

There was graphic evidence that the "people" were tired of condescension and impatient with grumbling or futile petitions. Hard feelings were bubbling just beneath the surface of British society, and they repeatedly erupted: with trade unions recruiting new members, strikes led to violent clashes and the beating of strikebreakers; brawls fueled by alcohol escalated into riots; Irishmen imported to do heavy labor in the factories or on the docks aroused vehement hostility, and Catholics were exposed to demagogic abuse sometimes followed by physical assaults. It was the people as attackers, not as victims, who troubled reformers in the great debate.

Then, in the summer of 1866, disorders sparked by the proposed reform bill offered added proof, at least to its opponents, that the people were not ready for absorption into the political process. The Reform Union, founded in 1864, had been agitating for a revision of the 1832 act; it was joined the following year by a crusading association, the Reform League. In 1866, the two organizations declared themselves willing, reluctantly, to support the rather modest bill that Gladstone had drawn up; after its defeat, they took to the streets. On July 23, they convened a protest rally in London, at Hyde Park. Alarmed, the home secretary ordered the gates to the park closed, but the most enterprising in the crowd pulled down the railings and rushed into forbidden ground, usually reserved for middle-class strollers. All they damaged was a few flowers and, of course, the railings, but some responded as though London had just gone through a revolutionary *journée*. The next day, Gladstone viewed the " 'field of battle' " and was shocked: "Alack, for the folly that made it."[26] But who had been the fool? The home secretary, for ordering the gates locked? The government, for slighting the people's grievances? The demonstrators, for their disorderly conduct? Gladstone did not decide.

Early in 1868, writing from what one might think the safe distance of almost two years, Matthew Arnold did decide, forcefully. He bemoaned the "riots" as a portentous symptom, not of culture but of anarchy. They had displayed the Englishman exercising his right "to do what he likes; his right to march where he likes, meet where he likes, enter where he likes, hoot as he likes, threaten as he likes, smash as he likes." If those of the "progressive party" were making light of these incidents as "a few transient outbreaks of rowdyism," Arnold thought a more alarmist line appropriate. The feeble response of the authorities had been deplorable. Forty years earlier his father, the great Thomas Arnold of Rugby, reflecting on popular unrest, had commended a simple remedy: "As for rioting, the old Roman way of dealing with *that* is always the right one; flog the rank and file, and fling the ringleaders from the Tarpeian Rock!" This opinion, Thomas Arnold's son sturdily agreed, "we can never forsake."[27]

Not everyone shared Arnold's fear and rage. But so much hysteria spent on so innocuous a cause, and by a proponent of sweetness and light, suggests that anxieties about the aggressive masses ran deep in cultivated circles. True, in *Culture and Anarchy,* Arnold was critical of the aristocracy, the "barbarians," and, even more, of the middle classes, the "philistines." But while the first troubled and the second repelled him, the lower orders, the "populace," loomed as the true danger to public order. It is curious though hardly surprising to see how often such a pessimistic estimate of human nature in politics depended upon judgments about class.

These alarms did not halt the agitation for reform, and in 1867, after convoluted parliamentary maneuverings in which Liberals and Conservatives outbid one another, Disraeli's bill, more far-reaching than Gladstone's draft, became law. The second reform act enfranchised most of Britain's urban working-men—the attempt of John Stuart Mill, then in the House of Commons, to extend the vote to women was solidly defeated—and roughly doubled the electorate. Among the antagonists of reform, Carlyle was predictably more depressed than anyone else. He found himself unable to work as he watched his country "getting into the *Niagara rapids* far sooner than I expected." The metaphor appealed to him; he adopted it for the title of a dark pamphlet, *Shooting Niagara, and After?* On their side, supporters of the bill purloined Carlyle's metaphor for their own purposes. English politics, Leslie Stephen wrote in 1868, was "befuddled," leaderless, and lacking common sense. "The Reform Bill will change all this and we will shoot Niagara. I am very glad of it, for we are terribly in want of an earthquake."[28] Carlyle's catastrophe was Stephen's opportunity. A more tentative appraisal would have been more fitting; while parliamentary politicians had made careful computations in the months of frenetic debates, the consequences of the democratization on which Britain had embarked lay veiled in uncertainty. That is what the prime minister, the earl of Derby, meant when he called the bill a leap in the dark.

It speaks for the political style current in Britain that the most adaptable among the Liberal opponents of reform chose to accept the inevitable. Much as they feared democracy, they determined to shape it. Their motto became "Let us educate our new masters!" Even Robert Lowe, the champion of inequality, came to adopt this line of thinking. He had made a controversial reputation in the early 1860s with a successful campaign to rationalize (which is to say, reduce) already skimpy government grants to schools, making the doling out of public funds for education dependent on measurable results. Cultural critics like Matthew Arnold—who, as a school inspector, had a special grievance—were appalled; they saw Lowe's decisions as fostering the kind of mindless recitation an inspector could easily quantify. It was to them the utilitarian nightmare that Dickens had pilloried in *Hard Times,* the fetishism of "facts, facts, facts."

In 1866 and 1867, as the menace of democracy seemed likely to swamp the country, Lowe found a larger target. He made some widely quoted speeches against the proposed extension of the suffrage, inside the House of Commons and out. "So far from believing that Democracy would aid the progress of the State," he said, "I am satisfied it would impede it." Proudly confessing himself a Liberal, he asserted that progress depends on "pure and clear intelligence alone." Lowe himself was extremely intelligent, with a cutting contempt for lesser minds that made him many enemies. And as an intelligent Liberal he regarded "as one of the greatest dangers with which the country can be threatened a proposal to subvert the existing order of things and to transfer power from the hands of property and intelligence, and to place it in the hands of men whose whole life is necessarily occupied in daily struggles for existence." His distaste for democracy was lifelong; as a young student he had already written a poem denouncing "the many-headed Monster." Unsettling personal experiences, which included exposure to the raw cultures of America and Australia and being wounded by a mob as he stood for the House of Commons, had scarcely endeared the many-headed Monster to him. Even after the Reform Act of 1867 had become history, he continued to put his thumb into the crumbling dike of a restricted franchise. The "educated and experienced" remained his ideal voters.[29]

But he was not content with lamenting a lost paradise. If the best voter is an instructed voter, it followed logically that the newly enfranchised must be instructed. And Lowe was nothing if not logical: "I am most anxious to educate the lower classes of this country in order to qualify them for the power that has passed, and," he prophetically added, "perhaps will pass in a still greater degree, into their hands." The failure to educate large numbers of citizens had long been a moral stigma on the nation. Now "that they have obtained the right of influencing the destinies of the country," it had become "a question of self-preservation," a "question of existence." He declared himself quite as anxious to reform the education of the upper classes by modernizing the curriculum, shifting it from the time-honored decorative but essentially useless classical training toward the sciences.[30] The Education Act of 1870, which established Britain's first national system of schooling, bore the mark of Lowe's thinking. It was a first step, no more, but in the democratic direction.

Lowe's call to educate the new masters of Britain was scarcely original. In June 1867, soliciting his fellow graduates of the University of London for their support in the coming election, Walter Bagehot reminded them, "After the first Reform Act the cry was, 'Register! Register! Register!' " After the second act, "the cry should now be, 'Educate! Educate! Educate!' " After all, "popular power" had come to enjoy "secure predominance."* The task was plain, and not evaded; by 1891, every child in Britain was educated free of charge.

Further enlargements of the electorate went hand in hand with improvements in education. In 1884, a third reform act smoothed out some anomalies left over from its predecessor. While the act of 1867 had granted the vote to householders in the towns, its successor extended the franchise to most males in the counties. Then, in 1885, a massive redistribution of seats further equalized the political weight of the vote no matter where the voter lived. When the Victorian decades ended, those on the dole, and all women, were still unenfranchised.† But Gladstone's ideal, and that of most British Liberals, to include the "capable citizen," had been realized. By 1885, Britain's capable citizens amounted to three adult males out of five.[31] And their vote was not merely secret; from the early 1880s on, it was also clean. The severe Corrupt and Illegal Practices Act of 1883 finally removed a notorious obstacle to political rationality. Political lures would now have to take a form different from getting voters drunk or paying them.

Democratic politics was many things, among them a kind of seduction, documenting once again the interplay of aggression with libido. It awakened and often gratified the electorate's hostile impulses, or at the very least, its desire for aggressive self-assertion. At the same time, it yoked followers to their leaders to produce a community rife with erotic overtones. Love for one's favorite politician was intensified by hatred for the opposition. This is not to minimize the rational, self-seeking dimension of modern election campaigns; candidates might promise to find a government post for a voter's brother-in-law, lobby for an army base in their district, or support tariffs to protect domestic products from foreign competitors. Bribery did not disappear, but it reversed direction;

---

*Bagehot to "My dear Hutton," June 24, 1867, *The Collected Works of Walter Bagehot,* ed. Norman St. John-Stevens, 15 vols. (1965–86), XIII, 616–19. This was not mere electioneering; as early as March, Bagehot had argued in the *Economist* that he preferred enfranchising "the really intelligent working classes of our great cities" rather than the "correspondent unintelligent classes of our petty bourgeois." "The New Reform Bill" (March 1867), ibid., VI, 366.

†Unmarried women and widows had the right to vote in certain local council and municipal elections, but the suffragists, of course, aimed higher.

instead of politicians bribing voters, now voters bribed politicians. Yet late-nineteenth-century office seekers were compelled to recognize that political enthusiasms were sustained by irrational feelings, feelings they could manipulate. This meant that oratory, an art hitherto cultivated as a gentleman's accomplishment exercised in the narrow, if strategic, confines of national legislatures, was now aimed at larger audiences. Candidates courted thousands of voters massed in gigantic halls or open fields to hear or (since most were out of earshot) to watch them in action.[32]

Democratic politics and Caesarism intersect at this point. The compelling, at times ominous, magnetism of demagogues in the decades in which mass politics was born had recognizable ancestors in Bonapartism. Indeed, in the late 1880s, republican France witnessed a ludicrous replay of earlier Caesarist politics, lending support to Marx's sardonic comment that in history everything happens twice, the first time as tragedy, the second time as farce. In 1886, in the midst of governmental instability, turmoil over domestic and foreign policy, and scandals in high places, General Georges Boulanger, considered a reliable partisan of the republican forces, was appointed minister of war. Enjoying his new prominence, Boulanger courted the public with parades, the soldiery with improved conditions, and the business community with uniformed strikebreakers. He succeeded; across the country, in by-election after by-election, voters chose this heroic, aggressive figure to represent them in the Chamber of Deputies. Emboldened by the outpouring of support, Boulanger expected to turn these local triumphs into a kind of national plebiscite that would make him the strong man of France. A fine figure in the saddle, he posed, literally, as the man on horseback destined to save his country and revenge it on the Germans. But unlike his Caesarist precursors, he was all show and no substance; threatened with a charge of treason, he fled to Belgium, and there, in 1891, already a forgotten man, he killed himself on the grave of his mistress. The love of dazzled Frenchmen had proved evanescent.

But love, we have seen, was an indispensable ingredient in Bonapartism. Devotees of the nineteenth-century Caesars adored their leaders beyond calculation, beyond reason. Napoleon I, for one, had never slighted the profits from such amorous politics even if maintaining the one-sided love affair proved hard work. A leader posing as a follower, he had been obliged to massage the populace, whether monitoring the price of bread, preaching the ideal of careers open to talent, or cultivating his image as a hardworking, ascetic, formidably gifted laborer in the vineyard of the public good. His message to the public, whether in military bulletins or newspaper propaganda, never changed: I am worthy of your love, for I am responsible for every triumph and innocent of every failure.

In the rule of Napoleon's wooden, far less eloquent nephew, the erotic element was less conspicuous but did underlie much of his support, even though it was often love of the nephew for his uncle's sake. Again, while worshipers heaped accolades on Bismarck to give him a semidivine stature, his human qualities, whether authentic or imaginary, were quite as marketable. Rulers, journalists and academics, schoolteachers, architects and painters, collaborated on his heroic image. They bestowed exalted titles on him; they sculpted gigantic and tasteless statues of his bulky figure; they recited flattering poems, wrote extravagant editorials, and delivered effusive orations on his birthday; they made adulatory visits to his country retreat; they sang his achievements in history books. Deliberately or not, they somehow lent all these tributes a very human touch, making him a veritable love object.

Reports of the effect that charismatic orators produced in the late-Victorian decades leave little doubt that they relied heavily, if not always consciously, on the work of Eros—or, better, on an inflammatory mixture of libido and aggression. Some of the erotic energy released in the audience by these performances was directed at the speaker—and they could become minor narcissistic orgies as the orator figuratively, or literally, stroked himself. The maverick English politician Joseph Chamberlain, a strange compound of fierce pugnacity, cerebral intellectuality, and suave persuasiveness, exemplifies the uses of love and hate on the speaker's platform. In March 1884, the brilliant social investigator Beatrice Potter watched Chamberlain, then lord mayor of Birmingham, seduce his audience. "At the first sound of his voice," she recorded in her diary, "they became as one man. Into the tones of his voice he threw the warmth of feeling which was lacking in his words, and every thought, every feeling, the slightest intonation of irony and contempt was reflected on the faces of the crowd. It might have been a woman listening to the words of her lover! Perfect response, unquestioning receptivity. Who *reasons* with his mistress?"[33]

True, Chamberlain was not just a demagogue; as an energetic and imaginative radical mayor he had earned his popularity. True, too, Beatrice Potter was even more in love with him than were his listeners in Birmingham. But her empathic testimony captures something of the atmosphere that Chamberlain could generate in public. In December 1887, he spoke in Toronto at a board of trade dinner, and, moved by the occasion, evoked the bond that tied Canada to the mother country. The "grand idea" of empire was "one to stimulate the patriotism and statesmanship of every man who loves his country." One eyewitness reported that the response to the speech—whose "grandeur and force," he insisted, "cold type" could not convey—had been "electrical." Men wept as "the audience was simply carried away in frenzied enthusiasm."[34] After the middle of the nineteenth century, with election campaigns wooing ever larger, ever more differentiated constituencies, such oratory became a cherished asset in the encounter of candidate with voter, of officeholder with ordinary citizen. However artificial the love affair often was, it was a love affair no less for that, and larded with aggression.

But the new democratic politics was not necessarily reduced to emotional appeals. In 1879 and 1880, Gladstone proved that a modern politician could attract voters by laboring to persuade rather than to excite them. In his famous Midlothian campaign, a series of speeches in which he contested a hitherto safe Conservative seat, he used reason as much as pathos, statistics as well as orotund phrases, explanations no less than exhortation, to make his point that the Tory government had to go. It was not the first time that Gladstone, or for that matter his great rival, Disraeli, had addressed audiences outside Parliament. But it was the first time that a British politician methodically canvassed his potential supporters. Gladstone, now seventy, gave no sign of fatigue as he maintained a schedule that would have exhausted most younger men; he traveled through Britain's north, across far-flung electoral districts, from cities to hamlets, speaking indoors and out, in halls and at railroad stations, often more than once a day, to students and farmers and solid middle-class burghers. They came by the thousands, crowding into auditoriums too small to hold them, standing in the snow to listen and to cheer. He spoke of the Tories' electoral tricks, of unsolved agricultural problems, of the pursuit of power, wealth, and knowledge in the contemporary world, and above all, with exceptional warmth, of Disraeli's and Lord Salisbury's callous and irresponsible foreign policy. The setting was perfect for a demagogue, but Gladstone was not disposed to exploit his magnetism. He had a moral case to make, and he made it.

To read Gladstone's Midlothian speeches is to enter a world of reasonableness, dignified and irate, a salutary distance from the brassy self-advertisement of Napoleon III's itinerant performances. To be sure, Gladstone did not disdain his trusted repertory of oratorical stratagems—the urgent warnings, the expressive repetitions, the resounding periods. He deprecated his performance: he was "daunted when I recollect, first of all, what large demands I have to make on your patience; and, secondly, how inadequate are my powers." He flattered his auditors: "We are comrades in a common undertaking." He overstated the desperateness of Britain's situation: "the most important crisis in our national history that has occurred during the last half-century."[35] These gambits leave no doubt that Gladstone's intercourse with his hearers was far from purely rational. On some deep level it was erotic, as the relations of leaders to led must always be. But at Midlothian he sublimated unconscious bonds between speaker and listeners as he appealed for support on the high grounds of common sense and decency. The Tories, Gladstone said over and over, had set aside both.

Gladstone was inviting his listeners to adopt his hostility to Tory policies, both domestic and foreign; struggling to forge a community of like-minded voters, he was at the same time creating a community of haters—or, more mildly and more precisely, of indignant supporters. He took care to avoid personalities and to express considerable respect for his opponents. But Gladstone was an angry man, had been for several years. In 1875, while keeping his seat in the House of Commons, he had retired from the leadership of the Liberal party and retreated to his country house, Hawarden, to think about his favorite subject—religion. But the spectacle of a Conservative government that he condemned as immoral would not let him rest; the earnestness that had dictated his self-imposed exile dragged him back into the turmoil of public life. "Good ends," he wrote in 1876 to Lord Granville, the leader of the Liberals in the House of Lords, "can rarely be attained in politics without passion: and there is now, the first time for a good many years, a virtuous passion."[36]

The virtuous passion that animated him—and many others—was fury at the massacre of thousands of Bulgarian Christians by their Turkish overlords, a fury exacerbated by what he read as the government's icily calculating strategy of appeasing the Turkish Empire. In three days in August 1876, stimulated by appalling reports, the indignation of other humanitarians, and his own revulsion, he dashed off a pamphlet, *The Bulgarian Horrors and the Question of the East,* that became an instantaneous best seller—a tribute to the level that political education had reached in the country. Some 40,000 copies were sold in four days and 200,000 before the month was out. The pamphlet divided the country as it had not been divided for years. Disraeli's flippant remark that British interests were "not affected by the question whether it was 10,000 or 20,000 persons who perished in the suppression," lent color to Gladstone's case.[37] His unprecedented Midlothian campaign was its logical culmination: rage translated into political action.

It was fitting somehow that Gladstone, that self-searching, self-tormenting, deeply devout statesman who had lived with politics for half a century should break the mold of traditional electioneering. After Midlothian, political campaigning would never be the same. In 1868, the year after the passage of the second reform act, Gladstone had jotted down some autobiographical observations in which he paid tribute to the altered political climate to which he, and his country, had to adapt. He noted "the constant seething of the public mind" and spoke, without disapproval, of the "silent changes, which are advancing in the very bed and basis of modern society." One of those changes was the "gradual transfer of political power from groups and limited classes to the community." Public opinion, he thought, was acting—rightly—to assert itself. "It is the office of law and of institutions to reflect the wants and wishes of our country." Leaders "exist for its sake, not it for theirs."[38] He felt compelled to respond to this new age.

After much thought he concluded that to go to the people, to cultivate the electorate systematically, was the proper response. Late in December 1879, drawing up his annual year-end balance sheet, he gave credit, as usual, to God. "For the last three and a half years," he wrote, "I have been passing through a political experience which is, I believe, without example in our parliamentary history." It had been "an occasion when the battle to be fought was a battle of justice humanity freedom law all in their first elements from the very root, and all on a gigantic scale. The word spoken was a word for millions, and for millions who for themselves cannot speak." He recognized that they were being taught to speak for themselves.[39] The "great principle of one man one vote," which John Morley, Gladstone's radical disciple, hailed at a conference of the National Liberal Federation some four years later, was waiting in the wings.[40] And it did not need a Caesar for a prompter.

≈ FOUR ≈

The Powerful, Weaker Sex

Old vinegar in new bottles—and at times the bottles, too, were old; the historian exploring nineteenth-century middle-class attitudes toward woman's proper share in bourgeois aggressiveness is bound to grow exasperated in the end. Much of the material is dreary and threadbare: dicta confidently uttered by clerics, philosophers and politicians, physicians and writers of books of advice, nearly all repeating each other and themselves. When, in 1891, the liberal French philosopher and politician Jules Simon weighed in with his contribution to the condition-of-woman question, he alerted his readers on the first page, "I have no hope of saying anything new."[1] This sort of apologia did not originate in the Victorian decades. Almost exactly a century earlier, in 1792, in her splendid diatribe vindicating women's rights, Mary Wollstonecraft had already declared with understandable impatience, "I do not mean to allude to all the writers who have written on the subject of female manners—it would, in fact, be only beating over the old ground, for they have, in general, written in the same strain."[2] To allude to all the nineteenth-century writers on women, most of them writing in the same strain, would be quite as unprofitable.

Still, the historian must record striking shifts from earlier thinking about women to a complex and evolving Victorian ideology. The French Revolution had generated long-lasting, if confusing and conflicting responses, and conservative governments tried to contain the fallout from that revolution, even to reverse its effects. Some principal combatants recognized that women, too, had been its victims and its beneficiaries. Millicent Garrett Fawcett, one of the earliest and most determined English suffragists, judged after decades in the trenches that the woman's movement "must be regarded as one of the results of the upheaval of the human mind of which the French Revolution was the most portentous manifestation. The awakening of the democratic spirit, the rebellion against authority, the proclamation of the rights of man, were almost necessarily accompanied by the growth of a new ideal concerning the position of women, by the recognition, more or less defined and conscious, of the rights of women."[3] After 1789, women's lives would never be the same.

The emergence of industrial society, large-scale business enterprise, and the modern professions complicated women's lives still further. Paradoxically, all of these squeezed bourgeois women out of visible economic activities. The Victorian years saw an appreciable retreat from outposts that women had begun to secure during the Enlightenment. The spectacular diffusion of prosperity and leisure time among the middling orders that accompanied these explosive upheavals allowed more and more husbands to keep their wives at home, and apparently most women did not protest against being kept there. The domestic circle had its charms.

But not for all. Currents of opinion ran in divergent directions, and the debates that engrossed the bourgeois century prominently included the question of woman—her role and her nature. Calls for the expansion of women's rights, still subdued before 1848 but drawing on the impetus of revolutionary expectations, clashed with a vigorous religious revival in the bourgeoisie and a no less vigorous cult of domesticity. Neither that revival nor that cult was invented upon the accession of Victoria in 1837. But especially among the middle classes, a sincere, often passionate commitment to pious values and pious observants, coupled with heartfelt praise of woman's essentially domestic character, markedly intensified in her reign.

Victorians everywhere constructed a wall between public and private spheres, and fortified it by mouthing the old commonplace about woman the mysterious sex. Thus they managed to be derisive about woman in the guise of awed admiration.[4] Thackeray, deploying that time-tested defense, asserted, "When I say that I know women, I mean I know that I don't know them. Every single woman I ever knew is a puzzle to me, as, I have no doubt, she is to herself."[5] It was as though, by concealing woman behind the veils of her enigmatic nature, men could evade the unpalatable truth that their mother was a sexual being. Proclaiming woman to be a dark problem, men were happily dispensed from searching for a solution.*

---

*Perhaps less unpalatable, but certainly little less disconcerting, was the realization that the mother had carried the man within her, giving him life and nourishment. In the course of these pages, I have called the idea of the mysterious woman a cliché, and so it was. But, like other clichés, it has a certain psychological reality.

These tendentious puzzlements never silenced debate in the nineteenth century. In 1822, in *De l'amour,* decades before the woman question grew into a formidable cultural issue, Stendhal flatly blamed men's despotism for women's all-too-conspicuous stupidity. "People concede that a little girl of ten has twenty times the cleverness of a young rascal of the same age. Why is she, at twenty, a great idiot, awkward, timid, and afraid of spiders, while the rascal is a man of wit and intelligence?" Obviously, the education of girls was "the fruit of chance and of the most absurd pride"; it left their "most brilliant faculties" idle and reduced them to domestic drudges, boring wax dolls, submissive sick nurses, slaves to their children. Stendhal's solution, which he thought would benefit men no less, was to allow women the same three or four hours of daily leisure that sensible men enjoyed. Nor would women with such a schedule lose their femininity: "The graces of women are in no way linked to ignorance."[6]

Wollstonecraft might have written this sentence, and it had as little immediate effect as any of her work. But it was a symptom of unease, a small cloud on the largely untroubled horizon of self-satisfied male ideologues—a horizon untroubled, that is, in their conscious minds. That cloud would grow as the decades went by. Like much else in these decades, statements about woman as the powerful, weaker sex were vehemently contested. While time-honored clichés continued to enlist sincere supporters, and engendered further clichés, they were also under attack. Some of the vinegar, then, was new. And not all of it proved to be vinegar.

I. Domesticity: Womanliness Defined

Prevalent Victorian perceptions of women were variations, most of them trite, on a single, simple thesis: the sexes differ as radically in mind as they do in body. Early in the century and late, this message permeated novels and poems, sermons and medical monographs, bourgeois autobiographies and books of advice. Yet its vast influence is no proof of its clarity. In 1915, after a century of irresolution and confrontations, Freud noted that it seemed "indispensable to be clear that the concepts 'masculine' and 'feminine,' whose meaning seems so unambiguous to popular opinion, belong among the most confused in the sciences."[1] Far from consistent in handling these treacherous terms, Freud did little to resolve the ambiguities he had noted. But his refreshing skepticism is a wry tribute to their staying power.

Most bourgeois found the polarization of the sexes too obvious to require much proof, even much discussion. For one thing, it buttressed the ideal of manliness, which derived most of its authority from the contrasting ideal of womanliness. In *Effi Briest,* his best-known novel, Theodor Fontane has his youthful, impulsive heroine characterize her suitor, the middle-aged official Baron von Instetten, as "very manly." And that, one of her friends suggests, is what counts. "Certainly it's what counts," Effi agrees. " 'Women womanly, men manly,'—that is, as you know, one of Papa's favorite sayings."[2] By 1894, when *Effi Briest* was published, this categorical formulation had long been familiar. It recalls the dictum of Turnvater Jahn, founder of German gymnastics, patriot, and demagogue, who had proclaimed early in the century, "Let man be manly, then woman will be womanly."[3] Both pronouncements quite explicitly reserve the privilege of aggression for the manly male, because he is male.

The writ of this invidious prescription ran across Western civilization. In 1847, a forceful American Southerner, James Henry Hammond, instructed his younger brother: "Women were meant to breed—men to do the work of the world."[4] Many voices like his, presuming to speak for middle-class culture, defined the virile qualities that mark a man as an exemplary specimen in counterpoint to the gentle qualities they saluted as woman's distinct endowment. The catalogue was recited through the century: man is active, vigorous, and self-assertive, the warrior on the battlefield of life; woman is passive, domestic, the soothing, healing, keeper of the home. These were the stigmata that ideologists of manliness professed—or wanted—to see everywhere.[5] What made the woman's movement so threatening was that it challenged these presumably God-given, eternally valid distinctions. Feminists male and female seemed intent on blurring them, or perhaps erasing them altogether. That is why the protests against women's gaining access to property, the professions, the vote, were so automatic, so fierce—so palpably anxious. The sexual innuendos that opponents of feminism lavishly scattered attest to that anxiety: females marching for suffrage were hens that crow; supportive men were male spinsters.[6]

In a massive compendium on design published in 1867, Charles Blanc demonstrated the pervasiveness of the manliness–womanliness dichotomy by his casual way of introducing it: "Design is the masculine sex of art; color is its feminine sex." Their combination is an erotic act. "The union of design and color is necessary to engender painting, just as the union of man and woman is to engender humanity. But," he quickly added, evidently anxious to safeguard male supremacy, "it is necessary that design preserve its superiority over color. If it is otherwise, painting rushes to its ruin; it will be undone by color just as humanity was undone by Eve."[7] The hoary accusation against the first woman had not lost its bite in Victorian times, though many writers put the complaint more politely. "Man and woman, what a beautiful contrast!" exclaimed the zoologist Konrad Guenther in an essay on man's battle for the female as manifested in the evolutionary process. "He, with frank forehead and with fresh self-confidence stepping into the struggle for life; she, leaning against him full of trust and managing his home with tender care."[8] Most Victorians were glad to believe that the differences between nineteenth-century Adams and Eves, as sharply etched as possible, were rooted in the biological facts of life.

The impressive career of this distinction, so convenient to its beneficiaries, played itself out in print with physicians and theologians providing rationales. It moved even philosophers to comment. In the few sentences that Hegel explicitly devoted to women in his *Philosophie des Rechts,* he laid down in his gnarled and emphatic way that "man has to take over struggle, enmity, hatred"—in a word, aggressiveness—while woman's destiny is "that of preserving the inner harmony of the spiritual and the ethical." Subsisting in that harmony, she "simply unfolds like a flower, without struggle and without resistance." It is man's duty to earn the family's livelihood, and to toil without female assistance, which he neither wants nor needs, in politics, science, and the arts. In contrast, "woman's appropriate circle is the family and private life, woman thrones in the family." After all, Hegel noted, offering a respectable home to a scornful banality, "it cannot be said of any woman that she made an epoch in world history." No woman had ever produced anything great. The male alone, in short, had earned the right to make overt aggression, constructive or destructive, his business.[9]

The nineteenth century supported this differentiation with two popular though seemingly inconsistent propositions; women already have all the power they can use, and outside the home, women are ill-equipped to exercise any power at all. That these two assertions clash somehow, and are nothing better than rationalizations reduced to a system, did not rob them of general support. Each apparently suited the cherished fantasies of men and, to the helpless irritation of feminists, of many women as well.[10] In fact, Victorian ideologues did not scruple to deploy both arguments together; they merged into one, just as they merged in men's unconscious into the covert but very real fear of woman. In their anxiety over the transformations haunting their century, men—and women—regressed to primitive, childlike ways of seeing the mother, the source of nourishment, as the source of mortal perils as well.

Wollstonecraft's acerbic remark about writings on women beating over old ground applies to these two alibis for the male monopoly on aggression. One could hear and read in treatises or jokes, in tones solemn or light, that men and women must occupy separate spheres because they have distinct natures, distinct capacities, and hence distinct tasks. One exemplary statement of this thesis, probably the most quoted, is a declamation by Tennyson in *The Princess,* as popular in its age as Coventry Patmore's badly overworked praise of woman as the angel in the house.* Tennyson first announces his position with a virile metaphor: "Man is the hunter; woman is his game." It followed logically, as his famous lines have it, that man is

> for the field and woman for the hearth:
> Man for the sword and for the needle she:
> Man with the head and woman with the heart:
> Man to command and woman to obey;
> All else confusion.[11]

With nature so legible, the moral and scientific case against subversive feminists seemed self-evident. It took a rare rebel like John Stuart Mill to meet such assertions—for they were assertions, not reasoned argument—with the reply that if the man's pugnacious superiority is indeed natural, too bad for nature. Most others, rejecting Mill as a fantast, gladly obeyed nature's dictates.

But to nervous Victorians nature appeared to be sending conflicting messages. For, in addition to showing that men are the superior sex, it seemed to be hinting, broadly, that male supremacy was actually a sham, since woman was really in control—secretly. That oxymoron—the power of the powerless—had enjoyed currency for many centuries; the Bible more than once paid wry tribute to woman, depraved woman. "All wickedness," as Ecclesiasticus has it, "is but little to the wickedness of a woman." Had she not prevailed in the Garden of Eden? Had she not brought about mankind's fatal Fall? The Church Fathers had taken up the refrain, inveighing against woman, the vessel of corruption, the source of sin, the sly submissive Eve.

Nineteenth-century opponents of woman's causes worked this indictment heavily, for all its antiquity.[12] In the late 1860s, in a notorious series of articles for the *Saturday Review,* that often uncivil London weekly catering to an educated, relatively conservative readership, Eliza Lynn Linton disparaged the painted, pleasure-seeking "advanced" girl of the period. Nor did she spare women who exercised power subtly and discreetly: "They may rule with a hand of iron, but the hand is sagely concealed in a glove of velvet. A man may be the creature of

---

*The title of Patmore's interminable poem *The Angel in the House* (1854–62), the exhaustive, often trite, history of the love and marriage of a masterful but chivalrous male and a superior female, has been made to serve as an all-purpose disdainful epithet, substituting for an analysis of the bourgeois housewife in the Victorian age. It is easily forgotten that the angel Patmore depicted (though with genteel circumlocutions) is remarkably unangelic in her sexual fervor—embodying a crucial, though normally overlooked, aspect of Patmore's erotic Christianity. For a further discussion of Patmore, see Peter Gay, *The Bourgeois Experience,* vol. II, *The Tender Passion* (1986), 291–97.

his wife's lofty projects, and yet dream all the time that he is altogether chalking out his own course." Trollope's Mrs. Proudie was untypical, Mrs. Linton thought, because she displayed her ascendancy over her husband so brashly. The influence of "wise wives" who "make bishops" is "not the less real because, unlike that of Mrs. Proudie, it is exerted chiefly behind the scenes." However shy and modest a girl may be, she will soon grow into "our master, changing our habits, moulding our tastes, bending our characters to her own." She does not need much to consummate her wily triumph: "A little love, a little listening, a little patience, a little persistence, and the game is won."[13] These articles, though excessive in their cynicism, struck a responsive chord.

The paradox of the powerful, weaker sex was epitomized for the Victorian age in a pair of lines—they are his only legacy to posterity—by a minor nineteenth-century poet, William Ross Wallace:

> For the hand that rocks the cradle
> Is the hand that rules the world.

A far better known poet, Byron's Irish friend Thomas Moore, had said much the same thing more mordantly some decades earlier in his significantly titled "Sovereign Woman":

> Disguise our bondage as we will,
> 'Tis woman, woman, rules us still.

The subject of woman's hidden powers fascinated not just poets, but philosophers, journalists, and pedagogues.* Early in the century, Hegel sought to unmask what he saw as aggressiveness concealed behind woman's parade of

---

*The roots of this idea reach deep into the eighteenth century. In 1761, Jean Jacques Rousseau offered a classic formulation. "Nature has armed" the timid sex with "modesty and bashfulness," qualities with which "the weak subdue the strong." Woman's "violence lies in her charms." *Émile,* in *Oeuvres complètes,* ed. Bernard Gagnebin, Robert Osmont, and Marcel Raymond, 4 vols. (1959–69), IV, 694. At the end of the century, Immanuel Kant explored female stratagems as a good Rousseauian. Only foolish men joke about feminine weaknesses; reasonable people understand that these so-called "weaknesses" are "the very levers" by which women "manage the male. They employ them to serve their designs." Kant was, like others, impressed with woman's mysteriousness: "The man is easy to explore, the woman does not betray her secret," incapable though she may be of keeping the secrets of others. He "loves *domestic peace* and cheerfully submits to her governance," but she "does not shy away from *domestic war,* which she conducts with her tongue, for which purpose nature gave her loquacity and emotional eloquence, which disarm the man." "Der Charakter des Geschlechts" (1798), *Die Anthropologie,* part II, in *Vermischte Schriften,* ed. Felix Gross (n.d.), 502.

vulnerability: femininity, "the community's eternal irony," transforms the general purpose of government into private ends, "perverting the general property of the state into a possession and ornament of the family." Scheming woman subverts communal purposes.[14]

These truisms summarized, and supported, a perspective on woman too comfortable to welcome rational refutation. But woman's power, many commentators were convinced, was greater in their own day than it had been in the distant past. In the mid-1850s, John Chapman, editor of the liberal *Westminster Review*, sketched woman's ever-growing influence through the ages as a chapter in humanity's moral progress. In barbarism and antiquity woman had been treated as a child, a laborer, and a defenseless dependent ministering to male lust. But with the passage of centuries, man's "lowest slave becomes the chief influence under which he lives, his inspiration in battle, his mental companion, the incarnation of beauty, love, devotion, holiness, the source and theme of poetry—compelling the noblest to worship at her shrine."[15] Tracing woman's history as an upward climb from servitude to freedom, so lovely to watch, became a favorite sport of journalists. It did not disconcert them that their case rested on the skimpiest of historical materials and that their cheerful account of woman's inspiring evolution was but one more stratagem for dodging contemporary issues. Plainly, to them, the woman as high priestess of the good and the beautiful did not need the superficial marks of power—higher education or the vote—to exercise supremacy.

In an unusually instructive text, the Reverend Horace Bushnell, a prominent Congregationalist theologian and prolific author, demonstrated how a self-proclaimed sympathizer with women's wrongs and admirer of their strength could mount a sustained defense of the male corner on aggressiveness. His *Women's Suffrage* begins by celebrating the female's essential superiority to the male and "the covert glory of the womanly nature." In conciliatory tones, Bushnell admitted that for centuries men had burdened women with inequitable laws and institutions, and clung to "foolish" prejudices. Successful experiments in coeducation at Oberlin and Antioch colleges, he thought, showed that women are perfectly competent to enter the liberal professions.[16]

So far Bushnell stood with the reformers, but then he deserted the cause. He was not, he stressed, a John Stuart Mill; men and women *do* differ from each other in character and endowment. Women are fit to study medicine, but not to practice surgery; nursing and pediatrics, in which they excel male physicians, seem more suitable. In the law, women can properly do research and frame documents, but litigation is not for them. His sexual panic is open: if woman is not to become a mere female man, she must stay away from "the wrangle, and debate, and vehement fight of a bar"; otherwise she will turn into a "virago."

Woman may find employment in the ministry, in literature, in some businesses, above all in dispensing charity, but the "roughest, tensest forms of creative labor" are man's province.[17] Thus reads nature's law.

In tune with other controversialists, Bushnell found nature a welcome rhetorical resource. His catalogue of sexual differences is heavily physiological. Men are taller than women, more muscular, with larger brains and a longer stride. Man has "some attribute of thunder," but woman is too finely made for such ruggedness. Man is "Force, Authority, Decision, Self-asserting Counsel, Victory," but woman represents the beauty principle.[18] The vote would destroy her exquisite femininity. Yet none of this implies that woman is a lesser being; her very subordination gives her "the truest and sublimest conditions of ascendency." Submitting to woman, man pays a tender and delicate homage. "Woman has her government as truly as man, only it is not political, not among powers, and laws, and public causes." Rather than demanding the vote and yearning to enter "the realm of force and aggression," she should recognize that she is already in power, governing by grace! Man "governs only the state, and she governs both the governors of the state and the people besides."[19]

Perceptive contemporaries recognized the weakness of Bushnell's case. Reviewing his book, William James endorsed the argument for woman's natural subjection as supported by the almost universal convictions of the day. But he objected to Bushnell's way of arguing from woman's dependence to woman's dominance; that only undid his authority.[20] But James's rather bland demurrer might as well have remained unwritten; the age was not yet prepared to discard argumentation like Bushnell's. In 1871, a scholarly Anglican divine, the Reverend John W. Burgon, sermonizing on woman's place, announced once more that "woman's strength is her weakness." She rules, or, rather, reigns, because she has vowed to obey. Indeed, when woman, "instead of being a gentle, modest, and *most* unselfish helper," becomes bustling and forward, she must expect to be treated as a rival. This was a threat posing as a worry: an aggressive woman (Burgon confessed more frankly than he knew) was an unwelcome competitor. "When, instead of rejoicing in the sacred retirement of her home and the strict privacy of her domestic duties, she is found to be secretly longing for the publicity of print and the notoriety of the platform," woman will discover that she has "unsexed herself," that she has made herself into an inferior kind of man, "with all his hardness" but "without his manliness." The loss will be hers; woman's presumed victory will be her actual defeat.[21] This ominous hint—typical of many—that men could be expected to take their revenge once put on the defensive suggests that for many nineteenth-century men, the sense of dominance was exceedingly precarious.

Much of this hectoring literature labored to reassure domestic women, build up their morale, and save them from the fanatics seducing them into discontent with their lot. A true woman does not really want to dirty her hands in public life; her mission is far too exalted for that. Among the most widely read, and most extravagant, supporters of this case for woman's divine assignment was Louis-Aimé Martin, a French litterateur as scholarly as he was devout. The subtitle of his swollen tract telegraphed his message "of the civilization of the human race by women." First published in 1834 and crowned with the *grand prix* of the Académie française, Martin's *Éducation des mères de famille* rapidly went through several enlarged editions; plainly, its appeal to mothers to "moralize their families and their country" by fostering the Christian spirit among the young spoke to a large, grateful readership. Only a mother can teach her children, and society, to be virtuous—that is the essential lesson of Martin's closely packed four hundred pages. Fathers are too busy in the world for this august task. "The most difficult thing in the world is not to do good, but to inspire it, above all to make it lovable. Should the man dispute woman the privilege of the patience and the long-suffering of love?" Surely not.[22]

Catholic France was not alone in applauding Martin's flattering portrait of woman the superior teacher of purity and virtue; Protestant England absorbed his ideas, suitably modified, through Sarah Lewis's *Woman's Mission* of 1839. A woman, Lewis wrote, can calmly observe men ostentatiously exercising public authority. After all, she has been entrusted with a worthier commission: to govern the world by governing the home. "There is no hyperbole in the phrase, 'Vainqueurs des vainqueurs de la terre'." Lewis praised Napoleon for having recognized that any reform of education must rely on the mothers, since maternal love is the purest of all sentiments, and the most powerful. "Most great men have had extraordinary mothers, and it seems, as though by some peculiar influence, the nature of the mother acts upon the son."[23]

In the enigmatic closing lines of *Faust,* part II, Goethe appealed to the "eternal-feminine" that "draws us upward." As the nineteenth century wore on, champions of women's rights became heartily tired of such poetic apostrophes. They had good reason for their fatigue; the whiff of incense hangs heavily over these accolades. It perfumed biographies no less than political and pedagogic polemics. In 1872, Henry Liebhart, a pious German poet and student of Christian missions, published *Edle Frauen,* a collection of adoring biographies of noble Christian women from early martyrs to Florence Nightingale. His book showed how a Victorian biographer could sustain the stereotype of woman the savior. In one noble woman's life after the other, it offered proof that "woman need not take the man's place, man need not become effeminate." Woman's "highest calling" is to be "*a genuine, godly woman.*"* All this dominion without the vote, without university education, without access to the professions or to equal treatment in legal proceedings, obtained through beauty and yielding tenderness alone!

Proffering this kind of argument, at once nervous and patronizing, men found ready allies among women. So alert and level-headed an educator as Catharine Beecher sought shelter in woman's protected status as she refused to join her more aggressive sisters' call for woman suffrage. "The moment woman begins to feel the promptings of ambition, or the thirst for power, her aegis of defense is gone. All the sacred protections of religion, all the generous promptings of chivalry, all the poetry of romantic gallantry, depend on woman's retaining her place as dependent and defenceless, and making no claims."[24] Nothing testifies more eloquently to the power of the dominant male ideology than this pathetic plea—by a woman—to keep the burden of aggressiveness from women's shoulders.

To general satisfaction, beloved heroines in nineteenth-century fiction informally documented this female power disguised by (or, rather, exercised through) impotence.† The novels of Charles Dickens are richly supplied with angelic female heroines, all decisively superior to men. They win the handsome hero by recognizing, in all honorable humility, the strategic advantages of silent waiting. David Copperfield's Agnes is only the most familiar among them. Dickens justified this view in a revealing aside in *Dombey and Son;* women's nature is "ever, in the mass, better, truer, higher, nobler, quicker to feel, and much more constant to retain, all tenderness and pity, self-denial and devotion, than the nature of men." In his fiction, women are more sensitive, more perceptive, more virtuous, than their male counterparts. "But there is much more Good in Women than in Men, however Ragged they are," he declared in a letter to the immensely rich philanthropist Angela Burdett Coutts. Later, when he was working with her to reform the lives of prostitutes, he waxed religious in his sentimental, non-denominational way about domestic woman as contrasted with her "unnatural" visible sister: "As if every home in all this

---

*Henry Liebhart, *Edle Frauen. Christliche Frauenbilder* (1872), 4. Not unexpectedly, this heady fantasy of woman's mission in the world invaded the arts. Early in the century, an English painter, the Reverend Matthew William Peters, painted *Sylvia,* a picture of a sensual, seminude young girl; an engraving of that work supplied an alluring caption from Thomas Otway's *Venice Preserved:* "O Woman, lovely woman! Nature made you to temper Man: we had been Brutes without you." This engraving of Peter's *Sylvia,* by J. R. Smith, hangs in the Fitzwilliam Museum, Cambridge, England.

†They were only one favorite type in nineteenth-century novels. As we shall see, another type, the spirited active young woman, emerged increasingly as the century wore on.

land were not a World, in which a woman's course of influence and action is marked out by Heaven!" And on an earthier note, in *David Copperfield,* Mr. Micawber, that philosophical clown, praises the "influence of Woman, in the lofty character of Wife."[25]

It was an old story; Shakespeare's King Lear had already disdained, in a desperate effort at manly self-control, "women's weapons, water drops." No question, the gentle sex was formidable indeed—or so its nineteenth-century admirers liked to say, untiringly. Dickens's Mr. Bumble, the corrupt work-house master in *Oliver Twist,* speaks for them all. Trying to shift blame for his depredations onto his wife, he is informed that he must take full responsibility, since "the law supposes that your wife acts under your direction." Bumble is amazed: "If the law supposes that," he says, "the law is a ass—a idiot. If that's the eye of the law, the law is a bachelor; and the worst I wish the law is, that his eye may be opened by experience—by experience."[26] Only a husband, Bumble knows, can appreciate the power of woman.

Bumble's cry of pain evokes the classic fictional portrait of a familiar fig-ure—the henpecked husband, wailing. True, nineteenth-century diaries and letters offer scattered evidence of wives governing, even bullying, their hus-bands. They did so commanding a varied repertory of techniques that included tears, hysterical seizures, and ostentatious displays of swooning vulnerability. In *that* weakness there was indeed strength. But in view of the obstructions con-fronting ambitious, or simply intelligent and self-respecting middle-class women, this paradox—the weak, powerful woman—reads like an exercise in hypocrisy. Until late in the nineteenth century, when feminists managed to break down some of the massive walls of male legal privilege, women remained frustrated in their bids to manage their property, act as witnesses in court, or control bank accounts of their own. A few scattered, heroic exceptions apart, they were barred from the vote, from higher education, and from the liberal professions. They found every step toward equality furiously contested, and forced their way forward, when they did, only after round upon round of defeats.

Still, hypocrisy—the practice of professing an ideal while consciously violat-ing it—is rarely an adequate explanation for social ideologies. The blatant con-tradiction between flowery word painting about domestic goddesses and the obstructions women faced every day is, rather, a clue to besetting problems below the threshold of awareness. The notion of female power radiating out from the hearth to the world, of recessive, modest mothers and wives determin-ing the careers of men, was an obscure recognition of a fact in male lives. It exhibited, in distorted, almost unrecognizable form, men's buried dependence on women, beginning with their mothers. Though a gross caricature of social realities, convenient and self-serving, the paradox was nevertheless deeply felt.

The array of furious sexual epithets that anti-feminists lavished on the very term "female emancipation" discloses their fierce distaste for an idea they found worse than offensive, profoundly alarming. We have already encountered one of their epithets for its advocates: hens that crow. There were more; they called feminists hermaphrodites, *hommes-femmes, hommesses,* their rage attesting to pervasive male anxieties over a threatened confusion of sexual roles. In her *Vindication of the Rights of Woman,* Mary Wollstonecraft had already observed that "from every quarter have I heard exclamations against masculine women."[27] Even when they did not use precisely this provocative language, many men perceived women agitating for emancipation as a castrating sisterhood.

The notable abundance of nineteenth-century paintings, stories, and poems depicting man-eating women documents this fear pervading bourgeois culture. There were potency-destroying female creatures borrowed from mythology and from Scripture; there were pitiless *belles dames sans merci* and blatantly murderous Messalinas, as fatal as any Delilah. An irresistible army of bloody-minded women, assisted by their male supporters, was on the march, certain to subvert the men's exclusive hold on the public sphere. It was in this atmosphere that nineteenth-century defenders of men's privileges clung to the conviction that women were already as aggressive as was good for them.

The second ideological proposition, the masterful perception of woman as too pure and vulnerable to function in the world, appears to reverse the vision of woman as a man-eating creature concealed behind a facade of ladylike submissiveness. But it served the same purpose: to keep her at home, securely locked away from the battlegrounds of scholarship, business, and politics. Its psychological roots intertwine with the notion that women already are stronger than men. Both propositions were scornful idealizations; as a few nineteenth-century women, hurting from all these compliments, shrewdly recognized, both wrapped contempt in lyrical, improbable caricatures. When all hyperbole has been stripped away, it becomes evident that the first saw woman as omnipotent mother; the second, as perpetual child.

John Ruskin's famous lecture "Of Queens' Gardens" gave the latter vision wide currency. Delivered in 1864 and published the following year, it deserves to be quoted as a representative statement of the case. Women are by no means inferior to men; they possess "queenly power." In any event, it is "foolish" to consider one sex superior to the other, for "each has what the other has not." Ruskin's catalogue of characteristic qualities holds no surprises. "The man's power is active, progressive, defensive. He is eminently the doer, the creator, the discoverer, the defender. His intellect is for speculation and invention; his energy for adventure, for war, and for conquest." How different woman's gifts: her "power is for rule, not for battle,—and her intellect is not for invention or creation, but for sweet ordering, arrangement and decision." Woman's "great function is Praise; she enters into no contest, but infallibly judges the crown of contest. By her office, and place, she is protected from all danger and temptation. The man, in his rough work in an open world, must encounter all peril and trial;—to him, therefore, the failure, the offence, the inevitable error: often he must be wounded, or subdued, often misled, and *always* hardened."[28]

Man, sword in hand, guards woman from all this misery; home is a "place of Peace," a "sacred place, a vestal temple, a temple of the hearth watched over by Household Gods." And the gods' representative is woman. To do justice to that shrine, home, she must be incorruptible, "incapable of error" and "infallibly wise."[29] The personal pathos in this highly colored address is only too apparent, delivered as it was by a lamentable failure as husband and lover, a man who had never consummated his marriage. But Ruskin's message proved very popular; he was only saying most musically what almost everyone believed. In his view, an anxious wish rather than an objective observation, woman sits in the center of her web like a beneficent spider, controlling her domain, which, it turns out, is all the world.*

This second perspective on women borrowed arguments from the first. In its straightforward way, it served the dogma of separate spheres with impeccable efficiency; merely to state the argument seemed to prove it. Behind the idealization of maternal woman stood the conventional perception, already explored, of the female as emotional and passive by nature, in fundamental contrast to the rational and active male. "The role that suits women best," the *Revue des deux mondes* had it in 1843, "is in the family. The domestic hearth"—*foyer*—"is their true country; public life is for them a kind of foreign terrain. It is in private life that they possess all their advantages." Surely one would prefer a

---

*In 1869, disregarding Ruskin's strictures against elevating one sex over the other, the popular British historian W. E. H. Lecky concluded that in "the great departments of virtue," at least, "women are superior to men." *History of European Morals from Augustus to Charlemagne*, 2 vols. (1869), II, 380. A few years earlier, Lecky had noted with approval that the medieval cult of the Virgin Mary had served to raise woman "for the first time" to her "rightful position, and the sanctity of weakness was recognized as well as the sanctity of sorrow." Woman was "no longer the slave or toy of man," and rose, through the Virgin Mother into an "object of a reverential homage." In short, "love was idealised," the "moral charm and beauty of female excellence" was fully felt, and, with that, "a new kind of admiration." *History of the Rise and Influence of the Spirit of Rationalism in Europe* (1866; 2 vols. in one, 1910), I, 78.

mother, a wife, or a sister who exercised her womanly talents to a woman who usurped man's role, developed odd habits, and violently uprooted herself from the circle of simple virtues![30]

This was not just a conventional Victorian statement; it was timeworn. While the age of big industry and business enterprise drew this differentiation most sharply, one of the most influential texts praising woman as the gentle sex dates back to the middle of the eighteenth century, to Rousseau's *Émile*. It consists of a few sentences at the very point where Rousseau lauds woman's alluring power, and serves as a wry commentary on his tribute. "Woman is specially made to please man," intended "to be subjugated." She "must make herself agreeable to man rather than provoke him."[31] Nor should she study abstract truths or difficult sciences for which she is not suited, but remain within her province by concentrating on practical matters. Woman observes, man reasons.

In her *Vindication,* Mary Wollstonecraft quoted some of these gems and briskly accused Rousseau of reducing women to "gentle, domestic brutes." She had read Rousseau closely and once admired him, though never for his sexual haughtiness. Women's "disorderly kind of education," she thought, failed to develop their native strength of mind; it schooled them in cunning and a preoccupation with seductive beauty. In a brilliant debating stroke, she likened women's affection for finery like red coats to the tastes of military officers, who, too, were "particularly attentive to their persons, fond of dancing, crowded rooms, adventures, and ridicule." Sturdily, she denied that human qualities are in any way linked to gender. There is no "sex in souls."[32]

For all her wit and forensic skills, Wollstonecraft was too scandalous to make many converts. A voracious reader and formidable logician, she packed much unconventional experience into her short life. She stepped out of her assigned sphere by writing novels and—far worse—polemical tracts, bore a child out of wedlock, married the radical social theorist William Godwin, and died in 1797, at the age of thirty-eight, giving birth to a daughter. This was not the sort of life a respectable middle-class woman was supposed to lead. Only several decades later did another rebellious female, the English feminist Frances Wright, agree with her. Writing to her good friend Lafayette in 1822, she observed, "I dare say you marvel sometimes at my independent way of walking through the world just as if nature had made me of your sex instead of poor Eve's. Trust me, my beloved friend, the mind has no sex but what habit and education give it."[33] But the tendentious notion she had labored to reason out of court continued to recruit vehement supporters. In 1874, the eminent English alienist Henry Maudsley asserted dogmatically that "there is sex in mind as distinctly as there is sex in body."[34] He was joining a long-raging controversy in which his side had the upper hand. To be sure, in 1850, in his vastly popular *Social Statics,* Herbert Spencer had already thrown an inconvenient rhetorical question at those who contended that woman's only sphere is the home: considering the talents woman has displayed in every department of human activity, we must ask, "Who shall say what her sphere is?"[35] But for all of Spencer's prestige, on this issue almost everyone sided with Maudsley. The dominant view remained that if aggressiveness reared its head in woman it had to be suppressed.

This stern conviction animated bourgeois discussion early and late. At times, indeed, extremists took the caricature beyond politeness. The founding father of French anarchism, Pierre Joseph Proudhon, radical only in the matter of private property, was among the most virulent of the misogynists who specialized in long-winded denunciations. "What distinguishes woman is the feebleness, or better, the inertia, of her intellect." She may be clever enough to apprehend a known truth but will never display any initiative. For Proudhon genius is "the virility of spirit," which, by definition, leaves women out entirely; it involves "the power of abstraction, of generalization, of invention, of conceptualization, of which the child, the eunuch, and the woman are equally destitute." It follows that woman has the choice of being a housewife or a courtesan. He preferred the housewife; she would need no elevated reasoning powers and—to expose Proudhon's subtext—she would be less dangerous to men.[36]

Not every detractor of woman's capacities felt compelled to be quite so brutal. Far more common was the practice of dismissing woman as a delightful bit of irresponsibility. Her supposedly flighty nature was in fact one favorite proof of the need to limit woman's sphere.[37] Writers on this interesting subject were fond of observing her inconstancy, her adorable and maddening indecisiveness in matters of taste, of opinion, above all of love. *Così fan tutte!,* Don Alfonso exclaims in Mozart's opera, and the two young men whose lady loves, as fickle as the rest, have just proved the old cynic right, join in the chorus: *Così fan tutte!* This beguiling, irreverent opera, too cynical and too disrespectful of bourgeois domestic virtues, experienced a long decline during the nineteenth century, but its informing sentiment never went out of fashion. Kant had already claimed that women cannot keep a secret; others consistently adduced female garrulity as a special case of woman's essential inconsequence. Who could deny that women substitute a stream, a very avalanche, of talk for logic or forceful action?

As the Victorian decades went by, more and more women protested against their dubious royal condition and their very real domestic bondage. A few rebelled outright. But a solid majority of women, schooled to acceptance, continued to shape their lives in a familial and social setting dictated by male preferences. They kept silent or professed to take pleasure—often did take pleasure—in whatever hidden powers fond husbands were willing to discover in them. Nineteenth-century advocates of women's rights worked hard to unmask the ideology as a sham—as it largely was. They worked no less hard to unmask its counterpart: the assumption of female inferiority, with its domestic dividends. It did not take them long to recognize that they had much to contend with; the arguments for a male monopoly over public aggressiveness drew insidious strength from their capacity to assume many plausible guises.

This versatile pair of alibis was bolstered by the training that prepared respectable girls for the world they would inhabit as married women. Educated mainly at home, and for home, drilled in altruism and self-sacrifice, they paid a heavy psychological price of which most of them did not become aware—directly. Propagandists for women's equality, working against the grain of securely anchored cultural ideals, faced vociferous resistance. That these ideals safeguarded carefully hoarded, often fragile, masculine self-esteem made the task all the harder. In 1830, the Owenite socialist Anna Wheeler candidly admitted that she was only too aware that her feminist preachments would draw upon her not only "the hate of most men" but also "that of the greater portion of the very *sex*" whose rights she was daring to advocate. Women were "willingly degraded," she wrote in a moment of deep discouragement, "passive and indifferent to the suffering of their species," ignorant of "rational liberty" and crippled by a "propensity for slavery."[38]

This willing self-abasement was too deeply ingrained to be quickly shaken off. The generation immediately following Wollstonecraft's virtually repressed her writings and her indignation. Condorcet's categorical demand that women be granted full equality with men had been drowned in the avalanche of revolutionary violence and the Napoleonic wars; Jeremy Bentham's analytical reflections, batting down one objection to woman suffrage after another, had remained unpublished.[39] The expressions of feminist sentiments that rose to audibility were sporadic, pathetic in their isolation. Little pockets of brave female aggression kept Wollstonecraft's ideas barely breathing. In 1798, the year after her death in childbirth, her friend Mary Hays had published *An Appeal to the Men of Great Britain in Behalf of the Women,* in which she pleaded the case for women's equality; her reward was to be charged with impertinence and visionary myopia. The popular line was the one taken by the novelist Maria Edgeworth, who urged that girls be taught more caution than boys, and that women learn to adapt to existing society.

Only the unhappy few scorned such counsels of prudence as unwarranted invitations to despair. In 1808, a short-lived Parisian periodical, *L'Athénée des dames,* edited by women for women, asked pugnaciously, "Whence the common view that man is superior to woman?" Its unequivocal answer: men had made that self-serving claim, and nobody had contradicted them. Men "continually boast about the quality of their soul, the profundity of their thought, and their steadiness in carrying through projects." But while this boast held true for some men, that was due more to their education than to their superior soul.[40] These were Wollstonecraft's views, in French. But while she had found it hard to stifle a laugh at seeing "a man start with eager and serious solicitude to lift a handkerchief, or shut a door, when the lady could have done it herself," most other women thought such chivalrous conduct grounded in their, and in man's, very nature.[41] And so men continued to pick up ladies' handkerchiefs and shut doors for them, and women gladly let them do it.

In fact, one woman reader bluntly warned *L'Athénée des dames* that its defiant analysis of man's presumed superiority would come back to haunt it: "People will ridicule your way of speaking and the insults they will address to you will more or less fall back on women in general. I think you are quite wrong to try putting into doubt the common view that the man is superior to the woman." Men will used woman's very rebelliousness to "prove our weakness and our inferiority."[42] *L'Athénée des dames* soon disappeared from the book stores, and for decades, champions of women's rights had good reason to berate their potential troops for their low self-esteem, their sheer failure to feel aggrieved.

Indeed, books for women perpetuated this failure. In *Home Life,* one typical example, Marianne Farningham, who wrote popular little tracts on the art of respectable living, argued that while the mother is "the one light and joy" of the house, the father is its true vital center. This bald assertion was too self-evident to require demonstration. "Mothers, sons, daughters, all have their places, but the father is, after all, the mainstay of the whole." Some modern households ignore this truth, but as a result are sadly damaged. "We hear a great deal about women's rights, but there are some men's rights which fare worse still." In another tract, *Girlhood,* Farningham defined the principal qualities of womanliness as dignity, devotion, and tenderness. "The motto of the Prince of Wales, 'I serve,' is written on every woman's heart."[43] The service Farningham was commending to women was service to men.

This literature of conscious self-denigration—almost self-flagellation—was very large and very trite.[44] Like men's self-congratulation it took many forms, some of them extravagant. The abolitionist American novelist and editor Lydia Maria Child twisted the fashionable notion that women are infantile into a racial analogy: "The comparison between women and the colored race is striking. Both are characterized by affection more than by intellect; both have a strong development of religious sentiment; both are exceedingly adhesive in their attachments; both, comparatively speaking"—and this was the critical point—"have a tendency to submission."[45] Again, in 1873, an English writer, Mrs. Elizabeth Stone, masquerading under the male pseudonym Sutherland Menzies, published a substantial two-volume study energetically opposing women's entry into the political arena. She pointed the moral on the opening page: women who invade that arena have only misery to show for it. They discover "too late that the strife has done them irreparable injury." Though they may perhaps be intellectually qualified for politics and diplomacy, their raids on public life would only diminish the social power they now enjoy. After all—and here one alibi once again folds into the other—women "now have more influence of a certain kind than men have; but if they obtain the influence of men, they cannot expect to retain the influence of women." It seems that "Nature"—here is nature again—has "established a fair distribution of power between the two sexes"; hence in the exciting, often sordid, game of politics, the woman's place "should be at the player's elbow, to warn and advise him," but not at the gaming table itself.[46]

Mrs. Stone had no wish, she protested, to reduce women to "humiliating inaction." They should observe public affairs closely and school themselves as solicitous seconds to "the companion of their existence." But nothing more, for "Nature herself" has "disqualified women from fighting." Their proper element is (of course) the home, where "their gentler presence" acts as a refining force, "so that strength should train itself to be submissive, rudeness should become abashed, and coarse passions held in check by the natural influence of women."[47] Ruskin had not said it any better.

This collective female self-portrait, an unstable but potent amalgam in which humility outweighs assurance, was diffused through respectable culture by a distinctive institution, the women's magazine. The observation that women have identifiable preferences in reading matter was, of course, not original with Victorian entrepreneurs; since the eighteenth century, magazines written for men had angled for female readers with special departments. A few ephemera apart, the first periodical explicitly addressed to women, The Ladies' Mercury, published in London, dates back to 1693. It had a few eighteenth-century successors, including a French magazine launched in 1759, the Journal des dames, which sought its readers among pious, learned, and fashionable ladies, and survived for some twenty years. In other countries as well, a handful of periodicals catering to women made a fleeting appearance, among them two outspoken monthly magazines that the German champion of woman's rights, Marianne Ehrmann, published between 1790 and 1795.[48] But it was in the nineteenth century, with innovations in techniques of printing and distribution and a rapidly expanding reading public, that this trickle turned into a torrent.

In France alone, no fewer than ninety-two women's periodicals were launched in the 1830s and 1840s. Most of these were Mayflies; for some, the premier issue was also the last, while others soldiered on for half a year, no more. Publishers' speculative ventures and broadsheets symptomatic for a time of effervescence had little staying power. But a number of journals for women evidenced a remarkable vitality, becoming standard items in French household budgets.[49] The English figures are somewhat less stirring, but in the 1830s alone, more than a score of women's magazines made their debut, and some of them far exceeded the five-year life-span that was usually the outer limit for periodicals of this sort. Publishing for women remained a risky business, but it had become attractive enough to interest astute businessmen looking for the profits that culture could provide.

Since woman readers differed not only from men but from one another, the magazines designed to rivet women's attention addressed the most divergent tastes. Fashion magazines lavishing advice on their audience about the dernier cri and decorated with plates showing outdoor, daytime, or evening wear, competed with sheets featuring innocuous short stories, wise saws, and brief biographies of contemporary worthies; earnest monthlies filled with recipes, household hints, and medical counsel coexisted with the rare political journal advocating women's causes. And since the aspirations of nineteenth-century women had a troubled history, a few of these publications began to devote space to larger issues. By the 1870s, though still prized as icons of perfect domesticity, the more restive among them managed to question that ideal. As latent mutinous impulses began to conflict with manifest traditional values, those magazines, published to sustain separate spheres, gingerly ventured to subvert that doctrine. This, too, enriched the debates about fundamentals that enlivened bourgeois culture among the Victorians.

Yet apart from a few notorious exceptions, down to the 1860s and even beyond, this modest feminism was still muted. The timidity of women's early rebelliousness is amply attested in the pages of *Godey's Lady's Book,* America's leading women's monthly magazine until the Civil War. It was founded in 1830 as *The Lady's Book* by Louis A. Godey, shrewd, genial, and shamelessly self-promoting. In 1837, he had the wit to enlist the services of Sarah Josepha Hale, an experienced and talented editor attuned to female tastes, who made *Godey's* a national favorite. With her advent, Godey's monthly flourished mightily, outstripped only in the 1860s by its principal rival, *Peterson's National Ladies' Magazine,* somewhat cheaper, slightly bulkier, and, with its larger typeface, kinder to its readers' eyes. Down to that time, *Godey's* circulation figures swelled year by year, reaching, in 1860, an impressive 150,000. And most of this triumph was its editor's doing.[50]

Sarah Hale was an extraordinary personage, living refutation of commonplaces about woman's natural incapacity for aggression. She retains a modest place in the history of American culture as the author of "Mary Had a Little Lamb" and the campaigner who persuaded Abraham Lincoln to proclaim Thanksgiving a national holiday. A prolific writer—novelist, poet, essayist, anthologist, compiler of cookbooks—and gadfly in behalf of diverse respectable causes, Mrs. Hale was, in her genteel, pious way, an editor of genius. Presiding over *Godey's,* she was a force that philanthropists and politicians chose not to overlook.

Her influence was intimidating even though—or, rather, just because—her thoughts on the cult of domesticity were perfectly safe. As writer and editor, she aimed above all to be inoffensive, to men no less than to women. Introducing her first editing venture, the *Ladies' Magazine,* she reassured husbands that nothing on her pages would make any wife "less assiduous in preparing for his reception" or tempt her to "usurp the station, or encroach upon the prerogatives of men."[51] Editing *Godey's Lady's Book,* she pursued the same policy, intoning hymns to the blessings of wifehood and motherhood, and of beneficent piety. The ideals of male supremacy and female domestic bliss are spread throughout her magazine—in the verse, the fillers, her regular editorials, her equally regular capsule book reviews, and above all in the fiction she carefully selected as her principal offering. Feeding her readers only digestible fare, she chose stories of self-sacrificing mothers, poems about laughing children, approving comments on men and women who allow God into their lives. Obviously, this is what the subscribers to her magazine—the "Ladies," as Godey invariably flattered them—really wanted. To judge from *Godey's,* these ladies were endowed with limited culture and undemanding tastes; quite unconsciously, it documents the pitiable level at which most young women's education was pitched in those years, a level Mrs. Hale consistently deplored but only mildly challenged and never substantially raised.

The engravings she lavished on her magazine, and even more, the fiction, carried Mrs. Hale's womanly agenda to untold thousands of readers.* She en-

---

*Consider *Home:* a father, returning to his house, embraces his infant daughter, who fervently kisses him while another daughter rushes to him flowers in hand and a third clings to her blissfully smiling mother; a small dog looking up affectionately completes the picture. The accompanying poem, "Home, or the Father's Return," by Professor W. J. Walter, tries to "describe the rapture

ticed major American writers, including Edgar Allan Poe and Nathaniel Hawthorne, to her monthly, but most of the stories and short novels she published
are stupefying in their mediocrity. Relentlessly didactic and predictable, they
cling to a debased idealism, a favorite literary style that in the mid nineteenth
century gradually gave way to realism—though one would never know that
from the fiction in *Godey's*. It is a style that George Sand, its exemplary practitioner, once described as the decision to turn away from nightmarish realities
and look only toward the beautiful: "That is woman's work."[52]

Godey's storytellers, normally women, applauded woman's work as bourgeois culture then chose to define it. The only aggression they allowed themselves was against aggressive females. Their principals all talk alike, in stilted,
elevated periods unlike any prose ever spoken by human beings. And their
resolute denial of all erotic excitement fits that verbal style seamlessly. *Godey's*
heroines sink on the hero's manly chest with a sigh; protagonists seal their
betrothal with a loving kiss; hero and heroine, once married, smile at the infants
they have somehow produced. But all these actions are purely mechanical;
every hint of passion has been drained out of them. What matters is the lesson:
the infinite superiority of love over money, the satisfactions that women experience as they make a home for their men.

Interestingly enough, those among *Godey's* protagonists most in need of
salutary lessons are female—though happily for the most part eminently teach-
able. Young women must be schooled through painful experiences to become
worthy wives. They are frivolous, capricious, too quick to make up their
minds—wrongly. In one aptly titled short story, "False Pride," a young snob,
Ellen, who disdains the honest poor and flatters the socially eligible, is educated
by her frank, lovable cousin Julia, endowed with "lofty, yet not unfeminine
independence." In the end, Ellen repents and winds up with the eligible young
man whom she has really loved all along.[53] In these stories, woman's reward for
resigning herself to—or, rather, joyfully embracing—her domestic fate is a
good husband.

At times, *Godey's* stories enforced their pedagogic point with grim, if gratifying, explicitness. "The Parlour Serpent," a particularly heavy-handed tale typical of many, employs poetic justice, that choice alibi for indulging the pleasures
of revenge. The serpent is an improbably vicious gossip and liar who specializes
in breaking up promising engagements and happy homes; her punishment is a

---

of this hour," which, he admits, "transcends the Poet's art"—certainly this poet's art—and "the
Painter's power." The scene, he concludes, would persuade "musty bachelors" to get married.
Godey's Lady's Book, XXIII (December 1841), 242.

terrible accident to her jaw that leaves her at first speechless and permanently disfigured. One did not need to be a trained logician to grasp the message.[54] Cautionary tales of women who disdain the authentic happiness of love in a cottage for the illusory delights of a luxurious establishment were great favorites in the circles devoted to *Godey's*. They liked to read about beautiful young women who prostitute themselves for money, particularly since so gross a word as "prostitution" never sullied the magazine's pages.

Another typical *Godey's* story, "Sweethearts and Wives," a disguised sermon on the hard-earned gratifications of domesticity brings, is explicit in another way. It tells of a young woman compelled to learn the difference between the joys of betrothal and the sober realities of marriage. Immature and willful, Agnes regularly fails to provide her beloved husband's breakfast or midday meal promptly enough, wasting time he cannot spare from his business. Finally, aware that she has somehow failed him, she begs William to tell her what is wrong, and he gladly obliges. Reproaching her gently though sententiously, he asks his Agnes to perform her domestic duties more efficiently, and she humbly promises that she will try harder. Her abject surrender gives him an opportunity to lecture his wife on the divine plan called Separate Spheres, and he imparts familiar wisdom for half a page and more.*

With the passage of years, *Godey's* remained *Godey's,* the old recipe with its cheerful browbeating tone in place. Its readership continued to increase; its issues grew fatter, its illustrations—engravings, fashion plates, sketches and floor plans of model houses—more abundant and glossier than ever. The stories, and most editorials, of the 1850s read like virtual copies of material printed a decade or more earlier.† *Godey's* did take a somewhat more assertive tone on one subject: woman's education. The sorely neglected dignity of the female sex was

---

*"In the wise order of Providence, there is a distinct and important difference in the relation of the sexes; and, particularly, in that which a man and his wife bear to each other. He is stronger, and his mind is a form receptive of more wisdom; she is weaker, and her mind is a form receptive of more affection. Thus they are radically different"—and so forth. T. S. Arthur, "Sweethearts and Wives," *Godey's Lady's Book,* XXIII (December 1841), 268.

†In 1852, *Godey's* published a repellent engraving, *January and May,* showing a lovely young woman, exquisitely dressed and with a stunning garland in her hair, on the arm of her decrepit husband creaking along on a stick. To reinforce its moral, the editor supplied this engraving with a commentary in the form of a story that rehashed the tale of youthful greed, "A Life of Fashion," published eleven years before. A stylish, beautiful young woman has been trained up from childhood to "*marry well,*" and she obeys her mother's calculating precepts by breaking with the man she loves to marry a gray-haired rich man. The punishment for selling her body is silent but unending regret, as she recalls her lover, who had been poor when they parted but has now risen to eminence and wealth. Alice B. Neal, "January and May," *Godey's Lady's Book,* XLIV (May 1852), 301–3; quotation at 301.

frequently under Mrs. Hale's pen; self-respect required women to rise above their status as decorations or drudges, and only education could provide the ladder on which they might climb to full recognition of their worth.[55] But the magazine's modest support of this cause was largely covered over by its systematic efforts at shoring up the doctrine of manly dominance and feminine subsidence into the home. And this was as close as *Godey's,* with its adamant evasion of controversy, ever came to allowing political issues to invade its pages.[56] In 1877, saying farewell to her magazine after four decades, over eighty now, Mrs. Hale recalled that when in 1828 she had accepted the invitation to edit the *Ladies' Magazine* in Boston, "my first object, in assuming my new position, was to promote the education of my own sex." She had never changed. Hence "there was not a volume" of her journal "which did not abound in appeals, in arguments, stories, songs, and criticisms bearing upon this subject of feminine education."[57] It seems not to have occurred to her that in *Godey's* she had done virtually nothing for that education, except to call for it.

To be sure, Sarah Hale gave ample house room in *Godey's* to the threadbare claim that women run the world.[58] Her wish was mother to the thought; she meant, of course, that they *should* run the world but did not yet do so. In her monthly column, "Editor's Table," she worried like other anti-feminists that zealous reformers were leading women astray. Mothers had a sacred duty to form their daughters, and in this department she thought them sadly deficient. They trained their daughters in how to run a household at the expense of developing their character and their intellect. She admitted that an education in domesticity was essential, but she wanted mothers to cultivate their daughters' heart and mind no less. And mothers had still another duty, equally sacred, equally at risk: to train up good men who would then, as legislators, undertake necessary reforms.[59] The female could influence men in many ways—impressing on them, for example, the urgency of temperance by depicting the horrid effects of the demon rum.[60] If woman does not cajole men into goodness, if she fails to point them toward high ideals, they will give way to their pugnacity and their inherent inclination toward gambling and political dealing. The rage against men that suffuses such appraisals was barely kept under control.

The cultural revolution, then, in whose birth Mrs. Hale thought she was assisting proved a circumspect affair. A plodding satire on the woman's movement that she published in *Godey's* in 1852 (and may have written herself) delineates the boundaries of her reforming energies. A group of anxious gentlemen given to hysterics at sharp noises and bearing such telltale names as "Wumenheyter" and "Easyled" meet to counteract a "treasonable" recent women's convention in Massachusetts. Their plan is to unite in an "effort to repel the proposed feminine aggression of their rights," which will result in "universal decapitation of the men" and an "Amazonian government." No castration (one might gloss the satire) without representation. The men met in convention deliver inane speeches and debate brave resolutions reaffirming their supremacy and their venerable privileges. But it is all hollow; in the end they meekly let themselves be led away by their wives. "Exeunt omnes, in wild confusion."[61] As Mrs. Hale said all her life, women should forget about their rights and remember their duties. They have no business with aggression.

As a famous editor with a guaranteed following, Mrs. Hale did not think it necessary to acknowledge, let alone bend to, the breezes of change. Feminists, in her view, were provocative, unsexed creatures. Their notions were simply absurd, calling not for refutation but for ridicule. *Godey's* in 1877, her last year, shows that the old verities still dominated her editorial policy. The time-tested alibis for male sovereignty—woman the secret power and woman the eternal child—retained their power to charm, at least for her faithful subscribers. Mrs. Hale's last volume still features stories about beautiful young women wrestling with the sordid temptations that wealthy suitors throw in their path. Those who resist end up happy; those who succumb pay the penalty of gilded solitude or abject death. And the volume still makes the case for woman's education, but also continues to offer, intent as ever on harnessing discontent, didactic tales extolling the pleasures of homemaking. "I have no patience with their woman's rights conventions," we read, "crying everlastingly for a right to vote, a right to make the laws, and the dear knows what not."[62]

By this time, though, a respectable party of women, and of men, had begun to think this sort of talk a little shopworn, if not yet wholly anachronistic. Women's rights conventions were no longer rare, no longer seemed eccentric. The reigning dogma about woman the homemaker continued very much in control, but it was finding spirited critics. "If there is any matter emphatically entitled to be considered 'a thing of the day,' it is this 'Woman Question,' " the American journalist Charles Astor Bristed wrote in 1870.[63] The question had forced itself onto the agenda.

2. A Time for Tentativeness

The woman question had in fact been closing in on the cultural agenda for some time. As early as 1850, Charlotte Brontë had noticed a change: "The girls of this generation have great advantages; it seems to me that they receive much encouragement in the acquisition of knowledge, and the cultivation of their minds." Men, she commented in the same year, "begin to regard the position of women in another light than they used to do; and a few men, whose sympathies are fine and whose sense of justice is strong, think and speak of it with a candour that commands my admiration."[1] Even Sarah Hale had observed this shift in cultural style and welcomed it; mockery or "bitter satire on every effort of female genius" had given way to serious discussion.[2] But she ignored the implications of this seriousness for her own work.

Others, though, did explore them. One striking instance of this reevaluation, tentative and inconsistent yet pregnant with the future, is the last chapter of Thomas Hughes's *Tom Brown at Oxford,* published in 1861. This sequel to *Tom Brown's Schooldays,* his best-selling plea for muscular if sportsmanlike manliness, garnered far fewer sales than its triumphant predecessor. But it exhibits one advocate of the manly doctrine prey to some second thoughts. Like other really gentle spirits, Hughes had clearly come to recognize that life is a matter of shadings rather than of absolutes, especially in the relations between the sexes. He concludes *Tom Brown at Oxford* with an earnest discussion between the hero and his wife. Tom of Rugby, having gone on to university and out into the world, is married now, and happily so. But as an impecunious social idealist, he finds his financial prospects dim. Anticipating a horseless and servantless future and married to a young woman who has always enjoyed both her riding and her domestic help, he feels humiliated at subjecting his Mary to these sacrifices.

He tells her all, but Mary's stalwart resolution to do without her accustomed amenities does not at first reassure him. She is "a brave, generous, pitying angel" who should be protected from the deprivations he is imposing on her. "It is a man's business. But why is a woman's life to be made wretched?" After all, "life should be all bright and beautiful to a woman. It is every man's duty to shield her from all that can vex, or pain, or soil." In this heartfelt speech, Tom Brown, though wrapping his appeal in expressions of sincere and magnanimous regret, is only keeping a well-worn Victorian verity alive. Mary Brown will have none of it. Women's souls are the same as men's, and women are strong enough to be in the wicked world and to labor, in their husbands' company, toward its reformation. "Why not put me on your own level?" she pleads. "Why not let me pick my way by your side? Cannot a woman feel the wrongs that are going on in the world?" Women "are not meant to sit in fine silks, and look pretty, and spend money, any more than you are meant to make it, and cry peace where there is no peace." She is realistic enough to recognize that in her time women are not free to be as active as men. But "if a woman cannot do much herself, she can honour and love a man who can."[3]

This peroration is a lame conclusion to Mary Brown's brave effort at self-assertion. But for all its incoherence and timidity, it suggests that after mid-century the doctrine of male supremacy, and with that the cult of domesticity, were in some danger. A rival ideal, that of the competent woman, her husband's partner, able to absorb the aggressions of the world and mete out a measure of aggression in her turn, was waiting in the wings. But the stage had not yet been cleared for its appearance; when accepted generalities about women started to crumble after the 1850s, they crumbled around the edges first.

The letters of that cool observer Elizabeth Barrett, written in the mid-1840s, before the tide began to turn, provide an incomparable glimpse of just how much men were still taking for granted, how much women seemed willing to endure, and how much work the feminists still had before them. Barrett must have seemed an improbable cultural critic; handicapped for years by delicate health and a dictatorial if well-meaning father, she wrote poetry and watched the human comedy from her invalid's couch. But she saw more than most others out in the world. In 1845—she was almost forty—she began corresponding with Robert Browning, and noted that what most people call love is really a kind of warfare, with one side enjoying all the strategic advantages. Again and again one sees "the growth of power on one side" and "the struggle against it, by means legal & illegal, on the other." The best counterattack that women can mount is guerrilla warfare. "I understand perfectly, how as soon as ever a common man is sure of a woman's affections, he takes up the tone of right & might," and "he *will* have it so . . . and he *won't* have it so."[4]

This male dictatorship, Elizabeth Barrett thought, extended as much to petty matters as to portentous ones, perhaps even more: "Did you ever observe," she asked Robert Browning, "a lord of creation knit his brows together because the cutlets were underdone, shooting enough fire from his eyes to overdo them to cinders?" Once, still a child, she had overheard an unforgettable conversation between two married women: "The most painful part of marriage is the first year," said one, "when the lover changes into the husband by slow degrees." When she and Browning started to correspond, half a year before they met, Elizabeth Barrett could still strike a note of conventional docility; asking him to criticize her poetry, she adopted "the humble, low voice, which is so excellent a thing in women."[5] But while she could echo what ordinary men and women believed, she was never comfortable with such humility. Nor did Browning want it; John Stuart Mill would have approved of his attitude toward women. Other reforming men and impatient women, less articulate than these two, were also of their party. The controversies over the rights and wrongs of women were anything but amiable conversations between equal partners; there was too much inherited baggage, too much tendentious pseudoscience, to permit good-tempered confrontations or rapid reform. But the debate was real, and as the century wore on, the balance between the debaters began to shift, slowly, toward the woman's side.

These decades sent out conflicting signals; the old ideas were far from ready

to yield to the new. Almost no one endorsing the doctrine of separate spheres—
and most men and women continued to endorse it—meant to imply equality
between the sexes. Indeed, the alibi of male supremacy in both of its principal
versions—as defense against woman's secret empire and as claim to man's indisputable superiority—displayed impressive staying power. In 1872, Maria Deraismes, a founder of French feminism, might angrily respond with a spirited
diatribe to Alexandre Dumas fils' *L'Homme-Femme,* a patronizing "analysis" of
mysterious woman, the conservative force. But her pamphlet, in which she
pitted Eve against Dumas, found few approving echoes.[6]

In her country and elsewhere, most literature of advice addressed to young
women continued to preach the blessings of docile domesticity, radical economic and social changes notwithstanding. In an editorial of 1897, the London
Times reiterated the doctrine once again, unequivocally, as though the likes of
Deraismes had never raised their voices in protest. "The sex difference is the
profoundest and most far-reaching that exists among human beings." Whether
men's equals in intelligence or not, "women in the mass will act after the
manner of women, which is not and never can be the manner of men." The
editorial was not arguing, but recording a simple, indisputable truth. It is striking that Samuel Butler, who thought highly enough of the female sex to attribute the authorship of the *Odyssey* to a woman, should quote this passage with
full approval.[7]

One signal clue to the potency of this attitude emerges in *He Knew He Was
Right,* a novel Trollope published in 1869. He did not intend this tale of a
disastrous marriage as a metaphor for the sickness at the heart of man's supremacy, a sickness whose most flamboyant symptom was the desperate effort to
keep that supremacy intact; disappointed in his inability to present the suffering
protagonist, Louis Trevelyan, sympathetically, he judged the book a failure.
But it virtually demands to be read as a grand metaphor. *He Knew He Was Right*
centers on a husband irrationally, later insanely, jealous of a harmless aging
acquaintance, Colonel Osborne, who holds no erotic attraction whatever for
his wife. Trollope takes care not reduce his anti-hero to a cardboard villain;
Trevelyan loves his wife, Emily, by his lights, and she exacerbates the strains in
their marriage by her resentful lack of empathy with his labile condition, her
failure to see the pathology driving his despotic conduct. But in essence, more
than he thought or his reviewers liked, Trollope takes the wife's side. The
husband claiming sovereignty is the unpardonable aggressor.

At first, as Trevelyan tries to assert his domestic mastery by insisting that she
stop seeing the colonel, his wife half resists, half complies. When he grows more
exigent, she grows more defiant; then, looking for incriminating information,
he hires a detective to spy on her. The whole ends tragically, with Trevelyan's

madness and death. Throughout, he has refused to yield an inch of his legal authority because a compromise, as Trollope sagely comments, would rob him of his cherished manly authority. The anxiety Trevelyan exhibits in psychotic form is the unconscious fear of female aggression—psychoanalysts call it castration anxiety—that many of his contemporaries felt less openly as they faced the advocates of women's rights. But, interestingly enough, Trollope complicates the issue by introducing a minor male character who, though affable with his spirited American fiancée, even submissive to her, asserts his power as a superior male when she tries to break their engagement: "In my own house I am master." His Caroline is relieved rather than offended at this show of force: "You must be master, I suppose, whether you are right or wrong."⁸ The old doctrine had a good deal of energy left in it.

Though banal, then—or precisely because it was banal—the self-serving male claim of an ineradicable distinction between the sexes retained much vitality. In the early 1890s, the republican French intellectual and public servant Jules Simon did not hesitate to underwrite once again the ideology that was struggling hard to keep its dominance: "What is the vocation of a man? It is to be a good citizen. And that of woman? To be a good wife and a good mother." Only fanatical feminists could quarrel with this truth. Woman, made for motherhood, organizes the household and—surely the heart of her task—"organizes happiness within it."⁹

Simon is an intriguing witness to the persistence of the old dispensation even among thoughtful Victorians who took pride in being thoroughly modern. And Simon *was* modern; his wife, like him, was an impassioned educational reformer—she was president of the Société pour l'enseignement professionel des femmes—and he seems not to have objected to her taking an active role in the French feminist movement. A productive philosopher and busy politician, a moderate freethinker with spiritual yearnings, he poured out books and articles on Plato and natural religion, on the travail of working women and the threat of clericalism. And he managed to combine all this scholarship and pampleteering with a prominent political career in the early years of the Third Republic.

In developing his social program, Simon could hardly overlook the women. He wanted them to be better educated than they were, and he endorsed the sensible view that the better educated a woman was, the better a wife and mother she would be. But within limits: while she ought to enjoy sound secondary schooling, she must not spend her days in a studio or in a shop.¹⁰ In a massive monograph on woman workers, *L'Ouvrière,* characteristic of his confident manner, he argued that a woman who leaves the household has abandoned her true mission. Grossly idealizing the workshop and factory of his time, in defiance of all the facts, as places of work bound to be salubrious, with pleasant company and good pay, he nevertheless asserted that "the woman who becomes a worker is no longer a woman." He was pleased to quote Jules Michelet's outbursts in support: "*L'ouvrière!* Sordid, impious word unknown to all languages, which no time before our iron age would have understood and which, by itself, outweighs all our so-called progress!" For Simon it was plain, as it had been for Michelet, that the woman who leaves the home destroys it.[11]

Not that Simon wanted to condemn women to the "anguish and misery" of idleness—the curse which, he thought, particularly haunts married women in the upper ranks of the bourgeoisie. In many middle-class families, where the husband condemns himself to hard labor, the wife, "virtuous spouse, tender mother, capable of devotion and sacrifice," spends time on visits, the piano, and embroidery. She needs employment—no question. But Simon's recipe for a married woman's best escape from idleness is "isolated work," work that will not take her away from her household. After all, any man studying his feelings will "recognize that the best that is in his heart and mind comes from his mother."[12] This, too, was a recurrent refrain. On Simon's logic, a respectable woman wasting precious hours in feminist meetings or literary pursuits when she should be seeing to her hardworking husband's comfort is, in the most basic sense, defying the command of nature.

Such accents occasioned no surprise in a nation that would cling to the ideal of woman the homemaker more tenaciously than most others. The French *foyer,* the consecrated hearth and home, and its presiding spirit, the *maîtresse de maison,* were anchored in bourgeois ways of life, perhaps more solidly even than the German domestic deity, the transfigured *Hausfrau.* In 1885, a characteristic French handbook surveying practical domestic problems, *Travaux manuels et économie domestique,* headed its catalogue of necessary wifely accomplishments with a chapter on the "duties of a *maîtresse de maison.*" In the preface, the authors enforced the old moral once again: "The domain of woman is her home."[13] Just the year before this manual was published, divorce, abolished in 1816, had been reinstated in French law after fierce, years-long combat in the press and the legislature. But other legal discriminations against women continued in force. France remained a sturdy center of resistance to feminist demands.*

Yet even female observers had to admit that these celebrations of domesticity seem not to have dispirited most French housewives. In France, they noted, probably more than elsewhere, acceptance of the wife's circumscribed domain was far from synonymous with submissiveness, especially because that domain

---

*It was in character that France should delay granting women the vote until 1944, acting a quarter century after Britain and Germany had yielded.

could be opened up to let her work side by side with her husband. And not just as a lowly clerk: "The bourgeois Parisienne," Clara Schreiber, an admiring Austrian woman visitor to France, marveled in 1885, "is not an article of luxury for the man, but a virtually indispensable necessity for the flourishing of his business." Six years later Mme M. S. Van de Velde, introducing French fiction to an English-speaking public, seconded this report. In France, she told her readers, assiduously sidestepping the aggrieved feminists who were having trouble making themselves heard, women "are admitted on a footing of perfect equality with men in business and commerce, consulted in politics, and listened to with consideration; they are excellent accountants, managers and book-keepers, and as active mercantile partners their services are invaluable to their husbands."[14] She forgot to mention, or perhaps did not care, that they were not voters.

The home, then, was the Frenchwoman's true empire. "In most French households," wrote an English traveler, Mathilda Betham-Edwards, in 1905, "women reign with unchallenged sway." This "feminine headship," she cautioned, should not be "summarily attributed to uxoriousness on the one side or to a masterful spirit on the other." The French bourgeoise "is never at a loss, never muddle-headed, always more than able to hold her own." Her secret is "concentration;" her power lies precisely in her confinement to the household or the family business, in her very abstinence from political rallies, ambitious philanthropy, or diversionary activities like sports. "Authority is her native element; the faculty of organization is here an intuitive gift." In a word, "alike château and cottage bow to one-sided law—to feminine ukase."[15] In short, aggression was fairly apportioned between Frenchmen and Frenchwomen.

Frenchwomen who rejected this genial verdict had every right to be disheartened. As late as 1908, Hubertine Auclert, who had founded the French woman-suffrage movement virtually single-handed some thirty-five years earlier, could still judge gloomily, "Frenchwomen have a sheep's docility that astonishes even the shepherds."[16] She was appalled, she had written in her feminist journal *La Citoyenne* in 1887, to see women taking "no interest in their own emancipation and employing their intelligence, their time, their money in augmenting masculine supremacy." All they did was to place "their arms laden with chains and their pocketbooks at the service of sovereign men."[17] She could have instanced all too many Frenchwomen who fitted her acidulous description. In 1884, Alice Durand, a popular French novelist writing under the pseudonym Henry Gréville, represented that majority in a lecture in Zurich: "Woman's right is duty." Man outdoes woman in intellect and knowledge, but woman surpasses man in her capacity for self-sacrifice and the loyal completion of her domestic tasks. "Woman's loveliest decoration is her wedding band."[18]

Auclert thought she understood why Frenchwomen might be victimized by such notions: unlike Englishwomen, who had learned to utilize the power inherent in clubs and circles, independent-minded women in France remained isolated. Whatever the reason, she remained persuaded that "the worst enemies of women are women."[19] Jules Simon, it seems, spoke for most of France.

He spoke for more than France. In other countries too the appeal to that sturdy alibi, nature, an inexhaustible debater's resource, remained a favorite weapon against malcontents campaigning for the radical enlargement of women's rights. And as in France, elsewhere too women made the case against themselves their own. In 1885, the German novelist Emilie von Mataja— known by the male pseudonym Emil Marriot—published a story, "Dem Manne gleich," in which she hauled out once again the unfailing lesson. An ambitious and intelligent young woman, Betty, is trapped into an affair with a man who, she discovers too late, has already married—for money—a rich old woman. Brooding over her experience, she sums up what her imprudence has taught her: woman is always man's victim because she is a born victim. " 'A lost cause!' thought Betty. This whole struggle for emancipation may mean a living for us, but true freedom would be ours only if we could shake off our weakness, our dependency, our impotence. And because Nature says 'No' to that, our lot will always remain the same."[20] But was it "Nature," or only Germany?

Marriot's doctrine of despair seems appropriate for a country in which the woman's movement, late to start and slow to blossom, had far more modest aspirations than it did in the United States, Britain, even France. The most outspoken German feminists, like Helene Lange, asked not for the vote or access to the professions, but for the better preparation of girls for their mission, wifehood and motherhood. A German association campaigning for universal suffrage was not founded until 1902. In this unpromising atmosphere, the handful of women pressing more extensive demands were held back by considerations of political prudence. As late as 1910, Kaiser Wilhelm II would tell his subjects that "our women" should "learn that the principal task of the German woman lies not in the field of assemblies and associations, nor in the achievement of supposed rights, with which they can do the same things as men, but in quiet work in the house and in the family."[21] While Germans vehemently criticized the emperor's impetuous interventions and bellicose rhetoric, on the issue of woman he had most of the country with him.

The argument for the natural segregation of women was loudly heard even in "advanced" Britain. In April 1892, shortly after Simon had set forth nature's law regulating man's and woman's proper place, the Liberal political leader Herbert Asquith told the House of Commons that "the inequalities which democracy requires that we should fight against and remove, are the unearned privileges and the artificial distinctions which man has made, and which man can unmake. They are not those indelible differences of faculty and function by which Nature herself has given diversity and richness to human society."[22] It was precisely the well-worn cliché that made his statement effective; faced with such rhetoric, doubters had to ask themselves whether they really wanted to argue with nature.

Yet in the 1870s and 1880s this sort of talk grew more defensive in tone. The first step was taken by men—and women—experimenting with new ideas about the female sphere without jettisoning the old, and without noticing the contradictions this caught them in. The German family weekly *Illustrirte Zeitung* is an illuminating instance of such intellectual muddle, a tribute to the human capacity for holding incompatible positions without a conscious sense of discomfort. The magazine appreciated women and despised them. Its "Frauenzeitung" devoted two or three columns to matters deemed particularly interesting to women. But many of its anecdotes were scornful: women are inordinately prying and talkative; American women are particularly prone to these irritating defects, but inquisitiveness also disfigures women in other countries; in Vienna, female typesetters work faster than the men, probably because they cannot wait to get to the end of the articles they are setting. Sustaining this critique of woman the chronic gossip with a show of classical erudition, the *Illustrirte* reminded its readers that in ancient Rome, Juvenal had already complained about women monopolizing literary conversations and talking incessantly, like so many chattering magpies. It reminded them, too, of the Chinese proverb "Woman's weapon is her tongue, hence she takes good care that it does not rust." In short, woman's nature exhibits itself everywhere, in every age. With all their garrulity, the *Illustrirte* added for good measure, women do faithfully keep one secret—their age.[23]

The fate that awaited reasonable women, the exceptions in their flighty sex, was, the *Illustrirte* held, sad to behold but predictable. A scheme for healthful clothing developed by the Rational Dress Society in London seemed a case in point; its call for loose, useful clothing and the abolition of veils, petticoats, corsets, and the rest of the modish vanities was bound to be futile. "A lot of water will still flow down the Seine, the Thames, the Donau and the Spree" before this sensible program becomes reality. "Women know perfectly well that they are tempting tuberculosis with their décolleté dresses and that they are crippling their noblest inner organs with their corsets, but they will renounce neither the one nor the other." Custom, fashion, and vanity "are more powerful than reason and morality."[24]

Woman, in a word, is irrepressibly childish. The *Illustrirte* offered instances: in recent years, certain ladies have extravagantly applauded the artists they adore, besieging them with flowers, tender poems, and ecstatic letters, and importuning them for locks of their hair. Again: in several confectioners' shops in Berlin, women openly display their hostility to men, staring at the hapless male who stumbles inside, or ignoring him. Compared to such all-too-typical females, men certainly shine as far more mature. In a long column of 1883, commenting on the festivities commemorating the four-hundredth anniversary of Martin Luther's birth, the *Illustrirte* proffered a bouquet of his pithy pronouncements on women. The great reformer had enjoined his listeners to cherish their wives, those marvelous gifts of God, but to remember that woman, always something of a child, must remain subject to man. The absence of flightiness in German women, the *Illustrirte* claimed, is an exceedingly rare exception; that is why foreign observers pay tribute to the pure morals and family sense of the *Hausfrau*.[25] Most women elsewhere provide less palatable food for thought.

With this dismal estimation of female nature, the *Illustrirte* saved its deadliest venom for emancipated women. We have already seen how much emotional resistance the term "female emancipation" aroused. The *Illustrirte,* which virtually spat out that epithet at least once each issue, certainly responded viscerally. It cautioned against a "radical party" among "emancipated ladies," a "revolutionary" wing whose "members are filled with an inextinguishable hatred for men, a hatred all the more dangerous in that it has taken over all the room of the love that had not favored the radical emancipated ladies." Here was another old story that died hard: it was the disappointed, dried-up spinsters who turned all their destructive impulses on men, because they had been too unattractive to get husbands of their own; such harridans would just as soon destroy "the whole male sex, so useless to them." Only a very few relatively sane feminists called for "the emancipated, but the womanly woman."[26] This was as far as the *Illustrirte* was prepared to go.

But in the magazine's nervous vision, the members of this slightly more rational group were far less effective in the political arena than the visionaries who called for absolute equality. *Their* influence was spreading like an epidemic across the civilized world—most notoriously in the United States and Britain but also as far away as India and Australia. To be sure, the *Illustrirte* observed with almost audible relief, a few American newspapers, and even that rebel George Sand in her last years, had alerted the public to this contagious disease, this "so-called woman's emancipation." And fortunately the "gigantic progress" that feminists claimed for the United States was a myth; not a single state or territory had granted full equality. Yet in that country, the female frenzy was nevertheless progressing with giant steps: "Women are conquering ever more and more terrain, and if the men there fail to show the necessary energy, the fair sex will pull out the rug from under them."[27] It needed watching.

The turbulent United States fascinated the *Illustrirte*. In 1884, summarizing a brochure, *Woman Suffrage,* by an American political pamphleteer, John C. Hertwig, it offered that curious mixture of warm appreciation and cold suspicion we have encountered so often. Women said Hertwig, are not inferior to men in spirit or intellect—of course not!—but the division of labor demands that they serve the family while their men serve the state. *"Womanhood"* teaches women that they have nothing to gain by the vote. The *Illustrirte* naturally applauded this stance, adding a warning against agitators for female emancipation. The glosses were hardly needed; it was no secret that the *Illustrirte* was appalled by the unwomanly fantasies of these "over-excited bluestockings."[28] Every page breathed aversion and anxiety.

But—and that is the telling inconsistency—all this derision did not keep the *Illustrirte* from saluting, if hardly in trumpet tones, those uncommon brave women who were beginning to force their way into public visibility here and there—at Somerville College, Oxford, at Uppsala University in Sweden, at the University of Toronto. These lonely pioneers were proving themselves as advanced students in academic specialties like archaeology, philology, mathematics, and classical languages; they were showing themselves no less effective as practitioners in carefully defined medical specialties, in pharmaceutics and botany, as commercial travelers, as architects, and even—though this was exceedingly rare—as bank presidents. Women performing skillfully on the piano were now overpowering male pianists with "squadrons" of "almost menacing numbers." Every few weeks, the *Illustrirte* would register the meager statistics of females studying medicine in Zurich or in Paris, or the handful of woman doctors in Russia.[29]

The magazine could even muster, in passing, a few kind words for Hubertine Auclert, despite her radicalism. And to provide an impartial view of "much maligned Parisian women," it printed a substantial report praising them as their husbands' valued business partners.[30] The *Illustrirte* conveniently forgot that precisely its own columns had "much maligned" women week after week, and not Parisian women alone. The stale caricatures in the "Frauenzeitung" pillorying women's innate defects raise the question of just where those prodigies, those young women with brilliant gifts for mathematics or banking, could have come from. Far from striking a tentative compromise between the fear of the new woman and admiration for her daring, the *Illustrirte* was regressing to sheer incoherence—the journal's response to a social ground swell it could not master.

But the *Illustrirte* was not alone; critics of feminism were spread across the intellectual landscape. Antique apocryphal anecdotes continued to amuse, and convince, ever new recruits. There was the one about the happy housewife and proud mother of sons who rejected the vote for women because, as she said, "I already control my sons' and my husband's votes."* This familiar and feeble paradox, so appealing before 1870, remained a staple into the twentieth century. In 1908 an English traveler, Violet Stuart Wortley, was gratified to note that in France, "though legally women occupy a much inferior status to men, in practice they constitute the superior sex. They are the 'power behind the throne' and both in the family and business relations undoubtedly enjoy greater consideration than English women."[31] Other observers, in other countries, also discovered women as powers behind the throne, endowed with a fateful mission. This, after all, was the time when Kipling could declare the female of the species more deadly than the male.

It is appropriate, then, that the notion of woman's secret empire should have been dramatized most suavely in England, as late as 1908. *What Every Woman Knows,* by James M. Barrie, is typical of its author's copious and, in his day, immensely popular, output; the comedy is cleverly constructed, flecked with playful touches, and perfumed by whimsy.[32] Barrie's life was governed by one heroine, his idealized mother. His adoration of her long survived her death; and she, far more than any other woman in his life, gave him a sufficient sense of woman's power over man. Like his most enduring creation, Peter Pan, Barrie never really grew up.

The deftly named heroine of *What Every Woman Knows,* Maggie Wylie, is a disguised tribute to maternal mastery. She is in her mid-twenties, lovable, plain and, under her modest self-depreciation, fiercely intelligent. Her family marries her off to a younger man, John Shand, an aspiring politician, self-educated and self-deluded, who thenceforth owes his entire career to his wife's backstage maneuvers. She sagely counsels him under the cover of demurely listening; she thoroughly rewrites, and drastically improves, his speeches, calling her rescue operations light editing; she saves him from calamitous political blunders without taking the slightest credit for her interventions. When, humorless and histrionic, Shand discovers what his loving, patient, and clever wife has done

*For a classic version of this stale joke, including a barely necessary interpretation, see *Godey's Lady's Book:* " 'I control seven votes; why should I desire to cast one myself?' said a lady who, if women went to the polls, would be acknowledged as a leader. This lady is a devoted, beloved wife, a faithful, tender mother; she has six sons. She *knows* her influence is paramount over the minds she has carefully trained. She *feels* her interests are safe confided to those her affection has made happy. She *trusts* her country will be nobly served by those whom her example has taught to believe in goodness, therefore she is proud to vote by her proxies." The editor enthusiastically endorsed this decision: "This is the way American women should vote, namely, by influencing rightly the votes of men." "Editor's Table," *Godey's Lady's Book,* XLIV (April 1852), 293.

for him, he despises himself. But she pleads with him to laugh with her: "It's nothing unusual I've done, John. Every man who is high up loves to think that he has done it all himself; and the wife smiles, and lets it go at that. It's our only joke. Every woman knows that."[33] That is Barrie's point. Maggie Wylie is not the only one who has tumbled to the secret of woman's empire. *Every* woman knows that.

But Maggie's joke is far from funny. In fact, the positive response to Barrie's rather unpleasant revelation of the reality behind the heavy veil of male supremacy is telling. Barrie's psychological history was, of course, peculiar to him; he exhibited the fate of the perpetual preadolescent with particular poignancy. Yet he was not simply dramatizing a rare idiosyncrasy. His portrait of a married couple—brazen male incompetence on one side, camera-shy female wisdom on the other—must have evoked in many men clusters of mental images, or vague memories, recalling the first and shaping love affair of their lives, with their mother. What Barrie thought every woman knew was something that most men knew, in their troubled unconscious.

Stories and caricatures that turn self-assured male attitudes on their head, and show the strong woman bullying her weak husband, were common in the nineteenth century. To be sure, writers and cartoonists liked to picture women like Olga, the pliant heroine of Anton Chekhov's story "The Darling," who slavishly adopts the opinions, even the character, of the men she marries. But they also profitably pictured women who tyrannize their lord and master in public no less than in private. In his first full-length play, *Ivanov,* almost as if to make up for the submissive Olga, Chekhov featured Lyebedev, an alcoholic landowner who leaves all significant financial decisions to his wife and is afraid of her. Zola delineated Mme Bourdelais, the canny shopper in *Au Bonheur des dames,* his novel about a Parisian department store, as a highly sensible woman who bosses her husband for his own good. Again, Samuel Butler introduced George Pontifex in *The Way of All Flesh* as a man whose wife "was said to be his master." And Theodor Fontane, ironically exposing the disparity between official ideology and sober actualities, had wicked fun with Frau Jenny Treibel in the novel named after her. The opinionated and obstinate wife of a wealthy Berliner, she speaks with becoming sentimentality about the "high pleasure of subordination" that constitutes women's "fairest happiness and is more or less synonymous with genuine love." But she lustily fights for, and normally gets, her own way.[34]

In what may be the most familiar portrayal of female sovereignty in the nineteenth-century novel, Trollope gave new meaning to the term "pillow talk." Mrs. Proudie, the henpecked bishop's ambitious wife in *Barchester Towers,* knows precisely what she wants—and he should want. Yet, while these imagined women stood for real wives in real bourgeois households throughout the Western world, the literary vignettes fasten on a certain type rather than a universal fact of Victorian life. They were all the more popular for being made so amusing and thus less threatening. But despite their realistic appearance, they lend only very limited credibility to the sweeping alibi for keeping females subdued on the ground that woman—every woman—is a master posing as a slave.*

Just as the legend of all-powerful woman survived into the latter days of Victoria's reign, so did its counterpart, the image of woman as gentle domestic angel. The old scornful idealization could count on a measure of devout support. Churchgoers in Protestant and Catholic countries alike derided talk of female emancipation as sheer impiety; they liked to invoke the awesome weight of Scripture to prove that God himself had prescribed a purely domestic role for women. St. Peter had laid it down: "Ye wives, be in subjection to your own husbands." And St. Paul had agreed; Christians throughout the centuries liked to echo his injunction that women keep silent in church. "And if they will learn any thing, let them ask their husbands at home: for it is a shame for women to speak in the church."[35] That should be enough, and for many religious bourgeois, it was enough.

Still more troubling to the campaign for woman's share in political action was the vocal antagonism from the left. For pressing, far from disinterested reasons, anti-feminism long remained a staple among progressives. In England, when the case for woman suffrage was raised once again in 1884 during the debates over a new parliamentary reform bill, Liberal members of Parliament objected on the ground that women were Tories by conviction, and once they had the vote, would overwhelmingly support the Conservatives. This cavil found even more aggressive expression in Catholic countries; anticlericals worried that women were only too disposed to rely on their confessors for their political opinions. On this issue, Jules Michelet had given late-Victorian radicals their cue. "Our wives and our daughters are raised," he observed at mid-century, "are governed *by our enemies*"—he meant priests, of course—"the enemies of the Revolution and of the future."[36] The consequences were unmistakable.

French Socialists and Radicals agreed, and insisted that women had to be

---

*Just one more instance of this alibi: In 1883, Freud, that amalgam of bourgeois conservative and revolutionary scientist, employed it to dismiss John Stuart Mill's demand that women should earn as much as men. "Any girl," he wrote his fiancée Martha Bernays, "even if with no right to vote or legal competence, whose hand a man kisses and for whose love he dares all, could have set him straight." Freud to Martha Bernays, November 15, 1883, Peter Gay, *Freud: A Life for Our Time* (1988), 39.

thoroughly educated—that is, weaned away from the church—before they could be entrusted with the vote.[37] The weaning seemed painfully slow. In 1877, Léon Richer, who, as founder of the French League for Women's Rights, boasted impeccable credentials, sounded the alarm: "Out of nine million women who have reached their majority, only several thousand would vote freely; the remainder would take their orders from the confessional." As late as 1907, after decades of republican efforts at secularizing the mind of French women, Georges Clemenceau, the undisputed chief of the Radical party, could still echo Michelet; women, he argued, are "completely impregnated with the sacristy." Without question, "almost all their influence is exerted to the benefit of the reactionary parties."[38] All that Hubertine Auclert, pleading for Frenchwomen's right to the ballot, could muster in reply was the accusation that republican orators like Clemenceau were being shortsighted, arrogant, and inconsistent; they wanted equality, but only for themselves.

In Germany, too, the principle that some humans are more equal than others held sway. In 1896, one of the country's first woman physicians, Hope Bridges Lehmann-Adams, pleading for the admission of women to medical school, returned to one of Wollstonecraft's cherished propositions: "Science has no sex."[39] But like her model, she was unable to disarm those intent on despising woman's intelligence. In 1900, Paul Julius Moebius, a Leipzig psychiatrist with literary ambitions, published an ill-tempered polemic, *Über den physiologischen Schwachsinn des Weibes,* which pushed the anti-feminist case as far as it could go. His argument was familiar, his virulence all his own. Gender matters, Moebius asserted—fundamentally. Woman is incurably inferior to man, in mind as much as in body. Relying on dubious anatomical claims, puerile questionnaires, and outmoded generalities, he concluded that "woman is a being halfway between child and man, and mentally she is so, too, at least in many respects."[40] Author of a study of Schopenhauer, Moebius proved himself that famous misogynist's loyal and intemperate disciple. The reason for woman's hopeless inferiority, he concluded, is that those parts of the brain essential to intellectual labor are less highly developed in her than in man. Anatomy—not education, training, environment—is destiny. Hence Moebius's provocative title, which proclaims the *physiological* feeblemindedness of women. After all, women's brains are smaller and weigh less than men's; even when asked to perform a task involving small motor skills, in which women presumably excel, a man will quickly surpass them.

It followed for Moebius that if men would only firmly inform women that they have no use for any feminist propaganda, the "unnatural" woman's movement would promptly wither away. "Nature is a severe lady and threatens violation of her regulations with harsh penalties." Moebius had no doubt—he never had any doubts: "*Instinct makes woman animal-like, dependent, secure and cheerful.*"[41] Moebius himself, for all the infuriated outcry of his critics, was certainly both secure and cheerful. He had reason to be; his pamphlet was widely and generously reviewed, and quickly went into several enlarged editions. Riding the crest of this favorable tide of opinion, Moebius's imaginative publisher supplied each succeeding version with excerpts from reviews, favorable and unfavorable, and from readers' letters, some of them quite savage. By 1906, the little book, much swollen, had reached its eighth edition.[42] Female imbecility was evidently a fashionable charge.

The longevity of Moebius's popularity unwittingly demonstrates the persistence of male fantasies about mighty, fatal woman, for only frightened men needed to believe so overemphatic and absurd a thesis. No wonder the Sphinx in modern dress, more lethal even than the figure of Greek legend, remained a favorite of poets, painters, and book designers. In her new incarnations, she usually appeared not as the victim of Oedipus, but as his conqueror. Even when she was not shown busy killing men, she stood for the mystery that is woman. It was only appropriate for the Sphinx to appear on the cover of *La Femme à Paris,* Octave Uzanne's lavishly illustrated survey of Parisian women in his time.[43]

Even the old canard that woman is a garrulous gossip kept a certain following toward the end of the Victorian decades. Theodor Fontane documented its survival in his novel *L'Adultera*. "The need to chatter," he had one of his characters say, is "the deepest need of woman's nature."[44] Such facile slanders had practical consequences; one argument against training women as physicians was that they would be unable to obey the rule of medical discretion.[45] The earnest ripostes of women, pathetically insisting that they were indeed trustworthy, serious, and discreet, must be read against these overbearing and wounding assaults. Women had been compelled to endure them for longer than they cared to remember.

3. A D——d Mob of Scribbling Women

Well before middle-class women could conquer, and defend, narrow beachheads in higher education and the liberal professions, they had found one highly visible career beyond housewifery, motherhood, teaching, and nursing: writing for money. Articles, poems, dramas, novels, books on travel, and books of advice were so many tokens of a calling arduously acquired and precariously enjoyed. By the first years of Victoria's reign, the female author was a familiar though not universally beloved figure, a protagonist in the great redefinition of roles that marked the age.

Many male writers, feeling crowded, damned these invaders as too self-assertive by far. Most female writers, less secure in the world, responded ambivalently. A few among them, proud of this interesting and honorable way of making a living, refused to be intimidated even if that meant offending the male establishment. These were the ones Samuel Johnson had baptized, in the mid eighteenth century, "Amazons of the pen." Yet even they, we shall see, had twinges of discomfort at their aggressive posture. Most writing women could not easily set aside the formidable barriers of male haughtiness and of stern familial distaste for female scribblers. What Anna Freud has called identification with the aggressor was a pervasive experience for them, as they denounced female colleagues for turning out popular trash, or modestly conceded that great literature remained the province of men. The only too familiar decision of many nineteenth-century woman writers to conceal their identity by sporting a masculine or sexually unrevealing pseudonym—George Sand, George Eliot, Currer Bell, Otto Stern, Ossip Schubin, E. Marlitt, Ouida—was overdetermined. But one powerful reason was the low self-esteem that made so many of them reluctant to claim their place among the makers of literature.

The careers of nineteenth-century woman writers, then, make for an illuminating test case in the history of aggression—of attack, counterattack, and only too often, more or less pathetic surrender to self-serving male verdicts. They are illuminating, too, because it is virtually impossible to disentangle the constructive from the destructive elements in the progress of Victorian women in the literary profession. What many authors and publishers resented as naked female aggressiveness, others welcomed as a source of new talent. It was by no means all embittered warfare over turf. Editors impressed by the sizable audiences that the most resourceful woman writers could command yielded to this profitable evidence of skill and talent. Readers, too, came to value the women who gave them pleasure, not in astonishment that women could do creditable work at all but simply because the work was creditable. In literature, as elsewhere, aggression in the Victorian age was a complex mixture of combat and accommodation. It will emerge that the truces were never final; old doubts about woman's competence kept reemerging in unexpected places. Woman writers discovered that some their supporters sounded suspiciously like their enemies.

A handful of women, mainly scandalous, had become prominent authors in the seventeenth century, and the age of Enlightenment saw a far more respectable troop of them: Fanny Burney in England, Sophie von La Roche in Germany, Madame de Staël in France. But it was in the Victorian decades that they established writing as a serious domestic industry. Women, W. R. Greg observed late in the 1850s, "are the chief readers of novels; they are also, of late at least, the chief writers of them." The reasons women drifted into this mode of gaining a livelihood were quite obvious at the time. The obstructions a woman poet or novelist faced were minor compared to those blocking her access to the liberal professions, let alone politics. She could write at home, inconspicuously, between chores; she required no capital, no training, no advanced education—just a table, writing paraphernalia, and a few stolen stretches of time. Women, Greg noted, "have nothing to do, and educated ones can wield a pen."[1] This is not untypical male response, uncharitable and a little nervous.

Literary men had long disliked woman writers. Ever since the late seventeenth century, when the amusing, licentious playwright and novelist Aphra Behn set a pattern, they had eyed authors of her sex as provocative aggressors. To be sure, Aphra Behn, with her explicit erotic writings, *had* been provocative. So had Mary Wollstonecraft, a century later, with her radical feminist program. Horace Walpole, in his sour way, spoke for the majority of males when he denounced her as a "hyena in petticoats."[2] The very spectacle of publishing females in what Samuel Johnson called the "Age of Authors" raised the vision of unwelcome potent rivals. At the least, men found them a remarkable phenomenon; around mid-century, Johnson, who liked educated women, worried over those scribbling Amazons who had "set masculine tyranny at defiance" and seemed "resolved to contest the usurpations of virility."[3] He was not a little surprised.

By the early nineteenth century, surprise was mingled with alarm. In 1807, looking at portraits by Karoline Bardua, a skillful professional painter, Goethe told a visiting friend, "Works of art by ladies are an occasion for astonishment every time, but never give us an opportunity for admiration."[4] Similarly, the writing female was still eccentric enough to arouse incredulity.* And insecure male authors translated their concern over aggressive woman writers into counteraggressive censoriousness. In December 1836, Charlotte Brontë, unpublished but intrepid, sent some of her poems to Robert Southey, the poet laure-

---

*A famous letter from Jane Austen to her nephew James Edward Austen, an aspiring author, subtly mirrors this attitude. She was sending sympathy upon hearing that he had misplaced some chapters of a book he was writing. With an appealing mixture of wit and tact, she pleaded innocent and added, "I do not think any theft of that sort would be really very useful to me. What should I do with your strong, manly, spirited Sketches, full of Variety and Glow? How could I possibly join them on to the little bit (two inches wide) of Ivory on which I work with so fine a Brush, as produces little effect after much labour?" One would never guess from this letter, admiring, without aspiring to, the manliness of her nephew's literary endeavors, that this was the year Jane Austen published her masterly *Emma*. But one can discern in it a woman's sensitive response to male vulnerabilities. December 16 [1816], *Selected Letters 1796–1817*, ed. R. W. Chapman (1955), 188–89.

ate. After a worrying silence, he sent a chilling reply, urging her to write poetry "for its own sake" and "not with a view to celebrity," and sternly cautioning her against daydreams. "Literature cannot be the business of a woman's life, and it ought not to be." Writing only interferes with woman's discharge of her destined work: "The more she is engaged in her proper duties, the less leisure will she have for it, even as an accomplishment and a recreation."[5]

This attitude did not fade easily. As late as 1911, the widely read French novelist Henry Bordeaux, speaking to a conservative woman's group, deplored modern woman's public self-display, which reduced the poor husband to the status of prince consort while the wife neglected her domestic responsibilities: "The housewife of today writes poetry or novels," having virtually abandoned her destined art—the culinary art. "It is dying, and she is writing novels." If Molière were to return to earth, he would condemn such bluestockings even more strongly than he had, two centuries earlier, in *Les Femmes savantes*.[6]

A few sympathizers did welcome this female self-assertion. "They are numerous, the literary *spinsters* of the United Kingdom," one French commentator, E.-D. Forgues, observed approvingly in 1860; he thought the "intervention of the feminine novel" a "salutary" influence on the young women who would shape the next generation, and envied the English for it.[7] "One of the most curious and most piquant chapters in the history of the world," the journalist Charles de Mazade observed two years later, "will be the one that retraces the sovereign power of women in its charm and its metamorphoses." True, women were not admitted to the Académie française, but they "elected" the members of the Académie, exercising their "charming sovereignty," and they wrote books![8] But most male writers instanced their female competitors as one more proof of abnormal militance.

This male anxiety was matched by the anxiety of woman writers. "If I were a lad, I would cheerfully deal out sword thrusts this way and that, and do literature the rest of the time," George Sand wrote in May 1835. "Not being a lad, I shall dispense with the sword and retain the pen, of which I shall avail myself in the most innocent way in the world."[9] About to launch a great career, she was strenuously experimenting with life and literature; two years earlier, she had published her Byronic novel *Lélia,* and her public was beginning to identify her with the pseudonym she had adopted the year before that. The psychological and cultural implications of her casual metaphor about sword and pen are dazzling. Not being a lad—in those years she was haunted by the doom of being a mere woman—she cowered, making herself as small, as "innocent," as she could; forever prevented by nature from wielding man's long, pointed weapon, she chose a substitute, long and pointed enough, and as wounding in its way as a sword. Writing, she was suggesting unselfconsciously, could be woman's game as much as man's, provided she armed herself with the instrument that seemed—metaphorically—a potent emblem of virility. These were the years when her critics liked to characterize George Sand as an aberrant being, a man-woman.

In this atmosphere of uneasiness and mutual recrimination, champions of literary women felt obliged to speak up for them. At mid-century, in a substantial survey of contemporary literature, Robert Prutz, a German playwright, poet, liberal publicist, and literary theoretician, welcomed them emphatically. Did not Europe's most lustrous laurels grace the brow of George Sand, not merely the greatest female author, but the greatest author? "It is impossible to take a tour around present-day literature without mentioning writing women. Women have become a power in our literature." Prutz saw this development as part of the great movement of liberation at work in the century.[10] Around the same time, G. H. Lewes, the literary critic and biographer who would soon become George Eliot's life companion, made the case for female novelists on biological grounds. Glancing at the novels of George Sand, Jane Austen, Charlotte Brontë, Mrs. Gaskell, and lesser writers, he concluded that "of all departments of literature, Fiction is the one to which, by nature and by circumstance, women are best adapted. Exceptional women will of course be found competent to the highest success in other departments; but speaking generally, novels are their forte."[11] This was an ambiguous tribute; the notion of a natural division of labor between males and females had long been used not to welcome professional women, but to patronize them. Anyone at all sympathetic to feminist aspirations was bound to find a bitter aftertaste in Lewes's kindly analysis of woman's literary vocation.*

But Lewes was exploiting commonplaces about woman's nature to subvert them, drawing unconventional consequences from conventional perceptions.

---

*More than two years earlier, reviewing Charlotte Brontë's *Shirley* with benign loftiness, Lewes had disregarded her earnest plea to be judged "as an *author,* not as a woman." He had "handled the question of sex," she protested to him in a letter, "so roughly—I even thought so cruelly." January 19, 1850. Elizabeth C. Gaskell, *The Life of Charlotte Brontë* (1857; World's Classics ed., 1919), 343. But Lewes believed, sounding much like everybody else, "The Masculine mind is characterized by the predominance of the intellect, and the Feminine by the predominance of the emotions." "The Lady Novelists," *Westminster Review,* LVIII (1852), 132. For untold decades, males taking pen in hand had drawn comfort from this tendentious polarity. Not long after Lewes's essay appeared, W. R. Greg made the same point all over again: "Novels constitute a principal part of the reading of women, who are always impressionable, in whom at all times the emotional element is more awake and more powerful than the critical." With their narrow experience, Greg concluded, female writers, though at times "really interesting and clear," are also "radically and inherently defective." "False Morality of Lady Novelists" [ca. 1858], *Literary and Social Judgments* (1873), 86, 89.

Precisely because women are more at home with feelings than men, "the advent of female literature promises woman's view of life, woman's experience; in other words, a new element." With her "greater affectionateness, her greater range and depth of emotional experience," woman will greatly benefit literature.* If a woman could not have written *Tom Jones* or *Vanity Fair,* a man could not have written *Pride and Prejudice.* Jane Austen was "the greatest artist that has ever written"; her "circle," though "restricted," was "complete." To read one of her novels "is like an actual experience of life."[12] Lewes knew no higher accolade.

This measured, somewhat dubious, appreciation put Lewes into a distinct minority. Even critics who professed to value women's literary talents were quick to lament their ineradicable frailties. In his reputable, once influential, history of modern German literature, Rudolf von Gottschall recognized the contribution of females to the current outpouring of fiction—within limits. "Writing women," with their "felicitous comprehension of social life, keen gift of observation, tact, charm of description," show a distinct aptitude for the novel of manners. But these qualities are "characteristic for the passive and reproductive talent of women." Most women could never aspire to produce great literature; most of their novels are disguised diaries.[13] This was appreciation as aggression.

With such admirers, woman writers scarcely needed detractors. But detractors were not lacking, and they included George Eliot. In 1856, herself about to venture into writing fiction after years of studying, editing, and reviewing, she chose to ridicule them in "Silly Novels by Lady Novelists." Her title obviously recalled, and challenged, Lewes's genial survey of several years back. In the piece, probably the most amusing she ever wrote, she wielded her wit with a polemical purpose. George Eliot did not object to "lady novelists" on principle; what annoyed her was that contemporary woman writers were clouding the pure stream of literature with a muddy avalanche of popular fiction. The novels George Eliot found most objectionable featured superhuman heroines, beautiful, learned, witty, religious. In the confections they graced, all was well—or, better, all would be well—in the best of all impossible worlds. The meretriciousness of these fictions stemmed, in her view, from their authors' sheer lack of worldly exposure. They were written in scented boudoirs by brainless la-

---

*Lewes, "The Lady Novelists," 131–32. Later in the century, Samuel Butler argued, even more drastically, that since men in ancient times had been principally occupied in hunting and fighting, women, occupied with "the arts of peace," were most likely the first authors. "If the truth were known, we might very likely find that it was man rather than woman who has been the interloper in the domain of literature." *The Authoress of the Odyssey* (1897; 2nd ed., 1922), 13.

dies.[14] George Eliot would not even grant silly lady novelists the alibi that "society shuts them out from other spheres of occupation." True enough, "society is a very culpable entity," but "where there is one woman who writes from necessity, we believe there are three women who write from vanity." Fortunately—and here, at last, George Eliot's pride as a woman intellectual broke through—great names attested that "women can produce novels not only fine, but among the very finest."[15] Surely, the history of aggression is a history of the subtlest mixed feelings.

In her clever and cruel performance, George Eliot failed to explore her promising diagnosis—women's enforced unworldliness—which penetrates to the core of women's disabilities. The experience of Victorian writing women was not just constricted but distorted. Especially in the first half of the century, virtually all educated women in Europe and the United States, even those growing up in households that fostered their reading and encouraged their literary experiments, were assigned their destiny: marriage and motherhood. They often found the fame and the modicum of fortune that came with writing best-selling novels an anomaly and a burden, scarcely eased by the gratuitous moralizing of more submissive woman writers frowning at them. "Literature," the didactic English author Jane West wrote just after 1800, "is with us an ornament, or an amusement, not a duty or profession; and when it is pursued with such avidity as to withdraw us from the especial purposes of our creation, it becomes a crime."[16] A male competitor could not have reproved female pugnacity more harshly than this.

The diaries and letters of these innocent transgressors were punctuated with little eruptions of guilt feelings, or a sense of being trapped in a hostile world. Women were assailed by regrets at what they read as their evasion, their very betrayal, of the domesticity that was their God-given assignment. Early in the century, prefacing a collection of her writings, the Scottish novelist Mary Brunton declared herself "positive that no part—no, not the smallest part—of my happiness can ever arise from the popularity of my book, further than as I think it may be useful." This was more than a becoming pose of modesty. "I would rather, as you well know, glide through the world unknown, than have (I will not call it *enjoy*) fame, however brilliant." Her desire for obscurity was not idiosyncratic; the lot of a woman writer, Brunton testified with a breathless profusion of dashes, was hard. "To be pointed at—to be noticed and commented upon—to be suspected of literary airs—to be shunned as literary women are, by the more unpretending of my own sex; and abhorred as literary women are, by the pretending of the other!—My dear, I would sooner exhibit as a rope dancer."[17]

Other intrepid but unloved rope dancers testified to the vertigo that beset

them. In the mid-1830s, after publishing such popular novels as *Hope Leslie,*
Catharine Maria Sedgwick recorded in her journal that her *"author's* existence
always seemed something accidental." Woman writers, often looking back to
an idealized father who had given them the run of his library, might take pride
in their intellectual prowess—their sophisticated learning, their grasp of French
and German. As the successful novelist Augusta J. Evans told a friend in 1862,
rebelliously, "To be 'feminine,' is scarcely a synonym for 'weak-minded, idi-
otic, or frivolous.' "[18] And yet, not a few of these writers envied men, for
obvious reasons. In 1851, Mary Virginia Terhune spoke for her troubled clan
when she exclaimed, "A man, darling, goes into the broad world to battle,
stimulated by the presence and influence of his fellows, his every action has a
witness and is censured or approved—while woman finds her warfare *within*—
Oh the battles agonizing and terrible that are fought within that penetralia! the
victories, unheralded save by angels who have seen and sympathized—and the
defeats after which she tries, still uncomplaining, perhaps smiling to the last."[19]
People like Terhune embodied a paradox haunting Victorian women active in
literature: the writer complaining in arresting prose at being a writer. "Envy,
malice, and all uncharitableness," the English poet Letitia Elizabeth Landon
grieved in 1836, "these are the fruits of a successful literary career for a
woman."[20] The game hardly seemed worth the few flickering candles it
bought.

   The rare works of fiction in which nineteenth-century woman writers presented a heroine professional, pen in hand, tend to portray her as a more or less
willing victim—ready, almost eager, to sacrifice fame to marriage. There is the
eponymous protagonist of Augusta Evans's *Beulah* of 1859, probably the most
lugubrious heroine in Victorian fiction, forever weeping. Despite her all-
pervading depression Beulah grows into a lovely, brilliant writer of philosophical and theological essays. But her guardian, whom she at long last will marry,
alerts her to the siren call of public acclaim: "Ambition such as yours, which
aims at literary fame, is the deadliest foe to happiness." Aggressiveness and
happiness are incompatible—for women: "Man may content himself with the
applause of the world, but woman's heart has holier idols." Obstinate, willful—
and weeping—Beulah resists the doctrine of separate spheres for another hundred pages before love conquers her appetite for celebrity. When the hero
challenges her to choose between two tyrants, ambition and himself, she does
not hesitate. "Well," she tells him, her cheeks burning and her lashes drooping,
"if I am to have a tyrant, I believe I prefer belonging to you." From then on,
Beulah will devote herself to her husband and make her campaign to convert
him to Christian piety her single mission.[21] That much for authorship.

   Talented nineteenth-century women faced the conflict between independence and domesticity, art and love, as a heartbreaking dilemma. In 1879, in *The Story of Avis,* a novel about a woman painter saddled with an unfaithful, unemployed husband and two small children, Elizabeth Stuart Phelps put the case vividly: "Women understand—only women altogether—what a dreary will-o-the-wisp is this old, common, I had almost said commonplace, experience, 'When the fall sewing is done,' 'When the baby can walk,' 'When housecleaning is over,' 'When the company has gone,' 'When we have got through with the whooping-cough,' 'When I am a little stronger,' then I will write the poem, or learn the language, or study the great charity, or master the symphony; then I will act, dare, dream, become."[22] It is this shackle on women's talents that George Eliot failed to appreciate. Feeling contempt for silly lady novelists, armed to carry her warfare to the world, she identified not with the victims of her culture but with its aggressors.

Not that the aggressors needed her help. In 1855, the year before Eliot heaped injury on insult, Nathaniel Hawthorne grumbled to his friend and publisher William Ticknor that the times were not right for the new romance he was contemplating. "America is now wholly given over to a d———d mob of scribbling women, and I should have no chance of success while the public taste is occupied with their trash—and should be ashamed of myself if I did succeed." These females were selling "by the 100,000."[23] To find harsh words for scribbling women became almost irresistible. As late as 1892, in his story "Greville Fane," Henry James drew drama from the contrast between the seriously committed but financially strapped male narrator and a relatively prosperous woman author. The narrator believes in "difficulty" and in literature that demands a "tremendous licking into shape," while she pours out three novels a year and has no literary ambitions whatever, never suspecting "that she had not contributed a sentence to the language."[24] James's weapon is suave irony, but his hurt at the triumph of female mediocrity pulsates just beneath the surface.

Few woman writers commanded the vast audience that Hawthorne imagined, but some, to his chagrin, really did. The single dreadful instance Hawthorne explicitly mentioned in his outburst, *The Lamplighter* of 1854, by Maria Cummins, sold some forty thousand copies in the first eight weeks after publication and at least fifty-five thousand copies in the first year; in comparison, *The Scarlet Letter* had sold, after six months, some five thousand copies—a total that Hawthorne, not spoiled in that department, found quite satisfactory.[25] He did not think he could—nor did he wish to—compete with the ladies.

Apparently it did not occur to Hawthorne that those who were paying good money for bad prose were not deserting him; most of them were new readers who would scarcely have found his probing fiction to their taste. Their invasion was not a usurpation of his territory. "Mr. Hawthorne, we are afraid," argued the prolific Scottish author Margaret Oliphant, no vulgarian, in 1855, "is one of those writers who aim at an intellectual audience, and address themselves mainly to such. We are greatly of opinion that this is a mistake and a delusion, and that nothing good comes of it. The novelist's true audience is the common people."[26] Whether we qualify her judgment as realistic or philistine, Mrs. Oliphant was observing a very real phenomenon. As leisure grew more widespread and ingenious inventions made paper cheaper, distribution easier, and printing more efficient, all sorts of reading materials became more accessible. The age was one of lending libraries and public libraries, of magazines thirsty for digestible fiction and light reading matter for tedious railroad journeys. The Victorian century was developing discrete reading publics, ever more sharply segregated by the quality of the literature each could enjoy.

In the 1850s, and beyond, the thousands were enjoying *The Lamplighter*. It is easy to see why that novel—Maria Cummins's first, published anonymously—was destined for bestsellerdom. It incorporated all the ingredients a not overly fastidious reader would devour amidst delicious tears: a sweet and beautiful heroine, a handsome hero, other lovable characters, and lessons on self-control and Christian forgiveness, the whole pervaded by an atmosphere of melting religiosity. But the picture of whole nations absorbed in trashy or hopelessly gushy novels is a caricature. Not all bourgeois consumers of print read novels; among books published before 1850, the most popular category was religious works.[27] Furthermore, in the popular fiction of the day, much of it written by women, the boundaries of literature and religion became oddly blurred; many novels were barely disguised sermons. Woman novelists competed not only with male novelists but with preachers. The prominent American Unitarian divine and author William Ellery Channing spoke in large company when he called the moralizing female novelist an "evangelist," a "teacher of nations."[28]

The priesthood of the woman novelist emerges forcefully in another American best seller of the day, *The Wide, Wide World* of 1850, by Susan B. Warner, which sold more than half a million copies by 1900.[29] The novel strikingly resembles *The Lamplighter:* the heroine is a much-abused, exquisitely miserable orphan whose religious impulses survive despite hardhearted relatives and worldly provocations; she, too, will marry happily and thank God for her good fortune. Reviewers, a fairly civilized lot, spoke scathingly of the book and its like, with their ludicrous "lachrymations."[30] Still, the lachrymations continued to outsell serious writers, easily. Male resentment at females elbowing their way into the profitable fiction market had some ground in reality.

The American best sellers of the 1850s demonstrate that pious sentimentality was being democratized; in the works that lady novelists were now scribbling for their receptive audiences, the heroines started out as pitiful orphans rather than high-society bluestockings. Nor did this literature find success only in the presumably unsophisticated United States. By 1855, Mrs. Oliphant could wryly comment on those "dreadful perfect little girls who come over from the other side of the Atlantic to do good to the Britishers," including Susan Warner's heroines.[31] Her complaint went unheeded; as her contemporaries marveled at the ever-expanding market for reading matter, the dreadful perfect American girls were welcomed in Britain as they had been at home.

They were no less welcome on the Continent. Tales of spotless, long-suffering, but resilient and ultimately conquering heroines filled the pages of magazines, the shelves of booksellers, and the catalogues of lending libraries. Doubtless the most popular among woman novelists satisfying this demand was the Thuringian Eugenie John, who wrote under the pseudonym E. Marlitt. She provides a fine instance of the mutual accommodation of a woman writer, a shrewd publisher, and bourgeois consumers of fiction; no one seems to have resented her doing a man's job better than most men. Featuring her work, *Die Gartenlaube,* the weekly in which all her fiction first appeared, prospered. The magazine's print run had been 5,000 copies in 1853, its first year, and exceeded 100,000 eight years later. But in 1866, the year after Marlitt had exploded in its pages, its circulation rose to 225,000 during the publication of her first serial novel, *Goldelse,* and two years later, subscriptions had climbed 25,000 more. From then on there was no stopping *Die Gartenlaube;* in 1878, the year its founder and first editor, Ernst Keil, died, it boasted a circulation of 375,000, and it kept its supremacy at least until 1887, the year of Marlitt's death.[32]

Marlitt's triumph, and Keil's, were quintessentially bourgeois triumphs. Keil explicitly aimed *Die Gartenlaube* at the *Mittelstand,* the sizable middling and lower segments of the German bourgeoisie. He wooed and won an audience among shopkeepers, self-employed craftsmen, minor bureaucrats, struggling professionals, thousands of German emigrants, and, of course, their families. These faithful readers, often keeping up their subscriptions through generations, were neither rich nor highly educated; the daring fare of the naturalists and the urbane experiments of avant-garde writers and artists were beyond their ken. Recognizing this, Keil astutely coupled moralizing and benign humor in *Die Gartenlaube* with cheerful, nonacademic articles, and matched the bluff heartiness of his editorials to the undemanding level of its fiction. In the first number, Keil sounded the note of cozy, good-humored intimacy that remained the magazine's signature for generations; he wanted his "little sheet" to be perused "in a quiet hour" and enjoyed "in the circle of your loved ones during long winter evenings, by the snug stove," and to provide a "knowledgeable guide" to the riches of human experience, all the while staying away from politics.[33] He gave his subscribers—who plainly delighted in cultivation, or were told they did—learning without tears; they were the kind of philistines who feel entitled to look down upon others, less exacting in their choice of literature, as philistines.

While Keil was a liberal nationalist who had been incarcerated for his political views, the ground tone of *Die Gartenlaube* was harmony, a commitment to peace and progress, with the emphasis on peace.* Despite its pronounced distaste for bigotry and particularism, *Die Gartenlaube* was almost from the start an exercise in denial; it touched on political issues and social problems gingerly, when it touched on them at all. Marlitt, with her energetic sallies against aristocratic arrogance and her defense of bourgeois aspirations, to say nothing of her anticlericalism, was more progressive than most of Keil's authors. Like other contemporary woman writers, she was no bland conformist.

Keil's recipe, with Marlitt an essential ingredient, never required serious amendment. Nor did the abrupt revelation that E. Marlitt was Fräulein John trouble him.† No need: she had an uncanny sense for German middle-class tastes. Producing her fiction with a bookkeeper's methodical rhythm—a novel every two or three years—Marlitt made her fortune, and considerably enhanced Keil's, with her luxuriant if thoroughly domesticated imagination. Diverted from a promising career as a singer by bouts of hysterical deafness, crippled by arthritis and chained to her desk, never married, she peopled her inventions with exciting fantasies that must have gratified her as they did her troop of devoted readers.[34] They were her revenge on fate.

It was a triumphant revenge; she became a model for her sister authors. The fiction of *Gartenlaube* novelists was nothing if not emotional. Their characters yield to the passions and act out the aggressions that the magazine's editors

---

*In the course of years, *Die Gartenlaube* changed; in the late 1860s, it jumped on the Bismarck bandwagon. Then, with Prussia's victory over France and the consequent founding of the German Empire, the liberal impulses that had informed the early *Gartenlaube* more or less discreetly gave way. But its public remained essentially intact. In 1895, the magazine illustrated an article about its printing plant with a vignette showing the window of the dispatch office. Among the people shown waiting there for the next issue or starting to read it, are a "lady" wearing a fashionable hat, "a woman of the people" wearing a kerchief, and "a gentleman" sporting a white mustache and bowler hat. Others on the scene include well-dressed young people and ladies in evidently comfortable circumstances. "Ein Donnerstag an der Expedition der 'Gartenlaube,'" *Die Gartenlaube,* XLIII (1895), 548.

†It is amusing, though scarcely surprising, that in his first communications with Eugenie John, Keil addressed her as "Herr Marlitt"; only when her pseudonym had been exposed did he claim—safely after the fact—that he had been "rather but not wholly surprised," because he had detected a certain "feminine warm and feminine refined pen" in her portrayal of woman characters. [Alfred John(?)], "Eugenie-John Marlitt. Ihr Leben und ihre Werke," *E. Marlitts Gesammelte Romane und Novellen,* 10 vols. (1889; 2nd ed., 1890), vol. X, *Thüringer Erzählungen,* 406.

consistently excised from its articles. They provided factitious crises for bourgeois readers intent on peace and quiet in the real world. Fathers curse sons;
sons kneel at the feet of their mothers; lovers shower passionate kisses on the
upturned faces of the beloved; handsome men overcome the stigma of hideous
mutilation through the love of good, beautiful maidens; fierce pride generates
appalling obstacles before pure young lovers; noble soldiers falsely accused of
treachery redeem their good name with superhuman feats of heroism.

Normally, *Gartenlaube* authors set the stage swiftly, after providing a bit of
Stimmung with humanized nature: before they introduced the protagonists,
they had sunshine dazzle, storms threaten, and birds wing their way into the
unknown. This symbolic freight, though ornate, was not heavy; authors
plunged rapidly into confrontations, and etched with brusque economy the
characters that would accompany the reader for some delectably tense weeks.
The *Gartenlaube* storytellers did not trouble themselves with the mixed motives
that drive real human beings. Every paragraph had to tell, every speech identify
its speaker as hero or villain. Working of features, quality of voice, style of
speech, settled—without delay and without appeal—the fictive actors' and ac-
tresses' roles in the tale. These novels do not lack development: a headstrong
young man learns to value the rectitude of his distant father; a cool heiress melts
under the glow of a poor but honest lover. But the suspense is at best mild, for
the conclusion has been programmed, and telegraphed, in the opening scene;
the alert reader cannot fail to guess that the stubborn hero will learn his lesson,
the rich heroine discover her heart.

Only—Marlitt did it better, much better. The eminent novelist Gottfried
Keller professed to find in her narrative flow, her gift for rendering moods, and
her descriptive powers, "something of the divine spark."[35] Still, her novels
predictably followed, and splendidly realized, the *Gartenlaube* program. They
begin in the required style with atmospheric word painting and move smoothly
to melodramatic moments. A heroine saves the hero's life, or his sanity. A suave
villain, whom the reader is invited to hiss, pursues the heroine with unwelcome
attentions. The author's greatest enemy is boredom.

Almost needless to say, a Marlitt heroine is as beautiful as an angel but
buoyant, energetic, affectionate, efficient, frank, and self-sacrificing. Her sensitive improvisations on the piano bring tears to strong men's eyes. Well-
educated or ignorant, she can moralize in paragraphs that could be inserted
without revision into a treatise on ethics. She dearly loves her family, who in
turn idolize her. When the hero in *Goldelse,* Marlitt's first major success, getting
to know his future wife, asks her whether she has ever felt the need for a friend,
she, "with a tone of deep feeling," replies, "No, for I have a mother." That
hero, in his mid-thirties, twice Golden Else's age, is no matinee idol, but

distinguished in his bearded dignity, manly and vigorous. And for all his appeal-ing inner strength, he is vulnerable enough to bring out the maternal side in her, the wish to pity and soothe him. The legend of powerful woman haunts Marlitt's pages.

In tune with the liberal German bourgeoisie, Marlitt's *Goldelse* does have its political moments. The protagonists are shadowed by deep mysteries and hints of noble blood coursing through bourgeois veins, but when it appears that Golden Else and her parents have a right to titles of nobility, they proudly reaffirm middle-class dignity: they refuse them. To top it all, when the hero, an aristocrat beyond doubt, marries poverty-stricken Golden Else, a few haughty noble personages are dismayed. But that only documents their decadence; goodness, bourgeois goodness, is all. In a late edition of his encyclopedic history of nineteenth-century German literature, Rudolf von Gottschall, himself a contributor to *Die Gartenlaube,* shrewdly observed that Marlitt retells the fairy tale of Cinderella—over and over.[36] In most of her novels, Marlitt traces the adventures of a beautiful, talented, usually penniless girl, of bourgeois origins or bourgeois sentiments, who ultimately marries above herself. Marlitt's plots, as *Die Gartenlaube* editorially celebrated them in 1871, delineate the victory of "harmless nobility of sentiment, the proud yet so modest dignity of a virginal femininity," a chaste German burgher femininity, over "rotted presumption and arrogant sanctimoniousness."[37] Some of Marlitt's heroines are aristocrats, but these are penniless waifs with titles, or are happily ignorant of their rank.

Whatever their inherited status, Marlitt's heroines testify to the kind of woman's power that nineteenth-century readers like to see. Each radically reforms the man she will marry, softening his asperity, reconciling him to life, awakening him to love. It is as though Marlitt had imported Jane Austen's proud Darcy without demanding that her counterparts to Elizabeth Bennet give up their prejudice in turn—being perfect from the start, they have no prejudices to give up. But Marlitt's leading ladies pay tribute to the reigning ideology; in the end each puts her trusting head on her hero's manly chest in fond surrender. Käthe, the pure, selfless, competent protagonist of Marlitt's *Im Hause des Kommerzienrats,* insists that as an active woman she needs to do more than practice her music and study languages, even at the risk of appearing "unwomanly." The man destined to become her husband raises no objections, but quickly adds that energetic though she may be, her true vocation is "not to stand at your desk, all alone, day after day, your head filled with figures and calculations."

Marlitt deployed her favorite formulas almost without variations, and so did her German imitators. In other countries, too, popular woman novelists drove their lovely creations toward the betrothal kiss that explains and cures everything. The exemplary heroine, only flawed (if she is flawed at all) by some venial defect, and glad to entrust her destiny to her chosen man, proved as irresistible to novel readers in France as in Britain, in Germany as in the United States. Bourgeois tastes did not differ all that much across frontiers.

It seems most likely that these stock characters, the perfect heroine and the imperfect hero, which so gratified the appetites of the reading public, did the same for their inventors, and not for Marlitt alone. But woman writers did not enter the literary profession simply to retaliate against men by taming them on paper. Their choice involved a supremely practical consideration; many women became writers because they needed the money. Johanna Schopenhauer, the most celebrated among the early-nineteenth-century German woman novelists, may serve as an example. She is principally remembered today as the mother of the philosopher Arthur Schopenhauer, but in her time he was mainly known as her son. The prosperous widow of a Danzig merchant, she settled in Weimar as Goethe's friend and made herself a popular hostess. But in 1819, the year the first volume of her best-selling novel, *Gabriele,* was published, the commercial house in which her fortune was invested went bankrupt. From then on, she poured out novel after novel, importuning her friends to give her favorable reviews and her publishers to raise her royalties.

Johanna Schopenhauer was an inspiring and far from isolated example. In England, Jane Austen, though from a comfortable clerical family, particularly welcomed the income from her novels, exiguous as it was, after her father's death. Harriet Martineau, that prolific author of children's tales, travel reports, improving novels, books on popular philosophy and political economy, made a living by her profession because she had to; when she was in her early twenties, her father's firm failed. And in the United States, Susan B. Warner, whose novel *The Wide, Wide World,* we know, became one of the century's publishing phenomena, started her literary career strictly for financial reasons; her father had suffered disastrous reverses, and her once affluent family had dropped into humiliating impecuniousness.[38] Even some of the most illustrious woman authors were impelled by need.

The pursuit of money, though, was rarely the dominant motive for literary work. Even the "heroine" of Henry James's "Greville Fane"—as we have seen, a best-selling and hopelessly third-rate woman novelist—purifies her quest for cash with a high ideal; "an industrious widow, devoted to her daily stint, to meeting the butcher and baker and making a home for her son and daughter," she persuades herself that the English novel needs her impassioned prose.[39] As the lives of great woman writers attest, this portrayal of intricate motives at work is realistic enough. No matter how pressing their pecuniary worries, many of them were genuinely driven by a burning sense of calling, by the lust for fame and the sheer pleasure of inventing imaginary worlds.

George Sand admirably exemplifies this overdetermination, and also the perils lying in wait for a woman seeking to assert her talent. Early in 1831 she escaped to Paris from a stressful marriage, and with her talent for literature she tried to secure her independence with the pen. She importuned the literary pundit Auguste de Kératry, novelist and politician, and made him listen to her novel in progress. Meanwhile, she did political journalism for the opposition paper *Figaro*. "One must live, after all," she wrote after two months in Paris, "and I am quite proud of earning my own bread." Proud or not, she had few illusions and bemoaned having to slave over casual pieces for a few francs: "That horrible trade of scribbler gives you an aversion to the very sight of ink and paper."[40]

Overwork and irritation were not the only antagonists George Sand had to battle. She found that hard as it was for anyone to gain a foothold as a professional writer, it was especially hard for a woman. Her open envy, mixed with rage, forms a troubling leitmotif in her letters and her autobiographical writings. To be sure, she could be severe on woman writers, just as George Eliot would later be. Indeed, for a time she adopted the critical perspective of the male literary establishment, deriding her friend Hortense Allart, better known for her lovers than for her novels, as a "pedant" at once "masculine" and a *"woman author."*[41] But such shots at her own troops did not assuage Sand's sense of oppression. In 1837, in her largely autobiographical *Lettres d'un voyageur,* she confessed, "You know that an immense pride devours me, but that this pride has nothing petty in it, nothing guilty"; it was a pride, she wrote to her friend Frédéric Girerd two years later, that "might have pushed me toward a heroic destiny, if I had not had the misfortune of being a woman." Her angry reminiscences of her first weeks in Paris in 1831 suggest that this anatomical misfortune obsessed her for years. She charged that Auguste de Kératry had told her to make not books but children. Whether literal truth or distorted memory, there is little doubt that her reconstruction dramatizes attitudes widespread in Parisian literary circles.[42]

At times she denigrated herself as a mere mercenary scribbler. "I am continuously writing books for love of gain," she told the great critic Sainte-Beuve late in 1833. But her love of literature was stronger still. "I have one goal, one task, let's say in one word, a passion," she observed. "The trade of writing is one of them, violent and almost indestructible. When it gets hold of a poor head, it can't be stopped."[43] While this excited profession of faith dates from the early days of her career, her violent passion never waned, even after she had made enough money to take sabbaticals from the writing table. Authorship provided pleasure, income, and a kind of redemption all at once.

The same complex of motives animated the no less prolific Scottish novelist, literary critic, and journalist Margaret Oliphant, once highly regarded. She discovered her vocation as a girl and kept on writing after her marriage. Her skill proved providential; in 1859, when she was just over thirty, her husband died, leaving the awkward legacy of three children and a thousand pounds in debts. In response, to support her children and the rest of what must have been an exceptionally unworldly family, she flooded the market with travel books, critical essays, biographies, and novels, sometimes more than a volume a year. In her cycle of agreeable provincial novels, the *Chronicles of Carlingford,* Mrs. Oliphant achieved a certain distinction with her wit and lack of sentimentality. True, the pressure to make money never left her. Even as a driven, fledging writer, she recalled, she had been criticized for "working too fast, and producing too much." Yet she insisted, persuasively and with transparent sincerity, "I have written because it gave me pleasure, because it came natural to me, because it was like talking or breathing, besides the big fact that it was necessary for me to work for my children." Financial pressures were never "the first motive."[44]

In short, even when the need for money drove woman writers, the serious artists among them derived nonpecuniary dividends from their work. Harriet Martineau for one professed to enjoy it. She "used to talk of *writing* being such a pleasure to her," Jane Carlyle reported.[45] Louisa May Alcott, famous for the classic *Little Women* and other chronicles of the March family, illustrates another striking reward—a psychological benefit: aggression in, and through, self-sacrifice. Her parents, weighing heavily on her exacting conscience, nailed her to the revolving wheel of duty. Her father, Bronson Alcott, was successively a peddler, a teacher, a food faddist, an abolitionist, and, almost on principle, a sponger; after failed attempts at running experimental schools and working the lecture circuit, he withdrew to his study to think deep Transcendental thoughts and write in his journal. Her mother, Abigail May Alcott, assisted worthy causes far beyond her income, adored her husband, applauded his eccentricities, and almost matched him in artlessness. In this rarefied atmosphere, Louisa May Alcott assumed the Victorian husband's role of breadwinner. She did sewing, taught school, nursed soldiers during the Civil War, and wrote and wrote.

Conflicts about sexual roles, even sexual identity, ran deep in her. "I was born with a boy's spirit under my bib and tucker," she confided to her journal in 1856; she was "more than half-persuaded" that she had "a man's soul, put by some freak of nature into a woman's body."[46] As an adolescent, that transparently autobiographical character Jo March acts like a tomboy. She walks about with her hands in her pockets, whistling, studying her boots "in a gentlemanly manner," emphatically regretting that "I can't get over my disappointment in not being a boy."[47] Her author had been, as it were, a boy for years. This was more than a private psychological bent; if society persisted in relegating true woman to wifehood and motherhood, a female out in the world earning money had to be something of a man. Nor was being doomed to femininity Louisa May Alcott's only disappointment. That she thought herself unloved by her emotionally abstracted father only intensified her devotion to forced labor. Like other children feeling shut out from parental affection, she apparently held herself responsible for her fate, heaping guilt upon her own head and longing for her father in secret.* The competence that set her apart from her parents was a bittersweet gift, a source of misery and of gratification. Matters would have been easier for a man.

But she loved writing. At times she found herself immersed in a rapturous fantasy world. Discovering her passion, Jo March, that stand-in for her creator, "would shut herself up in her room, put on her scribbling suit," a "black woollen pinafore on which she could wipe her pen at will." She would "fall into a vortex," and write away at her novel "with all her heart and soul, for till that was finished she could find no peace."[48] But for all this blissful absorption, erotic in its intensity, Louisa May Alcott sometimes wearied of her slavery to her family. In 1856 she confessed as much in her journal; she was "rather tired of living like a spider,—spinning my brains out for money." Then she would mildly retaliate against the author of her travail. "I am very well and happy," she wrote her father. "Things go smoothly, and I think I shall come out right, and prove that though an Alcott I can support myself." This cheerful bulletin barely conceals a hostile sting. It was a skirmish in the war between the sexes in the Victorian decades.[49]

But not a victory. What Louisa May Alcott really wanted to write was horror stories exploring somber underground regions of sexual and aggressive passions, even perversity. *Little Women* made her rich and famous, but that it should have been a publisher who suggested that she write a "girls' story," and her father who strongly seconded the plea, rather poisoned the book's success for its author. Always that sobering truth: a man would have been freer to choose. The exquisite pleasure of sending home large sums, settling the family's debts, was the best kind of revenge open to her.[50]

Still, women's opportunities for choice were improving. Witness the career

---

*Several of her novellas read like desperate pleas for her father's love. "Love and Self-Love" and "A Marble Woman; or, The Mysterious Model," to mention only two, are both about an emotionally starved young woman who, after improbable melodramatic episodes, wins the passionate love of a much older man who had once been coolly paternal to her.

of Fanny Lewald, which testifies at once to the travail and the expanding chances of a talented, persistent nineteenth-century woman writer in a man's world. Chiefly remembered today by historians of German feminism, Lewald was in her time a fashionable novelist, respected political polemicist, and widely read autobiographer; a few enthusiasts ranked her with George Sand and George Eliot. Her conquest of literature was a triumph of talent and energy over convention; her patient campaign for a room of her own is the leitmotif of her expansive self-portrait, *Lebensgeschichte*, of 1862. She knew her limitations. "I am only an artisan," she wrote in 1847, "not an artist."[51] But she accepted her gifts, and the world eventually gave her the opportunity to realize them.

Fanny Lewald's early life was that of a nineteenth-century bourgeoise. She was born in 1811 in Königsberg into a prosperous, cultivated Jewish family working hard at assimilation; her father changed his name from Markus to Lewald, and had Fanny, and her seven younger siblings, baptized. That beloved father was a paradox. A devotee of the Enlightenment, he superintended his children's education with care; at the same time, he was an exigent patriarch who demanded unconditional compliance to his wishes, and got it. But Fanny, for years unprepared to question—let alone defy—paternal authority, was quick-witted, political to the core, and increasingly impatient with the preparation for life imposed on her. After her schooling ended at fourteen—her two brothers would be sent to the university, but there was never any question of her joining them—she was assigned hours each day on "accomplishments": five hours doing needlework, two hours practicing the piano, and a set time for improving reading, which by paternal fiat excluded novels.

The latent crisis erupted in 1837, when she was twenty-six, as her parents presented her with a suitor she found unbearable. All her father's efforts at persuasion proved futile, and for six more years she kept up her tedious existence, dreaming of freedom and a literary career. Finally, after fatiguing domestic combat, she won her father's grudging permission to strike out on her own, on condition that if she *must* dabble in the disgraceful activity of writing for money, she publish all her work anonymously. What the father interpreted as unwarranted aggression, his daughter saw as a step toward self-realization. By 1840, she had begun to write, copiously, and she never stopped until her death in 1889.

Almost inevitably, her highly autobiographical fiction mirrored her tribulations and a long-pondered political position. Experience and reflection had made her a principled liberal; hence her novels of the 1840s are works of social engagement and explicit advocacy. She was convinced that a novel that has no precise relation to its time is bound to fail. In her first major effort, *Clementine*, published in 1843, she criticized marriages of convenience as worse than prostitution; in *Jenny,* of the same year, she boldly tackled the delicate theme of Jewish–Christian relations; in *Eine Lebensfrage,* of 1845, she advocated divorce. Though her inner storms abated, Fanny Lewald never abandoned touchy topics; her later novels deal sympathetically with women in search of professional independence in literature, music, and the theater. German feminism had found a voice.

Lewald's production included articles and books on the woman question, consistently calling for an end to legal restrictions and to male condescension.* Hers was a realized life, complete with a happy marriage to the scholar and author Adolf Stahr, who divorced his wife to marry her. She had mainly herself to thank—her intelligence, her resilience, her self-liberation from timidity. That her husband and a literary cousin assisted her shows that not all men shared her father's views on woman's self-assertion. Yet the appreciation she received was at best partial. Gottfried Keller praised Lewald for her "energy and her manly gift for experience."[52] In her time, male claims to innate superiority surfaced even in sincere tributes to woman.

It is a little astonishing that in this often infuriating situation, woman novelists and poets only seldom visited stern punishment on their male protagonists. Jane Austen's Mr. Darcy must shed his superb arrogance before he can claim his prize, Elizabeth Bennet. Charlotte Brontë's Mr. Rochester loses a hand and (temporarily) his eyesight, but his gain—Jane Eyre—makes his injuries worthwhile. George Eliot's Mr. Casaubon is an ineffectual creature, probably as impotent in bed as in his study, but then he is a foil for the vital Ladislaw, whom Dorothea will later marry. Romney, the hero of Elizabeth Barrett Browning's *Aurora Leigh,* is blinded, yet he remains the hero. A few other heroes are handled roughly, but for the most part the rage of woman writers was softened by success or concealed through repression.

Perhaps the most savage expression of female revenge fantasies against the male of the species—here repression failed—is a short narrative poem by the minor German poet Maria Janitschek. Published to widespread disapproval in 1889, "Ein modernes Weib" recounts the climactic encounter between a seducer and the woman he has unforgivably insulted. One evening, she appears at his rooms, dressed in deep mourning. Presenting a box holding two pistols, she challenges him to a duel. He stands amazed and then further infuriates her by

---

*No less an authority than John Stuart Mill warmly acknowledged her *Für und wider die Frauen* of 1870, a polemic in behalf of the emancipation of middle-class women. "Your book," Mill wrote Lewald, "is both convincing and persuasive, and is singularly free from the two contrary defects, one or other of which writings for the cause of women so often exhibit, of indiscreet violence and timid concession." March 1, 1870, *Collected Works of John Stuart Mill,* ed. J. M. Robson, 25 vols. (1963–86), vol. XVII, *Later Letters of John Stuart Mill,* 1703.

breaking into loud laughter. Men, he genially instructs her, do not fight duels with women. So, she responds bitterly, even in these "bright" times this is all the answer a man need offer a woman whose honor he has stained! Any other, he replies, would violate custom. This self-satisfied response propels her into action. Reminding him that she has grown up a modern woman, she shoots him down.[53]

The reader may reexperience the poet's feelings and share the easy satisfaction that poetic justice always provides. But "Ein modernes Weib" is highly unrepresentative. Whatever may have lurked in the unconscious of Victorian woman writers, they had persuasive evidence that they were slowly making their way. To be sure, male arrogance and female anxiety survived. So did the charge that women's inroads into the writing profession were somehow unnatural. Literary critics and historians found it hard to forgo comments on the graciousness, the purity, the poetic sensibility, that were so typical of woman writers—all halfhearted compliments that tried to confine them to the sphere of the sweet and the sentimental.

They would not stay in that prison. In some historic instances woman writers sported a distinct agenda; female Victorians, precisely like their male counterparts, used the novel as a pulpit from which to preach a favorite cause, whether women's emancipation or the abolition of slavery. A look at them should discredit the notion that nineteenth-century women forbade themselves aggressive self-assertion. Charlotte Brontë's *Jane Eyre* is much more than a manifesto in behalf of governesses, but it is also that. *Jo's Boys,* the concluding volume of Louisa May Alcott's trilogy, reflects among other things her fervent support of female self-respect and progressive coeducation. Again, *Die Waffen nieder,* a controversial, highly popular novel by the Czech aristocrat Bertha von Suttner, is a powerful plea for pacifism.[54] Elizabeth Barrett Browning's novel in verse, *Aurora Leigh,* explores the almost insoluble conflict between a woman's professional calling and the obligations she owes to love. "I too have my vocation,—work to do."[55]

Indeed, one need hardly be reminded that probably the most influential fiction of the century was Harriet Beecher Stowe's abolitionist novel *Uncle Tom's Cabin.* In 1852, the year of its publication, it sold some 300,000 copies in the United States, did even better in England, and proved an irresistible best seller in France; by the time the Civil War was under way, its sales had reached a staggering two million copies. The book added two memorable figures to American political folklore, Simon Legree and Uncle Tom, and its appearance impressed statesmen in the English-speaking world as an epoch-making event. President Lincoln was being patronizing, but not just being polite, when he famously saluted Harriet Beecher Stowe as "the little woman who wrote the book that made the great war."[56] Novels of this stripe were nothing if not politically confident, actuated by hatred of conditions their woman authors deemed intolerable.

With the passing decades, outright rejection of literary women softened into uneasy ambivalence. In 1884, in the liberal periodical *Die Nation,* the German critic Paul Schlenther published a series of short appreciative essays on female writers. He paid justified tribute to Annette von Droste-Hülshoff as "an authentic poet." Was she not among Germany's woman poets the greatest and, fortunately, not the last? But where to find them? Here the old sexual innuendo crept in: "Certainly not at the so-called authors' meetings where every fall, when the storks depart, a crowd of female authors with masculine names and even more masculine manners carouse in collegial fashion." Surely, "if the police did not prohibit this, such heroes of the pen would soon walk about in trousers, so that nothing would differentiate them any more from the great George Sand than genius and a woman's soul." In the same vein, the "Frauenzeitung" supplement of the *Illustrirte Zeitung* distinguished between two types of American woman authors: female journalists breathlessly supporting emancipation in a flowery style larded with personal attacks, and "a whole legion of ladies." The latter included "Francis Hodgson Burnett," "Louise Alcott," "Harriet Beecher-Stowe," and many others. "Writing is almost as epidemic in the ladies' world" of the United States as it is in England. But "the men do not begrudge them this pastime at all." They encourage their wives on Heine's principle that a woman author at least does no harm.[57]

All this sexual snobbery did not prevent nineteenth-century culture from doing masterful woman writers justice—almost. The reputations of the two most famous, George Eliot and George Sand, were towering. Marian Evans took her male pseudonym for complicated reasons, but almost certainly the fear of disdain by male reviewers played no part in her decision. A gifted male novelist, she knew, will be treated as shabbily as a female one.[58] But her hovering and protective companion, G. H. Lewes, playing literary agent for his single client, pleaded that her pseudonym remain protected at least until after *Adam Bede* was published. The mystery might be an advantage; and he recalled that once the author of *Jane Eyre* was known to be a woman, the reviewers' tone had changed. He conceded that nothing "adventitious" would long hurt "a good book."[59] But then one never knew.

The reception of George Eliot's work proved his caution misplaced. Dickens, who had guessed Eliot's identity before it was revealed, did not therefore stint his admiration. Nor did others. Eneas Sweetland Dallas, who reviewed her novels for the London *Times,* remained as enthusiastic when he knew her to be a woman as he had been when he thought her to be a man.[60] Through two decades of intensive and varied production, she was praised for her realism, her humor, her rich vocabulary, her capacity to render ordinary life, and was credited with extending the very boundaries of the novel. Inevitably she had her detractors, both temperate and carping. Some readers found *Felix Holt, the Radical* artificial or *Middlemarch* too long; some objected to her philosophical asides. But no one, not even the grudging *Saturday Review*, offered to dispute her greatness. Indeed, it called George Eliot's mind "really creative and original" without adding the expected spiteful gloss—"for a woman."[61] Henry James, discriminating and difficult, was an admirer, and so were Swinburne and Trollope, John Morley and Lord Acton.

Abroad, her reputation was naturally exposed to the vagaries of local tastes and parochial pressures. In France, it did not begin to soar until, in 1881, Ferdinand Brunetière published a powerful appreciation. But this slow start had nothing to do with her gender and everything to do with the chauvinistic rejection of foreign literature and the persistent authority of neoclassical criteria that found no room for George Eliot's realism. In Germany, Lady Blennerhasset was telling the reading public nothing new when she called Eliot, in a rather facile conclusion to a general survey of her life, "the great female genius of our modern days." The adjective was not meant as a slight.[62]

Yet, inescapably, George Eliot's forceful presence evoked conjectures about the share of masculinity and of femininity in her writings. Leslie Stephen's ironic commentary on this gossiping literary criticism, itself no mean accolade, suggests that the preoccupation was widespread. To be sure, Stephen himself did not quite escape the very speculations he treated so disdainfully. The "so-called masculine quality in George Eliot—her wide and calm intelligence," he judged, "was certainly combined with a thoroughly feminine nature." But though he remained committed to remnants of old-fashioned notions about the sexes, shortly after Eliot's death in 1880 he awarded her the title of greatest English novelist, and expected no one to contradict him.* In lapidary inscrip-

---

*"The poor woman was not content simply to write amusing stories. She is convicted upon conclusive evidence of having indulged in ideas; she ventured to speculate upon human life and its meaning," something, "according to some people, highly unbecoming in a woman and very inartistic in a novelist." For his part, Stephen was "rather glad to find ideas anywhere. They are not very common." Leslie Stephen, "George Eliot" (1881), *Hours in a Library*, 3 vols. (1874–79; new ed., 1892), III, 207–8. Female critics, too, wrestled with this issue. "George Eliot's books remain (with the exception of the 'Mill on the Floss') less definable in point of sex than the books of any other woman who has ever written," said Margaret Oliphant. "The history of her first great book," *Adam Bede*, "combined womanly prejudices so ineradicably with so much of the unscrupulous masculine intelligence." "*The Life and Letters of George Eliot* (George Eliot's Life As Related in Her Letters and Journals, Arranged and Edited by Her Husband J. W. Cross)," *Edinburgh Review*, CLXI (1885), 544.

tions, Samuel Johnson once said, a man is not upon oath. But Stephen was not just speaking well of the dead.[63]

Only in the 1890s, when subversive styles ranging from naturalism to symbolism seriously competed for the attention of readers, did a few critics mount a masculine counteroffensive. They regressed to venerable simplicities, and, retreating from hard-won insights, reduced Eliot to a typical female scribbler. In 1896, Arnold Bennett noted in his journal that while her "masculine" style could be "downright, aggressive, sometimes rude," it was never "genuinely masculine." On the contrary, "it is transparently feminine—feminine in its lack of restraint, its wordiness, and the utter absence of feeling for form which characterizes it."[64] The notion, it seems, had nine lives—one thinks of Gottschall's characterization of woman writers as typically compliant and reproductive. But, some lapses apart, most of those best equipped to judge Eliot's literary work found such distinctions irrelevant.

George Sand's reputation described a similar trajectory. No doubt, the notoriety she enjoyed and endured in the 1830s was bound up with her youthful political and sexual militancy. The lurid picture of her as the scandalous conqueror of the literary world, flouting dominant moral standards with her lovers, her cigars, her trousers, never quite faded. But Sand's fellow writers, craftsmen all, discounted the gossip and celebrated the honest, hardworking professional. "For forty-five years she was writing and publishing," Matthew Arnold said about her in 1877, the year after her death, "and filled Europe with her name." The catalogue of authors—men no less than women—who went to school to her amounts to a virtual who's who of nineteenth-century literature. It ranges from Heine, Balzac, and Charlotte Brontë to Whitman, Dostoevsky, and Hardy. Flaubert, writing to Turgenev after Sand's funeral, where he had "blubbered shamelessly," summed up informed opinion: "Why pity her? She lacked nothing and will remain a great figure." John Stuart Mill thought that her "style acts upon the nervous system like a symphony of Haydn or Mozart."[65] Literary critics drawing comparisons between George Sand and George Eliot—the pairing seemed natural to them—saw the two as "sisters in greatness."[66] Foreign literary establishments competed with one another in their cult of George Sand. The Germans hailed her, quite simply, as a towering figure. And among educated Russians, her greatness became almost proverbial. When Lyebedev, in Chekhov's *Ivanov,* seeks an admiring epithet to characterize his lovely daughter's intelligence, he calls her "quite a genius! a George Sand!"[67]

Sand's reputation drooped in the last decades of the century, more than Eliot's, as literary fashions changed. But it did not wane because she was a woman. The sexual innuendo to which she was long exposed, drawing sustenance from her provocative disregard of woman's God-given role, was to be expected with so visible a figure. She was the subject of sermons in pulpits and in periodicals no less than of enthusiastic reviews. In 1841, tapping that censorious vein, the *Foreign Quarterly Review* blamed the general decay of morals on Sand's "apodictic authority," with her "openly avowed hostility to marriage, borne out by a divorce from her husband, the adoption of her male attire, a cigar in her mouth, a whip in her hand, and her conversation with young men carried on in the familiar terms of tu and George." The whip especially was a useful accouterment; it broadly hinted at Sand's presumed sadism. A man-eating virago, she was only exercising her masculine aggressiveness on hapless lovers. Some six years later, in 1847, a pious English publication chastised Sand as "that great apostle of pantheism, 'semivir obscoenus' of France."[68] This denigration of a strong woman for really being a man, or half man, was only too familiar; what was perceived as female aggressiveness generated male counter-attacks.

Yet she was read, and not just by those hoping for mildly pornographic titillation. Readers whose stature gave their opinions deserved authority dwelt precisely on her spectacular combination of "manly" and "womanly" traits as ground for praise. Elizabeth Barrett Browning, who placed George Sand above all other French writers, wrote sonnets to her, and one of them, "A Desire," opens with the intriguing line "Thou large-brained woman and large-hearted man." Turgenev, who knew her well, exclaimed, "Such an absence of all low, petty or false sentiments—what a good fellow she was and what a fine woman!" Flaubert, who had known her even better, echoed his Russian friend: "One had to know her as I knew her to realise how much of the feminine there was in that great man, the immensity of tenderness there was in that genius."[69] From the late seventeenth century onward, we know, intrepid feminists writing long before feminism was a cause, or even a word, had asserted that the mind has no sex. Now, with major woman writers in evidence, this claim was gathering impressive support. An increasingly influential current of opinion in the Victorian decades held that great writing, whether by males or females, has no sex or, rather, felicitously combines the best of both. The lofty self-appraisal of the male as alone creative was being forced into retreat.

How far it had retreated emerges from the surging appreciation of woman writers as professionals. It was symptomatic of a new day that in 1898 the German writer Ernst Brausewetter thought it useful to assemble a two-volume collection of "master novellas" by German women, complete with biographical sketches of thirty-two of them. He had done his anthologist's work, he wrote, because the intellectual aspirations and achievement of women were growing increasingly significant in contemporary life. Brausewetter ruefully admitted that while people in Scandinavia were wholly aware of this, for many

Germans, "the literary activity of women still has something of a reputation for shallowness and lack of artistic preparation." But he hoped that his collection would help to undermine such prejudice.[70] The impartial test of competence had found its way into literary criticism.

In the previous decade, in 1887, Henry James had significantly tied this progress to the agitation for women's rights in other spheres. In the midst of earnest debate about the admission of women to a wide variety of fields previously closed to them, he wrote, "singularly little attention has been paid, by themselves at least, to the fact that in one highly important department of human affairs," that of literature, "their cause is already gained," gained so thoroughly that they can no longer rightfully complain of male intolerance. At least in the United States and in England, they have been "admitted, with all the honours, on a perfectly equal footing."* This was far too sunny a view; James chose to overlook subtler forms of condescension still alive in many a reader, many a reviewer. But in substance he summed up, if not the record, at least the drift, of the century.

4. Competence: Womanliness Redefined

Woman's competence: this paradigm would serve the Victorians as a bridge from the vision of woman as man's domestic angel to the competing vision of woman as man's accomplished partner. Competence proved to be the prerequisite for women's exercise of constructive aggression, a giant first step toward their exercise of mastery in the world. In the history of nineteenth-century women, beset as it is with ironies—the campaign to exalt women in order to keep them down, to dress up the cage as a pedestal—this is the most striking irony of all. Female competence was, after all, compatible with segregation of the sexes. The traditional ideal prescribed that a woman be adored for possessing skills—"accomplishments"—that made her agreeable in the drawing room or on the dance floor and, far more important, indispensable in the

---

*James, "Miss Woolson" (1887), *Partial Portraits* (1888), 177. James's fine discriminations among the varied receptions awaiting woman authors in different countries are valid. As late as 1901, Marie von Ebner-Eschenbach, Austria's most highly respected novelist, deftly parodied the patronizing attitude of her countrymen with a short story about a woman writer who has just received two reviews of her latest novel. Both praise her for doing work almost as good as a man's; one notes her characteristically feminine naive use of coincidence, while the other cannot do without the snide remark that woman writers lack inventiveness. Very few American or British reviewers would have sounded that way in 1901. See "Die Visite," *Ausgewählte Erzählungen,* 2 vols. (1968), II, 412.

kitchen and the nursery. The militant anti-feminists who denigrated "female emancipation" did champion competence of a sort, advocating better education for girls even as they objected to women's obtaining admission to universities, let alone the vote.

Yet, as the woman's movement began to secure numbers of influential converts, it redefined the very concept of competence to make it serve very different ends. It was on the field of competence that each of the feminists' battles was fought and each of their victories, such as they were, was won. Religious rationales, unconsciously supported by fear of change and of woman's hidden destructive powers, kept their honored place in the anti-feminist armory, but what ultimately mattered in the interminable debates were perfectly concrete questions: is woman physiologically and psychologically competent to teach school, run a business, manage her property, balance her checkbook, practice medicine, analyze social problems, make political decisions, perhaps even govern a country?

Gradually, opinion turned toward an enlarged view of female competence. Not without frequent backsliding: this was, we have seen, a painfully slow process. No doubt, it was assaults on the new ideas that the French journalist Louise de Salles had in mind when, in 1892, she defended the Parisienne against her detractors: The Parisian woman is thrifty. She "knows the places where one can shop cheaply; her secret is that she looks around a good deal." She knows how to make comparisons. She keeps her household accounts. She knows commerce; she is her husband's associate and friend, often at the cash register or keeping the books.[1] Frugality, shrewdness, the ability to bring order into domestic budgets—what could demonstrate woman's competence in action more cogently than these capacities?

Indeed, while the caricature of woman the adorable imbecile continued to haunt novels, operettas, and club talk, woman the sensible creature found new partisans, even among husbands. "My own impression," wrote Fenton John Anthony Hort, a professor of divinity at Cambridge, in 1871, "is that the helpless charmer theory finds favour with very few men except the supremely silly." As the father of two daughters, Hort spoke with feeling. Much of the talk about charmers was sheer conformity, the sort of thing men said because it was expected of them. "I doubt whether even the *Saturday Reviewers*," writing for that opinionated and anti-feminist weekly, "believe a quarter of their own rubbish." In fact, "men with the least stuff in them almost invariably hate" women who are nothing more than "decoratively prepared."[2] Hort's verdict—he was anything but a radical—was coming to seem plausible to many. From the 1880s on, the ideal of the vigorous, glowing outdoors woman competed with that of the delicate, shrinking female; sportswomen rejected the genteel game of croquet in behalf of its more athletic rivals, tennis and bicycling. In this fresher atmosphere, dress reformers designed clothes that would liberate women's bodies from stays and corsets, to wide approval.

To be sure, the competent woman was not an invention of the 1860s and 1870s; she had enjoyed some support during the very decades when the domestic ideology was on the ascendant. Writers of fiction had led the way, or at least obscurely glimpsed an image of a woman more interesting than the decorative doll or the domestic slave. Jane Austen's heroines are intelligent and thoughtful, all of them. Admittedly, in the society Austen depicted, woman's competence amounted largely to her household skills, social graces, and good character. But even before marriage, with their sphere of action confined mainly to the search for an eligible and worthy husband, these women display their competence admirably. Though the rules of the game prohibit them from taking the initiative in the mating dance, they can steer it to a desired outcome. An Austen heroine would never stoop to seductive manipulation, but she can show herself in the pleasing light of her true quality, her good sense, at its best.*

The men who love Jane Austen's heroines appreciate such gifts. "Men of sense, whatever you may chuse to say, do not want silly wives," Mr. Knightley says sententiously in *Emma;* his disappointment in the charming and clever Emma Woodhouse lies precisely in his recognition that she appears perversely unwilling to live up to her native intelligence.[3] And the silly women whom several among Jane Austen's characters marry, empty-headed creatures like Mrs. Bennet in *Pride and Prejudice* and Mrs. Palmer in *Sense and Sensibility,* confirm with the acute discomfort they give their husbands that Mr. Knightley speaks for his creator. So does one of Jane Austen's most intriguing inventions, Elinor Dashwood of *Sense and Sensibility;* unlike her impetuous and self-dramatizing sister Marianne, she typifies good sense. In contrasting these two styles of femininity, Jane Austen favored Elinor, rewarding her, after suitable complications, with the hero's proposal of marriage. The intelligent women in these novels never reach for full equality with men; Austen was a realist, not a

---

*In the famous twenty-third chapter of *Persuasion* (substituted for an earlier, tamer version), Jane Austen has Anne Elliot, the most intelligent and sensible of the book's characters, indirectly woo Captain Wentworth, the man whom she wants and who wants her, by allowing him to overhear her heartfelt praise of woman's fidelity, praise that finally clears up a disastrous misunderstanding between them. In real life, too, the presumably unshakable rule making the man the initiator of the ritual marriage dance was sometimes broken, or severely bent. Tennyson, after years of pursuing Emily Sellwood, had to be cajoled and maneuvered into marriage once she agreed to have him. His parents' wooing, the man timid and the woman aggressive, had taken a similar course. (See Robert Bernard Martin, *Tennyson: The Unquiet Heart* [1980] 23, 33, 329–36.)

utopian.[4] But they are the ancestors of the competent partners who emerged at the end of the century.

The sentimental tone that Dickens adopted with *his* heroines makes it easy to overlook that they, too, are competent—in their assigned niche. Even the much-maligned perfect Agnes in *David Copperfield* qualifies; she had received precocious domestic training as a little girl faithfully caring for her widowed and alcoholic father. Dickens's testimony is all the more instructive for the early history of the Victorian ideal of competence because he was so consistently and vociferously antagonistic to campaigns for women's rights. He had only contempt for "telescopic philanthropy," for reforming enthusiasts like Mrs. Jellyby, who criminally neglects her family to concentrate instead on relieving the sufferings of the remote African natives of Borrioboola-Gha. Those who descant on women's rights, Dickens sneered, think they are improving women's lot by encouraging them to usurp men's functions. Actually they are destroying what is already their own, their winning, lovable qualities. "A male female," he said, "is repulsive."[5]

Detesting the unnatural ambitions of such creatures, Dickens prized instead "quiet, unpretending, domestic heroism." For him, woman's effectiveness is tied to the hearth, where charm is not enough. David Copperfield's first wife, Dora, makes this point for him; she is delectable, infantile, unteachable, the incarnation of incompetence. But then his second wife, Agnes, is a walking exemplar of competence. Other idealized Dickens women, too, like Florence Dombey in *Dombey and Son* and Ruth Pinch in *Martin Chuzzlewit,* shine in the role of cook and cleaner and companion; they fetch pipes and tasty drinks as they sweetly but sensibly minister to men's comfort. In an early story, "The Nice Little Couple," Dickens introduced Mrs. Chirrup, "the prettiest of all little women," a model of neatness and efficiency: "In all the arts of domestic arrangement and management, in all the mysteries of confectionary-making, pickling, and preserving, never was such a thorough adept as that nice little body. She is, besides, a cunning worker in muslin and fine linen, and a special hand at marketing to the very best advantage," to say nothing of her accomplished way of carving joints.[6] This sketch was obviously meant to be lighthearted, but Dickens's amused, affectionate portrait places his ideal woman with deadly accuracy.

One representative reviewer said of Dickens that "his genius is his fellow-feeling with his race."[7] It speaks for that stature that while some critics found fault with his plots and, at times, with his political satire, virtually none of them took exception to his portrayal of women. Only an extremist, John Stuart Mill, countered Dickens's heated distaste for woman's aggression with an aggressive rebuttal. "That creature Dickens," he wrote his wife after happening upon *Bleak House,* "has the vulgar impudence in this thing to ridicule rights of women." Dickens's cheap caricature of feminism in Mrs. Jellyby's absent-minded, ridiculous behavior infuriated him. "It is done in the very vulgarest way—just the style in which vulgar men used to ridicule 'learned ladies' as neglecting their children and household etc."[8] This impulsive irritated response was highly unusual for its time—these, after all, were still the 1850s.

By mid-century, though, the teaching of domestic competence, anything but jocular or patronizing, had grown into a respectable small industry. Women's periodicals devoted more space than ever before to domestic advice, and books lavishing such advice became dependable sellers for venturesome publishing houses. The assiduity with which authors taught their readers how to run a household, offering the kind of methodical detail that is the lifeblood of such instruction, attests to a thirst for prosaic information that only grew with its supply.

Women's magazines continued to feature fiction for (and normally by) women, but they shifted attention in their nonfiction from innocuous elevating entertainments to the pedagogy of sober facts. While in the 1850s, each number of *Godey's Lady's Book* had included a didactic page or two on how to do fancy embroidery, and had printed two or three "receipts" for carrot pudding or tea cakes, in the next decade, it added a regular "Work Department." In a single number, for January 1864, Mrs. Hale included patterns for children's dresses, ornate letters for marking clothes, samples of embroidery, a household remedy for diphtheria, instructions on how to escape from a fire, directions for making pincushions, hairnets, and a screen for birdcages, and two closely printed pages of recipes. And she enriched this department with fifteen pages of illustrations, including half a dozen full-page engravings of fashionable dresses, in all some twenty-nine pages of information in digestible form. The emphasis was on solidity in the advice department, and on "novelties" in the pages showing ladies' clothes for all occasions.

Mrs. Hale kept this policy intact down to her last year at *Godey's.* The "Work Department" remained, supplemented by a small "Health Department" and three or four separate pages on fashions. Many of the instructions and some of the recipes call for considerable ingenuity. The recipes alone discredit the old stereotype of the shrinking Victorian gentlewoman calling for smelling salts in all situations that might compromise her blushing denial of life's realities. A column on how to make beef stock specifies, along with other explicit details, that the reader must "remove all the bones from a rump of beef, and tie the meat together with twine; then break the bones into pieces."[9]

Domestic competence called for a sturdy housewife who was untroubled by, or had conquered, ladylike squeamishness.

The impression that this tough-minded realism was accessible—in fact, indispensable—to bourgeois women is reinforced by Isabella Beeton's *Book of Household Management*. First serialized in her husband's *Englishwoman's Domestic Magazine* starting in 1859, and published in 1861 in a volume of over 1,100 pages, it suited the taste of middle-class Britain to perfection; it sold some sixty thousand copies within a year, and kept on selling. The public that this encyclopedia of domesticity aimed to serve was the core of the British middle classes, affluent enough to employ a housekeeper and a small staff of servants.

Mrs. Beeton celebrated, and inculcated, domestic competence in a firm tone, with meticulous detail and helpful illustrations. Her book is filled to bursting with recipes and with miscellaneous advice: how to superintend housekeepers, engage servants, inspect wet-nurses, cope with children's illnesses, and navigate the treacherous shallows of the law in buying a house, paying taxes, making a will. Mrs. Beeton had ventured on her monumental task, she revealed in her preface, only because of "the discomfort and suffering I had seen brought upon men and women by household mismanagement." She was alerting married women that husbands were now "so well served out of doors,—in their clubs, well-ordered taverns, and dining-houses," that their wives had to learn to compete with these temptations.[10] The moral was plain; a respectable woman could keep her man at home only by being competent.[11]

Mrs. Beeton took a high line from the outset: good household management is a sacred duty as much as an effective defense against the seductions of the club and the tavern. The epigraph she chose from Milton is a reminder that she was writing in a time of transition, with conventional views of woman still very much in the foreground:

> Nothing lovelier can be found
> In Woman than to study household good.

But she did not endorse domestic slavery; within the household, woman reigns supreme. Significantly, Mrs. Beeton devoted her first chapter to "the mistress." Just as significantly, she started with an energetic military metaphor: "As with the commander of an army, or the leader of any enterprise, so is it with the mistress of a house. Her spirit will be seen through the whole establishment; and just in proportion as she performs her duties intelligently and thoroughly, so will her domestics follow in her path. Of all the acquirements, which more particularly belong to the feminine character, there are none which take a higher rank, in our estimation, than such as enter into a knowledge of household duties." This sounds self-assertive enough, but her proof text, from Oliver Goldsmith's *Vicar of Wakefield,* must have struck the likes of John Stuart Mill as ominous: "The modest virgin, the prudent wife, and the careful matron, are much more serviceable in life than petticoated philosophers, blustering heroines, or virago queens."[12] In the army of nineteenth-century women, Mrs. Beeton was among the most articulate and influential officers decrying those who would emancipate them from domesticity.

For Mrs. Beeton this domesticity was at once an arduous and a rational activity. The mistress of the house must rise early, be neat, frugal, discreet, hospitable, sensibly dressed, genial about the faults of others, careful in forming friendships, a shrewd buyer of food and clothing. She must also be a prudent financial manager: "A housekeeping account-book should invariably be kept, and kept punctually and precisely"; the accounts, with every expense, no matter how small, painstakingly entered and classified, must be balanced at least once a month.[13] Mrs. Beeton's ideal housewife is quite as cool when she practices (or keeps informed about) the science of butchery. "The general mode of slaughtering oxen in this country is by striking them a smart blow with a hammer or poleaxe on the head, a little above the eyes. By this means, when the blow is skillfully given, the beast is brought down at one blow, and, to prevent recovery, a cane is generally inserted, by which the spinal cord is perforated." As for converting a pig into pork: "The best and most humane mode of killing all large hogs is to strike them down like a bullock, with the pointed end of a poleaxe, on the forehead, which has the effect of killing the animal at once; all the butcher has then to do, is to open the aorta and great arteries, and laying the animal's neck over a trough, let out the blood as quickly as possible."[14] Mrs. Beeton's recipe for making mock-turtle soup is no less graphic. She obviously had no patience with the fainting, queasy, fragile female.

Yet Mrs. Beeton cautioned her readers not to permit their mundane, often dull, activities to brutalize them or debase them into chattel. "Unless the means of the household be very circumscribed, and she be obliged to devote a great deal of her time to the making of her children's clothes, and other economical pursuits"—and this sort of impecunious housewife, we know, occupied the lowest fringe of Mrs. Beeton's readership—"it is right that she should give some time to the pleasures of literature, the innocent delights of the garden, and to the improvement of any special abilities for music, painting, and other elegant arts, which she may, happily, possess."[15] In this secular bible of the nineteenth-century British bourgeoisie, the man of the house remains very much the head of the house; his wife's accomplishments in reading or playing the piano are largely designed to keep him happy. At the same time, the mistress of the house, in Mrs. Beeton's book, is a respectworthy personage, even without the vote.

Radical feminists might regret their sisters' lack of political drive, but untold numbers of middle-class wives found it profoundly gratifying to superintend a crowded household, teach their children, and serve as a sounding board for their husbands' problems with business or scholarship. They were truly what the French called the *maîtresse de maison* or *ménagère*. Evoking thoughts of mastery and rational economy, these terms implied a confident, even exhilarated sense of control over a domain that, however restricted, was important to its mistress, and was seen to be important by others.

This sense of domestic mastery in action appears to good advantage in the fascinating autobiography of Judith Gautier, novelist, poet, collector of celebrities. In the mid-1860s, while she was an adolescent, she was suddenly propelled into the position of *ménagère* for her loving and indulgent father, the eminent poet and critic Théophile Gautier, a demanding "gourmet and gourmand." Her mother had suddenly been called away to attend to a medical emergency in the family, and "during her absence, I was put in charge of the management"— *gouvernement*—"of the house. I felt all the weight of such a responsibility, and applied myself as best I could to discharge the mission entrusted to me." Unfortunately, the Gautiers' favorite kitchen help had left to get married, and a succession of replacements had proved spectacular disasters. Managing was therefore left in Judith's youthful hands. "I took my new functions extremely seriously, applying myself with a good deal of attention, closely supervising the cook, and I quickly realized substantial economies." She went shopping for food at Les Halles, buying the freshest fish available at the most reasonable prices; she designed varied menus, "and my father was astonished to see that we spent less and ate better."[16] Judith Gautier's victorious air surely owes something to a sense of triumph over her absent mother and an intensified intimacy with her adored father. But it also reflects her satisfaction with a domestic assignment well done.

All the practical advice that the likes of Judith Gautier consumed was, of course, designed not to open the cage of domesticity but to beautify it. *Godey's* and Mrs. Beeton were not revolutionaries; they wanted to teach housewives to be better housewives. But their doctrine was not confined to the importance of making dinner, cleaning the house, and keeping the children out of trouble. It included the idea of self-cultivation, with the hope for marriage as an affectionate partnership dimly in the background. Once competence had been put into the forefront of discussion about woman's place, the argument from human nature, which had served the proponent of separate spheres so well, was conscripted by those who denied any fundamental difference between the sexes, except in function. This did not satisfy the most demanding feminists, but it was enough for those women who took pleasure in doing their work at home without having to endure the sentimental deification that instead of making them more estimable, really reduced them to sexless ladies and mindless domestics.

Then, late in the century, bourgeois women found grounds for satisfaction larger than wifery well done, as the ideal of true womanliness broadened to include competence beyond the kitchen, the nursery, and the drawing room. With the headlong expansion of trade, industry, and government, and with the explosive growth of law firms and retail outlets, managers developed a ravenous appetite for clerical help. Well before 1900, millions of bourgeoises across the Western world went to work in offices and stores, serving as bookkeepers, salesclerks, postmistresses. Unfortunately, all too many of the women "liberated" from domesticity had good reason to qualify their new satisfaction with wry, even cynical comments. They were exploited—and they were laughed at. Humor magazines and musical comedies in their defensive mood, and for that matter the self-lacerating "Frauenzeitung," allowed themselves repetitive jests about this modern phenomenon. Women gossiping on the job were, it seems, an irresistible target. As late as 1913, *Punch* published a particularly unpleasant cartoon showing an elderly man at a telegraph office exasperated by two female clerks too busy chatting to notice him; he attaches a huge crab to his umbrella, drops it between the two gossips, and frightens them into paying attention.[17]

Many of these jokes were directed against members of the new work force who had no husbands to neglect. The conspicuous presence of unmarried women gave rise, especially in England and in France, where the lot of such women was especially acute, to well-meaning discussions and desperate schemes for remedies. One favorite way to escape thinking about these women was to ridicule their claim that they had deliberately chosen single blessedness. Were they not unmarried because they could not persuade any man to marry them? But in fact Louisa May Alcott's journal entry, now much quoted—"liberty is a better husband than love to many of us"—was more than a rationalization, more than the gilding of a drooping lily.[18] Considering the risk of finding oneself tied to a cold or brutal husband and the ever-present danger of dying in childbirth, to say nothing of being reduced to drudgery, singleness was an acceptable style of life, with benefits of its own. Furthermore, virtually every employer was only too pleased to have women on his staff; he discovered that he could make them work harder and pay them less than men. Thus for most women the new opportunities brought a serious new grievance, one that obstinately survived disapproval, protests, even stabs at protective legislation.*

Women launched in more prestigious pursuits were somewhat more fortunate. They found unprecedented openings to demonstrate their competence in enterprises no longer domestic though not quite political. Nursing, teaching, and philanthropy involved them in what one might call semipublic life. Most of these women were dismayed to discover that, like the clerks, they were overworked and underpaid. Yet, though often cynically exploited, they helped to change the meaning of "womanliness" in the late Victorian decades, and made their contemporaries aware of it. Paying tribute to the most spectacular woman of the age, Florence Nightingale, Lord Stanley, the Tory secretary for India, said, "A claim for more extended freedom of action, based on proved public usefulness in the highest sense of the word, with the whole nation to look on and bear witness, is one which must be listened to, and cannot be easily refused."[19] To be sure, Nightingale was anything but representative. Wellconnected, single-minded, and domineering, a master at publicity, she could frighten cabinet ministers and influence legislation. But in more modest ways, other women, whether dispensing bandages, knowledge, or largesse, also claimed "more extended freedom of action." Idleness and delicacy, the two qualities detractors professed to find in the respectable Victorian lady, were precisely the qualities these women did without. Active as they were, they could not have afforded them.

The old reproach of strong-mindedness, leveled against women who let their intelligence show, thus became increasingly irrelevant. When one of John Stuart Mill's woman correspondents denied possessing that quality, Mill countered, sensibly enough, "I am sorry to find that you disclaim being strong-minded, because I believe strength of mind to be one of the noblest gifts that any rational creature, male or female, can possess."[20] But as we know, Mill was even more exceptional among mid-century men than Nightingale was among mid-century women. Far more representative was Ernest Legouvé. A distinguished French playwright, novelist, and autobiographer, honored in 1855 by election to the Académie française, he took a lifelong interest in woman's education, and saw his *Histoire morale des femmes,* first published in 1849, go

*Let one instance stand for literally thousands. During the Civil War era, the federal government of the United States found that "two women could be hired for the price of one man, and even when Congress, in 1865, raised women's salaries to $900, female clerks continued to represent a considerable saving. Senator Frederick Sawyer of South Carolina, speaking at an 1870 congressional debate on the merits of equalizing men's and women's salaries, summed it up this way: 'The truth is that those ladies were put into the Department of the Government as clerks because they were cheaper.' " Cindy Sondik Aron, *Ladies and Gentlemen of the Civil Service: Middle Class Workers in Victorian America* (1987), 71.

through several enlarged editions. And he wanted to see woman placed in the intermediate zone between the hearth and politics.

His book is of historical interest precisely because it is so commonplace and so inflexible. Legouvé voiced in 1882, in the eighth edition, precisely the opinions he had voiced over thirty years earlier. Women, he held, should make their mark with the qualities that distinguish them from men. He saw a role for them as teachers, even as writers. But if they should venture into authorship, they should speak only when they had something to say and fall silent after they said it. Their obligations as daughters, wives, and mothers outweighed everything else, even celebrity. A woman's destiny "can be summed up in a single word: to love."[21] By 1882, such once-progressive notions emitted a strangely musty aroma. If Mill's intransigence was prophetic, Legouvé's conciliatory attitude smelled of the past.

His views, though, expressed a broad consensus surviving into the 1880s. They demonstrated again, as Mrs. Hale had already demonstrated, that there was nothing very subversive in promoting woman's education. Yet such tepid support for learned women offended a militant manly minority that positively enjoyed seeing women as mindless playthings. "To my personal taste," says the heroine's husband in Fontane's novel *Cécile,* published in 1887, "ladies don't need to know anything." He was no hero to his inventor, but he had much company in real life. And in France, it seems, one could find cultivated men who liked their wives timid, ignorant, even stupid. "We want above all to keep women faithful to their husbands," said the minor novelist Edmond About in 1864. "So we hope that the girl will bring to the world an angelic provision of ignorance that will be immune to all temptations."[22]

Legouvé's reformism, then, was not much more than a mild protest against such draconian efforts to ensure woman's fidelity. His lordly permission—granting women the right to be teachers and authors, on sufferance—could hardly satisfy feminists who deprecated any limitation on women's activities as a craven compromise, at best a temporary halfway house. Their discontent was well founded; when nineteenth-century women went out to work, most of them found their energies forced into channels that men unwilling to make larger concessions had designed for them, channels men found appropriate—and thinkable.

It is striking, after all, that nursing and the rest were extensions of the domestic, the maternal—some effusively said, the angelic—roles that conventional wisdom had long assigned to women. Even men mortally afraid of amazons and viragos had little trouble visualizing a nurse with her soothing touch, a teacher with her gentle discipline, a dispenser of charity with her loving heart; these ladies were simply doing on a larger stage what they had been doing at home all along—and with more natural talent than any man. Many men were prepared to have these particular channels opened to women. Regarding themselves as sincerely in favor of seeing woman at work in the world, they would insist that she might be fit to be a curator in a museum but not its director, a musician in an orchestra but not its conductor, a gynecologist but not a surgeon, a lecturer in algebra but not a professor of mathematics. In *Cécile,* Fontane introduces a woman painter who chafes at the taboos that polite society has forced on her. "A lady is supposed to be a flower painter but not an animal painter," she protests. "That is what is demanded by the world, by decorum, by convention. A woman animal painter is at the frontier of the permissible."[23]

Hence it was only natural that in women's struggle for access to the professions, it was medicine that opened its doors to them, and even those doors opened with the most disagreeable creak. Plainly, the Victorians found a "doctoress" far more palatable, especially when her only patients were women and babies, than a woman attorney defending her client or a woman architect on a construction site. The first woman physician in the United States, Harriot Hunt, started practicing in 1835 after a private apprenticeship, but her contemporaries treated her more as a freak to be gawked at than a pioneer to be imitated. It took decades before women insisting on a physician's career were admitted to medical colleges; male medical students and senior physicians harassed the tiny minority in their classes, circulated petitions and provoked strikes against them, and published intemperate analyses of women's physical and intellectual defects. The physiological argument that conservative authorities deployed in opposing the admission of young women to colleges and universities was used even more forcibly against their training as doctors. Surely the being who menstruated was even more incapable of dissecting a cadaver than she was of studying Plato. At the end of the century, the number of woman physicians was still pitifully small. In 1883, there was just one woman doctor in the Netherlands; by 1900, there were some 258 in Britain. It was taken as an extraordinary sign of women's progress that by the same date, the United States had some 7,000 woman physicians, well under 6 percent of the medical population.

A catalogue of landmark dates signalizing woman's ever more visible display of competence across Western civilization, her progress from legal chattel to recognized person, reads superficially like a steady march of triumph. More closely studied, it reads very differently; what is remarkable is not the speed of this progress but its halting gait.[24] In 1845, Sweden granted women the right to hold property. In 1848, Samuel Gregory founded the New England Female Medical College, and in the same year, F. D. Maurice and Charles Kingsley opened Queen's College, a training institute for governesses, in London. In

1857, Britain's first modern divorce law granted women separated from their husbands the right to keep their earnings. In 1870, British women won the right to vote in school-board elections. In 1871, the first woman received her bachelor's degree at the Sorbonne. In 1873, after years of demeaning rebuffs, Girton College, the first women's college at Cambridge, was officially opened. In 1877, Italy admitted women as witnesses in court cases. In 1878, the University of London began to grant full degrees to women. In 1881, Frenchwomen gained the right to deposit and withdraw money without their husband's presence, though it took five more years before they secured the privilege of conducting these transactions without first obtaining their husband's consent. In 1884, a French law provided that in a case of adultery, the male and the female partners were to be treated as equals. In 1886, British law granted the mother the status of legal guardian for her children.

But what legislators left untouched matters more than what they chose to tackle. Revisions of the law in country after country testify to the tenacity of the patriarchal ideal and a systematic denial of realities. In 1868, the English feminist Frances Power Cobbe had pointedly asked whether the condescending way that the London *Times* had lumped together criminals, idiots, women, and minors, was really defensible.[25] Considering the laws under which she lived, her question was perfectly valid. John Stuart Mill asked it again a year later, just as cogently, in *The Subjection of Women*. Not until a year after Mill's classic text appeared did the Married Women's Property Act, later successively strengthened, remove some of the grossest legal inequities between the sexes in Britain.* Each of the historic moments in the lives of Victorian women records a victory long delayed and dearly bought.

More drastic changes were in the offing. In 1890, the new American state of Wyoming gave women the right to vote; it was followed three years later by Colorado and three years after that by Idaho and Utah. New Zealand and South Australia joined these pioneers in 1893 and 1894. The vote, of course, is what political feminists had wanted all along. They had been agitating for it from the start of the organized campaign for women's rights; the celebrated platform adopted at Seneca Falls, New York, in 1848, included a plank calling for uni-

---

*It is characteristic of the slowness with which the cause for women's rights was compelled to proceed that it took some fourteen years for the first Married Women's Property Act to become law after the reformist Law Amendment Society had proposed such an act and won the support of literally thousands of articulate English men and women. Those signing the petition calling for such a law in 1856 included, among many others, Elizabeth Barrett Browning, Elizabeth Gaskell, and Harriet Martineau, and it was introduced into both houses of Parliament by sympathetic legislators. In vain. See Caroline Frances Cornwallis, "The Property of Married Women," *Westminster Review*, LXVI (1856), 331–60.

versal suffrage. John Stuart Mill stated the case once again in his *Subjection of Women*, the most powerful plea for women's rights since Mary Wollstonecraft's *Vindication of the Rights of Woman*. Through the years, feminist movements were deeply split on matters of tactics and even of aims, but political feminists, no matter what other pressing issues emerged, continued to prod public opin-ion, and politicians, for full citizenship.

Their reasoning was straightforward and simple: only access to the political process, and with that, the prospect of a share in political power, could secure all the other rights for which women were rightfully clamoring. Anything short of that would keep them at the mercy of men and the victims of male aggres-sion. In their speeches and their manifestos, Hubertine Auclert and her follow-ers in France, Susan B. Anthony and her colleagues in the United States, and a small tribe of suffragists in Britain, forcefully insisted that without the vote, woman remains a slave. "Women who want civil rights," Auclert wrote in the journal *La Citoyenne* in 1883, "those who want divorce on an equal basis, the reform of marriage laws, integral education, the admission of women to remu-nerative employment, must combine more than anyone to conquer political power, for that power will give them the right to make the laws they desire."[26]

It was a measure of the distance that late-Victorian bourgeois women had traveled that they could take a self-critical view of what they had accomplished and still needed to accomplish. In 1890, A. Amy Bulley, an English writer on women's questions, surveyed women's political evolution in the *Westminster Review*. She was impressed by the great female campaign for a stake in power. Taking a leaf from Darwin's book, she argued that women had been least respected when the struggle for existence had been most ruthless. But now science and technology were relieving at least affluent women from the old drudgery, and this had inspired a rebellion against enforced domesticity. Unfor-tunately, the militants who mounted the platform had confirmed the feminists' reputation as self-proclaimed superior beings and humorless fanatics. But the vote would steady women rather than excite them further. Women with a mission were open to criticism, but it was only natural that they should, after centuries of oppression, "repay repression with repression, and force with force."[27] It was a sophisticated judgment: men's aggressions against women, compounded by efforts to retain intact their monopoly on aggression, had generated an aggressive response, with the final results not yet in sight.

The mounting respect for women's competence did nothing to weaken, let alone discredit, the demands of the nineteenth-century woman's movement. It was not a crusade of cranks, not—whatever its opponents might charge—an outlet for hysterics. Angry, anxious defenders of accepted legal and social ways continued to reject feminist proposals as unsettling, utopian, even worse: unnatural. They saw them, justly enough, as a defiance of established religious, ethical, and medical codes. But the most subversive planks in the platforms of Victorian feminists—the demands for equality before the law, access to higher education and the professions, the right to vote and to equal pay, an end to patronizing treatment in the home and in the marketplace—articulated solid, thoroughly documented grievances. "Equity," Herbert Spencer said categorically as early as 1850, "knows no difference of sex." The "law of equal freedom manifestly applies to the whole race—female as well as male." These statements entailed the obvious consequence that women deserved a better fate than men were meting out to them in Spencer's day. "That a people's condition may be judged by the treatment which women receive under it," Spencer said, "is a remark that has become almost trite."[28] On such a criterion, Victorian culture deserved low marks, though its performance improved with the decades.

Certainly the crusade to gain recognition for woman's competence was a painful process. To be sure, few husbands availed themselves of the extraordinary privileges reserved for them nearly everywhere—over their wife's money, children, activities, even her life. Contrary to the widely accepted myth about Victorian prudishness, many bourgeois couples discovered, and enjoyed, erotic equality in bed. Obligatory chivalry, however offensive to free spirits, softened the edges, as it perpetuated the hold, of male domination. But whether founded on law or on custom, the structure of this domination seemed built of solid stone until crusaders for women's rights began to hack away at it chip by chip.

It would be unhistorical, then, to end on too cheerful a note. The emotional investment in keeping man on top was too sizable and too cherished to be easily jettisoned. In 1879, Nora Helmer walked out of her doll's house and slammed the door behind her. But for years, Ibsen's famous heroine aroused more scandal than applause. Public debate continued as though little had happened in the real world, as though women had not demonstrated their professional skills as physicians or their robust health on the tennis court. Herbert Asquith, we know, lectured the House of Commons in 1892 on the "indelible differences" between men and women. Some four years later, conservatives in the German Reichstag drew from the same storehouse of threadbare ideas. Their defensiveness, really naked aggression, emerged as the deputies debated a bill on political organizations submitted by the Social Democrats. As matters stood, women were not permitted to join such organizations or to be present at their meetings. They could not legally attend even if there was no politics on the agenda. When the Social Democrats disapprovingly quoted St. Paul's injunction against women's speaking in church, their opponents taxed them with ignorance of Holy Scripture. "Gentlemen," said one deputy, "this sentence is founded on the organization and specific talents of woman." There is no way of eliminating the essential distinction between the sexes. Of course, woman has a soul; her exclusion from public life rests not on her "inferiority," but "on the fact that woman is different in nature." Another deputy agreed, blending the old arguments for woman's domestic destiny with those asserting her superiority to man: "The greatest glory of woman will always be that she has raised a race of competent children, a competent new generation. The greatest men have always boasted that they became what they are through their mother. Let things remain unchanged! *Men are what women make them,* says the Englishman, and I think: that's still valid today."[29]

There were loud bravos from the right, and general hilarity as one deputy, referring to the familiar saying "No fun without the ladies," commented that "the present law of associations violates this natural law." The prevailing mood in the chamber—except among the sponsors and supporters of the bill, which of course failed—smacked of the genial atmosphere in a men's club when the subject of woman came up: suggestive, slightly ribald, and at bottom anxiously humorous. But there were more and more middle-class men and women who did not think this sort of talk funny at all.

✖ FIVE ✖

The Bite of Wit

I. Varieties of Laughter

Compared to the warfare between men and women, making a joke, fabricating a pun, or writing a comedy may appear to belong to a radically remote psychological universe. Yet these disparate activities are grounded in very similar impulses. It is telling that common speech should link humor to such pugnacious acts as biting, slashing, cutting. Using the materials of its culture, humor offers splendid openings for the exercise—and the control—of aggression.

However mixed the motives underlying humor, its aggressive dimensions must claim preeminence. For one thing, it is, prominently, a form of boasting. Hobbes had long ago defined the "passion of laughter" as "nothing else but *sudden glory* arising from some sudden *conception* of some *eminency* in ourselves, by *comparison* with the *infirmity* of others, or with our own formerly." Nineteenth-century students of humor made this definition their own and offered imaginative variations on the theme of pointed invidiousness. In "De l'essence du rire," Baudelaire lent this claim to comparative eminence a dash of quasi-religiosity. It is a badge of human rebellion against the divine order. "Laughter comes from the idea of one's own superiority. Satanic idea if there ever was one! Pride and aberration!" He found a touch of insanity in this presumption: it is significant that madmen laugh and think themselves more worthy than all others; hardly any of them suffer from delusions of humility. Bergson, no doubt with Baudelaire in mind, agreed; the caricaturist's art "has something diabolical about it, raises up the demon the angel had felled."[1] For these writers, humor has an air of trying to storm the very heavens.

At the same time, Baudelaire sensed that the self-display of the humorist conceals troubling, even terrifying, inner uncertainties. He and other nineteenth-century observers elaborated this disenchanted perception into a psychology of defensive aggression. Laughter deriding others is only too often incense one burns at one's own self-constructed altar, an altar one knows to be rickety. "There is a symptom of weakness in laughter," Baudelaire wrote, a desperate hoping against hope. This, as the "satanic school" of the romantics had already hinted with its demonic characters, is "the primordial law of laughter," a "perpetual explosion" of rage and suffering which ties the triumphant laugher to the victim of his caustic joy. The comic, for Baudelaire, thus discloses nothing less than the essential contradiction inseparable from the human condition. "Laughter," he wrote, caressing the paradox, "is satanic, it is thus profoundly human." And since it is essentially human, "it is essentially contradictory," at once "a sign of infinite grandeur and an infinite misery." Echoes of Pascal! "It is the perpetual collision of these two infinites that releases laughter."[2]

The varieties of laughter cover so vast and varied a terrain that they all but frustrate mapping. Still, their forms are at least partly predictable as characteristic expressions of individual minds, class habits, and cultural styles. What is funny to one person, one time, or one nation may seem only crude or offensive to another. Just as each culture, it seems, has its favorite neurosis, so does each have its favorite impulses to being amused. "Our laughter is always the laughter of a group," Bergson reminded his readers in his famous essay *Le Rire*. His instance was "a man who was asked why he did not weep at a sermon when everybody was shedding tears, and replied, 'I don't belong to the parish.' " Bergson found this disclaimer revealing: "What that man thought would hold true even more of laughter."[3] The scatological jokes that convulsed nineteenth-century German *Bürger* were almost unknown among their English counterparts. Only a handful of humorists touched chords of mirth everywhere. Mark Twain's coarse-grained tales of the American frontier traveled without visible loss all the way to London and Paris, Berlin and Vienna.[4]

Certainly the psychological work done by wit and humor is heavily overdetermined. It may control, or salute, the sudden release of tension. It may express anxiety or alleviate it; bravado joking is a whistling past the graveyard of physical fear or social uneasiness. Humor may serve as a salutary act of regression—an agreeable holiday from frowning responsibility, a temporary retreat from earnestness that circumvents the punitive superego humans carry about with themselves. Even more, and significantly, humor may be a sly assertion of dignity or a piece of ferocious self-criticism—verbal aggression turned outward or inward.

To compound these complexities further, the producer and the consumer of humor are not necessarily on the same wavelength. An act of wit is a transaction, doomed to fail unless there is some relationship between teller and audience to let the spark of laughter leap from one to the other. But the dividends each derives may nevertheless differ radically. Being funny is Janus-faced; in marshaling a momentary community of laughers, it ingratiates the teller with a chosen audience, but at the same time and by the same means stigmatizes others as outsiders to be disliked or despised. Wit and humor give pleasure to some and pain to others as they mobilize love and hate. Their erotic and their aggressive work are inseparable, at times indistinguishable.

But laughter is not invariably hostile or destructive. There are innocent exercises of wit, performances without victims, providing unalloyed enjoyment with no malicious afterthoughts. Children's funny stories, tirelessly repeated, are often tests of verbal facility, rehearsals for the acquisition of cognitive competence. Recondite conceits and verbal pirouettes can be exuberant interludes in the day's drab business; so can the vast array of puns, as long as they do not grow compulsive enough to constitute a neurotic symptom. "Freedom generates jokes and jokes generate freedom," Johann Paul Friedrich Richter, the German novelist the world knows as Jean Paul, said early in the nineteenth century, and the freedom he had in mind was not political but inward: "A joke is a sheer play with ideas."[5] But this association of humor with that most envied of childlike activities, play, though not without its point, far from exhausts the matter; most humor is anything but a purely intellectual game or naive outburst. Very little, indeed, is simple about humor; the boundaries between playfulness and aggression are porous and indeterminate. Amusing verbal exuberance may cloak a determined quest for mastery; the most harmless-sounding jocular exhibitionism may be a disguised effort at sexual boasting.

Certain nineteenth-century humorists exemplified this complexity; their charming and imaginative productions could conceal a fierce edge. The pleasure that Lewis Carroll and Edward Lear, the two great makers of inspired nonsense humor, derived from their rhymes and their drawings, and the pleasure they gave others, look superficially like a childlike delight in genial verbal agility. But they deposited in their work the tensions of barely controlled murderous feelings. Their German counterpart Christian Morgenstern was only slightly gentler in his aggressiveness. Whatever the underlying obsessions and sexual conflicts of these three may have been, what matters here is that the public applauded their work and clamored for more. It enjoyed, and, however unconsciously, somehow participated in their acts of aggression.

The nineteenth century had more than an inkling of the hidden private sources and rich social functions of the comic. Alexander Herzen, that most literary of Russian revolutionaries, thought that "it would be extremely interesting to write the history of laughter."[6] Victorians found the subject absorbing; faithful to their self-conscious, self-exploratory style, they made massive efforts to trace laughter to its dark lair in human nature. What they discovered speaks to the history of nineteenth-century aggression: laughter was only too often awash in destructive energies. Typically, in 1858, noticing a new, much-enlarged edition of the celebrated *Joe Miller's Jest-book,* first published in 1739, the *Saturday Review* lamented that only about 20 of the 1,200 jokes contained in this new issue were worth telling; the rest "turn chiefly on the mistakes of Irishmen, the thriftlessness of sailors, the simple resource of calling one's opponent an ass, and on the hackneyed themes of matrimony, parsons, and lawyers"—hostile jokes nearly all of them.[7] Most of these jokes were, no doubt, exceedingly feeble, but as Mark Twain put it in *The Mysterious Stranger,* the only "really effective weapon" mankind has at its disposal is laughter. "Power, money, persuasion, supplication, persecution," can stir up hostility against humbugs. But laughter alone can blow them "to rags and atoms at a blast. Against the assault of laughter nothing can stand."[8] Satan speaks these lines, but he is speaking for his author.

Reflections on the problematic nature of humor had, of course, engaged inquiring spirits long before the nineteenth century. They go back to the ancient Greeks.[9] But the Victorian decades proved to be the time for sustained psychological commentary, speculative essays, and philosophical treatises on what makes people laugh. These explorations ranged from the quotable observations of Jean Paul in his *Vorschule der Aesthetik* of 1804 to Freud's more technical psychoanalytic theory of jokes, published in 1905. Hegel and Kierkegaard gravely incorporated discussions of the comic into their difficult texts. Hazlitt drew an important distinction in a subtle analytic essay, "On Wit and Humour," in 1819; Baudelaire published an impassioned, at moments inspired rumination on laughter and caricature in the 1850s. Spencer investigated the physiology of the facial distortion denoting amusement in the 1860s; Darwin followed suit in the 1870s, around the time that George Meredith was lecturing on comedy. Toward the end of the century, more solemn and more systematic, German explorers of humor—notably Friedrich Theodor Vischer and Theodor Lipps—ranged laughter under the rubric of aesthetic experience in their spe-

cialized treatises. Meanwhile, the eclectic psychiatrist Emil Kraepelin sought
the comical in unexpected intellectual contrasts, while psychologists like the
eminent American educator G. Stanley Hall and that omnivorous amateur
Havelock Ellis investigated the relationship of laughter to sexual excitement
and to physiological phenomena like ticklishness.

And they were alert to the aggressive component of laughter. Bergson called
it "a froth with a salt base. Like froth, it sparkles. It is gaiety itself. But the
philosopher who gathers up some of the taste, will find the substance thin
indeed, and a portion of bitterness."[10] It was this curious blend of gaiety and
bitterness that made humor all the more intriguing to its explorers in the age of
Queen Victoria—who, widespread reports to the contrary, was at times
amused, at least before her husband died. But though the study of humor was
highly cultivated, much puzzlement remained. "Psychologists are very fond of
attempting to define the nature of wit and humour," Leslie Stephen observed
near the end of the century. "Hitherto they have not been very successful."
Even so, students of humor had long known that laughter was no laughing
matter.[11]

It became a commonplace that humor is perhaps the only human activity that
scientific attention leaves limp and lifeless. "We murder to dissect," Wordsworth's famous critique of the analytic spirit, holds for all attempts to understand why something is funny. "An explanation," the Berlin humorist and
affable social critic Adolf Glassbrenner noted in his journal around 1844, "is the
death of a joke."[12] A symphony or a poem analyzed continues to provide
pleasure; analysis may in fact refine and enhance that pleasure. Not so with
humor: to explain the point, or the technique, of a joke is to banish laughter.

What lends the analysis of the comic such solemnity is not just the humorist's
well-advertised dismay at human nature or at the abuse of power. More generally, it is grave because humor is so firmly intertwined with aggressiveness.
Suffering, too, is somehow implicated. In the 1850s, Thackeray lent his well-
earned authority to that popular notion by depicting the clown as among the
most despondent of beings: "Harlequin without his mask is known to present a
very sober countenance, and was himself, the story goes, the melancholy patient whom the Doctor advised to go and see Harlequin—a man full of cares
and perplexities like the rest of us, whose Self must always be serious to him,
under whatever mask, or disguise, or uniform he presents it to the public."
Near the end of the century, Mark Twain said the same thing, still more
bluntly: "The secret source of Humor is not joy but sorrow. There is no humor
in heaven."[13]

But, as the Victorians also recognized, humor, often originating in sadness,
can boldly take aim at formidable, highly threatening targets. In the 1830s, the

English wit Thomas Love Peacock had already pointed out that "Rabelais, one of the wisest and most learned, as well as wittiest of men, put on the robe of the all-licensed fool, that he might, like the court-jester, convey bitter truths under the semblance of simple buffoonery."[14] Humor is a very human way of putting such truths on record. Not all of the time: it will turn out that wit, humor, the comic—aspects of laughter that nineteenth-century researchers learned to differentiate without denying their underlying affinities—are exceedingly ambiguous in their intentions and their effects, prudent and daring, conformist and rebellious in turn. For, to repeat, aggressiveness is of their very essence.* "Revenge is wicked, & unchristian & in every way unbecoming, & I am not the man to countenance it or show it any favor," wrote Mark Twain to his fiancée late in 1869. "But," he added, "it is powerful sweet, anyway."[15] And it was most powerful sweet when it was funny.

At times the aggression was palpable enough. Edward Lear directed some of his most violent limericks against himself, the nonconformist destroyed by his society:

> There was an Old Person of Buda,
> Whose conduct grew ruder and ruder;
>   Till at last, with a hammer,
>   They silenced his clamour,
> By smashing that Person of Buda.

Lewis Carroll, for his part, played the sadist instead of the masochist. *Alice in Wonderland,* with its temperamental and choleric characters, is the work of the eccentric who at twelve had written "Brother and Sister" and at twenty "The Two Brothers." These rhymes treat the most ghastly internecine hostilities with smiling and insouciant cruelty. In the earlier poem, brother and sister quarrel viciously until he borrows a frying pan from the cook to make his sister into an Irish stew. In the later poem, wish has become reality as a boy baits his fishhook with his younger brother:

> The fish hurried up by the dozens,
>   All ready and eager to bite,
> For the lad that had flung was so tender and young.

*While close students of laughter, such as Freud, carefully differentiated wit, humor, and the comic, I shall disregard these subtleties in this chapter to concentrate on the aggressive component in its various guises.

The victim's sister, her heart broken but resigned to her brother's fate, calmly comments that the fish, at least, had enjoyed this fratricide:

> It gave them an appetite.

Nor did the other consequences trouble her much:

> One of the two will be wet through and through,
> And t'other will be late for his tea!

It will not do, perhaps, to burden such surrealist absurdities with too heavy a weight of interpretation, but in any event their jocularity cannot expunge the bite of Lewis Carroll's wit. He set aside the constraints of civilization in the service of amusement.[16]

An even more persuasive testimonial to the savagery of humor is the poetry of the young W. S. Gilbert. Born into a well-to-do and cultivated family, he traveled widely in his youth and cast about for some years before he discovered his vocation as a maker of infectious light verse. Government service and the practice of law seemed drab to him and proved unprofitable, so he "stuck to literature," which meant contributing a stream of paragraphs and poems to humorous journals in London, mainly *Fun*.[17] His most memorable productions were his Bab ballads, which he decorated with vignettes that much resembled Thackeray's amusing illustrations. His name for the ballads was apt; "Bab" had been Gilbert's nickname as a small boy, and these poems uncannily resemble childhood fantasies translated into adult idiom, with repressed wishes and anxieties reemerging as broad, often bizarre, humor.

In his last years he recalled that at the age of two, in southern Italy with his parents, he had been kidnapped by brigands and then returned to his family, unharmed, for a small ransom.[18] Whether this memory reflects an actual event or developed as an early fantasy, melodramatic themes—infants switched after birth and children treated sadistically—were dominant in his lighthearted work, early and late. And whatever the facts, the casual brutality of his ballads, which vastly amused his readers, also a little obscurely frightened them.[19]

One can see why. One of Gilbert's ballads, "Gentle Alice Brown," is about an Italian robber's daughter; her inappropriate name displays the absurdity that was Gilbert's signature. Alice, we are told, confessed to her priest all sorts of crimes—kidnapping, burglary, forgery, murder—for which she was fined half-a-crown apiece. But she had also been making eyes at an infatuated handsome youth, and since her father intended her for one of his lieutenants, this was far more serious. The priest betrayed Alice's swain, her father murdered him, and her mother "dissected him before she went to bed," thus soothing Alice Brown's mind. Again, in "Annie Protheroe" Gilbert depicts "a gentle executioner" and his love, a postmistress, who would listen entranced to his reports, watch reenactments of his work or, when it rained,

> stop at home, and look,
> At his favourable notices, all pasted in a book,
> And then her cheeks would flush—her swimming eyes would dance with joy,
> In a glow of admiration at the prowess of her boy.

This was Gilbert's frivolous way with the predatory animal that sleeps in every man—and every woman.[20]

It found exemplary expression in "The Story of Gentle Archibald, Who Wanted to Be a Clown." Archibald started life as the sort of obedient creature that middle-class educators liked to produce. Even his humor was gentle, unaggressive:

> He was a mild, delightful boy,
> Who hated jokes that caused annoy.

In all, he was a cheerful, respectful son. But one extreme begets the other. One day, Archibald's father made the fatal mistake of taking him to a Christmas pantomime, and the boy was infected with the wish to become a clown. His family and his nurse remonstrated with him, in vain; his gentleness all gone, he thrashed the nurse, and driven by "some dreadful power unseen," proceeded to

> burn, and steal, and kill,
> Against his gentlemanly will.

He boiled his little sister Jane and painted his mother blue, and playing cruel jokes on the rest of his family, he

> Spread devastation round,—and, ah,
> He red-hot pokered his papa!

But it was all, Gilbert reassured his audience, in fun:

> He gave a wild, delighted scream,
> And woke—for, lo, it was a dream!

Still, Gilbert left little doubt that a "dreadful power unseen" lurks in the best-behaved of us.[21]

With vandalism and mayhem a matter of course in these ballads, their farcical treatment of cannibalism—biting wit at its most literal—is predictable; indeed, cannibalism became one of Gilbert's staple themes. In "The Two Ogres," he discovered cannibals in his own country, living in "Wickham Wold." One of these ogres eats only bad boys, as is natural, but the other, out of character, consumes only good ones. Challenged, he defends his tastes with an explanation that displays Gilbert's psychological acumen. Had he not been called, the ogre asks, to love the good?

> Why do I eat good children—why?
> Because I love them so!

Freud, analyzing the intertwining of libido and aggression, could have used these lines; they provide a world of insight into unconscious conflicts.[22]

At times Gilbert's violence struck his contemporaries as a shade excessive. In 1866, Mark Lemon, the editor of *Punch,* rejected one of his ballads, "The Yarn of the 'Nancy Bell,' " as "too cannibalistic."[23] His verdict seems not unreasonable if a little tender-minded. The yarn is about a wild-looking elderly sailor who, ever unsmiling, has one joke; he proclaims himself

> At once a cook, and a captain bold,
> And the mate of the *Nancy* brig,
> And a bo'sun tight, and a midshipmite,
> And the crew of the captain's gig!

Asked how he can be all these men at once, he tells a harrowing tale of being shipwrecked, leaving ten sailors marooned on a reef. Crazed with hunger, the survivors take to eating their comrades one after the other—and find many of them delicate morsels. In the end, only the teller of the tale, having last eaten the cook, remains to brood on his adventure and retell his painful joke.[24]

In retrospect, Gilbert displayed marked ambivalence about the mayhem he had spread over London's humor magazines and dismissed the Bab ballads as "but indifferent trifling." Yet in 1906, at a festive celebration of his seventieth birthday, he acknowledged their impact on the Savoy operettas, which had made Gilbert and Sullivan into a national treasure. His debt was beyond doubt: the aggression he unleashed, if in amusing guise, was his own. In a remarkable self-portrait, he depicted himself attired in a loud checked suit, frowning fiercely at the viewer—the comedian as curmudgeon. Then he scribbled aggressive confessions all around this sketch, and as if to underscore his self-proclaimed nastiness, he signed each of them. "I hate my fellow-man," reads one; "I loathe everybody," reads another; "confound everything," and "everybody is an ass." Beneath his feet, he wrote, "I am an ill-tempered pig, & I glory in it," and on the side one can find a most Bab-ballad-like declaration: "I like pinching little babies."[25] He probably did; he was touchy, quarrelsome, and fiercely competitive.

It is only natural, then, that Victorian psychologists and poets should regard aggressiveness as a highly significant ground for laughter. Consider Alexander Bain's *The Emotions and the Will* of 1859, a sensible and eclectic textbook in psychology. Laughter, that "remarkable perturbation of the system," Bain wrote, has many—often slight—causes, some of them purely physiological. But, more interesting, laughter also arises from psychological impulsions: "Self-complacency, and a feeling of triumph at some striking effect produced by self or others." To be sure, "kindly feeling" is among the reasons for laughter, but Bain kept his eye on less cordial sentiments, "the spectacle or notion of filthy, degraded, or forbidden things; the so-called ludicrous, which is usually the clash of dignity with meanness." For Bain, as for other explorers of the humorous domain, laughter is principally an act directed *against* something, or someone, else. It aims at "the degradation of some person or interest possessing dignity, in circumstances that excite no other strong emotion."[26] The line between a grin and a sneer is faint and easy to cross.

In his widely read lectures on comedy, George Meredith too paid tribute to this pugnacious side of the comic. He visualized comedy as the votary of Bacchus, as it "rolled in shouting under the divine protection of the Son of the Wine-jar." Wit, he argued, indulging in his characteristically involuted, allusive periods, desacralizes the subjects it chooses to attack. The modern comedy of manners, which had its rise in the frivolous reign of Charles II, has been "a combative performance, under a license to deride and outrage the Puritans." The wit of the English comic stage is "warlike"; its aim is "to wound," its essential attitude, "entirely pugilistic." Congreve's wit "is a Toledo blade, sharp and wonderfully supple for steel; cast for dueling, restless in the scabbard being so pretty when out of it." In short, if wit is to shine, it needs "an adversary."[27] To be sure, Meredith professed some uneasiness at the amoral implications of this attitude, but his lyrical evocation of the duellist at the ready, nervously awaiting the right moment to display his phallic prowess, suggests that he took pleasure in precisely this aggressive side of comedy.

But while Meredith saw no reason to dispute the prevalent definition of human nature as inherently pugnacious, he insisted that combative wit is effective only if it is cerebral. Reason alone provides the verbal duellist with appropriate targets. Hence the England of his time, at once puritanical, cynical, and sentimental, can only obstruct the flourishing of comedy. Above all, lachrymose self-indulgence blurs necessary distinctions and subverts rational criticism. The dominant excuses for false standards and trivial values are not the ally of moral seriousness but its nemesis, blocking the alert vision that keeps vice steadily in its sights. Only wit, cool and incorruptible, dares to plunge the sword of intelligent laughter into the heart of Folly.[28]

Meredith rather compromised the vigor of the comic spirit he valued so highly by defining it, in a noted flaccid phrase, as casting "an oblique light" on men's transgressions, "followed by volleys of silvery laughter." His professed critical intentions were rather more virile: "The laughter of satire is a blow in the back or the face. The laughter of comedy is impersonal and of unrivaled politeness, nearer a smile—often no more than a smile. It laughs through the mind, for the mind directs it; and it might be called the humor of the mind."[29] The smiling mental humor Meredith called for is inexorable as it punctures cant, pedantry, affectation, bombast, and hypocrisy. In his own best-known comic works, those long psychological novels on contemporary themes, Meredith was a rather inconsistent performer. But his message is unmistakable: though suave, wit is a warrior.

Other analysts of laughter were less disposed than Meredith to single out aggression as the fuel of wit, but none discounted it altogether. Not even the German aesthetician and essayist Friedrich Theodor Vischer, almost professionally cheery, could do without it. He distinguished between the truly comic, which is always "good-natured," and jokes, which may also be malicious and, if so, destructive of the sublime. The comic demonstrates through the work of amusing surprise that there is nothing unalloyed in this world; comic laughter frees the laugher from the "nightmare of life." Here the ugly, an essential ingredient in the comic, is both "painless and harmless." Still, the comic undeniably teaches painful lessons. "Nobody," Vischer wrote, in the unacademic style that marks him the man of letters, "remains unplucked, not even the person of the laugher himself." Pointed humor is most effective when its maker "has the mental freedom not to spare the *ego*," recognizes the frailty of his actions, and scoffs at himself.[30]

For Vischer this inward-turned aggression is not self-pity or masochism but self-knowledge; the laugher "experiences with deepest insight and in the very marrow of his being the contradictions" that afflict the world, "its evils and defects, the stupidity and baseness of men." This insight gives the self-critical laugher some hope that despite human wickedness, the good in the human spirit remains unbowed. Hence the true humorist's benign smile. Anticipating

Bergson, Vischer concedes that a deposit of bitterness always remains at the bottom of the cup. "Comedians have always been cynics."[31] But Vischer was good-humored about this cynicism; comedians prick the bubbles of self-conceit not from a sadistic pleasure in someone else's pain, but for the sake of truth and social amelioration. For Vischer, humorous aggression at its best is stylized, urbane, thoughtfully dosed, and carefully aimed.

Theodor Lipps, in his "psychological-aesthetic" treatise on the comic and on humor, attenuated aggression even further. He devoted much of his difficult text to debating fine points with other theorists. An influential aesthetician who reversed the common ranking of psychology and philosophy to make the second the servant of the first, Lipps was principally interested in classifying the genres of the comic; this was to assist him in sounding its work in the mind, and the peculiar affective mixture of pleasure and unpleasure that comic utterances generate. At once pugnacious and reasonable, Lipps praised the insights of pioneers like Kant, Bain, and Spencer; they had understood that the comic effect depends on "a contrast between a positive and a negative" element, and is generally released by the collapse of pretentiousness and dignity. Lipps saw more than a hint of pugilism in such deflationary labor, but he was slow to acknowledge that aggressive humor is the proper weapon for amending erring humanity. Aristophanic comedy, he wrote near the conclusion of his study, is the finest consummation that the incitement to laughter has ever attained. To dive, like Aristophanes, into the vortex of human nature is "the highest humor; that is, the deepest moral seriousness and the greatest mental freedom."[32]

In his civilized meditation on laughter, Henri Bergson seemed to keep the temperature even lower, disposed as he was to deny comic action any emotional springs at all. The comic emerges from a perception of incongruities like mechanical rigidity and inappropriate repetition. "It addresses itself to pure intelligence; laughter is incompatible with emotion," especially with sympathy—is, in fact, its greatest adversary. Hence the comic thrives in an atmosphere of indifference; its favorite condition is, in Bergson's memorable phrase, the momentary anesthesia of the heart. The fond smile at the mishap of a cherished person can appear only when we "forget that fondness, silence that pity."[33]

What is more, for Bergson laughter is not just a sheer personal outburst, but, rather, at once a product of culture and a commentary on it, a "*social gesture.*" He cites with approval Bain's well-known definition of the comic as an act of degradation but generalizes its scope: the gross enlargement of the small can be no less funny than the shrinking of the large. Whatever he saw as its transforming work, then, Bergson was compelled to acknowledge the aggressive components of laughter. The frigid, emotionless state of mind he postulated as its precondition turns out to be a kind of licensed clinical sadism. Laughter is "above all a corrective. Made to humiliate, it must give the person who is its object a painful impression. Through it, society avenges itself for the liberty one has taken with it." If it is not caustic, even cruel, it must fail.[34]

More probing on this point than Meredith, Bergson came to recognize that laughter is often indiscriminate and unjust. Like a "disease chastising excess, it will strike some of the innocent, spare some of the guilty." But that is in its nature. There is more than a touch of spite, then, and of malice, in all laughter. But Bergson was indulgent with this all-too-human ingredient; he offered the Darwinian alibi that in laughter nature is simply using "evil with a view to the good." This lofty perspective dispensed him from having to discriminate between the beneficial and the pernicious effects of aggressive humor. But that humor is aggressive was a truth he could not deny.[35]

For Meredith and Bergson, who took most of their evidence from comedy, and for philosophical psychologists like Vischer and Lipps, laughter was, as we have seen, a special case of the aesthetic experience. For Freud, committed to discovering the laws governing mental functioning, and malfunctioning, the pleasure in telling and hearing jokes was an element that fitted seamlessly into his developmental scheme, his theories of the dynamic unconscious and of dreams. "Is the subject of jokes worth all this effort?" he asked rhetorically, and answered that there was no doubt of it. "I can appeal to the fact that there is an intimate connection between all mental events." In the theories he evolved at the time of *Jokes and Their Relation to the Unconscious,* Freud was assigning unprecedented prominence to the sexual drive. Now, thinking about jokes, he did not propose to minimize the share of sexuality in them; sexual needs, or sexual problems, supply much laughter with its energy. At the same time, he gave ample room to aggressiveness—including sexual aggressiveness, that explosive mixture of love and hate—in the impulse to laugh. "A joke will allow us to exploit something ridiculous in our enemy which, because of obstacles standing in the way, we could not express openly or consciously."[36] The mind exercises its quarrelsome propensities in unsuspected territories, all the while, as it were, demurely protesting that it is only being funny or playful.

Characteristically, Freud's book on jokes had its origins in his clinical experience. His intimate of these years, Wilhelm Fliess, reading *The Interpretation of Dreams* in manuscript, had objected that Freud's dreamers were making too many jokes, implying that Freud had invented them. Freud could only plead innocent. He acknowledged his unfailing appetite for Jewish jokes, had in fact been collecting them for some time. But he had also quite independently been reflecting on laughter, and what mattered to him was the striking family resemblance of what he called the "joke work" and the "dream work." Some of the favored techniques of jokes are the very techniques that dreams employ to circumvent the internal censor.* Encouraged by this discovery, he pressed on, and *Jokes,* published in 1905, was the result. It drew freely on the little treasury of jokes he had been compiling, but even more, on his project to find for joking the most comprehensive psychological explanation. The act of joking, he concluded, yields pleasure of a special kind.

While Freud's analysis of jokes belongs to his theoretical preoccupations of the 1890s, his book on the subject also looks ahead to the basic revision of drive theory he would develop not long after the First World War. Well over a decade before he assigned to aggression a stature equal in dignity, perhaps superior in power, to the libido, he divided what he called "tendentious" jokes, those with a point to make beyond sheer verbal felicity, into two categories: *obscene* and *hostile.* Here was, in embryo, the structural theory of the 1920s, a theory that treated the mind as a battleground between the forces of love and aggression, or, in his more grandiose formulation, of life and death.

At the stage of his book on jokes, however, this grand theory was still far from Freud's mind. Rather, he was interested in discovering what makes people laugh. Since the effectiveness of a joke is not determined by its content— nothing, after all, is easier than to restate its message in drab expository prose at which nobody will laugh—he thought it appropriate to start with an exploration of technique. On this point, Freud could appeal to some impressive ancestors, including Shakespeare. He quoted Polonius's famous dictum that brevity is the soul of wit as an anticipation of the discoveries he had made about condensation in the joke work. But Polonius does not serve Freud just as a precursor, however unwitting, of psychoanalytic ideas; he also illustrates the uses of humorous techniques by making himself ridiculous precisely as he is trying to talk good sense. Trite and garrulous, Polonius persistently violates his own sound prescription of brevity, thus amusingly inverting—and involuntarily confirming—the rule he asserts. His loquacity, economy turned inside out, demonstrates that condensation is not the only device on which jokes rely. Their tool chest may be limited, but it is evidently large enough to satisfy the human need for surprise and variety and to provide pleasure for impulses that must otherwise go unsatisfied.

Substitute pleasure, after all, is what the joke essentially yields. Freud allowed himself to be relatively cursory on the substance of jokes, as if to say that their uses are scarcely a mystery. Jokes are regressions with a purpose; they disclose freely, on the model of the uninhibited child and under the privileges granted

---

*These techniques include, to use specialized terms, condensation, displacement, and exaggeration.

the jester, what adults have learned to suppress, or repress, from fear or politeness. On the plea that they are not to be taken seriously, jokes may avenge an insult by turning it wittily on the aggressor, deflate the pompous and the swollen by publishing their hidden defects, criticize an authority usually protected from challenge. Then, Freud noted, "the joke represents a rebellion against such authority, a liberation from its pressure."[37]

Freud saw the joke, then, whether hostile or obscene, as a devious, well-disguised agent of gratification. With sly indirections, it evades the roadblocks—the political, social, or religious barriers set up to restrict, or wholly inhibit, serious talk about delicate matters. Since society trains its children to rein in their aggressiveness, jokes represent a welcome outlet, often the only one, for repressed wishes. And, Freud commented with some justice, though more sternly than the evidence warranted, that since modern bourgeois have been excessively aggressive in taming aggressiveness, the joke can claim a privileged place in Victorian culture. Just as in the sexual domain looking becomes a substitute for touching and the dirty joke a substitute for looking, so in the area of aggression the hostile joke stands in for the desire, nearly always blunted or frustrated, to wound or kill one's enemies.

Whatever its aim, Freud analyzes the successful joke as a saving of inner resources. For the prohibitions that society imposes and the individual internalizes require for their maintenance a continuous expenditure of energy, an expenditure that the joke, and other sources of laughter, reduce. They are economical ways of enjoying once more the pleasures that socialization has compelled civilized humans to do without. That is why they constitute a return to those early euphoric days when "we were used to doing our psychological work in general with scanty expenditures, the mood of our childhood, when we did not know the comic, were incapable of jokes, and did not need humor to feel happy in life."[38] It is only on the surface that this conclusion seems harmless, remote from politics. After all—and rightly so—for Freud, as for his fellow investigators, much laughter was regression in the service of aggressiveness—whether personal revenge or social criticism.

2. Physicians to Society

Nineteenth-century humorists, theoreticians and practitioners alike, acknowledged one modern master of biting wit as supreme: Molière. He alone was fit to keep Aristophanes company. The aged Goethe praised him as a "pure human being," who "chastises mankind by drawing it as it truly is." Freud quoted favorite lines from his comedies casually and in passing, as though handling the coin current among the educated. Shaw, who read and recommended Molière all his life, flatly called him "the greatest dramatist who ever lived." And these were only three in an unending parade of admirers.[1]

All those scattering such tributes could cheerfully agree that Molière's laughter was supremely useful. Baudelaire spoke for them when he singled him out as the "best French expression" of lucid, utilitarian, and superbly effective humor. This verdict penetrates to the heart of Molière's perennial appeal and puts the most attractive face possible on aggression in laughter. Wit at its best—and Molière is wit at its best—assails foolishness and wickedness in the interest of suffering, deluded humanity. George Meredith argued this quite explicitly: "The comedy of Molière," that purest among comedians who has been "so clownishly mishandled," is "deeply conceived" and hence anything but impure. "Meditate on that statement," Meredith added, ever ready to throw himself into a didactic posture. "Never did men wield so shrieking a scourge upon vice; but his consummate self-mastery is not shaken while administering it." Molière's great comic villains are perfect butts for the humorist's lash: "Tartuffe and Harpagon, in fact, are made each to whip himself and his class— the false pietist and the insanely covetous." Setting these beautifully conceived puppets in motion, Molière "strips Folly to the skin, displays the imposture of the creature, and is content to offer her better clothing." And he does so with unimpeachable diction. "The source of his wit is clear reason"—for Meredith the highest imaginable commendation.[2]

This extravagant homage is not without its false notes; Molière, that fountain of pure language and pure reason, seems ill at ease wielding a shrieking scourge and stripping his victims. But early in the twentieth century, the brilliant and eccentric German playwright Carl Sternheim found images for his master Molière no less physical, no less strident. For Sternheim, whose chosen dramatic subject was "the heroic life of the bourgeoisie," Molière was the good *Bürger*. As "physician to his estate," he attended his patients not with "syrups and injections but with probe and saw." He would "reach into the intestines of the sick, press the poison from their overfull stomachs, their bloated veins." And then, exercising his "divine powers," he would perform works of love on his patients. "Softly flattering and persuasive, he breathed into them a fine fire of new youth." Molière, it seems, could not escape such inflamed rhetoric. He had, after all, shouldered the ungrateful burden of the humorist as social healer, confronting all-too-human failings as "physician to the body of his age."[3] The work of such a healer, driven to painful interventions before recovery can begin, is not for the squeamish.

Sternheim is Molière's most remarkable modern follower, bleaker than his idol, a grim if witty physician sitting by the bedside of what he has diagnosed as a very sick culture. From the opening lines of his short play *Die Hose*, the first in his loosely connected cycle of "bourgeois comedies," Sternheim unfolds a repertory of aggressions reaching far beyond the ludicrous, deliberately banal action to throw light on a world on the verge of disaster. *Die Hose*, first printed in 1910, was kept from the stage until the following year by Traugott von Jagow, Berlin's chief of police, a man with a good nose for the dynamite concealed beneath brisk dialogue and slight action. "There are," says the protagonist, Theobald Maske, at the end, "strange things behind the wallpaper of life." His name—"mask"—fiercely dramatizes the playwright's mission: to cut through the veils of contemporary culture. A curious sketch map of that culture emerges as, in successive plays, the Maskes rise from their lowly origins in the petty bourgeoisie to enter the aristocracy as ennobled industrialists.

Though a cold realist, Sternheim did not aspire to social realism. The event that sends *Die Hose* on its way is an insignificant, embarrassing incident: Luise Maske, Theobald's wife, loses her underpants in the street at the very moment the emperor is passing by. This kind of triviality, which frequently reappears in later dramas in this bourgeois cycle, is a calculated stratagem. Sternheim's fables are intentionally thin; his way of unmasking the Maskes and, through them, their society, depends rather on his unique diction. He gave his characters curt, hectic, baldly abbreviated speeches that omit definite articles and invert accepted sentence structure. This snarling, energetic, "telegraphic" style, unmistakably his, forces access to the sordid realities that mendacious social conventions have carefully buried: the sexual lust hiding behind sentimental avowals, the avarice masquerading as noble ambition, the Darwinian combat for profit and power pervading the most sacred family relations and polite social intercourse.

But Sternheim's audiences and interpreters were unsure just whom he was scourging. Some read his comedies as massive attacks on the middle class, others as wry tributes to it. Each had part of the truth; his caricature of the middling orders, much like the portrait of black-coated modern heroes that Baudelaire had drawn half a century earlier, was partly affectionate, partly sarcastic. Like many other good bourgeois late in the Victorian century, Sternheim was incurably ambivalent about his class. As an aristocratic anarchist, he loved what he hated.[4]

Sternheim had no hesitations about his self-imposed assignment as a modern Molière. With a Nietzschean contempt for the *juste milieu*, he was prodding bourgeois to reclaim their sources of vitality, discard their manicured, hypocritical social manner, and stand by their so-called vices. The question was whether his culture would survive long enough to take his cure. In the comedy *1913*, written that very year, only some months before the great war, one character presciently exclaims, "After us, collapse! We are ripe." In these desperate straits, the witty physician to his culture is bound to attack its malaise with all the medicine at his command.

This perception of the militant work of humor, genial in tone but severe in execution, lends credibility to Voltaire's old defense that there are times when one must tear down before one can build. "Laughter contains something revolutionary," Alexander Herzen insisted. As the Bavarian playwright, novelist, and *Simplicissimus* contributor Ludwig Thoma put it, "Satire has always been directed against the holders of power, or it was mere insipid wisecracking." This, as everyone knows, was also the view of George Bernard Shaw, one of the most aggressive and most self-conscious social physicians of the Victorian age and beyond. Eager to exploit and exacerbate what he called "the guilty conscience of the middle class," he made himself a demolition expert, assailing accepted values, accepted ideals, accepted certainties, with his disrespectful wit. His aim as a dramatist was, he frankly announced, to make the comfortable uncomfortable. Shaw made no secret, either, of the fact that his pungent critiques of musical and dramatic performances, as of society, were passionate political statements. He repudiated the title of objective critic and warned his readers that far from aiming at impartiality, he was laying siege to the Victorian theater, having cut his way into it, as he liked to say, at the point of his pen. Shaw's metaphor almost literally converts the laughter's pen into a sword.[5]

Through many centuries, social satirists supplied powerful evidence of this militancy at work. But it could be self-serving: ask the victims. Obviously, much depended on whom and what the humorist chose as targets of his aggressive impulses. Still, merely to identify the target of aggressive wit is not enough to permit the historian a conclusive verdict on the caliber of the attack. Not all the rich, powerful, and upwardly mobile, those natural victims of satire, are automatically in need of deflation. Nor are the wit's motives any more transparent. Humorous aggression is often the precipitate of personal needs shaping political attitudes, the ungainly child of rage or envy. And yet, unworthy or neurotic springs of action may produce deadly accurate critical perceptions.

Some such complex judgments are required for the work of Heinrich Heine, a supreme nineteenth-century wit. Heine's poetry and prose are a copious but never cloying banquet of virtuosity. Only in his excruciating last years, when he was confined to his "mattress-grave" in Paris, steadily in pain and partially paralyzed from the effects of a venereal disease, did his humor occasionally give way to pathos and his irreverence to a rather idiosyncratic Jewish piety, a truce with Yahweh. Until then the most consistent of performers, generously serving up unhackneyed images, conceits, and comparisons, Heine could not have written a boring sentence if he had tried. He sang of loss more than of love, of disillusionment more than of happy prospects, and, persistently, of politics. His was not a happy wit; it was the lament of the stranger longing for home, shaped into brilliant, deceptively simple melodies.

Heine was born in Düsseldorf in 1797, into a conflict of loyalties; the French troops that occupied the city had granted Jews civil rights their own German rulers had never dreamt of extending. From the start Heine translated such tensions into the stuff of wry reflection and sardonic verse. He was a Jew in a society in which Jews were poised between hopeful new prospects and terrifying old threats; as an aspirant to the glorious opportunities European culture had to offer, he was traversing treacherous terrain. He was a convert to Protestantism at a time when Jews and Christians alike were deeply suspicious of turncoats. He was a half-voluntary exile in Paris, feeling more at home abroad than in his native land, yet unable to forget its political travail or dismiss fond memories of its food and its landscape. He was an outspoken advocate of the poet's autonomy who accepted a clandestine pension from the regime of Louis Philippe. He was a radical critic of aristocracy and priesthood who vocally distrusted democratic movements and made political enemies among all parties. He was perennially short of money but insisted that he must make his own way as a man of letters. He was a scourge of sentimentality whose own poems proved a treasure-house of bittersweet sentiment to be set to music by Schubert and a score of lesser composers.

These paradoxes marked Heine's life. His need to assert himself, of which his notorious Mensuren were only one symptom, was blended with an urgent need to conform. No doubt his financial insecurity, made all the more galling by his dependence on a rich uncle's largess, had something to do with the contradictions in his conduct. But they were not determined by the pressure of economic necessity. In 1843, after more than a dozen years away in Paris, he came home to northern Germany to visit his mother and hear his native tongue once again; he confessed that he had been homesick. It was an emotion he ridiculed but could not exorcise. He told a sympathetic friend, falling naturally into the language of the duellist, that his satirical poem on Germany, *Deutschland. Ein Wintermärchen,* was "a biting challenge I have thrown down to the Teutomaniacs." But his political aggressiveness was punctuated with deep-seated nostalgia; in the poem, Heine compared himself, a little grandly, to Antaeus, the giant who, having touched his mother, his native soil, feels new strength growing within him.[6]

For this haunted man, abrasive wit was almost a condition of survival. Heine was a good hater.[7] He scattered hatred in all directions; his personal vendettas and his social criticism, though distinct in purpose and merit, were two vents for one need: aggression. He was aware of his reputation; in 1828, as he vigorously campaigned for a professorship in Munich, soliciting influential friends to intercede with Ludwig I, he voiced the pious hope that the king would find him milder than before.[8] But one use of his satire was to slake his thirst for revenge. Perhaps his most famous victim was a fellow poet, Count August von Platen. A fastidious aesthete and adept versifier, Platen excelled in *recherché* meters and esoteric forms like the Persian ghazel. His polished, formal verse was not pure artifice; it spoke only too loudly of his passion for other men. With all their burnished surfaces, his lines were confessions he extorted from himself, and his unconventional sexual tastes gave Heine his opening. He had been offended by some ungracious references to him in one of Platen's comedies, and, already irritated by his failure to secure the Munich professorship, he suspected Platen—wrongly—as one of the conspirators who had deprived him of the post.

Heine's reading of Platen was extreme, almost willfully misguided, but he could not wait to unleash his wit. He revealed his animus, and his strategy, from the outset in one of his travel reports, *Die Bäder von Lucca,* using as an epigraph a line wickedly truncated from Platen: "I am like the woman to the man." Thus launched, he pursued the attack with quotations from Platen's poems celebrating warm male friendships, scolding a beloved for his fickleness, agonizing over plans for tender meetings, and professed to find these effusions about sweet blond boys sickening. "One would think the author a man-crazed young maiden."[9]

This was not enough for Heine; he maliciously drew parallels between Platen and Nero and expressed mock sympathy for such wayward desires. At times, he noted, Platen concealed the gender of his beloved, acting like an ostrich with his head buried in the sand. He would have done better to hide his rear end and lift his head, but then, Platen was a man of the rear end. Yet for all this, Heine exclaimed righteously, Platen was a conceited, self-advertising rhymster who preened himself on being the poet of the age and dared to make vulgar jokes about "the baptized Heine."[10] For the self-appointed avenger who wrote these pages, aggression and humor were practically synonymous.

"I have done what belongs to my office," he wrote a friend in January 1830, after it was all over. As usually after executions, "there comes pity: I should not have hit him so hard." But executions cannot be gentle affairs. Nor have people "noticed that I only chastised him as the representative of a party. I did not want to attack that insolent male whore to aristocrats and priests on aesthetic grounds alone."[11] This was a fair comment on his performance; aesthetics played only a subordinate role in Heine's act of reprisal, the triumph of rage over reason.

This notorious episode, which dismayed Heine's admirers and heartened his detractors, was a damaging instance of his urge, at times irrepressible, to wound to the death. Much to Heine's chagrin, his well-wishers thought it in execrable taste, wit out of control. But on other occasions, particularly in his satires on fellow Germans, Heine's provocative shafts hit home. The German states of his day—he never tired of reciting the number "thirty-six" to call attention to the divisions afflicting his land—were in the grip of the post-Napoleonic restoration. After 1815, German universities were repeatedly purged of "demagogues," while scholars, publishers, cartoonists, journalists, even poets, cringed under the heavy hand of the censor. Publication in these police states, in which the mildest protest was suspect, almost invariably involved evasive tactics by the author, passages prudently dropped by the publisher, sentences deprived of their sting by the printer.

Before 1848, though, repression was too inefficient to stifle writers, and Heine found ways to be more uninhibited than most other satirists. His palette was well stocked and colorful; his most sustained metaphor depicted his compatriots as a people asleep, with himself the drummer inciting them to action. Waking up "the poor German Michel," the archetype of the Teuton, was weary work. He would "tweak him by the nose to rouse him from his giant's sound slumbers"—in vain. "Once, in despair, I tried to set his nightcap on fire, but it was so damp with the sweat of thought that it merely smoked gently— and Michel smiled in his sleep."[12] While the French and the Russians owned the land and the British the sea, the Germans dominated the airy realm of dreams alone.[13]

Heine's brave self-definition as the noisy drummer was at best halfhearted. Irony, which often served him as a cover for political despair, shadowed his calls to battle. In one of his topical poems, "Bei des Nachtwächters Ankunft zu Paris," he visualized a German visitor in Paris begging a night watchman—a man who guards sleepers—for news of home, only to receive bland reassurances that all is going well. This, the visitor concludes, must mean that all is going badly. The Cologne cathedral, to Heine's mind the embodiment of medieval superstition, is being completed; the constitutions that German rulers have been promising their subjects for decades are treasures buried as deep as the gold of the Nibelungen; patriots boast that the Rhine, the international river, will remain German forever; there is even talk of building a navy. In the end, censorship will wither away of itself—but only after publishers have been outlawed. In the laughter that Heine's sarcasm is intended to provoke, warfare against private and public enemies, against the world and the self, have practically blended into one.

Heine's assaults document how satisfying an outlet satire could be for the aggression that is humor. It had been so for centuries; nineteenth-century satirists had a rich tradition to pillage. Their onslaughts oscillated between the coarsest lampoons and the subtlest dissections, between cheap, safe slanders and suave, sometimes risky, stabs at the ruling orders. As with the admired ancestors—Aristophanes, Juvenal, Erasmus, Swift, and of course Molière—so with writers in the decades from Heine to Shaw, the principal targets of comic pugnacity were social types no less than political institutions: the parvenu and the convert, the bureaucrat and the lawyer, the insider and the outsider. Speaking at Yale in 1888 upon receiving an honorary master's degree, Mark Twain said, a little gravely as befitted the occasion, "Ours is a useful trade, a worthy calling." With "all its lightness, and frivolity, it has one serious purpose, one aim, one specialty, and it is constant to it—the deriding of shams, the exposure of pretentious falsities, the laughing of stupid superstitions out of existence." The humorist who "is by instinct engaged in this sort of warfare is the natural enemy of royalties, nobilities, privileges and all kindred swindles, and the natural friend of human rights and human liberties."[14] Mark Twain's bellicose vocabulary was right for his point.

This was the century that spawned humor magazines, which generally included social and political commentary in their repertory. In France, fortunate in such impressive craftsmen as Daumier and Gavarni, political satirists battled against superior odds from the very launching of the July Monarchy. *Punch,* the most cited, most widely imitated magazine of them all, was founded in London in 1841; *Fun,* less political and more receptive to crude humor, also originated in London, twenty years later. Germans laughed at the often sophomoric jokes of Munich's *Fliegende Blätter,* which first appeared in 1845, and of Berlin's more liberal *Kladderadatsch,* one by-product of the effervescence of the 1848 revolutions. Not until 1896 did the country get the satirical weekly it so obviously needed—*Simplicissimus,* a heady mix of vitriolic cartoons and no less vitriolic poems.

This satirical parade did not leave the United States behind. By the 1880s, it had *Puck* and *Judge,* both deriving from European models but finding much of their own to lampoon in the insolent corruption of the Gilded Age. The country boasted a master political cartoonist, Thomas Nast, whose ferocious drawings in *Harper's Weekly,* targeting the politicians ruling New York City, had the force of moral retribution and even some political effect. His caricatures made Boss Tweed of Tammany Hall an emblem of political wickedness, as unmistakable as the celebrated pear with which Daumier had memorably fixed the image of King Louis Philippe. Nast's Tweed is grossly rotund, sporting an outsized diamond stickpin in his shirt. At times he is Falstaff, at times an improbable but recognizable vulture—"Let us *prey,*" he tells his cronies—and once, even more famously, he has a fat money bag for a head.

By no means all the sallies of *Judge* and *Kladderadatsch* displayed much civic courage, and the humor of *Punch* grew markedly more conservative with the passing years. Its caricatures depicting the Irish as apelike, murderous monsters, and the jibes in New York's *Puck* at the expense of East European Jewish immigrants were hits at lower-class butts that exposed publishers and their artists to no risk. And in years of international tension—from the late century on, most of the time—humor magazines often hawked patriotism, inflaming rather than analyzing public excitement; *Punch* and *Simplicissimus* rivaled one another in chauvinistic self-righteousness. At times, nineteenth-century humorists were not physicians to their society, but its panders.

Disseminated to an ever-widening public, the novel, that favorite Victorian bourgeois entertainment, joined in the sport of satirical aggression. Early in the twentieth century the brothers Mann—Thomas with his Homeric epithets, somewhat obtrusive symbolism, and subtle ironies, Heinrich with his slashing sarcasms against leaders and followers—showed how much damage bourgeois writers could do to their own class with the bite of wit. Novelists before them had already found the range, among them Theodor Fontane with his bracing yet somehow gentle portrayals of Berlin parvenus, and Eça de Queiroz with his telling, very French anatomies of Lisbon's high society. By the time Marcel Proust, just before the First World War, invented that unforgettable couple the Verdurins, almost indecently rich, painfully fashionable, half-educated, snobbish, intolerant, and invincible, the novel had long established itself as a flexible vehicle for devastating humor.

The most conscious satirical novelist of the age was doubtless Thackeray. After more than a decade of somewhat unfocused journalism, he became almost overnight the witty conscience of English society with his first novel, *Vanity Fair,* the masterpiece he never equaled. He more than once vehemently protested against makers of moralistic fiction. Sermons belonged in church, statistics on crime or politics in newspapers and government reports. When "a comic moralist" comes rushing at his readers, taking "occasion to tell us that society is diseased," they are likely to protest against this "literary ambuscadoe." That was in 1845. Still, two years later, sobered by financial reverses, the pathetic madness of his wife, and the sheer process of growing older, he set himself up, no less vehemently, as a teacher dedicated to improving his public as he entertained it. "Our profession seems to me to be as serious as the Parson's own."[15]

Suiting his new mood, Thackeray equipped *Vanity Fair* with the trappings of the sermon. Its very title recalls that influential seventeenth-century preacher John Bunyan. And for its subtitle he chose, as we know, the ominous "A Novel without a Hero," a subtitle especially pointed because it replaced the neutral "Pen and Pencil Sketches of English Society" Thackeray had used when *Vanity Fair* first appeared in monthly installments. In one of the moralizing commentaries that punctuate the book, he fiercely alluded to people "Faithless, Hopeless, Charityless" who "are living and flourishing in the world," and who invite the moralist's keenest attention. "Let us have at them, dear friends, with might and main." Too many "quacks and fools" are successful and "it was to combat and expose such as those, no doubt, that Laughter was made."[16] He had come to acknowledge—in fact, insist—that laughter is a serious matter.

Certainly, *Vanity Fair* relentlessly exhibits its graver dimensions. Thackeray introduces himself as "the Manager of the Performance," who looks out at Vanity Fair and is overcome by "a feeling of profound melancholy" as he surveys "the bustling place." There is much activity to record: eating, drinking, fighting, dancing, smoking, lovemaking, stealing. It is all very oppressive. There are moments of cheer and of kindness, but the prevalent atmosphere is more "melancholy than mirthful." The only remedy is the corrective of humor. But will it do its work? Thackeray rather doubts it. "Ah! *Vanitas Vanitatum!*" It is on this note that he closes his show. "Which of us is happy in this world? Which of us has his desire? or, having it, is satisfied?—Come, children, let us shut up the box and the puppets, for our play is played out."[17] Here, truly, is Harlequin whom Thackeray sent to the doctor for his melancholia. He is Thackeray, the humorist, himself.

Flaubert's *Madame Bovary*, though written not just to satirize but to capture contemporary reality, also gives house room to aggressive wit, serving as a vent for its author's bilious detestation of his fellow humans. Flaubert was plainly uneasy about the place of satire in his fiction. He was persuaded that the Enemy—the bourgeois of his time—was so awesome in his stupidity and self-absorption that ridiculing him would be an exercise in redundancy. An objective portrayal would be enough to damn him without appeal. At the same time, Flaubert's appetite for attack was too exigent to be assuaged by mere realistic reportage, however damaging. As with Heine, so with Flaubert, psychological needs intersected with, and supplied fuel to, cultural commentary. The egregious Homais, local pharmacist, village worthy and busybody, walking treasury of platitudes, who blossoms as Emma Bovary proceeds to her catastrophe, is Flaubert's most venomous invention. It was essential to his literary strategy to have Homais emerge triumphant at the end. With the stage emptied by suicide and death, Homais stands tall, decorated with the cross of the Legion of Honor. The portion of bitterness that Bergson saw in laughter pervades the whole. This is Flaubert's laughter at its most sardonic.

But elsewhere his acrimony is tinged with ambivalence. Witness Flaubert's

unfinished novel, *Bouvard et Pécuchet,* about two pathetic bourgeois who traverse the wide world of middle-class clichés and half-educated ineptitude.
Since his youth, Flaubert had been collecting foolish and dogmatic commonplaces characteristic of the French bourgeois, and his last novel dramatizes the
Dictionnaire des idées reçues he apparently planned to incorporate into the second
volume, which he never wrote. His protagonists are two middle-aged copy
clerks—Parisians, be it noted, for in Flaubert's jaundiced perception, a bourgeois did not have to be a provincial to be stupid—who meet by chance and,
discovering affinities of taste, become fast friends. Conveniently coming into
money, they invest in a retirement house in Normandy, planning to devote the
rest of their days to catching up with the changing times and conquering the
world of knowledge. Having led lives of stifling routine, they now want to taste
the freedom that money and leisure have bestowed on them. They take up in
turn gardening, farming, distilling, chemistry, medicine, archaeology, sexual
love, metaphysics, religion, education, and fail spectacularly, yet somehow poignantly, over and over. The pratfalls Flaubert thinks up for them are an embarrassing vaudeville. Finally, grown old, the pair decide to return to their copying, the one thing they ever really learned.

   This satire is so devastating in its mordant detail that *Bouvard et Pécuchet* suffers
as literature while Flaubert displays his ingenuity and indulges his spleen. The
heroes are bourgeois stick figures, predictable victims, uncritically mouthing
received wisdom. Yet, as close readers have long noted, Flaubert partially subverted his intention of satirically exposing bourgeois idiocy in all its splendor.
As they lurch from disaster to disaster with their experiments and their attempts
at book learning, the two gain some perspective on their enterprise and some
insights into their society. They are no longer so gullible as they were when
they started their crusade for universal learning, no longer stupid enough to
miss the point that others are quite as stupid. It is as though a measure of serenity
had come to Flaubert's rescue, allowing him to forgive, if halfheartedly, the
characters he had invented in the most implacable spirit. His lifelong campaign
against the bourgeoisie faltered. Not without affection, mixing a touch of love
into his diet of hate, he called his butts "my idiots."[18] They were *his* idiots.

   Charles Dickens, a far more self-conscious humorist than Flaubert, commanded far greater resources of laughter. His comic portrayals, which lend his
novels much of their vitality, encompass both extremes in Freud's categories of
humor, the harmless and the tendentious. As his inimitable caricatures evolved
from the heartiness of the *Pickwick Papers* to the caustic sarcasm that darkens the
later novels from *Bleak House* onward, some of his attentive, generally admiring, reviewers wondered whether this progression constituted progress. With

characters like Sam Weller in *Pickwick* and Mr. Micawber in *David Copperfield,* they told Dickens, he had been most at home, spreading nothing but cheer; with such unrelieved human catastrophes as the neurotic capitalist Mr. Merdle in *Little Dorrit,* those hollow social climbers the Veneerings in *Our Mutual Friend,* and the rest of his cast of snobs, parasites, and hypocrites, Dickens had invaded the sober precincts of social criticism, alien terrain for him. In truth, the early genial Dickens was not quite so consistently good-tempered, the late Dickens not quite so morose, as superficial readings would suggest. He had already made resentful, tendentious jokes in *Pickwick* and would still make cheerful and innocent ones in *Our Mutual Friend*.

In short, while Dickens's aggressive use of humor intensified from the 1830s to the 1860s, his comic techniques never fundamentally changed. From the apprentice *Sketches by Boz* on, whether aiming to divert or to dismay, he regaled his vast public with ludicrous and menacing types springing to life with unduplicable facial tics, turns of speech, or modes of dress. Dickens hammered them into the reader's awareness by lavishing Homeric epithets on them and piling up clusters of adjectives. His sketch of the "bran-new" Veneerings, with its incessant reiteration of "new" until it sounds like a curse word, is justly famous.* Obviously Dickens intended with his catalogue of their bran-newness to strike at more than a single pair of detestable individuals; the Veneerings represent a prominent and socially destructive type. As Molière's Tartuffe is hypocrisy incarnate, so Dickens's newly rich couple still smelling of varnish stand for a modern social menace, the parvenu. The road from Dickens's Veneerings to Proust's Verdurins is short and straight.

To the end, Dickens's comic imagination continued to give pleasure, and the worlds he made retained extravagant touches of farce and melodrama. But as he discovered ever more grounds for anger and dismay, the balance of his satirical portrayals shifted from benign to hostile; distasteful, even hateful, specimens of folly and vice, etched in acid, elbowed their way toward center stage. In *Martin Chuzzlewit,* the youthful novel that his contemporaries declared to be his most

---

*"Mr. and Mrs. Veneering were bran-new people in a bran-new house in a bran-new quarter of London. Everything about the Veneerings was spick and span new. All their furniture was new, all their friends were new, their plate was new, their carriage was new, their harness was new, their horses were new, their pictures were new, they themselves were new, they were as newly married as was lawfully compatible with their having a bran-new baby." These sorry travesties of humanity boast, too, a new coat of arms and a "grand pianoforte with the new action"; and as becomes such freshly minted creatures, they keep everything, including themselves, "in a state of high varnish and polish." Of course they are precisely mirrored in their new furniture: "The surface smelt a little too much of the workshop and was a trifle sticky." Charles Dickens, *Our Mutual Friend* (1865; ed. Charles Dickens the Younger, 1908), 5–6 [book I, ch. 2].

hilarious, Dickens poured out samples of both types. On one side, Sairy Gamp, tippling, garrulous, with her imaginary companion Mrs. Harris and her mangled words of wisdom, is delightfully herself; on the other, Seth Pecksniff, schemer, plagiarist, orchestrator of scenes with himself cast as the hero, exemplifies the tribe of victimizers who reap what they have not sown.

Pecksniff is a gift to the student of aggressive feelings. Oleaginous, self-righteous, aggressive behind the guise of the benevolent martyr, a fraud to his fingertips, Pecksniff is a candidate for vengeful counteraggression, for delightful poetic justice. Hablot K. Browne—"Phiz"—drawing the climactic scene in which old Martin Chuzzlewit, at last alerted to Pecksniff's machinations, beats him to the ground with his cane, showed two books next to the fallen rhetorician: *Paradise Lost* and *Le Tartuffe*. Dickens, seconded by his illustrator, has transfigured the fate of an individual into a rather obvious moral allegory. To underscore his lessons, and anticipating Expressionist drama by half a century, Dickens at times identified his characters by their profession alone; in *Little Dorrit,* the financier Mr. Merdle entertains "Bishop magnates, Treasury magnates, Horse Guard magnates, Admiralty magnates"—potentates who speak only as "Bishop," as "Horse Guards," as "Treasury."[19] This making of abstractions, too, is aggression in action.

Dickens was a novelist, not a writer of tracts; his imagination took fire from characters in dramatic action. While he used individuals as representatives of types, he never slighted their distinctive characteristics; and obeying the same impulse for the concrete, Dickens endowed the institutions he detested with the qualities of real people. The Circumlocution Office in *Little Dorrit,* that bureaucratic maze incarnating the ideal of "HOW NOT TO DO IT," virtually achieves the stature of a character in its own right. It receives, digests, and generates a vast number of letters, petitions, memoranda (Dickens conscientiously enumerated each of them with chilling effect), all with the settled purpose of solving no problems, finding no solutions, relieving no distress.[20]

The Circumlocution Office is worse than torpor; it is designed to ward off all action whatever, with paralysis its fondest desire. The death drive institutionalized, it frustrates those few bureaucrats ready to break the mold and do something. So vividly realized is this odious creature, that it seems an act of supererogation on Dickens's part to introduce some of the personages employed in the impenetrable fortress that houses it. The ominously named Barnacles are the Circumlocution Office writ small; "sprightly" young Ferdinand Barnacle, who acts as the amused, and amusing, spokesman for his clan and its obstructionism, tells the hero of *Little Dorrit* with ingratiating candor why petitions never get anywhere and justice never gets done. His Office exists "with the express intention that everything shall be left alone. That is what it means. That is what it's for. No doubt there's a certain form to be kept up that it's for something else, but it's only a form. Why, good Heaven, we are nothing but forms! Think what a lot of our forms you have gone through."[21] Dickens, the enraged humorist spinning out this lampoon of modern bureaucracy, was all the more effective—and, some of his critics thought, all the more unfair—because he refused to be solemn.

The most satisfying match Dickens arranged between individual and type is probably Mr. Podsnap in *Our Mutual Friend.* Podsnap incorporates the most grievous of the defects infesting the respectable of his day: arrogance, insincerity, parochialism, philistinism. He is so self-assured that he is impervious to humorous deflation; he prospers right to the end of the novel. But from a psychoanalytic perspective, Podsnap seems highly neurotic, sporting symptoms that throw a lurid light on a society sick enough to tolerate, even to honor and reward, such a narcissist. Uncertain where he ends and the world begins, he has delusions of omnipotence. As a very rich and "eminently respectable man, Mr. Podsnap was sensible of its being required of him to take Providence under his protection. Consequently he always knew exactly what Providence meant. Inferior and less respectable men might fall short of that mark, but Mr. Podsnap was always up to it. And it was very remarkable (and must have been very comfortable) that what Providence meant, was invariably what Mr. Podsnap meant." He recognizes people and regions outside his boundaries—engaged as he is in "commerce with other countries" he can scarcely do less—but writes them off as congenitally inferior. Foreign countries are "a mistake"; Englishness is the supreme commendation in his vocabulary; the arts and literature at their best confirm his pedantic and ignorant excellence.[22]

Probably Dickens was only dimly aware that this caricature had clinical implications. But he showed the patient in action. Mr. Podsnap is obsessively regular in his habits, almost a living machine. He displays the kind of mechanical response to human exigencies that Bergson would later distinguish as a crucial ingredient in the comic: "The world got up at eight, shaved close at a quarter-past, breakfasted at nine, went to the City at ten, came home at half-past five, and dined at seven."[23] Whatever Dickens may have sensed, Mr. Podsnap certainly has no inkling that his conduct shows him to be a sick man; even more than other specimens in Dickens's cabinet of moral monsters, he is the prince of deniers. Unpalatable English realities on which foreigners and social reformers like to harp—poverty, oppression, injustice, indifference—do not exist; Mr. Podsnap waves them away with an expansive gesture. Subjects he does not want to see debated have a way of vanishing. "Happily acquainted with his own merit and importance, Mr. Podsnap settled that whatever he put behind him he put out of existence." He would say, "I don't want to know about it; I don't choose to discuss it; I don't admit it!"[24]

Podsnap's most memorable quality though, certainly the aspect of Podsnappery to enjoy the most enduring reputation, is his ostentatious prudishness. His daughter, almost eighteen when the Podsnaps enter *Our Mutual Friend*, continually reminds her father by her presumed fragility, her very existence, that "the question about everything was, would it bring a blush into the cheek of the young person?" The question is censorious but, as few have failed to notice, highly suspect: "There appeared to be no line of demarcation between the young person's excessive innocence, and another person's guiltiest knowledge."[25] Like other self-appointed guardians of propriety in fiction and fact, Podsnap deploys prudery as a more or less transparent guise for barely suppressed lechery.[26]

This strategy is most interesting to the historian of aggressive humor in nineteenth-century middle-class culture, for, ironically enough, while Dickens invented him to pillory an abhorrent exception in that culture, Podsnap has been distorted by critics of the bourgeoisie into its most typical emblem. In part, Dickens was himself responsible for this misreading. Did he not make sure that none of his writings would bring a blush to the cheek of the young person? Satirists of the bourgeoisie at times displayed the very failings they found unpardonable in their own class. Despite such inconsistencies, Dickens enlisted his aggressive humor in a moralistic campaign aimed at breaking through polished surfaces to reach—and perhaps correct—the evils of character and the vices of society he thought lurked beneath. That goal made him a representative Victorian. Most humorists of his day often behaved more like pastors than like physicians.

3. The Victim as Executioner

In December 1831, a lithograph appeared in Paris titled *Gargantua*. A vitriolic comment on the favoritism rampant in the recently installed regime of Louis Philippe, it was almost as coarse in its draftsmanship as in its message. The three Glorious Days that had brought him to the throne the previous July had quickly turned sour. In *Gargantua,* the king's enormously swollen figure, easily recognizable, sits in an armchair that is only too evidently a *chaise percée*. Heavily laden lackeys on a long steep ramp are carrying up to his grotesquely distended mouth quantities of gold pieces—the tribute extorted bit by bit from the submissive working poor, from ragged and crippled veterans. Swallowing and digesting these precious morsels, Louis Philippe is converting them, as they drop from what one writer delicately called "the lower orifices of his person," into medals, honors, and patents of nobility. To point up this corrupt linkage, plain to all but the most obtuse, the lithographer has drawn the Royal Exchange in the left background and Versailles on the right. And at bottom left, he has boldly inscribed his signature: "H. Daumier."[1]

When he committed himself to this aggressive strike, Daumier was just twenty-three, but no longer a raw beginner. Born in 1808 in Marseilles, he was raised and educated in Paris. Enjoying the company of other aspiring painters and sculptors as he copied plaster casts and masterpieces in the Louvre, he absorbed radical ideas with a quiet intensity that disconcerted his more ebullient fellows. He was soon going his own way, singularly fortunate in his chosen medium, lithography, still relatively new when he mastered it; the prepared stone permitted rapid, accurate, and cheap reproductions and thus proved convenient for a cartoonist responding to the news of the day. Daumier wanted to do more, and did more; whenever he could afford the time, he painted. But the satirical lithograph, whether inspired by bureaucratic chicanery, professional deformations, or marital squabbles, was his bread and butter. His alertness to the passing scene was acute; "one must be of one's time"—one of the few aphorisms reliably ascribed to him—was a claim for the aesthetic dignity of contemporary themes that Baudelaire, Manet, and Zola would echo in his lifetime. This small but influential fraternity of artists and writers saw the bourgeois as a figure of fun, a crafty menace—and an admirable maker of modernity.

By 1830, the year of revolution, Daumier still had much drawing to do before he would achieve his superb characterizations and the flowing line that gave him immortality. But the heady events and their disillusioning aftermath provided irresistible material, and Daumier set about translating his democratic convictions and his rage at corruption, cynicism, and oppression into political commentary. The revolution of 1830, we know, was fought in large measure over the freedom of the press, and the July Monarchy at first presented itself as hospitable to the open expression of opinion; the Charter of 1830 explicitly affirmed constitutional guarantees. But the honeymoon was short. Legislation in October waved the threat of fines and jury trials at offending journalists, and left the boundaries of freedom undefined. Legitimist polemicists on the right, like republicans on the left, tested those boundaries by savaging the regime, and the government actions against them attest to their daring miscalculations.

Daumier could flourish in this atmosphere. Charles Philipon, a minor painter and major journalistic entrepreneur, offered him steady work, first on the weekly sheet *La Caricature,* launched in November 1830, and later on the longer-lived daily *Le Charivari.* An audacious and irreconcilable republican, Philipon surrounded himself with talent and generated ideas for disrespectful cartoons; an ingenious inventor of political symbols, he discovered the telling resemblance of Louis Philippe's head to a pear and inspired Daumier to translate that bottom-heavy fruit into a devastating representation of the king. Foreshadowed in *Gargantua* and soon to become a staple in *Le Charivari,* the *poire,* savory with its slang meaning—"simpleton"—was the handy emblem of disenchantment translated into furious wit.

Not surprisingly, the purveyors of such wit faced prosecution upon prosecution. In its first years, the July Monarchy seems to have brought no fewer than 520 suits against the press, and Philipon's *La Caricature,* during its five-year existence, had to endure ten of these, and more than a score of confiscations. For Daumier, such dangers only lent zest; Philipon was a man to his taste, the inspired collaborator. One of Daumier's first topical cartoons, of December 1830, shows the king as a shepherd guarded by heavily armed soldier-dogs, shearing his docile sheep, the French people. It is a symptom of just how deep Daumier's—and Philipon's—disaffection ran only a few months after Louis Philippe's accession. The Charter of 1830, Thomas Love Peacock would say with pardonable exaggeration, looking back from 1836, "turned out a lie, and 'the best of republics' the beginning of the vilest and most sordid of tyrannies."[2]

By the time Philipon launched *Le Charivari* in December 1832, Daumier had been out of circulation for three months. *Gargantua* had been too much for the authorities. They promptly confiscated the print, and since he kept up his barrage against them with lithographs no less offensive even if far less scatological, they moved early in 1832 to try Daumier, his distributor, and his printer. Conviction of all three was a matter of course, and the sentence stiff: six months in prison, a fine of five hundred francs, and costs. The charge was "instigating hatred, contempt for the royal regime, and insulting the person of the king." These counts are an accurate description of the print but not of Daumier's taste. As students of his art have long noted, the grossness of *Gargantua,* and the literary allusion to Rabelais's outsized glutton, were rare in Daumier's work; the idea must have originated in his intimate political circle, perhaps from Philipon himself, from a fellow draftsman like the caricaturist Grandville, or from their intermittent collaborator Balzac.

Whatever the history of *Gargantua,* Philipon took it under his protective wing and secured it wide publicity. With affecting pathos he retailed the scene of Daumier's arrest "under the eyes of his father and mother, whose sole support he is"; with transparent innocence and mock piety, he described the print only to wonder how anyone could have mistaken the obese lump on the *chaise percée* for the distinguished personage of the French king.[3] But as we have just seen, this Voltairian tactic, confirmation by denial, though amusing in its way, did not save Daumier or Philipon from prison. Sainte Pélagie, where inconvenient opponents of the regime were held, was a meeting place for like-minded spirits more than a cruel place of confinement—if one was lucky enough to have thoughtful friends, robust health, and supplies of money. But it was damp and disagreeable, and a portent of worse to come.

Almost inevitably, then, for Daumier and Philipon the liberty to speak and draw, quite as much as the general course of the July Monarchy, became principal concerns. In a famous lithograph of 1834, *Don't Meddle with It!*, Daumier showed a sturdy printer, his hands made into powerful fists, standing on a broad rock marked "Freedom of the Press" and frowning at the threatening figure of what must be Louis Philippe. But the rock was crumbling; the government used every possible legal and administrative device to harass opposition journalists and publishers. It closed newspapers, confiscated prints, fined editors, and at times sent the lot to jail.

Journalists were not the only casualties of repression. In 1834, the government sent troops into Lyons to crush a strike, and then brutally suppressed a local rising in Paris called in sympathy for the casualties in Lyons. The massacre inspired one of Daumier's most enduring protests, *Rue Transnonain,* in which he abandoned humor altogether. With stark directness, he showed a disheveled bedroom with four bodies strewn about; the central figure is a father lying on top of his slain baby, bathed in blood. When the government proceeded to try, not the troops, but some of the insurrectionists, Daumier countered with another famous lithograph, portraying the threat to free speech in a different forum—a court of justice. The judge, viciously smiling, is in the chair; the scales, symbols of judicial evenhandedness, are askew; in the background, a victim has his head on the block and the executioner hovers near, axe in hand; in front is a defendant, his arms cruelly twisted by three toughs behind him. And the judge, holding out his hand in a gesture caricaturing reasonableness, tells the gagged and brutalized figure before him, "Go ahead, you are free to speak, you have the floor." Daumier was a sound prophet; in 1835, the government replaced its improvisations in repressiveness with precise edicts. An attempt on the king's life provided an excuse for laws that reintroduced censorship of the press, increased fines, facilitated convictions, and explicitly included in their purview sketches, engravings, lithographs, and all other forms of graphic representation. This was literally the end of *La Caricature,* but not the end of Philipon or Daumier.

Political satire, wit at its most wounding, engages entrenched enemies on a heavily defended but often fog-shrouded frontier. When a society pretends to even a shred of civility—and in the bourgeois century, most societies did—it is hard to predict just where or when oppositional humor will overstep the bounds of propriety or of the law. Thus, in Daumier's France in the early 1830s, which cartoon or poem would generate harassment or prosecution depended on the anxiety or servility of some public official, on the susceptibility of a crowned head to journalistic deflation, on the degree of tension pervading the domestic scene or diplomatic maneuverings. Only in 1835, with the new laws, did the July Monarchy clearly, and very firmly, draw the line between legitimate comment and impious slander, permissible criticism and insurrectionist incitement.

This spelled not the death of aggressive political humor in France, but its subtler management. Though the person of Louis Philippe was now sacrosanct, and politicians had ammunition enough to revenge themselves on their tormentors, the political elite of the July Monarchy remained a provocative target, not wholly taboo, for the exercise of biting wit. In 1836, adopting a suggestion of the ever-fertile Philipon, Daumier launched scores of lithographs using a familiar stage character, Robert Macaire, as their dubious hero. Appearing in widely assorted guises, Macaire stood, for the rebels, as the personification of the age. Speculator, auctioneer, banker, investor, lawyer, social lion, mercenary lover, fraudulent bankrupt, Daumier's Macaire is a grafter and a liar, an immoralist and a cynic, a most unprincipled trader and real-estate operator, a swindler to end all swindlers: the July Monarchy in person.

This was political wit by indirection, harder to censor than a direct challenge but less trenchant in its message. The government's sensitivity compelled Daumier to explore untried, not wholly welcome, avenues for his talents. During the dozen or so years that the July Monarchy lingered on, he developed popular series of prints that poured tame sarcasm over good bourgeois in bed or on holiday, over lawyers in complacent triumph or no less complacent defeat, over street crowds, provincials visiting Paris, theater audiences. In 1848, after the February Revolution had forced Louis Philippe from the throne, Daumier, the ex-king's great scourge, told the writer Champfleury that he was tired of attacking the king, now in ignominious exile. "An editor has commissioned a series, but I can't do it." Champfleury appreciated such gallantry: "In the midst of battle, under the pressure of political events, Daumier had employed pardonable weapons. But he considered them despicable against a defeated man."[4] No doubt, Daumier was a generous opponent. But he also discovered after February 1848 what many wielders of aggressive humor learn sooner or later: they need real targets for their arrows.

Daumier was only human. While he generally aimed his venom at those in a position to hurt him, he shared enough accepted prejudices to seek out victims far less capable of retaliating than Louis Philippe. His series directed against liberated women allied him with the very forces he had expended his sharpest wit to combat; he ridiculed bluestockings, advocates of the right to divorce, and female socialists. These new women appear under his pitiless pencil as harridans, supremely unattractive and irrational, noisy, demanding, obtrusive; they exploit their husbands as most contemporaries expected husbands to exploit their wives. Humorous aggression, we know only too well, may explode in almost any direction, and choose easy, defenseless targets as well as those who can strike back. Sadistic, aggressive humor, like an anti-Semitic joke told in times of Jewish suffering, amply attests to that.

Daumier, then, was a man of his time. But not only in his prejudices. Baudelaire hailed him as a subtle teacher instructing his fellows to laugh at themselves, a wise man and a satirist whose energetic depictions of evil and its consequences only demonstrated the goodness of his heart.* This was beautifully said, and surely the witty moralist aspiring to set up as physician to his society, must feel free to take all of human weakness for his province. But one cannot help wondering how much more Daumier would have concentrated his aggressions on the regime and the profiteers of his society if the laws of 1835 had not been passed and for years humorlessly enforced. The power of governmental repression prevents a nation from getting the aggressive political humor it deserves. Rather, it will get the humorous aggression its rulers can tolerate.

British political culture, too, experienced this tense conflict between the need for witty moralists and the ability to stand them. While it had no Daumier, Britain had somewhat gentler critics of its own, gentler not just because the country would not permit so harsh an indictment as *Rue Transnonain,* but because there was less need for it. Britain, it is true, was no stranger to the severe repression of humor which the authorities perceived to be blasphemous, libelous, or obscene. Nor was it a stranger to ferocious wit. It had enjoyed—if that is the right word—an outpouring of venomous political satire since the days of the French Revolution, and, to a more modest extent, even before. For sheer scurrility and grossness, James Gillray, moralizing in the sewer around the end

---

*Baudelaire was thinking in part of Daumier's irreverent treatment of Greek myths. Daumier's Agamemnon, Penelope, Narcissus, and the rest are flabby, middle-aged, thoroughly unheroic bourgeois or sensitive anorexic youths. Perhaps the most telling of these portrayals, *Menelaus Triumphant,* depicts Helen's cuckolded husband as a self-important, paunchy king striding along, bloody sword in hand, while the heavyset, fortyish Helen on his arm slightly behind him thumbs her nose at her boastful spouse. These lithographs, lampooning fashionable neoclassicism on the stage and on canvas and, at the same time, ill-bred obtuseness and self-conceit, are supreme documents in the gallery of nineteenth-century bourgeois self-criticism. Offenbach could not have done the deflation any better. This rude series Baudelaire thought "amusing and useful blasphemy," and he linked Daumier with Molière. "L'École paienne" (1852), *Oeuvres complètes,* ed. Y. G. LeDantec, rev. Claude Pichois (1961), 625; see also "Quelques Caricaturistes français" (1857), ibid., 1006–7. Baudelaire's poem "Vers pour le portrait de M. Honoré Daumier" dates from May 25–26, 1865. Ibid., 151.

of the eighteenth century, was unsurpassed. But Victorians found the decorous wit of George Cruikshank more appropriate. They liked the relatively benign assaults on snobs in Thackeray's prose and John Leech's drawings, and the mocking observations on social lions and sensitive creatures that were George du Maurier's specialty.

Victorian critical humor, then, was far from anemic; Cruikshank's sharply etched commentaries on morals and manners in the novels and comic almanacs he illustrated, contrasted the beauty of goodness, decency, and temperance with the corresponding, only too endemic vices. Douglas Jerrold, taking on political abuses in the early radical days of *Punch,* had a controlled vigor of his own. Dickens, we have seen, permitted himself satirical outbursts as savage as anything in Daumier, and around the turn of the century, Shaw harnessed his political rage to witty assaults on hypocrisy. "Man measures his strength by his destructiveness," the devil says in *Man and Superman.* "What is his religion? An excuse for hating me. What is his law? An excuse for hanging you. What is his morality? Gentility! an excuse for consuming without producing. What is his art? An excuse for gloating over pictures of slaughter. What are his politics? Either the worship of a despot because a despot can kill, or parliamentary cock-fighting."[5] But more typically, Victorian political satire was restrained, fantastic rather than furious. It invited knowing smiles more than righteous wrath.

This was the response that W. S. Gilbert aimed at after graduating from the Bab ballads. In his early work he had been quite unpolitical. But with *The Happy Land,* a satire of 1873, he entered a domain of disagreeable hazards and uncertain rewards. After the work had played to good houses for three days, the lord chamberlain closed it down. He was only doing his duty; in Britain the stage, unlike the press, labored under the constraints of censorship. The Theatres Act of 1843 specified that the lord chamberlain, having read the script, could refuse to license a play offensive to "good Manners, Decorum," or, for that matter, "the public Peace." The examiners who did the real work of reading were reined in by the vaguest of guidelines; plays portraying biblical characters, encouraging immorality, extolling vice, or parodying public figures were candidates for suppression. So imprecise a list could serve almost any prejudice, satisfy the most prudish of Podsnaps.

Hence the examiners' decisions, from which there was no appeal, were often capricious. A few of their verdicts could be anticipated, and after a time playwrights, producers, and theater owners learned the inclinations of the official who held their fate—or, to put it less portentously, their profits—in his hands. In the short autobiographical account that W. S. Gilbert published in 1883, when his most adroit political operetta, *Iolanthe,* was enjoying gratifying public acclaim, he recalled an incident that had marred his adaptation for the stage of Dickens's *Great Expectations:* in the line where Magwitch, the convict, tells Pip, "Here you are, in chambers fit for a Lord," the last two words were struck out and "Heaven" substituted "in pencil!"—presumably because "Lord" might be taken in a blasphemous sense.[6]

Avant-garde dramatists, like most cultivated playgoers, found the censors petty, philistine, sadly uninformed about the direction of modern drama. But censorship had its defenders, and not among the prissy or the unofficial guardians of morality alone. At parliamentary hearings in 1866 and again in 1909, the Theatres Act was eloquently supported by a curious alliance of devout publicists, theater owners, and even some playwrights. The first were vigilant in behalf of propriety; the second trusted that once a play had been licensed it would be safe from prosecution; the third were persuaded that dramatic representations have a more powerful impact on their audiences than do novels or paintings. The subversiveness of aggressive humor was by no means universally applauded.

Gilbert himself, though an occasional victim, did not support the abolition of the lord chamberlain's authority over the drama.[7] True, in some encore verses he wrote for Ko-Ko's famous song in *The Mikado* about the little list of nuisances one could do without, he included "all dramatic censors."[8] But his troubles over *The Happy Land* had been relatively trivial. In that play, Gilbert and a collaborator had broadly caricatured Gladstone, then prime minister, and two of his unpopular ministers, for presumed cowardice and betrayal of aristocratic principles. As a fairly consistent conservative, Gilbert was impatient with the Liberals' pacific foreign policy and their efforts to realize some of the democratic implications of civil service reform. His lampoon of Gladstone was a Tory's revenge, and being transparent, it violated the censor's prohibition against portraying living figures on the stage.* The public response to the lord chamberlain's action was predictable: critics of the ban ascribed it to partisan maneuvers placating the Liberal cabinet; its supporters were annoyed at Gilbert's lampoon of the prime minister. The press rehearsed once again the old question of whether the government's intervention was a valid exercise of

---

*Later, Gilbert learned to be more prudent—marginally so. Writing *H. M. S. Pinafore,* he intended to lampoon W. H. Smith, first lord of the Admiralty, in the comical incompetent character Sir Joseph Porter. Telling Arthur Sullivan on December 27, 1877, about the "splendid song" that could be written for this figure, he declared that he would introduce "no *personality.*" After all, "the fact that the First Lord in the opera is a *radical* of the most pronounced type will do away with any suspicion that W. H. Smith is intended." Of course, the ruse deceived no one—except perhaps the censors. Letter reproduced in Frederic Woodbridge Wilson, *An Introduction to the Gilbert and Sullivan Operas from the Collection of the Pierpont Morgan Library* (1989), 98.

power or an affront to the rights of freeborn Englishmen. Little happened; the authors slightly toned down the satire of Gladstone, and *The Happy Land* was allowed to reopen after a one-night hiatus. The solemn debate had enhanced the play's drawing power; it ran for seven months.

Aggressive political satire, then, was at some risk in Britain, at least on the stage. Yet in his historic collaboration with Arthur Sullivan, Gilbert made fun of virtually every institution of British political life—except the Queen. In 1882, the two reached the summit of their satire in *Iolanthe,* a fairy tale decorated with political patter songs and choruses that soon emancipated themselves from the operetta to achieve a certain immortality of their own. At the premiere, Gladstone, prime minister once again, was in the audience, as were the Prince of Wales and other glittering personages. All of them apparently enjoyed themselves hugely. The *Pall Mall Gazette* reported "enthusiastic acclamations" and indignation at "unnecessary applause" that disrupted the pleasure of close listening. Most reviewers liked *Iolanthe* very much, though some compared it a little unfavorably to those pieces of perfection *Patience* and *H. M. S. Pinafore.* Nearly all praised the acting as capital and most of the music as delightful.[9]

What mattered most was Gilbert's political wit, brilliantly pointed up by Sullivan's supremely apt score. Approving reviewers found *Iolanthe* cynical, scoffing, alive with irony and irreverence, and, we note, particularly popular with the upper bourgeoisie. They also remarked that it was aggressive. "Every shot told," wrote the *Pall Mall Gazette.* Only a handful felt uncomfortable with the squibs directed against respectable officials and no less respectable institutions; delighted audiences laughed heartily at the highly susceptible chancellor, the sheeplike members of Parliament voting as their leaders tell them to, the peers who serve their country best by doing nothing, and

> do not itch
> To interfere with matters which
> they do not understand.

In a long, thoughtful discussion in *The Theatre,* William Beatty-Kingston noted that Gilbert had introduced "pathos and politics" into *Iolanthe,* and that his passion "smacks of anger" while his politics were proving "bitterly aggressive."[10] This was well said; bourgeois aggression is written all over this fairy opera.

Where were the censors? It is true that Gilbert's lyrics credit men of blue blood with moral qualities usually reserved for the honest poor; true, too, that after the first night Gilbert and Sullivan decided to drop two political songs, one expressing a measure of sympathy for unfortunate slum dwellers, the other

Bab [W. S. Gilbert], "Gentle Alice Brown," *Bab Ballads* (1869). Typical of Gilbert's humor through total and startling incongruity: gentle Alice is the tough daughter of an Italian robber.

Bab [W. S. Gilbert], "The Yarn of the 'Nancy Bell'," *Bab Ballads* (1869). The garrulous elderly sailor (shades of Coleridge's ancient mariner!) describes himself as cook, captain, mate, bo'sun, midshipman, and crew of the captain's gig: stranded with these shipmates after a wreck, he had eaten them all.

THE IRISH FRANKENSTEIN

"The baneful and blood-stained Monster . . . . yet was it not my Master to the very extent that it was my Creature? . . . . Had I not breathed into it my spirit?" . . . . (*Extract from the Works of C. S. P-rn-ll, M.P.*)

John Tenniel, "The Irish Frankenstein," *Punch* (1882). The Irish politician Charles Stewart Parnell as Frankenstein crouches in horror before the monster he has made; it has stooped to political assassination.

Heinrich Heine as a poet in France. Engraving (1827) by Ludwig Grimm.

THE " BRAINS "

Thomas Nast, "The 'Brains,' " *Harper's Weekly* (1871). One of Nast's most celebrated renderings of William M. "Boss" Tweed of Tammany Hall.

Thomas Nast, "A Group of Vultures Waiting for the Storm to 'Blow Over.'—'Let Us *Prey*' " *Harper's Weekly* (1871). An equally famous assault: Tammany Hall in trouble.

Wilhelm Busch, *Eduards Traum* (1891). Note the "surgeon's" sadistic intensity.

Wilhelm Busch, "What comes from above is not always a good thing," *Fliegende Blätter* (1861).

Wilhelm Busch, "Das Pusterohr," *Über Land und Meer* (1868). Extreme retaliation, the punishment far exceeding the boy's crime of pestering a comfortable old man with his blowgun.

Wilhelm Busch, *Fipps, der Affe* (1879). An animal as the aggressor.

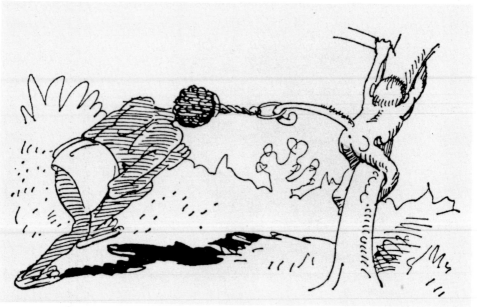

Wilhelm Busch, *Fipps, der Affe* (1879). More of the same.

Wilhelm Busch,
"Der Bauer und
sein Schwein,"
*Münchener Bilder-
bogen* (1862).
Cruel realism.

Wilhelm Busch, *Balduin Bählamm, der verhinderte Dichter*
(1883). The joys of dentistry without anesthesia.

"Happy New Year! The snipe were first rate." Wilhelm
Busch to "Nanda" Kessler, a young friend he had known
since her childhood (December 24, 1896). The drawing
represents a dream of Busch's, in which an angel pissed on
his tongue.

Wilhelm Busch, self-portrait (1894),
at age sixty-two.

**Und hilflos und mit Angstgewimmer
Verkohlt dies fromme Frauenzimmer.**

Wilhelm Busch, *Die Fromme Helene* (1872).
This is more than mischievousness: women,
too, Busch suggests, can be sadists.

**Hier sieht man ihre Trümmer rauchen.
Der Rest ist nicht mehr zu gebrauchen.**

Wilhelm Busch, *Die Fromme Helene* (1872).
"Pious Helen," who has even had an affair and
illegitimate twins with Cousin Franz, a priest,
drinks herself into a stupor and burns herself
to death.

Honoré Daumier, "Past, Present, and Future," *La Caricature* (1834). King Louis Philippe as a pear.

Honoré Daumier, "You have the floor, explain yourself," *La Caricature* (1835). Angry and self-explanatory.

Honoré Daumier, "The mother is in the heat of composition; the child is in the water of the tub," *Les Bas bleus* (1844). For all his radicalism, Daumier was no feminist.

Charles Booth, social researcher.

decrying snobbery in tones more acidulous than those of the songs that survived. But the decision to slim down *Iolanthe* seems to have been prompted by the wish to speed up the action rather than by fear of the lord chamberlain's wrath.[11] Where, then, were the censors?

Doubtless the immunity of *Iolanthe* had many causes. By the early 1880s, Gilbert and Sullivan had become something of an English institution, solid favorites among the upright theater-going public as purveyors of melodious, amusing, and clean entertainment. The social ties that both librettist and composer had successfully cultivated also did no harm. While neither their popularity nor their connections, so vividly dramatized by the first-night audience, were guarantees of impunity, they did reduce the threat of censorious intervention. Even more important, despite their sensitivity to what the pure in heart might consider blasphemous or obscene or too personal, Britain's ruling orders were less anxious than those of continental regimes. Buoyed up by a sense of security about the middling orders, they could cheerfully listen to the polite and lively lampoons that *Iolanthe* offered. Their worries lay elsewhere, with the remote—but, they thought, sinister—threat of mob violence.

Gilbert's satirical verses document the ambiguity that haunts much aggressive humor.[12] On the one hand, it supplied a vent for feelings and convictions not easily voiced in sober seriousness, and offered aid to the work of protest, even of rebellion. On the other hand, by making the protest lighthearted, the humorist removed some of its sting. The assaults of some implacable wits apart, humor soothes spirits as it rouses them; it splendidly illustrates the double meaning inherent in "the cultivation of hatred." To be sure, humor that cuts to the bone—the wit of a Daumier at his most pugnacious—puts the emphasis on the hatred rather than the cultivation. But Gilbert's humor was, when all is said, quite benign. It did not invite radical political reflection, let alone radical political action. Like Captain Corcoran, the well-mannered commander of H.M.S. *Pinafore,* Gilbert never used a big, big D——.

In sharp contrast, the German satirical weekly *Simplicissimus* did use it, often and emphatically, and aroused the authorities to fuming retaliation. They banned the periodical from railroad newsstands, fined and imprisoned its editors and contributors. The men of *Simplicissimus* could not have been surprised; much like their French counterparts, German political journalists had long been subject to alert and vindictive scrutiny. The draconian responses of the German states to popular protest, codified in the Karlsbad Decrees of 1819, had succeeded in crippling political humor. Censors harassed the makers and hawkers of caricatures, news sheets, and the mildest political poems. Policemen repeatedly searched the premises of printers and booksellers suspected of harboring subversive materials. Public officials worried over jokes, seen as dangerous by their very nature; as the count von Arnim-Boitzenburg, Prussia's minister of the interior, solemnly noted in 1844, a joke, "whether trivial or not trivial, is irrefutable."[13] Usually, the revolutionary potential of German political humor was visible to nervous bureaucrats alone, but they, of course, were the ones to determine what sort of laughter was legal and what was not.

This repressive system was discredited during the heady days of the German revolution of 1848 but was not dismantled. Governments continued to cast a jaundiced eye on humor, detecting subversive intentions in jokes, caricatures, comic broadsides. Just as before 1848, so in the 1850s and 1860s, the policeman assigned to public meetings and the censor scanning illustrated leaflets with trained suspiciousness were inclined to scent danger to the state, or to good morals, in the most inoffensive sally. During the 1850s, the editors and chief writers of *Kladderadatsch* were sent to the fortress at Spandau for critical animad-versions on the czar. Such episodes, making minor martyrs and providing free publicity, sent up the circulation of the journal and never quite blunted its verve, but they also amounted to pressure for self-censorship. Government actions functioned as stern warnings even to the case-hardened writers for *Kladderadatsch,* to say nothing of other journals tempted to play physician to their society; they anesthetized the atmosphere of political discussion. German *Festungen,* the fortresses to which the courts chose to sentence political offend-ers, were admittedly far less unsalubrious and depressing than regular prisons, but they were not spas. If German satirists apparently felt compelled to risk these forced holidays, they still did their best to avoid them.

Now and then, of course, aggressive humor found a way. "Berlin wit," Thomas Carlyle wrote in 1858, during one of his visits to Germany, has "more of bitter in it than of any other quality."[14] Still the state took care to keep the bitterness within secure limits. In 1874, the German Empire equipped itself with a press law that, much like its French ancestors, specified taboos and the penalties awaiting those who transgressed them. Incitement to class hatred and pornography were the most obvious offenses the law listed explicitly, but it did not omit insulting reflections on the person of the emperor—*Majestäts-beleidigung.* This was a smart hit at aggressive humor, shrewd recognition that a witty insult was no less illegal, and certainly more unsettling, than a heavy-handed one. In short, political satire was as susceptible to repression in imperial Germany as in imperial France, and for the same reason. It was, we recall, a brash insult offered to the king that had sent Daumier and Philipon to prison. *Simplicissimus* was to offend, and to suffer, for precisely the same transgression.

The stable of talented writers and artists whom the young, rich Rhinelander Albert Langen assembled in Munich in 1896 was to realize his fantasy of a truly satirical German journal. It proved irreverent enough to affront anyone and everyone: fat priests, hypocritical parsons, decadent youths, stupid Junkers, parvenu Jews—and the emperor himself. In his eight years on the throne, Wilhelm II had stamped his reign with a distinctive style. His intrusive "personal regime" struck *Simplicissimus* as nothing less than ominous, and provoked its staff to amusement, irritation, and a mounting concern.

The emperor was intelligent and quirky, garrulous and supremely tactless, mercurial in his moods, an opinionated dilettante who dabbled in science, education, art, architecture, domestic and international politics, and offered rash, often embarrassing comments on them all. He was modern in his commitment to world trade and technological innovation, feudal in his claims to divine right and unbridled authority—some close observers thought him close to outright megalomania.* These odd combinations, making him at once comical and threatening, turned him into an ideal butt for the satirist.

In the fall of 1898, Wilhelm II visited the Holy Land with great éclat, giving his detractors new cause for worry. This Near Eastern expedition, attended by nervous worldwide publicity, was a characteristic venture into informal and unwelcome imperialism, and Langen's stable did it sardonic justice. Thomas Theodor Heine, an artist of real stature and the most consistently biting of draftsmen, supplied for the special "Palestine" issue a cartoon depicting the specters of two crusaders, Geoffrey de Bourbon and the emperor Friedrich Barbarossa, in full regalia. Geoffrey is cautioning the emperor, who is doubling over with uncontrollable hilarity, to stop his filthy laughter: "Our crusades, after all, were of no use either."[15]

This was unkind enough, but it was a poem, "Im heiligen Land," by Frank Wedekind hiding behind the pen name Hieronymus, that brought the full weight of prosecution down on *Simplicissimus*. Wedekind, experimental playwright, sardonic poet, nightclub entertainer, was already enjoying a certain reputation among the cognoscenti; once his authorship was discovered, he acquired national notoriety. In his poem, King David rises from his grave and reaches for his harp to praise the Lord for the honor of being allowed to devote

---

*In 1894, one observer, the reputable German medievalist Ludwig Quidde, a democrat and pacifist, said so publicly in a devastating satire, with—for him—devastating effect. The protagonist of his *Caligula: Eine Studie über römischen Caesarenwahnsinn* (1894), though Quidde never mentioned the German emperor's name, was obviously, too obviously for comfort, based on Wilhelm II. Quidde's "Caligula" showed symptoms of insanity in his nervous restlessness, his histrionic maneuvers, his lust for slandering others, his talkativeness, and his fantastic desire for control of the seas. The study, a stunning exemplar of biting wit, essentially ruined Quidde's career; his colleagues boycotted him, and he spent the rest of his long life isolated from his profession. See Reinhard Rürup, "Ludwig Quidde," in H.-U. Wehler, ed., *Deutsche Historiker III* (1972), 124–47.

a psalm to the "Lord of nations." He welcomes Wilhelm (never, of course, mentioning him by name) and his entourage—"the gracious consort / Clerics, lackeys, excellencies / And innumerable policemen"—to the Holy Land. Historic places rejoice at having the German emperor among them and long to be photographed. How Golgotha, which once heard the last words from the Cross, will now boast at having heard the emperor's first! David wonders how Wilhelm can leave his country for so long, and attributes to the intelligence of German officials his ability to predict what will happen in his absence. As David's extravagant "psalm" progresses, it reaches for fresh absurdities in comical self-abasement: the emperor's visit fills millions of Christians with the deepest pride, and the Holy Land thanks him for having removed from it, at last, the disgrace of never having been visited by him. The poem ends with a stanza cataloguing the various uniforms Wilhelm II might wear in satisfying the Holy Land's yearning for that visit—a telling allusion to the emperor's histrionic penchant for displaying himself in one military outfit after another.[16]

Langen and his associates, even the attorneys they consulted, were satisfied with their work and thought the special issue wickedly funny. The government found it wicked but not funny, and initiated prosecution. Langen fled abroad and lived in Paris for five years, returning only after he had paid a heavy fine. Wedekind followed his publisher into half-voluntary exile but returned the next year to join Thomas Theodor Heine in a six-month stint in a *Festung*. The almost proverbial consequence of this sort of repression—free publicity for the offenders and their journal—followed here too; the "fury" of the authorities against the "guilty" journal, commented Korfiz Holm, Langen's trusted assistant, boosted its circulation within a month from some four or five thousand copies to about eighty-five thousand.[17] But such imprudent aggression against the father brought quick, pitiless counteraggression against the sons. Victims of repression who had turned executioner discovered that the bitten were biting back.

4. A Laughing, Cruel Sage

A fading alcoholic beauty overturns her oil lamp in a drunken stupor, incinerates herself, and drops into a boiling caldron in hell, where her cousin Franz, a priest and the father of her twins, is already waiting for her. A smooth-talking, bespectacled pedagogue, his suave plea to win the respectful attention of two boys having failed, takes a seasoned hazel switch from his coat and pitilessly beats his impudent and cynical charges into slavish compliance; at home, the boys copy the efficient educational discipline they have just undergone by whipping their dogs to secure *their* obedience. An exigent nearsighted husband who finds a hair in the soup his wife has prepared angrily seeks solace in his trusty bottle of rum, and engages her in a pitched battle, no holds barred, that turns out disastrously for him when she snatches off his glasses, making him tap around blindly; he severely burns his hand and his bottom on the red-hot stove, and gets a bloody nose when he runs smack into an open door. An irritating youth persists, without apparent provocation, in disrupting a gentleman's repose in his garden by blowing pebbles and feathered darts at him from behind a fence. The victim, who has been comfortably lounging in dressing gown and slippers, dunking a pretzel into a cup of tea, is mystified at first. Then, enlightened and enraged, he turns executioner and kills his assailant by shoving his blowpipe down his throat.[1]

We are in the world of Wilhelm Busch, Germany's most beloved nineteenth-century versifier, illustrator, and homely philosopher, a world of almost unmitigated aggression—and counteraggression. Freud, like uncounted other grateful readers, called him "our friend Busch."[2] Both the uncomplicated delight of his admirers—who quoted tags from him no less often than from Goethe, perhaps with greater pleasure—and the portentous puzzlement of his solemn interpreters long outlasted Busch's death in 1908.*

Busch's humor has not traveled well. While his drawings, vigorous and droll, may appeal to anyone, and his most famous tale, *Max und Moritz,* inspired a long-lived American comic strip, *The Katzenjammer Kids,* most of his allusions are best understood in their country of origin.[3] And his verse virtually defies translation. Yet Busch earned a starring role in the history of nineteenth-century bourgeois aggressive humor. He brilliantly demonstrated once again that in such humor the buried wishes to surpass and humiliate, to maim and murder, secure a socially acceptable outlet. After all, like his colleagues, Busch reassured everyone that wishing is not doing; fantasy is not reality. His merciless humor reenacted the jungle warfare of the unconscious, with the soothing assurance that no harm, and perhaps some good, would come of it. Busch was an inventive artist with pen and pencil. But in the ways that counted most, in his style of thinking, his experience was bourgeois experience, and he was pretty much like everyone else.

Certainly the German consciousness cheerfully domesticated Busch's lapi-

---

*From the 1870s on, once Busch began to acquire a reputation as a deep thinker, scholars gravely studied him as a poet and draftsman worthy of the attention of pedagogues and critics, even of philosophers. They swarmed over his work, writing dissertations on Busch's attitude toward animals or his debt to Schopenhauer or the secret sources of his wit. The body of ponderous scholarly exegesis that began to gather around Busch in his lifetime and picked up speed after his death is witness to the humorlessness of much writing about humor.

dary rhymed aphorisms about the rewards of immorality and the risks of matrimony, the poignancy of ambition and the ravages of alcohol, the equivocal pleasures of fatherhood and the disconcerting brevity of life. His breezy fables about wicked boys, clever dogs, tipsy bachelors, and thwarted artists did not just occupy a showy place on the bookshelves of German households; they were read and memorized. Given the inescapable differences in national styles of humor, no humorist could represent every nineteenth-century style of laughter with equal authority. But, always excepting Mark Twain, Busch spoke to, and for, as large a bourgeois public as any entertainer of his time.

Wilhelm Busch was something more than a purveyor of genial pleasure. The earnestness of his learned admirers imposed an awkward, heavy burden, but Busch himself took a grave view of the comic. One of his most frequently quoted poems recounts the last minutes in the life of a bird caught in birdlime. It flutters about frantically but is unable to free itself. As a black tomcat steals nearer and nearer to make an easy meal of it, the bird, resigned, decides to spend its final moments singing its song. "The bird, it seems to me," comments Busch in the closing line, "has a sense of humor."[4] This sounds psychoanalytic before its time: humor has, among other duties, the task of controlling anxieties, of mastering threats, by increasing their distance and reducing their dimensions. Whatever the precise meaning of laughter for Busch, the resolute cheerfulness of this philosophic bird suggests that for him its origins, like its effects, were anything but superficial. His humor, a feast of gaiety, discloses a vein of musing thoughtfulness, even melancholy.

It also discloses a disposition to violence often lapsing into sheer brutality—on paper. His friends found him gentle and generous, but his fantasy life, as it emerges in his drawings, must have been lurid in the extreme. His bluff and exuberant cruelty yielded in his later years to a measure of serene wisdom, but a barely sublimated urge to attack and draw blood retained its force through his work, which never lost a distinct provincial coarseness. He learned to be urbane in his ways but never urban; his most characteristic inventions, earthy and physical, recall his rural origins. Born in 1832 in the village of Wiedensahl, near Hannover, Busch repeatedly left but always returned to his native Lower Saxony. In a way a peasant might understand—though Busch's parents were bourgeois shopkeepers—the favored target of his pointed humor is the body, always vulnerable and often violated.

It was the world of Wiedensahl, then, with only faint touches of Munich or Frankfurt, that he recreated in his humorous tales; there are no bustling cities in them, no factories, no modern technological devices, no mass newspapers, only the most fleeting reference to the railroad.[5] His cast of characters consists principally of millers and village schoolteachers and barbers, Jewish peddlers, unpretentious small-town couples, gaping peasants, and—this was as modern as he would get—a small assortment of petty bourgeois like Tobias Knopp. Middle-aged, bald, and corpulent, Knopp searches the world for a wife, suffers many a humiliating if funny mishap, and, significantly, returns home to marry his housekeeper.

Busch's fidelity to Wiedensahl was not just nostalgic; his native soil served as a retreat from a life he feared he could not master. Like a neurotic Antaeus—like Heine—he needed to touch his mother earth. After the exuberant affability of his youth, the night-long debauches of beer and talk with a handful of intimates in Munich and Frankfurt in the 1860s, Busch became something of a recluse. "I don't drink beer," he asserted in 1875, when he was in his mid-forties, "I don't play cards, I don't like philistine sociability."[6] He increasingly retreated to Lower Saxony; his most unreserved attachments remained those to his brothers, nieces, and nephews, and to the landscape of his childhood. In his last years, he did not even answer letters from old companions.[7] His vice was a solitary one—smoking. And after the manner of the predestined bachelor, he invested his emotions in women who were safely unavailable to him. Not that he wholly evaded the erotic in his work; his illustrated tale *Der heilige Antonius von Padua* gave him a fine opportunity to choreograph a very ballet for a buxom, scantily clad, seductive female—the devil in guise of a dancer—trying to divert the saint from his "Christian calm."[8] And his impious "pious Helen," adulteress and dipsomaniac, hints at banked amorous passions in her creator. The nudes he drew (or at least the few he preserved) are at once academic and sensual.[9]

Yet for Busch sensual love, like his most extravagant aggressions, existed mainly on paper. If one of the perils to which he exposed his characters, mar-riage, he never experienced himself, many of the disappointments he visited on them were caricatured versions of his own. A guarded, private man, more candid about his digestive than his amatory problems, he kept his intimate life hidden away. His letters are often long and reflective, especially on religious questions, but they keep the mystery of his deepest feelings intact; the fragmen-tary self-portraits he consented to publish are cool and sparse. "We know nothing really about Shakespeare," he once observed, "nor about Homer. Mozart's grave is unknown. That's as it should be. What is good and significant about them is in their works. Let the other, the inferior and less lovable, disap-pear."[10] No doubt, as close readers have noticed, Busch's mordant portrayals of two failures, Balduin Bählamm the poet and Kuno Klecksel the painter, are flecked with autobiographical touches, attesting to Busch's self-critical stance toward his achievements as an artist. By and large, critics and collectors have treated his substantial output of oil paintings, landscapes and rural scenes in the darkest Dutch manner as a curiosity. His reticence, the saying goes, speaks volumes—and so, Busch's volumes must speak for him.

The eldest of seven children, Busch seems to have found the affective climate of his household sadly wanting. The very diction of the laconic recollections he wrung from himself in 1886 attests to a lingering malaise over his parents' strictness and exigence, and a longing for an embracing warmth evidently beyond their emotional range: "My father was a grocer; short, quirky, moderate and conscientious; continually anxious, never tender; inclined to fun but stern with foolishness." His mother matched her husband's mental temperature: "Quiet, diligent, pious, used to read after supper." Domestic and self-contained, preoccupied with the store, the couple never went anywhere. To relieve pressure on an overcrowded household, they farmed out their son Wilhelm, at nine, to live with relatives, where he remained for three years, an experience that was apparently traumatic for him. Busch's parents were slaves to duty, intent on reproducing themselves in their offspring. True, the father could mobilize a certain programmatic sentimentality; Busch recalled that when the nightingales sang, Johann Friedrich Wilhelm Busch wandered through the woods, alone. Yet he wanted his son to aspire to nothing higher than the modest eminence of a machinist. The boy's talent defeated him, however. In 1851, young Busch ventured forth to Düsseldorf to study painting at the Academy of Art; the following year, restless and in search of larger vistas, he struck out for Antwerp for further training and a close look at Dutch and Flemish masters. It was, he knew, a momentous decision. "May it be," he confided to his diary, almost prayerfully, "my second birthday."[11]

His second birth came not without cost. Less than a year later, exhausted from physical ailments and psychological strain, Busch was back in Wiedensahl, having executed the first of his flights to the familiar. There would be many other self-protective treks to his home base in Lower Saxony. But in 1854, he sallied forth into the world again, enrolling in Wilhelm von Kaulbach's Royal Academy of Art in Munich. While there, in 1858, he began to contribute sketches and caricatures to humorous periodicals like the *Fliegende Blätter* and the *Münchener Bilderbogen*. At first, he took most of his texts from others, but he soon emancipated himself to devise his own inimitable genre, the illustrated mock-moral fable in rhymed couplets. *Max und Moritz*, his first, dates from 1865; *Maler Klecksel*, the comical and pathetic tale about a frustrated painter, his last, from 1884. Then, in the quarter century that remained to him, he tried his hand at illustrated stories in prose, and continued to paint and write verse. His lyrical poetry, which he produced in great abundance, was not well received; he suffered, as he benefited, from being stereotyped as an entertainer. Yet an acquaintance with these poems is essential to any character sketch of the man and artist. For the most part short, untitled, of a deceptive simplicity, they echo Heine's technique and Heine's typical blend of detachment and engagement. Their humorous poignancy allows the poet to pose as the objective observer of the human animal while he reveals himself as a suffering sharer in the human predicament. Busch's laughter has more than a touch of Byron's *Don Juan* in it; he laughed that he might not weep.

In his lyrical verse, as in his better-known fables, he turned self-defense into attack, over and over. As he and his perceptive readers recognized from the start, he reveled in *Schadenfreude,* the malicious joy one takes in the discomfiture of others, the purest of impure pleasures. Looking back, he frankly confessed that he was only human, and felt refreshed as he watched "the little annoyances and stupidities of others." After all, "laughter is an expression of relative comfort. Franzel behind the stove enjoys being warm all the more as he sees Hansel outdoors, breathing into his reddish hands."[12] But Busch's was not a lonely pleasure; his vast, enthusiastic public treasured what he gave it and clamored for more.

Busch's first contribution to the *Fliegende Blätter* was an inane anecdote about two men walking on the ice on a bitterly cold day and one of them losing his head—literally. The theme must have found a gratifying reception, for Busch used it again soon after, in a cautionary cartoon, "Dreadful Consequences of Curiosity": a rustic sitting in a barber chair has his head cut off when he foolishly leaps forward to stare at circus animals being led past. Just before, Busch had concocted a comical melodramatic ballad in which two lovers end up impaled on a supernaturally large pencil.[13]

Obviously, decapitation and similar catastrophes appealed to Busch. In "Sad Result of a Neglected Education," he combined the themes of impalement and decapitation in a telling parody of prodding didactic verse. With the false solemnity that soon became his signature, Busch professed to lament the fate of a child bereft of moral and religious supervision. An unpleasant, spoiled seven-year-old named Fritz makes cruel fun of a tailor who, after bearing it patiently, lures the little pest to his house, cuts off his head, and disposes of the body in a lake. Fritz's mother, opening a fish to prepare it for dinner, finds her son's body inside, faints upon the kitchen knife, and dies. A Jewish peddler is falsely accused of the murder and hanged—Busch's graphic drawing turns this execution into another decapitation. The murderous tailor's conscience gets the better of him; he confesses and is condemned to death. But before *his* execution, he commits suicide in prison, with the very pair of shears he had used to decapitate little Fritz.[14]

Not all of Busch's victims perish; some are merely mutilated or temporarily disfigured. Two boys stealing honey are stung by angry bees, and their noses swell up to monstrous size. Noses were a favorite target of Busch's humor. In one of his laconic drawings, a man stumbles and falls onto a long, hot candle that bores into his nostril; in one of the longer tales, a mischievous captured raven takes an energetic bite out of its mistress's nose. And Herr Lehmann, back home after an alcoholic New Year's Eve party, tries to light a last cigar before going to bed, with predictable results; calamities pile up as he thrashes about his room, upsetting everything in sight, and with his candle severely burns his hair—and his nose.[15]

These misfortunes are not always altogether unmerited. In the tale of little Fritz, the Jewish peddler is hanged for a crime he has not committed, but the tailor *is* guilty. So are other of Busch's malefactors who come to a bad end. But this primitive poetic justice apart, Busch often punished his creations not on the compassionate legal scale that W. S. Gilbert had his Mikado proclaim, but on the harsher principle that the punishment should far exceed the crime. In one of Busch's early tales, two thieves who have invaded an apartment hide from the police in a closet, from which they emerge carrying sharply pointed umbrellas as improvised weapons. When they leap out of a second-story window in their attempt to escape, they disembowel one another, the tips of the umbrellas pushing right through their genitals. The scene reads almost like a caricature of a perverse sexual encounter. And in Busch, justified self-defense often takes the most extravagant form. His fable about a miller's brave daughter at home alone shows her resourcefully foiling three armed robbers who invade her house; she flattens one, rolls up the second, and—of course—decapitates the third.[16] Evidently, for Wilhelm Busch and his millions of readers, symbolic castration had its hilarious side.

These savage ephemera, ingeniously varied, are not just expressions of youthful high spirits. Busch seems to have had a lifelong obsession with painful penetration. Hot candles burn, serrated saws cut into nostrils, in his later work as they had in his earliest sketches; sharp objects—fishhooks, forks, knives, umbrellas—pushing through hands or ears or into the tender tissue of the bottom make their appearance in the 1880s no less than in the 1860s. Busch converted pencil and pen into sharp weapons in more ways than one. In *Maler Klecksel,* the painter fights a duel with a local art critic—their weapons an umbrella, a long pen, and a pointed pencil. The principal casualties in the all-out struggle are the painter's nose, stabbed through with the critic's pen, and the critic's rear end, punctured with the tip of his own pencil.[17] In Busch, no one is safe; he cares little for the bodily integrity of his characters as their noses are twisted off or burned by sealing wax, their ears torn, and their tails set aflame with lighted tapers.

Indeed, pain pervades Busch's work—and everyone laughed. Balduin Bählamm is subjected to the forceful though futile ministrations of a dentist joyfully straining to extract one of his teeth; Peter, the hapless narrator of a late story, *Der Schmetterling*, loses a foot in an operation the surgeon performs with lip-licking euphoria. And Busch made it plain that his sympathy with the creatures he put through these torments was no greater than that of the folk jeering at Bählamm upon his emergence from the dentist's ministrations, his cheek grotesquely swollen and his head swathed in a ludicrous bandage. Death, too, marks Busch's work, often in grisly and undignified guises: one formerly living being roasted to a crisp outline, another crumpled together like a blackened piece of paper, still another spread out on the floor in finely ground fragments grouped into a recognizable shape, to say nothing of one frozen into a large block of ice that shatters into little slivers. Not even an innocent, adventurous bird can hope to escape; Busch's irrepressible raven, getting drunk, entangles itself in a ball of knitting wool and is choked to death. Illustrating this tale, not one to pass up an opportunity, Busch showed the dead bird dangling from a table so that it looks like a hanged criminal.[18] His cruelty to animals is redeemed—if that is the right word—only by his impartial cruelty to humans.

The most unrelieved instance of Busch's humorous sadism, intensified by the heartlessness of a gloating victor, is his "Monsieur Jacques à Paris." This is one of Busch's few lapses into political aggression. The sketch was prompted by the Prussians' siege of Paris in late 1870, when the surrender of the ill-supplied capital was only a matter of weeks. The protagonist is a starving French patriot, reduced to smoking the seaweed from his mattress and eating a captured mouse, his cherished canary, and his dog's tail, which unfortunately reminds him of "that shape we used to call a sausage." As the Prussians approach, Monsieur Jacques invents explosive pills, which he tries out on the dog "with favorable results"—vividly shown in a cold-blooded illustration. Encouraged, Monsieur Jacques loads cutlets for Prussian soldiers with his lethal charge, but the cutlets instead blow apart two hungry *citoyens* who, uninvited, fall upon them. In despair, the inventor loads his boots with the explosive and blows himself up.[19] In the literature of German *Schadenfreude* over the enemy's plight during the Franco-Prussian war, only Richard Wagner's tasteless farce, *A Capitulation*, rejoicing like "Monsieur Jacques à Paris" over the starving of French civilians, reaches a lower level than this. It was a level to which Busch never quite descended again. Somehow, the stimulating, dimly erotic wartime atmosphere had weakened the checks on his raw aggressive impulses.

Busch's numerous and vocal partisans have been fairly defensive on the question of his inhumanity. They have insisted that those scenes of ferocious whippings, bloody impalements, and lovingly rendered human explosions do no psychological harm because they are so unreal. True, in 1880 Friedrich Theodor Vischer launched an unexpected criticism of Busch as a sly aggressor, but he conceded that the violence is amusing because it is so obviously fiction: "Where moderate guilt is punished by the most frightful, indeed the most extreme, consequences, a terrible death, the accent must fall on impossibility. It is too absurd to be thinkable. It makes us shudder, but it must, after all, be pure illusion, because it is not possible, and we laugh at the artist's crazy idea." Vischer offered in evidence Busch's concise fable about the bad boys of Corinth. Much like other bad boys in Busch's work, these two seek only to irritate—gratuitously. They annoy the long-suffering Diogenes by dousing him with water and rolling him in his barrel. But retribution soon comes, though it is impersonal fate, not human rage, that exacts a terrible revenge. The boys find themselves helplessly stuck on two nails protruding from Diogenes' rolling barrel, and are flattened out "like cakes." The reader, Vischer commented, shudders in horror and shakes with laughter, for such a result is physically unthinkable. Busch may depict pain most painfully, but he never lets his audience forget that it is seeing only a picture. His art, Vischer concluded, cancels causality; it is a cheerful insanity draped in the plastic mistiness of a dream.[20]

Vischer had a point; the impossible is Busch's stock in trade. It invades the very line of his drawings, as they portray, with extravagant and expressive distortions, acute distress or agonizing death and, less portentously, the passing of time or the spectacle of breathtaking virtuosity. Indeed, Vischer called Busch the "aptly inept" artist. Balduin Bählamm, smarting under the dentist's tugs at his diseased tooth, suddenly develops half a dozen legs as he writhes in pain. And when Busch's concert pianist moves from *"adagio con sentimento,"* which elicits a big tear from his listener, to *"fortissimo vivacissimo"* and *"finale furioso,"* he seems to have grown an unlimited number of fingers.[21]

Busch defied mundane reality most memorably in his first masterpiece, *Max und Moritz,* in which two preadolescent delinquents perform a series of seven surrealistic pranks. At least one of their schemes is utilitarian, aimed at stuffing their bellies with succulent meals. But the more notable ones are sheer *actes gratuits.* Max and Moritz saw through a bridge to give a tailor a nearly fatal dunking; they fill a teacher's pipe with powder which explodes to leave him singed and bald; they insert June bugs into their uncle's bed to give him an itchy night. In the end, captured as they senselessly slice open a farmer's sack of malt, they are taken to the mill, ground into little pieces, and eaten by geese—to no one's regret. One or two moralists objected that *Max und Moritz* inculcated disrespect for all that is respectworthy. After all, Busch had depicted the boys' victims—widow, teacher, tailor, uncle—as decent, well-liked, unprovocative.

But not even that sour minority found anything objectionable in Busch's most tasteless episodes. They seemed too absurd to court imitation.

This lack of concern is understandable, but its rationale was an oversimplification. Busch's humor seemed innocent not just because it was so unreal but also because it was so real. Humor, we know, can disarm harsh experience; it permits both its creators and its consumers to feel superior to misfortune—and to others. Even its palpable exaggerations (in fact, these very exaggerations) lend it a measure of deeper realism, for they surreptitiously exhibit the extravagant repressed fantasies of the child, or of the adult regressing in laughter.

Busch's humor was realistic in yet another respect. His culture, which he so impressively gratified, was intimately acquainted with the needs and workings of the body. People were freely exposed to digestive troubles and graver ailments at home, and to rodents, spiders, and insects; they were rarely spared the sight of mutilation and death.[22] I cannot repeat too often that the portrait of the respectable nineteenth-century bourgeois as a stranger to coarseness and addicted to squeamishness takes surfaces for essences. Little Fritz's mother, a good bourgeoise, is not too fastidious to cut open a fish, and uncounted numbers of real-life middle-class Victorian housewives were familiar with such operations. Hence the only shock that Busch's comical rendering of this world evoked was the shock of recognition. There was nothing strange, or even very imaginative, in illustrations showing bugs invading a bedroom in massive formation, bees beaten to pieces with a broom, spiders lowering themselves perilously over the open mouth of a sleeper, inebriated and horribly disfigured cripples hobbling about on their crutches.

That is why Busch did not think twice about describing to his two young "adopted nieces," well-bred girls in Frankfurt whom he had known since their infancy, the heartless way one fished for trout in his village. The water was let out of the pool in which they swam, so the trout were stranded on dry land. "They wiggled and would have liked to leap back into the water, but the word was: penknife ready! Pierced through the tail so that the blood flowed, and in the evening they lay in the pan and broiled and bubbled."[23] Life is cruel, and so is man, cruel and carnivorous, nine-tenths savage and one-tenth saint—if that. "Suffering, torture, has something atrociously attractive, it causes horror and delight at the same time," Busch the seasoned observer told a woman friend, recalling a bucolic scene he had often witnessed and would immortalize in one of his illustrations. "Have you ever noticed the expression of children watching a pig being slaughtered?—No?—Well, then call to mind the Medusa's head. *Death, cruelty, voluptuousness*—here they are united."[24]

These responses, Busch insisted, are complex. "I did not say: slaughter is

attractive, but I think I said: *horribly attractive*—fascination and revulsion; forward and back; corresponding to the two poles of our innermost being."* He
cautioned his friend Hermann Levi, the principal Munich conductor, that
"anyone who has ever seen the flashing eye of energetic bestiality is stalked by a
horrifying premonition that one peculiar scoundrel on the planet Uranus could
check the progress of salvation, that a single devil could be stronger than a
whole heaven full of saints."[25] Much like the aging Mark Twain, Busch had a
keen sense of the power of aggressive evil in human nature and employed his
humor as a way of managing and partly accepting its horrors—of managing and
accepting, not denying them.

Busch's preoccupation with anal humor displays the tough-minded, open-
eyed vulgarity prominent in himself and his readers. His quick sketch "Of the
Double Pair of Spectacles," a self-portrait showing him in a two-hole out-
house, defecating into one hole while vomiting into the other, was intended
only for his raucous friends in Munich. And he left unpublished too a pair of
drawings in which a man relieving himself in front of a fence is astonished to
have his excrement disappear; a sly farmer, grinning at his prank, has taken it
away on a shovel.[26] But Busch's more genteel excursions into scatology did
reach print; he enlisted bird droppings as a kind of humorous punctuation.
Gagging on a device of twisted string and tempting bait invented by Max and
Moritz, three frantically fluttering hens and a rooster hang themselves on the
branch of a tree; while each of the hens lays an egg as death approaches, the
rooster drops a small turd as his last offering.[27] Balduin Bählamm, seeking poetic
inspiration under a tree as he listens to a bird's lovely song, has his notebook
soiled when the bird relieves itself before flying away.[28] Near the end of his life,

---

*Busch to Maria Anderson, November 16, [18]75, Wilhelm Busch, *Sämtliche Briefe,* ed. Friedrich Bohne, 2 vols. (1968), I, 159. Clearly, the sadistic component in sensuality and the sensual
element in aggression did not need to be discovered by Freud. It says much about the atmosphere
in which psychoanalysis emerged that Busch casually anticipated some of its fundamental ideas.
Dreams, he wrote, are the "dubious amusements in the nursery and the servants' rooms of the
brain, after the father and head of the house has gone to bed." *Eduards Traum* (1891), in *Wilhelm
Busch Gesamtausgabe,* ed. Friedrich Bohne, 4 vols. (1959), IV, 159. And describing the way poetic
inspiration works, Busch noted that the poet, the Muse's son, sets to work as he grows discontented with his world and kneads himself another, more pleasing one—and it is his mother, Busch
added picturesquely and profoundly, who nourishes the poet from her ample bosom. See *Balduin
Bählamm, der verhinderte Dichter* (1883), ibid., 7–8. He was fully aware of sibling rivalry; in one of
his poems, an aunt tells her little nephew that the stork has just brought him a pretty brother,
whereupon the boy replies that he will get himself a heavy stone and throw it at his new sibling's
head. *Kritik des Herzens* (1874), ibid., II, 509. More fundamentally still, Busch told a correspondent
that human existence essentially consists of desire. Busch to Maria Anderson, July 6, 1875. *Briefe,* I,
148.

illustrating a *memento mori*—a quatrain about a wise man inspecting a skull—Busch showed that skull resting on a book signed with his initials, and sitting on it a raven that has just graced it with a dropping.[29] This was the affectionate "Uncle Wilhelm" who could thank young "Nanda" Kessler for a gift of snipe with a sketch showing an obese gourmand dreaming that an angel is pissing on his tongue.*

In sizable domains of experience, then, Busch's world was less antiseptic than that of later, presumably more liberated artists. Though the display of sexual excitement remained a tender subject for elevated moral disputes in the German Empire, though political criticism remained far from unobstructed, humorists could explore bodily functions with moderate restraint and no apologies. And aggressive humor was especially welcome if it chose for its butts ready figures of fun, like man-crazy spinsters and ineffectual uncles, oblivious lovers and foolish rustics, or objects of puzzlement and resentment, like Bavarians and Prussians, and, at times, priests and Jews.

Busch was never much of a political man. In 1863, cautioning a friend who planned to join a corps of volunteers to liberate the province of Schleswig-Holstein from Denmark, he objected to such an impassioned engagement on principle. Activists either enjoy fishing in troubled waters or wish to "drown their own inner confusion" through action. He had only contempt for such troublemakers. But others, "driven onward by enthusiasm for an ideal," worried him. The idealist "will have to atone for the effort of his intellect" with failures and disillusionment. "The happiness of the individual, in so far as it is attainable at all," he noted a little sententiously, "lies in his own head, in the harmonious cultivation of his personal capacities."[30]

This is a telling self-portrait. True, in the early 1870s, under the impress of German unification, Busch briefly deviated into politics. In "the excited time in which we live," he put his facile pen into the service of German chauvinism and Bismarck's anti-Catholic campaign; it was a moment when certain kinds of humor seemed in particular demand.[31] But he could not silence his misgivings; only after nagging by his publisher and friend Otto Bassermann did Busch ridicule what he thought to be corrosive forces in the new Reich. His illustrated exercise in anti-Catholic paranoia, *Pater Filuzius,* with its villainous con-

---

*Busch to "Nanda" Kessler, December 24, 1896, ibid., II, at p. 84. Busch's latrine humor was neither innovative nor radical. In 1843, the popular Berlin painter and cartoonist Theodor Hosemann had published a lithograph, *New Year's Greetings,* showing a worried-looking, pipe-smoking young man shitting ducats into a large pot. and around 1900, Thomas Theodor Heine drew for the urbane pages of *Simplicissimus* a class for diplomats in which aspirants are learning servility by climbing into a gigantic model of an anus. Busch's anality was not disreputable or even disrespectful. It was only very German.

spiratorial Jesuit accompanied by equally villainous allies, constitutes in company with "Monsieur Jacques à Paris" a detour from his life's course.*

Busch's attitudes toward Jews fit into this portrait. For some years, on his excursions to the city, he had associated intimately with Jewish literary men and musicians. Paul Lindau, a popular playwright and prolific reviewer, was one of them. Hermann Levi was another; their friendship even survived Levi's adoration of Wagner. Few of Busch's letters are more personal than the one he wrote Levi in December 1880, generously if guardedly responding to an outpouring of self-torturing religious doubts. "Here is the boat of faith, grace is ferryman; whoever calls out urgently will be ferried across. But I cannot call: my soul is hoarse; I have a philosophical cold."[32] This picturesque and detached demurrer was scarcely calculated to resolve anyone's religious quandary, but Busch's empathy with Levi's dilemma, coupled with the courteous refusal to compromise his own views, displays his attachment. When the two men met, they would discuss deep matters, and Levi would play the piano for his friend.

Yet these associations did not save Busch from occasionally employing the conventional stereotype of "the Jew": physically and morally repulsive, addicted to money, and very sly. The Jews who figure in Busch's irreverent alphabet for children and in the ballad of obnoxious little Fritz, both of 1860, are more crudely drawn, but also less emphatic, than his later caricatures. He drew one of these, depicting Schmulchen Schiefelbeiner, the year after he had himself photographed, in a studio, arm in arm with Levi under a large umbrella; the picture bears Busch's gloss: "Christian and Jew under one roof."† This affectionate souvenir and the ugly, hook-nosed, smirking Schmulchen seem to belong to two different worlds, especially since he is a gratuitous insertion in *Plisch und Plum,* the tale in which he makes his fleeting and offensive appearance. Measuring himself against Schmulchen, Busch concluded, with that touch of self-satisfaction that belongs to bigotry even at its mildest, that he and his kind were surely better looking than that.[33]

Busch's comical—not so comical—aggressions against Jews were more than

---

*In 1886, when a mediocre scribbler and tactless disciple, Eduard Daelen, publicly proclaimed *Pater Filuzius* the core of Busch's teachings and summit of his wit, Busch protested that he had been gravely misjudged. Except for a few things dictated by hunger, he said a little pathetically, and that one little tendentious anti-Jesuit piece, he had always worked for his private, his "most ruthless" pleasure. Busch to Friedrich August von Kaulbach, September 16, [18]86, ibid., I, 273.

†Photograph in Friedrich Bohne, *Wilhelm Busch. Leben, Werke, Schicksal* (1958), 153. Busch's easiness with his Jewish acquaintances was helped by the fact that none of them threatened to invade his terrain. "I wouldn't like to have a Jew for a competitor," he told a nephew in 1900. "But even so, I've known some pretty nice Jews—like Levi, Lindau, and several in Frankfurt." Fortunately, "they all aspired to a direction different from mine, and so I got along with them pretty well." Ibid., 190.

a private peccadillo. In them once again the individual intersects with his culture. To place these isolated episodes in their context is to circumscribe their hostility and recognize their inconsistencies. Many German anti-Semites resented the Jew because, they said, he insisted on retaining, and parading, his differences from the dominant culture; other German anti-Semites resented the Jew precisely for making strenuous efforts to erase these differences. Such resentments were symptomatic traces of partly unconscious responses to the most unsettling social upheavals. The German-Jewish quest for assimilation, or at least for civic and social equality, was after all only one element, and far from the most conspicuous, in the transformations Germans had to cope with after the late 1840s. In its ascendancy, Prussia swallowed up many smaller German states, including Busch's own Hannover, and the national unification of 1871 further compromised the autonomy of surviving entities like the kingdom of Bavaria. These political tremors, though far-reaching, were themselves eclipsed by social and economic earthquakes that threatened time-honored social distinctions, ideals of family life, religious observances, and moral certitudes.

As we know, most Germans, Busch among them, celebrated Bismarck's Reich as a consummation. For them Bismarck always remained "the great pilot" and "our hero."[34] He was right because he had won. The shape he had given his victory did fill some Germans with foreboding—but not Busch. During the war against France, he savagely lampooned the unreconstructed particularist, shown mourning the loss of independence and devastated by word of Prussian military successes.[35] In short, Busch was in accord with what he called in a letter of 1872 "the most recent wishes of the state."[36]

The cult of Bismarck, generally kept at the level of worship, could not silence the conflicts bubbling up beneath the surface of the Empire. When the young emperor Wilhelm II dismissed Bismarck in March 1890, most Germans were stunned and a little frightened, but somehow relieved as well. The liberal politician Eugen Richter tactlessly exclaimed, "Thank God, he's gone." But after the first shock, most showed a wounding indifference. The stock market, that barometer at once sensitive and heartless, dropped briefly at the news and then quickly regained the points it had lost. In his prose fantasy *Eduards Traum*, published the year after Bismarck's "retirement," Busch reflected on this collective ingratitude: "With politics, I bothered only just enough to know roughly what was going on. A few days ago, the greatest man in the nation left the driver's seat and dropped the reins of the world from his hands. Now, one should have thought, there'd be a clatter and a commotion. But no! Everyone kept on grumbling and bartering and fawning and played Skat or the piano or the lottery at Kohn's, and drained his short beer, just as before, and the great cart of everyday life kept rolling along the road, without creaking noticeably, as though it were greased with tallow."[37] Here spoke Busch in his unpolitical voice, unchanged in three decades.

Yet in some measure Busch shared the undercurrent of nervous concern over Germany's course. Precisely like others, he soothed anxiety by aggression, and humor was his weapon. The reassurance he once offered one of his nieces, a pianist who feared stage fright at her debut but then performed successfully, was his own refuge in anxiety-provoking situations: "Once the attack was launched, the anxiety was gone! Many a phantom, seen close up, disappears just this way." He knew all about this; he had "thoroughly studied" anxiety in his childhood years.[38]

Busch, then, was no fanatic and no breeder of fanatics. He was not obsessive, nor very consistent, about his dislikes. On the contrary, he conveyed in his letters, and taught in his published work, a stoical if cheerful resignation in the face of fate, the malice of objects, the defects of humanity, the ineluctable passage of time. The human animal, Busch remained persuaded, is incurably flawed. "As you know, on the matter of egoism," he wrote a friend when he was in his mid-twenties, "man is simply incorrigible."[39] As a good Protestant skeptic, he took leave to doubt the Roman Catholic cult of the saints. No human, he argued, is ever completely free from sin.[40] The elevated, somewhat forced correspondence he carried on in 1875 with a fervent Dutch admirer, Maria Anderson, displays a set of variations on this theme: "The noble is situated above the belt; the common, everywhere." Adversity is man's lot: "Whatever lives, suffers; suffers because it lives, and *wants* to live." Perhaps after a few billion years of Darwinian selection, reason will conquer desire, but not now, not yet. Life itself is the fundamental sin. "Repulsive pessimist! you will say, and be right."[41]

He said the same thing in print over and over: virtue must be taught; wickedness we commit on our own. This pensive perspective on life ran counter to the official strenuous optimism of his time. Still, it is worth repeating that original as Busch was with words and pictures, his unsurpassed popularity rested not on his isolation but on his representativeness. His aggressive imagination spoke to the imagination of others; his ruthless pleasure was the pleasure of millions. So too was his anxiety theirs. What amused and frightened him amused and frightened his public. This is the historic point of Busch's work; even those living in the kind of city that found no place in that work recognized themselves in his characters and laughed at their tribulations. In this crucial respect, his native village, Wiedensahl, was everywhere.*

---

*The essential conventionality of Busch's style of thinking is reflected in his commitment to the cane as the supreme educator. In Busch's works only boys are flogged. But his girls are as immoral

Busch was not a sadist. His mature satire is often gentle. In the Knopp trilogy of the mid-1870s, he took a rotund petty bourgeois through middle-aged bachelordom, happily henpecked marriage, fond paternity, rapid decline, and death; Busch smiled at his creature's foibles and his marital service, and expected no more than a smile from his readers in return, a smile not of derision but of empathy. Again, those last two illustrated fables in verse, *Balduin Bäh-lamm* and *Maler Klecksel,* are exercises in self-irony, their malice turned inward. Lack of talent, or lack of opportunity, keep a would-be poet a humble clerk and turn a would-be painter into a jovial innkeeper. The lesson these cautionary biographies can impart is simple: it is a sound idea—it is, in fact, necessary—to subject the pleasure principle to the reality principle. In his modest way, Busch the humorist had certain philosophical ambitions. Humorists often do. No doubt he was the most hilarious among Schopenhauer's admirers. But he was not much of an educator. His work was funny and poignant, at times both. And it stands as an extraordinary display of how to manage aggression by dissolving violence in laughter.

---

and vicious as their brothers. Even charming, innocent little Julchen, the Knopps's daughter, ruins her father's pen and and shaving knife, breaks his watch and his pipe, dunks her mother's knitting in the ink she has spilled on the floor, and cuts the tails off her father's formal coat. See *Tobias Knopp* (1875–77), in *Gesamtausgabe,* III, 163–70. One of Busch's most famous creations, "pious Helen," plagues the aunt and uncle with whom she lives with pranks rivaling the most depraved invented by his boys. She sews together her uncle's nightgown, producing bodily injuries and mayhem in his bedroom as he gropes blindly to put it on. She pulls the covers from her guardians' bed with an outsized fishhook on a long string, causing a quarrel between the two and impaling her uncle's toe on the hook. But she is only banished, to continue her nefarious ways as an adult. See *Die fromme Helene* (1872) ibid., II, 207–12, 230–41. But whatever the penalty appropriate for boy or girl, Busch viewed the inborn flaw in human nature as requiring strictness, often downright violence, for the sake of civilized conformity. And see above, pp. 182–83.

⤜ SIX ⤛

Uncertain Mastery

The range and the power of destructive aggressive impulses are almost unlimited. It is symptomatic of their formidable resources that every part of the body—the head, the mouth, the hand, the elbow, the foot—is adapted to carry out their commands. Even speech, we have seen, can be a weapon. But aggression has its constructive qualities as well, and the nineteenth century displayed them with impressive energy.

One conspicuous use is as counteraggression: striking back at bullies, refusing to take insults meekly, asserting oneself against overbearing competitors. Psychoanalytic studies have shown that for growing youngsters, this activating of aggressive impulses is highly adaptive, in fact imperative.* Nineteenth-century aggression was no exception; it effectively served the inventors, planners and statesmen, pedagogues, physicians and natural scientists, who conducted unprecedented crusades to master time, space, and scarcity. In his early years, Freud speculated about a distinct drive for mastery, which he called *Bemächtigungstrieb*. This conjecture, taken up by others after he abandoned it, blurs the sharp outlines of aggression as a destructive force, but it points to a consequential psychological and social reality. Aggression, common speech tells us, has to do with attack, and "attack" discloses certain positive implications. Normally it

*On this point, psychoanalysis was anticipated by Thomas Carlyle: "In all the sports of Children, were it only in their wanton breakages and defacements, you shall discern a creative instinct (*schaffenden Trieb*)." *Sartor Resartus* (1833–34; ed. Kerry McSweeney and Peter Sabor, 1987), 71 [book II, ch. 2].

refers to a hostile exploit—the assault of an army, the denunciation of a political opponent, the devastating review of a book; but it is also employed in appraising a skilled performance—music critics laud the attack of a violinist, dance critics that of a ballerina, for crispness and elegance. The German word for "attack," *Angriff,* exhibits its roots in the tactile act of grasping, of getting a grip on something, whether an enemy to be annihilated, a railroad network to be constructed, a symphony to be composed.

It is essential to recall, too, that mastery simply gives pleasure. The gratified sense of closure, of sheer relief, experienced when one finally understands the workings of an intricate machine, solves an intractable riddle, gets a demanding skill securely in one's grip, contrasts with its cheerless counterpart, frustration. Mastery, to be sure, is ethically neutral. The sadist, we have seen, finds joy in a mastery that his victims cannot be expected to share—unless, of course, they are masochists. And the martinet in uniform, or the exploitative manufacturer, takes pleasure in ordering his subordinates about, rewarding and punishing as he likes because he likes it. But the satisfactions of mastery need not be sinister. Virtue, despite its reputation, can be as enjoyable as vice.

Observant Victorians freely testified to the positive side of self-assertion and deplored its absence. As so often, novelists and poets anticipated the psychologists. George Eliot described the seductive Hetty in *Adam Bede* making butter so skillfully that her exigent aunt would let "it pass without severe criticism," since Hetty "handled it with all the grace that belongs to mastery." At the turn of the century, Thorstein Veblen called attention to an "instinct of workmanship," a ubiquitous human propensity giving "a taste for effective work, and a distaste for futile effort."[1] Whether independent drive or borrowed energy, inner urge or response to external pressure, disciplined aggression transformed the nineteenth-century world, and not always for ill.

Constructive aggressiveness explains much of the progressive thrust of the age and many of its strains. Over and over, observers commented, awestruck, on the rapid transformations of their time. Whether partisans of the new or its troubled critics, people characterized their century as a century of upheavals. If accepted definitions even of the criminal or the abnormal were questioned, no traditional way of seeing the world, or acting in it, was sacred. And the revolutions that shook Western culture were traumatic too for their beneficiaries; cheering on the innovators, many confessed to a vertigo generated by the disappearance of familiar landmarks.

Tumbling over one another, these new realities produced nervous responses. Stratagems of defense, partly unconscious, included regression from liberal open-mindedness, nostalgia for an idyllic past when the poor had doffed their caps to their betters, fearful clinging to strict rules of conduct, and psychological denials that were derisively, and unhelpfully, called hypocrisy. Statesmen, educators, preachers, frantically devised compromises and ambitious schemes for remedying the ills of industrial society, but their improvisations limped behind new needs and new demands. The excessive reactions of governments and affluent citizens to presumed revolutionary threats were symptoms of anxiety in a world out of control. Still, if alarm had been unanimous, the calls for a return to the old days would have been irresistible. The truth is that the agents of anxiety—those overpowering forces for change in politics, economics, science, morals, and social policy—were at the same time agents of self-confidence. Reactionaries and conservatives had to contest the ground with liberals and democrats who greeted the innovations as so many keys to a better life, so many roads to more secure mastery.

It is not possible, or necessary, to map all these roads. But several salient characteristics of the great nineteenth-century quest for mastery command our attention as we round out this study of aggression in Victorian bourgeois culture: the effort to cultivate hatred by diverting combativeness into productive channels, the application of science to daily life, specialization in the service of knowledge and action, and, finally, attempts to control the price of living in an age striving for mastery, a mastery that for all its achievements remained at best uncertain.

1. Equivalents, Moral and Other

We have had repeated reminders that Victorians were persuaded of the natural pugnacity in every human being. Hence, consistently enough, they sought ways of drawing the sting of that pugnacity by redirecting its aims. The search dominated their persistent, at times tremulous, campaigns to impose self-control on unruly passions, but as time went by, they did not remain satisfied with merely checking aggressiveness. Instead, they tried to mobilize it to build rather than destroy.

The first step, though, was to control combativeness, and after mid-century this came to seem a rational policy. In 1860, the *Saturday Review,* praising the home secretary's reluctance to move against the old anarchic sport of prize-fighting, congratulated him for accepting human nature. One way of dealing with the passion the lovers of boxing wanted to gratify would be to "deny its general existence, and to discourage and denounce its manifestations." But surely a better way was "to endeavor to regulate and improve a practice which we cannot extirpate." This was the aim Montague Shearman, an expert on English sports, had in mind when he defended soccer against the charge of brutality. It was rough, not brutal, and therefore socially productive. "The very function and final cause of rough sports is to work off the superfluous animal energy for which there is little vent in the piping times of peace."[1]

The same idea invaded matters graver than sports. In May 1876, at the Political Economy Club in London, William Gladstone ventured to remind his fellows "that the operations of commerce are not confined to material ends; that there is no more powerful agent in consolidating and in knitting together the amity of nations; and that the great moral purpose of the repression of human passions, and those lusts and appetites which are the great cause of war, is in direct relation with the understanding and application of the science which you desire to propagate."[2] Political economy, in this view, cultivates hatred by deflecting aggressive impulses into peaceful channels.

There were colonial administrators, supremely practical men, who consciously fostered the technique of subduing the lust for violence by diverting it into innocuous sporting channels. Around the turn of the century, the British resident in wildest North Borneo persuaded native tribes, hitherto devoted to blood feuds, to substitute a hotly contested regatta. "I felt," Charles Hose recalled, "that in order to suppress fighting and head-hunting, the normal young Bornean's natural outlet, it would be well to replace them by some other equally violent, but less disastrous, activity." Hence he proposed a local derby, "an annual race between the war-canoes of all the villages." It worked.[3] Again imaginative writers were the pioneers. Melville's inarticulate sailor Billy Budd, who has killed a superior, defends himself with a perceptive comment on the fatal failure of sublimation in him. "Could I have used my tongue," he stammers, "I would not have struck him."[4]

In a lecture of 1906, William James subjected the quest for the moral equivalent of violence to its most detailed, most searching examination. He warned his sympathetic audience that "the war against war is going to be no holiday excursion or camping party." The "military feelings" were too solidly established to fade unless a better ideal came along. As a psychologist, he wondered whether the continuing prosperity of war sentiment might not be partly due to certain shortcomings in the pacifist program, which gave the "militarist imagination" just grounds for resistance. The party of peace had failed to appreciate the opponent's aesthetic and ethical point of view.[5]

The ideals of self-sacrifice and manliness, then, retained a measure of validity. A world free from the scourge of war—which, James confessed, was his utopia—could not be effeminate and self-indulgent. "A permanently successful peace-economy cannot be a simple pleasure-economy." Rather, since the globe is not very hospitable, it is necessary to "make new energies and hardihoods continue the manliness to which the military mind so faithfully clings."

No doubt, "intrepidity, contempt of softness, surrender of private interest, obedience to command," must remain the rock on which states are built.[6] Virility was a standard James was reluctant to dismiss.

Modern man was, to James, a paradox; he cherished memories of war but would energetically oppose a new war started "in cold blood." Calling attention to the debate over fundamentals which, I have argued throughout, defined the Victorian age, James thought this ambivalence virtually unique to his time. The military instincts seemed as strong as ever, but criticism had considerably relaxed their ancient grip. Early societies had been hunting societies; they had prized killing, looting, and raping. The Greeks of the heroic age, jingoes and imperialists all, had gone to war for "pride, gold, women, slaves, excitement." The great Alexander, a pirate presiding over orgies of power and plunder, had been no exception, nor had the Romans. "The cruelty of those times is incredible." This history mattered because the nineteenth century, though nervous about the cost of war, had inherited the ancient sentiments.[7]

This innate pugnacity was an irrational disposition, untouched by proof of war's absurdity and horror. That horror, after all, was the fascinating thing. "War is the *strong* life; it is life *in extremis*"; millennia of peace would not breed these sentiments out of man. The only way to check the savage passion for conquest was to keep it chained and never let it get started. War might be a "gory nurse," but it was also "the romance of history." This unresolved conflict haunts James's argument. He refused to be tender-minded or sentimental, but proudly called himself a pacifist. The implications of inbred bellicosity appalled him: public opinion, intoxicated by the vision of war, drove complaisant governments into hostilities both uncivilized and unwise. This had been true of the Boer War, and true even more of the "squalid" and immoral Spanish-American War: once men gave the fighting instinct and the passion for mastery their opportunity, the unfortunate results were inescapable. The nations talked peace and prepared for war.[8]

James's substitutes for unchecked combativeness follow from this analysis: keep alive the manly spirit of competition and of service; recognize human nature without apology, but divert its aggressive propulsions to socially useful purposes; acknowledge the pleasure-giving element of battle but find new opponents, with "a conscription of the whole youthful population to form for a certain number of years a part of the army enlisted against *Nature*." Thus robustness and discipline would find targets worthy of their steel. "To coal and iron mines, to freight trains, to fishing fleets in December, to dishwashing, clothes-washing, and window-washing, to road-building and tunnel-making, to foundries and stoke-holes, and to the frames of skyscrapers, would our gilded youth be drafted off, according to their choice, to get the childishness knocked out of them, and to come back into society with healthier sympathies and soberer ideas." True to the Darwinian spirit, James celebrated the adaptive advantages to the conscripts. They would be better fathers and teachers; women would value them more highly. This experience, and only this, could be the moral equivalent of war.[9]

William James's lecture, published as a pamphlet in 1910, found thousands of approving readers.[10] Yet one of its most remarkable features is an absence. In a century virtually hypnotized by class, he was almost wholly silent on the subject. Combativeness was simply a universal instinct. On that view, *everyone* had to sublimate destructive urges, educated middle-class men not excepted. The volunteers he envisioned conquering nature—building roads and making tunnels—look like prosperous young bourgeois, so many Harvard men in overalls.

Unlike James, who called for the taming of his own class, most bourgeois cultural critics were satisfied that only the lower orders needed moral equivalents for their aggressiveness. It seemed obvious that the men and women with the smallest stake in their polity also have the smallest reserves of self-control. What was most urgent, then, was to devise pacifying activities analogous to James's moral equivalent—constructive outlets for the bellicosity the masses exhibited in drunken riots, unbuttoned festivities, wife-beating, sexual violence, and perhaps worst of all, irregular work habits. Mastery over a world growing more interdependent by the decade appeared out of reach without defensive strategies that would reduce savages in town and country to orderliness and sobriety.

With characteristic rhetoric, writers and orators intent upon this program resorted to metaphors drawn from mechanics. They particularly liked the graphic image of the "safety valve," visualizing the mind as a tightly closed vessel filled with dangerous volatile material which would explode if it was not allowed to escape. Around 1842, the English travel writer and journalist W. Cooke Taylor urged that "there must be safety-valves for the mind; that is there must be means for its pleasurable, profitable and healthful exertion." Those in power, he thought, had an opportunity, indeed an obligation, to put these devices into place. Some five years later, Robert Slaney, a progressive member of Parliament, warned that if the "neglected classes" were not provided with substitutes for their traditional rough amusements, they would flock to demagogues and "dangerous causes"; hence it was "alike wise and benevolent to provide, in regulated amusement for the many, safety valves for their eager energies." What he had in mind were organized sports, sanitized theatricals, and free public libraries.[11]

To Taylor and his fellows, skating and cycling were so many preventives against social disorder. Others prescribed devotional exercise. The Young Men's Christian Association, founded in London in 1844 and soon spreading to Canada and the United States, was an organization devoted, as the *Saturday Review* appreciatively observed in 1857, "to the task of providing harmless or useful occupations for the large class of young men who are exposed to the various temptations in London life." And in 1892, at the first German conference on leisure, the principal speaker, Viktor Böhmert, asserted that the "spread of discontent and subversive notions among the working classes" could be countered by social policies that implemented improvements in "recreation and sociability."[12]

Some would-be social engineers hunted after moral equivalents for violence in domains even more remote—not in physical but in mental exercise. One of these was the Quaker William Howitt. "The more our humble classes come to taste of the pleasures of books and intellect," he wrote in 1838, "and the deep fireside affections which grow out of the growth of heart and mind, the less charms will the outward forms of rejoicing have for them." Howitt's proposals were exceptionally refined; generally, reformers wanted to replace coarse amusements with respectable physical activity. Toward the end of the century, an English parliamentary committee investigating the poor physical condition of the working people, said it again: "If you provided them with footballs and made them kick footballs, they would not be so inclined to kick policemen in the street."[13] The proposed techniques varied, but the message was always the same; to regulate the habits of the masses involved finding civilized outlets for their riotous urges. Once in place, these substitutes would surely benefit everyone; the imposition of mannerliness and constructive vigor would generate class harmony, and this would profit not just the regulators but, quite as much, the regulated.

Radical critics, who distrusted all efforts at manufacturing harmony among the classes, did not believe in these promised windfalls for a moment; certainly the proletariat should not delude itself to expect them. To deny the grim—and necessary—reality of class struggle, or to work against it, was to draw the fangs of revolutionary social forces; all these bland equivalents could only force unilateral disarmament on the working class. In the *Communist Manifesto,* Marx and Engels sarcastically derided benevolent "Socialistic bourgeois" so "desirous of redressing social grievances." Casting their net of denunciation wide, they included among these mock socialists, "economists, philanthropists, humanitarians, improvers of the condition of the working class, organisers of charity, members of societies for the prevention of cruelty to animals, temperance fanatics, hole-and-corner reformers of every imaginable kind." What this motley humanitarian crowd really craved was "the existing state of society minus its revolutionary and disintegrating elements," as they clumsily tried to sell the world their love of self as love of others: "Free trade: for the benefit of the working class. Protective duties: for the benefit of the working class. Prison Reform: for the benefit of the working class." In sum: "the bourgeois is a bourgeois—for the benefit of the working class."[14] Marx and Engels, at least, were not impressed by the bourgeois conscience.

In face of such left-wing sniping, conservatives vilifying that conscience as maudlin and unmanly appeared tepid. Radicals denounced bourgeois reformism as Machiavellian, bourgeois outrage as cheap, bourgeois benevolence as an exercise in deceit. In their jaundiced view, nineteenth-century lovers of humanity crusading against abuses were awash in bad faith. Opponents of capital punishment could afford to appear humane: they had invented more efficient techniques for ensuring domestic and public compliance. And critics of flogging could scoff at time-honored disciplinary practices as unworthy and unaesthetic, convinced that soft modern methods were doing the work of repression with better results and less expenditure. If one could capture children, students, apprentices, even criminals, in the silken chains of guilt feelings, if one could fabricate submissive love for authority figures, the heavy artillery of harsh punishments could be profitably replaced by the subtler and cleaner weapons of control: psychological warfare. The bourgeois conscience was a fraud waiting to be unmasked. On this reading, the Victorian humanitarian style, anxious to bring pugnacity to heel, was only a cover for economic greed, political self-interest, and imperialistic lust for domination.

This derisive analysis, though it generated more distortions than it exposed, could muster plausible support. Spokesmen for the bourgeoisie—merchants, journalists, legislators—were often tempted to declare self-service to be social service. Some did so innocently, but others cynically gilded their sordid or exploitative dealings with pious humanitarian declamations or showy philanthropies. There were shrewd industrialists and businessmen across Europe and the United States who supported the temperance movement or endowed working-class clubs because they recognized that a sober work force would improve productivity and enhance their profits. English bankers, we have seen, agitated against capital punishment for forgery not from compassion so much as from the realization that a lighter penalty would induce jurors to convict makers of false banknotes more readily. And political leaders—notably Napoleon III and Bismarck—significantly enlarged the electorate, we know, not because they had been converted to democratic sentiments but because they expected to secure the loyalty of the newly enfranchised masses. For manipulators like these, the search after equivalents for bellicosity sprang principally from the appetite for, or anxiety over, profits and power.

Granted all this, the radical theory that proposed to unmask pious bourgeois and patriotic statesmen, raised to heights of sophistication in the nineteenth century, cannot explain the Victorians' penchant for curbing the wild animal within. At most, the will to deceive, conscious or unconscious, was a minor ingredient in a brew of mixed motives. Most social reformers abhorred hangings and the pillory as barbaric assertions of raw power unworthy of civilized societies. Philanthropists were literally sickened by the blighted quarters of Lyons and Birmingham, Berlin and Rome. These stinking warrens did more than offend the refined nostrils of bountiful lady visitors; humanitarians were brought to tears and spurred into action by the unhealthy conditions, the alcoholic misery, the hopeless prospects of slum denizens. The only way to rescue these victims of industrial society was to sober them up, teach them to read, give them healthful exercise in place of their savage entertainments. The unconscious reasons for the reformers' revulsion were often complicated; as Freud observed, we know, pacifists are often adults in flight from youthful sadistic desires. But the moving case they made in their speeches and manifestos, petitions to legislators, and letters to the editor, drew on heartfelt disgust at unsanitary conditions and ferocious punishments, prostitution and extreme want. That their reforms did not always hurt bourgois pocketbooks—though often enough they did—does not lessen the intensity or compromise the authenticity of the reformers' fervor. They really were offended by the unyielding conservatives of their day, really dismayed at the inhuman use of human beings.

The attentions of philanthropists and social scientists could be intrusive and patronizing, but taken as a whole, their attitudes boxed the compass of responses from the lordly to the egalitarian, the bossy to the cooperative.[15] Some reformers could not shed their naive confidence in the elevating power of palliatives. In 1881, the Noncomformist mayor of Bristol, Joseph Dodge Weston, a prosperous businessman and active worker in good causes, spoke at an exhibition in his city and used the opportunity to expound his recipe for producing social harmony: "He felt, he was sure all present felt, that if they could only make their artisan classes have more regard for their homes; if they could but teach them to introduce the elements of beauty in them, they should make the inmates far more comfortable and less likely to be tempted by outside excitements."[16] This was curing the plague with rose water. But those dedicated to relieving misery were as varied a crew as those they wished to relieve.

The unmasking strategies of radical critics, then, failed to sound the depths of middle-class indignation and dismay. Ridiculing the urge to civilize the lower orders, these critics ignored the genuine beliefs of the reformers. Devout philanthropists who endowed societies to distribute Bibles were usually good

Christians as intent on saving their own souls as those of the pagan working-class men and women on whom they lavished their missionary labors. Believing as most of them did in eternal hellfire, they thought the saving of souls supremely urgent and stood ready to give of their time, their strength—and their money—to this essential enterprise.

It became an article of faith on the left, in Protestant no less than in Catholic countries, that religion is the great enemy of progress, a drug producing social quiescence; it numbs the pain of social injustice and thus the willpower needed to see through, and shake off, the exploiter. Marx said so plainly in 1847: "The social principles of Christianity preach the need for a ruling and for an oppressed class"; they "preach cowardice, self-contempt, abasement, submissiveness, humility, in short, all the qualities of the canaille."[17] And we know how vigorously secular politicians in France—and in Italy no less—rejected calls for woman suffrage because they feared the reactionary influence of confessors on female penitents. But this does not prove that those who, like the Methodists, diligently spread religious doctrines and attitudes among the lower orders were in league with oppressors. The creed they preached to others was their own.

By the same token, most secular philanthropists supporting campaigns to spread the blessings of literacy were not intent on turning the lower orders into bourgeois much like themselves, only poorer and more docile; they valued the transforming power of reading as a force civilizing culture as a whole. These bourgeois founders of schools, organizers of working-class reading circles, publishers of inexpensive books on self-help, were training lower-class protesters and potential politicians who would use their schooling to think for themselves and to make demands their masters would find most inconvenient. "If the poor in this country," a British editor wrote in 1838, "are generally well informed—able to converse freely and rationally on many literary subjects—we owe it to the Sunday schools in which they have learned to read." The journalist who expressed this appreciation was writing in the *Northern Star,* a radical Chartist paper.[18]

The left-wing critics of the bourgeoisie failed, too, to see that civilizing the lower orders was not the monopoly of middle-class activists. The people of the "humble classes" did not form an undifferentiated mob lacking all resourcefulness. Thousands of artisans and steady laborers among them, unable and unwilling to aspire to middle-class status, took pride in their skills and their family life, and they readily acquiesced in the reformers' efforts to regulate untamed appetites. They did better than acquiesce; often taking the initiative, they called for schools and playing fields and joined the temperance crusade. Many workers, especially artisans in Catholic countries, were solidly religious and even politically conservative. The so-called lower orders, in short, were not simply passive consumers of bourgeois doctrine, malleable bits of clay allowing themselves to be seduced by shrewd manipulators into complicity with the capitalist system.

True, especially in the early phases of the industrial revolution, lower-class men and women in country after country resented the authorities' outlawing of the blood sports and rousing festivals that had so long provided relief from their drab daily lives. Many of them vigorously resisted imposition of the unvarying work discipline so essential to a bureaucratized industrial society that lived on schedules. The emergence of working-class consciousness in France, Britain, the German states, and elsewhere in the first half of the century testifies, of course, to the new conditions of work. But it testifies also to elements of cultural autonomy in the laboring masses. As the more militant among them organized into a network of social-democratic pressure groups, bourgeois reformers and proletarian radicals often found themselves at odds in the political arena. But in the great effort to master the world by mastering themselves they were often, at times to their surprise, involuntary allies.

A look at sports, especially after the 1860s, will clarify some of the subtleties attending the Victorian campaign to find pacific employment for aggressive impulses, its failures no less than its successes. Like other cultural phenomena, sports were national and cosmopolitan: the Germans were addicted to gymnastics, the British to soccer, the French to cycling, the Americans to baseball. Yet no tariff walls kept out imports; like goods and financial transactions crossing frontiers in the emerging world market, sports exemplified cultural diffusion. In particular, England, the unmatched originator, exported its inventions—complete with vocabulary—to receptive neighbors.

The representativeness of sports does not end there. Like the cities in which most sports were carried on, they expanded at explosive rates that the most infatuated enthusiast could not have predicted. Like the factories from which sports would recruit many of their practitioners and most of their spectators, they developed an ever finer division of labor; indeed, the mock combats of the age matched trade, banking, and the liberal professions in giving unprecedented prominence to the specialist. Like manual labor, sports were subject to authoritative rational rules; well before 1900, tennis players everywhere competed on courts of the same dimensions, with nets of the same height, while soccer teams across Western civilization fielded the same number of players and shot at goals of the same size. And like politics, sports had stars for the masses of spectators to adore, supplying a democratic age with the heroes after whom it yearned.

Sports mirrored the obsessiveness of bourgeois culture in their bulky rule books, their precise records of distances jumped or goals scored. More still: in an age that had for decades spouted egalitarian propaganda about careers open to talent and was starting to impose competitive examinations for government posts, sports staged contests in which merit alone was supposed to triumph. But not too much: the invidious class distinctions that continued to pervade Victorian society informed sports as well. Finally, like nearly all experience, sports drew on sexual emotions as well as open aggression; the erotic implications of grace or strength witnessed, and of movement experienced, were very real, despite the polite silence that surrounded them. In a word, sports, like the society of which they were so integral and so cherished a part, were shot through with contradictions.

The most important of these goes to the very heart of sports as a peaceful outlet for warlike urges. William James had thought to disarm the delights of pugnacity by substituting the delights of strenuous social service. The proposal seemed reasonable; since humans find it hard to give up a pleasure already experienced, such a sacrifice might come easier if another pleasure was offered in replacement. This was the psychology of that English parliamentary committee which expected that working-class men disposed to violence would not kick a policeman if they could kick a football instead. Cynical French industrialists seem to have been perfectly open about producing such equivalents; in Vienne on the Rhone, where they introduced rugby, locals said of the working population, "As long as they go to rugby games, they'll keep quiet." Suspicious working-class journalists and politicians were aware of the danger. They thought the ruling classes perfectly capable of turning professional sports into the opium of the masses. "Absorbing, from year's end to year's end, the minds of the great mass of the workers," the *Labour Leader* observed in 1904, sports might produce men "who can only obey their masters and think football."[19]

Other observers praised the civilizing effects of sports in more idealistic terms. In team games, A. Magendie, director of the École normale in Paris, wrote in 1893, "the strict obligation to keep one's temper, observe a certain decorum in one's words and gestures, behave correctly at all times, gradually accustoms the child to master himself and do what he thinks useful to his cause without infringing the rights of his comrades. Thus he acquires the strength of mind necessary to respect even the rights of his adversaries." A few optimists even found mass sports, with their hordes of impassioned supporters, pleasing exercises in self-control. "Public opinion," wrote Martin Cobbett, an English sportswriter, after 1900, "has grown into a stronger and gradually mighty power." Year by year, decade by decade, the voice of the people has worked "towards cleansing and purifying the country's manly amusements."[20]

These were charming but fanciful illusions; most journalists and observers took alarm at the behavior of the players on the field and the vicarious players in the stands. A healthful catharsis seemed only rarely a benefit of creating havoc, or merely viewing it. The heady spectacle of football players or boxers rough-ing up one another provoked not relaxed satiety, but a keener appetite for violence. In 1856, the *Saturday Review,* bemused by the continued popularity of prizefighting among the working classes, noticed that its votaries obtained psy-chological rewards—we would call them narcissistic supplies—from attending these "blackguard and brutal" battles. "They obviously want to be thought a bold, fierce, energetic generation, despising pain and fatigue, hating to do things by halves." Generally speaking, "they believe in the British lion as the be all and the end all of human excellence."[21]

Four years later, the same weekly, reporting on the famous bareknuckle championship fight between the outsized American bruiser J. C. Heenan and the far smaller but agile English boxer Tom Sayers, developed an unexpected—and revealing—sanguinary enthusiasm. Both fighters displayed great physical stamina in the fierce, apparently very exciting battle. Avidly watched by the cream of English high society, it lasted almost two and a half hours and ended only when the police broke it up because Heenan seemed to be choking Sayers on the ropes. "Never in the annals of pugilism were skill, coolness, judgment, variety of resource, pluck, and bottom displayed in such a wonderful degree as by Sayers in this splendid battle. Wherever manly courage and manly senti-ments prevail, his name will be held in honour."[22] The lust for virile and bloody displays was evidently not solely the property of navvies and publicans.

Not everyone defended violence in sports. In 1888, after soccer had become a mass sport in Britain, complete with organized leagues, cup competitions, and professional players, one French visitor, though himself addicted to sports, damned English football for its brutality: "It is a game of vulgarians. Far from developing civility, sang-froid, the spirit of justice, all the qualities that make, with dexterity and vigor, the true gentleman, one must admit that football rather arouses the low passions." In 1892, an informed English witness, Charles Edwardes, seconded this verdict. "The new football is a far more effectual arouser of the unregenerate passions of mankind than either a political gathering or a race meeting." Not that the players excited the spectators; rather, the spectators excited the players. There was unprintable jubilation or equally un-printable dejection, depending on the outcome of the game. There was much drinking and agitated dissection of the players' performance. "No mistake about it: the exercise is a passion nowadays and not merely a recreation."[23]

That soccer was also a business only increased the expenditure of energy; lust for victory was fed by hope for gain. Hely Hutchison Almond, a Scottish headmaster who defended fox hunting and corporal punishment, deplored the way professional soccer fostered unruliness. "A large part of the spectators," he wrote in 1893, "are manual labourers. They do not want exercise on Saturday afternoons, but they want rest, the open air, and some excitement which stirs their blood." Almond was a fanatical advocate of rough manly sports, but his ideal was play for sheer enjoyment rather than money, fame, or a cup; for the true amateur, soccer was nothing less than "a moral agent."[24] But Almond acknowledged that in his day, far from being an alternative to violence, mass sports were proving an incitement to it.

Some criticism of the rowdy language and rude gestures of crowds read like the snobbish disdain of an affluent onlooker observing the masses from the safe distance of his expensive seat. But some complaints were justified enough. Crowds at late-nineteenth-century soccer games, drunk with beer or excitement, often got out of hand. They screamed and cursed at players of the opposing team—or, if they performed badly, players of their own team—and at the referee. They invaded the pitch when one of their favorites was fouled, and after the game, on their way to the railroad station, they terrorized peaceful citizens living near the stadium. In 1892, England's Football League distributed a blunt poster for all member clubs to display: "Spectators and players are requested to assist in keeping order at all matches on this ground, and to prevent any demonstration of feeling against the referee, the visiting team, or any player. The consequence attending any misconduct of this kind may result in the closing of the ground for purposes of football. Such a course would not only entail great monetary loss, but would bring considerable disgrace to the Club."[25] A club might be able to live with the disgrace, but the monetary loss was something else. In late-Victorian culture, unchecked aggression could be expensive.

William James had envisioned a kind of open conspiracy for peace. But influential propagandists for sports put forward precisely the opposite goal. Their stand can be epitomized in the overworked statement, attributed—wrongly, it seems—to the duke of Wellington, that the battle of Waterloo was won on the playing fields of Eton.[26] Actually, the first polemicist to link physical fitness to military preparedness was a German we have encountered before, the eccentric patriot Friedrich Ludwig Jahn. He found his calling years before Waterloo, while the German states were bent under Napoleon's yoke. He was at first harassed by the authorities for his subversive nationalistic talk, but later much honored by his compatriots; his admirers bestowed on him a sobriquet that outlasted his life: "Turnvater," or "father of gymnastics." The author of rousing polemics that preached political unity and the purification of the German language, he marketed nostalgia for glorious Teutonic ideals that had been, he thought, sadly forgotten: fidelity, honesty, and bodily strength. For him, mastery was physical, or it was nothing.

A demagogic egalitarian, Jahn denounced Jews and Frenchmen with equal venom, but his reputation rests on his elaborate scheme of exercises. These quasi-religious morale builders were to be carried out in the open air by disciplined teams equipped with specially designed implements and identical uniforms. Jahn traveled across the German lands with his message, organized festivals, and mobilized enthusiastic disciples as robust and coarse as their master. Together, they committed themselves to the restoration of German strength and self-respect; collective gymnastics would be the agent of their country's revival. Jahn's program was William James's program turned upside down. He wanted to beat plowshares into swords.

Jahn, who died in 1852, did not live to see the realization of his most fervent wish, German unity; he once said wistfully that he had been born fifty years too soon. But his legacy, organized gymnastics bathed in a nationalistic aura, survived into the Empire. The first festival bringing together *Turner* from across the German lands was celebrated at Coburg in 1860, a decade before unification; it was treated in the press, properly enough, as a political far more than an athletic event. The liberal *Gartenlaube* hailed it as a "moral victory" for the German nation, with "a serious, high, national significance." Once the Empire was established, the accents of the gymnasts shifted toward a less political celebration of fitness, even though their spokesmen still ritually invoked Jahn's sacred name. In 1889, the year the seventh German gymnastics festival was held in Munich, some 400,000 Germans, united in 3,843 gymnastics clubs, were working out on the horizontal bar and the leather horse. Many of them simply enjoyed the sweat, the parades, the male companionship their activities provided.[27] These more temperate seekers after bodily health replaced muscle-flexing chauvinism with peaceful reasons for doing their exercises.

But precisely the historic occasion that allowed Germans to relax their militancy in sports forced that militancy upon the French. "Our neighbors," declared one writer in an 1882 *Gartenlaube* article on armed battalions of schoolboys in France, "have learned something from us." The situation was worrisome. The founding of the Reich had been one of the most traumatic humiliations in France's history. From then on, many French lovers of athletic combat saw war as sports by other means. On August 3, 1914, the day a military clash between France and Germany became inevitable, Henri Desgrange, a famous cyclist, originator of the Tour de France and editor of the vastly successful sports magazine *L'Auto,* exhorted his readers in his folksy way: "Mes p'tit gars français! Listen to me! . . . The Prussians are a bunch of bastards." The games Frenchmen had enjoyed in peacetime would now serve them in the trenches: "This is the big match that you have to play and you must use every trick that you've learned in sport." Evidently one of the things they had learned in sports, if one could believe Desgrange, was pitilessness. "When your bayonet is at their heart and they beg for mercy, don't give in. Run them through!"[28]

Publicists like Desgrange had been training French readers to such bellicosity for over forty years. Since their defeat, *revanche* had been a burning topic to which sportsmen, like others, returned obsessively. But their longing to regain France's lost provinces and reestablish its manhood among the nations raised unsettling doubts about the physical condition of the soldiers of the future. Anxiety over the dropping French population was compounded by anxiety over the people's deplorable lack of fitness. How was one to beat the German bastards with youngsters graduating from French schools as bespectacled and limp-wristed aesthetes?

During the Second Empire, educators had called for programs of physical education and legislators had decreed them, only to be frustrated by a lack of funds and of interest. Few schools had buildings suitable for gymnastics or games, fewer still had playing fields. But the dishonor of Sedan stimulated a willingness to introduce exercise into the schools and pay for it. Indifference was replaced by hysteria. In 1879, the president of the Club alpin français founded five years before, noted that while the club was still laboring "under the impact of patriotic grief," it hoped to become a "school of physical energy and moral vigor" to make young Frenchmen "more virile, more apt to bear military life, more prepared to face a long conflict without discouragement." Orators addressing banquets of sporting organizations all sounded that same note. They agreed with Magendie's curt pronouncement that "physical exercise" is "intimately linked to patriotic education."[29]

Philosophically minded Frenchmen joined in, making the connection between sports and pugnacity that William James deplored. In *La Morale des sports*, a solemn treatise of 1907, Paul Adam observed that in ancient Athens, "Force had been the mother of Spirit," and by *Esprit* Adam meant militancy. He also enlisted Nietzsche in his call for national manliness: "The taste for sports is a daily stimulant toward the will to power." Man, Nietzsche had said, must surpass himself. What a splendid maxim! Adam found no less splendid the Yankees' love for "excitement," defined as a feeling of satisfaction that "enhances corporal vigor and moral energy" in sports as in politics. Paradoxically, Adam also enlisted William James in his cause. Had James not epitomized the whole philosophy of sports in his theory of emotions, according to which gestures and actions create feelings? It was now time to "resurrect the heroism in the souls and bodies of Latin youth" that had distinguished French soldiers on the battle fields of Austerlitz and Jena.[30] Whatever one might think of Napoleon, he at least had beaten the Germans.

French sportsmen and spectators could no more sustain this patriotic intensity than could their German counterparts. Those who believed that sports might indeed tame aggressiveness could take comfort from that fact. True, French gymnasts who, ironically enough, took to this German import with a will after 1870, sounded like incarnations of Turnvater Jahn. In 1882, the members of a new club in Reims considered various names, among them the provocative "Le Souvenir," "Alsace-Lorraine," and, most bluntly, "La Revanche," only to settle on the rather more artful "La Sentinelle." And the Union des sociétés françaises de gymnastique, formed in 1873 and after some decades boasting a membership in the hundreds of thousands, took as its motto the patriotic request of General Chanzy: "Make me men, and we will make soldiers of them."[31] Anti-German pronouncements at the group's festivities were always sure of noisy applause. Yet, as more and more Frenchmen could afford to practice gymnastics, most did so to keep their muscles and their waists in shape. All they attacked was excessive weight.[32]

France's passion for cycling, identified with the country since the 1870s, was even more innocent of patriotic aggressiveness. At first, bicycles were beyond most people's means, but the price dropped in the 1890s after the new models with pneumatic tires were introduced, and the sport blossomed.[33] Bicycle manufacturers staged races, awarded prizes, and created folk heroes to advertise their product, turning the sport into mass entertainment. The velodromes built before 1900 in Paris and other large cities often accommodated crowds of fifteen thousand or more, all paying good money to watch the races.[34] And the famous Tour de France, a commercial venture to the core when it started in 1903, grew into a national festival. For most French cyclists and their enraptured spectators, the German enemy became a side issue. They had, in fact, developed different problems; around the turn of the century, physicians gravely worried about whether cycling might stimulate sexual desire or injure the genitals, and whether it should be permitted to women during menstruation or soon after intercourse. In 1900, after an unsparing investigation, Dr. Ludovic O'Followell allowed that there might be some risks in cycling, but he saw no evidence that it contributed to France's lamentable population decline. On the contrary, he thought, it brought families closer together and might thus help raise the birthrate.[35]

Whatever the conflicting motives agitating Victorian sportsmen, their sport could help effect the integration of classes—if it was affordable. Indeed, it worked so well that apprehensive socialists in several countries founded soccer and hiking clubs untainted by bourgeois members who might blunt the will to revolution. But the most conspicuously snobbish sports only exacerbated class divisions. Horseback riding, lawn tennis, rowing, polo, required expensive gear and a commitment of time and fees beyond the reach of the working classes and, for that matter, the petty bourgeoisie.

And some sports only seemed democratic. In 1871, the anonymous compiler of a cricket handbook noted that the sport beautifully developed physical skills, suited the English love of nature, and "added to this, there is the advantage of the free interchange of courtesy on the 'green turf' between class and class: there, even lords and labourers meet on common ground, and may for the nonce mingle freely together."[36] But this "Member of the Marylebone Club," that virtual dictator of cricket, conveniently forgot to mention that the free mingling stopped the moment the game was over and that the composition of the teams themselves, with their notorious distinction between gentlemen and players, amateurs and professionals—a practice that survived into the 1960s—emphasized English class divisions. Some sports, notably soccer, were democratized before the turn of the century. But others remained, until 1914 and after, the preserve of an elite. If sports did in some ways serve as moral equivalents for conflict, this did not hold true of class conflict.

With the shortening work week and the increase in disposable income, pressure mounted from lower-middle-class and working-class sports lovers, and the distinction between exclusive and demotic sports could not remain absolute. But Victorian gentlemen worked to sabotage the inescapable leveling down.* The mainstay of their defense against democratic sports was the cult of the amateur. The English did not invent the word, but they spread their definition of it across the civilized world. The ideal of the amateur imposed severe strains on officials and managers, to say nothing of the athletes themselves. As they faced growing masses of spectators clamoring for victories, teams tried to satisfy them by securing the services of the most accomplished athletes money could buy. Workingmen competing in team sports needed to be reimbursed for the time they lost on the job, and, spending a good deal of money, rival clubs tried to seduce the best players from their competitors or bribe them to perform below par. The cult of the amateur generated more hypocrisy than anything else in the history of modern sports.[37]

---

*British amateur soccer and rugby teams of the late nineteenth century refused on principle to participate in cup competitions; they ruined the spirit of the game. In the United States the issue surfaced in that bastion of gentlemanliness, Harvard University. In 1883, its Committee on Athletics ordered the Harvard Football Club dissolved because the game was "no longer governed by a manly spirit of fair play," but had become suffused with "a spirit of sharpers and roughs." The Club, having already arranged for a match against Yale in New York's Polo Grounds, refused, and it survived. William C. Rhoden, "College Athletics: Winning Games, Losing Perspective," *New York Times,* June 4, 1989, News of the Week in Review, 6.

The social implications of the cult are obvious; the amateur is the person who has both time and money to devote to his sport.[38] But proponents of the ideal did not like to dwell on this social reality. Pierre de Coubertin, the founder of the modern Olympic games, welcomed the salutary mixing of classes that, he thought, public-school and college sports had produced in England. He did not see—or did not say—that this genial camaraderie was largely restricted to the sons of the gentry and prosperous tradesmen; the lower orders were practically excluded from it.

Whatever its limitations in reality, Coubertin and other votaries saw the ethos of the amateur as part of the great nineteenth-century campaign in behalf of character. In 1894, at a meeting arranging for the Olympic games, he told the delegates that the neglect of the body since the Middle Ages had been an "immense error" with countless scientific and social consequences. An international festival of sports would redress the balance. "There are not two parts to a man, body and soul; there are three, body, mind, and character," and character is "not formed by the mind, but primarily by the body."[39]

Pierre de Coubertin embodies the complexities and contradictions that made nineteenth-century sports such a dubious ally in the crusade for self-restraint. In a stream of speeches, articles, and books, Coubertin reiterated the athletic creed that had first come to him in 1886, when he was twenty-three, on one of his trips to England. A French edition of Thomas Hughes's *Tom Brown's Schooldays*—"that moving and suggestive book"—became Coubertin's bible; like its hero, Coubertin found inspiration, indeed his vocation, on a visit to Rugby. The fantasy he developed there organized his life: he would teach the world to cultivate the body in free, joyous activity that would raise men's courage and moralize their whole being. Sports at Rugby "stop corruption at its birth by isolating it and preventing it from spreading, and, finally, arm nature for the struggle."[40] Pacific and martial metaphors jostled one another under Coubertin's pen all his life.

They enabled Coubertin, the scion of an ancient noble family, to extol prowess, that aristocratic virtue, and at the same time preach against the lust for victory. Sport had to be a *pure* pleasure, its pursuit the spontaneous expression of vitality. Like other champions of this gentlemanly ethos, Coubertin deprecated rage over defeat and exultation in victory; the game alone mattered. His was the Olympic credo: "The important thing is not winning but taking part, the essential thing in life is not conquering but fighting well." Hence he thundered against the professional spirit in sports, even though he recognized that a working-class athlete had to have some financial compensation. The modern Olympic games, which owed their existence to his patience and diplomacy, were to be a "republic of muscles."[41] Unlike many of the titled and snobbish amateurs with whom he associated, Coubertin was, in his way, a democrat.

He was also a lover of country and a lover of peace at the same time; he valued patriotism and detested nationalism. The upheavals in his France, he confessed late in life, had filled him with shame when he was a young man. "Nothing troubled my national amour propre more than the coexistence in my pocket of coins bearing different effigies." But this did not make him a chauvinist or a preacher of *revanche*. True patriotism, in his view, was love unspoiled by hatred. Fostering this love, the modern Olympic games should become agents of international understanding, "a potent if indirect factor in securing universal peace." The experience they provided differed decisively from that of tourism, which left the traveler as ignorant of the people he had visited as he was before he left home. Wars arose from misunderstandings. "We shall not have peace until the prejudices which now separate the different races shall have been outlived. To attain this end, what better means than to bring the youth of all countries periodically together for amicable trials of muscular strength and agility?"[42]

All agreed that so ambitious a program could never be realized by professionals. Only amateurs could keep the flame of fair play burning. Fairness demanded that one not take advantage of a referee's obstructed vision to foul an opponent, not enter the lists of combat with marked advantages, and not contest penalties.[43] During the hundred-kilometer bicycle race at the Olympic games of 1896, when a Greek racer needed his cycle serviced, a French competitor stopped until the repairs had been completed. Fairness demanded even more: stoical self-mastery. The fair-minded player did not glower or gloat; he was a good loser and (even more demanding) a good winner.[44] This was a prescription for gentlemen, one that nobody really expected the masses to master. The principal control of aggression in *their* sports was control over violence among the spectators. And that was a job for the police.

With all their much-deplored rowdiness, Victorian sports were exposed to a novel and impressive campaign, largely successful, to subject competitive games to rule. Here again sports were typical for wider nineteenth-century concerns; they found ways of cultivating aggression without losing its dividends in effort and energy. Not that the Victorians could rightfully claim to be the first to reduce mayhem to order; sports of earlier days, apparently so spontaneous and certainly so savage, had obeyed laws, however disheveled, of their own.[45] Boxing, for one, wildly popular in eighteenth-century England with the aristocrats who staked their favorite fighters and the mobs attending these sanguinary exhibitions, was conducted from the 1740s on under rules which forbade kicking an opponent, hitting him when he was down, or striking him below the belt. But—and this is where the Victorians came in—these rules did not provide sufficient protection against fouls, heavy betting, and other irregularities. The year 1866 saw the establishment of the Amateur Athletic Club, and the Queensberry Rules were formulated a year later. Repeatedly revised and widely adopted, they regulated the size of the ring, the length of rounds, the type of gloves, the kinds of blow permissible, the weight class to which a fighter was assigned. Modern boxing was born of a revolution.

So was the most widely played, and watched, sport in the world, soccer, which late-nineteenth-century England bestowed on untold millions of enthusiasts everywhere—except in the United States. An ancient sport, uncertain in its origins, it remained for centuries a democratic, often illegal diversion. By the eighteenth century a fairly primitive version, complete with predictable violence, had become a favorite entertainment of what England's middle classes called the "common people." But it was largely its enduring popularity among English public-school boys and, by mid-century, their influence at the old universities, that rescued it from obloquy and oblivion.

Since each public school was a sovereign commonwealth unto itself, each had its own treasured version of soccer, handed down across generations, including definitions of what constituted lawful riot. But with rapidly improved communications—the railroad transformed sports as it transformed virtually every other aspect of mid-nineteenth-century life—a unified set of rules became essential to permit Eton and Harrow, Oxford and Cambridge, to mount matches against one another. In the 1850s, a diplomatic compromise reconciled several idiosyncratic styles of soccer then in vogue. And in late 1863, to codify their proceedings, a number of these clubs sent representatives to London, to a meeting that the authors of a bulky four-volume history of soccer published in 1906 typically called the "opening of the Football Parliament."[46] Political skills were at a premium among these individualists tied to their own way of playing the game. But while they could agree on a central authority, the Football Association, they did so at heavy cost; advocates of the more physical version of the game walked out and worked toward an organization of their own; by 1871, their Rugby Football Union was in place.[47]

This split is of exceptional interest to the historian of moral equivalents for pugnacity, for the issue was the permissible forms and degrees of aggression. As readers of *Tom Brown's Schooldays* will remember, public-school football was not for the timid or the frail. Players bruised kneecaps, tripped opponents, squeezed necks, trampled feet. Nostalgic Old Boys regretted the banning of this delightful ferocity as a shameful surrender to effeminacy. They wanted to keep old-fashioned tripping and the venerable practice of "hacking"—the intentional kicking of shins—on the books. Only a game that included this open aggressiveness (said one of them, speaking for many) is "the true form of football." If "you do away with it, you will do away with all the courage and pluck of the game, and"—the ultimate insult—"I will be bound to bring over a lot of Frenchmen who would beat you with a week's practice."[48]

Rugby soon developed a substantial following of its own. It remained a more physical game than its chief competitor, but after mid-century, the bourgeois culture that left its mark on sports had moved beyond the boyish need to prove manliness by aiming a boot at an opponent's shin. This issue once settled, the legislators of soccer concentrated on refining the regulations that would discipline their sport. They had to confront, we know, the vexed issue of how to define an amateur in an age of mounting commercialism. And at a time when other sports, too, were methodically specifying the rules once left to chance, the governing body of soccer regulated in meticulous detail the size of the penalty area, the offside position, the right to handle the ball, and, by the mid-1870s, the authority of the referee.

The referee is a most instructive figure in Victorian culture. The second half of the era became the age of the referee; the Germans liked to call him the *Unparteiische*—the "nonpartisan man." In rowing and swimming, boxing and tennis, soccer and rugby and baseball, he rose to unprecedented summits of power. By 1880, the Football Association had authorized referees to send players off the field. "Our forefathers got on, and got on very well too," the sports historian William Pickford recalled in 1906, "without a referee." In a word, that official was a thoroughly modern institution. The game of football, Pickford added, "began without the 'Autocrat,' and it may end without him."[49] Pickford was, it turned out, a better historian than prophet.

In earlier days, a few public schools had appointed umpires to determine when a goal was scored, and had occasionally empowered them to maintain the fair conduct of the match. As large-scale professional soccer evolved in the last decades of the nineteenth century, first in Britain and then on the Continent, the referee's authority mounted. Contemporaries observed that the evolution of the modern referee had been striking. "Doubtless," Charles Edwardes wrote in 1892, "ere the game had grown to a mania among the people his position was a sufficiently responsible one. But it is now tenfold so. His relationship toward the players and the thousands of highly strung spectators somewhat resembles that of the Speaker in the House of Commons towards the members of Parliament." His duty was "to enforce the laws," and to decide "all disputed points." He was not to be questioned, and, the rule provided tersely, "his decision is final." The referee decided which aggression was legal, which beyond bounds.[50]

It soon emerged, to no one's surprise, that his profession was risky indeed. "I have seen him," Edwardes recalled, "retreat from the field after the match surrounded by the players themselves, who had the greatest difficulty to keep the yelling and blaspheming mob from getting hold of him and maltreating him as much as if he were a notorious welsher."[51] Stories abounded about enraged fans cursing referees, pelting them with muck and missiles, offering them violence after a match. In 1913, as the Scottish rugby team played against France in Paris, the patriotic mob of spectators watched feverishly, passionately hoping that their team might repeat the famous victory it had scored over Scotland two years before. When the English referee repeatedly, and it seems justly, penalized French players for fouls—the Scots were ahead—the fans shed all remnants of civilized self-control and shrieked the grossest insults at him. After the game, they stormed the field; the referee, who had kept his cool demeanor throughout, had to be walked from the stadium surrounded by a bodyguard of players and police.*

The referee, this majestic authority, stands as a commentary on human nature, one the Victorian well understood. To be sure, sporting contests need an impartial judge to make close judgment calls: whether a serve is in or out, whether a pitch is a ball or a strike, whether a punch is above or below the belt. But more: as the implacable, unbribable high priest of fairness, and the nemesis of cheaters and bullies, the referee stands as a reminder of inescapable imperfections. By definition, the sportsman able to handle his aggressive impulses and restrain his appetite for victory needs no guardian to keep him a gentleman. But a realistic appraisal of Victorian performance in sport after sport would turn up only a minority of such exemplary amateurs on the field or in the stands.

An optimist like Coubertin might retain faith that sports conducted on his principles are bound to promote social harmony and international understanding. There were times when this actually happened. Programs like William James's for replacing destructive passions with constructive equivalents sometimes produced gratifying results; such blueprints for securing mastery over the world by securing mastery over oneself were not utterly utopian. Rather, they were an admirable effort by a century intent upon making life more tolerable

---

*See Richard Holt, *Sport and Society in Modern France* (1981), 135–36. Catching this mood, around the turn of the century an English humorist imagined rules of football for the year 1950 that specified, "The field of play shall be surrounded on all sides by wire netting or iron bars," while the referee shall wear "a coat of bullet-proof armour" provided by the clubs, and have standing by "a motor-car or flying machine." What was more, "all clubs shall, before every game commences, insure the referee's life." William Pickford, "The Referee, Past, Present, and Future," in Alfred Gibson and William Pickford, *Association Football and the Men Who Made It*, 4 vols. (1906), III, 11.

than it had been. Yet history sternly teaches that these efforts were shot through with wishful thinking; they certainly failed as much as they succeeded.

2. The Empire of Fact

If evidence is wanted that the aggressive drive has its constructive uses, the drama of industrialization can supply it. Industrialization transformed the world in the nineteenth century and markedly increased man's control over his fate. It was the most concerted series of aggressions ever launched against ignorance, and against human resignation before the blind power of nature. Defying its narrow name, what the late nineteenth century called the industrial revolution went far beyond creating modern industry; it altered out of all recognition commerce, banking, transport, communications, administration, medicine, the relations of men to women and employers to employees. It was a revolution in knowledge that the Victorian century would master more completely, and would need more urgently, than any of its predecessors. In his account of human development, Freud put considerable stress on the child's increasing capacity for reality testing, for distinguishing between wishes and facts, between internal and external impulses. In the long and controversial history of the struggle for dependable knowledge, modern science occupies the summit with its competent, self-critical reality testing.

Since time out of mind, men have believed that knowledge is power; they have understood that they could not rely on intuition and improvisation alone as they attempted to master nature and themselves. Whether they worked to secure food and shelter, to build roads and cities, to prolong life, or to overcome enemies, they needed special, often esoteric lore. Propitiating the gods with sacrifices, seeking the counsel of priests, consulting an oracle, interpreting parables in a sacred text, falling back on a closely held craft secret, were ways of providing it. Inevitably, the prestige of these sources of knowledge fluctuated from century to century, culture to culture, even class to class. One man's wisdom was another man's superstition. Only the information generated by the modern sciences has given promise of commanding general assent. It is, after all cumulative, and boasts procedures of self-correction. And it has made a demonstrable difference to human lives, to which by the nineteenth century its devotees could proudly point.

In 1832, reflecting on these triumphs of the sciences, the famous English inventor Charles Babbage found use once again for an old saw: "The experience of the past, has stamped with the indelible character of truth, the maxim that '*Knowledge is power*.' "[1] All knowledge, even of the good or the beautiful, is useful by definition. But those aspiring to mastery needed a particular sort of knowledge. They looked for the precise data they could deploy in the undertakings of human life. "Why is knowledge of any kind useful?" the English positivist Frederic Harrison asked in 1862. Mere facts were not what was wanted. "All knowledge is imperfect, we may almost say meaningless, unless it tends to give us sounder notions of our human and social interests."[2] Except for aesthetes, all Victorians sounded that way. Even devout Christians, though troubled by the drift away from religion, subscribed to the proposition that theirs was the scientific century. The conviction was so common, and so commonplace, that it requires virtually no documentation. In the age of Pasteur, Edison, and Röntgen, it was rational to believe that science, which had presided over stunning innovations in technology and medicine, would keep up its revolutionizing work.

The supreme herald of the utilitarian scientific philosophy, Francis Bacon, had laid down his guidelines for the mastery of reality more than two centuries before. But, appropriately enough, the texts of his writings were definitively established in the nineteenth century; the age that abounded in scholarly editors did not overlook Bacon. "After three centuries," wrote the great German organic chemist Justus von Liebig in 1863, "his name glows like a shining star." The classic seven-volume collection of his works, edited by James Spedding and others between 1857 and 1874, has never been supplanted. Authoritative biographies and thoughtful analyses of his thought appeared during the same years. One eloquent testimonial to Bacon came from that powerful authority Charles Darwin. Studying plants and fossils with equal assiduity, he had started his first notebook in July 1837. "I worked on true Baconian principles, and without any theory collected facts on a whole-sale scale." It was only after stumbling on Malthus's book on population a year later that he "at last got a theory by which to work," but even then he remained faithful to his empiricism: "I was so anxious to avoid prejudice, that I determined not for some time to write even the briefest sketch of it."[3] Especially in his early investigations, Darwin found Bacon the most trustworthy of guides.

Bacon in fact seemed so authoritative a model that nineteenth-century commentators bravely enlisted him in their own intellectual or religious causes. In 1844 a devout Protestant lawyer from Maryland, Samuel Tyler, published a treatise on Bacon ostensibly animated by the "strong desire to vindicate a Method of Investigation," the "great doctrine" that "*experience is the only light to our path.*" But somehow that great doctrine supported Tyler's religious faith: "The Baconian Philosophy is emphatically the philosophy of protestantism."[4] But nothing documents Bacon's relevance to the Victorians more vividly than the attitude of William Whewell. A mathematical economist who diligently made propaganda for the scientific method, Whewell had grave doubts about Bacon's theory of induction, but nevertheless wrote his treatises in his shadow. And in 1845, as master of Trinity College, Cambridge, he presented to the fellows a statue of Bacon.* As he had spoken to the Enlightenment, in which so much of the Victorians' quest for mastery was rooted, Bacon also spoke to the Victorian century.†

Bacon's propaganda for a new way of thinking, perhaps the most thorough revolution any philosopher has ever proposed, is well known. He called for "a total reconstruction of the sciences, arts, and all human knowledge, raised upon proper foundations," that would awaken humanity from the dogmatic slumbers into which philosophers and theologians had lulled it. His method prescribed experimentation, the classification of knowledge, collective scientific investigation, and absolute submission to the truths of nature. "Nature to be commanded must be obeyed." This almost blasphemous program required insight into the prejudices—the "idols," Bacon called them—that regularly frustrate fertile research. For Bacon and his enthusiastic followers, the systematic exposure of calcified doctrine had to accompany inquiries into the mysteries of nature. Empiricism, to work, had to be critical empiricism. Once successfully applied, it would lead to "the enlarging of the bounds of Human Empire, to the effecting of all things possible." In a word, "The true and lawful goal of the sciences is none other than this: that human life be endowed with new discoveries and powers."[5]

This was the stance in Bacon's scientific ideology that the nineteenth cen-

---

*For Whewell on Bacon, see, for example, his observation to Augustus De Morgan, January 18, 1859: "I shall be amused if you succeed in persuading the world that Bacon had little to do with the modern progress of science." Isaac Todhunter, *William Whewell, D.D., Master of Trinity College, Cambridge,* 2 vols. (1876), II, 417; for the statue of Bacon, see ibid., I, 155. It can still be seen in the antechapel of Trinity, in the immortal company, among other graduates of the college, of Newton and Macaulay.

†The philosophes had hailed Bacon as an ancestor of the critical style of thinking that would explode theological and philosophical absurdities and prepare the way for the empire of fact. They were not sentimental about him; Voltaire acknowledged that Bacon "did not yet know nature." Still, he was "the father of experimental philosophy," who had "shown all the paths that lead to it." *Lettres philosophiques,* "XIIe Lettre" (1734; ed. Gustave Lanson, 2 vols., 1909), I, 154–55. Voltaire's favorite exhortation was an appeal to Bacon's philosophical style: "Au fait!" Like the other philosophes, he scorned the metaphysicians who built grandiose but empty systems, and yearned instead for what his contemporary Hume called the "science of man," a science built upon the very methods that the natural scientists were employing with such impressive results. For the Enlightenment, drawing this distinction between the pernicious "spirit of system" and the laudable "systematic spirit" was not just an innocent philosophical pastime. The knowledge the Enlightenment called for was at once a pacific instrument and a lethal weapon.

tury—at least Victorians committed to progress—most appreciated. In an expansive essay on Bacon, Macaulay assailed his character for his corrupt dealings as a public servant, but hailed his thought as the liberator of human capacities. In a breathtaking tribute, he listed the profits from the scientific philosophizing that Bacon had inaugurated: "It has lengthened life; it has mitigated pain; it has extinguished diseases; it has increased the fertility of the soil; it has given new securities to the mariner; it has furnished new arms to the warrior; it has spanned great rivers and estuaries with bridges of form unknown to our fathers; it has guided the thunderbolt innocuously from heaven to earth; it has lighted up the night with the splendour of the day; it has extended the range of the human vision; it has multiplied the power of the human muscles; it has accelerated motion; it has annihilated distance; it has facilitated intercourse, correspondence, all friendly offices, all despatch of business," and much else. Best of all, "it is a philosophy which never rests, which has never attained, which is never perfect. Its law is progress."[6]

Apologists for Bacon, like James Spedding, lapped up Macaulay's praise of their hero and tried to refute his strictures on Bacon's character. On the other side, social critics who questioned a philosophy that seemed obsessed with low, practical benefits derided Macaulay for his "materialism" and called him, as Matthew Arnold did, "the great Apostle of the Philistines."[7] The prosperous, steadily expanding nineteenth-century empire of fact had its eloquent detractors. But its supporters, by no means all of them philistines, proved no less eloquent. They insisted that the key to rational progress could be found precisely, and only, in the fact-driven science their critics found so deplorable. In 1828, upon the request of the Institution of Civil Engineers, a prominent self-educated English colleague, Thomas Tredgold, defined its field of expertise: "The art of directing the great sources of power in Nature for the use and convenience of man; being that practical application of the most important principles of natural philosophy which has, in a considerable degree, realized the anticipations of Bacon, and changed the aspect and state of affairs in the whole world."[8] Bacon remained the honored prophet of practical men.

When the Statistical Society of London was founded in 1834, it too declared its purposes in true Baconian style: "To procure, arrange, and publish facts calculated to illustrate the condition and prospects of society." By 1840, in its sixth report, the council sounded even more self-assured: "Statistics, by their very name are defined to be the observations necessary to the social or moral sciences, to the science of the *statist*, to whom the statesman and the legislator must resort for the principles on which to legislate and govern." To "estimate the condition of any people, and duly appreciate its causes, with the means of its modification, the 'physical geography' of the country which they occupy forms the first indispensable body of information." In short, the statistician's science "is the science of the arts of civil life."[9]

To their votaries it was clear that utter respect for, and tireless research into, facts had salutary social and even political consequences. Consider Charles Babbage, liberal, would-be reformer of Britain's scientific establishment, and inventor of genius; his designs for an "analytical engine" are an ancestor of the modern computer. In 1832, he ran for Parliament on the platform that his constituents could only profit from having a scientist, a man of facts, in the House of Commons. He advertised his "long pursued investigation of the laws of nature as displayed in the physical world," his "habit of regarding facts solely as facts, and of reasoning on those facts solely with a view to the elucidation of truth," and promised to carry his "wholesome habit" of first collecting facts and then rationally deducing conclusions from them into "political investigations." His audiences liked what they heard, murmuring, "Hear, hear!" Their applause did not translate into enough votes—Babbage just failed to get elected—but plainly there was nothing eccentric about his linking of the scientific method to social and political questions.[10]

Possibly the century's most poignant commitment to fact was a declaration by Thomas Henry Huxley. It has been much quoted. After the Huxleys' young son died, Charles Kingsley sent condolences, holding out a Christian's hope for a reunion. But Huxley, in the grip of a grief that brought him to the verge of a breakdown, sturdily rejected this chimerical consolation. He would not believe in immortality just because it might soothe his pain. "Science has taught to me the opposite lesson. She warns me to be careful how I adopt a view which jumps with my preconceptions, and to require stronger evidence for such belief than for one to which I was previously hostile." His business was "to teach my aspirations to conform themselves to fact, not to try and make facts harmonise with my aspirations." Huxley the pagan, using religious language to enforce his irreligious point, likened the teachings of science to the Christian sense of surrender to God's will. "Sit down before fact as a little child, be prepared to give up every preconceived notion, follow humbly wherever and to whatever abyss nature leads, or you shall learn nothing."[11] Huxley was too sophisticated a biologist—his reputation as Darwin's "bulldog" has unjustly obscured his stature as a man of science—to take this credo literally. His call to childlike reverence for fact essentially reflects his deep conviction that science is either objective or only a game. If it does not work as the nemesis of illusions, science is itself an illusion, mere wishful thinking dressed up in technical language.

One easily forgets that despite earnest efforts to escape from illusions, Huxley was writing in a century awash in them. Astonishingly ignorant, the Victorians needed more facts, ever more facts, than they had at their disposal. Dickens, in the opening sentences of *Hard Times,* wickedly mocked the hardhearted utilitarians who would uproot all poetry from life: "Now, what I want is, Facts. Teach these boys and girls nothing but Facts. Facts alone are wanted in life." His lampoon was supremely unjust; for the age, the cult of fact was not a fad but a necessity. Even the well-informed, and those who thought themselves well-informed, furiously divided on issues without mastering the most basic information about them. The international debate over Malthus's gloomy prediction that irresistible population increases must have tragic consequences for the food supply drew far more on passion than on accurate, or even approximate, numbers. The economists and politicians across Western civilization arguing over the advantages and liabilities of free trade knew little more. Both sides in the acrimonious dispute about Catholic emancipation in England had only the roughest guesses at just how many Roman Catholics lived in their country, or how many more might live there in the future.

Ignorance haunted the very pursuit of information. Early in the century, the decennial censuses launched by more and more countries provided social scientists with the most untrustworthy help.[12] For decades the American census, inaugurated in 1800, and its English counterpart of 1801, were too primitive, simply too erratic, to serve their announced purposes. The American census of 1840, for one, was a muddle and a scandal. Quite apart from sordid feuds over printing contracts, petty quarrels among politicians over turf, and paranoid popular resistance to answering intrusive questions, the skewed results were the inescapable consequence of vague instructions and statistical naiveté. And of racial bias: the politically most inflammable, and perfectly ludicrous, conclusion this census reached was that blacks in Northern states showed a far higher incidence of insanity than those in the South—an embarrassing "fact" for defenders of slavery to gloat over and abolitionists to explain away.[13] Contemporary statisticians were uncomfortably aware that facts can be manipulated, even manufactured. That acidulous observation attributed to Disraeli—"there are three kinds of lies: lies, damned lies, and statistics"—would not have angered them.

What the Victorians did not know, then, hurt them. Even more damaging were the legends they took for truths. As we have seen, statistics on crime and other social problems, though improving in volume and precision, provided only a rickety foundation for proposed remedies. The policies that nineteenth-century foreign offices developed for distant parts of the globe were based on the skimpiest data and made by ministers who had never seen the countries whose destinies they were shaping; Britain's fateful decision of 1882 to occupy Egypt is only one instance of the myopic leading the myopic. The bureaucrats and police chiefs, philanthropists and clerics, who carried on their nervous and confused campaigns against prostitution worked with figures that were far more fiction than fact, expressive witnesses to rich and murky inner lives.* The no less nervous, even more intensive crusade against masturbation, which the most respectable medical practitioners denounced as certain to produce lassitude, madness, and death, drew on a fanciful theory of the bodily economy that was a tribute to sheer misinformation as much as to deep-lying anxieties. And down to 1900 and beyond, reputable physicians advising married women on the rhythm method to prevent conception placed the period safest for sexual intercourse at the very time in the ovular cycle when a woman is in fact most likely to conceive; it was as though the doctors were unconsciously running a fertility clinic.[14]

The horrendous misreadings of woman's monthly biological rhythm, like the pathetic anxiety about "self-abuse," are stern reminders of the distance the late nineteenth century still had to travel before it could claim even partial mastery over the human body. On the other hand, there were heartening proofs that the revolution in knowledge did include medicine. The triumphs of Victorian medical science were often cited then, and have been cited since, as demonstrating that in some areas the Whiggish claims for continuous progress, so often ridiculed as naive, are justified. Macaulay's praise of Baconianism for lengthening life, mitigating pain, and extinguishing diseases came at mid-century; had he lived to draw this cheering balance sheet fifty years later, he would have been even more lyrical.

The extraordinary thing about the advances in medicine was not just how much physicians had learned but how quickly they had learned it. For decades after 1800, the causes of most diseases were embarrassing enigmas, only exacerbated by the slashing style of fashionable medical theorists competing with each other. All parties claimed to see in a darkness they would not acknowledge. In the Paris of the early Restoration, the commanding medical authority was François Joseph Victor Broussais, a fluent dogmatist who touted, to enormous audiences, his explanation of all diseases as lesions and inflammations. In Vienna during those years, "epidemicists," who attributed outbreaks of cholera to atmospheric conditions, dominated the medical debate. Everywhere the search for cures was hampered by the imprecision of diagnoses; typhoid fever and

---

*In the mid-nineteenth century, one excited self-appointed expert, the French litterateur Maxime du Camp, estimated that there were 120,000 prostitutes in Paris, while in London another, the investigative journalist Samuel Bracebridge, warned that some 80,000 were parading the streets; but after the turn of the century, Hans Ostwald, in a detailed study of Berlin's prostitutes, called the claim that in that city one woman in eight was a whore absurdly inflated. See Peter Gay, *The Bourgeois Experience,* vol. II, *The Tender Passion,* (1986), 352–90, esp. 357–58.

typhus, pneumonia and tuberculosis, were not distinguished one from the other. The germ theory of disease, that historic discovery, was adumbrated only in the late 1840s, by Semmelweis, and then established two decades later by Pasteur. And until a few rebels in the mid-1820s demonstrated that bleeding was really a licensed form of murder, most physicians commended it as the therapy of choice.

The most astute critic of bleeding was the eminent French physician Pierre Louis; his investigations leave little doubt that medical science was on the verge of a basic change in its style of thinking. His monograph discrediting bleeding rested on the latest statistical findings; his posture was one that a Huxley could applaud. Oliver Wendell Holmes, Sr., one of Louis's many reverential foreign pupils, described him as "modest in the presence of nature, fearless in the face of authority, unwavering in the pursuit of truth." It was this felicitous combination of attitudes that in 1832 moved Louis to found the appropriately named Société médicale d'observation, a medical society devoted to the respectful examination of facts. Five years later, the first volume of the society's journal included a characteristic statement of purpose: "L'examen des malades et la recherche des faits généraux."[15] These researcher-physicians were looking not just for facts but for general facts, for the network that raises facts to significant theories.

The increasingly close collaboration of physicians with natural scientists, chiefly chemists, made this search all the more fruitful.[16] In 1838, the German botanist Matthias Schleiden published a paper correctly stating that the tissues of plants are made up of cells. His friend the physiologist Theodor Schwann, fired up, generalized Schleiden's findings to all living organisms. Building on these discoveries, the pathologist Rudolf Virchow revolutionized the perception of disease and of epidemiology. In the same way, Joseph Lister's introduction of antisepsis to surgery, which saved untold numbers of lives, drew directly on the researches of Louis Pasteur.

By mid-century, intelligent and inquisitive physicians had gone beyond borrowing the findings of natural scientists to adopt their proven techniques of inquiry. The most dazzling instance of this cross-fertilization is Ignaz Semmelweis's investigation into the causes of the lethal ailment childbed fever—technically puerperal fever. It stands as a model of how to traverse the labyrinth of false clues to attain valid knowledge, and how to translate that knowledge into mastery—constructive aggression at its best. His story, made irresistible by Semmelweis's splendid detective work, venomous disputes, and pathetic career, has often been told. But as a textbook exemplar of the scientific method it deserves retelling.[17]

Semmelweis, a Hungarian, took his medical degree at the University of Vienna, and remained to specialize in obstetrics at the Vienna General Hospital. It was a disheartening assignment; he had too many opportunities to perform autopsies on mothers who had succumbed to childbed fever. They were dying in numbers that made the most callous bureaucrats take notice; in 1846, the city appointed a commission of inquiry. It was not a moment too soon; the official figures revealed that in 1844, the year Semmelweis graduated, some 260 mothers out of 3,157, or 8.2 percent, had died in the First Maternity Division, where he worked; two years later, the figure had risen to 11.4 percent. The actual number of casualties was much higher; probably one in five of the mothers in the First Division, perhaps as many as one in four, did not leave the hospital alive. But dying mothers were commonly transferred to other wards to conceal the frightful totals. Semmelweis spent much time and energy unmasking this defensive maneuver; the first step in his scientific research was to develop distrust of self-serving authorized pronouncements. His baffled senior colleagues were ready, as usual, with explanations, but could neither agree with one another nor offer any hope to their potential victims.

What made this plague even more mysterious was that the figures for the Second Maternity Division, located next to the First, were dramatically lower; only 2.3 percent of all mothers had died there in 1844, only 2.7 percent in 1846. To notice this disparity did not require brilliance, but to explain it did. Compounding the mystery was the fact that these appalling rates of death from childbed fever occurred nowhere but in the First Division; women delivered at home or in the streets survived with virtually no risk of falling victim to the fever. This fact, Semmelweis reasoned, made nonsense of the epidemicists' widely credited theory that the phenomenon was an epidemic on the order of cholera, with its own murderous, capricious rhythm. Nor was he impressed by the theory that an invisible miasma was causing these deaths: "atmospheric-cosmic-telluric" changes would affect women giving birth elsewhere as much as those unfortunate enough to find a bed in the First Division. Yet they did nothing of the sort. Neither Vienna's variable weather nor the course of the seasons matched the death rate in that murderous division.

One highly visible fact had given the commission of inquiry pause: the mothers in the First Division were attended by obstetricians and medical students; those in the Second, next door, by midwives. So the commission theorized that inexperienced medical students, handling their patients insensitively, subjected them to injuries that eventually proved fatal. Once again Semmelweis had a hypothesis to test, and it failed on three grounds: the traumas inevitably inflicted by birth itself were far harsher than those arising from the most inexpert examination; the midwives were no gentler with their patients than the students; and when the number of students in the ward was cut in half and those remaining were instructed to treat their patients considerately, mortality declined for a brief time only to rise again sharply.

Soon Semmelweis had two other hypotheses to scrutinize in his classic scientific style. A priest going to administer extreme unction to a dying patient in other wards would walk through the First Division, his portentous purpose announced by an attendant ringing a bell. Might this solemn procession frighten young mothers so badly that they fell ill and died? Admittedly, it was an unlikely scenario, but the disciplined Semmelweis refused to discard any hypothesis without testing it. He induced the priest to take a different route and the attendant to stop ringing his bell. But the mortality rate remained as high as before. A second hypothesis was a last resort. Noting that in the First Division women were delivered lying on their back while next door they were put on their side, he ordered that his patients be positioned like their neighbors. Nothing happened; the percentage of mothers dying of puerperal fever did not decrease.

The following year Semmelweis evolved a less implausible hypothesis. Its origins remain somewhat obscure. He himself attributed his revelation to a tragic accident: one of his cherished teachers, the forensic pathologist Jacob Kolletscha, died of an infection after puncturing his finger during an autopsy. As Semmelweis mourned this loss, his reflections gave him the decisive clue; Kolletscha had died of the same insult—blood poisoning—that was killing mothers in the First Division every day. Puerperal fever was not a distinctive disease with an independent etiology, but an invasion of a vulnerable body part by "cadaveric particles." Perhaps Semmelweis's long experience in dissecting cadavers, and intense discussions with his superiors, also prompted this conjecture; in any event, it was one he could test. The medical students assigned to his ward usually came to work after dissecting cadavers—a task that midwives did not perform—the foul odors of the autopsy room still clinging to them. At best they might casually splash their hands with water. Semmelweis ordered his staff to wash their hands in a solution of chlorinated lime. The results surpassed his wildest fantasies; in 1848, the figure for deaths caused by childbed fever in the First Division dropped to 1.27 percent, even below the 1.33 percent in the Second Division.

Semmelweis was to profit little from the tangible result that his scientific reasoning had brought. Though he never lacked admiring colleagues and an appreciative following, he refused to publish his controversial finding for a decade. A quirky and increasingly eccentric outsider, he abruptly returned to Hungary, growing angrier by the year and firing off injured and insulting letters to physicians he suspected of being too ignorant, or too stubborn, to adopt his life-giving idea. After descending into paranoia, he died in 1865, pathetically, in a Viennese insane asylum. But his role in enlarging the empire of fact was epoch-making.

Compared with the spectacular triumphs of science and medicine, the accomplishments of social scientists trying to master the changing world were bound to appear modest. In an unsettled and unsettling atmosphere they developed an ever more exigent appetite for accurate facts and helpful theories. Not without some gratifying results: the American census of 1850 was an improvement over its predecessor; the statistics on prostitutes were gradually shedding their imaginative extravagance. But much remained unsatisfactory; as late as the mid-1880s, the demanding social investigator Charles Booth, speaking with the authority of a dedicated student of poverty, still faulted all previous English censuses, including that of 1881, for their porous categories and inconsistent classifications. "The seeker after information," he sternly informed his fellow members of the Royal Statistical Society in May 1886, "is left to grope his way in the dark."[18]

Still, much was being done; social investigators and political economists— "moral statisticians" the age called them—diligently gathered information and boldly constructed theories to explain it. Enthusiasts among them saw a possibility in concentrating on the first at the expense of the second: if they could only clear their work of speculation and conjecture, those ungainly legacies of metaphysics, the facts would speak for themselves. But their subtler contemporaries knew that facts are not just hard little pebbles of truth which, when enough of them have been piled together, add up to a scientific law. Huxley, for one, recognized that isolated facts are mute. He was fully aware that the most diligent, most patient of empiricists, his friend Charles Darwin, had made progress in theorizing about evolution only after he had fitted the pieces of information he had collected over the years into the framework provided by a hypothesis.[19]

Auguste Comte, the most famous and most prolific propagandist for nineteenth-century positivism, had anticipated Huxley quite explicitly. Committed to the superiority of scientific over metaphysical—let alone theological— reasoning, Comte insisted that effective thinking must combine facts with theories; while theory depends on observation, observation is impossible without theory. The extravagances of Comte's later thought, his doctrinaire and absurd religion of humanity, gathered much unfavorable publicity. But the positivistic attitude was of signal importance to the nineteenth-century pursuit of mastery. It permitted physiologists and psychologists to free themselves from the shackles of philosophical systems and open themselves to nature, and to human nature, with as few preconceptions as possible.

The point, then, was not to deny theoretical commitments but to rid them of their ideological baggage. But the social scientists of the age would have been more than human if they had succeeded altogether. Few moral statisticians of the day breathed the thin, pure air of disinterested curiosity, that most highly sublimated form of human inquisitiveness. The virtually undiluted passion for knowledge that squeezes pleasure from intellectual clarity alone was reserved to the likes of Pasteur and Freud.[20] Motives, to be sure, did not in themselves determine results, but many social investigators found what they sought and allowed their fantasies about a good society to govern, or at least influence, their results. The two founders of family sociology in mid-century, Frédéric Le Play in France and Wilhelm Heinrich Riehl in Germany, both did their extensive, emotion-laden researches into the family from the conviction that family life was in severe danger in a world out of control. And both reached the pessimistic, anti-modern conclusions that had been implicit in their enterprise from the outset.[21]

Even the less tendentious students of society were driven by the desire to discover the truths about, and find remedies for, biological imbalances or social strains that were threatening to end in personal distress or to mobilize subversive energies. They detected signs of potential trouble everywhere: in the English Chartist movement of the late 1830s, the revolutions of 1848, the founding of the First International in 1864, the Paris Commune of 1871, to say nothing of the clamor for divorce, desertions from the churches, or the taste for the sordid in art or literature. Hence the investigators were not in the least apologetic about their attempts to link objective surveys with social purpose; what could be more useful than knowledge that alleviates extreme poverty and prevents revolutions? In 1877, the German economist and bureaucrat G. Embden defined a survey as "a *proceeding,* legally authorized, whose immediate task is to ascertain economic and social facts and their causal relationships, whose ultimate purpose is the preparation of legislative or administrative decisions, and whose principal *means* for the fulfillment of that task and the furthering of this purpose is the interrogation of witnesses and experts."[22] Fellow investigators in less bureaucratic cultures would have been less convoluted in their prose and put less emphasis on the government's share in initiating the search for social truths. But they, too, would have given utilitarian reasons for enlarging the empire of fact.

Even the incomparable Belgian statistician Adolphe Quetelet allowed a social agenda to invade his obsessive efforts at reducing the world to numbers. A generalist in a world of specialists, he was a gifted painter and accomplished poet. Trained as a mathematician, he first became prominent as a physicist and astronomer, and gained international stature with his "social physics." For decades after his death in 1874, his successors continued to debate the principal rules of analysis he had laid down, his method of amassing large numbers for their evidentiary power, and his construction of an artificial statistical entity, the average man. In a long career as the most influential quantifier of the century, Quetelet produced imposing tables on the weather and the climate, rates of birth and death, human stature and the disposition to crime and suicide; on physical, intellectual, and moral development; and on such complex causal relationships as the bearing of prosperity on population growth and of parents' age on the birthrate. His love affair with fact never wavered. "Instead of words facts are wanted," he wrote in 1829, "and sage observations instead of vague hypotheses and unfounded system." He could have written the same words forty years later. And he confidently predicted a bright future for facts and, with that, for social progress.[23]

Quetelet was a determinist. In an avalanche of papers and readable monographs he presented his statistical findings as demonstrations that apparently idiosyncratic personal decisions are subject to overriding laws, laws the statistician can discover.* Decades before Durkheim, Quetelet sank biography in sociology. Once the social physicist has amassed enough solid information, he can show the probability of an individual's "choosing" to enter a life of crime or commit suicide, to become addicted to strong liquor or remain sober. But this determinism, Quetelet protested a little defensively, did not make him a fatalist. The kind of collective knowledge he wished to propagate "enlarges, rather than reducing, the human soul's sphere of liberty." One who understands the quantitative laws of human conduct and development can bring a measure of influence to bear on the world. "Man possesses in himself moral forces that assure him the empire over all beings in the universe," and it is "through these moral forces," which distinguish humans from animals, that man "tends to approach a better condition."[24] His was a temperate—one might say, conservative—optimism.

In his fundamental work of 1835, *Physique sociale,* Quetelet was in fact extremely circumspect about man's "moral powers." While he thought humans

---

*Man's subjection to general laws was an essential element in the statisticians' faith. In 1860, the economist Nassau Senior told the Economics Section of the British Association for the Advancement of Science, "The science of statistics is far wider as to its subject matter," far wider than political economy. "It applies to all phenomena which can be counted and recorded. It deals equally with matter and with mind. Perhaps the most remarkable results of the statistician's labours are those which show that the human will obeys laws nearly as certain as those which regulate matter." "Statistical Science" (1860), in R. L. Smyth, ed., *Essays in Economic Method: Selected Papers Read to Section F of the British Association for the Advancement of Science, 1860–1913* (1962), 21–22.

capable of modifying the laws that apply to them, he cautioned that these powers only act very slowly. His readers must not give way to excessive hopes. "I cannot repeat too often"—and he did repeat it, in italics—that *"there is a price we pay with fearful regularity, that of prisons, hulks, and scaffolds; it is these above all that we must make an effort to reduce!"*[25] Knowledge was not only power; it was a door to freedom, but a narrow, a very narrow, door.

Quetelet's services to the venture of mastering industrial society transcended his native Belgium. He carried on a vast correspondence with social physicists in other countries, sought them out in conferences he arranged, earnestly lectured them on their rights and obligations as members of an international fraternity, and used data supplied by foreign experts. In *Physique sociale,* for one, he relied on material furnished by his English acquaintance Charles Babbage. He did more than preach; he acted. An indefatigable organizer no less than a genius with numbers, he secured cooperation among leading statisticians of advanced societies to move toward uniformity in methods and terminology; the first International Statistical Congress, held at Brussels in 1853, was largely his work. His election as its president was a deserved and self-evident tribute.[26]

In Quetelet's time, then, seekers after knowledge about society talked across national boundaries and, though at times reluctantly, borrowed ideas and methods from one another. Quetelet was not alone or even exceptional in this scientific cosmopolitanism. German social scientists went to England in the 1860s to study working-class conditions, and in the 1890s their English counterparts returned the compliment, studying Bismarck's social legislation on the spot. Such visits were not new; decades earlier, we recall, Tocqueville and Beaumont had examined American prisons and imported to France what they had learned.

Yet there were limits to this cordial internationalism. Social investigators discovered that their national experience shaped their methods for conducting research. German economists and sociologists, lagging after those of other countries in the systematic cultivation of acquaintance with their fellow citizens, noticed that their surveys differed markedly from those launched elsewhere. While in Britain amateur reformers, humanitarians both clerical and secular, had taken the initiative, in Germany it was the government or the university professors—themselves public servants—who were responsible for the surveys. Again, the type of investigation the Germans conducted resembled the French and Belgian model far more than the British. In Britain, royal commissions and private investigators alike took testimony from ordinary citizens to flesh out the advice of experts, but in Germany, the authorities were by and large content with sending out questionnaires to be filled out by local bureaucrats.[27] There were distinct national styles in social self-scrutiny, as there were in the proposed remedies.

The careers of two distinguished social scientists, the German economist Lujo Brentano and the English social explorer Charles Booth, illuminate these differences. Both were men flexible enough to learn from experience, but their experiences were not the same.

Brentano was born in 1844, not far from Frankfurt, into a distinguished Roman Catholic family; the poet Clemens Brentano was his uncle, the social critic Bettina von Arnim his aunt, the philosopher Franz Brentano his brother. He grew to maturity in the 1860s and 1870s, a time of shocks traumatic for an intelligent and ambitious young German of his background. Prime Minister Bismarck's successful defiance of the Prussian legislature in the early 1860s was a disturbing signal from a powerful neighbor showing no disposition to develop into a constitutional state. Prussia's quick victory over Austria in the war of 1866, followed by its annexation of territories like Frankfurt, was no less disturbing to Catholics, opening the unwelcome prospect of a Germany dominated by arch-Protestant Junkers. German industrialization, well under way before unification, speeded up after 1871 and displayed its symptoms, like its achievements, all the more dramatically. Brentano had to navigate his way, then, through problems of political authority jostling those of national integration, to say nothing of social questions. Starting as an unrepentant "Frankfurter" and observant Catholic, he took years to make peace with Prussianized Germany, to separate himself from the rigid political and religious faith of his family, and to throw himself into social problems.[28] His special brand of social liberalism was an acquired taste.

To Charles Booth liberalism came naturally. Born in 1840 in Liverpool, the son of affluent Unitarian parents, he grew up in an atmosphere of cultivated ease, practical philanthropy, and Liberal politics. He had all the advantages an English Nonconformist could hope for: sound progressive schooling, extended tours on the Continent and to the Holy Land, and an apprenticeship in the world of commerce, which he entered as a young man and throve in all his life. His lust for facts stood him in good stead as he mastered the intricacies of the shipbuilding industry, studying details of construction and transatlantic schedules with the meticulous care that later became his signature as a social scientist.

Like Brentano, Booth discarded the religion of his fathers, but unlike Brentano, he found this desertion very hard; in his late twenties, he underwent a time of religious questioning that amounted to a crisis. He had become ardently engaged with political and social reform, and thought the cheerful Unitarian benevolence of his family and his circle sadly wanting. Religion offered no salvation: "Science must lay down afresh the laws of life."* And that science meant, for Booth, social science.

Fortunately for his sanity, he found his vocation, one which, just as fortunately, he could afford to support: to apply in the study of poverty the respect for facts that was serving him so well as a businessman. His self-chosen task stretched out before him as the royal road toward solving what his wife Mary, the silent partner in his great enterprise, called "the problem of all problems." He settled in London to be near his future objects of research, cultivated philanthropists and reformers of all stripes, and read whatever he could lay his hands on. In the same cause, he took to wandering around the slums of London's East End, supping in cheap coffeehouses and visiting music halls. In his quest to master the problem of all problems, the poor became his obsession.

The mid-Victorian age had obviously not invented poverty. Since time out of mind, it had been the accepted condition of the large majority in Britain, as elsewhere. The voices of the discontented who asked for more had disturbed the peace now and then; bread riots and, more recently, political agitation kept the affluent on edge and propelled some of them into action. Already toward the close of the eighteenth century, humanitarians had taken occasional stabs at analyzing the lot of the lower orders and possibly alleviating it. The Society for Bettering the Conditions of the Poor, launched in 1796, announced that it would make "the inquiry into all that concerns the poor and promotion of their happiness a science." The following year, Sir Frederick Morton Eden published a three-volume study of the poor.[29] But for long years, attempts to understand and to relieve the needy remained quixotic enterprises. Right into the nineteenth century, few even among the poor questioned the fundamental assumption that the overwhelming mass of the British population had no choice but to be resigned to their fate on economic as on religious grounds.

*T. S. Simey and M. B. Simey, Charles Booth: Social Scientist (1960), 48. "No compromise is possible," Booth wrote around 1870. "It must be war to destruction between the old thought and the new, until the mind of man, freed from the trammels of this last form, as it has been of each previous form of theology, turns aside from destruction and finds new food for its faculties of worship in the recognised order around us and the great example of progress in order presented by the Human Race." Ibid. Booth's contemporaries, in the manner of their age, attributed his repeated breakdowns, which incapacitated him for months on end, to overwork. That is to take symptom for cause. True, he would work until exhaustion made him stop, spending long evenings at the office, making do with little sleep, taking ship at a moment's notice to the United States, where he had business interests. But the question is, of course, why he needed to drive himself as though he were a slave to an exacting master. The available material does not permit an answer.

Industrialization complicated the question. Transforming Britain into the first modern society, it sustained astonishing rates of population growth.[30] While it did not actually depopulate the countryside, Britons increasingly moved to the city, creating sprawling urban conglomerations across the landscape. Manchester, in 1801 a city of 70,000—this figure itself a striking increase from the 40,000 of twenty years before—doubled its population in the next thirty years. New roads, new canals, and from the 1830s on, the railroad, vastly improved transport and travel; inspired tinkerers, trained engineers, enterprising manufacturers, financial wizards, turned the country, as patriotic publicists said with pride, into the workshop of the world.

But the gains from this revolution were distributed very unevenly. For half a century, perhaps more, it ravaged large sectors of the working classes in town and, worse yet, in rural districts; only a minority, notably skilled workers finding employment in the new factories, profited even marginally. For the unskilled, and for artisans like handloom weavers and framework knitters, whom modern machinery was reducing to anachronisms, the specters of high bread prices and intermittent unemployment were ever threatening. Good harvests gave breathing space; bad harvests turned everyday misery into starvation. These were the victims of progress. Inhabiting the poisonous urban slums and the no less insalubrious villages, they were reduced to taking charity or to begging. They worked—when they had work—fourteen hours a day and compelled their children, often very young, to eke out the family income. Their plight provoked helpless protests and scattered disorders. Nor was popular discontent confined to the casualties of the new industrial order; the Chartist movement, with its program for political democracy, attests to that. Tinkering—informal attempts at mastery—largely failed.

Then, around mid-century, prosperity began to scatter its blessings more widely. In a famous series of lectures on the industrial revolution, delivered at Oxford in 1880 and 1881, Arnold Toynbee noted with pleasure that since the repeal of the corn laws, those much-debated agricultural tariffs, in 1846, the condition of the working classes had markedly improved. "Free Trade," he said, rather simplifying an exceedingly complicated issue, "has enormously increased the aggregate wealth of the country, and therefore increased the demand for labour." Free trade produced more regular employment, fewer economic fluctuations, and best of all, steadier bread prices. Several lesser causes, he thought, had contributed to this improvement, happily including higher moral standards. A succession of factory acts had restricted the hours of labor and the employment of women and children, and responsible trade unions and cooperatives had taught the poor the value of voluntary associations.[31] There were good grounds, then, for hoping that progress would continue.

Toynbee's lectures were a pioneering interpretation of the events that had made all things new in his country. But what he slighted was almost as important as what he chose to emphasize, and it was what he slighted that gave Booth his assignment. Inveterately optimistic, Toynbee failed to address the blight of extreme want, of a poverty persisting in face of all the resources that industrialization had liberated. Apart from a few hints about what emigration (and, more delicately, that repugnant remedy, contraception) might do for the very poor, Toynbee had virtually nothing to say about the bottom of the social pyramid in his own day. He was gratified to note that while in 1849 there had been 930,000 paupers in Britain, the number had shrunk to 800,000 in 1881—despite a population growth of 8 million.[32] This was the time when Booth was criticizing the very census on which Toynbee so confidently relied, and making himself ready to study the population about which Toynbee had so little to say.

Booth was entering a crowded field. For decades, dismayed, often angry observers had ventilated the "condition-of-England question." What they found most troubling, even more than the smoky industrial cities and the decline of trusted old values, was that modern nightmare, the urban slum. In early 1832, just before the passage of the Great Reform Act, the *Westminster Review* spoke sympathetically of "the oppressions and vexations, the wrongs of purpose and of carelessness, inflicted on the labouring classes of this country."[33] Then and later, royal commissions published reports—the famous blue books—on working conditions in mines and factories, on child labor, on trade unions. Social critics piled up indictments of industrial capitalism; when in 1845 Friedrich Engels published his powerful *Conditions of the Working Class in England in 1844,* he could draw on a sizable literature filled with hair-raising descriptions.

Meanwhile, the journalist Henry Mayhew walked around miserable neighborhoods gathering material for his anecdotal studies of London's street people, collected in the 1850s in *London Labour and the London Poor.* England was being swamped with information about poverty, and the pressures to relieve it multiplied. But while anxiety over the festering condition-of-England question continued to feed on social realities, the hope for its amelioration grew with the visible prosperity in the workshop of the world. Jesus' saying that the poor we shall always have with us, so comforting to employers paying subsistence wages, was beginning to sound a little hollow. Mastery seemed closer to hand than ever before.[34]

Neither the pessimism nor the optimism, neither fact-laden monographs nor moving vignettes, satisfied Booth. The available literature was valuable to him mainly for demonstrating that to blame the victim was neither humane nor accurate. If one had to be censorious, one should blame society, not the poor, for the slums. In some circles, paternalistic and moralistic notions still prevailed; among those who held to them, and whom Booth came to know well, were the leading spirits of the Charity Organization Society, who had been doing good deeds in London since 1869. They taught Booth what to avoid. Yet, however moralistic the volunteers working for the C.O.S., they did not disdain scientific methods of inquiry; evidently, modern techniques had begun to infiltrate even old-fashioned charitable bodies.[35] For Booth this was only a timid start. He had to know more.

During the early 1880s, he equipped himself to do so. Recent arresting exposés of appalling living conditions among the poor had troubled rather than gratified him. In late 1883, the *Pall Mall Gazette* had given wide circulation to *The Bitter Cry of Outcast London,* a stinging indictment by the Congregationalist minister Andrew Mearns, which painted a horrifying picture of the slums of London's East End that Booth had come to know so intimately.[36] Booth found this appeal to the emotions far from helpful. Two years later, he was pleased even less by the announcement of the socialist H. M. Hyndman, founder of the Social Democratic Federation, that as many as a quarter of London's inhabitants were living below the poverty line. That sort of talk, Booth feared, obscured the truth and could only lead to riots. Early in 1886, Booth called on Hyndman and bluntly accused him of sensationalism. He had no illusions about the gravity of social misery in London, he told Hyndman, but he would see for himself and refute these pernicious exaggerations.[37]

By the time of this encounter, Brentano was established as a respected economist, prolific author, and embattled partisan in debates on the *soziale Frage*, the German version of the condition-of-England question. As in Britain, so in Germany, only the question was new. Obviously, poverty was an old story, though most of the evidence for earlier times was anecdotal. Even in the eighteenth century, reports on conditions had been limited to a few local laments in times of trouble—precisely the sort of impressionistic vagueness that nineteenth-century social scientists were aching to remedy. It seems likely that around 1800 at least a quarter of the German population lived at the subsistence level. Much of the time they dipped below it. Wandering beggars, destitute invalids, widows dependent on local alms, were only the most pathetic exemplars of masses for whom poverty was the natural way of life. Even fully employed artisans normally spent more than half their wages on food, and, when harvests were bad, the price of bread would rise out of reach—with predictable consequences.

In Germany, as in other countries, after a time industrialization reduced the numbers of the poor but left thousands of casualties in its wake. Artisans were ruined by mechanization; the pathetic rising in 1844 of the Silesian weavers, driven to despair by foreign competition and cheap industrial output at home, was a shocking reminder that extremes of poverty among men and women— and children—willing to work was not yet a thing of the past. In Cologne in 1848—Brentano was a four-year-old boy then—25,000 people, more than a quarter of the population, were inscribed on the register of the poor; many others, including the "elite" among Cologne's 4,250 factory workers, barely managed to keep themselves afloat. In the same year, some two-thirds of Bremen's 17,000 families lived on or below the edge of destitution.[38]

As Germany industrialized, poverty grew more selective, but also more visible. In the age of urbanization, much of it moved from country to city. And while prosperous burghers had developed denial into a high art, they found it harder to shut out the reality of the slums than that of rural misery. Hence the massive urban blight gave the German bourgeois conscience, increasingly sensitized to the hardships of the less fortunate, a great deal to do. The Germans' collective sense of guilt, that prelude to action, was making influential recruits. A modern word, *Pauperismus,* quickly popularized, documents this new awareness. In an emotional article on pauperism, the 1846 edition of Brockhaus's encyclopedic dictionary denied that the condition could be attributed to the laziness, natural inferiority, or accidental misfortunes, of individuals; rather, the poor, however strenuously they worked, were doomed to a lifetime of struggle with poor health and the scourge of alcohol or other vices.[39] A whole agenda of reform was implicit in this colorful word painting, more accusation than definition. Brentano was ready to listen.

When, around the time of German unification, Brentano began to study the social question, the unskilled majority of the lower orders were perched, as always, over the abyss of disaster, forced to count on the income that their wives and children could generate to buy the bread and potatoes and coal they needed to get through the year. Even skilled workers remained at risk, exposed to the business cycles which periodically disrupted the spectacular growth of the German economy. They were insured against nothing; not protected against unemployment or old age, not against work-related injuries, not against sickness. These four horsemen were anything but chimeras invented by alarmists. While recurrent depressions put thousands out of work, the ravages of old age, which in those decades began for most in their forties, were even more devastating. Injuries on the factory floor, all too frequent in a time when safety devices were little regarded and largely unknown, were no less threatening.

And sickness meant catastrophe.* In the midst of the economic boom that brought wealth to many, millions of Germans kept on living lives of quiet desperation.

By the early 1860s, there were voices urging them to be less quiet. In 1863, the authoritarian socialist Ferdinand Lassalle founded a German workers' association, the Deutsche Allgemeine Arbeiterverband, no more than a hint that smoldering discontent might some day be mobilized; not long before his untimely death in the following year, he berated his working-class audiences for abjectly accepting their poverty and their lowly status. Not all of them were quite so passive; they called strikes and organized rudimentary trade unions. And in 1869, Wilhelm Liebknecht and August Bebel founded the militant Social Democratic Workers' party. In its first years, as the party fought its way forward in a repressive political atmosphere, it professed an ungainly amalgam of Lassallean and Marxist ideas. Only in 1891 did it adopt a revolutionary program purely Marxist in its rhetoric—at the very time that leading Social Democrats, Brentano noted with approval, were frankly or covertly throwing much of their ideological baggage overboard to constitute themselves a left-wing political party working within the system.

Within the system was of course where Brentano was at home, for all his unsettling ideas. Like many educated Germans, he was a fervent Anglophile. By 1868, when he visited England on a fateful study trip, he had decided on a career as a political economist, and he moved to the University of Berlin for his doctorate. His intellectual commitments were clarifying themselves; taking strong exception to the abstract theorizing that characterized most economic thinking, he adopted a historical view of the field. Unlike his chief in Berlin, the eminent statistician and liberal Ernst Engel, who thought the social question could be easily solved by granting workers co-ownership in industry, Brentano, less sanguine, put his hope in strong, independent trade unions.[40] During his visit to England, he had sought out sympathetic students of the labor movement and union leaders, who eased his access to factories across the country. While the "squalid conditions" of some workplaces appalled him, he was delighted with the cordial and collegial way that politicians of the rival parties dealt with each other. "What an enviable relationship between competing candidates,

*As the economist Gustav Schmoller, Brentano's friend and comrade-in-arms, put it in the 1880s, "Sickness descends on working-class families quite as unpredictably and destructively as a war that spreads over a neutral little country. If the sickness lasts for some time, nobody can save enough money for it in advance, nobody can have a sufficient reserve for the loss of wages and medical expenses. The normal result is the ruin of the whole family, which is obliged to carry its last to the pawn shop." In *Grundriss der allgemeinen Volkswirtschaftslehre,* 2 vols. (1900, 1904), II, 350.

when one thinks of German election campaigns!"[41] He soon discovered that
German professors were as pugnacious in their disputes as German politicians; a
disagreement among academics quickly became a *Streit*—a quarrel or row—
with no nonsense about sublimating aggression.

A few casual skirmishes apart, Brentano first felt the full force of German
verbal warfare in late 1871, when the journalist Heinrich Oppenheim derided
adherents of Brentano's economic school of thought as *Kathedersozialisten*—
"socialists of the lectern." The demagogic epithet stuck; Oppenheim had chosen it with care. A principled (or, better, unprincipled) admirer of the *laissez-
faire* preached by the Manchester school, he damned any government
intervention in the economy as socialism. His epithet was a libel. Neither
Brentano nor his allies were socialists; they never questioned the right to private
property, and advocated only strictly targeted, well-defined state action. Nor
were they cloistered academics. Quite the contrary; their whole effort was
directed at discovering the facts in order to make policy recommendations.

Indeed, Brentano and his fellow socialists of the lectern were good Baconi-
ans; perhaps, with their unremitting hostility to theorizing, too good.[42] Not
that contemporary economic theory was infallible; mid-century experience was
undermining the classical wages-fund theory, which held that market forces are
sure to frustrate all workers' attempts to rise above subsistence. But what was
needed to expose the failings of prevailing economic thinking was not just
empirical disconfirmation but better theory; and that, Brentano and his allies
were unwilling and unable to supply. Gustav Schmoller, the undisputed leader
of the school, advocated piling facts upon facts in extensive descriptive studies
before venturing toward conclusions.

In the fall of 1872, Brentano, Schmoller, and other like-minded spirits convened a conference in Eisenach to articulate a program of political economy at
once humane and realistic. In his opening address, defining the purpose of the
meeting, Schmoller enlisted the world spirit. Society as a whole, and every
well-meaning individual, must work to realize the great ideals of culture. This
was the supreme task of democratic development, "just as it appears to be the
great goal of world history in general."[43] If Booth had read these words he
would have objected to Schmoller's introducing a high-flying metaphysical
theory of history into a domain that would be better off without it.

The following year, back to earth, the socialists of the lectern founded an
association for social policy, the Verein für Sozialpolitik, to realize their social-
scientific plans. Though hampered by their inability to agree on a proper attitude toward political action, and by furious disputes over Bismarck's domestic
policies, the members of the Verein debated papers and published reports on
weighty topics like protectionism and trade unionism, local taxation, strikes,

and the methodology of social surveys. At best their discussions were productive, though increasingly they degenerated into combat. The impact of all this talk and print was uncertain. The Verein mustered a loyal following, especially among those in the nonacademic public not convinced that any piece of legislation regulating industry or aiding the unemployed was a fatal step toward communism. These sympathetic readers saw Brentano, Schmoller, and their brethren as valiant fighters against the revolutionary menace from Social Democrats, the selfish economic program of Junkers and robber barons, and that greatest of scourges—the favored servant of both—ignorance. In a letter to Schmoller, Brentano expressed his undying opposition to "socialist or absolutist despotism."[44] Only reliable knowledge could keep both at bay.

This statement sounds like a harmless oratorical generality. But it was part of a polemic, increasingly testy, that Brentano was conducting by mail with his close friend. While Schmoller continued to champion effective trade unions as a means to attack the social question, he also professed, unlike Brentano, faith in the state, even in Bismarck's so-called state socialism. The dispute mirrored irreconcilable positions in the Verein they had founded with such high hopes. When Bismarck forced through anti-socialist legislation in 1878, and the year after abandoned his free-trade political allies to embrace protectionism, members of the Verein stood on all sides of these inflammatory issues. In self-defense, they avoided such topics; concentrating instead on more manageable issues like the agrarian question, they found less and less to talk about.[45] For a time Brentano retreated from political agitation to historical scholarship. The decline in the fortunes of the Verein für Sozialpolitik supports the skeptical proposition that much of the time, the social science of the day did little more than find good reasons for advocating policies its practitioners liked on other grounds. Whatever it was, it was not yet a science.

For his part, Bismarck, whom the Verein had plied with advice, soon dispensed with it as he tackled the social question. With his workers' insurance legislation, Brentano remembered, he "took the wind out of its sails," as he had already done on other matters.[46] Obviously Bismarck did not miss the association's advice. Once he became enmeshed in pressing social issues, he ordered investigations into the condition of the working class that made him independent of the expert recommendations Brentano and his friends sought to offer him. Interestingly enough, he discovered that the vital statistics that moral statisticians and bureaucrats provided were inadequate for action. In the end, he relied on a few trusted subordinates, industrial magnates who had shown an interest in the social question, and on his political instincts. We know that his comprehensive program for social insurance was part of a larger political design. He seems to have felt a patronizing sympathy for the injured and the unemployed, but his principal reasons for advocating compulsory insurance were political, designed to win the working class away from the seductions of the Social Democrats and quietly prepare the way for more authoritarian institutions to replace the Reichstag.

During these years of controversy and frustration, and during the many years that remained to Brentano—he died in 1931, aged eighty-seven—he was neither idle nor passive. He had high, somewhat nervous, expectations of Wilhelm II, whose accession in 1888 promised a fresh course for social policy; the emperor's dismissal of the aged Bismarck two years later seemed a step in Brentano's direction. But Wilhelm's tough talk against "dangerous" radicals, his imperious interference in matters he knew nothing about, and his capricious shifts of front, proved these hopes sadly misplaced, and Brentano turned increasingly toward the left. As an economist, he wrote on tariff policy; as a liberal, he thundered against a bill that would have sent anyone interfering with strikebreakers to the penitentiary; as an academic mandarin, he defended freedom of research in the universities; as an Anglophile, he frequently returned to England, and devoted his last years to a bulky economic history of his favorite country.[47] With all his undiminished passion for scholarship, he did not like to think of himself as an unworldly professor; significantly he called his autobiography, published in his last year, My Life in the Struggle for the Social Development of Germany. It is hard to avoid the feeling that Brentano had spent his life in the wrong country; Booth would have been a splendid fellow citizen for him.

Booth's compassion for the poor was, if anything, more pronounced than Brentano's; his program for action, being more tightly focused, was more effective. We have seen that when he launched his study of London's slums in 1886, he was moved by indignation at sentimentalists, a desire to improve the lot of the destitute, and, above all, a confidence in science touching in its intensity. In Beatrice Webb's cool, distant judgment, he was the "most perfect embodiment" of "the mid-Victorian time-spirit—the union of faith in the scientific method with the transference of the emotion of self-sacrificing service from God to man." She was doing Booth less than justice; long before he completed his famous analysis of London's millions he had abandoned the mid-Victorian philanthropic ideal.[48] The findings of social science pointed him beyond patronizing benevolence.

Booth took his social science very seriously. In 1887, the second year of his survey, he told fellow statisticians that what sorely tried everyone concerned with the social question was "the sense of helplessness." Wage earners were helpless "to regulate or obtain the value of their work"; manufacturers and merchants were helpless because they "only work within the limits of competition"; legislators were helpless "because the limits of successful interference by change of law are closely circumscribed." This crippling sense of an inability to make a difference spawned "socialistic theories, passionate suggestions of ignorance, setting at naught the nature of man and neglecting all the fundamental facts of human existence." Dependable facts and sound theories were the only way out. "To relieve this sense of helplessness, the problems of human life must be better stated. The a priori reasoning of political economy, orthodox and unorthodox alike," he argued, sounding much like Brentano, "fails from want of reality. At its base are a series of assumptions very imperfectly connected with the observed facts of life. We need to begin with a true picture of the modern industrial organism, the interchange of service, the exercise of faculty, the demands and satisfactions of desire."[49] This is an instructive if obvious diagnosis: the quest for mastery is the antidote for impotence. Whatever the psychological mainsprings of Booth's crusade for truth, he was sure that action must follow, not determine, knowledge.

In fact, Booth proved anything but a naive Baconian in his efforts to state the problems of human life better than they had been stated before. He told Beatrice Potter—better known under her married name, Beatrice Webb—that deductive and inductive methods were equally necessary to him.[50] Facts, complicated as they were, had to have a framework. Still, even if discrete facts were meaningless, they were indispensable; despite all the investigations already in print, social scientists really knew little about the poor and even less about the very poor. His task was to map terra incognita.

As he drew that map, Booth was guided by his investigative principles. He was proud to say that his ideas had "taken shape gradually in the course of my work," and that he had started with "no preconceived ideas, no theory to work up to, no pet scheme."[51] Even if this is not a realistic account of anyone's intellectual itinerary, Booth was trying to follow Huxley in sitting down before fact as a little child. But there were so many of those facts! He was (to borrow his image) attempting nothing less than to photograph all London, starting appropriately enough with the East End, where a million of the city's poverty-stricken were concentrated.

Booth composed his vast photograph with a mere handful of assistants, on a work schedule that would have worn out anyone but a fanatic for truth. Working from the figures and categories of the 1881 census, suitably refined by his own classification of income levels, he constructed his basic procedures. To round out the data that questionnaires yielded, he and his co-workers drew on the wealth of information that local school inspectors had gathered in intensive interviews, and on statistics from official relief agencies and the police blotter. Then came the daunting task of organizing and classifying these masses of information. By 1889, only three years after Booth launched his investigation, the first volume of what later became *Life and Labour of the People in London* was ready for publication. By the time he completed his assignment in 1903, the whole ran to seventeen substantial volumes.

One way of reading the millions of words in this London survey is as something of an apology. Booth discovered that the irritating Hyndman had actually understated the extent and depth of London's poverty.[52] The fact was, and Booth did not conceal it, that those living below the poverty line amounted not to 25 percent but to slightly over 30 percent of those populating England's vast overgrown capital.[53]

It was his candor, combined with the overpowering quantities of statistics he threw at the reader and the moving descriptions he scattered through the survey, that secured Booth's authority as a collector and interpreter of facts. He was not satisfied with listening and counting and neutrally recording his data. As a vocal advocate of old-age pensions, finally instituted in 1908, he may claim a significant share in preparing the way for Britain's welfare state. But, most important for our purposes, even as he presented his findings as a social reformer who urged the government to ameliorate the poverty he had analyzed at such length, he was acting as an authentic social scientist, showing himself capable of changing his mind on an issue in which he had invested a great deal. The mounting conservatism of his last years—he died, much honored, in 1916—his impassioned individualism and distrust of trade unions, cannot lessen his place in the history of the social sciences. It was Booth, if anyone, who enlarged and secured the empire of fact, that potent agent of mastery.

3. The End of Renaissance Man

One ingredient essential to the nineteenth-century revolution in knowledge was a sharply intensified division of labor. Specialization left its mark on the cultural landscape everywhere; education and the professions were changed almost beyond recognition. But the new division of labor proved an ambiguous blessing. In promoting specialized training and rewarding specialized activities, it tightened man's mastery over the world, but shattered the Renaissance ideal of the well-rounded generalist. The burden of information was growing almost too unwieldy for any one person to master even in a single discipline, let alone several disciplines.

In this world, that versatile statistician Adolphe Quetelet, with his talent for painting, poetry, and a sizable gamut of natural sciences, stood as a reminder of heroic times gone by. But he too could not escape the demands of his age. With the passage of years, he found himself compelled to concentrate his efforts, even his interests, on a single field. Some French physicians might shine as competent painters or respectable poets.[1] A few extraordinary savants, like Hermann Helmholtz, who made signal contributions to medicine, biology, physics, mathematics, and the psychology of vision, ran against the stream of the century. Cultivated and accomplished amateurs like Brahms's good friend the distinguished German surgeon Theodor Billroth, who could have made a career as a piano virtuoso, were growing relatively rare.

Partisans of progress hailed this development as a necessary step away from helplessness; cultural critics lamented it as an irreparable loss. In the 1790s, Schiller had already offered an alarmed, and alarming, analysis of contemporary man as one-sided, alienated, conflict-ridden, one who had sold himself to material self-interest. "Eternally chained to a single small fragment of the whole, man forms himself only as a fragment." Hearing only "the monotonous sound of the wheel," he "never develops the harmony of his being." While Schiller was wary of the "Graecomania" then becoming fashionable, he invidiously contrasted the sickness of the moderns with the wholeness of the ancients. In classical times, as human powers were awakening, the senses and the spirit had not yet been fatally divided.[2]

The young Marx took up this theme for his own subversive purposes; in 1844, analyzing the degradation that industrial civilization inflicts on its worker victims, he blamed the division of labor, along with the accumulation of capital, for making the worker dependent on a monotonous, mechanical kind of labor. Reduced to a machine, he "becomes merely an abstract activity and a belly." Then in 1860, in his masterly *Civilization of the Renaissance in Italy,* Jacob Burckhardt allowed himself a wistful glance back at a time when *l'huomo universale* was more than a nostalgic fantasy. From the perspective of a troubled conservative, he recited the talents of one of these universal men, Leon Battista Alberti; athlete, scientist, mathematician, painter, sculptor, architect, musician, psychologist, essayist, poet, wit, student of manners, man of the world, he had filled all these roles with competence and elegance. And, though Alberti towered over his contemporaries, he was, Burckhardt thought, no match for Leonardo da Vinci, a man of proportions so colossal that "one will never more than divine them from afar."[3] The days that would permit such men to exist, Burckhardt intimated, were gone forever.

This was not the only way of looking at the new division of labor; early in the century, Goethe had read it more buoyantly. In the course of a long, remarkably productive life, he had made himself an unsurpassed poet, playwright, novelist, autobiographer, travel writer, philosophical scientist, art critic, letter writer, translator, conversationalist. Yet this modern Renaissance man, of all people, gave the novel of his old age, *Wilhelm Meisters Wanderjahre,* the subtitle *Die Entsagenden*—"The Renouncers." And what he made his leading characters learn to renounce was universality. "Unconditioned activity, of whatever sort it may be," action that will not recognize, let alone accept, proper limits, "leads to bankruptcy in the end." His was "the time of one-sidedness." Goethe's advice is conclusive: "Train yourself to become a competent violinist and rest assured that the conductor will gladly assign you your place in the orchestra." No doubt, "to confine yourself to *one* trade is best."[4] Mastery, Goethe said in one of his sonnets, only shows itself in the ability to restrict oneself. He evidently believed that if specialization is the price for the accumulation of knowledge, it is not too high. In his classic *Wealth of Nations* of 1776, Adam Smith had memorably anticipated this judgment by several decades.

The march of specialization was unstoppable. With the development of an international market economy in which goods and services were exchanged on the basis of marginal advantage, the profits from the division of labor became all the more evident. The principle, the German statistician Georg von Viehbahn wrote around 1860, "is gaining ever more ground with the utilization of auxiliary engines."[5] Hence, instructed by new experiences, some of Adam Smith's nineteenth-century readers refined his analysis. Perhaps most significantly, in the early 1830s, Charles Babbage made the important point that "the division of labour can be applied with equal success to mental as to mechanical operations." The principle of specialization that was doing so much for productivity in manufacturing had a more general application than had been recognized; the division of labor might be "usefully employed in preparing the road to some of the sublimest investigations of the human mind." Office clerks, industrial managers, high-level bureaucrats, and mathematicians were well advised to develop specialized competence for particular tasks.[6] For good or ill, the age of the expert was at hand. In 1893, Émile Durkheim underscored the specialist's importance in *De la division du travail social,* a landmark in modern sociology.

In this climate, the term "dilettante," once a complimentary name for well-born folk cultivating the arts and sciences for pleasure rather than profit, was metamorphosed into a derisive epithet. In 1799, Goethe wrote Schiller about that "horror, dilettantism," by which he meant the way that superficial amateurs were busying themselves with the arts. Goethe's admirer Carlyle made his Professor Teufelsdröckh denounce the man who has lost his sense of wonder before the miracles of the world as "a Dilettante and sandblind Pedant." And in *Middlemarch,* George Eliot had a German painter, Adolf Naumann, criticize the hero, Will Ladislaw, as "dilettantish and amateurish."[7] This reversal of attitudes put the once-uncontested ideal of a liberal classical education into question.

With the stakes even higher than they had ever been, nineteenth-century education became a cluster of battlefields on which commercial and technological interests provoked intense duels with the gentlemanly standard. Down to the time of the French Revolution, those who could afford it had been educated at home by tutors or sent to a school run by ecclesiastics. And eighteenth-century universities had remained in the hands of the faculties—divinity, law, and medicine—that had dominated higher learning since the Middle Ages. For all their much-deplored decay before the Revolution, they had turned out quantities of erudite clerics, attorneys, and physicians, but a remarkable number of leading scientists and inventors had worked outside the university system.[8] A handful of scattered, recently established technical schools imparted skills essential to the arts of design, agriculture, mining, and road building; the École des ponts et chaussées, established in France in 1747, was a pointer to the future. But these centers for practical training remained starved for funds and humble in status.

All this changed with the Revolution and its subversive heir, Napoleon I. In 1794, the revolutionary government put the training of engineers and natural scientists on a solid footing by founding the École polytechnique, which boasted strict entrance requirements, a demanding three-year course of study, and an outstanding faculty. The Polytechnique was one innovation of the Revolution that Napoleon supported and strengthened. It soon found imitators at home and in other countries, which paid homage to the original by adopting its name. In Milan in the late 1830s, when the philosopher Carlo Cattaneo started a journal that was to popularize the advances of contemporary science, he called it *Il politecnico*. But the massive achievements of the École polytechnique and its various copies only brought the tensions between classical education and technological training to the surface.

The first battlegrounds were the privileged secondary schools that served the Victorian elites—the *lycées* in France, the *Gymnasien* in Prussia, the public schools in England—all of them bastions of the upper bourgeoisie. As barriers more than roads to social mobility, their favorite device for maintaining the segregation of the middling from the lower orders was their classical curriculum. They fed their pupils a carefully restricted diet: much Greek and Latin, some mathematics and philosophy, with no nonsense about practical subjects. It was against this old program of instruction that the modernizers arrayed themselves.

The education wars of the Victorian age did not all turn on the demands of science and technology. Critics of existing primary education, everywhere under fire as reformers aimed at universal literacy, produced an array of proposed remedies. More unsettling still was the furious dissension over religion, that most refractory of issues. In the late 1820s, Quetelet had let himself be carried away by his passion for progress when he claimed that the "nineteenth century is characterized by only proceeding scientifically."[9] The age was by no means so securely wedded to science as Quetelet liked to think. In a time of spectacular scientific discoveries and rather more quiet crises of faith, bourgeois religiosity regained some of the ground lost during the Enlightenment and the French Revolution. Much of the interminable struggle over the minds of the young was fought out between clericals and secularists, or conservative divines and liberal dissenters. Religious parties, growing increasingly rancorous as they were increasingly embattled, were struggling for mastery—political mastery.* Yet religious issues, though divisive and time-consuming, never pushed the fight over "useful" subjects from center stage.

These controversies, in fact, ran simultaneously, and, a few awkward alliances apart, modernists and secularists usually found themselves in the same camp. In early-nineteenth-century England, members of the Established Church, committed to the traditional curriculum, monopolized the old universities as they had for centuries. The opening guns in the campaign to break the double hold of classicism and Anglicanism were fired from 1808 to 1810 in articles in the *Edinburgh Review* mainly by Sydney Smith, that unsurpassed wit and political polemicist. He employed Baconian rhetoric to mount his critique of Oxford and Cambridge; their principal task was to foster knowledge to relieve man's estate, and the universities, exclusive and pedantic, had signally failed to do their duty. It took outside pressure from reformers in and out of Parliament, and several decades, before scientific subjects finally crept into Oxford and Cambridge. It took no less time before Nonconformists and agnostics secured entry, and decades more before they were admitted to fellowships. Modernization was a tortuous process. It is a measure of growing impatience that in 1828, years before Oxford and Cambridge were forced to abolish religious tests and reluctantly embrace the sciences, reformers had defiantly founded the University of London, a center of higher learning both nonsectarian and committed to the modern courses that the old universities still disdained.

Education in France followed its own path toward the same end. French schools, including the universities, had been reduced to uniformity by a central-

---

*The picture is clouded by vastly different private commitments; while Darwin was an unbeliever who blamed bigots for the opposition his theories encountered, Pasteur was a good Catholic who reconciled his chemical research with devout attendance at mass.

ized bureaucracy since Napoleon's day, but that never silenced disputes over the place of religious instruction or of science in the curriculum. The old saw that there was not one France but two finds a certain support in the contests between French Catholics and French unbelievers for access to the ministry of education and public financial support. Fortunes wavered across the decades, but the *écoles laïques,* as modern in their offerings as in their disdain for religious lessons, had to await the advent of the Third Republic. Nor did they overcome priestly opposition even then; they vanquished it only with the absolute separation of church and state in 1905. Yet in France, as in other countries, while every step away from entrenched practices was contested, someone who had gone to school before the July revolution might have felt a stranger in the schools his grandsons attended.

The prolonged, public, often acrimonious debates over curriculum and funding, then, were the stuff of the Victorians' bid for mastery. One did not have to be a Jesuit to recognize that to control the schools was to control the future. But respectable bourgeois found this future exceedingly murky, as two conflicting ideals struggled for ascendancy, often within the same breast; the desire for a classical education, with the status it still bestowed, clashed with the desire for an educational machine that would produce the administrators, engineers, and scientists the century was calling for ever more clamorously.

The history of the nineteenth-century Prussian—from 1871, German—educational system, which foreign visitors exalted into a standard to be adopted at home, admirably documents this conflict. In view of the preeminence that German scientists attained from mid-century on, it is noteworthy that the system at first firmly denigrated specialization and expertise—on principle. Quite as noteworthy is the brave way the neo-humanist ideal rose from the ashes of disaster and humiliation. The foundations for Prussia's exemplary schools and universities were laid after the decisive defeats Napoleon inflicted on its troops in 1806. Stripped of territory, of funds, of honor, of allies, the Prussian monarchy listened for a scant few years to determined educational reformers, notably Wilhelm von Humboldt, who presided over the revamping of Prussia's schools. He was in charge of educational policy for less than a year and a half, from early 1809, but his influence long outlasted his moment in power.

Humboldt had, of course, not invented the neo-humanism that informed his thinking on education. The tendentious rediscovery of ancient Greece, which gave his pedagogic philosophy its distinctive drive, had been spread among educated Germans late in the eighteenth century by a small group of extraordinary scholars, poets, and visionaries who constructed a largely imagined antiquity as a model for their sadly imperfect age.* But, while Humboldt was not an intellectual innovator, the neo-humanist *Gymnasium* and the modern German university owe much to his clearheaded directives and polished advocacy.

Humboldt was a dilettante in the best sense of that rapidly deflating term, a sensitive critic, knowledgeable philologist, and efficient though reluctant public servant. An ideological classicist, he idealized the ancients to give his contemporaries a model to imitate. His educational program, elaborated in incisive policy papers and diplomatically worded memoranda to Friedrich Wilhelm III, reads like a sympathetic response to Schiller's lament over the fragmentation of modern civilization. He was adamantly opposed to utilitarianism; from elementary school through *Gymnasium* to the university, schooling should aim at achieving the harmonious cultivation of all human capacities. Specialized training, that mundane enterprise, could not be its business; teachers had to attend not to the needs of life, but to the texts and ideas that alone carry the civilizing message. Some knowledge and a certain cultivation should be common to all; one becomes a solid craftsman, merchant, or soldier only as an enlightened human being: in his much-quoted summary, "To have learned Greek could be as little useless for the joiner as it would be for the scholar to make tables."[10] Humboldt expected that this common possession would soften the crass contrasts then setting the higher against the lower orders.

These were not just fantasies. From around 1810, as the first *Gymnasien* were being built, right into the 1840s, pupils spent some 45 percent of their time on the classical languages.[11] Anachronistic as this curriculum was becoming, the education of French bourgeois boys and of their English counterparts was equally remote from the realities of the laboratory, railroad management, and the countinghouse. Worse, within Prussia itself education grew remote from Humboldt's ideal; the impassioned faith in the classics that had informed a generation of neo-humanists gradually faded. In too many *Gymnasien,* pedants were making new pedants.

---

*The undisputed founder of this seductive dispensation was the eccentric Johann Joachim Winckelmann, a poverty-stricken, learned amateur who virtually invented the history of art as a discipline. A student of ancient Greek art who never got to Greece, an infectuous enthusiast for classical beauty who fed his virtually erotic passion by contemplating Roman copies of Greek originals, he defined the neoclassical ideal for more than a generation. He was seconded by Johann Gottfried Herder, that compelling philosopher of culture who extolled ancient Greece as the golden age of humanity. Two of Humboldt's friends—Goethe, who found in ancient Greece dramatic inspiration, and Friedrich August Wolf, who was to become the most authoritative and most controversial student of Homer in his time—completed Humboldt's education in neo-humanism. And two German philosophers, Kant and Fichte, taught him that man's supreme task is to form himself into an autonomous being.

This was not Humboldt's only problematic legacy. His scheme was egalitarian, at least in theory. It proposed to admit and promote pupils on the basis of competence; aided by able colleagues, Humboldt devised meticulous examinations to discover talent among all of Prussia's young subjects. An examination, especially one free of corruption, is a deliberate affront to such time-honored ways to preferment as social connections, family rank, and financial resources. In the great struggle between the bourgeoisie and the aristocracy for political power, examinations served the middling orders well. We know how deeply troubled the upholders of tradition were in Britain in the late 1850s, when the government introduced competitive examinations as rational tests for public employment. The reformed civil service was not yet a haven for specialists; the reformers' ideal was still the classically trained generalist. Even so, the second half of the nineteenth century became an age of competition—to obtain a clerkship in a government office, to produce the most appealing architectural sketch or the best poem. In the future, asserted the liberal journalist, editor, and politician John Morley in 1867, the contest for reputation, even for power, "will lie between brains and numbers on the one side, and wealth, rank, vested interest, possession in short, on the other."[12]

Though no democrat, Humboldt insisted that merit alone should govern the selection of those fit to enjoy full cultivation, and pioneered that democratizing device the entrance examination. While the *Gymnasien* chiefly catered to a small minority—the sons of professional men, government officials, and prosperous merchants—they eventually aided the sons of petty tradesmen and respectable artisans in their strenuous efforts to climb a step or two up the social pyramid. Yet *Bildung*—cultivation—remained a mark of distinction more than a social leveler, if only because most Prussian families could not afford to pay the fees of the *Gymnasium* or do without their sons' contributions to the family's earnings.

Whatever the share of the *Gymnasium* in easing social mobility in Germany, its curriculum continued to slight practical needs until the end of the century. In 1882, after repeated and confusing shifts of policy in Prussia's educational bureaucracy, a new regulation reduced the hours devoted to the ancient languages, giving more time instead to mathematics, the natural sciences, history, geography, and French. Yet in 1897, Friedrich Paulsen, a respected philosopher, historian of German education, and partisan of reform, noted that the old struggle between the ancients and the moderns was reviving. "It comes to a head in the question: is the acquisition of the *Greek* language still the indispensable precondition for scientific study at a university?"[13] Paulsen thought not, and his position was finally translated into law in 1901, after vehement debates.

For decades the German universities, too, were in the grip of Humboldt's vision of harmonious cultivation. In 1807, soon after the Peace of Tilsit had robbed Prussia of its most highly esteemed university at Halle and of other centers of higher learning, Friedrich Wilhelm III recognized the political and intellectual dividends that a new university could yield. Historians have justly expressed admiration for a state which, poverty-stricken and beset by almost insoluble problems, still found the will and the money for higher education. In 1810, the University of Berlin opened its doors. It started modestly, with 250 students and twenty-four professors. But it made up in quality what it lacked in numbers, with a faculty roster reading like an academy of immortals in German scholarship. It included the romantic philosopher of religion Friedrich Schleiermacher; the classical philologist Friedrich August Wolf; the historian of law Friedrich Karl von Savigny; the physician and popularizer Christoph Wilhelm Hufeland; the nationalistic philosopher Johann Gottlieb Fichte; the ancient historian Barthold Georg Niebuhr. Hegel joined this galaxy in 1818. "Those were the days," Lord Acton wrote later, half admiring and half amused, "in which the familiar type of the German scholar was generated, of the man who complained that the public library allowed him only thirteen hours a day to read, the man who spent thirty years on one volume, the man who wrote upon Homer in 1806 and who still wrote upon Homer in 1870."[14] Acton was being unfair; the best German scholars were anything but the kind of dry-as-dust pedant who uses his erudition not as a key to knowledge, but as a defense against anxiety.

Still, the German universities lived paradoxical lives. Humboldt had believed that their contribution to intellectual progress depended on their ability to pursue inquiry untrammeled. And German professors elevated freedom to teach and learn into a fiercely defended ideology. However, as state institutions, subject to the minister of education, the universities needed continuing support from their government, whether Prussia or Bavaria—ever more urgently late in the century, when a massive increase in the number of students compelled professors to neglect their researches in favor of time-consuming teaching. This meant that they had powerful bureaucrats looking over their shoulders. Often, as Brentano and other guardians of academic freedom could testify, they did more than look.

Surprisingly, though, the veto that a *Kultusminister* could exercise over appointments and the pressures he could bring in behalf of unorthodox candidates or innovative programs were not unmitigated disasters for *Wissenschaft*. All depended on the politics of the professors, often as conservative in the academy as in the public arena, and on the agenda of the minister. Certainly in Prussia during the Empire, the minister of education was more liberal and more imaginative than many scholars under his authority. German professors often defined academic freedom as freedom to keep out socialists and Jews; as late as 1918, in his famous lecture in Munich on science as a vocation, Max Weber told his audience that accident and prejudice governed many appointments to professorships and that a Jew might as well give up hope. The much-touted German republic of scholars was an exclusive club, blackball at the ready.

Among the students, too, rhetoric and reality rarely coincided. Publicists portrayed them as so many disinterested lovers of knowledge, but that was sheer idealization. German students had access to lectures and seminars, but learning was not forced on them; rather, they had to seek it out. That even the University of Berlin could not quite dispense with the sophomoric side of higher education so familiar from its venerable counterparts—fraternities addicted to duelling and carousing, opportunistic cultivation of well-connected friends—was perhaps inevitable. But in the midst of this noisy, often trivial life, investigators conducted sober research, and with the passing decades the universities managed to attract the finest German natural scientists to their classrooms and their well-equipped, well-funded laboratories. German higher education adapted to the modern struggle for mastery late but impressively.

Indeed, the overwhelming majority of Germany's most prestigious scientists were, or became, professors.[15] Some, like the physicist Heinrich Hertz, received recognition through promotion from a position at a polytechnic institute to a chair at a university. Others, like Robert Koch, were treated like national treasures. Koch, a bacteriologist of unsurpassed technical ingenuity who discovered bacilli producing ailments all the way from anthrax to tuberculosis, wound infections to Egyptian ophthalmia, did his stunning early work with the microscope as a country doctor in provincial Posen, but in 1880 was lured to a post at the imperial office for health in Berlin. Four years later, he was honored with a high decoration, and the Reichstag voted him 100,000 marks for his services to public health. A specially endowed professorship at the University of Berlin followed in 1885, sweetened by resounding titles.

When Koch left that chair six years later, he did so to become director of the newly built Institute for Infectious Diseases, tailored to his research interests. Other, even greater, distinctions came his way. In 1905, he was awarded that supreme international honor, the Nobel Prize, and shortly after, the *Pour le mérite*—Germany's most exalted decoration—and the title *Wirklicher Geheimrat*. He was now an "Excellency."

Nor was Koch alone; the German states and the imperial government lavished prizes, medals, titles, even patents of nobility on their scientific stars, and, more to the point, prestigious chairs and up-to-date laboratories. Many of these thoughtfully calibrated rewards and honors came from Berlin. A call to the University of Berlin, young as it was, became the most prized accolade to which any scholar, including a natural scientist, could aspire. There Johannes Müller, an anatomist, embryologist, pathologist, and chemist as celebrated for his pupils as for his discoveries, accepted a chair in 1833, as did Rudolf Virchow in 1856, and, in 1871, that universal genius Hermann Helmholtz.

But Berlin was only the most potent among the magnets attracting Germany's scientists. "Berlin," wrote Paulsen, "will never be a German London nor a German Paris."[16] One could be happy in Göttingen or Tübingen, certainly in Munich. At mid-century, Maximilian II of Bavaria, intent upon raising the intellectual and scholarly tone in his capital, lured north German poets, historians, and scientists to that capital. In 1851, he succeeded in capturing the internationally renowned organic chemist Justus Liebig—he had been Baron Justus von Liebig since 1845—from Giessen, where he had held a chair for almost three decades. Experimenter, theorist, teacher, writer, all with equal distinction, Liebig had been revolutionizing agriculture across the world. In 1822 Louis I, the grand duke of Hesse-Darmstadt, had sent Liebig, then little more than a promising young scientist, to Paris to perfect his grasp of chemistry. There Wilhelm von Humboldt, impressed with Liebig's talents, put him in touch with the distinguished chemist Joseph Louis Gay-Lussac. In 1825 Humboldt exerted himself once again, securing an associate professorship at Giessen for Liebig, who was all of twenty-two. It was at Giessen that he made his discoveries in organic chemistry, and in his primitive, pioneering laboratory taught a generation of young scientists from as far away as Russia and the United States. What King Maximilian had for him was better company, a better-equipped laboratory, and better teaching conditions. Liebig was so content in Munich that in 1865, eight years before his death, he even rejected a call from Berlin.

Yet it was in Berlin that German natural scientists discredited the vitalistic philosophy of nature that had dominated, and retarded, German scientific progress until the early 1840s. Ernst Brücke, Emil Du Bois-Reymond, Hermann Helmholtz, all to make luminous names for themselves in physiology, optics, physics, jointly declared, defying romantic science, that only "common physical-chemical forces" are "active in the organism, and only the "physical-mathematical method" can produce dependable results. The metaphysical burden of nature mysticism once thrown off, German science, and with that, German technology, were on their way.[17] Even the German universities, if at times reluctantly and resentfully, yielded to the irresistible exigencies of the modern age.

In the sustained effort to master nature, then, German scientists took pride of place. Between 1901, when the Nobel Prizes were first awarded, and 1914, when the First World War broke out, fourteen of the forty-nine laureates in physics, chemistry, and medicine were Germans.[18] They did not need to envy the French their Pasteur or the English their Maxwell. And in applying their science they were second to none.[19] But in the political history of the Victorian bourgeoisie, their accomplishments were less impressive. Nearly all of them, we know, were public officials, and most were satisfied to serve their state without a murmur in exchange for noninterference in their academic affairs.

They were by no means all unpolitical men; the widespread legend of the unpolitical German explains too much and hence too little. Political inaction is itself a form of political action, support for the authorities in power, a brake on change. In nineteenth-century Germany, political interest and participation rose and fell in successive waves of excitement, frustration, and retreat, and professors were not exempt from these larger rhythms. During the revolutionary days of 1848, academics had stood among the vanguard of those calling for heroic reforms in the German states; the self-appointed Frankfurt parliament, sitting to write a constitution for Germany, was well stocked with professors. Again in the early 1860s, professors were among the most articulate liberal nationalists, preaching unification on the basis of a constitutional regime similar to that of Britain. It was only in the mid-1860s, after they had failed ignominiously, that academics abandoned the tribune to return to their lecterns.

But not all of them. The influential historian Heinrich von Treitschke, for one, supplied fuel for anti-Semitism with his much-quoted slogan, "The Jews are our misfortune." Theodor Mommsen, for another, vigorously answered Treitschke's diatribes and spoke out against the Reich that Bismarck had invented, and would dominate for two decades. In 1898, in a codicil to his will, Mommsen described himself as a consistent "animal politicum." He had "wished to be a citizen," but, he concluded poignantly, "that is not possible in our nation, in which the individual, even the best, cannot get beyond service in the ranks and beyond political fetishism."[20] Another activist academician, Rudolf Virchow, served as a progressive deputy, working for improved primary education and prodding Bismarck from the floor of the Prussian lower house to transform semi-absolutist Germany into a parliamentary regime. Still others, like Lujo Brentano, made proposals for social legislation their particular form of political action.

Those on the other side of the ideological fence joined patriotic societies supporting the construction of a larger navy or preparations for a new war with France. But a solid majority of the professoriate were content with giving their lectures, supervising their students, and writing their treatises; prudently they redefined the freedom they needed to breathe by narrowing its scope. In imperial Germany, more than in other countries, academic autonomy proved compatible with civic passivity, became in fact its regular companion. As researchers and experimenters, scholars and theorists, German academics—good bourgeois virtually all of them—made signal contributions to human mastery. But as citizens they failed to claim mastery over their own fate. The way they chose to confine their lives to their professional advancement was a kind of division of labor—scholarship to the scholar, politics to the politician. But it was also a fateful division of power.

Professionalization, that characteristic element in the nineteenth-century division of labor, was not free of similar ambiguities. It advanced mastery, but at a cost. Like the universities, the professions struggled for self-government but appealed to the state for legitimation: the state could offer them the autonomy they craved by extending them recognition; it could prescribe in detail, with the professionals' collaboration and in their interest, the rules under which practitioners were licensed to perform their mysteries. Such support would shield the professions—and their presumed beneficiaries, the public in need of their services—from the depredations of charlatans. Huddling under this sheltering umbrella, the professions labored to secure the right to police themselves. This paradoxical struggle for freedom under protection worked with relatively little tension, largely because bureaucrats, legislators, and professional men were usually of the same class—at times the same person. They understood each other.

The growing volume and increasing sophistication of knowledge in the Victorian decades made professionalization imperative. The old global names, though still common in informal discourse, proved too imprecise as the natural and the social sciences performed more finely differentiated work. William Whewell coined the all-embracing term "scientist" for any "cultivator of science in general" only in 1840.[21] But even in his time, a few geniuses apart, very few researchers were cultivating science in general. They divided up fields or, as in biochemistry, joined two formerly distinct fields. Liebig's epochal book of 1840, *Die Thier-Chemie; oder, Die organische Chemie in ihrer Anwendung auf Physiologie und Pathologie,* attests to both processes at once. It advertises in its very title both the triumph of specialization and the attempt of a remarkable generalist to leap across the frontiers of the new disciplines; Liebig was proposing, in what he called "animal chemistry," to apply organic chemistry to physiology and pathology.

These decades also fostered social scientists who concentrated on selected portions of their global discipline, calling themselves sociologists or political scientists; and historians began to think of themselves not as students of the past in general, but as intellectual or military or political historians. Official recognition of this transformation in the historical profession came in 1892, when

Harvard University established the first chair in economic history anywhere. Higher learning was joining the world. Other professions took the same route. In the short span between 1864 and 1888, the United States saw the founding of no fewer than ten associations of medical men, each concentrating on one part of the human body. Ophthalmologists, laryngologists, genito-urinary surgeons, could now speak to colleagues at their conventions and in their quarterlies.[22] The development was a matter for self-congratulation, but it also became a matter of some concern among professional men. In 1881, at the first session of the Berlin association of internal medicine, one internist, Ernst von Leyden, noted with evident disapproval, "Nowadays there are hardly any *physicians,* almost all are *specialists,* or one is a specialist, and a physician on the side."[23] He was trying to hold back the flood.

Most of the new professions, then, were carved out of traditional callings. The nineteenth-century engineer, now a civil, mechanical, or chemical engineer, was an up-to-date version of the skilled artisan and ingenious tinkerer who had built bridges and improved weaponry in earlier centuries; the nineteenth-century psychiatrist was a physician claiming a unique competence in a single domain of the healing art. At the beginning of that century, the gratifying title of profession had still been restricted to a historic trio—theology, law, and medicine—and in the steep social pyramid, the preacher, the lawyer, and (with some reservations) the physician had occupied enviable places. None of these callings was monolithic; each established an invidious hierarchy of rank and influence. English barristers looked down on attorneys as lesser men of the law; French physicians were perhaps even more contemptuous of the *officiers de santé,* medical practitioners without an M.D. degree; German academic theologians rarely consorted with lowly country parsons. But as scientific and technological imperatives eroded centuries-old attitudes of disdain and deference, they also shifted balances within the traditional professions. There were ever more professionals as the century went on, and, as old claims to prestige faced new contenders, ever more professions.

The rush to professionalization accompanied, and promoted, the Victorian way of mastering nature by obeying it. New specialized journals, all witnesses and aids to professional maturity, came into being almost every year. There had been scatterings of such publications in the late eighteenth century, but the avalanche started in the 1830s, especially in the natural sciences; the human sciences limped after. The *Historische Zeitschrift,* the first journal addressed exclusively to historians, was founded in Munich in 1859; the French launched their *Revue historique* in 1876, while the *English Historical Review* appeared in 1886 and the *American Historical Review* in 1895. Professional schools were another sign that a craft had elevated itself into an honored calling; in the United

States, the first university school of dentistry opened in 1867, while in 1881 businessmen founded the Wharton School of Finance and Commerce in Philadelphia.

The fragmentation of the British Association for the Advancement of Science, founded in 1831, is a vivid indicator that the end of Renaissance man had come. It started out with ten sciences grouped into six sections, but subdivided these and added to them when the need arose—and it arose frequently. In 1866, "biology" was still a comprehensive rubric, embracing physiology, zoology, botany, and anthropology; in 1893, physiology split off, followed in 1894 by anthropology and in 1895 by botany. Skeptics might define the expert, in that fatuous and familiar witticism, as a man who knows more and more about less and less. But the study of nature and society had come to require highly concentrated expertise, or expertise that cut its way across the old disciplines.

This evolution, stretched across Western civilization, was of absorbing interest to bourgeois everywhere. The professions were the preserve of educated men from the middling orders, claiming a right to respect on the basis not of birth or coarse commercial cleverness, but of proven competence and lengthy training. The very arduousness of the apprenticeship a modern profession imposed was offered as a guarantee of authentic achievement. A framed certificate or, better, a group of certificates, on the wall of the consulting room, embellished with elaborate calligraphy and Latin phrases, was an emblematic reminder to clients that they were in the presence of a personage who had earned his authority. It is characteristic of the century that a good bourgeoise would have an obstetrician, a professional from her own class, deliver her children rather than a midwife, a practitioner most likely from the lower orders, now increasingly compelled to seek her business among her own kind. If the nineteenth century has any right to be called the bourgeois century, the massive expansion of the professions had a great deal to do with it.

In the Victorian age, a profession was a guild of gentlemanly practitioners bound together by shared interests and institutions. It acquired, and displayed, its identity by devising procedures for training aspirants, criteria for admitting recruits to its ranks, and standards for measuring the conduct of its members. Its supreme claim to gentlemanliness was service to society; its supreme mark of success the acquisition of autonomy. It was by asserting their autonomy, we have seen, that the teachers of Boston tried to ward off criticism of their punitive practices from parents and state officials; they alone, they insisted, as members of a dignified profession, knew what was best.

It is only natural that, employing these self-protective stratagems, professional men made themselves the subject of envy and the target of ridicule. So they have been throughout history. They have exacerbated the aggressions against them with their air of superiority, parade of esoteric knowledge, and assertion of indispensability. Critics, even those not given to excessive carping, have summarized the overriding concerns of these experts as power, glamour, and income. This centuries-old public rage is perfectly intelligible: by his very existence the professional stands as a reproach to the ordinary folk who cannot do without him; he underscores their ignorance and their helplessness. Certainly the nineteenth century, far more dependent than its predecessors on professional men, did not let them escape unscathed. A look at Daumier's lithographs of lawyers—snobbish, heartless, passionate only about their fees—is a reminder of how vulnerable professional men still were to satire. Cynics interpreted talk about maintaining the highest quality of service and the need to root out charlatans as so much self-serving rhetoric.

These denigrators often hit real targets. But the self-interest of lawyers and doctors could, and at times did, coincide with the interest of the public. A patient could only benefit from being attended by a physician as thoroughly schooled as the medical learning of the time allowed, and as sensitive to his guild's ethical imperatives as was possible to human nature. George Bernard Shaw might rant, in his aggressive, cranky preface to *The Doctor's Dilemma,* against the "murderous absurdity" of the "medical service of the community," and find some good—which is to say, terrible—supporting examples. But there were physicians who applied the ethical rules they had been taught in medical school, determined "neither to neglect their duties for the sake of ease, nor to abuse their opportunities for the sake of gain." They felt obliged, in the words of the eminent ophthalmic surgeon R. Brudenell Carter, to "bring adequate skill and knowledge to the accomplishment of their work, to be true and just in their dealings."[24]

No doubt, the members of a profession had particular, selfish, loyalties, but they also had (and certainly claimed) higher ideals. The physicians whom Victorian novelists and playwrights imagined represent both extremes; for every fictional doctor who, like Georg Büchner's callous military physician in *Woyzeck,* saw patients as interesting guinea pigs, there was one like Trollope's Dr. Thorne, hardworking and empathetic. Taken as a whole, a profession could be self-centered and public-spirited at the same time.

The career of medical men in Victorian England may put some historical flesh on these sociological bones; it will confirm that part of the time mastery meant control of turf rather than control of disease. The assaults on the vulgar commercialism of quacks reflected not solely a conscientious concern for the sick, but also a determination to drive inconvenient, often strikingly effective competitors from the marketplace. Invidious distinctions had long governed the guild; around 1800, the country's health had been in the hands of three corporations—physicians, surgeons, and apothecaries. The doctors, monopolizing the top of the hierarchy, were organized into the Royal College of Physicians, which dated back to Henry VIII, and the age of its charter did their social standing no harm. This institution, owned and controlled by a narrow elite of Fellows, licensed doctors and disciplined its members, a task performed by its board of censors, Brudenell Carter judged genially, "with scrupulous fidelity."[25]

Standards of admission were strict: a practitioner was eligible for the honorable title of doctor only if he had graduated with a degree in arts and a doctorate of medicine from Oxford or Cambridge. He was recognized, Carter fondly thought, as "a man who had enjoyed every educational advantage which his time could afford, and who had drunk deeply of its best learning." This meant that his Latin was good enough for him to understand—and deliver—a Latin oration, and that he would not sully his hands in trade or sue remiss patients for his honorarium. "The bye-laws of the College aimed at maintaining the Fellows and Licentiates in the social position of gentlemen."[26] A doctor had his privileges no less than his obligations; he belonged to a select aristocracy within the clan. In 1850, among some 14,700 medical men in England, only 1,700 were recognized as physicians.[27]

Lesser mortals than the physicians, the surgeons had barely outworn the stigma of the plebeian company of barbers they had been compelled to keep for centuries. Even after their liberation, they were "scarcely more than handicraftsmen," doing the bloody physical labor that physicians disdained. In 1800, though, the surgeons of London had been granted a charter to form the Royal College of Surgeons, and membership was opened to all of England's surgeons in 1843. Those able to accumulate clinical experience in hospitals, the so-called "pure" surgeons, found their repute, and their income, mounting even if they had not attended any of the ancient universities, and, in Carter's words, "might be as ignorant as they pleased" in matters of general knowledge.[28] They were more fortunate than fellow surgeons who, lacking hospital connections, became simple country doctors, humble practitioners like the mild Dr. Chillip in *David Copperfield,* as vital to their patients as they were despised by their superiors. The apothecaries, too, were raised to professional status in the nineteenth century, complete with licenses, approved courses of study and examinations. They, like their betters, found themselves endowed with the most desired mark of respectability—a measure of self-regulation.

Complicated as all this sounds, the reality was far more complicated. Early in the century, the writ of one regulating body had run in London alone; that of others, across England and Wales but not in Scotland or Ireland. No fewer than nineteen bodies could determine medical qualifications, each in its own way, and the credentials they granted were all valid for the whole country.[29] The medical degrees offered by universities were anything but comparable, and the exclusive elites of Fellows in the corporations were frequently at odds with the rank and file of the membership. Empirics—unlicensed competitors—aroused the profession to displays of unseemly rage and panic.* There was audible discontent on the part of general practitioners, social reformers, the suffering public. But nearly all of their efforts, though sustained and energetic, failed to garner the necessary votes in Parliament for bills to regularize and enforce standards of medical practice; too much was at stake and too many conflicting interests were involved.

Until mid-century, then, confusion and embittered competition dogged Britain's medical men. The law finally passed in 1858 to establish the qualifications of physicians and surgeons was a first, relatively audacious, step out of the maze. It was a modest triumph for the ethos of professionalism, a necessary compromise. Like the Reform Act of 1832, the Medical Act of 1858 found critics calling out for revision practically from the day it received the royal assent. Still, it reduced conflicts among jurisdictions by clarifying licensing requirements, establishing a medical register, and spelling out procedures for striking an offender from the ranks. Then, in 1886, after some twenty more bills had failed, an important new Medical Act repaired many of the surviving deficiencies.

But the perplexities of the profession were hardly amenable to legislative remedies. While the social prestige of doctors rose markedly after mid-century, this did not silence snobbish references to them as less than full-fledged gentlemen, or persistent complaints about their unwillingness to provide adequate service for charity cases. In 1872, the English feminist Josephine Butler charged that "fashionable life, wealth, and honours, and the atmosphere of courts, are as injurious to the moral judgment and the spiritual life of doctors, as of other men."[30] And the overriding problem of making a living remained a ground for anxiety. Those without a prosperous practice—and this meant a good number of them—courted prison officials or the armed services for contracts, or, until late in the century, dispensed drugs to eke out their income. The gap between highly paid consultants and hard-pressed general practitioners, a source of angry

---

*"It excites the smile of contemptuous pity to witness the tumult and the terror which one enterprising and crafty Quack can raise in this land of science and of schoolmasters," the *Westminster Review* wrote severely in 1831, "to see the pomposity and the parade with which the druggist of a single nostrum is chased from county to county, and hunted down like some monster of unquenchable rapacity, amid all our colleges of health and all of our boast of enlightenment." "Professional Morality in 1831; or, The Lawyers' Defence of Medical Quackery," *Westminster Review*, XIV (1831), 463.

grievances, grew if anything wider late in the century. The guardians of the guild also worried over an unwelcome flood of medical students, and protected themselves by monopolistic practices like excluding graduates of foreign medical schools from the register.

To benevolent observers, such developments were the necessary price of progress. Advances in medical science, they insisted, were preserving health and shortening illnesses more effectively than ever. Assessing the Victorian age in 1905, Justin McCarthy concluded with some breezy comments on the march of civilization during the queen's sixty-four years on the throne. "The many benefits which the expansion of medical science" had "conferred upon humanity," notably anesthetics and antiseptics, deserved special comment. "There seems every reason to believe that the Victorian age will have left its deepest impression on the world's history by the beneficent triumphs which it has accomplished in the application of science in all its departments to the benefit of humanity and the progress of civilisation in the everyday life of men, women, and children in all classes from the highest to the lowest, from the richest to the poorest, from the prince to the peasant."[31]

This was a bracing peroration for an exhaustive retrospect, but it calls for a certain skepticism. McCarthy was no mere ideologue. He was right to call attention to exhilarating advances in medicine during the second half of the century. The heroic campaigns of the sanitary reformers in cleaning up the cities, so frequently derided as utopian fantasies and meddling socialism, had managed to check most epidemics.[32] Yet one need only think of Charles Booth's Londoners in the 1880s to wonder about the confident verdicts of these late Victorians, as self-deceptive as they were self-congratulatory. The medical profession had done much, but perhaps acted more in an effort to secure its own status and income than to improve the public's health.

The general state of that health, the exposure to infection, and life expectancy, in fact continued to vary drastically with class; the lower orders, housed in filthy slums, slaving in insalubrious and dangerous workplaces, eating poor, often tainted food, were far more susceptible than their better-off fellow citizens to the ravages of epidemics, to tuberculosis, measles, and scarlet fever. Far more often than middle-class parents, they watched their infants and small children die. The working class did profit from discoveries in medicine and hygiene, but in the matter of improving health, the nineteenth century was above all, in an unpleasant sense, the bourgeois century.[33]

And yet, limited as medical progress had been in the century, limited even in the classes it benefited most, whatever progress there was had been principally due to the Victorian cult of fact and the modern division of labor. And what held true for medicine held true no less for the other professions old and new.

Their achievements were spectacular but incomplete. The nineteenth century mounted a most determined effort at mastering the world. Its work stands as an impressive feat of harnessing aggression to constructive purposes. Yet even before the First World War shattered the sanguine hopes of bourgeois culture and dealt the theory of progress its death blow, the strains of mastery were visible everywhere. If the optimism of bourgeois had been wholly untroubled, why did they so ardently seek advice for every segment of their lives?

4. An Age of Advice and Neuroses

The century stretching from the defeat of Napoleon to the outbreak of the First World War has been called the Age of Steam, the Age of Nationalism—and the Age of the Bourgeoisie. Defensible names all, but it might well have been called, too, the Age of Advice. Among the telltale deposits left to its historians is a vast prescriptive literature on the art of living. Ventures in helpfulness, whether modest pamphlets, dramatized dialogues, substantial tracts, or didactic novels, inundated readers everywhere. Even French novelists, a species that more puritanical societies scarcely trusted, were disposed to improve rather than debauch their public. Making people better than they were, or at least less bad, blossomed into a sizable household industry in the nineteenth century; scratch a realist and you found a moralist in disguise.

While, as we know, nineteenth-century transformations were something of a tribute to the ability of bourgeois to harness aggressive impulses for social and private ends, the advice literature abundantly documents that many of them were also exceedingly anxious. They were anxious over the noisy lower orders, the abyss of immorality that the decline of religion appeared to be opening, the increase in bodily comforts that threatened to turn them into a race of ineffectual and effete epigones—anxious, in short, over whether they could manage a world apparently spinning out of control. The literature of advice was designed to help them gain, or keep, command.

To complicate matters, the century also had to cope with what respectable citizens denounced as pernicious counsel. In speeches, broadsides, and pamphlets, agitators were advising workers to act on their economic discontents, atheists were encouraging the young to desert the faith of their fathers, perhaps worst of all, troublemakers were handing out birth-control information. "Investigation brings to light the fact that there is in our midst a school of instruction in the art of avoiding parenthood," a scandalized Dr. Pomeroy, a Boston physician, observed in 1888. But he reassured himself with the thought that "the text-books and the recognized instructors" of this school "are not inviting to a pure and cultivated taste."[1] Perhaps not, but that school of rebels was worth watching.

The vast majority of advice-givers of course saw themselves as purer and more cultivated than these subversives; scores of parsons, educators, editorial writers, novelists—many of them women—broadcast household hints, moral prodding, medical wisdom, religious consolation, and instruction in social etiquette. Whether telling improving tales or adducing shocking statistics, they made up a formidable division in that great Victorian army battling the supreme enemy, ignorance. They, too, like the natural and social scientists, worshiped facts, though their facts often seem rather peculiar. In any event, they marched on, under the flags of wisdom—and of righteousness—on the defensive. Aiming above all to be understood, they dispensed their sermons in digestible language, spicing them with warnings against calamities in the wings and with vistas of a brighter future for the good and the obedient.

Disdainful romantics early on, and later, disaffected bohemians and dandies, derided the simplistic pieties, the sheer philistinism, of these cicerones to the good middle-class life. But their lofty objections spoke to a select handful, no more. Only two or three notorious birth-control pamphlets could hope to approach the circulation guaranteed the avalanche of uplift; the conventional improvers touched untold thousands of lives. Fleetingly, no doubt: the sheer amount and repetitiveness of advice suggests a high rate of recidivism in a public unwilling, or unable, to be consistently virtuous. Sniped at by critics who treated bourgeois virtues as bourgeois vices—thrift as stinginess, probity as hypocrisy—middle-class readers often returned to the literature on self-improvement in the wan hope of doing better next time.

Like so much else in the century, Victorian homilies had prestigious ancestors. From the late Middle Ages onward, and particularly since the Renaissance, didactic writers had proffered solemn counsel to princes and courtiers, pedagogues and literate citizens. Eminent scholars and no less eminent philosophers like Erasmus and Locke had not disdained teaching manners; amidst graver work, they had labored to school the young in the blessings of civility. Even Machiavelli's notorious masterpiece, *The Prince,* was in its tough-minded, sardonic way a secular sermon on the art of living—or, at least, of survival. The tempo of such purposeful counsel markedly increased in the century of the Enlightenment. Addison and Steele's *Spectator* and their German and French imitators urged gentleness and civilized rationality on receptive readers; philosophers of education like Rousseau, wrestling with the mysteries of human development, generated widely followed schemes of pedagogy; Christian philanthropists like Hannah More, troubled by the ravages of fashionable irreligion, made it their business to lead their audiences back to God with tracts and novels. The Victorian sermonizers democratized this literature, swelling a rivulet into a very Mississippi of advice.

As practical men and women, they tailored their publications to diverse audiences. They importuned or bullied young men and women, lovers about to marry, newlyweds, adolescents troubled in their religious beliefs, clerks eager to succeed in business, hostesses insecure about dinner parties, adults threatened by neurasthenia, pedagogues and physicians in a panic over the epidemic scourge of masturbation. But wide-ranging though its subjects and consumers, this literature appraising human nature at work propagated a single portentous vision. Virtually all of it depicted the human animal as torn between raw instincts—those mighty, almost irresistible incentives to sin and crime—and the powers of resistance, powers in need of cultivation, which alone held out hope for redemption. The advice industry's entrepreneurs thought good thoughts to wipe out the bad thoughts in their readers.

As may be imagined, no single mix of hope and despair could do for all of the improving authors. And too often, they could not compel even their own message into coherence. While these purveyors of verbal patent medicines to human nature were far more disposed to view with alarm than point with pride, many of them, with engaging inconsistency, proved relatively tolerant if not enthusiastic about the pleasures of sexual congress. They approved of woman's enjoying the supreme erotic experience as much as man did—always provided, of course, that she sought her carnal pleasures within the sacred silken ties of the marriage bond. Still, warnings outnumbered and far outweighed celebrations; exhorting, cajoling, prophesying, terrorizing their readers with instances displaying the appalling consequences of loose living or laziness—or, worse still, of "self-abuse"—these authors constituted themselves a cultural superego that would not be denied.

Anyone who surveys this vast and crowded field must be daunted by its riches and impressed by its astonishing uniformity.* There were, to be sure, characteristic variations from country to country, decade to decade. English authors stressed manliness more emphatically than others; German authors waxed more philosophical than their rivals abroad. The patriotic note grew increasingly audible from mid-century on, and was soon joined by laments over

---

*What follows, therefore, is a collective portrait. To keep the reader from being swamped by instances drawn from several countries and many decades, nearly all of them will be given in footnotes as running exemplifications of the points made in the text. Nothing would be easier than to match any set of them, many times over, with other instances equally telling and carrying the same weight.

decadence, which inspired the most strenuous exhortations. The ideals on which bourgeois were being lectured across Western civilization—dutifulness, temperance, good character—covered a broad range of difficult virtues. Yet all together, they proved variations on a single requirement: civilized people had to take control, and the most necessary kind of control was beyond question self-control.*

In the advice literature, self-control—more vividly, the Germans called it *Selbstbeherrschung;* the French, *empire sur soi-même*—appears as among life's most precious goods and the indispensable precondition for true maturity. Yet, since it is contrary to human inclinations, it is also among the hardest of lessons to impart. It demands nothing less than the triumph of reason over passion, of one's higher over one's lower nature. Self-control, said Nicholas Pain Gilman in a representative study sponsored by the American Secular Union, "should be taken to mean restraint of the lower self,—the animal, sensual, anti-social instincts and tendencies."[2] What children most need to learn they do not want to hear; what they want to hear they do not need to learn. As Freud would put it early in the twentieth century, the pleasure principle and the reality principle are usually at odds.†

---

*Consider an episode in *Home,* a didactic novel by one of America's favorite novelists, Catharine Maria Sedgwick. Mr. Barclay, a minister who rejects corporal punishment, disciplines his ten-year-old son for throwing a kitten into boiling water in a fit of rage, first lecturing him in language no human has ever spoken except in books of this type: " 'Go to your room, Wallace,' said his father. 'You have forfeited your right to a place among us. Creatures who are the slaves of passion, are, like beasts of prey, fit only for solitude.' " He then forbids Wallace to speak to anyone in the family, and forbids the members of the family to speak to him. He has turned his home into a penitentiary, complete with the silent treatment. In the end, utterly crushed, the boy gives in. After innumerable heartfelt prayers, he has become perfectly convinced that he has done grievous wrong and must control his passions from now on. *Home* (1835; 15th printing, 1841), 17.

†In "The Formation of the Will and the Discipline of Affects," a chapter in his two-volume treatise on ethics, Friedrich Paulsen defined "self-control" as the "virtue or competence" that regulates conduct by means of the rational will. *System der Ethik mit einem Umriss der Staats- und Gesellschaftslehre,* 2 vols. (1900), II, 10. Friedrich Wilhelm Foerster, a highly respected pedagogue, cosmopolitan and Christian thinker, made *Selbstbeherrschung* the indispensable quality in the formation of character. In *Lebenskunde,* a substantial, popular guide for the young, he gave it the longest chapter. One could live without railroads or the electric light, but not without self-control. *Lebenskunde. Ein Buch für Knaben und Mädchen* (1908; ed. 1912), 12. (By 1912, it had sold more than thirty thousand copies.) "*Control yourself,*" advised Charles Wagner, a French essayist on elevated topics like justice and the simple life, "Be master of yourself." *L'Ami. Dialogues intérieurs* (1902; 2nd ed., 1903), 202, 205. This lesson could not be inculcated too early. "*It is by authority that young children must be guided,*" exclaimed the French physician and school inspector Alfred Donné; it would accustom them to obedience—teach them, in other words, to internalize the ability to harness imperious wishes. *Mothers and Infants, Nurses and Nursing* (1846; tr. 1859), 226.

In the Victorian age these stern convictions required no proof and no defense. Everyone knew that humankind's only hope was the most energetic
intervention of reason seconded by the will, which would counsel and enforce
delay, moderation, prudence. The German moralist Ernst von Feuchtersleben,
aristocrat, poet, and physician, spoke for a wide consensus: "That all virtue is
self-command seems to me certain."[3] One had to tame the beast within.

Though there was nothing original in the Victorians' dramatization of the
mind as a battleground where primitive appetites wrestle with the restraining
hand of reason, their celebration of self-control can claim a noteworthy position of its own. The history of modern civilization down to the early twentieth
century was one of growing distance from unmediated feelings and spontaneous conduct. Cultivated men and women took the lead in erecting more and
more sophisticated defenses against the direct translation of instinctual desires
into action.[4] This development reached its summit among the Victorians; as we
have good reason to know, the very name "Victorian" has been taken as
synonymous with excessive defensiveness, variously denounced as gentility and
prudery.

We have seen that the criticism is largely unjustified; the Victorians were far
less squeamish, far more passionate, than their complacent and condescending
children later liked to imagine. Still, euphemism flourished as nineteenth-
century men and women constructed a culture of discretion and indirection.[5]
By and large they chose to speak daggers but use none. Just as the fork had come
to replace the hand at the dinner table to pick up food in the days of Erasmus,
and the handkerchief the fingers to deal with nasal discharge, so by the nineteenth century, the gratification of appetites whether erotic or aggressive had
been strenuously refined and sublimated, especially among the middling orders.
As bourgeois exigently pressed the drives into the service of "higher" things,
they found reason making ever more stringent demands on passion.

Nineteenth-century moralists took pains to justify their defensive rationalism
as something better than low calculation for gain. Nor was it cold. "Reason,"
the English physician George Moore wrote in 1848, "has desires of its own,
which lead to action."[6] Just as the bourgeois ideal of love strove to purify erotic
impulses with the lofty emotions of tenderness and enduring commitment, so
reasoned conduct was expected to raise itself above the vulgar contest for

---

But this was as difficult as it was imperative. See Alexander M. Gow: "The precepts of the moral
law are contrary to the natural inclinations of mankind." *Good Morals and Gentle Manners for Schools
and Families* (1873), 37. In the words of Sophie Bryant, a teacher of mathematics in the North
London Collegiate School for Girls, "Self-denial is the *sine qua non* of individual progress." *Short
Studies in Character* (1894), 7.

wealth or prestige. The treasured and conspicuous emblems of this civilized style were good manners at table, a piano in the parlor, a well-thumbed library, concert tickets and museum visits, a program to help others help themselves, and the public subscription to a favorite charity.

Naturally, temperance in all its meanings figured prominently in this idealized self-portrait. Temperance is, after all, precisely the ascendancy of reflection over desire. Even the rules of etiquette were enlisted in the struggle for temperate self-mastery.* The guidelines governing conduct in polite society, at least according to those who produced books about them, rose above snobbery and penetrated beneath artificial glitter to the core of middle-class virtuousness itself. "Good manners," Mrs. H. O. Ward declared in a bulky, highly successful compendium on manners and fashions, "facilitate intercourse, free us from impediments, aiding, as a railway aids travelling, by getting rid of all avoidable obstructions to the road." Where manners are bad, "no society can be improving." Significantly she uttered these dicta in a volume titled *Sensible Etiquette*.[7]

Temperance, of course, meant far more than politeness and social refinement. Its synomym was sobriety, a standard that called for abstention not only from intoxicating liquor but also from pernicious addictions like gambling. As authors praising sobriety insisted, moderation in sexual activity, in eating, drinking, and the general search for pleasure, was the royal road to that most inestimable of all commodities—good health. "Is it a wonder," Dr. Paul Paquin asked in 1891 in a book on the passions of the flesh, "that the heads of gormands, great eaters, and dyspeptics, often ache? or that such individuals suffer from loss of energy, from lassitude, pains in the muscles, stiffness, insomnia, pains in the kidneys, drowsiness after meals, auto-intoxication in fact?"[8]

Few physicians to society were quite so graphic, but such rhetorical questions were the staple of improving literature throughout the age. The vexing matter of temperance, or rather, intemperance, had long agitated reformers; the crusade to wean the laboring poor from alcohol was a classic preoccupation for Victorian humanitarians. They published books and pamphlets, held meetings and conferences, invaded working-class neighborhoods, in their effort to banish the specter.[9] And anxious preachers saw intemperance as a problem for the prosperous no less. Around mid-century Henry Ward Beecher proclaimed intemperance "the great social battle of the age," fought out "between the flesh

---

*"Civilization has its laws, civil, religious and social, binding upon the community," Mrs. Eliza Duffey, a favorite American moral guide, argued. "Etiquette may be considered as the by-laws of civilization, binding upon each individual of the community. Arbitrary as many of these by-laws may seem, they are all founded upon some good and sufficient reason." *The Ladies' and Gentlemen's Etiquette: A Complete Manual of the Manners and Dress of American Society* (1877), 16.

and the spirit." He worried about everyone, not just farmers and factory hands. "If you corrupt the working-class by drink; if you corrupt the great middle-class by drink; if you corrupt the literary and wealthy classes by drink, you have destroyed the commonwealth beyond your power to save it." The issue was plain: "Unless we can teach individuals and the masses self-respect and self-control, we are utterly ruined."* This was not an eccentric American point of view; instances from Britain and the Continent abound. Temperance was a synonym everywhere not just for sobriety, but for good health.

Health, in fact, was never far from Victorian prodders' minds. Medical encyclopedias and a menu of home remedies sold briskly. A virtually universal obsession and the leading theme in private correspondence, good health was supposed to provide a solid basis for rationality. It was at the same time its happy result. Resorting to the mercantile metaphors that came so easily to the pens of bourgeois counselors, Horace Mann asked why one should not "indulge an ambition to lay up a stock of health, as well as to lay up stocks of any other kind? Health is earned,—as literally so as any commodity in the market. Health can be accumulated, invested, made to yield its interest and its compound interest, and thus be doubled and redoubled." To give in to "allurements for the appetite" was to risk the kind of speculation that had ruined many a rich man.[10] Health was the best investment any young Victorian could hope to make.

On this crucial point, sports enthusiasts, sellers of quack remedies, and publishers of popular medical texts could heartily agree. No wonder warnings against lapses from sobriety were as bleak as they were frequent and ranged from frightening catalogues to nebulous threats.† Usually, the advice industry traded

---

*Beecher, "Intemperance the Great Social Battle of the Age," in Miss L. Penney, ed., *The National Temperance Orator* (1877), 189. In 1899, the Church of the Holy Communion in New York published a small book of addresses on personal purity, the observance of Sunday, and other pressing matters. In his lecture on temperance, the Right Reverend Henry C. Potter reminded his youthful listeners that "it is quite as much a vice with a great many of us to eat too much as to drink too much." One could never begin too soon to "apply the law of temperance to our indulgences, to our habits, to our recreations, to our appetites." Observing this law would make them "men of rule." "Temperance," in W. W. Moir, ed., *Some Things that Trouble Young Manhood* (1899), 100, 106.

†Through the 1830s and 1840s, Dr. William Alcott, a prodigious scatterer of advice, gloomily offered exhaustive bills of particulars. Drunkenness and gluttony, and the "unamiable," ruinous love of so-called "good eating and drinking," are the gravest offenses humans can commit against their sacred bodies. Addiction to tea or coffee, like addiction to alcohol, is a form of slavery. Water, so much ridiculed, is the best drink. Alcott even cautioned against bad eating habits like the rapid swallowing of large quantities of food, the failure to masticate thoroughly, and the "wretched practice" of suppers, that unnecessary fourth meal. *The Young Man's Guide* (1832; 16th rev. ed., 1845), 62–71.

in specificity, finding the beginning of wisdom in small things. The grim theory of the slippery slope was no invention of the Victorian age, but it flourished mightily there. The man "who indulges in one little draught of alcoholic drink, is in danger of ending a tippler," just as the man "who gives loose to one impure thought, of ending the victim of lust and sensuality."[11] For moral experts, rationality meant a continuous renewal of self-control, self-denial, self-overcoming. This was the shadow side of Humboldt's neo-humanist ideal of self-realization.*

One of the most dependable, but also most exacting, tests of temperance in action was the management of rage, that supreme inciter of impulsive aggression. Almost invariably, moral guides insisted that moderating one's anger, no matter how righteous, was imperative. One had to subject it, more forcefully than table manners, to rational rule. Those blessed with a gentle disposition would experience only moderate difficulty in obeying this injunction. But those given to irritability—and this seemed to be a solid majority—had to learn to rein it in. Alexander Gow, a writer of popular catechisms, summed up this counsel: "If we would learn to control our passions, we must commence with bridling our tongue." Dr. William Alcott had said so before: "He who has a violent temper, should always speak in a low voice, and study mildness and sweetness in his tones. If we find ourselves apt to be angry, we should endeavor to avoid the road which leads to it. The first thing to be done, is to govern our voice."[12] In self-imposed silence there was strength. Moralists agreed that the endangered individual best averted emotional chaos threatening from within not by taking precautions as emergency measures when aggressive urges were at the boiling point, but by making trained self-command into second nature.†

---

*In 1909, Friedrich Wilhelm Foerster summed up a century's wisdom about the management of appetite. It was all a matter of will. For hygienic and moral reasons, men and women had to learn to control their "drive for nourishment." Regrettably, fanatical campaigners against drunkenness were exposing a good cause to ridicule. "The drops we drink may not reduce us, or our offspring, to idiocy, but, still, they will influence our life's decisions, large and small, in a lower direction." *Lebensführung. Ein Buch für junge Menschen* (1909; ed. 1910), 43–48, 54–55.

†Sir John Lubbock, later Lord Avebury, banker, natural scientist, member of Parliament and indefatigable champion of moral improvement, thought this hackneyed counsel valuable enough to bear reiteration: "Above all, never lose your temper, and if you do, at any rate hold your tongue, and try not to show it." *The Use of Life* (1894), 33. In 1901, Dr. Mary Wood-Allen noted in her popular sex manual that "intense mental excitement, as a fit of anger or grief or even of intense joy, may be injurious in results." Since women are physically handicapped several days of the month, they should practice restraint with particular care: "The girl should cultivate a serene spirit and strong self-control at all times," especially when she is menstruating. *Ideal Married Life: A Book for All Husbands and Wives* (1901), 117. And Foerster reminded his young readers in a section

It is noteworthy how much the teachers of control over the passions enjoyed mercantile metaphors. Indeed, they were more than metaphors, for they amounted to sincere praise of the commercial virtues; the elevated commendation of reason often issued in a straightforward appeal to middle-class self-interest. In the 1830s, Dr. Alcott anticipated a flood of witnesses: "Nothing contributes more to despatch, as well as safety and success in business, than method and regularity." Men of business, and those who would follow their example, should keep books of memoranda, those instruments of reason, to know at a glance their assets and their liabilities. "Study therefore to live within your income. To this end you must calculate." Emerson gave this view an original twist: "The virtues," he wrote, "are economists." In turn, Ruskin thought the economists' virtues indebted to the ideal of rationality: "Economy, whether public or private, means the wise management of labor."[13]

This rationalistic attitude overran nineteenth-century fiction. Dickens's favorite character, David Copperfield, exploring the reasons for his success as a writer, instanced his sense of responsibility, his perseverance, and his "patient and continuous energy." He added, "I never could have done what I have done, without the habits of punctuality, order, and diligence, without the determination to concentrate myself on one object at a time."[14] Here is a brilliant description of disenchanted modern man, at once master and slave of rationality, and what matters is that Dickens offered it with approval.

Inescapably, treatises on conduct prominently included chapters on thrift, which was only self-command in another guise. Thrift called for the most demanding and most unpopular exercise of the will to which impatient humans could subject themselves: the postponement of pleasure. Thrift demanded forethought, judiciousness in saving and spending alike. Samuel Smiles, probably the most influential, certainly the most widely read, manufacturer of fluently written books of advice and inspiration in the Victorian age—often anthologies of elevating quotations and anecdotes—was bound to include a volume on the subject in his vast output. The ideal pervades his work. Thrift, he wrote in *Duty,* "assumed the dignity of labor, and urged men to economize in order to secure their independence; to provide for their families, with a view to the future; to live a clean, sober, and manly life; to avoid the horrible curse of drink, which keeps so many men and women poor; and to raise them up to an elevation of virtue, morality, and religion"—in short, win the war of life with the familiar weapon of self-determination, which really meant self-denial.[15]

---

characteristically titled "The Struggle with One's Tongue" that the great Julius Caesar, provoked to rage, would count to twenty before he spoke—"a splendid remedy." *Lebenskunde,* 19.

The sexual implications of exhortations to thrift, implications that nineteenth-century physicians were only too willing to spell out, were fairly obvious: just as a prudent man husbands his financial resources, so also will he expend his semen moderately, in careful regard for his readily depleted stock. On this delicate point, as so often, the need to master the sexual and the aggressive drives made common cause on the battlefield of existence.

In this dour Victorian theory of human nature, self-control and purposeful activity were two faces of a single coin. None of the writers crusading for sober, carefully cultivated restraint intended to license a life of passivity or meekness. They did not propose to train saints. Quite the contrary, they urged bourgeois to master their fate; the world, like a woman, was only waiting to be conquered. This meant unremitting toil in the almost limitless theater of action that nineteenth-century ingenuity and perseverance had opened up. Idleness drew the fire of earnest improvers almost as often, and quite as vehemently, as immorality.* In 1850, Henry Ward Beecher published a typical lecture on the topic, thundering not just against the "supine sluggard" but also against the "bustling do-nothing." Men "may walk much, and read much, and talk much, and pass the day without an unoccupied moment, and yet be substantially idle; because industry requires, at least, the intention of usefulness. But gadding, gazing, lounging, mere pleasure-mongering, reading for the relief of ennui—these are as useless as sleeping or dozing, or the stupidity of a surfeit." By contrast, industry, "the parent of thrift," is hearty and muscular, an unpolluted source of happiness.[16] To moral guides like Beecher, hedonistic activity was laziness by other means. But what he, like other physicians to society, hoped to

---

*Near the end of his famous biography of George Washington, M. L. "Parson" Weems, appraising his hero's character, found sincere religiosity, fatherly benevolence, noble patriotism, and above all tireless activity: "Of all the virtues that adorned the life of this great man, there is none more worthy of our imitation than his admirable industry." His youthful addiction to work had first led to Washington's preferment. "Oh! divine Industry! queen mother of all our virtues and of all our blessings! what is there of great or good in this wide world that springs not from thy royal bounty? And thou, O! infernal Sloth! fruitful foundation of all our crimes and curses!" *The Life of George Washington; with Curious Anecdotes, Equally Honourable to Himself, and Exemplary to His Young Countrymen* (ca. 1800; ed. 1849), 220–21, 227. In 1864, in a hortatory guide to life, the editor and essayist J. H. Friswell cited a bouquet of authorities to enforce his argument that of all hereditary sins, idleness is the most damaging. "Nowadays, many people are proud of doing nothing, and inflate themselves with wicked vanity, holding a prescriptive right to be indolent." This yawning snobbishness corrodes mind as much as body. The only thing that can overcome the ills of life is "Industry, the great opponent and conqueror" of the "rust of the mind" to which the lazy are exposed. *The Gentle Life: Essays in Aid of the Formation of Character* (1864; 2nd and 3rd ed., 1864), 253, 257.

promote was a grim felicity. Critics of the bourgeoisie gave the results he aimed at less cheery names than "happiness."

The flabbiness of the bourgeoisie, especially the more affluent, became a topic for censorious international concern in the nineteenth century. Calls for the exercise of the will—under rational command, of course, but energetic, schooled, persevering—topped the hierarchy of moral demands, in the United States, in Germany, and elsewhere. "I wish to preach," said Theodore Roosevelt, "not the doctrine of ignoble ease, but the doctrine of the strenuous life, the life of toil and effort, of labor and strife." In a book on the soul and body of the child, one French writer, Dr. Maurice de Fleury, warned that "indolence of mind goes along with indolence of the body," and both together are troubling symptoms of "low vitality." Edward Carpenter, an English propagandist for socialism, sexual liberation, and warm male friendships, could not withhold comment: "Among the middle and well-to-do classes especially," he wrote in 1894, "the conditions of high civilisation" induced "an overfed masculinity in the males and a nervous and hysterical tendency in the females."[17] None of these commentators had any illusions that doing battle with comfortable habits would be easy.[18]

This exaltation of activity assumed rationality and activity to be natural allies. That alliance was the overriding theme of Dr. George Moore's mid-century study *Man and His Motives*. Moore defined "self-management" as a mutually beneficial interweaving of thoughtfulness and emotionality. Reason lights up moral perceptions. "To be angry without sin," he noted, adverting, like so many others, to that touchstone of intimate aggression, "is the standard of perfection." And while Moore said much about self-restraint, his most deeply felt pages deal with the "love of action and power."[19] His argument became canonical. What was at stake in the fateful duel between labor and laziness was not simply social utility or religious duty, but life itself. Man needs activity or he will die.*

---

*See Jules Clément: "Man is made for work; it is the order of nature. Work is the soul of everything. *Traité de politesse et du savoir-vivre* (1879), 10. The Reverend G. S. Weaver put it more sententiously: "I take it that men and women were made for business, for activity, for employment." A "man with no Employment, nothing to do, is scarcely a man. The secret of making men is to put them to work, and keep them at it." Spoiled unemployed young men were "walking nuisances—pestilential gas-bags—fetid air-bubbles, who burst and are gone." *Hopes and Help for the Young of Both Sexes Relating to the Formation of Character, Choice of Avocation, Health, Amusement* . . . (1880), 122, 124, 126. "*Every virtuous life that has ever been lived has been a life of persistent effort,*" wrote an American educator, Edward P. Jackson. "Virtue is strength; vice is weakness. . . . Virtue is a constant resistance to force, which tends to draw the soul to its ruin; vice is the simple, passive

This prescription reads like a mixture of muscular Christianity and Social Darwinism, but Moore's book—published in 1848—shows that it predated both Charles Kingsley and Charles Darwin. "The infant no sooner moves its limbs, and feels that they are moved at its will, than it begins to enjoy itself in the use of its own power, for power is evinced only in action, and every action is a certainty—an advance in positive knowledge." No question, "the infantine motive is the motive of all. It is the love of power, or rather the pleasure of self-consciousness in the use of means, by which we obtain outward evidence of our own inward life and of the reality of things, in relation to ourselves."[20] Here are, in embryo, Nietzsche's will to power and Freud's early hypothesis of a drive for mastery.

The adulatory lives of financial tycoons and industrial magnates that flooded bookstores in Germany as in France, in Britain as in the United States—all these portraits of giants rising, of course, from humble beginnings to legendary riches—read like so many demonstrations of this thesis. Not until the turn of the century, when muckrakers in the United States, middle-class reformers in Britain, and socialists on the Continent dared to question the myth of mobility that these biographies tried to sell, did their appeal began to wane. But the doctrine that energy is richly rewarded in this life survived all the well-grounded assaults. As late as 1914, Georges Demeny, a professor of physical education for the city of Paris, in a book making propaganda for physical exercise, showed that Victorian praise of action had not yet gone wholly out of date. "Effort is the source of all work," whether cerebral or muscular; more, effort is life itself: *"L'effort, c'est la vie."* And effort can be trained into a salutary habit; Demeny substantially agreed with Theodore Roosevelt, Friedrich Wilhelm Foerster, and a legion of other moralists that success in life is wholly a matter of will. In an age of expansion and invention, man is the architect of his fortune and his will the father to power: *"Vouloir, c'est pouvoir."*[21]

Character, that magical word, intoned daily, encompassed all these cherished bourgeois ideals and anxieties. It meant realism, self-control, temperance, thrift, hard work, purposeful energy, and the rest—in short, aggression disciplined and sublimated. The troop of personal improvers, imparting their lessons in learned treatises and school lessons, in sermons and political forums, were all pedagogues teaching character. They spoke in virtual unison and in thoroughly schooled accents; the homilies they delivered after 1900 sound much like those

---

yielding to that force." It followed that industrious activity "is an indispensable condition both to health and happiness,—continued and regular activity." *Character Building: A Master's Talk with His Pupils* (1891), 28, 29, 171.

their grandfathers had delivered half a century earlier.

Rationality, then, had a potent competitor. Merchants of advice did not scruple to consider character more important than intelligence. This pronounced anti-intellectual preference was a widely held article of faith. One refrain in polemics on education was the charge that most pedagogues sinned in cultivating reason at the expense of the harmonious development of desirable qualities. The soul was a more elevated human endowment than the mind.* Around 1900, the French philosopher and pedagogue Alfred Fouillée asked rhetorically, suppose you have "taught the elements of the positive sciences— mathematics, astronomy, physics—in what respect will you have changed the heart and ensured the rule of justice? All you will have developed is the intelligence properly speaking; but to know is only one of our functions. An education of the feelings by means of literature, the arts, and history is not less necessary than the education of thinking, and the whole must culminate in the education of the will."[22] As everyone knew, this was precisely the aim of English education, especially of those famous public schools. There, the formation of moral perfection was taken to be more important than intellectual achievements.† The charge of philistinism that Matthew Arnold and others levied against the middle classes was tendentious in the extreme, but it was not groundless.

Clearly, one could learn to do right only by paying painstaking attention to character itself; secular philosophers agreed with clergymen on this important point.‡ John Stuart Mill, in his *System of Logic,* had proposed a psychological

---

*In his contribution to the question of how to educate German youth for a demanding world, Paul Güssfeldt, mountain climber, explorer, and friend to Kaiser Wilhelm II, thundered against the *"one-sided cultivation of the reason,"* an education that *"tears apart all harmony."* The schools should deliver over to adult life *"human beings* above all, strong, healthy, competent, energetic young citizens of the world who enter life full of joy and hope." *Die Erziehung der deutschen Jugend* (1890), 46, 59. Another German educator, A. Lammers, put it tersely: "Only the one whose head and arm are governed by a noble soul is truly strong." *Öffentliche Kinder-Fürsorge* (1885), 4.

†"The formation of character" in those schools, one study noted, was the essential aim of all pedagogy; they treated a "one-sided intellectual education" as a danger: "Moral is more important than intellectual perfection." Abel John Jones: *Charakterbildung in den englischen Schulen in Theorie und Praxis* (1906), 3, 5, 7. This view was not confined to the printed page. Speaking of Dickens's choice of associates, his intimate John Forster observed that "what was solid and beautiful in character, he rated higher than intellectual effort." *The Life of Charles Dickens* (1872–74; ed. J. W. T. Leys, 1928), 526. For an Italian instance, see Luigi Francesco Guerra, who stressed the "importanza dell' educazione de carattere" in *La filosofia della vita nel problema dell'educazione* (n.d.; 3rd ed., 1907), 21.

‡"The great purpose of our mortal existence," observed the Reverend Thomas M. Clark, an American, "is the formation of character." *Lectures on the Formation of Character* (1852), 12. In the 1860s, Clark's secular compatriot the publicist Edwin P. Whipple echoed his religious brother;

discipline, "Ethology," which aspired to being nothing less than "the Exact Science of Human Nature."[23] He would have found a more pleasing echo across the Channel than at home; no country attempted so elaborate a study of character as France, translating antique notions about the four humors into the modern-sounding discipline of characterology, minutely subdividing human beings into a number of predictable types. Mill at least was too skeptical to carry out the grand scheme he had first hatched as an ambitious young scholar. But even those repelled by the naive positivism of characterology did not quarrel with the notion that the understanding of character is the master key to knowledge and, with that, to goodness.

It seems only right that Samuel Smiles should have considered *Character* one of his principal publications; most of his books, whether biographies of exemplary English engineers or sermons on duty, thrift, and self-help, are really about character, its care and feeding. Literally scores of authors across Europe and the United States undertook, like him, to define character and prescribe for its proper unfolding. It cannot be repeated enough that they found the task of regulating vice even more pressing than that of fostering virtue. Behind the smiling facade of normality lurked the horrid beast of pathology, ever ready to spring. One author gave his homily against "social wine-drinking, card-playing, theatre-going, and dancing" the title *Better Not: A Discussion of Certain Social Customs.*[24]

Though individual nuances and national styles imposed various definitions of character—the French and the Germans were distinctly more chauvinistic in their attitudes than writers elsewhere—virtually all moralists in print defined character as the German poet Novalis had defined it early in the century, as "a completely fashioned will." Its components were as obvious as could be: character was an evolving amalgam of heritage and environment. But the sorting out of these two elements was anything but easy; some feared it to be almost beyond human powers.* Hence nothing was harder than making depend-

---

character, he said, is "the centre and heart" of being. Representative of an age in search of a science of society, Whipple thought that character, beyond offering scientific guidance to rational conduct, could itself be studied scientifically: "Whether it be small or great, evil or good," it "always represents a positive and persisting force, and can, therefore, like other forces, be *calculated,* and the issues of its actions predicted." *Character and Characteristic of Men* (1866), 3.

*John MacCunn, professor of philosophy at the University of Liverpool: "It is an impossible task to discriminate sharply between what is congenital and what is due to the influence of the environment." *The Making of Character: Some Educational Aspects of Ethics* (1900), 7. The German philosopher Bartholomäus von Carneri, speaking for a general consensus, did not find the task any easier: "That character is inborn, every thinking eye can observe among children. Cowardice like steadfastness, cunning like straightforwardness, truculence like good nature, honesty like insincer-

able predictions about, or paths toward, good character.

Students of character did think they could confidently assert that its two fundamental sources, endowment and experience, were by their very nature at odds. It was certainly essential to produce harmony between the native and the learned elements of character, lest private happiness and social tranquility be forfeited. This was not good news, since such harmony was extremely elusive; it required a most laborious conquest of inborn urges. And so we are back at the beginning—the one indispensable element in the formation of good character was self-restraint, however alien and repugnant to the child's original nature it might be. In *Character,* Smiles defined self-control as "only courage under another form," which "may almost be regarded as the primary essence of character." In short, "to be morally free—to be more than an animal—man must be able to resist instinctive impulse, and this can only be done by the exercise of self-control."[25] Paradoxical as it might sound, character was freedom won by submission to rule.*

The Victorian advice literature was a curious mixture of candor and denial. It frankly charted the obstacles to taming the pressures of primitive passion, and then minimized them. Yet dejection would not be silenced. A few authors openly confessed that education was a desperate war with no victory in sight. In a substantial study on character formation, John MacCunn admitted that "all development involves repression." Hence one had to inflict pain to extirpate pernicious dispositions like sensuality or the love of ease. His conclusion was depressing. It is not just that humans do what they ought not to do; "their malady lies deeper." Daily, hourly, "they are visited by feelings, desires, ideas, of which they would thankfully be rid."[26] No wonder that in this literature metaphors drawn from epidemics or warfare competed with more cheery metaphors from trade.

---

ity show themselves at a very early age." Yet he acknowledged that this rudimentary character is only a "sketch," open to modifications through the "school of life." *Der moderne Mensch. Versuch über Lebensführung* (1890; 5th ed., 1901), 122–23.

*Alexandre Martin's massive book on the education of character is typical. The child is a bundle of impulses; its impassioned demands show humans as aggressive and egotistical. "Moral beauty is only a promise"; education can make it a reality through self-restraint alone. Growing up is an apprenticeship for life, and character building a persistent, not always successful campaign to suppress wicked, and encourage benevolent, inclinations. Since "effort is inseparable from pain," it is as unpopular as it is necessary, but the will must be trained up into an inhibiting, repressive authority. Martin disclaimed any desire to be hard on children, but thought it essential not to give pleasure a large part in their lives. The tone of his confidence in the efficacy of effort belies its message. Martin laced his gloom with hope; it was his grandiloquent, platitudinous, hardworking optimism that made his treatise so representative a text. *L'Éducation du caractère* (1887), 49, 331.

The distrust of pleasure reached epidemic proportions. Again and again, books of advice observed that a life of self-indulgence is not a life of true pleasure at all; the self let loose is the enemy. The optimistic perorations some writers tacked onto these gloomy diagnoses were like a god from the machine. And when they concluded that man can remake himself—presumably after studying this literature diligently—they would quickly circumscribe the sweep of that prognosis by warning that the improvement must respect the bounds of human nature. And that, almost everyone acknowledged, allowed little room for maneuver.* Even Samuel Smiles, the most relentless optimist among these authors, betrayed a pronounced anxiety at the thought that savage passions might slip free from the leash of reason. Good models, he believed, may promote good character, but corrupt models are perhaps even more certain to leave their mark on the young. That is why character formation remains indispensable and self-control the royal road to good character. Without such rigor, wickedness will reign. "The most self-reliant, self-governing man is always under discipline; and the more perfect the discipline, the higher will be his moral condition."[27] With sufficient training, he thought, it would be fairly easy to resist sensual appetites and acquire the right habits. Somehow we do not believe in that ease, and wonder whether Smiles really believed in it himself.

The dire foreboding scattered through this literature evokes a perception of nineteenth-century culture as strewn with victims of their unchecked desires—of sensuality, selfishness, lethargy, greed, and ill-temper. This was not a mere symptom of hysteria; the casualties that moralists adduced to bolster their case, often with a certain relish, were the patients that physicians and pastors saw in their consulting rooms. The Victorian was the Age of Neuroses quite as much as the Age of Advice. The century, of course, had no monopoly on neuroses, however anxiously contemporaries lamented what they saw as the rise of nervous disorders. But the Victorians were more aware of them than any of their predecessors had been, and their awareness was typical of the self-consciousness that marked the age.

In the second half of the century, the preoccupation with nervous ailments grew into an obsession. In 1880, the American nerve specialist George M. Beard gave a name to what he, with many of his colleagues, feared as a danger-

---

*"Self-control, however difficult at first, becomes step by step easier and more delightful," said Sir John Lubbock. He saw "few truer triumphs, or more delightful sensations, than to obtain thorough command of oneself." Lubbock was whistling past the grimacing vision of human nature that he himself had conjured up. *The Pleasures of Life* (1887–89; ed. 1907), 20–21. Nicholas Pain Gilman concluded with equal uncertainty: "We can *remake ourselves* to an indefinite extent, inside the limits of human nature." *The Laws of Daily Conduct* (1891), 134.

ously increasing mental malaise: neurasthenia. "Modern nervousness is the cry of the system struggling with its environment."[28] The symptomatology of neurasthenia was as vague as it was comprehensive; it read like a catalogue of relatively minor irritations given major importance: blushing, insomnia, bad dreams, noises in the ears, and a score of other telltale signs that the machine was breaking down. The doctors diagnosing this growing threat to mental health offered conflicting opinions, but they tended to concentrate on what they called the hustle and bustle of modern life: the speed of travel and communications, the crowding in great cities, the exhausting, precise schedules that modern men (and, increasingly, modern women) were imposing on themselves, the nervous-making chatter of the mass press and popular politics. The sheer credulity and subjectivity of Beard and the others have come to seem almost funny. But as a cultural artifact, the panic over nervousness was in itself a symptom of the malaise the mind doctors hoped to cure.

In the 1890s Sigmund Freud, leaning on master diagnosticians like Jean Martin Charcot and making distinctive contributions of his own, brought a measure of order into the confused clinical picture. While the physicians, editorial writers, and educators who worried about the unexampled susceptibility to nervous problems had thrown them all into that leaky vessel "neurasthenia," Freud discriminated, and named, distinct types of nervous suffering—obsessional neurosis, anxiety hysteria, paranoia. His hunt for the etiologies of the neuroses he named shed much needed light on normal character formation and hence on adaptive styles of thinking and feeling. It was important for Freud to insist that the border between the normal and the neurotic is porous at best and easily crossed. "Perhaps," he once said, "we are all a little neurotic," and he was only half joking. In 1907, he pursued this line of thinking further. The reluctance of parents to give their children sensible information about sexuality and their eagerness to impose sexual abstinence on young adults—both principal props in the ruling ideology of the bourgeois family—were, he thought, pedagogic and moral catastrophes. They were calculated to generate mental traumas in childhood and to assure these traumas damaging if submerged survival in later life. He did not advertise prompt and honest early sexual enlightenment as a panacea, but he thought that it might reduce vulnerability to neurotic disturbances.[29]

Psychoanalysts, beginning with Freud himself, were puzzled about why a patient would "choose" one neurosis over another. Freud of course never wavered in his conviction that the analyst must seek the causes of a neurosis first and foremost in the patient's early inner conflicts; eventually, he developed a tentative timetable for the origins of mental distress and visualized the adult's neurotic problems as regressions to fixation points laid down in childhood years. Yet, while Freud was unwilling to grant the outside world a command-ing share in the making of a neurosis, he found it profitable to speculate about forces other than the clash of unconscious wishes with unconscious defenses as instigators of the sufferer's forced choice. His prescription of candor with chil-dren was cultural criticism as much as medical advice; while the patients lying on Freud's couch were victims principally of themselves and their families, their symptoms had poignant resonances with the time—and the class—to which they belonged and which made their erotic and aggressive life so hard for them. Gender and religious affiliation were only two such external contributors to neurosis; with fellow members of his Wednesday Psychological Society, he wondered more than once whether women and Jews were not peculiarly ex-posed to neuroses. Part of the neurotic's difficulties, he commented, stems after all from his clashes with others.[30]

These tentative explorations underlay Freud's sense of himself as a sexual reformer; it was only logical that in 1908, while still musing over the "choice" of neurosis, he should publish his important paper " 'Civilized' Sexual Morality and Modern Nervous Illness," complete with sardonic quotation marks in its title. In offering a psychoanalytic diagnosis of how the erotic norms of his fellow bourgeois contributed to nervousness, he found himself in the usual small minority. The physicians and publicists who lamented the tender, often shattered, psyches which they thought increasingly haunted their society per-sisted in the belief that their urban, industrial culture had exacted its exorbitant cost, producing a generation of exceedingly nervous men and women.

Their villains were those whom Beard had already accused, from the restless tumult of city life to the ever-accelerating velocity of communication and transport. "These days of high-pressure steam," Mrs. Loudon, editor of *The Ladies' Companion,* had written at mid-century, "when time and space seem really annihilated," whirl everyone "along at railway speed." A decade earlier, Ernst von Feuchtersleben had introduced his *Zur Diätetik der Seele,* probably the most widely read nineteenth-century German tractate in popular philosophy, with the flat assertion, "Our time is rapid, stormy, and irresponsible." Mark Twain stood on well-tilled ground when he commented on "the drive and push and rush and struggle of the raging, tearing, booming nineteenth cen-tury."[31]

But Freud, while he agreed with other physicians on the symptoms of the disease called modernity, rejected their diagnoses. Not the strains of urban life were at fault, but the undue restrictions on sexual information and activity. And the nineteenth-century bourgeoisie, more than other classes, was cultivating precisely these pernicious evasions. While little working-class girls were likely to masturbate without a sense of guilt and to mature into adult sexual beings with a minimum of psychic damage, their middle-class playmates who engaged in the same erotic self-exploration were exposed to all sorts of neurotic suffering from adolescence onward.

These conjectures invite the startling supposition that the susceptibility of the nineteenth-century bourgeoisie to neuroses was at least in part generated by their cultural style. It is surely too much to claim that a culture imposes one neurosis rather than others. Any attempt to link a single type of mental malaise exclusively to one class and one age must fail in face of the enormous repertory open to individual development and the mass of interlaced psychological tributaries entering the stream of each life history; the hysterics whom Jean Martin Charcot presented in his famous demonstrations at the Salpêtrière in Paris included a sizable representation of working-class males. But allowing for a generous sampling of exceptions, it seems plausible to see the prevailing mores of a class propelling vulnerable individuals along specifiable developmental paths. The nineteenth-century bourgeoisie did have its own recognizable preferred neurotic style, and that style was obsessional-compulsive neurosis.

One did not have to be an obsessive neurotic to be a nineteenth-century bourgeois, but it helped. It is interesting how proud Freud was of having been the first to isolate and name this ailment.[32] The Victorian century was, we have seen, obsessed with control and an abiding fear of its loss. Good manners, respect for privacy, self-restraint—all the bourgeois virtues their critics denigrated as bourgeois defects—were stratagems designed to discipline the chaos of experience and master the pressures of the passions. From the inevitably self-serving perspective of middle-class propagandists, other classes were indifferent, even hostile, to this programmatic sobriety; aristocracies acted with superb and selfish willfulness, the lower orders with an animal-like inability to postpone the immediate gratification of lust and rage.

Bourgeois saw nervousness as an intimate enemy, fostered and doing its damage at home. Hysteria and obsessional neurosis, the classic neurotic disorders on which psychoanalytic therapy concentrated, were subverters of the precarious order that the century had sought to buttress with its commitment to thrift, hard work, duty, and propriety. Hysteria defied self-control; obsessional neurosis mimicked it. The hysteric rebelled against cherished familial and social rules with histrionic displays, inappropriate emotional attachments, flamboyant physical symptoms lacking all physical basis—defensive mechanisms mobilized to escape harsh realities. And the obsessive neurotic parodied accepted rules with an almost insane preoccupation with trivia, irritating bouts of indecision, ironclad rituals and ceremonies—odd ways of draining aggressive impulses of their affective power.

Both these neuroses, then, were savage comments on nineteenth-century bourgeois ideals. And obsessive-compulsive neurotics caricatured these ideals most trenchantly. Their ailment was a mockery, in point after point, of the rational character the Victorian bourgeoisie prized and labored so earnestly to rescue from the grip of unruly human impulses. The Rat Man, Freud's best-known patient in this genre and one of its most-discussed exemplars, suffered from disavowed, deeply repressed feelings of hostility toward the two persons he loved most—his father and a woman he thought of marrying—and these feelings reemerged in distasteful, even horrifying, fantasies and irrational ritual gestures. His interminable brooding, his doubts and compulsive thoughts, mimicked the middle-class determination to subject everything to critical thought. His ruminations were the disheveled double of careful reflection. By the same token, his staring attention to detail, especially to inessentials, his repetitive, irksome making of lists and schedules, were a grimacing counterfeit of the bourgeoisie's trained disposition to take pains and overlook nothing. The ritual observances of obsessive-compulsive neurotics, without which they cannot begin a task, go to sleep, or fall in love, are farcical reenactments of the much-praised middle-class respect for the rules governing all domains of life.

Similarly, the Rat Man's fatigued enslavement to duty and his inability to relax burlesqued the idealized bourgeois infatuation with energy and industry. Indeed, on the rare occasions that such neurotics carry out their solemnly professed intentions, they do not experience the exhilaration that is bound to flood more fortunate humans when their appetite for achievement has been gratified. In any case, accomplishment, however unrewarding, is rare for the obsessive, who is hypnotized by technique at the expense of effective work. Both this neurosis and the less-disturbed neatness which it travesties have the same aim: to outwit the wickedness that beckons on every hand, control erotic desire, and checkmate aggression. Hence obsessiveness was the most character-istic mental maladaptation of Victorian life.

Freud's discovery of obsessional neurosis, which gave him so much pleasure, received considerable attention among psychiatrists. In 1903, Pierre Janet, his once-famous French rival, published an exhaustive two-volume monograph on obsessions, in which he meticulously examined a rich menu of symptoms. In passing, Janet listed among the causes of this neurosis the "absurd education of young Frenchmen whom one permits to dream before their dictionaries during interminable hours of study and whom one prohibits all movement and all practical exercise," instead of teaching them how to face life's problems with decisiveness.[33] Freud, with his critique of bourgeois sexual mores, was far more searching, far more sweeping, in his cultural analysis.

This discovery fit Freud's time and class even better than he recognized. Witness Max Weber's memorable portrait of that cultural debacle the obsessive capitalist. He is the driven businessman who cannot dream of taking a holiday, let alone retire. Surrounded, almost suffocated, by tokens of his opulence, he is an emotional disaster, caught in the meshes of mechanical reason, a nail-biting devotion to numbers, and worried punctuality. In that representative man, the profit motive has emancipated itself in the manner of a symptom from its servitude to higher ends. Planning for profit, even scheming for sexual conquest, no longer serves to buy pleasure. For all his displays of affability, no one is more dispirited at heart than the capitalist in the grip of his compulsion, sentenced to his routine like the proverbial squirrel in its treadmill. He no longer knows why he persists in his sisyphean labors, except that he can do no less, and nothing else. He stands as the supreme exemplar of the inauthentic rationalist, a suffering individual representing a social type. Elaborating this appalling portrait of the bourgeois imprisoned in the iron cage of modern life, Weber reached back into the eighteenth century for instances, notably Benjamin Franklin, whose utilitarian maxims had entered the mainstream of nineteenth-century thinking about time, money, and getting ahead.[34]

Weber's famous critique canonized decades of discontent with a culture that could foster, and celebrate, such a type. Carlyle, who denounced the rule of Mammon and the phallus as twin evils of his day, was only the first to exclaim against the compulsive man in the saddle. Marx and Engels made him their butt in the *Communist Manifesto*. Charlotte Brontë abused the "mercantile classes" for thinking "too exclusively of making money," and being dead to "chivalrous feeling, disinterestedness, pride in honour." John Stuart Mill testily denigrated them as devoted to the "sabbathless pursuit of wealth."[35] These drudges, antibourgeois polemicists argued, made their mundane routine—meals, walks, holidays, their very love life—conform to the most relentless timetables, reduced marriages to cynical business deals and friends to so much merchandise. Virtual robots, they subjected the most solemn human experiences to a frigid calculus. And while it was fashionable for educated Europeans to delude themselves that these human automatons were found only in America, moralists in Britain and Germany, France and Italy, reminded their readers that the Old World provided ample prototypes for them as well. If capitalism was rationality in action, then so much the worse for capitalism—and for rationality.

These warnings strongly suggest that in the Victorian century, the ideal of constructive, and the reality of destructive, aggression were often at a great distance from one another. The ideal was plain and contested mainly at the margins. Good burghers were enjoined to restrain their aggressive urges in dealing with the dependent and the weak, to moderate their desires for physical gratification and self-indulgent displays of temper, and to sublimate their volcanic instinctual inclinations by conquering nature, enjoying the products of higher culture, and improving the human lot. Aggression was to be rational-ized, subjected to testing and sensible self-command, and pointed toward what contemporaries defined as constructive goals. But much of the time bourgeois achieved the sublimation of aggression on a level far lower than this. As these chapters have documented, it was easy to cloak aggressiveness in moralistic rationalizations. Many proper Victorians, no better than others before or after them, found ways to make their reason serve, rather than master, the insatiable demands of their passions—though not without suffering the expense of guilt feelings and psychological conflicts.

The bourgeois who thought it necessary to defend these failures appealed to the imperfections of human nature. But this appeal, though universal in tone, was narrowed by class feelings. While bourgeois gladly admitted that they shared most of their essential qualities with other classes, they claimed certain elements as particularly their own. There was a distinct bourgeois experience, and it was not limited to obsessional neuroses.* To be sure, the defense mech-anisms, those psychological maneuvers that help humans to confront the world, inhabit aristocrats and peasants and working people no less than middle-class men and women. But among the Victorian middling orders, these mechanisms were burdened with a particularly onerous role. Bourgeois constituted a class, after all, that put aggressive displays, whether of gun, muscle, or word, at a severe discount. Hence they pressed the defensive stratagem of reaction forma-tion, for one, into stressful service to convert sadistic passions into crusades against cruelty to animals or children, and they employed the key defense of repression to tuck unacceptable wishes, whether sexual or aggressive, out of sight. As we know only too well, they did not always succeed, but their culture bears the marks of strenuous and persistent efforts.

The discipline that tracked these psychological stratagems and the full mea-sure of human savagery to their lair in the unconscious, and fitted them, after some false starts, into a powerful theory of the mind, was of course psychoanal-ysis. It is of particular relevance to a study of the nineteenth-century middle classes not just as a method of investigation but as a sign of its times. With its founder and virtually all of its later practitioners drawn from the middle classes, it was supremely bourgeois. So, despite a smattering of aristocrats and working-

---

*In *The Tender Passion,* I quote at some length a letter that Freud sent to his fiancée Martha Bernays that is worth recalling here. He tells her that the "rabble" live without constraint while the middle classes "do without" to keep their integrity intact. We bourgeois, he adds, "economize with our health, our capacity for enjoyment, our excitement," and this proves that " 'the common people' judge, believe, hope, and work quite differently from us. There is a psychology of the common man that is rather different from ours." August 29, 1883, Sigmund Freud, *Briefe 1873–1939,* ed. Ernst L. Freud (1960), 49.

class analysands, were its patients. And so was its much-misunderstood ideal of the mature adult.

Freud, we have just seen, was highly critical of what he condemned as excessive repression in the class of which he was at once an ornament and a subverter. But he never argued, or implied, that anyone should take the inner freedom he valued as a license to uninhibited sexual and aggressive conduct. Quite the contrary: well-analyzed persons were, to his mind, those who had explored the range of proper conduct, had judiciously widened its limits, and worked within the moral sphere they had carved out for themselves with their analyst's discreet assistance. While Freud found fault with the unreasonably strict superego he saw as characteristic for the nineteenth-century bourgeoisie, he did not advocate relaxing the famous bourgeois conscience into self-indulgence. Where id was, he once put it memorably, there ego shall be. Freud was, in fact, remarkably unanalytic about morality; as a good bourgeois he was confident that a decent adult would find the question of right and wrong easy to answer.

His view that the human animal is forever beset by clashing desires and prohibitions, stumbling in its dealings with aggression and sexuality, is original and compelling. But it is not altogether satisfactory as cultural criticism. Freud's insight into the bourgeois experience of his time was rather more sardonic than the facts warranted. While he focused on the pathology of self-control, on repressed psychological conflicts making for hysterical or obsessive suffering, he read the patients on his couch as typical exemplars rather than as marginal figures in bourgeois culture. He felt entitled to do this because he regarded neurotics as not very different from "normal" people. The consequence seemed inescapable: aggressiveness, whether let loose or inhibited and unacknowledged, made only victims. But this view insufficiently appreciated the degree to which Victorian bourgeois had tamed aggression, to say nothing of the positive role that aggressive impulses played in their great campaign for mastery. Sublimated aggression could collaborate with Eros to build cities, speed travel, enhance comfort, improve communications, lengthen life.

EPILOGUE

August 4, 1914

In the morning hours of August 4, 1914, German troops invaded neutral Belgium and made an all-European war a certainty. During the previous week, the century-old concert of Europe had begun to unravel: Austria had declared war on Serbia on July 28, Germany on Russia on August 1 and on France two days later. But the Germans' strategic move, designed to outflank the French armies, brought Britain into the conflict. August 4 doomed the great compromises that had largely held national antagonisms in check through the long nineteenth century.

After June 28, when the Habsburg archduke Franz Ferdinand and his consort were assassinated at Sarajevo by young Bosnian Serb nationalists, angry emotions hovered near the boiling point, and when earnest attempts at mediation failed, they bubbled over into catastrophe. A contagious hatred of the enemy spread as an irresistible alibi for aggression. Military leaders were not alone in lusting for confrontation. "This country," the British ambassador reported from Vienna late in July, "has gone wild with joy at the prospect of war with Serbia, and its postponement or prevention would undoubtedly be a great disappointment." In Berlin, on August 1, after the government proclaimed the mobilization of its armed forces, untold thousands gathered to cheer Wilhelm II, greeting him with jubilation and patriotic songs. They had been demonstrating their will to war for a week. On the other side, in Russia, the Austrian threats against Serbia triggered popular hostility vehement enough to force a truculent policy. Were the government to tolerate the Habsburg empire's moves in the Balkans, Russia's foreign minister, Sergei Sazonov, declared, "there would be a revolution in this country."[1] Virtually all the decision makers in these fateful weeks boasted impeccable aristocratic credentials, but they could count on, or felt compelled to reckon with, popular pressures for war, from respectable bourgeois no less than from mobs in the streets.

Through July, as the bourgeois era teetered on the verge of death, the German emperor, Austrian diplomats, and bellicose Russian patriots took a tough line that made a peaceful resolution to the crisis increasingly remote. Wilhelm II, anxious not to appear indecisive, thought that a conciliatory tone would "awaken an impression of weakness." Austria-Hungary's prime minister, Count Istvàn Tisza, told Emperor Franz Josef that any hesitation would "heavily injure the way friends and foes judge of our energy and capacity for action."* Russian politicians itching for war belabored more pacific compatriots as un-Slavic. Much like aging *roués* protesting their virility, men with their finger on the trigger rejected any settlement lest the world despise them as an inferior breed, as unmanly. As so often, the panic fear of showing weakness generated destructive displays of strength.

The mood prevailing at the outbreak of hostilities and in the following months has often been described, usually with a certain amazement, even shock. Understandably enough; the war discovered unsuspected reservoirs of hatred. Masses of volunteers, including thousands of over-age bourgeois filled with high sentiments, rushed to the colors. Law-abiding citizens harassed stranded foreigners and persecuted the courageous—or foolhardy—smattering of pacifists. Families saddled with names that might remind militants of the Wicked Others rebaptized themselves to reassure their countrymen of their politically correct attitudes. Men educated to know better regressed to foaming chauvinism with a kind of savage joy: intellectuals lent their names to manifestos declaring the other side to be barbarians, while dignified professors returned honorary degrees granted them by universities in enemy countries and placed their scholarship at the service of tendentious war propaganda.[2]

The intensity of this fever naturally varied somewhat from individual to individual and from country to country, but it infected all manner of men: democrats and monarchists, radicals and reactionaries, atheists and Christians. Poets, philosophers, and preachers were nearly unanimous in welcoming the war as a supreme opportunity for moral regeneration. The Germans were perhaps most emphatic in their zeal to abuse the enemy—primitive Russia, decadent France, perfidious Albion. Especially perfidious Albion: indulging in what

---

*Fritz Fischer, *Griff nach der Weltmacht. Die Kriegspolitik des kaiserlichen Deutschlands 1914/18* (1961; 3rd ed., 1964), 79. See also ibid., 65. The cause of manliness was adduced as a justification for making war even in behalf of others; on August 6, 1914, Kaiser Wilhelm II, in a proclamation to the German people, gave as one of the reasons for Germany's belligerence that the enemy did not want his country to "stand, in resolute fidelity, by our ally," Austria-Hungary, "which is battling for its reputation as a great power, and with whose humiliation our power and honor, too, would be lost." "Aufruf an das deutsche Volk," *Reden des Kaisers,* ed. Ernst Johann (1966; 2nd ed., 1977), 106.

Freud has called the narcissism of small differences, they reserved their most unmeasured denunciations for Britain, the nation they had most admired and had most earnestly expected to stay neutral. The curt prayer *Gott strafe England*—"God punish England"—was elevated into a national formula, while Ernst Lissauer's "Hymn of Hate," which minimized the villainy of France and Russia to concentrate its venom against Britain, found impressive public resonance. In return, the British and the French invented and spread atrocity stories about invading Huns raping Belgian women and slaughtering Belgian babies. The war hysteria gripped normally sober adults like a religious revival; all the belligerents piously appealed to the Divinity for aid and persuaded themselves that He was on their side.[3]

Not even psychoanalysts, schooled in the ways of irrationality and presumably immune to its worst ravages, could escape this epidemic—at least during the early phase of hostilities. From Berlin, Karl Abraham and Max Eitingon sent Freud "dazzling news" and crowed about the "incomparably splendid beginning" of the march to victory as German armies battled their way toward Paris. Freud himself could not wholly resist, and surprised himself with patriotic rhetoric as he referred to "the success of 'our' war loan" and the "chances of 'our' battle of millions." By late 1915, he had mustered enough distance to be appalled at the spectacle debasing all reason and decency. "Science itself," he noted, "has lost its dispassionate impartiality."[4] Had he fully absorbed what he had already learned about human aggression, he would have been no less saddened but less astonished.

In short, the war released aggressive impulses of which people had been unconscious in calmer times, and would probably have been ashamed. To be sure, war enthusiasts did not consider themselves brutes, heartened as they were by skillful propagandists who dressed up aggressive cravings as exalted sentiments. It was notable—a few intrepid satirists made the point at the time—that the publicists most energetically engaged in the sport of killing the enemy with words committed their murders many miles behind the front, safe in some government office. To hear noncombatant poets and playwrights tell it, the bourgeois century now being buried in the trenches had been a singularly uninspiring affair: unmanly, materialistic, conformist, a stranger to the ideals for which a man might willingly fight and die. Perhaps worst, the century had been boring. "War!" exclaimed Thomas Mann, one of those heroes of the pen, in November 1914, "it was purification, liberation we felt, and an enormous hope"; its coming had provided a tremendous sense of relief: "How could the artist, the soldier in the artist, not praise God for the collapse of a peaceful world with which he was fed up, so exceedingly fed up!"[5] Mann's outburst, far from eccentric, was echoed with equal conviction by bellicose officers, routine-ridden bureaucrats, cloistered pedants, and unpolitical artists.

Most merchants of hate were ignorant of what modern war entailed; arm-chair generals by the thousands cultivated fantasies about soldiers clashing in chivalrous tournaments, brief encounters. They were certain that the war would be over by Christmas; all that remained to be settled was whether it would end with Allied troops in Berlin or German troops in Paris. Propagandists pointing to the enemies' frightening war aims, commercial or industrial adventurers promising lavish returns from victory, did their part to numb the voices of sanity, voices in any case quickly suppressed and only slow to re-awaken as the slaughter went on, and on.

The war had not come wholly without warning. For decades, imaginative novelists and underemployed military men had forecast sanguinary conflicts between nations and races. Some of these dreamers wrote to castigate human self-destructiveness, others to belabor a bourgeois order badly in need of a fighting tonic. Together, they sketched vast battles and invented fanciful weapons for readers greedy for such horrors on paper: submarines, flying machines, chemical warfare. This literature reflected, and fostered, ingrained bellicose attitudes, whether drawn from a Social Darwinist defense of conflict in human affairs or an avant-garde irritation with effeminate commercial civilization. The pacifist ideology, though it had enlisted eloquent advocates, was feeble in comparison; spokesmen for pugnacity, schooled to see mortal violence as a great teacher, apparently had a solid majority behind them.

Oliver Wendell Holmes, Jr., spoke for that majority in 1895. "War, when you are at it, is horrible and dull.—It is only when time has passed that you see that its message was divine." He conceded that he was recommending a most unpalatable remedy to alleviate the bourgeois crisis of courage. "I hope it may be long before we are again to sit at that master's feet." Yet war remained the ultimate didactic device necessary to modern civilization, necessary because men had become "snug, over-safe," blissfully unaware that their "comfortable routine is no eternal necessity of things, but merely a little space of calm in the midst of the tempestuous untamed streaming of the world, and in order that we may be ready for danger." Heroism, Holmes believed, was in shameful retreat in an effete society overwhelmed by self-indulgence, and impatient with discipline or self-sacrifice. Hence the spectacle of polo players battling it out filled him with delight. "If once in a while in our rough riding a neck is broken, I regard it, not as a waste, but as a price well paid for the breeding of a race fit for headship and command." Even the Mensur had its virtues: "I rejoice at every dangerous sport which I see pursued. The students at Heidelberg, with their sword-slashed faces, inspire me with sincere respect."[6] Holmes was not a brutal man, and his were familiar accents in the age of Theodore Roosevelt. But no doubt such calls for combat weakened the forces arrayed against it.

Still more ominously, relations among the major powers had been shadowed by worrisome strains for some years. Blustering leaders, most noisily Wilhelm II of Germany, had hinted at great conflicts to come. By 1914, European states were equipped with formidable arsenals, with each country's military policies spurring on the military policies of its potential enemies. And there were points of tension that might trigger military conflict—between France and Germany, between Germany and Britain, among the nationalities in the Austro-Hungarian empire, between Russia and Austria. In fact, the Balkans had seen open military confrontations in 1912 and 1913. Europe before 1914 was a threatened and nervous world.

At the same time, as recently as 1913, European diplomats had managed to contain the Balkan conflicts, and there was no inherent reason that they might not do so again. Their pacific work was buttressed by the interweaving of trade among nations. As early as 1879, William Graham Sumner had declared that the civilized world was a "unit" where "the barriers of race, religion, language, and nationality are melting away under the operation of the same forces which have to such an extent annihilated the obstacles of distance and time."[7] The decades that followed appeared to bear out Sumner's sanguine assessment. The years from the early 1870s to the mid-1890s were a time of mixed economic signals, mislabeled a great depression, but thereafter Europe and the United States experienced a period of sustained, at times explosive, growth. The standard of living rose, investments boomed, new technology—the automobile and the airplane—transformed communications and transportation. All of this, and more, solidified the flourishing world economy, a vast and ever more tightly knit network of trade, banking, industrial production. In this atmosphere, most economic interests were in the party of peace. So were religious and political interests. The great world religions transcended national boundaries in inspiration and following, and so did the socialist movements, significantly gathered in an organization, and boasting a hymn, called the "International."

And yet, cosmopolitan sentiments collapsed in July and early August 1914, as in the battle of loyalties nationalism blotted out all the others. Love of one's country and hatred for its enemies proved the most potent rationalization for aggression the long nineteenth century produced. It secured the dubious distinction of being the alibi of alibis. A human life is a life of multiple roles. A man is—all at once—a worker, a Roman Catholic, a Frenchman, a good husband and father, a stamp collector, a supporter of the local soccer team. Most of the time, these diverse identifications coexist peacefully. But there may be moments of crisis when a choice becomes imperative, and in the summer of 1914 the choice was a militant nationalism. Its most spectacular casualty was the organized international workers' movement, which showed itself helpless before patriotic appeals and patriotic excitement. For years, socialist parties had vowed to disrupt any effort by their governments to send workers into a slaughter from which only the capitalists would profit. This war against war was hampered by reservations; the German Social Democrats, for one, would not promise to sit by if Russia, that hated tyranny, assaulted its western neighbors. The rigorous proposal that workers everywhere call a general strike if the powers should mobilize their armies was therefore watered down in favor of well-meaning declarations of opposition to war and promises to work for peace.

Then came Sarajevo. For weeks, socialist leaders frantically negotiated to avert war. But once war had been declared, they abruptly turned patriot, discarding their commitment to the workers of the world. True, only a few of them were passionate converts to aggression. The Social Democratic deputies who unanimously voted for war credits in the Reichstag on August 4 were in fear of their lives, and had, besides, persuaded themselves that Germany was fighting a defensive war against Russia.* French socialists, for their part, supported the war because the Germans had committed aggression against their country. But whatever the extenuating circumstances, nationalism triumphed, even among those for whom it had long been a word of reproach.

With the coming of the war, the shapers of opinion systematically nurtured this nationalistic fervor in their speeches, handouts, and military bulletins. When the Kaiser told his people that he no longer knew parties, only Germans now—"*Ich kenne keine Parteien mehr, Ich kenne nur noch Deutsche*"—he was creating a passionate national community. The French followed suit, resurrecting for this grave occasion an old saw declaring the country in mortal peril—*La patrie en danger*. An embodied, unified nation was calling upon all citizens to sacrifice domestic comforts, vacation trips, the usual profits, and even the lives of sons and brothers and husbands.

The very extravagance of these demands allowed all within the magic circle

---

*The Social Democratic functionary Gustav Noske later admitted that his party had voted for the credits to avoid "being beaten to death in front of the Brandenburg Gate." A. Joseph Berlau, *The German Social Democratic Party, 1914–21* (1950), 73. It should be added that some Europeans never sang hymns of hate. In 1915, the Englishman Graham Wallas wrote to his German friend the Revisionist Socialist Eduard Bernstein, "Sometimes I hope that when peace comes you and I may meet and shake hands, and tell each other that we have never had one thought of each other that was not kind, and then sit down to consider whether we can help in any way to heal the wounds of civilization." Peter Gay, *The Dilemma of Democratic Socialism: Eduard Bernstein's Challenge to Marx* (1952), 277.

of a nation to cluster together as one large family, to live within the comforting hug of undifferentiated mutual love. This bath of shared emotions linked one-time adversaries—labor and capital, Bavarians and Prussians, Jews and Christians—as though internal enmities no longer mattered, indeed no longer existed. And they welcomed that national embrace not just because it bridged familiar gulfs and repressed familiar hostilities, but also because in doing so it authorized aggression. August 1914 once again demonstrated the old truth that a community of lovers is at the same time a community of haters. Chauvinism is fed by fury as much as by affection, is in fact unthinkable without fury. And chauvinism, that massive collective indulgence in primitive ways of thinking and feeling, is the pathological version of nationalism.

The modern alibi of nationalism differs from old-fashioned patriotism and even from national consciousness in its sheer political energy, its pointed will to aggression. The ancient feeling of pride in one's birthplace was its remote ancestor, and it had forerunners also in early modern times. It speaks through Shakespeare's lofty lines in *Richard II* praising "this dear dear land," his England, "this other Eden, demi-paradise."[8] But into the age of the Enlightenment, the competing ideal of cosmopolitanism still had a strong appeal to the educated. For Voltaire and the other philosophes, the "fatherland" was the select community of the propertied, the sophisticated, and the irreligious, a large salon that laughed at national boundaries. Like Benjamin Franklin, they believed that where liberty was, there was their country.[9]

This attitude tenaciously survived into the nineteenth century. Schiller's "Ode to Joy," which Beethoven famously set to music in his Ninth Symphony, sent a "kiss to the whole world." Indeed, the best-known eighteenth-century heralds of nationalism, Rousseau and, even more, Johann Gottfried von Herder, had been too closely linked to the cosmopolitan Enlightenment to preach chauvinism. Every *Volk,* Herder argued, is an organic, distinctive, divinely appointed repository of characteristics that differentiate it from all the others. It blossoms in poetry, folklore, customs, above all in language. Conflict among nations was, for him, the most dismal of prospects. This quasi-religious vision of collective individualism, which left its mark on Herder's nineteenth-century admirers, was compatible with the recognition of contributions each nation makes to the grand symphony that is humanity. Aggressive nationalism needed less philosophical, more immediate impulsions than Herder's prose—and found them in the upheavals of the French Revolution and Napoleon's reshaping of Europe.

Nineteenth-century nationalism was a complex response to this epic sequence of events. French armies carried the ideal of citizenship and the impulses for self-determination across central Europe. But while a few "German Jacobins" supported the invaders, Napoleon's military conquests largely generated nationalistic passions of a radically opposite sort: Germans must rise up to expel the French oppressor. It was symptomatic of German nationalism that it arose as a militant retort to severe narcissistic injuries; turning passivity into furious activity, the Germanic ideology developed a savage animus. In important ways, hatred of the foreigner who had humiliated them was not the consequence of the Germans' love of country, but its cause.

Despite the desperate efforts of the post-Napoleonic settlements to root out this populist effervescence in the German states, the passion for national unity continued to flicker among organized students and outspoken professors. It was an essential plank in the platform of German liberals, whose demands survived broken pledges, police surveillance, draconian measures against provocative speakers advocating national unification. They survived even the failed bourgeois revolutions of 1848 and the pathetic Frankfurt parliament. It was not until the mid-1860s that Bismarck ruthlessly disrupted the alliance between nationalism and liberalism, and produced German unity by disrupting it.*

Before the fantasies of German patriots were realized with the establishment of the Empire, nationalistic sentiments had proved their power to redraw the map of Europe. In 1830 they had fostered the successful insurrection of the Belgians against Dutch domination, and in 1831 they had dominated the unsuccessful insurrection of the Poles against their Russian masters. Later, in 1867, they dictated that great compromise the *Ausgleich,* giving Magyars a significant measure of autonomy in the Austro-Hungarian empire, and in 1870 they reaped the benefits of persistent agitation with the founding of a united kingdom in Italy.

Nationalistic sentiments, then, had been a political force for more than a century before August 1914. In 1882, an anonymous author known only as "Un diplomate" judged, rightly, that "the principle of nationalities has taken a great ascendancy in politics, and from various sides people are tending to assure it an even greater influence." The word " 'fatherland,' by itself, exercises a magical power." Again, writing in the early 1890s, the German orientalist and novelist Georg Ebers declared, "Love for our native land was indelibly imprinted on my soul, and lives there joyously." It would make him happy to give

*Given the importance of language in the making of nationalistic sentiments, it is notorious that the question of just how many Germans the united Germany of the future was to embrace remained for decades a subject of the most impassioned disputes. Bismarck's *kleindeutsche* solution, joining the northern German states to Prussia but leaving Austria independent, was fervently applauded by many, but bitterly opposed by those who thought that Germany must include *all* German speakers within its frontiers.

up all he held dear "for the freedom and greatness of Germany."[10] These writers spoke for millions.

The usual caution against facile generalizations is, of course, in order here; obviously each country, each group, indeed each decade, told this story of passionate affection and aversion in its own way. Nationalistic aspirations were unequivocal in their goals: national identity and national prestige. But the nationalists battled diverse adversaries: dynastic monarchs and feudal institutions, arbitrary censors and ultramontane clerics, neighboring powers, linguistic rivals and obstinate ethnic minorities within their own borders. They could struggle against persecution or initiate it. And across the century, though nationalism always remained a mixture of political postures, it largely shifted from its position as a liberal, even radical, ideology to the reactionary side. Patriots in the new states—notably Germany and Italy—shouted for a place in the sun, as though the recent unification of their countries had liberated untested chauvinist energies; patriots in the older states—above all, Britain and France—joined the chauvinist chorus as they confronted new competitors. The stridency of the controversialists late in the century astounded their more moderate contemporaries.[11]

This much is clear: any comprehensive definition of Victorian nationalism must respect its conflict-ridden emotional nature, recognizing it as a potent amalgam of libido and aggression. And that definition must take into account the massive popular response that nationalism generated. It was cultivated—in many places, first imagined—by professors, preachers, poets, and artists, those self-appointed storytellers to their culture. These prophets were nearly all bourgeois; divided as the politically alert middle classes might be, they supplied the vanguard for this ideology.[12] Finnish philologists discovered the uniqueness of their language; Danish theologians preached the religion of Danishness; Russian historians discovered, or invented, unmatched virtues in their past; German folklorists read admirable national qualities into fairy tales; Italian publicists reminded their readers of glorious Renaissance days crying out for a resurgence. All these scholars and fantasts—some were both at once—fed national pride and, often enough, national arrogance. But their ideology matured into a political force only after they had disseminated their romance of national history or national folklore to a wider public. Unruly mobs in search of windows to smash, clubmen conspiring to organize backing for militaristic policies, orderly citizens voting for a patriotic slate, were the foot soldiers of nationalism. And that necessary conjunction between massive propaganda and massive support arose only with, and after, the French Revolution.

Nationalistic movements, then, evolved in highly individual ways. This cannot be the place to rehearse their careers, from Serbia to Ireland, Norway to

Italy; the political history of the nineteenth century is wrapped up in their fortunes. What unites them is that in each an aggrieved dwelling on rights long denied, or a no less aggrieved alarm at threatening neighbors, supplied the alibi for aggressive conduct.* If the decades from the 1820s to the 1840s were, as many liked to say, the springtime of nations, it was a spring generally overcast and nearly always stormy. Exiled nationalists, from the Polish poet Adam Mickiewicz in Lausanne and Paris to the Italian romantic revolutionary Giuseppe Mazzini in Marseilles and London, battled in lectures, editorials, and manifestos against the foreign oppressors of the fatherland. They fought, too, as political refugees will, with fellow exiles whose diagnoses of past political failures and prescriptions for a national future differed from their own.

At times, nationalistic sentiment took a milder form, amounting to little more than a sticking out of elbows to enhance one's self-respect, without gravely wounding the self-respect of others. Norwegian nationalism may serve as an instance of this largely civilized aggression. In 1814, after chafing under Danish overlordship for centuries, the Norwegians found that the Danish government had unceremoniously handed them over to Sweden—without taking the trouble to ask them. Their new situation gave them a measure of autonomy and a constitution of their own, but they wanted more. Nationalistic resentments had not been unknown to them in the eighteenth century, but it was the French Revolution and, even more, their country's new identity that provided Norwegian patriots with the impetus they craved. Danish and German romanticism supplied formulas they could apply to their own situation, and over the next decades, enthusiasts went into isolated mountain villages to find their proof texts. They collected folk tales, ballads, and melodies, all satisfactorily establishing Norwegian cultural uniqueness. A competent student of local dialects, Ivar Aasen, published a grammar of the Norwegian folk language in 1848, and a comprehensive dictionary two years later. Together, these two forbidding reference works served as building blocks for a characteristic national language, distinct from the Danish that educated Norwegians had used in the past.

Patriotic historians of Norway expanded this enterprise in self-definition. In the course of more than a decade, from 1852 to 1863, Peter A. Munch pub-

---

*In the 1830s, the Poles developed an interesting passive—one might say masochistic—variant. The charismatic Lithuanian mystic Andrzej Towianski preached against revolutionary action; the suffering the Polish people were enduring was divinely ordained, and they would enjoy a new dispensation only if they persisted in self-sacrifice and humility. This strange messianism enjoyed a considerable vogue among Polish political exiles; some, like the poet Juliusz Slowacki, pushed the theme of sacrifice so far as to liken Poland to Christ, and to see Poland's fate, like Christ's, as one of crucifixion and resurrection. But this yearning to surrender rather than fight is a rare exception in the nationalistic camp.

lished a thoroughly documented if highly tendentious eight-volume *History of the Norwegian People,* which provided his readers with a usable past. All this learned labor was not immune to fanciful speculations based on Norse mythology and place names; scholars claimed that the Norwegian people had migrated from the "north," while the Swedes and Danes had come from the "south." And this somehow established the superiority of Norwegians. An assiduously cultivated attachment to their countryside, its snow-topped mountains and tranquil fjords, further promoted their search for identity and their call for liberation. The "Norwegian party" was filled with rage against those who would impose "foreign" culture on them. "Norwegian actors, Norwegian dramas, Norwegian music. A Norwegian theater in Norway's capital," ran one of their incendiary slogans around mid-century. "To hell with the corrupters of language, the corrupters of taste, the vagabonds!"[13]

But while Norwegian nationalists pointedly celebrated their own folk and affected distaste for Danish culture, others, like the cultivated poet, painter, and philosopher Johan Welhaven, preferred a quasi-cosmopolitan Scandinavianism. Leader of the Party of the Intelligentsia, he pointed disdainfully at the poverty of indigenous culture and the absurd fantasies of superpatriots. To him, national pride meant a confident sense that Norwegians no longer needed to feel inferior to Danes or Swedes.[14] These disputes were mainly combats of words among men of words; there were a few fisticuffs and some infuriated threats, but nothing more.

In the lands governed by the Austrian crown, rancor was not so well controlled. The stakes were higher, the temptations for aggressive action greater; in an age of noisy national movements, the multinational Habsburg empire was an anachronism. Some eleven nations were uneasily held together by residual loyalties to the dynasty, displays of armed force, and sheer habit. While German-speaking Austrians were a distinct minority in that sprawling central and eastern European domain, they were the undisputed ruling elite; graciously, they extended select privileges to such Austrian possessions as the Kingdom of Hungary or to restless Czechs. Troublesome as this dated dynastic style of domination came to seem after the age of Napoleon, the Habsburgs boasted such impressive military muscle and bureaucratic personnel that a few concessions to the most clamorous demands sufficed to keep the empire intact.

Oddly enough, the empire was aided in its effort to survive the nationalistic onrush of its peoples by ugly divisions among the nationalists. Magyars, protesting against the power of German-speaking Austrians in their state, at the same time denied Hungary's sizable minorities the rights they claimed for themselves. One man's nationalism, it seemed, was another man's demagogy. In a decree of 1830, and in subsequent decrees, the Hungarian diet made Hungarian (rather than Latin or German) the official language of lawyers, bureaucrats, and teachers, thus disqualifying the languages spoken by the kingdom's Croats, Serbs, and Romanians.[15] Magyar nationalists struggling to secure their hold thoroughly understood how to deploy language, the instrument and very emblem of national identity, as a weapon.

In other sectors of the Habsburg empire, other nationalities, living uncomfortably with, or next to, each other, clashed no less angrily over conflicting designs for the future. Czechs quarreled with Slovaks, while in the south Serbs and Croats were, at times literally, at one another's throats. In the parliament in Vienna, nationalistic deputies made unseemly, almost surrealistic scenes; they interrupted, insulted, screamed at one another, and cavalierly disregarded the presiding officer's bell as they battled over delicate questions of language and domination.

After the 1870s, the alibi of nationalism entered a new phase. The ferocious battles among competing patriots in the Austro-Hungarian empire were not exceptional. Irish nationalists continued to cultivate a catalogue of grievances more explosive than they could safely handle. French nationalists grew increasingly vocal about wiping out the shame of Sedan by retaking their lost provinces from the Germans. In their turn, German nationalists brooded on the power of the British navy and the choking sensation of being encircled by hostile powers. Yet many of the European nationalists' goals had been met, and it was precisely at this point that chauvinism, even in the "satisfied" nations, flourished as never before.

The irony is only apparent; the appetite for aggressiveness seemed more or less inexhaustible. As J. A. Hobson noted in 1901, in the midst of the Boer War, there was really nothing new in that "inverted patriotism whereby the love of one's own nation is transformed into the hatred of another nation, and the fierce craving to destroy the individual members of that other nation." But there was one new ingredient: democratic politics. Since the easily roused emotions of the masses had become a public force, nationalism had taken on a different face. Hobson thought primitive "jingoism," the virulent form that nationalistic hatreds had assumed in the late nineteenth century, both an expression of democratic culture and a problem for it. The credulity of ordinary newspaper readers, to whom the popular press prostituted itself, was only a tempting step away from open destructiveness. "The modern newspaper," Hobson observed with the disdain many radicals reserve for the democratic mob, "is a Roman arena, a Spanish bull-ring, and an English prize-fight rolled into one. The popularization of the power to read has made the press the chief instrument of brutality." It is "the chief aim of civilization and of government to repress" those "lusts of blood and physical cruelty" that lurk in everyone.

But as "the business man, the weaver, the clerk, the clergyman, the shop assistant, can no longer satisfy" their "savage cravings, either in personal activity or in direct spectacular display," the press gratifies aggressiveness by providing vicarious excitement.[16]

This is a superior instance of psychological muckraking. The very existence of Hobson's little book confirms what must be apparent by now: the most vehement advocates of alibis for aggression did not have things all their own way; their rationalizations were continually being engaged in demanding debate. As these pages have shown, the liberation of aggressive urges was evidently highly pleasurable; still, the exacting superego of the bourgeoisie spoiled much of the pleasure by raising uncomfortable ethical and religious, scientific and political, questions. The most thoughtful in the middle classes showed a certain awareness of complexity and a certain appreciation of ambiguity and questioned the easy commonplaces from which these alibis drew their strength.

This awareness and this appreciation characterize what we may call the liberal temper. It is not a political category; there were nineteenth-century liberals who lacked its distinctive qualities, while some contemporary conservatives possessed them. The liberal temper is a capacity for tolerating the maddening twists, delays, uncertainties, and disappointments attendant upon life in an open society, coupled with a gift for testing and accepting reality, to say nothing of a feeling for the absurdities of existence. It is, after all, telling (as Hobson had pointed out) that the first thing the jingo loses is his sense of humor. The liberal temper notes, and does not lament, the many shades of gray that make up the human experience. As the last trait to be developed—children, born conservatives, are strangers to it—it is also the first to be set aside; not an attitude easily acquired, it is an attitude easily lost.

The liberal temper is so precarious because it is steadily under pressure from more primitive demands—for quick decisions, simple answers, forceful action, above all instant gratification. The threat—for most, the promise—of regression lurks everywhere. Most people find that hitting out, whether calculated or spontaneous, yields greater satisfactions than holding in, at least in the short run; smiting the other's cheek is more delightful than turning one's own. And yet, though a tender plant, the liberal temper had sunk sturdy roots in nineteenth-century bourgeois culture. Not every battle with imperious impulse was lost. Mastering aggression without denying it, translating destructive wishes into productive occupations, heeding the call of desire with all the grace and rationality in one's power—at their best, bourgeois were liberals of that sort.

But could they prevail against the urgencies of aggressiveness? In retrospect, the First World War came to appear a predictable calamity; a favorite, much-overused metaphor likened the Europe of 1914 to a powder keg ready to explode, with Sarajevo supplying the spark. No doubt August 4, 1914, was the most signal defeat the bourgeois world suffered in modern times. But it was not written in the stars. The fatalist notion that aggression was bound to triumph over prudent rationality slights the role of contingency in human affairs. Misunderstandings among diplomats, an inability to read danger signals, events developing a momentum of their own, sheer stupidity—that much underrated force in history—drove the world toward August 4, 1914, as surely as the greed of imperialists or the swagger of emperors.

In fact, the history of the nineteenth-century bourgeoisie is rich in instances when it managed to blunt or sublimate aggressive impulses to make for a livable, civilized culture. Its struggle to master aggression, whether with love, humor, or punishment, or by making human life more human, brought at best a partial victory. The cultivation of hatred was never an unambiguous affair; as noted early on, it curbed aggression and intensified it. Considering the problematic nature of the human self, forever threatened with internal civil war, it would have been utopian to hope for more.

APPENDIX

Theories of Aggression

As I noted in the Introduction, the nineteenth century was virtually unanimous in seeing the human as an aggressive animal, and I quoted contemporaries from Georg Büchner to William James and beyond to that effect. Some Victorians, to be sure, had reservations about this popular verdict; the history of Freud's hesitant acceptance of aggression as an equal partner—or rival—to libido in mental life attests to that. Yet from early on Freud also paid wry tribute to the grip of aggressiveness on human thought and action.

We are no longer so sure about man's Fall, whether scriptural or metaphorical. Psychoanalysts, sociologists, and ethologists, the last freely translating their observations of animal behavior into sweeping conclusions about human nature, have been debating the ultimate sources of aggressiveness for some decades, with an asperity that may itself rank as a document in the history of human aggression. The ethologists, with Konrad Lorenz in the vanguard, have postulated an innate aggressive drive and pleaded in behalf of its adaptive evolutionary qualities. For all his disclaimers, Lorenz sees human as endowed with a certain quantity of aggressiveness, which if not discharged, must raise fatal mischief. While his rather less naive and far less folksy disciples, politic in embracing some of their critics' objections, have modified Lorenz's bald assertions, they cannot quite do without them. They do grant that man is not just a naked ape, given to murder whenever the impulse gets too strong and the opportunity too tempting. "My basic premise," Irenäus Eibl-Eibesfeldt, perhaps the most prominent spokesman for the ethologists, has categorically asserted, "is that if a certain behavior pattern or disposition is inherited, this by no means implies that it is not amenable to conditioning."[1] Still, he insists that a sizable quantity of aggressiveness is an undeniable—and at its best an indispensable—ingredient in the evolutionary baggage that humans drag through life.

Rejecting this biological determinism even in its softened form, irate denigrators of ethology—and of its recent offspring, sociobiology—have proposed
an equally uncertain, though far more humane, philosophical anthropology of
their own. Suspecting as they do (not wholly without cause) that the ethologists' and sociobiologists' perspectives barely conceal a conservative, even reactionary program for ruthless *laissez-faire* in the political and economic struggle
for survival, they have constructed an uncompromising environmentalism.
They deny the existence of preprogrammed drives—aggressive or any other.
Defending their territory, the politics of decency, with commendable warmth,
they have tried to secure space for the work of moral pedagogy and remedial
social action. This passion has dictated their fervent tributes to the malleable
qualities of the child, susceptible to relentless external influences from the moment of birth. Children, they say, are quickly shaped into recognizable, distinct
bits of humanity, into members of a class, a region, a nation, a race, a religious
community.

These liberals have a solid point. No doubt particular ways of exhibiting—or
repressing—vitality or competitiveness, hostility or hatred, are learned. If this
were not so, no history of aggression registering variations from age to age, class
to class, country to country, would be possible. Yet this school of thought has
failed to sound the stubborn innate core of human nature, thus perpetuating the
fallacy that the sociologist Dennis Wrong has felicitously called "the oversocialized conception of man."[2]

In truth, though exposed to threats and promises, though apparently putty in
the hands of family, school, neighborhood, and a wider world, the maturing
human being retains deeply buried but potent impulses—impulses that remain
beyond the grasp of outside pressures, and fiercely resist them. In the developing person, plasticity and rigidity alike are at work. The point, for the historian
as for other students of humanity, is to investigate and specify as clearly as
possible the respective shares of each. One of Freud's central self-assigned tasks
was to define realistically the balance between the claims of nature and nurture.
The balance was so elusive, he knew, because much of mental life goes on, as it
were, behind the individual's back.[3]

Since Freud's thinking has helped to shape this volume, like its predecessors,
his views on aggression deserve attentive scrutiny. On the surface it seems that
in their claims for heredity, the psychoanalysts anticipated the ethologists. But
to minimize the differences between these two schools of thought would be
unfortunate. Though firmly committed to the proposition that human nature is
securely rooted in biology, Freud made the anthropologists' description of man
as the social animal his own.[4] From the early 1890s on, as he began to advance

psychological explanations for psychological manifestations—even, by analyzing conversion symptoms in hysteria, psychological explanations for physiological manifestations—he paid tribute to the impact of experience on the mind. Freud admired Darwin greatly, as much as Lorenz and his pupils later did. But he read Darwin's work very differently from them. To him, it was a cautionary tale far more than a celebration. Unlike the ethologists, Freud treated aggression as a signal danger to the very survival of civilization. The epic struggle between life and death (as envisioned in his late so-called structural system) is a combat to the end; mankind, he argued, can exorcise the threat that aggression poses only through the supreme efforts of love. Unlike Konrad Lorenz, Freud did not take wicked pleasure in fantasies of dealing out floggings and uppercuts.

Freud's aversion to the human capacity for mayhem only increased with the years. Yet for all the decades he tinkered with his theories of aggression, he never really unambiguously defined its nature—at least not to the complete satisfaction of his colleagues and successors. Beginning with his earliest psychoanalytic researches, he had given conspicuous room in the psychic economy to rage, hatred, sheer destructiveness. His early theory, soon abandoned, that all neuroses originate in traumatic experiences like rape or seduction suffered in childhood, underscored his uneasy appreciation of the share of violence in human erotic life. And there is no evidence that after he abandoned this so-called seduction theory in 1897, his awed respect for the power of aggressiveness slackened in any way. After all, he recognized aggression in the very foundations of the Oedipus complex, that passion play of mingled affection and aversion, childish lust and jealousy. Before 1900, he had learned, sitting behind the couch, what poets had long known: love and hate are inextricably enmeshed. The convenient term "ambivalence," which Freud would borrow from the Swiss psychiatrist Eugen Bleuler, admirably condenses this tense interplay of opposites. As he elaborated his delineation of the Oedipus complex, Freud discovered significant traces of aggressiveness in emotional domains where it might be supposed to have no place. Chapter upon chapter in this book demonstrates that his sense of the ubiquity of aggression was well grounded.

In short, years before he elevated aggression into an equal with its immortal adversary, libido, Freud was far from trivializing the versatility and energy of hostile impulses. They lurked, he knew, in the analysand's resistance to the analyst's interpretations, in pointed jokes, in mantled death wishes against loved ones, in adolescent fantasies about slaying giants, in the ferocious assaults of a stern conscience upon the primitive urge toward pleasure. The atrocities and unending slaughter of the First World War would only confirm ideas which, he claimed in December 1914, psychoanalysts had long held, basing themselves on "a study of the dreams and mental slips of normal people" no less than on "the symptoms of neurotics." Plainly, the "primitive, savage and evil impulses of mankind have not vanished in any individual, but continue their existence, although in a repressed state" and only wait for "opportunities to display their activity."[5]

Psychoanalysts had no problem with Freud's somber view of human nature in action. But when, in 1920, he speculated in print that human existence is dominated by the combat of two titanic forces, Eros and Thanatos, few of his adherents followed him all the way. In Freud's stark, symmetrical dualism, the constructive forces of life confront the subversive forces of death. Aggression, in this scheme, is the public voice of the death drive, itself remote and silent. To be sure, Freud's late blueprint of mental structure and functioning, which among other things threw searching doubts on the primacy of the pleasure principle in human motivation, was a triumph of theoretical clarification. But his play with speculative biology, and his grandiose vision of two outsized rivals wrestling for the soul of humanity and the very future of civilization, moved him a risky distance from the clinical terrain in which he had been most at home and had made his historic discoveries.

While Freud in his later years repeatedly asserted that he could no longer think about life and death in any other way, most other psychoanalysts, though considering themselves good Freudians, found the logical and evidentiary problems presented by Thanatos to be unsurmountable. It was mainly the child analyst Melanie Klein and her enthusiastic admirers who would retain the death drive as a profoundly necessary insight into the human condition. The others rejected the picturesque mythological titans, while retaining the theory of conflicting drives. Freud's "*death instinct*," the psychoanalyst David Rapaport wrote in 1957, "is as dead as a doornail"; yet he immediately added, candidly revealing the continuing puzzlement troubling his profession, "the problem of the origin and development of *aggressive drives* is still unsolved."[6]

This agnostic school of thought now dominates psychoanalytic thinking. But there is a third school, far smaller but no less respectable, which has rejected the concept of an aggressive drive as too imprecise, encompassing as it does the most diversified cluster of feelings and actions. These psychoanalysts refuse also to recognize aggression as a pendant to the sexual drive, since its pressure is neither spontaneous nor continuous and is far more varied in its effects than the incitements of Eros. In a magisterial article of 1971, Leo Stone, surveying the situation, saw aggression "and its psychological functions and representations," as "the aggregate of diverse acts, having diverse origins, and bound together, sometimes loosely, by the nature of their impact on objects rather than by a demonstrably common and unitary drive." Stone noted that "aggression is often integrated with basic and unequivocal instincts such as hunger (where killing is archaically inevitable), and the various phases of sexuality." Inescapably, then, "there are varying degrees and varying forms of aggression." Hence, "when a hoodlum shoots an enemy, when an overprotective mother refuses to allow her child to go swimming with his peers, when an inveterate Don Juan accomplishes habitual, loveless seductions, or when a person deliberately omits to greet an acquaintance," we are confronted with a wealth of motives and actions far too disparate to fit comfortably under a single umbrella. Some acts of aggression arise from anxiety and others from rage, some from narcissistic self-promotion and others from sexual needs or hunger, still others from sheer pleasure in exercising one's bodily powers.[7]

Such candid and refreshing pluralism, a triumph of the welter of experience over the neatness of theory, can only appeal to historians, professionally committed as they are to celebrating the uniqueness of each event. Stone's openness to diversity respects the essential untidiness of mental life and the continuous intermingling of libido with aggression to which I called attention at the beginning of this book. What is more, the interpreter of aggression soon discovers that it makes greater demands on him than sexuality because, unlike sexuality, it traverses no autonomous developmental lines, being parasitic, in its history, on libidinal evolution.* Nor, unlike sexuality, can aggression boast of specific executive organs. To be sure, we know that every part of the body can be enlisted, whether in fantasy or reality, in erotic excitement and consummation; conventional sexual intercourse plots the rising rhythm of sensations across diverse bodily zones, to culminate in genital union. But it does culminate there; in both male and female some fairly specialized organs seem virtually designed to accommodate the principal erotic pleasures. In contrast, it is impossible to determine in advance which part of the body is best adapted to carry out an act of aggression. Even speech, so often the eloquent servant of love, can, as common idioms reveal, bite or cut, hit or slash, like so many weapons.

I have found Stone's pluralism refreshing and congenial, and have taken it as a caution against dogmatism or oversimplification. Yet though aware of the risks, I have continued to employ the general concept aggression in this comprehensive, though far from complete, survey of nineteenth-century bourgeois

*"Long before the beginning of independent analytic studies of aggression," Anna Freud wrote in a characteristically lucid paper, "the aggressive nature of infantile sexuality was taken for granted, as evidenced by the cannibalistic tendencies and fantasies on the oral level; the sadistic, tormenting, possessive attitudes characteristic of the anal stage; and the domineering, thrusting qualities of phallic sexuality." "Comments on Aggression," International Journal of Psycho-Analysis, LIII (1972), 184.

culture, since its manifestations, however varied, bear significant family resemblances. Still, aggression is indeed protean, and even has, as Freud was reluctant to recognize, its positive dimensions. It is not just at home all over the body; its repertory is in no way exhausted by the lust to insult, maim, or kill. Indeed, in recent years, psychoanalysts have begun to explore the adaptive functions of aggressiveness, and have come to see it as an educator for life no less than as an agent of death. It can be, as chapter 6 documents in detail, the fuel for essential civilized and civilizing work.

To give but one instance of the positive coloring that aggression can assume: In March 1862, the London *Inquirer,* a Unitarian weekly, ran a front-page editorial—really an exhortation—titled, simply, "Aggression." No longer on the defensive, the editorial writer noted, good Unitarians had much land to conquer, and the "signs of the times" helped to strengthen "our new resolve to do good *aggressive* work," not to be harsh but to be effective. "Let that be our watchword for 1862, and our solemn pledge, every Church for itself, every minister for himself. We have great truths to tell, we have a free spirit to make known, we have a spirit of evil to cast out." To be sure, "the aggression we advocate has nothing to do with debate," but everything to do with "*affirmation.*" In short, the editorial went on in ringing tones, "Let the word for this year be, then, *Aggression*—not for our own sake, not for our party's sake, but for the truth's sake."[8]

It was this line of thinking that led Freud in his early days to postulate a *Bemächtigungstrieb*—a "drive toward mastery." He envisioned it as independent of the sexual drives with which it might conclude temporary alliances, and in no way intent on harming, diminishing, or demolishing the objects it seeks to master. This urge, he speculated, might explain the widely observed disposition to translate passivity into activity, to master unpleasurable experiences by rewriting the script of life in play or fantasy in which victim becomes master. The little girl who has suffered in the dentist's chair will come home to play dentist, and this time *she* is the white-coated adult dealing out pain. But after adopting his stunning myth of Eros in permanent conflict with Thanatos, Freud found no room for such an independent drive, and reduced the will to mastery, when he mentioned it at all, into a derivative of the death drive working under the dictates of sexuality.

For all the aesthetic charm of this great simplification, the palpable human pleasure in mastery calls out for recognition, and as the reader knows, I have given it house room in these pages. Solving a tantalizing puzzle, climbing an unclimbable mountain, gaining proficiency in an obscure tongue, inventing a labor-saving device, are all in their way aggressive acts. Hence a few psychoanalysts, notably Ives Hendrick, impressed with the sheer human joy in functioning, have taken Freud's early hints seriously enough to posit an "instinct to master."[9]

This postulate may violate the principle of parsimony: one might derive the pleasure in mastery from the collaboration of the drives with which psychoanalysts tend to work, or from a more benign, or at least more differentiated, aggressive drive than Freud was ultimately ready to accept. But whether mastery is a derived amalgam or an independent drive, the observation that it gives pleasure does not contradict Freud's well-known theory of culture, which holds that all societies require their members to postpone, to compromise, often to sacrifice, instinctual wishes for the sake of ensuring common survival and storing up energies for the conquest of nature. I cannot repeat too often that the invention of tools to extract and refine natural resources, the establishment and improvement of rapid communications, the development of techniques easing the exchange of goods and services, the founding of institutions to distribute necessities and, for those better situated, comforts and luxuries, all exemplify the kind of "attack" on the world in which the nineteenth century was preeminent. They were attacks aimed at reducing pain and increasing pleasure on the solid ground of reality rather than in the cloud land of fantasy. "The aim of the instinct to master," Hendrick suggests, "differs from sadism or any other of the sexual or sexualized instincts" as it drives people "to control or alter a piece of the environment" by skillfully employing "perceptual, intellectual, and motor techniques." The drive to master, then, works as "the incentive to the development and exercises of the ego functions which are mentally and emotionally experienced as the need to perform work efficiently."[10]

In the absence of conclusive agreement among psychoanalysts on the drives, Hendrick's proposal has found some sympathetic but quite tentative allies. After all, as late as 1932, Freud called the theory of the drives "our mythology"; the drives, he said, are "sublime in their indefiniteness."[11] David Rapaport, taking an interest in Hendrick, suggested in 1961 in an impressive paper that it was time to rethink aggressiveness as "a complex derivative of activity."[12] Other psychoanalysts, like the ego psychologist Heinz Hartmann, though skeptical, have similarly looked for sources of mental energy located in the ego and serving neither sexuality nor aggression. Before them, in the 1940s, the astute psychoanalyst Otto Fenichel reasoned that "while the existence and importance of aggressive drives cannot be denied," there is really "no proof that they always and necessarily came into being by a turning outward of more primary self-destructive drives. It seems rather as if aggressiveness were originally no instinctual aim of its own, characterizing one category of instincts in contradistinction to others, but rather a mode in which instinctual aims sometimes are striven for, in response to frustrations or even spontaneously." For Fenichel, in short, aggression is a summary name for many ways of doing many things.[13] Such thinking forms the background of a reasonable suggestion by the English psychoanalyst Joseph Sandler that it is proper to postulate a *"capacity* to be aggressive" which works itself out in a wide variety of circumstances, mobilized by whatever is experienced as unpleasurable, whether external pressures or internal impulses.[14]

This is where psychoanalysts now stand. Their very inconclusiveness about aggressive feelings, thoughts, and conduct should serve to discourage premature and simplistic verdicts. It should, too, expose as sheer caricatures of complicated realities both the pastel portrait of humans as wholly malleable and the ethologists' biological determinism. Analysts' uncertainties point rather to what George Eliot once beautifully called "the half tints of real life."[15] One person's work for mastery, after all, is another person's work for demolition.* I have written this book to show that the nineteenth century was an age of aggressive destruction and construction both, an age in which respectable culture made more determined efforts than ever to cultivate hatred—and needed to.

*There are times, as Voltaire wrote more than two centuries ago, when one must destroy in order to build. We hear a nineteenth-century echo of that proposition in the early 1830s, from the English novelist Edward Bulwer-Lytton. "The age then," he wrote, "is one of *destruction:* disguise it as we will, it must be so characterized; miserable would be our lot were it not also an age of preparation for reconstruction." *England and the English* (1833; ed. Standish Meacham, 1970), 319.

NOTES

In citations of Freud titles, *Gesammelte Werke* denotes Sigmund Freud, *Gesammelte Werke,* ed. Anna Freud et al., 18 vols. (1940–68), and *Standard Edition* denotes Sigmund Freud, *Standard Edition of the Complete Psychological Works,* tr. and ed. James Strachey et al., 24 vols. (1953–74).

Introduction

1. Ernst John, *Büchner* (1958), 86. In his remarkable play of the same year, 1832, *Dantons Tod,* Büchner repeated the question almost word for word and added a despairing commonplace about man as a mere puppet, pulled on wires by unknown powers.

2. November 16, 1859, Edmond and Jules de Goncourt, *Journal; mémoires de la vie littéraire 1851–1896,* ed. Robert Ricatte, 22 vols. (1956–58), III, 168.

3. William James, *The Varieties of Religious Experience: A Study in Human Nature* (1902), 366, 338.

4. Georg Simmel, *Soziologie. Untersuchungen über die Formen der Vergesellschaftung* (1908), 261, 262.

5. The principal proponent of this view was the psychoanalytically sophisticated psychologist and anthropologist John Dollard. See John Dollard, Leonard Doob, Neal E. Miller, O. H. Mowrer, and Robert R. Sears, in collaboration with Clellan S. Ford, Carl Iver Hovland, and Richard T. Sollenberger, *Frustration and Aggression* (1939).

6. Heine: among other instances, *Die Romantische Schule* (1835), in Heinrich Heine, *Sämtliche Schriften,* ed. Klaus Briegleb et al., 6 vols. (1968–76), III, 366, 362, 471; James: Jacques Barzun, *A Stroll with William James* (1983), 25.

7. See Ernest Jones, *The Life and Work of Sigmund Freud,* vol. II, *Years of Maturity, 1901–1919* (1955), 12.

8. In the first two volumes of this series, *Education of the Senses* (1984) and *The Tender Passion* (1986), I have explored these issues in detail, and have argued that among bourgeois couples happy sexual consummations were in fact far more frequent and far more passionate than usually supposed.

BOURGEOIS EXPERIENCES, III:
Mensur—the Cherished Scar

1. " 'Three Men in a Boat,' " Jerome wrote with understandable resentment in his autobiography, "brought me fame, and had it been published a few years later"—after the United States had become party to an international copyright agreement—the book "would have brought me fortune also. As it was, the American pirate reaped a great reward." It had sold "well over a million copies" in the United States. *My Life and Times* (1926), 109, 76.

2. "Military Terrorism in France," *Saturday Review*, VI (May 22, 1858), 526–27. In response to this caricature of Tocqueville's far subtler concern over the tyranny of the majority looming over the United States, one might note that duelling was heavily concentrated in the antebellum South, and that the American clergy inveighed against the practice in sermon after sermon—literally dozens of them were published, perhaps showing by their very repetitiousness that their message had not been fully absorbed.

3. "Literary Duelling," *Saturday Review*, VI (October 30, 1858), 419.

4. Jerome K. Jerome, *Three Men on the Bummel* (1900; ed. 1982), 203–4.

5. Ibid., 204–5.

6. Ibid., 205–6.

7. Ibid., 206–7. The psychoanalyst might note that this cherished scar, the *Schmiss,* is a heavily overdetermined emblem. It is a passport to social preferment, a symbol of aggression rightfully exercised, and at the same time a conspicuous mark of penance for oedipal victory, a payment for entering the world of the fathers.

8. Ibid., 207–8.

9. Ibid., 208. In his autobiography, Jerome recalled that he had "sat upon the blood-splashed bench" and watched youngsters fitted for "the 'greatest game of all,' as Kipling calls it"—war. "I hated the stupidity, the cruelty of the thing." He insisted, speaking of hunting, "Killing has never attracted me." But Jerome, though something of a philistine, was far from insensitive to his less creditable emotions. Much as the prewar bellicosity of the chauvinist British press had repelled him, August 1914 transformed him for a time: "I heard of our declaration of war against Germany with cheerful satisfaction. The animal in me rejoiced. It was going to be the biggest war in history. I thanked whatever gods there be that they had given it in my time." *My Life and Times,* 268, 227, 276. For Jerome, as for most of his nineteenth-century predecessors, humans were cruel animals barely restrained by their leash, civilization.

10. Jane Austen, *Sense and Sensibility* (1811; ed. Tony Tanner, 1969), 220 [ch. 31]. There are hints at duels as a possible resolution of a matter of honor in Austen's *Pride and Prejudice* as well.

11. William Howitt, *The Student-Life of Germany* (1841), vi, 441.

12. Ute Frevert, "Die Ehre der Bürger im Spiegel ihrer Duelle. Ansichten des 19. Jahrhunderts," *Historische Zeitschrift,* CCXLIX (1989), 555.

13. Even when the nostalgia for "feudalism" reached almost grotesque heights in late-nineteenth-century German society, aristocrats remained a minority within a minority. Only a relative handful of German university students joined *Corps* or *Burschenschaften* committed to the duel. In 1873, at Marburg, a university noted for its exceptionally active fraternity life, a little more than a third of all students belonged to corporations requiring the duel in their statutes; by 1913, they numbered one in six. Even at "aristocratic" Bonn, as Jerome called it, the student duellers declined from about 8 percent in the late 1880s to less than 5 percent just before the outbreak of the First

World War. Berlin, during the same decades, counted just under 4 percent of duelling fraternity men in a sizable and rapidly growing student population.

14. *Stenographische Berichte über die Verhandlungen des Reichstags*, vol. 294 (1914), 235th session, 8088–90.

15. Ibid., 8090.

16. Max Weber, "Agrarstatistische und sozialpolitische Betrachtungen zur Fideikommissfrage in Preussen" (1904), *Gesammelte Aufsätze zur Soziologie und Sozialpolitik* (1924), 390n.

17. Detlev Grieswelle, "Zur Soziologie der Kösener Corps 1870–1914," in Karsten Bahnson et al., *Student and Hochschule im 19. Jahrhundert. Studien und Materialien* (1975), 346–65.

18. Harnack: Agnes von Zahn-Harnack, *Adolf von Harnack* (1937; ed. 1951), 43; "*Burschen*": Adolf Kussmaul, *Jugenderinnerungen eines alten Arztes* (1899), 125–26.

19. *Schokoladisten* and Goethe: see Friedrich Schulze and Paul Ssymank, *Das deutsche Studententum von den ältesten Zeiten bis zur Gegenwart* (1910), 143; Thomas: see *The Making of a Feminist: Early Journals and Letters of M. Carey Thomas*, ed. Marjorie Housepian Dobkin (1979), 155.

20. See Georg von Below, *Das Duell und der deutsche Ehrbegriff* (1896), and Heinrich Geffcken, *Fehde and Duell* (1899), passim.

21. Howitt, *Student-Life of Germany*, 443–45.

22. Medieval origins: see W. Fuhrmann, *Geschichte der studentischen Fechtkunst* (1901), vol. III in the Burschenschaftliche Bücherei, esp. 7–13; different pedigree: see Georg von Below, *Das Duell in Deutschland. Geschichte und Gegenwart* (1896).

23. See Wilhelm Fabricius, *Die deutschen Corps. Eine historische Darstellung mit besonderer Berücksichtigung des Mensurwesens* (1898; ed. 1926), 96–98.

24. See Peter Krause, *"O Alte Burschenherrlichkeit." Die Studenten und ihr Brauchtum* (1979; 3rd ed., 1980), 105.

25. See David McLellan, *Karl Marx: His Life and Thought* (1973), 17.

26. See Thomas Nipperdey, *Deutsche Geschichte, 1800–1866. Bürgerwelt and starker Staat* (1983), 280.

27. Heinrich Heine, *Die Harzreise* (1824), in *Sämtliche Schriften*, ed. Klaus Briegleb et al., 6 vols. (1968–76), II, 146.

28. Eduard Wedekind, *Studentenleben der Biedermeierzeit. Ein Tagebuch aus dem Jahre 1824*, ed. H. H. Houben [ca. 1927], Introduction, p. 8; April 21, p. 23; July 1, 2, 3, pp. 95, 98, 99–100.

29. See Peter Loewenberg, "Theodor Herzl: Nationalism and Politics," *Decoding the Past: The Psychohistorical Approach* (1983), 107. "I regarded it all as an aping of German student mores," the Zionist leader Nahum Goldman recalled with energetic disapproval many years later. As a student at Heidelberg he had been a member of a Zionist fraternity. *Mein Leben als deutscher Jude* (1980; ed. 1983), 75.

30. J. B. Engl, "Zurechtweisung," *Simplicissimus*, III (1898–99), 156.

31. Breslau manifesto: Adolf Asch and Johanna Philippson, "Self-Defence at the Turn of the Century: The Emergence of the K.C.," *Leo Baeck Institute Yearbook*, III (1958), 122–39; number of Jewish duellers: see Arthur Ruppin, *Die Juden der Gegenwart* (1904), 231.

32. See Nipperdey, *Deutsche Geschichte*, 475.

33. Friedrich Paulsen, *Aus meinem Leben. Jugenderinnerungen* (1909), 139–41, 145.

34. Otto Julius Bierbaum, *Stilpe. Ein Roman aus der Froschperspektive* (1897; ed. 1963), 120.

35. See Walter Bloem, *Der krasse Fuchs* (1906), 162–63.

36. Gregor Samarow, *Die Saxoborussen* (1885; 4th ed., 1903), 114.

37. See Bierbaum, *Stilpe*, 120.

38. Bloem, *Der krasse Fuchs*, 162–63.

39. However, James went on to say, again echoing current views, "The woman in turn subjugates the man by the mystery of gentleness in beauty." *The Varieties of Religious Experience: A Study in Human Nature* (1902), 363–64.

40. Bierbaum, *Stilpe*, 120–21.

41. Wilhelm II: Grieswelle, "Zur Soziologie der Kösener Corps," 348; "all forgotten": Heinrich Rosenberg, *Duell, Ehre und Herr Egenter. Ein Wort der Erwiderung* (1875), 10. Rosenberg is responding to Egenter's pamphlet *Ueber Duell und Ehre. Mit besonderer Berücksichtigung auf Studentenduelle* (2nd ed., 1875).

42. Bloem, *Der krasse Fuchs*, 158–59.

43. "In the sexual life of puberty," Freud noted, "the stimuli of early years and the inhibitions of the latency period wrestle with one another." "Selbstdarstellung" (1925), *Gesammelte Werke*, XIV, 62; "Autobiographical Study," *Standard Edition*, XX, 37.

ONE: Alibis

1. Webb: Peter d'Alroyd Jones, *The Christian Socialist Revival, 1877–1914: Religion, Class, and Social Conscience in Late-Victorian England* (1968), 85–86n; Shaw: George Bernard Shaw, Introduction to Charles Dickens, *Hard Times* (ed. 1912), in George H. Ford and Lauriat Lane, Jr., *The Dickens Critics* (1961), 126.

2. Walter Bagehot, "Charles Dickens" (1858), *Literary Studies (Miscellaneous Essays)*, ed. Richard Holt Hutton, 3 vols. (1st ed., 2 vols., 1879; 2nd ed., 1902–5), II, 158.

1. The Apotheosis of Conflict

1. Adam Smith, *An Inquiry into the Nature and Causes of the Wealth of Nations* (1776; ed. Edwin Cannan, 1937), 343.

2. John Adams, *Letters to John Taylor, of Caroline, Virginia, in Reply to His Strictures on Some Parts of the Defence of the American Constitutions* (1814), in *The Works of John Adams, Second President of the United States*, ed. Charles Francis Adams, 10 vols. (1850–56), VI, 516.

3. See Herbert Spencer, *The Man versus the State* (1884), 79–82.

4. R. J. White, Introduction to James Fitzjames Stephen, *Liberty, Equality, Fraternity* (1873; 2nd ed., 1874; ed. White, 1967), 4.

5. Herbert Spencer, *Social Statics; or, The Conditions Essential to Human Happiness Specified, and the First of Them Developed* (1850; American ed., 1865), 353–54.

6. Ibid.

7. Spencer as "towering intellect": Robert H. Thurston, "Inaugural Address," to the American Society of Mechanical Engineers (1880), in Henry Nash Smith, ed., *Popular Culture and Industrialism, 1865–1890* (1967), 30; greatest living philosopher: see Léon Dumont, "Le Transformisme et les causes finales," *Revue scientifique*, 2nd series, XI (1876), 372. Linda L. Clark, *Social Darwinism in France* (1984), 39; equal of Newton: see Richard Hofstadter, *Social Darwinism in American Thought, 1860–1915* (1944; 2nd ed., 1955), 31.

8. See Charles Darwin, *Autobiography* (1887), in *Autobiographies of Darwin and Huxley*, ed. Gavin de Beer (1974), 64.

9. Spencer, *Social Statics*, 80.

10. Ibid., 180.

11. Spencer, "Some Regrets," *Facts and Comments* (1902), 7. In this chastened mood he instructively inveighed against the musical virtuoso's "pre-occupation with self," which tramples upon

the composer's intentions and reveals "not love of the music rendered but desire for the applause which brilliant rendering will bring." Spencer, "The Corruption of Music," ibid., 27–28.

12. Spencer, "State-Education," ibid., 82–83, 92–93.

13. Spencer, "Re-Barbarization," ibid., 172–88; Spencer, "Imperialism and Slavery," ibid., 158.

14. Herbert Spencer, *Autobiography*, 2 vols. (1904), II, 472, 479.

15. Spencer, *The Man versus the State*, 70.

16. Laveleye made the charge in a letter to the editor of the *Contemporary Review* in 1885. Both his letter and Spencer's reply are quoted in Robert C. Bannister, *Social Darwinism: Science and Myth in Anglo-American Thought* (1979), 51.

17. "Darwin's Origin of Species," *Saturday Review*, VIII (December 24, 1859), 775.

18. Walter Bagehot, *Physics and Politics; or, Thoughts on the Application of the Principles of 'Natural Selection' and 'Inheritance' to Political Society* (1872 [first published as a series of articles in the late 1860s]; American ed., 1873), 44.

19. Adams: *The Education of Henry Adams* (1918; ed. James Truslow Adams, 1931), 225, 231, 284; French writer's concession: Dr. P. Duverney, obituary of Darwin, quoted in Clark, *Social Darwinism in France*, 91.

20. English Christians: see George St. Clair, *Darwinism and Design; or, Creation by Evolution* (1873); Brentano: see Peter Gay, *Freud: A Life for Our Time* (1988), 29.

21. Henry Drummond, *The Ascent of Man* (1894), 4, 195.

22. See Ernst Haeckel, *The Riddle of the Universe* (1899; tr. Joseph McCabe, 1900; ed. 1929), 63, 252.

23. Charles Darwin, *On the Origin of Species by Means of Natural Selection; or, the Preservation of Favoured Races in the Struggle for Life* (1859; ed. John W. Burrow, 1968), 68.

24. Charles Darwin, *The Descent of Man, and Selection in Relation to Sex*, 2 vols. (1871), I, 168; II, 403.

25. See Benjamin Kidd, *Social Evolution* (1894), 54–56.

26. Clémence-Auguste Royer, "Des rapports de principes généraux de l'histoire naturelle avec la solution du problème social" (1872), quoted in Clark, *Social Darwinism in France*, 34.

27. Clark, *Social Darwinism in France*, 31, 108–11.

28. See ibid., 106–13.

29. Émile Zola, "Ébauche" for *Au Bonheur des dames* (1883), in *Les Rougon-Macquart. Histoire naturelle et sociale d'une famille sous le second Empire*, ed. Armand Lanoux and Henri Mitterand, 5 vols. (1960–67), III, 1680.

30. Zola, *Au Bonheur des Dames*, ibid., 457 [ch. 3].

31. Zola, "Ébauche" for *Au Bonheur des dames*, ibid., 1680. For the erotic aspects of this novel, see Peter Gay, *The Bourgeois Experience*, vol. II, *The Tender Passion* (1986), 312–19.

32. See Alfred Kelly, *The Descent of Darwin: The Popularization of Darwinism in Germany, 1860–1914* (1981), 112–14.

33. Friedrich von Hellwald, *Culturgeschichte in ihrer natürlichen Entwicklung bis zur Gegenwart* (1875; 2nd ed., 1876), 37; Julius Lippert, *Kulturgeschichte der Menschheit in ihrem organischen Aufbau*, 2 vols. (1886–87), passim.

34. Otto Ammon, *Die Gesellschaftsordnung und ihre natürlichen Grundlagen. Entwurf einer Sozial-Anthropologie zum Gebrauch für alle Gebildeten, die sich mit sozialen Fragen befassen* (1895; 2nd ed., 1896), 248, 154, 17.

35. Georg von Gizycki, "Darwinismus and Ethik," *Deutsche Rundschau*, XLIII (April–June 1885), 261.

36. Friedrich Nietzsche, *Jenseits von Gut und Böse. Vorspiel einer Philosophie der Zukunft* (1886), in *Werke*, ed. Karl Schlechta, 3 vols. in 5 (1972), III, 175 [aphorism 259].

37. Kelly, *Descent of Darwin*, 23, 102.

38. Carnegie on the law of competition: "It is here; we cannot evade it; no substitutes for it have been found; and while the law may sometimes be hard for the individual, it is best for the race, because it insures the survival of the fittest in every department." Andrew Carnegie, "The Gospel of Wealth" (1888), *The Gospel of Wealth and Other Timely Essays*, ed. Edward C. Kirkland (1962), 16; Rockefeller addressing a Sunday school: "The growth of a large business is merely a survival of the fittest." Hofstadter, *Social Darwinism*, 45. Hill, speaking out against government regulation of railroad rates: "Competition is the test which proves the survival of the fittest." The "laws of trade," Hill said, are as certain as the "laws of gravity." Henry F. Pringle, *Theodore Roosevelt: A Biography* (1931), 417.

39. Koenraad W. Swart, *The Sense of Decadence in Nineteenth-Century France* (1964), 158.

40. Darwin to Charles Lyell, January 4, 1860, *The Life and Letters of Charles Darwin, Including an Autobiographical Chapter*, ed. Francis Darwin, 3 vols. (1887; ed. 1919), II, 56–57.

41. Bagehot, *Physics and Politics*, 43–44, 43, 81.

42. Ibid., 74–75, 161.

43. Ibid., 200, 194–95.

44. Thomas Henry Huxley, "Evolution and Ethics," a Romanes Lecture (1893), *Evolution and Ethics and Other Essays* (1903), 83, 80, and passim. In the preface he added in 1891 to his intelligent short book *Darwinism and Politics, with Two Additional Essays on "Human Evolution"* (1889), David G. Ritchie said emphatically, "*The theory of Natural Selection (in the form in which alone it can properly be applied to human society) lends no support to the political dogma of laissez faire*" (p. iii).

45. Hofstadter, *Social Darwinism*, 73.

46. As recalled by William Lyon Phelps, later an equally popular Yale professor, in "When Yale Was Given to Sumnerology" (1925). Hofstadter, *Social Darwinism*, 54.

47. See William Graham Sumner, *Folkways: A Study of the Sociological Importance of Usages, Manners, Customs, Mores, and Morals* (1907), 18.

48. Sumner, "Rights" (written between 1900 and 1906, published posthumously), *Earth-Hunger and Other Essays*, ed. Albert Galloway Keller (1913), 79; "The Boon of Nature" (1889), *Earth-Hunger*, 234–36; "The Influence of Commercial Crises on Opinions about Economic Doctrines" (1879), *The Forgotten Man and Other Essays*, ed. Keller (1919), 225; "State Interference" (1887), *War and Other Essays*, ed. Keller (1911), 213. It is appropriate to cite Sumner's views from every part of his writing career since they changed only marginally across the years.

49. Sumner, "On the Case of a Certain Man Who Is Never Thought Of" (1884), *War*, 248.

50. Sumner, "Purposes and Consequences" (written between 1900 and 1906, published posthumously), *Earth-Hunger*, 73; "The Absurd Effort to Make the World Over" (1894), *War*, 210.

51. See Sumner, "Do We Want Industrial Peace?" (1889), *War*, 239, 242.

52. Sumner, "Earth Hunger or the Philosophy of Land Grabbing" (1896), *Earth-Hunger*, 51, 47, 64, 62.

53. Sumner, "The Conquest of the United States by Spain" (1898), *Earth-Hunger*, 334.

54. Sumner, "War," *War*, 15, 29, 35, 36.

55. Thus the marquis de Nadaillac observed anxiously in the mid-1880s, "The fate of a nation depends on its military preponderance, and that preponderance, all too often, on the number of men it can muster for the field of battle. . . . In the battles of industry, no less ardent, no less implacable, one must produce rapidly, one must produce a great deal, and the number of young

and vigorous arms will assure the economic victory." *Affaiblissement de la natalité en France, ses causes et ses conséquences* (1885; 2nd ed., 1886), v–vi, 2. See Gay, *Bourgeois Experience*, vol. I, *Education of the Senses* (1984), 265–71.

56. Frank Norris, *Vandover and the Brute* (written in 1895; published posthumously in 1914), 230–31.

57. Carnegie: Thomas C. Cochran and William Miller, *The Age of Enterprise: A Social History of Industrial America* (1942; rev. ed., 1961), 143; Rockefeller: John D. Rockefeller, *Random Reminiscences of Men and Events* (1909), 65–66.

58. Harold C. Livesay, *Andrew Carnegie and the Rise of Big Business* (1975), 72.

59. Carnegie, "The Advantages of Poverty" (1891), *The Gospel of Wealth*, 66–67.

60. The two articles originally appeared in 1888, in the June and December issues of the *North American Review* under the blander title "Wealth." When they were reprinted in the *Pall Mall Gazette* in London, the editor, William T. Stead, chose the far more evocative title under which they have become known.

61. Carnegie, "The Gospel of Wealth," 19, 27, 31.

62. See ibid., 29–30, 21.

63. *Autobiography of Andrew Carnegie* (published posthumously, ed. John C. Van Dyke, 1920), 272; see also 270.

64. Rockefeller, *Random Reminiscences*, 20–21, 11, 140, 58, 62.

65. In the fall of 1907, Rockefeller said again what he had said before: he considered himself merely "a trustee of the property of others through the providence of God committed to my care." Oakland, California, *Tribune*, October 8, 1907, quoted in George E. Mowry, *The Era of Theodore Roosevelt, 1900–1912* (1958), 45.

66. Other philanthropists sounded very much like Carnegie and Rockefeller. Philip D. Armour, Chicago's most aggressive and wealthiest meat packer, and a formidable philanthropist, founded the Armour Institute, a kind of preparatory school for impecunious boys and girls, and professed to be working really for them. "We run the packing business," he said, "the grain business, the glue factory, and the railroad to make money for these boys and girls." Arthur Warren, "Philip D. Armour: His Manner of Life, His Immense Enterprises in Trade and Philanthropy," *McClure's Magazine*, II (1893–94), 294–95.

67. Rockefeller, *Random Reminiscences*, 20, 152.

68. Rockefeller: Theodore Roosevelt to David Scull, president of Bryn Mawr, August 16, 1907, *The Letters of Theodore Roosevelt*, sel. and ed. Elting E. Morison, with John M. Blum and Alfred D. Chandler, Jr., 8 vols. (1951–54), V, 755; Carnegie: Theodore Roosevelt, *An Autobiography* (1913), 209.

69. Hofstadter, *Social Darwinism*, 72.

2. The Convenient Other

1. See Richard Hofstadter, "Cuba, the Philippines, and Manifest Destiny" (1952), rev. in *The Paranoid Style in American Politics and Other Essays* (1965), 152n.

2. "Manuskript H," enclosed with letter from Freud to Wilhelm Fliess, January 24, 1895, Sigmund Freud, *Briefe an Wilhelm Fliess 1887–1904*, ed. Jeffrey Moussaieff Masson, assisted by Michael Schröter and Gerhard Fichtner (1986), 110.

3. Chekhov to Alexei Suvorin, February 6, 1898, *Letters of Anton Chekhov*, tr. Michael Henry Heim in collaboration with Simon Karlinsky, ed. Simon Karlinsky (1973), 316.

4. See J. H. Elliott, *Imperial Spain, 1469–1716* (1963), 216.

5. Benjamin Constant, *De l'esprit de conquête et de l'usurpation dans ses rapports avec la civilisation européenne* (1813; 3rd ed., 1814), 121–22.

6. François Guizot, *The History of Civilization from the Fall of the Roman Empire to the French Revolution* (1829–1832; tr. William Hazlitt, 4 vols. in 2, 1887), II, 151.

7. See ibid., I, 16.

8. Hippolyte Taine, *History of English Literature* (1864; 2nd ed. 1866; tr. H. Van Laun, 1873), 23.

9. Ibid., 35, 565.

10. Robert Blake, *Disraeli* (1967; ed. 1968), 186.

11. Robert Knox, *The Races of Men: A Philosophical Enquiry into the Influences of Race over the Destiny of Nations* (1850; 2nd ed., 1862), 8, 6. Both of these statements have been much quoted.

12. Joseph Arthur de Gobineau, *Essai sur l'inégalité des races humaines* (1853–55; ed. Hubert Juin, 1967), 28, 29.

13. See Stephen Jay Gould, *The Mismeasure of Man* (1981), 85, 92.

14. Ibid., 99; see also 82–107.

15. Friedrich Max Müller, *Biographies of Words and the Home of the Aryas* (1888), 245, 120.

16. Gobineau, *Essai sur l'inégalité*, 58.

17. Herman Melville, *The Confidence-Man: His Masquerade* (1857; ed. Hershel Parker, 1971), 124 [ch. 25].

18. Georges Vacher de Lapouge, *L'Aryen: Son rôle social* (1899), 511; Wilhelm II reported in Léon Poliakov, *The Aryan Myth: A History of Racist and Nationalist Ideas in Europe* (1971; tr. Edmund Howard, 1974), 260.

19. Lapouge, *L'Aryen,* 465–66. The history of modern anti-Semitism, which has for painfully obvious reasons received much attention, fits the thesis of these pages to perfection. In the course of the nineteenth century, the medieval caricature of the Jew as Christ-killer waned as racial anti-Semites began to draw another, if anything more lethal, caricature, the Jew by racial endowment always the same, no matter what his family history, his environment, his convictions.

20. Ibid., 373.

21. Charles Dilke, *Problems of Greater Britain* (1890), 2. This work is a substantially revised and enlarged edition of *Greater Britain,* first published in 1868.

22. "Aryan prejudices": Freeman to Professor Dawkins, October 15, 1881, W. R. W. Stephens, *The Life and Letters of Edward A. Freeman,* 2 vols. (1895), II, 234; Freeman to F. H. Dickinson, December 4, 1881, ibid., 242; Freeman to Rev. N. Pinder, March 24, 1882, ibid., 253. Irishmen killing Negroes: Freeman to F. H. Dickinson, December 4, 1881, ibid., 242. Resemblance to "big monkeys": Freeman to Professor Dawkins, October 15, 1881, ibid., 234. Jews controlling press, "Hebrew heads": Freeman to Rev. N. Pinder, March 24, 1882, ibid., 253.

23. See L. P. Curtis, Jr., *Anglo-Saxons and Celts: A Study of Anti-Irish Prejudice in Victorian England* (1968), passim. The Tenniel cartoon, "The Irish Frankenstein," from *Punch,* is reproduced on page 60.

24. James Russell Lowell, *The Biglow Papers,* First Series (1848), in *The Poetical Works of James Russell Lowell,* rev. Marjorie R. Kaufman (1978), 185.

25. See J. A. Hobson, *The Psychology of Jingoism* (1901), 75.

26. "by their tails": Ivo Banac, *The National Question in Yugoslavia: Origins, History, Politics* (1984), 293; "the nineteenth century": Vladam Georgevitch [Djordjević], *Die Albanesen und die Grossmächte* (1913), 4.

27. Thomas Carlyle, "Occasional Discourse on the Negro Question," *Fraser's Magazine,* XL

(December 1849), 670–71. The title was later changed, and the essay is usually referred to by this revised title—"The Nigger Question."

28. Ibid.

29. Ibid. Carlyle's "Negro Question" anticipated Dickens's savage caricature, in *Bleak House*, of Mrs. Jellyby, the telescopic philanthropist who grossly neglects her family to pursue improbable charities for an obscure African tribe.

30. John Stuart Mill, "The Negro Question," *Fraser's Magazine*, XLI (January 1950), 29.

31. See Geoffrey Dutton, *The Hero as Murderer: The Life of Edward John Eyre, Australian Explorer and Governor of Jamaica, 1815–1901* (1967), 283.

32. Harrison: Christine Bolt, *Victorian Attitudes to Race* (1971), 84; Beesly: ibid., 83; Huxley: Dutton, *The Hero as Murderer*, 355.

33. For one anti-imperialist text, see a work by the prominent Methodist preacher and widely traveled missionary John Beecham: *Colonization: Being Remarks on Colonization in General, with an Examination of the Proposals of the Association which has been formed for Colonizing New Zealand* (1838), 3–4. Such voices of reason and restraint grew fainter with each decade.

34. Josiah Strong, *Our Country: Its Possible Future and Its Present Crisis* (1885), 175. The version of racism to which Strong subscribed was atypical: he saw positive value in "race mixture"—the mixture not of blacks and whites, but of Europeans with various ethnic backgrounds. In *Social Evolution*, the Social Darwinist Benjamin Kidd argued that the difference between the "restless, aggressive, high-pitched life" of the white races and that of the "careless, shiftless, easily satisfied negro of the United States or West Indies" was indelible and only growing larger (p. 56). Thomas Hughes, author of *Tom Brown's Schooldays*, was in full agreement, and his response documents how convenient this sort of ideology could be. "I was greatly delighted with the treatment [in Kidd's *Social Evolution*] of the 'nigger' problem, and to be fortified in my faith that our occupation of India and Egypt is only 'a part of the cosmic order of things which we have no power to alter'!" Hughes to George Macmillan, March 3, 1894, D. P. Crook, *Benjamin Kidd: Portrait of a Social Darwinist* (1984), 89.

35. Carl Peters, "Kolonialpolitische Korrespondenz," in Hans-Ulrich Wehler, *Bismarck und der Imperialismus* (1969; 4th ed., 1976), 333.

36. Carl Peters, *Die Gründung von Deutsch-Ostafrika* (1906), 253.

37. Ibid., 252.

38. Roundell: Bolt, *Victorian Attitudes to Race,* 105; Jameson: Robert I. Rotberg, with Miles F. Shore, *The Founder: Cecil Rhodes and the Pursuit of Power* (1988), 431.

39. Sydney Olivier, a British socialist and distinguished public servant who was intimately acquainted with these issues (he was to become governor of Jamaica), wrote before the First World War, "Under all these diverse conditions one complaint on the part of the White is constant: that the Black man is lazy." *White Capital and Coloured Labour* (1910), 6.

40. The commissioners looking into these charges had amassed "one long narrative of the most gruesome atrocities, which includes a lengthy list of murders, mutilation of limbs, acts of cannibalism, rape, and deaths caused by floggings administered with unexampled severity." Barbara Emerson, *Leopold II of the Belgians: King of Colonialism* (1979), 249.

41. P. Leutwein, "Anhang. Die Unruhen in Deutsch-Südwest-Afrika," in "Simplex africanus," comp., *Mit der Schutztruppe durch Deutsch-Afrika* (1905), 197.

42. Horst Drechsler, *Südwestafrika unter deutscher Kolonialherrschaft. Der Kampf der Herero und Nama gegen den deutschen Imperialismus (1884–1915)* (1966; 2nd ed., 1984), 156.

43. Ibid., 159.

44. George Dunlap Crothers, *The German Elections of 1907* (1941), 179.

45. Walter Bagehot, *Physics and Politics* (1872; American ed., 1873), 190–91.

46. Hartmann, 1878: Robert Hartmann, *Verhandlungen der Berliner Gesellschaft für Anthropologie, Ethnologie und Urgeschichte,* ed. Rudolf Virchow, X (1878), 303; Hartmann, 1876, and Mortillet: Jacques Barzun, *Race: A Study in Superstition* (1937; rev. ed., 1965), 103.

47. William James, *The Varieties of Religious Experience: A Study in Human Nature* (1902), 77; Josiah Royce, "Race Question and Race Prejudice," *International Journal of Ethics,* XVI (April 1906), 285.

48. Salomon Reinach, *L'Origine des aryens (histoire d'une controverse)* (1892), 81, 36, 71, 40, 7, 73, 47, 90.

49. William Graham Sumner, "War," *War and Other Essays,* ed. Albert Galloway Keller (1911), 12, 11.

50. Ibid., 24–25.

51. William Gladstone, "The Sclavonic Provinces of the Ottoman Empire" (1877 lecture), *The Gladstone Diaries,* ed. M. R. D. Foot and H. C. G. Matthew, 11 vols. so far (1968–   ), vol. IX, *1875–1880* (1986), xv.

52. Jean Finot, *Le Préjugé des races* (1905; 2nd ed., 1906), 5, 15, 24–32, 354–62, 505. The book went through four French editions and was quickly translated into German, Spanish, and English. In 1907, President Theodore Roosevelt was reading and citing it as an authority on depopulation. See Roosevelt to Albert Shaw, April 3, 1907, *The Letters of Theodore Roosevelt,* sel. and ed. Elting G. Morison, with John M. Blum and Alfred D. Chandler, Jr., 8 vols. (1951–54), V, 637.

53. Anatole France, *Sur la pierre blanche* (1903; ed. 1950), 25.

54. Franz Boas, "Changes in Bodily Form of Descendants of Immigrants" (1912), *Race, Language and Culture* (1940), 68.

55. I am drawing in this paragraph on C. Vann Woodward's classic *The Strange Career of Jim Crow* (1955; 3rd rev. ed., 1974).

56. Ibid., 20.

57. See ibid., 45–46.

58. Lewis H. Blair, *The Prosperity of the South Dependent upon the Elevation of the Negro* (1889), 60.

59. Woodward, *Strange Career of Jim Crow,* 96.

60. Ibid., 67.

61. Ibid., 81.

3. Manliness: Ideal and Trauma

1. Charles Kingsley, "Heroism," *Sanitary and Social Lectures and Essays* (1880), 225–26.

2. February 14, 1831, Johann Peter Eckermann, *Gespräche mit Goethe in den letzten Jahren seines Lebens,* in Johann Wolfgang von Goethe, *Gedenkausgabe der Werke, Briefe und Gespräche,* ed. Ernst Beutler, 27 vols. (1948–71), XXIV, 448.

3. William James, *The Varieties of Religious Experience: A Study in Human Nature* (1902), 142n.

4. Henry James, *The Bostonians* (1886; intro. Lionel Trilling, 1952), 289.

5. See Paul Bourget, "La Maladie de la volonté—une guérison," *Oeuvres,* 9 vols. (1899–1911), I, 497–99.

6. Otto Julius Bierbaum, Introduction to A. von S. [pseud.], *Felix Schnabels Universitätsjahre oder der deutsche Student. Ein Beitrag zur Sittengeschichte des neunzehnten Jahrhunderts* (1895; ed. 1907), xiii, xv.

7. G. Stanley Hall, *Adolescence: Its Psychology and Its Relations to Physiology, Anthropology, Sociol-*

ogy, Sex, Crime, Religion and Education, 2 vols. (1904), I, 216–18; Georges Sorel, *Reflections on Violence* (1906; tr. T. E. Hulme, 1915), 82; Gustav Ratzenhofer, *Soziologie. Positive Lehre von den menschlichen Wechselbeziehungen* (1907), 108–9.

8. Anthony Trollope, *The Duke's Children* (1880; ed. Hermione Lee, 1983), 20, 15 [chs. 3, 2].

9. E. T. A. Hoffmann, "Don Juan. Eine fabelhafte Begebenheit, die sich mit einem reisenden Enthusiasten zugetragen," *Fantasiestücke in Collots Manier* (1814), in *Sämtliche Werke,* ed. Leopold Hirschberg, 14 vols. (1922), VII, 71–83; quotation at 73.

10. Grace Greenwood, *Haps and Mishaps of a Tour in Europe* (1854), 1–2.

11. Since the first observer was Walt Whitman, his appraisal may be explained by an understandable tendentiousness. See Richard Ellmann, *Oscar Wilde* (1988), 170. The second observer, expressing the opposite view, was the mother of one of Wilde's friends at Oxford, Bodley. Ibid., 178n. (See also ibid., 206, for a reference to Wilde's "manly chest.")

12. Byron to [John Cam Hobhouse], November 16, 1811, *Lord Byron: Selected Letters and Journals,* ed. Leslie A. Marchand (1982), 56.

13. Thomas Babington Macaulay, *The History of England from the Accession of James II,* 5 vols. (1849–61; American ed., n.d.), I, 306; Walter Bagehot, *Physics and Politics* (1872; American ed., 1873), 61.

14. Charles Dickens, *The Life and Adventures of Martin Chuzzlewit* (1843–44; ed. P. N. Furbank, 1968), 263, 353, 660 [ch. 12, 17, 37]. Anthony Trollope was, if anything, even more generous with this accolade. See esp. *Doctor Thorne* (1858; ed. David Skilton, 1980), 12, 166, 271, 318, 371 [ch. 1, 12, 20, 24, 28]. Other Trollope novels, like *The Prime Minister* (1876) would yield even larger harvests.

15. "Haunted," *Plays and Poems of W. S. Gilbert,* pref. Deems Taylor (1932), 928.

16. William James to John C. Gray, November 23, 1899, *The Letters of William James,* ed. by his son Henry James, 2 vols. (1920), II, 108.

17. Basil Willey, "J. A. Froude," *More Nineteenth Century Studies: A Group of Honest Doubters* (1956), 110, 133. The victim would later become a prolific English historian and outspoken religious doubter. In the preface to her novel *Cecil,* the fashionable English novelist Catherine Gore, clearly worried about her reviewers' fairness and good will, tries to forestall them by describing them as "nothing generous,—nothing manly in their nature." *Cecil; or, The Adventures of a Coxcomb,* 3 vols. (1841), I, vi.

18. See Henry James, "The Picture Season in London" (1877) and "The Grosvenor Gallery" (1878), *The Painter's Eye,* ed. John L. Sweeney (1956), 144–47, 161–64. In contrast, it is exceedingly difficult to discover what James had in mind when he applauded Jean Louis Ernest Meissonier's paintings for showing "the *manliest finish conceivable.*" "The Wallace Collection in Bethnal Green" (1873), ibid., 75.

19. "On Men and Pictures: A Propos of a Walk in the Louvre" (June 1841), *The Works of William Makepeace Thackeray,* Centenary Biographical Edition, 26 vols. (1910–11), XXV, 261.

20. The words are *"bestimmt, gedrängt, schmucklos und männlich."* Gisela Dischner, *Caroline und der Jenaer Kreis* (1979), 83.

21. Thomas Babington Macaulay, "Machiavelli" (1825), *Critical and Miscellaneous Essays* (rev. ed., 7 vols. in 5, 1879), I, 97–98.

22. Gomperz to Ferdinand von Saar, September 18, 1902, *Theodor Gomperz. Ein Gelehrtenleben im Bürgertum der Franz-Josefs-Zeit. Auswahl seiner Briefe und Aufzeichnungen, 1869–1912* (ed. Heinrich Gomperz; newly ed. Robert A. Kann, 1974), Österreichische Akademie der Wissenschaften. Philosophisch-Historische Klasse, Sitzungsberichte, vol. CCVC, 358.

23. William James to Margaret James, May 26, 1900, *Letters,* II, 130.

24. Linton: George Somes Layard, *Mrs. Lynn Linton, Her Life, Letters and Opinions* (1901), 260; "manly breast": Dickens, *Martin Chuzzlewit*, 746 [ch. 43].

25. Benjamin Disraeli, *Sybil; or, The Two Nations* (1845; World's Classics ed., 1926), 29 [book I, ch. 5].

26. Heinrich Heine, *Die Romantische Schule* (1835), in *Sämtliche Schriften*, ed. Klaus Briegleb et al., 6 vols. (1968–76), III, 379.

27. Morris to Aglaia Coronio, March 1875, E. P. Thompson, *William Morris: Romantic to Revolutionary* (1955), 204.

28. Charles Wagner, *Courage* (1892; tr. 1984), 151, 156. In 1856, the British Chartist Robert Lowery wrote resentfully, "It is in the very nature of the intelligent and virtuous to feel self-respect, and the claims of manhood as man." He was objecting to superior spirits too snobbish to extend the suffrage to craftsmen. Brian Harrison, *Peaceable Kingdom: Stability and Change in Modern Britain* (1982), 193.

29. *Oliver Cromwell's Letters and Speeches, with Elucidations*, in *The Centenary Edition of the Works of Thomas Carlyle*, 30 vols. (1898–1923), VI, 265.

30. Georg Moritz Ebers, *The Story of My Life from Childhood to Manhood* (1893; tr. Mary J. Safford, 1893), 141.

31. Joseph Ruggles Wilson to Thomas Woodrow Wilson, December 22, 1877, Edwin A. Weinstein, *Woodrow Wilson: A Medical and Psychological Biography* (1981), 44.

32. Ludwig Gurlitt, *Erziehung zur Mannhaftigkeit* (1907), 6–7; Friedrich Wilhelm Foerster, *Lebensführung. ein Buch für junge Menschen* (1909; ed. 1910), 53, 96; Hall, *Adolescence*, I, 218 (though he quickly adds, that bad as overpugnacity is, "a scrapping boy is better than one who funks a fight"); Thackeray, Preface, *The History of Pendennis* (1848–50), in *Works*, III, iv.

33. Francis Galton, "Eugenics: Its Definition, Scope and Aims" *Sociological Papers*, 2 vols. (1905–6), I, 45–46.

34. The book's English and American editions are listed in Edward C. Mack and W. H. G. Armytage, *Thomas Hughes: The Life of the Author of "Tom Brown's Schooldays"* (1952), 294–95.

35. Thomas Hughes, *Tom Brown's Schooldays* (1857; ed. 1913), 5, 20 [part I, ch. 1, 2]. For the match, see part I, ch. 5.

36. Ibid., 55, 158 [part I, ch. 3, 8].

37. Ibid., 121, 195, 123, 144 [part I, ch. 7; part 2, ch. 1; part I, ch. 7, 8].

38. Thomas Hughes, *Tom Brown at Oxford* (1861; ed. 1914), 99–100 [ch. 11]. In 1858, Hughes added a preface to *Tom Brown's Schooldays* in which he reprinted a long letter from a friend who had criticized the book for not denouncing bullying more sternly. Hughes's response was not wholly responsive, but a sign that he was aware of a problem: "Boyishness in the highest sense is not incompatible with seriousness,—or earnestness, if you like the word better." Preface, *Tom Brown's Schooldays* (ed. 1858), xlvii.

39. Thomas Hughes, *The Manliness of Christ* (1879), 9.

40. Ibid., 9–11.

41. Ibid., 34, 138.

42. Ibid., 27.

43. See ibid., 36.

44. John Martineau, Kingsley's loyal disciple and close friend, whose "tender recollections" Kingsley's widow later printed, discovered in his master "with all his man's strength," a "deep vein of *woman*," a "nervous sensitiveness, and intensity of sympathy," and, what was more, a "tender, delicate, soothing touch." *Charles Kingsley: His Letters and Memories of His Life*, ed. by his wife, 2 vols. (1876; ed. 1879), I, 240. W. R. Greg saw this side of Kingsley quite as clearly. There

was a certain "tenderness" in Kingsley, he thought, that was, though not profound, "manly, prompt, and genuine." "Kingsley and Carlyle" (1860), *Literary and Social Judgments* (1873), 119.

45. See Kingsley, "Heroism," 231, 237–38, 252.

46. Elizabeth Barrett Browning to Mrs. Martin [September 2, 1852]. *The Letters of Elizabeth Barrett Browning,* ed. Frederic G. Kenyon, 2 vols. (1897), II, 83; Elizabeth Barrett Browning to Mary Russell Mitford, August 20, 21, 1855, ibid., 134.

47. Thackeray, *Vanity Fair* (1848), in *Works,* I, 369 [ch. 30].

48. Stifter to Gustav Heckenast, December 17, 1860, *Adalbert Stifters Leben und Werk in Briefen und Dokumenten,* ed. K. G. Fischer (1962), 464.

49. "The Suppressed Sex" (1868), quoted in Lee Holcombe, *Victorian Ladies at Work: Middle-Class Working Women in England and Wales, 1850–1914* (1973), 9–10.

50. Thackeray, "Small Beer Chronicle" (July 1861), *Works,* XX, 135–36.

51. Thackeray, *Pendennis, Works,* III, 102, 595, 785 [ch. 7, 57, 75]. In this and the preceding two paragraphs, I am indebted to the pioneering study by Mario Praz, *The Hero in Eclipse in Victorian Fiction* (1952; tr. Angus Davidson, 1956).

52. Peter Gay, *Style in History* (1974), 122n.

53. Bülow to Eduard von Welz, February 2, 1875, *Briefe und Schriften,* ed. Marie von Bülow, (1895–96; 2nd ed., 1896–1908), vol. V (1904), *1872–1880,* 250–51. Here is the central portion of this almost untranslatable statement in the original: "Die Zeiten des Lakaienthums, des Waschlappenthums, des Kaninchenthums, des Molluskenthums für den Künstler und den leider bisher unter ihnen—den Künstlern—am meisten nachhinkenden, am stärksten durch Charakterlosigkeit hervorragenden Musiker—sind vorüber."

54. Bülow to Louise von Welz, June 6, 1877, ibid., 409.

55. *Mary Chesnut's Civil War,* ed. C. Vann Woodward (1981), 86.

56. This thoroughly unbourgeois attitude was fairly widespread. In 1812, when Sam Houston joined the American army to fight in the war against Britain, his mother handed him a musket and told him: "Never disgrace it; for remember, I had rather all my sons should fill one honorable grave, than that one of them should turn his back to save his life." As a token of her earnestness, she handed her son a gold ring that had "Honor" engraved in it. Bertram Wyatt-Brown, *Southern Honor: Ethics and Behavior in the Old South* (1982), 51.

57. See John K. Campbell, *Honour, Family and Patronage: A Study of Institutions and Moral Values in a Greek Mountain Community* (1964), 269–70.

58. See Thomas Mann, *Buddenbrooks. Verfall einer Familie* (1901), part 3, ch. 15. For more poignant representation of this sort of *mésalliance* between a young aristocrat and a working-class woman in Berlin, see Theodor Fontane's charming and touching novel *Irrungen, Wirrungen* (1888).

59. Kingsley to Sir Henry Taylor, December 26, 1868, *Letters,* II, 214.

60. Oliver Wendell Holmes, Jr., "Memorial Day," *Occasional Speeches,* comp. Mark DeWolfe Howe (1962), 10.

T.R.: Extremist of the Center

1. David McCullough, *The Path between the Seas: The Creation of the Panama Canal, 1870–1914* (1977), 490.

2. Richard Hofstadter, *The American Political Tradition and the Men Who Made It* (1948), 205.

3. David McCullough, *Mornings on Horseback* (1981), 15.

4. Ibid., 29–30. No student of T.R. has neglected the incident. For one brilliant brief exploration, see Hofstadter, *American Political Tradition,* 207.

5. See ibid., 209–10.

6. Henry Adams, *The Education of Henry Adams* (1918; ed. James Truslow Adams, 1931), 417–18.

7. Henry F. Pringle, *Theodore Roosevelt: A Biography* (1931), 494.

8. "appear to do": Lodge to T.R., September 27, 1902, *Selections from the Correspondence of Theodore Roosevelt and Henry Cabot Lodge, 1884–1918,* 2 vols. (1925), I, 532; hitting his quarry: Pringle, *Theodore Roosevelt,* 345.

9. Theodore Roosevelt, *An Autobiography* (1913), 57.

10. Adams, *Education of Henry Adams,* 166; Roosevelt, *Autobiography,* 57.

11. McCullough, *Mornings on Horseback,* 260.

12. "ashamed": T.R. to William Tudor, March 28, 1898, Joseph Bucklin Bishop, *Theodore Roosevelt and His Time Shown in His Own Letters,* 2 vols. (1920), I, 88; "parlor Jingoes": T.R. to Sturgis Bigelow, March 29, 1898, ibid., 103.

13. T.R. to Amos Pinchot, November 3, 1916, *The Letters of Theodore Roosevelt,* sel. and ed. Elting E. Morison, with John M. Blum and Alfred D. Chandler, Jr., 8 vols. (1951–54), VIII, 1122.

14. T.R. to John Albert Sleicher, February 25, 1906, ibid., V, 167. This was a frequent refrain, especially during his presidency and after. See T.R. to Frank A. Munsey, January 16, 1912, ibid., VII, 481; and T.R. to Arthur Hamilton Lee, December 26, 1907, ibid., VI, 875.

15. T.R. to F. S. Oliver, August 9, 1906, ibid., 352; T.R. to Henry Lee Higginson, March 28, 1907, ibid., 633; T.R. to William Howard Taft, March 9, 1909 (upon leaving the White House), ibid., VI, 1543; T.R. to Nicholas Murray Butler, September 20, 1907, ibid., V, 797; T.R. to Henry White, November 27, 1907, ibid., 859.

16. George E. Mowry, *The Era of Theodore Roosevelt, 1900–1912* (1958), 111.

17. T.R. to George Horace Lorimer, May 12, 1906, *Letters,* V, 263.

18. "The World Movement" (1910), *The Works of Theodore Roosevelt,* ed. Hermann Hagedorn, 20 vols. (1926), XIV, 275.

19. Preface to Edward, Duke of York, "The Master of Game" (1904), ibid., 482.

20. T.R. to George Otto Trevelyan, March 9, 1905 (just after his inauguration for a second term), *Letters,* IV, 1132.

21. T.R. to Kermit Roosevelt, October 2, 1903, *Theodore Roosevelt's Letters to His Children,* ed. Joseph Bucklin Bishop (1919), 60–61; T.R. to Theodore Roosevelt, Jr., October 4, 1903, ibid., 63.

22. T.R. to Gertrude Tyler Carow (his mother-in-law), October 18, 1890, *Letters,* I, 234.

23. T.R. to Edward Sanford Martin, November 26, 1900, ibid., III, 1443.

24. Theodore Roosevelt, "A Colonial Survival" (1892), *Works,* XIV, 372. Hofstadter has noted this important passage. in *American Political Tradition,* 209.

25. T.R. to Owen Wister, April 27, 1906, *Letters,* V, 222. An astute American lawyer, William Nelson Cromwell (who was deeply involved in the murky legal, financial, and diplomatic prehistory of the Panama Canal), knew exactly what would please the president when he praised T.R. in late 1903 for his "virile and masterful policy." Pringle, *Theodore Roosevelt,* 318.

26. Theodore Roosevelt, "Biological Analogies in History," a Romanes Lecture (1910), *Works,* XIV, 103.

27. Theodore Roosevelt, "The Search for Truth in a Reverent Spirit" (1911), ibid., 419.

28. Theodore Roosevelt, "Washington's Forgotten Maxim" (1897), address to the Naval War College, ibid., XV, 255–56.

29. See Theodore Roosevelt, "Biological Analogies in History," *Works,* XIV, 65–106, esp. 69–70.

30. Theodore Roosevelt, "Social Evolution" (1894), ibid., 107, 112.

31. "Dagos": T.R. to John Hay, September 2, 1904, *Letters,* IV, 917; "Creatures," "jack rabbits": T.R. to John Hay, August 17, 1903, ibid., 567; "inferior to the whites": T.R. to Owen Wister, April 27, 1906, ibid., V, 226; Tower family: T.R. to Henry Cabot Lodge, September 11, 1899, ibid., I, 1069; "diminishing birth rate": Pringle, *Theodore Roosevelt,* 471.

32. Theodore Roosevelt, Eighth Annual Message to Congress, December 8, 1908. *Works,* XVII, 579–80.

33. "abhor a corruptionist": T.R. to Ray Stannard Baker, November 28, 1905, *Letters,* V, 100; French Revolution: see T.R. to Samuel Sidney McClure, October 4, 1905, ibid., 45.

34. "passions of men": T.R. to George Otto Trevelyan, August 18, 1906, ibid., 366; "jealousy and hatred": T.R. to the novelist Winston Churchill, August 18, 1906, ibid., 378; "human soul": T.R. to James Schoolcraft Sherman, October 8, 1906, ibid., 452.

TWO: Pathologies

1. Charles Holmes to Annie E. Slade, April 16, 1865, Holmes Family Papers, Box 1. Yale University Library, Manuscripts and Archives.

2. Ibid.

3. Ibid.

4. Ibid.

5. Ibid.

1. In Search of Civilized Rationales

1. Johann Wolfgang von Goethe, *Dichtung und Wahrheit,* in *Gedenkausgabe der Werke, Briefe und Gespräche,* ed. Ernst Beutler, 27 vols. (1948–71), X, 576.

2. Ernest Bertrand, "Essai sur la moralité comparative des diverses classes de la population et principalement des classes ouvrières," *Journal de la Société de statistique de Paris,* XIII (October 1872), 271, 268.

3. See Peter Alexeivich Kropotkin, *The Conquest of Bread* (1892; ed. and tr. 1906), ch. 8, "Objections."

4. Louis Günther, *Die Idee der Wiedervergeltung in der Geschichte und Philosophie des Strafrechts. Ein Beitrag zur universalhistorischen Entwicklung desselben,* 2 vols. (1889–91), II, x. In 1839, a member of a Prussian commission studying the penal law argued that "in the opinion of the common people," quite as much as in the criminal's own mind, punishment should be "an act of retribution." Richard J. Evans, "Öffentlichkeit und Autorität: Zur Geschichte der Hinrichtungen in Deutschland vom Allgemeinen Landrecht bis zum Dritten Reich," in Heinz Reif, ed., *Räuber, Volk und Obrigkeit. Studien zur Geschichte der Kriminalität in Deutschland seit dem 18. Jahrhundert* (1984), 219.

5. "With remarkable consistency, myths tell of the origins of man in a fall, a crime that is often a bloody act of violence." Walter Burkert, *Homo Necans: The Anthropology of Ancient Greek Sacrificial Ritual and Myth* (1972; tr. Peter Bing, 1983), 21–22.

6. Theodor Mommsen, *Römisches Strafrecht* (1899), 901.

7. Immanuel Kant, *Grundlegung zur Metaphysik der Sitten* (1785), in *Werke in sechs Bänden,* ed. Wilhelm Weischedel (1960–64), IV, 598 [par. 36]; see also *Metaphysik der Sitten. Rechtslehre,* part II, *Das öffentliche Recht,* ibid., 455.

8. Claude-Joseph Tissot, *Le Droit pénal étudié dans ses principes, dans ses usages et les lois des divers*

peuples du monde; ou, Introduction philosophique et historique à l'étude du droit criminel, 2 vols. (1860; 3rd. ed., 1888), passim; quotation at II, 591.

9. Thomas Babington Macaulay, The History of England from the Accession of James II, 5 vols. (1849–61; American ed., n.d.), I, 383–85 [ch. 3].

10. The Times (London), March 11, 1846, p. 3. Philip Collins notes that Dickens quoted this passage in the same year and was not convinced by it—not yet. Dickens and Crime (1962; 2nd ed., 1964), 226.

11. Patricia O'Brien, The Promise of Punishment: Prisons in Nineteenth-Century France (1982), 3. Some years after, Harriet Martineau said much the same thing in Britain: "The treatment of the Guilty is all important as an index to the moral notions of a society." Martin J. Wiener, Reconstructing the Criminal: Culture, Law, and Policy in England, 1830–1914 (1990), 4. And several decades later, in Germany, George Jellinek wrote, "The penal law is perhaps the best measure of culture there is." Die sozialethische Bedeutung von Recht, Unrecht, und Strafe (1908), 114.

12. "Model Prisons" (1850), The Centenary Edition of the Works of Thomas Carlyle, 30 vols. (1899–1923), XX, 52, 55, 56.

13. Charles Dickens, The Personal History of David Copperfield (1850; ed. Trevor Blount, 1966), 921–29; quotation at 922 [ch. 61].

14. The Mikado, in Plays and Poems of W. S. Gilbert, pref. Deems Taylor (1932), 382 [act II].

15. See Zucker, "Einige criminalistische Zeit- und Streitfragen der Gegenwart," Der Gerichtssaal, XLIV (1891), 1. He was quoting Gustav Geib, Lehrbuch des deutschen Strafrechts (1861–62), 312.

16. Bernhard Düsing, Die Geschichte der Abschaffung der Todesstrafe in der Bundesrepublik Deutschland (1952), 90–91.

17. Charles de Secondat, Baron de Montesquieu, De l'esprit des lois (1751), in Oeuvres complètes, ed. Roger Caillois 2 vols. (1949–51), II, 327 [book VI, ch. 16]; Cesare Beccaria, Dei delitti e delle pene (1764; ed. Franco Venturi, 1965), 19 [ch. 6]. Readers of Charles Kingsley's once-famous children's book The Water Babies (1863) may recall the severe Mrs. Bedonebyasyoudid, and note that proportionality can have harsh contours. It all depends on who defines it.

18. Gustave de Beaumont and Alexis de Tocqueville, Du système pénitentiaire aux États-Unis, et de son application en France, 2 vols. (1833; 2nd ed., 1836), I, 166.

19. Jeremy Bentham, The Theory of Legislation, from the original French edition of Étienne Dumont (1802; tr Richard Hildreth, 1864; ed. C. K. Ogden, 1931), 76.

20. Beccaria, Dei delitti e delle pene, 11–12 [chs. 1–2].

21. Voltaire, Commentaire sur le livre des délits et des peines (1766), in Oeuvres complètes, ed. Louis Moland, 52 vols. (1877–85), XXV, 572–73.

22. In 1739, David Hume had argued that "the science of man," hitherto sadly neglected, was beyond question "the only solid foundation for the other sciences." Its object was nothing less than "human nature." A Treatise of Human Nature: Being an Attempt to Introduce the Experimental Method of Reasoning into Moral Subjects (1739–40; ed. L. A. Selby-Bigge, 1888), xx.

23. See Hermann Mannheim, Introduction to Pioneers in Criminology (1960), 1.

24. Tissot, Le Droit pénal, I, 221–22, 227; Günther, Die Idee der Wiedervergeltung, I, 5; Jellinek, Die sozialethische Bedeutung von Recht, 98.

25. James Fitzjames Stephen, Liberty, Equality, Fraternity (1873; 2nd ed., 1874; ed. R. J. White, 1967), 148, 152. A few years later, Stephen reiterated this view in his authoritative history of criminal law. See A History of the Criminal Law of England, 3 vols. (1883), II, 81.

26. Moreau-Christophe: Gordon Wright, Between the Guillotine and Liberty: Two Centuries of the Crime Problem in France (1983), 66; Lotze: Ted Honderich, Punishment: The Supposed Justifications (1969; rev. ed., 1971), 29n.

2. Between Prisons and Pathos

1. W. R. Greg, "The Correction of Juvenile Offenders," *Edinburgh Review*, CI (April 1855), 383–84.

2. Ibid.

3. Gordon Wright, *Between the Guillotine and Liberty: Two Centuries of the Crime Problem in France* (1983), 63.

4. "Reformatory Schools," *Saturday Review*, VI (September 11, 1858), 250.

5. "The Knotty Problem," *Saturday Review*, II (June 7, 1856), 120. Some fifty years earlier, the *Saturday Review* wrote, people had discovered that the inherited system "was no longer endurable to modern feeling, and would no longer bear the searching scrutiny of modern reason." In consequence, as the "tendency of the age set strongly in the direction of mercy and forgiveness," statesmen had rendered some penal procedures "a little less shocking." Thus "we abolished hanging—we shrank from whipping—common prudence, common decency, and common humanity induced us to improve our prisons till they became, almost inevitably, places of comparative comfort." But, a few "theoretical jurists" apart, no one had established where the "principles" of the old jurisprudence had gone astray, let alone how one might construct a better one. Ibid.

6. Lynds: Gustave de Beaumont and Alexis de Tocqueville, *On the Penitentiary System in the United States and Its Application in France* (tr. Francis Lieber, 1833; ed. Herman R. Lantz, 1964), 163; Sue: see Wright, *Between the Guillotine and Liberty*, 67; German visitor: R. [pseud.], "Das Zellengefängniss der jugendlichen Verbrecher in Paris," *Die Gartenlaube*, XII (1864), 472.

7. A note from ca. 1773—three years before Bentham published his first book, *A Fragment on Government*. Élie Halévy, *The Growth of Philosophical Radicalism* (1901–4; tr. Mary Morris, 1928), 55.

8. Jeremy Bentham, *The Theory of Legislation*, from the original French edition of Etienne Dumont (1802; tr. Richard Hildreth, 1864; ed. C. K. Ogden, 1931), 354.

9. Ibid.

10. John Stuart Mill, "Bentham" (1838), *Dissertations and Discussions Political, Philosophical, and Historical*, 2 vols. (1859), I, 332.

11. Samuel Gridley Howe, *Report of a Minority of the Special Committee of the Boston Prison Disciplinary Society, Appointed at the Annual Meeting, May 27, 1845* (1846), 68.

12. Ibid., 15.

13. Gustave de Beaumont and Alexis de Tocqueville, *Du système pénitentiaire aux États-Unis, et de son application en France*, 2 vols. (1833; 2nd ed., 1836), I, 352.

14. Beaumont and Tocqueville, *On the Penitentiary System in the United States*, 164.

15. Howe, *Report of a Minority*, 25.

16. "Treatment of Crime—Deterring Punishments," *Saturday Review*, III (January 17, 1857), 47.

17. *Archives*: Ruth Harris, *Murders and Madness: Medicine, Law, and Society in the "Fin de Siècle"* (1989), 87; Napoleonic decree: see ibid., 138.

18. This is Isaac Ray's summary. *A Treatise on the Medical Jurisprudence of Insanity* (1838; 5th ed., 1871), 45.

19. Ray, Preface to the fifth edition, ibid., iii.

20. See, for example, Cesare Lombroso, *Crime: Its Causes and Remedies* (1899; tr. Henry P. Morton, 1911), xiii, 432, 426. Actually, one of Lombroso's best-known disciples, Enrico Ferri, was responsible for this coinage. Another disciple, the criminologist and historian William Ferrero, became Lombroso's son-in-law.

21. Ibid.

22. Havelock Ellis, "Criminal Anthropology (Criminal Psychology, Criminal Biology, Criminology, etc.)," in D. Hack Tuke, *A Dictionary of Psychological Medicine*, 2 vols. (1892), I, 288–92;
Hippolyte Taine, letter of 1887 to Lombroso, quoted by Lombroso in *Crime*, 428; Gabriel Tarde,
quoted in Harris, *Murders and Madness*, 86.

23. W. Douglas Morrison, Introduction to Cesare Lombroso and William Ferrero, *The Female
Offender* (1893; tr. 1895), vii.

24. Harris, *Murders and Madness*, 121.

25. Louis Proal, *Passion and Criminality in France: A Legal and Literary Study* (1900; tr. A. R.
Allison, 1901), 679.

26. Hans Gross, "Vorwort des Herausgebers," to Bruno Meyer, "Homosexualität und Strafrecht," *Archiv für Kriminal-Anthropologie und Kriminalistik*, XLIV (1911), 249–54.

27. See Émile Durkheim, *The Division of Labor in Society* (1893; tr. George Simpson, 1933), ch.
2; Ferdinand Tönnies, "Das Verbrechen als soziale Erscheinung," *Archiv für soziale Gesetzgebung
und Statistik*, VIII (1895), 329–44; Fritz Heine, "Sociale Rechtswissenschaft," *Freie Bühne für
modernes Leben*, I (March 19, 1890), 195.

3. The Bourgeois Conscience at Work

1. Alexander Innes Shand, *Half a Century; or, Changes in Men and Manners* (1888), 330.

2. Those murdered included Czar Alexander II and President Garfield, both assassinated in
1881; in addition, Irish secret societies and anarchists practicing propaganda of the deed claimed
other victims. *The Friends and Capital Punishment. 1883* (1883), 3–4.

3. For these four paragraphs, Charles E. Rosenberg, *The Trial of the Assassin Guiteau: Psychiatry
and Law in the Gilded Age* (1968), is authoritative; quotations at 227–28, 221.

4. See Robert A. Nye, *Crime, Madness, and Politics in Modern France: The Medical Concept of
National Decline* (1984), ch. 8; the cartoons are reproduced on pp. 274 and 275.

5. See Gordon Wright, *Between the Guillotine and Liberty: Two Centuries of the Crime Problem in
France* (1983), 172–73.

6. Hans Gross, "Anmerkung des Herausgebers," *Archiv für Kriminal-Anthropologie und Kriminalistik*, IX (1902), 15–16; Ernst Lohsing, "Abschaffung der Todesstrafe," ibid., 1–15; Paul Näcke,
"Gedanken eines Mediciners über die Todesstrafe," ibid., 321, 319, 323.

7. See Ernst Lohsing, "Todesstrafe und Standrecht," ibid., X (1903), 305–20.

8. See Ernst Lohsing, "Der Kampf um die Todesstrafe. Bemerkungen zur Juristentagdebatte,"
ibid., XLII (1911), 243–56; Schüle, "Der Kampf um die Todesstrafe," ibid., XLIII (1912), 303;
Ernst Lohsing, "Wider die Todesstrafe. Zur Abwehr gegen Prof. Dr. Schüle," ibid., XLVII
(1912), 300–306.

9. See N. M. Curtis, *Capital Crimes and the Punishments Prescribed Therefor by Federal and State
Laws and Those of Foreign Countries, with Statistics Relating to the Same* (1894), 6–11. This pamphlet,
compiled for the Judiciary Committee of the House of Representatives, also indicates that the
federal government shared with the states the authority to hand down death sentences, mainly for
piracy, but most of these sentences were commuted.

10. K. D'Olivecrona, *De la peine de mort* (1866; tr. Jules-Henri Kramer, 1868), 5; Francis Bishop,
"Thou Shalt Not Kill," a Paper upon the Law of Capital Punishment (1882), 1; Näcke, "Gedanken
eines Mediciners über die Todesstrafe," 317.

11. There is something distinctly defensive about these productions, on both sides; on occasion,
their authors liked to hide behind what they described as the urgent requests of their parishioners.

The Reverend William Patton, D.D., observed in an introductory paragraph to his homily on capital punishment, *Capital Punishment Sustained by Reason and the Word of God, Being the Substance of a Sermon Preached in the Spring Street Presbyterian Church, New York* (1842), that "the author has yielded to the many and urgent solicitations for its appearance in print, with the hope that it may aid in settling the agitated mind of the public on the main subject of discussion." The title page noted, "Published by Request." Similarly, a writer on the other side, A. D. Mayo, minister of the Congregational Society of Liberal Christians in Cleveland, put on the title page of *The Death Penalty: A Sermon Preached at Concert Hall on Sunday Morning, June 3, 1855* (1855), "Printed by Request of the Congregation." False modesty? Or recognition that they had really nothing new to say?

12. William Patton, *Capital Punishment Sustained by Reason and the Word of God*, 5, 30–31; John N. McLeod, *The Capital Punishment of the Murderer, an Unrepealed Ordinance of God; a Discourse* (1842), 13, 22. The copy of McLeod's pamphlet in the Yale University Library bears on its cover the handwritten legend "Rev. Dr. Patton with the respect of the Author."

13. Joseph F. Berg, *A Plea for the Divine Law against Murder* (1846), 13, 43.

14. Ibid., 15–16.

15. Moritz Müller, *Der unbedingte Ausspruch, dass die Todesstrafe eine Sünde vor Gott und Menschen sei, ist weiter nichts als ein leeres Gerede* (n.d.).

16. See two articles by Charles Dickens in *Household Words*: "Pet Prisoners," April 27, 1850; and "The Murdered Person," October 11, 1856.

17. George B. Cheever, *Capital Punishment. Argument, in Reply to J. L. O'Sullivan, Esq., in the Broadway Tabernacle, on the Evenings of January 27th, and February 3d and 17th* (1843), 29.

18. A. D. Mayo, *The Death Penalty*, 3 and passim. Sermonizing on capital punishment, the Reverend J. Weiss of New Bedford took as his text Luke 10:36, 37, in which Jesus invidiously compares an uncharitable priest and an equally uncharitable Levite with the good Samaritan coming upon a man who had been robbed and beaten and left on the side of the road, half dead: "Which now of these three, thinkest thou, was neighbor unto him that fell among the thieves? And he said, he that showeth mercy on him." Weiss, *Shall We Kill the Body, or Save the Soul? A Sermon upon Capital Punishment, Preached April 22, 1849* (1849), 3.

19. Henry S. Patterson, *A Brief Statement of the Argument for the Abolition of the Death Punishment in Twelve Essays* (1844), 2, 4.

20. Charles Lucas, *De la ratification à donner par l'Assemblée Nationale au décret d'abolition de la peine de mort en matière politique* (1848), 31; Lucas, *Du système pénal et du système répressif en général, de la peine de mort en particulier* (1827), 145; Lucas, *Le Droit de légitime défense dans la pénalité et dans la guerre et les congrès scientifiques internationaux réclamés par les trois réformes relatives au système pénitentiaire, à l'abolition de la peine de mort et à la civilisation de la guerre* (1873), 84–85.

21. Charles Neate, *Considerations on the Punishment of Death* (1857), 1, 37. Reviewing Neate's little book, the *Saturday Review*, predictably, remained unrepentant in its support of the death penalty as the supreme deterrent. Yet it paid Neate the tribute, unusual in its treatment of abolitionists, of praising the exceptionally able way he had argued for his position. "Mr. Neate on Capital Punishment," *Saturday Review*, III (April 25, 1857), 375–76.

22. Charles Phillips, *Vacation Thoughts on Capital Punishment* (1856; 4th ed., 1858), 99–141; "Mr. Phillips on Capital Punishment," *Saturday Review*, II (November 15, 1856), 635–37, quotation at 637.

23. Karl Josef Mittermaier, *Die Todesstrafe nach den Ergebnissen der wissenschaftlichen Forschungen, der Fortschritte der Gesetzgebung und der Erfahrungen* (1862), 110, 110n; D'Olivecrona, *De la peine de mort*, 151; Howard Association, *Summarised Information on Capital Punishment* (n.d.), 348.

24. Moritz Müller, *Der Zweck erfordert das Mittel! Eine volksphilosophische Betrachtung über die Todesstrafe* (1870), 12–13. For the sword of Damocles, see Cesare Lombroso, *Crime: Its Causes and Remedies* (1899; tr. Henry P. Horton, 1911), 427. George B. Cheever anticipated Müller's views by more than two decades, putting the case succinctly: "There is nothing that can possibly check the spirit of murder, but the fear of death." *Capital Punishment,* 45.

25. Franz von Holtzendorff, *Das Verbrechen des Mordes und die Todesstrafe. Criminalpolitische und psychologische Untersuchungen* (1875), 122; see also Mittermaier, *Die Todesstrafe,* 104–6. As early as 1840, Mittermaier had already published an impressively detailed comparative study on the death penalty, *Die Todesstrafe nach dem neuesten Stande der Ansichten in England, Nordamerika, Frankreich, Belgien, Dänemark, Schweden, Russland, Italien und Deutschland über die Abschaffung dieser Strafart.*

26. David D. Cooper, *The Lesson of the Scaffold: The Public Execution Controversy in Victorian England* (1974), 35, 41; see also John Macrae Moir, ed., *Capital Punishment; Based on Professor Mittermaier's 'Todesstrafe,'* (1865), 29–30.

27. J. C. Bucknill, *Unsoundness of Mind in Relation to Criminal Acts* (1854: 2nd ed., 1857), 136, quoted in Roger Smith, *Trial by Medicine: Insanity and Responsibility in Victorian Trials* (1981), 28.

28. Edward Livingston, *Capital Punishment: Argument of Edward Livingston* (1847), 7.

29. Curtis, *Capital Crimes,* 12–13.

30. Louis P. Masur, *Rites of Execution: Capital Punishment and the Transformation of American Culture, 1776–1865* (1989), 96, 95.

31. Robert Rantoul, "House, No. 36. Commonwealth of Massachusetts. House of Representatives, Jan. 14, 1835," 16.

32. Lucas, *De la ratification à donner par l'Assemblée Nationale,* 45.

33. Cobden, Bright, Ewart, all in Cooper, *Lesson of the Scaffold,* 85.

34. "Public Executions," *Saturday Review,* II (August 9, 1856), 337; Wright, *Between the Guillotine and Liberty,* 169.

35. Karl von Holtei, *Vierzig Jahre,* 8 vols. (1843–50), I, 130–33.

36. Ibid.

37. Byron to [John Murray], May 30, 1817, *Byron's Letters and Journals,* ed. Leslie A. Marchand, 12 vols. (1973–82), V, 229–30.

38. Thackeray to his mother, July 18, 1840, *The Letters and Private Papers of William Makepeace Thackeray,* ed. Gordon N. Ray, 4 vols. (1945–46), I, 453; "Going to See a Man Hanged," *Fraser's Magazine* (August 1840), *The Works of William Makepeace Thackeray,* Centenary Biographical Edition, 26 vols. (1910–11), XXVI, 417–34.

39. Dickens, "A Letter to the Daily News," February 28, 1846; see Louis Blom-Cooper, ed., *The Law as Literature* (1961), 382–87.

40. The hostility was mutual. In 1849, Dickens characterized the "total abolitionists" as "utterly reckless and dishonest," while in the same paragraph calling the conduct of spectators at a public hanging "indescribably frightful." Dickens to W. W. F. de Cerjat, December 29, 1849, *The Letters of Charles Dickens,* vol. V, *1847–1849,* ed. Graham Storey and K. J. Fielding (1981), 683.

41. Paul Lindenberg, "Polizei und Verbrechertum in Berlin. Moabit," *Die Gartenlaube,* XL (1892), 734–35.

42. William Wordsworth, "Sonnets upon the Punishment of Death" (1841), sonnet VIII, lines 4–5.

43. See esp. Victor Brombert, *Victor Hugo and the Visionary Novel* (1984), 38, 250.

44. Hugo to M. Bost, November 17, 1862, *Écrits de Victor Hugo sur la peine de mort,* ed. Raymond Jean (1979), 171.

45. See Victor Brombert, *The Romantic Prison: The French Tradition* (1978), 88–89; Joseph Frank,

Dostoevsky: The Seeds of Revolt, 1821–1849 (1976), 109–10; Zola to Jean-Baptistin Baille (end of August–beginning of September 1860), Émile Zola, *Correspondance,* ed. B. H. Bakker, vol. I, *1858–1867* (1978), 230–34, 234n.

46. Victor Hugo, *Le Dernier Jour d'un condamné* (1829; ed. Roger Borderie, 1970), 358–61. On the basis of internal evidence, Victor Brombert has persuasively speculated that the prisoner's crime must have been parricide. But Hugo deliberately leaves the reader in the dark. Brombert, *Victor Hugo,* 32–33.

47. Zola to Jean-Baptistin Baille [end of August–beginning of September 1860], *Correspondance,* I, 231.

48. Hugo, Preface of 1832, *Le Dernier Jour d'un condamné,* 376, 403.

49. Brombert, *Victor Hugo,* picture insert between pp. 48 and 49.

4. The Pleasures of Pain

1. Gustav Stephan, *Die häusliche Erziehung in Deutschland während des achtzehnten Jahrhunderts* (1891), 133.

2. For *Fliegende Blätter,* see Walter Hävenick, *'Schläge' als Strafe. Ein Bestandteil der heutigen Familiensitte in volkskundlicher Sicht* (1964), 58. One so-called humorous illustration from the 1880s in another German periodical shows children playing school; one little girl, the teacher, holds a doll and lifts up its skirts to beat its bottom with a bunch of branches. "Die kleine Schulmeisterin," *Das neue Blatt,* XIII (1882), 78.

3. See "Abenteuer eines Junggesellen" in the trilogy *Tobias Knopp* (1875–77), in *Wilhelm Busch Gesamtausgabe,* ed. Friedrich Bohne, 4 vols. (1959), III, 29.

4. Busch, "Der kleine Pepi mit der neuen Hose" (1860), ibid., I, 92; "Der zu wachsame Hund" (1862), ibid., 150; "Der Bauer und das Kalb" (1863), ibid., 249; *Bilder zu Jobsiade* (1872), ibid., II, 304; "Schnurrdiburr oder die Bienen" (1869), ibid., 21; "Die Drachen" (1881), ibid., III, 442–45; *Plisch und Plum* (1882), ibid., 495. There are others.

5. Busch to Maria Anderson, April 23, [18]75, Wilhelm Busch, *Sämtliche Briefe,* ed. Friedrich Bohne, 2 vols. (1968), I, 140.

6. Morrill Wyman, *Progress in School Discipline. Corporal Punishment in the Public Schools. Addressed to the Citizens of Cambridge* [Massachusetts] (1867), 37.

7. Lyman Cobb, *The Evil Tendencies of Corporal Punishment as a Means of Moral Discipline in Families and Schools, Examined and Discussed* (1847), 7.

8. Henry Salt, "The Hymn of the Flagellomaniacs," *Consolations of a Faddist* (1906), 28.

9. Michel de Montaigne, "Of the Education of Children," *Complete Essays* (1580–95; ed. and tr. Donald A. Frame, 1958), 122–23 [book I, ch. 26]; Montaigne, "Cowardice, Mother of Cruelty," ibid., 523 [II, 27]. Montaigne plainly regarded this psychological insight as something of a commonplace: he opens the essay on cowardice with "I have often heard it said. . . ."

10. Salt, "Hymn of the Flagellomaniacs," 28.

11. Cobb, *Evil Tendencies of Corporal Punishment,* 9.

12. Horace Mann, "Report for 1839," *Annual Reports on Education,* ed. Mary Mann (1868), 57.

13. "actual rod": Association of Masters of the Boston Public Schools, *Remarks on the Seventh Annual Report of the Hon. Horace Mann, Secretary of the Massachusetts Board of Education* (1844), 121; "arm that wields them": Horace Mann, *Reply to the "Remarks" of Thirty-One Boston Schoolmasters on the Seventh Annual Report of the Secretary of the Massachusetts Board of Education* (1844), 133, 135.

14. Wyman, *Progress in School Discipline,* 11–12; Henry A. Drake, Chairman, Boston School Committee, *Report on Corporal Punishment in the Public Schools of the City of Boston* (1867), 6.

15. Ibid., 6, 24, 7, 22, 24.

16. Julius Beeger, "Die Disciplinargewalt der Schule," *Allgemeine Deutsche Lehrerzeitung*, no. 28 (July 9, 1876), 233, 231, 232.

17. Ibid., 232. "*In every case a judgment must be made about public education,*" Beeger said, "*the teachers are the competent experts*"; if a complaint against a punitive teacher should get into the courts, the judges must be advised by "*experts, that is to say, active teachers.*" Ibid., 233.

18. Ibid., 234; for the other epithets, see Wolfgang Scheibe, *Die Strafe als Problem der Erziehung* (1972), 177.

19. Eduard Sack, *Gegen die Prügel-Pädagogen* (1878), 13, 39. One of the witnesses Sack enlisted in his behalf was the celebrated German liberal and rationalist pedagogue Adolf Diesterweg, who had voiced his revulsion against flogging in no uncertain terms.

20. Sack was not the only one to notice. In the mid-1860s, an anonymous Austrian pamphleteer listed among the reasons for abolishing flogging that it was unworthy of the state, proved invariably ineffective, damaged victims physically and mentally—and led "to the most critical legal inequality." *Gegen die Prügelstrafe* (1866), 8. And as late as 1911, a contributor to a handbook on social policy for Germany's youth condemned legal corporal punishment as open to "the suspicion of class justice." [Nikolaus Hermann] Kriegsmann, "Prügelstrafe," *Encyklopädisches Handbuch des Kinderschutzes und der Jugendfürsorge*, ed. Th. Heller et al., 2 vols. (1911), II, 131.

21. Heinrich Heine, "Nachbemerkung zu dem Aufsatz: Körperliche Strafe" (1828), *Sämtliche Schriften*, ed. Klaus Briegleb et al., 6 vols. (1968–76), II, 648. In England the irony was pushed even further: it was mainly the sons of the upper classes who were still being flogged, while pupils in other schools were spared that punishment. But this distinction was limited to schoolboys. Advocates of flogging in imperial outposts certainly wanted to confine this punishment to the natives. In 1890, for example, Cecil Rhodes, then beginning his tenure as prime minister of Cape Colony, proposed a law subjecting native laborers to flogging for failure to work hard enough. See Robert I. Rotberg, in collaboration with Miles F. Shore, *The Founder: Cecil Rhodes and the Pursuit of Power* (1988), 359–60, 401, 450, 456.

22. Bartholomäus von Carneri, *Der moderne Mensch. Versuch über Lebensführung* (1890; 5th ed., 1901), 28; September 28, 1847, *The Gladstone Diaries*, ed. M. R. D. Foot and H. C. G. Matthew, 11 vols. so far (1968–   ), vol. III, *1840–1847* (1974), 656.

23. Wyman, *Progress in School Discipline*, 7; see also *Gegen die Prügelstrafe*, 6–7.

24. Wyman, *Progress in School Discipline*, 7–10.

25. Alfons Jannisek, *Das Recht des Lehrers zur Vornahme körperlicher Züchtigungen mit besonderer Rücksicht auf seine strafrechtliche Verantwortlichkeit* (1911), 16–22; quotation at 20.

26. Bavaria: Wilhelm Emnet, "Über das Züchtigungsrecht in der bayerischen Volksschule," *Die christliche Schule*, I (1910), 111; Prussia: W. Olsen, "Die körperliche Züchtigung in den höheren Schulen," *Monatsschrift für höhere Schulen*, IX (January 1910), 170. By this time, flogging had been removed from the lawbooks as an acceptable criminal penalty.

27. "The Flogging Question," *Saturday Review*, VIII (October 8, 1859), 422.

28. John Chandos, *Boys Together: English Public Schools, 1800–1864* (1984), 239; see also 245–46.

29. Jacques Claude Demogeot and Henri Montucci, *De l'enseignement secondaire en Angleterre et en Ecosse*, (1867), 40–43—written at the behest of the French ministry of education; Hippolyte Taine, *Notes sur l'Angleterre* (1872; 14th ed., 1910), 145.

30. Chandos, *Boys Together*, caption in picture insert between pp. 128 and 129.

31. John Morley, *The Life of William Ewart Gladstone*, 3 vols. (1903), I, 42.

32. Carlyle: *Sartor Resartus* (1833–34; ed. Kerry McSweeney and Peter Sabor, 1987), 82 [book

II, ch. 3]; Stephen: R. J. White, Introduction to James Fitzjames Stephen, *Liberty, Equality, Fraternity* (1873; 2nd ed., 1874; ed. White, 1967), 5.

33. C. Kegan Paul, *Memories* (1899), 41. The floggings, which he describes in painful detail on pp. 41–42, were designed as "an ingenious piece of cruelty."

34. In *Pride and Prejudice,* the two flightiest of the Bennet sisters casually gossip to the sensible Jane and Elizabeth, returned from a brief absence, about recent news of the regiment stationed nearby: "Several of the officers had dined lately with their uncle, a private had been flogged. . . ." Jane Austen, *Pride and Prejudice* (1813; ed. Tony Tanner, 1972), 105 [ch. 12]. Thackeray, with all his ambivalence about cruelty, could bring himself to approve stoutly of a good thrashing now and then. He puts many of his fictional characters through that kind of correction; Foker, Pendennis's dandyish and enterprising schoolmate, is a "youth who had been deservedly whipped." *The History of Pendennis* (1848–50), in *The Works of William Makepeace Thackeray,* Centenary Biographical Edition, 26 vols. (1910–11), III, 38 [ch. 3]. Dickens, no doubt unaware of the sinister erotic overtones he was evoking, seems to endorse flogging with the nonchalant tone he takes in describing the cherubic Mr. Wilfer in *Our Mutual Friend:* he is "so boyish" in "his curves and proportions, that his old schoolmaster" coming upon him "might have been unable to withstand the temptation of caning him on the spot." Charles Dickens, *Our Mutual Friend* (1865; ed. Charles Dickens the Younger, 1908), 29 [book I, ch. 4]. These are only a handful of appetizers from a vast English menu, and they make flogging sound perfectly commonplace.

35. Others were the diplomat, war correspondent, novelist, playwright, and poet Maurice Baring and the liberal Anglo-German aesthete and patron of the arts Harry Graf Kessler.

36. See Randolph S. Churchill, *Winston Churchill,* vol. I, *Youth, 1874–1900* (1966), 45–56.

37. Fry's observations are from a fragmentary autobiography that Virginia Woolf quotes in extenso in her *Roger Fry: A Biography* (1940), 34.

38. Woolf, *Roger Fry,* 32; Maurice Baring, *The Puppet Show of Memory* (1922), 74; Harry Graf Kessler, *Gesichter und Zeiten. Erinnerungen* (1935; ed. 1962), 122, 132, 135.

39. Woolf, *Roger Fry,* 32–33.

40. Ibid., 33. This is not the only time that such an accident happened during a flogging. In his polemic against corporal punishment, Eduard Sack recalled a scene in which a pleasure-bent teacher was intent on breaking a pupil's resistance: "Wanting under all circumstances cries of pain and tears, he struck pitilessly at a boy with a terrible scourge woven together from strong cords. The strong boy endured it silently, although all his fellow pupils were weeping and shouting to him to scream. At last he slid with a hair-raising bellow from the bench. The children, horrified, jumped onto the table, for the teacher, too, had fallen down and was screaming while the boy was only wheezing. For, as he slid from the bench he had bitten deeply into the leg of the teacher. What is more, another misfortune had happened to the boy." *Gegen die Prügel-Pädagogen,* 41.

41. Woolf, *Roger Fry,* 33.

42. For an excellent brief appraisal of this "philosophy," see Mario Praz, *The Romantic Agony* (1933; 2nd ed., tr. Angus Davidson, 1951), 104–6.

43. Leopold von Sacher-Masoch, *Venus im Pelz* (1869; ed., with study, by Gilles Deleuze, 1980), 138.

44. Sigmund Freud, *Drei Abhandlungen zur Sexualtheorie* (1905), in *Gesammelte Werke,* V, 59; *Three Essays on the Theory of Sexuality,* in *Standard Edition,* VII, 159. On this point, Freud cites Havelock Ellis, who, in turn, leans on Krafft-Ebing and three other sexologists. Krafft-Ebing thought that cases in which a thoroughgoing sadist practiced masochistic rituals at the same time were intriguing but rare. Richard von Krafft-Ebing, *Psychopathia Sexualis mit besonderer Berücksich-*

tigung der conträren Sexualempfindung. Eine medicinisch-gerichtliche Studie für Ärzte und Juristen (1882; 11th enlarged ed., 1901), 162.

45. Dostoevsky, *Crime and Punishment* (1866; tr. Jessie Coulson, 1964), 154 [part II, ch. 7].

46. January 4, 1843, *Gladstone Diaries*, III, 250. Gladstone goes on to speculate, "May not such virtue often exist, as shall find [,] when the lower faculty is punished or straightened, a joy in the justice and in the beneficial effects of that chastisement, which shall do more than compensate and counteract even at the moment the suffering of the punishment itself. . . ." He seems here to be anticipating Freud's much later notion of the pleasure the punitive superego derives from the pain the ego suffers under the superego's prodding.

47. "America on the High Seas," *Saturday Review*, IX (January 21, 1860), 79.

48. In 1904, the Swiss psychiatrist Auguste Forel paid Krafft-Ebing a tribute that no one disputed and no one begrudged him; the question of the "sexual drive directed at inadequate objects," Forel wrote, had been "studied most thoroughly by Krafft-Ebing." *Die sexuelle Frage. Eine naturwissenschaftliche, psychologische, hygienische und soziologische Studie für Gebildete* (1904; 4th and 5th ed., 1906), 248.

49. A. James Hammerton, "Victorian Marriage and the Law of Matrimonial Cruelty," *Victorian Studies*, XXXIII (1990), 276n.

50. See Richard D. Altick, *Victorian Studies in Scarlet: Murders and Manners in the Age of Victoria* (1970), 286. Only five wives were executed for murdering their husbands.

51. The first modern divorce bill became law in 1857. From then on, as A. James Hammerton, a careful student of court records, has concluded, "contrary to popular belief, among those appearing in the court, upper-class men were as likely as those lower in the social scale to strike their wives with pokers and similar weapons, throw them downstairs, beat them during pregnancy, enforce sexual intercourse after childbirth, and indulge in marital rape or enforced sodomy." "Victorian Marriage," 276.

52. Dr. Matthaes, "Zur Statistik der Sittlichkeitsverbrechen," *Archiv für Kriminal-Anthropologie und Kriminalistik*, XII (1903), 316–18.

53. See Hammerton, "Victorian Marriage," 275–79.

54. Robert Rantoul, "House, No. 36. Commonwealth of Massachusetts. House of Representatives, Jan. 14, 1835," 6.

55. Dostoevsky, *Crime and Punishment*, 418 [part VI, ch. 5]. Late in the eighteenth century, in his classic *Commentaries*, Blackstone quoted the great seventeenth-century English jurist Sir Matthew Hale to the effect that "rape is a most detestable crime," but "an accusation easy to be made, hard to be proved," and "harder to be defended by the party accused, though innocent." William Blackstone, *Commentaries on the Laws of England*, 4 vols. (1765–69), IV, 215.

56. Hubert Lauvergne, *Les Forçats considérés sous le rapport physiologique, morale et intellectuel, observés au bagne de Toulon* (1841), 378, 401, 398.

57. Albert Bournet, *De la criminalité en France et en Italie. Étude médico-légale* (1884), 119.

58. A few French medical experts, the prolific Ambroise A. Tardieu among them, did take an interest in what Tardieu called "assaults on morals"—mainly the rape of children, including father-daughter incest. See his *Étude médico-légale sur les attentats aux moeurs* (1857; 5th ed., 1867). Several of his colleagues contributed to his collection of case histories.

59. See Thomas Hardy, *Tess of the d'Urbervilles* (1891; ed. Scott Elledge, 1965; 2nd ed., 1979), 62 [ch. 11].

60. Marie von Ebner-Eschenbach, *Unsühnbar* (1890; ed. Burkhard Bittrich, 1978), 64 [ch. 10].

61. John Galsworthy, *The Man of Property* (1906; ed. 1951), 264 [part III, ch. 4].

62. "the reader's imagination": W. Starke, *Verbrechen und Verbrecher in Preussen 1854–1878. Eine*

kulturgeschichtliche Studie (1884), 173; "throughout the neighbourhood": "The Queen vs. Job Lawrence," *The Times* (London), April 7, 1850, p. 6; "during the day": "The Charge against a Clergyman," ibid., November 17, 1850, p. 3.

63. "The Tables Turned," ibid., February 17, 1850, p. 6; "Guildhall," ibid., February 21, p. 8.

64. "Guildhall," ibid., February 27, 1850, p. 7; also February 28, 1850, p. 8; and March 3, 1850, p. 5.

65. "I cannot conceive": *"POLICE,"* ibid., February 21, 1850, p. 8; "reverend defendant": "The Charge of Rape against a Clergyman": ibid., November 10, 1850, p. 3; see also November 17, 1850, p. 3.

66. "The Queen v. Job Lawrence," ibid., April 7, 1850, p. 6.

67. Tailor named Henry Digby: "Indecent Conduct," ibid., August 18, 1850, p. 8; "transported for life": "David Harrington," ibid., October 27, 1850, p. 6. What was true of high Victorian days was just as true earlier. When, in 1818, Thomas De Quincey was writing for the *Westmorland Gazette,* rape cases were given a good deal of prominence, and the attractive looks of the victims received a measure of lip-licking attention. See Grevel Lindop, *The Opium Eater: A Life of Thomas De Quincey* (1981), 229.

68. Augustine, *The City of God* (after 412; tr. Marcus Dods, n.d.), 22 [book I, ch. 17.]

69. See Albert Bayet, *Le Suicide et la morale* (1922), passim, and an unpublished paper by Lisa Lieberman, "The Suicide Discourse in Nineteenth-Century France." Clerics intent on rescuing the souls of parishioners from eternal damnation, drew careful (if analytically dubious) distinctions between the felony of defiant, unrepentant self-destruction and the ultimately innocent act of doing away with oneself in a moment of incurable depression. The sermon that the High Church cleric G. F. Biber published in 1865 under the intriguing title *The Act of Suicide as Distinct from the Crime of Self-Murder* is a characteristic instance of the apologetic literature.

70. Falret, See Jean-Pierre *De l'hypochondrie et du suicide* (1822); Étienne Esquirol, *Des maladies mentales considérées sous les rapports médical, hygiénique et médico-légal,* 3 vols. in 2 (1838), I, 639, 655. In the book, the chapter on suicide (pp. 526–676), is dated 1821.

71. Among many titles, most noteworthy are *Du suicide considéré comme maladie* (1845), by the physician Charles Bourdin, and *Du suicide et de la folie suicide* (1856; 2nd ed., 1865), by the prolific French alienist Alexandre Brierre de Boismont. In a bulky survey of more than five thousand suicides, which included the notes many of them had left behind, Boismont again endorsed this medical view.

72. Émile Durkheim, Preface to *Le Suicide* (1897), viii–ix.

73. Enrico Morselli, one of the two or three most prestigious mid-nineteenth-century students of suicide and a fervent admirer of English empiricist social science, duly cautioned against such temptations: "Statistics may be compared to a two-edged weapon, murderous to the inexperienced or malicious who wishes to use it in his own fashion. It is always easy to lay down laws and then model one's own researches upon them and make facts bend to our own preconceptions and *a priori* reasoning." *Suicide: An Essay on Comparative Moral Statistics* (1879; tr. 1882), 11–12.

74. Thomas Masaryk, *Suicide and the Meaning of Civilization* (1881; tr. William B. Weist and Robert G. Batson, 1970), 3.

75. A. Baer, *Der Selbstmord im kindlichen Lebensalter. Eine social-hygienische Studie* (1901), 49; Hans Rost, *Der Selbstmord als sozialstatistische Erscheinung* (1905), 113; Rost, *Der Selbstmord in den deutschen Städten* (1912), 55, 56.

76. Masaryk, *Suicide and the Meaning of Civilization,* 169. It is no wonder that in his careful statistical study of self-murder in the nineteenth century, the German Jesuit H. A. Krose cited Masaryk approvingly for seeing "in the irreligiosity of our time the principal cause of the waxing

inclination to suicide." There surely could be no question that "the most important and effective preservative against suicide is religion." *Der Selbstmord im 19. Jahrhundert nach seiner Verteilung auf Staaten und Verwaltungsbezirke* (1906), 140–41, 167.

77. Durkheim, *Le Suicide*, viii, 171.

78. Ibid. Compare Freud's celebrated credo closing *The Future of an Illusion* of 1927: "No, our science is no illusion. But an illusion it would be to believe that we could get anywhere else what it cannot give us." *Die Zukunft einer Illusion*, in *Gesammelte Werke* XIV, 380; *Standard Edition*, XXI, 56.

79. See Durkheim, *Le Suicide*, 264–311.

THREE: Demagogues and Democrats

1. Redefinitions

1. Benjamin Constant, "De la liberté des anciens comparée à celle des modernes" (1819), *Cours de politique constitutionelle, ou collection des ouvrages publiés sur le gouvernement représentatif*, ed. Edouard Laboulaye, 2 vols. (1861), II, 542.

2. R. N. B[ain], "Görtz, Georg Heinrich von," *Encyclopedia Britannica* (11th ed., 1910–11), XII, 262.

3. Dominique Bagge, *Les Conflits des idées politiques en France sous la Restauration* (1952), 113.

4. Tocqueville to Gustave de Beaumont, March 23, 1853, Alexis de Tocqueville, *Selected Letters on Politics and Society*, ed. Roger Boesche, tr. James Toupin and Roger Boesche (1985), 285; Tocqueville to Louis de Kergorlay, June 29, 1831, ibid., 54–55.

5. Gervinus: Georg Gottfried Gervinus, "The Course and Tendency of History since the Overthrow of the Empire of Napoleon I," *Introduction to the History of the Nineteenth Century* (1853; tr. Moritz Sernan, assisted by Rev. J. M. Stephens, 1853), 14, 16, 17; Sybel: Folkert Haferkorn, *Soziale Vorstellungen Heinrich von Sybels* (1976), 110.

6. Alexis de Tocqueville, *Souvenirs* (written 1850; published posthumously, 1893; ed. Luc Monnier, 1942), 16.

7. Friedrich Engels, *The Condition of the Working Class in England in 1844* (1845; tr. Florence K. Wischnewetzky, 1885; ed. 1891), 95n; "On Historical Materialism," in Karl Marx and Friedrich Engels, *Basic Writings on Politics and Philosophy*, ed. Lewis S. Feuer (1959), 63.

8. Tocqueville to Hippolyte de Tocqueville, December 4, 1831, *Selected Letters*, 66.

9. James Anthony Froude, *Thomas Carlyle: A History of the First Forty Years of His Life, 1795–1835*, 2 vols. (1882), II, 205–6.

2. The Long Birth of Political Culture

1. See Archibald S. Foord, *His Majesty's Opposition, 1714–1830* (1964), 1.

2. Disraeli: Robert Blake, *Disraeli* (1967; ed. 1968), 181–82; Palmerston: ibid., 323.

3. Bolingbroke argued that government by a party "must always end in the government of a faction," for "faction is to party what the superlative is to the positive; party is a political evil, and faction is the worst of all parties." Henry St. John, Viscount Bolingbroke, *The Idea of a Patriot King* (1749; ed. 1965), 46.

4. Madison warned against the "mischief of faction," which only checks and balances could cure (*Federalist*, no. 10). Hamilton agreed. A "successful faction may erect a tyranny on the ruins of

order and law" no 21). It is a contagious disease that "must be expected to infect all political bodies" (no 26). *The Federalist* (1787–88; ed. Jacob E. Cooke, 1961), 56–58, 131, 168.

5. See esp. "Of Parties in General" (1741), *Essays, Moral, Political, and Literary*, in *The Philosophical Works of David Hume*, ed. T. H. Green and T. H. Grose, 4 vols. (1875; ed. 1882), III, 127–28; "Of the Parties of Great Britain" (1742), ibid., 139; "Of the Coalition of Parties" (1758), ibid., 464.

6. Edmund Burke, *Thoughts on the Present Discontents* (1770), in *The Writings and Speeches of Edmund Burke*, ed. Paul Langford, vol. II, *Party, Parliament, and the American Crisis, 1766–1774* (1981), 314–18; quotation at 317.

7. Henry Adams, *History of the United States of America during the Administrations of Thomas Jefferson and James Madison*, 9 vols. (1889–91; repr. 1930), I, 82.

8. "Declaration of the Rights of Man and Citizen," August 27, 1789, in John Hall Stewart, *A Documentary Survey of the French Revolution* (1951), 114. A follow-up, "Decree on the Fundamental Principles of Government," was issued on October 1, 1789. Ibid., 115.

9. See Stewart, *Documentary Survey*, 431.

10. While, obviously, the French Revolution was far more than an oedipal revolt, this all-too-simple (though not completely absurd) psychoanalytic explanation has imposed itself even on historians who reject Freudian categories.

11. See William Wordsworth, *The Prelude*, book XI, lines 113–15; Burke to Charles-Jean-François Depont [November 1789], *The Correspondence of Edmund Burke*, vol. VI, *July 1789–December 1791*, ed. Alfred Cobban and Robert A. Smith (1967), 41. For expressions of enthusiasm and of aversion in England, the texts in *The Debate on the French Revolution, 1789–1800*, ed. Alfred Cobban (1950), are ample.

12. Marat: William Doyle, *The Oxford History of the French Revolution* (1989), 120, 228; Girondins: see Alphonse Aulard, *Histoire politique de la Révolution Française* (1901; 5th ed., 1913), 395; Robespierre: see Doyle, *Oxford History*, 191.

13. Morris to Thomas Pinckney, December 3, 1792, *A Diary of the French Revolution*, ed. Beatrix Cary Davenport, 2 vols. (1939), II, 581.

14. Morris to Thomas Jefferson, September 10–16, 1792, ibid., 542.

15. Charles de Rémusat, "La Révolution Française," *Critiques et études littéraires, ou passé et présent* (1st ed. titled *Passé et présent. Mélanges*, 1847; new enlarged ed., 1859), 102.

16. See "Proclamation to the French Nation, 19 Brumaire, Year VIII" (November 10, 1799): *Letters and Documents of Napoleon*, sel. and tr. John Eldred Howard, vol. I, *The Rise to Power* (1961), 313; Napoleon I in conversation with Lucien and Joseph Bonaparte, 1803: Théodore Iung, *Lucien Bonaparte et ses mémoires, 1775–1840*, 3 vols. (1882–83), II, 407–8.

17. James Fenimore Cooper, *The American Democrat* (1838; ed. George Dekker and Larry Johnston, 1969), 225–26.

18. William James to William M. Salter, September 11, 1899, *The Letters of William James*, ed. by his son Henry James, 2 vols. (1920), II, 100.

19. Benjamin Constant, a manuscript dating between 1802 and 1806, in Stephen Holmes, *Benjamin Constant and the Making of Modern Liberalism* (1984), 275.

20. Charles de Rémusat, *Mémoires de ma vie*, ed. Charles H. Pouthas, 5 vols. (1958–67), vol. I, *Enfance et jeunesse. La Restauration libérale (1797–1820)*, 278.

21. François Guizot, *Des moyens de gouvernement et d'opposition dans l'état actuel de la France* (1821), viii–ix, 4, 295.

22. See Rémusat, "Du choix d'une opinion" (1823), *Critiques et études littéraires*, 165; Rémusat, *Mémoires de ma vie*, vol. II, *La Restauration ultra-royaliste. La Révolution de Juillet (1820–1832)*, 59;

Rémusat, "Sur la situation du gouvernement" (written in 1818), *Critiques et études littéraires,* 77; Rémusat, "Du moeurs du temps" (1825–26), ibid., 337.

23. André Jardin and André-Jean Tudesq, *La France des notables. L'Évolution générale, 1815–1848* (1973), 116.

24. J. P. T. Bury and R. P. Tombs, *Thiers, 1797–1877: A Political Life* (1986), 18–19.

25. Rémusat, *Mémoires de ma vie,* vol. III, *Les Luttes parlementaires. La Question d'Orient. Le Ministère Thiers-Rémusat (1832–1841),* 47.

26. Alfred Cobban, *A History of Modern France,* vol. II, *From the First Empire to the Second Empire, 1799–1871* (1961; 2nd. ed., 1965), 98.

27. Karl Marx, *The Class Struggles in France, 1848–1850* (1850; ed. C. P. Dutt, 1935), 34.

28. Ibid.

29. Jardin and Tudesq, *La France des notables,* 167.

3. Modern Caesars

1. "Bernard Shaw and the Heroic Actor" (1907), *The Bodley Head Bernard Shaw: Collected Plays with Their Prefaces,* 7 vols. (1970–74), II, 310; Victor Duruy, *History of Rome and of the Roman People* (1879–85; tr. M. M. Ripley and W. J. Clarke, 8 vols. in 16, 1883–86), III, 550n.

2. "The Caesars" (1832), *The Works of Thomas De Quincey* (1878), VII, 7–8. I owe this gem to Frank M. Turner.

3. Duruy, *History of Rome,* III, 155–56, 546.

4. See Theodor Mommsen, *Römische Geschichte,* 3 vols. (1854–56; 2nd ed., 1857), III, 609, 445, 447, 448, 456, 457.

5. See James Anthony Froude, *Caesar: A Sketch* (1879), 1, 7. Even Trollope who in 1880, shortly before his death, published a two-volume plea for Cicero, was more intent on defending Cicero than on attacking Caesar, and cited Mommsen with deep respect. See Anthony Trollope, *The Life of Cicero,* 2 vols. (1880), II, 206. For another English admirer of Caesar, who had taken this view even before Mommsen, see the Anglican divine Charles Merivale, *The Roman Triumvirates* (1876; 4th ed., 1885), 161, 169; and Merivale, *A General History of Rome from the Foundation of the City to the Fall of Augustulus, B.C. 753 to A.D. 476* (1875), 311, 353.

6. G[oldwin] S[mith], "The Roman Empire of the West" (review of four lectures by Richard Congreve published under that title in 1855), *Oxford Essays, 1856,* contributed by the Members of the University (1856), 295–96, 311.

7. Henri de Ferron, *Théorie du progrès,* 2 vols. (1867), II, 440–43.

8. See Louis Napoleon Bonaparte, *Des idées napoléoniennes* (1839), in Napoleon III, *Oeuvres,* 5 vols. (1856–69), I, 36n.

9. Louis de Fontanes, *Parallèle entre César, Cromwel, Monck et Bonaparte* (1800), 13.

10. Napoleon Bonaparte, *Précis des guerres de César,* dictated to M. Marchand (1836), 212, 208, 214, 218.

11. Napoleon III, *Histoire de Jules César,* 2 vols. (1865), I, 8, 10; II, xxx.

12. Pierre Vésinier, *La Vie du nouveau César. Étude historique,* 2 parts in 1 vol. (1865), I, vii. *"Eh bien!"* Vésinier exclaimed, "strange thing: that man who has attracted the attention of his contemporaries for such a long time is one of the least known of our epoch; many today still find him an insoluble problem, a political sphinx whose enigmas have not been solved, an indecipherable charade whose password has not been found." Ibid., iii–iv. By 1865 this was a familiar complaint. In a generally positive study of the emperor published in the third year of his reign, Charles Phillips

(writing as "A Man of the World") outlined the "problem" of studying Louis Napoleon's character as difficult: "For a long time its solution seemed impossible. Frigidly affable and repulsively polite, he avoided either offence or familiarity, but seemed instinctively to coil up his nature from observation. In phrase and demeanour, all that became his birth, still *the man* was perfectly opaque." *Napoleon the Third* (1854), 10.

13. Louis Napoleon to his mother, July 24, 1821, F. A. Simpson, *The Rise of Louis Napoleon* (1909), 332.

14. "You can understand," he wrote his mother, "all that I felt in seeing the spot where the fate of France was decided, and where the star of the Emperor set for ever." November 14, 1832, ibid., 335. For the Rubicon, see J. M. Thompson, *Louis Napoleon and the Second Empire* (1955), 26.

15. François Guizot, *Des moyens de gouvernement et d'opposition dans l'état actual de la France* (1821), 228–29. "As long as Buonaparte only purified and moderated the revolution, he served France. As soon as he claimed to substitute himself for the revolution, as soon as he saw in us only machines of war and servitude against Europe and against ourselves . . . he showed himself the most fatal of usurpers." Ibid., 239. Needless to say, the nephew accepted only the first half of this judgment.

16. Louis Napoleon, *Des idées napoléoniennes*, 5, 28.

17. Ibid., 123, 172.

18. Napoleon I in conversation with Las Cases, April 22–25, 1816, Emmanuel, comte de Las Cases, *Mémorial de Sainte-Hélène. Journal de la vie privée et des conversations de l'empéreur à Sainte Hélène*, 8 vols. in 4 (1823), II, 83. For Napoleon's cynicism, as shown in conversations in the early 1800s, see *The Mind of Napoleon: A Selection from His Written and Spoken Words*, ed. and tr. J. Christopher Herold (1955), 5; and Claire de Vergennes, comtesse de Rémusat, *Mémoires 1802–1808*, ed. Paul de Rémusat, 3 vols. (1881), I, 183.

19. April 3, 1829, Johann Peter Eckermann, *Gespräche mit Goethe in den letzten Jahren seines Lebens*, in Johann Wolfgang von Goethe, *Gedenkausgabe der Werke, Briefe und Gespräche*, ed. Ernst Beutler, 27 vols. (1948–71), XXIV, 337. Stendhal was more observant on this point than Goethe. He acknowledged that Napoleon Bonaparte had no use for "institutions rooted in public opinion." Geoffrey Strickland, *Stendhal: The Education of a Novelist* (1974), 105.

20. Simpson, *Rise of Louis Napoleon*, 191.

21. The republican general Louis Cavaignac, a declared favorite among the candidates for the presidency, garnered fewer than 1.5 million votes. Cavaignac, whom later critics would call "the butcher of June" for harshly putting down civil unrest in Paris in 1848, had many sincere admirers. When he died in 1857, the *Saturday Review* lamented his passing: "The intelligence falls most mournfully on the ear. . . . Of Cavaignac himself, no one has said a word but good." "General Cavaignac," *Saturday Review*, IV (November 7, 1857), 414.

22. Louis Napoleon to the legislative assembly, September 26, 1848, *Oeuvres*, III, 22.

23. Louis Napoleon, "À ses concitoyens," early December 1848, ibid., 24–28, quotation at 25; see also Louis Napoleon to the legislative assembly, December 20, 1848, ibid., 31. Here is one instance of Louis Napoleon recycling his statements. In his proclamation of December 2, 1851, he said, "If you believe that the cause of which my name is the symbol is still yours—that is to say, a France regenerated by the revolution of '89 and organized by the Emperor—proclaim it in sanctioning the powers I am asking for." Ibid., 275. In the preamble to the constitution promulgated on January 14, 1852, he spoke of present-day French society as "nothing but a France regenerated by the revolution of '89 and organized by the Emperor." Ibid., 288.

24. Roger Price, *The French Second Republic: A Social History* (1972), 215; Karl Marx, *The Class Struggles in France, 1848–1850* (1850; ed. C. P. Dutt, 1935), 72.

25. Louis Napoleon, "Proclamation au peuple français," June 13, 1849, *Oeuvres,* III, 83.

26. Louis Napoleon, at Sens, inaugurating the section of the railroad from Lyons, September 9, 1849, ibid., 107–8.

27. Tocqueville doubted that one so covetous for power as Louis Napoleon would willingly resume private life after serving for four years and made it his cardinal task to dissuade the president from establishing a "bastard monarchy." In a dramatically understated scene, he described how the president, that modern Sphinx, listened quietly but gave no hint of what he was thinking: "The words one addressed to him were like stones one throws down a well; you hear the sound they make but you never know what becomes of them." Alexis de Tocqueville, *Souvenirs* (written 1850; published posthumously, 1893; ed. Luc Monnier, 1942), 201, 209.

28. Louis Napoleon to the legislative assembly, October 31, 1849, *Oeuvres,* III, 112–13.

29. Louis Napoleon, to the legislative assembly, November 4, 1851, ibid., 223.

30. Charles Forbes de Montalembert to Monseigneur Dupanloup, December 9, 1851, "Notes et lettres de Montalembert (1848–1853)," part II, ed. André Traunoy, *Revue historique,* LXXXVI (1946), 432.

31. For this text, see Louis Napoleon, *Oeuvres,* III, 300. He had not written this document but it was pasted together in his spirit.

32. "Notes et lettres de Montalembert (1848–1853)," 433.

33. For this paragraph, see John M. Merriman, *The Agony of the Republic: The Repression of the Left in Revolutionary France, 1848–1851* (1978), passim.

34. The first plebiscite, in 1800, confirmed the constitution Napoleon had imposed after appointing himself first consul; the second, in 1802, buttressed his more exalted post of consul for life; the third, in 1804, legitimized his new imperial title. The figures are truly overwhelming and wholly unbelievable. In 1800: 3,011,007 voted yes, 1,562 no; in 1802: 3,600,000 yes, 8,374 no; in 1804: 3,572,329 yes, 2,569 no.

35. Sand to Giuseppe Mazzini, May 23, 1852, in Price, *French Second Republic,* 322.

36. Dedication of statue, August 8, 1858, Napoleon III, *Oeuvres,* V, 66.

37. Thompson, *Louis Napoleon,* 319.

38. See David H. Pinkney, *Napoleon III and the Rebuilding of Paris* (1958), 6 and passim.

39. In 1860, the *Saturday Review,* which like other English journals had long pursued the emperor with choice epithets, noted severely that "the household of NAPOLEON III must consist not of hired servants but of bought serfs." "The Suppression of the *Univers,*" *Saturday Review,* IX (February 4, 1860), 137.

40. Tocqueville had foreseen it all eighteen years earlier. "This government," he wrote a month after Louis Napoleon's coup, "established by one of the greatest crimes known in history," was sure to be "dragged fatally into wanting territorial expansion, spheres of influence, in other words, into war." And in that war, he added, "it will surely find death." Tocqueville to Henry Reeve, January 9, 1852, Alexis de Tocqueville, *Selected Letters on Politics and Society,* ed. Roger Boesche, tr. James Toupin and Roger Boesche (1985), 284.

41. Bismarck in conversation with Robert von Keudell, summer 1864, Otto von Bismarck, *Gesammelte Werke,* ed. Wolfgang Windelband and Werner Frauendienst, 15 vols. (2nd ed., 1924–35), VII, 90.

42. See Bismarck to Leopold von Gerlach, May 11, 1857, ibid., XIV, 469.

43. Bismarck to Leopold von Gerlach, May 2, 1857, ibid., 464–65. See also Bismarck to Gerlach, May 30, 1857, ibid., 470.

44. Otto von Bismarck, *Gedanken und Erinnerungen,* 2 vols. (1898; complete ed., 1911), I, 19.

45. Bismarck to his fiancée, June 15, 1847, *Gesammelte Werke,* XIV, 95.

46. Erich Eyck, *Bismarck. Leben und Werk,* 3 vols. (1941–44), I, 130.

47. Bismarck in conversation, January 28–February 18, 1874, Robert Lucius von Ballhausen, *Bismarck-Erinnerungen* (1920), 39–40.

48. "point of annihilation": Benda to Rudolf von Bennigsen, August 1878, quoted in *Bismarck und die preussisch-deutsche Politik 1871–1890,* ed. Michael Stürmer (1970; 3rd ed., 1978), 130; "must destroy him": Eyck, *Bismarck,* I, 115.

49. Bismarck in rage: the Prussian historian Gustav Adolf Harald Stenzel, quoted in Eyck, *Bismarck,* I, 147; "even quite ruthlessly": Bismarck to Otto von Manteuffel, February 15, 1854, *Gesammelte Werke,* I, 427.

50. Bismarck the woodsman: see his "Ansprache an die Vertreter der Lehrkörper der Universitäten und Technischen Hochschulen des Deutschen Reiches," April 1, 1895 (Bismarck's eightieth birthday), ibid., XIII, 555; "natural to man": Bismarck in conversation with Robert von Keudell, mid-March 1862, ibid., VII, 44; "acquire any new ones": Bismarck to Albrecht von Roon, November 20, 1873, ibid., XIV, 1507; "battlefield": Bismarck to Bernhard von Bülow, December 1, 1877, ibid., VIc, 97.

51. "and is weakness": Bismarck to Rudolf von Delbrück, June 3, 1872, ibid., XIV, 1455; "passive in this fight": Bismarck, in Protocol of the Ministry of State, April 3, 1873, *Bismarck und die preussisch-deutsche Politik,* 63.

52. "terror without end": Bismarck to Robert Lucius von Ballhausen, May 31, 1875, Ballhausen, *Bismarck-Erinnerungen,* 74; *"to go with me"*: Bismarck at a session of the Staatsministerium, October 6, 1877, Erich Foerster, *Adalbert Falk* (1927), 384.

53. Blood not likely to flow: Bismarck to his wife, September 23, 1848, *Gesammelte Werke,* XIV, 113; "barricadists": Bismarck to his brother, November 2, 1848, ibid., 115; "war to the knife": Ballhausen, *Bismarck-Erinnerungen,* 335; "manly self-assurance": Bismarck to the Prussian Second Chamber, October 24, 1849, *Gesammelte Werke,* X, 56. On January 11, 1879, Christoph von Tiedemann, for some years Bismarck's secretary in the imperial chancellery, noted after a meeting with his chief, "The prince in a very martial mood, believes that in the course of the year, one will have to work a great deal with gunpowder." Bismarck was talking about nothing more martial than the resistance he was encountering to his proposals on tariffs and taxes. Tiedemann, *Aus sieben Jahrzehnten. Erinnerungen,* vol. II, *Sechs Jahre Chef der Reichskanzlei unter dem Fürsten Bismarck* (1909), 326.

54. "swindle": Bismarck to his brother, April 18, 1849, *Gesammelte Werke,* XIV, 127; "republican-pagan education": Bismarck to Leopold von Gerlach, November 25, 1853, ibid., 328; "civilized world": Bismarck to Kaiser Wilhelm I, April 4, 1872, *Bismarck und die preussisch-deutsche Politik,* 50; "demagoguery": Bismarck to King Ludwig II of Bavaria, August 12, 1878, *Gesammelte Werke,* XIV, 1587; "enemies of the state": Bismarck to Count Karl von Tauffkirchen, February 16, 1872, ibid., VIc, 18, and Bismarck to Bernhard von Bülow, November 21, 1873, ibid., 53.

55. "growling dog": Bismarck in conversation with Robert Lucius von Ballhausen, May 1871, Ballhausen, *Bismarck-Erinnerungen,* 11; "takes them for merits": Bismarck to Heinrich von Puttkamer, Heinrich von Friedberg, and Ballhausen, March 3, 1883, *Bismarck und die preussisch-deutsche Politik,* 193; "incompetence and megalomania": ibid., 195; "and impudence": Bismarck to Otto von Manteuffel, December 2, 1854, Eyck, *Bismarck,* I, 250; "of the anti-Christian": Bismarck to Hermann Wagener, June 30, 1850, *Gesammelte Werke,* XIV, 159.

56. "Laskerei": Adalbert Falk's diary, October 29–30, 1878, Foerster, *Falk,* 490; "Jew-boy": Falk's diary, March 10, 1878, ibid., 485.

57. This episode is reported in detail in Eyck, *Bismarck,* III, 378–80.

58. Bismarck to his wife, September 19, 1849, *Gesammelte Werke,* XIV, 143.

59. Speaking to the Prussian diet in April 1848, after the government had reestablished control in the streets, Bismarck publicly decided to vote against an address of thanks for the happy turn of events. The "Crown itself," he said sharply, "has thrown earth on its own coffin." He would give thanks only if a "united German fatherland" emerged from what had happened. At that moment, he writes, he was so deeply moved that he had to stop speaking, "falling into a fit of weeping." *Gedanken und Erinnerungen*, I, 50. A second occasion came in 1866 after the Prussian victory over Austria, when Bismarck, alone among all of Wilhelm's advisers, urged a nonvindictive peace. Exhausted by illness and his isolation, he had to leave the council and go to the next room, where he was overcome by a "violent fit of weeping." Ibid., II, 62.

60. "and bottles": Bismarck to his fiancée, February 13, 1847, *Gesammelte Werke*, XIV, 57; "vomiting": Eyck, *Bismarck*, I, 267; "malicious willfulness": Bismarck to his fiancée, May 24, 1847, *Gesammelte Werke*, XIV, 91; "fall into ruins": Bismarck to his wife, January 21, 1871, ibid., 1389; "in my nature": Bismarck to his sister, August 26, 1848, ibid., 112.

61. Bismarck to his fiancée, February 23, 1847, ibid., 65–69; quotation at 67. In the same remarkable confessional letter, displaying the frankness that was his signature, he admitted that as a boy he had hated and deceived his mother—and he had never quite forgiven her. See the somewhat bowdlerized version in ibid., 65–69, and some previously unpublished excerpts in Lothar Gall, *Bismarck. Der weisse Revolutionär* (1980; ed. 1983), 30.

62. A humorously boastful letter from his student days reads more like a wry acknowledgment of his pervasive uncertainty than a burst of sheer vitality. Writing from his provincial estate, he asks his friend Gustav Scharlach to come and visit: "I invite you to commit *adulterium* with a young *mulier facilis et formosa*, to drink as much potato brandy as you wish and break your neck hunting as often as you like. You will find here a stall-fattened militia officer, a mustache who swears and curses that the earth trembles, who cherishes a just revulsion against Jews and Frenchmen, and who thrashes dogs and servants in the most brutal manner when he has been tyrannized by his wife." April 7, 1834, *Gesammelte Werke*, XIV, 4.

63. "none at all": Eyck, *Bismarck*, I, 30; "superiors": Bismarck to Gustav Scharlach, January 9, 1845, *Gesammelte Werke*, XIV, 31; "untamed passions": Bismarck to Heinrich von Puttkamer [ca. December 21, 1846], ibid., 46.

64. See A. J. P. Taylor, *Bismarck: The Man and the Statesman* (1955), 86; Gall, *Bismarck*, 373. "My two greatest difficulties," Bismarck told the English writer J. Whitman in October 1891, after his retirement, "were, first to get King Wilhelm into Bohemia, and then to get him out again." Ibid., 368.

65. Bismarck in conversation with Moritz Busch, January 5, 1886, *Gesammelte Werke*, VIII, 541–42. Earlier, on October 22, 1880, he had told his physician, E. Cohen, that "he was no absolutist. Everyone who has been a cabinet minister for a few years could not advocate absolutism. He would be for unlimited publicity, which he thought even more valuable than parliamentarism. . . . There should be just two parties, for and against the government." Ibid., VIII, 384, 393.

66. It was precisely this identification that his Catholic parliamentary adversary Ludwig Windthorst objected to when he pointedly told Bismarck, "The prime minister is not the state, and so far, no cabinet minister has dared to call his opponents also opponents of the state." Eyck, *Bismarck*, III, 97.

67. See Bismarck to Robert Lucius von Ballhausen, November 3, 1879, *Gesammelte Werke*, XIV, 1621.

68. Bismarck's thought about a coup: see Otto Pflanze, "Bismarcks Herrschaftstechnik als Problem der gegenwärtigen Historiographie," *Historische Zeitschrift*, CCXXXIV (1982), 583; "Brumaire": Albrecht von Roon to Edwin von Manteuffel, December 1862, Michael Stürmer,

Regierung und Reichstag im Bismarckstaat 1871–1880. Cäsarismus oder Parlamentarismus (1974), 310; "to develop more": Bismarck to the cabinet, December 5, 1884, Ballhausen, *Bismarck-Erinnerungen,* 306; "far-reaching plans": ibid., 307.

69. See Protocol of the Ministry of State, March 2, 1890, *Bismarck und die preussisch-deutsche Politik,* 297–99.

70. Louis Napoleon, "Du système électoral" (ca. 1843), *Oeuvres,* I, 400.

71. Bismarck in conversation with Victor von Unruh, mid-March 1859, *Gesammelte Werke,* VII, 38.

72. Ludwig Dehio, "Die Taktik der Opposition während des Konflikts," *Historische Zeitschrift,* CXL (1929), 300n.

73. Bismarck to Count Robert von der Goltz, March 30, 1866, *Gesammelte Werke,* V, 429. On March 24, 1866, he wrote to Prince Heinrich von Reuss, "The masses are more honestly interested in the order of the state than the leaders of the classes one could privilege by introducing some property qualification into the right to vote." Ibid., VII, 177.

74. Walter Gagel, *Die Wahlrechtsfrage in der Geschichte der deutschen liberalen Parteien 1848–1918* (1958), 40. In his memoirs, Bismarck noted that his proposal to introduce universal manhood suffrage was an instrument in foreign policy as well, warning off outsiders from any attempts to "put their fingers into our national omelette." *Gedanken und Erinnerungen,* II, 78.

75. "bourgeois classes": Gall, *Bismarck,* 352; "*parliamentarism*": Bismarck in conversation with Baron Richard von Friesen, *Gesammelte Werke,* VII, 177; "the Reichstag deputies": Bismarck to Ludwig II, August 12, 1878, ibid., XIV, 1587. Bismarck argued that after long experience he had recognized the "artificial system" of "indirect and class elections" as "dangerous," because it keeps "the highest powers in the state out of touch with the sound elements that form the core and the mass of the people." Heinrich von Sybel, *Die Begründung des deutschen Reiches durch Wilhelm I,* 7 vols. (1889–1984), IV, 318.

76. Eyck, *Bismarck,* II, 155.

77. Engels to Karl Marx, April 13, 1866, Karl Marx and Frederick Engels, *Selected Correspondence, 1846–1895* (1934; tr. Dona Torr, 1942), 205–6.

78. Eyck, *Bismarck,* III, 368.

79. See Max Weber, "Wahlrecht und Demokratie in Deutschland" (1917), *Gesammelte politische Schriften* (1921; ed. Johannes Winckelmann, 1958), 233.

80. Weber, "Parliament and Regierung im neugeordneten Deutschland. Zur politischen Kritik des Beamtentums und Parteiwesens," section I, "Die Erbschaft Bismarcks" (1918), ibid., 307.

81. Bismarck to Arthur Hobrecht, mayor of Berlin in the 1870s, May 25, 1878, *Gesammelte Werke,* VIc, 121. In a passing observation about the "Caesarism" of what he disdainfully called Russian chauvinism, he intimated that his own political thinking was on a very different plane. Bismarck to Kaiser Wilhelm I, September 7, 1879, *Die grosse Politik der europäischen Kabinette 1871–1914,* ed. Johannes Lepsius et al., 40 vols. (1922–27), III, 461.

82. Mommsen to Lujo Brentano, January 3, 1902, Albert Wucher, *Theodor Mommsen. Geschichtsschreibung und Politik* (1956), 157.

4. Human Nature in Politics

1. Graham Wallas, *Human Nature in Politics* (1908; 3rd ed., 1915), 112.

2. William Blackstone, *Commentaries on the Laws of England,* 4 vols. (1765–69), I, 171. The dictum was much quoted, but not because there was anything new in this reasoning; Blackstone was virtually plagiarizing Montesquieu's *Esprit des lois* of mid-century, and Montesquieu had taken

no particular pride for originality in serving up so patent an argument. See Chilton Williamson, *American Suffrage from Property to Democracy, 1760–1860* (1960), 10–11.

3. Franklin D. Scott, *Sweden: The Nation's History* (1977; ed. 1988, with an epilogue by Steven Koblik), 403.

4. Lowe: F. B. Smith, *The Making of the Second Reform Bill* (1966), 81; Macaulay: "A Speech Delivered in the House of Commons on the 3rd of May, 1842," *The Works of Lord Macaulay Complete,* ed. Lady Trevelyan, 8 vols. (1866), VIII, 221.

5. Robert J. Goldstein, *Political Repression in Nineteenth Century Europe* (1983), 3.

6. Williamson, *American Suffrage,* 260.

7. Henri Pirenne, *Histoire de Belgique,* 7 vols. (1900–1932), vol. VII, *De la révolution de 1830 à la guerre de 1914* (1932), 65.

8. Ibid., 97.

9. Theodore S. Hamerow, *The Social Foundations of German Unification, 1858–1871: Struggles and Accomplishments* (1974), 211–12.

10. Douglas Johnson, *Guizot: Aspects of French History, 1787–1874* (1963), 75.

11. "I should not have had the least objection to our extending the suffrage," Guizot wrote in 1858, "if it had been likely to strengthen our cause, but it promised us nothing but danger or embarrassment." Recalling the revolution of 1830, he spoke disparagingly of "the masses of the people of both towns and country, who neither cared nor understood anything about the consti-tutional system." Expansion of the governing elite to include more than the intelligent friends of the Orleanist constitution he served would have prompted "revolutionary longings, Bonapartist memories, or the constitutional ignorance and indifference." Guizot to Henry Reeve, November 4, 1858, ibid.

12. Dominique Bagge, *Les Conflits des idées politiques en France sous la Restauration* (1952), 140; François Guizot, *De la démocratie en France* (1849), 73, 7, 5, 10–11.

13. Hippolyte Taine, *Du suffrage universel et de la manière de voter* (1872), 8, 14–15, 58–59.

14. Ludwig Dehio, "Die Taktik der Opposition während des Konflikts," *Historische Zeitschrift,* CXL (1929), 280n.

15. Gottschalk to Moses Hess, May 5, 1848, Gustav Mayer, *Friedrich Engels. Eine Biographie,* 2 vols. (vol. I, 1920; 2nd ed., with vol. II, 1934), I, 298.

16. For a thorough summary of the debates, from which these quotations are taken, see Walter Gagel, *Die Wahlrechtsfrage in der Geschichte der deutschen liberalen Parteien 1848–1918* (1958), 8–16.

17. Sybel in 1862: ibid., 295; Sybel in 1869: to H. E. von Holst, July 4, 1869, Folkert Haferkorn, *Soziale Vorstellungen Heinrich von Sybels* (1976), 110–11.

18. Norman Gash, *Politics in the Age of Peel: A Study in the Technique of Parliamentary Representa-tion, 1830–1850* (1953), 10.

19. In 1831, Cobbett told his listeners that the 1830 revolution had broken out in France "*only because a reform was not made in time!*" The application to his own country was too obvious to be missed. G. D. H. Cole, *The Life of William Cobbett* (1924; ed. 1947), 381.

20. Henry Brougham, *Speeches on Social and Political Subjects, with Historical Introductions,* 2 vols. (1857), II, 357.

21. Gash, *Politics in the Age of Peel,* 15, 17.

22. "The composition of the House of Commons in 1833," R. K. Webb has written, "was little different from what it was in 1831, nor did it change significantly before the last quarter of the century." While the rather steep property qualifications for membership in Parliament were significantly modified in 1838 and finally dropped twenty years later, "members were still unpaid and the cost of serving was likely to be high." So were the expenses of contested elections. "The

country expected its representatives to be independently wealthy, and most of them were. The House remained overwhelmingly the preserve of the landed classes. There were no more businessmen in the first reformed Parliament than had been there before 1832." *Modern England from the Eighteenth Century to the Present* (1968; 2nd ed., 1980), 213.

23. See Smith, *Making of the Second Reform Bill*, 29–49.

24. "Present Aspects of Parliamentary Reform" (1859), *The Collected Works of Walter Bagehot*, ed. Norman St. John-Stevas, 15 vols. (1965–86), VI, 262.

25. George C. Brodrick, "The Utilitarian Argument against Reform," *Essays on Reform* (1867), 7.

26. July 24, 1866, *The Gladstone Diaries*, ed. M. R. D. Foot and H. C. G. Matthew, 11 vols. so far (1968–   ), vol. VI, *1861–1868* (1978), 454.

27. Arnold, *Culture and Anarchy* (1869; 2nd ed., 1875; ed. J. Dover Wilson, 1932), 76, 77, 203. As Wilson notes (pp. viii–ix), in the second edition Arnold deleted the passage about the Tarpeian Rock.

28. Carlyle: James Anthony Froude, *Thomas Carlyle: A History of His Life in London, 1834–1881*, 2 vols. (1890), II, 374–75; Stephen: Christopher Harvie, *The Lights of Liberalism: University Liberals and the Challenge of Democracy, 1860–86* (1976), 140.

29. D. W. Sylvester, *Robert Lowe and Education* (1974), 28–31.

30. Ibid., 120, 34.

31. H. C. G. Matthew, "Rhetoric and Politics in Great Britain, 1860–1950," in P. J. Waller, ed., *Politics and Social Change: Essays Presented to A. F. Thompson* (1987), 36.

32. See ibid., 34–58, esp. 34–44.

33. Beatrice Potter, March 16 [1884], *The Diary of Beatrice Webb*, ed. Norman MacKenzie and Jeanne MacKenzie, vol. I, *1873–1892, Glitter Around and Darkness Within* (1982), 107–8. For the personal relationship between Potter and Chamberlain, see Peter Gay, *The Bourgeois Experience*, vol. II, *The Tender Passion* (1986), 110–14.

34. J. L. Garvin, *The Life of Joseph Chamberlain*, vol. II, *1885–1895, Disruption and Combat* (1933), 333–34. Describing the impact of Chamberlain's speeches in the mid-1880s, the time when Beatrice Potter heard him, Garvin says (without disapproval), "Everywhere he aroused fighting enthusiasm at his meetings. Now his invective was his force. . . . Addressing Conservatism now as well as Liberal Unionists, he met hate with hate. Denouncing dynamiters, assassins, separatists, agrarian outrage, parliamentary intimidation, he employed a new and sulphurous power of incitement. Chamberlain, now and many a time henceforth, made his audiences bay" (p. 253).

35. William Gladstone, "Third Midlothian Speech," November 27, 1879, *Political Speeches in Scotland, November and December 1879* (1879), 96; "Hawick Speech," November 24, 1879, ibid., 20; "Second Midlothian Speech," November 26, 1879, ibid., 60.

36. Peter Stansky, *Gladstone: A Progress in Politics* (1979), 126.

37. Richard T. Shannon, *Gladstone and the Bulgarian Agitation, 1876* (1963), 23.

38. William Gladstone, "A Chapter of Autobiography" (1868), *Gleanings of Past Years, 1843–79*, vol. VII, *Miscellaneous* (1879), 98–102.

39. December 28, 1879, *Gladstone Diaries*, IX, 471.

40. Andrew Jones, *The Politics of Reform, 1884* (1972), 4.

FOUR: The Powerful, Weaker Sex

1. Jules Simon, *La Femme du vingtième siècle* (1891; 4th ed., 1892), 1.

2. Mary Wollstonecraft, *A Vindication of the Rights of Woman, with Strictures on Political and Moral Subjects* (1792; ed. Charles W. Hagelman, Jr., 1967), 158.

3. Lee Holcombe, *Victorian Ladies at Work: Middle-Class Working Women in England and Wales, 1850–1914* (1973), 3.

4. As early as 1698, in his *Essay upon Projects,* Daniel Defoe had already charged his fellow men with mistreating women in word and deed; had they the educational advantages men enjoyed, their apparent inferiority would soon disappear. Later, the philosophes made some brave stabs at probing beneath social appearances to underlying realities, judging women not on conduct dictated by cultural pressures but on their inherent, unrealized possibilities. Yet the philosophes' thinking about women was hampered by remnants of conventionality and by mixed feelings they could neither sort out nor altogether escape. Denis Diderot's *Encyclopédie* is a study in ambivalence; some of its articles depict the ideal woman as a housewife, pious, thrifty, gentle, submissive, while others denounce the legal disabilities and perfunctory education of women as unnatural and obtuse. Men who fancied themselves destined to rule over women, some encyclopedists asserted, were ignoring evidence showing them to be as intelligent, competent, and energetic as men. David Hume, much like Defoe before him, described marriage as "an engagement entered into by mutual consent," and denounced the "male tyranny" that "destroys the nearness of rank, not to say equality, which nature has established between the sexes." But he had no quarrel with the musty notion that woman is "little to be understood." "Of Polygamy and Divorce" (1741), *The Philosophical Works of David Hume,* ed. T. H. Green and T. H. Grose, 4 vols. (1875; ed. 1882), III, 231, 234, 234n; Hume to William Mure of Caldwell, November 14 [1742], *The Letters of David Hume,* ed. J. Y. T. Greig, 2 vols. (1932), I, 45. Diderot, in a much-quoted phrase, said it more poetically: "The symbol of woman in general is that of the Apocalypse, on whose forehead is written: Mystery." *Sur les femmes* [1772], in *Oeuvres complètes,* ed. J. Asségat and Maurice Tourneux, 20 vols. (1875–77), II, 260.

5. "On Love, Marriage, Men, and Women, I," *Sketches and Travels in London,* in *The Works of William Makepeace Thackeray,* Centenary Biographical Edition, 26 vols. (1910–11), IX, 306. As late as the 1920s Freud could still famously ask Marie Bonaparte, his analysand and friend, "What does woman want?" Peter Gay, *Freud: A Life for Our Time* (1988), 501.

6. Stendhal, *De l'amour* (1822; ed. Henri Martineau, 1938), 220, 223.

1. Domesticity: Womanliness Defined

1. Sigmund Freud, *Drei Abhandlungen zur Sexualtheorie* (1905; addition of 1915), in *Gesammelte Werke,* V, 121n; *Three Essays on the Theory of Sexuality,* in *Standard Edition,* VII, 219n.

2. Theodor Fontane, *Effi Briest* (1894), in *Sämtliche Werke,* ed. Edgar Gross et al., 24 vols. (1959–75), VII, 173–74 [ch. 1].

3. Friedrich Lienhart, *Neue Ideale, nebst Vorherrschaft Berlins* (1901; ed. 1913), 16.

4. James Henry Hammond to Marcellus Hammond, September 5, 1847, Bertram Wyatt-Brown, *Southern Honor: Ethics and Behavior in the Old South* (1982), 191.

5. In 1903, in a series of sermons on the duties of men to women, a French priest, the abbé de Gibergues, summed it all up: "Men and women will be to each other as the head and the heart. To man intelligence, reason, reflection, wisdom, majesty, strength, energy, resolution, authority. To

woman delicacy, sensibility, grace, sweetness, goodness, tenderness, discreet attention, devotion, enthusiasm, communicative warmth." *Les Devoirs des hommes envers les femmes; instructions aux homme du monde prêchées à St. Philippe-du-Roule et à St. Augustin* (1903), quoted in James E. McMillan, *Housewife or Harlot: The Place of Women in French Society, 1870–1940* (1981), 9.

6. I have explored this panicky rhetoric in some detail in "Offensive Women and Defensive Men," ch. 2 of the first volume of this series, *Education of the Senses* (1984).

7. Charles Blanc, *Grammaire des arts du dessein* (1867; 3rd ed., 1876), 21–22.

8. Konrad Guenther, *Der Kampf um das Weib in Tier- und Menschenentwicklung* (1909), 14. Charles Dickens began one of his fairy tales with this genial picture: "There was once a King, and he had a Queen, and he was the manliest of his sex, and she was the loveliest of hers." "Holiday Romance. Part II, From the Pen of Miss Alice Rainbird [age seven]," in *Yesterday's Children: An Anthology compiled from the Pages of 'Our Young Folks,' 1865–1873*, ed. John Morton Blum (1959), 166.

9. Friedrich Hegel, *Philosophie des Rechts* (lectures of 1819–20), ed. Dieter Henrich (1983), 137–39.

10. As several writers on nineteenth-century woman's movements have observed, the term "feminism" did not come into general use in France and England until the early 1890s. But the word itself is older, and "feminism" and "feminist" are convenient expressions.

11. Alfred, Lord Tennyson, *The Princess*, section v, lines 147, 427–31.

12. In contrast, the German Social Democrat August Bebel devoted a chapter in *Die Frau und der Sozialismus* (1883) to the tragic fate of woman in the Christian centuries and took undisguised pleasure in quoting with disapproval the most misogynistic outbursts of the Church Fathers.

13. Eliza Lynn Linton, articles for the *Saturday Review* reprinted in *Modern Women* (1888): "Ambitious Wives," 198–205 passim; "Feminine Influence," 177–87 passim; "Man and His Master," 215–24 passim.

14. Friedrich Hegel, *Phänomenologie des Geistes* (1807; ed. Johannes Hoffmeister, 1952), 340.

15. John Chapman, "The Position of Woman in Barbarism and among the Ancients," *Westminster Review*, LXIV (1855), 379.

16. Horace Bushnell, *Women's Suffrage: The Reform against Nature* (1869), Acknowledgment (unpaged) and 11; see also 13.

17. Ibid., 17–27 passim.

18. Ibid., 50–51. Bushnell took pleasure in quoting extensively from an article in the *Nation* which holds that just as men and women differ in form and features, so do they differ in mental and moral qualities: "They take the same views of nothing." Bushnell agreed with the *Nation* that science verifies the old verities about the sexes: "One is passive, the other active; one emotional, the other moral; one affectionate, the other rational; one sentimental, the other intellectual." Differences in occupations and standards between men and women have been decreed by nature. Ibid., 36–37.

19. Ibid., 59, 58, 64, 175.

20. See "*Women's Suffrage*, by Horace Bushnell and *The Subjection of Women*, by John Stuart Mill" (1869), *The Works of William James*, ed. F. H. Burkhardt et al., 19 vols. (1975–88), vol. XVII, *Essays, Comments and Reviews*, 247–48.

21. John W. Burgon, *Woman's Place* (1871), 9–10. Thirty years earlier, T. H. Lister in the *Edinburgh Review* had anticipated this threat. Reviewing half a dozen books on women, he noted that some "champions of female rights" were unfortunately prepared to infringe "upon that important law which prescribes a division of duties." After all, man's intellectual, literary, and aesthetic superiority to woman is a fact of life. And if women were granted real power, they would

suffer substantial loss, notably in men's deference. "Do they owe this treatment to their strength or to their weakness? Undoubtedly to the latter." Once women are "made ostensibly powerful" and "a sense of competition" between the sexes emerges, the "spirit of chivalry" will quickly disappear. "Women, as a class, cannot enjoy, at the same time, the immunities of weakness and the advantages of power." *Women in Public: Documents of the Victorian Women's Movement, 1850–1900,* ed. Patricia Hollis (1979), 8.

22. Louis-Aimé Martin, *Éducation des mères de famille; ou, De la civilisation du genre humain par les femmes* (1834; 4th ed., 1842), 3, 68, 85.

23. [Sarah Lewis], *Woman's Mission* (1839; 17th English and 4th American ed., 1854), 26.

24. *The Limits of Sisterhood: The Beecher Sisters on Women's Rights and Woman's Sphere,* ed. Jeanne Boydston, Mary Kelley, and Anne Margolis (1988), 231.

25. "than the nature of men": Charles Dickens, *Dombey and Son* (1848; ed. Alan Horsman, 1974), 29 [ch. 3]; "however Ragged they are": Dickens to Angela Burdett Coutts, September 24, 1843, *The Letters of Charles Dickens,* vol. III, *1842–1843,* ed. Madeline House, Graham Storey, and Kathleen Tillotson (1974), 572; "marked out by Heaven!": Dickens to Coutts, May 17, 1849, *Letters,* vol. V, *1847–1849,* ed. Graham Storey and K. J. Fielding (1981), 542; "lofty character of Wife": Dickens, *The Personal History of David Copperfield* (1850; ed. Trevor Blount, 1966), 474 [ch. 28].

26. Charles Dickens, *The Adventures of Oliver Twist* (1838; ed. Humphry House, 1949), 399 [ch. 51].

27. *Hommesses:* Deborah L. Silverman, *Art Nouveau in Fin-de-Siècle France: Politics, Psychology, and Style* (1989), 63; Wollstonecraft, *Vindication,* 33.

28. "Of Queens' Gardens," *Sesame and Lilies* (1865), in *The Works of John Ruskin,* ed. E. T. Cook and Alexander Wedderburn, 39 vols. (1903–12), XVIII, 111, 121–22.

29. Ibid., 121–22.

30. Paulin Limayrac, "Les Femmes moralistes," *Revue des deux mondes,* 13th year (October 1843), 52. Fifteen years later, the journal favorably noticed poems on young mothers by M. A. de Beauchesne, and quoted at length from one: "When we hear the very name 'mother' our heart expands, for it is the most aromatic name ever to perfume sad humanity, the sweetest song and the one most listened to." V. de Mars, *"Le Livre de jeunes Mères,* par M. A. de Beauchesne," *Revue des deux mondes,* 28th year (September–October 1858), 973.

31. Jean Jacques Rousseau, *Émile,* in *Oeuvres complètes,* ed. Bernard Gagnebin, Robert Osmont, and Marcel Raymond, 4 vols. (1959–69), IV, 693.

32. Wollstonecraft, *Vindication,* 54, 82–83, 55, 104.

33. Wright to the marquis de Lafayette, February 11, 1822, William Randall Waterman, *Frances Wright* (1924), 74. The assertion goes back to a famous pamphlet of 1673 by the Cartesian writer François Poulain de la Barre, *De l'égalité des deux sexes.* "L'esprit," he wrote, "n'a point de sexe." See Liselotte Steinbrügge, *Das moralische Geschlecht. Theorien und literarische Entwürfe über die Natur der Frau in der französischen Aufklärung* (1987), 19–21.

34. Henry Maudsley, *Sex in Mind and in Education* (1874), 7. For details concerning the debate, see Peter Gay, *The Bourgeois Experience,* vol. I, *Education of the Senses* (1984), 213–25.

35. Herbert Spencer, *Social Statics; or, The Conditions Essential to Human Happiness Specified, and the First of Them Developed* (1850; American ed., 1865), 188.

36. *De la justice dans la révolution et dans l'Église* (1858; complete ed., 1860), in *Oeuvres complètes de P.-J. Proudhon,* ed. C. Bouglé and H. Moysset, 14 vols. (1923–38), XII, 197. Later, the French novelist Barbey d'Aurevilly, a monarchist and Catholic notorious for his slashing polemics, was as rabid on the subject as Proudhon before him. In "Fragments sur les femmes" he asserted that

women in power are a guaranteed source of corruption, and that all of them are wicked, without exception: "From one woman to another, not a single virtuous woman. All of them scoundrels, more or less." And, almost needless to say, mysterious scoundrels: "Woman's nature, inexplicable." "Fragments sur les femmes," *Pensées détachées* (1889), in *Les Oeuvres complètes de Jules Barbey d'Aurevilly,* ed. Joseph Quesnel, with assistance from Mlle Read, 15 vols. (1926–27), VII, 191, 196.

37. Sir Walter Scott once described woman as "Uncertain, coy, and hard to please / And variable as the shade / By the light quivering aspen made." *Marmion,* canto VI, stanza 30.

38. Barbara Taylor, *Eve and the New Jerusalem: Socialism and Feminism in the Nineteenth Century* (1983), 62–63.

39. See Claire Tomalin, *The Life and Death of Mary Wollstonecraft* (1974), 104–5.

40. Evelyn Sullerot, *Histoire de la presse féminine en France, des origines à 1848* (1966), 119.

41. Wollstonecraft, *Vindication,* 100.

42. Sullerot, *La Presse féminine en France,* 123.

43. Marianne Farningham [Marianne Hearn], *Home Life* [1869], 15, 10–11, 13; Farningham, *Girlhood* (1869), 23.

44. Consider, for example, *Woman's Own Book,* a compact compendium of advice to young married women. The anonymous author, almost certainly a woman, bestowed intimate attention on recipes and beauty hints (one of them on how to increase the size and improve the shape of one's breasts), but found room for moralizing instructions. Wives must learn to make themselves effective seconds to their husbands. As so often, this call for feminine subservience accompanies grandiose claims: "There is no earthly relation that involves greater responsibility, or demands higher wisdom, than that suggested by the name of MOTHER." But woman's immediate, most conspicuous task is that of being a helpmeet. Her man is, after all, her life. "Frequently love, to a man, is only an episode; to a woman, it is always a history." The man, *Woman's Own Book* told its readers, divides love "with fame, fortune, honor, sometimes with pleasure. She, in giving that, gives her all." A "wife can help her husband [most], perhaps, by BEING CONTENT." *Woman's Own Book* (1873), 103, 90, 90–91, 130, 131, 97.

45. Willie Lee Rose, "Reforming Women," *New York Review of Books,* XXIX (October 7, 1982), 45.

46. Sutherland Menzies, *Political Women,* 2 vols. (1873), I, vii–ix.

47. Ibid., xx.

48. The English *Lady's Magazine,* founded in 1770, which offered an attractive menu of stories, poems, fashions, practical hints, sheet music, and news, lived far longer. Its American counterpart, bearing the same name—the sincerest form of flattery—first appeared in 1792; it concentrated on "female excellence alone."

49. See the list in Laure Adler, *À l'aube du féminisme: Les Premières Journalistes (1830–1850)* (1979), 215–19, which, though extensive, may not be quite complete.

50. See Frank Luther Mott, *A History of American Magazines,* vol. I, *1741–1850* (1930), 581.

51. Ruth E. Finley, *The Lady of Godey's: Sarah Josepha Hale* (1931), 39.

52. George Sand, *My Life,* tr. Dan Hofstadter (1980), 218.

53. Mary W. Hale, "False Pride: A Tale of Every Day Life," *Godey's Lady's Book,* XXII (January 1841), 7–11; quotation at 8.

54. See Mrs. C. Lee Hentz, "The Parlour Serpent," ibid., 26–34. Another emphatic moral tale, "A Life of Fashion," relies on poetic justice quite as much. A mercenary but fascinating, and (of course) beautiful young woman is determined to capture a fortune. She marries an unprepossessing, tightfisted, white-haired millionaire—he is over sixty—whom she expects to outlive by many years as a rich, attractive widow. To her dismay, her husband dies at ninety-six, leaving her a

miserable, aged widow, with "the frosts of nearly sixty winters" having "withered the roses of her cheek and whitened the dark beauty of her raven locks." Emma C. Embury, "A Life of Fashion," ibid., 22–25.

55. See Sarah Josepha Hale, "New Year's Eve," ibid., 44–46.

56. Similarly, Ernst Keil, editor of Germany's favorite family periodical, *Die Gartenlaube,* insisted in its first number that it would stay far away from "disputatious politics." *Die Gartenlaube,* I (1853), 1.

57. Sarah Josepha Hale, "Fifty Years of My Literary Life," *Godey's Lady's Book,* XCV (December 1877), 522. In this short account of her career, she noted with real pride (showing lamentable ignorance of earlier efforts, mainly in France and England) that before she took over the *Ladies' Magazine,* "a magazine edited by a woman for women had never been conducted, so far as I know, either in the Old World or the New."

58. "Oh! ever sacred be the ties," Mary Augusta Coffin rhymed, "That nature's laws impart; / 'Tis man must rule the multitude, / But woman sways *his* heart." "Woman's Rights Illustrated," *Godey's Lady's Book,* XXII (February 1841), 78. The epigraph to this versified argument was Mrs. Hale's: "The world's proud empire leave to man, / But by maternal love, / Oh! raise his hopes, his aims, to share / Your heritage above."

59. See Hale's column, "Editor's Table," in *Godey's Lady's Book,* XXII (February 1841), 95, and XLIV (January 1852), 88. In 1852 she enlisted the celebrated orator Daniel Webster to make her point for her. "It is to the inculcation of high and pure morals," he exclaimed, that "in a free republic, woman performs her sacred duty, and fulfills her destiny." "Influence of Women," ibid., 90. See also, in *Godey's Lady's Book,* "Formation of Character," XXII (April 1841), 160, and Hale, "Editor's Table," XXIII (December 1841), 294.

60. On the perils of alcohol, see Hale, "Editor's Table," *Godey's Lady's Book,* XXII (March 1841), 142, and XLIV (May 1852), 404.

61. "From Our Own Reporter, Chericot: Men's Rights Convention at ———. Extraordinary Proceedings, Exciting Scenes, and Curious Speeches," *Godey's Lady's Book,* XLIV (April 1852), 268–73.

62. Effie Effindale, "The Young Housekeeper," *Godey's Lady's Book,* XCIV (January 1877), 39.

63. Frank Luther Mott, *A History of American Magazines,* vol. III, *1865–1885* (1938), 90.

2. A Time for Tentativeness

1. Charlotte Brontë to George Smith, March 16, 1850, Patricia Beer, *Reader, I Married Him: A Study of the Women Characters of Jane Austen, Charlotte Brontë, Elizabeth Gaskell and George Eliot* (1974), 29; Charlotte Brontë to Mrs. Gaskell, August 27, 1850, ibid., 30.

2. Sarah Josepha Hale, "Editor's Table," *Godey's Lady's Book,* XLIV (March 1852), 228.

3. Thomas Hughes, *Tom Brown at Oxford* (1861; ed. 1914), 478.

4. Elizabeth Barrett to Robert Browning, July 4, 1846, *The Letters of Robert Browning and Elizabeth Barrett Browning, 1845–1846,* ed. Elvan Kintner, 2 vols. consecutively paginated (1969), 844.

5. Elizabeth Barrett to Robert Browning: April 7, 1846, ibid., 599; January 11, 1845, ibid., 4.

6. See Maria Deraismes, *Eve contre Monsieur Dumas fils* (1872).

7. Samuel Butler, *The Authoress of the Odyssey* (1897; 2nd ed., 1922; ed. 1967), 11.

8. Anthony Trollope, *He Knew He Was Right* (1869; ed. P. D. Edwards, 2 vols. in one, 1974), II,

247, 249 [ch. 81]. For Trollope's disappointment in the novel, see *An Autobiography* (1883; World's Classics ed., 1953), 275–76.

9. Jules Simon, *La Femme du vingtième siècle* (1891; 4th ed., 1892), 67.

10. See Jules Simon, *Dieu, patrie, liberté* (1883), 304.

11. Jules Simon, *L'Ouvrière* (1861), vi, v. While this is a study of working-class women, his strictures explicitly hold for bourgeois women as well.

12. Ibid., 8.

13. Mme G. Schéfer and Mme Sophie Amis, *Travaux manuels et économie domestique à l'usage des jeunes filles* (1885), 7, 5.

14. Clara Schreiber, *Eine Wienerin in Paris* (1885), summarized and quoted in *Illustrirte Zeitung*, no. 2171 (February 7, 1885), 149; M. S. Van de Velde, *French Fiction of Today*, 2 vols. (1891), II, 166.

15. Mathilda Betham-Edwards, *Home Life in France* (1905), 89–90.

16. Steven C. Hause, *Hubertine Auclert: The French Suffragette* (1987), 5. In the 1860s John Stuart Mill, the unrivaled feminist of the century, had already bitterly noted, "The greater part of what women write about women is mere sycophancy to men." *The Subjection of Women* (1869), in John Stuart Mill and Harriet Taylor Mill, *Essays on Sex Equality*, ed. Alice S. Rossi (1970), 153 [ch. 1]. Far more typical than Mill's reaction was the farcical proposal for a "Girls' Holiday Occupation Institute" by Charles Dickens's friend Wilkie Collins in Dickens's periodical *All the Year Round*. This institute would rectify the hollow excuse for an education that many young women were still receiving with "a Physical-Education Class; a Cookery Class; a Household-Bill-auditing Class; a Shirt-button-Supervision Class; and a Mangy-Gossip-Suppression Class." Here is the damaging stereotype of garrulous, superficial woman, a neat specimen of gratuitous male aggression, in full flower. "My Girls," *All the Year Round*, II (February 11, 1860), 370–74.

17. Hubertine Auclert. *La Citoyenne. Articles de 1881 à 1891*, ed. Edith Taïeb (1982), 102–3.

18. The lecture is summarized approvingly in "Frauenzeitung," *Illustrirte Zeitung*, no. 2129 (April 19, 1884), 338. The "Frauenzeitung" supplement was so successful among its "woman readers" that in the summer of 1884, the *Illustrirte* decided to enlarge it, with a story written expressly for each issue. See ibid., no. 2140 (July 5, 1884), 21.

19. Hause, *Hubertine Auclert*, 137.

20. Emil Marriot [pseud.], "Dem Manne gleich," in "Frauenzeitung," *Illustrirte Zeitung*, no. 2210 (November 7, 1885), 464.

21. Richard J. Evans, *The Feminist Movement in Germany, 1894–1933* (1976), 23.

22. Brian Harrison, *Separate Spheres: The Opposition to Women's Suffrage in Britain* (1978), 57.

23. For these instances, see "Frauenzeitung," *Illustrirte Zeitung*, of the following dates. Inquisitiveness: no. 2144 (August 2, 1884), 123; Vienna: no. 2117 (January 26, 1884), 78; Juvenal: no. 2155 (October 18, 1884), 397; Chinese proverb: no. 2156 (October 25, 1884), 402; age kept secret: no. 2089 (July 14, 1883), 42.

24. "Frauenzeitung," *Illustrirte Zeitung*, no. 2071 (March 10, 1883), 218.

25. For these instances, see "Frauenzeitung," *Illustrirte Zeitung*, of the following dates. Flowers, poems, and letters: no. 2194 (July 18, 1885), 73; ignoring men: no. 2076 (April 14, 1883), 322; Luther: no. 2106 (November 10, 1883), 430; German women: no. 2111 (December 15, 1883), 562, and no. 2124 (March 15, 1884), 227.

26. "Frauenzeitung," *Illustrirte Zeitung*, no. 2204 (September 26, 1885), 315.

27. For these instances, see "Frauenzeitung," *Illustrirte Zeitung*, of the following dates. American newspapers: no. 2107 (November 17, 1883), 452; "woman's emancipation": no. 2139 (June 28, 1884), 555; "rug from under them": no. 2142 (July 19, 1884), 74.

28. John C. Hertwig, *Woman Suffrage* (1883), 7–8; quotation at 12; "Frauenzeitung," *Illustrirte Zeitung,* no. 2145 (August 9, 1884), 147–48; ibid., no. 2142 (July 19, 1884), 74.

29. For these instances, see "Frauenzeitung," *Illustrirte Zeitung,* of the following dates. Somerville College: no. 2077 (April 21, 1883), 342; Uppsala: no. 2087 (June 30, 1883), 558; Toronto: no. 2166 (January 3, 1885), 77; archaeology: no. 2148 (August 30, 1884), 219; philology: no. 2161 (November 22, 1884), 578; mathematics: no. 2135 (May 31, 1884), 464; classical languages: no. 2149 (September 6, 1884), 244; medicine: no. 2162 (November 29, 1884), 548; pharmaceutics: no. 2095 (August 25, 1883), 166; botany: no. 2145 (August 9, 1884), 148; commercial travelers: no. 2121 (February 23, 1884), 158; architects: no. 2120 (February 16, 1884), 138; bank presidents: no. 2086 (June 23, 1883), 539; pianists: no. 2072 (March 17, 1883), 238; medical students in Zurich: no. 2104 (October 27, 1883), 390; medical students in Paris: no. 2115 (January 12, 1884), 38; woman doctors in Russia: no. 2136 (June 7, 1884), 486.

30. Hubertine Auclert: see "Frauenzeitung," *Illustrirte Zeitung,* no. 2167 (January 10, 1885), 53; businesswomen: ibid., no. 2171 (February 7, 1885), 149.

31. Theodore Zeldin, *France, 1848–1945,* vol. I, *Ambition, Love and Politics* (1973), 346.

32. Barrie detested the epithet "whimsical"; in a speech to drama critics he proposed "inoffensive" as a substitute. William Lyon Phelps, Introduction to *Representative Plays by J. M. Barrie* (n.d.), viii–ix.

33. J. M. Barrie, *What Every Woman Knows* (1908; ed. 1928), 159–60.

34. Samuel Butler, *The Way of All Flesh* (1903; ed. 1916), 1 [ch. 1]; Theodor Fontane, *Frau Jenny Treibel* (1892), in *Sämtliche Werke,* ed. Edgar Gross et al., 24 vols. (1959–75), VII, 151 [ch. 14].

35. 1 Peter 3: 1; 1 Corinthians 14:35.

36. Steven C. Hause, with Anne R. Kenney, *Women's Suffrage and Social Politics in the French Third Republic* (1984), 16. The opposition to women's rights was only too pleased to enlist George Sand among its supporters. As the "Frauenzeitung" triumphantly reported in 1884 upon publication of Sand's correspondence of the 1860s, in her later years that celebrated radical had turned away from her feminism; participating in politics, she had come to believe, would prevent a woman from fulfilling her wifely and maternal duties. See *Illustrirte Zeitung,* no. 2139 (June 28, 1884), 555.

37. Indeed, it was generally accepted that the French law of 1879 establishing secondary schools for girls was designed precisely for that purpose. "In truth, what is involved" in that law, *La Civilisation* noted on November 24, 1880, "is to win woman away from the influence of Christianity." Mona Ozouf, *L'École, l'Église et la République 1871–1914* (1963), 104.

38. Hause, with Kenney, *Women's Suffrage,* 16–17.

39. James C. Albisetti, *Schooling German Girls and Women: Secondary and Higher Education in the Nineteenth Century* (1988), 183.

40. Paul Julius Moebius, *Über den physiologischen Schwachsinn des Weibes* (1900; 8th ed., 1906), 28.

41. Ibid., 42, 34.

42. As late as 1927, Freud thought it necessary to refute Moebius's provocative thesis of woman's feeblemindedness. See *Die Zukunft einer Illusion,* in *Gesammelte Werke,* XIV, 371; *The Future of an Illusion,* in *Standard Edition,* XXI, 48. In 1904, Freud had lectured critically on Moebius's pamphlet to his brethren at the B'nai B'rith, and in 1908, he had attacked it in his paper " 'Civilized' Sexual Morality and Modern Nervous Illness." "Die 'kulturelle' Sexualmoral und die moderne Nervosität," in *Gesammelte Werke,* VII, 162; *Standard Edition,* IX, 199.

43. See Octave Uzanne, *La Femme à Paris: Nos contemporaines. Notes successives sur les Parisiennes de ce temps, dans leur divers milieux, états et conditions* (1894).

44. Theodor Fontane, *L'Adultera* (1882), in *Sämtliche Werke*, IV, 38 [ch. 7]. The speaker is, of course, a character in a novel, and by no means a lovable one, and there is no reason to assume that Fontane endorsed his view. But plainly it was current enough to be put into a character's mouth.

45. See Albisetti, *Schooling German Girls*, 186.

3. A D——d Mob of Scribbling Women

1. W. R. Greg, "False Morality of Lady Novelists" [ca. 1858], *Literary and Social Judgments* (1873), 89.

2. Walpole to Hannah More, January 24, 1795, *Horace Walpole's Miscellaneous Correspondence*, ed. W. S. Lewis and John Riely, 48 vols. (1937–83), XXXI, 397. No wonder, too, that an anonymous American journalist writing in the *Lady's Magazine* should object in 1792 to woman writers as essentially unfeminine: "We admire them more as authors than esteem them as women." Frank Luther Mott, *A History of American Magazines, 1741–1850* (1930), 66.

3. Samuel Johnson, *The Adventurer*, no. 115 (December 11, 1753), in *The Works of Samuel Johnson in Nine Volumes* (1825), IV, 109–10.

4. Goethe in conversation with Heinrich Meyer, April 30, 1807, *Gespräche 1752–1817*, in Johann Wolfgang von Goethe, *Gedenkausgabe der Werke, Briefe und Gespräche*, ed. Ernst Beutler, 27 vols. (1948–71), XXII, 446.

5. Elizabeth C. Gaskell, *The Life of Charlotte Brontë* (1857; World's Classics ed., 1919), 124–25.

6. Lisa Tiersten, "Sisterhood of Shoppers: Bourgeois Women and Consumer Culture in Late-Nineteenth-Century Paris," Ph.D. dissertation, Yale University (1991), 183.

7. E. D. Forgues, "Le Roman de femme en Angleterre. Miss Mulock," *Revue des deux mondes*, 30th year (January–February 1860), 797, 831.

8. Charles de Mazade, "Les Femmes dans la société et dans la littérature. Mme. de Sévigné, Mme. de Staël, Mme. Swetchine," *Revue des deux mondes*, 32nd year (March–April 1862), 76–77.

9. George Sand to Adolphe Guéroult [May 6, 1835], *Correspondance*, ed. Georges Lubin, 23 vols. so far (1964–   ), II, 879.

10. Robert Prutz, *Die deutsche Literatur der Gegenwart, 1848–1858*, 2 vols. (1859), II, 249–53; quotation at 249.

11. G. H. Lewes, "The Lady Novelists," *Westminster Review*, LVIII (1852), 133.

12. Ibid., 134.

13. Rudolf von Gottschall, *Deutsche Nationalliteratur des 19. Jahrhunderts* (1855; 6th ed., 4 vols., 1892), IV, 568–69.

14. "Silly Novels by Lady Novelists" (1856), *Essays of George Eliot*, ed. Thomas Pinney (1963), 303–4. George Eliot was of course not the only woman writer to denigrate writing women. In 1852, four years before Eliot's assault, Alice B. Neal caustically called attention to a new development: "But just now the needle seems to be for the first time threatened by a powerful rival; the work-box is replaced by the desk, and the portfolio has usurped the corner sacred to the tambour-frame. In other words, authorship is the mania of our ladies.." "American Female Authorship," *Godey's Lady's Book*, XLIV (February 1852), 145.

15. Eliot, "Silly Novels by Lady Novelists," 323–24.

16. Claire Tomalin, *The Life and Death of Mary Wollstonecraft* (1974), 247.

17. Janet Todd, *The Sign of Angellica: Women, Writing and Fiction, 1660–1800* (1989), 4–5.

18. Sedgwick and Evans in Mary Kelley, *Private Woman, Public Stage: Literary Domesticity in Nineteenth-Century America* (1984), 100–101, 186.

19. Ibid., 30.

20. Alison Adburgham, *Women in Print: Writing Women and Women's Magazines from the Restoration to the Accession of Victoria* (1972), 248.

21. Augusta J. Evans, *Beulah* (1859), 401, 500, 510.

22. Elizabeth Stuart Phelps, *The Story of Avis* (1879; repr. 1977), 272–73.

23. Hawthorne to William Ticknor, January 19, 1855, *The Centenary Edition of the Works of Nathaniel Hawthorne*, ed. William Charvat et al., 19 vols. so far (1962–   ), XVII, 304.

24. Henry James, "Greville Fane" (1892), *The Complete Tales of Henry James*, ed. Leon Edel, 12 vols. (1962–64), VIII, 438, 436.

25. See Henry Nash Smith, *Democracy and the Novel: Popular Resistance to Classic American Writers* (1978), 7. The copy of *The Lamplighter* in the Sterling University Library at Yale, dated 1854, the year of publication, bears the legend "Fifty-Fifth Thousand" on the title page.

26. [Margaret Oliphant], "Modern Novelists—Great and Small," *Blackwood's Edinburgh Magazine*, LXXVII (May 1855), 565.

27. R. K. Webb has reminded us that "of the roughly 45,000 books published in England between 1816 and 1851, well over 10,000 were religious works, far outdistancing the next largest category—history and geography—with 4,900, and fiction with 3,500." "The Victorian Reading Public," *The New Pelican Guide to English Literature*, ed. Boris Ford, vol. VI, *From Dickens to Hardy* (1958; 2nd ed., 1982), 199.

28. Ann Douglas, *The Feminization of American Culture* (1977; ed. 1978), 130.

29. Smith, *Democracy and the Novel*, 7.

30. See Henry Nash Smith, "The Scribbling Women and the Cosmic Success Story," *Critical Inquiry*, I (1974), 49.

31. [Oliphant], "Modern Novelists—Great and Small," 567.

32. See *Die Gartenlaube als Dokument ihrer Zeit*, ed. Magdalene Zimmerman (1963; abr. 1967), 12–13; Gabriele Strecker, *Frauenträume, Frauentränen. Über den deutschen Frauenroman* (1969), 23–25.

33. Ernst Keil, editorial in *Die Gartenlaube*, I (1853), 1.

34. In her intemperate assault on "modern" woman, Eliza Lynn Linton wrote about such novelists, "Women's heroines, except in the case of the best artists, are conceptions borrowed, not from without but from within." The heroine's "triumph is the representation of her own delicious dreams." "Women's Heroines," *Modern Women* (1888), 137, 136.

35. Strecker, *Frauenträume, Frauentränen*, 28.

36. See Gottschall, *Deutsche Nationallitteratur*, IV, 594.

37. A. Fr., "Der Frauenliebling im Festgewande," *Die Gartenlaube*, XIX (1871), 805.

38. Schopenhauer: see Stephan Koranyi, "Nachwort" to Johanna Schopenhauer, *Gabriele* (1819–20; ed. 1985), 411–12; Martineau: see R. K. Webb, *Harriet Martineau: A Radical Victorian* (1960), 40, 59, 312–14; Warner: see Kelley, *Private Woman, Public Stage*, 90–91, 148–52.

39. Henry James, "Greville Fane," 437.

40. Sand to Jules Boucoiran [March 4, 1831], *Correspondance*, I, 825; Sand to Frédéric Girerd, November 1839, ibid., IV, 810.

41. Sand to Laure Decerfz, April 1, 1833, ibid., II, 291.

42. George Sand, *Lettres d'un voyageur* (1837; ed. 1971), 132; Sand to Frédéric Girerd, November 1839, *Correspondance*, IV, 810. The matter remains murky. In her letters, Sand spoke affectionately of Kératry, describing him as hospitable, a "good man," a "worthy man," and as one from whose "protection for the sale of my little novel" she expected a great deal. Sand to Maurice and Casimir Dudevant [February 4, 1831], ibid., I, 798; Sand to Jules Boucoiran [February 12,

1831], ibid., I, 801. At the same time, she noted tartly, "I have seen Kératry again and have had enough. Alas! One should not see celebrities too close up!" Sand to Jules Boucoiran [March 4, 1831], ibid., I, 819.

43. Sand to Charles Augustin Sainte-Beuve, November 13, 1833, ibid., II, 434; Sand to Jules Boucoiran (March 4, 1831), ibid., I, 817. Henry James, rarely caught out on such matters, got George Sand wrong when he reported, "She affirms that her natural indolence was extreme, and that the need of money alone induced her to take her pen into her hand." "George Sand," *French Poets and Novelists* (1878; 2nd ed., 1884), 166.

44. *Autobiography and Letters of Mrs. Margaret Oliphant* (1899; ed. Mrs. Harry Coghill, 1974), 44, 4.

45. Webb, *Harriet Martineau*, 41.

46. "bib and tucker": October 1856, *The Journals of Louisa May Alcott*, ed. Joel Myerson and Daniel Shealy (1989), 79; "a woman's body": interview with Louise Chandler Moulton quoted in Elaine Showalter, Introduction to Louisa May Alcott, *Little Women* (1868–69; ed. 1989), xiii.

47. Alcott, *Little Women*, 2 [ch. 1].

48. Ibid., 265 [ch. 27].

49. "out for money": Alcott, *Journals*, 81; "support myself": Alcott to her father, November 29, 1856, *The Selected Letters of Louisa May Alcott*, ed. Joel Myerson and Daniel Shealy (1987), 26.

50. Alcott's diaries and letters are repositories of contained fury, mainly against one man, the oedipal father she loved and hated. While Cheney estimates that more than a million copies of her novels were sold and that she realized more than $200,000, this accounting slights the emotional cost that having to endure fame and fortune, to say nothing of being father to her family, extracted from Louis May Alcott. She made her debut as a published writer in 1854, at twenty-two, with a collection of fairy tales, *Flower Fables*. The little book was, she proudly told her mother, her "first-born." It brought her $32, which she handed to her family. Ednah Dow Cheney, *Louisa May Alcott* (1889; intro. Ann Douglas, 1980), 397–98; quotation at 76. In 1863, when she earned nearly $600 "by writing alone," she turned over about $500 to her parents and sisters. And at the end of 1868, suddenly a famous author, she gave more; with a royalty check of $8,500 for the first part of *Little Women*, she paid off all of her family's long-term debts. Martha Saxton, *Louisa May: A Modern Biography of Louisa May Alcott* (1977), 261; see also 291.

51. Marieluise Steinhauer, *Fanny Lewald, die deutsche George Sand. Ein Kapitel aus der Geschichte des Frauenromans im 19. Jahrhundert* (1937), 3.

52. Ibid., 107–8.

53. Maria Janitschek, "Ein modernes Weib" (1889), in Gisela Brinker-Gabler, ed., *Deutsche Dichterinnen vom 16. Jahrhundert bis zur Gegenwart. Gedichte und Lebensläufe* (1978), 240–41.

54. The book, Rudolf von Gottschall wrote shortly after its appearance in 1889, "is one of the most brilliant polemics against war ever written, all the more effective and convincing because it does not just advance reasons, but describes the horror and inhumanity of war in all its repellent guises and with a truly intrepid pen." *Deutsche Nationalliteratur*, IV, 693.

55. Elizabeth Barrett Browning, *Aurora Leigh*, book II, lines 460–66; quotation at line 466. This is not the speaker's last word, but it remains a powerful claim.

56. James McPherson, *Battle Cry of Freedom: The Civil War Era* (1988), 88–90.

57. Paul Schlenther, "Von dichtenden Frauen," *Die Nation*, II (1884–85), no. 8, 101, and see ibid., no. 9, 116–18, and no. 11, 144–46; "Frauenzeitung," *Illustrirte Zeitung*, no. 2102 (October 13, 1883), 322–23. Misspellings in original.

58. See Eliot, "Silly Novels by Lady Novelists," 322.

59. Lewes to John Blackwood [December 2, 1858], *The George Eliot Letters*, ed. Gordon S.

Haight, 7 vols. (1954–55), vol. II, *1852–1858* (1954), 506. By then, Blackwood, George Eliot's publisher, was in on the secret.

60. Dallas opened his assessment of *Adam Bede* with a trumpet flourish. "There can be no mistake" about the matter: "It is a first-rate novel, and its author takes rank at once among the masters of the art." *The Times* (London), April 12, 1859, p. 9. When he turned to *The Mill on the Floss,* after Marian Evans's secret was out, he began, " 'George Eliot' is as great as ever." Ibid., May 19, 1860, p. 10. As for *Silas Marner:* "To George Eliot belongs this praise—that not only is every one of her tales a masterpiece, but also they may be opened at almost any page, and the eye is certain to light upon something worth reading." Ibid., April 29, 1861, p. 12.

61. "Romola," *Saturday Review,* XVI (July 25, 1863), 124–25.

62. France: John Philip Couch, *George Eliot in France: A French Appraisal of George Eliot's Writings, 1858–1960* (1967), 1; Germany: Lady Blennerhasset, countess von Leyden, "George Eliot," *Deutsche Rundschau,* XLIV (July–September 1885), 362. In 1893, Hedwig Bender, in what appears to be the first German biography of George Eliot, began her tribute—it was nothing less—with expressions of wholly unreserved esteem: "The number of women who deserve the rank and title of true imaginative writer, imaginative writer by the grace of God, is not very large. But among them George Eliot indisputably takes one of the first places, perhaps, at least as novelist, the very first and highest." *George Eliot. Ein Lebensbild* (1893), 3.

63. Robert Louis Stevenson found Eliot a "high" and "rather dry lady," who had unfortunately conjured up that "melancholy puppy and humbug Daniel Deronda," that "Prince of Prigs." Still, "hats off all the same, you understand: a woman of genius." Jane Miller, *Women Writing about Men* (1986), 279.

64. May 13 [1896], *The Journals of Arnold Bennett,* 3 vols. (1932–33), I, 7–8. The year before, George Saintsbury, a critic and literary historian whose opinions carried imposing weight for decades, had been even more misogynistic, resorting to well-worn clichés. Like Charlotte Brontë, he declared, George Eliot did not possess "in any great degree the male faculties of creation and judgment. Both, and Miss Evans especially, had in no ordinary degree the female faculty of receiving, assimilating, and reproducing." *Corrected Impressions: Essays on Victorian Writers* (1895), 162.

65. Arnold on Sand: Patricia Thomson, *George Sand and the Victorians: Her Influence and Reputation in Nineteenth-Century England* (1977), 117; Flaubert to Ivan Turgenev, June 25, 1876, *Flaubert and Turgenev, a Friendship in Letters: The Complete Correspondence,* ed. and tr. Barbara Beaumont (1985), 103; John Stuart Mill, *The Subjection of Women* (1869), 204.

66. Sidney Colvin, review (1876) of George Eliot's *Daniel Deronda,* quoted in Thomson, *George Sand and the Victorians,* 152.

67. Anton Chekhov, *Ivanov,* act III, scene 5.

68. Thomson, *George Sand and the Victorians,* 20, 24.

69. Turgenev to Gustave Flaubert, June 18, 1876, *Flaubert and Turgenev,* ed. and tr. Beaumont, 102; Flaubert on Sand: Curtis Cate, *George Sand* (1975), 731.

70. Ernst Brausewetter, *Meister-Novellen deutscher Frauen,* 2 vols. (1898), I, xii.

4. Competence: Womanliness Redefined

1. Lisa Tiersten, "Sisterhood of Shoppers: Bourgeois Women and Consumer Culture in Late-Nineteenth-Century Paris," Ph.D. dissertation, Yale University (1991), 266.

2. Hort to Miss March Phillipps, October 28, 1871, M. Jeanne Peterson, *Family, Love, and Work in the Lives of Victorian Gentlewomen* (1989), 35.

3. Jane Austen, *Emma* (1816; ed. Ronald Blythe, 1966), 90 [ch. 8].

4. Toward the conclusion of *Pride and Prejudice*, after Elizabeth Bennet has overcome her prejudice against Mr. Darcy, her father, giving his consent, warns her, "I know that you could be neither happy nor respectable unless you truly esteemed your husband," by which he means, "unless you looked up to him as a superior." There is no need for Elizabeth to assure her father that she does indeed look up to Darcy; she has no choice. Jane Austen, *Pride and Prejudice* (1813; ed. Tony Tanner, 1972), 385 [ch. 59].

5. "male female": Michael Slater, *Dickens and Women* (1983), 316.

6. "domestic heroism": Dickens to Angela Burdett Coutts, September 10, 1845, *The Letters of Charles Dickens*, vol. IV, *1844–1846*, ed. Kathleen Tillotson (1977), 375; Mrs. Chirrup: Dickens, "The Nice Little Couple": *Sketches by Boz* (1836; ed. 1957), 584–87.

7. E. P. Whipple, "Novels and Novelists: Charles Dickens" (1849), in Philip Collins, ed., *Dickens: The Critical Heritage* (1971), 238. Other writers on Dickens, including his friend and biographer John Forster, silently stole this characterization. See ibid., 293n.

8. Mill to Harriet Taylor Mill, March 20, 1854, *Collected Works of John Stuart Mill*, ed. J. M. Robson, 25 vols. (1963–86), vol. XIV, *Later Letters of John Stuart Mill*, 190.

9. "Miscellaneous Cooking: Common Beef Stock," *Godey's Lady's Book*, XCIV (February 1877), 181–82; for equally unblushing advice from *Godey's* on how to carve a chicken, see XCIV (January 1877), 85; and for preparation of a lobster, see XCIV (April 1877), 367–68. For more on the Victorian gentlewoman's exposure to life's realities, see Peter Gay, *The Bourgeois Experience*, vol. I, *Education of the Senses* (1984), ch. 5, "Carnal Knowledge."

10. Isabella Beeton, *The Book of Household Management* (1861), iii.

11. The competition any *Hausfrau* faced from the outside world was obviously a burning issue elsewhere, too; just after 1900, a Mme M. Sage, in a compendium of domestic science addressed to her French compatriots, made the wife responsible for her husband's straying: "If the man deserts the home so often, that is because the home is not the nest that it should be, and that through the woman's fault." Blaming the victim remained good sport. *La Science et les travaux de la ménagère* (1901; 2nd ed., 1902), 4.

12. Beeton, *Household Management*, title page and p. 1.

13. Ibid., 6; see also 1.

14. Ibid., 275, 371.

15. Ibid., 9.

16. Judith Gautier, *Le Collier des jours*, vol. II, *Le Second Rang du collier* (1909), 188, 262–64.

17. "Invention for Attracting the Notice of Post-Office Ladies. (Patent Applied For)," in Lee Holcombe, *Victorian Ladies at Work: Middle-Class Working Women in England and Wales, 1850–1914* (1973), at p. 177.

18. February 14, 1868, *The Journals of Louisa May Alcott*, ed. Joel Myerson and Daniel Shealy (1989), 165.

19. Holcombe, *Victorian Ladies at Work*, 74.

20. Mill to Caroline Liddell, May 6, 1866, *Collected Works*, vol. XVI, *Later Letters*, 1163–64. This letter may have actually been written by Mill's stepdaughter Helen Taylor, who was in Mill's confidence just as her mother had been. But if so, she was expressing his views.

21. Ernest Legouvé, *Histoire morale des femmes* (1849; 8th ed., 1882), 380.

22. Theodor Fontane, *Cécile* (1887), in *Sämtliche Werke*, ed. Edgar Gross et al., 24 vols. (1959–75), IV, 154 [ch. 7]; About: Theodore Zeldin, *France, 1848–1945*, vol. I, *Ambition, Love and Politics* (1973), 355.

23. Fontane, *Cécile*, 146 [ch. 6].

24. For details of the slow progress to gain legal rights and admission to higher education and such professions as medicine, see Gay, *Education of the Senses,* 174–88.

25. Frances Power Cobbe, "Criminals, Idiots, Women, and Minors," *Fraser's Magazine,* LXXVIII (December 1868), 777–94.

26. Hubertine Auclert, *La Citoyenne. Articles de 1881 à 1891,* ed. Edith Taïeb, 133.

27. A. Amy Bulley, "The Political Evolution of Women," *Westminster Review,* CXXXIV (1890), 1–8 passim.

28. Herbert Spencer, *Social Statics; or, The Conditions Essential to Human Happiness Specified, and the First of Them Developed* (1850; American ed., 1865), 173, 179.

29. February 8, 1896. *Stenographische Berichte über die Verhandlungen des Reichstags,* IX, Legislatur-periode, IV. Session, 1895–1897, vol. 2, 831–41.

FIVE: The Bite of Wit

1. Varieties of Laughter

1. *Human Nature, or the Fundamental Elements of Policy* (1650), in *The English Works of Thomas Hobbes of Malmesbury,* ed. Sir William Molesworth, 11 vols. (1839–45), IV, 46 [ch. 9]; Charles Baudelaire, "De l'essence du rire et généralement du comique dans les arts plastiques" (written in 1852, published in 1855), *Oeuvres complètes,* ed. Y. G. LeDantec, rev. Claude Pichois (1961), 980; Henri Bergson, *Le Rire. Essai sur la signification du comique* (1900; ed. 1950), 20.

2. Baudelaire, "De l'essence du rire," 980–82. Hobbes had anticipated this modern psychologi-cal analysis by two centuries. Laughter, that "*sudden glory*," he observed astutely, is "incident most to them, that are conscious of the fewest abilities in themselves by comparison whereof they suddenly applaud themselves"; much superior laughter, in short, is nothing better than "a sign of pusillanimity." *Leviathan* (1651; ed. Michael Oakeshott, 1947), 36.

3. Bergson, *Le Rire,* 5.

4. Freud heard Mark Twain in 1898 and gratefully remembered his performance more than thirty years later. See *Das Unbehagen in der Kultur* (1930), in *Gesammelte Werke,* XIV, 485–86n; *Civilization and Its Discontents,* in *Standard Edition,* XXI, 126n.

5. Quoted in Sigmund Freud, *Der Witz und seine Beziehung zum Unbewussten* (1905), in *Gesam-melte Werke,* VI, 7; *Jokes and Their Relation to the Unconscious* in *Standard Edition,* VIII, 11.

6. Mikhail Bakhtin, *Rabelais and His World* (1965; tr. Hélène Iswolsky, 1968; ed. 1984), 92. Herzen had been anticipated by Thomas Love Peacock, who proposed, as "an interesting and amusing inquiry," to "trace the progress of French comic fiction, in its bearing on opinion, from the twelfth century to the Revolution." "French Comic Romances" (1836), *Memoirs of Shelley and Other Essays and Reviews,* ed. Howard Mills (1970), 209.

7. "Old Jokes," *Saturday Review,* VI (September 18, 1858), 275.

8. Mark Twain, *The Mysterious Stranger* (version published posthumously in 1916), in *The Mysterious Stranger and Other Tales* (1922), 132 [ch. 10].

9. The analysis of comedy goes back to Plato and Aristotle, while the ancient Romans perfected satire—an aggressive style of humor if ever there was one—which they had learned from the Greeks. At mid-seventeenth century, Thomas Hobbes offered trenchant and, we have seen, eminently quotable aphorisms on laughter, and before 1700, John Dryden had studied the history of satire. James Beattie, the Scottish essayist, poet, and common-sense philosopher, published *An*

Essay on Laughter and Ludicrous Composition in 1764; other eighteenth-century scholars, both physicians and moralists, wrote dignified Latin dissertations on the subject.

10. Bergson, *Le Rire*, 152–53.

11. Leslie Stephen, "George Eliot" (1881), *Hours in a Library,* 3 vols. (1874–79; new ed., 1892), III, 215. "A book on laughter is not a book for laughter," Denis Prudent Roy had announced succinctly, early in the century, in the preface to his *Traité médico-philosophique sur le rire* (1814).

12. Mary Lee Townsend, *Forbidden Laughter: Popular Humor and the Limits of Repression in Nineteenth-Century Prussia* (1992), 191.

13. William Makepeace Thackeray, *The English Humorists of the Eighteenth Century* (1853), 1; Mark Twain, "Pudd'nhead Wilson's New Calendar," *Following the Equator,* 2 vols. (1897; ed. 1924), I, 101.

14. Peacock, "French Comic Romances," 209.

15. Mark Twain to Olivia Langdon, December 27 [1869], *The Love Letters of Mark Twain,* ed. Dixon Wecter (1949), 132.

16. "Person of Buda": *A Book of Nonsense* (1846), in *The Complete Nonsense of Edward Lear,* ed. Holbrook Jackson (1947), 14; "Brother and Sister," *The Complete Works of Lewis Carroll,* intro. Alexander Woolcott (n.d.), 702–3; "The Two Brothers," ibid., 716–20, quotations at 716 and 720.

17. "William Schwenck Gilbert: An Autobiography," *The Theatre,* n.s., I (January–June 1883), 217, 219.

18. See Edith Browne, *W. S. Gilbert* (1907), 9–10; Leon E. A. Berman, "The Kidnapping of W. S. Gilbert," *Journal of the American Psychoanalytic Association,* XXXIII (1985), 133–48.

19. Max Beerbohm, in an admiring appreciation, called the Bab ballads the very epitome of absurdity, at once sane and uncontrolled: "So soon as he had determined to be silly, Mr. Gilbert let himself go—took the bit between his teeth, charged wildly forward." "A Classic in Humour" (1905), in John Bush Jones, ed., *W. S. Gilbert: A Century of Scholarship and Commentary* (1970), 64.

20. "Gentle Alice Brown," *Plays and Poems of W. S. Gilbert,* pref. Deems Taylor (1932), 1012–16; "Annie Protheroe," ibid., 1054–59.

21. "The Story of Gentle Archibald," ibid., 1204–8. This poem was printed in the periodical *Fun,* but was not included in *Bab Ballads.*

22. "The Two Ogres," ibid., 1021–25.

23. "Gilbert, Sir William Schwenck," *Dictionary of National Biography,* ed. Sir Sidney Lee, second supplement, vol. II (1912), 107–8.

24. "The Yarn of the 'Nancy Bell,' " *Plays and Poems of W. S. Gilbert,* 957.

25. "indifferent trifling": Gilbert to Edward Bruce Hindle, January 29, 1885, Morgan Library; acknowledgment of *Bab* ballads' impact: see Fredric Woodbridge Wilson, *An Introduction to the Gilbert and Sullivan Operas from the Collection of the Pierpont Morgan Library* (1989), 12; self-portrait: ibid., at p. 10.

26. Bain, *The Emotions and the Will* (1859; 2nd ed., 1865), 248. Freud quoted from this passage in *Witz,* 228n; *Jokes,* 200n.

27. George Meredith, "An Essay on Comedy," two lectures first delivered as "The Idea of Comedy and the Uses of the Comic Spirit" (1877), in Wylie Sypher, ed., *Comedy* (1956), 5, 7, 18.

28. See ibid., 16, 32–33.

29. Ibid., 48, 47.

30. Friedrich Theodor Vischer, *Das Schöne und die Kunst. Zur Einführung in die Aesthetik. Vorträge,* ed. Robert Vischer (1897; 3rd ed., 1907), 190, 188, 183, 191.

31. Ibid., 191, 181.

32. Theodor Lipps, *Komik and Humor. Eine psychologisch-ästhetische Untersuchung* (1898), 39–42, 264.

33. Bergson, *Le Rire,* 106, 3.

34. Ibid., 15, 150.

35. Ibid., 151, 152.

36. Freud, *Witz,* 113; *Jokes,* 103.

37. Ibid., 114–15; 105.

38. Ibid., 269; 236. Quite independently of Freud, Bergson, too, pointed to the early origins of adult humor: "The more we advance in our study of the methods of comedy, the better we understand the role played by childhood memories." *Le Rire,* 61.

2. Physicians to Society

1. Goethe: January 29, 1826, Johann Peter Eckermann, *Gespräche mit Goethe in den letzten Jahren seines Lebens,* in Johann Wolfgang von Goethe, *Gedenkausgabe der Werke, Briefe und Gespräche,* ed. Ernst Beutler, 27 vols. (1948–71), XXIV, 173; Shaw: Archibald Henderson, *Bernard Shaw: Playboy and Prophet* (1932), 555. Other admirers include Vischer, who cited the "witty Molière" for his imaginative way of moving his characters about the stage only to have them collide with stunning eclat; Lipps, who praised Molière's problematic hero of the *Misanthrope,* Alceste, as an exemplary comic hero; and Bergson, who called up in evidence a parade of Molière's superb comic doctors. Friedrich Theodor Vischer, *Das Schöne und die Kunst. Zur Einführung in die Aesthetik. Vorträge,* ed. Robert Vischer (1897; 3rd ed., 1907), 182; Theodor Lipps, *Komik und Humor. Eine psychologisch-ästhetische Untersuchung* (1898), 259; Henri Bergson, *Le Rire. Essai sur la signification du comique* (1900; ed. 1950), 36–37, 41, 43. Earlier, William Hazlitt had exalted Molière as "unquestionably one of the greatest comic geniuses that ever lived; a man of infinite wit, gaiety, and invention," comparable to Shakespeare. *Lectures on the English Comic Writers* (1819), 49–50, 57. To quote just one lesser figure, the pseudonymous Coquelin Cadet [Ernest Alexandre Honoré Coquelin]: "We will never grow weary" of Molière's laughter. *Le Rire* (1887; 4th ed., 1887), 145–46.

2. Charles Baudelaire: "De l'essence du rire et généralement du comique dans les arts plastiques" (written in 1852, published in 1855), *Oeuvres complètes,* ed. Y. G. LeDantec, rev. Claude Pichois (1961), 987; George Meredith, "An Essay on Comedy," in Wylie Sypher, ed., *Comedy* (1956), 17.

3. Carl Sternheim, "Molière, der Bürger" (1912), *Gesamtwerk,* ed. Wilhelm Emrich, 10 vols. in 11 (1963–76), VI, 16–17; Sternheim, "Molière" (1917), ibid., 31.

4. See Peter Gay, *Freud, Jews and Other Germans: Masters and Victims in Modernist Culture* (1978), 146–49.

5. Herzen: Mikhail Bakhtin, *Rabelais and His World* (1965; tr. Hélène Iswolsky, 1968; ed. 1984), 92n; Thoma: to Reinhold Geheeb (editor of *Simplicissimus*), January 26, 1919, Friedl Brehm, *Immer gegen die Machthaber: Ludwig Thoma und der Simplicissimus* (1966), 23; George Bernard Shaw: *The Quintessence of Ibsenism* (1891; ed. 1912), 3.

6. Heine to Caroline Jaubert, December 16, 1844, *Heinrich Heine, Briefe,* ed. Friedrich Hirth, 6 vols. in 2 (1949–50; ed. 1965), part II, 557; see also Heinrich Heine, *Deutschland. Ein Wintermärchen* (1844), in *Sämtliche Schriften,* ed. Klaus Briegleb et al., 6 vols. (1968–76), IV, 579 [ch. 1].

7. Freud, seeking to demonstrate the absurdity of the Christian call for universal love, quoted, in his *Civilization and Its Discontents,* a particularly pointed passage from Heine the hater, with full approval: "I possess the most peaceable disposition. My wishes are: a modest cottage, a thatched

roof, but a good bed, good food, very fresh milk and butter, flowers before my window, a few handsome trees before my door; and if the good Lord wants to make me completely happy, he will let me live long enough to have the pleasure of seeing some six or seven of my enemies hanged on those trees. Before their death, with a tender heart, I shall forgive them all the wrong they did me in my life—yes, one must forgive one's enemies, but not before they have been hanged." This is aggressive wit at its most untamed. *Das Unbehagen in der Kultur* (1930), in *Gesammelte Werke*, XIV, 469–70n; *Standard Edition*, XXI, 110n.

8. See Heine to Baron Johann Friedrich von Cotta, June 18, 1828, *Briefe*, part I, 364.

9. Heinrich Heine, *Die Bäder von Lucca* (1830), in *Sämtliche Schriften*, II, 392, 445. Just beneath the epigraph, borrowing the mask of an indignant commoner, he quoted Beaumarchais's Figaro defying Count Almaviva: "If the count wants to dare a dance, / Let him say so, / I'll make music for him." Ibid., 392.

10. Ibid., 467.

11. Heine to Varnhagen von Ense, January 3, 1830, *Briefe*, part I, 412.

12. Heine, *Ludwig Börne. Eine Denkschrift* (1840), in *Sämtliche Schriften*, IV, 36.

13. See Heine, *Deutschland. Ein Wintermärchen*, 592. This was a lament that Schiller had uttered, only more earnestly, four decades earlier. His poem *Der Antritt des neuen Jahrhunderts*, dated 1801, ends with a grim quatrain: "You must flee from life's pressures / Into the holy quiet rooms of the heart; / Freedom lives only in the realm of dreams / And the beautiful blossoms only in song."

14. Hartford *Courant*, June 29, 1888, quoted in Justin Kaplan, *Mr. Clemens and Mark Twain: A Biography* (1966), 147.

15. William Makepeace Thackeray, "Lever's St. Patrick's Eve—Comic Politics" (April 3, 1845), and Thackeray to Mark Lemon, February 1847, both in Gordon N. Ray, "*Vanity Fair*: One Version of the Novelist's Responsibility" (1950), in Ian Watt, ed., *The Victorian Novel: Modern Essays in Criticism* (1971), 252, 255.

16. William Makepeace Thackeray, *Vanity Fair* (1848; ed. 1864; ed. Joseph Warren Beach, 1950), 79 [ch. 8].

17. Thackeray, "Before the Curtain," ibid., xxix; ibid., 730 [ch. 67].

18. See Victor Brombert, *The Novels of Flaubert: A Study of Themes and Techniques* (1966), 158–81.

19. Charles Dickens, *Little Dorrit* (1857; ed. John Holloway, 1967), 292–300 [book I, ch. 21].

20. Ibid., 145–65 [book I, ch. 10]; quotation at 145.

21. Ibid., 804 [book II, ch. 28].

22. Charles Dickens, *Our Mutual Friend* (1865; ed. Charles Dickens the Younger, 1908), 121 [book I, ch. 11].

23. Ibid.

24. Ibid., 120. Denial is precisely the policy too of Podsnap's female counterpart, Mrs. General, in *Little Dorrit*. The companion hired by the Dorrits, newly come into wealth, to lend tone to their establishment, she teaches her charges, "A truly refined mind will seem to be ignorant of the existence of anything that is not perfectly proper, placid, and pleasant." *Little Dorrit*, 530 [book II, ch. 5].

25. Dickens, *Our Mutual Friend*, 122 [book I, ch. 11].

26. Anthony Comstock, the nemesis of pornography in late-nineteenth-century America, who seems to have been obsessed with the obscene, was a splendid exemplar of the type. See Peter Gay, *The Bourgeois Experience*, vol. I, *Education of the Senses* (1984), 359, 377–78.

3. The Victim as Executioner

1. For "orifices of his person," Arsène Alexandre, *Honoré Daumier, l'homme et l'oeuvre* (1888), 46.

2. Thomas Love Peacock, "French Comic Romances" (1836), *Memoirs of Shelley and Other Essays and Reviews*, ed. Howard Mills (1970), 212.

3. Charles Holme, ed., *Daumier and Gavarni*, with critical and biographical notes by Henri Frantz and Octave Uzanne (tr. Edgar Preston and Helen Chisholm, 1904), D vi.

4. Champfleury [Jules Husson], *Histoire de la caricature moderne* (n.d.; ed. 1865), 102.

5. *Man and Superman*, in *The Bodley Head Bernard Shaw: Collected Plays with Their Prefaces*, 7 vols. (1970–74), II, 654 [act III]. While this is the devil speaking, in much of this long speech he is speaking for Shaw.

6. "William Schwenck Gilbert: An Autobiography," *The Theatre*, n.s., I (January–June 1883), 222–23.

7. See John Palmer, *The Censor and the Theatres* (1913), 180–82.

8. Gilbert's handwritten verse is reproduced in Fredric Woodbridge Wilson, *An Introduction to the Gilbert and Sullivan Operas from the Collection of the Pierpont Morgan Library* (1989), 66.

9. *Pall Mall Budget, Being a Weekly Collection of Articles Printed in the Pall Mall Gazette*, XXIX (December 1, 1882), 8; for other representative comments, see *Punch*, LXXXIII (December 9, 1882), 268–69; *Saturday Review*, LIV (December 9, 1882), 764–65; *The Academy*, XXII (December 8, 1882), 404–5.

10. *Pall Mall Budget*, XXIX (December 1, 1882), 8; *Iolanthe*, in *Plays and Poems of W. S. Gilbert*, pref. Deems Taylor (1932), 269 [act II]; Wilson, *Introduction to the Gilbert and Sullivan Operas*, 21.

11. See Leslie Baily, *Gilbert and Sullivan: Their Lives and Times* (1973), 75–79.

12. When in 1901 Liberals asked Gilbert for permission to cull his *Iolanthe* libretto for ammunition against the House of Lords, he indignantly refused to have it exploited "for electioneering purposes." And, quite by the way, he offered a lesson in differentiating between the opinions of an author and those he lends his creations: "They do not at all express my own views. They are supposed to be the views of the wrong-headed donkey who sings them." Still, enthusiastic audiences took his work as a gentle form of social criticism. Christopher Hibbert, *Gilbert and Sullivan and Their Victorian World* (1976), 147.

13. Norbert Dittmar and Peter Schlobinski, eds., *Wandlungen einer Stadtsprache. Berlinisch in Vergangenheit und Gegenwart* (1988), 187. I owe this passage to Mary Lee Townsend.

14. Thomas Carlyle, *Journey to Germany, Autumn 1858*, ed. R. A. E. Brooks (1940), 42.

15. *Simplicissimus*, III (1898–99), no. 31.

16. Ibid.

17. Ann Taylor Allen, *Satire and Society in Wilhelmine Germany: "Kladderadatsch" and "Simplicissimus" 1890–1914* (1984), 41.

4. A Laughing, Cruel Sage

1. See *Die fromme Helene* (1872), in *Wilhelm Busch Gesamtausgabe*, ed. Friedrich Bohne, 4 vols. (1959), II, 286–87; *Plisch und Plum* (1882), ibid., III, 500–507; "Die Brille" (1870), ibid., II, 158–69; "Das Pusterohr" (1867–68), ibid., I, 499–505.

2. Freud to Carl G. Jung, July 1, 1907, Sigmund Freud / C. G. Jung, *Briefwechsel*, ed. William McGuire and Wolfgang Sauerländer (1974), 77.

3. William Randolph Hearst, who had made his first trip to Europe at ten, came back laden with German illustrated tales, including Busch's most famous production, *Max und Moritz*, and appar-

ently later suggested that Rudolph Dirks, an enterprising young artist, adapt them to American tastes. See Stephen Becker, *Comic Art in America: A Social History of the Funnies, the Political Cartoon, Magazine Humor, Sporting Cartoons and Animated Cartoons* (1957), 15–16.

4. Busch, "Es sitzt ein Vogel auf dem Leim," *Kritik des Herzens* (1874), in *Gesamtausgabe*, II, 495.

5. I am much indebted on this point to comments by Ernst Prelinger.

6. Busch to Maria Anderson, April 26 [18]75, Wilhelm Busch, *Sämtliche Briefe*, ed. Friedrich Bohne, 2 vols. (1968), I, 141. As we saw earlier in this chapter, Heine explicitly likened himself to Antaeus. Busch would have had every right to do so.

7. See Paul Lindau to Busch, July 1, 1907, complaining of shabby treatment during "the last decades"(!). Ibid., II, 320.

8. Busch, *Der heilige Antonius von Padua* (1870), in *Gesamtausgabe*, II, 122.

9. See, for one instance, the drawing reproduced in Ulrich Beer, *". . . gottlos und beneidenswert." Wilhelm Busch und seine Psychologie* (1982), 67.

10. Gert Ueding, *Wilhelm Busch. Das 19. Jahrhundert en Miniature* (1977), 26.

11. Busch, "Was mich betrifft" (1886), *Gesamtausgabe*, IV, 205; diary entry, June 26, 1852, Friedrich Bohne, *Wilhelm Busch. Leben, Werk, Schicksal* (1958), 37.

12. Busch, "Von mir über mich" (1894), *Gesamtausgabe*, IV, 210.

13. See Busch, "Der harte Winter" (1859), ibid., I, 12–13; "Schreckliche Folgen der Neugierde, dargestellt an einem Bauern in der Barbierstube" (1860), ibid., 71; "Schreckliche Folgen eines Bleistifts. Ballade" (1860), ibid., 68–71.

14. See Busch, "Trauriges Resultat einer vernachlässigten Erziehung" (1860), ibid., 75–81.

15. See Busch, "Die kleinen Honigdiebe" (1859), ibid., 28–33; "Ein interessanter Fall" (1860), ibid., 72; "Hans Huckebein, der Unglücksrabe" (1867), ibid., 492; "Der vergebliche Versuch" (1867), ibid., 446–51.

16. See Busch, "Zwei Diebe" (1866), ibid., 424–32; "Die kühne Müllerstochter" (1868), ibid., 534–41.

17. See Busch, *Maler Klecksel* (1884), *Gesamtausgabe*, IV, 118–26.

18. See Busch, *Balduin Bählamm, der verhinderte Dichter* (1883), ibid., 60–66; *Der Schmetterling* (1895), ibid., 259–60; "Hans Huckebein," 498.

19. Busch, "Monsieur Jacques à Paris während der Belagerung im Jahre 1870" (1870–71), *Gesamtausgabe*, II, 137–47.

20. Friedrich Theodor Vischer, "Satyrische Zeichnung" (1846), with the addition "Neuere deutsche Karikatur" (1880), *Altes und Neues* (1882), 120–29; quotations at 122. He is referring to Busch, "Diogenes und die bösen Buben von Korinth" (1862), *Gesamtausgabe*, I, 157–63.

21. Vischer, "Neuere deutsche Karikatur," 128; Busch, *Balduin Bählamm*, 65; "Ein Neujahrskonzert" (1865), *Gesamtausgabe*, I, 403–10.

22. See, for example, a spider heading for an open mouth, in Busch, "Es kömmt nicht immer nur das Gute von oben" (1861), ibid., 95; and a fly minus a leg, "Die Fliege" (1861), ibid., 117. It is characteristic of Busch and his culture, that he, so reticent a correspondent, found it perfectly proper to discuss openly with his sister-in-law his poor digestion and its consequences, or to praise, to a close woman friend, the compulsive cleanliness of Haarlem: "Scarcely does a horse lift its tail just a little, someone already stands there and holds a shovel under it." See Busch to Johanne Busch, November 19 [18]71, *Briefe*, I, 70, 73; Busch to Johanna Kessler, November 9, 1873, ibid., 115.

23. Busch to "Nanda" and "Letty" Kessler, Christmas Eve, 1873, ibid., 116.

24. Busch to Maria Anderson, November 6 [18]75, ibid., 157.

25. Busch to Hermann Levi, December 13, 1880, ibid., 215.

26. See "Von der doppelten Brille" and two drawings from a sketchbook (none of them dated), *Wilhelm Busch–Buch. Sammlung lustiger Bildergeschichten,* ed. Otto Nöldeke and Hermann Nöldeke [ca. 1930], 84, 253.

27. See Busch, *Max und Moritz* (1865), in *Gesamtausgabe,* I, 347.

28. See Busch, *Balduin Bählamm,* 46.

29. See Busch, "Sorglos," *Hernach* (1908), in *Gesamtausgabe,* IV, 391.

30. Busch to Otto Bassermann, December 12 [18]63, *Briefe,* I, 29.

31. Busch to Carl Müller, February 19, 1871, ibid., 62.

32. Busch to Hermann Levi, December 13, 1880, ibid., 215.

33. Here is Schmulchen Schiefelbeiner: "Short his trousers, long his coat / His nose as crooked as his stick / Eyes black and soul gray / Hat pushed back and expression crafty." Busch, *Plisch und Plum,* 479.

34. Busch to Franz von Lenbach, February 3 [18]92, *Briefe,* I, 347; Busch to Franz von Lenbach, April 7 [18]94, ibid., II, 26.

35. See Busch, "Der Partikularist" (1870–71), *Gesamtausgabe,* II, 148–53.

36. Busch to Otto Bassermann, August 7 [18]72, *Briefe,* I, 81.

37. Busch, *Eduards Traum,* 181.

38. Busch to Grete Meyer, January 24, 1900, *Briefe,* II, 157.

39. Busch to Friedrich Warnecke, February 26, 1856, ibid., I, 10.

40. See Busch to Moritz Schwarzenberg, August 12 [18]70, ibid., 56.

41. Busch to Maria Anderson: January 27, 1875, ibid., 130; February 11, 1875, ibid., March 22, 1875, ibid., 135; April 16, 1875, ibid., 139.

SIX: Uncertain Mastery

1. George Eliot, *Adam Bede* (1859; foreword F. R. Leavis, 1961), 91 [book I, ch. 7]; Thorstein Veblen, *Theory of the Leisure Class* (1899; ed. 1931), 15.

1. Equivalents, Moral and Other

1. "Lessons of the Prize Ring," *Saturday Review,* IX (April 28, 1860), 526; Montague Sherman, *Athletics and Football* (1887), 369.

2. Political Economy Club, *Revised Report of the Proceedings at the Dinner of 31st May 1876 Held in Celebration of the Hundredth Year of Publication of the "Wealth of Nations"* (1876), 42–43.

3. Charles Hose, *Natural Man: A Record from Borneo* (1926), 148; see also W. McD[ougall], "A Savage Peace-Conference," *The Eagle: A Magazine Supported by the Members of St. John's College,* XXI (1900), 70–82. I owe this reference to Richard Tuck.

4. *Billy Budd, Foretopman,* in *Shorter Novels of Herman Melville,* intro. Raymond Weaver (1928), 299.

5. William James, "The Moral Equivalent of War," *Memories and Studies* (1911), 267, 274.

6. Ibid., 287–88.

7. Ibid., 268, 269–71.

8. Ibid., 269, 272, 275.

9. Ibid., 290, 291.

10. Some thirty thousand copies were distributed, according to Ralph Barton Perry, *The Thought and Character of William James,* 2 vols. (1935), II, 278.

11. Taylor: *Notes of a Tour in the Manufacturing Districts of Lancashire* (1842), quoted in Peter Bailey, *Leisure and Class in Victorian England: Rational Recreation and the Contest for Control, 1830–1885* (1978), 37; Slaney: *A Plea for the Working Classes* (1847), quoted in ibid., 35–36.

12. Y.M.C.A.: "Exeter Hall on Popular Amusements," *Saturday Review*, III (March 21, 1857), 263; Böhmert: Jürgen Reulecke, " 'Veredelung der Volkserholung' and 'edle Geselligkeit.' Sozialreformerische Bestrebungen zur Gestaltung der arbeitsfreien Zeit im Kaiserreich," in Gerhard Huck, ed., *Sozialgeschichte der Freizeit: Untersuchungen zum Wandel der Alltagskultur in Deutschland* (1980), 143.

13. Howitt: *The Rural Life of England,* 2 vols. (1838), quoted in Hugh Cunningham, *Leisure in the Industrial Revolution, c. 1780–c.1880* (1980), 88; parliamentary committee: Geoffrey Pearson, *Hooligan: A History of Respectable Fears* (1983), 108.

14. Karl Marx and Friedrich Engels, *Communist Manifesto* (1848; tr. Samuel Moore, 1888, ed. A. J. P. Taylor, 1967), 113–14 [part III, ch. 2].

15. Here are two instances, one from each extreme. In 1867, an American expert surveying the network of charities in France objected to independent associations for workingmen because what they needed to be taught were "habits of order, economy, and forethought," which they obviously lacked. [William Richards Lawrence], *Charities of France in 1866: An Account of Some of the Principal Charitable Institutions in That Country* (1867), 164. Others understood the lower orders better. In 1904, in a study of social-welfare institutions across Europe, Karl Singer insisted that no charitable organization could function unless it had the active "*cooperation* of the circles to be benefited"; the working classes had to be invited to participate in shaping and managing their own relief. *Soziale Fürsorge, der Weg zum Wohltun* (1904), 2, 13.

16. H. E. Meller, *Leisure and the Changing City, 1870–1914* (1976), 179.

17. Karl Marx, "Der Kommunismus des Rheinischen Beobachters," *Deutsche-Brüsseler Zeitung,* September 12, 1847, in D. Ryazanov and V. Adoratskij, eds., *Marx–Engels Gesamtausgabe,* Erste Abteilung, 6 vols. (1927–32), VI, 278.

18. Walter Laqueur, *Religion and Respectability: Sunday Schools and Working Class Culture 1780–1850* (1976), 96. Laqueur observes (p. 239) that "the puritan ethic was . . . not the monopoly of the owners of capital; it was the ideology of those who worked as against those who did not," and cut across class lines.

19. "keep quiet": Yves Lequin, "Une Nouvelle Culture dans le premier vingtième siècle," in Maurice Agulhon et al., *Histoire de la France urbaine,* vol. IV, *La Ville de l'âge industriel, le cycle haussmannien* (1983), 444; "think football": Paul Smith, "Saturday Afternoon Fever," *Times Literary Supplement,* April 4, 1980, 379.

20. A Magendie, *Les Effets moraux de l'exercise physique* (1893), 190; Martin Cobbett, "Sports and 'Sports,' " *Sporting Notions of Present Days and Past,* ed. Alice Cobbett (1908), 1–2.

21. "Prizefighting," *Saturday Review,* II (November 22, 1856), 658.

22. "The Fight for the Championship," *Saturday Review,* IX (April 21, 1860), 498.

23. Philippe Daryl [Paschal Grousset], *Renaissance physique* (1888), 65; Charles Edwardes, "The New Football Mania," *The Nineteenth Century: A Monthly Review,* XXXII (1892), 622–23.

24. Hely Hutchison Almond, "Football as a Moral Agent," ibid., XXXIV (1893), 906, see also Richard Holt, *Sport and the British: A Modern History* (1989), 81.

25. Wray Vamplew, "Ungentlemanly Conduct: The Control of Soccer-Crowd Behaviour in England, 1888–1914," in T. C. Smout, ed., *The Search for Wealth and Stability: Essays in Economic and Social History Presented to M. W. Flinn* (1979), 144. As the records of organized English soccer show, the League meant it: between 1895 and 1912, it ordered twenty-four closures, and banned a number of teams from exciting and profitable cup matches. See ibid., 151.

26. The saying remained immensely and internationally popular. At the start of the next century, Raoul Fabens quoted it once again, crediting the duke of Wellington. See *Les Sports pour tous* (1905), 21,

27. Arnold Schloenbach, "Das erste allgemeine deutsche Turn- und Jugendfest in Coburg vom 17. bis 19. Juni," *Die Gartenlaube*, VIII (1860), 430–32; see also E. Euler, "Deutsche Turnfeste," ibid., XXXIII (1885), 442–44; Euler, "Das siebente deutsche Turnfest in München," ibid., XXXVII (1889), 557–59.

28. "something from us": M. Zettler, "Die neue französische Jugendwehr," ibid., XXX (1882), 608; "Run them through!": Richard Holt, *Sport and Society in Modern France* (1981), 195.

29. "without discouragement": Eugen Weber, "Gymnastics and Sports in Fin-de-Siècle France: Opium of the Classes?" *American Historical Review*, LXXVI, 1 (February 1971), 72; Magendie, *Les Effets moraux*, 194. The sort of exercise that could be related to the war they expected became a favorite among athletic, and would-be athletic, Frenchmen. In the names they gave themselves, and in their manifestos, clubs devoted to strenuous walking, to rifle practice, or to rigorous gymnastics, stressed their patriotic sentiments and their military usefulness. Addressing the Union des sociétés françaises de gymnastique of the Seine in 1898, Octave Gréard, vice rector of the Académie de Paris, recalled that they been "born, nearly all, under the impact of our disasters," and were all still "imbued with the same duty." Weber, "Gymnastics and Sports," 73. He did not need to spell out for his audience what that duty was; it lay beyond France's eastern borders.

30. Paul Adam, *La Morale des sports* (1907), 6, 12–13, 130, 133, 7. These militaristic attitudes were, of course, not confined to Frenchmen and Germans. In 1860 the *Saturday Review*, commenting on the Oxford–Cambridge boat race, mused that looking at these rowers, "one feels tolerably tranquil upon the subject of national defence." With rowing clubs springing up wherever there is water, "half the business of making every able-bodied citizen a soldier is done even before the drill-sergeant begins his duty." "The University Boat Race," *Saturday Review*, IX (April 7, 1860), 433.

31. Holt, *Sport and Society in Modern France*, 47.

32. "By the 1880s many who joined such gymnastic societies did so in the hope of losing weight or, more simply, because they provided convenient occasions for members to meet, wives to chat, and children to admire their fathers' prowess." Weber, "Gymnastics and Sports," 73.

33. There were about 130,000 bicycles in France in 1893, and almost three times as many, 375,000, five years later; by 1914, the number had reached almost three million. Many of these bicycles served as transportation, but thousands of Frenchmen—and visible numbers of Frenchwomen—joined clubs to do a little racing. In 1889, the Union vélocipédique de France, founded in 1882, had 10,000 members; four years later, its membership stood at 44,000.

34. See Holt, *Sport and Society in Modern France*, 81–103.

35. See Ludovic O'Followell, *Bicyclette et organes génitaux* (1900), passim.

36. Introduction to *Cricket; and How to Play It*, "By a Member of the Marylebone Club" [1871], vi.

37. There were subtleties here: a university student invited to participate in a tournament in a distant city would retain his amateur standing even if his family, or a fatherly friend, met his expenses. But it was understood that he was to accept no gifts for his performance, whether in money or in kind, even if—especially if—these tangible temptations were disguised as reimbursement for expenses.

38. Exceptions were rare and notable; the winner of the first modern marathon race at the Olympics, Spiridon Loues, was a Greek shepherd. What mattered was that Loues nobly refused all

the presents—money, free meals, gold watches—that his ecstatic compatriots tried to shower on him.

39. John J. MacAloon, *This Great Symbol: Pierre de Coubertin and the Origins of the Modern Olympic Games* (1981), 173.

40. Pierre de Coubertin, "L'Éducation anglaise," address to the Société d'économie sociale, April 18, 1887, *La Réforme sociale. Bulletin de la Société d'économie sociale et des Unions de la paix sociale,* 2nd ser., III (January–June 1887), 644.

41. MacAloon, *This Great Symbol,* 141.

42. Pierre de Coubertin, *Les Batailles de l'éducation physique. Une Campagne de vingt-et-un ans, 1887–1908* (1909), 1; MacAloon, *This Great Symbol,* 262.

43. A famous English amateur soccer team, the Corinthians, founded in 1883, recruited all its players from graduates of public schools and the ancient English universities; in play, the Corinthians refused to take advantage of a penalty they had been awarded or to defend their goal when they thought a penalty against them was deserved.

44. Olympic bicycle incident: see Marie Thérèse Eyquem, *Pierre de Coubertin: L'Épopée olympique* (1966), 153; fairness: see Eric Dunning and Kenneth Sheard, *Barbarians, Gentlemen and Players: A Sociological Study of the Development of Rugby Football* (1979), 153.

45. Into the early nineteenth century, Bretons played *la soule,* a sanguinary ancestor of modern rugby, contested as if life literally depended on victory. Informally recruited teams, sometimes sizable, wrestled with one another in the open fields to keep a large ball out of the opposition's hands. This was, one contemporary judged, "not an ordinary amusement but a heated and dramatic game in which the players fight, strangle each other and smash each other's heads." But, though it was a "game that allows one to kill an enemy without losing one's right to Easter communion," the players had to take "care to strike as though by accident." As the "blood flows," a kind of "drunkenness seizes the players, the instincts of wild beasts seem to be aroused in the hearts of men, the thirst for murder seizes their throats, drives them on and blinds them." Émile Souvestre, *Les Derniers Bretons* (1836; 2nd ed., 2 vols., 1858), I, 125–32.

46. Alfred Gibson and William Pickford, *Association Football and the Men Who Made It,* 4 vols. (1906), I, 36.

47. In 1895, the Rugby Football Union itself split over the issue of amateurism versus professionalism. The "aristocratic," largely upper-middle-class amateurs wanted to keep the sport in their own hands, while the opposing faction, organizing as the Rugby League, openly made commitments to professional players and thus opened the door to lower-class athletes.

48. Holt, *Sport and the British,* 86.

49. Pickford, "The Referee, Past, Present, and Future," in Gibson and Pickford, *Association Football,* III, 1, 3.

50. Edwardes, "The New Football Mania," 628. See also Pickford, "The Referee, Past, Present, and Future," 4–6.

51. Edwardes, "The New Football Mania," 629.

2. The Empire of Fact

1. Charles Babbage, *On the Economy of Machinery and Manufactures* (1832; 4th enlarged ed., 1835), 358.

2. Frederic Harrison, "The Use of History" (1862), *The Meaning of History and Other Historical Pieces* (1894), 11, 14.

3. Justus von Liebig, *Ueber Francis Bacon von Verulam und die Methode der Naturforschung* (1863), 1; Charles Darwin, *Autobiography* (1887), in *Autobiographies of Darwin and Huxley,* ed. Gavin de Beer (1974), 71. As Darwin's notebooks reveal, he had at least some conjectures to guide him from the beginning.

4. Samuel Tyler, *A Discourse of the Baconian Philosophy* (1844; 2nd ed., 1846), 7, 15. In 1856, the German historian of philosophy Kuno Fischer, in a substantial, not uncritical appraisal of Bacon's life and thought, concluded that his "philosophy is the most vital and wholly unaffected expression of realism." *Franz Baco von Verulam. Die Realphilosophie und ihr Zeitalter* (1856), xiii.

5. Francis Bacon, "Proemium," *The Great Instauration* (1620), in *Selected Writings,* ed. Hugh G. Dick (1955), 424; Bacon, Aphorism III, *Novum Organum* (1620), in *Selected Writings,* 462; Bacon, *New Atlantis* (1624), in *Selected Writings,* 574; Bacon, Aphorism LXXXI, *Novum Organum,* 499.

6. "Lord Bacon" (1837), *The Works of Lord Macaulay,* 12 vols. (1898), VIII, 616. Macaulay put the speech into the mouth of an admirer of Bacon. Kuno Fischer criticized this lengthy verdict as unduly separating practical from theoretical philosophy. *Franz Baco von Verulam,* 358–80.

7. John Clive, *Macaulay: The Shaping of the Historian* (1973), 486.

8. W. H. G. Armytage, *A Social History of Engineering* (1961; 4th ed., 1976), 124.

9. "Sixth Annual Report of the Council of the Statistical Society of London," *Journal of the Statistical Society of London,* III (1840), 1–2.

10. Anthony Hyman, *Charles Babbage: Pioneer of the Computer* (1982), 85.

11. Huxley to Charles Kingsley, September 23, 1860, Leonard Huxley, *Life and Letters of Thomas Henry Huxley,* 2 vols. (1900), I, 218–21.

12. The immediate precursors of these elaborate counting exercises dated back to the mid-eighteenth century; in 1764 Voltaire had warmly praised the Swedes for undertaking "the useful enterprise of knowing the resources of their country thoroughly." Voltaire to *Gazette littéraire de l'Europe* [October 1764], *Correspondance,* ed. Theodore Besterman, 16 vols. (1963–89), VII, 880.

13. See Patricia Cline Cohen, *A Calculating People: The Spread of Numeracy in Early America* (1982), ch. 7.

14. Masturbation: see Peter Gay, *The Bourgeois Experience,* vol. I, *Education of the Senses* (1984), 295–309; safe period: see Carl N. Degler, *At Odds: Women and the Family in America from the Revolution to the Present* (1980), 213–15. Readers of *Education of the Senses* (esp. 84–85) will recall how Mabel Loomis Todd conceived her daughter Millicent: using a homemade theory of "safety," she had intercourse with her husband precisely in a way that did not protect her at all from getting pregnant. But then, she had the excuse of being an amateur.

15. Erwin H. Ackerknecht, *Medicine at the Paris Hospital, 1794–1848* (1967), 102, 104.

16. Governments, with France in the vanguard, understood the utility of such alliances. A pure scientist like Pasteur was explicitly instructed not to slight practical applications of his work. He had little quarrel with this injunction, and his record confirms that in assisting the French wine, beer, and silk industries, he followed it to the letter.

17. I have constructed this narrative from Ignaz Philipp Semmelweis, *An Etiology, Concept and Prophylaxis of Childbed Fever* (1860; tr. K. C. Carter, 1983); Carl G. Hempel, *Philosophy of Natural Science* (1966), 3–8; Sherwin B. Nuland, "The Enigma of Semmelweis: An Interpretation," *Journal of the History of Medicine,* XXXIV (1979), 255–72; Erna Lesky, *The Vienna Medical School of the Nineteenth Century* (1965; tr. L. Williams and I. S. Levij, 1976), 181–92.

18. Charles Booth, "Occupations of the People of the United Kingdom, 1801–81" (read before the Royal Statistical Society, May 18, 1886), *Journal of the Royal Statistical Society,* XLIX (June 1886), 318.

19. In some brief autobiographical jottings, Huxley paid tribute to Darwin's "sagacity" and his

"untiring search after the knowledge of fact, his readiness always to give up a preconceived opinion to that which was demonstrably true." "Speech at the Royal Society Dinner" (1894), *Notebook: "Thoughts and Doings,"* in *Autobiographies,* ed. Gavin de Beer, 112. Half a century before Huxley, amused at the pretensions of fellow statisticians who wanted to exclude all "opinion" from their work, one R. John Robertson wrote, "No mere record and arrangement of facts can constitute a science. Facts," he argued, "can be interpreted only in the light of theories"; after all, "theories are facts as viewed by the most powerful minds." Theodore M. Porter, *The Rise of Statistical Thinking, 1820–1900* (1986), 40.

20. Pasteur's papers and letters breathe his supreme passion for knowledge. "I have already told you," he wrote to a friend of his youth, Charles Chappuis, in 1851, "that I am on the verge of mysteries, and that the veil which covers them is getting thinner and thinner. The nights seem to me too long, yet I do not complain, for I prepare my lectures easily, and often have five whole days a week that I can devote to the laboratory. I am often scolded by Madame Pasteur, whom I console by telling her that I shall lead her to posterity." René Dubos, *Louis Pasteur: Free Lance of Science* (1960; ed. 1976), 40. The word "beauty" recurs in Pasteur's writings. Freud, working out his psychoanalytic theories in the late 1890s, also experienced deep aesthetic pleasure in his scientific activity. On one of his buoyant days, when insight crowded insight, he wrote his intimate friend Wilhelm Fliess, to whom he confided everything at that time, that he could not convey to him "any notion of the intellectual beauty of the work." Freud to Fliess, October 3, 1897, Sigmund Freud, *Briefe an Wilhelm Fliess 1887–1904,* ed. Jeffrey Moussaieff Masson, assisted by Michael Schröter and Gerhard Fichtner (1986), 289.

21. For Le Play and Riehl, see Gay, *Education of the Senses,* 423–30.

22. G. Embden, "Wie sind Enquêten zu organisieren," *Das Verfahren bei Enquêten über sociale Verhältnisse. Drei Gutachten,* in *Schriften des Vereins für Sozialpolitik,* XIII (1877), 1.

23. Adolphe Quetelet, "Recherches statistiques sur le Royaume des Pays-Bas," quoted in Porter, *Rise of Statistical Thinking,* 45.

24. "sphere of liberty": Adolphe Quetelet, *Sur la statistique morale et les principes qui doivent en former la base* (1848), 109; "a better condition": Quetelet, *Physique sociale; ou, Essai sur le développement des facultés de l'homme* (1835; enlarged ed., 2 vols., 1869), I, 146, 146n.

25. Ibid., II, 316–17.

26. Francis Galton, the father of that dubious human science, eugenics, a brilliant statistician to whom the discipline owes some remarkable technical innovations, was only the most celebrated nineteenth-century student of man to be in Quetelet's debt; it was largely to Quetelet that Galton owed his conviction that the range of human heredity and human actions can be reduced to numbers and plotted on revealing curves.

27. See Anthony Oberschall, *Empirical Social Research in Germany, 1848–1914* (1965), 3–5, 16–17.

28. "I grew up," Lujo Brentano recalled in old age, "in the practice of an uncritical faith, politically so conservative that, whenever I read about the demands of a people for a constitution, even this seemed to me revolutionary." *Mein Leben im Kampf um die soziale Entwicklung Deutschlands* (1931), 24.

29. Asa Briggs, *The Age of Improvement, 1783–1867* (1959), 16.

30. In 1751, it was estimated that some 7.5 million people lived in Great Britain; half a century later, according to the first census, 3 million had been added, and after that, the rate of increase each decade was about 20 percent; the census of 1831 counted over 14 million people, that of 1851 almost 21 million.

31. Arnold Toynbee, *Lectures on the Industrial Revolution in England* (1884; ed. 1956), 117. (The speculative historian Arnold Toybee was this Toynbee's nephew.)

32. See ibid., 84.

33. "Art. XIII—*Houses in Danger from the Populace*. By E. G. Wakefield,—London, Effingham Wilson, 1831," *Westminster Review*, XVI (1832), 219.

34. In 1854, visiting the Crystal Palace in London, H. T. Buckle, whose *History of Civilization in England* was much read, exclaimed to a friend over "the bright promise of reward to man's genius, and of continued triumph over the blind powers of Nature." In ecstasy over progress, he quoted Hamlet: "What a piece of work is man! How noble in reason! how infinite in faculty!" He did not persuade the skeptical friend, a Miss Shirreff, who reported these remarks; still, he spoke for many. A. H. Huth, *The Life and Writings of H. T. Buckle*, 2 vols. (1880), I, 78.

35. In the astute retrospect of Booth's invaluable collaborator Beatrice Potter (better known under her married name, Beatrice Webb) the C.O.S. was "one of the most typical of mid-Victorian social offsprings." This "much-praised and much-abused organization" worked on three principles: "patient and persistent service" by the rich; accepting "personal responsibility" for the consequences of giving charity; and "as the only way of carrying out this service and fulfilling this responsibility, the application of the scientific method to each separate case of a damaged body or a lost soul." Beatrice Webb, *My Apprenticeship* (1926; ed. 1971), 206, 208.

36. "The churches are making the discovery," Andrew Mearns wrote, "that seething in the very centre of our great cities, concealed by the thinnest crust of civilization and decency, is a vast mass of moral corruption, of heartbreaking misery and absolute godlessness, and that scarcely anything has been done to take into this awful slough the only influences that can purify or remove it." *The Bitter Cry of Outcast London* (1883), 1.

37. See H. M. Hyndman, *The Record of an Adventurous Life* (1911), 331–33; T. S. Simey and M. B. Simey, *Charles Booth: Social Scientist* (1960), 68–70.

38. See Wolfram Fischer, *Armut in der Geschichte: Erscheinungsformen und Lösungsversuche der 'Sozialen Frage' in Europa seit dem Mittelalter* (1982), 58, 61.

39. See Wilhelm Abel, *Massenarmut und Hungerkrisen im vorindustriellen Deutschland* (1972; 2nd ed., 1977), 304–5.

40. See Brentano, *Mein Leben*, 44.

41. Ibid., 45–46.

42. In his autobiography, Brentano quoted a passage from Bacon's *Novum Organum* on the right way of scientific investigation, and asserted that he and his colleagues, who had gone through "the school of the statistician Engel," were following Bacon's lead. Ibid., 74.

43. Ibid., 79.

44. Brentano to Gustav Schmoller, November 4, 1878, James J. Sheehan, *The Career of Lujo Brentano: A Study of Liberalism and Social Reform in Imperial Germany* (1966), 83.

45. "The policy of protection had split the Verein at its Frankfurt congress of 1879 into two camps, so that, for the sake of staying together, questions of commercial policy could not be placed on the agenda for more than a decade. As for the anti-socialist law, opinions confronted one another even more violently." Brentano, *Mein Leben*, 122. Not all was pure loss; the Verein asked the rising sociologist Max Weber to study the living conditions of agricultural workers in eastern Germany, and Weber became, not only a loyal member of the Verein but Brentano's lifelong friend.

46. Ibid.

47. It is telling that Beatrice Potter, the most carping of observers, should find Brentano, with whom she debated the advantages and failings of socialism, "attractive and sympathetic." September 7, 1890, *The Diary of Beatrice Webb*, ed. Norman MacKenzie and Jeanne MacKenzie, vol. I, *1873–1892, Glitter Around and Darkness Within* (1982), 340.

48. Webb, *My Apprenticeship*, 243, 257.

49. Charles Booth, "The Inhabitants of Tower Hamlets (School Board Division), Their Condition and Occupations" (read before the Royal Statistical Society, May 17, 1887), *Journal of the Royal Statistical Society*, L (June 1887), 376.

50. See Simey and Simey, *Charles Booth*, 77–78.

51. Charles Booth, *Life and Labour of the People in London*, first series, *Poverty* 4 vols. (1902), I, 165.

52. The apology was implicit; as Hyndman recalled, Booth "had not the courtesy at the time to inform me of the result of his inquiry, or to withdraw the imputations he had personally made upon me and the body to which I belong. Nor has he ever done so to this day." *The Record*, 333.

53. It should be noted that of the 30.7 percent below the poverty line only around one in four was destitute; most were more or less regularly employed as unskilled laborers, making a bare living. But when they compared their lot to that of more prosperous Londoners, they saw themselves falling ever further behind.

3. The End of Renaissance Man

1. See Theodore Zeldin, *France, 1848–1945*, vol. I, *Ambition, Love and Politics* (1973), 41–42.

2. Friedrich Schiller, *Über die aesthetische Erziehung des Menschen in einer Reihe von Briefen* (1795), in *Sämtliche Werke*, ed. Gerhard Fricke and Herbert G. Göpfert, 5 vols. (1960–62), V, 584.

3. See Karl Marx, "Economic and Philosophical Manuscripts," *Early Writings*, tr. and ed. T. B. Bottomore (1964), 72; Jacob Burckhardt, *Kultur der Renaissance in Italien: Ein Versuch* (1860; ed. Walter Goetz, 1925), 132; see also Peter Gay, *Style in History* (1974), 157.

4. Johann Wolfgang von Goethe, *Wilhelm Meisters Wanderjahre; oder, Die Entsagenden* (1829), in *Goethes Werke*, ed. Erich Trunz, 14 vols. (1948–69), VIII, 286 [book II], 37 [book I].

5. Georg von Viebahn, *Statistik des zollvereinten und nördlichen Deutschlands*, in *Deutsche Sozialgeschichte. Dokumente und Skizzen*, vol. I, *1815–1870* (1973), 238.

6. Charles Babbage, *On the Economy of Machinery and Manufactures* (1832; 4th enlarged ed., 1835), 191, 201. In the opening chapter of his *Wealth of Nations*, Adam Smith gave a celebrated example: the manufacture of pins. On his own an unskilled worker without machinery could barely expect to make a single pin a day. But with the eighteen specialized operations the industry had introduced, a small factory with only ten operatives could turn out in one day some 48,000 pins. See *An Inquiry into the Nature and Causes of the Wealth of Nations* (1776; ed. Edwin Cannan, 1937), 3–5.

7. Goethe to Friedrich Schiller, July 20, 1799, *Goethes Briefe und Briefe an Goethe*, ed. Karl Robert Mandelkow, 6 vols. (1964; 3rd ed., 1988), II, 385 (Goethe, with Schiller and his friend Johann Heinrich Meyer, even worked on an essay, "Über den Dilettantismus"); Thomas Carlyle, *Sartor Resartus*, (1833–34; ed. Kerry McSweeney and Peter Saber, 1987), 54 [book I, ch. 10]; George Eliot, *Middlemarch* (1871–72; ed. Bert G. Hornback, 1977), 132 [ch. 19].

8. Gibbon's precise indictment of Oxford as the home of torpor and ignorance—"I spent fourteen months at Magdalen College; they proved the fourteen months the most idle and unprofitable of my whole life"—may have been overdrawn, but not by much. *The Autobiography of Edward Gibbon* (1794; ed. Dero A. Saunders, 1961), 72.

9. Adolphe Quetelet, "Recherches statistiques sur le Royaume des Pays-Bas," quoted in Theodore M. Porter, *The Rise of Statistical Thinking, 1820–1900* (1986), 45.

10. Wilhelm von Humboldt, "Bericht der Sektion des Kultus und Unterrichts an den König" (December 1809), *Werke in fünf Bänden*, ed. Andreas Flitner and Klaus Giel (1960–81), IV, 218; see

also "Unmassgebliche Gedanken über den Plan zur Einrichtung des Litthauischen Stadtschulwe-sens" (September 22, 1809), ibid., 189.

11. In 1824 one of the true believers in the supremacy of ancient Greek culture, the classicist Karl Wilhelm Baumgarten-Crusius, reiterated Humboldt's doctrine: "The purpose of learned instruction in the schools is the development and the formation of *humanness*." The study of German and, even more, of the ancient languages, was intended to cultivate "spiritual human beings above all, not burghers who make money." Hence Greek, "for the inner spiritual world," and Latin, "for external life," should be taught from the first class on. *Briefe über Bildung und Kunst in Gelehrtenschulen* (1824), 51, 56, 77.

12. Christopher Kent, *Brains and Numbers: Elitism, Comtism, and Democracy in Mid-Victorian England* (1978), 34.

13. Friedrich Paulsen, *Geschichte des gelehrten Unterrichts auf den deutschen Schulen und Universitäten vom Ausgang des Mittelalters bis zur Gegenwart. Mit besonderer Rücksicht auf den klassischen Unterricht* (1885; 2nd ed., 2 vols., 1896–97), II, 442.

14. Lord Acton, "German Schools of History" (1886), *Historical Essays and Studies,* ed. John Neville Figgis (1907), 370.

15. The scientists did not, however, do all their most original work within the university setting. Recognizing the limitations of academic departments, and organizing unprecedented coopera-tion, they saw to it that the government established, and generously funded, scientific institutes. Thus the Physikalisch-Technische Reichsanstalt came into being in 1887, while the immensely productive Kaiser Wilhelm Gesellschaft, which in turn set up research institutes for specialized tasks, dates from 1911.

16. Friedrich Paulsen, *An Autobiography* (1909; ed. and tr. Theodor Lorenz, 1938, the first full edition), 425.

17. Siegfried Bernfeld, "Freud's Scientific Beginnings," *American Imago,* VI (1949), 169–74. "In the world of science," Friedrich Paulsen recalled, of the mid-century, "there were profound changes." A "thirst for facts took the place of the thirst for general thoughts. *Natural-scientific* research arose and began to throw powerful excitements into life." *Geschichte des gelehrten Unter-richts,* 444–45.

18. These figures do not include Max Planck, who had developed his quantum theory as early as 1901 but did not win the Nobel Prize until 1918, and Albert Einstein, who enunciated his epochal special theory of relativity in 1905 but did not become a Nobel laureate until 1921.

19. Thus Thorstein Veblen appraised the German in 1915, in his brilliant and quirky study *Imperial Germany and the Industrial Revolution:* "It used to be one of the stock aspersions on the German community that it was top-heavy with a redundance of learned men. Fault-finding on this score has ceased since the latter part of the century, the learned class having been found useful and the demand for men proficient in the sciences having fully caught up. Meantime the character of this learning, or rather the direction of it, has changed somewhat, the change resulting on the whole in a pronounced shift toward those branches of knowledge that have some technological or commercial value" (p. 77).

20. Alfred Heuss, *Theodor Mommsen und das 19. Jahrhundert* (1956), 282.

21. William Whewell, *Philosophy of the Inductive Sciences, Founded upon Their History,* 2 vols. (1840), I, 113.

22. See Burton J. Bledstein, *The Culture of Professionalism: The Middle Class and the Development of Higher Education in America* (1976), 85.

23. Hans-Heinz Eulner, "Das Spezialistentum in der ärtzlichen Praxis," in Walter Artelt and Walter Rüegg, eds., *Der Arzt und der Kranke in der Gesellschaft des 19. Jahrhunderts* (1967), 17.

24. "of the community": "Preface on Doctors" (1911), *The Bodley Head Bernard Shaw: Collected Plays with Their Prefaces*, 7 vols. (1970–74), III, 226; "the sake of gain": Sir James Paget, quoted in R. Brudenell Carter, "The Medical Profession," in E. H. Pitcairn, ed., *Unwritten Laws and Ideals of Active Careers* (1899), 251; "in their dealings": Carter, "The Medical Profession," 251.

25. Ibid., 205.

26. Ibid.

27. See M. Jeanne Peterson, *The Medical Profession in Mid-Victorian London* (1978), 8n.

28. Carter, "The Medical Profession," 206, 207.

29. See Peterson, *The Medical Profession*, 213–14.

30. Brian Harrison, "Women's Health and the Women's Movement in Britain: 1840–1940," in Charles Webster, ed., *Biology, Medicine and Society, 1840–1940* (1981), 33.

31. Justin McCarthy, *A History of Our Own Times from the Diamond Jubilee 1897 to the Accession of Edward VII*, 2 vols. (1905), II, 371, 375–76. These volumes continue McCarthy's expansive *History of Our Own Times*, 5 vols. (1879–97).

32. So wary and unsentimental a student of Britain's health in the Victorian decades as F. B. Smith concludes that "though some of the Victorians' actions were misguided, like their fierce fumigation procedures, and others were proved less successful than they expected, like compulsory vaccination, they acted, and did in the long run save the lives of millions." *The People's Health, 1830–1910* (1979), 425.

33. While a solid Edwardian bourgeois could reckon on some fifty years of life, his working-class compatriot averaged thirty-six; about a quarter as many among the affluent as among the poor were likely to develop tuberculosis; while a mere 4 percent of infants born to the well-to-do died before they were a year old, more than 30 percent of infants born in the slums died during that time. See Paul Thompson, *The Edwardians: The Remaking of British Society* (1977), 27.

4. An Age of Advice and Neuroses

1. H. S. Pomeroy, *The Ethics of Marriage* (1888), 58.

2. Nicholas Pain Gilman, *The Laws of Daily Conduct* (1891), 53n.

3. Ernst von Feuchtersleben, Preface to second edition, *Zur Diätetik der Seele* (1841; 2nd ed., 1879), 18.

4. Early in the eighteenth century, Alexander Pope had already noted in his *Essay on Man*, "Two Principles in human nature reign; / Self-love, to urge, and Reason, to restrain." Without a measure of egotism, man would not be active, but egotism without the restraint of reason is a prescription for disaster: "Self-love, the spring of motion, acts the soul; / Reason's comparing balance rules the whole." *Essay on Man*, epistle 2, lines 53–54, 59–60. Plato's analysis of the human soul as tripartite—rational, courageous, passionate—anticipates much modern discussion.

5. For detailed evidence, see Peter Gay, *The Bourgeois Experience*, vol. I, *Education of the Senses* (1984), passim.

6. George Moore, *Man and His Motives* (1848), 276.

7. Mrs. H. O. Ward [Mrs. Clara Sophia (Jessup) Bloomfield-Moore], *Sensible Etiquette of the Best Society, Customs, Manners, Morals and Home Culture. Compiled from the Best Authorities* (1878), 182.

8. Paul Paquin, *The Supreme Passions of Man; or, The Origin, Causes, and Tendencies of the Passions of the Flesh* (1891), 37.

9. "There is grief in the cup!" begins one favorite nineteenth-century temperance poem; then, "There is shame in the cup!" and "There is death in the cup!" "In the Cup," in Miss L. Penney,

ed., *The National Temperance Orator: A New and Choice Collection of Prose and Poetical Articles and Selections, for Public Readings, Addresses, and Recitations* (1877), 11.

10. Horace Mann, *A Few Thoughts for a Young Man: A Lecture, Delivered before the Boston Mercantile Literary Association, on Its 29th Anniversary* (1850), 22–23. In a sermon preached at Rutgers College in 1900 by the Reverend Henry Evertson Cobb we read, "O men, believe that every muscle put in play in healthful exercise, every restraint put upon prodigal appetites and enervating passions, every conquest of self-indulgence, every victory for self-control, puts a tempered sword into your hand against the subtle enemy of future days!" *Victories of Youth, the Defense of Manhood* (1900), 8.

11. William Alcott, *The Young Man's Guide* (1832; 16th rev. ed., 1845), 92–93.

12. Alexander M. Gow, *Good Morals and Gentle Manners for Schools and Families* (1873), 39; Alcott, *Young Man's Guide*, 94–95.

13. Alcott: ibid., 116, 122; Emerson: Theodore Munger, *On the Threshold* (1881), 78; Ruskin: ibid.

14. Charles Dickens, *The Personal History of David Copperfield* (1850; ed. Trevor Blount, 1966), 671 [ch. 42].

15. Forethought: see Munger, *On the Threshold*, 82; Samuel Smiles, Preface to *Duty, with Illustrations of Courage, Patience, and Endurance* (1882), 5.

16. Henry Ward Beecher, *Industry and Idleness, with Twelve Causes of Dishonesty, to Which Are Added Six Warnings* (1850), 6, 17. Horace Mann was, if anything, even more rigorous: "No matter what may be the fortunes or the expectations of a young man, he has no right to live a life of idleness. In a world so full as this of incitements to exertion and of rewards for achievement, idleness is the most absurd of absurdities and the most shameful of shames." *A Few Thoughts for a Young Man*, 48–49.

17. Theodore Roosevelt, "The Strenuous Life" (delivered 1899), *The Strenuous Life: Essays and Addresses* (1900), 1; Maurice de Fleury, *Le Corps et l'âme de l'enfant* (1899), 86; Edward Carpenter, *Marriage in a Free Society* (1894), 11.

18. "We live in an ease-loving, pain-hating age," a time when "elementary virtues" like devotion, service, and self-denial "are apt to be esteemed too lightly." Sophie Bryant, *Short Studies in Character* (1894), 7. To Foerster work was "divine service" when it stood under the signs of fidelity, love, reliability, and conscience. *Lebensführung. Ein Buch für junge Menschen* (1909; ed. 1910), 24.

19. Moore, *Man and His Motives*, 112, 117.

20. Ibid., 272.

21. Georges Demeny, *L'Éducation de l'effort; Psychologie—physiologie* (1914), 1, 3, 223.

22. Alfred Fouillée, *La France au point de vue morale* (1900), 203–4.

23. *A System of Logic* (1843), in *Collected Works of John Stuart Mill*, ed. J. M. Robson, 25 vols. (1963–86), VIII, 870 [book VI, ch. 5, §5].

24. J. H. Vincent, *Better Not: A Discussion of Certain Social Customs* (1883); quotation at 3–4.

25. Samuel Smiles, *Character* (1871; ed. 1872), 165. He made the same point elsewhere: "Character is made up of small duties faithfully performed—of self-denials, of self-sacrifices, of kindly acts of love and duty." *Duty*, p. 29.

26. John MacCunn, *The Making of Character: Some Educational Aspects of Ethics* (1900), 33, 36, 212. "The conflict between good and evil," Edward P. Jackson acknowledged, "is ever in progress." *Character Building: A Master's Talk with His Pupils* (1891), 31.

27. Smiles, *Character*, 167.

28. George M. Beard, *American Nervousness, Its Causes and Consequences: A Supplement to Nervous*

Exhaustion (Neurasthenia) (1881), 138. For details on Beard and late-nineteenth-century nervousness, see Gay, *Bourgeois Experience*, vol. II, *The Tender Passion* (1986), ch. 6, "The Price of Repression," esp. 340–48.

29. Sessions of January 30 and December 18, 1907, *Protokolle der Wiener Psychoanalytischen Vereinigung*, ed. Hermann Nunberg and Ernst Federn, 4 vols. (1976–81), I, 94, 256–57. See also ibid., 89, 92–95; II, 18, 127, 240, 247n; III, 36.

30. See Freud, "Zur Ätiologie der Hysterie" (1896), *Gesammelte Werke*, I, 456–58; "The Aetiology of Hysteria," *Standard Edition*, III, 219–20; and "Die Disposition zur Zwangsneurose" (1913), *Gesammelte Werke*, VIII, 441–52; "The Disposition to Obsessional Neurosis," *Standard Edition*, XII, 313–26.

31. J.W.L. [Mrs. Loudon]: editorial in *The Ladies' Companion at Home and Abroad*, I (March 16, 1850), 168; Von Feuchtersleben, *Zur Diätetik der Seele*, 21; Mark Twain: Allen Guttmann, *From Ritual to Record: The Nature of Modern Sports* (1978), 15. For further material, see Gay, *The Tender Passion*, 329–52.

32. See Freud, "L'Hérédité et l'étiologie des névroses" (1896), *Gesammelte Werke*, I, 411; "Heredity and the Aetiology of the Neuroses," *Standard Edition*, III, 146.

33. Pierre Janet, *Les Obsessions et la psychasthénie*, 2 vols., vol. II in collaboration with Dr. F. Raymond (1903), I, 626.

34. See Max Weber, *The Protestant Ethic and the Spirit of Capitalism* (1904–5; tr. Talcott Parsons, 1930), passim, esp. 155–83 [ch. 5].

35. Charlotte Brontë: *Shirley* (1849; ed. Andrew Hook and Judith Hook, 1974), 183 [ch. 10]; Mill: "De Tocqueville on Democracy in America [II]" (1840), *Collected Works*, vol. XVIII, *Essays on Politics and Society*, 194. Mill's phrase is from an essay by Francis Bacon.

EPILOGUE: August 4, 1914

1. Oron J. Hale, *The Great Illusion, 1900–1914* (1971), 300, 304.

2. Anthropologists and psychologists, wrote Sigmund Freud in 1915, had felt it "necessary to declare the adversary inferior and degenerate" or to diagnose his "mental or spiritual sickness." "Zeitgemässes über Krieg und Tod" (1915), *Gesammelte Werke*, X, 324; "Thoughts for the Times on War and Death," *Standard Edition*, XIV, 275.

3. Looking back, Freud drily commented that the assured way both the Allies and the Central Powers had claimed "a special personal intimacy with the Almighty" had done little for God's reputation. Sigmund Freud, Introduction to Freud and William C. Bullitt, *Thomas Woodrow Wilson: A Psychological Study* (1966; ed. 1968), xiii–xiv.

4. Peter Gay, *Freud: A Life for Our Time* (1988), 347–57; quotations at 349 and 355.

5. Thomas Mann, "Gedanken im Krieg," *Neue Rundschau*, XXV (November 1914), 1475.

6. Oliver Wendell Holmes, Jr., "The Soldier's Faith," *Occasional Speeches*, comp. Mark DeWolfe Howe (1962), 80–81. James Bratt first called my attention to this passage.

7. William Graham Sumner, "The Influence of Commercial Crises on Opinions about Economic Doctrines" (1879), *Essays of William Graham Sumner*, ed. Albert Galloway Keller and Maurice R. Davie, 2 vols. (1934), II, 48.

8. A certain sense of wounded national pride speaks in the famous last chapter of Machiavelli's *The Prince*, in which he prods the Medici to liberate Italy from the "barbarian" invaders. And national pride speaks in modern chauvinist tones in William Hogarth's famous satirical picture *The Gate of Calais: O the Roast Beef of Old England*, which shows plump French friars and ragged

French sentries staring—the priests with connoisseurs' smiles and the soldiers with starvelings' envy—at a haunch of English roast beef just unloaded. A cultivated English patrician like Horace Walpole could deride Hogarth's contemptuous caricature of the French, hungry or bloated, as nothing better than a stooping "to low images and national satire" that would "please his vulgar customers." Fair appraisal or cheap shot, Hogarth fully grasped the dividends of making invidious comparisons with other nations in order to establish the superiority of one's own. Frederick Antal, *Hogarth and His Place in European Art* (1962), 3.

9. Samuel Johnson's celebrated definition of patriotism as the last refuge of a scoundrel strongly suggests an awareness that the loudly proclaimed love of nation concealed some unattractive demagogic possibilities. Gotthold Ephraim Lessing called for men who could rise above the "prejudices" of "peoplehood"—*Völkerschaft*—and would know the point where "patriotism ceases to be a virtue." "Zweites Gespräch," *Ernst und Falk. Gespräche für Freimaurer* (1778), in *Lessings Werke,* ed. Franz Bornmüller, 5 vols. (n.d.), V, 590. David Hume had already argued, in an essay typical of his calm good sense, that "the vulgar are apt to carry all *national characters* to extremes; and having once established it as a principle, that any people are knavish, or cowardly, or ignorant, they will admit of no exception, but comprehend every individual under the same censure." "Of National Characters" (1748), *Essays, Moral, Political, and Literary,* in *The Philosophical Works of David Hume,* ed. T. H. Green and T. H. Grosse, 4 vols. (1875; ed. 1882), I, 244.

10. "Un diplomate," *Essai sur les principes des nationalités* (1882), 1; Georg Moritz Ebers, *The Story of My Life from Childhood to Manhood* (1893; tr. Mary J. Safford, 1893), 244.

11. In 1885 Alfred von Kremer, an Austrian Egyptologist, historian of Islamic culture, and public servant—he had been minister of trade from 1880 to 1881—tried to discuss the idea of nationality in a reasonable way, but despaired of success; the debate, he wrote sadly, was dominated by "party men, enthusiasts and fanatics of one persuasion or another." His dismay was widely shared. Kremer, *Die Nationalitäts-Idee und der Staat. Eine culturgeschichtliche Studie über den Einfluss der nationalen Ideen, besonders auf Staaten mit gemischter Bevölkerung* (1885), xi.

12. In 1861, *Die Gartenlaube* wondered whether the Polish people would be able to sustain a free nation-state in the absence of "the necessary ingredient, the forceful bearer of freedom, a capable middle class"—*tüchtiger Bürgerstand.* Miroslav Hroch, "Das Bürgertum in den nationalen Bewegungen des 19. Jahrhunderts. Ein europäischer Vergleich," in Jürgen Kocka, ed., *Bürgertum im 19. Jahrhundert. Deutschland im europäischen Vergleich,* 3 vols. (1988), III, 339n.

13. Andreas Elviken, *Die Entwicklung des norwegischen Nationalismus* (1930), 103.

14. See Harald Beyer, *A History of Norwegian Literature* (1933; ed. 1952, ed. and tr. Einar Haugen, 1956), 149.

15. See Robert A. Kann, *A History of the Habsburg Empire, 1526–1918* (1974; corr. ed., 1977), 288, 304.

16. J. A. Hobson, *The Psychology of Jingoism* (1901), 1–2, 29.

APPENDIX: Theories of Aggression

1. Irenäus Eibl-Eibesfeldt, *Love and Hate: The Natural History of Behavior Patterns* (1970; tr. Geoffrey Strachan, 1971), 3.

2. Dennis H. Wrong, "The Oversocialized Conception of Man in Modern Sociology" (1961), *Skeptical Sociology* (1976), 37. I have explored this issue in *Freud for Historians* (1985), ch. 5.

3. As the psychoanalyst Hans W. Loewald has put it, "The infant and child equipped at birth only with certain automatic mechanisms for maintaining himself in equilibrium with the environ-

ment, increasingly becomes confronted with external conditions of an extremely complex nature. These complex external conditions . . . are not merely sets of 'biological' events, but events of different orders of integration which we call psychological, cultural, social." "The Problem of Defense and the Neurotic Interpretation of Reality" (1952), *Papers on Psychoanalysis* (1980), 21–22.

4. "The drives or 'instincts' of psychoanalysis," Dennis Wrong has written in full agreement with Freud, "are not fixed dispositions to behave in a particular way; they are utterly subject to social channeling and transformation and could not reveal themselves in behavior without social molding." For the psychoanalyst, then, "man is indeed a social animal" but not "entirely a *socialized* animal. His social nature is itself the source of conflicts and antagonisms that create resistance to socialization." "Oversocialized Conception of Man," 45. See also Wrong, "Postscript 1975" and the companion essay, "Human Nature and the Perspective of Sociology" (1963), *Skeptical Sociology,* 47–54, 55–70.

5. Freud to Frederic van Eeden, a Dutch poet and psychopathologist, December 1914, Ernest Jones, *The Life and Work of Sigmund Freud,* vol. II, *Years of Maturity, 1901–1919* (1955), 368.

6. "Response to Robert M. White's Review of Heinz L. and Rowena R. Ansbacher's *The Individual Psychology of Alfred Adler*" (1957), *The Collected Papers of David Rapaport,* ed. Merton M. Gill (1967), 683.

7. Leo Stone, "Reflections on the Psychoanalytic Concept of Aggression," *Psychoanalytic Quarterly,* XL (1971), 195, 238, 199.

8. *The Inquirer* (London), March 22, 1862, p. 217. I owe this reference to R. K. Webb.

9. Ives Hendrick, "Work and the Pleasure Principle," *Psychoanalytic Quarterly,* XII (1943), 311.

10. Ibid., 314.

11. Sigmund Freud, "Angst und Triebleben" (1932), *Neue Folge der Vorlesungen zur Einführung in die Psychoanalyse,* in *Gesammelte Werke,* XV, 101; "Anxiety and Instinctual Life," *New Introductory Lectures on Psycho-Analysis,* in *Standard Edition,* XXII, 95.

12. Rapaport, "Some Metapsychological Considerations Concerning Activity and Passivity" (1961), *Collected Papers,* 533; see also Gill's editorial comment, ibid., 532.

13. Otto Fenichel, *The Psychoanalytic Theory of Neurosis* (1945), 59.

14. Joseph Sandler, in "Panel on 'Aggression,' " chaired by Martin H. Stein, *International Journal of Psycho-Analysis,* LIII (1972), 14.

15. Eliot to Mrs. Peter Alfred Taylor, February 1, 1853, *The George Eliot Letters,* ed. Gordon S. Haight, vol. II, *1852–1858* (1954), 86.

BIBLIOGRAPHICAL ESSAY

This bibliographical essay is highly selective, stripped more or less to essentials, precisely because the literature on the subjects covered in this volume is so mountainous. I have consulted far more sources—monographs, biographies, comprehensive histories, archival materials—than I discuss in this essay, and concentrated in it on the titles that have proved most informative and most stimulating—whether moving me to assent or to disagreement. Since I have already indicated my indebtedness to psychoanalytic theories in *Education of the Senses* (especially pp. 463–66 and 469), I am not repeating my tribute here.

As in the Notes, Freud titles have been slightly abridged: *Gesammelte Werke* denotes Sigmund Freud, *Gesammelte Werke,* ed. Anna Freud et al., 18 vols. (1940–68), and *Standard Edition* denotes Sigmund Freud, *Standard Edition of the Complete Psychological Works,* tr. and ed. James Strachey et al., 24 vols. (1953–74).

BOURGEOIS EXPERIENCES, III:
Mensur—the Cherished Scar

German texts on the Mensur, generally sympathetic to the duelling mentality, are not necessarily apologetic. The best of them show its integration into student life and customs. See especially Friedrich Schulze and Paul Ssymank, *Das deutsche Studententum von den ältesten Zeiten bis zur Gegenwart* (1910). Peter Krause, *"O Alte Burschenherrlichkeit." Die Studenten und ihr Brauchtum* (1979; 3rd. ed., 1980), and the earlier P. Seiffert, *Geschichte und Entwicklung der studentischen Verbände* (1913), are useful. Werner Klose, *Freiheit schreibt auf eure Fahnen: 800 Jahre deutsche Studenten* (1967), is popular and comprehensive. Ssymank's *Bruder Studio in Karikatur and Satire* (1929) offers amusing and instructive glimpses of German students under the pens of cartoonists and caricaturists. W. Fuhrmann, *Geschichte der studentischen Fechtkunst* (1901), is a concentrated history of student duelling. On the most exclusive student associations, Wilhelm Fabricius, *Die deutschen Corps. Eine historische Darstellung mit besonderer Berücksichtigung des Mensurwesens*

(1898; ed. 1926), retains its value. An excellent monograph on a most select *Corps* is H. Gerhardt, *Hundert Jahre Bonner Corps* (1926). Detlev Grieswelle, "Zur Soziologie der Kösener Corps 1870–1914," in Karsten Bahnson et al., *Student und Hochschule im 19. Jahrhundert. Studien und Materialien* (1975), 346–65, is an informative socio-historical essay. See also in Bahnson the essays by Grieswelle, "Antisemitismus in deutschen Studentenverbindungen des 19. Jahrhunderts," 366–79, and Christian Helfer, "Formen und Funktionen studentischen Brauchtums im 19. Jahrhundert," 159–72. K. Endemann, *Der deutsche Student und die sexuelle Ethik* [ca. 1900], is an early exploration of the erotic background of German student life; more needs to be done.

The literature in English tends to be more critical; witness Konrad H. Jarausch, *Students, Society, and Politics in Imperial Germany: The Rise of Academic Illiberalism* (1982), passim, esp. ch. 5, "The Hidden Curriculum." Charles E. McClelland, *State, Society and University in Germany, 1700–1914* (1980), firmly places the German university in its social context. Going beyond its title, R. G. S. Weber, *The German Student Corps in the Third Reich* (1986), has good material on earlier years and very full notes. See also Gary D. Stark, "The Ideology of the German *Burschenschaft* Generation," *European Studies Review*, VIII, 3 (July 1978), 323–48. Jewish duelling fraternities are discussed in Adolf Asch and Johanna Philippson, "Self-Defence at the Turn of the Century: The Emergence of the K.C.," *Leo Baeck Institute Yearbook*, III (1958), 122–39. The comments of Thomas Nipperdey, *Deutsche Geschichte, 1800–1866. Bürgerwelt und starker Staat* (1983), esp. 278–82, are terse but much to the point.

Among nineteenth-century testimonies to the Mensur, the (justly) best-known is William Howitt, *The Student-Life of Germany* (1841). See also the diary of Heine's friend Eduard Wedekind, *Studentenleben der Biedermeierzeit. Ein Tagebuch aus dem Jahre 1824,* ed. H. H. Houben [ca. 1927]. Many widely quoted German autobiographies touch on the Mensur; the most revealing are perhaps Adolf Kussmaul, *Jugenderinnerungen eines alten Arztes* (1899); Friedrich Paulsen, *An Autobiography* (1909; ed. and tr. Theodor Lorenz, 1938); Werner von Siemens, *Lebenserinnerungen* (1892); and Heinrich Laube, *Erinnerungen 1810–1840* (1909). F. Eichholz, *Der Paukarzt* (1886), the reminiscences of a physician who specialized in tending victims of the Mensur is chilling and interesting. Arthur Schnitzler, a critic of the Mensur who understood it thoroughly, conjures up the atmosphere in *My Youth in Vienna* (1968; tr. Catherine Hutter, 1971), and in some of his most effective short stories, notably "Der Sekundant" and "Leutnant Gustl." I have drawn on atmospheric novels on the subject, like Walter Bloem, *Der krasse Fuchs* (1906), in the text. For Max Weber's attitude toward the duel, see Marianne Weber's remarkable *Max Weber: A Biography* (1950; tr. Harry Zohn, 1975). What remains a desideratum is a study of how German women really felt about "their" men getting themselves cut up. Otto Julius Bierbaum, *Stilpe. Ein Roman aus der Froschperspektive* (1897; ed. 1963), is light-hearted satire but nothing more.

Most historians of duelling have rightly stressed its aristocratic heritage but have underestimated its adoption by bourgeois, especially by the German *Bildungsbürgertum,* in the nineteenth century. This holds true even for the best modern survey, V. G. Kiernan, *The Duel in European History: Honour and the Reign of Aristocracy* (1988). Kiernan's far-ranging history may be supplemented with a scholarly work by François Billacois, *The Duel: Its Rise and Fall in Early Modern France* (1986; tr. Trista Selous, 1990). Ute Frevert has offered splendid correctives to the literature taking aristocratic appearances for the whole of reality (they gratifyingly confirm my conviction that the Mensur is relevant to the history of nineteenth-century bourgeois culture): "Bürgerlichkeit und Ehre. Zur Geschichte des Duells in England und Deutschland," in Jürgen Kocka, ed., *Bürgertum im 19. Jahrhundert. Deutschland im europäischen Vergleich,* 3 vols. (1988), III, 101–40; "Die Ehre der Bürger im Spiegel ihrer Duelle. Ansichten des 19. Jahrhunderts," *Historische Zeitschrift,* CCXLIX (1989), 545–82 (with a fascinating account of Heine's duels on pp. 554–57); and her substantial, persuasive synthesis, *Ehrenmänner. Das Duell in der bürgerlichen Gesellschaft* (1991).

For duelling in the antebellum South, see Bertram Wyatt-Brown, *Southern Honor: Ethics and Behavior in the Old South* (1982), passim. Jerome K. Jerome's autobiography, *My Life and Times* (1926), is candid about the author's ambivalence about cruelty and war, and hence indispensable to a reading of his encounter with a Mensur. Finally, though they do not deal with duelling explicitly, the essays in *The Invention of Tradition,* ed. Eric Hobsbawm and Terence Ranger (1983), illuminate, often wryly, the way that "ancient" rituals can be manufactured.

ONE: Alibis

The literature on Spencer is beginning to do justice to his place in Victorian intellectual life. His bulky *Autobiography,* 2 vols. (1904), repays rereading. David Duncan, *Life and Letters of Herbert Spencer,* 2 vols. (1908), is a classic post-Victorian life and letters. John W. Burrow has a thoughtful essay on Spencer (ch. 6) in *Evolution and Society: A Study in Victorian Social Theory* (1966). See also Jay Rumney, *Herbert Spencer's Sociology: A Study in the History of Social Theory* (1934; ed. 1966); and J. D. Y. Peel, *Herbert Spencer: The Evolution of a Sociologist* (1971). Arnold M. Paul persuasively argues that Spencer's impact, at least on American lawyers, has been exaggerated: *Conservative Crisis and the Rule of Law: Attitudes of Bar and Bench, 1887–1895* (1960). There are some telling reminiscences and appraisals of Spencer in Beatrice Webb, *My Apprenticeship* (1926; ed. 1971). I am indebted to Richard Hofstadter's brilliant and pioneering *Social Darwinism in American Thought, 1860–1915* (1944; 2nd ed., 1955), though my reading of Spencer somewhat differs from his.

The literature on Darwin and Darwinism is becoming unmanageable. Darwin's terse, much-quoted *Autobiography* (1887), in *Autobiographies of Darwin and Huxley,* ed. Gavin de Beer (1974), is relatively impersonal—revealing precisely because it is so unrevealing. *The Correspondence of Charles Darwin* (1985–   ), an indispensable source, is now being authoritatively edited by Frederick Burkhardt and Sydney Smith. As this volume went to press, 7 volumes, reaching to 1859, had been published. Until this splendid series is completed, the older compilation by Francis Darwin, *The Life and Letters of Charles Darwin, Including an Autobiographical Chapter,* 3 vols. (1887; ed. 1919), and Francis Darwin and A. C. Seward, ed., *More Letters of Charles Darwin: A Record of His Work in a Series of Hitherto Unpublished Letters,* 2 vols. (1903), must serve for the later years. Among modern lives, Gertrude Himmelfarb, *Darwin and the Darwinian Revolution* (1959), is fluently written, but tendentiously skeptical about his science. Gavin de Beer, *Charles Darwin: Evolution by Natural Selection* (1963), is the work of an expert; Loren Eiseley, *Darwin's Century: Evolution and the Men Who Discovered It* (1958), is highly accessible. See also Peter Brent's very substantial *Charles Darwin: A Man of Enlarged Curiosity* (1981). Ronald W. Clark, *The Survival of Charles Darwin: A Biography of a Man and an Idea* (1984), benefits from modern scholarship and goes beyond the man to his impact. One significant side effect of that impact, on literature, is well studied in Leo J. Henkin, *Darwinism in the English Novel, 1860–1910* (1940); Lionel Stevenson, *Darwin among the Poets* (1932); Georg Roppen, *Evolution and Poetic Belief: A Study in Some Victorian and Modern Writers* (1956); and above all in George Levine, *Darwin and the Novelists: Patterns of Science in Victorian Fiction* (1988), a suggestive text. In similar vein, Gillian Beer, *Darwin's Plots: Evolutionary Narrative in Darwin, George Eliot and Nineteenth-Century Fiction* (1983), is sophisticated and rewarding.

For the precursors and spread of Darwin's ideas, and resistance to them, *Forerunners of Darwin: 1745–1859,* ed. Bentley Glass, Owsei Tempkin, and William L. Straus, Jr. (1959), is useful; it contains some fifteen dependable essays on evolutionism from Buffon to Schopenhauer, including three by the master Arthur O. Lovejoy. The generous anthology *Darwin and His Critics: The Reception of Darwin's Theory of Evolution by the Scientific Community,* ed. David L. Hull, boasts a long introduction. D. P. Crook, *Benjamin Kidd: Portrait of a Social Darwinist* (1984), is a biography of one important follower, reaching beyond its subject. Peter J. Bowler, *The Eclipse of Darwinism: Anti-Darwinian Evolution Theories in the Decades around 1900* (1983), analyzes critiques of Darwin, but shows no real "eclipse." As for "Darwin's bulldog," the old expansive biography by Leonard Huxley, *Life and Letters of Thomas Henry Huxley,* 2 vols. (1900), though still worth reading, should be supplemented by Mario A. diGregorio's informative *T. H. Huxley's Place in Natural Science* (1984). *The Wider Domain of Evolutionary Thought,* ed. David Oldroyd and Ian Langham (1983), contains some helpful papers. Ernst Mayer's encyclopedic and authoritative *The Growth of Biological Thought: Diversity, Evolution, and Inheritance* (1982) deserves to be consulted.

The fascinating, often disturbing, career of Darwin's ideas—or what passed for them—at home and abroad has attracted some admirable scholarship. For an interesting early French appraisal, there is A. de Quatrefages, *Charles Darwin et ses précurseurs français: Étude sur le transformisme* (1870). For recent scholarship, see Greta Jones, *Social Darwinism and English Thought: The Interaction between Biological and Social Theory* (1980); Cynthia Eagle Russett, *Darwin in America: The Intellectual Response, 1865–1912* (1976); *Evolutionary Thought in America,* ed. Stow Persons (1968); and Robert C. Bannister, *Social Darwinism: Science and Myth in Anglo-American Thought* (1979). Linda L. Clark, *Social Darwinism in France* (1984), is excellent; it may be supplemented by Pietro Corsi, *The Age of Lamarck: Evolutionary Theories in France, 1790–1830,* rev. and tr. Jonathan Mandelbaum (1988). Alfred Kelly, *The Descent of Darwin: The Popularization of Darwinism in Germany, 1860–*

1914 (1981), covers the field. It is a corrective for Wilhelm Bölsche, *Ernst Haeckel. Ein Lebensbild* (1900), which idealizes Germany's popularizer of Darwinism out of all recognition. Hofstadter's *Social Darwinism,* cited above, is extremely illuminating.

William Graham Sumner deserves closer study than he has had; his complexities remain insufficiently explored. The pages in Hofstadter, *Social Darwinism,* are sparkling but not conclusive. Albert Galloway Keller's four collections of Sumner's occasional essays are handy: *War and Other Essays* (1911), *Earth-Hunger and Other Essays* (1913), *The Challenge of Facts and Other Essays* (1914), and *The Forgotten Man and Other Essays* (1919). Keller also edited a two-volume selection with Maurice R. Davie, *Selected Essays of William Graham Sumner,* 2 vols. (1924); his *Reminiscences (Mainly Personal) of William Graham Sumner* (1933) is also useful. See in addition Harris E. Starr, *William Graham Sumner* (1925), and the more recent work by Maurice R. Davie, *William Graham Sumner: An Essay of Commentary and Selections* (1963). Robert Green McCloskey, *American Conservatism in the Age of Enterprise, 1865–1910* (1951), is a justly appreciated study but rather too emphatic on Sumner's conservatism. Clifford H. Scott, *Lester Frank Ward* (1976), is a good account of Sumner's great adversary. Israel Gerver has edited a handy selection, *Lester Frank Ward* (1963), from a voluminous output.

On Walter Bagehot, author of the classic *Physics and Politics,* see Alastair Buchan, *The Spare Chancellor: The Life of Walter Bagehot* (1959), above all ch. 8. It supplements and largely supersedes Mrs. Russell Barrington's traditional *Life of Walter Bagehot* (1914). I have learned from John W. Burrow, "Sense and Circumstances: Bagehot and the Nature of Political Understanding," in Stefan Collini, Donald Winch, and John W. Burrow, *The Noble Science of Politics: A Study in Nineteenth-Century Intellectual History* (1983), 161–81. For Bagehot's emotional life, see my "Bourgeois Experiences, II: Counterpoint," in *The Bourgeois Experience,* vol. II, *The Tender Passion,* (1986), 3–43. The critical edition, *The Collected Works of Walter Bagehot,* ed. Norman St. John-Stevas, 15 vols. (1966–86), is admirable in its treatment of the texts and its long explanatory annotations.

John D. Rockefeller offered unapologetic glimpses of his life and ideas in *Random Reminiscences of Men and Events* (1909). He has been exhaustively covered by Allan Nevins in *Study in Power: John D. Rockefeller, Industrialist and Philanthropist,* 2 vols. (1953), a revision of his *John D. Rockefeller: The Heroic Age of American Enterprise,* 2 vols. (1940), thoroughly documented but apologetic to the point of adoration. Joseph Frazier Wall's almost equally substantial *Andrew Carnegie* (1970) is more detached. Harold C. Livesay, *Andrew Carnegie and the Rise of Big Business* (1975), says the essential in brief compass. The *Autobiography of Andrew Carnegie* (published posthumously, ed. John C. Van Dyke, 1920) has some nuggets. Carnegie's famous articles setting forth his philanthropic creed have been well edited by Edward C. Kirkland: Andrew Carnegie, *The Gospel of Wealth and Other Timely Essays* (1962). For the world of these industrial magnates, see above all Kirkland, *Dream and Thought in the Business Community, 1860–1900* (1956); Merle Curti and Roderick Nash, *Philanthropy in the Shaping of American Higher Education* (1965); and Thomas C. Cochran and William Miller, *The Age of Enterprise: A Social History of Industrial America* (1942; rev. ed., 1961). John A. Garraty, *The New Commonwealth, 1877–1890* (1968), judiciously surveys the period. Irvin G. Wyllie,

The Self-Made Man in America: The Myth of Rags to Riches (1954), provides some fascinating sidelights. Some of the titles cited in the section on Theodore Roosevelt, below, and in the section on advice literature in the listings for chapter 6, are also relevant here.

The pessimistic side of evolutionism has been canvassed by Koenraad W. Swart, *The Sense of Decadence in Nineteenth-Century France* (1964), and A. E. Carter, *The Idea of Decadence in French Literature, 1830–1900* (1958). On the most notorious prophet of degeneration, see P. M. Baldwin, "Liberalism, Nationalism, and Degeneration: The Case of Max Nordau," *Central European History*, XIII, 2 (June 1980), 99–120. See also, for Nordau, George Bernard Shaw's slashing counterattack, "A Degenerate's View of Nordau" (1895; rev. as *The Sanity of Art*, 1908). Jean Pierrot, *The Decadent Imagination, 1880–1900* (1977; tr. Derek Coltman, 1981), is interesting and dependable. Among the most ambitious titles in this literature is the imaginative, wide-ranging study by Daniel Pick, *Faces of Degeneration: Aspects of a European Disorder, c. 1848–1918* (1989). He and the others should be read in tension with Richard Gilman, *Decadence: The Strange Life of an Epithet* (1979), which virtually dismisses decadence as a "freelance epithet." Though a useful corrective, the book does not discredit the idea that the *fin de siècle* did betray a certain anxiety about decline, based in part on a peculiarly depressing reading of Darwin's ideas.

The most accessible introduction to nineteenth-century racial theories is Jacques Barzun's banquet of quotations, gracefully put into context: *Race: A Study in Superstition* (1937; rev. ed., 1965). Hugh A. MacDougall, *Racial Myth in English History: Trojans, Teutons, and Anglo-Saxons* (1982), ably traces these myths back to medieval writers. Amid the bulky literature on nineteenth-century racism, L. P. Curtis, Jr., *Anglo-Saxons and Celts: A Study of Anti-Irish Prejudice in Victorian England* (1968), stands out for its psychological insights, offered without psychoanalytic terminology. An equally insightful (and equally unanalytic) older text is J. A. Hobson, *The Psychology of Jingoism* (1901), a powerful polemic inspired by the Boer War. There are suggestive (though hardly conclusive) psychoanalytic speculations in O. Mannoni, *Prospero and Caliban: The Psychology of Colonization* (1950; 2nd ed. tr. Pamela Powesland, 1964). For a full examination of the complexities of racial prejudgments in early America, with comments on Europe, Winthrop Jordan, *White over Black: American Attitudes toward the Negro, 1550–1812* (1968), remains impressive. It can be read in conjunction with Roy Harvey Pearce, *Savagism and Civilization: A Study of the Indian and American Mind* (1953; rev. ed., 1988), on the attitude of whites toward Indians. See also the learned study by Philip Mason, *Prospero's Magic* (1962).

Daniel J. Kevles, *In the Name of Eugenics: Genetics and the Uses of Human Heredity* (1985), is a readable and persuasive indictment of the "scientific" work of Francis Galton, Karl Pearson, and their successors. No less devastating and no less thorough, for Germany, is Peter Weingart, Jürgen Kroll, and Kurt Bayertz, *Rasse, Blut und Gene. Geschichte der Eugenik und Rassenhygiene in Deutschland* (1988), which devotes ample pages to the years before 1914. Stephen Jay Gould's assault on racist "science," *The Mismeasure of Man* (1981), is popular in tone but powerful in substance and has left its mark on these pages. These texts show that indignation need not cripple efforts at historical objectivity. On Aryanism, Léon Poliakov, *The Aryan Myth: A History of Racist and Nationalist Ideas in Europe* (1971; tr. Edmund Howard, 1974), has much essential information. One of the earliest refutations of this myth, still worth reading for more than its historical interest, is Salomon Reinach, *L'Origine des aryens (histoire d'une controverse)* (1892). Even more conclusive refutations came from the great cultural anthropologist Franz Boas. His most important prewar paper is doubtless "Changes in Bodily Form of Descendants of Immigrants," *American Anthropologist*, n.s. XIV (1912), 530–62, handily compressed in *Race, Language and Culture* (1940). His late *Anthropology and Modern Life* (1928) sums up a lifetime of work. For an appreciation (and an indication of the large literature Boas has inspired), see Alexander Lesser, "Boas, Franz," *International Encyclopedia of the Social Sciences,* ed. David L. Sills, 17 vols. (1968), II, 99–110. See also F. H. Hankin, *The Racial Basis of Civilization* (1926), and the social psychologist Otto Klineberg's *Race Differences* (1935). The thesis of Ashley Montagu, *Man's Most Dangerous Myth: The Fallacy of Race* (1945; 4th ed., 1964), is explicit in its title. One anti-racist statement, particularly interesting in view of its source, is by the knowledgeable British administrator and author Sydney Olivier, who was also a Fabian socialist: *White Capital and Coloured Labour* (1910).

For nineteenth-century anthropology, a hotbed of racist speculation, see the collection of authoritative papers by George W. Stocking, Jr., *Race, Culture, and Evolution: Essays in the History of Anthropology* (1968); in singling out "French Anthropology in 1800" (pp. 13–41); "The Dark-Skinned Savage: The Image of Primitive Man in Evolutionary Anthropology" (pp. 110–32); and the appreciation "Franz Boas and the Culture Concept in Historical Perspective" (pp. 195–233), I do not mean to slight the others. Stocking's synthesis, *Victorian Anthropology* (1987) is admirable. Christine Bolt, *Victorian Attitudes to Race* (1971), is most serviceable. See also the authoritative biography by Francis Schiller, *Paul Broca: Founder of French Anthropology, Explorer of the Brain* (1980). For Hippolyte Taine's complex views, see the excellent chapter in René Wellek, *A History of Modern Criticism, 1750–1950,* 8 vols. so far (1955–92), IV, 27–57.

Racist ideas in sixteenth-century Spain, the country that pioneered in devising tests for racial "purity," are elegantly explored in J. H. Elliott, *Imperial Spain, 1469–1716* (1963). The pages in Américo Castro's justly famous *The Structure of Spanish History* (1948; rev. text tr. Edmund L. King, 1954), 521–44, remain compelling. The most detailed scholarly examination of *limpieza de sangre* is A. A. Sicroff, *Les Controverses des statuts de 'pureté de sang' en Espagne du XVe au XVIIe siècle* (1960). In fairness I should note that *some* sixteenth-century Spaniards, notably the celebrated Bartolomé de Las Casas, resisted the dominant ideology. For the context, Lewis Hanke, *The Spanish Struggle for Justice in the Conquest of America* (1949), is indispensable. See also Charles Gibson, *Spain in America* (1966).

The handiest, most convincing—and most succinct—history of the Eyre affair is Bernard Semmel, *Jamaican Blood and Victorian Conscience* (1963); the British edition was published in 1962 under the title *The Governor Eyre Controversy,* and a paperback edition appeared in 1969 under the title *Democracy versus Empire.* Geoffrey Dutton, *The Hero as*

Murderer: The Life of Edward John Eyre, Australian Explorer and Governor of Jamaica, 1815–1901 (1967), is a well-researched but excited and to my mind wrongheaded defense of Eyre, which paints his adversaries as hypocrites. Bolt, *Victorian Attitudes to Race,* cited just above, has a good chapter on Eyre. Robert I. Rotberg, with Miles F. Shore, *The Founder: Cecil Rhodes and the Pursuit of Power* (1988), is an exhaustive modern biography, complete with reasonable psychoanalytic conjectures. A fine companion piece is Phyllis Lewsen, *John X. Merriman: Paradoxical South African Statesman* (1982), a biography of Rhodes's great adversary. Among several biographies of the private owner of the Congo, Barbara Emerson, *Leopold II of the Belgians: King of Colonialism* (1979), is especially well-informed and fair-minded. The sober monograph by George Dunlap Crothers, *The German Elections of 1907* (1941), throws necessary light on the German colonial mood. See also the (unintentionally) revealing compilation by the pseudonymous "Simplex africanus," *Mit der Schutztruppe durch Deutsch-Afrika* (1905), complete with a self-serving appendix on the extermination of the Hereros by Lieutenant P. Leutwein. However skeptical I am of scholarship emerging from what was once the German Democratic Republic, I have found Horst Drechsler's *Südwestafrika unter deutscher Kolonialherrschaft. Der Kampf der Herero und Nama gegen den deutschen Imperialismus (1884–1915)* (1966; 2nd ed., 1984) solidly documented despite its rhetoric. The same holds true of Fritz Ferdinand Müller, *Kolonien unter der Peitsche* (1962). Jon M. Bridgman, *The Revolt of the Hereros* (1981), is scholarly, economical, and devastating—on the Germans.

The vast literature on imperialism inevitably touches on racism. Among the titles I have read through the years (with varying degrees of assent) I single out the first three chapters of Phillip Darby, *Three Faces of Imperialism: British and American Approaches to Asia and Africa, 1870–1970* (1987), and Henri Brunschwig, *French Colonialism, 1871–1914: Myths and Realities* (1960; rev. version tr. William Glanville Brown, 1966), terse but mindful of psychological elements. *The History and Politics of Colonialism, 1870–1914,* ed. L. H. Gann and Peter Duignan, the first volume of their *Colonialism in Africa 1870–1960* (1969), gathers well-informed essays on all aspects of British, French, German, Belgian and other imperialistic expansion. Richard Hofstadter, "Cuba, the Philippines, and Manifest Destiny" (1952), rev. in *The Paranoid Style in American Politics and Other Essays* (1965), 145–87, is (like all his work) immensely suggestive. For a very substantial, and sobering, study of the religious apologetic side of imperialism—the fulfillment of a mission—see Karl Hammer, *Weltmission und Kolonialismus. Sendungsideen des 19. Jahrhunderts im Konflikt* (1978). For the hostile view of German imperialism, Hans-Ulrich Wehler, *Bismarck und der Imperialismus* (1969; 4th ed., 1976) is most remarkable. Two intelligent general studies still repay reading: Richard Koebner, *Empire* (1961), and George Lichtheim, *Imperialism* (1971).

I believe I am entitled to call C. Vann Woodward's crisp, pathbreaking *The Strange Career of Jim Crow* (1955; 3d rev. ed., 1974) a classic. It informs my comments on American racism after the Civil War. Lewis H. Blair's amazing plea for racial equality, *The Prosperity of the South Dependent upon the Elevation of the Negro* (1889), is available in a modern edition under the title *A Southern Prophecy,* ed. C. Vann Woodward (1964). See, in this connection, Thomas F. Gossett, *Race: The History of an Idea in America*

(1963), and the more specialized book by Barbara Miller Solomon, *Ancestors and Immigrants: A Changing New England Tradition* (1956).

When I began gathering material on Victorian manliness years ago, historians showed little interest in it as a phenomenon—or symptom—worthy of research. Recently, it has become downright fashionable. This not to overlook useful older texts. Richard Slotkin's massive *Regeneration Through Violence: The Mythology of the American Frontier, 1600–1860* (1973) has interesting sidelights on American manliness. *The American Man,* ed. Elizabeth H. Pleck and Joseph H. Pleck (1980), presents articles grouped chronologically on subjects ranging from sodomy in seventeenth-century New England to the cult of toughness in foreign policy in the Vietnam years. Mark C. Carnes, *Secret Ritual and Manhood in Victorian America* (1989), details the fantasy world in which lodge brothers were enmeshed to maintain a primitive manly ideal. The anthropologists have made most interesting contributions. Witness the rich comparative study of manliness, David D. Gilmore, *Manhood in the Making: Cultural Concepts of Masculinity* (1990), which documents both expected differences and the overwhelming prevalence of the manly ideal across classes, professions, and cultures. For the antebellum South, Bertram Wyatt-Brown, *Southern Honor: Ethics and Behavior in the Old South* (1982), also cited earlier, is the authority. See, as well, Julian Pitt-Rivers, "Honor," *International Encyclopedia of the Social Sciences,* VI, 503–11; Ray Raphael, *The Men from the Boys: Rites of Passage in Male America* (1988); and Michael Herzfeld, *The Poetics of Manhood: Contest and Identity in a Cretan Mountain Village* (1985). Two older, well-known studies are J. G. Peristiany, *Honour and Shame: The Values of Mediterranean Society* (1966), and John K. Campbell, *Honour, Family and Patronage: A Study of Institutions and Moral Values in a Greek Mountain Community* (1964); both have much of value for this section. And see Peter N. Stearns's eclectic *Be a Man! Males in Modern Society* (1979).

For England, much preoccupied with the subject, I am particularly indebted to Stefan Collini, "Manly Fellows: Fawcett, Stephen, and the Liberal Temper" (1989), rev. in *Public Moralists: Political Thought and Intellectual Life in Britain, 1850–1930* (1991), ch. 5. See also the relevant passages in Boyd Hilton's impressive *The Age of Atonement: The Influence of Evangelicalism on Social and Economic Thought, 1795–1865* (1988), which connects manliness to an influential aspect of English religiosity. It can be profitably read with Norman Vance, *The Sinews of the Spirit: The Ideal of Christian Manliness in Victorian Literature and Religious Thought* (1985). All this literature has drawn—as have I—on David Newsome, *Godliness and Good Learning: Four Studies on a Victorian Ideal* (1961), an appealing and candid text, though psychologically unsophisticated.

William James touched on manliness often, even in *The Varieties of Religious Experience: A Study in Human Nature* (1902). In the secondary literature, see Ralph Barton Perry, *The Thought and Character of William James,* 2 vols. (1935), despite its age still valuable; Jacques Barzun, *A Stroll with William James* (1983), which contains ripe reflections by an aficionado, presented with the author's customary stylishness, and Gerald E. Myers, *William James: His Life and Thought* (1986), a very substantial, even leisurely, intellectual biography. For some sensitive psychoanalytic approaches to James's life and

thought, particularly plausible in view of his early depressive phase, see especially Howard M. Feinstein, *Becoming William James* (1984); and two papers by Cushing Strout,
"William James and the Twice-Born Sick Soul," *Daedalus*, XCVII (Summer 1968),
1062–82, and "The Pluralistic Identity of William James: A Psychohistorical Reading of
The Varieties of Religious Experience," *American Quarterly*, XXIII (1971), 135–52.

For the man who wrote *The Manliness of Christ*, see Edward C. Mack and W. H. G.
Armytage, *Thomas Hughes: The Life of the Author of "Tom Brown's Schooldays"* (1952),
and George J. Worth's brief life, *Thomas Hughes* (1984). But a more penetrating biography would be welcome. Meanwhile, there is Boyd Hilton, "Manliness, Masculinity,
and the Mid-Victorian Temperament," in Lawrence Goldman, ed., *The Blind Victorian:
Henry Fawcett and British Liberalism* (1989), 60–70. Devotees of manliness in Victorian
literature—and even more, its opponents—are delineated in Mario Praz's masterly *The
Hero in Eclipse in Victorian Fiction* (1952; tr. Angus Davidson, 1956). On the definition of
manliness and its problems, Sigmund Freud, *Drei Abhandlungen zur Sexualtheorie* (1905),
in *Gesammelte Werke*, V, 27–145; *Three Essays on the Theory of Sexuality*, in *Standard
Edition*, VII, 123–243, remains important.

For American "manly" novelists, see James Lundquist, *Jack London: Adventures, Ideas,
and Fiction* (1987); Joan D. Hedrick, *Solitary Comrade: Jack London and His Work* (1982);
and Donald Pizer, *The Novels of Frank Norris* (1966). All histories of American literature
give them space; among the most informative remains Alfred Kazin, *On Native Grounds:
An Interpretation of Modern American Prose Literature* (1942; ed. 1956).

Other relevant titles are cited in the section on sports in the listings for chapter 6,
below.

I have drawn the material for my pages on T.R. principally from *The Works of
Theodore Roosevelt*, ed. Hermann Hagedorn, 20 vols. (1926), and *The Letters of Theodore
Roosevelt*, sel. and ed. Elting E. Morison, with John M. Blum and Alfred D. Chandler,
Jr., 8 vols. (1951–54), a splendid monument to a garrulous American and to diligent
scholars. A few other gems have been saved in *Theodore Roosevelt's Letters to His Children*,
ed. Joseph Bucklin Bishop (1919), a charming collection, and *Selections from the Correspondence of Theodore Roosevelt and Henry Cabot Lodge, 1884–1918*, 2 vols. (1925). Among
T.R.s' voluminous writings, *The Winning of the West*, 4 vols. (1889–96), is exceptionally
revealing about attitudes toward manliness and toward race. See also Theodore Roosevelt's characteristic *An Autobiography* (1913).

Understandably, T.R. has attracted the attention of biographers. Among the many
lives, Henry F. Pringle's opinionated *Theodore Roosevelt: A Biography* (1931) holds up
remarkably well. David McCullough, *Mornings on Horseback* (1981), is a vigorous and
persuasive account taking T.R. through his youth and early political career; though it
covers the same ground, it is psychologically more penetrating, I think, than Carleton
Putnam's fine *Theodore Roosevelt: The Formative Years, 1858–1886* (1958). John M. Blum's
lucid and terse *The Republican Roosevelt* (1954; 2nd ed., 1977) is an almost wholly
convincing evaluation of T.R. the political leader; I have learned much from the book
even as I disagreed with its verdict. I trust I have not been overly influenced by Richard

Hofstadter's mordant chapter, "Theodore Roosevelt: the Conservative as Progressive," *The American Political Tradition and the Men Who Made It* (1948), 203–33. George E. Mowry, *The Era of Theodore Roosevelt, 1900–1912* (1958), is a most useful survey. For a psychoanalytic appraisal, necessarily speculative, see two articles by Glenn Davis: "The Early Years of Theodore Roosevelt: A Study in Character Formation," *History of Childhood Quarterly*, II, 4 (Spring 1975), 461–92, and "The Maturation of Theodore Roosevelt: The Rise of an 'Affective Leader,' " *History of Childhood Quarterly*, III, 1 (Summer 1975), 43–74.

TWO: Pathologies

The crucial concept of the normal, without which of course the pathological cannot be defined, has been explored in Georges Canguilhem, *Le Normal et le pathologique* (1966; 2nd ed., 1972). For biographical essays on the founders of the "science" of criminology (of varying lengths and merit), see *Pioneers in Criminology,* ed. Hermann Mannheim (1960); it contains, among others, chapters on Beccaria, Bentham, and Henry Maudsley. Its long and useful (if overly defensive) chapter on Cesare Lombroso should be read in conjunction with Maurice Parmalee, "Introduction to the English Version," in Lombroso, *Crime: Its Causes and Remedies* (1899; tr. Henry P. Horton, 1911); Hermann Mannheim, "Lombroso and His Place in Modern Criminology," *Sociological Review,* XXVIII (1936), 31–49; and illuminating pages in Daniel Pick, *Faces of Degeneration: Aspects of a European Disorder, c. 1848–1918* (1989), also cited earlier. Élie Halévy's classic *The Growth of Philosophical Radicalism* (1901–4; tr. Mary Morris, 1928), which includes the utilitarians' ideas on punishment in its purview, has lost none of its luster, though its tribute to the triumph of *laissez-faire* now seems excessive. John Stuart Mill's "Bentham" (1838) included in many collections, is indispensable reading. The historian cannot neglect the charge that Bentham was essentially a totalitarian thinker, asserted most forcibly in the hard-hitting, one-sided essay by Gertrude Himmelfarb, "The Haunted House of Jeremy Bentham" (1965), adapted in *Victorian Minds: A Study of Intellectuals in Crisis and of Ideologies in Transition* (1968), ch. 2. Himmelfarb is referring to Bentham's blueprint for a model prison, the "Panopticon."* No doubt his rationalism

---

*In the 1780s and 1790s, Bentham grew enamored of this "simple idea in Architecture." It would have delivered convicted criminals to overseers with powers virtually unmatched in their control of human beings. The Panopticon, as its name makes plain, would have been so constructed that an inspector, standing at the hub of a great wheel of stone and iron, could see at a glance what was going on in all the spokes. Bentham thought so highly of this idea that he recommended its application to other institutions, like workhouses, insane asylums, and schools, all in the name of utility, and convinced himself that his plan was a vast improvement over current ways of housing criminals, and would be cheap. He was fortunate that he could never persuade his government, or any other, to fund the project, and a Panopticon was never built. Still, the idea had a certain impact on prison construction. The maximum-security prison built between 1876 and 1881 in the Moabit district in Berlin, with its a central hall and five wings radiating out from it,

had its cranky side, but this miserable scheme is not the core of Bentham's thought, which, for all its dry rationalism, had a significant humane streak. For one influential English historian of the law, see George Feaver, *From Status to Contract: Sir Henry Maine, 1822–1888* (1969), and R. C. J. Cocks, *Sir Henry Maine: A Study in Victorian Jurisprudence* (1988).

On the impulse to revenge, see (in addition to the material in the Appendix) two short psychoanalytic studies: Theodor Reik, *Geständniszwang und Strafbedürfnis: Probleme der Psychoanalyse und der Kriminologie* (1925), and Franz Alexander and Hugo Staub, *Der Verbrecher und sein Richter: Ein psychoanalytischer Einblick in die Welt der Paragraphen* (1929). They have been conveniently brought together under the title *Psychoanalyse und Justiz* (1974). The classicist Walter Burkert's *Homo Necans: The Anthropology of Ancient Greek Sacrificial Ritual and Myth* (1972; tr. Peter Bing, 1983) is very suggestive. On the history of the urge for revenge, the old study by Louis Günther, *Die Idee der Wiedervergeltung in der Geschichte und Philosophie des Strafrechts. Ein Beitrag zur universalhistorischen Entwicklung desselben,* 2 vols. (1889–91) still has much of value. For a more modern, no less bulky study, see H. von Hentig, *Die Strafe,* 2 vols. (1954–55).

Much recent scholarly literature on the theory and practice of nineteenth-century prisons has been inspired by the work of Michel Foucault. To my mind willful and often perverse, it has set the tone of the debate. His key text is *Discipline and Punish: The Birth of the Prison* (1975; tr. Alan Sheridan, 1977). Foucault breathed fresh air into the history of penology and severely damaged, without wholly discrediting, traditional Whig optimism about the humanization of penitentiaries as one long success story. I share Gordon Wright's severe assessment.* For Foucault and his followers, overcommitted rationalists all, social control—the forcible or, better, the manipulative use of resources to keep the masses quiet, if not contented—lurks behind every pronouncement, every act, of those who run society, whether aristocrats or bourgeois. They are—thus Foucault—preoccupied, almost obsessed, with the hidden hand of power. But this plays down contin-

---

seems derived from the Panopticon. Paul Lindenberg, in "Polizei und Verbrechertum in Berlin. Moabit," *Die Gartenlaube,* XL (1892), 731–35, a report complete with an evocative drawing, even used the almost inescapable cliché: the "internal iron of the prison appears like a gigantic spider's web, in which the spider itself is not missing" (p. 732).

*"For Foucault, as for the Marxists, the Enlightenment reformers were impelled by bourgeois interests clothed in humanitarian phrases. The reformers' concern was the rising threat to property manifested in the changing crime pattern from violence to theft. . . . The bourgeoisie, in Foucault's version, was also determined to close those legal loopholes . . . that favored the poorer classes, and to widen those loopholes that would be useful for enterprising businessmen. Even more fundamental, according to Foucault, was the bourgeoisie's urge to create what he calls 'the disciplinary society,' adapted to the needs of an industrial age. . . . The dazzling brilliance of his work has made him a cult-figure, and his ideas are echoed in a number of recent monographs on the crime problem." But "Foucault boldly asserts his ideas as facts, and just as boldly attributes motives to the criminal-justice reformers. . . . To take Enlightenment ideas as no more than a reflection, a dependent variable, of economic change is to take hypothesis for fact." *Between the Guillotine and Liberty: Two Centuries of the Crime Problem in France* (1983), 21–22.

gency, complexity, the sheer anxiety or stupidity of power holders, let alone their authentic idealism, and the tendency of institutions to establish their own agenda.

The most authoritative studies of nineteenth-century prisons, though not untouched by Foucault, have allowed the evidence to overpower ideology. Witness Patricia O'Brien, *The Promise of Punishment: Prisons in Nineteenth-century France* (1982), a soundly reasoned and fully documented study. I read Martin J. Wiener's lucid and sophisticated *Reconstructing the Criminal: Culture, Law, and Policy in England, 1830–1914* (1990) too late to take it into account in the text, but was happy to note the convergence of our readings. Klaus Doerner, *Madmen and the Bourgeoisie: A Social History of Insanity and Psychiatry* (1969; tr. Joachim Neugroschel and Jean Steinberg, 1981), though not innocent of Foucault, criticizes him for oversimplifying a complex history (p. 70) and limiting himself to "a merely reactive anti-Enlightenment position" (p. 14). For a debate with Foucault, see the stimulating collection of essays *L'Impossible Prison. Recherches sur le système pénitentiaire au XIXe siècle,* ed. Michelle Perrot (1980), with essays by the editor among others and comments by Maurice Agulhon and Foucault; Catherine Duprat's long "Punir et guérir. En 1819, la prison des philanthropes" (pp. 64–122) is of special interest.

Gustave de Beaumont and Alexis de Tocqueville, *Du système pénitentiaire aux États-Unis, et de son application en France,* 2 vols. (1833; 2nd ed., 1836), remains more than a document for its time. The modern English edition of this classic, *On the Penitentiary System in the United States and Its Application in France* (tr. Francis Lieber, 1833; ed. Herman R. Lantz, 1964), is worth consulting. Among other rebels against Whiggish optimism is Michael Ignatieff, author of *A Just Measure of Pain: The Penitentiary in the Industrial Revolution, 1750–1850* (1978), a dramatic, indignant, and informative history of the emergence of the modern prison in England, though rather overemphatic on the issue of power.

Philosophical views have been intelligently and tersely studied by Ted Honderich in *Punishment: The Supposed Justifications* (1969; rev. ed., 1971). Stanley E. Grupp, ed., *Theories of Punishment* (1971), collects an interesting series of papers on punishment as retributive, deterrent, rehabilitative, and "integrative." For the background to the nineteenth century, see above all the scholarly treatise by J. M. Beattie, *Crime and the Courts in England, 1660–1800* (1986), and Heinz Reif, ed., *Räuber, Volk und Obrigkeit. Studien zur Geschichte der Kriminalität in Deutschland seit dem 18. Jahrhundert* (1984), whose discrete essays largely concentrate on lower-class criminality. The shifting responses of one alert nineteenth-century observer are explored in Philip Collins's indispensable *Dickens and Crime* (1962; 2nd ed., 1964). See the excellent study by James A. Colaiaco, *James Fitzjames Stephen and the Crisis of Victorian Thought* (1983), for that crusty English historian and theorist of the law; it is well supplemented by K. J. M. Smith, *James Fitzjames Stephen: Portrait of a Victorian Rationalist* (1988). Stephen's important treatise *Liberty, Equality, Fraternity* (1873; 2nd ed., 1874), has been well edited by R. J. White (1967).

The issue of diminished responsibility has generated a pile of commentaries across the years. Abraham S. Goldstein, *The Insanity Defense* (1967), an admirable synthesis, draws on the rich legal, and no less rich psychological, literature. Sheldon Glueck's humane

Mental Disorder and the Criminal Law: A Study in Medico-Sociological Jurisprudence (1925) retains its classic stature. Glueck, *Law and Psychiatry: Cold War or "Entente Cordiale"?* (1962), is a ripe summing up. Henry Weihofen, *Mental Disorder as a Criminal Defense* (1954), is also an authoritative text, to be supplemented by another of his books, *The Urge to Punish: New Approaches to the Problem of Mental Irresponsibility for Crime* (1956). See also Roger Smith, *Trial by Medicine: Insanity and Responsibility in Victorian Trials* (1981). Among recent historians of mental illness and the law, Foucault has understandably enjoyed a certain vogue, though not an uncritical one. Robert A. Nye, *Crime, Madness, and Politics in Modern France: The Medical Concept of National Decline* (1984), is a full treatment, sympathetic but not slavish to revisionist views. I have learned, especially about quarreling schools of French criminologists, from Ruth Harris, *Murders and Madness: Medicine, Law, and Society in the "Fin de Siècle"* (1989). See also Jan Goldstein, *Console and Classify: The French Psychiatric Profession in the Nineteenth Century* (1987), for a thorough mapping of the terrain. For the United States, there is David J. Rothman's provocative *The Discovery of the Asylum: Social Order and Disorder in the New Republic* (1971). And see U. R. Q. Henriques, "The Rise and Decline of the Separate System of Prison Discipline," *Past and Present*, no. 54 (February 1972), 61–93. A number of Victorian prison directors, chaplains, and physicians left interesting memoirs. See among many the tough, but not brutal, short reminiscences *Thirty Years' Experience of a Medical Officer in the English Convict Service* (1884), by John Campbell, who warns against "mistaken sympathy" (p. 6).

J. Imbert, *La Peine de mort. Histoire—actualité* (1967), offers a serviceable conspectus of capital punishment through history. And see Leon Shaskolsky Sheleff, *Ultimate Penalties: Capital Punishment, Life Imprisonment, Physical Torture* (1987). For an economical but comprehensive statistical comparison of capital punishment across the "civilized" world (which comes out in the end for its retention), see Arthur MacDonald, "Death Penalty and Homicide," *American Journal of Sociology*, XVI, 1 (July 1910), 88–116. There is a well-managed anthology of Victor Hugo's persistent attacks on the death penalty, *Écrits de Victor Hugo sur la peine de mort,* ed. Raymond Jean (1979). In this context, Victor Brombert, *Victor Hugo and the Visionary Novel* (1984), is indispensable.

On the move toward abolition of the death penalty in the United States, see the fully documented study by Louis P. Masur, *Rites of Execution: Capital Punishment and the Transformation of American Culture, 1776–1865* (1989). In briefer compass, David Brion Davis, "The Movement to Abolish Capital Punishment in America, 1787–1861," *American Historical Review*, LXIII, 1 (October 1957), 23–46, is excellent. Charles E. Rosenberg's gripping *The Trial of the Assassin Guiteau: Psychiatry and Law in the Gilded Age* (1968) demonstrates how Guiteau could not escape the death penalty once President Garfield succumbed to his wounds. For Germany, see Bernhard Düsing, *Die Geschichte der Abschaffung der Todesstrafe in der Bundesrepublik Deutschland* (1952), which starts much earlier. For France, there is Gordon Wright's slender but not thin *Between the Guillotine and Liberty: Two Centuries of the Crime Problem in France* (1983). Britain is well served by Leon Radzinowicz, *A History of English Criminal Law and Its Administra-*

tion from 1750, 5 vols., the last with Roger Hood (1948–86), which is eloquent and exhaustive. On the debate over public versus secluded hangings, David D. Cooper, *The Lesson of the Scaffold: The Public Execution Controversy in Victorian England* (1974), is illuminating.

Heinz Lange's dissertation (longer than most such German products), *Theorie und Praxis der Erziehungsstrafe im achtzehnten Jahrhundert* (1932), offers many true horror stories about eighteenth-century views and practices of corporal punishment, which the nineteenth century was so reluctant to discard. Gustav Stephan, *Die häusliche Erziehung in Deutschland während des achtzehnten Jahrhunderts* (1891), contains much that is still valuable. Walter Hävenick, *'Schläge' als Strafe. Ein Bestandteil der heutigen Familiensitte in volkskundlicher Sicht* (1964), is a folklorist's examination of domestic corporal punishment. For a compelling history of the slow move away from corporal punishment in Prussia between the 1790s and 1848, see Reinhart Koselleck, "Exkurs I: Über die langsame Einschränkung körperlicher Züchtigung," *Preussen zwischen Reform und Revolution. Allgemeines Landrecht, Verwaltung und soziale Bewegung von 1791 bis 1848* (1967), 641–59. Alfons Jannisek, *Das Recht des Lehrers zur Vornahme körperlicher Züchtigungen mit besonderer Rücksicht auf seine strafrechtliche Verantwortlichkeit* (1911), brief but well organized, explores the legal considerations bearing on corporal punishment in the schools. While the German secondary literature is surprisingly (perhaps not so surprisingly) large, other countries, too, have been studied. For a look at the United States before the Civil War, see Richard H. Brodhead, "Sparing the Rod: Discipline and Fiction in Antebellum America," *Representations*, XXI (Winter 1988), 67–96; too prone to attribute motives, it provides a wealth of information. On the use of flogging as a weapon of imperialism, see Robert I. Rotberg, with Miles F. Shore, *The Founder: Cecil Rhodes and the Pursuit of Power* (1988), also cited earlier. The subject of beating pupils in English public schools has been receiving serious attention. See above all John Chandos's documented *Boys Together: English Public Schools, 1800–1864* (1984), with full bibliography. Jonathan Gathorne-Hardy, *The Unnatural History of the Nanny* (1972), which does not neglect child-beating, is informal but informative. Strikingly, if involuntarily, illustrating the long reign of gentility in historical scholarship, Edward C. Mack is all discretion on flogging in his two substantial volumes, *Public Schools and British Opinion, 1780–1860: An Examination of the Relationship between Contemporary Ideas and the Evolution of an English Institution* (1938) and *Public Schools and British Opinion since 1860. The Relationship between Contemporary Ideas and the Evolution of an English Institution* (1941). For the leading anti-flogger, there is George Hendrick, *Henry Salt: Humanitarian Reformer and Man of Letters* (1977).

From these pedagogic considerations to sadomasochism is but one step. There is less really useful writing on Sade than one might think. Gilbert Lely, *The Marquis de Sade: A Biography* (1952–57; tr. Alec Brown, 1961), is a detailed, tolerant life that often proceeds like a chronology, day by day. Walter Lennig, *De Sade in Selbstzeugnissen und Bilddokumenten* (1965), is a short enthusiastic defense, almost a glorification. *Marquis de Sade, Selections from His Writings*, chosen by Paul Dinnage, with an essay by Simone de

Beauvoir, "Faut-il brûler Sade?" (1949; Sade tr. by Paul Dinnage, Beauvoir by Annette Michelson, 1951), has usable extracts—but whenever the text becomes really unsavory, the offending passages are left in French. Mario Praz, "The Shadow of the 'Divine Marquis,' " ch. 3 in *The Romantic Agony* (1933; 2nd ed., tr. Angus Davidson, 1951), is a model of good sense. For sexual irregularities, sadistic and masochistic, in the British Empire, and for related exploits, see Ronald Hyam, "Empire and Sexual Opportunity," *Journal of Imperial and Commonwealth History*, XIV, 2 (January 1986), 34–89, and Hyam's longer study, *Empire and Sexuality: The British Experience* (1990). On teasing, a derivative of sadism, see the discussion by a Victorian witness, Frederick L. Burk, "Teasing and Bullying," *Pedagogical Seminary*, IV, 3 (April 1897), 336–71, and a psychoanalytic paper by Margaret Brenman, "On Teasing and Being Teased; and the Problem of Moral Masochism," *Psychoanalytic Study of the Child*, VII (1952), 264–85. *Child Abuse: An Agenda for Action*, ed. George Gerbner, Catherine J. Ross, and Edward Zigler (1980), tackles a hitherto largely repressed topic and includes historical material.

The ur-masochist has been earnestly dealt with in Eberhard Hasper, *Leopold von Sacher-Masoch* (1932), but Hasper plays down what matters—the masochism. Reinhard Federmann, *Sacher-Masoch oder die Selbstvernichtung* (1961), contains *Venus im Pelz* and two other stories, each followed by biographical analysis. A study by Gilles Deleuze accompanies a modern edition of Sacher-Masoch's *Venus im Pelz* (1869; ed. 1980). Ian Gibson, *The English Vice: Beating, Sex and Shame in Victorian England and After* (1978), covers the desire to be beaten, which foreigners quite unjustly thought an English monopoly, with evident pleasure but careful documentation. Among psychoanalytic papers, the one most relevant to me was Charles Brenner, "The Masochistic Character: Genesis and Treatment," *Journal of the American Psychoanalytic Association*, VII (1959), 197–226. See also Martin H. Stein, "Report of Panel on the Problem of Masochism in the Theory and Technique of Psychoanalysis," *Journal of the American Psychoanalytic Association*, IV (1956), 526–38. Freud's paper on the subject still serves as a guideline: "Das ökonomische Problem des Masochismus" (1924), *Gesammelte Werke*, XIII, 369–83; "The Economic Problem of Masochism," *Standard Edition*, XIX, 157–70. On pornography, see Peter Gay, *The Bourgeois Experience*, vol. I, *Education of the Senses* (1984), 358–79. H. Montgomery Hyde, *A History of Pornography* (1964), provides a general survey.

Until recently, the subject of rape has been virtually taboo for historians and most other scholars. Among nineteenth-century treatises, Ambroise A. Tardieu, *Étude médico-légale sur les attentats aux moeurs* (1857; 5th ed., 1867), is emotional but full of matter; around the end of the Victorian age, the *Archiv für Kriminal-Anthropologie und Kriminalistik*, which I have used freely, broke the German silence. The best analysis I have come across is A. Nicholas Groth, with H. Jean Birnbaum, *Men Who Rape: The Psychology of the Offender* (1979), a subtle, humane book which distinguishes among the causes of rape and stresses the rapist's aggressive motivation. Susan Brownmiller, *Against Our Will: Men, Women and Rape* (1976), deserves pride of place among (rightly) indignant feminist writers on the subject, but her treatment of Freud is singularly unfair—a point effectively made by John Forrester, "Rape, Seduction and Psychoanalysis," in

Sylvana Tomaselli and Roy Porter, ed., *Rape* (1986), 57–83, a book that also includes other worthwhile papers. Anna Clark's slim *Women's Silence, Men's Violence: Sexual Assault in England, 1770–1845* (1987), shows that the historian can extract *some* materials on that vexed problem from the public press. (In my text, I demonstrate the same point by glancing at the London *Times* of the mid-nineteenth century. In fact, Victorian newspapers were far less reticent about rape than the scholarly fraternity.) Jean-Claude Chesnais's valuable *Histoire de la violence en occident de 1800 à nos jours* (1981; rev. ed., 1982) has a helpful chapter on the topic (pp. 170–95), with statistics, but richer on the twentieth century than on the nineteenth. The debate over whether or not Tess of the d'Urbervilles was raped continues, in part because Hardy, worried over the censorious public, kept rewriting the novel, particularly this scene. Irving Howe takes the negative in *Thomas Hardy* (1966; ed. 1985), 116–17, J. T. Laird the affirmative in "Developments in the Printed Versions" (1975), included in a critical edition of *Tess of the d'Urbervilles* (1891; ed. Scott Elledge, 1965; 2nd ed., 1979), 375. Peter C. Hoffer and N. E. H. Hull, *Murdering Mothers: Infanticide in England and New England, 1558–1803* (1984), concentrates on earlier periods, but does supply pertinent material on victimized women taking the lives of others. A. James Hammerton's important article "Victorian Marriage and the Law of Matrimonial Cruelty," *Victorian Studies*, XXXIII (1990), 269–92, includes wife-beating. Clearly much more needs to be, and can be, done.

The literature on self-murder is growing rapidly. Jack D. Douglas, *The Social Meaning of Suicide* (1967), offers an astringent sociological critique of the famous theories of Durkheim, with interesting chapters on his successors. Jacques Choron, *Suicide* (1972), largely analytical, has a historical introduction. In the bulky literature on Émile Durkheim, there is above all Steven Lukes, *Émile Durkheim, His Life and Work: A Historical and Critical Study* (1972). *Essays on Sociology and Philosophy by Émile Durkheim with Appraisals of his Life and Thought,* ed. Kurt H. Wolff (1960), collects over a dozen papers on Durkheim in addition to some little-known texts by the master himself. See also the long essay in Raymond Aaron, *Main Currents in Sociological Thought,* vol. II, *Durkheim, Pareto, Weber* (1967; tr. Richard Howard and Helen Weaver, 1967), 11–117. Albert Bayet, *Le Suicide et la morale* (1922), a formidable French thesis, has been widely used for its coverage of changing attitudes. Among the texts antedating Durkheim, the most detailed and statistically sophisticated treatment is Alexandre Brierre de Boismont, *Du suicide et de la folie suicide* (1856; 2nd ed., 1865). I cannot praise too highly Olive Anderson, *Suicide in Victorian and Edwardian England* (1987); a model of rigorous scholarship, it disposes of myths and offers persuasive countertheories. I am grateful to Lisa Lieberman for sending me an unpublished paper, "The Suicide Discourse in Nineteenth-Century France." See also her "Romanticism and the Culture of Suicide in Nineteenth-Century France," *Comparative Studies in Society and History,* XXXIII, 3 (July 1991), 611–29. And see Stanley W. Jackson's sober account, *Melancholia and Depression: From Hippocratic Times to Modern Times* (1987). Patricia O'Brien's fascinating "The Kleptomania Diagnosis: Bourgeois Women and Theft in Late Nineteenth-Century France," *Journal of Social History,* XVII, 1 (1983), 65–77, throws some lurid light on mental disorders, mainly depressive, among the French middle classes. On Thomas Masaryk, see *T. G. Masaryk (1850–1937)*, ed. Robert B. Pynsent (1990), which canvasses his life and ideas.

This is not the place to discuss theorists of social control at length. This may suffice: In their refusal to take surfaces for substance, these critical students of social history resemble the historian who deploys psychoanalysis as an auxiliary discipline. After all, psychoanalysis is a science of suspicion, searching for clues to penetrate beyond manifest to latent meanings and to resolve the recondite mysteries of drives and defenses. But, for all their apparently acrobatic leaps of interpretation, historians utilizing Freud's discoveries are pledged to remain faithful to the material at hand. There is yet another difference between psychoanalytic historians and those discovering the hidden hand of the controlling manipulators everywhere: the former look for the unconscious grounds of action, while the latter are fixated on the operations of the conscious mind and therefore intent on exposing discreditable, self-serving springs of action concealed behind noble-sounding pronouncements and even noble actions. Theirs is a world of conspiracies, of bourgeois industrialists, merchants, and politicians conniving during discreet lunches to train the working masses in docility and scotch in them any thoughts of going out on strike, let alone starting a revolution, by feeding them the Bible and throwing them crumbs of social legislation. Such an analysis is not wholly out of place—as this text shows, nineteenth-century Caesars, whether French or German, were all too ready to deploy stratagems that would preserve their political power and the economic well-being of their supporters. The difficulty with this type of analysis is not that it refuses to take manifest motives literally; psychoanalysis, as I have just noted, does the same thing. No doubt, the opponents of the death penalty betray a certain amount of pleasure in their recitals of horror stories. But psychoanalysts do not end here; unlike the advocates of social control, they are not satisfied with denunciation.

THREE: Demagogues and Democrats

Common consent has justly nominated Alexis de Tocqueville as the most profound observer of nineteenth-century politics. The best English-language edition of his masterwork on the United States—first published, as two volumes, in 1835 and 1840—is *Democracy in America*, ed. J. P. Mayer and Max Lerner, tr. George Lawrence (1966). Alexis de Tocqueville, *Selected Letters on Politics and Society,* ed. Roger Boesche, tr. James Toupin and Roger Boesche (1985) contains some remarkable letters. His *Souvenirs* (written 1850; published posthumously, 1893; ed. Luc Monnier, 1942) is moving and informative. André Jardin, *Tocqueville: A Biography* (1984; tr. Lydia Davis, with Robert Hemenway, 1988), is solid and unpretentious. Among commentaries the most interesting are George W. Pierson's classic *Tocqueville and Beaumont in America* (1938), and Roger Boesche, *The Strange Liberalism of Alexis de Tocqueville* (1987), which sets right some widespread misreadings. *The Two Tocquevilles: Father and Son* (ed. and tr. R. R.

Palmer, 1987) contains fascinating interpretations of the advent of the French Revolution by the elder Tocqueville and his more famous son.

For general analyses of political parties, see the old study by Moisei Ia. Ostrogorskii, *Democracy and the Organization of Political Parties,* 2 vols. (1902), which deals magisterially with party politics in England and the United States; a condensed and revised version appeared in 1910. The modern study by Maurice Duverger, *Political Parties: Their Organization and Activity in the Modern State* (1951; 2nd ed., tr. Barbara North and Robert North, 1962), remains indispensable. Robert Michels, *Political Parties: A Sociological Study of the Oligarchical Tendencies in Modern Democracy* (1911; tr. Eden Paul and Cedar Paul, 1959), contains the famous bleak prognosis that party democracy is inevitably doomed. But a slim volume by E. E. Schattschneider, *Party Government* (1942), defends parties vigorously.

On liberalism in general, the old comprehensive and comparative study by Guido de Ruggiero, *The History of European Liberalism* (1925; tr. R. G. Collingwood, 1927), retains value for its sweep. L. T. Hobhouse, *Liberalism* (1911), offers a terse, appealing statement. And see Frederick Watkins, *The Political Tradition of the West: A Study in the Development of Modern Liberalism* (1948). For Germany, James J. Sheehan, *German Liberalism in the Nineteenth Century* (1978), is compelling. On the Austro-Hungarian empire, there is Georg Franz, *Liberalismus. Die deutsch-liberale Bewegung in der Habsburgischen Monarchie* [ca. 1955]. Peter Gay, "Liberalism and Regression," *Psychoanalytic Study of the Child,* XXXVII (1982), 523–45, offers a psychoanalytic interpretation aiming at the broader implications of what I call, in the Epilogue, the liberal temper. For eighteenth-century ideas that underlie modern liberalism, I refer to my study *The Enlightenment: An Interpretation,* vol. I, *The Rise of Modern Paganism* (1966), and vol. II, *The Science of Freedom* (1969).

On the politics of opposition, Ghita Ionescu and Isabel de Madariaga, *Opposition: Past and Present of a Political Institution* (1968), is short but fundamental. For England, Archibald S. Foord, *His Majesty's Opposition, 1714–1830* (1964), could not be bettered. See also Caroline Robbins's important article, " 'Discordant Parties': A Study of the Acceptance of Party by Englishmen," *Political Science Quarterly,* LXXIII (December 1958), 505–29. Going back to the inescapable prehistory of Victorian party politics, J. H. Plumb's survey of the early days of opposition in England, *The Growth of Political Stability in England, 1675–1725* (1967), is exhilarating; it needs to be read in the light of Linda Colley's spirited *In Defiance of Oligarchy: The Tory Party, 1714–60* (1982). An informal treatment of a minor (but not unimportant) matter is Patrick Howarth, *Questions in the House: The History of a Unique British Institution* (1956). For Bolingbroke on opposition, see Quentin Skinner, "The Principles and Practice of Opposition: The Case of Bolingbroke versus Walpole," in Neil McKendrick, ed., *Historical Perspectives: Studies in English Thought and Society in Honour of J. H. Plumb* (1974). For Hume, Norman Kemp Smith, *The Philosophy of David Hume: A Critical Study of Its Origins and Central Doctrines* (1949), remains *the* authority. Victor G. Wexler, *David Hume and the History of England* (1979), throws light on Hume's political thought; more directly on that thought, there are John B. Stewart, *The Moral and Political Philosophy of David Hume* (1963), and Duncan Forbes, *Hume's Philosophical Politics* (1976). For interpretations of Burke, I have relied on Alfred Cobban, *Edmund Burke and the Revolt against the Eighteenth Century* (1929; 2nd ed., 1960), which intriguingly links Burke to English romantic thought. Stanley Ayling, *Edmund Burke: His Life and Opinions* (1988), is a full biography. Richard Hofstadter, *The Idea of a Party System: The Rise of Legitimate Opposition in the United States, 1780–1840* (1969), typically lucid, reaches into English history as well.

As everyone knows, the French Revolution has spawned, and continues to spawn, the most contentious appraisals. The bicentennial of 1989 produced an outpouring, most of it decidedly hostile—more hostile than seems to me necessary. The assault on the ideology of French professional historians, many of them inspired by Marxism, was launched by François Furet, especially in *Interpreting the French Revolution* (1978; tr. Elborg Forster, 1981). Simon Schama, *Citizens: A Chronicle of the French Revolution* (1989), has its author's characteristic verve and gift for the telling anecdote, but its obsession with the revolutionists' violence raises questions about his interpretation. William Doyle, *The Oxford History of the French Revolution* (1989), though far from sympathetic, is sound and reliable, and grants the Revolution tragic stature. See also D. M. Sutherland, *France, 1789–1815: Revolution and Counter-Revolution* (1985), up-to-date and unhysterical. Among left-wing readings, Georges Lefebvre, *The French Revolution* (1951; tr. Elizabeth Moss Evanson, 2 vols., 1962–64), remains the most scholarly and most judicious. Lefebvre, *The Coming of the French Revolution* (1939; tr. R. R. Palmer, 1947), though still a pleasure to read, should be supplemented with (and somewhat modified by) William Doyle, *Origins of the French Revolution* (1980; 2nd ed., 1988). Among a plethora of biographical approaches to revolutionary worthies, G. G. van Deusen, *Sieyes: His Life and His Nationalism* (1932); J. M. Thompson, *Robespierre*, 2 vols. (1935); and R. R. Palmer, *Twelve Who Ruled: The Committee of Public Safety during the Terror* (1941), more the biography of an institution than of its members, remain worth reading, even if somewhat overtaken by time.

One innovation (not wholly free of faddism but important for students of nineteenth-century politics) is the emphasis on "political culture," particularly songs, emblems, and festivals. The prehistory of the political culture of the French Revolution has been discussed in *The French Revolution and the Creation of Modern Political Culture*, vol. I, ed. Keith Michael Baker, *The Political Culture of the Old Regime* (1987), which is followed by vol. II, ed. Colin Lucas, *The Political Culture of the French Revolution* (1987). Lynn Hunt, *Politics, Culture, and Class in the French Revolution* (1984), has domesticated recent French scholarship, such as Mona Ozouf's fascinating *Festivals and the French Revolution* (1976; tr. Alan Sheridan, 1988) and the pioneering researches of Maurice Agulhon, especially *Marianne into Battle: Republican Imagery and Symbolism in France, 1789–1880* (1979; tr. Janet Lloyd, 1981). Emmet Kennedy, *A Cultural History of the French Revolution* (1989), offers an intriguing survey of a much-covered age from new angles. Michel Vovelle's essay *La Mentalité révolutionnaire: Société et mentalités sous la Révolution française* (1985), is a readable instance of the French interest in "mentalities." For the unreconciled right, Jacques Godechot, *The Counter-Revolution: Doctrine and Action, 1789–1804* (1961; tr. Salvator Attanasio, 1971), does the necessary. For the Jacobins after the fall of Robespierre, see Isser Woloch's richly documented *Jacobin Legacy: The Democratic Movement under the Directory* (1970).

All histories of the century necessarily touch on the lasting impact of the French Revolution at home and abroad. See, in particular, Geoffrey Best, ed., *The Permanent Revolution: The French Revolution and Its Legacy, 1789–1989* (1988), with (among other contributions) fine essays by Conor Cruise O'Brien, "Nationalism and the French Revolution" (pp. 17–48), and Eugen Weber, "The Nineteenth-Century Fallout" (pp. 155–81). For Germany, a principal "beneficiary" of the Revolution as an export, see the impressive study by Jacques Droz, *L'Allemagne et la Révolution française* (1949), which rather minimizes German nationalism; it should be read in conjunction with T. C. W. Blanning's specialized *The French Revolution in Germany: Occupation and Resistance in the Rhineland, 1792–1802* (1983). For Britain, *The Debate on the French Revolution, 1789–1800*, ed. Alfred Cobban (1950), is an intelligently chosen anthology of excerpts.

The best edition of *The Federalist* is by Jacob E. Cooke (1961). Among scholarly writings on this masterpiece of political persuasion, Douglass Adair has made some outstanding contributions, especially "The Tenth Federalist Revisited," *William and Mary Quarterly*, 3rd ser., VIII, 1 (January 1951), 48–67, and " 'That Politics May Be Reduced to a Science': David Hume, James Madison, and the Tenth *Federalist*," *Huntington Library Quarterly*, XX, 4 (August 1957), 343–60. See also Fletcher Wright, "*The Federalist* on the Nature of Political Man," *Ethics*, LIX, 2, part II (January 1949), 1–31; the judicious study by Drew R. McCoy, *The Last of the Fathers: James Madison and the Republican Legacy* (1989); and my discussion of *The Federalist* on pp. 555–68 and 704–5 of *The Science of Freedom*, cited above. For the birth of political parties in the United States, there is Hofstadter, *The Idea of a Party System*, also cited above. And see Joseph Charles, *The Origins of the American Party System: Three Essays* (1956). For prerevolutionary politics, Bernard Bailyn, *The Ideological Origins of the American Revolution* (1967), and *The Origins of American Politics* (1968), are impressive. I also profited from the sturdy common sense of Richard B. Morris, *The American Revolution Reconsidered* (1967).

Historians have rather neglected the French Restoration; the most substantial treatment is Guillaume de Bertier de Sauvigny, *The Bourbon Restoration* (1955; tr. Lynn Case, 1966), a reasoned defense. For a terse synthesis, see the relevant chapters (1–4) in André Jardin and André-Jean Tudesq, *Restoration and Reaction, 1815–1848* (1973; tr. Elborg Forster, 1983). Alfred Cobban, *A History of Modern France*, vol. II, *From the First Empire to the Second Empire, 1799–1871* (1961; 2nd ed., 1965), is aphoristic and refreshing. Among the memoirs, those of Charles de Rémusat, all ed. Charles H. Pouthas, are most enjoyable and informative: *Mémoires de ma vie*, vol. I, *Enfance et jeunesse. La Restauration libérale (1797–1820)* (1958), and vol. II, *La Restauration ultra-royaliste. La Révolution de juillet (1820–1832)* (1959). The political machine *Aide-toi, le Ciel t'aidera* is fully and fairly described in Pouthas, *Guizot pendant la Restauration. Préparation de l'homme d'état (1814–1830)* (1923), 369–79; the rest of the volume, too, is extremely valuable. For the most complex liberal of the period, see above all Stephen Holmes, *Benjamin Constant and the Making of Modern Liberalism* (1984), and Biancamaria Fontana, *Benjamin Constant and the Post-Revolutionary Mind* (1991), which stresses Constant's preoccupation with modern alienation.

For the July Monarchy, David H. Pinkney, *The French Revolution of 1830* (1972), which throws doubts on the accepted notion that Louis Philippe presided over a "bourgeois monarchy," is suggestive but problematic. Chapters 6–9 of Jardin and Tudesq, *Restoration and Reaction,* cited just above, are valuable. The concluding chapters of vol. II of Rémusat's *Mémoires,* also cited just above, are relevant to the July Revolution and the immediate aftermath; this volume is followed by vol. III, *Les Luttes parlementaires. La Question d'Orient. Le Ministère Thiers-Rémusat (1832–1841)* (1960), and vol. IV, *Les Dernières Années de la monarchie. La Révolution de 1848. La Seconde République (1848–1851)* (1962). The most useful recent biographies of French politicians are J. P. T. Bury and R. P. Tombs, *Thiers, 1797–1877: A Political Life* (1986), and Douglas Johnson, *Guizot: Aspects of French History, 1787–1874* (1963). A series of topical essays, John M. Merriman, ed., *1830 in France* (1975), goes beyond the title date; one of the papers, Christopher H. Johnson, "The Revolution of 1830 in French Economic History" (pp. 139–89), is outstanding. See also the important study by Alan B. Spitzer, *The French Generation of 1820* (1987).

For the reputation of Julius Caesar through the ages, two well-known books by Friedrich Gundolf, more rhapsodies than scholarly exploration, are worthwhile mainly for suggesting texts to consult: *Caesar. Geschichte seines Ruhms* (1924) and *Caesar im neunzehnten Jahrhundert* (1926), which ranges from Napoleon to Nietzsche. The earlier book begins with a long tormented sentence that underscores Gundolf's reasons for finding Caesarism relevant: it is good to be reminded of "the great man" in a time when "the need for the strong man becomes audible, since, tired of fault-finders and gossips, one makes do with sergeants instead of leaders"—*Führer* (p. 7). Far more rational is Zwi Yavetz, *Julius Caesar and His Public Image* (1979; tr. anon., 1983). Sigmund Freud, *Massenpsychologie und Ich-Analyse* (1921), in *Gesammelte Werke,* XIII, 71–161; *Group Psychology and the Analysis of the Ego,* in *Standard Edition,* XVIII, 67–143, is a noble though fragmentary pioneering essay on the psychoanalytic social psychology of leadership—and followership.

The history of nineteenth-century Caesarism is intertwined with the suffrage—its reach, import, and manipulation. Alistair Cole and Peter Campbell, *French Electoral Systems and Elections since 1789* (1989), is short and reliable. Chilton Williamson, *American Suffrage from Property to Democracy, 1760–1860* (1960), lucidly surveys opinions and practices. So does Walter Gagel, *Die Wahlrechtsfrage in der Geschichte der liberalen deutschen Parteien 1848–1918* (1958). See also Robert J. Goldstein's sweeping survey of suffrage restrictions (and restrictions on free press and opinion), *Political Repression in Nineteenth Century Europe* (1983). On the old but ever new idea of the people's wisdom, George Boas, *Vox Populi: Essays in the History of an Idea* (1969) is an illuminating, "old-fashioned" exercise in the history of ideas. Frank M. Turner, "British Politics and the

Demise of the Roman Republic, 1700–1939," *The Historical Journal*, XXIX, 3 (1986), 577–99, includes interesting comments on Caesarism in Victorian Britain.

In the veritable library of biographies and monographs clustering around Napoleon I, J. M. Thompson, *Napoleon Bonaparte: His Rise and Fall* (1953), retains its sensible authority. Louis Bergeron, *France under Napoleon* (1972; tr. R. R. Palmer, 1981), is an original mapping of the society Napoleon found and remade. The title of Jean Tulard, *Napoleon: The Myth of the Saviour* (1977; tr. Teresa Waugh, 1984), promises more than the book delivers. Book V of Jacques Godechot's exhaustive *Les Institutions de la France sous la Révolution et l'Empire* (1951) does yeoman work for the Napoleonic years. The anthology *The Mind of Napoleon: A Selection from His Written and Spoken Words,* ed. and tr. J. Christopher Herold (1955), proved a gold mine. Among older biographies, Pierre Lanfrey, *The History of Napoleon I,* 4 vols. (1867–75; tr. anon., 2nd ed., 1886), which ends at 1804, is outstanding among the hostile lives. For the principal debaters, see the attractive study by Pieter Geyl, *Napoleon, For and Against* (1947; tr. Olive Renier, 1949). Napoleon's stealing of the plebiscite of 1800, never a secret, has been impressively documented by Claude Langlois, "Le Plébiscite de l'an VIII; ou, Le Coup d'État du 18 pluviose an VIII," *Annales historiques de la Révolution française,* XLVI (1972), 43–65, 231–46, 390–415. For Stendhal's view of Napoleon, see in particular Geoffrey Strickland, *Stendhal: The Education of a Novelist* (1974), passim, esp. 99–107. The cult has been well analyzed (even if the final word has not yet been said) by J. Lucas-Dubreton, *Le Culte de Napoléon 1815–1848* (1960), and Frédéric Bluche, *Le Bonapartisme. Aux origines de la droite autoritaire (1800–1850)* (1980). The emperor's literary following has been well tracked by Maurice Descotes, *La Légende de Napoléon et les écrivains français du XIXe siècle* (1967). Napoleon's letters, collected by a commission headed by J. B. P. Vaillant in *Correspondance,* fill 32 vols. (1858–69). For a sour nineteenth-century view of Caesarist "Bonapartist liberals" who, for all their protestations, "did not escape its contagion" (p. 68), see Paul Thureau-Dangin, *Le Parti Libéral sous la Restauration* (1876).

The Nephew put editors (not named on the title page) to work on his *Oeuvres,* 5 vols. (1856–69); though not complete, and servile in its brief annotations, the collection is valuable. For the short-lived republican interlude preceding the Second Empire, there is Roger Price, *The French Second Republic: A Social History* (1972). Frederick A. de Luna, *The French Republic under Cavaignac 1848* (1967), is more favorable to "the butcher of June" than other historians have been. The establishment of Napoleon III's authoritarian regime is most satisfactorily canvassed in John M. Merriman, *The Agony of the Republic: The Repression of the Left in Revolutionary France, 1848–1851* (1978). For the life of Louis Napoleon, see above all J. M. Thompson, *Louis Napoleon and the Second Empire* (1955), cool and well-informed, to be supplemented by Theodore Zeldin, *The Political System of Napoleon III* (1958), which draws almost exclusively on unpublished sources. The two volumes of F. A. Simpson's uncompleted biography, *The Rise of Louis Napoleon* (1909) and *Louis Napoleon and the Recovery of France, 1848–1856* (1922; 2nd ed., 1930), are well-informed if rather indulgent. See also William E. Echard, *Napoleon III and the Concert of Europe* (1983), which mounts a defense of the emperor's foreign-policy initiatives. Patricia Mainardi, *Art and Politics of the Second Empire: The Universal Expositions of*

1855 and 1867 (1987), examines the imaginative uses of propaganda. Alain Plessis, *De la fête impériale au mur des fédérés, 1852–1871* (1973), is brisk and reliable for the age. David H. Pinkney has studied the "Haussmannization" of Paris in his authoritative *Napoleon III and the Rebuilding of Paris* (1958). H. Gollwitzer, "Der Caesarismus Napoleon III. im Widerhall der öffentlichen Meinung Deutschlands," *Historische Zeitschrift,* CLXXIII (1952), 23–75, has good material on the question of the emperor's Caesarism and the Germans' perception of it.

For Bismarck, who must rival Luther and Goethe in the competition for most-written-about German, see the thoughtful, expansive life by Lothar Gall, *Bismarck: The White Revolutionary* (1980; ed. 1983; tr. J. A. Underwood, 1986), which has clearly mastered all the materials. It is rivaled, and with respect to clarity and distance surpassed, by Otto Pflanze's lifework, *Bismarck and the Development of Germany,* 3 vols. (1990; the first edition of vol. I, reaching to 1871, appeared in 1963). "Bismarck's Character"—vol. II, ch. 2, of Pflanze's biography—is a penetrating psychoanalytic exercise. Gall and Pflanze should be complemented by the liberal Erich Eyck's classic *Bismarck. Leben und Werk,* 3 vols. (1941–44). A monument in the anti-Bismarck tradition, it concentrates on the Iron Chancellor's more shocking traits, like his vindictiveness (see above, pp. 256–57, for one instance, found in Eyck and Pflanze but not in Gall). Eyck summed up his conclusions in lectures at Oxford, published as *Bismarck and the German Empire* (1950). The Deutsche Historische Museum, which in 1990 organized the great exhibition on Bismarck in Berlin, was also responsible for the substantial catalogue: *Bismarck: Preussen, Deutschland und Europa,* intro. Lothar Gall (1990); it sets Bismarck firmly within his world. A. J. P. Taylor, *Bismarck: The Man and the Statesman* (1955), is vintage Taylor, breezy, opinionated, and comprehensive on Bismarck's mental problems. Among the reminiscences published by Bismarck's intimates, I found most informative Robert Lucius von Ballhausen, *Bismarck-Erinnerungen* (1920), and Christoph von Tiedemann, *Aus sieben Jahrzehnten. Erinnerungen,* vol. II, *Sechs Jahre Chef der Reichskanzlei unter dem Fürsten Bismarck* (1909). Bismarck's celebrated autobiography, *Gedanken und Erinnerungen,* 2 vols. (1898; and many editions), is impressive but self-serving and more revealing than its author bargained for. Bismarck's own writings—articulate letters, speeches, memoranda and dispatches—are indispensable; they are collected in *Gesammelte Werke,* ed. Wolfgang Windelband and Werner Frauendienst, 15 vols. (2nd ed., 1924–35). But Gall, who has examined the holographs, has shown that the editors cut from the letters some of Bismarck's more damaging self-revelations, about his feelings toward his mother, for instance (see Gall, *Bismarck,* German ed., 735). Michael Stürmer has edited an anthology of well-chosen pronouncements, official and private, *Bismarck und die preussisch-deutsche Politik 1871–1890* (1970; 3rd ed., 1978). The top administration under his aegis has been ably studied in Rudolf Morsey, *Die oberste Reichsverwaltung unter Bismarck 1867–1890* (1957).

Bismarck's Caesarism continues to be heatedly debated. Gall vigorously disputes any relevance of the category, notably in "Bismarck und der Bonapartismus," *Historische Zeitschrift,* CCXXIII (1976), 618–37. So does Pflanze, in "Bismarcks Herrschaftstechnik als Problem der gegenwärtigen Historiographie," *Historische Zeitschrift,* CCXXXIV

(1982), 561–99. In sharp contrast, Michael Stürmer affirms the charge, in "Staatsstreich-gedanken im Bismarckreich," *Historische Zeitschrift*, CCIX (1969), 566–615, and in his vigorous, even slashing, *Regierung und Reichstag im Bismarckstaat 1871–1880. Cäsarismus oder Parlamentarismus* (1974). Weighing this conflict of authorities, I have come down on Stürmer's side. David Blackbourn's unhackneyed, revisionist observations on Bismarck and his Germans are illuminating; in his *Populists and Patricians: Essays in Modern German History* (1987), see especially "Bismarck: the Sorcerer's Apprentice" (pp. 33–44), "The Discreet Charm of the German Bourgeoisie" (pp. 67–83), and "The Politics of Demagogy in Imperial Germany" (pp. 217–45). Bismarck's program of social legisla-tion, covered in all the major biographies, became a model to other countries; E. P. Hennock, *British Social Reform and German Precedents: The Case of Social Insurance, 1880–1914* (1987) documents its impact on Britain.

On the weakness of the liberal opposition to Bismarck in the critical days of the early 1860s, Ludwig Dehio, "Die Taktik der Opposition während des Konflikts," *Historische Zeitschrift*, CXL (1929), 279–347, is outstanding. So is Margaret Lavinia Anderson's biography of Bismarck's principal Catholic adversary, *Windthorst: A Political Biography* (1981). For one eminent critic of Bismarck, see above all a series of essays by Wolfgang Mommsen, *Max Weber and German Politics, 1890–1920* (1974; tr. Michael S. Steinberg, 1984). Reinhard Bendix, *Max Weber: An Intellectual Portrait* (1960), is a straightforward account of Weber's development. See also the sophisticated essays by Wolfgang Schluchter, *Rationalismus der Weltbeherrschung. Studien zu Max Weber* (1980). Arthur Mitzman, *The Iron Cage: An Historical Interpretation of Max Weber* (1970), is a psychohis-torical assessment in which Weber appears as an archetypal German; though controver-sial, his presentation is persuasive. For a second critic, there is the excellent study by Albert Wucher, *Theodor Mommsen. Geschichtsschreibung und Politik* (1956). Alfred Heuss, *Theodor Mommsen und das 19. Jahrhundert* (1956), is a suggestive interpretation. Lothar Wickert, *Theodor Mommsen: Eine Biographie,* 4 vols. (1959–80) is not exciting, but reli-able.

The most satisfying general history of England, giving politics the widest possible meaning, is to be found in chapters 3–10 of R. K. Webb, *Modern England from the Eighteenth Century to the Present* (1968; 2nd ed., 1980). Élie Halévy, *A History of the English People in the Nineteenth Century* (1913–26; tr. E. I. Watkin and D. A. Barker, 1924–29; 2nd ed., 1949–51), is magnificent. Unfortunately Halévy did not live to inter-pret the mid-Victorian years, from 1841 to 1895, but the five volumes he did write remain a treasure trove of sound information and sound judgment. Halévy's celebrated thesis that Methodism saved England from revolution, advanced in *England in 1815,* the first volume of this work, is explored in Bernard Semmel, *The Methodist Revolution* (1973). G. M. Young, *Victorian England: Portrait of an Age* (1936; ed. G. Kitson Clark, 1977), which does not neglect political life, is subjective, brilliant, irritating—and justly celebrated. Much can be learned from Kitson Clark's long essays, notably *The Making of Victorian England* (1962) and *An Expanding Society: Britain, 1830–1900* (1967). One other history of the period, Asa Briggs, *The Age of Improvement, 1783–1867* (1959), going from the 1780s to the 1860s, is outstanding. Harold Perkin's interesting *The Origins of Modern English Society, 1780–1880* (1969) traces the rise of class society. The important, rather neglected, subject of local politics is analyzed in Derek Fraser, *Urban Politics in Victorian England: The Structure of Politics in Victorian Cities* (1976). The no less important subject of the press is well covered in Stephen Koss, *The Rise and Fall of the Political Press in Britain*, vol. I, *The Nineteenth Century* (1981). Brian Harrison, *Peaceable Kingdom: Stability and Change in Modern Britain* (1982), is a collection of beautifully reasoned essays stressing the centrist theme in English political life.

For the Reform Act of 1832, Michael Brock, *The Great Reform Act* (1973), is authoritative. Joseph Hamburger, *James Mill and the Art of Revolution* (1963), tracks the reformers' push for the bill. The politics of the period is illuminated in Norman Gash's splendid *Politics in the Age of Peel: A Study in the Technique of Parliamentary Representation, 1830–1850* (1953), elaborated in his great two-volume biography: *Mr. Secretary Peel: The Life of Sir Robert Peel to 1830* (1961) and *Sir Robert Peel: The Life of Sir Robert Peel after 1830* (1972); see also Gash's magisterial *Reaction and Reconstruction in English Politics, 1832–1852* (1965). J. F. C. Harrison, *The Early Victorians, 1832–51* (1971), is brisk and wide-ranging.

For the decades between the reform acts of 1832 and 1867, W. L. Burn, *The Age of Equipoise: A Study of the Mid-Victorian Generation* (1964), offers a comprehensive look. Geoffrey Best, *Mid-Victorian Britain, 1851–75* (1971), is compressed but imaginative. Dorothy Thompson, *The Chartists: Popular Politics in the Industrial Revolution* (1984), amply records the radical agitation of the late 1830s and 1840s. Oliver MacDonagh, *Early Victorian Government, 1830–1870* (1977), analyzes the increasing engagement of the state in many aspects of British life. Although the myth persists, J. Bartlett Brebner's important article "Laissez Faire and State Intervention in Nineteenth-Century Britain," *Journal of Economic History*, VIII (1948), supplement, 59–73, long ago conclusively demolished the notion that the state in mid-nineteenth-century Britain was a virtually invisible night watchman. The impact of Palmerston, the prime minister who dominated politics at mid-century, has been canvassed in Donald Southgate, *"The Most English Minister . . .": The Policies and Politics of Palmerston* (1966). That work, like Jasper Ridley's *Lord Palmerston* (1970), is being superseded by Kenneth Bourne's study; the first volume, *Palmerston: The Early Years, 1784–1841* (1982), has already appeared. On the influential administrative reformers, Royston Lambert, *Sir John Simon, 1816–1904, and English Social Administration* (1963), is standard. For the Reform Act of 1867 and the agitation that led up to it, see F. B. Smith's precise *The Making of the Second Reform Bill* (1966). Christopher Harvie, *The Lights of Liberalism: University Liberals and the Challenge of Democracy, 1860–86* (1976), studies the intellectual background of supporters before, during, and after the debate. The competitive rhetoric around the bill is analyzed by several authors, including Asa Briggs, in Helmut Viebrock, ed., *Robert Lowe, John Bright. Reden zur Parlamentsreform 1866/67* (1970). For one of the most articulate opponents of reform, see D. W. Sylvester, *Robert Lowe and Education* (1974). Another unhappy witness was Matthew Arnold. The most widely accessible—but not really satisfactory—edition of his famous *Culture and Anarchy* (1869; 2nd ed., 1875), first a series of articles, is by J. Dover Wilson (1932). Lionel Trilling in a sense rediscovered the man for the twentieth century in his elegant *Matthew Arnold* (1939). Park Honan, *Matthew Arnold: A Life* (1981), is ample and well researched; Stefan Collini, *Arnold* (1988), despite its enforced brevity perceptively touches all the bases. Bagehot's journalistic comments on domestic politics and foreign affairs are assembled in vols. V–VIII of *The Collected Works of Walter Bagehot,* ed. Norman St. John-Stevas, 15 vols. (1966–86), also cited earlier. For the third reform act, see Andrew Jones, *The Politics of Reform, 1884* (1972).

Gladstone has been the commentators' dream. Essential for a grasp on his reading, convictions, and character is the astonishing journal he kept faithfully every day: *The Gladstone Diaries,* ed. M. R. D. Foot and H. C. G. Matthew, 11 vols. so far (1968–   ), reaching to December 1886. The early pages of Matthew's "Rhetoric and Politics in Great Britain, 1860–1950," in P. J. Waller, ed., *Politics and Social Change: Essays Presented to A. F. Thompson* (1987), throw welcome light on Gladstone the orator. On that subject, see also the collaborative bilingual effort, with commentaries (and texts in the original), Helmut Viebrock and Hans Jochen Schild, eds., *Rhetorik und Weltpolitik, William Ewart Gladstone, Joseph Chamberlain, Bernard Graf von Bülow* (1974). Gladstone's celebrated Midlothian campaign has been saved for posterity in his *Political Speeches in Scotland, November and December 1879* (1879). The election following that campaign is traced in Trevor Lloyd, *The General Election of 1880* (1968). Richard T. Shannon on Gladstone's return to politics after his "retirement," *Gladstone and the Bulgarian Agitation, 1876* (1963), is first-rate. For all the abundance of biographies, John Morley's traditional *The Life of William Ewart Gladstone,* 3 vols. (1903), by now a document to its time, retains a certain authority. S. G. Checkland, *The Gladstones: A Family Biography, 1764–1851* (1971), ably places the man within his intimate setting. Georgina Battiscombe, *Mrs. Gladstone* (1956), is a useful supplement. Erich Eyck, *Gladstone* (1938), is the tribute of a German liberal to an English counterpart. Peter Stansky, *Gladstone: A Progress in Politics* (1979), brief but meaty, concentrates on key moments in Gladstone's political career. The initial volumes of two biographies in progress incorporate the latest scholarship: Richard T. Shannon, *Gladstone,* vol. I, *1809–1865* (1982), and H. C. G. Matthew, *Gladstone, 1809–1874* (1986)—a most penetrating study.

On Gladstone's great rival, the old standard W. F. Monypenny and G. E. Buckle, *The Life of Benjamin Disraeli, Earl of Beaconsfield,* 6 vols. (1910–20), with its vast bulk, is a throwback to Victorian biography. It has been largely superseded by Robert Blake's substantial one-volume *Disraeli* (1967; ed. 1968), highly sympathetic but striving for objectivity; this may be read in tandem with the first five chapters of another work by Blake, *The Conservative Party from Peel to Churchill* (1970). See also the rather disenchanted analysis by Paul Smith, *Disraelian Conservatism and Social Reform* (1967). For Disraeli as an orator, there is *Disraeli. Rede im Kristallpalast am 24. Juni 1872,* ed. Helmut Viebrock (1968).

H. J. Hanham, *Elections and Party Management: Politics in the Time of Disraeli and Gladstone* (1959; 2nd ed., 1978), deals with politics during the great rivalry in masterly fashion. Two monographs by John Vincent, *The Formation of the British Liberal Party, 1857–68* (1966) and *Pollbooks: How Victorians Voted* (1967), are helpful; they should be read along with Robert M. Stewart, *The Foundation of the Conservative Party, 1830–1867*

(1978). D. A. Hamer, *The Politics of Electoral Pressure: A Study in the History of Victorian Reform Agitations* (1977), impressively charts the fortunes of political-reform lobbies. *The Conscience of the Victorian State,* ed. Peter Marsh (1979), attractively traces the moral motives of the age, real enough; it includes chapters—naturally—on Gladstone, but also on the utilitarians, Nonconformists, Tories, and imperialists. A good companion essay is P. H. J. H. Gosden, *Self-Help: Voluntary Associations in Nineteenth-Century Britain* (1974). On the vast subject of imperialism, C. C. Eldridge, *England's Mission: The Imperial Idea in the Age of Gladstone and Disraeli 1868–1880* (1973), is excellent. See also the impressive, still compelling, exercise in revisionist scholarship by Ronald Robinson and John Gallagher, with Alice Denny, *Africa and the Victorians: The Official Mind of Imperialism* (1961).

Though ultimately a failure, the maverick radical-turned-imperialist Joseph Chamberlain was the most interesting English politician around the turn of the century. J. L. Garvin and Julian Amery, *The Life of Joseph Chamberlain,* 6 vols. (1932–68), is very full but apologetic. Denis Judd, *Radical Joe* (1977), is far more succinct and far less admiring. On a special topic, the split Chamberlain produced in the Liberal ranks, see Michael Hurst, *Joseph Chamberlain and Liberal Reunion: The Round Table Conference of 1887* (1967). H. C. G. Matthew, *The Liberal Imperialists: The Ideas and Politics of a Post-Gladstone Elite* (1973), eminently repays study. A highly subjective but penetrating view of this seductive speaker emerges in the journal of Beatrice Potter (as she then was): *The Diary of Beatrice Webb,* ed. Norman MacKenzie and Jeanne MacKenzie, vol. I, *1873–1892, Glitter Around and Darkness Within* (1982). *Rhetorik und Weltpolitik,* cited above, contains an interesting section on Chamberlain.

FOUR: The Powerful, Weaker Sex

Since the emergence of the new feminism in the 1960s, the tone of writing on the position of women in the past has often been acrimonious. Nineteenth-century women did indeed have legitimate grievances, and their chroniclers' indignation and tendentious excess have been accompanied by some valuable insights. But at the same time, scholars (including feminists) have also generated less spectacular and more dependable studies. In the heroic years, even solid historians produced anthologies with titles like *Clio's Consciousness Raised: New Perspectives on the History of Women*—ed. Mary S. Hartman and Lois W. Banner (1974). We have moved on. It is symptomatic that the publishers of a recent anthology, *The Woman Question: Society and Literature in Britain and America, 1837–1883,* ed. Elizabeth K. Helsinger, Robin Lauterbach Sheets, and William Veeder, 3 vols. (1983), advertise it as showing that "contrary to traditional belief, there was no single Victorian attitude toward women," a point I wrote this chapter to prove. For my work on female rights—and wrongs—and female sexuality in life and scholarship from a psychoanalytic perspective, see *The Bourgeois Experience,* vol. I, *Education of the Senses* (1984), chs. 2 and 3. And for Freud's views of female sexuality, see my discussion in *Freud: A Life for Our Time* (1988), also cited earlier (pp. 501–22); Sarah Koifman, *The Enigma of Woman: Woman in Freud's Writings* (1980; tr. Catherine Porter,

1985); and Zenia Odes Fliegel, "Half A Century Later: Current Status of Freud's Controversial Views on Women," *Psychoanalytic Quarterly*, LXIX (1982), 7–28.

Priscilla Robertson, *An Experience of Women: Pattern and Change in Nineteenth-Century Europe* (1982), surveys, calmly enough, Victorian women in France, Germany, Britain, and Italy. Among several meritorious anthologies, I leaned most on *Victorian Women: A Documentary Account of Women's Lives in Nineteenth-Century England, France, and the United States*, ed. Erna Olafson Hellerstein, Leslie Parker Hume, and Karen M. Offen (1981). An old study, Moisei Ia. Ostrogorskii, *The Rights of Women: A Comparative Study in History and Legislation* (tr. under the author's supervision, 1893), still repays reading for its portrayal of the situation at the turn of the century. Mary S. Hartman, *Victorian Murderesses: A True History of Thirteen Respectable French and English Women Accused of Unspeakable Crimes* (1977), is amusing and absorbing; in discussing her case histories, Hartman anticipated many insights of later writers. Emily James Putnam's old *The Lady: Studies of Certain Significant Phases of Her History* (1910; ed. 1960), which follows genteel women through the ages, is not too old, nor too ladylike, to lack interest today. *The Psychology of Women: Ongoing Debates*, ed. Mary Roth Walsh (1987), intriguingly pits psychologists' and psychoanalysts' views on mothering, sexuality, and much else against one another.

Mary P. Ryan, *Womanhood in America from Colonial Times to the Present* (1975; 2nd ed., 1979) is a detailed review. Frances B. Cogan's revisionist *All-American Girl: The Ideal of Real Womanhood in Mid-Nineteenth-Century America* (1989), dissents from the prevailing caricature of the Victorian American woman as a slave to the cult of "true womanhood," and stresses her health and activity. For an exemplar of what she is revising, see the influential essays of Barbara Welter, *Dimity Convictions: The American Woman in the Nineteenth Century* (1976). Carl N. Degler, a leading historian of women, sums up a long stretch of American female experience in *At Odds: Women and the Family in America from the Revolution to the Present* (1980), which includes sexual life as well as predictable topics like child rearing and domesticity. On women who chose not to marry, Lee Virginia Chambers-Schiller, *Liberty a Better Husband: Single Women in America, the Generations of 1780–1840* (1984), is vigorous. Cindy Sondik Aron, *Ladies and Gentlemen of the Civil Service: Middle Class Workers in Victorian America* (1987), usefully describes women and men in an integrated workplace, offices of the federal government, after the Civil War. In *"Doctors Wanted: No Women Need Apply": Sexual Barriers in the Medical Profession, 1835–1975* (1975), Mary Roth Walsh explores a far less palatable area, in which professional misogyny flourished. Nancy F. Cott, *The Bonds of Womanhood: "Woman's Sphere" in New England, 1780–1835* (1977), reaches back into earlier days for comparisons. While I dissent from the more categorical formulations of Ann Douglas, I learned from *The Feminization of American Culture* (1977; ed. 1978), which deals with what Douglas sees as the prevailing sentimentalization of status and of religious creeds. Rosemary Radford Ruether and Rosemary Skinner Keller, eds., *Women and Religion in America*, vol. I, *The Nineteenth Century* (1981), collects some valuable articles. Lois W. Banner, *American Beauty* (1983), studies the captivating (and revealing) shifts of fashions in female beauty from the early days of the republic to recent times. It can be read in conjunction with Ellen K. Rothman's eminently satisfying *Hands and Hearts: A History of Courtship in America* (1984), and with a study of romantic love—more common than supposed—by Karen Lystra, *Searching the Heart: Women, Men, and Romantic Love in Nineteenth-Century America* (1989). John S. Haller and Robin M. Haller, *The Physician and Sexuality in Victorian America* (1974), has sidelights on perceptions of gender.

On some exceptional American women: Bell Gale Chevigny, *The Woman and the Myth: Margaret Fuller's Life and Writings* (1976), presents excerpts from Fuller's works and the responses of her contemporaries. David M. Kennedy, *Birth Control in America: The Career of Margaret Sanger* (1970), is a careful biography, to be read with Linda Gordon, *Woman's Body, Woman's Right: A Social History of Birth Control in America* (1976). Kathryn Kish Sklar, *Catharine Beecher: A Study in American Domesticity* (1973) is extremely astute. The writings of Beecher and her sisters have been excerpted in *The Limits of Sisterhood: The Beecher Sisters on Women's Rights and Woman's Sphere,* ed. Jeanne Boydston, Mary Kelley, and Anne Margolis (1988). *The Making of a Feminist: Early Journals and Letters of M. Carey Thomas,* ed. Marjorie Housepian Dobkin (1979), provides access to the thought of a remarkable intellectual and academic administrator. Faye E. Dudden, *Serving Women: Household Service in Nineteenth-Century America* (1983), on female domestics, throws light by reflection on middle-class women. So, more sadly, does Ruth Rosen's pioneering *The Lost Sisterhood: Prostitution in America, 1900–1918* (1982).

The pages of *Godey's Lady's Book* from the 1830s on offer an indispensable glimpse into the preoccupations of middle-class, middle-brow American women. For her editor, Sarah Josepha Hale, see the brief autobiographical retrospect, "Fifty Years of My Literary Life," in the last issue of *Godey's* she edited, XCV (December 1877), 522–23. Isabelle Webb Entrikin, *Sarah Josepha Hale and Godey's Lady's Book* (1946), is efficient; Ruth E. Finley, *The Lady of Godey's: Sarah Josepha Hale* (1931), is cheery, determinedly informal, and well illustrated. Frank Luther Mott, *A History of American Magazines,* vol. I, *1741–1850* (1930), and vol. II, *1850–1865* (1938), provide the necessary background for *Godey's;* see especially, in the first volume, 350–51, 509–23, and 580–94. And see Cynthia L. White, *Women's Magazines, 1693–1968* (1970).

For women in late-nineteenth-century France, James E. McMillan, *Housewife or Harlot: The Place of Women in French Society, 1870–1940* (1981), part I, is most relevant. M. William Oualid, *L'Évolution intellectuelle féminine. Le Développement intellectuel de la femme. La Femme dans les professions intellectuelles* (1937), abounds in statistics and comparative data. Linda L. Clark, *Schooling the Daughters of Marianne: Textbooks and the Socialization of Girls in Modern French Primary Schools* (1984), fortunately starts in mid-nineteenth century. The key theme of education for women in France before some important reforms is explored in Marie-François Lévy, *De mères en filles: L'Éducation des françaises 1850/1880* (1984); it complements Françoise Mayeur's more detailed *L'Éducation des filles en France au XIXe siècle* (1979). Both stress the religious upbringing of middle-class girls at home. And see Mona Ozouf, *L'École, l'Église et la République 1871–1914* (1963), a brief, solid treatment. Rambert George, *Chronique intime d'une famille des notables au XIXe siècle* (1981), has illuminating details. On prostitution, Alain Corbin, *Women for Hire: Prostitu-*

tion and Sexuality in France after 1850 (1978; tr. Alan Sheridan, 1990), is impressive if, to my mind, too committed to Foucault.

Among histories of German women, Ute Frevert, *Frauen-Geschichte. Zwischen bürger-licher Verbesserung und neuer Weiblichkeit* (1986), stands out. John C. Fout, ed., *German Women in the Nineteenth Century: A Social History* (1984), has useful essays, with a long introduction by the editor on the current state of research. On medical attitudes, see a fine essay by Ute Frevert, "Ärzte and Frauen im späten 18. und frühen 19. Jahrhundert. Zur Sozialgeschichte eines Gewaltverhältnisses," in Annette Kuhn, ed., *Frauen in der Geschichte*, vol. II (1982), 177–210. Marion Kaplan has markedly advanced our knowl-edge of Jewish women in Germany, notably with *The Jewish Feminist Movement in Germany: The Campaigns of the Jüdischer Frauenbund 1904–1938* (1979); with "For Love or Money: The Marriage Strategies of Jews in Imperial Germany," *Leo Baeck Institute Yearbook*, XXVIII (1983), 263–300, a splendid essay; and with a synthesis, *The Making of the Jewish Middle Class: Women, Family, and Identity in Imperial Germany* (1991). James C. Albisetti's informative *Schooling German Girls and Women: Secondary and Higher Education in the Nineteenth Century* (1988), goes beyond its title. In the late eighteenth century, women began to practice journalism; see Sabine Schumann, "Das 'lesende Frauenzim-mer': Frauenzeitschriften im 18. Jahrhundert," in Barbara Becker-Cantario, ed., *Die Frau von der Reformation zur Romantik* (1980), 138–69. Karen Hausen, ed., *Frauen suchen ihre Geschichte. Historische Studien zum 19. und 20. Jahrhundert* (1983), includes, among other interesting articles, an enlightening essay by Gisela Bock, "Historische Frauenfor-schung: Fragestellung und Perspektiven" (pp. 22–60), which candidly shows how deeply German research into woman's history has been indebted to American work—and passions.

Among anthologies documenting Englishwomen, Patricia Hollis, ed., *Women in Pub-lic: Documents of the Victorian Women's Movement, 1850–1900* (1979), offers excellent selections. Janet Murray, ed., *Strong-Minded Women and Other Lost Voices from Nine-teenth-Century England* (1982), an expansive gathering of texts, is more sober than its melodramatic title. Outstanding amidst the profusion of collections are the pathetic-sounding *Suffer and Be Still: Women in the Victorian Age* (1972) and the far more hearten-ing *A Widening Sphere: Changing Roles of Victorian Women* (1977), both edited by Martha Vicinus. Her apparently growing optimism suggests a certain progress not so much for women, but for women's studies. Leonore Davidoff and Catherine Hall, *Family For-tunes: Men and Women of the English Middle Class, 1780–1850* (1987), offers persuasive generalizations about the way talented Victorian bourgeois men and women made their lives. M. Jeanne Peterson, *Family, Love, and Work in the Lives of Victorian Gentlewomen* (1989), is beautifully informed. See also Suzanna Shonfield, *The Precariously Privileged: A Professional Family in Victorian London* (1987). Joan Perkin, in an angry but instructive survey, *Women and Marriage in Nineteenth-Century England* (1989), supplies ample infor-mation about the "male chauvinist" laws under which Englishwomen were compelled to live. A more specialized treatment of this knotty theme is Lee Holcombe, *Wives and Property: Reform of the Married Women's Property Law in Nineteenth-Century England* (1984). Judith Rowbotham, *Good Girls Make Good Wives: Guidance for Girls in Victorian*

Fiction (1989), well surveys improving literature. It should be read with Carol Dyhouse's study of socialization, *Girls Growing Up in Late Victorian and Edwardian England* (1981). Lee Holcombe, *Victorian Ladies at Work: Middle-Class Working Women in England and Wales, 1850–1914* (1973), admirably covers a neglected topic. But see also Jean Donnison, *Midwives and Medical Men: A History of Inter-Professional Rivalries and Women's Rights* (1977), which demonstrates how nineteenth-century men excluded women from one possible working career. Martha Vicinus, *Independent Women: Work and Community for Single Women, 1850–1920* (1985) discusses women for whom home and children were not the vital center. F. K. Prochaska, *Women and Philanthropy in Nineteenth-Century England* (1980), places women dealing out charity in their social environment. John R. Gillis, *For Better, for Worse: British Marriages, 1600 to the Present* (1985), devotes significant space to the Victorians. Theresa M. McBride, *The Domestic Revolution: The Modernisation of Household Service in England and France, 1820–1920* (1976), is a succinct and—with its cross-Channel comparisons—revealing study. Stella Mary Newton, *Health, Art and Reason: Dress Reformers of the Nineteenth Century* (1974), gets good mileage from an apparently minor subject. The darkest side of Victorian womanhood is explored in an impressive monograph by Judith R. Walkowitz, *Prostitution and Victorian Society: Women, Class, and the State* (1980). See also, on this topic, Paul McHugh, *Prostitution and Victorian Social Reform* (1980).

Feminism is important enough to deserve separate treatment. Two feminist classics, at once polemical masterpieces and literary gems, have left their mark on this chapter: Mary Wollstonecraft, *A Vindication of the Rights of Woman, with Strictures on Political and Moral Subjects* (1792; ed. Charles W. Hagelman, Jr., 1967), and, of course, Virginia Woolf, *A Room of One's Own* (1929). Wollstonecraft is well served by Claire Tomalin, *The Life and Death of Mary Wollstonecraft* (1974); Woolf—to mention only a few titles— by Quentin Bell, *Virginia Woolf: A Biography*, 2 vols. in 1 (1972); Lyndall Gordon, *Virginia Woolf: A Writer's Life* (1984); and a venturesome effort by Shirley Panken, *Virginia Woolf and the "Lust of Creation": A Psychoanalytic Exploration* (1987).

The conspectus by Richard J. Evans, *The Feminists: Women's Emancipation Movements in Europe, America and Australasia, 1840–1920* (1977), provides a good introduction. Marianne Weber's wide-ranging survey, *Ehefrau und Mutter in der Rechtsentwicklung* (1907), shows what feminists were up against. For one intercountry examination of their campaigns, see William L. O'Neill, ed., *The Women's Movement: Feminism in the United States and England* (1969), selected texts with a long introduction. Miriam Schneir, ed., *Feminism: The Essential Historical Writings* (1972), draws principally on England and America, but also has some continental selections. Nancy F. Cott, *The Grounding of Modern Feminism* (1987), examines the years early in the twentieth century when the term "feminism" emerged.

For American feminism, see Eleanor Flexner, *Century of Struggle: The Woman's Rights Movement in the United States* (1959; new pref., 1972), which sensibly treats a vital theme; so does Aileen Kraditor, *The Ideas of the Woman Suffrage Movement, 1890–1920* (1965). Rosalind Rosenberg, *Beyond Separate Spheres: Intellectual Roots of Modern Feminism*

(1982), examines nineteenth-century woman social scientists who questioned prevailing pieties about female nature. For the woman's movement in France, see Claire G. Moses, *French Feminism in the Nineteenth Century* (1984), especially well informed, and enthusiastic, on the influence of the Saint-Simonians. On Frenchwomen and the vote, the detailed monograph by Steven C. Hause, with Anne R. Kenney, *Women's Suffrage and Social Politics in the French Third Republic* (1984), is most satisfactory; it belongs with Hause's study of France's leading feminist, *Hubertine Auclert: The French Suffragette* (1987). For Germany, Richard J. Evans, *The Feminist Movement in Germany, 1894–1933* (1976), is a reliable history. An anthology of writings by German women seeking to improve their lot before 1848, *Frauenemanzipation im deutschen Vormärz. Texte und Dokumente,* has been edited by Renate Möhrmann (1978). For portraits of pioneering German feminists, see Anna Plothow, *Die Begründerinnen der deutschen Frauenbewegung* (1907). Chapters 1–4 of Werner Thönnessen, *The Emancipation of Women: The Rise and Decline of the Women's Movement in German Social Democracy, 1863–1933* (1969; tr. Joris de Bres, 1973), offer a brisk romp on a special topic.

English nineteenth-century feminism has been well covered. See Sheila R. Herstein, *A Mid-Victorian Feminist, Barbara Leigh Smith Bodichon* (1985). Barbara Taylor, *Eve and the New Jerusalem: Socialism and Feminism in the Nineteenth Century* (1983), is a substantial history, with relevance beyond its announced program. The prehistory of the nineteenth-century woman's movement in England, by no means irrelevant to later developments, has been ably studied in Hilda L. Smith, *Reason's Disciples: Seventeenth-Century English Feminists* (1982), and Katharine M. Rogers, *Feminism in Eighteenth-Century England* (1982). The early chapters of Carol Dyhouse, *Feminism and the Family in England, 1880–1939* (1989), intelligently consider the strain that ideology put on traditional family values. The anti-feminists have been judiciously handled in Brian Harrison, *Separate Spheres: The Opposition to Women's Suffrage in Britain* (1978). The famous key text by John Stuart Mill, *The Subjection of Women* (1869), rightly the icon of feminists, has been repeatedly reprinted, most conveniently in John Stuart Mill and Harriet Taylor Mill, *Essays on Sex Equality,* ed. with a long introductory essay by Alice S. Rossi (1970).

The nineteenth-century woman writer, a striking cultural phenomenon, continues to be the subject of wide debate. A pioneer in the feminist reading of her history was Ellen Moers, *Literary Women: The Great Writers* (1976; ed. 1977). But probably the most aggressive (and possibly the most influential) recent polemic has been Sandra M. Gilbert and Susan Gubar's bulky *The Madwoman in the Attic: The Woman Writer and the Nineteenth-Century Literary Imagination* (1979). It opens with a pun to show nineteenth-century woman writers as an oppressed species in a patriarchal society—the pen is a metaphorical penis—and largely remains on that level through its many pages. The rhetorical temperature of Gaye Tuchman, with Nina E. Fortin, *Edging Women Out: Victorian Novelists, Publishers, and Social Change* (1989), is far lower, but for all its array of statistics and recondite social-science vocabulary, the authors fail to make their case that men, once they tumbled to the success of woman novelists, took over and eased them out. Earlier, Elaine Showalter argued, in *A Literature of Their Own: British Women Novel-ists from Brontë to Lessing* (1977), that English woman writers have historically been forced to live in a separate imaginative world. The evidence of male condescension (and male jealousy) throughout the century is beyond dispute; it is equally plain that many woman writers, often taking male pseudonyms or concealing their identity, felt driven to internalize male standards—I offer ample instances of all this in the text. But the lot of what Hawthorne called the d——d mob of scribbling women was far more complex than these volumes indicate. For a scathing but thoroughly reasoned criticism of the unscholarly attitudes that underlie, and the stylistic disasters that attend, such tenden-tious productions, see Helen Vendler, "Feminism and Literature," *New York Review of Books*, XXXVII (May 31, 1990), 19–25.

The work of historians, including feminists, effectively sets forth some of the com-plications in the picture. Janet Todd's lively *The Sign of Angellica: Women, Writing and Fiction, 1660–1800* (1989), though it concentrates on earlier writers, makes a valuable contribution to our understanding of the emerging woman writer as a professional. It may be supplemented with Eva Figes, *Sex and Subterfuge: Women Writers to 1850* (1982), which, like Todd's book, concentrates on England. For the same period and the same country, see also Alison Adburgham, *Women in Print: Writing Women and Women's Magazines from the Restoration to the Accession of Victoria* (1972). Adburgham, *Silver Fork Society: Fashionable Life and Literature, 1814–1840* (1983), examines the novels of high life that woman writers then specialized in. Guinevere L. Griest, *Mudie's Circulating Library and the Victorian Novel* (1970), makes a good case for the cultural power of lending libraries over the lives of readers—and writers. Kathleen Blake has argued, in *Love and the Woman Question in Victorian Literature: The Art of Self-Postponement* (1983), that En-glish woman writers felt compelled to choose between sexual fulfillment and literary excellence; though she is not altogether persuasive, hers is an interesting position.

The literature on individual writers is strong if at times tendentious. But see R. K. Webb's objective *Harriet Martineau: A Radical Victorian* (1960). Margaret Oliphant left a touching self-portrait, *Autobiography and Letters of Mrs. Margaret Oliphant* (1899; ed. Mrs. Harry Coghill, 1974). See also Merryn Williams, *Margaret Oliphant: A Critical Biography* (1986). Dorothy Mermin, *Elizabeth Barrett Browning: The Origins of a New Poetry* (1989), is both feminist biography and literary criticism. And see *The Letters of Robert Browning and Elizabeth Barrett Browning, 1845–1846*, ed. Elvan Kintner, 2 vols. (1969). Daniel Karlin has used this correspondence to good purpose in *The Courtship of Robert Browning and Elizabeth Barrett* (1985). For the Brontës, individually and collectively, there are W. A. Craik, *The Brontë Novels* (1968), and Winifred Gérin's studies of the sisters: *Anne Brontë* (1959), *Charlotte Brontë* (1967), and *Emily Brontë* (1971). For Charlotte Brontë, I should add an adventurous long essay by John Maynard, *Charlotte Brontë and Sexuality* (1984). William S. Peterson, *Victorian Heretic: Mrs. Humphry Ward's "Robert Elsmere"* (1976), is a felicitous appraisal, which in recording the respect with which editors and publishers approached Mrs. Ward, once again disproves the myth of the woman writer shunted aside. The greatest nineteenth-century English woman writer was, of course,

George Eliot.* From the outpouring of comment, I confine myself to a few titles. The first serious biographical study was by her husband: *George Eliot's Life as Related in Her Letters and Journals,* ed. J. W. Cross, 3 vols. (1885; rev. one-volume ed., 1887). The biographical appreciation by Leslie Stephen, *George Eliot* (1902), is more than a document for its time. Beyond question, the authoritative life is Gordon S. Haight, *George Eliot: A Biography* (1968). Haight's splendid edition, *The George Eliot Letters,* 7 vols. (1954–55), is indispensable. He has epitomized it in *Selections from George Eliot's Letters* (1985). *George Eliot: The Critical Heritage,* ed. David Carroll (1971), is a handy collection of reviews. Among literary appraisals, I learned most from Joan Bennett, *George Eliot: Her Mind and Her Art* (1948), and Barbara Hardy, *The Novels of George Eliot* (1959) and *Particularities: Readings in George Eliot* (1983). Gillian Beer's enjoyable *George Eliot* (1986) stresses the woman question. Sally Shuttleworth, *George Eliot and Nineteenth-Century Science: The Make-Believe of a Beginning* (1984), tackles the novelist from an uncommon perspective. For her fame abroad, there is John Philip Couch, *George Eliot in France: A French Appraisal of George Eliot's Writings, 1858–1960* (1967).

For woman writers in Germany, H. Spiero, *Geschichte der deutschen Frauendichtung seit 1800* (1913), may serve as a compact introduction. The autobiography of a German woman novelist extremely popular in her day, Fanny Lewald, *Meine Lebensgeschichte* (1861–62; ed. and abr. Gisela Brinker-Gabler, 1980) is revealing. See also the same editor's useful anthology *Deutsche Dichterinnen vom 16. Jahrhundert bis zur Gegenwart. Gedichte und Lebensläufe* (1978). Marieluise Steinhauer, *Fanny Lewald, die deutsche George Sand. Ein Kapitel aus der Geschichte des Frauenromans im 19. Jahrhundert* (1937), is, considering its date of publication, remarkably free of Nazi taint. For the most successful of all commercial German woman writers, see the anonymous "Eugenie-John Marlitt. Ihr Leben und ihre Werke," probably by Alfred John, in *E. Marlitts Gesammelte Romane und Novellen,* 10 vols. (1889; 2nd ed., 1890), vol. X, *Thüringer Erzählungen.* For the magazine that made Marlitt famous, see the anthology *Die Gartenlaube als Dokument ihrer Zeit,* ed. Magdalene Zimmermann (1963). Gabriele Strecker, *Frauenträume, Frauentränen. Über den deutschen Frauenroman* (1969), is informal but informative. To this should be added Gustav Sichelschmidt, *Liebe, Mord und Abenteuer. Eine Geschichte der deutschen Unterhaltungsliteratur* (1969), which places woman writers in their social context.

Leading nineteenth-century American woman writers have been subjected to ex-

---

*Eliot's only rival was doubtless Jane Austen. Since she occupies only a marginal place in this book, I shall content myself with a few texts most important to me, aware that the critical literature about Austen is threatening to become unmanageable. I have learned from Barbara Hardy's civilized *A Reading of Jane Austen* (1975), far less contextual than the splendid exploration by Marilyn Butler, *Jane Austen and the War of Ideas* (1975), which unhesitatingly places her author in a world of clashing opinions. Butler's introduction to the paperback edition (1987) offers a spirited critique of the interpreters who have, to her mind, idealized, patronized, or tendentiously misread her. Ian Watt, ed., *Jane Austen: A Collection of Critical Essays* (1963), gathers some influential modern appraisals, including contributions by Virginia Woolf, Edmund Wilson, and Lionel Trilling's essay on *Mansfield Park.*

haustive analysis in Mary Kelley, *Private Woman, Public Stage: Literary Domesticity in Nineteenth-Century America* (1984), from which I have profited. On the emergence of the best seller, whether by men or women, Henry Nash Smith, *Democracy and the Novel: Popular Resistance to Classic American Writers* (1978), is succinct and authoritative. Smith, "The Scribbling Women and the Cosmic Success Story," *Critical Inquiry*, I (1974), 47–70, was important for this chapter. Ednah Dow Cheney, *Louisa May Alcott* (1889; intro. Ann Douglas, 1980), worshipful but with good material, has been largely superseded by Martha Saxton, *Louisa May: A Modern Biography of Louisa May Alcott* (1977). The scholarly volumes of *The Selected Letters of Louisa May Alcott*, ed. Joel Myerson and Daniel Shealy (1987), and *The Journals of Louisa May Alcott*, also ed. Myerson and Shealy (1989), are indispensable. For Alcott's true literary passion, see *A Double Life: Newly Discovered Thrillers of Louisa May Alcott*, ed. Madeleine H. Stern (1989). *Little Women* testifies to her blissful absorption in writing.

In France, more than anywhere else except the United States, women became journalists and editors. The story is well told in Evelyn Sullerot, *Histoire de la presse féminine en France, des origines à 1848* (1966), and in Laure Adler, *À l'aube du féminisme: Les Premières Journalistes (1830–1850)* (1979). Elyane Dezon-Jones, *Les Écritures féminines* (1983), surveys the scene. And see a short general article by Philip Spencer, "The French Reading Public about 1850," *Modern Language Review*, XLV (1950), 473–77. On the adventurous countess who wrote under the pseudonym Daniel Stern, see Jacques Vier, *La Comtesse d'Agoult et son temps*, 6 vols. (1955–63), and the intellectual study by Suzanne Gugenheim, *Madame d'Agoult et la pensée européenne de son époque* (1937). And on a once-famous poet, see Charles Du Bos, *La Comtesse de Noailles et le climat du génie* (1949). That leaves the giant, George Sand, now discussed more as a historical than as a literary phenomenon. (It is characteristic that Martin Turnell, *The Novel in France* [1950], with seven chapters devoted to French novelists from Mme de La Fayette to Marcel Proust, has no place for her, and only mentions her once in passing.) Among recent biographies in English, Joseph Barry, *Infamous Woman: The Life of George Sand* (1977), is perhaps most satisfactory. Barry also has published a substantial anthology, *George Sand in Her Own Words* (1979), which serves as an introduction to her voluminous output. See also Renée Winegarten, *The Double Life of George Sand: Woman and Writer* (1978), and Curtis Cate, *George Sand* (1975). One recent French biography deserves mention: Francine Mallet, *George Sand* (1976). Sand's *Oeuvres autobiographiques*, garrulous but most instructive, have been edited by Georges Lubin, 2 vols. (1970–71). Even more instructive is her vast *Correspondance*, also ed. Lubin, 24 vols. so far (1964–   ), an almost incredible output even for the letter-intoxicated Victorian century. Given Sand's solid reputation abroad, especially in Britain, Patricia Thomson, *George Sand and the Victorians: Her Influence and Reputation in Nineteenth-Century England* (1977), and Paul G. Blount, *George Sand and the Victorian World* (1978), are worth reading. Henry James's appreciation, "George Sand," in his *French Poets and Novelists* (1878; 2nd ed., 1884), 149–85, has much weight.

The matter of how women are represented in nineteenth-century fiction has generated wide controversy. A classic in the denunciation of male overlordship, an angry book much imitated, is Françoise Basch, *Relative Creatures: Victorian Women in Society and the Novel* (1972; tr. Anthony Rudolf, 1974). Hazel Mews, *Frail Vessels: Woman's Role in Women's Novels from Fanny Burney to George Eliot* (1969), though tough-minded, does without rage. Patricia Thomson, *The Victorian Heroine: A Changing Ideal, 1837–1873* (1953), convincingly suggests that across the decades, woman characters in women's novels mirrored certain "advanced" attitudes. Patricia Beer, *Reader, I Married Him: A Study of the Women Characters of Jane Austen, Charlotte Brontë, Elizabeth Gaskell and George Eliot* (1974), is terse and witty. See also Ruth Bernard Yeazell's interesting *Sex, Politics and Science in the Nineteenth Century Novel* (1986). In *Man and Woman: A Study of Love and the Novel, 1740–1940* (1978), A. O. J. Cockshut proffers his expected insights. A refreshing turnabout is Jane Miller, *Women Writing about Men* (1986). For France, there is M.-A. Martin, *La Jeune Fille française dans la littérature et la société (1815–1914)* (n.d.), which is popular and lacks references.

FIVE: The Bite of Wit

Humor has long attracted psychologists. One modern selection of their writings on this subject is Jeffrey H. Goldstein and Paul E. McGhee, eds., *The Psychology of Humor: Theoretical Perspectives and Empirical Issues* (1972), a substantial, often highly technical anthology. Another, no less interesting, is Antony J. Chapman and H. C. Foot, eds., *Humor and Laughter: Theory, Research, and Applications* (1976). For psychoanalytic views—some of them strictly orthodox, others eclectic—see a provocative essay (historical, experimental, and theoretical) by Norman N. Holland, *Laughing: A Psychology of Humor* (1982), and Jacob Levine, ed., *Motivation in Humor* (1969), which contains papers on humor and anxiety, drive discharge and humor, and—particularly relevant to this chapter—humor and aggressiveness. See also Aver Ziv, *Personality and Sense of Humor* (1984), which succinctly surveys various functions of humor, including, again, its aggressive dimension. Anton Ehrenzweig's influential *The Psycho-Analysis of Artistic Vision and Hearing: An Introduction to a Theory of Artistic Perception* (1965; 2nd ed., 1965) has a relevant treatment: ch. 8, "The Inarticulate ('Baffling') Structure of the Joke." Freud's classic *Der Witz und seine Beziehung zum Unbewussten* (1905), vol. VI of *Gesammelte Werke*; *Jokes and Their Relation to the Unconscious*, vol. VIII of *Standard Edition*, goes beyond jokes. I have dealt with Freud's views on jokes in "Serious Jests," *Reading Freud: Explorations and Entertainments* (1990), 133–51.

Not surprisingly, humor has been a gold mine for anthologists. The most helpful anthology, for me, proved to be Pierre Mille, ed., *Anthologie des humoristes français contemporains* (1912; ed. 1923), an excellent gathering of excerpts. See also Walter Jerrold and R. M. Lenard, eds., *A Century of Parody and Imitation* (1913), a well-edited collection which concentrates on nineteenth-century poetry. Dwight Macdonald, ed., *Parodies: An Anthology from Chaucer to Beerbohm—and After* (1960), which has a sizable section on the Victorian years, is a very funny book. Satire, too, has brought out the critics. I mention only James Sutherland, *English Satire* (1962), and the brief, well-illustrated comparative study by Matthew Hodgart, *Satire* (1969). Ann Taylor Allen, *Satire and*

Society in Wilhelmine Germany: "Kladderadatsch" and "Simplicissimus," 1890–1914 (1984), deftly analyzes the fate of humorous political aggressiveness in the early years of Wilhelm II's reign. Dorothy George, *Hogarth to Cruikshank: Social Change in Graphic Satire* (1967), is authoritative on English satirical cartoons up to the mid-nineteenth century.

Of the many works on the great nineteenth-century humorists discussed in the text, just a few can be mentioned here. On Heine, Jeffrey L. Sammons, *Heinrich Heine: A Modern Biography* (1979), ably sums up advanced scholarship, including his own. Barker Fairley, *Heinrich Heine: An Interpretation* (1954) is, as usual, impressive. S. S. Prawer, *Heine's Jewish Comedy: A Study of His Portraits of Jews and Judaism* (1983), is very bulky and does the subject full justice. *Heine in Deutschland. Dokumente seiner Rezeption 1834–1956,* ed. Karl Theodor Kleinknecht (1976), opens up a painful subject: the Germans' views of that uncomfortable gadfly.

The literature on George Bernard Shaw is vast. Among older biographies, Archibald Henderson, *Bernard Shaw: Playboy and Prophet* (1932), remains interesting; it is being superseded, however, by the three-volume life by Michael Holroyd, *Bernard Shaw,* of which vols. I and II are relevant here: *1856–1898: The Search for Love* (1988), and *1898–1918: The Pursuit of Power* (1989). Special studies from which I have profited include a vigorous essay by Eric Bentley, *Bernard Shaw, 1856–1950* (1947; ed. 1957), and Martin Meisel, *Shaw and the Nineteenth Century Theater* (1963; ed. 1968).

Mark Twain, surely the most thoroughly examined American humorist, is best approached through the biography by Justin Kaplan, *Mr. Clemens and Mark Twain: A Biography* (1966), which has lost none of its luster. The great battles over Mark Twain that enlivened the twenties and thirties—Van Wyck Brooks's grim *The Ordeal of Mark Twain* (1920; rev. 1933) versus Bernard De Voto's cheery *Mark Twain's America* (1932)—have largely died down, in good part because of the erudite work of scholars like Henry Nash Smith; see especially his *Mark Twain: The Development of a Writer* (1962). More recently, Guy Cardwell, *The Man Who Was Mark Twain: Images and Ideologies* (1991), has concentrated on the darker side of this author's private life. Constance Rourke, in her highly regarded *American Humor: A Study of the National Character* (1931), fills in the background, as do Walter Blair and Hamlin Hill in *America's Humor: From Poor Richard to Doonesbury* (1978), which devotes two chapters to Mark Twain.

W. S. Gilbert's terse "William Schwenck Gilbert: An Autobiography," *The Theatre,* n.s., I (January–June 1883), 217–23, tells very little. Edith Browne, *W. S. Gilbert* (1907), though still interesting, has been largely superseded by recent work. See Christopher Hibbert, *Gilbert and Sullivan and Their Victorian World* (1976), and Leslie Baily, *Gilbert and Sullivan: Their Lives and Times* (1973). John Bush Jones, ed., *W. S. Gilbert: A Century of Scholarship and Commentary* (1970), gathers an array of interesting materials. Fredric Woodbridge Wilson, *An Introduction to the Gilbert and Sullivan Operas from the Collection of the Pierpont Morgan Library* (1989), reproduces some significant documents. Leon E. A. Berman, "The Kidnapping of W. S. Gilbert," *Journal of the American Psychoanalytic Association,* XXXIII (1985), 133–48, studies an episode in Gilbert's early life to which the application of psychoanalytic expertise is appropriate. It is applied, too, in Berman, "Gilbert's First-Night Anxiety," *Psychoanalytic Quarterly,* XLV (1976) 110–27, and A.

Brenner, "The Fantasies of W.S. Gilbert," *Psychoanalytic Quarterly* XXI (1952), 373–401. Arthur Jacobs, *Arthur Sullivan: A Victorian Musician* (1984), a fine biography, necessarily sheds light on Sullivan's favorite librettist. See also Elwood P. Lawrence, " 'The Happy Land': W. S. Gilbert as Political Satirist," *Victorian Studies,* XV (1971), 161–83; and James F. Stottler, "A Victorian Stage Censor: The Theory and Practice of William Bodham Donne," *Victorian Studies,* XIII (1969), 253–82.

For Christian Morgenstern, there is the sober and thorough comparative study by Ernst Kretschmer, *Die Welt der Galgenlieder. Christian Morgenstern und der viktorianische Nonsense* (1983), which pits this author against Lewis Carroll and Edward Lear; and Kretschmer's brief *Christian Morgenstern* (1985). The dazzling, eccentric (almost untranslatable) playwright Carl Sternheim is little known outside Germany. Hellmuth Karasek, *Sternheim* (1965), is a brief introduction. And see the "Vorwort" by Wilhelm Emrich in his edition of Carl Sternheim, *Gesamtwerk,* 10 vols. in 11 (1963–76), I, 5–19, which captures Sternheim's complexity.

Daumier has never been neglected. See Armand Dayot, *Les Maîtres de la caricature française au XIXe siècle* (1888); Champfleury [Jules Husson], *Histoire de la caricature moderne* (n.d.; ed. 1865); and Charles Holme, ed., *Daumier and Gavarni,* with critical and biographical notes by Henri Frantz and Octave Uzanne (tr. Edgar Preston and Helen Chisholm, 1904). James Parton, *Caricature and Other Comic Arts in All Times and Many Lands* (1878), is chiefly of historical interest. The best modern studies I have come across are Jean Adhémar, *Honoré Daumier* (1954); Robert Rey, *Honoré Daumier* [ca. 1965]; and Roger Passeron, *Daumier* (1979; tr. Helga Harrison, 1981). Oliver W. Larkin's lucid biography, *Daumier: Man of His Time* (1966), surrounds the great caricaturist with his French world. Among exhibition catalogues, I have found *Honoré Daumier 1808–1879. Bildwitz und Zeitkritik,* ed. Gerhard Langemeyer et al. (1980), most satisfactory.

Easy and enjoyable access to *Punch* is provided by *The Best of Mr. Punch: The Humorous Writings of Douglas Jerrold,* ed. and intro. Richard M. Kelly (1970). For *Simplicissimus,* there is the dependable monograph by Allen, *Satire and Society in Wilhelmine Germany,* cited above, complete with a most helpful bibliographical essay. For Berlin humor before 1848, see Mary Lee Townsend: *Forbidden Laughter, Popular Humor and the Limits of Repression in Nineteenth-Century Prussia* (1992).

The edition of Busch's works is the *Wilhelm Busch Gesamtausgabe,* ed. Friedrich Bohne, 4 vols. (1959). Bohne is also responsible for a splendid edition of Busch's complete letters—*Sämtliche Briefe,* 2 vols. (1968), fully annotated and with evocative illustrations. The *Wilhelm Busch–Buch. Sammlung lustiger Bildergeschichten,* ed. Otto Nöldeke and Hermann Nöldeke [ca. 1930], has useful unpublished material. Most of Busch's drawings have been collected by Hugo Werner in *Das Gesamtwerk des Zeichners und Dichters,* 6 vols. (1959). By far the most felicitous attempt to render Busch's laconic humor into English verse (an ungrateful, almost impossible assignment) is *The Genius of Wilhelm Busch: Comedy of Frustration,* ed. and tr. Walter Arndt (1982). Among several lives, Bohne, *Wilhelm Busch. Leben, Werk, Schicksal* (1958), though a bit pious, is standard. Joseph Kraus, *Wilhelm Busch in Selbstzeugnissen und Bilddokumenten* (1970), is a very short, well-documented, and fair-minded biography. Fritz Winther, *Wilhelm Busch als*

Dichter, Künstler, Psychologe and Philosoph (1910), published shortly after Busch's death, is mainly of historical interest today. Characteristic of the exegetes who take Busch extremely seriously, treating him (as their very titles reveal) as a laughing sage and disciple of Schopenhauer, are Roelof Deknatel, *Wilhelm Busch: Der lachende Philosoph des Pessimismus* (1940); Hans Balzer, *Nur was wir glauben, wissen wir gewiss: Der Lebensweg des lachenden Weisen* (1954); and Joseph Ehrlich, *Wilhelm Busch der Pessimist. Sein Verhältnis zu Arthur Schopenhauer* (1962). Fortunately, since I first began to work on Busch in the early 1970s, less respectful and more penetrating studies have appeared. Gert Ueding, *Wilhelm Busch. Das 19. Jahrhundert en Miniature* (1977), offers a perceptive critical (and even vaguely psychoanalytic) analysis; Peter Bonati, *Die Darstellung des Bösen im Werk Wilhelm Buschs* (1973), is less portentous than its title might indicate; and there is a suggestive essay by the psychologist Ulrich Beer, *". . . gottlos und beneidenswert." Wilhelm Busch und seine Psychologie* (1982). See also Ulrich Mihr, *Wilhelm Busch: der Protestant, der trotzdem lacht. Philosophischer Protestantismus als Grundlage des literarischen Werks* (1983). All of these are in German. For a solid (if, in my judgment, too apologetic) life in English, see Dieter P. Lotze, *Wilhelm Busch* (1979). More generally, see Wolfgang Kayser, *The Grotesque in Art and Literature* (1957; tr. Ulrich Weisstein, 1963). By far the best treatment of Busch in English is ch. 11 in David Kunzle's outsized *The History of the Comic Strip: The Nineteenth Century* (1990).

For criticisms of Busch's kind of humor during his lifetime, see Friedrich Theodor Vischer, "Satyrische Zeichnung" (1846), with additional material in "Neuere deutsche Karikatur" (1880), both in *Altes und Neues* (1882); and Vischer, *Kritische Gänge,* 2 vols. (1844; 2nd ed., 6 vols., 1860–73). There are helpful comments on the subject in Fritz Schlawe, *Friedrich Theodor Vischer* (1959). See also Julius Duboc's hostile observations on Busch's *Max und Moritz,* excerpted in K. H. Hoefele, ed., *Geist und Gesellschaft der Bismarckzeit, 1870–1890* (1967). And for Busch's best Jewish friend, see Peter Gay, "Hermann Levi: A Study in Service and Self-Hatred," *Freud, Jews and Other Germans: Masters and Victims in Modernist Culture* (1978), 189–230, esp. 202–8. Another of Busch's Jewish friends, the drama critic Paul Lindau, expressed himself interestingly on Busch in his monthly *Nord und Süd,* IV (1878), 257–72. For *The Katzenjammer Kids,* the brief comments by Stephen Becker, *Comic Art in America: A Social History of the Funnies, the Political Cartoon, Magazine Humor, Sporting Cartoons and Animated Cartoons* (1957), esp. 15–16, are relevant.

SIX: Uncertain Mastery

For William James, see above, pp. 613–14. The subject of sports, long overlooked by the historical profession, has suddenly, and rightly, blossomed as a theme for social historians. The most significant lead has been given by Norbert Elias. (In the light of Elias's theoretical work, Carl Diem's ambitious history of sports, *Weltgeschichte des Sports,* 2 vols. [1960; vol. II rev. 1971], though comprehensive, looks positively primitive.) Among Elias's distinguished contributions, see the essays collected, along with papers by his pupil and collaborator Eric Dunning, in *Quest for Excitement: Sport and Leisure in the Civilizing Process* (1986). Dunning has collaborated with Kenneth Sheard in *Barbarians, Gentlemen and Players: A Sociological Study of the Development of Rugby Football* (1979), a social history that goes beyond a single sport. See also the collection *The Sociology of Sport*, ed. Dunning (1971), which is representative of the modern literature. Apart from Elias, the most notable invitation to think seriously—and historically—about sports is Allen Guttmann's long essay *From Ritual to Record: The Nature of Modern Sports* (1978). The authors represented in Donald G. Kyle and Gary D. Stark, eds., *Essays on Sport History and Sport Mythology* (1990), among them Guttmann himself, Kyle, Richard D. Mandell, Steven A. Riess, and Stephen Hardy, come to terms, and take some issue, with Guttmann's views. Another complex response to Guttmann is *Ritual and Record: Sports Records and Quantification in Pre-Modern Societies,* ed. John Marshall Carter and Arnd Krüger (1990), which in its concern with quantification, is also relevant to the following section of this chapter. Among general histories, Richard D. Mandell, *Sport: A Cultural History* (1984), is enormously ambitious in its coverage, at once nostalgic and scathing about modern sports. See also a similar effort by William J. Baker, *Sports in the Western World* (1982). For earlier times, Dennis Brailsford, *Sport and Society: Elizabeth to Anne* (1969), is one intriguing contribution. The largely hidden roots of sports in antiquity have received erudite attention; witness the conspectus by H. A. Harris, *Sport in Greece and Rome* (1972). David Sansone, *Greek Athletics and the Genesis of Sport* (1988), defying such formidable classicists as Walter Burkert, argues that ancient sports and modern athletics are much alike. For psychoanalytic considerations (still fairly rare), see especially A. R. Beisser, "Psychodynamic Observations of a Sport," *Psychoanalytic Review,* I (1961), 69–76, and Beisser, ed., *The Madness in Sports: Psychoanalytic Observations* (1967). Richard G. Spies, "War, Sports and Aggression: An Empirical Test of Two Rival Theories," *American Anthropologist,* n.s. LXXV (1973), 64–86, comes to the conclusion (on very limited evidence) that the "cultural pattern model" is more plausible than the psychoanalytic "drive discharge model." More work needs to be done.

For French sports, see the well-informed interpretation by Richard Holt, *Sport and Society in Modern France* (1981); not confined to that French favorite, cycling, it canvasses popular attitudes from patriotism to hooliganism. And see also the appealing paper by Eugen Weber, "Gymnastics and Sports in Fin-de-Siècle France: Opium of the Classes?" *American Historical Review,* LXXVI, 1 (February 1971), 70–98. Richard Holt, *Sport and the British: A Modern History* (1989), admirably packs an ample helping of social history into a moderate compass. John Hargreaves, *Sport, Power and Culture: A Social and Historical Analysis of Popular Sports in Britain* (1986), tries to link sports to power from an interesting, not wholly persuasive, radical perspective. H. A. Harris, *Sport in Britain: Its Origins and Development* (1975), is a short—too short—overview. More impressive is Tony Mason, *Association Football and English Society, 1863–1915* (1980). The expansive Alfred Gibson and William Pickford, *Association Football and the Men Who Made It,* 4 vols. (1906), abounds in anecdotes and portraits; while it does convey the flavor of soccer, the whole is more a document of its time than an analysis of it. On soccer violence, see the excellent article by Wray Vamplew, "Ungentlemanly Conduct: The Control of Soccer-Crowd Behavior in England, 1888–1914," in T. C. Smout, ed., *The Search for Wealth and Stability: Essays in Economic and Social History Presented to M. W. Flinn* (1979), 139–54. Vamplew's full-length analysis of athletes playing for money is as rewarding in its scholarship as it is witty in its title: *Pay Up and Play the Game: Professional Sport in Britain, 1875–1914* (1988). The first essays in the collection edited by Richard Holt, *Sport and the Working Class in Modern Britain* (1990), esp. Douglas A. Reid, "Beasts and Brutes: Popular Blood Sports, c. 1780–1860," 12–28, are relevant here. Despite some cavils, I found J. A. Mangan's attempts to tie the cult of the athlete to public schools and to imperialism stimulating; see his *Athleticism in the Victorian and Edwardian Public School: The Emergence and Consolidation of an Educational Ideology* (1981) and *The Games Ethic and Imperialism: Aspects of the Diffusion of an Ideal* (1986). Kathleen McCrone, *Playing the Game: Sport and the Physical Emancipation of English Women, 1870–1914* (1988), offers interesting sidelights on the role of sports in cultural change.

For German sports, see the trenchant observations of Norbert Elias, *Studien über die Deutschen. Machtkämpfe und Habitusentwicklung im 19. und 20. Jahrhundert* (1989). The pithy reflections of Christian Graf von Krockow, *Sport und Industriegesellschaft* (1972), are a thoughtful German contribution. Carl Koppehel, *Geschichte des deutschen Fussballsports* (1954), recounts the history of Germany's favorite sport. Henning Eichberg, *Der Weg des Sports in die industrielle Zivilization* (1979), is a good general treatment.

The history of America's national sport has been well introduced by Harold Seymour, *Baseball: The Early Years* (1960), and responsibly explored in Peter Levine, *A. G. Spalding and the Rise of Baseball: The Promise of American Sport* (1985). David Voigt, *American Baseball: From Gentleman's Sport to the Commissioner System* (1966), covers a longer stretch of history. Ronald A. Smith illuminates a significant aspect of competitive American games in *Sports and Freedom: The Rise of Big-Time College Athletics* (1988); ch. 7, "The Americanization of Rugby Football: Mass Plays, Brutality, and Masculinity," is also relevant to the topic of manliness. Thomas G. Bergin, *The Game: The Harvard Football Rivalry, 1875–1983* (1984), written from a Yale perspective, transcends nostalgic anecdotes. For a sociological analysis, see David Riesman and Reuel Denny, "Football in America: A Study in Cultural Diffusion," *American Quarterly*, III (1951), 309–25. Melvin L. Adelman, *A Sporting Time: New York City and the Rise of Modern Athletics, 1820–1870* (1986), is a useful account of track and field. Robert J. Higgs, *Laurel and Thorn: The Athlete in American Literature* (1983), and, even more, Christian K. Messenger, *Sport and the Spirit of Play in American Fiction: Hawthorne to Faulkner* (1983), demonstrate in their reading of novels and stories how exalted a place sports occupy in the psyche of many Americans. James C. Whorton, *Crusaders for Fitness: The History of American Health Reformers* (1982), is also relevant.

The maker of the modern Olympic games has been well served by Marie-Thérèse Eyquem, *Pierre de Coubertin: L'Épopée olympique* (1966). John J. MacAloon, *This Great Symbol: Pierre de Coubertin and the Origins of the Modern Olympic Games* (1981), is less a full biography—though chronological in form—than an informative analysis of Coubertin's ideology and his experiences with the Olympics. Despite the comprehensiveness of these volumes, Eugen Weber, "Pierre de Coubertin and the Introduction of Organised Sport in France," *Journal of Comtemporary History*, V (April 1970), 3–26, remains well worth reading. Of Coubertin's own numerous writings, the one of greatest importance is doubtless *Les Batailles de l'éducation physique. Une Campagne de vingt-et-un ans, 1887–1908* (1909). For the Greek origins of the games, still open to impassioned debate, see Wendy J. Raschke, ed., *The Archaeology of the Olympics: The Olympics and Other Festivals in Antiquity* (1988).

Most of these volumes necessarily touch on leisure—another recent discovery of social historians—so intimately tied to sports. I have profited most from H. E. Meller, *Leisure and the Changing City, 1870–1914* (1976), which is principally, but not only, about Bristol. I learned from Peter Bailey, *Leisure and Class in Victorian England: Rational Recreation and the Contest for Control, 1830–1885* (1978), though I do not share its political stance. See also Hugh Cunningham, *Leisure in the Industrial Revolution, c. 1780–c. 1880* (1980). The Germans have been exploring the matter mainly in short takes. See Gerhard Huck, ed., *Sozialgeschichte der Freizeit: Untersuchungen zum Wandel der Alltagskultur in Deutschland* (1980), esp. (among other intriguing contributions) Jürgen Reulecke, " 'Veredelung der Volkserholung' und 'edle Geselligkeit.' Sozialreformerische Bestrebungen zur Gestaltung der arbeitsfreien Zeit im Kaiserreich" (pp. 141–60). Reulecke and W. Weber, eds., *Fabrik, Familie, Feierabend. Beiträge zur Sozialgeschichte des Alltags im Industriezeitalter* (1978), also repays perusal. On France, there is an unmanageable wealth of material. Eugen Weber, *France: Fin de Siècle* (1986), somewhat slights the three-star attractions that were once the staple of cultural history, but its observations on the leisure of ordinary men and women—popular entertainment, travel, cycling, and the rest—are instructive and amusing. Several chapters in Theodore Zeldin, *France, 1848–1945*, 2 vols. (1973–77), are of interest, esp. in part II of vol. II, which examines taste. Michael B. Miller, *The Bon Marché: Bourgeois Culture and the Department Store, 1869–1920* (1981), takes a famous Parisian emporium as a jumping-off point for larger considerations. See also Rosalind H. Williams, *Dream Worlds: Mass Consumption in Late Nineteenth-Century France* (1982), and, principally for its illustrations, Charles Rearick, *Pleasures of the Belle Epoque: Entertainment and Festivity in Turn-of-the-Century France* (1985). And see also the fine historical survey, Maurice Agulhon et al., *Histoire de la France urbaine*, vol. IV, *La Ville de l'âge industriel, le cycle haussmannien* (1983).

All modern scholarship on Francis Bacon is indebted to the seven-volume biography by his nineteenth-century editor James Spedding, *The Life and Letters of Bacon* (1861–74). The terse late-nineteenth-century life by R. W. Church, *Bacon* (1884), remains worth reading. While Isaac Todhunter, *William Whewell, D.D., Master of Trinity College, Cambridge*, 2 vols. (1876), the first serious biography of Bacon's great Victorian student, admirer, and critic, retains much of value, it must be supplemented with Menachem Fisch, *William Whewell: Philosopher of Science* (1991). Among recent interpretations, Charles Whitney, *Francis Bacon and Modernity* (1986), seeks to place Bacon in the context of the modern sensibility without (I think) wholly escaping certain fashionable formulations. He rightly accepts the German philosopher Hans Blumenberg's appraisal, in *The*

Legitimacy of the Modern Age (1966; tr. Robert Wallace, 1983), of Bacon as an archetypal modern. Anthony Quinton, *Francis Bacon* (1980), packs an amazing amount of information and interpretation into a duodecimo package. Anthony F. C. Wallace's essay *The Social Context of Innovation: Bureaucrats, Families, and Heroes in the Early Industrial Revolution As Foreseen in Bacon's "New Atlantis"* (1982) is most interesting. Adolphe Quetelet, *L'Oeuvre sociologique et démographique. Choix de textes,* ed. Marc Lebrun (1974), with long excerpts and short comments, is useful. A substantial, deservedly much-quoted essay by Paul F. Lazarsfeld, "Notes on the History of Quantification in Sociology—Trends, Sources and Problems," *Isis,* LII, part 2 (June 1961), 277–333, places Quetelet in his scientific culture at welcome length. Beyond that, recent work has been surprisingly thin. One exception is Charles C. Gillispie, "Intellectual Factors in the Background of Analysis by Probabilities," in A. C. Crombie, ed., *Scientific Change: Historical Studies in the Intellectual, Social, and Technical Conditions for Scientific Discovery and Technical Invention from Antiquity to the Present* (1963), 431–53. Anthony Hyman, *Charles Babbage: Pioneer of the Computer* (1982), deals fully with that spectacular English inventor and scientific politician. Theodore M. Porter, *The Rise of Statistical Thinking, 1820–1900* (1986), is an important monograph. And see Michael J. Cullen, *The Statistical Movement in Early Victorian Britain: The Foundations of Empirical Social Research* (1975). R. L. Smyth, ed., *Essays in Economic Method: Selected Papers Read to Section F of the British Association for the Advancement of Science, 1860–1913* (1962), contains some splendid addresses. For Thomas Henry Huxley, see above, p. 608. Patricia Cline Cohen, *A Calculating People: The Spread of Numeracy in Early America* (1982), has left its mark on this section.

Ignaz Semmelweis, that pathetic medical pioneer, has been captured in ch. 9 of Sherwin B. Nuland, *Doctors: The Biography of Medicine* (1988), smoothly written, scholarly and gripping; it can be read with Nuland, "The Enigma of Semmelweis: An Interpretation," *Journal of the History of Medicine,* XXXIV (1979), 255–72. Erna Lesky, *The Vienna Medical School of the Nineteenth Century* (1965; tr. L. Williams and I. S. Levij, 1976), has pages on Semmelweis (pp. 181–92) that give him his due. Semmelweis's own crucial text is *An Etiology, Concept and Prophylaxis of Childbed Fever* (1860; tr. K. C. Carter, 1983).

James J. Sheehan, *The Career of Lujo Brentano: A Study of Liberalism and Social Reform in Imperial Germany* (1966), concentrates on the essential. Brentano's autobiography, *Mein Leben im Kampf um die soziale Entwicklung Deutschlands* (1931), is more political than intimate. Anthony Oberschall, *Empirical Social Research in Germany, 1848–1914* (1965), has sound material but is tantalizingly short. The English reformer I have juxtaposed with Brentano has been thoroughly canvassed in T. S. Simey and M. B. Simey, *Charles Booth: Social Scientist* (1960). Michael J. Cullen, "Charles Booth's Poverty Survey: Some New Approaches," pp. 155–74 in *The Search for Wealth and Stability,* cited p. 646, offers a sensible critique of Booth's investigative procedures. H. M. Hyndman, *The Record of an Adventurous Life* (1911), describes his historic encounter with Booth. Beatrice Webb (then Beatrice Potter), Booth's close collaborator, is more sympathetic though not sentimental in *My Apprenticeship* (1926; ed. 1971) and in her journal, *The Diary of Beatrice Webb,* ed. Norman MacKenzie and Jeanne MacKenzie, vol. I, *1873–1892, Glitter around and Darkness Within* (1982), both also cited earlier. On the issue that agitated both Brentano and Booth, see for an early text B. Seebohm Rowntree, *Poverty: A Study of Town Life* (1906), and for a later one the study by Wilhelm Abel, *Massenarmut und Hungerkrisen im vorindustriellen Deutschland* (1972; 2nd ed., 1977). Wolfram Fischer, *Armut in der Geschichte: Erscheinungsformen und Lösungsversuche der 'Sozialen Frage' in Europa seit dem Mittelalter* (1982), is very short but meaty. The famous provocative analysis by Thorstein Veblen, *Imperial Germany and the Industrial Revolution* (1915), which attributes Germany's strong showing in the industrial race to the country's late start, should not be overlooked.

Two volumes by Eduard Spranger provide the best access to German neo-humanist schooling in the early nineteenth century: *Wilhelm von Humboldt und die Humanitätsidee* (1909) and *Wilhelm von Humboldt und die Reform des Bildungswesens* (1910). Peter Berglar, *Wilhelm von Humboldt in Selbstzeugnissen und Bilddokumenten* (1970), is succinct and candid. Klaus Sochatzy, *Das neuhumanistische Gymnasium und die rein-menschliche Bildung. Zwei Schulreformversuche in ihrer weiterreichenden Bedeutung* (1973), tracks Humboldt's program at work in local schools. See Margaret Kraul, *Gymnasium und Gesellschaft im Vormärz. Neuhumanistische Einheitsschule, städtische Gesellschaft und soziale Herkunft der Schüler* (1980), for the social origins of the pupils; the substantial study by Karl-Ernst Jeismann, *Das preussische Gymnasium in Staat und Gesellschaft. Die Entstehung des Gymnasiums als Schule des Staates und der Gebildeten, 1787–1817* (1974), on the early history of the system Humboldt's created; and the same author's slender but well-selected anthology *Staat und Erziehung in der preussischen Reform 1807–1819* (1969). The first four chapters of W. H. Bruford, *The German Tradition of Self-Cultivation: "Bildung" from Humboldt to Thomas Mann* (1975), on Humboldt, Goethe, and Schleiermacher, are not as searching as they might be, but offer suggestions. For the history of university reform, the bulky, several times revised account by the philosopher and reformer Friedrich Paulsen, *The German Universities: Their Character and Historical Development* (1885; tr. Edward Delavan Perry, 1895), is indispensable for its historical information, conveyed with the passionate partisanship of an activist. And see Paulsen, *An Autobiography* (ed. and tr. Theodor Lorenz, 1938), also cited earlier, which incorporates not only his posthumous *Jugenderinnerungen* (1909) but memoirs and annals not previously published in German. For an American perspective on prestigious German higher education, there is Carl Diehl, *Americans and German Scholarship, 1770–1870* (1978).

Among the numerous monographs on mid-nineteenth-century university reform in Britain, Christopher Kent, *Brains and Numbers: Elitism, Comtism, and Democracy in Mid-Victorian England* (1978), which ably discusses the influential educational radicals, is noteworthy. See also the far-ranging history by W. H. G. Armytage, *Four Hundred Years of English Education* (1964), esp. chs. 4–9. A brief sociological monograph, Joseph Ben-David, *The Scientist's Role in Society: A Comparative Study* (1971), cuts back and forth across Europe.

On doctors and health we have been well served. For physicians in England, M. Jeanne Peterson, *The Medical Profession in Mid-Victorian London* (1978), is a model of its kind. Roy Porter, *Health for Sale: Quackery in England, 1660–1850* (1989), at once informative and entertaining, leaves no doubt that sheer self-interest often guided the medical profession's attempt to root out charlatans. British health is notoriously difficult to research, but F. B. Smith, *The People's Health, 1830–1910* (1979), successfully explores elusive data to follow English men—and women—from infancy through adolescence, adulthood, and old age. See also a substantial essay by Brian Harrison, "Women's Health and the Women's Movement in Britain: 1840–1940," in Charles Webster, ed., *Biology, Medicine, and Society, 1840–1940* (1981), 15–71. The grim picture of the lower orders in Gareth Stedman Jones, *Outcast London: A Study in the Relationship between Classes in Victorian Society* (1971), serves as a corrective for complacency.

For the general medical picture, Nuland, *Doctors,* has been mentioned on p. 648. The growth of the psychiatric profession in France has been charted by Jan Goldstein, *Console and Classify: The French Psychiatric Profession in the Nineteenth Century* (1987), also cited earlier. Among histories of medicine in France, I am particularly indebted to Erwin H. Ackerknecht, *Medicine at the Paris Hospital, 1794–1848* (1967).

On specialization, Jean Donnison, *Midwives and Medical Men: A History of Inter-Professional Rivalries and Women's Rights* (1977), also cited before, is valuable. So are two works by W. H. G. Armytage: *A Social History of Engineering* (1961; 4th ed., 1976), which cuts a wide swath across countries and ages, and his *The Rise of the Technocrats: A Social History* (1965). Specialization in German medicine has been treated exhaustively, in more than 720 pages, by Hans-Heinz Eulner, *Die Entwicklung der medizinischen Spezialfächer an den Universitäten des deutschen Sprachgebiets* (1970), which omits nothing, from ophthalmology to gynecology, internal medicine to dentistry. For the United States, see *The Organization of Knowledge in Modern America, 1860–1920* (1979), ed. Alexandra Oleson and John Voss. One ambitious attempt to define professionalization as a bourgeois phenomenon is the energetic (but, to me, not really persuasive) argument by Burton J. Bledstein, *The Culture of Professionalism: The Middle Class and the Development of Higher Education in America* (1976). W. J. Reader, *Professional Men: The Rise of the Professional Classes in Nineteenth-Century England* (1966), is more prudent. Alexander Carr-Saunders and P. A. Wilson, *The Professions* (1933), is a pioneering report. See also the illuminating essay by Stefan Collini, "Their Title to be Heard: Professionalization and Its Discontents," ch. 6 of *Public Moralists: Political Thought and Intellectual Life in Britain, 1850–1930* (1991), also cited earlier. The history of inventions offers relevant sidelights. For a theoretical approach, there is H. G. Barnett, *Innovation: The Basis of Cultural Change* (1953). See also Christine MacLeod, *Inventing the Industrial Revolution: The English Patent System, 1660–1800* (1988), for the early period; and for the central years, H. I. Dutton, *The Patent System and Inventive Activity during the Industrial Revolution, 1750–1853* (1984).

The significance of time and quantity is explored in a suggestive but not conclusive essay by G. J. Whitrow, *Time in History: Views of Time from Prehistory to the Present Day* (1988). Carlo M. Cipolla, *Clocks and Culture, 1300–1700* (1967) deals admirably with the prehistory of modern perceptions. David S. Landes, *Revolution in Time: Clocks and the Making of the Modern World* (1983), is an elegant long essay by a clock enthusiast who happens to be a distinguished economic historian. Cohen, *A Calculating People,* cited above, has an excellent chapter (ch. 6) on the census of 1840.

On advice literature, some titles already listed—like Irwin G. Wyllie, *The Self-Made Man in America: The Myth of Rags to Riches* (1954); Judith Rowbotham, *Good Girls Make Good Wives: Guidance for Girls in Victorian Fiction* (1989); and many of the other titles in the section on chapter 4, "The Powerful, Weaker Sex"—are relevant here. See Gary Scharnhorst with Jack Bales, *The Lost Life of Horatio Alger, Jr.* (1980), for the specialist in rags to riches. Richard Weiss, *The American Myth of Success: From Horatio Alger to Norman Vincent Peale* (1969), esp. chs. 1–4, is very informative. The generous anthology *English Popular Literature, 1819–1851* (1976) has a useful section ("Admonitory") and an equally useful introduction, both by its editor, Louis James. On the greatest model builder of them all, *The Autobiography of Samuel Smiles, L.D.D.,* ed. Thomas Mackay (1905), should be read in conjunction with Aileen Smiles, *Samuel Smiles and His Surroundings* (1956), a fair-minded appraisal; with Asa Briggs's lively chapter (ch. 5) in *Victorian People: An Assessment of Persons and Themes, 1851–67* (1955); and with the introduction by Thomas Parke Hughes to his edition of Smiles, *Selections from Lives of the Engineers with an Account of their Principal Works* (1966). For that mid-Victorian best seller the *Book of Household Management,* there is Sarah Freeman, *Isabella and Sam: The Story of Mrs. Beeton* (1978). Unfortunately, I came upon Ruth Bernard Yeazell's original *Fictions of Modesty: Women and Courtship in the English Novel* (1991), which has exhilarating pages on the advice literature, too late to do more than applaud it.

For Germany, the prehistory of nineteenth-century bourgeois styles has been covered better than the history itself; see, for example, the collection of snippets from the fifteenth to the early nineteenth century edited by Paul Münch, *Ordnung, Fleiss und Sparsamkeit. Texte und Dokumente zur Entstehung der 'bürgerlichen Tugenden'* (1984), and Wolfgang Ruppert, *Bürgerlicher Wandel. Die Geburt der modernen deutschen Gesellschaft im achtzehnten Jahrhudert* (1981; ed. 1983). For France, see the helpful pages in Theodore Zeldin, *France, 1848–1945,* vol. I, *Ambition, Love and Politics* (1973), 285–362. The classic book of advice on how to love and to marry was Gustave Droz's phenomenally successful *Monsieur, madame et bébé* (1866). Adeline Daumard's authoritative survey, *Les Bourgeois et la bourgeoisie en France depuis 1815* (1987), is essential reading. But the topic of advice needs more work.

EPILOGUE: August 4, 1914

The outbreak of the First World War has been studied so intensely that a few representative titles must suffice. On the unending controversy around just who was responsible for Armageddon, the pamphlet *The Outbreak of the First World War* (1958), ed. Dwight E. Lee, gathers the main contending views. Oron J. Hale, *The Great Illusion, 1900–1914* (1971) ably surveys the critical years before August 4, 1914. A. J. P. Taylor's detailed and spirited history of great-power accommodation and rivalry, *The Struggle for Mastery in*

Europe, 1848–1918 (1954), remains worth consulting. Walter Laqueur and George L. Mosse, eds., *1914: The Coming of the First World War* (1966), brings together articles on the foreign and military policies, and the war aims, of the powers. And see Laurence Lafore, *The Long Fuse* (1965). Roland N. Stromberg, *Redemption by War: The Intellectuals and 1914* (1982), is thorough and disheartening about philosophers, poets, artists, and political leaders—right, center, and left—who should have known better. John Williams, *The Other Battleground: The Home Fronts—Britain, France and Germany, 1914–1918* (1972), satisfactorily continues the story. On German aggressive attitudes before war was declared, the long introductory section of Fritz Fischer's famous controversial *Germany's Aims in the First World War* (1961; abr. and tr. anon., 1967), is indispensable. In *Voices Prophesying War, 1763–1984* (1966), I. F. Clarke entertainingly (and a little frighteningly) records the sizable output of prewar publications imagining the great conflict to come. William Ashworth, *A Short History of the International Economy since 1850* (1952; 2nd ed., 1962), says the essential on world economic ties. It can be read with the early chapters in W. W. Rostow, *The World Economy, History and Prospect* (1978). And see David S. Landes, *The Unbound Prometheus: Technological Change and Industrial Development in Western Europe from 1750 to the Present* (1969), a comprehensive survey. The beloved French pacifist and patriotic socialist Jean Jaurès, murdered before the outbreak of hostilities, has been celebrated in Harvey Goldberg, *The Life of Jean Jaurès* (1968). For the collapse of socialism in the face of nationalism, see above all James Joll, *The Second International, 1889–1914* (1955).

Historiographers of nationalism like to say that the two scholars who put the subject on a scientific footing were Carlton J. H. Hayes and Hans Kohn. The former epitomized his early researches in *Essays in Nationalism* (1926) and *The Historical Evolution of Modern Nationalism* (1931). The latter published *The Idea of Nationalism: A Study of Its Origins and Background* in 1944, and *The Age of Nationalism: The First Era of Global History* in 1962. His *The Mind of Germany* (1965) also belongs in this company. To these pioneers (in many respects superseded), I want to add Friedrich Meinecke, *Cosmopolitanism and the National State* (1908; tr. Robert B. Kimber, 1970), an old and old-fashioned but still suggestive history of the rise of German national sentiment down to the time of Bismarck. Alfred Cobban, *The Nation State and National Self-Determination* (1945; expanded ed., 1969), also remains worthwhile. The substantial survey by Salo Wittmayer Baron, *Modern Nationalism and Religion* (1947; 2nd ed., 1960), focuses on a somewhat neglected aspect of the topic.

Sozialstruktur und Organisation europäischer Nationalbewegungen, ed. Theodor Schieder with the collaboration of Peter Burian (1971), instructively discusses historiographical problems raised by nationalism. Anthony D. Smith, *Theories of Nationalism* (1971), seeks to anchor the phenomenon historically and to provide definitions. K. R. Minogue's terse *Nationalism* (1968) stays with the modern world. Elie Kedourie, *Nationalism* (1960), has been justly praised for its analytic acumen. So, with equal justice, has Hugh Seton-Watson, *Nations and States: An Enquiry into the Origins of Nations and the Politics of Nationalism* (1977). Miroslav Hroch, *Social Conditions of National Revival in Europe: A*

Comparative Analysis of the Social Composition of Patriotic Groups among the Smaller European Nations (1968; tr. Ben Fowkes, 1985), is an interesting attempt to distinguish stages of nationalism. Amid this wealth, Benedict Anderson, *Imagined Communities: Reflections on the Origin and Spread of Nationalism* (1983; 2nd ed., 1991), still manages to add new and intriguing ideas about the cultural foundations of nationalism. Linda Colley's important article "Whose Nation? Class and National Consciousness in Britain, 1750–1830," *Past and Present*, no. 113 (November 1986), 97–117, raises questions beyond its narrow announced topic.

For France, see Carlton J. H. Hayes's now-old *France: A Nation of Patriots* (1930). Eugen Weber, *The Nationalist Revival in France, 1905–1914* (1968), charts the disappearance of liberal nationalism. The standard history of the Austrian domains is Robert A. Kann, *A History of the Habsburg Empire, 1526–1918* (1974; corr. ed., 1977); given the enormous variations in the multinational empire, it is, however bulky, all too brief. A good supplement is the exhaustive collection of papers on the nationalities—German and non-German—under Habsburg sway, ed. R. John Rath et al.: *The Nationality Problem in the Habsburg Monarchy in the Nineteenth Century: A Critical Appraisal,* in *Austrian History Yearbook,* III (1967), parts 1 and 2. For the volatile Czech situation, see Joseph Chada, *The Czech National Revival: The Age of Romanticism* (1934), a useful short treatment. Ivo Banac's impressive monograph *The National Question in Yugoslavia: Origins, History, Politics* (1984) reaches, especially in the early chapters, into prewar Europe.

For Norway, see above all Andreas Elviken, *Die Entwicklung des norwegischen Nationalismus* (1930), a brief monograph emphasizing the eighteenth-century background, and Oscar J. Falnes, *National Romanticism in Norway* (1933), one of several monographs sponsored by Carlton J. H. Hayes.

Acknowledgments

As often in the past, I have been sustained in writing this book by friends, colleagues, students, commentators on lectures, and by foundations which have munificently supported my work. I cannot hope to discharge, but want gratefully to record, my debts.

I am deeply obliged to the Research Division of the National Endowment for the Humanities, an independent federal agency, for a substantial grant stretching from 1989 to 1992, which provided much of the free time I needed to write this book. Without the repeated aid of the N.E.H., this series of volumes would have been virtually unthinkable. Jack Censer and Frances Gouda eased my way through the administrative maze in the most unbureaucratic manner possible. I want also to thank the Harry Frank Guggenheim Foundation for going out of its way to liberate most of the matching funds the N.E.H. had provided. As always, money has been time. A welcome triennial term's leave from Yale further speeded up my work. I should add that Yale administrators have been most helpful with advice in the complex matter of applications and budgets. Alice Oliver patiently explored possibilities with me, much to my benefit; more recently, I have profited from the assistance of Suzanne Polmar and Sally Tremaine.

I have been fortunate in being invited to try out my thoughts on aggression in lectures across the years—this book has been long in the making. Back in 1976, I lectured on Wilhelm Busch at Dartmouth College, and in 1978 I repeated the performance, in a revised version, at Colgate University. My first opportunity to discuss aggression comprehensively came at Syracuse University in 1980; I published the paper, "Aggression and Culture: A Psychoanalytic Perspective," in the Fall 1981 issue of the *Syracuse Scholar*. The four Freud Lectures I gave in 1981 under the sponsorship of the Western New England Society for Psychoanalysis and the Whitney Humanities Center at Yale University contain material I have incorporated into this book. In May 1981, at the spring meeting of the American Psychoanalytic Association in San Juan, Puerto Rico, I presented an important paper (important to me) called "Liberalism and Regression"; published the next year in *Psychoanalytic Study of the Child,* it explores the deep relationship of cultural strains to aggressive conduct. Then, in the intervening years, I concentrated on volumes I and II of this series and on my Freud biography, to take up aggression again in 1988. In May, I spoke at a conference in Osterbeek, the Netherlands, on aggression in humor; later that month, it was the turn of Wilhelm Busch at the Wellcome Institute in London. Shortly after, I gave a lecture on manliness before the History Faculty of Cambridge University, and in the following month, on aggression and the historian at the Psychoanalytic Institute of New England, East in Boston. Aggression was the theme once more in January 1989 at the Chicago Psychoanalytic

Institute, while in March of that year, at a public lecture in Amherst, Massachusetts, I offered a revised version of the talk on aggression and the historian. The following month, at Butler University in Indianapolis, I addressed the general topic "Victorianism: Myths and Realities." The tempo picked up in 1990: In January, I presented a paper on Wilhelm Busch before my colleagues at the Western New England Society for Psychoanalysis, an occasion made memorable to me by Ernst Prelinger's brilliant commentary. In April, I ventured to try out my (unconventional) ideas about "scribbling women" in the History and Literature program at Harvard. In the same month, I participated in a conference on aggression sponsored by the Toronto Psychoanalytic Society, contributing a paper titled "The Cultivation of Hatred." In June, I delivered a paper, in German, on aggression and the historian before the Berlin branch of the Deutsche Psychoanalytische Gesellschaft. Then, in October, I spoke at the University of Amsterdam on aggression and, on the occasion of receiving the first Amsterdam Prize for History, to the Dutch Academy of Arts and Sciences on the task of cultural history, in an address which touched on my methods in this series of books. In November, at the American Philosophical Society in Philadelphia, my topic was "Humor: The Bite of Wit," and the following month, at the winter meeting of the American Psychoanalytic Association in New York, I addressed a plenary session on the Mensur. Finally, late that month, I spoke at the American Historical Association, also in New York, at a session dedicated to R. K. Webb, on Thomas Hughes and manliness. These encounters, in both formal and informal ways, have borne fruit for me. With real pleasure, I record my gratitude to historians in Amsterdam—Maarten Brands, Herman Beliën, and Willem Melching—who invited me to lecture at their university on my chapter on humor, and to offer related seminars. They made my stay, in May and June 1992, a truly memorable one.

I want to repeat what I said in an earlier volume: a book such as this is a conversation and a collaboration. Let me acknowledge here—and I trust I have not forgotten anyone—my conversation partners and collaborators. I am beholden to them all, even if I have not always taken their good advice. Walter Arndt, that unmatched translator of Wilhelm Busch, talked Busch with me at Dartmouth; Jeff Auerbach lent me an unpublished paper on women's magazines; Ivo Banac passed on outrageous racist remarks from Serbia and helped clarify my ideas on nationalism; Jacques Barzun kindly traced some elusive quotations on racism; John Blum helped with Theodore Roosevelt—and I trust he will take my pages on T.R. in good part; James Bratt, in a graduate paper, provided valuable material on Oliver Wendell Holmes, Jr.; Richard Brodhead had interesting comments about corporal punishment; Bill Cronon talked with me about the West, and Nancy Cott about Victorian women; David Brion Davis supplied me with his articles on capital punishment; John Demos steered me to Catharine Sedgwick's *Home* and has over the years given me his wisdom on psychoanalysis and history; Robert Dietle, at many enjoyable lunches, helpfully went over my argument with me; John A. Gable, of the Theodore Roosevelt Association, answered my questions about T.R.; Hank Gibbons and I have been talking and corresponding for years, much to my benefit; Sir Ernst Gombrich provided comments on Wilhelm Busch; Bob Herbert led me to Charles Blanc; Juri Hwang had in her senior essay a fine passage from Eliza Lynn Linton; Carter Jefferson took time to supply me with the French originals of quotations in his book on Anatole France; Jim Jordan of W. W. Norton helped with ethology; Fred Kaplan sent me a fascinating essay by Carlyle; David Large supplied interesting offprints; Lisa Lieberman lent me unpublished material on suicide that supplemented her dissertation; Colin Matthew spent a splendid day with me at Oxford, talking Gladstone; Mark Micale has long listened and commented on my ideas about history informed by psychoanalysis; Shep Nuland and I had lunches on doctors—Semmelweis and others; Denis Paz sent me material on popular violence; Otto Pflanze solved some intractable puzzles about Bismarck; Michèle Plott was helpful about women in France; Ernst Prelinger taught me about the psychoanalytic implications of Wilhelm Busch and much else; Ferrel Rose provided details on Marie von Ebner-Eschenbach; Lisa Tiersten expanded on her dissertation for my benefit; Mary Lee Townsend, former student and now good friend, sent relevant (and hilarious) materials on Berlin humor; Richard Tuck led me to moral equivalents in the South Seas; Frank M. Turner found, among other things, a beautiful passage in Thomas De Quincey; Hans-Ulrich Wehler has supplied me with his provocative offprints for years; Richard Weiss earned my gratitude for sending me his book on the American myth of success; Meike Werner supplied material on German woman students and the Mensur; Fredric Woodbridge Wilson guided me through the W. S. Gilbert papers at the Pierpont Morgan Library.

I want to record, too, good talk or correspondence with Geoffrey Best, David Bromwich, Peter Brooks, Gilda Buchbinder, Linda Colley, Peter Demetz, Judy Forrest, Jack Garraty, Debbie Glassman, Ingeborg Glier, Tom Greene, Charles Hanly, Geoffrey Hartman, Paul Kennedy, Jeff Merrick, Jerry Meyer, Hillis Miller, Arthur and Marleen Mitzman, Elting Morison, Lynn Whisnant Reiser, Reinhard Rürup, Jean Strouse, and Henry Turner.

While I was working on this book, Janet Malcolm and Gardner Botsford, Gladys Topkis and Vann Woodward, showed me over and over, as they have through the years, what friendship can mean; all I can do is to thank them.

My undergraduate assistants for the past five years—Becky Haltzel, Mario Koshon, Christina Erickson—have proved informed and skilled beyond their years; besides tracking down footnotes and finding books, they have helped with my actual researches.

As before, so now, the staff at W. W. Norton were at once cordial and helpful. I want to thank above all Esther Jacobson for the patient and attentive copy-editing for which she is rightly famous, Toni Krass for improving the design of the book, and Amy Cherry and Jennifer Di Toro for making my life easier.

Last but by no means least, I have been exceptionally lucky in my readers, as I have been throughout my writing life. More than readers, they too have joined in the conversation across the years. David Cannadine, Stefan Collini, John Merriman, and Bob Webb read these pages with a mixture of care and imagination, saving me from mistakes and suggesting improvements. One of my readers, Don Lamm, publisher, editor, and friend, proved unsurpassed in all these roles. My wife, Ruth, my most consistent reader, attacked my prose (in the constructive sense of that phrase) at least twice, removing infelicities and fostering concision. I am deeply grateful to her, as I am to the others.

PETER GAY

Index

Colonialism: racism and, 85–90; sexual desire and, 86; as distant reality, 87–88. *See also* Imperialism

Colorado, women granted vote in, 364

Comedy. *See* Humor; Satire

Comedy of manners, 377

Committee for the Diffusion of Information on the Subject of Capital Punishments, 161–62

Competition, conflict: scientific justifications for, 4, 38–40, 47; as alibi for aggression, 35, 38–68; government regulation of, 40, 42–43; industrialist opposition to, 62. *See also* Social Darwinism

Comte, Auguste, 457

Congo Free State, 87–88

Congress, U.S., 221

Congreve, Richard, 377; Caesar praised by, 238–39

Conservatives, 83; socialism as source of worry for, 79; vs. liberals on punishment, 135–37, 141

Constant, Benjamin: on racial justifications of oppression, 72; on idealization of ancient politics, 214–15; on freedom from politics, 224; on Napoleon I's political legacy, 229; freedom of the press advocated by, 230; on voting rights, 271–72

Constitution, U.S., 67, 228; *The Federalist* written in support of, 267n.

Contraception. *See* Birth control

Corporal punishment, 181–94; description of cartoons of, 182–83;

rationales for, 182–83, 192; in U.S., 183, 184–86, 189; opponents of, 183–90, 431; religion and, 187, 192; class and, 188; abolition of, 189–90; fictional portrayals of, 193, 194; sexual pleasure and, 194

Corrupt and Illegal Practices Act (1883) (England), 282

Cortès, Donoso, 247

Coubertin, Pierre de, 442–43

Counteraggression, children's use of, 424

Counterphobic behavior, 117

Courvoisier, François, public hanging of, 176–77

Coutts, Angela Burdett, 298

Craies, W. F., "Capital Punishment," 166n.

Crime: reform movements and, 141–60; juvenile, 142–44, 151; sanity and, 152–53, 163–64; nature-nurture question and, 154–55; Lombroso's studies on, 155–56; as social phenomenon, 160. *See also* Murder; Punishment; Rape

"Criminalistics," 159

Criminologists, popularization of term, 139

Crispi, Francesco, 237

Cromwell, Oliver, 102

Cruikshank, George, 402

Cults of personality. *See* Caesarism

Culture: racial categorization and, 75–76; sports as representative of, 434–35

Cummins, Maria, popularity of novel by, 335, 336

Curtis, N. M., capital punishment study of, 173

Cuvier, Georges, races categorized by, 72

Cycling, 434, 440

Daelen, Eduard, 420n.

Dallas, Eneas Sweetland, 348

"Dangerous classes," legend of, 181

Dante Alighieri, 237

Darwin, Charles, 4, 45–50, 84, 371, 457; *Origin of Species*, 38–39, 45, 46, 48n., 49, 54, 55; Marx's admiration of, 39n.; *The Descent of Man*, 45, 47; religious interpretations of, 45–46; social philosophy of, 47–48; English satirizing of, 48; French followers of, 49–51; Social Darwinism opposed by, 54; on Bacon, 448; on religion, 476n.; Freud on, 531. *See also* Social Darwinism

Daudet, Alphonse, 49

Daumier, Honoré, 250, 487; political satire by, 396–400; background of, 397; imprisonment of, 398; anti-feminist satire by, 400–401; Greek myths satirized by, 401n.

Death drive: aggression as public voice of, 532; will to mastery as derivative of, 534

Death penalty. *See* Capital punishment

Declaration of the Rights of Man, 222

Demeny, Georges, 502

"Demi-bourgeois," 272

Democracy: aristocratic anxieties about, 79; European clamor for, 217–18; bourgeois

Ray, Isaac, *Treatise on the Medical Jurisprudence of Insanity*, 152, 153

Reade, Winwood, *The Outcast*, 48n.

Reality principle, pleasure principle and, 423, 494

Recidivism, 151

Recipes, graphic details in, 356, 358

Referees: power of, 445; aggression against, 446

Reform Act (1832) (England), 228, 274–77, 464, 489

Reform Act (1867) (England), 268, 274, 277–82

Reform Act (1884) (England), 274

Reformatory schools, 144

Rehabilitation, 156; as rationale for punishment, 133, 134, 137, 150–51, 157–58

Reinach, Salomon, 260n.; on Aryan racial theories, 91, 93

Relativism, in Enlightenment, 71

Religion: and theory of evolution, 45–46, 48–49; racism and, 68n., 69, 92; missionaries and, 69, 83, 86, 87; and philosophies of punishment, 137–38; capital punishment and, 168–70; corporal punishment and, 187, 192; suicide and, 207, 210; politics as, 222; women's suffrage and, 325–26, 433; in women's writings, 336; as enemy of progress, 433, 476

Rémusat, Charles de: Napoleon I praised by, 226; on Restoration, 229; political action advocated

by, 230–31; in Restoration and July Monarchy, 231, 233

Renaissance "Man," end of, 472–91

Renan, Ernest, 50

Republican party (U.S.), 125

Restoration, French, 229–32, 233, 268, 271

Retribution, as rationale for punishment, 133–34, 137, 140

Revenge, punishment as, 128–30, 146, 167, 170

Rhode Island, capital punishment in, 162–63

Richelieu, Cardinal, 215

Richer, Léon, women's suffrage opposed by, 326

Richmond *Times*, 95

Richter, Eugen, 421

Riehl, Wilhelm Heinrich, 458

Ringseis, Johann Nepomuk, Mensur opposed by, 18–19

Rites of passage, 32, 112

Robespierre, Maximilien François Marie Isidore de: declaration of rights proposed by, 222–23; execution of, 225–26

Rockefeller, John D., 53, 62, 121; corrupt business practices of, 64; as philanthropist, 64–65

Rogers, Samuel, 99

Roman Catholic Church, 255; as state church of France, 232; French secondary schools of, 246; in England, 275, 277, 279

Roman Catholic reformatories, 144

Romania, capital punishment abolished in, 167

Rome (ancient), 320; punishment as sacred act in, 133; war in culture of, 428

Romieu, Auguste, 99, 246

Roon, Albrecht von, 261

Roosevelt, Theodore, 114, 116–27, 501; on race suicide, 61, 125; Carnegie and Rockefeller denounced by, 65, 121; birth of, 116; bourgeois aggression epitomized by, 116; counterphobic behavior of, 117; asthma suffered by, 117, 118; paradoxical character of, 117, 126–27; autobiography of, 117n., 118; compulsive volunteering of, 118; teenage epiphany of, 118; as president, 118, 120, 123, 125, 127; symbolic action favored by, 118–19; hunting as pastime of, 119, 120, 121–22; political career of, 119–20; deaths of mother and wife of, 120; in Spanish-American War, 120, 123–24; on tender side of manliness, 122–23; on just vs. unjust war, 123; Social Darwinism and, 123, 124; Nobel Peace Prize of, 124; race and, 124–25

Root, Elihu, 121

La Roquette prison, 143

Rosenberg, Heinrich, 31

Rost, Hans, 209n., 210

Rothschild, Baron Lionel de, 277

Rough Riders, 120, 124

Roundell, Charles, 87

Rousseau, Jean Jacques, 139, 492, 520; masochism of, 196; on woman's hidden

Self-laceration, aggression as, 36–37

Sellwood, Emily, 354n.

Semites, "Aryans" compared with, 77, 80

Semmelweis, Ignaz: childbed fever research of, 454–56; death of, 457

Seneca Falls convention (1848), 5

"Separate but equal" doctrine, 95

Separation, violent quarrels as grounds for, 201

Seward, William, 69

Sexual desire: as elemental spring of action, 57; colonialism and, 86; qualities contributing to, 98; manliness and, 98–99

Sexuality: aggression and, 7–8, 30, 31–32, 197–98, 202, 529, 531–33; link between humor and, 7–8, 372; in adolescence, 31–32; scientific studies of, 199; sports and, 435; infantile, 533n.

Sexual pleasure, pain and, 191, 194–99

Shakespeare, William, 68n., 237; on brevity as soul of wit, 381; *Richard II*, 520

Shand, Alexander, 161

Shaw, George Bernard: on consciousness of sin, 37; manliness ideal criticized by, 110n.; *Caesar and Cleopatra*, 237; Molière praised by, 383; polemical aims of, 385; hypocrisy attacked by, 402; on medical profession, 487

Shearman, Montague, on controlling aggression through sports, 426–27

Sibling rivalry, 418n.

Simmel, Georg, on innateness of aggression, 4

Simon, Jules, 288; on women's domestic role, 316–17; feminist activities of wife of, 317

Simplicissimus, 16, 25, 389, 390, 419n.; government response to, 405–7

Sin, consciousness of, 37

Skin color, racial categorization by, 72

Slaney, Robert, 429

Slavery, British abolition of, 82

Slowacki, Juliusz, 523n.

Smiles, Samuel, 101; advice literature of, 499, 504, 505, 506

Smith, Adam: competition in philosophy of, 39–40; *Wealth of Nations*, 474

Smith, Goldwin, on Caesar, 238–39

Smith, Sydney, 476

Sneyd-Kynnersley, H. W., corporal punishment as administered by, 193–94, 196

Soccer, 434, 436–37, 444–45

Social Darwinism, 39–68, 153, 165; definition and roots of, 39, 41, 45, 47; Spencer and, 41–42, 45; Huxley and, 56; in literature, 49–53, 60, 61–62; in U.S., 51, 53, 56–58; ambivalence and confusion in, 51–52, 53–54; in Germany, 51–53, 60; philanthropy and, 53, 58, 62–65; opposition to, 54–57; middle class acceptance of, 60; psychological need gratified by, 67–68; racism and, 74, 75, 78n.,

85, 86; Roosevelt and, 123, 124; criminal reform and, 154–55

Social Democratic party (Germany), 16, 263, 264, 366, 519

Social Democratic Workers' party (Germany), 467, 469, 470

Social engineering, as impulse for criminal reform, 138, 139–40

Social insurance, 67

Socialism, socialists, 63, 79; women's movement and, 325–26; German social science and, 467–70

Social science, 457–72; importance of theory in, 457–58; national culture and, 460–61; specialization in, 484

Société médicale d'observation, 454

Society for Bettering the Conditions of the Poor, 462

Society for German Colonization, 86

Society for the Abolition of Capital Punishment, 162

Society for the Diffusion of Knowledge Respecting the Punishment of Death and the Improvement of Prison Discipline, 161–62

Sociobiology, 530

Sociology, family, 458

Socrates, 215

Solomons, Joseph, 205–6

Sorbonne, first woman granted degree at, 364

Sorel, Georges, 97–98

South Africa, 87

South Carolina, segregation in, 95

Southey, Robert, Brontë's
writing discouraged by,
329–30
Spain, mania for racial
purity in, 71
Spanish-American War, 59,
120, 123–24, 428
Specialization, 472–91; in
education, 472, 475–84;
by professionals, 472,
484–91; as ambiguous
blessing, 472–74
Spectator, 138, 492
Spedding, James, 448, 450
Spencer, Herbert, 4, 41–45,
58, 61, 65, 84, 85, 379;
Hobbes criticized by, 40;
"survival of the fittest"
phrase coined by, 41;
Social Statics, 41, 42, 43,
44, 67, 303; U.S.
reputation of, 41, 42, 56,
57, 61, 63, 65; Social
Darwinism and, 41–42,
45; death of, 42; on role
of government, 42–43;
Facts and Comments, 43;
antiwar sentiments of, 44;
on origin of organized
society, 214n.; universal
suffrage supported by,
278n.; sexual equality
advocated by, 366; on
physiology of laughter,
371
Sphinx, as symbol of
woman's mystery, 327
Sports: women in, 353–54;
as means of controlling
aggression, 426–47; class
and, 429–30, 435,
440–43; national tastes in,
434; regulation of, 434,
443–45; cultural
representativeness of,
434–45; sexual
implications of, 435;
behavior of spectators of,

435, 436–37, 443, 446;
violence in, 435–37,
444–45, 446; military
preparedness and, 437–38;
nationalism and, 438–40,
443; amateurism and,
441–43; fairness in, 443;
referees in, 445–46
Square Deal, 127
Staël, Madame de, 271, 328
Stahr, Adolf, 346
Standard Oil, 64, 66
Stanley, Lord, 361
State. *See* Government
Statistical Society of
London, 450
Statistics: emergence of
science of, 450–51;
Disraeli on, 452;
Quetelet's work on,
458–60
Steele, Joseph, 138, 492
Stendhal, women's
education advocated by,
290
Stephan, Gustav, on
corporal punishment, 181
Stephen, James Fitzjames,
149; on innateness of
aggression, 40–41; on
retribution, 140–41; on
punishment, 192
Stephen, Leslie, 111, 280;
on Eliot, 349; on defining
humor, 372
Stern, Otto, 328
Sternheim, Carl, as social
satirist, 383–85
Stifter, Adalbert, 109
Stone, Elizabeth, women's
political role opposed by,
306
Stone, Leo, on aggression,
532–33
Stowe, Harriet Beecher,
Uncle Tom's Cabin,
347–48
Strafford, Earl of, 216

Strauss, Salomon, 14
"Strenuous life,"
Roosevelt's use of phrase,
117
Strong, Josiah, *Our Country*,
85
Struggleforlifeurs, 49–50
Student duels. *See* Mensur
Sue, Eugène, blinding of
murderers advocated by,
145
Suffrage. *See* Voting rights;
Women's suffrage
Suicide, 207–12; as sin, 207;
in Stoic and Epicurean
doctrines, 207; as crime,
207, 208; religion and,
207, 210; as social
problem, 208–12;
statistics on, 209n., 210;
of children, 210
Sumner, Charles, 112
Sumner, William Graham,
63, 65, 123; on four
elemental springs of
action, 57; economic
philosophy of, 58; antiwar
philosophy of, 59–60;
racism questioned by,
91–92; Roosevelt's
criticism of, 121; globalist
views of, 518
Superego, 32, 37, 513;
society as, 112; birth of,
133
Supply and demand, law of,
43
Supreme Court, U.S.: social
conservatism of, 67;
"separate but equal"
decision of, 95
"Survival of the fittest,"
phrase coined by Spencer,
41
Suttner, Bertha von, 347
Sweden: capital punishment
abolished in, 167; voting
rights in, 268; women's